ROUTLEDGE HANDBOOK
OF LEISURE STUDIES

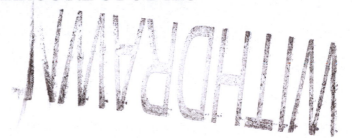

This landmark publication brings together some of the most perceptive commentators of the present moment to explore core ideas and cutting edge developments in the field of Leisure Studies. It offers important new insights into the dynamics of the transformation of leisure in contemporary societies, tracing the emergent issues at stake in the discipline and examining Leisure Studies' fundamental connections with cognate disciplines such as Sociology, Cultural Studies, History, Sport Studies and Tourism.

This book contains original work from key scholars across the globe, including those working outside the Leisure Studies mainstream. It showcases the state of the art of contemporary Leisure Studies, covering key topics and key thinkers from the psychology of leisure to leisure policy, from Bourdieu to Baudrillard, and suggests that leisure in the twenty-first century should be understood as centring on a new 'Big Seven' (holidays, drink, drugs, sex, gambling, TV and shopping). No other book has gone as far in redefining the identity of the discipline of Leisure Studies, or in suggesting how the substantive ideas of Leisure Studies need to be rethought. The *Routledge Handbook of Leisure Studies* should therefore be the intellectual guide of first choice for all scholars, academics, researchers and students working in this subject area.

Tony Blackshaw is Reader at Sheffield Hallam University, UK. He has published works on a broad range of themes in Leisure Studies which include the following: *Leisure Life: Myth, Masculinity and Modernity* (Routledge, 2003), *The Sage Dictionary of Leisure Studies* (with Garry Crawford) (Sage, 2009) and *Leisure* (Routledge, 2010).

ROUTLEDGE HANDBOOK OF LEISURE STUDIES

Edited by Tony Blackshaw

LONDON AND NEW YORK

First published in paperback 2015
First published 2013
by Routledge
2 Park Square, Milton Park, Abingdon, Oxon OX14 4RN

Simultaneously published in the USA and Canada
by Routledge
711 Third Avenue, New York, NY 10017

Routledge is an imprint of the Taylor & Francis Group, an informa business

British Library Cataloguing in Publication Data
A catalogue record for this book is available from the British Library

Library of Congress Cataloging in Publication Data
Routledge handbook of leisure studies / edited by Tony Blackshaw.
  pages cm
1. Leisure--Social aspects--Handbooks, manuals, etc.
2. Recreation--Social aspects--Handbooks, manuals, etc.
I. Blackshaw, Tony, 1960–
GV14.R68 2013   790.01--dc23
2012043937

ISBN: 978-0-415-69717-0 (hbk)
ISBN: 978-1-138-92461-1 (pbk)
ISBN: 978-0-203-14050-5 (ebk)

Typeset in Bembo and Minion Pro
by Bookcraft Ltd, Stroud, Gloucestershire

MIX
Paper from
responsible sources
FSC® C013056
www.fsc.org

Printed and bound in Great Britain by
TJ International Ltd, Padstow, Cornwall

CONTENTS

Contents

Contents

Contents

Contents

ILLUSTRATIONS

Figures

Tables

ACKNOWLEDGEMENTS

The *Routledge Handbook of Leisure Studies* is a truly collaborative work. I am grateful to all the contributors for their dedication, professionalism and expertise. I am grateful in particular to Peter Bramham and Chris Rojek who both kindly went beyond the normal call of duty. Others I want to thank include the anonymous reviewers of the original book proposal; for their insightful comments I am appreciative. I am also grateful to Judith Oppenheimer and would like to thank her for her scrupulous reading and copy-editing of all the chapters. I am especially indebted to Simon Whitmore, the Senior Commissioning Editor for Sport and Leisure at Routledge, without whom the *Handbook* would not exist. It was his idea and he has engaged the project with enormous interest and support from its inception. Simon is an exemplary editor and one of the world's true gentlemen. As ever, I want to thank Fiona, without whose love and support I would never have been able to complete the project. Finally, I wish to dedicate my work on this *Handbook* to Peter Bramham, John Capenerhurst, Jonathan Long, Chris Rojek and John Spink, whose teaching, tutelage and writing introduced me to the study of leisure and helped to establish it in my educated imagination. Their wisdom will always be appreciated.

CONTRIBUTORS

Feona Attwood is a Professor in the Media Department at Middlesex University, UK. Her research is in the area of sex in contemporary culture; and in particular, in obscenity; sexualization; sexual cultures; new technologies, identity and the body; and controversial media. She is the editor of *Mainstreaming Sex: The Sexualization of Western Culture* (2009), *porn.com: Making Sense of Online Pornography* (2010) and (with Vincent Campbell, I.Q. Hunter and Sharon Lockyer) *Controversial Images* (in press) and the co-editor of journal special issues on Controversial Images (with Sharon Lockyer, *Popular Communication*, 2009), Researching and Teaching Sexually Explicit Media (with I.Q. Hunter, *Sexualities*, 2009), and Investigating Young People's Sexual Cultures (with Clarissa Smith, *Sex Education*, 2011).

Alan Bairner is Professor of Sport and Social Theory at Loughborough University, UK. He is the author of *Sport, Nationalism and Globalization: European and North American Perspectives* (SUNY Press, 2001), editor of *Sport and the Irish: Histories, Identities, Issues* (University College Dublin Press, 2005) and co-editor (with Gyozo Molnar) of *The Politics of the Olympics: A Survey* (Routledge, 2010). He has written extensively on the relationship between sport and national identity. He serves on the editorial boards of the *International Review for the Sociology of Sport* and the *International Journal of Sport Policy* and is advisor to the Taiwan Society of Sport Sociology.

David Bauckham is Senior Lecturer at the University of Brighton, UK. For over a decade he has been photographing and writing about the history of football grounds and lower league football culture, and his work has been widely published within this genre.

Tom Baum is Professor of International Tourism and Hospitality Management at the University of Strathclyde in Glasgow. He holds BA and MA degrees in Education from the University of Wales and a PhD in Tourism Labour Market Studies from the University of Strathclyde. Tom has worked in tourism education and training for over 30 years, as a research manager within the public sector, an educator in the university sector and as consultant to public and privately funded projects across five continents. He has published extensively in this area and the wider context of people and work within hospitality and tourism. Tom's research has a strong focus on human resource development themes in the sector within the context of developing and transition economies and he also has an active interest in volunteering as work in events and tourism.

Joy Beatty is an Associate Professor of Organizational Behavior at the University of Michigan–Dearborn, USA. She completed her PhD at Boston College. Her research areas are diversity and management education. Among her peer-reviewed publications she has published in *Journal of Management Inquiry* on the relationship between work and leisure. Her current research addresses time and technology, and how electronic calendars are changing people's perception and experience of time. She serves on the editorial board of *Academy of Management Learning and Education*, and on the executive committee of the Gender and Diversity in Organizations division of the Academy of Management (US).

Andy Bennett is Professor of Cultural Sociology and Director of the Griffith Centre for Cultural Research at Griffith University in Queensland, Australia. He has authored and edited numerous books, including *Popular Music and Youth Culture*, *Cultures of Popular Music*, *Remembering Woodstock*, and *Music Scenes* (with Richard A. Peterson). He is Editor-in-Chief of the *Journal of Sociology*. He is a Faculty Fellow of the Center for Cultural Sociology, Yale University, an Associate Member of PopuLUs, the Centre for the Study of the World's Popular Musics, Leeds University, and a member of the Advisory Board for the Social Aesthetics Research Unit, Monash University.

Tony Blackshaw is Reader at Sheffield Hallam University in the UK. He has published works on a broad range of themes in Leisure Studies which include the following: *Leisure Life: Myth, Masculinity and Modernity* (Routledge, 2003), *New Perspectives on Sport and 'Deviance': Consumption, Performativity and Social Control* (with Tim Crabbe) (Routledge, 2004), *The Sage Dictionary of Leisure Studies* (with Garry Crawford) (2009) and *Leisure* (2010) in Routledge's Key Ideas series.

Johan Bouwer is currently acting Rector Magnificus of NHTV Breda International University of Applied Science, Netherlands. Formerly he was Director of Research and Senior Researcher in Meaning and Leisure at the same university. He received his PhD from the Free University in Amsterdam in 1992. During the period 1997–2008 he was successively chair in Spiritual Care in Health Care Institutions at Groningen University and the PThU in Kampen, Netherlands.

Steven Bradbury is a Senior Research Associate at the School of Sport, Exercise and Health Sciences at Loughborough University, UK. Steven has conducted research for a range of sports and football agencies, including: Sport England, Sports Scotland, Sports Leaders UK, the English FA, the Football Foundation, the Professional Footballers' Association, Kick It Out, Football Against Racism in Europe and UEFA. His recent published work includes an examination of racism, resistance and minority participation in amateur football, the effectiveness of anti-racist strategies in professional football, and an analysis of the representation and structural discrimination of minorities as players, coaches and in leadership positions in football in Europe.

Peter Bramham is a Research Fellow, and former Reader, in the Carnegie Faculty at Leeds Metropolitan University in the UK. His publications include: *Understanding Leisure* (with John Capenhurst, Les Haywood, I.P. Henry, Frank Kew and John Spink) (Nelson Thornes, 1995); *Leisure and the Urban Process* (Routledge, 1989); *Leisure Policies in Europe* (CABI, 1993) and *Leisure Research in Europe* (CABI, 1996) (all edited with Ian Henry, Hans Mommaas and Hugo van der Poel). His most recent work includes *Sport, Leisure and Culture in the Postmodern City*, a study of Leeds, edited with Stephen Wagg (Ashgate, 2009) and also *The New Politics of Leisure and Pleasure* (Palgrave Macmillan, 2011).

Oona Brooks is a Lecturer in Sociology/Criminology at the University of Abertay, Dundee in Scotland. Her research interests include gender inequalities, gendered identities, sexual violence and alcohol. Previously, Oona has worked as a researcher for the Scottish Centre for Crime and Justice Research (University of Glasgow), the Department of Applied Social Science (University of Stirling) and the Institute for Social Marketing (University of Stirling).

Garry Chick holds a PhD in cultural anthropology and is currently Professor and Head of the Department of Recreation, Park and Tourism Management as well as a Professor in the Department of Anthropology at the Pennsylvania State University, USA. He is a past editor of *Leisure Sciences* and *Play & Culture* and a past president of the Association for the Anthropological Study of Play and the Society for Cross-Cultural Research. Recent publications include 'Leisure and Cultural Complexity' (*Cross-Cultural Research 45*: 59–81) and 'Culture as a Variable in the Study of Leisure' (*Leisure Sciences 31*: 26–45, 2009).

Garry Crawford is Professor in Sociology at the University of Salford, UK. His research focuses primarily upon audiences and consumer patterns and, most specifically, sport fans and video gamers. He is the author of *Consuming Sport* (2004) and *Video Gamers* (2011), and the co-author of *Introducing Cultural Studies* (2nd edn 2008, with B. Longhurst, G. Smith, G. Bagnall, and M. Ogborn), the *Sage Dictionary of Leisure Studies* (2009, with T. Blackshaw), and co-editor of *Online Gaming in Context* (2011, with V.K. Gosling and B. Light). Garry is Director of the University of Salford Digital Cluster, Publications Director of the British Sociological Association, and review editor for *Cultural Sociology*.

Chas Critcher is Visiting Professor in Media and Communications at Swansea University and Emeritus Professor of Communications at Sheffield Hallam University, UK. Since writing *The Devil Makes Work* (1985) and co-editing *The Sociology of Leisure: A Reader* (1995), he has continued to write occasionally on aspects of leisure. Recently this work has overlapped with his other main research interest in moral panics, evident in the authorship of *Moral Panics and the Media* (2003) and the editing of *Critical Readings in Moral Panics and the Media* (2006). His current research interests focus on applying the concept of moral regulation to various social contexts, including those of leisure.

Jon Dart is Senior Lecturer in Leisure Policy and Sociology at Leeds Metropolitan University, UK. He entered higher education as a mature student and completed his PhD on leisure and home-based work at Leeds Metropolitan University. He has previously worked at McMaster University (Canada) and Trinity and All Saints College (Leeds).

Chris Gratton is Professor of Sports Economics and Director of the Sport Industry Research Centre (SIRC) at Sheffield Hallam University, UK. He currently has five academic sports books in print, the latest being *The Economics of Sport Broadcasting*, published in 2007. Chris's main areas of research include: the economic benefits of major sports events; measuring the economic importance of sport; and the analysis and modelling of large sports participation surveys. He has represented the UK on the EU Workshop on Sport and Economics since 2006.

Maureen Harrington has a PhD in Sociology from University of California, Santa Barbara (1988). Born in London, Ontario, Canada, she has lived in Queensland, Australia, since 1995. Her research ranges across volunteering in sport, women's work, leisure and family lives, and gender and family leisure. Her current research is on family leisure, children's sport, notions of healthy lifestyles and risk.

David Harris is Professor of Leisure and Education at University College Plymouth St Mark and St John, UK. His research interests have resulted in publications in distance education and electronic teaching, in social theory, and in Cultural Studies and Leisure Studies. He has taught a range of undergraduate and postgraduate students using conventional and electronic means. Further details of interests and publications can be found on his personal website: http://www.arasite.org/

Karla A. Henderson is a Professor in the Department of Parks, Recreation and Tourism Management at North Carolina State University (USA). She has written numerous journal articles, book chapters, and textbooks on topics related to gender, diversity, research methods, leisure philosophy and theory, and curriculum development. Henderson has received the National Recreation and Park Association (NRPA) Roosevelt Excellence in Research Award as well as the NRPA Literary Award. She was the 2010 recipient of the World Leisure George Torkildsen Literary Award. Henderson is a member of the Academy of Leisure Sciences and the American Academy of Park and Recreation Administrators.

Kirsten Holmes BA, MA, PhD is Senior Lecturer at the School of Marketing, Curtin University, Australia. She has over 15 years' experience researching in the area of volunteerism and leisure and is the co-author (with Dr Karen Smith) of *Managing Volunteers in Tourism: Attractions, Destinations and Events* (Elsevier, 2009). She is a member of Volunteering Australia's research advisory group and Volunteering Western Australia's research committee.

Jason Hughes is Senior Lecturer in Sociology and Deputy Head of the School of Social Sciences at Brunel University. His research interests span a range of concerns but include: the sociology of consumption; the sociology of the body and health; emotions, work and identity; figurational sociology and sociological theory; moral panics and regulation. His first book, *Learning to Smoke* (University of Chicago Press, 2003) was winner of the 2006 Norbert Elias prize. More recently he has completed, together with Eric Dunning, a major study of the work of Norbert Elias titled *Norbert Elias and Modern Sociology: Knowledge, Interdependence, Power, Process* (Bloomsbury, 2013). He has also recently published a number of edited books, including *Visual Methods* (Sage, 2012) and *Internet Research Methods* (Sage, 2012); and co-edited books, including *Moral Panics in the Contemporary World* (Bloomsbury, 2013) and *Communities of Practice: Critical Perspectives* (Routledge, 2007).

Grant Jarvie is currently Chair of Sport at the University of Edinburgh and Visiting Research Professor with the University of Toronto. He has served as Vice-Principal and acting Principal with one Scottish university. He was awarded an Honorary Doctorate in 2009 in recognition for his efforts to forge international cooperation and academic developments between universities. He is an Honorary Professor of the University of Warsaw. He has held established chairs and been dead of departments and research centres in different UK universities including Stirling, Warwick and Heriot-Watt. His research has covered aspects of sport, health and education in other countries including Denmark, China, South Africa, Kenya, Taiwan and France.

Margaretha Järvinen is Professor at the Department of Sociology, University of Copenhagen, Denmark, and at SFI – the Danish National Centre for Social Research. Her research interests include alcohol and drug use, youth studies, qualitative methods and general sociological theory. Among her most recent works related to substance use are: 'From Recreational to Regular Drug Use' (with S. Ravn), in *Sociology of Health and Illness* (2011); 'The Normalization of Cannabis Use' (with J. Demant), in *Health, Risk and Society* (2011); 'Governing Adolescent Drinking' (with J. Østergaard), in *Youth and Society*; 'Approaches to Methadone Treatment', in *Sociology of Health and Illness* (2008); and *Youth Drinking Cultures* (ed. with R. Room, 2007).

Douglas A. Kleiber is Professor of Leisure Studies, Gerontology and Lifespan Developmental Psychology at the University of Georgia. He holds academic degrees in psychology and educational psychology and has taught at Cornell University and the University of Illinois in previous positions. He is a past President of the Academy of Leisure Sciences and has also received both Sapora and Roosevelt awards. His research addresses the optimization of leisure in adaptation to developmental transitions. He is the author of *Leisure Experience and Human Development* (Basic Books) and co-author of *A Social Psychology of Leisure* (Venture Publishing).

Alan Law is Associate Professor of Sociology at Trent University, Ontario, Canada, specializing in the Sociology of Leisure, and holds degrees in Business, Recreation Administration and Sociology. Law's interests in tourism sociology primarily centre on relations of distributive justice between and within visitor and host communities at cultural, economic and political levels. Past studies have pursued classic gentrification themes common in resort development. Work underway targets the role of the welfare state in regulating 'belonging' in gentrifying tourism regions (sifting the lazy), which serves as a natural bridge to new interests in labour market conditions of outdoor adventure workers.

Jonathan Long is Professor in the Carnegie Research Institute at Leeds Metropolitan University, UK. He has directed some 50 research projects for external clients. His experience embraces all stages of the research process from design to dissemination, using both quantitative and qualitative techniques. He is the author of *Researching Leisure, Sport and Tourism: The Essential Guide* (Sage), was a founding member of the Editorial Board of *Leisure Studies*, and is now on the board of both *Managing Leisure* and the *Journal of Policy Research in Tourism, Leisure and Events*. He is an Academician of the Academy of Social Sciences.

Dominic Malcolm is Senior Lecturer in the Sociology of Sport in the School of Sport, Exercise and Health Sciences at Loughborough University, UK. His research on the historical and sociological aspects of cricket and the critical sociological analysis of sports medicine is underpinned by a theoretical framework informed by the work of Norbert Elias. His co-edited books *Sport Histories* and *Matters of Sport* expand upon and develop Elias's theories in relation to sport. He is also author of the *Sage Dictionary of Sports Studies* (2008), *Sport and Sociology* (2012), *Globalizing Cricket: Englishness, Empire and Identity* (2013), and editor of *The Social Organization of Sports Medicine* (with P. Safia, 2012).

Roger C. Mannell is a psychologist and Professor of Leisure and Health Sciences at the University of Waterloo in Canada. He studies and writes about the determinants of lifestyle choices and health, and the role of leisure in coping with negative life events such as bereavement, challenges of care giving, and time pressure and stress experienced by adolescents and parents. Roger co-authored the book *A Social Psychology of Leisure* and has received the Allen V. Sapora Research Award and NRPA's Theodore and Franklin Roosevelt Research Excellence Award. He is a Fellow of the Academy of Leisure Sciences and has served as its president.

Louise Mansfield is Senior Lecturer in the Sociology of Sport and works within the Centre for Sport, Physical Education and Activity Research (SPEAR) at Canterbury Christ Church University, UK. Her research focuses broadly on the gendered and sexualized experiences of women in sport and leisure. She has published on the relationships between feminisms and the work of Norbert Elias and on the application of Elias's approach in understanding the historical development of sport and leisure, fitness and competing femininities, and the stigmatization of fat in fitness cultures. The health and well-being aspect of her research embraces a Health at Every Size approach (www.healthateverysize. org.uk) and has extended into exploring leisure and the politics of the environment. Her most recent research explores women and sport development and is evolving to include an international development perspective in understanding women's experiences of netball in Malawi.

Toby Miller is the author and editor of over 30 books, has published essays in more than 100 journals and edited collections, and is a frequent guest commentator on television and radio programmes. His teaching and research cover the media, sports, labour, gender, race, citizenship, politics, and cultural policy, as well as the success of Hollywood overseas and the adverse effects of electronic waste. Miller's work has been translated into Chinese, Japanese, Swedish, German, Spanish and Portuguese. His latest books are *Television Studies: The Basics* (2010), *The Contemporary Hollywood Reader* (2009), and *Makeover Nation: The United States of Reinvention* (2008).

Simon Mussell is Visiting Research Fellow in the Centre for Social and Political Thought at the University of Sussex, UK. His research interests include the critical theory of the Frankfurt School (especially the work of Theodor W. Adorno), political aesthetics, affect theory, modern and postmodern culture, and the philosophy of film. His current research examines the role of emotion and feeling within the social and political theory of the Frankfurt School.

Geoff Nichols is a Senior Lecturer at the Management School at the University of Sheffield, UK, where he has worked since 1990. He has been researching sports' volunteering since 1996 and contributed to three national surveys. He has also researched event volunteers and a volunteering legacy of the 2002 Commonwealth Games. He presently chairs the Sports Volunteering Research Network in the UK.

Matthew Nicholson is Associate Professor in the Centre for Sport and Social Impact at La Trobe University, Melbourne, Australia. Matthew's research focuses on policy development and practice, sport and the media and the contribution of sport and volunteering to social capital. His most recent publications include *Sport and Policy: Issues and Analysis* (2010), *Sport Management: Principles and Applications* (2nd edn) (2009), *Sport and Social Capital* (2008) and *Sport and the Media: Managing the Nexus* (2007), all published with Elsevier, UK, *A National Game* (2008, Penguin-Viking) and *Participation in Sport: International Policy Perspectives* (2011, edited, Routledge) and *Australian Sport: Better by Design?* (2004, Routledge).

Steve Redhead is Professor of Sport and Media in the Faculty of Education, Charles Sturt University, Bathurst, Australia. He is the author or editor of fifteen books, including *We Have Never Been Postmodern: Theory at the Speed of Light* (2011), *The Jean Baudrillard Reader* (2008), *Paul Virilio: Theorist for an Accelerated Culture* (2004) and *The Paul Virilio Reader* (2004), all published by Edinburgh University Press, and *Repetitive Beat Generation* (2000) published by Canongate. *We Have Never Been Postmodern* and *The Jean Baudrillard Reader* are also published as e-books by Edinburgh Scholarship Online. He is editor of Berg's Subcultural Style book series. His personal website is www.steveredhead.com.

Gerda Reith is Professor of Social Science and Director of the Gambling Research Group at the University of Glasgow, UK. Her research focuses on the role of social, cultural and environmental factors in the development of different types of risky or addictive consumption, with a particular focus on gambling behaviour. She has written extensively on these areas from both UK and international perspectives, and her book *The Age of Chance: Gambling in Western Culture* was awarded the Philip Abrams Prize for 2000. She is currently carrying out research into gambling-related behaviour on a number of ESRC-funded projects.

Greg Richards is Professor of Leisure Studies at Tilburg University in the Netherlands. He has conducted extensive research on cultural and creative tourism over the past 20 years, producing major texts on *Cultural Tourism in Europe* (1996); *Cultural Attractions and European Tourism* (2001); *Tourism and Gastronomy* (2002); *The Global Nomad: Backpacker Travel in Theory and Practice* (2004); *Cultural Tourism – Global and Local Perspectives* (2007); *Tourism, Creativity and Development* (2007); *Eventful Cities: Cultural Management and Urban Regeneration* (2010); and *Research Methods in Cultural Tourism* (2010).

Ken Roberts is Professor of Sociology at the University of Liverpool, UK. His books include *Leisure* (1970), *Contemporary Society and the Growth of Leisure* (1978), and *Leisure in Contemporary Society* (2nd edition, 2006). He is a former Chair of the World Leisure Organization's Research Commission, and also a former President of the International Sociological Association's Research Committee on Leisure. He is a founder member and now honorary life member of the Leisure Studies Association. His most recent books are *Key Concepts in Sociology* (2009) and *Youth in Transition: Eastern Europe and the West* (2009).

Victoria Robinson is Reader in Sociology at the University of Sheffield, UK. She has published widely in the areas of extreme sports, sexuality and gender, and men and masculinities. Her books include *Masculinities in Transition* (Palgrave) and *Everyday Masculinities and Extreme Sport: Male Identity and Rock Climbing* (Berg). She is currently writing a book on rock climbing in the USA for Greenwood Publishers and is co-editor for a new international Palgrave book series on sex and gender.

Chris Rojek is Professor of Sociology and Culture at Brunel University, UK. His first book on leisure, *Capitalism and Leisure Theory*, was published in 1985 and he has since written five others, the most recent of which is *The Labour of Leisure* (Sage, 2010). He has also published widely on the subjects of celebrity and popular culture.

Dave Russell has long-established interests in the history of leisure, with particular reference to music, sport and the construction of regional identities. He is the author of *Popular Music in England, 1840–1914: A Social History* (1997, 2nd edn), *Football and the English* (1997) and *Looking North: Northern England and the National Imagination* (2004), as well as numerous essays and articles on the history of popular culture. He retired from Leeds Metropolitan University, UK as Professor of History and Northern Studies in 2010.

Alexander Sager is Assistant Professor of Philosophy and University Studies at Portland State University, USA. He is one of the general editors of the two-volume *Broadview Guide to Social and Political Thought*. He has taught and lectured on the philosophy of leisure and his article 'A Plea for (the Philosophy of) Leisure' appeared in the October/November 2010 issue of *Philosophy Now*.

David Scott is a Professor in the Department of Recreation, Park and Tourism Sciences at Texas A&M University, USA. He received his doctorate from the Pennsylvania State University in 1990. His research focuses on leisure constraints; use and non-use of park and recreation services; and recreation specialization and serious leisure. Articles of his have appeared in several scholarly journals, including *Applied Behavioral Science Review, Environment and Behavior, Journal of Leisure Research, Journal of Park and Recreation Administration, Human Dimensions of Wildlife, Leisure Sciences,* and *Society and Leisure.* He is the former editor of the *Journal of Leisure Research.*

Erin K. Sharpe is Associate Professor in the Department of Recreation and Leisure Studies at Brock University, St. Catharines, Canada, where she has worked since 2001. Her teaching and research revolves most centrally around relationships between leisure and community, community development and, more recently, international development. Past work has explored the relationships between leisure and social change in the context of festivals, as well as critical analyses of community sport, volunteering, and local governance. She is currently engaged in critical reflexive analyses of development practice in both a local and international context.

Clarissa Smith is Reader in Sexual Cultures at the University of Sunderland, UK. Her research focuses on pornography and sexual representations and practices. Her publications include *One for the Girls! The Pleasures and Practices of Pornography for Women* (2007), (with Michael Higgins and John Storey) *Cambridge Companion to Contemporary British*

Culture (2010), and (with Niall Richardson and Angela Werndly) *Studies in Sexualities: Theories, Representations, Practices* (forthcoming).

Karl Spracklen is Professor of Leisure Studies in the Carnegie Faculty of Sport and Education, Leeds Metropolitan University, UK. Previously to this, he worked as a National Development Manager for Sporting Equals, a project funded by the Commission for Racial Equality and Sport England to promote ethnic diversity in sport. His research interests include racism in sport, the construction of social identity, leisure theory, authenticity and extreme metal. He is a Verifier for the Equality Standard for Sport. Since 2009 he has been Chair of the Leisure Studies Association. He has published widely on the sociology of leisure: his recent books include *The Meaning and Purpose of Leisure* (Palgrave, 2009) and, with Jonathan Long, *Sport and Challenges to Racism* (Palgrave, 2011).

Robert A. Stebbins, FRSC, received his PhD in 1964 from the University of Minnesota, USA. Professor Stebbins has published 43 books and written over 200 articles and chapters. He has authored *Serious Leisure: A Perspective for Our Time* (Transaction, 2007), *Personal Decisions in the Public Square: Beyond Problem-Solving into a Positive Sociology* (Transaction, 2009), *Leisure and Consumption: Common Ground/Separate Worlds* (Palgrave Macmillan, 2009), and *The Idea of Leisure: First Principles* (Transaction, 2012). Stebbins is an elected fellow of the Academy of Leisure Sciences, the Royal Society of Canada, and the World Leisure Academy.

Nick Stevenson is Reader in Cultural Sociology at the University of Nottingham, UK. He is the author of *The Transformation of the Media* (Longman, 1999), *Understanding Media Cultures* (Sage, 2001), *Making Sense of Men's Lifestyle Magazines* (Polity, 2001), *Culture and Citizenship* (Sage, 2001), *Cultural Citizenship* (Oxford University Press, 2003), *David Bowie* (2006, Polity) and *Education and Cultural Citizenship* (Sage, 2011).

Bob Stewart is Associate Professor in the School of Sport and Exercise at Victoria University in Melbourne, Australia and an Affiliate of the Institute of Sport, Exercise and Active Living (ISEAL). He is co-author of *A National Game: The History of Australian Rules Football* (Penguin Viking, 2008) and co-author of *Sport Management: Principles and Applications* (Butterworth-Heinemann, 2009). Bob is currently completing a manuscript on drugs and sport, which will be published by Routledge in 2013 under the title of *Rethinking Drug Use in Sport: Why the War Will Never Be Won*.

Peter Taylor is Professor of Sport Economics at Sheffield Hallam University, UK; co-director of the Sport Industry Research Centre; editor of *Managing Leisure: An International Journal*, a trustee for the 7 Hills Leisure Trust, Sheffield, and a Companion of the Chartered Institute for the Management of Sport and Physical Activity. He is technical consultant to Sport England's National Benchmarking Service for Sports and Leisure Centres. He has recently edited a sixth edition of *Torkildsen's Sport and Leisure Management*.

William R. Torbert is known as a transformational leader, teacher, consultant, and scholar who has pioneered Developmental Action Inquiry, a theory and practice that interweaves expanding personal awareness, leading organizational change, and assessing outcomes scientifically. Professor Emeritus of Management at Boston College, he has authored many books and articles, including *The Power of Balance: Transforming Self, Society and Scientific Inquiry* and *Action Inquiry: The Secret of Timely, Transforming Leadership* (Berrett-Koehler, 2004), and the 2005 *Harvard Business Review* article 'The Seven Transformations of Leadership'. Currently, he serves as Principal of Action Inquiry Associates and the Action Inquiry Fellowship, and offers by-invitation Alchemists' Workparties.

Marco van Leeuwen is Lecturer in Philosophy and Coordinator of the academic 'International Leisure Sciences' programme at NHTV Breda International University of Applied Sciences, Netherlands. He received his PhD from the Radboud University Nijmegen in 2009, on the topic of embodied and embedded cognition. His research interests include the philosophy of leisure, meaningful experience and modern media.

A. J. Veal is Adjunct Professor in the School of Leisure, Sport and Tourism in the University of Technology, Sydney, Australia, and worked previously in the universities of Birmingham and North London. He is past president of the Australian and New Zealand Association for Leisure Studies (ANZALS) and of the UK Leisure Studies Association. He is author or joint author/editor of a number of books, including: *Leisure, Sport and Tourism, Politics, Policy and Planning* (3rd edn, CABI, 2010); *The Olympic Games: A Social Science Perspective* (2nd edn, CABI, 2007); *A Handbook of Leisure Studies* (Palgrave-Macmillan, 2006); *Research Methods for Leisure and Tourism* (4th edn, FT/Prentice Hall, 2011); *Free Time and Leisure Participation: International Perspectives* (2nd edn, CABI, 2005); *Australian Leisure* (4th edn, Pearson Australia, 2013); and *Work and Leisure* (Routledge, 2004).

John K. Walton, Ikerbasque: the Basque Foundation for Science; Instituto Valentín de Foronda, University of the Basque Country UPV/ EHU, Vitoria-Gasteiz, Spain. He has published extensively on the history of tourism, especially coastal resorts, in various countries, especially Britain and Spain, and he edits the *Journal of Tourism History* for Routledge/ Taylor & Francis. His recent books include *The British Seaside: Holidays and Resorts in the Twentieth Century* (Manchester University Press, 2000); *The Playful Crowd: Pleasure Places in the Twentieth Century* (with Gary Cross: New York: Columbia University Press, 2005); *Riding on Rainbows: Blackpool Pleasure Beach and Its Place in British Popular Culture* (St Albans: Skelter, 2007); and *Constructing Cultural Tourism: John Ruskin and the Tourist Gaze* (with Keith Hanley: Bristol: Channel View, 2010).

Stephen Wearing is Associate Professor at the University of Technology, Sydney (UTS). He has also taught as Visiting Fellow at a number of universities in his 25-year career at UTS, including Wageningen University, Netherlands, and Newcastle University and Macquarie University in Australia. Stephen specializes in the social sciences in natural resource management. His research and publications range across the areas of the sociology of leisure and tourism. He has been project director for a range of social sciences in natural resource management projects and research and a team leader for a variety of ecotourism, volunteer tourism and outdoor education activities internationally. His latest book, *Tourism Cultures: Identity, Place and Traveler* (Sage, 2010), contributes to the growing area of 'critical tourism studies', a movement that seeks to bring an alternative commentary and new theoretical thinking to the understanding of tourism in contemporary society.

Henry Yeomans is Lecturer in Criminology and Criminal Justice at the University of Leeds, UK. His research focuses on the legal and moral frameworks which have governed the consumption of alcohol in England and Wales from the eighteenth century onwards. He has published widely in this area and, in 2012, was awarded the Sage Prize for Innovation and/or Excellence for his article 'What did the British Temperance Movement Accomplish? Attitudes to Alcohol, the Law and Moral Regulation' (published in *Sociology*).

INTRODUCTION

Tony Blackshaw

How do scholars of Leisure Studies define the current identity of their subject field, which is communal and soaked in history, to map out, as it were, a comprehensive analytical and theoretical account of the themes that currently sustain it, as well as the variety of critical perspectives and the key figures that are inspiring these? That is one reason why I have spent a good part of the last two years compiling the chapters that comprise the *Handbook of Leisure Studies*, which has been written in accordance with a basic objective: simply to put together the best edited collection that there is on Leisure Studies by bringing together some of the most perceptive commentators of the present moment in the subject field – the core ideas and cutting edge developments and their implications – in the hope that it will inspire a new generation of readers.

The *Handbook of Leisure Studies* is intended to be both a critical source of knowledge and a guide to further reading that displays the richness and scope of Leisure Studies at the beginning of the twenty-first century. The key to any good handbook lies in its selection of topics. It was extremely difficult to decide what to include and what to leave out, given the scope of the study of leisure. The main criteria were to include the key contemporary ideas and the major thinkers from the world stage, both past and present, along with their key ideas, theories and concepts. To this extent, this *Handbook* is a body of work that presents a scholarly account and critique of Leisure Studies from a multidisciplinary perspective, and it includes chapters by some of the leading figures and some of the best of the emerging new talent in the subject field today. As their titles suggest, some of the chapters investigate topics from the perspective of a particular academic discipline, but most of them do so at the intersection of several.

The *Handbook of Leisure Studies* is written for the scholar, student and general reader alike. It contains 49 chapters of varying length and scope. It also consists of six parts: 'Key disciplines'; 'Key thinkers'; 'Leisure as a socio-cultural phenomenon'; 'The Big Seven leisure pursuits'; 'Uses of leisure'; and 'New directions'.

The organization of the six parts is quite simple. Part I introduces the reader to some of the fundamental perspectives in Leisure Studies. As its title suggests, Part II, 'Key thinkers', deals with the major intellectual figures who have inspired and continue to inspire the subject field. Part III is an attempt to analyse leisure as a social and cultural phenomenon, as a 'socio-cultural constructed reality', as it were. Whether focusing on leisure activities and pursuits as sites of freedom or constraint or a combination of both, the chapters that appear in this part recognize that these must always be interpreted in social and cultural terms. In other words, leisure must always be studied from the perspectives of sociology and cultural studies. Part IV deals with 'The Big Seven leisure pursuits'. As is well known in Leisure Studies, at the beginning of the 1970s, in attempting to define leisure, Ken Roberts wrote about the Big Five leisure pursuits: gambling; sex; alcohol; television; and annual holidays (Critcher and Bramham, 2004; Blackshaw, 2010). Each of these has held its own, but to the Big Five have also been added the Big Two of drug taking and shopping, and also the rewiring of traditional leisure activities and pursuits through information technology and the internet. The chapters that comprise Part V introduce and analyse a variety of themes critical to understanding the uses of leisure. The final section of the *Handbook*, Part VI on 'New Directions', features a selection of chapters that explore and on occasion revisit some of the ideas and themes which have had the most significant impact in Leisure Studies in the last few years. The goal here, as in the other sections of the *Handbook*, is one of critical engagement with current developments in the subject field, which by its very nature is selective, rather than of easy categorization, which feigns to be exhaustive.

Each of the chapters is self-contained, and they can of course be read in any order. But taken as a whole, this *Handbook* offers a meticulously researched and hugely absorbing volume, focusing on the topics which have led the discursive formation known as Leisure Studies to where it is today. Many of the chapters bear witness to individual authors' conception of leisure and Leisure Studies and more often than not reveal the authors' own ideological preferences.

Yet there is no overarching narrative in the *Handbook* – not even in this introduction. There is no meta-interpretation of the current state of play in Leisure Studies here. I have already had something to say about this in my extended critical essay *Leisure* (Blackshaw, 2010), which explores what modern leisure has been, is and might be; provides some insights about varieties of leisure and the different perspectives that have been used over the years to interpret these; and above all else aims to convey a sense of wonder about the many uses of leisure.

If there is an overarching principle for the *Handbook of Leisure Studies*, it is the central importance of this last aim. This observation notwithstanding, Leisure Studies constitutes a vast subject field to deal with and certain editorial choices had to be made. With the exception of a small number of obvious omissions, which occur for reasons beyond my control, it is hoped that the resulting *Handbook* reflects the vitality and scope of contemporary Leisure Studies. Of course, some readers may still feel that particular topics or some intellectual figures that have shaped Leisure Studies are missing, but the intention was always, as I have pointed out already, to be selective rather than exhaustive. The overriding goal has been one of critical engagement.

To assemble a resource of this magnitude has been a formidable challenge. In spite of the impossibility of dealing with every issue in contemporary Leisure Studies, this *Handbook* brings together critical explorations of a wide range of the topics and the intellectual figures who have framed them. The *Handbook of Leisure Studies* represents a collective work which is a powerful testimony to the rich exchange of ideas that is Leisure Studies today. It is my privilege to have been the mere assembler of a volume that is, as they say, much more than the sum of its parts.

References

Blackshaw, T. (2010) *Leisure*. London and New York: Routledge.

Critcher, C. and Bramham, P. (2004) 'The Devil Still Makes Work', in J. T. Haworth and A. J. Veal (eds) *Work and Leisure*. London: Routledge.

PART I

KEY DISCIPLINES

1

PHILOSOPHY OF LEISURE[1]

Alexander Sager

At its core, philosophy of leisure is an investigation into part of the good life. As such, it is a branch of moral and political philosophy. Philosophy of leisure enquires into the ends that should be pursued for their own sake, the role of social institutions in supporting valuable ends, and the virtues that people ought to cultivate so as to best avail themselves of their free time. It is in this spirit that this chapter examines the meaning of leisure, traces its philosophical development, and discusses its moral and political significance. The chapter begins by doing two things: it offers a definition of leisure and distinguishes it from related concepts. In the following section it briefly traces the historical development of the idea of leisure in the Western philosophical tradition. The discussion then turns to leisure's ethical implications. The final part of the chapter explores the politics surrounding leisure.

Understanding leisure

We have an intuitive understanding of when an activity involves leisure. Hiking in the mountains, enjoying BBQ and beer with friends, and reading a detective novel are leisure activities. Catching up with work that you've been putting off on Friday evening, sitting in rush-hour traffic, and scrubbing the bathroom are not leisure pursuits. Nonetheless, leisure is not easy to define. It belongs to a cluster of concepts that includes idleness, rest, free time, play, and work (to which it is often mistakenly opposed). The English word *leisure* has its roots in the Latin *licēre*, 'to be permitted'. The concept of leisure descends from the Greek word *skholē* (Latin: *scola*) – the etymology of 'school' – and describes a state of freedom from necessity. To be at one's leisure is to be free to pursue activities of value.

Free time is necessary for leisure, but not what characterizes it. Free time is a precondition to freely develop the skills and knowledge that allow for the pursuit of leisure, but not all free time involves leisure. A harried manager using her lunch break to run errands is not at leisure even though she has chosen how to use this time. Furthermore, leisure differs from idleness or laziness. We may follow Paul LaFargue (1883) and Bertrand Russell (2004) in praising laziness, but the trust-fund baby who dulls his boredom with OxyContin is not at leisure.

Much of what passes for leisure in our society is in fact rest. The ancient Greeks distinguished leisure from amusement (*paidia*) and recreation (*anapausis*). Amusement and recreation allow people to recover from work *and* from strenuous leisure. Leisure is reserved for the most valuable activities, activities chosen for their own sake, not for respite from the grind of life. For this reason, we would be mistaken to identify idleness with leisure. The common reader deciphering a difficult text, the striker aiming the ball toward the corner of the net, and the chef braising a fillet of salmon in preparing a meal for friends are not idle.

Play is another activity which is discussed in relation to leisure. Despite psychological and sociological accounts that reduce it to the function of socialization and learning, much play has no immediate function outside of itself (Huizinga, 1950). Though 'amateur' is sometimes taken as a synonym for dilettante, it still retains some of its French meaning of 'lover of'. The amateur engages seriously and passionately in an activity for its own sake without financial remuneration. Games may build community, sharpen our minds, or strengthen our bodies, but we often play for the sake of the game. In fact, games do not qualify as leisure if they are obligatory. The child prodigy forced to practise for hours on the golf course and the systems analyst who suffers through an aerobics class on doctor's orders are not at leisure. In his *Treatise*, David Hume writes of the passion of 'curiosity or the love of truth' that rests not only on the acquisition of true belief, but in the activity of the mind overcoming the challenges to understanding. He compares philosophy with hunting and gaming, noting that we come to value the end of the game because we value the activity, not because of its independent value.

Whether an activity is a leisure activity depends on why it is chosen. Reading philosophy may be leisure if it is done in the pursuit of wisdom, but will become onerous if it is done for the sake of a grade. Because the purpose of the activity and whether it is freely chosen defines an activity as leisure, work is not necessarily opposed to leisure. When a professional poker player earns a living, poker may not be a leisure activity. The reason is not that she is being paid – a recreational poker player betting on line may make money. Rather, professionals often lack leisure because their activity is obligatory. The professional tennis player cannot miss a game because she does not want to travel, feels tired, or has made other plans. Leisure activities, if performed merely for the sake of a wage, become labour.

We should be careful, though, of drawing too sharp a line between leisure and non-leisure activities. Many of our pursuits are complex and they may be simultaneously chosen because they are valuable in themselves and valuable as an end to something else. Athletic activity may be valuable for its own sake and because of its health benefits, which are also good in themselves. Artists may simultaneously create works of art for their intrinsic value and for remuneration. The best jobs may obligate us to perform activities that we also value for their own sake and that provide us with the freedom to complete tasks creatively.

A genealogy of leisure

In the Western tradition, philosophy of leisure has its origin in ancient Greek philosophy. In particular, Aristotle's views of leisure dominated Western culture until the Renaissance and remain highly influential today.

Today, leisure is often defined as the opposite of the more dominant term of work. For the ancient Greeks, leisure was the dominant term; work was defined as *askolia*, the absence of leisure, due to the need to complete necessary tasks. Plato thought the philosophical life of contemplation superior to the life of governing the community or to the pursuit of wealth. Philosophy or the love of wisdom required leisure. In the *Republic*, he set out a curriculum to prepare youth with potential talent for philosophy to acquire the capacity for reflection on the good. Education includes gymnastics, music, arithmetic, geometry, and, finally, dialectic. Notably, Plato stresses that the education should not be authoritarian or obligatory, since this undermines the autonomy of the learner (*Republic*, 536d)

Aristotle's *Nicomachean Ethics* (NE) is an investigation into the nature of happiness or flourishing (*eudaimonia*). We pursue some ends for the sake of something else, earning money to purchase goods or eating nutritious food for the sake of health. Aristotle's ethics depend on his conception of human nature. For Aristotle, everything has its proper function. Plants grow and animals feel. Humans are distinct because they possess reason. Aristotle attempts to identify the highest end, the end that we pursue for its own sake and not for the sake of anything else. The human good – its highest end – will be 'an activity (*energeia*) of the soul in accordance with reason' (NE 1098a, trans. Crisp) and the best life will be one in which we exercise our distinctly human virtues.

Aristotle considers and dismisses the claim that pleasure is the highest end and focuses on two possibilities: the political life and the life of intellectual contemplation. At the end of the *Nicomachean Ethics* he concludes that contemplation of the divine is the highest end because of its self-sufficiency. The distinction between the liberal and servile arts emerges here. For Aristotle, human flourishing is possible only with leisure to pursue such ends. Artisans and slaves cannot be virtuous because they lack the leisure necessary to engage in activities that are valuable in themselves. Liberal arts – grammar, rhetoric, dialectic, geometry, arithmetic, music, and astronomy – are not useful, in the sense that they aim at knowledge for its own sake and have no straightforward application to other tasks. In contrast, servile arts such as carpentry, engineering, and accounting are part of vocational training.

Despite the importance of intellectual contemplation in ancient Greek thought, Greek ethics cannot be separated from the *polis*. Aristotle admires the political life and recognizes the importance of civic virtue, which also depends on leisure. Civic virtue cannot be achieved without respite from acquiring food and shelter. Moreover, responsible political participation requires reflection and communication, striving to move beyond one's own self-interested ends to an understanding of the good of the community. A society without leisure will have citizens who are poorly informed and apathetic, unable to govern themselves according to what is good.

The Romans largely followed Aristotle in maintaining the dominance of leisure over work: leisure or *otium* is pursued for its own sake, whereas the negation of leisure is *negotium*. Though Romans such as Cicero sometimes saw leisure primarily in terms of rest from the important business of governance, Seneca retains much of Aristotle's account. Reflecting in his essay *De Otio* (On Leisure) on the charges of impiety that led to Socrates' execution and Aristotle's flight from Athens, he argued that the wise man must choose a life of leisure over the political life because no state will tolerate him. The early stages of the rise of Christianity also preserved many aspects of the ancient conception of leisure. In the Gospels, Jesus says of the fowls of the air that 'They sow not, neither do they reap nor gather into barns; yet your Heavenly Father feedeth them. Are ye not much better than they?' (Matt. 6:26, KJV). St Augustine's *beata vita* (blessed life) is the contemplation of God. St Thomas Aquinas preserved many aspects of Aristotle's thought in advocating for the contemplative life (*vita contemplativa*) (Pieper, 1998).

Nonetheless, as the medieval period develops we see a shift away from the Aristotelian ideal of leisure. For Aristotle, work was a necessity best passed on to slaves, women, and artisans so that citizens could engage in the more valuable activity of theoretical reason. He would have found incomprehensible the monastic life with its rigid division of time and its valuation of physical labour, and the exhortation of the Benedictine Order to pray and work (*ora* and *laboura*).

In the late medieval period and early Renaissance we begin to witness a transformation in the understanding of contemplation and in how work is valued. The ideal of theoretical contemplation present in Aristotle and Aquinas is increasingly subordinated to instrumental and technocratic reasoning. The task is no longer to observe nature, but to reshape and control it. Roger Bacon's experimental method in optics and his view that scientific experimentation should be used for the good of the community anticipates Francis Bacon's conviction that science should transform nature and society so as to alleviate human misery. Bacon's *New Atlantis* sets out a utopian society founded on the application of science. The requirement in Thomas More's *Utopia* that everyone work in agriculture and the trades is distant from Plato's *Republic*, in which the labour of the artisan class provides the guardians with the leisure to pursue a specialized education that may enable them to contemplate the good.

Along with the shifts in thinking about the nature and purpose of contemplation, a fundamental change occurs in the attitude toward work. This occurs most starkly in the Protestant Reformation, especially in Calvinism (Weber, 2002). Martin Luther and John Calvin criticized the monastic life, which they identified with idleness, and found the Christian calling to rest in labour. As we reach the early modern period, we see the rise of the labour theory of value, with its origins in John Locke and its development by Adam Smith and David Ricardo. Locke claimed that we create value from nature by mixing it with our labour; Ricardo held that the value of a commodity is the amount of labour that goes into producing it.

By the twentieth century, the rejection of ancient ethics based on the objective end chosen for its own sake becomes personified in *Homo economicus* (economic man), the model of humans as self-interested, rational actors pursuing their subjectively defined ends. For *Homo economicus*, there is no objectively determined highest end and the ultimate arbitrator of value is the individual. The political function of leisure disappears in favour of the productive worker guided by bureaucratic and technocratic management.

The rise of the work society has alarmed many theorists, but the Aristotelian conception of leisure relies on a view of human nature and of the natural order that is no longer tenable: Aristotle saw us as having a distinct function of reason that distinguishes us from plants that grow and animals that move. Our end is the exercise of this intellectual function. Darwin's insight that human beings evolved through the gradual, random process of descent with modification calls into question Aristotle's account of the highest good of intellectual contemplation. It suggests the need for an account of value that is compatible with the contemporary scientific world-view.

Furthermore, Aristotle's social prejudices and limited understanding of the possibilities of labour pose an obstacle to applying his insights on leisure. Aristotle's conception of leisure rested on a society in which a minority were freed from necessity due to the labour of slaves and workers (and women) who performed onerous tasks so the minority could engage in politics and intellectual contemplation. John Dewey contended in *Democracy and Education* that the division between a life of labour and a life of leisure had its basis in a dualism between theory and practice that mirrored the division between citizens and slaves, workers, and women.

One way of salvaging Aristotle's insights on leisure once we reject his aristocratic hierarchies and his account of the highest end is to reflect more carefully on the value of work. Aristotle was correct to observe that much work is performed for the sake of something else and serves to stunt, rather than develop, human capacities. Nonetheless, it does not follow that work need be or should be opposed to leisure. Indeed, Plato's treatment of *technē* (craft or skill) attributes considerable knowledge to its practitioners – unlike the sophist, the physician, horse trainer, and smith at least know specific things Aristotle acknowledges the importance of theoretical understanding in some crafts (*technē*) such as medicine.

The Marxian tradition follows Hegel in emphasizing the value of work (Sayers, 2005). In the Hegelian tradition, work is chosen for its own sake and is fundamental to human nature. For Hegel, work distinguishes human beings from other animals. It does not simply aim to fulfil immediate needs, but involves a self-conscious transformation of the natural and the social world that forms people's personal and social identity. Work is not external or separate to us; rather, it is creative, involving intellectual activity as well as physical labour for self-realization. Through work, we dissolve barriers separating us from the natural world and forge relationships with other people.

The Marxian complaint is that under capitalism and scientific management people are alienated from their labour. One source of alienation is the degradation of work itself through the division of labour that reduces labour to a series of simple, repetitive tasks. Organizational hierarchies and compartmentalization further limit workers' autonomy, depriving them of the opportunity to develop and exercise skill and creativity. Moreover, capitalism deprives workers of the value of their labour by selling products for a profit. Labour is torn from the social processes that give it meaning and becomes another commodity to be bought and sold (Braverman, 1988).

The Marxian tradition helps us to see that labour's value depends on the opportunities for people to realize valuable purposes. Labour conflicts with leisure if economic necessity or authority imposes it on workers and if it is limited to mind-numbing routines. When people creatively work toward valuable ends, not merely for sustenance, labour becomes leisure. Marx believed that the gains in production through mechanization and the coming socialist revolution would lead to a world in which labour was no longer enslaved to necessity.

More modestly, in the liberal democratic tradition, Dewey advocated that education break down the division between liberal and vocational studies with the goal of transforming the workplace so as to better support human flourishing. He also revived the Aristotelian theme of leisure's role in civic virtue. For Dewey, education should lead to citizens capable of governing themselves, jointly striving to solve social problems through democratic discussion.

Today we share with Dewey the need to articulate a philosophy of leisure that overcomes the opposition between work and leisure and provides guidance for evaluating social institutions and the ideal of citizenship. To do this, we need to turn to ethics and political philosophy.

The ethics of leisure

Leisure raises central questions about the good life. Leisure is not reducible to free time or to the freedom to follow one's whims; rather, it arises when people undertake activities that are valuable for their own sake. But the question of what is valuable for its own sake raises contentious issues about the nature of value.

A theory of leisure needs to explain what grounds comparative judgements about the value of activities. On what basis can we justifiably say that one activity is better than another? One candidate for the basis of value is psychological hedonism. In *The Rationale of Reward*, Jeremy Bentham argued that the standard of value ultimately rests on individuals' experience of pleasure, infamously remarking that 'Prejudice apart, the game of push-pin is of equal value with the arts and sciences of music and poetry'. Since the individual is the ultimate arbitrator of value, there are no grounds for dispute with someone who sincerely prefers push-pin to poetry.

Bentham's position has influenced social scientists who strive to avoid controversial value judgements in their theories. Economists, for instance, often use subjective preference satisfaction as the basis of value. They refuse to address questions about whether some preferences are better but, rather, look for ways to evaluate aggregated preferences, holding that, all other things being equal, distributions in which more people are able to satisfy their preferences are better.

Philosophers of leisure should be uneasy with theories that base value entirely on what people happen to prefer. People's preferences have many sources, including faulty information and failures in reasoning. Preferences often conflict, and sometimes we act from preferences that we would rather not have. For example, many smokers would like to quit, but are unable to overcome their addiction. Furthermore, people socialized in oppressive circumstances often come to endorse 'adaptive preferences' in which they come to prefer oppressive social roles. For example, feminists have drawn attention to how women in patriarchal societies often come to accept gender roles in which they take a subordinate place in the family and even tolerate physical and psychological abuse.

Beyond concerns about the weight we should give to the mere fact that people prefer some things over others, many of us are confident that some preferences are better than others. In *Utilitarianism*, John Stuart Mill responded to Bentham that his version of psychological hedonism ignores a distinction between 'higher' and 'lower' pleasures: pleasures that require the intellect and the imagination have more value for human beings than do mere bodily pleasures. A life devoted to passive consumption of prime-time television is inferior to a life of scientific collaboration. John Rawls develops Mill's insight in what he calls the 'Aristotelian Principle', which maintains that human beings receive the most enjoyment through activities sufficiently complex and challenging to allow them to realize their capacities (Rawls, 1999).

Mill and Rawls are committed to a moral theory called perfectionism that urges people to strive toward human excellence by developing their talents. Perfectionism has its roots in the thought of Plato and Aristotle and its advocates include philosophers as diverse as Spinoza, Kant, Hegel, Marx, Nietzsche, and T.H. Green. Leisure demands freedom to develop the talents or faculties that allow the pursuit of intrinsically good activities that contribute to human flourishing. Perfectionism mandates that we should seek not mere happiness, but human excellence.

Though perfectionist views are widely shared, it is challenging to specify exactly what enables us to judge some activities as being better than others. Ancient Greek ethics relied on an account of human nature that specified objectively good ends. Contemporary biology does not see species as aiming at an objective good; instead, the good of an organism is based on random mutation and selection in a particular environment. This raises an obstacle to the attempt to base morality on human nature and to arguments that there is a best life toward which we should all strive. Theorists who want to base their account of the good life on human nature need to explain how this is possible.

In his response to Bentham, John Stuart Mill followed David Hume in 'The Standard of Taste' in holding that we should appeal to a 'competent judge' who has experienced the activities under consideration. Mill believed that human beings, if educated so that their capacity for enjoyment is not stunted, would be naturally inclined to prefer some activities over others. Some contemporary perfectionists have attempted to ground their views on an account of human nature (Hurka, 1996). Others have argued that some things possess objective value independent of people's recognizing this (Parfit, 1986).

Philosophers of leisure are likely to find virtue ethics, with its roots in ancient philosophy, congenial. Virtue ethics contrasts with approaches to ethics that emphasize rules, decision-procedures, or the weighing of actions to determine how much good they promote. Instead, it enquires into the habits or dispositions that we should cultivate so as to identify and pursue activities of value. It emphasizes the development of moral reasoning, imagination, and judgement. Also, virtue ethics emphasizes the importance of exercising the virtues. It sees ethics not simply as a set of rules for acting rightly or achieving good ends, but also as stressing the value of activity for its own sake.

Philosophers of leisure are not only interested in abstract questions of value. Philosophy of leisure also has many applications in applied ethics. If we agree that some activities are better than others, philosophers of leisure should examine and evaluate particular activities and practices. The examination of the good life is incomplete if it fails to ask how people spend their lives.

First, philosophers of leisure needs to ask what makes an activity valuable for its own sake. Though we are convinced that some activities are better than others, what is it that gives them value? Rawls and other perfectionists have noted that the most rewarding activities have a level of complexity and challenge, but much more needs to be said. What sorts of complexity are best? What should we conclude about the value of hunting and of competitive sports, including combat sports and extreme sports with a high risk of injury? What should we think of intoxication when socializing with others, a practice that is not only widespread, but endorsed by luminaries such as Socrates, Hume, and Kant? How has technology transformed leisure? Detailed descriptions and interpretations of leisure activities and their value for participants are needed. Philosophers need to explore the empirical literature on recreation and psychological studies, including positive psychology (Csíkszentmihályi, 1996).

Second, philosophers of leisure should ask about the relations people should cultivate. Human beings are social animals, and few, if any, activities occur in isolation. Some do. For example, to read *Anna Karenina* alone with a glass of Cabernet Sauvignon is to participate in literary and viniculture traditions. However, most of our activities occur with friends, family, and co-workers, so philosophy of leisure overlaps with the philosophies of love, sex, and work. What sorts of relations should we cultivate and how should we sustain them?

Careful consideration should be given to how leisure activities structure human relationships, as well as relationships with other animals and the natural environment. What, for example, should we think about hierarchical divisions in martial arts and team sports, the relationship between coaches and athletes, or the role of family members in encouraging leisure activities? What do the insights of feminist ethics and epistemology reveal about the role of leisure in reinforcing and reifying gender roles? Is the rise of online socialization on Facebook and Twitter to be celebrated or deplored? These questions demand careful study if they are to be answered with the nuance required.

Leisure and politics

The philosophy of leisure also has implications for the design of political institutions, including schools and universities. The Universal Declaration of Human Rights states that 'Everyone has the right to rest and leisure, including reasonable limitation of working hours and periodic holidays with pay' (Article 24). Since rights entail duties, this suggests that a just society must provide opportunities for leisure. The inclusion of leisure as a human right is sometimes disputed on the grounds that it lacks the importance and urgency of more fundamental rights such as life, liberty, security of person, and freedom from slavery and torture.

The objection that leisure lacks the level of importance to qualify as a human right is mistaken if it is essential for human flourishing. Though rights that protect us from physical violence and guarantee us with food and work may seem more basic, a life without leisure is not a good life. Though stability and the provision of sufficient resources are preconditions to leisure, this does not undermine the conviction that all humans should enjoy freedom from necessity in order to develop their talents.

In fact, leisure is more fundamental than it may appear. For instance, the right to participate politically depends on leisure. Leisure is necessary for civic virtue; without it, citizens will be unable to inform themselves about politics so that they can participate effectively. Moreover, political theorists in the civic republican tradition have argued that human development occurs through dialogue with fellow citizens. The mutual exchange of reasons and arguments allows us to clarify our values and to jointly rule each other as political equals. This exchange is fundamental to what it means to be a human being.

Nonetheless, granting leisure the status of a human right could unduly impose duties on people to guarantee other people's leisure. Perfectionism as a political philosophy maintains that political authorities are responsible for establishing policies and institutions that lead to human flourishing (Wall, 2007). It is possible to be a moral perfectionist and reject political perfectionism on the grounds that it conflicts with the liberal position that governments should be as neutral as possible toward people's substantial views about the good life. The role of the government is not to develop people's excellence; rather, it should provide a background of laws that allow people to decide for themselves how they wish to live their lives.

This liberal concern can be assuaged by noting that the right to leisure is a right to conditions that enable leisure. It is one of the 'economic, social and cultural rights' encompassed by Article 22 of the Universal Declaration of Human Rights 'indispensable for [the dignity of every member of society] for the full development of his [*sic*] personality'. Since the corresponding duty to respond to human rights falls predominantly on social and political institutions, governments must provide an environment that will enable people to pursue perfectionist ends.

But perfectionist ends vary more widely than basic human needs. Some people may want to study philosophy, while others may prefer to scale mountains. Some seek spiritual enlightenment; still others aim at physical perfection. People might be willing to delegate these sorts of decisions to a democratic procedure which funnels resources to the projects of diverse groups. This may be true, but do they have an obligation to do so? After all, they may object to some pursuits on moral, aesthetic, or other grounds and prefer not to take any part in them. For instance, need all members the public support the leisure pursuits of big game hunters, or the art of Andres Serrano? But if not, why should they be required to support publicly funded philosophy, ballet, or Olympic sports?

The human right to leisure needn't guarantee that everyone pursue any form of leisure. Rather, it is committed to guaranteeing sufficient opportunities to enjoy a reasonably broad set of leisure activities. Amartya Sen and Martha Nussbaum's capabilities approach may be congenial to the philosophy of leisure, since a capability is a real opportunity to do things that one values (Nussbaum, 2011; Sen, 2011). A plausible set of government obligations with regard to leisure may be fairly general, including the guarantee of labour rights that limit working hours, provide sufficiently high salaries, and conditions congenial to human flourishing.

Considerations of distributive justice are also pertinent. Leisure opportunities are unevenly distributed, with parts of the population condemned to unrelenting drudgery for survival. Philosophers of leisure need to address how social and economic inequalities deprive many people of the opportunity to develop their faculties and engage in intrinsically valuable activities. They will also ask about the fair distribution of public facilities and opportunities for recreation.

Attention to leisure in politics may have its most direct impact on education. When we recall the origins of leisure in *skholē* (school), we should recognize that people will not be able to use their free time in a valuable way if they don't develop from an early age the capacity to do so. Education plays a major role, since youth must develop reasoning skills that allow them to discriminate between activities and to enjoy difficult pleasures. Philosophy of leisure is at odds with prominent trends that emphasize the role of education in promoting human capital. It also condemns approaches to education that cultivate blind loyalty to the community. In their place, it endorses a system of education that encourages children to develop into citizens who can freely choose valuable activities in their leisure time. Philosophers of leisure need to reflect on the appropriate content for education at different stages and the methods and practices most likely to help children to acquire dispositions that will make them fit for leisure.

As with moral philosophy, political philosophers of leisure should turn their attention to concrete observations about how social and political institutions promote or hinder human flourishing. Political philosophers concerned with leisure would consider urban planning and architecture to be major social and political topics. They would ask how our environment, including buildings and landscape, contribute to our ability to freely pursue intrinsically valuable ends. They would discuss not merely how leisure is an individual activity, engaged in in isolation, but how it impacts on and is impacted upon by the larger world.

Finally, philosophers would join sociologists, labour economists, and psychologists in the study of work. How can we transform more work into leisure? How can we reduce the number of hours devoted to necessary tasks? Too much of our labour feeds conspicuous consumption, the creation of need, and the futile attempt to keep up with the Joneses. Attention to the philosophy of leisure reorients political thought toward questions of the good life and asks how we can create societies where equal citizens are free to devote as much of their time as possible to the pursuit of intrinsically valuable ends.

Note

1   I am grateful to Angela Coventry, Brian Elliott, and David Weber for comments on a draft of this chapter.

References

Braverman, H. (1988) *Labour and Monopoly Capital: The Degradation of Work in the Twentieth Century*. New York: Monthly Review Press.

Csíkszentmihályi, M. (1996) *Finding Flow: The Psychology of Engagement with Everyday Life*. New York: Basic Books.

Huizinga, J. (1950) *Homo Ludens: A Study of the Play-Element in Culture*. Boston, MA: The Beacon Press.

Hurka, T. (1996) *Perfectionism*. New York: Oxford University Press.

LaFargue, P. (1883) *The Right to Be Lazy*. (C. Ker, trans.) Chicago: Charles H. Kerr Publishing Company.

Nussbaum, M. (2011) *Creating Capabilities: The Human Development Approach*. Cambridge, MA: Harvard University Press.

Parfit, D. (1986) *Reasons and Persons*. New York: Oxford University Press.

Pieper, J. (1998) *Leisure: The Basis of Culture*. South Bend, IN: St. Augustine's Press.

Rawls, J. (1999) *A Theory of Justice,* (rev. ed.) Cambridge, MA: Harvard University Press.

Russell, B. (2004) *In Praise of Idleness and Other Essays*. London: Routledge.

Sayers, S. (2005) 'Why Work? Marx and Human Nature', *Science & Society* 69 (4) 606–616.

Sen, A. (2011) *The Idea of Justice*. Cambridge, MA: Belknap Press of Harvard University Press.

Wall, S. (2007) *Liberalism, Perfectionism, and Restraint*. New York: Cambridge University Press.

Weber, M. (2002) *The Protestant Ethic and the Spirit of Capitalism and Other Writings*. (P. Baehr and G.C. Wells, trans.). Harmondsworth: Penguin. (Original work published 1904–5).

2

THE MAKING OF MODERN LEISURE: THE BRITISH EXPERIENCE *c.*1850 TO *c.*1960

Dave Russell

Historical periods are always intellectual constructs rather than objective categories. The period considered here contains numerous sub-divisions, and might easily have been extended, certainly at its beginning, or shortened; the years from about 1870 to 1950 found the culture under discussion at its most pronounced. No fundamental discontinuities are posed between the 'traditional'/'pre-industrial' age that preceded it or the 'post-modern'/'post-industrial' one that followed. Industrialization did not create leisure as a new category, with a buoyant middle-class commercial leisure culture clearly identifiable in eighteenth-century Britain and a more popularly rooted one emerging from around the 1780s (Burke, 1995; Borsay, 2006: 8–16; Harvey, 2004). Similarly, many elements of the twenty-first-century leisure landscape would have been broadly familiar in the nineteenth century. Overall, however, the century or so from 1850 – best viewed, arguably, as a very long Victorian age – has a powerful degree of coherence. Driven by a mature industrial economy and continuing urbanization, the middle years of the nineteenth century ushered in a dynamic new phase in the history of leisure, defined by a set of trajectories in which all sectors of leisure provision, and not least the commercial one, grew dramatically: patterns of leisure activity became ever more national and marked by a passage from 'class' to 'mass'; were structured by the rhythms of urban and industrial rationality rather than by rural ritual and task orientation; and became ever more privatized. The culture thus created was far from exhausted in the 1960s, but the social, economic and cultural changes of that decade undeniably pointed to a far more fragmented and increasingly globalized leisure world (Marwick, 1998).

The practical demands imposed by an essay of this type have resulted in much compression. The term 'leisure' is used to denote a wide range of activities carried out in time free from work and domestic and civil obligations, although this common-sense usage is accompanied by an acute awareness that leisure needs to be defined and treated as something of distinctive value rather than merely what remains when other apparently more central concerns have been considered (Borsay, 2006: 1–8). Personal expertise and the need for a manageable focus mean that the 'British experience' explored here is largely, although not exclusively, that of the northern English industrial working class. Once again, this is accompanied by a full acceptance of the need to study other geographical areas and other social classes. Above all, virtually every confident generalization disguises counter-trends and exceptions. The falls in working hours and rises in real wages documented below were always dependent on occupation, age, gender, health and innumerable other variables. Regional differences could be striking, even within national leisure industries – cinema admissions in Scotland and northern England in the 1950s, for example, were double those in East Anglia and the south-west of England – and family cultures could impact hugely on individual leisure careers. Harry Mortimer, a leading twentieth-century brass bandsman, recalled of his child-hood music making, 'I don't think that I was even asked if I wanted to learn – it was as much a matter of course as cleaning my teeth or polishing my boots' (Kynaston, 2009: 199; Russell, 1997b: 221). Beneath its general contours, the history of leisure holds innumerable other compelling narratives.

Demand and supply

Writing the history of leisure can feel akin to an exercise in total history, with virtually every aspect of human life impinging in some way on its production or consumption. A list of the factors underpinning the expansion of leisure time and activity would certainly include population growth, generally, and the expansion of urban centres, specifically; the role of organized religion as patron and, in contradistinction, the relative social libera-tion that resulted from long-term secularization; the improvements in housing quality that rendered the home an ever richer site of entertainment; and the technological developments that provided both an infrastructure – especially in terms of rail and road transport – essen-tial to a modern leisure culture and its specific tools such as cinematographic equipment, wireless and television. As evidenced by publications as disparate as *The Lady Cyclist* (1895) and *Model Railway Constructor* (1934), improvements in printing technology, coupled with rising functional literacy, were similarly important.

Of greatest importance, however, was the combined impact of an increase in, and regu-larization of, non-work time, and a rise in real incomes. In 1850, the 'normal' working week for the labouring classes in regular employment saw attendance from 6 a.m. to 6 p.m., punctuated by a two-hour lunch-break, from Monday to Saturday. There were innumerable exceptions, with skilled craftsmen and artisans in particular utilizing their greater levels of control over the means of production to enjoy shorter days, a 'weekend' created by observa-tion of the customary holiday of 'Saint Monday' and a flexibility which allowed for a task-orientated approach whereby exceptionally long hours were worked in order to generate a significant period of free time (Reid, 1976 and 1996). Others, notably the employees of Yorkshire woollen and worsted mills, faced considerably longer hours (Bienefeld, 1972: 8–81). Between *c.*1850 and 1961 the duration of the mean normal week fell by 30% from 60 to 42 hours (Reid, 2000: 751; *Social Trends*, 1971: 64). Although overtime and other practices meant that actual hours worked were always higher than these figures suggest, the secular trend was clear and its cumulative effect was dramatic. By 1920, an employee might expect to work, effectively, one full day a week less than his or her 1850 counterpart, and two by the early 1960s.

These reductions came in four concentrated bursts in the early 1870s (establishing the 54-hour week); immediately after the First (48 hours) and Second World Wars (44 hours) and between 1960 and 1966 (40 hours). In each case an unusually buoyant economy, coupled with low unemployment rates, provided the optimal context for the collective bargaining, backed by the threat or actuality of strike action, which proved to be the critical engine for change. Trade union battles for shorter hours were ultimately concerned with guaranteeing regularity of employment, by controlling either the labour supply or output (Bienefeld, 1972:

216–26). Nevertheless, workers undeniably prized their leisure time and, as it increased over the period, saw the altered balance between work and free time as increasingly important to their lives and those of their families.

Although Saint Monday survived for decades in some areas, Saturday became the preferred location for popular leisure by the 1870s. The spread of the Saturday half-holiday, initially stimulated by the 2 p.m. finish imposed upon textile mills by the 1850 Factory Act, actually saw many workers exchange a full day's 'play' on Monday for a half-day on Saturday. Fines, threats of dismissal and even lock-outs were used to force the change (and the parallel process of outlawing the older task orientation) in some contexts but workers were often willing to exchange a longer customary holiday, always potentially at risk, with a shorter guaranteed one (Reid, 1976: 1996). Saturday afternoons became the focus for sport, as evidenced by the dramatic emergence of popular team sports from the 1870s, its evenings focus for an ever-widening range of commercial activity. By the early 1920s, Saturday takings at the Bradford Alhambra regularly represented over 30% of the variety theatre's entire weekly income.

In the mid-nineteenth century, longer periods of working-class holiday-making remained highly subject to regional and occupational variation, although Christmas, Easter and Whitsun generally saw their highest concentration. Over the course of the nineteenth century, particularly in the textile communities of Lancashire, where regularity of employment and a 'family' wage boosted by higher levels of female labour proved crucial stimuli, the traditional annual wakes week (essentially a parish feast) saw significant sections of the working population migrate to the seaside, their holidays funded by weekly payments into savings clubs that were testament to the existence of a distinctive and pleasure-tinged form of working-class self-help (Poole, 1983; Walton, 1981). A small number of employers did provide paid holidays, but it was in the inter-war period, with the labour movement again at the fore, that the concept, as expressed in both statutory provision such as the 1938 Holidays with Pay Act and the (more important) voluntary collective agreements, became increasingly accepted within British society. Approximately one million manual workers had some form of paid holiday in 1920, four million by 1939 and at least ten million by 1945; by the 1950s it was effectively a universal entitlement (Jones, 1986: 17–20; Barton, 2005: 107–97; *Social Trends*, 1971: 78).

Increased free time was of limited value unless accompanied by a growth in personal wealth sufficient to allow some level of expenditure on non-essential items, and the second half of the nineteenth century, and especially its final two decades, proved critical in this regard for large numbers of the British working class. Falling basic commodity prices caused real wages for workers to rise by about 80% between 1850 and 1900, with approximately half of that increase falling in the last twenty years of the century (Bienefeld, 1972: 184; Benson, 1994: 12). Despite its economic vicissitudes, a 16% rise in real wages has been suggested for the inter-war period, while rates approximately doubled between 1951 and 1974, with 1959 to 1964 alone seeing a 19% increase (Jones, 1986: 13; Bernstein, 2004: 308). Initially, new forms of commercial leisure were not always sufficiently advanced to benefit from this situation, with rises in the mid-1870s effectively funding instead the highest-ever recorded levels of drink consumption in England and Wales (Dingle, 1972: 618). However, even in periods of stagnating or falling incomes, such as the 1900s, workers came to see some expenditure on leisure as essential and showed a willingness to budget accordingly, trading one outgoing against others if necessary. This essentially positive account of working-class living standards must be accompanied by a cautionary note. The opulent worker sometimes encountered in critiques from both the political right and left was largely a mythical figure, and 'cheap luxuries', to use George Orwell's phrase – his list in 1937 included 'the movies, the radio, strong tea and the football pools' – typified the popular leisure experience; poverty prevented a significant minority from aspiring even to many of these (Orwell, 1962: 80–1; Davies, 1992).

While these limits must be acknowledged, the changed socio-economic context allowed for a previously unimaginable expansion of popular leisure provision, located essentially within the respective commercial, voluntary/community and state sectors (Hill, 2002). Distinctions between them were not always neat, with the public house, for example, serving as a crucial staple of commercial leisure in its own right and a nursery for other forms (most notably the music hall), but also a headquarters for numberless voluntary organizations, especially sporting ones. Accepting the broad categorization, however, the state sector was undoubtedly the smallest. At national level its function largely involved the enabling of local state provision, with the 1845 Museums Act and 1850 Public Libraries Act notably important early examples (Cunningham, 1980: 104–5). Wider commercial considerations meant that resort towns were more alert than most to the potential of rates-supported amenities, although a small number of industrial communities showed great inventiveness. In the 1910s and 1920s, the Dunbartonshire town of Kirkintilloch ran its own cine-variety shows and used the profits to organize galas, lectures and operatic evenings as well as a clothing bank (Brown, 1996: 213).

The commercial leisure world undoubtedly greets the historian with far greater force. English professional football was in its infancy in the 1880s, with the 12-strong Football League attracting about 600,000 supporters in its inaugural 1888–89 season. By 1948–49, albeit in a post-war setting marked by ravenous consumption of public entertainment, its 88 clubs drew a combined attendance of 41.2 million. By the late 1930s, perhaps 100 million people attended Britain's dance halls annually and some 38 million its greyhound stadia, while cinema reached a peak *weekly* average attendance of 31.4 million in 1946 (Clapson, 1992: 146; Cook and Stevenson, 1996: 135; Russell, 1997a: 131; Nott, 2002: 158). It was, however, the vast and complex voluntary sector that probably provided the largest element of daily leisure life. Its more visible, formal manifestations grew collectively over the period, although the rhythms of individual sectors were distinctive. Brass banding reached its peak around 1900 and declined from that point, whereas football clubs continued to grow in number; 1,000 largely amateur clubs were affiliated to the Football Association in 1888 and by 1937 that number had risen to 37,000 (Russell, 1997a: 30, 77). The Boy Scout movement founded by Baden-Powell in 1907 had 152,000 members by 1913 and 438,000 by 1938, while the Boys' Brigade, originating in Glasgow in 1883, had 158,000 adherents by that stage. In the 1950s the organization generated a football league comprising some 200 teams in its home city, exemplifying how voluntary leisure institutions could generate their own creative dynamic (Springhall, 1977: 138–9; Taylor, 2008: 130.) Finally, impossible to measure but inordinately important, lay the dense networks of informal voluntary leisure activities ('community leisure' might better capture such activity) carried on above all in the street – 'the new commons of the industrial poor' – until the large-scale arrival of cars from the 1950s (Bailey, 1978: 15). Gossiping, gambling, parading, playing games and dancing – hundreds performed the Charleston in a Newcastle street in 1927 – were amongst the numerous pastimes open to even the poorest members of society, often enjoyed in their own right and not merely as a substitute for more expensive alternatives (Davies, 1992: 109–67; Reid, 2000: 762).

Experiencing leisure

Urban settings generally provided a far fuller leisure life than did rural ones, which were simply unable to match the facilities available in larger communities (Cunningham, 1990: 302–5). For all the importance of location, however, age, class and gender were the key determinants of how and with whom individuals enjoyed themselves. Occupying a moment in the life cycle when disposable incomes were likely to be the highest, personal obligations the lowest and physical prowess the best developed, younger adults were ideally placed to enjoy the benefits of much existing provision, and were invariably the target of the new. The extent to which they, or other age groups, could benefit depended nevertheless upon the other two variables. At its crudest, class equated to money; the cheapest membership of a southern English Edwardian shooting syndicate was approximately equivalent to the annual income of a highly skilled artisan (Lowerson, 1993: 39). More subtly, leisure provided a form of cultural capital the deployment of which spoke eloquently of status, achievement and aspiration. Class was thereby performed in the leisure arena as almost nowhere else, inevitably resulting in the erection and maintenance of suitable social barriers. Seaside towns usually exhibited a clear 'social tone', often flowing from initial landholding structures but consciously reinforced and sometimes determined by accommodation prices, provision of civic amenities and the choice of visitor encouraged (Walton, 1983: 187–215). Sports stadia, music halls and theatres were marked by pricing differentials designed to minimize too promiscuous a degree of cross-class social intercourse, and even in the rather more democratic commercial entertainment sector of the 1920s and onwards, pricing policies created hierarchies within the ranks of local cinemas and dance halls. While financial barriers usually sufficed for the purposes of social zoning in the commercial sector, voluntary societies often sought recourse in formal regulations. Nineteenth-century sport was deeply veined by class, as athletics and rowing clubs sought to exclude artisans and labourers via membership clauses, gentlemen 'amateur' cricketers to distinguish themselves from professional 'players' by changing in separate dressing rooms and entering the field of play by separate gates, and amateur footballers to fight professionalism with bans, expulsions and constant changes to competition rules; such social apartheid was especially deeply entrenched and long lasting in English Rugby Union (Holt, 1989: 74–134; Collins, 2009: 96–129). 'Subordinate' social groups also operated exclusionary strategies, albeit of a less formal nature. Many public houses, dance halls and even cinemas were made safe from 'outside' interference by dint of their location in places where the bourgeoisie rarely trod, but, in more mixed territories, the construction of a distinctly plebeian social tone often served as an effective social filter.

A focus on inter-class divisions should not obscure those present within classes. The complexities of intra-working-class status hierarchies were highly visible within public houses; in Edwardian Salford 'workers other than craftsmen would be frozen or flatly ordered out of those rooms in which journeymen gathered … "he's only a tap-room man" stood as a common slur' (Roberts, 1973: 19). Neither should it disguise the fact that some activities drew individuals from a very wide social spectrum into genuinely close partnership: this was perhaps especially the case in forms of 'serious' leisure in which the erection of arbitrary barriers could prove highly counter-productive. Large provincial choral societies certainly absorbed talent wherever they found it, consequently exhibiting a social composition spanning the skilled working to the upper middle class; the fact that most choral singers enjoyed the shared thread of respectability that came from initial training in church and chapel choirs was crucial in facilitating this particular example of pan-class mixing (Russell, 1997b: 250–58). Class barriers were probably crossed most frequently, however, through adherence to cultures that could be shared without close contact. As the very need for social zoning indeed demonstrates, many leisure activities did not map directly onto social class, even though different social groups might encounter or 'use' them in distinctive ways. Serious literature, opera and Shakespeare had many working-class enthusiasts; variety theatres, cinemas and dance music many within the middle class; and the growth of the gramophone, radio and television certainly created at least the potential for the existence of common cultures (Rose, 2001). Leisure reproduced and reinforced the structures of class, but class in modern Britain was rarely found in neatly sealed containers.

Much of the academic history of leisure has been about men precisely because they had the greatest access to it; not for nothing was leisure often referred to as the 'bread-winner's reward'. Even to the 1960s and beyond, women's leisure was still often distinctively structured as private, informal, prone to interruption, and to marry domestic activity such as sewing and cooking with recreational interests (Langhamer, 2000). Lower levels of participation in the full-time labour force, lower wage levels and an extremely limited sense of entitlement to what was earned meant that women invariably had less money for leisure than did males. Their free time was similarly limited by domestic obligation and the social policing that dictated appropriate behaviour for the nation's mothers, helpmates and moral guardians. In early twentieth-century Salford, some dance halls closed on Friday nights on the assumption that young female patrons would be assisting with family chores (Roberts, 1973: 37, 232). Even apparently 'improving' recreation could be suspect. At the beginning of the period, violin playing was discouraged in many middle-class households because the facial distortions that occurred during performance were deemed to 'unsex' the performer, while women's involvement in sport was often restricted by disabling assumptions about the limits to their physical capacities and the danger posed to their reproductive systems (Hargreaves, 1994; Gillett, 2000: 77–108). It must be acknowledged that women neither necessarily resented the leisure culture that they were allotted nor fought against it. Women were indeed often central to their own policing, at the heart of the numerous philanthropic societies seeking to offer moral guidance; providing some of the most vocal medical proponents of conservative exercise regimes; and, as mothers, friends and relations, often forming the chorus that reproduced domestic ideology in daily life. When the amateur racing cyclist Beryl Burton sought to return to competitive sport after giving birth in 1956, it was her mother-in-law who hinted strongly at the 'bad mothering' underpinning Burton's decision to reduce time spent in child-care by taking her infant daughter to training sessions (Russell, 2008: 798).

Women's opportunities for leisure undeniably increased significantly across the century from 1850, albeit on a particular set of terms. Possibilities were probably always greatest for unmarried women in their teens and early twenties, a vital moment of relative freedom in the female leisure life cycle. Middle-class women were, arguably, the major beneficiaries, joining choirs, tennis and golf clubs and much else on a far greater scale than did their working-class sisters, while within the commercial sector institutions seen as utterly beyond the pale for middle-class women (and many working-class ones) were heavily sanitized in order to reap the enormous economic dividend that came from this immense surplus army of leisure and the aura of respectability that it conferred. 'Music hall' evolved into 'variety' over the late nineteenth and early twentieth centuries, with national syndicates building ever more luxurious and grandiosely decorated premises in which drink moved from the auditorium to less visible and avoidable bars and where performances were monitored for moral suitability (Bailey, 1986; Kift, 1996). Following the opening of the continental European-style Hammersmith Palais in 1919, the popular dance hall, very much a hidden feature of earlier urban life, emerged to become one of Britain's key leisure forms (Nott, 2002: 148–67). Even the public house attracted some middle-class women in the inter-war period as large, hotel-style premises began to emerge along arterial roads (Jennings, 2007: 205–7, 224–6).

The politics of leisure

The whole field of leisure, not just that relating to women, was a major site of cultural contestation, with the habits of young, working-class males invariably deemed particularly problematic (Beaven, 2005; Tebbutt, 2012). The resultant conflict and debate was always heavily flavoured by class, but cannot be entirely reduced to it. Many of the socialist and religious communities within the working class were as dispirited by popular recreation as any critic from higher up the social scale (Jones, 1986: 133–63; Waters, 1990: 97–130). Within the middle class, some enthusiastically embraced the very pleasures, such as horse-racing, that their peers abhorred (Huggins, 2000: 68–87). Neither can this issue be seen as a straightforward opposition between the 'roughs' and 'respectables' within each class. As Peter Bailey has shown of working-class culture, a single individual could move swiftly and comfortably between temperate rationality and excessive conviviality as situation and strategy demanded (Bailey, 1979).

Although activities including Sabbath abuse, popular blood sports, gambling and a general unease about the carnivalesque nature of much popular leisure drew extensive condemnation, drink was always the principal concern, both a cause of genuine and sometimes valid anxiety and the standard tool of social analysis through which working-class life was so often viewed (Harrison, 1994). Although the drink question remained important in the twentieth century, especially in nonconformist strongholds, a combination of factors, including the licensing controls introduced in the First World War, the increased options for popular expenditure and improved housing conditions, saw significant shifts in drinking culture – convictions for drunkenness, a useful indication of trends, fell in England and Wales from 209,000 in 1903 to 52,000 by 1939 – and concerns receded somewhat (Chaplin, 2009: 77). If the twentieth century had a central leisure 'problem' it was the supposed threat of the growing mass media, especially the electronic forms of cinema, radio and television, and it was often expressed in the guise of anti-Americanism. American popular culture was certainly criticized in its own right, not least in the challenge that it was believed to offer to social and racial hierarchies. Hollywood films of the inter-war years worried some because of their frequent celebratory and democratic focus on ordinary people, while, when faced with rock 'n' roll in 1956, the *Daily Mail* wondered 'whether this is the negro's revenge' (Pearson, 1983: 24). The sheer scale of America's incursion into British culture made it an inevitable enemy, but it undoubtedly stood proxy for wider fears about mass communications more generally, in which passive and impressionable audiences were imagined as falling prey to ideological persuasion from powerful technologies that penetrated deeply into people's daily lives (Nott, 2002: 209–11; Glancy, 2006).

Concerns about the disruptive potential of leisure led to a degree of state intervention (Borsay, 2006: 42–73). Although a limited body of repressive or restrictive parliamentary legislation was passed, central government often preferred to establish control at one remove, a tactic increasingly deployed in the twentieth century. Both direct state control and free market liberalism were rejected in favour of public bodies such as the British Board of Film Censors (1912) and the British Broadcasting Corporation (BBC) (1927), bound to the government by numerous subtle linkages; the requirement that parliament had to renew the BBC's licence fee every ten years was an effective disciplinary tool. Where these structures proved inadequate, powerful networks of informal influence were invoked, as when, in 1938, a newsreel made by the American Paramount Company that was critical of appeasement was withdrawn after combined pressure from the British government and the American Embassy (Aldgate, 1979: 84–90; Scannell and Cardiff, 1991: 23–71). Much of the legislation directed at popular leisure and much of the implementation of national regulation took place at a local level. In Scotland, the 1892 Burgh Police Act, which survived in part until as late as 1976, allowed local councils to intervene, if they chose, against 'every major and minor leisure activity imaginable' (Brown, 1996: 218–23).

For much of the period, however, the attempt to control or reform popular leisure often came from within civil society in the form of the 'rational recreation' that had originated as a self-regulatory mechanism within a late eighteenth-century middle class that was nervous about its usage of new leisure time. From the 1820s and 1830s, the virtues of useful and improving pastimes were increasingly extolled to a wider audience (Bailey, 1978). Middle-class sponsorship of popular rational recreation was driven by guilt, an urge for social control and a shrewd understanding of the value of giving modest rewards in order to defend larger privileges, but also by a genuine desire to bestow cultural benefits which the working class appeared to have been denied. Although enthusiastic endorsements of its principles always far outweighed actual provision, its legacy was still extraordinarily rich, embracing for example national bodies such as the juvenile temperance organization the Band of Hope (1849) and the Club and Institute Union (1862), the building of major public parks and the founding of the most modest of mutual improvement societies. Although a diminishing force by 1914, it was still frequently invoked even in the mid-twentieth century, and its wider ambitions for cultural diffusion can be clearly glimpsed in the philosophy of the early BBC (Scannell and Cardiff, 1991: 7–10).

Attempts to control and reform popular leisure met with only the most qualified success. Legislation, backed by the intervention of the police and even the military, could be effective. Large set-piece events such as street football matches or fairs were probably the easiest to remove, and certain activities such as bull baiting and dog fighting were undoubtedly reduced, although never eradicated (Delves, 1981: 90–1). However, local elites were not always willing to endorse such suppression – indeed, they sometimes continued patronage of controversial events – and the resources available to the state were simply never large enough to allow for the truly effective monitoring of daily leisure life. The police, as the result partly of corruption but mainly of simple expediency, often colluded with publicans and street bookmakers over misdemeanours, taking sufficient action to pacify vocal critics but not so much as to alienate substantial sections of the working-class community or overload the legal system. Significantly, Scotland's Burgh Police Act was invoked less frequently from the 1930s, not least because courts became cluttered with minor prosecutions and appeals (Brown, 1996: 223). Self-surveillance within communities by active reformers and institutions such as the local press proved a valuable reinforcement to police operations (Croll, 2000). Government action against the drink trade was often limited and hesitant, checked by the trade's political and economic power and a reluctance to damage tax revenues, while, at a local level, councils were frequently unwilling to attack commercial popular entertainments that, while offending moral reformers, represented legitimate business interests (Kift, 1996: 181). Occasionally, legislation inadvertently stimulated the very problem that it sought to eradicate. The Scottish magistracy's opposition to the sub-division of public houses into small bars led to the creation of premises that were easily observed, but denuded of the privacy required by many female and skilled working-class male patrons. Pubs thereby

22

tended to become the territory of more hardened drinkers, with the probable result that 'aggression and drunkenness became worse' (Fraser, 1990. 243). The sections of the 1960 Betting and Gaming Act that were designed to prevent Britain becoming 'a casino country' left loopholes allowing over 1,000 gaming clubs and 3,000 bingo clubs to exist in England and Wales by 1967.

The impact of rational recreation was also less dramatic than its admittedly often Panglossian advocates desired or claimed. Where class interests coincided, it could be highly effective. The 'taming' of Whitsuntide in Victorian Oxfordshire, which turned several days of feasting strongly flavoured by alcohol and blood sports into a one-day event combining moderate drinking (or none at all) with cricket, brass bands and all the fun of the fête, resulted from a sharing of agendas, if not ideologies, by local churches and working-class friendly societies (Howkins, 1973). Undoubtedly, many individuals did embrace rational recreational provision but they were often adept at enjoying or capturing the facilities offered while ignoring or resisting any accompanying ideological thrust. The history of the Club and Institute Union (CIU) is an exemplary case. Although its middle- and upper-class founders intended working men's clubs to be temperance-orientated gathering places where different social classes could meet over mutually improving activities, the CIU's liberal attitude to beer sales allowed the generation of sufficient income to allow the working-class membership to engineer a self-sustaining independence by the mid-1880s. Far from transcending class, the working men's club became one of the most closed and deeply embedded elements of working-class social life (Jackson, 1972: 40–71; Bailey, 1978: 106–23).

Working-class resistance to the ideological blandishments of social superiors (and of some social peers) is a reminder that, even if many workers would not have described or perceived their leisure experience in quite these terms, this apparently rather marginal and innocent area of life was shot through with political significance. The history of the CIU would suggest that popular leisure tended in a counter-hegemonic direction, and the cultural activities of organized labour and the left, the challenge to bourgeois respectability often posed from the popular stage and the possibilities for utopian fantasy opened up by fiction, film and television would offer support for such a position. However, a strong alternative case can be made. Leisure was never the opiate of the people, but it had at least the capacity to minimize the likelihood of significant challenges to the social and political status quo. The leisure arena was always a place of informal political education, with those arguing for a powerful popular imperialist and militarist sentiment within British life finding much sustenance for their case in the songs of the Victorian and Edwardian music hall, juvenile fiction, 1930s feature film and the manifestos of many uniformed youth movements (Mackenzie, 1986). Perhaps more importantly, it also had the potential to bring satisfactions and rewards to its consumers and participants, ranging from the small moments of relief and release that it frequently offered to a rather more substantial range of social, emotional and financial rewards. Achievements in the recreational sphere could confer considerable status within the wider social world; betting was never entirely a 'mug's game'; prize money was available to all manner of competitors in all manner of competitions; and Britain always possessed an army of part-time employees, from casual staff in public houses, dance halls and cafes to semi-professional sportsmen and club and music-hall entertainers, for whom leisure was an invaluable source of income. Leisure could certainly provide a powerful form of work discipline, with regular attendance at the workplace, and overtime working often essential to the servicing of recreational interests (Cross, 1993). It was, too, potentially a rival to working-class political and industrial organizations, challenging them for time, commitment and money and offering more rapid and usually more tangible reward (McKibbin, 1984).

Such relationships between popular leisure and popular politics are, however, ultimately easier to assert than to demonstrate and it is appropriate to conclude not with speculation, no matter how well informed, but with an acknowledgement of an obvious but fundamental truth. Throughout the period, leisure practices clearly mattered profoundly in the lives of ordinary people, allowing them, in Douglas Reid's words, to achieve or receive 'a massively expanded realm of choice about how to develop their humanity outside the necessity of making a living' (Reid, 2000: 807). How they did that, and with what consequences, remains a subject of enormous historical significance.

References

Aldgate, A. (1979) *Cinema and History*. London: Scolar Press.

Bailey, P. (1978) *Leisure and Class in Victorian England. Rational Recreation and the Contest for Control, 1830–1885*. London: Routledge and Kegan Paul.

Bailey, P. (1979) '"Will the real Bill Banks, please stand up?". Toward a Role Analysis of Mid-Victorian Working-Class Respectability', *Journal of Social History* 12 (3) 336–53.

Bailey, P. (ed.) (1986) *Music Hall. The Business of Pleasure*. Milton Keynes: Open University Press.

Barton, S. (2005) *Working-Class Organisations and Popular Tourism, 1840–1870*. Manchester: Manchester University Press.

Beaven, B. (2005) *Leisure, Citizenship and Working-Class Men in Britain, 1850–1945*. Manchester: Manchester University Press.

Benson, J. (1994) *The Rise of a Consumer Society in Britain, 1880–1980*. London: Longman.

Bernstein, G. (2004) *The Myth of Decline. The Rise of Britain since 1945*. London: Pimlico.

Bienefeld, M.A. (1972) *Working Hours in British Industry. An Economic History*. London: Weidenfeld and Nicolson.

Borsay, P. (2006) *A History of Leisure*. Basingstoke: Palgrave Macmillan.

Brown, C. (1996) 'Popular Culture and the Continuing Struggle for Rational Recreation', in T. Devine and R. Finlay (eds) *Scotland in the Twentieth Century*. Edinburgh: Edinburgh University Press, 210–30.

Burke, P. (1995) 'The Invention of Leisure in Early Modern Europe', *Past and Present* 146: 136–50.

Chaplin, P. (2009) *Darts in England, 1900–1939. A Social History*. Manchester: Manchester University Press.

Clapson, M. (1992) *A Bit of a Flutter. Popular Gambling and English Society, c. 1823–1961*. Manchester: Manchester University Press.

Collins, T. (2009) *A Social History of English Rugby Union*. London: Routledge.

Cook, C. and Stevenson, J. (1996) *The Longman Companion to Britain since 1945*. London: Longman.

Croll, A. (2000) *Civilizing the Urban: Popular Culture and Public Space, Merthyr c.1870–1914*. Cardiff: University of Wales Press.

Cross, G. (1993) *Time and Money. The Making of Consumer Culture*. London: Routledge.

Cunningham, H. (1980) *Leisure in the Industrial Revolution*. London: Croom Helm.

Cunningham, H. (1990) 'Leisure and Culture', in F.M.L. Thompson (ed.) *The Cambridge Social History of Britain*, vol. 2. Cambridge: Cambridge University Press, 279–340.

Davies, A. (1992) *Leisure, Gender and Poverty. Working-Class Culture in Salford and Manchester, 1900–1939*. Buckingham: Open University Press.

Delves, A. (1981) 'Popular Recreation and Social Conflict in Derby', in E. Yeo and S. Yeo (eds) *Popular Culture and Class Conflict, 1590–1914*. Brighton: Harvester Press, 89–127.

Dingle, A.E. (1972) 'Drink and Working-Class Living Standards in Britain, 1870–1914', *Economic History Review* 25 (4) 608–22.

Fraser, W.H. (1990) 'Developments in Leisure', in W.H. Fraser and R.J. Morris (eds) *People and Society in Scotland*, vol. 2, 1830–1914. Edinburgh: John Donald Publishers, 236–64.

Gillett, P. (2000) *Musical Women in England, 1870–1914*. Basingstoke: Macmillan.

Glancy, M. (2006) 'Temporary American Citizens? British Audiences, Hollywood Films and the Threat of Americanisation in the 1920s', *Historical Journal of Film, Radio and Television* 26 (4) 461–84.

Hargreaves, J. (1994) *Sporting Females. Critical Issues in the History and Sociology of Women's Sports*. London: Routledge.

Harrison, B. (1994) *Drink and the Victorians*. Edinburgh: Keele University Press.

Harvey, A. (2004) *The Beginnings of a Commercial Sporting Culture in Britain, 1793–1850.* Aldershot: Ashgate.

Hill, J. (2002) *Sport, Leisure and Culture in Twentieth Century Britain*. Basingstoke: Palgrave.

Holt, R. (1989) *Sport and the British. A Modern History*. Oxford: Clarendon Press.

Howkins, A. (1973) *Whitsuntide in Nineteenth Century Oxfordshire*. History Workshop Pamphlet, no. 8.

Huggins, M. (2000) *Flat Racing and British Society, 1790–1914. A Social and Economic History*. London: Frank Cass.

Jackson, B. (1972) (ed.) *Working Class Community*. Harmondsworth: Penguin.

Jennings, P. (2007) *The Local. A History of the English Pub*. Stroud: Tempus.

Jones, S.G. (1986) *Workers at Play. A Social and Economic History of Leisure, 1918–1939*. London: Routledge and Kegan Paul.

Kift, D. (1996) *The Victorian Music Hall. Culture, Class and Conflict*. Cambridge: Cambridge University Press.

Kynaston, D. (2009) *Family Britain, 1951–57*. London: Bloomsbury.

Langhamer, C. (2000) *Women's Leisure in England, 1920–1960*. Manchester: Manchester University Press.

Lowerson, J. (1993) *Sport and the English Middle Class*. Manchester: Manchester University Press.

Mackenzie, J. (1986) *Imperialism and Popular Culture*. Manchester: Manchester University Press.

McKibbin, R. (1984) 'Why Was there No Marxism in Great Britain?', *English Historical Review* 99 (391) 297–331.

Marwick, A. (1998) *The Sixties. Cultural Revolution in Britain, France, Italy and the United States, c.1958–1974*. Oxford: Oxford University Press.

Nott, J. (2002) *Music for the People. Popular Music and Dance in Interwar Britain*. Oxford: Oxford University Press.

Orwell, G. (1962) *The Road to Wigan Pier*. Harmondsworth: Penguin (Originally published 1937).

Pearson, G. (1983) *Hooligan. A History of Respectable Fears*. London: Macmillan.

Poole, R. (1983) 'Oldham Wakes', in J.K. Walton and J. Walvin (eds) *Leisure in Britain, 1780–1939*. Manchester: Manchester University Press, 71–98.

Reid, D.A. (1976) 'The Decline of Saint Monday, 1766–1876', *Past and Present* 71 (1) 76–101.

Reid, D.A. (1996) 'Weddings, Weekdays, Work and Leisure in Urban England: the Decline of Saint Monday Revisited', *Past and Present* 153 (1) 135–63.

Reid, D.A. (2000) 'Playing and Praying', in M. Daunton, (ed.) *The Cambridge History of Urban Britain, vol. 3, 1840–1950*. Cambridge: Cambridge University Press, 745–807.

Roberts, R. (1973) *The Classic Slum. Salford Life in the First Quarter of the Twentieth Century*. Harmondsworth: Penguin.

Rose, J. (2001) *The Intellectual Life of the British Working Class*. New Haven, CT: Yale University Press.

Russell, D. (1997a) *Football and the English. A Social History of Association Football in England, 1863–1995*. Preston: Carnegie Publishing.

Russell, D. (1997b) *Popular Music in England, 1840–1914. A Social History*. Manchester: Manchester University Press.

Russell, D. (2008) 'Mum's the Word. The Cycling Career of Beryl Burton, 1956–1986', *Women's History Review* 18 (5) 787–806.

Scannell, P. and Cardiff, D. (1991) *A Social History of British Broadcasting, vol.1, 1922–1939. Serving the Nation*. Oxford: Blackwell.

Social Trends (1971). London: Her Majesty's Stationery Office.

Springhall, J. (1977) *Youth, Empire and Society*. London: Croom Helm.

Taylor, M. (2008) *The Association Game. A History of British Football*. Harlow: Pearson Education.

Tebbutt, M. (2012) *Being Boys*. Manchester: Manchester University Press.

Walton, J.K. (1981) 'The Demand for Working-Class Seaside Holidays in Victorian England', *Economic History Review* 34 (2) 249–65.

Walton, J.K. (1983) *The English Seaside Resort. A Social History, 1750–1914*. Leicester: Leicester University Press.

Waters, C. (1990) *British Socialists and the Politics of Popular Culture, 1884–1914*. Manchester: Manchester University Press.

3

FEMINIST LEISURE STUDIES

Origins, accomplishments and prospects

Karla A. Henderson

Introduction

When I was growing up in rural America, over 50 years ago, I was what most people would call a tomboy. I especially had a passion for baseball and I worked persistently to get good by throwing a rubber ball against my family's barn and hitting it, at first with a big stick and then eventually with a real bat. I was better than anyone in my primary school. The boys got to sign up for 'Little League Baseball', and I wanted to play too. But when I boldly asked the coach if I could try out for the team, he laughed and said maybe I could play girls' softball when I got into high school. My feminist consciousness was raised that day, although I could not put it into words until much later in my life. Women and their involvement in sports and leisure, at least in the Western world, have come some distance since the 1950s. This story is mine and this chapter reflects my perspective regarding the origins, accomplishments, and prospects for feminist research about leisure, women, and gender. Every feminist leisure scholar has a somewhat different story and would likely interpret scholarship in varying ways. I offer this chapter, however, as one perspective that is open for further expansion, discussion, and discourse.

Although the study of leisure became visible in the latter half of the twentieth century, feminist perspectives on women's leisure have been present in Leisure Studies only since the early 1980s. During these three decades the topics, methods, and analyses have evolved. The earliest studies focused largely on the disadvantages of being female in relation to personal and fundamental issues surrounding leisure opportunities. Today, perspectives for analyses are more complex, with a focus on social structure, gender, and power relations pertaining to leisure. Further, multiple methods have been applied to study leisure, women, and gender from feminist perspectives. The purpose of this chapter is to highlight the contributions of feminist approaches to better understanding leisure and leisure behaviour.

Clarifying feminisms

Feminism is an ideology and a social political movement. Describing and defining feminisms may appear somewhat unnecessary at this juncture. However, since this chapter is about the contributions of feminisms, I want to be clear about multiple perspectives. Recognizing the forms of feminism may be important, since one single definition does not encompass all the possibilities. A description that I once saw on a poster attributed to Rebecca West (1913), written during what has been described as the first wave of feminism, stated:

> I myself have never been able to find out precisely what feminism is: I only know that people call me a feminist whenever I express sentiments that differentiate me from a doormat.

In addition to this simple statement, however, feminism has been viewed from various philosophical perspectives. In earlier work with my colleagues (Henderson, Bialeschki, Shaw, and Freysinger, 1989; 1996), we identified three primary perspectives describing feminisms: liberal, socialist, and radical. Liberal feminism aligns itself with political connections to individualism. Therefore, the core relates to the importance and autonomy of the individual and the equality and freedom that should be offered to all humans. Socialist feminism is somewhat related to Marxism but takes the analysis beyond capitalism to recognize that patriarchy is a critical contributor to women's oppression. To this extent, socialist feminism acknowledges the connections between the material conditions of society and social structures and ideologies. Radical feminists suggest that the oppression of women is the root of all oppression and that patriarchal domination must be overcome through transformation of the systems that have defined gender and power. Thus, radical feminists would say that simply advocating for equality between men and women, regarding leisure or any other dimension of life, only serves to perpetuate an oppressive system.

At the turn into the twenty-first century, post-structuralism gained popularity among scholars studying leisure (e.g., Aitchison, 2000; Wearing, 1998). Advocates of this perspective focused on deconstructing traditional texts (e.g., language, meanings, symbols) and structures (e.g., education, work, leisure) so as to challenge established categories. Post-structuralism offered a way of studying how knowledge is produced, and critiqued structuralist premises related to the assumption of one scientific truth. For example, a post-structuralist approach might emphasize that being a woman may have numerous meanings, which could all have implications for leisure. History and culture condition the study of underlying assumptions and structures, which are subject to biases and misinterpretations. Further, gender-power relationships are critical to consider from post-structuralist perspectives (Aitchison, 2005). A post-structuralist approach also mandates that to understand a concept such as leisure requires questioning the systems that produced the knowledge. Questioning has been the foundation for much of the feminist research about women and leisure over the past three decades.

Morgan (1984) argued that feminism has been evident in every culture and every period of history since the subordination of women began. Three evolving waves of feminism, mainly pertaining to the US, have been discussed (Walker, 1995). I point out these waves to show the dimensions of feminism and how its evolution has implications for current and future examinations of leisure, women, and gender. First-wave feminism, arguably, began in the late eighteenth century and ended in the US with the ratification of the 20th Amendment to the Constitution, which gave women the right to vote. First-wave feminism addressed primarily how women were human beings, as noted in the above quote attributed to West, and how they should be able to vote and not be treated like a man's property. The second wave of feminism emerged in the mid-twentieth century and focused on gender equality related to political, legal, and economic rights based primarily on variations of liberal, and to some degree to socialist and radical, feminisms (Aitchison, 2005). The criticism often levelled at this second wave, however, was that it focused on white middle-class heterosexual women. The presence of a third wave of feminism today is arguable in terms of its necessity. Although it builds on second-wave feminism, it also seeks to assure that black women, non-heterosexual, low-income, and women in developing countries are part of the conversation, and emanates primarily from postmodern and post-structuralist premises. These waves are also reflective of how feminists studying leisure emerged as part of systems aimed at equity and social justice.

Two other words central to feminism that can be briefly clarified are 'woman' and 'gender'. To be female means to have specific biological structures and functions. However, to be defined as a woman comes not only from those biological characteristics but also from social constructions of the meanings of gender. Gender is the social construction, including the cultural connections associated with one's biological sex. It refers to how society defines expectations and behaviours associated with being female (i.e., femininity) or male (i.e., masculinity). Gender is an ongoing process and not an inborn biological trait. Further, gender dictates behaviours that are produced and reproduced through people's actions (Henderson, 1994), as well as the power relations in society. The focus of this chapter is on leisure, women, and gender, which includes how performing gender has implications for the leisure of both women and men. As I will explain shortly, feminists have focused both on women and on gender in their research about leisure.

Regardless of how feminism might be embodied, all perspectives in some way point to a critique of social structures influencing gender, and can provide a mechanism for social change and the transformation of current ways of thinking. The question of interest in this chapter addresses what contributions feminisms have made to a better understanding of leisure and leisure behaviour. Examining the evolution and content of applications of feminism in the study of leisure, women, and gender is a good starting-place.

The stages of feminist analyses applied to leisure, women, and gender

The basis of feminism had its origins in women's rights. The foundational examination of women's leisure evolved from recognizing the social justice issues surrounding the oppression and diminished quality of life for women as well as for other traditionally disadvantaged groups. Tetrault (1985) originally proposed feminist phase theory, which Henderson (1994) and Aitchison (2001) adapted into five stages to describe the past and potential of leisure research. The next stages of this research are evolving in new ways, described as gender justice by Aitchison (2013) and as intersectionality by Henderson and Gibson (2013).

The first phase or stage was termed *invisible women* in the leisure literature. As noted earlier, little research about women existed in the leisure literature until the early 1980s, even though leisure research publications had begun over a decade earlier (e.g., *Journal of Leisure Research* in 1969). Fortunately, the first issue of *Leisure Studies*, published in 1982, had two articles about women that were written by women (i.e., Deem, 1982; Glyptis and Chambers, 1982). Studies about leisure, women, and gender now constitute about 10% of the research studies published in the primary English-language journals (Henderson and Gibson, 2013).

The second stage was labelled compensatory or *add women and stir*. Women were acknowledged as potentially missing from the leisure literature but were discussed as an addition to the real discussion of traditional views of leisure (e.g., leisure as non-work time). Wimbush and Talbot (1988) critiqued this compensatory stage to suggest that including women was important, but the analyses must go beyond simply noting that women should be considered, to also examine power relationships that existed. The problem with this compensatory phase was that some questions were raised about the ghettoization of research about women's leisure (Deem, 1999). For example, when research about women was a separate session at an academic conference, often results from this research were not part of the mainstream of the leisure literature.

The third phase was described as dichotomous *sex/gender differences*. These studies, both in the past and currently, focus on differences between males and females. These analyses may refer to gender differences but are sometimes about biological sex differences and not gender structures. Such studies may provide interesting insights if they move beyond simply identifying differences (i.e., treating sex or gender as more than just an independent variable), to interpret the meanings of those differences. The scholarship that underpins these studies can also serve to reinforce the status quo if the historical, cultural, and social contexts are not explored. Examining differences can be important in addressing issues of distributive justice if it moves beyond those differences being considered solely the conclusions of the research.

The study of *women-only* from articulated feminist perspectives is a stage that remains important in examining the nuances of leisure more broadly, especially for diverse groups of women. In this phase, the leisure of women is examined not in relation to men but in order to understand the importance and meaning of leisure pertaining to women in different life contexts. This approach also allows for the taken-for-granted aspects of women's lives to be explored, such as their everyday leisure (e.g., family relationships). Understanding the experiences of different groups of women also can serve as a way to interpret the meanings of leisure in more nuanced ways related to multiple identity characteristics, in addition to gender.

The discussion of *gender* and its applications was identified as a fifth stage, as evidenced by explorations of gender roles, gender relations, masculinity, and femininity in the leisure literature. This phase focuses on how cultural meanings and connections are associated with expectations regarding the social construction surrounding one's biological sex. This analysis goes beyond socialization to also address unequal power relations based on gender, which reflects emerging post-structuralist analyses.

As discussed later in this chapter, these five stages have opened the door for the next possible stages, linking post-structuralism and third-wave feminism to address the interaction of gender with other identity markers such as race, class, sexual identity, disability, and culture (Henderson and Gibson, 2013). Similarly, Aitchison (2003; 2005; 2013) has also suggested that the next stage of feminist research about leisure, women, and gender relates to examinations of the social-cultural nexus leading to policy analysis. This examination of the stages of research illustrates how studying women and gender from feminist perspectives has shown a progression and growth in epistemology, and has offered a means to correct and transform social policy and practice.

The growth of topics and themes in feminist studies of leisure

Another way to summarize the accomplishments of the feminist examinations of leisure is to articulate the topics and themes about women and gender that have appeared in the published literature. Henderson and her colleagues have provided five integrative reviews that overview the literature about leisure, women, and gender in the major English journals for the past 30 years (i.e., Henderson, 1990, 1996; Henderson, Hodges, and Kivel, 2002; Henderson and Hickerson, 2007; Henderson and Gibson, 2013). Table 3.1 provides a matrix of the findings from these five systematic reviews. Summaries of these findings show the convergence as well as divergence of themes about leisure, women, and gender uncovered in the literature.

Table 3.1 An examination of leisure research about women and gender from 1980 to 2010

	1980–89	1990–95	1996–2000	2001–5	2006–10
Number of articles	Not available	75 (6 years)	74 (5 years)	67 (5 years)	101 (5 years)
Percentage solely qualitative	Not available	Not available	60%	62%	64%
Topics/themes					
Inclusion	Common world in inequality	Multiple and varied meanings	Intersection of gender with other identity markers		Necessity of social inclusion
Interpersonal	Social importance of leisure for women				Friendship and social support
Family and roles	Containers of the home and non-structured activities	The more roles the less leisure	Family roles		Extended view of family relationships
Nature of activity, time, and space	Nature of leisure/ fragmentation	Leisure as a positive and negative context	Claiming leisure space	Importance of active leisure	Women and physical/ mental health
Beyond constraints	Lack of entitlement	Constraints more salient for some groups of women	Negative aspects of leisure in women's lives	Structural social forces/ constraints in context	Resistance and empowerment
Epistemology		Significance of gender analysis	Hegemonic significance of gender	Resistance and leisure/ use of critical theory	Feminist perspectives expanded
Beyond ethnocentricity			Globalization of women's leisure		Cultural descriptions

The sources for these five integrative reviews included studies from nine primary English-language refereed journals: *Annals of Leisure Research, Journal of Leisure Research, Journal of Park and Recreation Administration, Leisure/Loisir, Leisure Sciences, Leisure Studies, Society and Leisure/ Loisir et Société, Therapeutic Recreation Journal*, and *World Leisure Journal*. The contents of all articles with the keywords of women, men, girls, boys, feminism, gender, or related words such as widow, caregiver, family, gay, masculinity, or lesbian in the title, the abstract, or among the listed keywords were identified. Those articles that dealt with professional issues regarding women, recreation, careers, and leadership were not included, as the authors chose to focus on leisure behaviour as the context, and not on management issues. Although additional papers have been delivered at conferences and included in book chapters, only these widely accessible refereed journal articles were used. Further, the reviews delimited the work to the English language not because no other work was occurring outside English-language journals, but because translations from other languages were not easily available. These journals have a North American bias, admittedly, but they do offer some context for comparisons of topics and themes about leisure, women, and gender since the early 1980s.

The number of articles about leisure, women, and gender seems to be growing. Some of the increase from 2006 to 2010 may also be related to broader definitions of family and a small but growing presence of articles addressing men's leisure as well as lesbian, gay, bi-sexual, transgendered, and non-heterosexual identities. Also, the *sine qua non* of this research has focused on qualitative methods, although a great range existed in comparing the analyses done since 1996. The relationships between epistemology and methods are central to the construction of both knowledge and power (Aitchison, 2005) and will be discussed later in this chapter with regard to a summary of the contributions of feminist research.

The themes in this leisure literature seemed to evolve from a singular focus on finding the meaning of leisure for women (i.e., a common world) to recognizing the range of meanings associated with leisure, women, and gender (i.e., importance of social inclusion). The research has gone from fairly descriptive explanations about women and leisure to greater theoretical critiques of the sources and implications of leisure for not only women but women and men in different life contexts.

As Table 3.1 shows, several broad themes have persisted and evolved in importance over the years. This matrix of themes is not mutually exclusive, but provides something of a visual framework for identifying the topics as they have developed. Three themes have been particularly stable over the years. One is the gendered roles of women related to the importance of home and the family. A second relates to the examination of constraints described in the initial review as lack of entitlement. As constraints have been examined over the years, the focus has changed from the negative implications of constraints to a focus on resisting constraints and finding empowerment in leisure. Third, an identification of the nature of leisure, starting from the fragmented nature of women's leisure, has evolved into identifying the possibilities of leisure for health.

Two other areas seem to have emerged since the first review. The first is gender analysis as it relates to explanations of leisure behaviour for women. The early writing, although often discussed in terms of gender roles, focused solely on women and their leisure. In the past 20 years gender has emerged related to the implications of feminist perspectives on continuing to understand leisure, as well as to highlight internal reflections on how women and gender should be studied. This perspective also addresses how feminist approaches can include men. Second, although a limitation of these reviews has been the ethnocentrism focused on the English language, more studies reflecting the globalization of women's leisure and the cultural descriptions have become evident in the twenty-first century.

This body of literature over this period has continued to reflect the thinking of feminist researchers as well as of individuals involved in ongoing examinations of the meanings of leisure and leisure behaviour from diversity perspectives. This research has provided identifiable contributions to the field of Leisure Studies and, perhaps more importantly, has pointed toward future directions for research from feminist perspectives.

Contributions to Leisure Studies

Eichler (1980) suggested that feminist research at its best should serve as a critique of existing research, a correction of the biases that have existed, and a groundwork for the transformation of social science and society (e.g., through future research, policies, and practice). A characteristic of feminist research is putting women at the centre of the analysis. Further, feminism also addresses the deconstruction of research in order to ascertain what is not in the literature and where feminist or gender analyses would be helpful.

In reflecting on the leisure literature, the challenge is to explicate how feminist research focused on women and gender has addressed aspects of critique, correction, and transformation. Feminist research into Leisure Studies, however, has not occurred in a vacuum. Research about other areas such as diversity and inclusion has complemented this research. Nevertheless, several directions in which feminist research has led leisure research may be worth considering further: epistemology and methodology; leisure behaviour and constraints; professional development; globalization, intersectionality; and equity and social justice.

Epistemology and methodology

Feminist researchers as well as others have openly disputed the assumption that science is objective and value free. Dispassionate and disinterested research cannot occur in a feminist framework if the goals are critique, correction, and transformation. Although most feminist scholars would agree that a feminist *methodology* does not exist, the influence that feminist researchers have had on epistemologies and expanding methods cannot be denied.

Epistemology refers to ways of knowing and understanding the social realities of the world. The inclusion of the study of women was the first example of how leisure-research epistemology was enhanced by feminists. Feminist epistemology has been instrumental in emphasizing that identifying differences in gender or any other identity marker without examining the social and power structures in operation is not useful. Further, feminist epistemologies have also emphasized the idea of praxis (hooks, 1989), in that theory and application must occur together in order for change to occur.

Most feminist researchers believe in the value of empirical research. However, many of them believe that logical positivism has not always been the best way to study women. The most important aspect is asking the appropriate questions, which can then be followed by choosing the best methods. In the 1980s and early 1990s, quantitative survey-based research seemed to be the accepted method for doing leisure research (i.e., at least in North America), and women were largely invisible in this research or were described in relation to sex differences only (Henderson, 1994). As Table 3.1 shows, in the analysis of research on women, qualitative approaches, and especially in-depth interviews, have been the most used in the 30 years of articles reviewed about leisure, women, and gender.

Although qualitative methods are often justified when little is known about a topic, the continued use of these approaches to study women may indicate that qualitative data have ongoing importance in giving individuals *voice* (Henderson *et al.*, 1996) and allowing for reflexivity in the research conducted by women. The diversity of populations investigated requires opportunities for new voices. For example, although not limited to feminist researchers, the use of autoethnography has emerged in the literature about women and leisure (e.g., Raisborough and Bhatti, 2007). As more has been learned about leisure, women, and gender, the nature and quality of experiences has often been more fully explained with the continued use of qualitative data. The approaches and mixing of data in feminist research studies have highlighted the diversity of questions asked as well as the many possible *ways of knowing*. Although qualitative data have been dominant, the utility of quantitative methods for feminist research (e.g., Westmarland, 2001) and in studies of leisure and gender (Shaw, 2010) cannot be underestimated.

Feminist researchers studying leisure have also pointed to the importance of who is writing research and the relationships that they may have to the individuals being studied. For example, many feminist researchers have advocated for changing the terming of those being studied from subjects to participants (Aitchison, 2005). This change in terminology also reflects the desire of feminists to make research a less hierarchical process. The use of the first person in presenting research is another means for representing how research cannot be value free if it is to result in social change as an important tenet of the research. Feminist research epistemology and methodology have also provided the connections between structural explanations and post-structuralist approaches. This openness has also provided a way to examine the broader cultural opportunities in studying leisure, women, and gender.

Epistemology, methodology, and methods related to leisure have been expanded by the contributions of feminist researchers. These contributions have added to the discourse of leisure by emphasizing how the everyday experiences of women and men are described, practised, enacted, perpetuated, and resisted. These contributions have also served to show how the personal and the political cannot be disconnected when examining leisure behaviour.

Leisure behaviour and constraints

Leisure has been understood in expanded ways because of feminist research, particularly in relation to traditional assumptions about what leisure is and issues surrounding constraints. Both of these areas have sometimes been more the concern of North American researchers than of researchers in other parts of the world (Ravenscroft, 2005). However, the challenges presented by feminists with regard to assumptions about leisure and leisure constraints can be considered.

One idea that is mostly taken for granted today concerns the *definitions* of leisure as the opposite of (paid) work or as unobligated time. The simplicity of defining leisure in either of these ways several decades ago did not reflect the roles of women related to family and household unpaid duties. The paradox of definitions was that either women had no leisure, since none of their time was unobligated, or since some women did not work outside the home, all their time at home was considered free time and, thus, leisure.

This feminist critique of the definitions of leisure was also reflected in describing leisure as recreation or activity. Earlier ideas about activity included largely structured male-defined activities that occurred outside the home, such as sports and outdoor pursuits. Feminists offered that activities could be explained more broadly as they related to everyday home pursuits and social activities. Feminists also reframed how the choice and freedom tradition-ally associated with leisure were socially constructed. These redefinitions have implications for better understanding leisure as well as for further examining masculinity and gender roles for men.

The study of constraints has benefited from a broader examination of the meanings related to feminist perspectives. Much of the study of women's leisure, at least in the early years, was the study of constraints in various forms (e.g., Glyptis and Chambers, 1982; Henderson, 1990), although the terminology of constraints was not always used. In North America, a major paradigm of research about constraints emerged with empirical models that explained how constraints to leisure worked (Jackson, 2005). Although women's leisure sometimes fitted the models, feminists often questioned whether the models really did include the context of women's lives, and especially the societal structures that were omnipresent. Shaw and Henderson (2005) described this relationship between gender research and constraints research as an *uneasy alliance.*

Shaw and Henderson (2005) questioned several premises of the constraints models from feminist perspectives. One concern related to the over-reliance on examining individual behaviour without considering structural inequalities that often contributed to perceived and actual constraints. They also described, as did Samdahl and Jekubovich (1997), the value of using qualitative data and grounded approaches in order to better understand the context of people's lives and to contextualize leisure. Feminists such as Samdahl (2005) and Shogan (2002) questioned the definition of constraints that suggested that constraints always resulted in non-participation. These researchers contended that constraints could be positive in how they led to negotiating experiences of leisure in more meaningful ways. Shaw (2001), in particular, pointed out how women's leisure could be associated with resistance. Resistance suggested that acknowledging constraints could lead women to resist structures that impacted on their individual lives, but more importantly, resistance could be applied collectively by women to change society. This view of constraints, coming mainly from feminists, also reinforced the need to examine multiple systems of oppression beyond individual disadvantages, which pointed to the opportunities that globalization and intersectionality provided.

Globalization

Most feminists have long accepted the idea that as long as any woman is oppressed, all women are oppressed. Therefore, the examination of women in many cultures is necessary if transformations regarding the status of women are to occur anywhere. Henderson and Gibson (2013) noted the growing and continuing focus on gender and leisure in the non-Western countries, and particularly in Middle Eastern and Asian countries. Although some of the conceptual perspectives adopted for studies in the West may be relevant, a *one size fits all* approach will not work in explaining the social structures and values inherent with regard to women and gender in other countries. Just as the exploration of women's leisure resulted in broader perspectives about leisure behaviour and constraints in general, feminist research projects emerging from non-Western countries can help in rethinking traditional assumptions about leisure for both women and men. Leisure is dynamic, and these feminist interpretations from non-Western perspectives can further strengthen the potential value associated with leisure for all people.

The perceived ethnocentricity of leisure (Roberts, 2010) is being addressed globally to some extent by the opening of doors for broader definitions of leisure within cultural contexts. Feminists (e.g., Samdahl, 2010) have pointed out that inequities and globalization must be taken into account and must be more than just recognizing multiple identities and experiences. However, women may not be able to address the influence of gender on leisure until working together as equals enables the recognition of how differences also matter. These analyses will require additional work to examine varying degrees of access to power and resources. Efforts to address the ethnocentricity of leisure and the contributions of global perspectives must come from all leisure researchers in the future.

Professional development

It would be remiss of me not to acknowledge how feminists have also addressed the role of women in the professions related to leisure, recreation, parks, sport, and tourism. This relates indirectly to Leisure Studies but does reflect the practice of management as well as local and national policies. As noted earlier, the integrative reviews conducted by myself and my colleagues (e.g., Henderson, 1990) excluded research about women in the profession. However, the contributions of feminism to applications in the field of practice are worthy of summary.

In the US, Bialeschki and Henderson (1984) first examined women's personal and professional spheres. At this time, women appeared to be more visible in the leisure services profession, and studying their status was important. A decade later Henderson and Bialeschki (1995) examined women's career development (i.e., job satisfaction, personal and family issues, and equity concerns), based on the work of Frisby (1992). Other research about women as leisure services professionals during the 1990s came from Canada (e.g., Frisby and Brown, 1991), the United Kingdom (UK; e.g., Aitchison *et al.*, 1999), and the US (e.g., Anderson and Shinew, 2001; Shinew and Arnold, 1998).

Examining women included documenting employment representation and the quality of women's experiences in the workplace. For example, Shinew and Arnold's (1998) work in the US showed gender-related obstacles in gaining promotion. Anderson and Shinew (2001) discovered inequity with men in the recreation field in relation to salary, respect from subordinates, and level of participation in management. Aitchison *et al.* (1999) specifically examined perceptions of (in)equity within sport and leisure management in the UK, evaluated practices and policies related to inequity, and suggested necessary steps to assure opportunities for equity in the workforce. Henderson, Grappendorf, Bruton, and Tomas (2013) most recently examined the career development of women who were members of the National Recreation and Park Association. Their research concluded that women were generally satisfied with their jobs, but that senior managers were more satisfied than women in the other levels of employment. All women surveyed rated family/work/leisure balance issues as important. Gender equity issues were identified particularly with regard to ongoing unconscious discrimination. The results from Henderson *et al.* (2013) were compared to the work of Henderson and Bialeschki conducted almost two decades before and showed only small positive changes in women's career development opportunities.

Some of this research focused on the distributive justice of women in the field, but Aitchison (2005) has advocated for a social-cultural nexus consideration related to materiality in the form of organizational structures, organizational cultures, and policies as well as cultural aspects pertaining to women's (and men's) perceptions, attitudes, and appearances. The role of women in the workforce has been explored from numerous perspectives but the contributions offered by feminists to the field of leisure services are important. The situation has been adequately described but future research will need to address strategies for making workplaces friendlier for all individuals, regardless of gender, race, or class.

Intersectionality

The summary of the research about women and gender since Henderson and Bialeschki's (1995) has continually recognized the differences among women. Women are not a homogeneous group with the same life experiences. Further, feminist researchers have shown how impossible developing any grand theory might be. Although the term 'intersectionality' has rarely been used in the leisure literature, its conceptual presence reflects emerging contributions to exploring the interaction of gender, race, and class as well as other identities such as sexuality and ability. Henderson and Gibson (2013) suggest that this idea of intersectionality may be the next logical stage/phase of feminist research in feminist Leisure Studies.

Intersectionality focuses on interconnections among the multiple dimensions of social categories such as gender, race, age, sexuality, ability, and class. Intersectionality addresses the privilege of dominant groups and emphasizes the limits of current perspectives and classification systems for understanding any human activity such as leisure. Further, intersectionality asserts that forms of oppression such as sexism, racism, classism, colonialism, or homophobia do not act independently of one another, and these interactions contribute further to social inequality and powerlessness. Intersectionality also emphasizes how feminism is a broader project that addresses more than just gender and women. Feminist researchers studying leisure, for example, must take into account racism, imperialism, or any other form of oppression that limits the leisure opportunities of any individual.

McCall (2005) described intersectionality as a major paradigm that can influence research. McCall and others (e.g., Choo and Ferree, 2010; Knudsen, 2007) have also emphasized the complexity of the idea. Henderson and Gibson (2013) uncovered that social inclusion was a theme of the most recent review of published literature about leisure, women, and gender. Knudsen described this acknowledgement of inclusion as *additive* intersectionality, which focuses on the socio-cultural categories but not necessarily their influence on one another. The next step is to also focus on perspectives that emphasize the power implications and the ways in which gender, sexuality, nationality, or any other category might be intersecting. Different social categories not only affect one another, but work together to exert a combined influence on individuals at social, structural, and systemic levels.

Feminist research has set the stage for moving into the acknowledgement and application of intersectionality as an essential epistemology for better understanding leisure. Despite the infancy of operationalizing what intersectionality means, possibilities exist for using the applications and implications of intersectionality in Leisure Studies in critical and reflective ways. This emerging opportunity also complements the way that feminist research has contributed and can further contribute to social justice.

Equity and social justice

The most significant contribution, and potential for feminist Leisure Studies in the future, to my mind, is the emphasis on social and environmental justice not only for women but for other groups around the world who may not have adequate opportunities for leisure. The feminist agenda calls for a transformation of society, and much needs to be done in relation to broad elements of gender justice.

Feminist researchers are not alone in these concerns related to social justice from a gender perspective. For example, Kivel, Johnson, and Scraton (2009: 489) highlighted 'the fluidity of identity and identity categories ... that shift the paradigm of how we study race and the leisure experience'. McDonald (2009) described the use of intersectional mapping to challenge how diversity is conceptualized and how whiteness works, and Stewart, Parry, and Glover (2008) described enhancing leisure research to address values and ideologies that can lead to social justice. The application of this type of inclusive thinking will be important in further examining the social context of leisure, developing methods to examine oppression and power, discovering new knowledge, and informing action to address social justice and change. Feminists have worked to illuminate the tension between the recognition of diversity *and* the commonality of experiences (Henderson and Shaw, 2006), which can lead to greater justice and quality of life for all individuals.

Concluding thoughts

Feminist research since the early 1980s has served as the conscience of Leisure Studies. In analysing leisure, feminists have asked where the women are. The use of critical perspectives has raised questions about why leisure is what it is. Most of the feminist research has described the complexity of leisure behaviour, but has also attempted to recognize how leisure has personal, social, cultural, economic, and political implications in women's and men's lives. This feminist research has helped to open up baseball opportunities for farm girls like me, as well as contributing to the well-being of women and other traditionally powerless groups from global perspectives. Empowerment is a goal of leisure, and feminists have made clear that oppression and exclusion cannot be overlooked.

Feminists, further, have led the way in thinking about how the study of leisure can be more inclusive and how leisure cannot be separated from society. Leisure is in culture and leisure is culture. Feminist researchers were among the first in the leisure field to widely employ qualitative approaches, which are now common in the leisure literature regarding a variety of topics. Feminists have made clear how the study of leisure will always be incomplete and fluid. Although the world is largely postmodern and the possibilities of grand theory are remote, feminists have reminded leisure researchers that structural inequities cannot be ignored. Feminists have not asked anyone to abandon the past completely, but they have implored leisure researchers to add to (and potentially transform) how scholars know about leisure, what is known, and the possibilities for social justice.

References

Aitchison, C. (2000) 'Poststructuralist Feminist Theories of Representing Others: A response to the "crisis" in leisure studies discourse', *Leisure Studies* 19: 127–144.

Aitchison, C. (2001) 'Gender and Leisure: The codification of knowledge', *Leisure Sciences* 23: 1–19.

Aitchison, C. C. (2003) *Gender and Leisure*. London: Routledge.

Aitchison, C. C. (2005) 'Feminist and Gender Research in Sport and Leisure Management: Understanding the social-cultural nexus of gender-power relations', *Journal of Sport Management* 19: 422–441.

Aitchison, C. C. (2013) 'Gender and Leisure Policy Discourses: The cultural turn to social justice', in V. Freysinger, S. Shaw, K. Henderson, and D. Bialeschki (eds) *Leisure, Women, and Gender*. State College, PA: Venture Publishing, pp. 521–40.

Aitchison, C., Brackenridge, C., and Jordan, F. (1999) *Gender Equity in Leisure Management*. Reading, UK: Institute of Leisure and Amenity Management.

Anderson, D. M. and Shinew, K. J. (2001) 'A National Examination of Gender Equity in Public Parks and Recreation', *Journal of Leisure Research* 33: 470–491.

Bialeschki, M. D. and Henderson, K. A. (1984) 'The Personal and Professional Spheres: Complement or conflict for women leisure services professionals', *Journal of Park and Recreation Administration* 2: 45–54.

Choo, H. Y. and Ferree, M. M. (2010) 'Practicing Intersectionality in Sociological Research: A critical analysis of inclusions, interactions, and institutions in the study of inequalities', *Sociological Theory* 28 (2) 129–149.

Deem, R. (1982) 'Women, Leisure, and Inequality', *Leisure Studies* 1: 29–46.

Deem, R. (1999) 'How Do We Get Out of the Ghetto? Strategies for the research on gender and leisure for the twenty-first century', *Leisure Studies* 18: 161–177.

Eichler, M. (1980) *The Double Standard*. New York: St. Martin's Press.

Frisby, W. (1992) 'Women in Leisure Service Management: Alternative definitions of career success', *Loisir et Société/Society and Leisure* 15 (1) 155–174.

Frisby, W. and Brown, B. (1991) 'The Balancing Act: Women leisure service managers', *Journal of Applied Recreation Research* 16: 297–321.

Glyptis, S. and Chambers, D. (1982) 'No Place Like Home', *Leisure Studies* 1: 247–262.

Henderson, K. A. (1990) 'The Meaning of Leisure for Women: An integrative review of the research', *Journal of Leisure Research* 22 (3) 228–243.

Henderson, K. A. (1994) 'Broadening an Understanding of Women, Gender and Leisure', *Journal of Leisure Research* 26 (1) 1–7.

Henderson, K. A. (1996) 'One Size Doesn't Fit All: The meanings of women's leisure', *Journal of Leisure Research* 28 (3) 139–154.

Henderson, K. A. and Bialeschki, D. (1995) 'Career Development and Women in the Leisure Services Profession', *Journal of Park and Recreation Administration* 13: 26–42.

Henderson, K. A. and Gibson, H. (2013) 'An Integrative Review of Women, Gender, and Leisure: Increasing complexities', *Journal of Leisure Research* 45 (2) 115–135.

Henderson, K. A. and Hickerson, B. D. (2007) 'Women and Leisure: Premises and performances uncovered in an integrated review', *Journal of Leisure Research* 39: 591–610.

Henderson, K. A. and Shaw, S. M. (2006) 'Leisure and Gender: Challenges and opportunities for feminist research', in C. Rojek, A. Veal, and S. Shaw (eds) *Handbook of Leisure Studies* (pp. 216–230). London: Routledge.

Henderson, K. A., Bialeschki, M. D., Shaw, S. M., and Freysinger, V. J. (1989) *A Leisure of One's Own: A feminist perspective on women's leisure*. State College, PA: Venture Publishing, Inc.

Henderson, K. A., Bialeschki, M. D., Shaw, S. M., and Freysinger, V. J. (1996) *Both Gains and Gaps: Feminist perspectives on women's leisure*. State College, PA: Venture Publishing, Inc.

Henderson, K. A., Hodges, S., and Kivel, B. (2002) 'Context and Dialogue in Research on Women and Leisure', *Journal of Leisure Research* 34 (3) 253–271.

Henderson, K. A., Grappendorf, H., Bruton, C., and Tomas, S. (2013) 'The Status of Women in the Parks and Recreation Profession in the US', *World Leisure Journal* 55 (1) 1–14.

hooks, b. (1989) *Feminist Theory: From margin to center*. Boston, MA: South End Press.

Jackson, E. L. (ed.) (2005) *Constraints to Leisure*. State College, PA: Venture Publishing.

Kivel, B. D., Johnson, C. W., and Scraton, S. (2009), '(Re)Theorizing Leisure, Experience and Race', *Journal of Leisure Research* 41: 473–493.

Knudsen, S. (2007) Intersectionality – A theoretical inspiration in the analysis of minority cultures and identities in textbooks. Retrieved from: http://www.caen.iufm.fr/colloque_iartem/pdf/knudsen.pdf

McCall, L. (2005) 'The Complexity of Intersectionality', *Signs: Journal of Women in Culture and Society* 30 (3) 1771–1800.

McDonald, M. G. (2009) 'Dialogues on Whiteness, Leisure and (Anti)Racism', *Journal of Leisure Research* 41 (1) 5–21.

Morgan, R. (ed.) (1984) *Sisterhood is Global*. New York: Anchor Press/Doubleday.

Raisborough, J. and Bhatti, M. (2007) 'Women's Leisure and Auto/Biography: Empowerment and resistance in the garden', *Journal of Leisure Research* 39 (3) 459–476.

Ravenscroft, N. (2005) 'The Ontology of Exclusion: A European perspective on leisure constraints research', in E. L. Jackson (ed.) *Constraints to Leisure* (pp. 321–335). State College, PA: Venture Publishing.

Roberts, K. (2010) 'Is Leisure Studies "Ethnocentric"? If so, does this matter?' *World Leisure Journal* 52 (3) 164–176.

Samdahl, D. M. (2005) 'Making Room for "Silly" Debate: Critical reflections on leisure constraints research', in E. L. Jackson (ed.) *Constraints to Leisure* (pp. 337–349). State College, PA: Venture Publishing.

Samdahl, D. M. (2010) 'Is Leisure Studies "Ethnocentric"? It takes more than optimism: A view from Athens, Georgia, USA', *World Leisure Journal* 52 (3) 185–190.

Samdahl, D. M. and Jekubovich, N. J. (1997) 'A Critique of Leisure Constraints: Comparative analyses and understanding', *Journal of Leisure Research* 29: 430–452.

Shaw, S. M. (2001) 'Conceptualizing Resistance: Women's leisure as political practice', *Journal of Leisure Research* 33: 186–201.

Shaw, S. M. (2010, September) The state of research about leisure, women, and gender. Paper presented at the 11th World Leisure Congress. Chuncheon, South Korea.

Shaw, S. M. and Henderson, K. A. (2005) 'Gender Analysis and Leisure: An uneasy alliance,' in E. L. Jackson (ed.) *Constraints to Leisure* (pp. 23–34). State College, PA: Venture Publishing.

Shinew, K. and Arnold, M. L. (1998) 'Gender Equity in the Leisure Services Field,' *Journal of Leisure Research* 30: 177–194.

Shogan, D. (2002) 'Characterizing Constraints of Leisure: A Foucaultian analysis of leisure constraint', *Leisure Studies* 21 (1) 27–38.

Stewart, W. P., Parry, D. C., and Glover, T. D. (2008) 'Writing Leisure: Values and ideologies of research', *Journal of Leisure Research* 40: 360–384.

Tetrault, M. L. (1985) 'Feminist Phase Theory: An experience-derived evaluation model', *Journal of Higher Education* 56: 364–384.

Walker, R. (ed.) (1995) *To Be Real*. New York: Anchor Books.

Wearing, B. (1998) *Leisure and Feminist Theory*. London: Sage Publications.

Westmarland, N. (2001) 'The quantitative/qualitative debate and feminist research: A subjective view of objectivity' [28 paragraphs]. *Forum Qualitative Sozialforschung/Forum: Qualitative Social Research*, 2 (1), Art. 13, http://nbnresolving.de/urn:nbn:de:0114-fqs0101135.

Wimbush, E. and Talbot, M. (eds) (1988) *Relative Freedoms*. Milton Keynes, UK: Open University Press.

4

PSYCHOLOGY OF LEISURE

Roger C. Mannell and Douglas A. Kleiber

Introduction

Psychological perspectives have been influential in Leisure Studies and these perspectives are primarily those of social psychology with some influence from personality and developmental psychology. The psychology of leisure is concerned with how people choose to fill and structure their free or leisure time with behaviour and experience, why they make these choices, and the impact of these choices on well-being. The psychology of leisure is also concerned with the relationship between what people do in their leisure and what they do in the other domains of their lives, such as work, family, and community (Mannell and Kleiber, 1997).

There has been much speculation about and many claims have been made for the beneficial psychological effects of leisure; however, before the early 1970s little systematic research had been reported. Around this time, a number of North American and British scholars began to promote and contribute to the psychological study of leisure (for reviews see Iso-Ahola, 1995; Argyle, 1996). Since then there has been a significant growth of interest in leisure as a psychological phenomenon outside of North America and Britain, with contributions from many areas of the world (Kleiber, Walker, and Mannell, 2011). Much of this research has been curiosity driven, but particularly in North America, where Leisure Studies scholarship has been typically located in university departments of parks and recreation, and a great deal of it reflects efforts to provide knowledge for evidence-based education and leisure-service practice (Mannell, 1984a; Ingham, 1987; Mannell, Kleiber, and Staempfli, 2006). Since the early 1990s, understanding the benefits of leisure (Driver and Bruns, 1999), including well-being (Mannell, 2007) and health promotion (Godbey *et al.*, 2005) as well as the constraints to participation in leisure and its potential benefits (Jackson, 2005), have strongly influenced psychologically oriented research within Leisure Studies.

In the discipline of psychology, leisure as a phenomenon in its own right has been largely ignored, although leisure settings have provided useful testing grounds for the study of basic psychological, particularly social-psychological, processes throughout psychology's history (Mannell *et al.*, 2006). The classic 'Robbers Cave' studies carried out by Muzafer Sherif and his associates (1961) used the leisure setting of children's summer camps to examine the role of group membership in the development of leadership and intergroup conflict. Leisure settings such as beaches (e.g., Moriarity, 1975) and bars (e.g., Gueguen, 2010) also have been used to study basic psychological processes such as altruism and interpersonal attraction. However, in recent years there has been some growth in psychological research outside of Leisure Studies published in non-leisure studies journals in which leisure activities and choices are used as variables to better understand a range of phenomena such as adolescent socialization (e.g., Schmid, 2012), mental health (e.g., Toker and Biron, 2012), self and identity (e.g., Carter and Gilovich, 2012), and electronic media and social support (e.g., Trepte, Reinecke, and Juechems, 2012).

The psychological study of leisure is also becoming more of an international enterprise (Mannell *et al.*, 2006), paralleling the globalization of mainstream psychology itself (Quiñones-Vidal *et al.*, 2004; Pickren, 2012). Concern with the limitations of transferring psychological ideas and research findings from North American and European to other cultural contexts (Yang *et al.*, 2003) has led to increased interest in developing indigenous psychologies reflecting cultural differences. Similar reservations have been voiced about uncritically imposing Western ideas about leisure globally (Iwasaki *et al.*, 2007). There is, however, growing international interest in using psychological perspectives to study leisure and its relationships to other phenomena. For example, leisure motivation and stress coping (Murray and Nakajima, 1999) and constraints (Lee and Scott, 2009) have been studied in Japan; the leisure motives of students in Canada and China (Walker and Wang, 2008); and free time use and quality of life in Korea (Cho *et al.* 2009).

With the maturing of the study of the socio-cultural and cross-cultural dimensions of leisure (Stodolska and Yi, 2003; Walker, Deng, and Dieser, 2005), psychological leisure researchers are also beginning to explore the cultural universality–relativity of Western theories of leisure behaviour. For example, Walker *et al.* (2005) have illustrated the way in which social-psychological cross-cultural analysis can be used to acquire a more informed picture of not only how, but why, the meaning of leisure and people's reactions to it might differ from one culture to another. Also, Iwasaki (2007) has argued that the development of culturally universal propositions about leisure's contributions to the quality of life are possible, but are dependent on researchers using research methods that are sensitive to international and cross-cultural differences. This type of thinking is aligned with contemporary thinking in mainstream psychology (see Hoshino-Browne, Zanna, Spencer, and Zanna, 2004).

Approaches to the psychological study of leisure

Social psychology

Social psychology is the scientific study of the behaviour and experience of individuals in social situations. Social psychologists attempt to understand how the actual, imagined, or implied presence of others influences the thoughts, feelings, and behaviours of individuals. In other words, what is going on in the person and the social environment interact to affect perceptions or misperceptions of social reality, which influence behaviour and experience (Ross and Nisbett, 1991). Lewin (1935) expressed this 'interactionism' perspective in his classic statement that behaviour is a function of the person and the environment, that is, $B=f(P, E)$. He believed that it is the person–environment unit that determines behaviour and that the individual cannot be separated from the environment because 'they interpenetrate one another in such a complex manner that any attempt to unravel them tends to destroy the natural unity of the whole and to create an artificial distinction between organism and environment' (p. 83). Researchers adopting this approach assume that people's understanding of situations is the result of an active, constructive process. Consequently, the impact of any 'objective' situation depends on the personal and subjective meanings that people attach to that situation.

Although not usually made explicit, a great deal of social-psychological leisure research is based on this interactionism premise. Dominated by survey and questionnaire methods, leisure researchers have relied on people's self-reports, in other words their subjective assessment of their social environments. For example, in research on leisure constraints, typically, study participants are asked to report the number and intensity of the constraints that they experience. These perceptions of constraints may, and likely do, differ from the actual level of constraint encountered, and are 'constructed' as a result of the interaction between internal psychological dispositions (e.g., expectations, beliefs, attitudes, moods, memories) and the external objective social situations in which constraints are encountered.

It is important to note, however, that there are other views of interactionism in psychology that have influenced the psychological study of leisure and involve examining the way in which relatively stable personality differences affect both how people perceive social situations and, subsequently, their response to them. This idea of 'person by situation' interactionism (Endler, 1983), which involves separating the 'person' and the 'situation', will be discussed later, along with personality approaches to the psychological study of leisure.

From 1974 to the present, a number of books have been published describing psychological research on leisure, and in particular promoting the use of social-psychological theory and its primarily post-positivist epistemology and characteristic use of quantitative research methods (Kleiber *et al.*, 2011). Some of the earliest leisure social-psychological research focused on understanding why people participate in outdoor recreation (see Manning, 1999), and concepts such as attitude, motivation, and satisfaction and mood, as well as social context, were used to explain a wide range of leisure behaviours (see Iso-Ahola, 1995). Early research also was concerned with ways to conceptualize and measure leisure as a psychological state and experience, and considerable progress has been made in that regard (for a review see Kleiber *et al.*, 2011).

Social-psychological theory and research published in Leisure Studies journals and edited books has increased and used ideas such as substitution, constraints and affordance, social influence and behaviour change, stress and coping, and physical, mental, and spiritual health and well-being to aid in understanding leisure. As well, the influence of leisure on family and interpersonal relationships, unemployment, work, work–life balance, and sense of community have been studied (see Kleiber *et al.*, 2011), and there has been growth in research on leisure and gender (see Henderson, Hodges, and Kivel, 2002), sexual orientation (e.g., Mock and Hummel, 2012), potentially negative life events such as caregiving (e.g., Dupuis, 2000), disability (e.g., Hutchinson, Loy, Kleiber, and Dattilo, 2003), and cross-cultural similarities and differences (e.g., Walker, Deng, and Dieser, 2005).

In spite of the growth of research, concerns have been raised over the years that much of it is atheoretical (Henderson, Presley, and Bialeschki, 2004). However, mainstream social-psychological theories have been used (e.g., psychological reactance, attribution, planned behaviour, cognitive dissonance, intrinsic motivation and self-determination theory, flow and complexity, stress–coping, self-efficacy, social exchange, and learned helplessness) and, in some cases, these theories have influenced the development of leisure-specific social-psychological theories in Leisure Studies. For example, the theory of intrinsic motivation and self-determination has been used extensively, and leisure-specific social-psychological theories built on ideas of intrinsic motivation include models of leisure experience (Neulinger, 1974) and tests of them (see Iso-Ahola, 1980). Psychological reactance theory has been used to explain and design tests of the influence of perceived freedom on flow in leisure activities (Mannell and Bradley, 1986) and as the basis for the theory of the substitutability of leisure behaviour (Iso-Ahola, 1986). The theory of transactional stress coping has been used in developing new theory about the role of leisure in coping with stress (Iwasaki, 2003). Also, theories of affordance and self-efficacy have been used (e.g., Kleiber, Wade, and Loucks-Atkinson, 2005; Loucks-Atkinson and Mannell, 2007) to extend leisure-constraint theory by describing the social-cognitive processes underlying the perception and operation of constraints to participation.

One area where the social-psychological study of leisure has not been in step with mainstream social psychology is in the extensive use of laboratory research methods. The experimental control over variables and settings allowing the management of extraneous influences and the identification of causal mechanisms are credited with the success of social psychology (Reis and Gosling, 2010). In the social psychology of leisure research, survey methods have dominated and only a relatively small number of laboratory, field, and quasi-experiments have been reported. However, other non-laboratory methods such as time-use diaries and experiential sampling have been used effectively and have led to advances in leisure researchers' ability to conceptualize, measure, and examine leisure experience and behaviour from a social-psychological perspective (Kleiber *et al.*, 2011).

Personality psychology

A personality approach to the study of leisure involves examining stable psychological dispositions as causes of leisure behaviour and experience. Also, leisure has been studied as an influence on personality, and on identity formation in particular (e.g., Collinson and Hickey, 2007). Personality dispositions may be learned, inherited, or a result of both types of influences, and personality is inferred from the enduring patterns of thought, feeling, and behaviour that people express in different circumstances. It also refers to the ways in which people are similar to and different from one another (Pervin, 1990). Personality dispositions are typically called traits. There have been a large number of personality traits identified; however, they can be reduced to five fundamental factors: extroversion, agreeableness, conscientiousness, neuroticism, and openness to experience. Often called the Five Factor Model or Big Five, these five traits have been found to be relatively consistent across cultures (McCrae and Costa, 1999)

Leisure researchers have attempted to predict leisure behaviour based on individual differences in traits. The study of relationships between personality and leisure interests and activities has been popular, in part due to the ease of measurement of traits using paper-and-pencil tests or inventories. Early research on personality and leisure was carried out to help outdoor recreation managers to identify the characteristics of recreationists interested in their sites and activities. Escape, affiliation, achievement, exploration, and social recognition were some of the personality-based individual differences identified (Knopf, 1983). However, early research was criticized as atheoretical, since trait measures were often used indiscriminately to find any personality characteristic related to leisure-activity participation, whether it made sense or not. However, meaningful associations have been found between specific traits and leisure-activity participation. For example, chess players were found to be more unconventional and to have a stronger need for order (Avni, Kipper, and Fox, 1987), and higher levels of internet use among young adults have been associated with extroversion, neuroticism, psychoticism, loneliness, and self-esteem (Hills and Argyle, 2003). In fact, the trait of extroversion has been found to be associated with many types of leisure involvements. People who spend a great deal of time playing computer fantasy games like *Dungeons and Dragons* appear to be less extroverted than the norm (Douse and McManus, 1983). Brandstätter (1994) found that, compared to introverts, extroverts more often used the freedom of leisure for stimulating and social activities. Also, high-adventure participants such as mountain climbers are typically high on extroversion (Egan and Stelmack, 2003), and extroversion is associated with experiencing greater boredom during leisure (Barnett and Klitzing, 2006).

Leisure researchers have also proposed and developed measures of leisure-specific personality traits. Playfulness is a personality construct that has been measured reliably in children (Barnett and Kleiber, 1984), adolescents (Staempfli, 2007), and young adults (Barnett, 2007), and in later life playfulness appears to be related to leisure choices characterized by unconventionality and fun (Yarnal, Chick, and Kerstetter, 2008). A measure of people's capacity to entertain themselves, that is, fill their leisure with mental, physical, or social activity that is personally satisfying, has been developed (Mannell, 1984b). Good self-entertainers have been found to be less likely to be bored during free time (Barnett and Klitzing, 2006) and more satisfied with their lives when they have substantial amounts of free time available (Mannell, 1984b). A related personality trait has been measured with the intrinsic leisure motivation scale (Weissinger and Bandalos, 1995) and people with high scores have also been found to be less likely to experience boredom during their leisure. These individuals have a strong desire to experience self-determination, competence, deep involvement, and challenge while engaging in leisure pursuits.

However, in spite of direct links found between people's personality traits and their leisure behaviour, the influence of personality characteristics such as the leisure-intrinsic motivation orientation have been shown to vary, depending on the social context (Iwasaki and Mannell, 1999). In fact, the importance of taking the social situation into account in understanding the influence of personality on behaviour and experience is extremely important and has been demonstrated in a number of other studies of leisure behaviour. Tang (1986), in a laboratory experiment, found that study participants' behaviour and experience were best predicted when both social situation (work versus leisure context) and personality dispositions (Type A versus Type B) were taken into account. Recreationists' intentions to obey rules in outdoor recreation areas were shown to depend on both personality and situational factors (Gramann and Bonifield, 1995), and in a study of recreation centre participants, peer influence interacted with the trait of adventurousness to predict inappropriate sexual activity (Person, Kerr, and Stattin, 2004).

Another aspect of leisure and personality of interest to researchers is related to the likelihood that people's leisure behaviour may more accurately reflect their personalities than at any other time in their daily lives, due to the greater freedom of choice and fewer constraints operating. For example, Diener, Larsen, and Emmons (1984) found that people's personalities were more likely to influence their choice of activities in leisure settings than in work settings. Mannell and Bradley (1986) found that when the social setting was highly unstructured and there were few guidelines and expectations for behaviour, as in many leisure settings, people who had a more internal locus of control (i.e., believe generally that they have high levels of control) became more psychologically involved in a laboratory game when they were given more freedom to choose the game, as compared to those with an external locus of control (i.e., who believe generally that they have little control over the things that happen to them).

Regardless of the approach taken in conceptualizing personality and its interaction with the social situation, researchers continue to be fascinated by personality-based explanations of leisure behaviour. Currently, personality approaches are being used to provide insights into new and emerging forms of leisure such as internet use and online gaming (e.g., Orchard and Fullwood, 2010).

Developmental psychology

A developmental perspective suggests that the internal psychological dispositions that people 'carry' around with them and the social situations that influence leisure behaviour and experience change throughout life. Age has been shown to be a highly relevant conditioning circumstance of leisure interests, activities, and experience over the lifespan. Interest in leisure socialization and the influence of life changes on leisure have continued to grow (Kleiber, 1999) and greater attention is starting to be given to the role of leisure in childhood and adolescent development (Hutchinson, Baldwin, and Caldwell, 2003). Furthermore, researchers are examining the ways in which leisure activity and experience contribute to adjusting to life events, both predictable (e.g., parenthood, retirement) and unpredictable (e.g., unemployment, widowhood).

The strongest case for chronological age alone being a determinant of leisure behaviour is in the evolution of childhood play. Starting with Jean Piaget (1962) and Erik Erikson (1963), and in subsequent work by many others (Bjorklund, 2007; Elkind, 2007; Brown, 2009), the biological development of the child is now seen to be characterized by changes in play orientation, unfolding quite naturally as children transition from solitary, practice-oriented play, through imaginative play, and ultimately into cooperative game play – play that reflects evolution in cognitive, emotional, social, and even moral development. However, the development of leisure attitudes, preferences, and behaviour patterns from childhood on is almost entirely socially constructed rather than biologically driven and this leisure socialization has been a research subject for over 30 years (Kelly, 1977, 2011). Essentially, this work has been about the social influences, particularly parents, peers, and institutions that foster leisure interests and skills in both active and passive ways. The processes of identification, imitation, and modelling are largely responsible for leading children forward into leisure activity and experience, while the internalization of leisure values and commitment to activities and interests allows a greater degree of self-regulation and personal choice with age. Self-socialization also occurs to the extent that children and adolescents use leisure activities to become part of the larger world and learn its rules (Kleiber, 1999).

There is some predictability, if not inevitability, in the issues and tasks confronting developing individuals in a given culture that influence leisure behaviour and experience as well as the role that leisure can play in dealing with those issues and tasks. What remains especially at issue from a developmental perspective is the question of autonomy and self-direction versus social accommodation, which often makes leisure – a context pre-eminently reflective of relative freedom – 'contested terrain' for the evolution of self-expression and sociability. For example, adolescence has been recognized as a critical period for identity development. The dialectical dynamics of identification and individuation are often worked out in weekend and after-school leisure activity choices that reflect both conformity and resistance to the interests of peers, parents, and other adults, as well as self-discovery influenced by the inspiring images of others, need for social recognition, involvement with others, and individual moments of joy and pleasure (Caldwell and Darling, 1999; Kleiber, 1999; Larson, 2000).

When leisure is examined as an agent of socialization over the entire life span, the resolution of developmental tasks and issues involved with the experience of parenthood, unemployment, retirement, etc. can be aided by leisure involvements. That is, leisure can serve as a palliative condition in modulating developmental change. Certainly, with predictable, normative transitions such as retirement, marriage, or the birth of a child, the 'free space' of leisure may afford the context for managing the demands and expectations of role changes while maintaining continuity of other roles or aspects of them. The same may also be said of non-normative life events, particularly negative life events, where the distress associated may be mitigated through the distraction of leisure activities or through the resumption of some form of stability (Kleiber, 1999; Kleiber, Hutchinson and Williams, 2002). If events such as an injury, a divorce, or the loss of a significant other disrupt people's lives, familiar activities can help to repair the disruptions, which may be both psychological and social.

Cross-cultural differences in the developmental influences and consequences of leisure socialization have not received significant attention as yet. However, even in Western cultures, where most of the research has been completed, historical changes modify the social circumstances and opportunities that shape socialization for successive generations and can create distinctive cohort effects. For example, patterns of modernization and social complexity have given rise to a period in between adolescence and young adulthood, at least in Western societies, called 'emerging adulthood' (Arnett, 2000), where commitments and entry into an adult establishment period are delayed and the exploratory aspects of adolescent identity formation are extended and commonly reflected in experimentation with drugs, sexuality, and social and political affiliations. Also, a lengthened lifespan afforded by better health and wealth has created a post-retirement 'third age'. Consequently, previous assumptions of continuity of leisure interests and relaxation of social and personal ambitions appear to be giving way to other priorities such as increased expectations for innovation, experimentation, and re-examination of life purposes. This third age is also leading some to reconstruct work to be more intrinsically satisfying and leisure-like as part of a restructuring of developmental priorities among the 'young old' (Freedman, 1999; Vaillant, 2002; Nimrod and Kleiber, 2007; Kleiber and Nimrod, 2008).

The field of gerontology itself has been a major contributor over the years to the developmental psychology of leisure (for reviews, see Gibson and Singleton, 2011). It has been a source of theoretical development, where prevailing models of successful aging (e.g. Baltes and Carstensen, 1996) have put emphasis on leisure activity as a source of healthy engagement, on the one hand, and later life leisure as a context for disengagement, selection, and present-centredness, on the other (see Kleiber, 1999; Tornstam, 1997).

Finally, even those relatively predictable developmental changes in play patterns in childhood are being influenced by evolutions in media, technology, and the priorities of parents (Mannell, Kaczynski, and Aronson, 2005; Elkind, 2007; Brown, 2009). Clearly, developmental approaches are critical to understanding the changing nature of leisure behaviour and experience over the life course, and leisure's ongoing impact on development and socialization.

Conclusions

This discussion of the psychology of leisure has explored developments that have occurred primarily in the field of Leisure Studies where the focus is on explaining the choices that people make in using their free time, and the influence of these choices on their lives. Clearly, psychological approaches have been popular in Leisure Studies and considerable progress has been made, including the growth of international research. Psychological leisure research has been primarily social-psychological in recognition of the fact that most leisure behaviour and experience occur in the various social contexts that comprise daily life. However, the psychology of leisure has been informed by personality and developmental perspectives as well. Researchers continue to be fascinated by personality differences in leisure behaviour, particularly with respect to new and emerging forms of leisure. In the case of developmental perspectives, although there are long-standing traditions for understanding socialization 'into' and 'through' leisure (e.g., Rapoport and Rapoport, 1975; Kelly, 1977; Kleiber and Kelly, 1980), it is only in the last couple of decades that such research has been extended throughout the lifespan. With the ageing population and changing demographics, it will likely continue.

In spite of the growth of psychological interest in leisure as a potentially influential concept in other fields, there is little formal recognition of the psychology of leisure as a distinct field of study outside of Leisure Studies. Even areas of study more closely aligned with Leisure Studies with psychological traditions, such as tourism and sport and exercise, constitute relatively separate fields of study with limited cross-fertilization with the psychology of leisure. Consequently, it is not surprising that researchers in other fields who incorporate leisure concepts and variables into their research appear unaware of the field and do not see their work as necessarily contributing to a psychology of leisure. Rather, leisure appears to be seen as a domain of human behaviour that can be useful in understanding issues and problems that are germane to those fields. As well, some types of leisure behaviour, particularly newly emerging forms, such as online gaming and gambling, are receiving greater attention from psychologically oriented scholars outside of Leisure Studies, and this research is being published in non-leisure journals. The US, Canadian, and British psychological associations have divisions devoted to the psychology of law, religion, media, health, environment, etc. as well as exercise and sport. The psychology of leisure is not represented in these organizations. These other psychological subfields typically support one or more journals dealing exclusively with their theory and research. No such journals exist for the psychology of leisure. Most psychological leisure research in Leisure Studies is published along with other social science research on leisure in the major leisure sciences or studies journals. Although this lack of identity may be a sign of immaturity for the psychology of leisure, it is not entirely negative, since a separate identity might contribute to a segmentation of Leisure Studies and an erosion of its multidisciplinary nature – a feature of Leisure Studies that is greatly valued by those interested in leisure as a phenomenon in its own right and not just as a variable that might help to explain other phenomena. However, if the psychology of leisure is to flourish and attract scholars from a variety of fields, such developments may be necessary to enhance its identity.

References

Argyle, M. (1996) *The Social Psychology of Leisure*. London: Penguin.

Arnett, J. J. (2000) 'Emerging Adulthood: A Theory of Development for the Late Teens through the Twenties', *American Psychologist* 55: 469–480.

Avni, A., Kipper, D., and Fox, S. (1987) 'Personality and Leisure Activities: An Illustration with Chess Players', *Personality and Individual Differences* 8: 715–719.

Baltes, M. M., and Carstensen, L. L. (1996) 'The Process of Successful Aging', *Aging and Society, 16*: 398–404.

Barnett, L. A. (2007) 'The Nature of Playfulness in Young Adults', *Personality and Individual Differences* 43: 949–958.

Barnett, L. A. and Kleiber, D. A. (1984) 'Playfulness and the Early Play Environment', *Journal of Genetic Psychology 144*: 153–164.

Barnett, L., and Klitzing, S. (2006) 'Boredom in Free Time: Relationships with Personality, Affect, and Motivation for Different Gender, Racial and Ethnic Student Groups', *Leisure Sciences 28*: 223.

Bjorklund, D. (2007) *Why Youth is Not Wasted on the Young: Immaturity in Human Development*. Malden, MA: Blackwell.

Brandstätter, H. (1994) 'Pleasure of Leisure – Pleasure of Work: Personality Makes the Difference', *Personality and Individual Differences 16*: 931–946.

Brown, S. (2009) *Play*. New York: Avery/Penguin.

Caldwell, L. L. and Darling, N. (1999) 'Leisure Context, Parental Control, and Resistance to Peer Pressure as Predictors of Adolescent Partying and Substance Use: An Ecological Perspective', *Journal of Leisure Research 31*: 57–68.

Carter, T., and Gilovich, T. (2012) 'I Am What I Do, Not What I Have: The Differential Centrality of Experiential and Material Purchases to the Self', *Journal of Personality and Social Psychology 102*: 1304–1317.

Cho, H. K., Lee, K. Y., Lee, Y. S., Kim, O. S., Lee, S. M., Hong, D. S., Cho, H.S., and Kim, Y. K. (2009) 'Time Use and Quality of Life of the Korean Rural Poor', *Social Indicators Research 93*: 223–227.

Collinson, J. A., and Hickey, J. (2007) '"Working Out" Identity: Distance Runners and the Management of Disrupted Identity', *Leisure Studies 26*: 381–398.

Diener, E., Larsen, R. J., and Emmons, R. A. (1984) 'Person x Situation Interactions: Choice of Situations and Congruence Response Models', *Journal of Personality and Social Psychology 47*: 580–592.

Douse, N. A., and McManus, I. C. (1983) 'The Personality of Fantasy Game Players', *British Journal of Psychology 84*: 505–510.

Driver, B. L., and Bruns, D. H. (1999) 'Concepts and Uses of the Benefits Approach to Leisure', in E. L. Jackson, and T. L. Burton (eds) *Leisure Studies: Prospects for the Twenty-First Century* (pp. 349–369) State College, PA: Venture Publishing.

Dupuis, S. (2000) 'Institution-Based Caregiving as a Container for Leisure', *Leisure Sciences 22*: 259–280.

Egan, S., and Stelmack, R. M. (2003) 'A Personality Profile of Mount Everest Climbers', *Personality and Individual Differences 34*: 1491–1494.

Elkind, D. (2007) '*The Power of Play*. Cambridge, MA: Da Capo Press.

Endler, N. S. (1983) 'Interactionism: A Personality Model, but not yet a Theory', in M. M. Page (ed.) *Nebraska Symposium on Motivation* (pp. 155–200). Lincoln, NB: University of Nebraska Press.

Freedman, M. (1999) *Prime Time: How Baby Boomers Will Revolutionize Retirement and Transform America*. Cambridge, MA: Perseus.

Gibson, H., and Singleton, J. (eds) (2011) *Leisure, Aging and Well-Being*. Champaign, IL: Human Kinetics.

Godbey, G. C., Caldwell, L. L., Floyd, M., and Payne, L. L. (2005) 'Contributions of Leisure Studies and Recreation and Park Management Research to the Active Living Agenda', *American Journal of Preventative Medicine 28*: 150–158.

Gramann, J. H., and Bonifield, R. L. (1995) 'Effect of Personality and Situational Factors on Intentions to Obey Rules in Outdoor Recreation Areas', *Journal of Leisure Research 27*: 326–343.

Gueguen, N. (2010) 'The Effect of a Woman's Incidental Tactile Contact on Men's Later Behavior', *Social Behavior and Personality: An International Journal 38*: 257–266.

Henderson, K. A., Hodges, S., Kivel, B. D. (2002) 'Context and Dialogue in Research on Women and Leisure', *Journal of Leisure Research 34*: 253–271.

Henderson, K. A., Presley, J., and Bialeschki, M. D. (2004) 'Theory in Recreation and Leisure Research: Reflections from the Editors', *Leisure Sciences 26*: 411–425.

Hills, P., and Argyle, M. (2003) 'Uses of the Internet and their Relationships with Individual Differences in Personality', *Computers in Human Behavior 19*: 59–70.

Hoshino-Browne, E., Zanna, A. S., Spencer, S. J., and Zanna, M. P. (2004) 'Investigating Attitudes Cross-Culturally: A Case of Cognitive Dissonance among East Asians and North Americans', in G. Haddock, and G. R. Maio (eds) *Contemporary Perspectives on the Psychology of Attitude* (pp. 375–399). Hove, England: Psychology Press.

Hutchinson, S. L., Baldwin, C. K., Caldwell, L. L. (2003) 'Differentiating Parent Practices Related to Adolescent Behavior in the Free Time Context', *Journal of Leisure Research 35*: 396–422.

Hutchinson, S. L., Loy, D. P., Kleiber, D. A., and Dattilo, J. (2003) 'Leisure as a Coping Resource: Variations in Coping with Traumatic Injury and Illness', *Leisure Sciences. Special Issue: Leisure, Stress, and Coping 25:* 143–161.

Ingham, R. (1987) 'Psychological Contributions to the Study of Leisure – part two', *Leisure Studies 6:* 1–14.

Iso-Ahola, S. E. (1980) *The Social Psychology of Leisure and Recreation.* Dubuque, Iowa: Wm. C. Brown Company Publishers.

Iso-Ahola, S. E. (1986) 'A Theory of Substitutability of Leisure Behavior', *Leisure Sciences 8:* 367–389.

Iso-Ahola, S. E. (1995) 'The Social Psychology of Leisure: Past, Present, and Future Research', in L. A. Barnett (ed.) *Research about Leisure: Past, Present, and Future Research* (2nd ed., pp. 65–96). Champaign, IL: Sagamore.

Iwasaki, Y. (2003) 'The Impact of Leisure Coping Beliefs and Strategies on Adaptive Outcomes', *Leisure Studies 22:* 93–108.

Iwasaki, Y. (2007) 'Leisure and Quality of Life in an International and Multicultural Context: What are Major Pathways Linking Leisure to Quality of Life?', *Social Indicators Research 82:* 233–264.

Iwasaki, Y., and Mannell, R. C. (1999) 'Situational and Personality Influences on Intrinsically Motivated Leisure Behavior: Interaction Effects and Cognitive Processes', *Leisure Sciences 21:* 287–306.

Iwasaki, Y., Nishino, H., Onda, T., and Bowling, C. (2007) 'Leisure Research in a Global World: Time to Reverse the Western Domination in Leisure Research?', *Leisure Sciences 29:* 113–117.

Jackson, E. L. (ed.) (2005) *Constraints to Leisure.* College Park, PA: Venture Publishing.

Kelly, J. R. (1977) 'Leisure Socialization: Replication and Extension', *Journal of Leisure Research 9:* 121–132.

Kelly, J. R. (2011) *Leisure* (5th ed.). Boston, MA: Allyn and Bacon.

Kleiber, D. A. (1999) *Leisure Experience and Human Development.* New York, NY: Basic Books.

Kleiber, D. A., and Kelly, J. R. (1980) 'Leisure, Socialization, and the Life Cycle', in S. E. Iso-Ahola (ed.), *Social Psychological Perspectives on Leisure and Recreation* (pp. 91–137). Springfield, IL: Charles C. Thomas

Kleiber, D. A., and Nimrod, G. (2008) 'Expressions of Generativity and Civic Engagement in a "Learning in Retirement" Group', *Journal of Adult Development 15:* 76–86.

Kleiber, D. A., Hutchinson, S. L., and Williams, R. (2002) 'Leisure as a Resource in Transcending Negative Life Events: Self-Protection, Self-Restoration, and Personal Transformation', *Leisure Sciences 24:* 219–235.

Kleiber, D. A., Wade, M., and Loucks-Atkinson, A. (2005) 'The Utility of the Concept of Affordance for Leisure Research', in E. Jackson (ed.) *Constraints to Leisure* (pp. 233–243). State College, PA: Venture Publishing, Inc.

Kleiber, D. A., Walker, G., and Mannell, R. C. (2011) *A Social Psychology of Leisure* (2nd ed.). State College, PA: Venture Publishing, Inc.

Knopf, R. C. (1983) 'Recreational Needs and Behavior in Natural Settings', in I. Altman and J. F. Wohlwill (eds) *Behavior and the Natural Environment* (pp. 205–240). New York, NY: Plenum Press.

Larson, R. (2000) 'Toward a Psychology of Positive Youth Development', *American Psychologist 55:* 170–183.

Lee, S., and Scott, D. (2009) 'The Process of Celebrity Fan's Constraint Negotiation', *Journal of Leisure Research 41:* 137–156.

Lewin, K. (1935) *Dynamic Theory of Personality.* New York, NY: McGraw-Hill.

Loucks-Atkinson, A., and Mannell, R. C. (2007) 'The Role of Self-Efficacy in the Constraints Negotiation Process: The Case of Individuals with Fibromyalgia Syndrome', *Leisure Sciences 29:* 19–36.

Mannell, R. C. (1984a) 'A Psychology for Leisure Research', *Society and Leisure 7:* 13–21.

Mannell, R. C. (1984b) 'Personality in Leisure Theory: The Self-as-Entertainment Construct', *Loisir et Société/Society and Leisure 7:* 229–242.

Mannell, R. C. (2007) 'Health, Well-Being and Leisure', *World Leisure Journal 49:* 114–128.

Mannell, R. C., and Bradley, W. (1986) 'Does Greater Freedom Always Lead to Greater Leisure? Testing a Person x Environment Model of Freedom and Leisure', *Journal of Leisure Research 18:* 215–230.

Mannell, R. C., and Kleiber, D. A. (1997) *A Social Psychology of Leisure.* State College, PA: Venture Publishing.

Mannell, R. C., Kaczynski, A. T., and Aronson, R. M. (2005) 'Adolescent Participation and Flow in Physically Active Leisure and Electronic Media Activities: Testing the Displacement Hypothesis', *Loisir et Société/Society and Leisure 28*: 653–675.

Mannell, R. C., Kleiber, D. A., and Staempfli, M. (2006) 'Psychology and Social Psychology and the Study of Leisure', in C. Rojek, S. M. Shaw, and A. J. Veal (eds) *A Handbook of Leisure Studies* (pp. 109–124). New York: Palgrave Macmillan.

Manning, R. E. (1999) *Studies in Outdoor Recreation: A Review and Synthesis of the Social Science Literature in Outdoor Recreation.* Covallis, OR: Oregon State University Press.

McCrae, R. R., and Costa, P. T. (1999) 'A Five-Factor Theory of Personality', in L. A. Pervin, and O. P. John (eds) *Handbook of Personality: Theory and Research.* (2nd ed., pp. 139–153). New York: Academic Press.

Mock, S. E., and Hummel, E. M. (2012) 'Sexual Minority Adults at a Seasonal Home Campground: An Examination of Common, Unique, and Diverse Leisure Motivations', *Leisure Sciences 34*: 155–171.

Moriarity, T. (1975) 'Crime, Commitment, and the Responsive Bystander: Two Field Experiments', *Journal of Personality and Social Psychology 31*: 37–376.

Murray, C., and Nakajima, I. (1999) 'The Leisure Motivation of Japanese Managers: A Research Note on Scale Development', *Leisure Studies 18 (1)* 57–65.

Neulinger, J. (1974) *Psychology of Leisure: Research Approaches to the Study of Leisure.* Springfield: Charles C. Thomas.

Nimrod, G., and Kleiber, D. A. (2007) 'Reconsidering Change and Continuity in Later Life: Toward an Innovation Theory of Successful Aging', *International Journal of Aging and Human Development 65*: 1–22.

Orchard, L. J., and Fullwood, C. (2010) 'Current Perspectives on Personality and Internet Use', *Social Science Computer Review 28*: 155–169.

Person, A., Kerr, M., and Stattin, H. (2004) 'Why a Leisure Context is Linked to Norm-Breaking for Some Girls and Not Others: Personality Characteristics and Parent–Child Relations as Explanations', *Journal of Adolescence 27*: 583–598.

Pervin, L. A. (1990) 'A Brief History of Modern Personality Theory', in L. A. Pervin (ed.) *Handbook of Personality: Theory and Research* (pp. 3–18). New York: The Guilford Press.

Pickren, W. E. (2012) 'Internationalizing the History of Psychology Course in the USA', in F. T. L. Leong, W. E. Pickren, M. M. Leach and A. J. Marsella (eds) *Internationalizing the Psychology Curriculum in the United States* (pp. 11–28). New York: Springer.

Quiñones-Vidal, E., Lozpez-García, J., Peñarañda-Ortega, M., and Tortosa-Gil, F. (2004) 'The Nature of Social and Personality Psychology as Reflected in JPSP, 1965–2000', *Journal of Personality and Social Psychology 86*: 435–452.

Rapoport, R., and Rapoport, R. N. (1975) *Leisure and the Family Life Cycle.* London: Routledge.

Reis, H. T., and Gosling, S. D. (2010) 'Social Psychological Methods Outside the Laboratory', in S. T. Fiske, D. T. Gilbert, and G. Lindzey (eds) *Handbook of Social Psychology.* New York: John Wiley and Sons.

Ross, L., and Nisbett, R. (1991) *The Person and the Situation: Perspectives of Social Psychology.* New York: McGraw-Hill Publishing.

Schmid, C. (2012) 'The Value "Social Responsibility" as a Motivating Factor for Adolescents' Readiness to Participate in Different Types of Political Actions, and its Socialization in Parent and Peer Contexts', *Journal of Adolescence 35*: 533–547.

Sherif, M., Harvey, O. J., White, B., Hood, W. R., and Sherif, C. W. (1961) *Intergroup Conflict and Cooperation: The Robbers Caves Experiment.* Norman, OK: Institute of Group Relations, University of Oklahoma.

Staempfli, M. B. (2007) 'Adolescent Playfulness, Stress Perception, Coping and Well-Being', *Journal of Leisure Research 39*: 393–412.

Stodolska, M., and Yi, J. (2003) 'Impacts of Immigration on Ethnic Identity and Leisure Behavior of Adolescent Immigrants from Korea, Mexico and Poland', *Journal of Leisure Research 35*: 49–79.

Tang, T. L. (1986) 'Effects of Type-A Personality and Task Labels (Work vs. Leisure) on Task Preference', *Journal of Leisure Research 18*: 1–11.

Toker, S., and Biron, M. (2012) 'Job Burnout and Depression: Unraveling their Temporal Relationship and Considering the Role of Physical Activity', *Journal of Applied Psychology 97*: 699–710.

Tornstam, L. (1997) 'Gerotranscendence: The Contemplative Dimension of Aging', *Journal of Aging Studies 11*: 143–154.

Trepte, S., Reinecke, L., and Juechems, K. (2012) 'The Social Side of Gaming: How Playing Online Computer Games Creates Online and Offline Social Support', *Computers in Human Behavior 28:* 832–839.

Vaillant, G. (2002) *Aging Well*. New York: Little, Brown.

Walker, G. J., and Wang, X. (2008) 'A Cross-Cultural Comparison of Canadian and Mainland Chinese University Students' Leisure Motivations', *Leisure Sciences 30:* 179–197.

Walker, G. J., Deng, J., and Dieser, R. B. (2005) 'Culture, Self-Construal, and Leisure Theory and Practice', *Journal of Leisure Research 37:* 77–99.

Weissinger, E., and Bandalos, D. L. (1995) 'Development, Reliability and Validity of a Scale to Measure Intrinsic Motivation in Leisure', *Journal of Leisure Research 27:* 379–400.

Yang, K., Hwang, K., Pedersen, P. B., and Daibo, I. (eds) (2003) *Progress in Asian Social Psychology: Conceptual and Empirical Contributions*. Westport, CT: Praeger Publishers/Greenwood Publishing.

Yarnal, C. M., Chick, G., and Kerstetter, D. (2008) '"I Did Not Have Time to Play Growing Up ... So This is My Play Time. It's the Best Thing I Have Ever Done for Myself": What is Play to Older Women?' *Leisure Sciences 30:* 235–252

5

ECONOMICS OF LEISURE

Chris Gratton

Introduction

Few economists have used the concept of leisure extensively. Most standard economics text-books will have only one entry in the index for the word 'leisure'; and this entry will refer to the income/leisure trade-off model that we discuss in the first section of this chapter. The primary reason for this is that whereas academics studying leisure spend their time looking at what people do in their leisure time, economists see leisure as what is left over after we have done both paid and unpaid work. From their perspective, it is a residual.

Even though economics as a subject has tended to ignore leisure, a small number of economists have not. Three economists, Becker (1965), Linder (1970) and Scitovsky (1976), made a major contribution to the way that economics can help us to understand leisure behaviour. The second section of the chapter will look at what these economists have had to say about leisure.

The income/leisure trade-off

Neo-classical economic analysis assumes that the allocation of time between work and leisure is driven by individuals' decision making. Rational utility-maximizing consumers are faced with a continuous choice over how to allocate their time, principally between leisure, paid work and 'obligated time' (for such activities as housework, hygiene and sleeping). Paid work is treated as disutility, and consumers need compensation in terms of income to persuade them to give up their leisure time. If we assume that obligated time is a constant, the key choice for individuals is between paid work and leisure – the income/leisure trade-off. Any time spent in leisure means losing potential earnings, so that the opportunity cost, or *price of leisure* is the forgone earnings. If people behave rationally, they will enter the labour market and continue to work only as long as the benefits from income outweigh the benefits from leisure time.

If a decision is made to enter the labour market, it implies that the initial hours of paid work are worth more than the hours of leisure that they replace. The next decision concerns how many hours to work. The more hours the consumer works, the more valuable each hour of leisure time becomes that is left, as leisure time becomes increasingly scarce. Eventually there will come a point when the additional income earned from an additional hour of work (i e , the hourly wage rate) is not sufficient to compensate for the loss of another hour of leisure time. The optimum trade-off between time spent at work and time spent at leisure will be at the point when the valuation of an hour of leisure time is equal to the wage rate. Working longer hours than this optimum would mean that the consumer was irrationally choosing to forsake leisure time that was worth more than the income from the extra work.

This mechanism of choice has been used in economics to analyse individual decisions concerning whether or not to work, whether to take part-time or full-time employment, whether to work more hours in a week (overtime) or whether to take a second job (moon-lighting). The crucial point, though, is that the economist's interest is in the labour market and how many hours the worker spends in it. Leisure is not the main interest in this model.

A crucial part of the analysis is how people react to a change in the hourly rate of pay, the price of leisure time. Over time, rates of pay usually rise, even in real terms. How does this affect the income/leisure choice? In neo-classical economics theory there are two contrasting influences caused by a change in a price: the substitution effect and the income effect. Firstly, because the price of leisure time is rising there is an inducement to take less leisure time and devote more time to work. This is the normal demand relationship: for any commodity, as the relative price rises, we demand less of it. This is the substitution effect.

Secondly, because rates of pay for all *existing* work hours are higher, total income will rise even if the amount of time spent at work does not change. Some of this extra income may be used to 'buy' more leisure time, by working fewer hours. If leisure time is a 'normal good', which in economics means that demand for it rises as incomes rise, then we would expect demand for leisure time to rise as rates of pay rise. This is the income effect.

Thus we have two effects pulling in opposite directions, and the net effect on the demand for leisure time is uncertain. Whether leisure time increases or decreases as wage rates rise is an empirical question. We need to look at the evidence.

Two qualifying observations should be made about the indicators used to represent work and leisure-time allocations. First, leisure time is rarely measured directly. Leisure time is more typically assumed to be the residual in any given time period after paid work time has been measured. Second, the assumption that time not in paid work is leisure time ignores obligated time. There are also 'grey areas' in the use of time that are partly obligated and partly leisure, such as eating, shopping, travelling and DIY. At the simplest level of analysis these obligated or partly obligated time allocations may be assumed to be constant, but this may not be correct.

Over the long term, the basic working week (excluding overtime) in the UK has been falling. From an average of over 44 hours a week in 1950, it fell to around 40 in the late 1960s (Gratton and Taylor, 2000). Thereafter it declined at a much slower rate. One estimate for 2000 is of a basic working week of 37 or 37½ hours for manual workers and 35–37 hours for non-manual workers (IDS, 2000). A different picture emerges, however, when overtime is taken into account.

One of the features of the UK labour market has been the predominance of overtime working. In the early 1990s half of men in manual jobs worked an average of ten hours a week of paid overtime, and 30% of female manual workers worked an average of six hours a week of paid overtime. The scale and length of paid overtime working for non-manual workers is typically lower.

Despite the long, paid overtime hours of manual workers, it is not those at the bottom end of the income distribution that are working the longest hours in the UK, as might have been expected. Those who are contributing most to a so-called 'long hours culture' in the UK are the better-educated, the higher-paid, those in middle and senior management. Gershuny (1996), Britain's most prominent economic researcher into time allocation, reports evidence from the British Household Panel Survey to indicate that those with the highest monthly income have clearly the longest working hours. He estimates that for men, on average, excluding the unemployed, the highest-paid 20% of the workforce work ten hours longer per week than do the lowest-paid.

The Institute for Employment Studies (Kodz, Kersley and Strebler, 1998) reported that one in four UK employees regularly worked more than 48 hours a week, exceeding the European Union's Working Time Directive. One in five worked an extra 14 hours a week over their contracted hours, with managers, professionals and specialist occupations the most typical of those working such long hours. Nine out of ten people in this study blamed increased workloads as a major cause of long-hours working.

An Institute of Management survey (Charlesworth, 1996) also reinforced Gershuny's findings. A random sample of 3,000 managers returned 1,073 questionnaires. Of these, 12% were of chief executive/managing director status, a further 36% senior management, and 25% junior management. Of this sample 47% were aged between 45 and 54. Thus the sample included a high proportion of people at the top end of the jobs hierarchy. Nearly six in ten respondents claimed that they always worked in excess of their official working week. Among the sample, 49% regularly took work home, with 18% always doing so; whilst 41% of the sample regularly worked at weekends, with 14% always doing so. More than eight in ten of respondents reported that their workload had increased over the past year, with 47% stating that it had increased greatly.

Furthermore, it is apparent that for many managers and professionals, working longer hours is not a simple substitution effect whereby leisure time is 'bought' by a premium pay rate. A study on work–life balance in the UK (Hogarth, Hasluck and Pierre, 2000) reported that more than one in three employees who worked in excess of their standard or fixed hours of work received neither additional pay nor time off in lieu for any additional hours worked. The most common incidence of this was for senior managers: in two-thirds of workplaces they were neither paid nor had time off in lieu of additional hours.

This impression is reinforced by the Department for Education and Employment (DfEE, 1999) report on results from the Labour Force Survey in the winter of 1997/98. This indicated that whilst 23% of male workers and 12% of female workers worked paid overtime during the period covered, 18% of men and 20% of women worked unpaid overtime. Only 2% worked both paid and unpaid overtime. Whilst it was manual occupations that topped the list of those working paid overtime, it was managers and professionals who were most likely to be working unpaid overtime.

Survey evidence has provided a consistent picture that the amount of work and leisure time being experienced is often not what individuals actually want. In the Institute of Management survey (Charlesworth, 1996) 60% of British managers found it difficult to find enough time for relaxation, for hobbies/interests and time for their partner. Another survey, commissioned by the Chartered Institute of Personnel and Development (Compton-Edwards, 2001), researched a sample of 291 people who worked longer than 48 hours in a typical week in 1998 and continued to do so in 2000. The results suggest that most of such 'long hours' workers feel that they have struck the wrong work–life balance, 56% saying that they have dedicated too much of their life to work, whilst 54% claimed that they suffered from mental exhaustion or always feeling drained and 43% experienced difficulty sleeping. Fewer than half the sample (47%) claimed that working long hours was entirely their own choice, with 43% sometimes working long hours reluctantly and 10% working long hours reluctantly most or all of the time. Clearly, even in this sample, known to work long hours for years, work time is not always a matter of choice.

Gershuny (1996) reports evidence to show that there is a clear preference amongst those working the longest hours to reduce their working hours. A staggering 57% of women in the top 20% of income earners and of working hours wanted to reduce their working hours in 1994/95. As you move up the hierarchy of either income or working hours the preference for reducing working hours grows. The preference for reducing working hours rises more steeply for women than for men. Part of the reason for the higher preferences of women for shorter working hours may be the length of time that they also spend on domestic unpaid work outside the workplace.

Gershuny (1997) shows that although there has been a slight reduction in women's house-work (cleaning, clothes washing and cooking) time since 1961, there has been a sharp rise in time spent on shopping and domestic travel and, perhaps more surprisingly, a massive rise in the amount of time that both women and men spend on childcare. Even though family size has declined, Gershuny's evidence suggests that childcare time has almost doubled for both men and women in every category. He found that full-time employed women with children in 1995 appeared to devote more time to children than even non-employed mothers did in 1961.

Overall though Gershuny's evidence does suggest that in addition to increasing working hours there is also increasing time committed to other domestic chores, so they cannot simply be assumed to be constant.

The evidence for the UK suggests that the standard economic theory of individual employees' work/leisure time decisions being made in response to rates of pay is too simple. The main expectation from the standard theory (given an assumption that leisure is a normal good), that a strong income effect will cause work time to contract as rates of pay rise in the long term, has not been realized in the last 25 years in the UK, particularly for higher-level, full-time occupations. Furthermore, individual preferences in work/leisure time allocations can often not be realized.

Gershuny (1999) attempts an overall summary of time allocations for the UK in the period 1961 to 1995, using data from time-budget studies. This presents trends for all people in the age band 20–60 years. The results for those in full-time employment are as follows:

- paid work time falling from 1961 to 1985; then rising from 1985 to 1995
- unpaid work time falling from 1961 to 1975, rising sharply from 1975 to 1985, then more or less constant from 1985 to 1995
- paid and unpaid work time combined falling from 1961 to 1985, then rising from 1985 to 1995.

The reason why leisure time has not expanded post-1985 for those in full-time employment is not necessarily that leisure is an inferior good (where, as incomes rise, less is demanded), although for some employees this may be the case. In practice, the more persuasive evidence is that many preferences of employees, both for reduced work time and work at more flexible times, are being frustrated by labour market constraints. The economic theory that workers have a choice over their working hours is simply not supported by the evidence. The evidence presented above casts serious doubt on the validity in practice of the one part of standard economic theory that deals with leisure: the income/leisure trade-off model.

Beyond the income/leisure trade-off model

Some economists have produced a more comprehensive economic approach to the study of leisure than simply the decision on how much leisure time to have. Becker (1965) introduced a novel approach to consumer demand that is particularly relevant for the demand for leisure. His approach treats consumption as household production, which demonstrates that any activity undertaken by an individual or household, even a pure leisure activity, involves inputs of market goods and time.

Becker terms these activities 'composite commodities'. Each composite commodity involves different inputs of market goods and time, so that when the price of time or market goods alters, the effect on consumption of different activities will be varied.

In the long run, as real wage rates increase, the price of time rises relative to the price of market goods. Time is a finite input to household production, whereas market goods can be continually expanded. The change in relative prices causes consumption patterns to alter. Once again, substitution and income effects operate to give a change in the optimum consumption pattern.

As the relative prices of time and market goods change, household production and consumption also alter to a different package of time-intensive and goods-intensive commodities. As wage rates rise, if the substitution effect dominates, the end result is falling consumption of time-intensive commodities. In practice, the household and individual face not just the two-dimensional choice represented, but a multi-dimensional choice between composite commodities of varying degrees of time intensity and goods intensity. What the individual chooses depends on the relative strengths of the substitution and income effects, as in the conventional analysis.

The sophistication of this approach is to show that the demand for leisure time is, in fact, composed of many demands for different types of commodities with differing degrees of time intensity and goods intensity. As time becomes relatively scarcer and more expensive, household production and consumption of goods-intensive activities will increase relative to more time-intensive activities. It is still possible for consumption of time-intensive activities to rise, however, since the conventional income effect may ensure that it does. However the dominant pressure is for goods-intensive activities to increase, i.e., the substitution effect. This can be seen in the increasing goods inputs and reduced time input in many so-called 'leisure' activities which may be seen as inferior – for example, cooking, shopping, washing and cleaning – when contrasted with the maintained, and often increased, time input in more enjoyable leisure activities, such as holidays.

Linder (1970), in his book *The Harried Leisure Class*, also explores the changing value of time and concludes that leisure is becoming less self-determined and less 'leisurely'. The dominant tendency of increased affluence causes increased consumption of goods-intensive activities and this traps the consumer into maintenance of this increased goods input in the household production process. Furthermore, the same affluence encourages an increased array of leisure-time activity choices. These pressures result in time becoming even more scarce, and this brings about the 'harried leisure class'. Other writers bemoan the decreasing leisureliness of leisure time – in particular the emergence of an 'anti-leisure' attitude, filling non-work time with greater amounts of compulsive activities, complete with such work-related traits as anxiety, externally imposed conditions and time consciousness.

Scitovsky (1976), in his book *The Joyless Society*, criticizes the neo-classical theory of consumer demand, indicating that at best it can contribute only to a partial analysis of consumer behaviour. He particularly criticizes the assumption of a given set of preferences, the model of a rational consumer who knows what he wants and fails to achieve it only for lack of means. For Scitovsky, in order to understand demand one has to understand the motivational force behind behaviour; that is, we need to investigate how preferences are formed. To do this, his starting-point is psychology, and in particular the theory and concept of arousal.

The level of arousal has a lot to do with general feelings of satisfaction or dissatisfaction. Too much arousal and too little arousal are both unpleasant. Scitovsky uses the example of solitary confinement of prisoners as a case of low arousal and stimulus deprivation leading to pain, nausea, confusion and general feelings of unpleasantness. Similarly, the over-arousal felt by an executive faced with too much extremely demanding work can lead to stress, fatigue, anxiety and physical illness.

Thus, too little and too much stimulation and arousal are both unpleasant. Psychologists argue that there exists an optimum level of total stimulation and arousal which, when reached, gives rise to a sense of comfort and well-being. Below this optimum, a person is likely to feel boredom; above it, they are likely to feel anxiety and tension. If the arousal level falls below the optimum level, or rises above it, these feelings provide an inducement to attempt to bring the arousal level back to the optimum. The greater the divergence of the present position from the optimum, and the longer the duration of this divergence, then the greater the inducement to attempt to return to the optimum level. Thus this theory of optimal arousal provides the motivation for human behaviour.

The theory of optimal arousal as a basis for the analysis of behaviour is broader than the economic approach, although there is a considerable overlap. Economists see consumer demand as want satisfaction. If an individual is deprived of food, he experiences discomfort in hunger (i.e., he becomes over-aroused). Consumption of food relieves the discomfort and lowers his arousal level back towards its optimum level. Pleasure (utility) results from the comfort of returning to an optimum level of arousal from the heightened level caused by hunger. Comfort is the feeling that results from being at the optimal level of arousal; pleasure, on the other hand, results from moving towards the optimal level from a non-optimal level. Scitovsky uses the analogy between speed and acceleration (or deceleration) to explain the difference between comfort and pleasure.

When we are deprived of the essential elements of human existence (food, clothing, shelter), then we 'demand' these essentials and receive pleasure from the satisfaction of these demands. However, this is not the only source of pleasure. Pleasure flows from the change in arousal level rather than the state of being at a particular level. Pleasure will also follow from moving from a low level to a higher one: the relieving of boredom. Some activities are so stimulating that they raise arousal levels too high (i.e., beyond the optimum level), causing anxiety and tension, but pleasure still follows when the activity finishes and arousal levels fall back towards the optimum.

Scitovsky criticizes economists for considering only the want-satisfaction (lowering too-high arousal) aspects of demand and completely ignoring stimulation-seeking behaviour (raising too-low arousal). It is this latter aspect that relates his theory to demand for leisure, or, in the following quote, sport:

> The simplest remedy for too low arousal is bodily exercise. Not only is bodily exercise a good weapon against boredom it is also pleasant. It seems most pleasant when it fully engages our skill and powers … Competitive sports and games are popular because the pleasantness of exercise is maximised by the full exertion of our strength and skills

called forth by competition. Higher animals also engage in playful combat and other forms of competitive behaviour.

(Scitovsky, 1976)

The basic source of stimulation is experience that is new, unexpected or surprising. New and surprising experience is always stimulating, but if it is completely outside the bounds of our previous experience it can be so stimulating as to be disturbing. As Scitovsky indicates: 'what is not new enough and surprising enough is boring: what is too new is bewildering. An intermediate degree of newness seems the most pleasing.' What an individual considers 'new' obviously depends on his previous experience. What is stimulating to one person may be boring to another; not because of differences in tastes, but because of differences of experience. The nursery slope can be terrifying to the person on skis for the first time, and yet boring to the expert.

Danger or threat is the most obvious source of stimulation, but we need to broaden our view of what we mean by a threat, as Scitovsky explains:

Each of us, through the accumulation of personal experience, develops a view of the world, starting from day one. And that view is the basis of the strategy we use for living – for surviving. Which would be fine if it were not for the fact that the world changes all the time and so threatens to render our strategy obsolete. For that reason we must continually update our world view, by perceiving new information, processing it, and relating it to our previously accumulated fund of knowledge which it will complete and modify. By doing this we update our strategy of survival.

(Scitovsky, 1976)

In this quote, Scitovsky is introducing the concept of 'skilled consumption'. The perceiving and processing of new information is 'skill acquisition', and the more skills acquired, then the greater the opportunity for pleasure through stimulation. Enjoyment of novelty requires learning.

The main question that Scitovsky addresses in *The Joyless Economy* is why, in the USA, increasing affluence does not seem to have led to increasing happiness. He argues that a major reason for this is that there has been too much emphasis on the acquisition of production skills and not enough on the acquisition of consumption skills. Consequently, American consumers seek pleasure through want satisfaction rather than stimulation seeking, since they do not possess the skills to 'enjoy' the stimulation. However, once the basic demands for material goods have been met, there is less and less opportunity for pleasure through want satisfaction. Hence the overall picture of an affluent but bored, joyless society.

The overall point of Scitovsky's analysis is that stimulation seeking is the motivator behind many if not most leisure demands. Not all leisure activities require a high degree of consumption skill. Scitovsky makes the point that America's three most popular leisure-time activities – watching television, shopping and driving for pleasure – are low-skill activities. But such low-skill leisure activities are likely to produce low satisfaction levels.

Thus Scitovsky's approach can be adopted to provide the basis of a theory of demand for leisure. As a society becomes more affluent, there is less and less potential for pleasure through want satisfaction (i.e., wishing to earn money to purchase goods and services that by themselves give pleasure) and a major avenue to pleasure comes through stimulation seeking. Such stimulation can be obtained through interesting and challenging work, again conflicting with the economists' categorization of work as disutility. However, for many it is through their leisure activities that we would expect to see stimulation-seeking behaviour.

Low-skill leisure activities can be stimulating when tried for the first time, but repetition can quickly make the experience boring. Hence the tendency for the demand for leisure activities in general to be volatile as consumers move in and out of the market. We often see rapid growth in demand for a new leisure activity (e.g., the cinema in the 1930s), only to see an equally rapid decline in demand as the novelty effect wears off and other new leisure experiences emerge (e.g., television) to widen the spectrum of leisure-time choices facing the consumer.

For activities that provide the potential for skilled consumption, the same leisure activity can continue to be stimulating, since, as the consumer's skills develop, the nature of his enjoyment also changes. The competitive sportsperson may move to higher and higher levels of competition and may even find that excitement and stimulation increase the more skilled he becomes and the higher the level of competition he enters. Within the broad field of sport, however, demand will be heterogeneous, since participants will have different backgrounds, experiences, interests and skills. What is stimulating to a football participant may be boring or uninteresting to the golfer. The demand for leisure is not a homogeneous demand. Different people develop different consumption skills – which allows the hetero-geneity of leisure demands that is a major characteristic of leisure.

Scitovsky's *Joyless Economy* was a critique of the economic approach to consumer demand. It was effectively saying that a lack of consumption skills can lead to consumers choosing to buy goods and services that do not maximize their utility. The book, however, did provide leisure researchers with a new approach to understanding the economics, or economic psychology, of leisure behaviour. His approach suggests that in order to maximize the satis-faction we get from leisure we may need to invest in the consumption skills that will allow enjoyable stimulation-seeking behaviour. Going back to the Becker model of household production, consuming leisure does not only require the time input for the act of consump-tion. There is an additional time input that is required which is the time input to invest in the acquisition of the consumption skills that enable maximum satisfaction to be obtained from the consumption of leisure. This makes the time input much more important to the enjoyment of leisure. In order to really enjoy our leisure, we have to 'work' at it.

Conclusions

Conventional economic analysis has not given much time or space to the economics of leisure. The word 'leisure' appears only in the model of choice of working time. Economics perceives the labour market as a completely flexible market allowing people to work as many hours as they wish and to have as much leisure as they wish. In economic theory every indi-vidual achieves a perfect work–life balance.

The evidence presented in this chapter from the last 15 years of the twentieth century and the early years of the twenty-first is that many people in work are now working many more hours than they would ideally like. For these people, leisure time is an increasingly scarce commodity. For those out of work, in particular young people, they are not working as many hours as they would like. Very few people seem to have the amount of work and leisure time that they would freely choose. The labour market does not seem to work in the way that economic theory suggests it does.

This is very important for those interested in leisure research, since leisure time is the crucial input into the household production of leisure in the Becker framework. In Linder's analysis, leisure time is such a valuable input that we try to substitute as many goods for time as we can and the end result is a harried leisure class. In Scitovsky's analysis, satisfaction from leisure is maximized by investing time in acquiring consumption skills, and so leisure time becomes even more important. Skilled leisure consumption can provide the stimulation that generates high levels of satisfaction and well-being.

There is no comprehensive economic theory of leisure, but this chapter has highlighted the contribution of those economists who have come closest to developing such a theory.

References

Becker, G. S. (1965) 'A Theory of the Allocation of Time', *Economic Journal*, 75 (299), 493–517.

Charlesworth, K. (1996) 'Are Managers under Stress? A Survey of Management Morale', *Institute of Management Research Report*, September.

Compton-Edwards, M. (2001) 'Married to the Job?', *Chartered Institute of Personnel and Development*, March.

DfEE (1999) 'Overtime Working', *Labour Market Trends*, 107, 4 April.

Gershuny, J. I. (1996) 'High Income People Want Less Work', *ESRC Research Centre on Micro-Social Change*, Working Paper, University of Essex.

Gershuny, J. I. (1997) 'Time for the Family', *Prospect*, 56–57, January.

Gershuny, J. I. (1999) 'Leisure in the UK across the 20th Century', *Working Paper 99-3*, Institute for Social and Economic Research.

Gratton, C. and Taylor, P. D. (2000) *The Economics of Sport and Recreation*. London: Taylor & Francis.

Hogarth, T., Hasluck, C. and Pierre, G. (2000) *Work–Life Balance 2000: Baseline Study of Work–Life Balance Practices in Great Britain*. Department for Education and Employment.

IDS (2000) 'Hours and Holidays 2000', *IDS Studies* 697, October.

Kodz, J., Kersley, B. and Strebler, M. (1998) *Breaking the Long Hours Culture*. Institute for Employment Studies, Sussex University.

Linder, S. (1970) *The Harried Leisure Class*. New York: Columbia University Press.

Scitovsky, T. (1976) *The Joyless Economy*. New York: Oxford University Press.

6

LEISURE MANAGEMENT

Moving with the times

Peter Taylor

Why manage leisure?

It may seem a strange question to ask, but is there a need to manage people's leisure? Leisure is freely chosen and is a concept at the opposite end of the spectrum from work; whilst management is most associated with work. Some of the most obvious leisure activities seem, on the face of it, to occur without the 'interference' of management, such as walking in mountains, by lakes or on the coast, or just relaxing or reading a book. These activities do not seem to require expensive facilities, services, programmes and staff in order to enjoy them.

However, look a little deeper and it is evident that every leisure activity requires management, if only to provide the circumstance and opportunity. For example, mountains require footpaths, signage, accommodation and catering. Furthermore, an infrastructure of transport is needed to access the mountains. And for many people it is necessary to provide sufficient information so that they can plan the experience – the travel, accommodation, walking routes etc. Part of the problem with defining leisure is that it is multi-dimensional, and the more this concept is explored, the more management-relevant considerations emerge.

A similar issue occurs in defining the leisure economy: to do so requires consideration of the leisure-relevant aspects of many other industries, such as transport, accommodation, food and drink, and media. This list includes housing too, because houses are a major venue for leisure and any leisure activities taking place in the home are supported by conventional industrial management activity to produce leisure goods and services used in the home, such as home entertainment, computers, reading materials, gardening equipment and DIY materials. In short, all leisure functions require managing.

The multi-dimensional nature of leisure has led to increasing fragmentation in the study of its management. Whilst leisure management was a fairly coherent subject 40 years ago, in recent decades there has been an increasing fragmentation of leisure management into constituent activity elements. These include sports management, arts management, heritage management, countryside management, tourism management, hospitality management and entertainments management. There are, however, many overlaps between these different activities, and the management of them shares a lot of common functions and theories. Therefore, the discussion of leisure management that follows largely abstracts itself from differences between the management of different leisure activities.

What is leisure management?

According to Taylor (2011: 7), the management of leisure comprises 'planning the products, services, facilities and other infrastructure that combine to give people leisure; managing the available resources to produce high quality services; monitoring and improving the resulting outcomes in the form of participation in and enjoyment of leisure activities; and it stretches to contributing to possible impacts of sport and leisure on people's health, quality of life and sense of community'.

The first three elements of this definition relate to classical management theories (which are reviewed later), i.e., identifying a scientific approach to management which attempts to improve the effectiveness and efficiency of leisure supply. The last element raises an important consideration – that the 'management' of leisure stretches beyond the responsibility of suppliers of leisure goods and services, to reach the societal level of social infrastructure and community impacts. When government, therefore, intervenes in leisure markets with regulation, or with its own supply of leisure facilities and services, it does so in an attempt to 'manage' people's leisure, for society-wide reasons.

The term 'management' can be distinguished from 'administration' in that the latter is a narrower process of developing and maintaining procedures, or in other words, it is largely concerned with organization. Management, on the other hand, is equally concerned with planning, commanding, controlling and coordinating.

Management theories

The meaning of the term 'management' has evolved through several phases of theories, all of which contribute to a contemporary understanding of what management is.

Classical management

The foundation of management sciences is commonly credited to Frederick Taylor, who pointed to scientific systems which facilitate the improvement of efficiency in organizations. Classical management theory developed a 'rational goal model' with the principal objective of efficiency being dependent on the structure and operation of organizations. Leading proponents of classical management theory were Taylor and Henri Fayol. Max Weber is also associated with these theories, adding the important concept of bureaucracy, through which the continuous organization of functions is bound by rules which establish authority; this is necessary in large organizations to ensure consistent service quality. Classical management theory identifies five key management processes: planning, organizing, commanding, coordinating and controlling. It embraces such features as time and motion studies, standardized operational procedures, division of labour and individual incentives such as piece rates. Structurally, this requires hierarchical chains of command, which are now often criticized, particularly by advocates of later theories, for their formality and bureaucracy. However, many organizations still display the classic hierarchical structures and command-and-control management processes. Furthermore, contemporary management literature still typically contains chapters on planning, organizing, leading and controlling – e.g. Boddy and Paton (2011).

The human relations model

This model developed in the early twentieth century, partly in response to criticisms of the rigid implications of classical management theory. It focused on the motivations and needs of the individuals in organizations and was inspired by such writers as Mary Parker Follett, Elton Mayo and Abraham Maslow. This movement concentrated on managerial effectiveness rather than on the efficiency of organizations, with good interpersonal relationships being important for the effectiveness of organizations. It is more democratic and less authoritarian than classical management theory, with networks being important for analysing problems and implementing solutions. The human relations model also arose from concern for the adverse effects of supervision on staff morale and productivity. The ramifications of this approach to management are clearly with us today, given the importance in most organizations of human resources management and development. An example of literature in this model is Peters and Waterman (1982), in which there is a greater emphasis on intuitive, human perspectives and less emphasis on rational goals.

The behaviourist view

This view of management developed the human relations movement to advocate the benefits of more informal and flexible organizational structures, and greater employee involvement. Whilst human relations principles could co-exist with classical management theory to some extent (good interpersonal relations are possible in hierarchical structures), a behaviourist theory represents a more radical structural difference from classical theory. Frederick Herzberg's motivation–hygiene theory is arguably the best-known example. This emphasizes the importance of motivators and dissatisfiers in influencing staff satisfaction, with motivators such as achievement, recognition, responsibility, personal development and job enrichment capable of increasing staff satisfaction; whilst dissatisfiers or hygiene factors such as working conditions, salary, status and job security are only capable, at best, of preventing dissatisfaction.

Open systems models

This was the next major development in management, involving a much more flexible approach to organizational performance which views organizations as depending on the wider environment for inputs such as energy, materials, people and finance (Boddy and Paton, 2011). The transformation of these inputs into outputs takes place through such activities as production, marketing, planning, organizing and research and development. This system disaggregates into sub-systems for people, finance, technology, structure, business processes etc. No one theory guarantees organizational effectiveness, which depends on what is an appropriate mix for the specific internal and external environments of the time. This gives rise to 'contingency theory', whereby appropriate decisions depend on the circumstances of the moment. A manifestation of this approach is the concept of the 'learning organization', with flexibility and adaptability essential to managing in a fluid environment (Cole and Kelly, 2011). Interestingly, such a systems approach is less evident than are its predecessors in leisure management literature.

The shift to customer orientation

In the second half of the twentieth century management theory developed specific branches which correspond to business sub-systems – the main examples being human resources management, marketing management, financial management, strategic management and information management. Towards the end of the century this disaggregation continued, with a focus on organizational effectiveness, including specialist theories of organizational culture, quality management, performance management, organizational excellence and stakeholder relationships, to name a few. In leisure management literature the increasing focus on functional sub-systems was quickly apparent, with many applied leisure texts specific to such disciplines as marketing, finance and human resources management. A particular focus in leisure management literature is customer orientation. This focus began in the context of marketing theory but then spread to the more general theory of quality management. In this approach, customer needs are the foundation for the design and delivery of products and the structure and processes in organizations.

Management disciplines

Leisure management is complex because it involves two multi-disciplinary concepts: leisure and management. Management covers a range of disciplines and skills that are required to run organizations effectively and efficiently, which are reviewed below. Leisure is a subject that has been analysed, mostly separately, by economists, sociologists, psychologists, geographers, political scientists, philosophers and management scientists. Combine the two sets of disciplines, and the permutations are numerous.

Leisure management is composed of a number of disciplines, each comprising its own sets of theories, principles and skills, which are most often analysed separately. Relevant disciplines include finance, marketing and human resources management, as well as elements of law and economics. However, in practice, leisure managers will face problems and issues which often do not require single-discipline analysis but are more likely to involve a number of these perspectives. Whilst specialism by managers in any one of these disciplines is not unusual, especially in larger leisure organizations – e.g. finance, marketing, human resources – a good leisure manager should have a strong awareness of all relevant management disciplines.

Human resource management

Leisure is often termed a 'people business' because of the importance of customers, and also because the main purpose of staff is to satisfy customers' demands. Human resource management (HRM), according to Wolsey, Minten and Abrams (2012), is 'an holistic series of management functions designed to elicit maximum performance from employees'. Citing other authors, they identify eight HRM practices: planning, recruitment, screening, orientation, training and support, performance management, recognition and retention. To these micro, personnel management functions, Wolsey *et al.* (2012) add strategic HRM, through which personnel management is linked to the strategic objectives of an organization.

Because leisure is largely a service industry, leisure staff are resources that are critical to organizational performance. The relationship between staff and managers is a fundamental aspect of human resource management, and a key theoretical concept in analysing this is the psychological contract. Not all aspects of the relationship between management and staff can be encapsulated in written rules and procedures – much of this relationship is governed by tacit expectations on both sides. Wolsey *et al.* (2012: 2) quote Richard Branson, who emphasizes that 'if you start off with a happy well-motivated workforce you're much more likely to have happy customers'. Reviewing other evidence of what influences organizational performance, they conclude that 'one of the main mediating factors affecting individual, group and organizational performance is the ability of the manager to engender a sense of belonging, purpose, enthusiasm and team spirit consistent with organizational values and strategic objectives'.

Marketing

Knowledge of the customer is increasingly considered to be the essential pre-requisite of good management. This is not surprising, because without customers a leisure organization would have only costs. Important concepts of marketing include mission and vision, market research, marketing strategies, market positioning, segmentation and the use of the marketing mix to meet the objectives of marketing plans. The marketing mix is the core set of marketing tools, and, in the case of leisure services marketing, this includes: designing the right products (and brands); deciding the right prices; locating the service in the right places for its market; appropriate promotion to create awareness of and attraction to the service; ensuring that the right people with appropriate training are positioned at the 'customer face'; maintaining high-quality physical evidence of the service – i.e. attractive, tangible service attributes such as the design and cleanliness of the service setting and equipment; reliable and effective processes in the interaction between the customer and the provider – from booking, through service provision, to post-service communication; and generating and maintaining effective sponsorship – particularly important in certain parts of the leisure industry, e.g. sport and the arts.

Arguably, the most important development of marketing theory towards the end of the twentieth century is relationship marketing. Consuming leisure is often not a one-off experience but a process of repeated consumption, often formalized with membership arrangements. Creating the best possible relationship with customers is vital to the success of leisure organizations, and this is where marketing interfaces fundamentally with human resource management – in a people business such as leisure, happy staff will generate happy customers.

Marketing is not simply the province of commercial management – ensuring that the appropriate products are supplied in the right places, at the right prices, with sufficient promotion of the opportunities to relevant people, is all just as relevant to public sector services, social enterprises and voluntary organizations as it is to a commercial business. Social marketing is increasingly employed by public agencies to get their message across and ensure that policies and provision are having an impact. And all suppliers of leisure need to ensure a good relationship with their customers/clients/members – so the principles of relationship marketing are universally valid.

Financial management

An understanding of financial management is important as an essential context within which all managers operate. But knowledge of this context is typically not enough for a contemporary leisure manager: management accounting principles enable managers to act appropriately in order to improve financial performance, because all managers are responsible to the bottom line, in any sector. It is not important for all leisure managers to be able to construct accounts: that is a specialist function. But it is important for leisure managers to be able to use their accounts to make appropriate decisions (Wilson and Joyce, 2008). Financial information underpins many of the important decisions made by managers – such as deciding what resources to use in supplying a service, deciding what prices to charge, deciding what legal identity is best for the organization and deciding whether and how to expand or contract a service.

Important structural components for financial management are the key elements of financial statements, i.e., the balance sheet, showing the organization's assets and liabilities; the profit and loss account; and the cash flow statement. The construction of these instruments is conditioned by rules and regulations because financial information has to be reported in a consistent, transparent and accurate manner – this is good corporate governance.

As well as accurate reporting of recent financial transactions and positions – the province of financial accounting – it is important for all organizations to use financial information in looking to the future – the role of management accounting. So all organizations will produce budgets, forecasting their finances for the next year. And financial information is necessary in order to make decisions on controlling costs, increasing revenues and also on capital investment decisions.

Sound management requires the analysis of financial indicators in order to both fully understand previous operations and inform future management decisions. Ratio analysis is an important branch of financial management and entails the construction and interpretation of financial ratios in order to represent an organization's profitability, liquidity, asset utilization, defensive positioning and investment return. It would be a mistake to think that ratio analysis is relevant only to commercial leisure businesses – many ratios are relevant to public sector and third sector organizations.

Law

Law is another inescapable consideration for managing leisure. Because of the essential interface between leisure staff and customers, it is vital for leisure managers to be aware of their legal responsibilities and how their decision making is constrained by the law. As with finance, leisure managers are not expected to be legal experts, but an understanding of the law as a vital context for their decision making is necessary. The essential principles which a leisure manager needs to know include legal liability and negligence, because managers have a duty of care to staff, volunteers and customers alike, and they are responsible for their employees' actions. Health and safety legislation and anti-discrimination legislation also impose further responsibilities on managers with respect to both staff and customers.

Young people are an important set of leisure consumers and, in the UK at least, working with children is increasingly conditioned by legislation, particularly in regard to the supervision of young people and vulnerable adults. Other aspects of the law that it is important for a leisure manager to be aware of include employment law, contract law and licensing.

The last thing that a leisure manager wants is to be sued for negligence by an aggrieved customer or hauled up before a tribunal because of legal action taken by a member of staff. Good leisure management requires anticipation of risks, calculation of risks and risk management to avoid or minimize risks. By such means legal action, and the large amounts of time and cost that it would entail, is avoided.

Interdisciplinary subjects

Leisure management in practice is not just multi-disciplinary but also interdisciplinary, and includes such interdisciplinary subjects as planning, programming, strategic management, quality and performance management, entrepreneurship and enterprise. These subjects are briefly reviewed below, but this is an illustrative rather than a complete selection. Clearly, compartmentalism is endemic to the study of leisure management because even interdisciplinary subjects such as these are studied and written about separately, in the main. And the list is growing – subjects such as quality management and enterprise are relatively new to the list, whilst other specialist interdisciplinary subjects include facilities management and events management.

Planning

Planning has several important perspectives for leisure management. First, government plays a key role in establishing planning legislation and regulations, which are enforced nationally, regionally and locally – in England alone there are over 400 planning authorities. Planning regulations are designed to steer rational and sustainable development in urban and rural areas, and to prevent inappropriate development.

Second, localities engage in planning processes, which are determined partly by national planning policy and guidance and partly by local needs and pressures. Veal (2010) suggests that local planning processes are ideally of a rational-comprehensive type, which he summarizes in a flow model comprising: the brief; the values and goals; the planning approach; an environmental appraisal; development of options; evaluation of options; strategy and objectives; implementation; and monitoring – with stakeholder consultation necessary at many of these stages. However, Veal also points out that such an ideal process is rarely if ever followed – in practice, limited options are considered, with limited information, in a process that is best described as 'disjointed incrementalism'. Nevertheless, just because ideal theory is not followed in practice does not undermine its theoretical value, and a rational planning process is very much the aspiration in standard planning advice for leisure managers.

Third, from an organizational perspective, planning involves such techniques as demand forecasting, public and/or customer consultation and the design of business plans. Business planning has a literature of its own and, like a systems approach, it typically comprises a collection of sub-system plans for operations, finances, marketing and people.

Programming

Programming is a distinctive feature of leisure management, and many aspects of sport, the arts and entertainments are designed around programmes for facilities and services. These are organized by activities, geographical areas, time periods (i.e. seasonal programmes), outcomes (e.g., beginner, skill development, advanced level) and/or types of customers. Programming is a structural form of organizational planning and delivery. There are a variety of different possible programming strategies, from expressed demand led, which is entirely market driven, to a prescriptive authoritarian approach directed by a key stakeholder.

Typical programming theory identifies a rational approach, similar to planning more generally. Taylor (2011) describes this as a process of interpreting local policy; assessing current and potential demand; assessing organizational resources for delivering programmes; setting specific objectives, planning the programme, implementing it, and evaluating it.

Strategic management

Strategic management is the process of planning, implementing and evaluating a strategy for the future direction of an organization (Parent, O'Brien and Slack, 2012) in order to stimulate superior performance through value creation. It is less concerned with day-to-day operations and more concerned with accomplishing the mission and longer-term objectives for successful operation. It is, in essence, a long-term process of establishing competitive advantage.

The principles of strategic management, as with other management subjects, follow a scientific-logical thread of establishing the organization's mission and values; assessing external and internal environments (e.g., through a SWOT analysis and a competitor analysis); establishing strategic objectives; designing strategic direction after evaluating strategic options (i.e. strategic positioning); conducting functional implementation of the strategy; and reviewing progress against the strategy. This approach has many synergies with marketing management and also with enterprise. Key issues in strategic management include strategic leadership, environmental fit, strategic positioning and intrapreneurship (the process of creative development within organizations).

Quality management and performance management

Quality management and performance management are two contemporary interdisciplinary perspectives on management which are closely related. Quality management focuses mainly on management and operational processes in order to ensure that organizational improvement is a continuously evolving ethos. Total quality management systems are now commonplace in the sport and leisure industry, as in other industries. Two systems in the UK – Quest and the Culture and Sport Improvement Toolkit – are designed specifically for sport and leisure organizations. However, there are numerous other quality awards available that are designed to improve organizational performance. Many of these systems have a common root – the European Foundation for Quality Management Excellence Model. The essential components of this model consist of enabling factors – leadership, policy and strategy, partnerships and resources – which, when processed, lead to various results – for people, customers and society. A typical quality award system requires self-assessment by relevant stakeholders of the enabling factors, processes and results, typically accompanied by a verification process – for example, mystery customer visits and assessor visits.

Performance management is more focused on outcomes. It consists of the specification of measurable objectives, selection and measurement of appropriate performance indicators and, typically, benchmarking the resulting performance against other, similar organizations. This process provides sufficient information for managers to take appropriate decisions to improve performance, especially when the data benchmarks are accompanied by process benchmarking in order to identify what processes have generated excellent performance in the best-performing organizations. As with other approaches to management, both quality management and performance management follow in the scientific management tradition, although they are flexible enough to accommodate human resources and systems approaches, provided the relevant performance can be measured accurately and consistently.

Entrepreneurship and enterprise

Entrepreneurship is an essential set of managerial skills which facilitates enterprise, the creation of new business developments. This is as relevant to leisure management as any other type of business. It is often misconceived as being relevant only to the commercial sector, but it incorporates many aspects of good management practice in any sector – indeed it is the essence of social enterprises. Enterprise is also not simply the creation of completely new businesses by individuals; it incorporates innovation and new business developments in existing organizations. It is at the heart of change management.

The characteristics of entrepreneurs are relatively easy to identify but difficult to analyse – i.e., attributes such as hard working, proactive, resilient, risk taking, assertive, problem solving, and resourceful. They are the subject of popular non-fiction at newsagents and they are the subject of serious academic investigation. Much debate centres on the question of whether entrepreneurs are born with innate skills or are the products of their environments. Nevertheless, management education in leisure, as well as generic management courses, typically contains at least one component promoting entrepreneurial skills and techniques for stimulating enterprise.

Enterprise involves a set of principles and techniques, including feasibility assessment, business start-up financing, business planning, investment appraisal and managing risk. It has a close relationship with many other management disciplines, particularly finance, marketing and human resource management.

Multi-sector management

Leisure management is valid in all three main sectors: public; private profit making; and the third sector. Gone are the days when public sector leisure management was simply a matter of administration – organizing systems that do not change – because, increasingly, public sector leisure is competing directly with commercial leisure organizations. Similarly, the boundaries between the commercial sector and the third sector are blurring, particularly with the rise of social enterprises – i.e., non-profit commercial organizations.

Such changes form an important dynamic context to a discussion of leisure management, with a changing balance between the three sectors in leisure. In the UK, arguably the most dynamic recent change is the development of charitable trusts running many public sector leisure facilities and services. Similarities and differences in management between sectors, and the blurring of the distinctions between them, are distinguishing points of analysis for leisure management as a discipline. Each sector brings its own management agenda to the table, despite the grey areas between them. In particular, public sector leisure management is mindful of the external benefits and costs of leisure activity – i.e., effects which are not priced in market transactions. This consideration leads not only to public sector supply but also public sector regulation of commercial leisure activity – e.g., health and safety, child protection. Third sector management includes such considerations as governance of voluntary organizations, and service effectiveness for exclusive memberships in the voluntary sector; and also managing partnerships with the public sector, which often supplies funding to social enterprises.

Leisure management is changing to fit its context – e.g., accommodating changing political priorities in the public sector, accommodating changing consumer tastes and preferences in the commercial sector, and accommodating changing financial environments in the third sector.

Is leisure management different from other industries?

Thus far, the premise of this review has not distinguished leisure management or any of the derived activity specialisms (sports, arts, tourism etc.) from generic management principles. The distinctiveness of leisure management has been portrayed as being dependent on the particular application of common principles which can just as easily be applied to other industries. However, some authors in various aspects of leisure management claim that their subject is different from generic management disciplines because their business is different.

In sport management, for example, Trenberth (2012: 10) claims, 'the debate continues as to whether sport is a business like any other and should be treated as such. The answer is no, it isn't.' In sport the business is claimed to be unique because of the unpredictable outcome of the sporting product, the need for regulation in order to ensure competitive balance, and the intangible and subjective nature of the sporting product. These distinctive features emanate from the elite end of the market – principally professional sport and the attraction of spectators – which comprises a relatively small part in terms of market size. They do not apply to the larger, mass-participation market, where generic management principles are readily applied in the literature (e.g., Gratton and Taylor, 2000). Furthermore, there are those who argue that what professional sport lacks is the application of sound, generic management principles, particularly from financial management.

The claim that arts management is unique also rests on the distinct characteristics of the elite end of the market. A principal tension in arts management is between the arts as a commercial activity that has to pay its way, and artistic integrity, which depends on creative talents and critical acclaim, almost regardless of market demand. This means that a common feature of arts management is a division between a commercial manager and an artistic director (Wong, 2010). This characteristic is also evident in professional sport, with dual management by technical coaches and commercial managers – but in elite sport this derives from the specialized technical nature of human resource development. The dual management in the arts leads to enduring ambivalence towards conventional management principles, which many artists view with, at best, suspicion or, at worst, hostility.

Heritage management and countryside recreation management share a similar claim to difference from generic management principles, based on a dual responsibility to conservation and education, on the one hand, and for visitor management, on the other hand. A core management issue is achieving an appropriate balance between conservation and access. This balance has shifted as public resources have declined, with an increasing emphasis on gaining commercial revenue by applying generic management principles to visitor management, particularly marketing, quality management and stakeholder management (Hall and McArthur, 1998).

In countryside recreation management, developing environmentalism has seen conservation become of increasing importance to commentators in the academic and political domains (e.g., Shoard, 1980). This has coincided with the increasing promotion of access to the countryside for recreation purposes, both by commercial tourism interests and, in the UK, by government legislation. The arbiter is planning legislation, although Crowe (2011) points out that the tensions between conservation and recreational use of the countryside are overstated – much greater threats to the environment come from agriculture, urban development and pollution.

There are less evident arguments to suggest that tourism and hospitality management are different from generic management, probably because they are primarily the concern of commercial businesses.

Conclusion

The segmentation of management into a variety of disciplines and interdisciplinary subjects is, it is suggested, a matter of convenience and clarity. A genuinely interdisciplinary approach to leisure management can probably be found only in real management situations and, in the literature and education, in case studies.

Several themes run through this review of leisure management, e.g., a scientific, positivist approach, logical processes, engagement with customers. A pattern develops of leisure management principles which entail: understanding the business environment, particularly the market; setting appropriate organizational objectives; designing a structure and strategy for operations; implementing plans to realize the strategic objectives; organizing operations and adapting to internal or external circumstances; monitoring and evaluation; feedback, review and change.

These general principles are not unique to leisure. Regardless of attempts to identify the unique characteristics of specific parts of leisure, this author is of the opinion that, fundamentally, leisure is no different from other multi-sector activities, such as education, health and housing. The quest for efficient and effective service provision should be shared by all providers, whatever sector they are in and whatever objectives they are pursuing.

References

Boddy, D. and Paton, S. (2011) *Management: An Introduction*, 5th edition. Harlow: Pearson Education Ltd.

Cole G. A. and Kelly, P. (2011) *Management Theory and Practice*, 7th edition. Andover: Cengage Learning EMEA.

Crowe, L. (2011) 'Leisure and the Natural Environment', in P. Taylor (ed.), *Torkildsen's Sport and Leisure Management*. Oxon: Routledge.

Gratton, C. and Taylor, P. (2000) *Economics of Sport and Recreation*. Oxon: Routledge.

Hall, C. M. and McArthur, S. (1998) *Integrated Heritage Management*. London: The Stationery Office.

Parent, M., O'Brien, D. and Slack, T. (2012) 'Strategy and Planning in the Context of Sport', in L. Trenberth, and D. Hassan (eds) *Managing Sport Business: An Introduction*. Oxon: Routledge.

Peters, T. J. and Waterman, R. (1982) *In Search of Excellence*. New York: Harper and Row.

Shoard, M. (1980) *The Theft of the Countryside*. London: Temple Smith.

Taylor, P. D. (2011) *Torkildsen's Sport and Leisure Management*. Oxon: Routledge.

Trenberth, L. (2012) 'The Sport Industry', in L. Trenberth, and D. Hassan (eds) *Managing Sport Business: An Introduction*. Oxon: Routledge.

Veal, A. J. (2010) *Leisure, Sport and Tourism: Politics, Policy and Planning*, 3rd edition. Wallingford: CABI.

Wilson, R. and Joyce, J. (2008) *Finance for Sport and Leisure Managers*. Oxon: Routledge.

Wolsey, C., Minten, S. and Abrams, J. (2012) *Human Resource Management in the Sport and Leisure Industry*. Oxon: Routledge.

Wong, D. (2010) *Arts Management*, 2nd edition. Oxon: Routledge.

7

LEISURE POLICY

The example of sport

Matthew Nicholson and Bob Stewart

Leisure, including one of its core sub-sets, sport, is a fundamental part of the day-to-day experiences of people living in any society. In modern societies, time, money and space are allocated to an array of activities that range from reading online newspapers, shopping for fashion-wear or visiting art galleries, to doing aerobics, playing netball or attending professional football games. While these examples are disparate, they all share the family resemblance of being activities that are done in non-paid-work time settings and spaces, and that we, for the most part, choose to do. In contemporary societies with high levels of commodification, the drive to ever more intensive consumption means that these experiences occupy more time, are more intense, are more self-consciously undertaken and, arguably, mean more to us than ever before. Leisure has become something far more important than a respite from the daily chores of life or a way of letting off emotional steam. As Stebbins (2007) noted, leisure can often be deadly 'serious'. As such, the traditional role of leisure policy, which sees governments regulating leisure and using it in direct and indirect ways to encourage societal health and well-being, has shifted as leisure has been commodified and has become more about personal meaning – most particularly in the ways in which it is provided, marketed, consumed and measured.

This chapter will first of all explore the relationships between leisure, sport and government intervention, as a way of contextualizing the example of sport as a domain of leisure policy. It will then introduce the concept of the sport policy dichotomy, which is used to examine the way in which the governments of many of the world's developed and increasingly developing nations have focused on elite sport and mass sport participation as the two primary aspects of sport policy. In the course of this it will become evident that many national governments have used sport policy to cut through the 'hyperreality' of leisure commodification and prioritize instrumental outcomes. The chapter then explores elite sport policy and mass-participation policy in more detail, in order to illustrate the specific focus of national governments and the relative importance of these two policy areas. Finally, some brief conclusions are drawn that argue that sport policy supports activities that are more akin to work than play and prioritizes economic and political development more than sport for sport's sake.

Leisure, sport and government intervention

The state has a vested interest in people's use of leisure. This is not primarily because it wants people to strike a good work–life balance, nor that it is interested in people pursuing activities that have an intrinsic value for the participant. Rather, the state sees its role as facilitating those leisure activities that seem to provide better social outcomes than others, and considers that it is its civic responsibility to restrict leisure pursuits that it believes have socially problematic outcomes, as well as to incentivize those that have socially beneficial outcomes (Rojek, 2010: 134–135). All governments need to regulate access to scarce resources. Resources have to be rationed, which for most nation-states is done through a combination of market mechanisms, pseudo markets, the welfare state and the interaction of demand, supply and prices. However, there are often cases where markets do not operate in the best interests of society; these cases are known as 'market failure', which occurs when the full benefits of markets are not realized. Market failure can occur for a number of reasons, including an under-supply of socially desirable products, an over-supply of less-desirable products and cartel-type arrangements that produce anti-competitive behaviour such as market sharing, price fixing and misleading advertising (Baldwin *et al.*, 2012). Market failure also occurs when the outputs, even if they were viewed as highly desirable in the first instance, subsequently exacerbate the risk of accident, injury or illness, which immediately implies that leisure practices, like high-speed motor sports, mountaineering, base-jumping, boxing and the martial arts, require firm regulation.

The under-supply problem facing governments arises in situations where there are 'external' or social benefits in addition to private benefits. Private benefits represent the value that consumers obtain from the immediate 'purchase' of a good or service – hiking and bushwalking, for example – while social benefits are the value that society, or the community in general, obtains from the production of a good or service, which in this case might be a healthier and more productive community. In cases where social benefits can be demonstrated – which in this instance might be a fitter and more energized workforce – society would be better served by allocating additional resources to those activities. Where private investors lack a sufficient profit incentive to supply more bushwalking spaces to the market, it will be left to government to fill the breach and to use taxpayers' money to regulate supply by funding additional infrastructure and services.

From a government perspective the over-supply of products that produce external costs in addition to private benefits is also a problematic issue to deal with. External costs include workplace accidents and environmental pollution associated with the production process; advertising that makes unsubstantiated claims about product features; and the marketing of products that impose unforeseen risks on their users. These scenarios not only impose costs on others, and potentially threaten them with harm, but are also inequitably distributed, since the burden of costs and harms is often shifted from the producer to the consumer.

In essence, governments regulate the leisure sector because of the social benefits that it can deliver and its capacity to generate significant social costs if left unregulated. Despite the problems embedded in the development of regulatory models that aim to make a positive difference to people's lives, all regulatory models work on the assumption that individuals, groups, neighbourhoods, communities, regions, provinces and nations will be better off with them, rather than without them. It is also assumed, though often with less certainty, that the most-preferred regulatory options will deliver better outcomes than the less-preferred or discarded options. The problem for policy makers is to design regulatory models and policies that, while limiting the costs and harms associated with specific behaviours, do not, at the same time, deny society the opportunity of securing the pleasures and benefits that these behaviours might also deliver. The policy idea of giving space for people to secure the benefits, while simultaneously limiting the harms, underpins a variety of social practices. This is especially the case where there are strong moral objections to the practice; excessive alcohol consumption, illicit drug use, prostitution, pornography and gambling immediately come to mind in this respect. On the other hand, there are also cases where the public becomes agitated about insufficient consumption, and over the past 50 years this agitation has been especially severe about problems associated with sedentary behaviour.

In the case of sport and the benefits that it can deliver to society, direct participation as 'players' is clearly the most significant place to start, since a mass of evidence shows that physically active societies are fit, healthy and productive. Many arguments have been mounted to support the view that sport also provides significant social benefits, and consequently deserves government support in order to ensure that the welfare of the whole community is maximized. The potential benefits are multi-fold, and include improved community health, a fall in medical costs, a reduction in the crime rate, the inculcation of 'character', the development of ethical standards through the emulation of sporting heroes, greater civic engagement and the building of social capital (Cameron and MacDougall, 2000; Long and Sanderson, 2001; Nicholson and Hoye, 2008). Recent research into social capital building suggests that it not only expands social networks but also produces 'safer neighbourhoods and healthier and happier communities' (Productivity Commission, 2003: 17–19). Moreover, the benefits linked to social capital are extended when sports groups and clubs 'look outward and encompass people across diverse social cleavages' (Putnam, 2000: 22). This bridging or inclusive social capital can be contrasted with bonding social capital, which characterizes sport groups and clubs with a narrow ethnic, social or occupational base. In the case of elite and spectator sports, the potential benefits include tribal identification with a team or club, social cohesion, a sense of civic and national pride, international recognition and prestige, economic development and the attraction of out-of-town visitors and tourist dollars (Cooke, 1994; Houlihan, 1997).

Additionally, a case can be made for government assistance to sport on the grounds that it is more often than not a public or collective good. Public goods are those goods where one person's consumption does not prevent another person's consumption of the same good. For example, a decision to walk in the park, visit a surf beach or identify with a winning team or athlete will not prevent others from doing the same. Indeed, the experience may be enhanced by others being in proximity. This is a non-rival feature of the good. Public goods are also goods where, in their purest form, no one can be prevented from consuming the good. Again, a walk in the park, a visit to the beach and identifying with a winning team meet this criterion. This is a non-excludable feature of the good. Public goods can provide substantial benefits throughout the whole of society and are usually not rationed through high prices. However, they are not attractive to private investors, since there is no assurance that all users will pay the cost of the provision of the benefit. Where the number of so called free-riders exceeds the number of paying consumers, there is no incentive for private operators to enter the public good market (Baldwin *et al.*, 2012). In this instance it is argued that government should invest.

The sport policy dichotomy

Sport, like leisure, is not homogeneous. Rather, sport consists of myriad activities, pursuits and experiences. There have been many attempts to categorize sport and to distinguish it from related activities like play, games, contests and athletics (Pearson, 1979:

159–183). When the various theories of sport are conflated, three defining themes emerge (Guttmann, 1978). First, it must have some physical dimension to it. Second, it should normally have a competitive element to it: that is, there is a contest in which there are winners and losers. Third, the activity has to be structured. Thus, sport is usually viewed as a regulated, rule-bound physical activity played in a competitive setting (Loland, 2002). This definition is perhaps unnecessarily restrictive, privileging particular types of sports in particular types of settings, but it is useful in the context of government policy interventions in leisure and sport.

Figure 7.1 provides a graphic illustration of the sport landscape, itself contained within the broader leisure environment (Stewart, Nicholson, Smith and Westerbeek, 2004). It divides sport into five distinct yet interrelated segments: 'spontaneous sport'; 'recreational sport'; 'exercise sport'; 'regional and community competitive sport'; and 'high-performance sport'. In Figure 7.1 it is evident that within the sport landscape or continuum there is a core of competitive sport that begins with community, school and local sport and culminates in elite sport, which includes national sport leagues, national championships and international sport events. There is also a strong link between the 'regional and community competitive sport' and 'high-performance sport' segments, as young talent in particular is channelled into the elite end of the competitive sport core, while retired elite athletes frequently return to the community and local core. This 'regional and community competitive sport' segment is what policy makers and sport administrators refer to as the 'talent pool'. In other words, athletes and coaches first experience competitive sport in community sport clubs, where they are trained and develop into aspiring high-performance participants. The

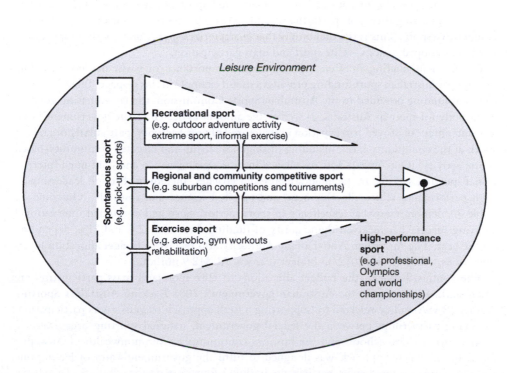

Figure 7.1 A typology of sport practice (Stewart, Nicholson, Smith and Westerbeek, 2004)

'high-performance sport' segment often appears to operate, via the activities of professional sporting clubs and institutes of sport, as an autonomous and independent set of organizations, whereas in reality it is highly dependent on the 'regional and community competitive sport' segment to supply athletes and coaches, as well as officials, administrators and volunteers.

Importantly, the links between the segments in Figure 7.1 also illustrate the constant shift between 'recreational sport' or non-competitive sport and 'regional and community competitive sport' as older players become less competitive and new entrants want more intense competition and structure. There are also links between 'spontaneous sport' and 'regional and community competitive sport' as young children engaged in what some might term 'pick-up' sport develop skills, commitment and enthusiasm to take part in more competitive sport contexts. Figure 7.1 also links 'exercise sport' with 'regional and community competitive sport', although the direct flow of athletes between these segments is not as apparent as the other linkages that are highlighted. It is more likely that athletes either are participating in exercise sport as a self-contained and instrumental activity, or divide their time between 'exercise sport' and 'regional and community competitive sport' as a way of cross-training, improving their performance or simply because they enjoy both.

In terms of the purpose of this chapter, it is important to note that the 'high-performance' and 'regional and community competitive sport' segments in Figure 7.1 have become the dominant domains for sport policy, although this is only a relatively recent development. Houlihan (2005: 163) argued that 'few governments in the 1960s gave any explicit budgetary or ministerial recognition to sport', but that 'by the mid-1990s sport was an established feature in the machinery of government in the most economically developed countries'. As Nicholson, Hoye and Houlihan (2011: 1) argued, 'over the last thirty years the governments of most developed nations have implemented sport policies focussed on two key pillars – supporting elite sport performance and increasing rates of participation in organized competitive sport'. This is the dichotomy that characterizes sport policy within most of the world's developed nations – elite sport and mass participation.

Government funding is often a proxy for the importance of particular policies. The example of Australian sport funding provides a useful example in this respect. Table 7.1 shows the total funding provided to the Australian Sports Commission, the coordinating government body for sport in Australia, as well as the amount allocated to the government's two key outcomes: 'improved participation in structured physical activity, particularly organized sport, at the community level, including through leadership and targeted community-based sports activity' (Outcome 1) and 'excellence in sports performance and continued international sporting success, by talented athletes and coaches, including through leadership in high performance athlete development, and targeted science and research' (Outcome 2). Table 7.1 demonstrates that 'excellence in sports performance and continued international sporting success' has received the majority of funding, between 62% and 71%, depending on the year. The Australian Anti-Doping Authority also receives a budget allocation for its operations, which in the 2012/13 budget year was AU$12.9 million.

The contrast between the budget allocations to elite sport and mass participation are often stark. For example, the Australian government's 2001 Backing Australia's Sporting Ability (BASA) policy referred to 'supporting a fresh approach to grass-roots participation, involving partnerships between the federal government, national sporting organizations, local sporting clubs, schools and the business community' (Commonwealth of Australia, 2001: 6). This new approach was designed to fulfil the government's aim of having one million more registered sport participants within a four-year period, 2001–5. To achieve this aim and execute the programme, the Australian Sports Commission was allocated

Table 7.1 Australian Sports Commission annual allocations, 2005/6–2012/13 (AU$ million)

	2005/6	2006/7	2007/8	2008/9	2009/10	2010/11	2011/12	2012/13
Total	168,631	192,428	204,409	219,785	222,044	248,032	268,693	268,143
Outcome 1*	57,666	66,971	72,895	78,236	78,171	72,217	97,841	101,942
Outcome 2*	110,965	125,457	131,514	141,549	143,873	175,815	170,852	166,201

Notes:
* Outcome 1 at 2012/13: improved participation in structured physical activity, particularly organized sport, at the community level, including through leadership and targeted community-based sports activity. Outcome 2 at 2012/13: excellence in sports performances by Australians. The figures within the table relate only to government allocations and do not include Australian Sports Commission revenue from other sources, such as the sale of services and products, nor do they include cash reserves.

Source: Parliament of the Commonwealth of Australia (2012, 2011, 2010, 2009, 2008, 2007, 2006, 2005)

AU$12 million. By contrast, during the same period, Rowing Australia, the sport's national governing body, was allocated more than AU$12 million to fund its elite sport programmes and scholarships (Stewart, Nicholson, Smith and Westerbeek, 2004).

High-performance sport

Government policies that support high-performance or elite support, in particular Olympic-level athletes and coaches, are recognition that sport provides almost boundless potential opportunities for status and national image making in an increasingly global and mediated world. Sporting success within many nations is inextricably bound to perceptions of national worth and the potential of engaging with the rest of the world. This engagement is usually achieved through major events such as the Olympic Games or the FIFA World Cup. The small nation of Qatar is a perfect example of the way in which nations perceive that sport can be used as both the catalyst and an on-going tool for engaging with the rest of the world, in this case particularly the non-Arab world. Qatar took a significant step when it hosted the 2006 Asian Games, the second-biggest multi-sport event after the Olympic Games. In reference to these Games, Muhammad al Malki, President of the Qatar Sports Press Committee, was quoted as saying that 'sport is the shortest way to be part of the world. It's the language between nations' (Hoye, Nicholson and Houlihan, 2010). Since then, Qatar has successfully bid for the 2022 FIFA World Cup, an event that will further increase its global profile.

Hosting major sport events, or competing well in them, has increasingly been viewed by developed and developing nations as an important source of political capital. As such, the major part of government sport budgets in many developed nations is directed to elite sport performance, particularly through the funding of elite sport institutes and support for elite athletes, coaches and sport scientists. However, it is not often clear exactly what benefits a nation receives from hosting major sport events, or by being regarded as one of the nations 'to beat'. Hall (2006: 59) argued that mega events are an extremely significant component of place promotion 'because they may leave behind social, economic and physical legacies which will have an impact on the host community for a far greater period than that in which the event took place'. More often than not these legacies are used by nations and cities in bid documents, and by politicians and policy makers captivated by sport's symbolic power, but they are only ever potential legacies, dependent on the capacity of a nation's or city's human capital to convert the potential into reality. Almost inevitably, politicians, policy makers and proponents of sport's unlimited potential retreat to arguing for sport's capacity to create what Crompton (2001) referred to as 'psychic income', the benefits that accrue to the collective morale of residents. Not surprisingly, there is a paucity of research that demonstrates this impact.

In many developed nations, sport policies have coalesced around four key themes: elite sport development; anti-doping or drug control; improving the capacity of the sport system, particularly national governing bodies; and increasing mass participation (Hoye, Nicholson and Houlihan, 2010). The first three are directly aligned. Government investment in high-performance sport is in many respects worthless without concomitant investment in anti-doping and drug control, as the national prestige and status gained through elite sport success is likely to be tarnished via positive drug tests and their ensuing scandals. The World Anti-Doping Agency (WADA) was formed in 1999, jointly funded by the International Olympic Committee and a group of national governments. As Smith and Stewart (2008) argued, WADA's policy model is predicated on four assumptions about the role of sport in modern society and its responsibilities to its key constituents: first, the need to set a good example; second, the need to ensure a level playing field; third, the need to protect the health of athletes; and fourth, the need to preserve the integrity of sport. The first, second and fourth elements of the policy model are all designed to protect the institutions of high-performance sport, including national governments and elite institutes of sport, particularly their on-going credibility and status.

Similarly, government investment in elite sport development relies on the performance of national governing bodies and organizations. As such, national governments are aware that improvements to the sport system in areas such as governance and strategic planning are essential if investment in elite sport development is to be maximized. As Hoye, Nicholson and Houlihan (2010: 4) noted, 'the interest in management improvement that emerged in the 1980s and 1990s engendered more business-like and commercial approaches to managing sport. The consequences of these developments included the dilution of traditional democratic approaches to representative governance processes and a shift to a model encouraging people with business, marketing and entrepreneurial experience to be appointed to boards. Such development served to reinforce the largely instrumental paradigm evident in government priorities and the subservience of other policy concerns to elite performance, rationality and professionalization.'

Sport participation

Nicholson, Hoye and Houlihan's (2011) edited collection on national sport-participation policies demonstrated that sport has universal appeal. This is illustrated by the evolution of unique and varied national sporting cultures and pursuits, substantial investment in sport events and infrastructure by the public and private sectors and what amounts to near-saturation coverage of elite and professional sport across multiple media forms. However, the collection also demonstrated that this universal appeal has not translated into mass participation, which has been an issue that national governments have been grappling with since the early 1970s in particular. Watching sport, either live or mediated, has continued to grow in popularity as the public and private sectors have invested in the staging of major events, the construction of new stadia and the development of new forms of sport content distribution, such as pay (or cable) television and the internet. By contrast, in most nations sport-participation rates have either stagnated or declined. As Nicholson, Hoye and Houlihan concluded, the reasons for this global trend in sport participation are many and varied and include:

lifestyle changes, particularly in Western developed nations; urban design trends and increasing population density, which has resulted in less open space and public amenity; persistent economic disadvantage, particularly among developing nations, which results in low levels of disposable income and, for many who are in employment, long working hours; a reduction in the amount and frequency of physical education mandated within the curriculum at all year levels; the growth of broadcast coverage of elite and professional sport and the penetration of pay television networks; an increase in the number of families in which both parents work and the pressure this places on available leisure time for adults and their children; changes in shopping hours; pressure on voluntary sport clubs, particularly as NGBs [National Governing Bodies], governments and interested third parties have introduced more stringent compliance requirements; growth of other leisure options; and potentially a failure of sport to adapt their offerings to cater to changing needs in the marketplace, especially in relation to the young.

(2011: 298)

The benefits that sport governing bodies and governments ascribe to sport, such as improving general fitness, health, social inclusion and crime rates, remain relatively unchallenged, despite the fact that the social benefits of sport and physical activity are far less well researched than the physical or physiological benefits. Issues of efficacy and the size of impact aside, it appears that, despite these reasonably well-articulated benefits, sport participation is a relatively abstract concept for many national governments. Whereas elite sport development policies are well supported financially, have clear targets (e.g., gold medals at Olympic Games or World Championships), strong programmes (e.g., elite institutes of sport) and are well supported politically, mass-participation policies have relatively little money allocated to them, are subject to unrealistic targets, have little programmatic detail and enjoy little or no political support.

The efficacy of sport-participation policies is threatened and undermined by several factors: first, governments setting unrealistic targets; second, the absence of reliable sport-participation data; third, the short-term nature of sport-participation policies and programmes; and fourth, a reliance on national governing bodies of sport to deliver sport-participation programmes. While it is true that sport policies often hinge on achieving targets, the sport policy dichotomy reveals that the area of sport participation is far more complex. The elite sport system is set up to cope with these targets far more effectively; elite institutes and national governing bodies are familiar with performance targets that focus on the number of medals or the number of athletes to make finals or semi-finals. Targets in the sport-participation area, by contrast, do not focus on a specific cohort of committed and highly trained athletes. Rather, they typically apply to the entire population. As Houlihan (2011) illustrated, these often-grandiose sport-participation targets are pragmatically revised (either the number of participants is decreased or the time period is extended) by governments, which causes further uncertainty.

Perhaps the most problematic aspect of sport-participation policy making is its short-term nature. Whereas elite sport, particularly in Western developed nations, has enjoyed long-term political and policy support (thirty or forty years in some nations), sport-participation policies have typically been of three to four years in duration, and often as short as one year (Nicholson, Hoye and Houlihan, 2011). Sport-participation policies are often changed as a result of a change of government, a new political ideology or agenda, a financial downturn or a new set of ideas about how sport might be used to contribute to a range of complex economic and social problems. In the case of England, sport-participation policy has shifted from 'contributing to tackling the complex social problems associated with community fragmentation, educational underachievement and anti-social behaviour, to improving the nation's health and in particular tackling the problem of overweight and obesity, and most recently to providing support for the pursuit of Olympic medals' (Houlihan, 2011).

Conclusion

The foregoing discussion has demonstrated how sport policies have a tendency to prioritize some types and uses of sport over others. In the main, elite sport and the systems and infrastructure that support it have been given the highest priority. However, it is clear that the elite or high-performance sport domain more often resembles work than play, while it uses and is subjected to the same efficiency mechanisms as economic production. Elite athletes are subject to training regimes that are carefully planned and monitored, often by teams of coaches, sport scientists and administrators. In most cases these athletes are paid for their skills and effort, as professional sportsmen and women in international leagues and circuits or as athletes supported by national governments and governing bodies. The industry in which these athletes work supports and is supported by an array of broadcasters, sponsors and investors (including owners, local, state and national governments). As such, it is highly commercialized and business orientated, and government policy in the area of high-performance sport is often predicated on direct and indirect economic benefits. It is also clear that the high-performance sport policies of national governments also support the mediation and consumption of sport, a valuable yet relatively sedentary form of leisure.

Sport and non-sport government policies that attempt to use sport as a way of enabling physical activity and health, urban regeneration and economic development or social inclusion are invariably interested in capitalizing on sport's ability to be used, to borrow Coalter's (2007) apt analogy, as 'fly paper'. In this respect sport has the capacity to contribute to ameliorating a range of problems associated with the global overweight and obesity epidemic, the ghettoization of urban areas or the disconnection and disaffection of young people, for example. In all these cases, government policies are not directed at encouraging sport for sport's sake but, rather, are directed at using sport's ability to attract participants, funding, media coverage and general interest to solve what are often complex and intractable problems.

Sport policies that relate to mass participation are also instructive in terms of government priorities and political agendas. These policies typically illustrate that governments are more concerned with measurable outputs, which lead in turn to pressing political outcomes. Mass participation in sport is often about increasing the talent pool from which high-performance participants are selected, or enabling other outcomes, such as health and social inclusion. National sport-participation policies are very rarely, if at all, about encouraging sport because it is fun and might provide enjoyment.

References

Baldwin, R., Cave, M. and Lodge, M. (2012) *Understanding Regulation: Theory, Strategy and Practice.* Oxford: Oxford University Press.

Cameron, M. and MacDougall, C. (2000) 'Crime Prevention through Sport and Physical Activity', *Trends and Issues in Crime and Criminal Justice* 165: 1–6.

Coalter, F. (2007) *A Wider Social Role for Sport: Who's Keeping the Score?* London: Routledge.

Commonwealth of Australia (2001) *Backing Australia's Sporting Ability: A More Active Australia.* Canberra: Australian Government Publishing Service.

Cooke, A. (1994) *The Economics of Leisure and Sport*. London: Routledge.

Crompton, J. (2001) 'Public Subsidies to Professional Team Sport Facilities in the USA', in C. Gratton and I. Henry (eds), *Sport in the City: The Role of Sport in Economic and Social Regeneration*. London: Routledge.

Guttmann, A. (1978) *From Ritual to Record: The Nature of Modern Sport*. New York: Columbia University Press.

Hall, C. (2006) 'Urban Entrepreneurship, Corporate Interests and Sports Mega-Events: The Thin Policies of Competitiveness within the Hard Outcomes of Neoliberalism', in J. Horne and W. Manzenreiter (eds) *Sports Mega-Events: Social Scientific Analyses of a Global Phenomenon*. Oxford: Blackwell Publishing.

Houlihan, B. (1997) *Sport Policy and Politics: A Comparative Analysis*. London: Routledge.

Houlihan, B. (2005) 'Public Sector Sport Policy: Developing a Framework for Analysis', *International Review for the Sociology of Sport* 40 (2) 163–185.

Houlihan, B. (2011) 'England', in M. Nicholson, R. Hoye and B. Houlihan (eds) *Participation in Sport: International Policy Perspectives*. London: Routledge.

Hoye, R., Nicholson, M. and Houlihan, B. (2010) *Sport Policy: Issues and Analysis*. Oxford: Butterworth-Heinemann.

Loland, S. (2002) *Fair Play in Sport*. London: Routledge.

Long, J. and Sanderson, I. (2001) 'The Social Benefits of Sport: Where is the Proof?', in C. Gratton and I. Henry (eds) *Sport in the City: The Role of Sport in Economic and Social Regeneration*. London: Routledge.

Nicholson, M. and Hoye, R. (eds) (2008) *Sport and Social Capital*. London: Butterworth-Heinemann.

Nicholson, M., Hoye, R. and Houlihan, B. (eds) (2011) *Participation in Sport: International Policy Perspectives*. London: Routledge.

Parliament of the Commonwealth of Australia (2005) *Appropriation (Parliamentary Departments) Bill (No. 1) 2005–2006*.

Parliament of the Commonwealth of Australia (2006) *Appropriation (Parliamentary Departments) Bill (No. 1) 2006–2007*.

Parliament of the Commonwealth of Australia (2007) *Appropriation (Parliamentary Departments) Bill (No. 1) 2007–2008*.

Parliament of the Commonwealth of Australia (2008) *Appropriation (Parliamentary Departments) Bill (No. 1) 2008–2009*.

Parliament of the Commonwealth of Australia (2009) *Appropriation (Parliamentary Departments) Bill (No. 1) 2009–2010*.

Parliament of the Commonwealth of Australia (2010) *Appropriation (Parliamentary Departments) Bill (No. 1) 2010–2011*.

Parliament of the Commonwealth of Australia (2011) *Appropriation (Parliamentary Departments) Bill (No. 1) 2011–2012*.

Parliament of the Commonwealth of Australia (2012) *Appropriation (Parliamentary Departments) Bill (No. 1) 2012–2013*.

Pearson, K. (1979) *Surfing Subcultures of Australia and New Zealand*. University of St Lucia: Queensland University Press.

Productivity Commission (2003) *Social Capital: Reviewing the Concept and its Policy Implications*. Canberra: Commonwealth of Australia.

Putnam, R. (2000) *Bowling Alone: The Collapse and Revival of American Community*. New York: Simon and Schuster.

Rojek, C. (2010) *The Labour of Leisure*. London: Sage.

Smith, A. and Stewart, B. (2008) 'Drug Policy in Sport: Hidden Assumptions and Inherent Contradictions', *Drug and Alcohol Review* 27 (2) 123–129

Stebbins, R.A. (2007) *Serious Leisure: A Perspective for Our Time*. New Brunswick, NJ: Transaction Publishers.

Stewart, B., Nicholson, M., Smith, A. and Westerbeek, H. (2004) *Australian Sport: Better by Design? The Evolution of Australian Sport Policy*. London: Routledge.

8

RESEARCH POSITIONS, POSTURES AND PRACTICES IN LEISURE STUDIES

Jonathan Long

Introduction

In accord with one contemporary research style, this paper is in part a personal story of a journey through what I have previously referred to as inter-paradigmatic space (Long, 2007). As narratives are now accepted as a more credible form of research it might be possible to present this chapter purely as a series of reflections on a career in research during which fields and habitus have continually locked horns. I shall refrain from surrendering entirely to that temptation. However, to deny the significance of personal experience would be perverse, and it is worth emphasizing that any piece of social science writing must involve elements of individual narrative, whether or not it is recognized as such. To deny that would be akin to positivist attempts to assert an objectivity that cannot be. Of course I shall have to return to such a value-laden statement at various times in this chapter, but it is in accord with calls for reflexivity (e.g., Dupuis, 1999; Watson and Scraton, 2001) that have come to the fore over the past two decades. And if I didn't know it before, my research into racism has screamed the importance of appreciating the need for reflexivity. However, if pressed, I would still position myself somewhere close to the kind of critical realist position of Ramazanoglu and Holland (2002: 72), who maintain that 'reality exists independently of people's consciousness of it, but the connections between what is real, what is thought and what is experienced cannot be easily disentangled'.

Is there really anything special about leisure that would suggest a different methodological debate from the rest of the social sciences? As a relatively new arrival, it is likely to draw heavily on other subject areas. But not being part of an established discipline facilitated multi-disciplinary (then inter-disciplinary and trans-disciplinary) approaches, which, in the words of *1066 and All That*, 'was a good thing'. There is, of course, the subject matter itself, where apparent relative autonomy in leisure might encourage a different ontological position among its researchers. Easily overlooked by critical theory, it is at the heart of post-modernist theories, the very arena of cultural formulations, lifestyles and the construction of personal identities. But leisure itself has proved difficult to define (Parry and Long, 1990) and a slippery concept to address adequately in empirical research. The obvious conceptual confusion around leisure has even been evident in sub-categories like sport, with the obvious shortcomings of the oft-quoted definition from the Council of Europe (2001). Such definitional slippage may well have frustrated a sense of advance.

Nonetheless, committed though I am to the field of Leisure Studies, I doubt that there is anything peculiar to it that might necessitate an approach to research that is distinct from other areas of study in the social sciences. Leisure scholars have not been particularly forthcoming in contributing to methodological debates in the social sciences, but when they do they rehearse similar arguments. Equally, though, it is no less important for leisure scholars to deliberate the nature of the world and their experiences, how they find out about those and what their responsibilities are in doing so.

As the field has developed over the years leisure researchers have put a wide range of techniques to work as distinct approaches have emerged. These have ranged from nomothetic attempts to replicate the scientific method to idiographic writings verging on solipsism; from empiricist data gathering and positivist research like that evidenced by psychometric scaling and multivariate statistical analysis, through Marxist and other critical approaches to the more messy ethnographic and narrative approaches of those anxious to throw off the structures and strictures of grand theory. I recall Henderson (1991: 24) aligning herself with Guba (1987) and insisting:

> you cannot at one time believe that the world is both round and flat. You cannot believe that theory can be confirmed at the same time as it is being generated. Therefore, researchers must make hard decisions about what they believe about the reality of leisure and the delivery of leisure services. No possibility exists for mixing paradigms although it has been attempted with the outcome of creating a great deal of philosophical confusion.

However, by the millennium her position had shifted such that 'there are no totally right or wrong approaches. For leisure researchers the expansion beyond binary thinking to more intellectual diversity provides a strong anchor' (Henderson, 2000: 49). Moreover, 'despite the objections of a few purists [*sic*] we see examples of how qualitative and quantitative data can be linked' (Henderson, 2000: 50).

Whether a researcher is inclined to Durkheim's treatment of facts as things that have to be discovered or considers knowledge to be something that is constructed, the choice of research methods is fundamental. However, I have never had the certainty possessed by some that there is a single path to truth. Indeed, I am suspicious of those who make privileged truth-claims for their particular model of research, and I confess a leaning towards the methodological polytheism of writers like Bourdieu rather than engagement in the pitched battles between positivism and hermeneutics that I see around me. Similarly I am equally distressed by quantitative researchers who allow the numbers to become their truth, forgetting the people and processes that they are supposed to represent, and by radical theorists content with extraordinarily casual empirical 'study'. That is why I warm to Wacquant's (1998: 219) description of Bourdieu's willingness to embrace a range of techniques, not as a cavalier disregard for epistemology but as involving:

> Equal epistemic attention to all operations, from the recollection of sources and the design of questionnaires to the definition of populations, samples and variables, to coding instructions and the carrying out of interviews, observations and transcriptions. For every act of research, down to the most mundane and elemental, engages in full the theoretical framework that guides and commands it.

It would be an ill-conceived exercise in a chapter of this size to try to put together the definitive 'how to guide' for leisure research. Instead, reflections on a personal journey through multiple methods accompany a consideration of contemporaneous developments in the wider field of Leisure Studies. The chapter also addresses how different research traditions have developed in different research environments, reflecting different disciplines and paradigmatic rivalries (Rojek, 1985; 1993). If I were writing this from outside the Anglophone world I might, of course, write a very different chapter. But I am where I am and, as such, will venture some observations later on the different styles of research conducted in the United States (US) and the United Kingdom (UK). In doing this I want to consider whether the more purposeful, scientific approach to research in the US has allowed researchers to build more successfully on what has gone before than has been possible for researchers in the UK.

Historical shifts

I am a product of the particular moments of the research worlds I have inhabited, so I make it very clear that this is a story told from where I sit. No doubt the story told of the development of leisure research would be different had I been operating at different moments of that development, working in a different country, or employed in the commercial sector. Throughout there has been a struggle to resolve the tension between the posturing of some virtuous 'pure' academics, on the one hand, and the populist, anti-intellectualism of some practitioners, on the other.

I count myself fortunate to have been taught the statistical techniques of the quantitative revolution in geography at a time when they were beginning to be questioned from a range of alternative perspectives. I then honed my empirical investigation in a research centre examining leisure and tourism practices, gradually trying to introduce more analyses from the perspective of critical social science. When I first became involved with leisure research in the second half of the 1970s, the idea of studying leisure was still relatively new in the UK. Local and central government and related agencies were trying to plan for and shape people's leisure behaviours and were data hungry. Tomlinson (1989) rather dismissively referred to empirical researchers who 'were happy to chug away producing head-counting surveys of what people did'. He saw their work as being atheoretical, and there was some truth in that; it reflected the efforts of a new field to gather 'baseline data', but for a while at least it was part of a project that aimed to model behaviour in order to allow the prediction that was thought necessary for planning. The (post) positivist belief in measurement was evident in the search for scientific solutions.

This gradually evolved into attempts by some (including myself) to offer a more critical interpretation of leisure in the context of a range of social issues, which reflected what Coalter (1997), following Jackson and Burton (1989), referred to as the 'leisure in society' model. At that time the planning orientation of approaches servicing central and local government and associated agencies was criticized by critical theorists for perpetuating the status quo rather than promoting social change, which required a focus on what could be rather than on what was. Coalter (1997) identified them as viewing 'society in leisure'. Sadly, some of those critical theorists appeared to scorn the use of empirical data more generally (see, for example, Clarke and Critcher, 1985) for fear that a few facts might get in the way of a good [sic] theory (I have more sympathy with their political project than their methodological stance). The next major wave of critical theory within leisure research was introduced by feminists. Of course, like the neo-Marxists, they were anything but a homogeneous group.

84

However, while I was never clear about what was peculiar to feminist methodology, it did return attention to the importance of engaging with people in order to tell the stories of women. There were many who inherited from neo-Marxists an intent to secure a political role for their research. Perhaps more significantly in terms of their contribution to reorienting research methods, they challenged researchers to consider (and redress) the imbalance of power between the researcher and the researched, and they also fuelled the move towards more general acceptance of qualitative techniques. In recent years similar cries have been heard from the advocates of critical race theory (CRT) (Hylton, 2012).

Since the introduction to public policy of a business culture, with its targets and performance indicators, the concern of practitioners with 'monitoring' has driven an interest in positivist approaches again, albeit with periodic calls to examine logic models or programme theories. At the same time leisure scholars have been trying to get to grips with, and contribute to, the development of a body of post-modernist and post-structuralist theory. That has been evidenced in two quite distinct strands of research. One seemed reluctant to go beyond commentary and semiotic interpretation of texts, with only a passing concern for real-world investigations for fear that the evidence might reveal the persistence of class-based deprivation rather than the brave new world in which all could buy the identity they chose. The other championed a wider array of research techniques using auto-ethnography, visual techniques and narrative approaches (including poetic representation, ethnodrama, confessional tales and story-telling), often making their own use of semiotics (e.g. Smith and Sparkes, 2012).

I too have advocated such approaches, but also fear for what they might represent (I shall return to that in the conclusion). In arguing for 'reclaim[ing] the label of storytelling for something that gives expression to "truths" otherwise unheard' (Long and Carless, 2010), we acknowledged the pressure on practitioners and researchers to listen to the most strident voices. The challenge, then, is for researchers to make sure that none is overlooked and to adopt a mind-set in which what we never previously imagined can be heard. Just as with CRT, the goal is typically to move voices from the margin to the centre. We insisted that this had to involve 'not just hearing, but actively listening to the stories with a view to facilitating change' (Long and Carless, 2010: 223). Naturally, some stories are still more tellable than others (Smith and Sparkes, 2008), because of power relations between researcher and researched, because of cultural expectations or because of the articulateness of those included in the research. This last calls for the adoption of a variety of research techniques. For example, we have used mental mapping and photo-elicitation techniques in an attempt to redress the difficulties of working with research participants who may not have English as their first language.

Cultural variations

Greiffenhagen *et al.* (2011) challenge the view that quantitative and qualitative researchers employ different modes of reasoning. In their empirical work they found both 'camps' being logical and systematic for some of the time, just as they might be intuitive and interpretive at others. And Iso-Ahola (2009: 304) seems to have surprised himself by observing that 'many scholars (e.g. Stebbins) have used qualitative methods exclusively and yet have developed theories that are powerful in their explanation'. From his post-positivist position Iso-Ahola sees the ability to produce generalizable knowledge as the key, and certainly there are some qualitative researchers who instead eschew that challenge.

Nonetheless, when we were setting up the journal *Leisure Studies* at the beginning of the 1980s it was partly in the belief that leisure research in the UK had developed along a rather different path from research in America, home of the *Journal of Leisure Research* (*JLR*) and *Leisure Sciences*. The latter was only just getting off the ground, so our judgement was based mainly on *JLR*, conference presentations and visiting academics. Over the subsequent years of my involvement with *Leisure Studies* that assessment seemed to hold. It was one that saw social psychology being used by geographers, economists and sociologists in the US who sought to import into the social sciences many of the quantitative techniques and approaches of the scientific method in order to examine motivations and benefits. In the UK, research was more likely to adopt a critical social science approach, using qualitative techniques to address sociological concepts in examining the political dimensions of leisure.

Writing in the fortieth anniversary issue of *JLR*, Witt (2009: 293) comments that:

> It is hard to imagine now that there was once considerable controversy concerning the value and appropriateness of quantitative verses [*sic*] qualitative methodologies and concerns that review panels had a quantitative bias, therefore providing a roadblock to publication of quality articles that used qualitative methodologies.

Looking at the early articles that the editors chose to republish in that celebratory issue it is not hard to imagine as we are greeted by chi-square, rankings, percentages, correlation, factor analysis, hypothesis testing, scaled responses, analysis of variance ... The only reason that the more sophisticated multivariate techniques are less prominent than they are today is because the computing power simply was not available to crunch large data sets through complex matrix algebra. Witt continues by asserting that:

> So much has changed. The journal has provided a home for articles where the key issue is the appropriateness of the methodologies employed rather than the assumption that quantitative approaches are superior.
>
> (p. 293)

My impression of cultural variation was essentially supported by Coalter's (1997) comparison of Leisure Sciences and Leisure Studies. He appeared to attribute this distinction in part to Gans's (1988) assertion about 'Americans being concerned with obtaining personal control over the general environment in order to minimize threat and unwanted surprise seem[ing] close to the spirit of positivist methodologies' (Coalter, 1997: 265). The goal of this 'normal science' (Kuhn, 1962) is to build upon previous contributions by incrementally filling the gaps. In contrast, from my interpretation of Kuhn's thesis, the diversity of approach in the UK suggested that I was working in a pre-paradigm research environment, whereas Rojek (1985; 1993) preferred to see it as a multi-paradigmatic stage. Despite being smaller in scale, Leisure Studies in the UK had less methodological coherence than its counterpart in the US. That seems to suggest a superior position for American leisure, but writers like Goodale (1990: 296) bemoaned it becoming 'increasingly positivist, operationalist and reductionist'. Kelly (2000: 75) similarly complained that with this model of 'normal science' (Kuhn, 1962) leisure research was operating 'in a bounded world [where] there are no emotions, no bodies, no inequities, no social and economic forces, no conflict and no change'.

I remember well having to argue strongly for the use of qualitative techniques (alongside quantitative) in our study of the changing significance of leisure around retirement (Long, 1987). But that was in 1979, and within a few years such techniques were not seen as being particularly untoward, whereas it was the millennium when, in the special issue of the *JLR*, several contributors commented on the 'epistemological revolution that has taken place in the social sciences', resulting in a move 'away from positivism and the social psychology framework that shaped research through the past several decades' (Samdahl, 2000: 127).

By way of illustration of how I see the difference, let me refer to work we did on leisure and social networks within the community. Working in the US, Stokowski (1994: 90) had argued that future leisure research

> must refine measurements of interactional criteria such as reciprocity and tie strength, and, more importantly, must devote greater effort to analyzing specific structural variables, including network size, density and relational distance.

In rather different vein we (Blackshaw and Long, 1998: 246) concluded that:

> When leisure research is about people and their relationships it needs to be about more than points and lines on a chart. One cannot literally interview a friendship, but combinations of research styles can be used to elucidate the meanings of sociality in the social world. Conversations in the field may lack the reassuring rigour of graph theory, but close interrogation of the consequent text may reveal much more about the mosaic of contemporary community life and how people actually experience leisure.

I would have to be a particularly bad researcher to argue that all leisure researchers in the US would naturally concur with Stokowski and all UK researchers would align themselves with our assessment; it is a question of balance.

Research methods as reflected in the journals

Having told the story about historical shifts and cultural distinctions as it appeared to me, it behoves me to address whether there is any supporting evidence. To that end we conducted a small exercise to examine the content of two US-based journals and two UK-based journals. Although 'based' in these countries they are all 'international journals attracting submissions from around the world', so to suggest that they publish, respectively, American or British research would be mistaken. However, we know that journals tend to attract and select papers in their own image. The journals selected were:

- the *JLR* – to the best of my knowledge the longest-running leisure journal, the child of the National Recreation and Park Association in the US
- *Leisure Sciences (LSc)* – itself now running for more than thirty years and also starting in the US
- *Leisure Studies (LSt)* – the journal of the Leisure Studies Association has also been in publication for thirty years
- *Managing Leisure (ML)* – a newer journal that was established with the intention of speaking more directly to the needs of leisure professionals and practitioners.

Our[1] interest was restricted to the disciplinary base and research methods represented by the papers published in these journals. Clearly, there are difficulties in representing the complexity of research in any categorization, and a balance had to be sought between capturing important distinctions and presenting a manageable number of categories:

1   geography, environmental/urban studies, planning
2   sociology and social policy
3   economics, management and business
4   political science
5   psychology
6   history
7   philosophy
8   pedagogy, education studies
9   unassigned.

Although it is not uncommon for researchers to assert a multi- or inter-disciplinary approach, we tried to identify the primary discipline; the final category therefore relates mainly to those papers that are atheoretical and a few that are genuinely transtheoretical. As there are plenty of instances of geographers, sociologists and economists using social psychology and many similar hybrids, such judgements are anything but straightforward. The allocation was made on the basis of the background of the research team, the theory and concepts used and the authors cited.

The same kind of approach was adopted for the assessment of research methods, so the last category refers only to those papers where none of the previous categories dominated:

1   review
2   theoretical
3   quantitative – descriptive statistics/content analysis
4   quantitative – statistical testing
5   quantitative – multivariate analysis and modelling
6   qualitative – interviews/narratives
7   qualitative – ethnographic/participant observation/case studies
8   qualitative – semiotics/texts/content analysis
9   mixed method.

The volume of inter-disciplinary research and the use of mixed methods are therefore both under-represented by the tables. Some contributors to the journals would be horrified at this impressionistic assessment. I share some of that concern, but in cases of confusion the judgement of a second researcher was given.

A sample of volumes was selected, starting with the two most recent volumes and their equivalents in each decade, back to early issues of *Leisure Sciences* (and the first volume of *Leisure Studies* [1982]). So this is clearly only a partial picture. There are those other years, other leisure (related) journals, and those leisure articles more closely aligned with one of the parent disciplines can be placed in journals devoted to those disciplines. Table 8.1 confirms the significance of psychology in the leisure research in America. Indeed, it tends to underestimate the significance of psychology, as many of the geographers and sociologists were making free use of social psychology (in addressing motivation and satisfaction, for example). There have been times though when the balance has shifted towards sociology, which also has a strong presence in both *JLR* and *Leisure Sciences* but does not dominate in the way it does in *Leisure Studies*. As might be expected from its name, *Managing Leisure* is dominated by economics, business and management. Variation from one volume to the next makes it hard to discern any broader temporal shifts, though after its first decade *Leisure Sciences* does seem to have a larger sociological presence. The original decision to have separate categories for history, philosophy and pedagogy seems misplaced, given the small number of articles in which those disciplines are dominant.

Table 8.1 Disciplinary base of four journals

		Discipline								
		Geography/ environment	Sociology	Economics/ management	Policy	Psychology	History	Philosophy	Pedagogy	Unassigned
JLR	2011	3	4	1	1	11				5
JLR	2010	3	11			10			1	3
JLR	2001	3	6	4		9		1		
JLR	2000★	2	7	2		3				1
JLR	1991	1	8	4		8				
JLR	1990		7	1		9			1	2
JLR	1981	3	6			14				3
JLR	1980	3	7	2		13				3
JLR	Total (%)	18 (10)	56 (30)	14 (8)	1 (1)	77 (41)		1 (1)	2 (1)	17 (9)
LSci	2011	4	10	1		7				
LSci	2010	4	7	2		8		1		2
LSci	2001	1	8	2		6				
LSci	2000		7	1		6				1
LSci	1991	3	8	4		5				
LSci	1990	5	4	9		4	1			1
LSci	1981	6	5	1	3	12				1
LSci	1980	7	4	2		2				
LSci	Total (%)	30 (18)	53 (32)	22 (13)	3 (2)	50 (30)	1 (1)	1 (1)		5 (3)
LSt	2011	7	12		2	3				1
LSt	2010	2	16	1	1	1			1	
LSt	2001	1	7	1	2	3	1	1		1
LSt	2000	2	11	1		1		2		
LSt	1991	2	9		2	3				
LSt	1990	1	10	2		1	1			
LSt	1982	4	14		2	1		2		
LSt	Total (%)	19 (14)	79 (59)	5 (4)	9 (7)	13 (10)	2 (1)	5 (4)	1 (1)	2 (1)
ML	2011	1	2	14					1	1
ML	2010	1	1	9	2	5				
ML	2001	4	2	7	2					
ML	2000	1	6	6						1
ML	Total (%)	7 (11)	11 (17)	36 (55)	4 (6)	5 (8)			1 (1)	2 (3)

Notes:
★ Excludes special issue.
Percentages may not sum to 100, due to rounding errors.

Table 8.2 confirms the significance of multivariate quantitative techniques in American leisure research, but also suggests that there is now rather more acceptance of qualitative techniques there. There is very little use of quantitative techniques in *Leisure Studies*, where there is greater reliance on reviews, purely theoretical offerings and qualitative techniques. Unsurprisingly, *Managing Leisure* features much more quantitative work.

Table 8.2 Research methods in four journals

Journal	Year	Review	Theory	Descriptive statistics	Statistical testing	Multivariate modelling	Qualitative interview	Ethnographic	Semiotics	Mixed method**
JLR	2011	1	1	2	2	9	3	1	1	5
JLR	2010	1	1		1	11	7	2	1	4
JLR	2001	1	3	1	1	8	1	1	1	6
JLR	2000*			1	1	6	3	1		3
JLR	1991	1			1	13		1		5
JLR	1990	8		1	1	8				2
JLR	1981		1	7	7	9		1	1	
JLR	1980	3		1	3	18				3
JLR	Total (%)	15 (8)	6 (3)	13 (7)	17 (9)	82 (44)	14 (8)	7 (4)	4 (2)	28 (15)
LSci	2011					12	2	4		4
LSci	2010	1	1	1	1	7	6	3		4
LSci	2001	3	2		1	8	1			2
LSci	2000		2		1	9	2			1
LSci	1991	1	3	2	2	9	1	1		1
LSci	1990	5	5	1	1	9		1		2
LSci	1981		5	3	12	7				1
LSci	1980	3	2		1	6				3
LSci	Total (%)	13 (8)	20 (12)	7 (4)	19 (12)	67 (41)	12 (7)	9 (5)	0	18 (11)
LSt	2011	4				1	4	6	5	5
LSt	2010	2	3			1	10	4	1	1
LSt	2001	1	5	2	2	1	2		4	
LSt	2000	5	4	2			2	1		3
LSt	1991	1	5			3	2	2	2	1
LSt	1990	1	5	3		1	1	2		2
LSt	1982	12	6				1	1		3
LSt	Total (%)	26 (19)	28 (21)	7 (5)	2 (1)	7 (5)	22 (16)	16 (12)	12 (9)	15 (11)
ML	2011	2		5	1	6	1	1		3
ML	2010				4	6	6	1		1
ML	2001	3		5		1		2	1	3
ML	2000	5		6		1	1			1
ML	Total (%)	10 (15)		16 (24)	5 (8)	14 (21)	8 (12)	4 (6)	1 (2)	8 (12)

Notes:
* Excludes special issue.
** Many studies may present themselves as mixed method; this category was used only when it was not possible to assign one of the other categories as the main approach.
Percentages may not sum to 100, due to rounding errors.

Just as sociology that owes a lot to social psychology and the sociology of critical theory appear in the same category in Table 8.1, the same methodological category in Table 8.2 may encompass quite different techniques and styles of approach. For example, more diverse qualitative techniques like video diaries, photo-elicitation and creative writing make occasional appearances in more recent years. And at the beginning of the period many of the papers using qualitative techniques still bore the hallmarks of the positivist approaches that they were trying to escape, but against which they were still being judged. Equally, ever more sophisticated mathematical modelling may appear in the same category over the years in *JLR*, *Leisure Sciences* (and *Managing Leisure*). However, despite the increasing sophistication of statistical techniques, papers still commonly conclude with caveats around the confidence that can be attached to findings.

The link to policy and practice

At some stage someone has to take the step from understanding people's experiences to formulating policy and devising practice. There has been some tension in the relationship between research (or should I say 'researchers'?) and policy/practice (Best, 2009). Every researcher knows that politicians and policy professionals should take more notice of research, yet research commissioned to inform policy has long been looked down upon by academia as an inferior form of intellectual endeavour amidst concerns that policy makers may be concerned that 'their policies are underpinned by the "right" kind of evidence' (Best, 2009: 175). In the UK the recent preoccupation with evidence-based policy and research impact has prompted a revaluation of this relationship (see Silk *et al.*, 2010, for a challenge to this research 'turn').

After a long struggle by leisure scholars, it is not unusual to see the social value of sport/arts/recreation/tourism recognized in policy circles. However, some time ago I observed that we were short of research evidence to substantiate that. Long and Sanderson (2001) and observations by fellow scholars since then suggest that subsequent advances have been marginal. The obvious difficulties in identifying precise measures, isolating cause and effect, establishing true added value and accounting for opportunity costs, assessing sustainability and calculating negative side-effects are easier to rehearse than to resolve. In the light of that, Coalter (2007) follows Pawson (2006) in suggesting that our research efforts should not be about determining whether or not an outcome is successful, but about identifying which processes are most likely to deliver a successful outcome in which circumstances.

As one senior member of an agency said recently in an interview that I was conducting, 'I can't be expected to suggest we should base policy on an ethnographic study of five people in the East End of London'. Perhaps not, though I seem to remember that the, albeit larger, study by Young and Wilmott (1957) on *Family and Kinship in East London* was quite influential in policy/government circles. It is not hard to see the appeal for policy makers of research that apparently allows for generalization of a study's findings of apparently precise measurement. However, surely there is a place too for ethnographic research that takes seriously the senses, emotions and embodiment (Thurnell-Read, 2011). For example, city managers might gain a better appreciation of how to deal with 'stag tourism' from Thurnell-Read's participative study that evokes the multi-sensory experience of taste, noise, smell, bravado, elation, amusement, embarrassment and disgust. The point is that it would be unwise to base research on any single study, even the most expensive piece of research using complex multivariate modelling, especially when it is not clear what is being measured. And that may account for the growing fashion for systematic reviews.

As the volume of work in any given area of leisure research expands, it makes sense to ask what those studies show in the aggregate; hence the interest in trying to review systematically the available evidence. The gold standard is widely regarded as being set by the Cochrane procedures,[2] which are seen to be rigorous, objective and reliable in their implementation of a scientific process. However, when viewed from a different perspective they have a number of shortcomings:

- being dependent on a culture that is far more likely to report successful/positive outcomes than negative or no relationships
- employing a restrictive definition of what constitutes knowledge, an emphasis on controlled trials that leads to the rejection of alternatives like surveys and qualitative research
- small-scale, theoretically informed studies being relegated down the hierarchy are likely to be excluded
- focusing on outcomes overlooks the significance that process has for policy.

The key issue here is what rules are established for inclusion, which more commonly result in exclusion. This is especially so if trying to apply the criteria of Cochrane reviews to leisure research, as the Cochrane approach gives primacy to randomized controlled trials. For example, in conducting their Cochrane review of material published in English about interventions that sporting organizations had implemented to promote healthy behaviour, Priest *et al.* (2008) managed to find 'no rigorous studies' after reviewing 1,591 studies, despite extending the criteria beyond randomized controlled trials to include controlled trials more generally. So that was it, job done. The review process led to nothing apart from a reference to *Driving Up Participation*, the papers commissioned by Sport England (2004) that identified an abundance of qualitative information on barriers to participation. Reviewers need to protect policy makers from poor research, but the interests of policy makers are not best served by their being denied access to what can be learnt from good research, purely on the grounds that it does not conform to the rules of the review procedure. If the research riches lie not in controlled trials but in qualitative studies supplemented by quantitative surveys, any responsible reviewer must surely embrace such studies. Fortunately, there are researchers wrestling with the challenge of how to assess the contribution of qualitative studies within a systematic review.

In the UK the Department for Culture, Media and Sport recently commissioned the Culture And Sport Evidence (CASE) programme[3] about engagement in culture and sport, central to which has been a process of systematic review. In appearing to opt for a more rigorous approach, the CASE reviews rejected a large body of research by insisting that in order to be included studies had to have at least a comparator design. This sacrificed a more nuanced understanding of available knowledge by confusing data with knowledge. It also meant that, because of the distinction in research styles, the majority of evidence being used as the basis of policy in the UK came from the different cultural context of the US.

Conclusions

Nice as it would be to assume that decisions about the research methods selected by leisure scholars were the consequence of erudite debate, we have to recognize that they may also be the result of the skills/attributes of individual researchers (some do not do numbers, others do not like people), the cultural context in which they are working (the way things are done around here) or the resources available (leisure research rarely commands big budgets, so inexpensive techniques typically have to be adopted). The procedures of systematic review introduced in the previous section invite questions not just about how we know, but about what is considered legitimate knowledge. Such matters become particularly important if funders, clients and academics dogmatically privilege particular methods at the expense of others that may be equally valuable.

Earlier in this chapter I expressed my concern over those quantitative researchers who become so preoccupied with the mathematical formulations that the numbers become the truth, without any recourse to the people they supposedly represent. Such arguments have been well rehearsed, particularly in the US, where qualitative leisure researchers have felt more oppressed by the yoke of the scientific method; and so, purely in the interests of balance, you understand, let me voice concerns about two approaches to qualitative research for which I can see the appeal but about which I am wary. The first is the siren call of those who want to promote a purely narrative approach so that we, as researchers, do not intercede and corrupt the analysis of the person(s) we have encountered 'out there'. This is not dissimilar to the scientist's insistence that the researcher should maintain an objective distance and not contaminate the experiment. If we recognize that people may tell a different story, depending upon the researcher in front of them, there can be no *a priori* truth–claim for their narrative. As has been observed:

> While any good researcher should respect the interpretations of others (respondents) derived from the 'realness' of their experience, a good researcher should also have acquired a breadth and depth of data and refined a set of skills. If this means claiming a privileged position for the researcher's interpretations, so be it; we should be suspicious of those researchers who deny such claims.
>
> (Long and Wray, 2003: 175)

Although I make no claim to be a great theoretician, and indeed often go out of my way to contest their abstractions, it would seem strange to deny the frameworks and tools of understanding that we have so assiduously acquired, in favour of a more raw account. In making that claim I certainly do not wish to gainsay the view of standpoint theorists, that the perspective from the lives of the less powerful is likely to be very different from the perspective of the more powerful (usually, researchers are in the latter category), so I have to satisfy myself that I am not taking for granted my white, middle-class, patriarchal training and assuming that my consequent analysis must necessarily be correct. Researchers have to use their skills and understanding of people, structures and theory in order to operate as research engines (Long and Wray, 2003) capable of processing data with integrity.

My second, related concern is with those who encourage us to present our findings through the medium of creative writing. Despite being prompted by a desire to capture a different ontology, epistemologically it is not so different from conventional qualitative research, where data gathered through participation, observation and interview are fashioned into a new account; so why should I be wary? My concern here is simply that few social researchers are great novelists or great poets, and the accounts offered can appear banal (forgive me for not offering references here). Now, if I could write poetry like Carol Ann Duffy ...

In editing a special issue of *Methodological Innovations Online*, Mason and Davies (2011) reflect on a theme common to their companion papers of how to disrupt boundaries in research. They suggest that to do this 'we need to see not only how we go about our investigations, but the thing itself that we are seeking to investigate, as multi-dimensional' (Mason and Davies, 2011: 2). This accords with calls for leisure research to address intersectionality. My reading suggests that while qualitative researchers may have a more refined conceptual analysis of this, the methodological advantage lies with quantitative researchers with their multivariate techniques; qualitative researchers have yet to devise appropriate mechanisms to keep up with their leisure theory.

With an eye to the future, Savage and Burrows (2007) have cautioned sociological researchers that the pre-eminent position they commanded because of their data-capture techniques and the knowledge they produced can no longer be guaranteed in an age of 'knowing capital'. Whereas previously sociologists had developed a suite of methodological tools for empirical research, now large amounts of social data are routinely collected for commercial purposes and data from publicly funded research is expected to be made available to all for analysis. Beyond claims for sophisticated social theory, they call for the repertoires of empirical sociology to be rethought with an interest in the politics of method which would 'link narrative, numbers and images in ways that would engage with, and critique, the kinds of transactional analysis that now proliferate' (Savage and Burrows, 2007: 896). Part of that reorientation would be to demand access to data that are currently held privately by government and, particularly, by commercial organizations. It is possible that leisure research, being one of the less prominent areas of research, is sheltered from the early icy blasts of the winds of such change, but we need to keep a weather eye to the future.

Particularly as leisure scholars, we need to address the complexities of research in the web, not just in terms of the technical challenges of sampling and data gathering, but in terms of what we encounter there. It is an environment where people can in one instant be more truthful than in their face-to-face encounters, and in the next invent a completely different persona for themselves.

Although Henderson (1991) and Guba (1987), above, were following Kuhn (1962) in arguing that it is not possible to inhabit more than one paradigm, I have found it rewarding to explore inter-paradigmatic space in researching leisure without adopting the identity of a Second Life avatar. However, as a researcher hoping to make a difference, I have to remind myself that choice of methods should be like Tyson's (2003: 20) choice of theory:

> It is the understanding of lived oppression – the struggle to make a way out of no way – which propels us to problematise dominant ideologies in which knowledge is constructed.

For Willis and Trondman (2002: 398), this must acknowledge the results of unequal power. They urge researchers to 'make explicit embedded logics, so that social actors become more agents of their own will but within some sociological frame, somehow understood, conditioning and setting its limits of possibility – changing the social within the social'. This applies not just to what we study, but to the academy within which we operate. As we try to increase the impact of leisure research I enter a plea to researchers not to forget why politics is important.

Notes

1   The assistance of Ronnie Richards in this exercise was extremely useful.
2   http://www2.cochrane.org/reviews.
3   http://www.culture.gov.uk/what_we_do/research_and_statistics/7275.aspx.

References

Best, J. (2009) 'What Policy-Makers Want from Research; What Researchers Want to Tell Them', *Journal of Policy Research in Tourism, Leisure and Events* 1 (2) 175–178.

Blackshaw, T. and Long, J. (1998) 'A Critical Examination of the Advantages of Investigating Community and Leisure from a Social Network Perspective', *Leisure Studies* 17 (4) 233–248.

Clarke, J. and Critcher, C. (1985) *The Devil Makes Work: Leisure in Capitalist Britain*. London: Macmillan.

Coalter, F. (1997) 'Leisure Studies, Leisure Sciences: Different Concepts Same Crisis?' *Leisure Sciences* 19 (4) 255–268.

Coalter, F. (2007) *A Wider Social Role for Sport: Who's Keeping the Score?* London: Routledge.

Council of Europe (2001) *The European Sports Charter* (revised). Brussels: Council of Europe.

Dupuis, S. (1999) 'Naked Truths: Towards a Reflexive Methodology in Leisure Research', *Leisure Sciences* 21 (1) 43–64.

Gans, H. (1988) *Middle American Individualism: The Future of Liberal Democracy*. New York: Free Press.

Goodale, T. (1990) 'Perceived Freedom as Leisure's Antithesis', *Journal of Leisure Research* 22 (3) 296–302.

Greiffenhagen, C., Mair, M. and Sharrock, W. (2011) 'From Methodology to Methodography: A Study of Qualitative and Quantitative Reasoning in Practice', *Methodological Innovations Online* 6 (3) 93–107.

Guba, E. (1987) 'What We Have Learned about Naturalistic Evaluation', *Evaluation Practice* 8 (1) 23–43.

Henderson, K. (1991) *Dimensions of Choice: A Qualitative Approach to Recreation Research*. State College, PA: Venture Publishing.

Henderson, K. (2000) 'False Dichotomies, Intellectual Diversity and the "Either/Or" World: Leisure Research in Transition', *Journal of Leisure Research* 32 (1) 49–53.

Hylton, K. (2012) 'Talk the Talk, Walk the Walk: Defining Critical Race Theory in Research', *Race, Ethnicity and Education* 15 (1) 23–41.

Iso-Ahola, S. (2009) 'The Flagship Journal and its Role in Advancing New Knowledge and the Field of Inquiry', *Journal of Leisure Research* 41 (3) 301–305.

Jackson, E. and Burton, T. (eds) (1989) *Understanding Leisure and Recreation: Mapping the Past, Charting the Future*. State College, PA: Venture Publishing.

Kelly, J. (2000) 'The "Real World" and the Irrelevance of Theory-Based Research', *Journal of Leisure Research* 32 (1) 74–78.

Kuhn, T. (1962) *The Structure of Scientific Revolutions*. Chicago: University of Chicago Press.

Long, J. (1987) 'Continuity as a Basis for Change: Leisure and Male Retirement', *Leisure Studies* 6 (1) 55–70.

Long, J. (2007) *Researching Leisure, Sport and Tourism: The Essential Guide*. London: Sage.

Long, J. and Carless, D. (2010) 'Hearing, Listening and Acting', in M. O'Sullivan, and A. MacPhail (eds) *Young People's Voices in Physical Education and Youth Sport*. London: Routledge.

Long, J. and Sanderson, I. (2001) 'The Social Benefits of Sport – Where's the Proof?' in C. Gratton and I. Henry (eds) *Sport in the City*. London: Routledge.

Long, J. and Wray, S. (2003) 'It Depends Who You Are: On Asking Difficult Questions in *Leisure Research*', *Loisir et Société* 26 (1) 169–182.

Mason, J. and Davies, K. (2011) 'Introduction to the Special Issue', *Methodological Innovations Online* 6 (2) 1–4.

Parry, J. and Long, J. (1990) 'Immaculate Conceptions', in S. Parker (ed.) *Leisure, Labour and Lifestyles: International Comparisons, Volume 2 Work Leisure and Lifestyles*. Brighton: Leisure Studies Association.

Pawson, R. (2006) *Evidence-Based Policy: A Realistic Perspective*. London: Sage.

Priest, N., Armstrong, R., Doyle, J. and Waters, E. (2008) 'Interventions Implemented through Sporting Organisations for Increasing Participation in Sport'. Cochrane Database of Systematic Reviews (Issue 3): Art. No.: CD004812. DOI: 004810.001002/14651858.CD14004812.pub14651853.

Ramazanoglu, C. and Holland, J. (2002) *Feminist Methodology: Challenges and Choices*. London: Sage.

Rojek, C. (1985) *Capitalism and Leisure Theory*. London: Tavistock.

Rojek, C. (1993) 'After Popular Culture: Hyperreality and Leisure', *Leisure Studies* 12 (4) 277–289.

Samdahl, D. (2000) 'On the Future of Leisure Studies', *Journal of Leisure Research* 32 (1) 125–128.

Savage, M. and Burrows, R. (2007) 'The Coming Crisis of Empirical Sociology', *Sociology* 41 (5) 885–899.

Silk, M., Bush, A. and Andrews, D. (2010) 'Contingent Intellectual Amateurism, or, the Problem with Evidence-Based Research', *Journal of Sport and Social Issues* 34 (1) 105–128.

Smith, B. and Sparkes, A. (2008) 'Changing Bodies, Changing Narratives and the Consequences of Tellability: A Case Study of Becoming Disabled through Sport', *Sociology of Health and Illness* 30 (2) 217–236.

Smith, B. and Sparkes, A. (2012). 'Narrative Analysis in Sport and Physical Culture', in K. Young and M. Atkinson (Eds.), *Qualitative Research on Sport and Physical Culture* (pp. 79–99). Bradford: Emerald.

Sport England (2004) 'Driving up Participation: The Challenge for Sport'. Academic Review Papers Commissioned by Sport England as Contextual Analysis to Inform the Preparation of the Framework for Sport in England. London: Sport England.

Stokowski, P. (1994) *Leisure in Society: A Network Structural Perspective*. New York: Mansell.

Thurnell-Read, T. (2011) '"Common-Sense" Research: Senses, Emotions and Embodiment in Researching Stag Tourism in Eastern Europe', *Methodological Innovations Online* 6 (2) 39–49.

Tomlinson, A. (1989) 'Whose Side Are They on? Leisure Studies and Cultural Studies in Britain', *Leisure Studies* 8 (2) 97–106.

Tyson, C. (2003) 'Epistemology of Emancipation', in G. Lopez and L. Parker (eds) *Interrogating Racism in Qualitative Research*. New York: Peter Lang.

Wacquant, L. (1998) 'Pierre Bourdieu', in R. Stones (ed.) *Key Sociological Thinkers*. Basingstoke: Palgrave.

Watson, B. and Scraton, S. (2001) 'Confronting Whiteness? Researching the Lives of South Asian Mothers', *Journal of Gender Studies* 10 (3) 265–277.

Willis, P. and Trondman, M. (2002) 'Manifesto for Ethnography', *Cultural Studies <=> Critical Methodologies* 2 (3) 394–402.

Witt, P. (2009) 'A Long Journey to Somewhere: JLR at 40', *Journal of Leisure Research* 41 (3) 293–295.

Young, M. and Wilmott, P. (1957) *Family and Kinship in East London*. London: Pelican.

PART II

KEY THINKERS

9

THEODOR W. ADORNO, THE CULTURE INDUSTRY AND LEISURE

Simon Mussell

Introduction

Anyone serious about the study of either culture or leisure and the various cultural and leisure practices undertaken in capitalist societies must have some familiarity with the arguments put forward by the German philosopher, sociologist, musicologist and cultural critic, Theodor W. Adorno (1903–69), in his seminal 'culture industry' thesis. While the influence of this thesis is undeniable, its content is provocative, sometimes unsettling and always uncompromising. The aim of this chapter is to provide the reader with a critical overview of Adorno's work and what it has to offer leisure scholars. After outlining some biographical details to contextualize the author and his approach, the chapter begins by exploring the main tenets of the culture industry thesis. Building on this groundwork, it goes on to explore what Adorno had to say about leisure (and 'free time'). In the subsequent section, the chapter rehearses some of most notable criticisms directed at Adorno's work. Finally, the chapter offers some responses to these criticisms, as well as asking how Adorno's pioneering insights might be (at least partially) salvaged for those interested in developing scholarly understandings at the intersection between Culture Studies and Leisure Studies in our contemporary 'postmodern' landscape.

Who was Theodor W. Adorno?

Theodor Ludwig Wiesengrund was born on 11 September 1903 in Frankfurt am Main. His father, Oskar Wiesengrund, was a Jewish wine merchant and his mother, Maria Calvelli-Adorno, was a Catholic professional singer from Corsica. On the advice of Friedrich Pollock (a colleague at the Institute for Social Research in Frankfurt), Theodor Wiesengrund adopted his mother's maiden name (Adorno) during the late 1930s while in exile from Nazi Germany. Adorno demonstrated from a young age an interest in and aptitude for music and philosophy. In his teenage years, Adorno had tutorials with Siegfried Kracauer (who became an influential critic and film theorist in the Weimar Republic) and familiarized himself with the works of Georg Lukács and Ernst Bloch. Adorno attended the University of Frankfurt and took classes in philosophy, sociology, psychology and music. In 1924, at the age of 21, he received his doctorate with a critique of Edmund Husserl's phenomenology. In the mid-1920s, Adorno lived in Vienna for a while, during which time he studied composition with Alban Berg and attended lectures by Karl Kraus (Jarvis, 1997: 4). Through his friend Max Horkheimer, Adorno became acquainted with members of the Institute for Social Research (Institut für Sozialforschung) and other leading thinkers of the day – including Leo Löwenthal, Friedrich Pollock, Ernst Bloch, Bertolt Brecht, Kurt Weill, Walter Benjamin and Herbert Marcuse. In 1931, Adorno took up a teaching position at the University of Frankfurt, but he was forced into exile two years later. Horkheimer eventually resituated the Institute in New York, but Adorno fled to Oxford. By the middle of the 1930s, Adorno had discarded his ambitions for composition and instead focused his energies on social philosophy and cultural critique.

By 1938, Horkheimer had organized for Adorno to work for Paul Lazarsfeld at the Princeton Radio Project. A reluctant Adorno left European shores to take up the post. In November 1941, Adorno moved from New York to California to join Horkheimer. At the time, Los Angeles was home to an interesting group of German émigrés – intellectuals, artists, composers and writers, including Thomas Mann, Arnold Schoenberg, Bertolt Brecht, Fritz Lang and Hanns Eisler. While in exile, Adorno worked on a range of projects, most notably his collaborative effort with Horkheimer entitled *Dialectic of Enlightenment*, which would become a canonical text in 'critical theory'. Adorno also developed the 'F-scale', an analytical device for identifying various personality types and assessing their amenability to fascism.

In 1949, Adorno, Horkheimer and Pollock returned to Frankfurt to re-establish the Institute. In the remaining twenty years of his life, Adorno produced dozens of books, essays and articles on a vast array of subjects, the most notable of which were *Negative Dialectics* (1966) and the posthumously published *Aesthetic Theory* (1970).

The political unrest at the University of Frankfurt in the late 1960s put Adorno in a difficult situation. While most of the student activists were extremely receptive to his provocative and complex theoretical works, which offered deft and contemporary analyses of the crises and contradictions of capitalism, they soon became impatient and frustrated with Adorno's apparent unwillingness to support practical or direct action. Following numerous disruptions to his lectures, Adorno became increasingly depressed, and found no solace from the communications he had with his friend and colleague Herbert Marcuse. Writing from Berkeley, Marcuse was adamant that the students must be fully supported, and that to fail to do so would be to side with the state. In a short piece written towards the end of his life, entitled 'Resignation', Adorno argued vociferously for the power and necessity of critical thinking, particularly in the face of myopic actionist demands. He refused to be 'terrorized into action' (Adorno, 1991: 202), and elsewhere lamented: 'When I made my theoretical model, I could not have guessed that people would want to realize it with Molotov cocktails' (cited in Jay, 1984: 55).

In a state of exhaustion, Adorno, accompanied by his wife Gretel, travelled to Switzerland in the summer of 1969. Against the orders of the family doctor, the couple embarked upon a mountain excursion, during which Adorno suffered chest pains that forced them to return to their hotel. The pains recurred later that day, after which Adorno was taken to the local hospital as a precautionary measure. The next day, 6 August 1969, Gretel set out to visit him at the hospital, only to discover that her husband had died after suffering a sudden heart attack. The funeral took place in Frankfurt on 13 August 1969, with over two thousand mourners in attendance (Müller-Doohm, 2009: 474–480).

The culture industry

> Cultural entities typical of the culture industry are no longer *also* commodities, they are commodities through and through.
>
> (Adorno, 1991: 100)

When reading Adorno's cultural theory it is essential to keep in mind his theoretical concerns and political persuasions, not to mention his unwavering disdain for purely descriptive or 'positivistic' social science. In contrast to the more prevalent and government-sponsored methodologies often found today – which predominantly promote a disinterested, 'objective' and empirically grounded account – Adorno's social theory seeks to relate cultural phenomena to their wider contexts and effects. One of the main aims of his work is to survey the social, historical and economic conditions within which cultural production occurs, as well as to analyse the ways in which particular forms of culture either promote or preclude the possibilities for social transformation and emancipation. In order to achieve this larger 'macro' perspective on cultural production and consumption, Adorno developed a thesis concerning what he and his senior colleague Max Horkheimer came to call the 'culture industry'.

Adorno and Horkheimer constructed and used the term 'culture industry' (*Kulturindustrie*) as a deliberately confrontational and oppositional one. Adorno recalls the motivations for this decision in the essay 'Culture Industry Reconsidered':

> In our drafts we spoke of 'mass culture'. We replaced that expression with 'culture industry' in order to exclude from the outset the interpretation agreeable to its advocates: that it is a matter of something like a culture that arises spontaneously from the masses themselves, the contemporary form of popular art. From the latter the culture industry must be distinguished in the extreme.
>
> (Adorno, 1991: 98)

The first point of note here is the intriguing juxtaposition of two words that are ordinarily deemed mutually incompatible. Just as work is routinely contrasted with leisure (and there will be more on this distinction later), so culture is often construed as being inherently non-industrial. Culture is traditionally perceived as an important site for diverse human praxis, expression, freedom, creativity and spontaneity, while industry is normally thought of in terms of instrumentality, repetition, automatism, technology and mechanized production. Compounding these nouns into one provocative phrase – the culture industry – allowed its authors to swiftly and powerfully invoke the ways in which culture is created and regulated along the very same industrial lines of other capitalist modes of production, distribution and exchange. However, while certain culture industries may well operate Fordist-style production processes, such a literal rendering of the term 'industry' is not the main reason behind Adorno's usage. Instead, by invoking the term Adorno wants to draw attention to the many ways in which culture becomes reduced, rigidly controlled, managed, shaped, pre-formed, pre-digested and marketed so as to negate its critical, spontaneous and unpredictable elements. The industrialization of culture makes priorities of categorization, routinization and demographics. Each cultural entity must be easily categorized within extant genres and rehearse established conventions, so that they may be consistently reproduced and distributed to their target audiences.

Marked differentiations such as those of A and B films, or of stories in magazines in different price ranges, depend not so much on subject matter as on classifying, organizing, and labeling consumers. Something is provided for all so that none may escape.

(Adorno and Horkheimer, 1997: 123)

As a result of this top-down blanket provision, any grander notions of autonomy, spontaneity, expression, unfettered communication and playful purposelessness – those positive aspects associated with non-industrialized forms of culture and leisure – are reduced to pure semblance amid the culture industry, if not expunged altogether. Existing no longer as a repository for the varied hopes, dreams and promises of humanity, culture is instead fully integrated into and placed in the service of the capitalist economy: 'The entire practice of the culture industry transfers the profit motive naked onto cultural forms' (Adorno, 1991: 99). Only those cultural goods that can be shown to make a considerable profit will end up being mass produced and thereby exchanged on a scale large enough to adequately remunerate their producers/owners. Indeed, Adorno argues that the capacity for cultural products to be exchanged and exchangeable is now of more importance than any qualitative distinctions, genuine utility or particularity. *Exchange-value* (i.e. the value of something when placed within an exchange relation with other commodities) has come to be the primary value for all cultural artefacts, over and above any intrinsic *use-value*:

> Everything is looked at from only one aspect: that it can be used for something else, however vague the notion of this use may be. No object has an inherent value; it is valuable only to the extent that it can be exchanged.
>
> (Adorno and Horkheimer, 1997: 158)

The ubiquity of exchange value (or the 'exchange principle', as Adorno also calls it) robs culture of the possibility of autonomous and spontaneous development, for the culture industry tightly regulates its output in order to affirm and reproduce the status quo. The mass cultural objects produced under such conditions are either entirely homogeneous – as if made from the same mould – or thinly veiled replicas – that is, consisting of ultimately the same content but with minor or superficial modifications that are exaggerated in an attempt to feign novelty and difference:

> What parades as progress in the culture industry, as the incessantly new which it offers up, remains the disguise for an eternal sameness; everywhere the changes mask a skeleton which has changed just as little as the profit motive itself since the time it first gained its predominance over culture.
>
> (Adorno, 1991: 100)

The 'eternal sameness' or standardization of cultural goods is not just manifested at the productive level; it can also be observed at the consumptive level. Indeed, the categories of production and consumption are tightly coordinated. In an early (and slightly overlong) essay entitled 'On the Fetish Character of Music and the Regression of Listening' (1991 [1938]), Adorno argues that the culture industry presents consumers of music with a succession of familiar and predictable motifs, melodies, harmonies, sounds, chord progressions and lyrical content. On encountering a popular musical piece, the listener is rendered a passive consumer inasmuch as she has nothing to do but receive the object in its pre-digested state. The content comes already schematized – that is to say, when cultural goods merely conform to and reaffirm established categories and generic conventions, there is 'nothing left for the consumer to classify' (Adorno and Horkheimer, 1997: 125). The need for critical cognitive input in order to synthesize the phenomena confronting us is removed. As consumers, we are spared the 'burden' of active engagement and genuine reflection, leaving us (supposedly) free to enjoy ourselves through repetition, relaxation and playful distraction from the daily grind.

As a rejoinder to Walter Benjamin's positive invocation of *distraction* (in the perception of film by cinemagoers) outlined in his classic study *The Work of Art in the Age of its Technical Reproducibility* (Benjamin, 2008), Adorno writes pejoratively of 'deconcentration' as playing a central role in the regression of listening. His claim is that the 'uncompelling and superficial nature of the objects of refined entertainment inevitably leads to the inattentiveness of the listeners' (Adorno, 1991: 38). He continues:

> Deconcentration is the perceptual activity which prepares the way for the forgetting and sudden recognition of mass music. If the standardized products, hopelessly like one another except for conspicuous bits such as hit lines, do not permit concentrated listening without becoming unbearable to the listeners, the latter are in any case no longer capable of concentrated listening. They cannot stand the strain of concentrated listening and surrender themselves resignedly to what befalls them, with which they can come to terms only if they do not listen to it too closely.
>
> (Adorno, 1991: 49)

Later, we will consider some of the most strident criticisms of the culture industry thesis, but as a brief prefatory remark it is fair to presume that one may sense an underlying tone of paternalism and elitism in the above passage. Indeed, it can often appear as if – quite contrary to his overt Hegelian-Marxist predilections – Adorno is no better than a traditional cultural conservative, looking down upon 'mass' culture from a lofty and cantankerous position of privilege. But this view is mistaken because, fundamentally, Adorno is simply *de-naturalizing* our habitual modes of listening. He is making the claim, and trying to demonstrate through technical analyses of musical products, that how we listen, and what we listen to, are socially conditioned and historically specific. It is not a matter of 'high' versus 'low' art, since each exists in a relation to the other, and both are subject to the same industrial techniques and market demands. All culture is commodified under capitalism. The rightful target, then, of Adorno's critique is not the victimized 'masses' at all but, rather, the culture industry itself, that is, the cultural producers who wilfully degrade or constrain people's listening habits and destroy the possibilities for any autonomy and spontaneity. As Adorno puts it:

> [The regression of listening] does not mean a relapse of the individual listener into an earlier phase of his own development, nor a decline in the collective general level … Rather, it is contemporary listening which has regressed, arrested at the infantile stage … [T]heir primitivism is not that of the undeveloped, but that of the forcibly retarded.
>
> (Adorno, 1991: 46)

The deleterious effects of the regression of listening – and of the culture industry's continual reproduction of the ever-same – are worrying for Adorno because of their implicit conservatism and de-politicization. A cultural environment that is unflinchingly affirmative, repetitive, infantile and unchallenging, on Adorno's account, is hardly worthy of being considered 'culture' in any meaningful sense. The clichéd melodies and lyrics that (still) inhabit the great majority of popular songs are replicated in the pre-digested sound bites that substitute authentic conversation and political discourse. In Adorno's words, 'In an all-embracing system conversation becomes ventriloquism. Everyone is his own Charlie McCarthy' (Adorno, 2005: 137). With neither the time nor the inclination needed to respond autonomously to various social phenomena, individuals are absolved of the responsibility of thinking for themselves; instead they are made to feel content with simply imitating the pre-approved experiences and arguments tendered by the culture industry, not concerning themselves with any kind of expression that might pose a threat to the existing order of things. Such is the apathy and helplessness fostered and reinforced by the culture industry. The consequences of this enforced resignation can be clearly delineated in the realm of leisure and free time.

Leisure and 'free time'

[F]ree time depends on the totality of social conditions, which continues to hold people under its spell. Neither in their work nor in their consciousness do people dispose of genuine freedom over themselves.

(Adorno, 1991: 187)

So what role does leisure play in Adorno's social theory? In an essay simply entitled 'Free Time', Adorno outlines his position on and critique of 'free time' under late capitalism. He begins by briefly drawing a distinction between 'free time' (*Freizeit*), on the one hand, and 'leisure' (*Muße*), on the other. Since leisure in its more traditional understanding denotes 'the privilege of an unconstrained, comfortable life-style', it should be seen as 'qualitatively different' from 'free time'. The latter, according to Adorno, is rightly understood as inextricably linked to and determined by the demands and patterns of work: 'Free time is shackled to its opposite' (Adorno, 1991: 187). Only by reinforcing a strict division of labour (which includes the false division between labour and leisure) can the concept of 'free time' even come into being.

The falsity of the division between work and leisure can be seen in the fact that there exist *leisure industries* made up of companies specializing explicitly in the provision of leisure, not only on a mass scale but also through all manner of niche markets. As with the culture industry, the variety of leisure pursuits on offer is bewilderingly vast so that nobody can claim they are not catered for. However we may choose to spend what little free time is granted us, one thing is made abundantly clear: do not allow any thoughts about your work life to enter into your free time, and vice versa. Or, as Adorno bluntly puts it, 'Work while you work, play while you play – this is a basic rule of repressive self-discipline' (Adorno, 2005: 130). No ground whatsoever is given to the inkling that perhaps, in some alternative arrangement of society, it may no longer be necessary to so rigidly divide one's labour time and leisure time in such a way. Again, there is an inherent conservatism and de-politicization involved in the many leisure practices undertaken in our ostensibly free time. In liberal democratic societies, it is understood that people cannot be put to work for lowly wages without some other forms of (paltry) compensation – one of which is the limiting of working hours per week, guaranteeing a certain level of non-working time. Yet, in Adorno's account, the borders surrounding our working lives are extremely porous. Our working practices are inseparable from free time: 'Amusement under late capitalism is the prolongation of work. It is sought as an escape from the mechanized work process, and to recruit strength in order to be able to cope with it again'

(Adorno and Horkheimer, 1997: 137). Most leisure activities are undertaken merely in order to recuperate and rejuvenate, in the process replenishing our energy levels so that we may once again functionally fulfil our role in the workplace. Any fleeting moment of enjoyment experienced during free time is held up as a fragment proving that working so hard and for so long is not so bad after all. For Adorno, this is how a liberalized workforce learns to perpetuate its own subjugation.

> Because, in accordance with the predominant work ethic, time free of work should be utilized for the recreation of expended labour power, then work-less time, precisely because it is a mere appendage of work, is severed from the latter with puritanical zeal … On the one hand one should pay attention at work and not be distracted or lark about; wage labour is predicated on this assumption and its laws have been internalized. On the other hand free time must not resemble work in any way whatsoever, in order, presumably, that one can work all the more effectively afterwards. Hence the inanity of many leisure activities.
>
> (Adorno, 1991: 189–190)

What is more, on Adorno's view, while people almost certainly retain a nagging aware-ness of the external forces and relations that reproduce and direct their lives in certain (often undesirable) ways, they are also only too conscious of the strife, dangers and difficulties involved in genuinely attempting to alter these existing conditions and 'throw off the yoke that weighs upon them'. In the light of this recognition, Adorno argues, it is no surprise that people 'prefer to be distracted by spurious and illusory activities, by institutionalized vicarious satisfactions, than to face up to the awareness of how little access they have to the possibility of change today' (Adorno, 1991: 194). As a compensation for the realization that radical social transformation is highly unlikely, if not utterly impossible, we occupy our free time by accumulating minor pleasures – the football match, the gallery visit, the restaurant meal, reading a book or magazine, and so on. In such activities, the workaday world infil-trates. Think of how the looming Monday morning mars the Sunday evening. We start to wonder how much 'value for money' we are getting from an overpriced football match with few goals. We visit a gallery and want an artwork to immediately 'give us' something, and readily complain to others if it does not do so, since presumably time is money. According to Adorno, all leisure experiences are tainted with the same methods of quantification that predominate in our working lives. No 'investment' of our time and energy is given without thorough pre-planning and calculation.

As we saw in the culture industry, while spontaneity and autonomy have lost none of their allure, the possibility of their realization is routinely thwarted by the intrusion of working practices into free time. The very freedom implied by the idea of free time is made to remain an impossibility by its absolute subordination to work: 'no spark of reflection is allowed to fall into leisure time, since it might otherwise leap across to the workaday world and set it on fire' (Adorno, 2005: 130).

Criticism

Having now familiarized ourselves with the central tenets of Adorno's culture industry thesis, as well as his critique of 'free time', it is worthwhile considering some of the criticisms that his work has received before evaluating, by way of conclusion, the extent to which Adorno's theses maintain their relevance in our 'postmodern' age.

The sheer scope and ferocity of Adorno's attacks on the culture industry have (unsurprisingly) prompted a number of critical responses in the years since their original formulation. There are two features of the culture industry thesis that seem to provoke the greatest animosity: (1) the overly strong claim regarding the *homogeneity* of mass culture; (2) the supposed *passivity* of cultural consumers. While these two angles are different, if not entirely independent, they are often compounded in the critiques aimed at Adorno.

In reaction to Adorno's argument against the homogeneous output of the culture industry, Peter Uwe Hohendahl observes that 'mass culture does not confront us as a unified system speaking with one voice; its obvious variety in organization, recipients, style, and formal structures calls for a different explanation' (Hohendahl, 1995: 143). In contrast to the monolithic account put forward by Adorno, critics call for culture to be understood in terms of its ceaseless heterogeneity. As Douglas Kellner notes, there is a 'variety of cultural artifacts offering diverse pleasures and oppositional form and content' (Kellner, 2002: 106). By confining the potential for even minimal points of resistance and autonomy to a handful of high modernist artworks, Adorno severely limits his analysis, and, what is more, in doing so he excludes almost everything else as being irrevocably detrimental to society and individuals alike. Defending certain objects of 'high' art also does nothing to temper the oft-repeated charges of elitism aimed at Adorno. One such charge comes from Jim Collins (1987), who sees in Adorno a culturally conservative mandarin prioritizing authentic (high) art over against inauthentic (low) mass culture. I will respond to these critical points in the concluding section in order to discern what is worth salvaging from the culture industry thesis.

In addition to showing how Adorno does not adequately recognize the levels of plurality and difference in culture, many detractors take issue with the alleged passivity of cultural consumers in his account. It could be argued that Adorno's politically motivated analyses significantly overestimate the direct top-down influence of the culture industry, as well as its ability to completely rigidify experience, control or pacify audience responses and thoroughly pre-form consciousness in order to uphold the status quo. Stuart Hall and others at the Centre for Contemporary Cultural Studies (CCCS) in Birmingham contributed much to the field of cultural studies and sought to rectify what they saw as an overly pessimistic and deterministic analysis on the part of Adorno and his Frankfurt School colleagues. The CCCS investigated how culture is experienced, symbolically understood (coded/decoded) and communally and individually (re)appropriated, particularly by subordinate groups in society. The focus on cultural reception was not without a critical edge – most members of the Centre were left-leaning politically – but its goal was to emphasize and encourage the inclusive and democratizing impulses of popular culture rather than to dismiss the latter out of hand.

Another critic offering a similar rejoinder to Adorno is the sociologist John Thompson (1990), who draws attention to what he calls the 'fallacy of internalism'. In Thompson's view, this fallacy of internalism at the core of Adorno's thesis consists of focusing too much on the structure and content of cultural products and the forces of cultural production, which has the two-fold effect of diminishing the moment of reception in cultural consumption and exaggerating the extent to which 'individuals have been integrated into the existing social order' (Thompson, 1990: 108). Such an approach, so the argument goes, fails to properly analyse the diverse and often unpredictable ways in which cultural artefacts and practices are actually utilized, refashioned, interpreted and experienced at the everyday level. While these counter-arguments usually originate from the discourses and sub-disciplines of sociology – such as media and cultural studies – similar criticisms have been voiced much closer to Adorno's theoretical home in the guise of so-called second- and third-generation critical theorists of the Frankfurt School, namely, Jürgen Habermas and Axel Honneth. Echoing Stuart Hall's (1981: 232) invocation that 'ordinary people are not cultural dopes', Habermas states that the proliferation of reception studies has 'done away with the image of passive consumers … who are manipulated by the programs offered to them' (Habermas, 1996: 377). Likewise, Honneth follows Habermas' lead in criticizing Adorno's overly bleak portrayal of consumers as 'helpless victim[s] of an all-pervasive media reality' (Honneth, 1991: 78).

Whether taken together or individually, these constitute some important challenges to the validity and utility of Adorno's cultural theory. As such, by way of concluding it is worth offering some potential responses to the above criticisms in order to see what of Adorno's work can be redeemed in our contemporary context.

Discussion and conclusions

When confronted with the apparently diverse cultural landscape of postmodernity, the culture industry thesis can come across as somewhat outmoded, what with all its talk of homogeneity, standardization and the ever-same. Of course, at the time of Adorno's writing (roughly from the early 1930s until 1969) cultural output was more tightly regulated and controlled by a few major conglomerates, which would have allowed for little deviation from established norms. However, Adorno never denied that a considerable degree of surface plurality can be offered by the culture industry. In this way, one should think twice before dismissing his thesis as unfairly or inaccurately reductive. The ostensible diversification and hybridization of culture that we witness today does not necessarily mean that ours is a more critical, open and autonomous culture. Instead, one might argue, the ever-expanding technological and cultural integration of all manner of experience is gladly provided so as to carefully manage the levels of genuine plurality and spontaneity within culture. In this regard one need only think of the degrees of 'cultural capital' (to borrow a term from Pierre Bourdieu) now invested in different commodities – fair trade, organic and ethnic foods, yoga, 'exotic' travel destinations, reading groups, museum and gallery visits, vintage items, arts and crafts, and so on. Thus, while the variety of cultural goods and services on offer cannot be denied, its contribution to an authentically autonomous and emancipated cultural sphere remains up for debate. Adorno's critical theory is still an invaluable analytical tool in this respect.

Furthermore, the multiplicity of postmodern culture(s) is often heralded as collapsing once and for all the distinctions between 'high' and 'low' culture, thereby democratizing cultural production and consumption – making writers like Adorno seem woefully anachronistic and elitist in the process. Yet, as early as the 1930s, Adorno claimed that both high and low art are commodified and degraded through the culture industry. In a letter to his friend Walter Benjamin from 1936, Adorno famously remarks that high and low are 'torn halves of an integral freedom, to which, however, they do not add up' (Adorno, 1999: 130). While high art tries to be edifying and renounces a false pleasure, low art aims at fulfilling immediate desires that are industrially manufactured. The guilt of high art lies in its broken promise of happiness (since art cannot fulfil what it promises in a false world), whereas the guilt of low culture is born of its wilful subordination to empirical reality, its 'selling out', as it were. What is more, even cultural works that attempt to subvert their status as commodified are swiftly brought under the industry's watchful gaze and neutralized as a result:

The total interconnectedness of the culture industry, omitting nothing, is one with total social delusion. Which is why it makes such light work of counter-arguments … That all cultural products, even non-conformist ones, have been incorporated into the distribution-mechanisms of large-scale capital … denies deviationary longings their subject matter in advance.

(Adorno, 2005: 206–207)

Even in a supposedly permissive postmodern culture, art occupies an unenviable and aporetic position. If art relinquishes its claim to autonomy 'it sells out to the established order, whereas if it tries to stay strictly within its autonomous confines it becomes equally co-optable, living a harmless life in its appointed niche' (Adorno, 1984: 337). In Adorno's radical critique, only through major social and political transformation could a reconciled and truly free culture become a real possibility. As such, merely celebrating our postmodern simulation (and fetishization) of difference and superficial plurality is perhaps not such a robust refutation of Adorno's work after all.

Another criticism noted was that of the perceived passivity of consumers in Adorno's theory. No element of the thesis has been challenged more rigorously than the claim that individuals are powerless in the face of what a domineering culture industry imposes on them. It is probably wise to accept that people generally are not entirely passive in their cultural experiences and indeed often appropriate a product's meanings and effects to subversive or alternative ends. Adorno himself acknowledges that he has often deliberately 'exaggerated the somber side' (Adorno, 1998: 99) in the hope of provoking in his readers critical thoughts and reactions. Moreover, the culture industry cannot have it all its own way:

What the culture industry presents people with in their free time … is indeed consumed and accepted, but with a kind of reservation … It is obvious that the integration of consciousness and free time has not yet completely succeeded. The real interests of individuals are still strong enough to resist, within certain limits, total inclusion.

(Adorno, 1991: 196–197)

An air of mistrust and suspicion surrounds people's engagements with prescribed culture, which, so the argument goes, creates dissent and resistive activity in consumers.

However, the staunch Adornian might aver that a superficially multivalent and self-critical industry functions more smoothly than a traditionally monolithic one, for the former invokes a pseudo-democratic movement, re-establishing itself as the true voice of the people. In our contemporary context, one might think of the many different forms of comedy and satire that permeate the media landscape. Much of this comedic output is *prima facie* highly critical of capitalism, media moguls, corrupt politicians, conservatism, popular culture and so forth. Yet in these comedic formats one can often observe the effective deployment of distance, disavowal and irony, all of which serve to neutralize whatever political or critical potential they might have otherwise manifested. Today, everything is fair game because, ultimately, it remains 'just a joke'. Nothing changes as a result of such self-proclaimed (and industrially approved) 'subversion'. As the late Bill Hicks once said in an outburst directed at advertising and marketing executives who are wont to reduce everything to the profit motive: 'Bill's going for that righteous indignation dollar, that's a big dollar, huge market. A lot of people are feeling that indignation – we've done research.' The culture industry might be said to be at its most influential when it can comfortably incorporate all dissenting voices into its ideological melting pot, no matter how critical they may appear to be. Ever more layers of cultural consumption are created and reproduced to cater for all discerning viewers, of all stripes, so that no individual is without their allotted type.

Adorno's prognoses may be extremely bleak, but in returning to his ideas in order to try to get to grips with our postmodern situation we may find an important and timely corrective to excessively sanguine and uncritical accounts of contemporary cultural and leisure practices. As a result, we can see that there is still much of value in Adorno's admittedly stark perspectives on the culture industry. That his varied reflections on culture and leisure are frequently uncomfortable and challenging for us is a sure sign of their straining to resist being entirely commodified and incorporated into the very system that they set out to criticize and undermine. Returning to and engaging productively with Adorno's critical theory should be an attractive proposition for anyone interested in keeping alive hopes for a genuinely diverse culture in which people are free to pursue leisure interests under conditions of their own choosing.

References

Adorno, T.W. (1973 [1966]) *Negative Dialectics* (E.B. Ashton, trans.). New York, NY: Continuum.

Adorno, T.W. (1984 [1970]) *Aesthetic Theory* (C. Lenhardt, trans.). London: Routledge and Kegan Paul.

Adorno, T.W. (1991 [1938]) 'On the Fetish Character in Music and the Regression of Listening', in J.M. Bernstein (ed.) *The Culture Industry: Selected Essays on Mass Culture*. London: Routledge.

Adorno, T.W. (1991) *The Culture Industry: Selected Essays on Mass Culture* (J.M. Bernstein, ed.). London: Routledge

Adorno, T.W. (1998) *Critical Models: Interventions and Catchwords* (H.W. Pickford, ed.). New York: Columbia University Press.

Adorno, T.W. (2005) *Minima Moralia: Reflections on a Damaged Life* (E. Jephcott, trans.). London: Verso.

Adorno, T.W. and Horkheimer, M. (1997) *Dialectic of Enlightenment* (J. Cumming, trans.). London: Verso.

Benjamin, W. (2008) *The Work of Art in the Age of Its Technological Reproducibility, and Other Writings on Media* (M.W. Jennings, B. Doherty and T.Y. Levin, eds). Cambridge, MA: Belknap Press.

Collins, J. (1987) *Uncommon Cultures: Popular Culture and Post-Modernism*. New York: Routledge.

Habermas, J. (1996) *Between Facts and Norms* (W. Rehg, trans.). Cambridge, MA: MIT Press.

Hall, S. (1981) 'Notes on Deconstructing the Popular', in R. Samuel (ed.) *People's History and Socialist Theory*. Boston, MA: Routledge.

Hohendahl, P.U. (1995) *Prismatic Thought: Theodor W. Adorno*. Lincoln, NE: University of Nebraska Press.

Honneth, A. (1991) *The Critique of Power: Reflective Stages in a Critical Social Theory* (K. Baynes, trans.). Cambridge, MA: MIT Press.

Jarvis, S. (1997) *Adorno: A Critical Introduction*. Cambridge: Polity.

Jay, M. (1984) *Adorno*. Cambridge, MA: Harvard University Press.

Kellner, D. (2002) 'Adorno and the Dialectics of Mass Culture', in N.C. Gibson and A. Rubin (eds) *Adorno: A Critical Reader*. Oxford: Blackwell.

Müller-Doohm, S. (2009) *Adorno: A Biography* (R. Livingstone, trans.). Cambridge: Polity.

Thompson, J.B. (1990) *Ideology and Modern Culture: Critical Social Theory in the Era of Mass Communication*. Stanford, CA: Stanford University Press.

10

THE LEISURE CLASS

From Veblen to Linder to MacCannell

David Scott

On several occasions I have heard colleagues say that the sociology of leisure, and Leisure Studies more generally, lacks a solid theoretical foundation. I contend there are at least three powerful archetypes for understanding leisure in contemporary society, each representing thoughtful models of how moderns behave. The first comes from Thorstein Veblen's (1899) *The Theory of the Leisure Class* (Veblen, 1934). Veblen's classic work is grounded in the idea that people use leisure to seek status. Veblen used the term 'emulation' to describe a deep-seated motive that drives people to grade themselves (and others) in regard to worth. Conspicuous consumption and conspicuous leisure are two mechanisms people use to create favorable impressions. The second archetype comes from Staffan Linder's (1970), *The Harried Leisure Class*. Status was of secondary importance to Linder. A key premise of his work was that as the pace of work becomes frenetic so does leisure. Moderns pursue leisure and consumption with an eye toward maximizing the yield on time. Given the plethora of goods and experiences that people can afford, they are constantly reminded that time is scarce. The final model is based on the work of Dean MacCannell. In *The Tourist: A New Theory of the Leisure Class*, MacCannell (1976) begins with the assumption that differentiation in contemporary society has resulted in acute alienation as people feel disconnected from stable communities and institutions. For MacCannell, the tourist is a metaphor for the human condition as people are driven to seek authentic experiences. Leisure is about people's endless quest for self-discovery and meaning. In this chapter I examine the relevance of these three scholars' ideas for understanding leisure in contemporary societies.

The Theory of the Leisure Class

Nothing succeeds like the appearance of success.

(Christopher Lasch)

Originally published in 1899, Thorstein Veblen's *The Theory of the Leisure Class* is probably the first major sociological explanation of leisure, and certainly among the first works to examine the function of consumption in everyday life. As a point of departure, Veblen assumed that people strive for status and to elevate their social position in the eyes of others. Veblen used the term *pecuniary emulation* to describe a 'pervading trait of human nature' by which people seek favourable comparisons with others. Emulation is what drives people to grade themselves and others in terms of worth; this results in their avoiding individuals judged to be inferior in social stature, and mimicking the attitudes and behaviors of individuals thought to be respectable or prestigious. Although Veblen's work is largely a criticism of the leisure class of nineteenth-century America, he recognized that emulation was practised across all socio-economic levels: 'Members of each stratum accept as their ideal of decency the scheme of life in vogue in the next higher stratum, and bend their energies to live up to that ideal' (p. 84).

Veblen's ideas shed insight into the origins of stratification processes. Veblen argued that the beginnings of class differences stem from importance ascribed to different employments. Jobs held in high regard were exploitive in nature; unworthy employments smacked of drudgery and were deemed 'debasing and ignoble'. Although status differences based on employment remained pervasive during Veblen's lifetime, he recognized that social position was conferred increasingly simply on the basis of wealth. Veblen noted that wealth provided a 'customary basis of repute and esteem' (p. 28) and had become 'intrinsically honourable' (p. 29). Today, wealth is an important indicator of social class throughout the world and people can readily be arranged in a hierarchy from rich to poor.

Importantly, Veblen inferred that status did not automatically accrue to people who had wealth. Rather, they earned status by exhibiting their wealth: 'Wealth or power must be put in evidence, for esteem is awarded only on evidence' (p. 36). One way in which they did this was by engaging in conspicuous leisure, which Veblen defined as 'non-productive consumption of time' (p. 43). The idea here is that people engage in leisure activities and hone their skills in ways that confirm that they are in fact exempt from productive work and are able to afford being idle. Leisure in this sense sprang from a belief that productive work was debasing. Veblen offered several examples of skills and activities that would signify that an individual could afford to be idle: 'knowledge of the dead languages and the occult sciences; of correct spelling; of syntax and prosody; of the various forms of domestic music and other household art; of the latest proprieties of dress, furniture, and equipage; of games, sports, and fancy-bred animals, such as dogs and race-horses' (p. 45). People also announced their social position by displaying 'manners and breeding, polite usage, decorum, and formal and ceremonial observances generally' (p. 45). In sum, conspicuous leisure included a wide range of skills and knowledge that verified that a person had the financial means to not engage in paid employment.

This leads to an often-overlooked point: conspicuous leisure required considerable time and energy. Manners provided Veblen with a vehicle for driving home his point. He argued that displaying good manners 'requires time, application, and expense, and can therefore not be compassed by those whose time and energy are taken up with work. A knowledge of good form is *prima facie* evidence that that portion of the well-bred person's life which is not under the observation of the spectator has been *worthily spent* [italics added] in acquiring accomplishments that are of no lucrative effect' (p. 49). The acquisition of manners and other skills required a specialized education, which involved 'a laborious drill in deportment and an education in taste and discrimination as to what articles of consumption are decorous and what are the decorous methods of consuming them' (p. 50). Clearly, much effort went into developing skills and knowledge in order to show proof positive that one had leisure.

Veblen also argued that people advertised their wealth through what he called conspicuous consumption – goods and services purchased and displayed for the express purpose of showing off one's wealth and social position. Although goods have practical value and provide comfort to the consumer, Veblen contended that many goods are procured because they are 'a mark of prowess and perquisite of human dignity' (p. 69). Stated differently, status is gained by being able to buy and show off goods and services that are excessive and too expensive for others to acquire. According to King (2009), the entire Gilded Age in the United States rested on conspicuous consumption. Following the Civil War, exclusivity and outward appearances drove elites to pay inordinate amounts of money for clothes, jewelry, artwork, servants, travel, carriages and yachts, homes, and hosting parties and balls.

Women's clothing provides a useful example of conspicuous consumption. During Veblen's lifetime, elite women were raised to be dependent on men and were objects of display. As such, their clothing was often highly impractical and adorned in ways to show that they were exempt from productive work and thus beholden to the men in their lives. According to Veblen, 'the high heel, the skirt, the impracticable bonnet, the corset, and the general disregard of the wearer's comfort which is an obvious feature of all civilized women's apparel' reflected conspicuous consumption in the decoration of women's clothing (p. 181). Today, many women continue to wear clothes that are impractical, expensive, and provide evidence of their subservient position (Mestrovic, 2003). Some women's clothing is often worn once (e.g., a prom or wedding dress) while other clothing is worn for a relatively short period of time and discarded with the introduction of new fashions. Thus, for many women, clothing functions primarily as adornment and secondarily as affording comfort.

Although the display of status can be achieved by either conspicuous leisure or conspicuous consumption, there are several reasons why people in Western societies today rely progressively more on the latter to advertise their social position. One reason is that most people have to work to make a living. Few have independent means to spend their lives in pastimes that have little outward productive value. A related reason is that employment has become highly valued as an end in itself. David Riesman (1953) observed that *The Theory of the Leisure Class* had immediate shock value and many elites sought to distance themselves from practices that smacked of pretentiousness. A life of leisure thus became a sign of wealth unjustly earned.

Perhaps the most important reason for the ascent of conspicuous consumption is that we live in societies that are now highly mobile and where interactions are ephemeral. Veblen recognized over a century ago that, as societies became differentiated and fast-paced, conspicuous consumption would become far more efficient than conspicuous leisure to convey one's social position: 'In order to impress these transient observers, and to retain one's self-complacency under their observation, the signature of one's pecuniary strength should be written in characters which he who runs may read' (p. 87). For all these reasons, status seeking today is far more likely to be expressed through consumption than through skills and knowledge acquired during leisure time.

Veblen recognized that people look upon many of the goods and services that they consume as necessities. Furthermore, once people achieve a particular standard of living, that standard takes on the form of 'habit' and they are reluctant to recede from it. Many university and college students today, for example, grow up feeling entitled to a wide range of goods and services. In the United States, for example, numerous college students own their own automobiles and personal computers, have credit cards in their own names, live in luxury condominiums, belong to private fitness clubs, own pedigree dogs, and travel to exotic places during spring break. These same students would no doubt feel deprived and less privileged if they were to go through school with less. Likewise, Veblen noted that standards of emulation are continually evolving, which gives rise to gradual dissatisfaction with current goods: 'But as fast as a person makes new acquisitions, and becomes accustomed to the resulting new standard of wealth, the new standard forthwith ceases to afford appreciably greater satisfaction than the earlier standard did' (p. 31). Thus, the college students noted above will graduate to more luxurious automobiles, homes, and vacation destinations, and will increasingly deprecate the very goods which they were once loath to live without.

Veblen offered one other provocative insight with regard to consumption: people's tastes and definitions of beauty are shaped by 'the expensiveness of the articles' (p. 127). This means that goods that are expensive and in relative short supply will be deemed more beautiful, tasteful, and fashionable. By way of example, Veblen noted that fashionable people regarded silver spoons as more beautiful and delicate than wrought-iron spoons simply on the basis of the expense that went into making them. Many people today make similar judgments regarding a whole range of consumer items. They are willing to pay exorbitant prices for designer jeans, luxury automobiles, and gourmet foods because they equate quality with expense. Simultaneously, fashion-minded consumers will sometimes purchase leather-bound books to decorate their homes or offices. These books cost far more than ordinary books and are highly valued because of the expense that went into manufacturing them.

In many ways, Veblen's classic work remains as relevant today as it was when it was first published over a century ago. Yet surprisingly few leisure researchers today use Veblen's ideas to explain leisure phenomena. This seems extraordinary, given just how pervasive conspicuous consumption is in contemporary society. Likewise, leisure continues to be a site where individuals seek to display their status and to distance themselves from individuals and groups deemed undesirable. Veblen continues to provide researchers with theoretical guidance about how status influences a whole range of leisure behaviour, including our choice of activities, friends, and tourism destinations. And his book may also help to explain how some people seek to live more simply and sustainably. Researchers can use the book to understand the challenges that these individuals face as they seek to distance themselves from wasteful consumptive practices.

The Harried Leisure Class

What worries you masters you.

(Haddon W. Robinson)

In his provocative book, *The Harried Leisure Class* (1970), Staffan Linder makes his central theme clear from the outset: the pace in modern societies is quickening and our lives are becoming steadily more hectic. An economist by training, Linder presents ideas that have profound sociological significance. A key assumption of his work is that leisure and non-work time mirror work time in pace and productivity. Linder noted, 'Just as working time becomes more productive when combined with more capital, so consumption time can give a higher yield when combined with more consumer goods' (p. 4). Linder argued that people apply in their behavior what he called a *shadow price* 'to consumption time ... [and] this price will go up in step with the productivity of work time' (pp. 4–5). This means that as the pace of work speeds up, people seek to make leisure more productive by increasing 'the yield per time unit in consumption' (p. 78).

Like Veblen, Linder believed that consumption was integral to understanding how people behave in contemporary societies. Both Veblen and Linder assumed that a higher standard of living is associated with increased purchasing power. Linder, however, minimized how consumption was related to status and instead focused on how consumption made life more harried. Consumption in Linder's work contributes to a feeling of time scarcity. The reason for this is that the more goods and services people purchase, the more demand there is to consume them. This leads to a key idea from Linder's work: *consumption takes time*. Given the glut of goods and services that people can afford in contemporary societies, it becomes highly problematic to devote sufficient time to them all. Members of the harried leisure class are constantly reminded that time is scarce. A feeling of time scarcity results in people's striving to increase the yield on time. An esoteric phrase that Linder used to describe this process was *accelerated consumption*.

Linder put forward several ways in which people strive to increase the yield on leisure time. One way was to substitute new and more expensive products for older and less expensive ones. As their incomes increase, consumers may upgrade, for example, their television sets, wardrobe, golf clubs, cell phones, computers, automobiles, clothes, exercise equipment, and dinner ware. Whereas Veblen argued that consumer goods like these are integral to pecuniary emulation, Linder contended that expensive goods are simply a way to accelerate consumption. Although consumer goods can also be seen as a symbol of time lost to work, in Linder's work the purchase of expensive goods is thought to create equilibrium on the yield of time spent in different areas of life.

Another way that Linder claimed people seek to maximize the yield on leisure is by engaging in *simultaneous consumption*. As the phrase indicates, this is 'when a consumer tries to enjoy more than one consumption item at a time' (p. 79). Several examples from the contemporary world give evidence of the ubiquity of this form of accelerated consumption. An exercise regimen can be made more productive by listening to music, watching television, or reading. The yield on outings or trips to parks can be maximized by taking photographs and/or sending text messages to family and friends. Likewise, organizers of sporting events incorporate music and dance demonstrations, giveaways, contests, and a variety of other ancillary activities that help attendees feel that they are getting the most from their participation.

Linder theorized that activities and goods that facilitate simultaneous consumption are likely to rise in popularity. The pervasiveness of television supports this premise. According to a Nielsen (2009) survey, the average American watches over four hours of television daily, while two-thirds of Americans regularly watch television while eating dinner. The prominence of television in America and elsewhere stems from the fact that it requires relatively low attention and allows users to do so many other things concurrently. While watching television, participants can dress, shave, eat meals, smoke, knit, fold laundry, do crossword puzzles, talk on the telephone, surf the internet, send text messages, and spend 'quality time' with friends and family.

Finally, Linder thought that people could accelerate consumption through *successive consumption* – enjoying 'one commodity at a time, but each one for a shorter period' (p. 79). The idea here is that people devote less time to individual consumer items. Other researchers (e.g., Rifkin, 1987; Robinson and Godbey, 1997) have reformulated this principle and concluded that time scarcity results in people 'speeding up' the time that it takes to engage in everyday activities. Rifkin underscored how efficiency pervades everyday life: 'It is the primary way we organize our time and has burrowed its way into our economic life, our social and cultural life, and even our personal and religious life' (p. 127). To this end, members of the harried leisure class expect speedy results when they cook, exercise, travel, and seek information. A company called getAbstract© helps subscribers to become 'better educated' by offering five-page summaries of books, which can be read in 10 minutes. The summaries are marketed as the 'fastest way to expand your business knowledge.'

Technology has played a central role in the speed-up of leisure. Two decades ago, compact disc players all but eclipsed record players and cassette players as vehicles for listening to music. Whereas older entertainment systems required frequent album or tape changes, compact disc players could be pre-programmed in ways that eliminated the time it took to change music selections. Portable media players today are now making compact disc players seem antiquated. Music selections are available literally at one's finger-tips and have reduced the time it takes to consume music. Similar technology advancements have reduced the time it takes to watch television shows and movies. Video cassette recorders (VCRs) allowed people to tape television shows and watch them in a fraction of the time by fast-forwarding through commercials. DVDs and digital streaming have now eclipsed VCRs because of their ability to reduce the amount of time that it takes to download desired television shows and movies.

Linder predicted that as the number of goods and services increase there is likely to be an overall decline in the quality of decision making. Difficulties associated with making informed decisions are exacerbated by a proliferation of technology that has increased the amount of available information and the speed with which information is disseminated. The Internet and cable television, in particular, bombard people with news from across the globe and an avalanche of choices about how they can spend time and money. Although an information explosion makes people more cognizant of issues worldwide, many people feel overwhelmed by the quantity of information that they inevitably encounter. James Gleick (1999) captured this sentiment in a book entitled *Faster*. He cannily noted that the 'Information Age does not always mean information in our brains.' He added, 'We sometimes feel that it means information whistling by our ears at light speed, too fast to be absorbed' (p. 87).

The leisure class that Linder described is one where time is increasingly scarce, and lives feel put upon, as people seek to maximize the yield on leisure and everyday activities. Linder's ideas are as important today as when they were published over 40 years ago. Furthermore, Linder anticipated several deleterious consequences associated with the speed-up of time. One of these was that people will forsake developing their minds spiritually and culturally. Because religious and cultural activities are not amenable to either simultaneous or successive consumption, Linder predicted that people would increasingly regard them as unproductive pursuits. Many pastimes of the harried leisure class require little in the way of skill development and thought. A second consequence that he predicted was that there would be greater hardships for people who have special needs, including small children and older adults. In their efforts to save time, members of the harried leisure class are likely to hire specialized care-givers for their young children and aging parents. The quality of such care is open to question. Finally, as consumers face inevitable time pressures to maintain the goods that they have acquired, it becomes more efficient to let products wear out and simply replace them. This has fuelled what Linder called a 'use-and-throw' system, whereby consumers no longer expect products to last. According to Linder, such a system means that the Earth's natural resources – including clean air and water – will be continually exploited and defiled to meet the unceasing needs of members of the harried leisure class.

The Tourist: A New Theory of the Leisure Class

Reality is nothing but a collective hunch.

(Lily Tomlin)

Dean MacCannell provides a third archetype for understanding leisure in contemporary society. First published in 1975, *The Tourist* is first and foremost a sociological examination of the role and function of *tourism* in post-industrial societies. As noted by MacCannell, tourists are actual 'sightseers, mainly middle-class, who are at this moment deployed throughout the entire world in search of experience' (p. 1). Had MacCannell conceived the tourist as a mere sightseer, his work might warrant little more than a footnote among leisure researchers. In fact, this is not the case – MacCannell argued that the tourist represents 'one of the best models available for modern-man-in-general' (p. 1). In this second sense of the term, the tourist is a metaphor for modern people's quest for meaning amidst anxiety over increased differentiation and the inauthenticity of post-industrial life. As a leisure class, tourists are driven by a need to search for authentic experiences in the lives of others.

As a point of departure, MacCannell argued that modernization is characterized by *social structural differentiation*. Post-industrial societies, he stated, 'constantly subdivide and reorganize [themselves] in ever-increasing complexity' (p. 11). On the one hand, differentiation brings about freedom as it breaks down hegemonic class divisions, race relations, and gender roles. People in post-industrial societies are accorded choices and opportunities unavailable to individuals in more traditional cultures. According to MacCannell, however, differentiation comes at a cost, as it is a primary source for 'contradiction, conflict, violence, fragmentation, discontinuity and alienation that are such evident features of modern life' (p. 11). At the same time, traditional ideas about what constitute virtue and evil are increasingly contested. This leads to a major supposition in MacCannell's work: modernization has resulted in deep-rooted feelings of instability and inauthenticity. Members of contemporary societies are faced with vexing questions about meaning and how they fit within the grand scheme of things. MacCannell argued, 'For moderns, reality and authenticity are thought to be elsewhere; in other historical periods and other cultures, in purer, simpler lifestyles' (p. 3).

This leads MacCannell to argue that sightseeing, in the broadest sense of the term, is '*ritual performed to the differentiation of society* … [and] a kind of collective striving for a transcendence of the modern totality, a way of attempting to overcome the discontinuity of modernity, of incorporating its fragments into unified experience' (p. 13). Modern tourism, according to MacCannell, has arisen in step with a modern consciousness that is dislocated from the past and traditional ways of doing things. Whereas religion and work once provided a foundation for morality and meaning, identity and purpose are increasingly sought in leisure. Individual acts of sightseeing are interpreted as acts of *self-discovery*. In sum, MacCannell's leisure class is one that is in search of authenticity, significance, and purpose.

Not surprisingly, travel to faraway sites is a major focus of MacCannell's work. Tourist destinations, or public places more generally, 'embody the representations of good and evil that apply universally to modern man in general' (p. 40). MacCannell assumed that authenticity and traditional ways of life could be glimpsed in faraway places that had not yet been ravaged by modernization. Travel to remote locations, particularly those felt to be primitive and historic, provides tourists a glimpse of the 'real life' of others. Experiences like this ostensibly help tourists to better understand themselves and their place in society.

Yet MacCannell understood that modernization was so ubiquitous that even remote places and people were not immune to its effects. Indeed, the effects of modernization have not slackened in the 35 years since the publication of *The Tourist*. The Internet, cell phones, fast food restaurants, and Western apparel have made their appearance in far-flung destinations and have made it increasingly difficult for tourists to discern authentic patterns of life. Tourism providers recognize the tensions surrounding modernization and, in the words of MacCannell, go to extremes to *stage authenticity* in order to ensure that tourists experience the 'real life' of the locals. Travellers to Tjapukia Aboriginal Cultural Park in Queensland, Australia can pay to see an 'authentic' aboriginal dance, spear-throwing, fire-making and hunting demonstrations. The activities, however, are merely performances by members from several aboriginal tribes, as few aboriginal Australians today engage in these activities as part of their everyday routine. Many tourists, of course, accept the raw fact that performances like this are staged, and may even feel cheated. Yet tourists, according to MacCannell, remain certain that authenticity exists beyond staged performances and remain ever vigilant that they will happen upon bona fide locals doing what locals are supposed to do.

However, the tourist is not simply a sightseer travelling to remote places in search of authentic lifestyles. As I have already noted, MacCannell believed that the tourist was a metaphor for modern people's quest for meaning and identity and this quest infuses leisure in contemporary society. Acts of self-discovery extend to the social groups and social worlds with which we align ourselves on a daily basis. A case in point is the worldwide fascination with reality television. Viewers are invited to watch seemingly ordinary people act in relatively unscripted situations. Followers of reality television are tourists to the extent that they believe that the characters and action in the shows that they watch embody authentic lifestyles that are distinct from their everyday experience. This means that people's search for significance occurs within lifestyle groupings that transcend time and space.

It is also important to note that this search for meaning and authenticity occurs relatively unfettered by traditional social class ties and cleavages. In this way, MacCannell's ideas represent a dramatic shift away from Veblen's strict emphasis on social class as a primary organizer of social life. According to MacCannell, people in contemporary society are 'released from primary family and ethnic group responsibilities' and increasingly coalesce 'around world views provided by cultural productions' (p. 30). For my purpose here, cultural productions include a wide range of leisure venues and activities to which diverse groups of people gravitate. Writing in 1976, MacCannell pointed to rock musicians' groupies and tour groups as examples of people coming together around a cultural production where traditional ideas about boundary maintenance are permeable. The cult movie classic, *The Rocky Horror Picture Show*, provides a familiar and colourful example of a cultural production that has attracted (primarily) youth from disparate backgrounds. The film continues to be played at midnight in dozens of theatres worldwide. Several studies have documented how people from different backgrounds have coalesced around dancing, card games, dog breeding, college football, and other leisure pastimes (Baldwin and Norris, 1999; Brown, 2007; Gibson, Willings, and Holdnak, 2002; Scott and Godbey, 1992). Unlike MacCannell, these studies stopped short of explaining people's participation in these and other activities as acts of self-discovery.

MacCannell also noted that cultural productions themselves are often dislodged from their historical antecedents and become objects of interest to members of the leisure class. Furthermore, people often become 'interested only in the model or the life-style, not in the life it represents' (p. 32). Many white people throughout North America and Europe, for example, have developed a passionate interest in rap and hip-hop music without grasping how the music evolved in African American culture as a form of resistance to the dominant white culture. A similar phenomenon is at play when upper middle-class Europeans take on aspects of Rastafarian culture. They can be seen dressing up and listening to reggae music that is characteristic of Rastafarian culture, all the while not comprehending the cultural and religious origins of the Rastafari movement and ideology. The exportation of the American Civil War to the United Kingdom provides another interesting example. British Civil War re-enactors regard their involvement in this facet of American history with the utmost seriousness (Hunt, 2004), yet they have embraced a lifestyle that can only be described as alien.

MacCannell's leisure class is one that has developed in lock-step with modernization. Post-industrial societies have laid waste to conventional social divisions, thereby providing people with limitless options for how to spend their time. Unconstrained by traditional expectations and conventions, moderns are left to their own resources to fashion a meaningful lifestyle. MacCannell's tourist is an apt metaphor of contemporary leisure – we are all tourists to the extent that self-discovery and authenticity are sought in pastimes that are culturally and historically disconnected from our everyday life. As I have tried to show, MacCannell's ideas are applicable to a broad array of leisure behaviors, and not just travel to faraway places. For all these reasons, MacCannell's ideas about leisure stand alongside those presented by Veblen and Linder as compelling depictions of human behavior in contemporary societies.

Concluding thoughts

The psychologist Kurt Lewin was purported to have said, 'There is nothing so practical as a good theory.' The use of solid, theoretical frameworks in the sociology of leisure can best be described as skinny. My goal in this chapter has been to present three classic works that may provide current and future scholars' tools for understanding contemporary leisure. The works of Veblen, Linder, and MacCannell provide compelling theories and explanations of the leisure habits of people living in affluent societies. Veblen's ideas are the oldest, but his ideas continue to help us to recognize how status seeking and emulation are linked to patterns of consumption and leisure. Linder's ideas about the speed-up of time are equally astute. The harried leisure class is oriented to accelerating consumption and maximizing the yield on free time. MacCannell's work affirms that modernization has undermined traditional prescriptions for living. For MacCannell, members of today's leisure class are tourists who are fixated on self-discovery and authenticity.

The ideas that these classics provide to understanding contemporary leisure are often at odds. Linder and MacCannell can be thought of as contemporaries – their works were published a mere six years apart (1970 and 1976). While both authors were keenly interested in the impacts of modernization, their conclusions led them down different paths. Nevertheless, their works alongside that of Veblen provide scholars with persuasive and complementary treatises of leisure in contemporary society. Collectively, the works of Veblen, Linder and MacCannell continue to be relevant as explanations of modern leisure and should provide current and future leisure scholars with strong theoretical guidance as they seek to make sense of leisure in everyday life.

References

Baldwin, C. K. and Norris, P. A. (1999) 'Exploring the Dimensions of Serious Leisure: "Love me – Love my dog!"', *Journal of Leisure Research* 31 (1) 1–17.

Brown, C. A. (2007) 'The Carolina Shaggers: Dance as Serious Leisure', *Journal of Leisure Research* 39 (4) 623–647.

Gibson, H., Willings, C. and Holdnak, A. (2002) '"We're Gators … not just Gator fans": Serious Leisure and University of Florida Football', *Journal of Leisure Research* 34 (4) 397–425.

Gleick, J. (1999) *Faster: The Acceleration of Just About Everything*. New York: Pantheon Books.

Hunt, S. J. (2004) 'Acting the Part: "Living History" as a Serious Leisure Pursuit', *Leisure Studies* 23 (40) 387–403.

King, G. (2009) *A Season of Splendor: The Court of Mrs. Astor in Gilded Age New York*. Hoboken, NJ: John Wiley and Sons Inc.

Linder, S. B. (1970) *The Harried Leisure Class*. New York: Columbia University Press.

MacCannell, D. (1976) *The Tourist: A New Theory of the Leisure Class*. Berkeley, CA: University of California Press.

Mestrovic, S. (2003) *Thorstein Veblen on Culture and Society*. London: Sage Publications.

Nielsen Company (2009) 'Television, Internet and Mobile Usage in the U.S. A2/M2 Three Screen Report'. 1st Quarter 2009. Available at http://kr.en.nielsen.com/site/documents/ A2M23ScreensFINAL1Q09.pdf.

Riesman, D. (1953) *Thorstein Veblen: A Critical Interpretation*. New York: Charles Scribner's Son.

Rifkin, J. (1987) *Time Wars: The Primary Conflict in Human Society*. New York: Henry Holt.

Robinson, J. P. and Godbey, G. (1997) *Time for Life: The Surprising Ways Americans Use Their Time*. University Park, PA: Pennsylvania State University Press.

Scott, D. and Godbey, G. C. (1992) 'An Analysis of Adult Play Groups: Social versus Serious Participation in Contract Bridge', *Leisure Sciences* 14 (1) 47–67.

Veblen, T. (1934) *The Theory of the Leisure Class*. New York: Modern Press. (Original work published in 1899).

11

NORBERT ELIAS AND LEISURE STUDIES

Dominic Malcolm, Louise Mansfield and Jason Hughes

Almost all text-books purporting to introduce the sociology of sport contain sections on the work of Norbert Elias and subsequent researchers who identify themselves as figurational sociologists. Almost all introductions to, and critiques of, Elias's work devote key sections to his writings on sport. This is no doubt partly a consequence of Elias being 'one of the pioneers of the sociology of sport' (Dunning, 2002: 213). Elias was conscious of his role in this regard, reflecting on his collaboration with Dunning by saying, 'I think we helped a little' to make sport a respectable subject for academic study (Elias, 1986a: 19) – indeed, while otherwise something of a serial monogamist when it came to publication, Elias published extensively with Dunning (Waddington and Malcolm, 2008). Although Elias's prominence in the sociology of sport stands in sharp contrast to his centrality to the sociology of leisure and Leisure Studies, as we will show, Elias neither neglected leisure through his empirical focus on sport, nor envisaged their study to be mutually exclusive. Indeed it is characteristic of Elias's more general approach that such dichotomous thinking, and academic divisions, are counter-productive to the generation of socially useful knowledge

Comparison with Bourdieu is illustrative in outlining Elias's orientation towards sport and leisure. Both Elias and Bourdieu have been described as 'unusual' amongst leading social theorists to treat sport and leisure as important areas of investigation and to have applied their central theoretical concepts to the empirical study of these practices (e.g. Jarvie and Maguire, 1994; Tomlinson, 2004). Both stand as relatively early examples of authors who sought to combine, to use Bourdieu's phrasing, 'immense theoretical ambition with extreme empirical modesty' (Bourdieu in Wacquant, 1989: 51); to treat the everyday aspects of life as sociologically significant; and to take such areas as sport, art, and shifting 'tastes' as legitimate objects of social analysis. In this respect, Elias and Bourdieu share a considerable degree of common ground with regard to their sociological practice (Dunning and Hughes, 2013). Indeed, mirroring Elias's self-reflection, Bourdieu has similarly claimed that he 'is virtually alone among major sociologists – Elias being the other one – to have written seriously on sports' (Bourdieu and Wacquant, 1992: 93). While we might take issue with the degree to which the respective authors seriously engaged with sport and leisure (Malcolm, 2012), more pertinent for present purposes is the degree to which their theoretical insights have been embraced in the respective fields. Our central aim in this chapter is to illustrate how

Elias has influenced the Leisure Studies field. However, a supplementary aim is to highlight the considerable potential for scholarly development in this area.

We cannot, within the limits of this chapter, present a detailed overview of Elias's entire sociological approach. Indeed, this task has been done well elsewhere (Loyal and Quilley, 2004; Mennell, 1992; Van Krieken, 1998). Moreover, given that Elias's most well-known, and arguably most significant, book, *The Civilizing Process*, was voted seventh in the International Sociological Association's 'Most Influential Books of the Twentieth Century', such an overview should by now be unnecessary. However, whilst, as Liston (2011: 161) rightly observes, *The Civilizing Process* 'has become synonymous with Elias's figurational sociology', Elias's contribution to sociology is more extensive than the influence of a single book. Rather, one should consider his work as a series of conceptual arguments that interweave and represent a comprehensive theory of human society. With an emphasis on breaking the divide between theory and evidence, Elias developed his theoretical framework as he engaged in sociological research. Thus, the theoretical and conceptual discussions that suffuse *The Civilizing Process* come to the fore, and are developed and refined in different ways in other works such as *The Society of Individuals* (1991a), *The Court Society* (1983), *The Germans* (1996), *Mozart: Portrait of a Genius* (1993), *Involvement and Detachment* (1987a), *The Symbol Theory* (1991), *What is Sociology?* (1978) and *The Established and the Outsiders* (Elias and Scotson, 1994). Elias's thinking extended to the social construction of: identity (particularly, but not solely, in relation to established and outsider groups); science as both a social institution and a forum for the development of knowledge; time as a means of human orientation; and the process of death and dying. Throughout, Elias undertook an 'analysis of the historical development of emotions and psychological life ... in relation to the connections ... with larger scale processes such as state formation, urbanization and economic development' (van Krieken, 1998: 353).

Sport, as noted above, and leisure, as illustrated below, were important elements of Elias's broader theory. While *The Civilizing Process* explored the relationship between social development (*sociogenesis*) and developments in personality structures (*psychogenesis*) primarily in relation to France and Germany, 'Elias's work on sport constituted his main attempt to contribute to the understanding of English social development' (Dunning, 1992: 98). But Elias's historical sensitivity alerted him to the temporal and contextual specificities of the definition of sport, and thus to the potential pitfall of drawing a false dichotomy between sport and leisure. Tellingly, some of Elias's (1986b) early research explored what he called the 'sportization' of fox hunting in the eighteenth century, an activity that few would now describe as either a sport or sporting.

However, if we concern ourselves with the theoretical underpinnings more than with the empirical focus we can see that Elias's sociological approach involves at least five overlapping principles: (1) human societies can be understood in terms only of long-term processes of change; (2) human life is characterized by interdependent relations which are diverse and shifting and underpinned by ever-changing, frequently asymmetrical, balances and ratios of power; (3) human societies are characterized by different degrees of, and a dynamic interplay between, internal and external social controls, with the increasing internalization of the latter in relatively complex societies; (4) human acts involve processes in which intentional action contributes to unintended or unplanned patterns of relationships; (5) human beings have degrees, balances and blends of emotional involvement in, and detachment from, the 'contexts' of which they form an integral part. As we explore Elias's influence on the Leisure Studies field we will seek to highlight the degree to which a relatively consistent commitment to these principles is evident.

The chapter commences by reviewing Elias's theoretical analyses of sport and leisure before exploring the various ways in which these ideas have been developed and applied. We do this by looking at how Elias's (and Dunning's) ideas have been used to explore firstly leisure, exercise and emotion, and secondly the interdependence of sport and social identity. We then address a conceptual development – the notion of the quest for exciting significance – and related empirical studies, before finally focusing on two forms of leisure – smoking and birdwatching – which (a) demonstrate the importance of research located within an understanding of long-term historical processes and (b) represent a distinct departure from sport/exercise/physical activity and thus show the applicability of Elias's ideas to all forms of leisure.

Elias on leisure

Elias's initial works in the field, while ultimately representing key developments to his theoretical corpus, were fundamentally more analyses of leisure in general than of sport more narrowly. In 1967, Elias and Dunning presented a paper titled 'The Quest for Excitement in Unexciting Societies' at the annual BSA conference; it was subsequently published as 'The Quest for Excitement in Leisure' (Elias and Dunning 1969), and provided the opening chapter and inspired the title for Elias and Dunning's (1986a) *Quest for Excitement: Sport and Leisure in the Civilizing Process* (hereafter *Quest*) – a text which would subsequently become acknowledged as Elias's 'major statement' on the area (Giulianotti, 2004: 146). In 1969 Elias and Dunning presented a paper at a symposium in Magglinger (Switzerland) that would subsequently be published as 'Leisure in the Spare-time Spectrum' (1971a) revised and reprinted in *Quest*. Elias's first empirical studies directly focused on leisure – his analyses of sport in ancient Greece (Elias, 1971) and of folk football in medieval Britain (Elias and Dunning, 1971b) appear to have been developed subsequently.

The notion of a 'Quest for Excitement' extends Elias's (2000) argument in *The Civilizing Process*, that one could empirically observe a change in the *habitus* of people in Western European societies since the Middle Ages. In conjunction with processes of state formation (and the twin monopolies over violence and taxation in particular), people were increasingly expected, and increasingly internalized the expectation, to exhibit more regular and even self-control over emotions and behaviour. In complex modern societies, characterized by relatively extensive networks of interdependency, it became socially advantageous to curb spontaneous emotional outbursts. Those who fail to do so tend to be hospitalized or criminalized. What Elias and Dunning call public and private crises (e.g. a successful harvest, a funeral) characteristically invoke more muted emotional displays of celebration or grief. Consequently, 'In advanced industrial societies, leisure activities form an enclave for the socially approved arousal of moderate behaviour in public' (Elias and Dunning, 1986b: 65).

Elias and Dunning's work on leisure challenged two assumptions that were at that time commonly held, and which remain enduring. First, in line with Elias's broader rejection of the false dichotomies which characterized Western sociological thinking (e.g. between agency and structure), they rejected the mutual exclusivity of work and leisure. Consequently they introduced the notion of a spare-time spectrum which consisted of three overlapping and fusing categories: spare-time routines (e.g. eating, washing, cleaning, domestic administration); 'intermediary' activities which are orientating or self-fulfilling (e.g. voluntary work, religious activities, technical or challenging hobbies); and leisure activities (sociable activities such as partying, and mimetic/play activities such as sport, the theatre etc.). These categories were distinguished by their progressively greater degree of de-routinization. Thus, Elias and Dunning could describe 'lovemaking' as a spare-time routine, but 'de-routinising love relations' as a leisure activity.

Second, Elias and Dunning rejected the Aristotelian-informed notion of catharsis, which suggested that people sought in their leisure time to 'relax' through the dissipation of the tensions created in their 'work' lives. Instead they argued that people actively pursue pastimes which generate stress tensions. Hence music concerts and dramas build to a crescendo, sports competitions culminate in victory or defeat. Stress tensions result from de-routinization.

Elias and Dunning point out that their use of 'unexciting' is somewhat ironic, for contemporary societies offer a wide range of opportunities for pleasure seeking. However, these opportunities are of a particular type, and thus Elias and Dunning pose two related questions:

1   What are the characteristics of the personal leisure needs developed in the more complex and civilized societies of our time?
2   What are the characteristics of the specific types of leisure events developed in societies of this type for the satisfaction of these needs?

(Elias and Dunning, 1986b: 74)

Their answers lead them to focus on the category of mimetic activities in particular. They note that a peculiar feature of leisure is that people tend to seek those emotions – fear, anxiety, anger, sadness – which we otherwise avoid in 'real life'. People do this, they reason, because in the mimetic sphere of activities such unusual levels of emotion are not 'seriously perturbing and dangerous'; rather, they are 'transposed into a different key. They lose their sting' (Elias and Dunning, 1986b: 80). A delicate balance between routine (which provides security) and de-routine (which provides insecurity and playful risk) is key. Such 'controlled and enjoyable de-controlling of restraints on emotions' is enhanced in collective activities (e.g. watching films in the cinema or taking part in team sports or group leisure activities), for this makes the sport/leisure experience meaningful, mutually reinforcing and distinctive.

Elias and Dunning (1986a) and others examining sport and leisure in the spare-time spectrum have tended to focus on the nature of mimetic activities which differ widely in terms of type, but which also have a set of common characters spatially and temporally defined. Mimetic activities operate as a theatre for the expression and relatively unrestrained flow of emotions, and a sphere for the elicitation of pleasurable excitement imitating real-life experiences but without the associated risks. In studies of rugby and association football (Dunning and Sheard, 2005), boxing (Sheard, 1997) and cricket (Malcolm, 2002) Elias's thinking about civilizing processes is brought into sharp relief to understand the sportization of English folk pastimes. It is the long-term, very gradual but perceptible internal pacification of English society, marked more prominently in the eighteenth century, that shapes the changing character of the sport forms noted previously. Increasingly regulated and requiring relatively restrained uses of violence as the importance of physical *skill* superseded that of force, the aristocracy's cultural activities acquired a novel structure. These sports forms gradually increased in popularity with groups across the social spectrum. The opportunities they afforded for people to exhibit a relatively restrained social habitus served as a basis for acquiring social status. Sport-leisure activities, then, are sites for the making, remaking and expression of individual and collective behaviours and identities in particular spatial and temporal landscapes. Leisure pursuits are not social contexts where there is an absolute freedom to act as one might want. Rather, mimetic activities allow for socially permitted actions and affects within certain limits (Maguire, 1992, 2011).

As prominent as mimetic activities are in Elias and Dunning's analysis, the authors stress that such de-routinization is not solely confined to this part of the spare-time spectrum. They discuss, for instance, the importance of relatively high levels of overt emotionality in sociability and the role of alcohol in facilitating this. They refer to the role of laughter as a 'means of counterbalancing the strains and stresses of impulse-control' (Elias and Dunning, 1986b: 61). They locate their argument within a broader sociology of the emotions, identifying three interlocking levels of emotion – social pressure, conscience and affection – which underpin an individual's commitment to the family unit. In noting that the latter disproportionately guides leisure behaviour, they critique the 'assumption fairly widespread in contemporary sociology ... that the norms of every society are monolithic and all of a piece' (Elias and Dunning, 1986b: 101). Perhaps most importantly, the 'Quest for Excitement' essay concludes by noting that entertainment, culture, arts and sports are normally studied in separation, and that while their differences need to be acknowledged, a fuller theory of leisure, the emotions and social life requires that we also consider their commonalities. Tellingly, Elias's conclusion to his 'Introduction' to *Quest* draws a distinction between professional sport and leisure sport, and argues that the former may lead to skilled but ultimately joyless performances; and he is critical of the scholarly dominance and social importance of sport relative to leisure per se.

Thus, incorporated in this work we can see Elias and Dunning's concern to understand the long-term processes of change which shape leisure, the blends of emotional involvement and detachment which characterize different aspects of social life, and the dynamic interplay between internal and external social controls, with the increasing internalization of the latter in relatively complex societies.

Leisure, exercise and emotion

Two premises of Elias's approach to understanding leisure – (1) that personal and social restraints and control of overt emotional expressions (of some kind) characterize human societies; and (2) that pleasurable excitement is sought out in leisure activities – form the foundation of some work on leisure in exercise contexts (Maguire and Mansfield, 1998; Mansfield, 2002, 2007, 2008). In conditions of broadening and increasingly stricter controls over human emotions, and the gradual but perceptual lessening of opportunity for public expressions of excitement in response to public and private crises, sociable physical activity – such as that seen in exercise to music classes – may provide participants with opportunities not afforded elsewhere in their daily lives. During exercise, excitement can be variously felt in relation to: psychological desire to participate, which itself may well be experienced in varying degrees of narcissistic (deriving pleasure from seeing oneself), fetishist (deriving pleasurable fascination from the spectacle or object) and voyeuristic (deriving excitement from illicitly watching others) satisfaction; physiological sensation in the form of a burning feeling in the muscles when exercising with enough intensity, popularly known as 'the burn' (see reference to Elias's notion of the 'hinge' discussed later in this chapter); and socio-cultural or communal enjoyment that can come with high-energy movement to loud music and the opportunity that it brings to express resounding shouts, cheers, claps and whoops with a great deal of free abandonment.

The interwoven aspects of psychological, biological and sociological emotional expression and experience are central to Elias's idea about the mimetic sphere of leisure (Maguire, 2011). Exercise to music classes have some essential structural characteristics that reflect the character of mimetic activities as a 'make-believe' setting, allowing the relatively unrestrained flow of emotions and eliciting a range of pleasures and excitement connected to 'real life', but operating in an environment with a relatively low risk of negative judgements to those emotional displays. In particular, there is the capacity for loud vocal expressions, which illustrates the exercise context as an environment for the decontrolling of emotion with the social consent of others through communal passionate expression (Maguire and Mansfield, 1998). There is an argument that exercise to music classes – predominantly, although not exclusively, a female activity – involve engagement in exercises principally founded on improving heterosexual attractiveness and desire, sexual 'performance' and sexual pleasure, and thus provide a socially sanctioned environment for collective 'sex exercises' (Mansfield, 2011). Pleasure may be more or less sought and experienced in exercise contexts. Exercise to music does not provide for a totally free arena for emotional outbursts. Indeed, the vocal, emotional and sexual expressions are bound by emotional scripts, a 'feeling vocabulary' (Elias, 1987b), which determine the type, extent and precise character of behaviour and emotion in the class. Vocal expressions are 'in time' to the music, bodily movements are precisely choreographed and the pattern of the class (its timing, flow and timetabling) are ritualized, highly organized and routine.

In Elias and Dunning's (1972) typology of spare-time activities, then, exercise to music is principally of a mimetic leisure type. However, one could argue also that such exercise overlaps to an extent with the routinized spare-time activity type focused on caring for one's body, the relatively informal sociable, 'leisure-*gemeinschaften*' type of activity offering a degree of open emotionality and friendliness. Moreover, exercise to music carried out in private (using home exercise DVDs, for example) is partly characterized by the intermediary spare-time activity type of self-fulfilment (Elias and Dunning, 1986b: 97). This account therefore illustrates that the spare-time spectrum is not a list of discrete leisure types, but an analytical tool for understanding leisure in relation to the embodiment of a 'controlled decontrolling of restraints and emotions' and the balance between the embodiment of 'routinisation and de-routinisation' (Elias and Dunning, 1986b: 96).

Leisure and identity

Elias's ideas have been used for articulating how sport and leisure can be central to processes of identification and to the production and reproduction of difference and distinction. Such work can be located within contemporary debates about identity which focus on understanding a variety of issues, including subjectivity, difference, inequality and social justice. In short, Elias's work has been useful for some sport and leisure scholars seeking to answer questions about identity (who we/they are) and identification (the processes by which we give meaning to ourselves and others). Central to Elias's thinking in this regard is the importance of examining the complexities of power, interdependence and social change in understanding identification in social life more broadly. Smith's (1998, 2000) analysis of British non-elite road runners illustrates the complex configurations of masculinities reflected in the life course of middle-aged (30–60 years) male runners in relation to wider social changes in the labour market in Britain and changing gender relations which have led to a comparative loss of power and status for middle-class men across the generations. In Smith's work, such mid-life men are relatively disadvantaged, as compared to previous generations of men. They have relatively few opportunities to experience and express a traditional sense of masculine identity in the work-place or in family life. Running long distances in training and race environments provides the men with a sense of self-respect and admiration from others based on their physical prowess and achievement. Running is thus perceived by Smith to be a site for the subtle expression of traditional masculine ideals.

The examination of gendered identities and habituses in sport and leisure in the work of Colwell (1999), Mansfield (2007, 2008), Liston (2006, 2007) and Velija and Malcolm (2010) – and indeed the extensive analysis of football hooliganism, for which figurational sociologists are particularly noted (e.g. Dunning *et al.*, 1988) – illustrates the fruitfulness of thinking of people in constant motion: being in 'process' rather than simply going 'through a process' (Elias, 1978: 118). This is a key feature of a range of figurational work examining the psychogenesis and sociogenesis of identity formation by individuals and societies in relation to sport, globalization and national identity (Maguire, 1999; Malcolm, 2013); sport and race (Dunning, 1999; Malcolm, 2001); and physical education (Green, 2002). The argument that self- and we-images are always constructed and reconstructed over time, at different levels and within groups of interdependent people provides a basis for conceptualizing identity as always multi-layered. Furthermore, the precise characteristics of identification will vary according to the manner and extent to which socio-cultural factors are interwoven into a person's habitus or second-nature, the deeply ingrained subconscious nature of modes of behaviour, tastes and feelings of a particular group.

The dynamic and multi-layered character of identification discussed by Elias is connected to 'the mutual conditioning of processes of meaning and power' (Mennell, 1994: 180). The making of identity in leisure practices has been referred to as 'the leisure–identity nexus' (Mansfield and Chatziefstathiou, 2010: ix) and is characterized by 'power games' which refer to the processes through which people struggle for 'position and dominance' and against subordination. People give meaning to their leisure lives, laying claim to a sense of self-hood, often on the basis of 'membership status', a criteria-based, fluid and contested process marked out by struggles over meanings, belonging, self and otherness. Such power struggles are central to the legitimation of identities and are thus significant in understanding the status hierarchies that frame processes of identification. Tension, conflict and consensus mark out the production and reproduction of status hierarchies. The precise expression of such power struggles and the making and remaking of selfhood – in other words the overall character of the 'leisure–identity nexus' – varies according to the social conditions under examination (Mennell, 1994: 185). In Elias's terms, identity formation in sport and leisure involves personal and group meaning making and the search for distinction through public self-presentation.

Quest for exciting significance in leisure

There has been one major theoretical development building on Elias and Dunning's 'Quest for Excitement'. In elucidating a framework for the study of sport and the emotions, Maguire presents a 're-reading' or 'rethinking' of Elias, arguing that Elias and Dunning underplayed the processes through which identity formation in sport and leisure involves the quest for self-realization and the presentation of self. Maguire (1992: 109) expands upon Elias's consideration of the connection between biological and social development, and learned and unlearned processes in human identification – what Elias calls 'the hinge' (1987b: 351–2) – to argue that 'sport involves the quest for "exciting significance"'. The arousal of pleasurable forms of excitement elicited through sport and leisure, emphasized by Elias and Dunning (1986b), is developed in Maguire's (1992, 2011) discussion to focus on the connection between emotional experience, meaning and identity formation. Maguire's (1992: 107) account explains that contemporary leisure is marked by a historically specific 'affect economy (Affektshaushalt)' involving both the creation and release of an emotional repertoire, with various intended and unintended consequences. Whatever the precise character of these emotional experiences in leisure, the quest for exciting significance prevails, such that excitement is centrally connected to a rewarding experience that becomes habitual and that serves to produce and reproduce a sense of self. Leisure-based emotions and excitement, then, come from the meaning experienced in the taking part.

Atkinson (2008) harnesses the very idea of exciting significance in a case study of triathlon in Canada. The gruelling training and competition experiences of swimming, cycling and running are explained as a middle-class quest for exciting significance elicited through the mental and physical pain that is suffered by participants. For Atkinson (2008: 165), triathlon is characterized by the formation of 'pain communities' in which people experience 'intense social and emotional stimulation through "suffering" athletically'. Triathletes mutually identify with the capacity to endure and enjoy athletic pain which is status enhancing and which becomes a distinguishing part of the character of individual participants and the group. A type of wilful suffering is exciting, personally significant and centrally important to being part of the group. The quest for exciting significance is a key part of the self-realization aspect of identity formation through triathlon. As Atkinson (2008: 170) explains it, triathletes have a sense of 'social calling' to engage with others who seek out a shared desire to be 'physically and socially "special"'.

Atkinson similarly conceives of professional wrestling as a 'double mimetic ... a mock sport within a make-believe world of professional sport ... [It] seeks to de-routinize the now "mundane" mimesis created by professional sport' (2002: 62). Promoters of wrestling create this impression by aligning it closely to the structure and format of professional sport (a form of routinization), while injecting elements of surprise and uncertainty within an otherwise relatively predictable 'script'. Furthermore, wrestling provides flamboyant styles of violence which are structured according to specific norms of legitimacy. Ironically, the extreme forms of violence are probably acceptable only because the audience is aware of their 'fake' character, but nonetheless this de-routinization is a primary source of tension-excitement.

The example of mixed martial arts (MMA) shows similar processes to Atkinson's study of wrestling, but in many ways acting in reverse, for the rather more 'real' violence in MMA has led its existence to be relatively socially contentious. However, Sanchez Garcia and Malcolm (2010) argue that a primary stimulus to the emergence of MMA was the relative routinization of other fighting events. The hybridization of fighting styles inherent to MMA injected an additional element of uncertainty and novelty into proceedings as fighters with very different skills were pitted against one another. Thus the development of MMA has been characterized by tension-balance oscillations within what might best be characterized as a zone of stress tensions, between which too great levels of violence become repugnant and too low levels of intensity make such activities routine and dull. When early, relatively high levels of violence were challenged by abolitionists, promoters resorted to spectacularizing violence and making cosmetic changes so as to *promote the appearance* of de-routinization and thus generate greater tension. Sanchez Garcia and Malcolm conclude that 'the unique combination of intentional and open conflict means that by definition combat sports exist, and will always exist, on the margins of "real" and "mock" fighting, and thus on the margins of modern sport' (Sanchez Garcia and Malcolm, 2010: 55). As with triathlon and 'fake' wrestling contests, the popularity of this leisure form stems from the controlled de-controlling of emotional controls in a context which has meaning for the identity of those (participants and spectators) involved – a quest for exciting significance.

Leisure and leisure commodities in the long-term perspective

At its core, Elias's framework embraces a thoroughgoing commitment to the importance of analysing social processes over multiple generations. While there is not scope to elaborate on Elias's rationale for this commitment (see e.g. Elias, 1978), in this final section we address two leisure-related studies which epitomize this commitment: Hughes's (2003) analysis of smoking and Sheard's (1999) analysis of birdwatching.

Smoking

Hughes (2003) has undertaken one of the few figurational studies of leisure commodities. He analyses the long-term development of tobacco use in the West, developing a model of the sociogenesis of present-day patterns of consumption and use. Hughes's central line of argument is that the use of tobacco – what it is understood and employed to do 'to and for' the people who consume it – fundamentally shifts over time. Following Elias, Hughes argues that material tobacco, the primary mode of its consumption, the practices and understandings surrounding its use, its 'purposes' and how its 'effects' are 'experienced' by users must all be understood as long-term processes. Thus, significantly, while it is now common to use the term 'smoking' to refer to the consumption of tobacco, it is noteworthy that a number of substances – phencyclidine (PCP), crack cocaine, cannabis etc. – have characteristically been smoked as the primary mode of their consumption. Conversely, over the last few millennia, tobacco has been licked, blown, ocularly absorbed, drunk (tobacco juice), ingested, snuffed, topically applied and anally injected, to name but a few of the ways it has been used.

Employing a developmental perspective, Hughes finds that such changes in the primary mode of consuming tobacco are in themselves markedly significant. Pre-Columbian Amerindian tobacco use typically involved the consumption of strains and varieties of tobacco that were much stronger than those of latter-day 'Western' cigarettes. Tobacco was, more than any other psychoactive substance, used extensively in shamanistic ritual. There is a wealth of documented evidence to suggest that the tobacco used in the 'old world' was fully capable of inducing hallucinations, and many early (bewildered) colonial accounts of *'godlesse'* natives using the substance in order to fall into 'death-like' trances: a key component of Amerindian cosmology holds that only 's/he who overcomes death is capable of defeating' it. Understandings and practices surrounding tobacco and its use in pre-Columbian America varied widely, but a common theme was that tobacco was a sacred plant that hinged together the physical and spiritual world. Tobacco-induced intoxication was thus a means of 'communing with the spirits'; and the tobacco plant thus had enormous symbolic potency.

Early European use contrasted starkly to present-day practices. Early smokers were referred to as tobacco 'drinkers' or 'dry drunks', not simply because no other model than alcohol existed with which to make sense of the practice, but because the forms of tobacco in use were far more capable of inducing intoxication. Hughes observes a shift towards, over the longer term, the use of progressively less potent and 'milder' forms of tobacco; an accompanying set of processes involving an increasing elaboration of codes of etiquette surrounding tobacco use; and increasing regulation over the supply of tobacco and the licentiate 'use' and 'abuse' of tobacco, culminating in an emergent temperance movement akin to that surrounding the use of alcohol.

At the risk of over-simplifying the set of complex, and in certain respects contradictory, processes, Hughes's argument is that over the long term there has been a shift away from the use of tobacco to 'lose control' and 'escape normality' – i.e. de-routinization – and a move towards the use of tobacco to maintain control and to 'return to normality'. A core driver of these changes, he suggests, is changing standards of behaviour – in Elias's language, the *social constraint towards self-constraint* – of the type that accompany civilizing processes. Thus, for example, snuffing became a popular mode of consuming tobacco among the secular upper classes in many parts of seventeenth century Europe. While it was considered to be the height of refinement – an opportunity to display a well-turned wrist, or an ornate snuff-box – snuffing involved the transgression of other emergent sensitivities. Typically, it involved the expulsion of mucous, the placing of fingers into orifices and a repeated transient loss of control through sneezing. Increasing social pressure for more 'civilized' forms of tobacco, Hughes suggests, undergirded a move towards progressively 'milder' and 'cleaner' forms of tobacco and modes of consuming these. Thus, for example, early filter cigarettes were tipped not so as to remove unwanted carcinogens, but to prevent the unsightly habit of spitting out soggy cigarette ends. Significantly, modern cigarettes came to be understood as a 'psychological tool', an 'instrument of self-control', and of corporeal control more generally. Early cigarette adverts, typically targeted at women, made great play of the associations between cigarette smoking and weight control. 'Reach for a Lucky instead of a sweet', 'Avoid that future shadow', and more recently brands such as Virginia 'slims', and various 'lights', all played on associations with physical lightness. These trends continued throughout the twentieth century – a transition which, in a manner akin to developments relating to exercise to music activities, seemed to address increasing public concern over the health risks of smoking.

Birdwatching

The analytical parallels with the seemingly very distinct activity of birdwatching are not only striking but illustrate the flexibility of an approach which has frequently been criticized for its inflexibility. Sheard (1999) argues that birdwatching can be understood only as a long-term development of hunting. Initially humans interacted with birds largely because the latter constituted an important source of food (both meat and eggs). He illustrates the degree of interdependence between hunting for birds, the scientific study of birds and the conservation of birds. The roots of ornithology and bird preservation lie in the Renaissance and Tudor practice of hunting birds and collecting stuffed specimens. Prior to the development of photographic and optical equipment, the only way to identify and classify a bird was to kill it first. 'It is apparent ... that for many people watching and photographing birds become acceptable substitutes for, or alternatives to, killing them' (Sheard, 1999: 188).

Animal preservation laws first appeared in Britain in the early nineteenth century, and the Society for the Prevention of Cruelty to Animals was established in 1824, followed by the Society for the Protection of Birds in 1889. But only certain types of societies, Sheard argues, develop notions of animal rights and incorporate pressure groups dedicated to their protection. In societies where humans express empathy for the suffering of animals, activities such as hunting become infrequent and mimetic versions such as birdwatching develop. Thus, 'nearly all the elements of the hunt are present in birdwatching, with chasing and stalking especially evident' (Sheard, 1999: 190). Birdwatchers, like hunters, require a good aim in order to 'shoot' birds with their cameras. Thus, taken in long-term perspective, birdwatching exhibits many of the characteristics of a 'civilized' sport.

But, as with the fighting-based sports discussed above, particular forms of birdwatching (which Sheard calls 'twitching') have redeveloped in reaction to the routinization of birdwatching in post-war Britain. Sheard describes how the activity became more democratized, both demographically, due to increased affluence, and in the sense that technological advances deskilled birdwatching. Bird reserves became increasingly managed to cater for increased numbers of birdwatchers, and while birdwatching was initially a relatively solitary activity it became more clubbable, sociable and family oriented. Increasingly, 'hides' were provided, which led to a more sanitized and less active birdwatching experience. 'Controlled, routinized watching increasingly replaced the pleasures of the chase' (Sheard, 1999: 195). Consequently increasingly competitive forms of birdwatching – twitching – came into existence. Such developments involved a re-emphasizing of 'the chase' and movement, with an increasing value attached to the technical skill of detecting and 'shooting' birds (photographically), such that, ultimately, 'greater hunt excitement was re-injected into … an increasingly pacified activity' (Sheard, 1999: 197).

Conclusions

The central significance of this study of birdwatching to this chapter is that it illustrates the importance to figurational sociologists of a historical orientation (and therefore connections also to the control of violence, Elias's *The Civilizing Process*, and notions of a controlled decontrolling of emotional controls as part of a 'quest for excitement'). In addition, the case of birdwatching also returns us to one of the central themes highlighted in our prior discussion of Elias and leisure. Specifically, such activities need to be viewed as part of the spare-time spectrum described by Elias and Dunning (1971a, 1986b), for while Sheard emphasizes the mimetic aspects of birdwatching, one cannot ignore either the role of sociability or the overlap between mimetic and technical, challenging and self-fulfilling aspects which could more properly be defined as an 'intermediary' activity. Returning to the opening theme of this chapter, although the work of Elias and figurational sociologists has gained far greater recognition in relation to the sociology of sport, the grounds for seeing sports participation as just one manifestation of a broader range of leisure practices (including sports spectatorship, exercising and smoking), and recognizing, as Elias would, these leisure activities as variously interdependent in different temporal and spatial contexts, is compelling.

References

Atkinson, M. (2002) 'Fifty Million Viewers Can't be Wrong: Professional wrestling, sports–entertainment and mimesis', *Sociology of Sport Journal* 19: 47–66.

Atkinson, M. (2008) 'Triathlon, Suffering and Exciting Significance', *Leisure Studies* 27 (2) 165–180.

Bourdieu, P. and Wacquant, L. (1992) *An Invitation to Reflexive Sociology*. Cambridge: Polity Press.

Colwell, S. (1999) 'Feminisms and Figurational Sociology: Contributions to understandings of sport, physical education and sex/gender', *European Physical Education Review* 5 (3) 219–240.

Dunning, E. (1992) 'A Remembrance of Norbert Elias', *Sociology of Sport Journal* 9: 95–99.

Dunning, E. (1999) *Sport Matters: Sociological Studies of Sport, Violence and Civilization*. London: Routledge.

Dunning, E. (2002) 'Figurational Contributions to the Sociological Study of Sport', in J. Maguire, and K. Young (eds) *Theory, Sport and Society*. Oxford: Elsevier Science, 211–238.

Dunning, E. and Hughes, J. (2013) *Norbert Elias and Modern Sociology: Knowledge, Interdependence, Power, Process*. London: Bloomsbury Academic.

Dunning, E. and Sheard, K. (2005) *Barbarians, Gentlemen and Players: A Sociological Study of the Development of Rugby Football*. Abingdon: Routledge.

Dunning, E., Murphy, P. and Williams, J. (1988) *The Roots of Football Hooliganism: An Historical and Sociological Study*. London: Routledge & Kegan Paul.

Elias, N. (1971) 'The Genesis of Sport as a Sociological Problem', in E. Dunning (ed.) *The Sociology of Sport: A Selection of Readings*. London: Frank Cass, 88–115.

Elias, N. (1978) *What is Sociology?* London: Hutchinson.

Elias, N. (1983) *The Court Society.* Oxford: Blackwell.

Elias, N. (1986a) 'Introduction', in N. Elias and E. Dunning (eds) *Quest for Excitement: Sport and Leisure in the Civilizing Process*, Oxford: Blackwell, 19–63.

Elias, N. (1986b) 'An Essay on Sport and Violence', in N. Elias and E. Dunning (eds) *Quest for Excitement: Sport and Leisure in the Civilizing Process*, Oxford: Blackwell, 150–174.

Elias, N. (1987a) *Involvement and Detachment.* Oxford: Blackwell.

Elias, N. (1987b) 'On Human Beings and Their Emotions: A process sociological essay', *Theory, Culture and Society*, 4: 339–61.

Elias, N. (1991) *The Symbol Theory.* London: Sage.

Elias, N. (1991a) *The Society of Individuals.* Oxford: Blackwell.

Elias, N. (1993) *Mozart: Portrait of a Genius.* Cambridge: Polity Press.

Elias, N. (1996) *The Germans.* Cambridge: Polity Press.

Elias, N. (2000) *The Civilizing Process* (revised edition). Oxford: Blackwell.

Elias, N. and Dunning, E. (1969) 'The Quest for Excitement in Leisure', *Society and Leisure* 2: 50–85.

Elias, N. and Dunning, E. (1971a) 'Leisure in the Sparetime Spectrum', in R. Albonico and K. Pfister-Binz (eds) *Sociology of Sport: Theoretical Foundations and Research Methods.* Basle: Magglinger Symposium.

Elias, N. and Dunning, E. (1971b) 'Folk Football in Medieval and Early Modern Britain', in E. Dunning (ed.) *The Sociology of Sport: A Selection of Readings.* London: Frank Cass, 116–132.

Elias, N. and Dunning, E. (1986a) *Quest for Excitement: Sport and Leisure in the Civilising Process.* Oxford: Blackwell.

Elias, N. and Dunning, E. (1986b) 'Quest for Excitement in Leisure', in N. Elias, and E. Dunning *Quest for Excitement: Sport and Leisure in the Civilizing Process.* Oxford: Blackwell, 63–90.

Elias, N. and Scotson, J. (1994) *The Established and the Outsiders.* London: Sage.

Giulianotti, R. (2004) 'Civilizing Games: Norbert Elias and the sociology of sport', in R. Giulianotti (ed.) *Sport and Modern Social Theorists.* Basingstoke: Palgrave Macmillan, 145–160.

Green, K. (2002) 'Physical Education Teachers in their Figurations: A sociological analysis of everyday philosophies', *Sport, Education and Society* 7 (1) 65–83.

Hughes, J. (2003) *Learning to Smoke: Tobacco Use in the West.* Chicago: University of Chicago Press.

Jarvie, G. and Maguire, J. (1994) *Sport, Leisure and Social Thought.* London: Routledge.

Liston, K. (2006) 'Women's Soccer in the Republic of Ireland: Some preliminary sociological comments', *Sport in Society* 7 (2/3) 364–384.

Liston, K. (2007) 'Revisiting the Feminist–Figurational Sociology Exchange', *Sport in Society* 10 (4) 623–645.

Liston, K. (2011) 'Sport and Leisure', *The Sociological Review* 59: 160–180.

Loyal, S. and Quilley, S. (2004) *The Sociology of Norbert Elias.* Cambridge: Cambridge University Press.

Maguire, J. (1992) 'Towards a Sociological Theory of the Emotions: A process sociological perspective', in E. Dunning and C. Rojek (eds) *Sport and Leisure in the Civilizing Process.* London: Macmillan, 96–120.

Maguire, J. (1999) *Global Sport: Identities, Societies, Civilizations.* Cambridge: Polity.

Maguire, J. (2011) 'Welcome to the Pleasure Dome: Emotions, leisure and society', *Sport in Society* 14 (7/8) 913–926.

Maguire, J. and Mansfield, L. (1998) '"No-body's Perfect": Women, aerobics and the body beautiful', *Sociology of Sport Journal* 15 (2) 109–137.

Malcolm, D (2001) '"It's not Cricket": Colonial legacies and contemporary inequalities', *Journal of Historical Sociology* 14 (3) 253–275.

Malcolm, D. (2002) 'Cricket and Civilizing Processes: A response to Stokvis', *International Review for the Sociology of Sport* 37 (1) 37–57.

Malcolm, D. (2012) *Sport and Sociology.* London: Routledge.

Malcolm, D. (2013) *Globalizing Cricket: England, Empire, Identity.* London: Bloomsbury Academic.

Mansfield, L. (2002) 'Feminist Thought and Figurational (Process) Sociology', in J. Maguire and K. Young (eds) *Theory, Sport and Society.* London: JAI Elsevier Science, 317–335.

Mansfield, L. (2007) 'Involved-Detachment: A balance of passion and reason in feminisms and gender-related research in sport, tourism and sports tourism', *Journal of Sport and Tourism* 12 (2) 115–141.

Mansfield, L. (2008) 'Reconsidering Feminisms and the Work of Norbert Elias for Understanding Gender, Sport and Sport-related Activities', *European Physical Education Review* 14 (1) 93–121.

Mansfield, L. (2011) '"Sexercise": Working out heterosexuality in Jane Fonda's fitness books', *Leisure Studies* 30 (2) 237–255.

Mansfield, L. and Chatziefstathiou, D. (2010) 'Introduction to Leisure, Identities and Authenticity', in L. Mansfield and D. Chatziefstathiou (eds) *Leisure, Identities and Authenticity*. Brighton: LSA, v–xvii.

Mennell, S. (1992) *Norbert Elias: An Introduction*. Oxford: Blackwell.

Mennell, S. (1994) 'The Formation of We-Images: A process theory', in C. Calhoun (ed.) *Social Theory and the Politics of Identity*. Oxford: Blackwell, 175–198.

Sanchez Garcia, R. and Malcolm, D. (2010) 'De-civilizing, Civilizing or Informalizing? The international development of mixed martial arts', *International Review of the Sociology of Sport* 45 (1) 1–20.

Sheard, K. (1997) 'Aspects of Boxing in the Western "Civilizing Process"', *International Review for the Sociology of Sport* 32 (1) 31–57.

Sheard, K. (1999) 'A Twitch in Time Saves Nine: Birdwatching, Sport and the Civilizing Process', *Sociology of Sport Journal* 16 (2) 181–205.

Smith, S. (1998) 'Athletes, Runners and Joggers: Participant-group dynamics in a sport of "individuals"', *Sociology of Sport Journal* 15 (2) 174–192.

Smith, S. (2000) 'British Nonelite Road Running and Masculinity: A case of "running repairs"?' *Men and Masculinities* 19: 187–210.

Tomlinson, A. (2004) 'Pierre Bourdieu and the Sociological Study of Sport: Habitus, capital and field', in R. Giulianotti (ed.) *Sport and Modern Social Theorists*. Palgrave Macmillan: Basingstoke, 225–240.

van Krieken, R. (1998) *Norbert Elias*. London: Routledge.

Velija, P. and Malcolm, D. (2010) '"Look, it's a Girl": Cricket and gender relations in the UK', with P. Velija, in D. Malcolm, J. Gemmell, and N. Mehta (eds) *The Changing Face of Cricket: From Imperial to Global Game*. London: Routledge, 199–212.

Wacquant, L. (1989) 'Toward a Reflexive Sociology: A workshop with Pierre Bourdieu', *Sociological Theory* 7 (1) 26–63.

Waddington, I. and Malcolm, D. (2008) 'Eric Dunning: This sporting life', in D. Malcolm and I. Waddington (eds) *Matters of Sport: Essays in Honour of Eric Dunning*. London: Routledge, 1–11.

12

MICHEL FOUCAULT AND LEISURE[1]

Toby Miller

Michel Foucault is an emblem of post-structuralism, postmodernism, and associated theoretical and artistic movements. For those on the left, his displacement of the concept of ideology with discourse has delivered us from the Marxist split between base and superstructure 'under' a given mode of production.

In terms of Foucault's contribution to thinking about leisure, arguably the core aspect is anti-psychological. He interrogates the discourse of the human and the conditions of its emergence, arguing that people become individuals through discourses and institutions of culture. They undergo a simultaneous internalization and externalization, individuation and collectivization. It may well be that subjection derives from forces connected to production, class conflict or ideology. But Foucault maintains that the loci and logic of governance are not merely to be found amongst the interests or persuasions of the class that controls it, because government operates at a micro level as well as through and because of general economic forces.

Foucault rejects deterministic accounts of interiority in his skepticism about the psy-function and its account of basic needs (such as work and leisure). This clearly runs counter to the visionary perspective in the study of leisure, which links it to consciousness, values, and civilization in a heritage that runs from classical Greek philosophy to contemporary social psychology. It also distances him from the pragmatic tradition, which applies rational public policy to ameliorate inequalities, though there has been an uptake of Foucault by cultural-policy technocrats (Rojek, 2012: 3; Miller and Yúdice, 2002).

So what is Foucault's criticism of these assumptions about human needs for, *inter alia*, leisure? His term 'the psy-function' describes a shifting field of knowledge and power over the mind. It is comprised of psychoanalysis, psychology, psychotherapy, psychiatry, social psychology, criminology, and psycho-pharmacology, and their success in sites of discipline – educational, military, industrial, recreational, and carceral (Foucault, 2006: 85–86, 189–90). The idea that recreation might be qualitatively different from, and richer than, these other experiences of life is inimical to such an account.

Foucault sought to uncover how mental conditions came to be identified as problems in need of treatment through forms of demographic problematization that functioned as techniques, economies, social relations, and knowledges. They were the means whereby 'some real existent in the world' became 'the target of social regulation at a given moment'

(Foucault, 1994: 123; 2001: 171). He defined madness, for instance, as 'the absence of work' (Foucault, 1995) rather than a psychological condition.

Foucault argued that struggles for power take place over:

> the status of the individual: on the one hand, they assert the right to be different, and they underline everything that makes individuals truly individual. On the other hand, they attack everything which separates the individual, breaks his links with others, splits up community life, forces the individual back on himself and ties him to his own identity in a constraining way.
>
> (Foucault, 1982: 781, 777–78)

In the words of the late liberation psychologist Ignacio Martín-Baró, 'there does not first exist a person, who then goes on to become socialized'. Rather, the 'individual becomes an individual, a human person, by virtue of becoming socialized' (Martín-Baró, 1996: 69). The raw stuff of human beings, then, is not individuals: people *become* individuals through the discourses and institutions of culture, in an oscillation between the law, economy, and politics, with the psy-function operating as a switching-point between people's proclivities and aptitudes (Foucault, 2006: 58, 190). The same applies to discourses about assumed basic needs, such as the practice of leisure.

This micro level of analysis centres on the formation of public subjects – people as invoked by leisure policy, in this case. The determining logics applied to these subjects do not necessarily provide intelligible accounts of action if they are always led back to the economic or the psychological. In short, Foucault's account of the social redisposes dialectical reasoning away from the grand stages of history or psyche and towards an analysis of conjunctures. Leisure Studies can benefit from Foucault's direct consideration of consumption and pleasure and his more generalized address of ethical self-formation and the government of people (McNamee, 2000).

More direct articulations between Foucault and leisure derive from his address of sport in the context of early Western philosophy's quest for an ethics of the self that would inculcate and evaluate fitness to rule others. In ancient Greece and Rome, the body was the locus of a combat with pleasure and pain that disclosed the inner truth of people and schooled the mastery needed to control their drives (Foucault, 1986). Austerity and hedonism could be combined through training:

> The metaphor of the match, of athletic competition and battle, did not serve merely to designate the nature of the relationship one had with desires and pleasures, with their force that was always liable to turn seditious or rebellious; it also related to the preparation that enabled one to withstand such a confrontation.
>
> (Foucault, 1986: 72)

Xenophon, Socrates, and Diogenes held that sexual excess and decadence came from the equivalent of sporting success. In sex and sport, triumph could lead to failure, unless accompanied by regular examination of the conscience, and physical training. Carefully modulated desire in both spheres became a sign of the ability to govern. Aristotle and Plato favoured regular, ongoing flirtations with excess, as tests as well as pleasures. This ethos was distinctly gendered: the capacity of young men to move into positions of social responsibility was judged by charioteering and man-management. Their ability to win 'the little sports drama' was akin to dealing with sexually predatory older males (Foucault, 1986: 72–77, 104,

120, 197–98, 212). Clearly, this history brings into question the separation of work from leisure just as conclusively as latter-day commodification, corporatization, and post-industrialization do. It therefore encourages us to query the notion of transcendent psychological needs and the basis for a separation of employment from fun.

Roman sexual ethics attached additional anxieties to the body and leisure because spirituality had emerged. It complicated exercises of the self as ways of preparing men to govern:

> increased medical involvement in the cultivation of the self appears to have been expressed through a particular and intense form of attention to the body. This attention is very different from that manifested by the positive valuation of physical vigor during an epoch when gymnastics and athletic and military training were an integral part of the education of a free man. Moreover, it has something paradoxical about it since it is inscribed, at least in part, within an ethics that posits that death, disease, or even physical suffering do not constitute true ills and that it is better to take pains over one's soul than to devote one's care to the maintenance of the body. But in fact the focus of attention in these practices of the self is the point where the ills of the body and those of the soul can communicate with one another and exchange their distresses; where the bad habits of the soul can entail physical miseries, while the excesses of the body manifest and maintain the failings of the soul. … The body the adult has to care for, when he is concerned about himself, is no longer the young body that needed shaping by gymnastics; it is a fragile, threatened body, undermined by petty miseries.
>
> (Foucault, 1988: 56–57).

In place of personal excesses, which had preoccupied fourth-century BC Athens, first-century AD Rome was principally concerned with the finitude of fitness and life. Arguments were imbued with 'nature and reason', and exercises of the self joined this more elevated search for truth (Foucault, 1988: 238–39). Foucault's studies indicate how leisure has been central to social control, in two senses. On the one hand, it is subject to individual controls for managing desire. On the other, it is subject to collective methods for managing families (Foucault, 2003: 251).

Dave Andrews (1993), Samantha King (2008), Ben Carrington (2010), Brooke Johnson (2010), and C. L. Cole (1998) have all drawn on Foucault. Their work indicates how his methods can be providential for political economy, feminism, and critical race theory as applied to leisure, from basketball to advertising and from celebrity feminism to social activism. They maintain the non-humanist base to Foucault, and his commitment to discourse and power, without losing the significance of social movements and the political economy.

But numerous progressive scholars are ambivalent or condemnatory in their evaluations of Foucault's legacy for understanding leisure. Feminist critiques and Gramscian-inflected ideas of hegemony have provided vital means of attacking the prior dominance of reactionary celebrations and instrumentalizations of leisure. For many analysts working in these traditions, Foucault is endowing power with an agency of its own, while eviscerating subjects from history (see Gruneau, 1993 and 1999).

Trotskyite Jean Marie Brohm, a central figure in leftist theorizations of leisure, scorns the eclecticism that mixes and matches Foucault with Marx because primacy 'must' be given to means and modes of production and class struggle (Brohm and Bui-Xuan, 2005). Before he turned to the right, John Hargreaves (1986: 135) decried 'the danger of a Foucaultian analysis of consumer culture' because of 'the implication that control programmes actually achieve their desired effects'. Ian R. Henry (2001: 3) argues that there has been virtu-ally no Foucauldian influence on studies of leisure policy. Garry Robson's recuperation of Millwall Football Club fans from the dustbin of racist proletarian masculinism (Robson, 2000: 71–72, 77) criticizes the supposed 'passivity' inscribed on people by Foucault. Valda Burstyn (1999: 33) says that gendered leisure power is tied to the expression of interests, rather than being multifaceted, as per Foucauldian feminism. Chris Rojek (2012), while not critical of Foucault per se, and arguably an early proponent of his work within Leisure Studies, laments the hasty exclusion of Marxism from the field after the decline of state socialism, given the clear determinations of money and class on the rich world, especially since the crisis that began in 2008.

But active if socially marginalized subjects are very present in Foucault: the mad, the ill, the deviant, the incarcerated, the racialized, and the gendered. And he took public political actions in support of those groups, participating in numerous social movements and contrib-uting to public debate (Foucault, 1980; 1989; 1991; 2003).

As we have seen, the subject is neither a point of origin in Foucault nor a destination, because subjects vary with time and space. This is an affront to conceptions of conscious-ness that posit the reasoning person at the heart of social activity, whether they be psycho-logical or political. But it does not in any way preclude politics, choice, or social-movement activism. If there were no room for agency, why have so many feminists, queers, medical professionals, prison activists, and post-colonial critics found value in Foucault's work and persona?

Both protagonists and antagonists suggest that Foucault's work was opposed to grand narratives. As a consequence his influence is deemed either baleful or useful, based on the analyst's views of power and discourse (Wiggins and Mason, 2005: 48; Markula and Denison, 2005: 166; Morgan, 1995). At some times Foucault is valorized for decentring traditional norms of writing and agents of history. At others, he is derided for encouraging sectarian social movements and irrationality. This idealist version of Foucault says that he discounts the real in favour of a focus on language, licensing a free play of the signifier. But while Foucault was attracted by philosophy at the limit, he was vitally concerned with the manufacture and governance of rules – and their inevitability.

Industrialized and post-industrialized societies alike subject people to bodily and ethical regimes that equate body and mind. The body is a 'site of condensation for a whole range of social anxieties' in an era of self-responsibility. Moral panics and calculations of risk are diurnal forms of social control and calculation, rendering the disciplined body a key analytic tool (King, 2005: 25–26). This Foucauldian insight has proven especially fruitful in engaging the impact of masculinity on leisure (Mangan, 1999; Miller, 2001; Pringle, 2005; Blackshaw, 2003).

The work of governments in normalizing leisure has historically been crucial: policing holidays in order to standardize vacations and regularize recreation as play and spectator-ship; securing the conditions of existence for a partial commodification that makes sport governed rather than classically competitive; and allocating resources to leisure as a diplo-matic symbol and domestic training mechanism. The state is also concerned with leisure as a route to improved urban public health, military fitness, and the diversion of rebellious politics. From Chancellor Hitler and Marshal Pétain to President Carter, modern heads of state have initiated physical-fitness tests in order to invigorate and ideologize the young; for example, rational recreation, the human-relations movement, and their affines are part of a long heritage emphasizing the paradox that productive workers must be entertained as well as disciplined.

Scholars have found value in Foucault's work to help in analysing such developments. Numerous investigations have been made of school sports, marching, drills, gymnastics, and physical education (PE). David Kirk (1998) has demonstrated how gendered regimes of corporeal regulation, individualization, and differentiation underpinned PE in colonial and post-colonial Australia, intersecting with eugenics, racism, and national efficiency and fitness. Beyond white-settler histories, Foucault's work has also stimulated inquiry into the South Asian body disciplined through leisure (Mills and Dimeo, 2003). Despite his misgivings, John Hargreaves (1986) argued that the cardinal values of contemporary school sport and PE programmes are disciplinary, and Burstyn (1999: 78–79, 99) uses Foucault's history of the body. Jean Harvey and Robert Sparks (1991) show how PE and gymnastics in the late nineteenth century dovetailed with bio-power, Susan Brownell (2000) looks at China disciplining its citizenry through sport, and Helena Wulff (2003) examines the nationalist rhetoric of Irish dance as social control.

And there are numerous other sites of Foucauldian influence in work on leisure: studies of football[2] 'hooligans' that reject both their romantic annunciation as working-class scions and their criminalization via moral panics (Armstrong and Young, 1997: Armstrong, 1998); assessments of the panoptic design of contemporary football stadia (Giulianotti, 1999: 80–82); accounts of masculinist domination and feminist resistance and critique (Jennifer Hargreaves, 1994; Duncan, 1994; Montez de Oca, 2005; Rahilly, 2005; Pringle, 2005; Chisholm, 1999 and 2002; Miller, 2001); interrogations of women's football and cultural citizenship (Giardina and Metz, 2005); and analyses of racism and leisure (Ismond, 2003; King and Springwood, 2001; Gardiner and Welch, 2001; Carrington, 2010).

Cole (1998) suggests that bodies at play appear to embody free will, self-control, health, productivity, and transcendence (also see MacNeill, 1998). Patricia Vertinsky (1998) highlights the medicalization of women's bodies in the Victorian era, which still permeates health-and-fitness promotion campaigns. Since the Second World War, additional factors have made bio-power crucial. The contest for international sporting supremacy between the former protagonists in the Cold War, developments in pharmaceutical research, increasing commodification, and the dominance of instrumental rationality have seen biomedical science applied to enhance performance and identify deviance. Shari Lee Dworkin and Faye Linda Wachs (2009) use Foucault to investigate HIV panics and athletes (also see Pronger, 1998). King (2001) questions the corporate social-responsibility ethos of companies that use fitness to elevate their public standing.

Away from the governance of leisure, its codification, there are said to be new and powerful liberties, ripe for their utopian humanistic plucking by Foucauldianism. A deregulated, individuated world supposedly makes consumers into producers, frees the disabled from confinement, encourages new subjectivities, rewards intellect and competitiveness, links people across cultures, and allows billions of flowers to bloom in a post-political cornucopia. It's a kind of Marxist/Godardian wet dream, where people fish, film, frolic, fornicate, and finance from morning to midnight. Production is discounted, labour forgotten, and consumption sovereign. Leisure overdetermines work.

These cybertarian ideas of leisure say that deregulated, individuated media making turns consumers into producers and subcultural rebels – this includes blogging or posting videos online to riff on commercial culture or right-wing demagoguery, clicking on a link for virtual anti-war or environmental activism, mocking bourgeois manners, goading the law from cyberspace, or simply celebrating alternative lifestyles. 'Prosumers', putatively freed from social convention, experiment with new subjectivities, find rewards for intellect and competitiveness, and network with people across cultures in a post-political cornucopia (Zwick *et al.*, 2008; Ritzer and Jurgenson, 2010).

The idea of a proactive leisure consumer is quite capacious, though its claims don't stand up once we understand the limits imposed by technology and the political economy that the consumer inhabits. For example, the possibilities for green leisure can be seen in media commodities' material effects on the planet (Maxwell and Miller, 2012). And as Andrew Ross says of prosumption, it refers to consumers who undertake work that producers used to pay for (2009).

Conclusions

This chapter has offered a brief tour of Foucault's relevance for thinking about leisure by looking at three principal elements of his work. The first was Foucault's problematization of the psy-function, which helps us to bring into question the essentialism underpinning the doctrines of fundamental human needs that inform theories and policies of leisure. The second field of work was his engagement with ancient Greek and Roman philosophy to see how bodies at play were sites for learning and demonstrating the capacity for leadership, where model forms of citizenship could be encapsulated. Here, the major implication is that, regardless of prevailing modes of production, distinctions between work and leisure have always been problematic and leisure is as much a form of governance as its supposed other. The third domain was associated scholarship and activism, where we saw that the wide array of researchers inspired by Foucault's work casts doubt on accusations that his work is theoreticist or that it regards people as passive rather than active.

Notes

1 This chapter draws on Miller, 2009. I should say at the outset that I am not an expert in the study of leisure or tourism. Many of the sources used here are from the narrower sphere of sport and the wider one of culture. I hope that the result is nevertheless of use to readers.
2 I refer here to real football, not the 60-minute stroll 16 times a year that laughably claims the name in the Yanqui lexicon.

References

Andrews, D. (1993) 'Desperately Seeking Michel: Foucault's Genealogy, the Body, and Critical Sport Sociology', *Sociology of Sport Journal* 10 (2) 148–67.
Armstrong, G. (1998) *Football Hooligans: Knowing the Score*. Oxford: Berg.
Armstrong, G. and M. Young. (1997) 'Legislators and Interpreters: The Law and "Football Hooligans"', in G. Armstrong and R. Giulianotti (eds) *Entering the Field: New Perspectives on World Football*. Oxford: Berg, pp. 175–91.
Blackshaw, T. (2003) *Leisure Life: Myth, Masculinity, and Modernity*. London: Routledge.
Brohm, J. M. and G. Bui-Xuan. (2005) 'Nouveau millénaire, défis libertaires', <1libertaire.free.fr/Brohm05.html>.
Brownell, S. (2000) 'Why Should an Anthropologist Study Sports in China?', in N. Dyck (ed.) *Games, Sports and Cultures*. Oxford: Berg, pp. 43–63.
Burstyn, V. (1999) *The Rites of Men: Manhood, Politics, and the Culture of Sport*. Toronto: University of Toronto Press.
Carrington, B. (2010) *Race, Sport and Politics: The Sporting Black Diaspora*. Los Angeles, CA: Sage.
Chisholm, A. (1999) 'Defending the Nation: National Bodies, U.S. Borders, and the 1996 U.S. Olympic Women's Gymnastic Team', *Journal of Sport & Social Issues* 23 (2) 126–39.
Chisholm, A. (2002) 'Acrobats, Contortionists, and Cute Children: The Promise and Perversity of U.S. Women's Gymnastics', *Signs* 27 (2) 415–50.
Cole, C. L. (1998) 'Addiction, Exercise, and Cyborgs: Technologies of Deviant Bodies', in G. Rail (ed.) *Sport and Postmodern Times*. Albany: State University of New York Press, pp. 261–276.

Duncan, M. C. (1994) 'Sports Photographs and Sexual Difference: Images of Women and Men in the 1984 and 1988 Olympic Games', *Sociology of Sport Journal* 7 (1) 22–43.

Dworkin, S. L. and F. L. Wachs. (2009) *Body Panic: Gender, Health, and the Selling of Fitness*. New York: New York University Press.

Foucault, M. (1980) 'Body/Power', *Power-Knowledge: Selected Interviews and Other Writings 1972–77*, ed. C. Gordon. New York: Pantheon.

Foucault, M. (1982) 'The Subject and Power', trans. L. Sawyer, *Critical Inquiry* 8 (4) 777–95.

Foucault, M. (1986) *The History of Sexuality: Volume 2 The Use of Pleasure*, trans. R. Hurley. New York: Vintage.

Foucault, M. (1988) *The History of Sexuality: Volume 3 The Care of the Self*, trans. R. Hurley. New York: Vintage.

Foucault, M. (1989) 'The Discourse of History', trans. J. Johnston, *Foucault Live (Interviews, 1966–84)*, ed. S. Lotringer. New York: Semiotext(e).

Foucault, M. (1991) *Remarks on Marx: Conversations with Duccio Trombadori*, trans. R. J. Goldstein and J. Cascaito. New York: Semiotext(e).

Foucault, M. (1994) 'Problematics: Excerpts from Conversations', in R. Reynolds and T. Zummer (eds) *Crash: Nostalgia for the Absence of Cyberspace*. New York: Third Waxing Space, pp. 121–27.

Foucault, M. (1995) 'Madness, the Absence of Work', trans. P. Stastny and D. Şengel, *Critical Inquiry* 21 (2) 290–98.

Foucault, M. (2001) *Fearless Speech*, ed. J. Pearson. Los Angeles, CA: Semiotext(e).

Foucault, M. (2003) *'Society Must be Defended': Lectures at the Collège de France 1975–1976*, trans. D. Macey, eds M. Bertani and A. Fontana. New York: Picador.

Foucault, M. (2006) *Psychiatric Power: Lectures at the Collège de France, 1973–74*, trans. G. Burchell, ed. J. Lagrange. Basingstoke: Palgrave Macmillan.

Gardiner, S. and R. Welch. (2001) 'Sport, Racism and the Limits of "Colour Blind" Law', in B. Carrington and I. McDonald (eds) *'Race', Sport and British Society*. London: Routledge, pp. 133–49.

Giardina, M. D. and J. L. Metz. (2005) 'All-American Girls? Corporatizing National Identity and Cultural Citizenship with/in the WUSA', in M. L. Silk, D. L. Andrews, and C. L. Cole (eds) *Sport and Corporate Nationalisms*. Oxford: Berg, pp. 109–26.

Giulianotti, R. (1999) *Football: A Sociology of the Global Game*. Cambridge: Polity.

Gruneau, R. (1993) 'The Critique of Sport in Modernity: Theorising Power, Culture, and the Politics of the Body', in E. Dunning, J. A. Maguire and R. E. Pearton (eds) *The Sports Process: A Comparative and Developmental Approach*. Champaign, IL: Human Kinetics, pp. 85–109.

Gruneau, R. (1999) *Class, Sports and Social Development*, rev. ed. Champaign, IL: Human Kinetics.

Hargreaves, Jennifer. (1994) *Sporting Females: Critical Issues in the History and Sociology of Women's Sports*. London: Routledge.

Hargreaves, John. (1986) *Sport, Power and Culture: A Social and Historical Analysis of Popular Sports in Britain*. Oxford: Polity Press.

Harvey, J. and R. Sparks. (1991) 'The Politics of the Body in the Context of Modernity', *Quest* 43 (2) 164–89.

Henry, I. (2001) *The Politics of Leisure Policy*, 2nd ed. Houndsmill: Palgrave.

Ismond, P. (2003) *Black and Asian Athletes in British Sport and Society: A Sporting Chance?* Houndsmill: Palgrave.

Johnson, B. (2010) 'A Few Good Boys: Masculinity at a Military-Style Charter School', *Men and Masculinities* 12 (5) 575–96.

King, C. R. and C. F. Springwood. (2001) *Beyond the Cheers: Race as Spectacle in College Sport*. Albany, NY: State University of New York Press.

King, S. (2005) 'Methodological Contingencies in Sports Studies', in D. L. Andrews, D. S. Mason, and M. L. Silk (eds) *Qualitative Methods in Sports Studies*. Oxford: Berg, pp. 21–38.

King, S. (2008) *Pink Ribbons, Inc.: Breast Cancer and the Politics of Philanthropy*. Minneapolis: University of Minnesota Press.

Kirk, D. (1998) *Schooling Bodies: School Practice and Public Discourse*. London: Leicester University Press.

McNamee, S. (2000) 'Foucault's Heterotopia and Children's Everyday Lives', *Childhood* 7 (4) 479–92.

MacNeill, M. (1998) 'Sex, Lies, and Videotape: The Political and Cultural Economies of Celebrity Fitness Videos', in G. Rail (ed.) *Sport and Postmodern Times*. Albany: State University of New York Press, pp. 163–84.

139

Mangan, J. A. (1999) 'The Potent Image and the Permanent Prometheus', in J. A. Mangan (ed.) *Shaping the Superman: Fascist Body as Political Icon of Aryan Fascism*. London: Frank Cass, pp. 11–22.

Markula, P. and J. Denison. (2005) 'Sport and the Personal Narrative', in D. L. Andrews, D. S. Mason, and M. L. Silk (eds) *Qualitative Methods in Sports Studies*. Oxford: Berg, pp. 165–84.

Martín-Baró, I. (1996). *Writings for a Liberation Theology*, trans. A. Aron, P. Berryman, C. Forster, A. Wallace, T. Sloan, and J. Carroll, ed. A. Aron and S. Corne. Cambridge, MA: Harvard University Press.

Maxwell, R. and T. Miller. (2012) *Greening the Media*. New York: Oxford University Press.

Miller, T. (2001) *SportSex*. Philadelphia: Temple University Press.

Miller, T. (2009) 'Michel Foucault and the Critique of Sport', in B. Carrington and I. McDonald (eds) *Marxism, Cultural Studies and Sport*. London: Routledge, pp. 181–94.

Miller, T., and G. Yúdice. (2002) *Cultural Policy*. London: Sage Publications.

Mills, J. and P. Dimeo. (2003) '"When Gold is Fired It Shines": Sport, the Imagination and the Body in Colonial and Postcolonial India', in J. Bale and M. Cronin (eds) *Sport and Postcolonialism*. Oxford: Berg, pp. 107–22.

Montez de Oca, J. (2005) '"As Our Muscles Get Softer, Our Missile Race Becomes Harder": Cultural Citizenship and the "Muscle Gap"', *Journal of Historical Sociology* 18 (3) 145–72.

Morgan, W. W. (1995) '"Incredulity toward Metanarratives" and Normative Suicide: A Critique of Postmodernist Drift in Critical Sport Theory', *International Review for the Sociology of Sport* 30 (1) 25–45.

Pringle, R. (2005) 'Masculinities, Sport, and Power: A Critical Comparison of Gramscian and Foucauldian Inspired Theoretical Tools', *Journal of Sport and Social Issues* 29 (3) 256–78.

Pronger, B. (1998) 'Post-Sport: Transgressing Boundaries in Physical Culture', in G. Rail (ed.) *Sport and Postmodern Times*. Albany, NY: State University of New York Press, pp. 277–98.

Rahilly, L. (2005) 'Is *RAW* War? Professional Wrestling as Popular S/M Narrative', in N. Sammond (ed.) *Steel Chair to the Head: The Pleasure and Pain of Professional Wrestling*. Durham, NC: Duke University Press, pp. 213–31.

Ritzer, G. and N. Jurgenson. (2010) 'Production, Consumption, Prosumption: The Nature of Capitalism in the Age of the Digital "Prosumer"', *Journal of Consumer Culture* 10 (1) 13–36.

Robson, G. (2000) *'No One Likes Us, We Don't Care': The Myth and Reality of Millwall Fandom*. New York: Berg.

Rojek, C. (2012) 'Is Marx Still Relevant to the Study of Leisure?' *Leisure Studies* DOI: 10.1080/02614367.2012.665942.

Ross, A. (2009) *Nice Work if You Can Get It: Life and Labor in Precarious Times*. New York: New York University Press.

Vertinsky, P. (1998) '"Run, Jane, Run": Central Tensions in the Current Debate about Enhancing Women's Health through Exercise', *Women & Health* 27 (4) 81–111.

Wiggins, D. K. and D. S. Mason. (2005) 'The Socio-Historical Process in Sport Studies', in D. L. Andrews, D. S. Mason, and M. L. Silk (eds) *Qualitative Methods in Sports Studies*. Oxford: Berg, pp. 39–64.

Wulff, H. (2003) 'The Irish Body in Motion: Moral Politics, National Identity and Dance', in N. Dyck and E. P. Archetti (eds) *Sport, Dance and Embodied Identities*. Oxford: Berg, pp. 179–96.

Zwick, D., S. K. Bonsu, and A. Darmody. (2008) 'Putting Consumers to Work: "Co-creation" and New Marketing Governmentality', *Journal of Consumer Culture* 8 (2) 163–96.

13

LEISURE AT THE END OF MODERNITY

Jürgen Habermas on the purpose of leisure

Karl Spracklen

Introduction

Although Habermas' writings range from political science to epistemology and ethics, the fundamental Habermasian concern is to protect the project of modernity and provide a new critical approach to understanding society. For Habermas (1962), the critical work of Adorno and Gramsci can be reconciled with liberal ideas about freedom by recognizing the tension between two irreconcilable rationalities: communicative rationality, which stems from human interaction and the free exchange of ideas (for example, through leisure choices in the private and public spheres); and instrumental rationality, which is a product of capitalism and the emergence of the modern nation-state. Habermas balances historiographical caution about writing metanarratives with a desire to introduce and explain the slow submergence of the lifeworld of civic society, the Enlightenment project, by non-communicative and instrumental rationalities. Just as communicative rationality produces free, communicative action and leisure (Habermas, 1984; 1987), instrumental rationalities constrain the ability of individuals to rationalize and act on anything other than commodified things: so instrumental rationality leads to instrumental action, which leads to commodified leisure and passive consumption. This chapter will explore these ideas and demonstrate how they can be used by leisure theorists and researchers at the end of modernity. I will explore Habermas' own writings on leisure, and then use examples from contemporary leisure research to demonstrate the efficacy of Habermasian critical theory for Leisure Studies (Spracklen, 2009).

Habermas

Jürgen Habermas was a product of the radical European politics of the twentieth century. A citizen of Germany, Habermas grew up seeing the rise and fall of Hitler and the emergence of a Europe and a Germany divided into regions aligned with the 'democratic' West and the Communist Soviet Union. Habermas was educated in the critical theory developed by the Frankfurt School, and his own theoretical work is a direct development of the post-Marxist account of modernity in critical theory. In *Dialectic of Enlightenment*, Adorno and Horkheimer (1944) argued that modernity had resulted in the loss of individual freedom, the loss of agency and the victory of modern capitalism. Popular culture had been appropriated by fascism and capitalism in order to keep the masses enslaved and ignorant of their exploited situation – a situation described as hegemony in the writings of Gramsci (1971). For Adorno (1947; 1967), modern, commercialized sports and leisure forms were simply capitalist tools of oppression, with no redeeming value. Critical theory took Marxist critiques of capitalism and extended the arguments to their logical end: modern nation-states, universities, political parties and culture all operated to serve the interests of capitalism as efficiently as possible.

In the work of Adorno and Horkheimer, the Enlightenment had served to construct an epistemology of reason that justified the excesses of modernity and the rationalizing evils of capitalism and totalitarianism. While Habermas accepted some of this argument, he was determined to defend the Enlightenment and the idea of progress in philosophical terms. His entire career can be viewed as a long argument with his Frankfurt School peers, an attempt to reconcile a belief in truths such as justice and progress with his awareness that much of modernity is beholden to the structures of nation-states and global capitalism. In *The Structural Transformation of the Public Sphere*, Habermas (1962) explores the historical origins of the Enlightenment and its role in the development of the public sphere. Habermas discusses the emergence of proto-public spheres in ancient Greece and suggests that the failure of these public spheres in pre-modernity was a consequence of the lack of political freedoms. In Western Europe, the emergence of towns and civil society in the Renaissance is a precursor to the Enlightenment. New bourgeois classes emerge in towns that have access to capital and education; the revolutions in religion, natural philosophy and printing all lead to demands for greater liberty. For Habermas, the public sphere is the part of society that emerges as a result of these greater liberties: people meet in coffee shops to discuss politics and philosophy; they read newspapers and political manifestos; and they identify themselves with the public, the people who have freedom and education to think for themselves and to demand more rights from the emerging nation-states that they live in. The public sphere, then, produces democracy, equality and social justice, and the Enlightenment for Habermas remains something that created lasting ideals about liberty. It is in the interests of the ruling classes to belittle the achievement of the Enlightenment: the overthrow of traditions; the challenge to religious authority; the extension of democracy; the call for equality; and the rational justification of freedom that is enshrined in the *Declaration of the Rights of Man*.

In his later work, Habermas warns of the dangers of losing the public sphere and civil society and the threats posed to the public sphere by late modernity's twin evils: the bureaucratic nation-state and global capitalism. In *The Philosophical Discourse of Modernity* (Habermas, 1985) he describes the different ways in which the idea of modernity becomes an all-encompassing shroud, befogging the reason of the public sphere. In *Time of Transitions* (Habermas, 2001) he sees reason under attack from new forms of totalitarianism such as religious fundamentalism and nationalism. The social democratic settlement of post-war West Germany (along with the formation of the European Union) is, for Habermas, a product of discussion and reason, and serves for him as a good example of his idea of the civil society and the public sphere – the weakening of this settlement and the growing globalization of power is, for Habermas, a troubling symptom of the loss of the public sphere. When decisions on fiscal policies are made to serve the profit making of off-shore banks and unaccountable transnational corporations, something is clearly dysfunctional in the public sphere. Elsewhere, he has been strongly critical of the postmodern turn in social theory, where relativism and sophistry seemingly replace the commitment to social justice (Habermas, 2003).

Habermas on rationalities and actions

What Horkheimer described as objective reason is, for Habermas, only possible where there is a free interaction of ideas and debate (Habermas, 1984; 1987). That interaction is what Habermas calls communicative action, which is necessary for the unimpeded functioning of communicative rationality (Pedersen, 2008). If actors have the freedom to act in a demo-cratic, communal manner, treating each other with respect and testing each other's claims, then it is possible to make sense of the world in a way that is classically rational, and the Enlightenment project is saved. William Outhwaite has shown that Habermas' approach to communicative action is predicated on a hermeneutics of language that is grounded in the analysis of speech. As Outhwaite explains:

> Habermas's central idea is remarkably simple. It is that every standard use of language to make statements involves certain presuppositions: that what the speaker says is true, that it is sincerely meant, and that it is normatively appropriate. Joking apart, talking about things, including ourselves, only has a point if we are serious about it and can at least envisage the possibility of reaching agreement, as autonomous and equal partners in discussion. I can make you believe what I want by hypnosis, or by deception, or by perhaps appealing to authority, but this isn't playing the game: our discussion in this case is merely a simulated one.
>
> (Outhwaite, 2005: 11–12)

We can see that Habermas' idea of communicative rationality is an idealized model of the democracy of Athens, a reflection of the demands of Thomas Paine and other political philosophers for a public society based on a free and fair exchange of ideas leading to actions based on the common good of that society (Honneth and Joas, 1991). As Brand argues, Habermas' communicative rationality begins with more than one individual actor and a mutually agreed set of rules about discourse, language and meaning (Brand, 1990).

Progress in the public sphere, then, works through mutual agreement of those rules, and actions that support and establish communicative rationality. For Habermas, Adorno's conception of rationality is too subjective: either the product of the work of one individual, or the product, following Marx, of a collective subject (Habermas, 1987). In one sense, it could be argued that Habermas is attempting to retain a Marxist account of society while also preserving faith in reason. Communicative rationality is emergent, contingent on actors and action, and dependent on consensus over the hermeneutics of language. Furthermore, communicative action takes place in what Habermas calls the lifeworld, which 'comprises a stock of shared assumptions and background knowledge, of shared reasons on the basis of which agents may reach consensus' (Finlayson, 2004: 52). The lifeworld shares many simi-larities to Cohen's symbolic community (Cohen, 1985), or perhaps Bourdieu's habitus–field nexus (Bourdieu, 1984). All three are based on the notion of shared principles, discourse, agreements on meaning and the objectification of the social. But there is one difference between the lifeworld and these other imaginary constructions of belonging: the lifeworld is the totality of our social world, not just a small set of our ontological environment. Habermas' concept owes its origins to the work of Karl Popper, who tried to make a distinc-tion between the worlds of physical objects, mental states and cultural products (Thompson and Held, 1982). The lifeworld is the world of the latter, a symbolic construction of the first two worlds. Ideally, the lifeworld is constructed out of communicative rationality, which leads to principles of progress, fairness and ethics being part of that world. So Habermas argues in his analysis of discourse ethics and morality: the lifeworld is where reason and discourse shape laws about equality, for example, which can be seen in the way in which racial discrimination has been slowly challenged and criminalized in many liberal democracies (Habermas, 1983; 1991).

There is, then, a simple seductiveness about the theory of communicative action and communicative rationality. The latter is an ideal of objective, unfettered reasoning, drawing on structural realist ideas of meaning and language, which in turn inherit older notions of rationality from Kant and Plato. The former is the way in which the latter is acted out in discourse: free from constraint, democratic, fair and consensual in its rules and outcomes. In an ideal world, the lifeworld would be built solely from such stuff, and progress and truth would be assured to all those in it.

Against the lifeworld of communicative action and rationality, Habermas presents in *The Theory of Communicative Action* what he calls the system: a symbolic construction that is created entirely from the workings of instrumentality on modernity. Instrumentality is purposive rationality and action, things done and ways of seeing the world imposed on us by the goal-seeking behaviour of actors and institutions that wish to limit our choice and our ability to get in the way of their goal seeking. As Finlayson (2004) argues, this instrumentality itself establishes an instrumental rationality: the subjective reason of Horkheimer, where the freedom of communicative rationality and action is curtailed for the greater good of some other enterprise. Habermas is here in debt to Weber and Adorno, who had both identified the way in which modernity is a product of increasing rationalization, industrialization and capitalization; and also Gramsci, whose work independently of Adorno had articulated the way in which power is used to establish hegemonic constraints on people's freedoms to choose. With Horkheimer in *Dialectic of Enlightenment*, Adorno had argued that the Enlightenment had been turned from a way to freedom to a way to slavery precisely because of its nurturing of instrumental rationality and reason. Gramsci (1971) had demonstrated that instrumentality went hand in hand with the increasing centralization of power and hegemony of the capitalist elite over all forms of life, including culture. Instrumentality comes from two sources in modernity, as Habermas describes in the extract above from *The Philosophical Discourse of Modernity*, drawing on the earlier work of Weber: from the power of capitalism and its all-embracing pursuit of economic goals; and from the rise of the modern nation-state and its interference with and limitations on the freedoms of individuals.

Both capitalism and the modern nation-state create systems that limit our freedoms and choices, and our ability to make communicative rational decisions and actions. Capitalism has become an accepted good of liberal democracy, and the theory of the free market is the exemplar of liberalism. Yet economic power is clearly used in a way that is counter to the principles of communicative rationality. It is instrumentally rational to support the appropriation of small, self-owned shops by larger supermarket conglomerates. The conglomerates can (possibly) bring cheaper goods and convenience to customers; and at the same time the profit imperative can keep its shareholders happy. Yet the closure of locally owned, independent shops is not good for the local communities that they serve: it reduces choice, social capital and democratic discourse. It is not communicatively rational to rip out the hearts of villages and small towns in order to squeeze another halfpenny of dividend to the bankers who own the supermarkets. However, it is clearly instrumentally rational to pursue those profit margins for short-term gains, without any reason to think of long-term concepts such as the environment, sustainability and the well-being of producers and consumers.

Habermas on leisure

Habermas (1962) suggests that in modernity there is a transformation of traditional social structures into ones dictated by instrumentality: so the old, private space of the family is colonized by the rationality of commodification, and codes of honour are replaced by shopping lists; in turn, leisure becomes measured by the timing of television programmes. Habermas says that leisure behaviour becomes an ersatz copy of communicative, rational behaviour, a shallow, meaningless replacement for the public sphere of the Enlightenment. Habermas is not dismissing all leisure activity, only that which is imposed on people by those in power as a hegemonic trick to make the people forget about the power of public discourse and reason. With the shrinking of the public sphere, Habermas writes (1962: 159): 'private people withdrew from their socially controlled roles as property owners into the purely personal ones of their noncommittal use of leisure time … Leisure behavior supplies the key to the floodlit privacy of the new sphere, to the externalization of what is declared to be the inner life. What today, as the domain of leisure, is set off from an occupational sphere that has become autonomous, has the tendency to take the place of that kind of public sphere that at one time was the point of reference for a subjectivity shaped in the bourgeois family's intimate sphere.'

The theme of leisure behaviour continues, when Habermas contrasts the bourgeois culture of the Enlightenment with the empty leisure lives of us moderns, caught as we are in a realm of instrumental consumption. In making the contrast, Habermas also elucidates the distinction between affairs (action) self-directed by individuals pursuing private interests, and affairs (action) that unite individuals into a critical, communicative public sphere. In the Enlightenment, Western Europe was for a brief moment shaped by the latter: now, as in the last 150 years or so, caught as we are in a lifeworld colonized by instrumentality, our public sphere and our capability of free, communicative action, is limited. How we use our leisure time is indicative of our inability to choose freely or wisely; leisure defined as something apolitical or frivolous (something to do to keep us amused from boredom, as hundreds and thousands do every lunchtime when making friends on Facebook, perhaps) is itself evidence of the drain of critical thinking from the public sphere.

> So-called leisure behavior, once it had become part of the cycle of production and consumption, was already apolitical, if for no other reason than its incapacity to constitute a world emancipated from the immediate constraints of survival needs. When leisure was nothing but a complement to time spent on the job, it could be no more than a different arena for the pursuit of private business affairs that were not transformed into a public communication between private people.
>
> (Habermas, 1962: 160)

The early stages of modernity, the rise of the nation-state and the homogenization and globalization of capitalism lead inexorably, for Habermas, into the present times and our late modern dilemmas of freedom, free will and constraint. Here Habermas is at his most pessimistic, and most in debt to his mentors Adorno and Horkheimer. His strong criticism of the leisure activities of the culture consumers reads like a British Leisure Studies paper written in the 1980s by Bramham or Critcher: leisure is not only denuded of any political philosophy, but in its shallow, instrumental form it limits and constrains the ability of people to realize that they are limited and constrained. As he continues (Habermas, 1962: 163): 'In the course of our [the twentieth] century, the bourgeois forms of sociability have found substitutes that have one tendency in common despite their regional and national diversity: abstinence from literary and political debates.' That is, the twentieth century has seen a decline in the engagement of people with critical, communicative debates about the nature and direction of politics, a decline equated by Habermas with the decline in discourses about the meaning and value of literature (and indeed other forms of high culture). What was crucial, for Habermas, about the critically debating public in the Enlightenment public sphere was its reliance on private reading and learning, which allowed for the intellectualization of the critical, public debate. In contemporary society, however, Habermas writes (1962: 163), 'the leisure activities of the culture-consuming public, on the contrary, themselves take place within a social climate, and they do not require discussions'. There is in instrumentalized leisure and culture an absence of both private cogitation and public discourse.

In the second volume of *The Theory of Communicative Action*, Habermas (1987) returns to leisure only briefly. But the section where he does mention leisure is instructive, as it comes where he is sketching the consequences of the colonization of the lifeworld by the systems of instrumental rationality. Here Habermas describes how leisure, culture, recreation and tourism are key areas of struggle between the communicative free-thinking of the lifeworld and the brutal commodification and consumption of capitalism:

> The thesis of internal colonization states that the subsystems of the economy and state become more and more complex as a consequence of capitalist growth, and penetrate ever deeper into the symbolic reproduction of the lifeworld. It should be possible to test this thesis sociologically wherever the traditionalist padding of capitalist modernization has worn through and central areas of cultural reproduction, social integration, and socialization have been openly drawn into the vortex of economic growth and therefore of juridification. This applies not only to such issues as protection of the environment, nuclear reactor security, data protection, and the like, which have been successfully dramatized in the public sphere. The trend toward juridification of informally regulated spheres of the lifeworld is gaining ground along a broad front – the more leisure, culture, recreation and tourism recognizably come into the grip of the laws of the commodity economy and the definitions of mass consumption, the more the structures of the bourgeois family manifestly become adapted to the imperatives of the employment system, the more the school palpably takes over the functions of assigning job and life prospects, and so forth.
>
> (Habermas, 1987: 368)

Despite the briefness of the discussion, Habermas' use of leisure in *The Theory of Communicative Action* provides the justification for leisure theory, Leisure Studies and an on-going empirical programme in leisure, sport and tourism that critically investigates the struggle over the meaning and purpose of leisure. The pessimism about art does not rule out leisure and culture being places where communicative rationality can produce communicative action; but for leisure and culture to be places where communicative action can take place, there has to be a public (externalized) sphere in which debates about meaning can take place. Just as in his earlier work, leisure can only be morally instructive if it plays a communicative role, or is the product of such communicative rationality. Where leisure is a product of consumption and commodification, the end-point of some instrumentally rational system, such as global capitalism, it becomes less useful as a space, form or activity that gives individuals meaning and purpose. Then there is only the circus, at which we are entertained and made to forget our dreams of freedom and democracy.

Leisure research using Habermasian frameworks

Habermasian frameworks have been used in a range of leisure research to explore the ways in which leisure is both about freedom and about constraint. In the rest of this chapter, three research projects that use Habermas will be explored.

The tension between communicative rationality and instrumentality is used by Morgan (2006) in his book *Why Sports Morally Matter* to make a justification for the importance of sports participation. Morgan is concerned with the professionalization of modern sport and the way in which modern sport has become driven by commerce. For many sociologists, historians and philosophers of sport this professionalization and commercialization of sport has destroyed the ethical value of sports activity, which was, historically, founded on ideas of amateurism, fair play and participation. Morgan agrees with those who say that sport has become too commercial and professionalized, and has no problem with the notion that modern, professional sport has become part of the entertainment industry. This is, he argues, a bad thing for the ethics of sport – but it is not the end of sport as an ethical sphere. Morgan argues that there is still the potential for sports participation to be something that instils social, moral and political values. This, he says, is due to the communicatively active nature of sports participation: people choose to take part in sports, choose to be communicative in their engagement in sport and choose to adhere to internal rules about fair play. This Habermasian communicative value of sports participation – its role as a public sphere, a part of the lifeworld ranged against the instrumentality of commercialized sport – gives it, for Morgan, a vital role to play in the future development of modern society.

Scambler (2005), in *Sport and Society: History, Power and Culture*, draws on his wider sociological interests in reflexive critical sociology. Elsewhere, Scambler (2002) uses Habermas' idea of the lifeworld of communicative action being swamped by the forces of global capitalism to examine the instrumentalization of health. In the modern nation-state, interventions in health are increasingly medicalized, but not without resistance from those who use their agency to act in a communicative way to counter such medicalization. In his research project on sport (Scambler, 2005), Scambler criticizes previous attempts to theorize sport and power for failing to address the agency of individuals involved in sport. He also critiques previous theoretical frameworks for their failure to explain the paradox of modern sport: the importance it plays in people's lives and identities, and the subjugation of modern sport to the monopolies of nationalism, patriarchy and capitalism. Sport is used by individuals to make sense of their lives, while it is simultaneously abused by the hegemonic forces that hold real power in late modernity. For Scambler, Habermas is crucial in helping to make sense of what is actually going on in modern sport. He is cynical of those who suggest that sport is somehow postmodern, that there is an endless diversity of choice and a weakening of hegemonic structures. As he puts it:

> There is a real risk of the postmodernization of contemporary movements of opposition, that is, of the 'ironic' neutering of organized opposition to lifeworld colonization by its incorporation in a culture-ideology of consumerism consonant with the vested interests of a resurgent and strongly globalized capitalist-executive and its allies in disorganized capitalism. This is why [Habermas] … sees most postmodern or post-structuralist perspectives, for all their capacity to disinhibit, as insidious forms of neo-conservatism; and why, relatedly, he seeks to reconstruct and revive the project of modernity, noting its proven capacity, all too seldom realized, to emancipate.
>
> (Scambler, 2005: 182)

The final research project that applies Habermas to leisure is that of Spracklen (2009; 2011a; 2011b). In *The Meaning and Purpose of Leisure*, Spracklen (2009) attempts to challenge postmodern theories of leisure and tries to reconcile debates about agency and structure in Leisure Studies. Habermas is drawn upon to explain the so-called 'paradox of leisure' – that it is clearly related to agency but also a product of instrumentality. For Spracklen, leisure is something essentially communicative in nature, but that communicative nature has been undermined by the emergence of instrumental forms of leisure: leisure that is commercialized and commodified, which is provided by the state or by transnational corporations in order to keep consumers docile (but content). Spracklen draws on examples from modern sport, pop music and the tourism industry to show that leisure activities at this moment in late modernity are sites for communicative resistance and instrumental colonization: so, for example, 'extreme metal' music fans use their music scene to find communicative space to resist instrumentality, but they are also constrained by the hegemonic discourse of the music industry. In *Constructing Leisure*, Spracklen (2011a) uses Habermasian rationalities as a framework to analyse the meaning and purpose of leisure at different periods of history and pre-history, countering the notion that leisure is an invention of modernity (and breaking with Habermas by applying his philosophical history of modernity to pre-modern situations). Finally, Spracklen (2011b) uses Habermasian rationalities and actions to critically analyse whisky tourism and the search for authenticity in Scottishness. Following an account of whisky distilleries and their visitors, and discussions among whisky enthusiasts, he concludes:

> Pace Habermas ... existential authenticity operates in a communicatively rational way, but the rational discourse of authenticity in tourism is, as MacCannell (1973) noted, essentially instrumental in nature. These incommensurate rationalities remain unresolved. One can see, then, that discourses around Scottishness in whisky and whisky tourism both define something felt as real in communicative experience and something consumed through the apparatus of Habermasian instrumentality. The discourses traced in this paper demonstrate the way in which authenticity is marketized, how whisky tourists are still caught in a dialectic of control. It is at once the commodification of leisure expressed in the brochure and the dream of liberty and the choice of the open road in a hundred Hollywood movies: as Cohen (1988) argues, the tension between desires, expectations of something tangibly authentic and the reality of the tourist's commodified experience. Tourism then returns us to the paradox of leisure: the way in which it is both freedom and choice and constraint and commodification.
>
> (Spracklen, 2011b: 114)

We can see, then, that Habermas' ideas can be very important in helping leisure researchers to resolve structure and agency, explore late modernity and analyse the meaning and purpose of leisure in our everyday lives.

References

Adorno, T. (1947) *Composing for the Films*. New York: Oxford University Press.
Adorno, T. (1967) *Prisms*. London: Neville Spearman.
Adorno, T. and Horkheimer, M. (1944) *Dialectic of Enlightenment*. London: Verso.
Bourdieu, P. (1984) *Distinction: A Social Critique of the Judgment of Taste*. London: Routledge.
Brand, A. (1990) *The Force of Reason: An Introduction to Habermas' Theory of Communicative Action*. London: Allen and Unwin.

Cohen, A. (1985) *The Symbolic Construction of Community*. London: Tavistock.

Cohen, E. (1988) 'Authenticity and Commoditization in Tourism', *Annals of Tourism Research* 15. 371–386.

Finlayson, J. (2004) *Habermas: A Very Short Introduction*. Oxford: Oxford University Press.

Gramsci, A. (1971) *Selections from Prison Notebooks*. London: Lawrence and Wishart.

Habermas, J. (1962) *The Structural Transformation of the Public Sphere*. Cambridge: Polity.

Habermas, J. (1983) *Moral Consciousness and Communicative Action*. Cambridge: Polity.

Habermas, J. (1984) *The Theory of Communicative Action, Volume One: Reason and the Rationalization of Society*. Cambridge: Polity.

Habermas, J. (1985) *The Philosophical Discourse of Modernity*. Cambridge: Polity.

Habermas, J. (1987) *The Theory of Communicative Action, Volume Two: The Critique of Functionalist Reason*. Cambridge: Polity.

Habermas, J. (1991) *Justification and Amplification*. Cambridge: Polity.

Habermas, J. (2001) *Time of Transitions*. Cambridge: Polity.

Habermas, J. (2003) *Truth and Justification: Philosophical Essays*. Cambridge: Polity.

Honneth, A. and Joas, H. (1991) *Communicative Action: Essays on Jürgen Habermas's 'The Theory of Communicative Action'*. Cambridge: Polity.

MacCannell, D. (1973) 'Staged Authenticity: Arrangements of Social Space in Tourist Settings', *American Journal of Sociology* 79: 589–603.

Morgan, W. (2006) *Why Sports Morally Matter*. London: Routledge.

Outhwaite, W. (2005) *The Habermas Reader*. Cambridge: Polity.

Pedersen, J. (2008) 'Habermas' Method: Rational Reconstruction', *Philosophy of the Social Sciences* 38: 457–485.

Scambler, G. (2002) *Health and Social Change: A Critical Theory*. Maidenhead: Open University Press.

Scambler, G. (2005) *Sport and Society: History, Power and Culture*. Maidenhead: Open University Press.

Spracklen, K. (2009) *The Meaning and Purpose of Leisure*. Basingstoke: Palgrave.

Spracklen, K. (2011a) *Constructing Leisure*. Basingstoke: Palgrave.

Spracklen, K. (2011b) 'Dreaming of Drams: Authenticity in Scottish Whisky Tourism as an Expression of Unresolved Habermasian Rationalities', *Leisure Studies* 30: 99–116.

Thompson, J. and Held, D. (1982) *Habermas: Critical Debates*. Basingstoke: Macmillan.

14

CHRIS ROJEK

Peter Bramham

Introduction

This chapter outlines the contribution of this important writer in the field of Leisure Studies. It focuses on his six major leisure textbooks *Capitalism and Leisure Theory* (1985), *Ways of Escape* (1993), *Decentring Leisure* (1995), *Leisure and Culture* (2000), *Leisure Theory* (2005a) and *The Labour of Leisure* (2010a). During the last two decades, he has been similarly prolific in cultural studies and has reflected upon diverse topics such as celebrity (2001a; 2012) and national identity (2007) in addition to writing books on Frank Sinatra (2004) and Stuart Hall (2002) and more recently on music (2011a; 2011b). This is no idle coincidence, as Chris Rojek is determined to bury leisure within the wider context of culture. His substantive contribution to Leisure Studies is twofold: it has been secured by a distinctive mapping of shifting debates in Leisure Studies and also by raising new questions in order to open up new lines of enquiry. I suggested a decade ago that Rojek should then be heralded as one of the founding fathers of postmodern perspectives on leisure, whatever that nomenclature may signify (Bramham, 2002), but, at the time, it was a mantle he was reluctant to bear. His later publications, as befits any leading contemporary social theorist, have changed emphasis and he subsequently has sought to establish an 'action approach' to leisure. However, one does not need to be Sherlock Holmes in order to detect his postmodern interests. For instance, to quote Tony Blackshaw: 'Here was a dramatic irony: by the mid-1990s, postmodernism had lost its magnesium-flare fame, but at the very moment some in sociology were gleefully driving a stake through its heart, Rojek was using it to give the study of leisure a blood transfusion' (Blackshaw, 2012: 2). It is worth mentioning that the title of Blackshaw's recent interview with Rojek sits comfortably with these new, sharp times, as it casts Rojek as '*The Man* [italics added] from Leisure', whereas critics would happily dismiss him as just 'That Man from Leisure' or, more cruelly, as 'That Man from Leisure Studies'.

There is a further irony too, which overrides divisions between the worlds of mainstream sociology and the more marginal networks of Leisure Studies. Despite writing extensively about postmodern celebrity culture, Rojek himself has achieved celebrity status, certainly in Leisure Studies networks, as well as in the wider and the more prestigious field of cultural studies. But, as is often the case with celebrity, the heroes or heroines start at the margins and fight their way to the centre. Often having something different and important to say, celebrities are 'newsworthy' and particular events embellish stories, reputations and gossip. But this is no fairy story, as celebrities, especially in academia, generate envy and opposition as well as interest; hence they are continually pressed to explain and justify themselves. This involves the need for celebrities to clarify their position, or at the very least to say or tweet something, especially if there is some controversy out there to cast their celebrity gaze upon. But if celebrity is about anything, it is about status position: it is about positioning oneself in relation to any other celebrities or stars in the galaxy.

Taking and maintaining a position becomes a categorical imperative for celebrity, and Rojek's presence within Leisure Studies is one of increasingly explicit engagement with moral, political and environmental issues. His myriad national and international conference appearances and keynote presentations provide a traditional platform to test out ideas and promote current interests and predilections. But, like Zygmunt Bauman, he uses less conventional means, such as published interviews, streamed panel discussions and YouTube clips, to spread his ideas about sociology, culture and leisure. But, unlike all his contemporaries, with the exception of Anthony Giddens, his role in the commercial sector as commissioning editor for publishers Routledge and Sage has provided a crucial opportunity for him to expand his ideas on social theory. The number and breadth of publications are simply staggering: for example, his collaboration with Eric Dunning at Leicester University, Mike Featherstone at the Theory, Culture and Society Centre, Nottingham Trent University, with Bryan Turner, particularly when at Cambridge University, and now at Brunel University. These are perhaps important avenues to explore in some future analysis towards a sociology of knowledge which locates intellectuals in the history of academic disciplines and their functioning within the diverse networks that make up Leisure Studies. Mapping such processes of academic inclusion and exclusion often becomes starkly judgemental and is clearly a dangerous business. Nevertheless, Rojek has consistently sought to develop a coherent sociology of leisure and has been a resilient player in developing debates about Leisure Studies as a field of study. However, there remains a reluctance to engage with Rojek's work. The reasons for this ambivalence about his contribution to Leisure Studies are complex but, in short, he directly challenges most of the domain assumptions and conventional wisdoms embedded in this field of study.

A star is born

The 1980s and 1990s were inauspicious times to start an academic career in the UK because neo-liberal ideas of new managerialism, marketization and commercialism where forcing change on old and new universities alike. Thatcherism, sustained during the Thatcher, Major and Blair years, distrusted unionized professionals within the public sector and so demanded more regulation and monitoring of standards and performance through the CNAA[1] and later the QAA.[2] Traditional, secure academic tenure was challenged by the RAE,[3] as academics had to demonstrate prestigious publications in peer-reviewed academic journals and extensive research funding. New researchers had to shape up to more flexible work practices and heavy teaching loads rather than sharing and enjoying the more secure academic tenure of their older-established university colleagues. Right from the start, Rojek had read and fully understood the runes of Thatcherism, and also the workings of the academy; he was determined both to play the game and to win. At that time he was (and still is) certainly breathtakingly prolific, and for good reason:

My job at the Queen's College was a fixed term opportunity. I thought it expeditious to build up my publications record in order to prepare for the awful day when I would be forced to reapply for my job. In just under four years, I completed one book, began work on another two, signed a contract for a fourth and published over twenty articles in a variety of academic journals.

(Rojek, 1993: x)

But a key question is to decide what sort of sociology of leisure was produced, to relate Rojek's work to C. Wright Mills's (1970) demand for sociology to exhibit 'sociological imagination'. There is also room to speculate on the reasons for the magnitude of Rojek's impact and the ambivalence encountered in reactions to his work.

In his first major excursion in the field of Leisure Studies, he displays what will be the hallmark of all later contributions. In 'Emancipation and Demoralisation: Contradicting Approaches in the Sociology of Leisure', Rojek (1983) maps out two contrasting approaches to leisure: one of positivist empiricism and the other the Frankfurt School of cultural materialism. Both are seen as flawed and he proposes as one solution deployment of the developmental theory of Elias to examine the emotional content of leisure and also to introduce a power perspective of leisure as a process of accommodation and opposition by different groups.

From the outset, his work is transgressive and subversive in questioning 'conventional wisdom' which associates leisure with free time and freedom. Both need to be contextualized, and any quest for a universal theory of leisure is both illusory and idealistic ... one cannot dislocate free time or quality of experience from its context. This is a position that he reasserts in his last leisure text-book, about emotional intelligence and emotional labour:

> Emotional intelligence and emotional labour are, I think, core concepts for the analysis of leisure forms and practice. This is because the display of credibility, relevance and competence in our 'voluntarily' chosen 'free' time activities speaks to others about who we are, what we hold to be valuable and how we can make a difference.
>
> (Rojek, 2010a: 4)

Consequently, Rojek rides roughshod over philosophers and social theorists who search for any universal theory of leisure. They all fall foul of Wittgenstein's criticisms of the fallacy of essentialism – as free-floating intelligentsia seeking to demarcate the essential features or characteristics of leisure. Leisure is shaped by history and there can be no 'timeless' theories of leisure. Leisure is a distinctive form of human experience and not a derivative of work. Nor is leisure necessarily 'good', a site for accumulation of pleasure or human freedom, as founding fathers seem to imply. Leisure is now recast in broader cultural terms as an effect of systems of legitimation.

Writing in the mid-1980s, in *Capitalism and Leisure Theory* Rojek berates leisure researchers who work within the dominant tradition of social formalism. This approach myopically searches for data on leisure forms and encourages measurement of variables within patterns of leisure participation. It emulates the natural sciences and treats leisure as something 'out there', as an unproblematic social fact that can be objectively measured within a scientific positivist perspective. It has one obsession, and that is quantification. It is empiricism per se with no sociological imagination. This division between Leisure Sciences and Cultural Studies is seen by many to be causing the 'crisis' in Leisure Studies: see, for example, the arguments of Aitchison (2000), Coalter (1999) and Tomlinson (1989); but, as I have argued elsewhere, fields of study are more susceptible to crisis than are more traditional disciplines (Bramham, 2006)

Social formalism offers us theories of 'leisure without society'. It is a study of 'society without sociology'. Rojek makes no bones about this: 'I shall argue that the main defects in social formalism, the dominant research tradition in the sociology of leisure, arise from the failure to situate leisure relations in the context of the history and the general power structure of capitalist society' (Rojek, 1985: 3).

The key concepts of power and capitalism imply that Rojek will settle comfortably within the parameters of Marxist sociology. Indeed, his characterization of major structural tendencies or organizational forms of modern leisure only confirms this position. He maps out *privatization, individualization, commercialization* and *pacification* as defining characteristics of modern leisure accounts. But Rojek is not committed to Marxism as a mode of analysis, and even less so as revolutionary emancipatory praxis. Marxists and neo-Marxists may be framing the right sorts of questions, but they usually come up with the wrong answers. In the 1980s, the politics of the left no longer seem credible so, following Anthony Giddens, some new form of life politics must be placed on the agenda, with growing significance for the future of leisure (2001b).

In the penultimate chapter of his first book, Rojek assesses the contribution of figurational sociology to understanding leisure. Indeed, there are clear theoretical resonances in this early work with figurational sociology. At an earlier stage of his career, he decided not to embark on PhD research under supervision by Eric Dunning, but completed his MPhil at Leicester University. His intellectual debt to figurational sociology found expression in the early 1990s as co-editor of a book entitled *Sport and Leisure in the Civilising Process* (Dunning and Rojek, 1992). Figurational sociology was later criticized and reassessed by him as one sociological approach amongst many. The framing of new rules for leisure research mirrors the influential work of Giddens in *New Rules of Sociological Method* (1976); and co-incidentally, Giddens studied at Leicester University and his theory of structuration explores similar themes to Elias's work. Rojek helpfully concludes with four main rules for leisure:

1 Leisure activity is an adult phenomenon which is defined in opposition to the play world of children.
2 Leisure practice is an accomplishment of skilled and knowledgeable actors.
3 The structure and development of leisure relations is an effect of the legitimating rules of pleasure and unpleasure.
4 Leisure relations must be sociologically examined as dynamic, relatively open-ended processes.

(Rojek, 1985: 180–181)

Routes of escape for Leisure Studies

Rojek's next major sortie into the scientific community of leisure scholars came with a collection of papers, *Leisure for Leisure* (1989). One abiding residue of this book was its somewhat hostile review by Professor Alan Tomlinson, working within the cultural studies tradition. He characterized the contributors as constituting a Glasgow–Leicester axis, implying that they sought hegemonic control over Leisure Studies. It is clear that this hostile review was for Rojek a chastening experience, and provided personal and damaging evidence of the multi-paradigmatic rivalry in Leisure Studies. Indeed, it is neither forgotten nor forgiven.[4] But controversy courts celebrity and Rojek's book on Stuart Hall (2002) has been fiercely criticized by some, but not without some vigorous response.[5] Again, it sometimes appears that his work on leisure is treated as a stalking horse or a catalyst for others to articulate their own theories.[6]

Accounting for paradigmatic rivalry in Leisure Studies underpins Rojek's theoretical work, as he frequently provides authoritative overviews of the state of leisure theory in UK Leisure Studies, often published in edited compilations for North American markets in Leisure Studies or Leisure Sciences.[7] Over the years, the precise categorization of paradigmatic traditions varies, yet all the usual suspects are there – social formalism, the politicization of leisure within cultural studies and feminism, alongside more recent postmodernist discourses. At this stage there is a lack of clarity about Rojek's own vantage-point: how can or does one write an overview of the sociology of leisure? Such themes have been explored in *Leisure Research in Europe* (Mommaas, van der Poel, Bramham, and Henry, 1996). For example, how does one theorize involvement with and detachment from competing paradigms in Leisure Studies? This is especially pressing when postmodern developments in social theory demand the deconstruction of dominant discourse. At this stage, the driving force of Rojek's position betrays his figurational roots as he seeks to void naïve dualisms of agency and structure, of the individual and society, 'the twin blights of essentialism and reification' (Rojek, 1989: 9), of work and leisure. He restates 'Leisure relations must be studied as relations of power. However they must also be studied as relations which are both constraining and enabling' (ibid.: 8). This dualism of constraint and choice lies at the heart of his own work but such framing and conceptualization are seen as fundamental weakness in the work of others: as, for example, in his criticisms of Clarke and Critcher (1985) in *The Devil Makes Work*.

Whilst he was teaching sociology at Queen's College, Glasgow, Rojek's own PhD, under the tutelage of David Frisby, was focused much more on modernity, influenced by work on the 'modern' by writers such as Simmel, Kracauer and Benjamin. The publication of *Ways of Escape* in 1993 proved an important milestone or turning-point in Rojek's intellectual journey. It signifies his distance from any neo-Marxist research agenda around class and capitalism or figurational approaches to civilized society, or feminist positions on patriarchal society. Indeed, he directly challenges Marxist cultural studies on several counts: its positing of a universal ontology, of the necessity to labour as a shared common experience; the scope of resistance and struggle inside consumer capitalism; equally, its failure to grasp the changes taking place in class structures, work organization and media consumption. Yet powerful structural processes shape lives and leisure choices:

> However, we confront these attractions as members of a particular class, race, nation and civilization. And were we able truly to abandon these identity values we could no longer function. Our escape attempts are therefore themselves artificial. They are encoded activities with structural parameters. There is no escape.
>
> (Rojek, 1993: 12)

Change in modernity could mean that class, elite, statist or corporatist types of moral regulation would not apply and were no longer viable. In Zygmunt Bauman's terms (1987; 1991; 1992), nation states were no longer in authoritative control. There were no legislators able to sustain credible 'invented traditions'[8] imposing a history and shared culture on all but rather global processes; or what Appadurai (1990) terms 'flows' were transforming citizens into consumers, prey to the babble of diverse experts proffering advice on lifestyles. The book therefore engages with key debates of late 1980s postmodernism. Rojek argues that two key ideas of modernity are circulation and consumption. Quoting Benjamin (1983), Rojek asserts that 'we live in *"the ruins of the bourgeois world"'* (1993: 45). It is within these continuities and discontinuities that Rojek focuses on the development of the nation-state and its involvement in licensing, policing and stereotyping. As Giddens (1999) would argue later in his Reith lectures, Rojek posits that gender relations become more democratic, more informalized and that women exercised more power through consumption, not least leisure shopping in department stores. However, driving forces of change within modernity such as de-differentiation gradually undermine bourgeois divisions or polarities of work/leisure, reason/nature, body and mind and so on: 'De-differentiation is nothing but the pursuit of the contradiction of modernity. Postmodernism, it might be said, is the acceptance of these contradictions – not as necessities or impediments, but as conditions to work with' (Rojek, 1993: 188). Consequently, the sureties of the bourgeois world dissolved. Modernity stressed unfinished aspects of experience; life had an accidental character ... one of ambiguity, illusion, diversity and opposition. Indeed, Rojek criticizes structuralist accounts for failing to challenge contradictions in experience and not developing a phenomenology of leisure. This is a task that he later takes on himself.

Rojek illustrates disintegration of the bourgeois world through a brief discussion of the ordering of nature as an escape area, the subsequent organization of tourism and the dissolution of home interiors as a means of escape. He also maps out Lash and Urry's arguments about disorganized capitalism and postmodern challenges to an authoritative universal rationalist discourse and Baudrillard's suggestion that reality has been replaced by representation. The implications for leisure and tourism – they are consumption activities – posttourism is no quest for the self; they are part of de-differentiation – work spaces become leisure spaces and leisure activities become more work-like; they challenge the right of nation-states to rule and regulate; they acknowledge inauthenticity. Rojek identifies leisure as spectacle and sensation by exploring four types: black spots, fatal attractions, heritage sites and literary landscapes. He expands John Urry's arguments (1990; 1995) about the post-tourist's quest for playfulness, the search for inauthenticity and intertextuality, ... the growing interest in different facets and interpretations of tourist sites and sights. Rojek also provides brief commentary on four 'escape areas' – the beach, the hotel, historical monuments and wilderness.

Centring on Rojek

Any assessment of Rojek's unique contribution to Leisure Studies could safely start in 1995 with *Decentring Leisure: Rethinking Leisure Theory.* If previous writing teased out latent and neglected theories of modern leisure, this book represents his decisive engagement with the 'postmodern turn' in social theory, certain aspects of which he himself later dismissed as 'decorative sociology' (Rojek and Turner, 2000). The book's title signifies critical engagement with postmodern perspectives. Its subtitle acts as a harbinger of change of vantage-point so as to gain full purchase on Leisure Studies. It would be too strong to suggest that here is an epistemological break, as has been suggested in other writers such as Marx and Bauman.[9] As ever, Rojek demands that leisure must be contextualized and must be related to determinate social formations. There is no such thing or space as essential leisure, with its own unique laws, management practices, propositions and rhythms; so nothing could be *centred* on leisure. Leisure Studies operate at a discursive level. It offers a cultural problematic. Under modernity, leisure meant freedom, release and escape, whereas under postmodernity those traditional meanings are challenged and deconstructed.

In the second part of the book, entitled 'Modernity and Leisure', Rojek deploys the heuristic device of separating modernity 1 from modernity 2, although acknowledging the two formations as interdependent. This device is identical to Giddens' (1984) distinction between modernity and late modernity or to Bauman's (1988; 1992) categories of modernity and postmodernity. As befits postmodern times, writers skirt history and thereby avoid fierce debates about periodization, i.e. whether modernity had shifted into a new formation and established postmodernity. In modernity 1, Rojek defines leisure as an essential element of social order; it is integrative, regulated and moral. He then summarizes five separate theories of leisure: conservative, (Marxist) moral regulation, the Protestant ethic, conspicuous consumption and the civilizing process. In chapter 4, 'Mechanisms of Regulation', he draws on Michel Foucault to provide an account of the 'carceral networks of power' which are also forms of recognizing individuals. Medicalized and sexualized discourses are languages of power written into people's lives to 'normalize' behaviour. Foucault (1983) recognized three forms of power – institutional (involving ethnic, national, religious rules), economic (involving class) and subjective (involving personal struggles against subjectivity and submission).

The micro-politics of leisure in modernity is one of regulation, order and control. Following Foucault and others, power is embodied and grounded within the healthy, normal body, controlled by the gaze of others. To use concepts derived from Giddens (1991), during the later part of the nineteenth century modernity was about sequestration of deviant experience, its institutionalization and medicalization. People were organized into the lifecycle, into appropriate gender roles within the family, with a clear sexual division of labour and normalized sexual identities, valuing heterosexuality. Leisure became a symbol of personal merit and health. Leisure was an important site for emulation and consumption; following Bourdieu's concepts of cultural capital and competence became important arenas for social evaluation, for exercise of social taste, for distinction. In modernity, bureaucracies, particularly within the nation-state, were important mechanisms for organizing leisure time, managing access to leisure spaces and national heritage. Modernity 1 offered citizens controlled nature. Leisure spaces, such as countryside, national parks and urban recreation grounds were nonludic, controlled and managed.

If modernity 1 was all about order, rationality and recreation, modernity 2 was about change, irrationality and pleasure. Rojek captures these disintegrating, destructuring processes of modernity 2 by summarizing Nietzsche's four propositions about modernity. First, the rational order of modernity is an illusion; second, change is inevitable; third, change must be positively embraced and affirmed; fourth, modernity 2 demands a celebration of unavoidable divisions and fragmentations. Leisure under modernity 1 was purposive and rational; for example, character-building outdoor pursuits offered hygienic and healthy countryside recreation. In modernity 2, leisure becomes postmodern; shopping, promenading *flâneurie* – browsing, wandering, watching, wishing, and opening oneself up to the sensations and rhythms of the city.

Chapter 6 reasserts Rojek's demand for a phenomenology of leisure … to place experiences of the naïve or native subject at the centre of analysis. It provides a strong indication of his future concentration on the social psychology of leisure, developed in his two textbooks, *Leisure Theory* (2005a) and *The Labour of Leisure* (2010). Phenomenology has as its focus both the individual and everyday life, what is left over from mainstream institutions. It is the untidy world of subjectivity, of love, friendships and humour. In modernity 2 there are growing processes of individualism and privatization, as there are growing feelings of risk and insecurity, a collapse of public trust and collective fraternity. Modernity 2 focuses on the psychology of the consumer, on *wanting* rather than *having*, on incompleteness, arbitrariness, fragmentation and indifference. The modern citizen, self-confident, self-developed, embedded in stable networks of neighbourhood supports, has gone, vital communities are nowhere and no longer to be seen.

The final part of *Decentring Leisure* is entitled 'Postmodernism and Leisure'. For Rojek, writing in 1995, postmodernity includes the de-differentiation of high and popular culture, the collapse of a 'progress' view of history, the debunking of science, the superimposition of the local/national by the global and the politics of impression rather than problem solving. Following Bauman (1992), Rojek argues that postmodernism refers to a change in social consciousness. It is an expression of disquiet about the ideas of modernity, a self-reflexivity, a stepping away from modernity. Modernity has crumbled because of the feminist movement, international tourism, restructured markets, the politicization of gays, the collapse of the USSR, increased environmental awareness and new communications technology.

The postmodern term 'decentring' was taken from Derrida's phenomenology in his argument that meaning was located not in reality or in things but in language. The *presence* of concepts such as leisure was also marked by their *absence*. We understand freedom because we understand constraint, and so with other dualisms of agency and structure, individual and society, work and leisure, male and female. What then follows is Rojek's authoritative pen-picture of postmodern changes; key changes in knowledge and grand narrative, in authority, in culture, in communication and in the economy.

So the term 'postmodern leisure' is now cast as an oxymoron. The postmodern is about flexibility, irrationality and play, whereas leisure was a modernist, bounded and rational experience. Postmodern culture is characterized by hyperreality and hypermobility, by restlessness and disengagement. Individuals carry polysemic identities; fixed commitments are resisted in postmodern life. As Bauman tellingly argued, the icon of late nineteenth-century modernity was the camera, the family portrait, shared kinship, fixed in particular locality. In the late twentieth century, the definitive icon of postmodernity is the erasable videotape recorder, the camcorder or, more recently, the iPhone and iPad.

Rojek concludes *Decentring Leisure* with the question, what is the legacy of postmodernism? For him, postmodern analysis corrected the modernist notion that leisure was segmented from the rest of life, was a charmed realm of self-fulfilment. It also reverses the tendency to oppose authentic experience with inauthenticity. It challenges any notion of an integrated self. Postmodern analysis acknowledges identity politics, the difference and divisions of ethnicity, gender and class. It highlights failures of government, of public policies; consequently, it destabilizes elitist authority structures and those cultural missionaries keen to bind citizens into the 'imaginary community' of the nation-state. The final chapter raises the question of whether leisure constitutes an individual or societal need. Doyal and Gough (1984) argued that societal needs were production, reproduction, communication and political authority. So should there be a politics of liberation to reconcile individual and societal needs?

Rojek's next book,[10] *Leisure and Culture* (2000), offers a compilation of conference presentations in diverse global locations and stands witness to not only Rojek's professorial and international status but also his determination to secure Leisure Studies within broader debates about culture. The papers can also be read as transitional work towards a more coherent exposition of an 'action analysis' of leisure (Rojek, 2005c). Rojek seeks to explore those domain assumptions grounded in the philosophical view of human nature, captured by the phrase *Homo ludens*. He accuses all three major traditions in Leisure Studies – functionalism, critical Marxism and feminism – of lacking any anthropological view of culture.

Rojek restates his challenge to any *Homo faber* view of humanity – which he sees as historically specific to modernity. With post-Fordism – de-industrialization, flexibilization and feminization of labour and, not least, the attractive media techno-culture embedded in non-work – work is no longer central to individuals, communities or classes. So it should be no surprise that identity politics creates fissures in the homogeneous blocks of common culture, constructed around class or the nation-state. Following Huizinga's *Homo Ludens*, Rojek argues that language, communication and play are at the centre of human culture. Industrial societies stress over-regimentation, calculability and rationality, whilst leisure remains a site for transgression and change, for challenging everyday culture and compulsion. So, logically, the culture of leisure is essential for a clear understanding of rule-breaking deviance.

In the penultimate chapter, Rojek pushes at the boundaries of Leisure Studies by categorizing types of 'dark' leisure – liminal leisure, moral transcendence and edgework and, finally, surplus energy. In Durkheimian vein, liminal leisure and surplus energy in traditional societies are seen as functional for social order. In differentiated pluralistic societies they do not serve that collective function. Indeed, and this is one of Rojek's many insights: leisure is all about liminality, testing diversity and difference, clear expressions of self-reflexivity. If people are culturally and materially constrained, they seek escape. Some forms of fantasy and escape threaten both self and others, as in abnormal leisure forms. Not only does free time provide the context within which deviant activities take place, but leisure researchers should be well placed to challenge determinist medical models of compulsion and addiction. So Rojek does not shy away from discussing pornography and, iconoclastically, serial killing. He maps out three types of abnormal forms which he classifies an invasive, mephitic and wild leisure ... drawing eclectically on parties, raves, motorcycle riots, inner-city disorders and soccer hooliganism.

Leisure and Culture (2000) casts a much wider historical net than any of Rojek's previous works, which, as we have seen, focus on nineteenth- and twentieth-century capitalism, on modernity and postmodernity. This is no doubt because of his commitment to develop an anthropological perspective on leisure. In the very first chapter, 'From Ritual to Performative Culture', he argues that all societies must organize time and space for economic and social survival but there is and has always been a surplus of energy and unused resources. The problem of leisure is how to use this surplus. Human history is not so much about scarcity, poverty and inequality but, rather, about abundance, conspicuous consumption and transgression.

In traditional societies, culture is grounded in a cyclical collective time-frame. Play is a means to religious ritual and conformity. People, as human bodies, are always 'occupied', performing activities/rituals for the collective clan. In industrial society, 'vacant' bodies mean that individuals seek to kill free time, avoid commitments, create lifestyles and restlessly fill space. Modernity then offers a diverse pluralistic culture, yet it is replete with pressures to perform in standard ways, to organized and carefully scripted roles. Modern industrial life is characterized by relentless techniques of Goffmanesque impression management, especially in work, performing against criteria of relevance which demarcate what constitutes a legitimate performance. Although leisure is uniformly defined and presented as the antithesis to performative work, it is not. This paradox informs the direction of the rest of the book; how best to understand leisure?

Rojek argues that leisure is a status-positioning activity that places us culturally in relation to others. He revisits the contribution that Veblen's concept of a leisure class may make to our understanding of class, leisure and culture. Commodities shift from use value to exchange value to denotional value. Having explored some of Veblen's weaknesses in understanding the cultural processes of emulation and consumption, Rojek reviews Bourdieu's contribution of the relativism of taste and cultural competence and refers to the new service class and the growing importance of cultural intermediaries in consumer culture.

In the final chapter, Rojek reviews the post-work argument, which has three major aspects – cybernation of work processes, growing media and cultural consumption and increased self-reflexivity, with mass higher education. He rejects Andre Gorz' solutions and his politics of work and time. He demands that leisure policies acknowledge the transgressive elements in leisure. This is qualified by an acknowledgement of the frailty of the human body and of the natural environment, so that leisure policies must be based on values of care and respect for others. Rojek powerfully concludes that personal engagement is necessary, especially in a performative culture.

The political becomes personal

This demand for personal engagement reasserts itself in Rojek's writings five years later. The book *Leisure Theory: Principles and Practice* (2005a) represents a concerted effort to occupy the middle ground of Leisure Studies by developing an 'action approach' to the study of leisure. Rojek wants to avoid the Scylla and Charybdis of leisure theory … the dragons of agency and structure, freedom and constraint, atomistic individualism and romantic organicism. All are basic myths set out to reconcile the contradictions and dilemmas of social organization. At times the book's policy exhortations read and sound like Anthony Giddens' 'Third Way' as the author demands that care for the self, care and respect for others and care of the environment must be three key values to guide leisure policy and practice. Indeed, his demand for active citizenship and life politics, with rights and responsibilities driving towards empowerment, distributive justice and social inclusion, is far more principled and theoretically cogent than anything that New Labour or Coalition government politicians have promised or delivered so far in the UK.

The ambition of the book is mapped out in the introduction. All societies face economic, cultural and political problems, with leisure functioning to provide *identity formation, representations of solidarity,* and *control* and *resistance* within consumer culture. Previous theoretical perspectives reveal how people are positioned in leisure forms and practices and, most importantly, how power relations permeate motivations and experiences of leisure. Leisure forms must be analysed in the context of risk and active citizenship, yet they are both hedonistic and relaxing.

Rojek maps out an/the 'action approach' to leisure, which is developed and deployed as a heuristic device so as to focus on motivation, location and context. As both context and location are mutually reinforcing, it is important not to privilege either the one or the other, i.e. location privileges the actor's motivations and personal choices, whereas context privileges cultural constraints and traditions that shape leisure. It is therefore essential to Rojek's argument to acknowledge (and theorize) that all social actors are both embodied and emplaced. All people are trapped both existentially and physiologically within decaying bodies, and these and ourselves in turn are placed and positioned in cultural locations and contexts.

Chapter 3, on 'Coding and Representation', draws on Stuart Hall's work which sees the public sphere as encoded by the mass media; social science must deconstruct articulated messages of ideology, particularly ethnocentrism. Chapter 4 describes the importance of the life course in people's biographies and the historical importance of generations. Later chapters deal with the structuralist complaints of action perspectives, namely the latter's failure to theorize power and the processes of class, race and gender. The latter three are conceptualized as regulative mechanisms, although leisure spaces are thought to be more relaxed and less regulated. The axial power circuits of society are relationships between production and consumption and the management of aggression and sexuality. Class power is reconceptualized as predatory strata exercising control over economic resources, whereas oppositional blocks may challenge existing hierarchies, regulation and divisions of the surplus. Rojek deploys Foucault's Janus-faced version of power which can be both liberating and constraining, but naturally the important question is how, when and why this dualism mediates and articulates social networks. Chapter 7 is entitled 'Leisure Functions', and function is recast in the action lexicon to the determinate orientation in leisure practice that arises from the condition of individual embodiment and emplacement in relation to location and context. For Rojek, Pierre Bourdieu's concept of habitus is central. Class and conspicuous consumption represent leisure; leisure practice is a declaration and status-positioning activity, with branding and lifestyle regimes colonizing leisure.

The penultimate chapter of the book, 'Location Principles', is more about the appropriate methodology for researching leisure. If ideological interpellation and position provide the rules and resources for action, leisure researchers are encouraged to focus on the trinity of meaning, form and structure. These three relate to the social regime of power. The two circuits of production and consumption, and aggression and sexuality, constitute the context in which leisure trajectories are pursued. One needs to place cultural and leisure practices into location (places) and contexts (regimes) of power.

The final chapter is aptly named 'Central Problems'. In more Weberian mode Rojek discusses the importance of fact/value distinctions, the need for reflexivity and professional independence, the rationalizing process of McDonaldization and interpretive challenges facing leisure scholars.

In the last of his six books on leisure, Rojek returns to explore yet again the iconic domain assumptions in Leisure Studies: voluntarism, freedom and choice. But he remains an iconoclast: 'One of the attractions of studying leisure is that it addresses people's free-time behaviour. Or to alter the payload of the term in a manner that is more apposite for the central arguments in the book, it explores what people plan and do when they believe themselves to be free' (Rojek, 2010a: 1). Drawing on sociology's interest in the processes of individualization, clearly articulated in the works of Giddens (1991), Beck (Beck and Beck-Gernsheim, 2002) and Bauman (2005), Rojek too gains his inspiration from social psychology, with the concepts of emotional intelligence and emotional labour which, as was pointed out at the beginning of this chapter, he believes are pivotal concepts for any analysis of contemporary leisure forms and practice.

But Rojek maintains that there are real differences in respect to freedom, choice and life satisfaction – these three are qualities of citizenship enmeshed in cultural codes, rendering them attractive and desired characteristics in the conduct of life, and, importantly, relate to how they are represented in relation to power and 'governmentality', a concept closely linked to Foucault's discourses about medicine, penology and the history of ideas.

The next chapters of the book evaluate the idealized landscape of the leisure society thesis, articulated in the 1970s. Rojek demands that Leisure Studies rethink concepts in relation to globalization, deregulation, emotional intelligence and emotional labour. The traditional formations of modernity – grounded in markets, state and society – have been shifted by globalization, new social movements and environmental challenges. One topic neglected by leisure scholars has been the growth of global corporate power, and Rojek spends some time spelling out the cultural significance of 'neat capitalism', which offers smart, 'stateless' solutions to pressing social, cultural and political questions. These conglomerates are headed by celebrity moral entrepreneurs who, learning the lessons from the 1960s cultural revolution, speak up for the 'silent majority' who have been messed around by the nanny state. With lifestyle branding strategies and access to web and social networking sites on the Internet, leisure practices emphasize emotional intelligence with both coaching and counselling opportunities for both legitimate and illicit leisure, such as pornography, illegal downloading of intellectual property and drug abuse.

The subsequent chapters go over more ground – the deregulation of leisure lifestyles during the 1980s, with the corrosive postmodern challenges to traditional structuralist meta-narratives, and next the roots of modern individualized leisure in the 1880s with 'muscular Christian' visions of rational recreation and healthy well-being. Another chapter re-examines the separate competing paradigms within Leisure Sciences and Leisure Studies, and their diverse methodological research traditions. Rojek argues that the eclecticism of his balanced 'action approach' offers leisure scholars the way out of the paradigmatic jam. The next chapter, on the state, seeks to translate emotional intelligence and emotional labour in the realm of citizenship and civil society and Rojek proceeds to compare corporations that sell unhealthy leisure (e.g. cigarettes and alcohol) with 'neat capitalism' that acknowledges that social responsibility and environmental awareness are central to progressive business practice. The final chapter challenges the simple syllogism that less work means more leisure and more leisure means more freedom. Leisure is a regime, not a vacuum for voluntarism. To quote Rojek's last lines:

> Leisure is a school for life. The end of schooling is to maintain and enhance competence, relevance and credibility. The successful attainment of this end requires perpetual emotional intelligence and emotional labour. Freedom is for the birds.
>
> (Rojek, 2010a: 176)

Conclusion

This chapter has sought to provide a review of Rojek's key ideas and arguments. It cannot do justice to the complexity and diversity of his work, nor to its sheer weight, embedded in various international journals. Over the past three decades Rojek has developed theoretical debates around interpreting and understanding postmodern cultures and their possible relevance for leisure. Rojek occupies a decisive place in Leisure Studies, since he has consistently sought to establish a sociology of leisure with its roots buried in cultural studies.

Notes

1   The Council for National Academic Awards operated from 1965 to 1992.
2   The Quality Assurance Agency (for Higher Education) was established in 1997.
3   The Research Assessment Exercise, conducted every five years. The last report appeared in 2008.
4   See in his later book, *Leisure and Culture* (Rojek, 2000).
5   See, for example, his response 'On a Rant by a Little Musketeer: A Reply to Bill Schwarz' (Rojek, 2005b).
6   See, for example, his guest article 'Leisure and Emotional Intelligence' and the varied commentaries by international academics in *World Leisure Journal 52* (4) 240–278 (2010b).
7   For example, his substantial contributions to leisure handbooks such as Jackson and Burton (1999); Jackson and Burton (1989); Rojek (1989a); Rojek (2010b); Rojek, Shaw, and Veal (2006).
8   See Hobsbawm and Ranger's (1983) compilation about 'invented traditions' in the UK, Europe, India and Africa.

9 See arguments of an 'early' and 'late' Marx in Althusser and Balibar (1970) and of Bauman Mark 1 and Mark 2 in Blackshaw (2005).
10 As mentioned in his Acknowledgement, 'This is the first book I have written in the congenial circumstances of the Theory, Culture and Society Centre at Nottingham Trent University' (Rojek, 2000: viii).

References

Aitchison, C. (2000) 'Poststructural Feminist Theories for Representing Others: A Response to the Crisis in the Leisure Studies Discourse', *Leisure Studies 19* (3) 127–144.

Althusser, L., and Balibar, E. (1970) *Reading 'Capital'* (B. Brewster, trans.). London: New Left Books.

Appadurai, A. (1990) 'Disjuncture and Difference in the Global Cultural Economy', in M. Featherstone (ed.) *Global Culture, Nationalism, Globalization and Modernity* (pp. 295–310). London: Sage.

Bauman, Z. (1987) *Legislators and Interpreters: On Modernity, Post-Modernity, and Intellectuals*. Cambridge: Polity Press.

Bauman, Z. (1988) 'Is there a Postmodern Sociology?', *Theory, Culture and Society 5* (2/3) 217–237.

Bauman, Z. (1991) *Modernity and Ambivalence*. Cambridge: Polity.

Bauman, Z. (1992) *Intimations of Postmodernity*. London: Routledge.

Bauman, Z. (2005) *Liquid Life*. Cambridge: Polity.

Beck, U., and Beck-Gernsheim, E. (2002) *Individualization: Institutionalized Individualism and its Social and Political Consequences* (P. Camiller, trans., 2001). London, Thousand Oaks, New Dehli: Sage.

Blackshaw, T. (2005) *Zygmunt Bauman*. London and New York: Routledge.

Blackshaw, T. (2012) 'The Man from Leisure: An Interview with Chris Rojek' *Cultural Sociology 26* (1) 1–17.

Bramham, P. (2002) 'Rojek, the Sociological Imagination and Leisure', *Leisure Studies 21* (3/4) 221–234.

Bramham, P. (2006) 'Hard and Disappearing Work: Making Sense of the Leisure Project', *Leisure Studies 25* (4) 379–390.

Clarke, J., and Critcher, C. (1985) *Devil Makes Work: Leisure in Capitalist Britain*. Basingstoke: Macmillan Press.

Coalter, F. (1999) 'Leisure Sciences and Leisure Studies: The Challenge of Meaning', in E. Jackson and T. Burton (eds) *Leisure Studies: Prospects for the Twenty-First Century* (pp. 507–519). State College, PA: Venture Publishing, Inc.

Doyal, L. and Gough, I. (1991) *A Theory of Human Need*. Basingstoke: Macmillan.

Dunning, E., and Rojek, C. (1992) *Sport and Leisure in the Civilizing Process: Critique and Counter-Critique*. Basingstoke: Macmillan.

Foucault, M. (1983) 'The Subject and Power', in H. Dreyfus and P. Rabinow (eds) *Michel Foucault: Beyond Structuralism and Hermeneutics*. Chicago: Chicago University Press.

Giddens, A. (1984) *Constitution of Society: Outline of the Theory of Structuration*. Cambridge: Polity Press.

Giddens, A. (1991) *Modernity and Self-Identity*. Cambridge: Polity Press.

Giddens, A. (1999) 'Runaway World' [Radio Podcast], *Reith Lectures*. UK: BBC.

Hobsbawm, E., and Ranger, T. (eds) (1983) *The Invention of Tradition*. Cambridge: Cambridge University Press.

Jackson, E., and Burton, T. (eds) (1999) *Leisure Studies: Prospects for the Twenty-First Century*. State College, PA: Venture Publishing, Inc.

Jackson, E. L., and Burton, T. L. (1989) *Understanding Leisure and Recreation: Mapping the Past, Charting the Future*. State College, PA: Venture Publishing.

Mills, C. W. (1970) *The Sociological Imagination*. Harmondsworth: Penguin.

Mommaas, H., van der Poel, H., Bramham, P., and Henry, I. (eds) (1996) *Leisure Research in Europe: Methods and Traditions*. Wallingford, Oxford: CAB International.

Rojek, C. (1983) 'Emancipation and Demoralisation: Contradicting Approaches in the Sociology of Leisure', *Leisure Studies 2* (1) 83–96.

Rojek, C. (1985) *Capitalism and Leisure Theory*. London and New York: Tavistock.

Rojek, C. (1989a) 'Leisure and Recreation Theory', in E. Jackson and T. Burton (eds) *Understanding Leisure and Recreation* (pp. 69–88). State College, PA: Venture Publishing.

Rojek, C. (1989b) *Leisure for Leisure: Critical Essays*. Basingstoke: Macmillan.

Rojek, C. (1993) *Ways of Escape: Modern Transformations in Leisure and Travel*. Basingstoke: Macmillan.

Rojek, C. (1995) *Decentring Leisure*. London: Sage Publications.

Rojek, C. (2000) *Leisure and Culture*. Basingstoke: Macmillan.

Rojek, C. (2001a) *Celebrity*. London: Reaktion.

Rojek, C. (2001b) 'Leisure and Life Politics', *Leisure Sciences 23*: 115–125.

Rojek, C. (2002) *Stuart Hall*. Oxford: Polity.

Rojek, C. (2004) *Frank Sinatra*. Cambridge: Polity Press.

Rojek, C. (2005a) *Leisure Theory: Principles and Practice*. Basingstoke: Palgrave Macmillan.

Rojek, C. (2005b) 'On a Rant by a Little Musketeer: A Reply to Bill Schwarz', *International Journal of Cultural Studies 8* (4) 486–503.

Rojek, C. (2005c) 'An Outline of the Action Theory to Leisure Studies', *Leisure Studies 25* (1) 13–25.

Rojek, C. (2007) *Brit-Myth: Who Do the British Think They Are?* London: Reaktion Books.

Rojek, C. (2010a) *The Labour of Leisure: The Culture of Free Time*. London: Sage Publications.

Rojek, C. (2010b) 'Leisure and Emotional Intelligence', *World Leisure Journal 52* (4) 240–252.

Rojek, C. (2010c) *Leisure Studies*. Los Angeles, CA: Sage.

Rojek, C. (2011a) *Pop Music, Pop Culture*. Cambridge: Polity.

Rojek, C. (2011b) *Popular Music*. Los Angeles; London: Sage.

Rojek, C. (2012) *Fame Attack: The Inflation of Celebrity and Its Consequences*. London: Bloomsbury Academic.

Rojek, C., and Turner, B. (2000) 'Decorative Sociology: Towards a Critique of the Cultural Turn', *Sociological Review 48* (4) 629–648.

Rojek, C., Shaw, S., and Veal, A. (eds) (2006) *A Handbook of Leisure Studies*. Basingstoke: Palgrave Macmillan.

Tomlinson, A. (1989) 'Whose Side Are They On? Leisure Studies and Cultural Studies in Britain', *Leisure Studies 8*: 97–106.

Urry, J. (1990) *The Tourist Gaze*. London: Sage.

Urry, J. (1995) *Consuming Places*. London: Routledge.

15

TWO SOCIOLOGISTS

Pierre Bourdieu and Zygmunt Bauman

Tony Blackshaw

Introduction

The sociology of Pierre Bourdieu, the great social theorist of *Distinction* (Bourdieu, 1984), has always made a consistent appeal to leisure scholars. He is one of the most studied sociologists in Leisure Studies, and his 'theory of practice' (Bourdieu, 1977) is widely taught on undergraduate and postgraduate courses. And to a remarkable extent he has become Leisure Studies' key sociologist. This is hardly surprising, since throughout his academic career he undertook numerous studies – taste, high culture, symbolic rivalry, photography, sport, education, *skholē* – so as to raise some compelling questions relating to the study of leisure. In marked contrast, the sociology of Zygmunt Bauman has until recently largely been ignored in Leisure Studies. This should not surprise us either, since he is not a leisure scholar. On the face of it there could hardly be a greater contrast than between the two key thinkers. On the one hand, Bourdieu's Gallic, empirically informed social theory which brings myriad notions to bear for leisure scholars to apply in their own studies. On the other, Bauman's Polish-British, desk-based sociological hermeneutics that simply demands of its readers that they be alert to 'the continuous and changing aspects of life strategies [which should always be traced] back to the social figurations they serve (in a dialectic process of reciprocal determination) – and forward, to the patterns of daily life in which they find expression' (Bauman, 1992: 11). But the two key thinkers are not altogether dissimilar: both are trying in their own inimitable ways to offer a way of thinking sociologically that is made to the measure of a world in which the rationalization of objects (and human subjects) through standardization, abstraction and Fordist mass production has been superseded by a world of rationalization through cultural difference, reflexive individualization and consumerism. This observation notwithstanding, it is the central argument of this chapter that Zygmunt Bauman is the more important, challenging and useful of the two sociologists for understanding leisure in contemporary societies. In order to substantiate this critique, the final third of the chapter offers a discussion of my various applications of Bauman's work, and especially the theory of liquid leisure (Blackshaw, 2010). The preceding section identifies and discusses Bauman's specific way of thinking sociologically about leisure. The chapter begins by outlining Bourdieu's key ideas and how these have been applied to leisure, before exposing the limits of his sociology for Leisure Studies.

Pierre Bourdieu: the triumvirate of field, habitus and capital

Like Adorno (see Chapter 9 in this volume), Bourdieu is critical of the economic determinism found in the more unsophisticated versions of Marxist analyses of leisure. His thinking requires that we move towards a more general theory of social inequality in consumer-based societies where social classes are 'united by the way they spend their money, not the way they earn it' (Bauman, 1988: 36). In this sense, Bourdieu's social theory of *Distinction* is an explicit attempt to understand the nature of social class and social class divisions in a complex world in which production has largely given way to consumption. Accordingly, he offers what is essentially a treatise on taste. For Bourdieu (1984), social class, like gender and 'race', needs to be understood as much by its *perceived* existence as through its *material* existence in the classical Marxist sense. To make this synthesis he draws on a theoretical toolkit featuring the concepts of field, habitus and capital.

Fields reflect the various social, cultural, economic and political arenas of life, which form their own microcosms of power endowed with their own rules. Leisure is structured in this way. Power struggles emerge in leisure fields as a result of the belief of social actors that the capital(s) of the field are worth fighting for. To draw on one example, the question is not just whether Italian opera is superior to Chinese opera, but also 'the series of institutions, rules, rituals, conventions, categories, designations, appointments and titles' which constitute the objective hierarchy of opera 'and which produce certain discourses and activities' (Webb, Schirato and Danaher, 2002: 21–22). Analogous to fluctuations in the stock market, the 'currency' or rates of exchange attached to particular capitals in particular fields are also vulnerable to change, as these are continually contested.

In order to synthesize the relationship between the individual and society, or more precisely, his or her relationship with a highly differentiated consumer world constituted by these fields of power, Bourdieu draws on Marcel Mauss's use of the concept of habitus. Bourdieu (2000) suggests that the habitus is an embodied internalized schema which is both structured by and structuring of social actors' practices, attitudes and dispositions. The habitus also constitutes and is constituted by social actors' practical sense of knowing the world and it is through their 'feel for the game' of the leisure field in question – in our example the world of opera – that they come to see that world and the position of themselves and others in that world as unexceptional. Vital to understanding this 'perfect coincidence' is the idea of the social actor's *doxa* values or 'doxic relation' to that field and world, which Bourdieu identifies with that tacitly cognitive and practical sense of knowing what can and cannot be reasonably achieved. In this sense, the *habitus* constitutes only an 'assumed world', captured as it is through the confines of the individual social actor's 'horizon of possibilities' (Lane, 2000: 194).

In leisure, the practices, attitudes and dispositions which social actors both adopt and embody ultimately depend on the extent to which they can position themselves in any given field and their particular 'endowment of capital'. For Bourdieu, a capital

> is any resource effective in a given social arena that enables one to appropriate the specific profits arising out of participation and contest in it. Capital comes in three principal species: economic (material and financial assets), cultural (scarce symbolic goods, skills, and titles), and social (resources accrued by virtue of membership in a group). A fourth species, symbolic capital, designates the effects of any form of capital when people do not perceive them as such ... The position of any individual, group, or

institution, in social space may thus be charted by two coordinates, the *overall volume and the composition of the capital* they detain.

(Wacquant, 1998: 221)

What this suggests is that 'the profits of membership' offered by leisure are not available to everybody in the same way. This is because, as Ball (2003: 4) asserts, the point of all 'capitals' is that they are resources to be *exploited* and it is their exclusivity in the battle for distinction that gives them their value. In other words, people who realize their own capital through their leisure interests do so specifically because others are excluded.

Bourdieu explains this process through his theory of cultural capital, which identifies the forms of value associated with culturally authorized consumption patterns and tastes. Bourdieu identifies three separate strands of cultural capital – (1) *incorporated*, which is seen as indistinguishable from habitus and confined to the embodied experiences and knowledge of class groups across the life span; (2) *objectivated*, which is independent of individuals and located in material culture and its value in the market-place; and (3) *institutionalized*, which is located within establishment structures, such as appointments, titles, awards and so on, and their implicit and explicit relations of power. Despite their distinctions, these different forms of cultural capital should be seen as co-existing within specific cultural fields defined by their own institutions, conventions and dispositions.

According to Bourdieu, social capital, like cultural capital, has two decisive features: on the one hand, it is a tangible resource made by advantage of social networks, and on the other, it has a symbolic dimension, which contrives to hide networks of power woven into the fibres of familiarity. In the event, Bourdieu's understanding of capital suggests that it is related to the extent, quality and quantity of social actors' networks *and* their ability to mobilize these, which is always governed by the mutual understanding that any given leisure field is an arena of struggle and it is the battle for distinction that gives capital its qualities. The upshot of this 'battle for distinction' is that it ends up symbolically approving the leisure interests of the most powerful, e.g. opera, ballet, classical music etc., and disapproving those of the weakest groups, e.g. shopping, sport, pop music etc. What this tells us is that the world of leisure is made up of different sites of symbolic rivalry. As Skeggs (2009) argues, the battle for distinction in leisure is also often accompanied with 'a gaze', or a 'look that could kill', that embodies a symbolic reading of who has and who hasn't the right to certain kinds of leisure, and which makes those who are perceived as unworthy feel 'out of place'. This is what Bourdieu calls symbolic violence.

Embodiment, symbolic violence and leisure

One of Bourdieu's major themes in this regard is people struggling with their own embodiment, with the fact of having bodies in the modern sense. If how a body looks makes some individuals happy, it can also make others unhappy with their bodies, particularly when they feel that they fail to match the social norm. This can persuade some individuals to pretend that things are not as they are or encourage them to pursue leisure pursuits which will give them a better 'look'. It can also lead some individuals to follow conventions which, while they complement some bodies, must be stretched over others; this can also lead to a situation where those (deviants) who contravene the social norm are over-identified with and through their bodily 'look' and deportment. In other words, and as Bourdieu would say, violence is exercised upon individuals in symbolic rather than in physical ways.

166

Symbolic violence is the non-physical, emotional violence which is exercised upon individuals with their complicity that plays a key role in underlining the socially reproductive nature of the status quo (Bourdieu, 1989). Individuals are represented as the reproducers of 'objective meaning' who 'do not, strictly speaking, know what they are doing that what they do has more meaning than they know' (Bourdieu, 1977: 79). Symbolic violence works to ensure the reproduction of class and gender *dispositions* and the habituses *most* advantageous for maintaining the order of things. In other words, symbolic violence is one of the tools which enables the activator class to impose a *cultural arbitrary* as an arbitrary power – it does this by making class and other inequalities seem both natural and necessary.

As Blackshaw and Long (2005) argue, put directly in terms of leisure policy, symbolic violence has the larger effect of normalizing the marginality of the weakest groups, who are treated as inferior and denied the kind of trust that they could manage public resources for themselves. This in turn not only limits their opportunities for social mobility but also 'naturalizes' their inadequacy, since how they see and experience the world is not taken into account. This delineation of the world, as Bourdieu writes, works thus:

> Like a club founded on the active exclusion of undesirable people, the fashionable neighbourhood symbolically consecrates its inhabitants by allowing each one to partake of the capital accumulated by the inhabitants as a whole. Likewise, the stigmatised area symbolically degrades its inhabitants, who, in return, symbolically degrade it. Since they don't have all the cards necessary to participate in the various social games, the only thing they share is their common excommunication. Bringing together on a single site a population homogeneous in its dispossession strengthens that dispossession, notably with respect to culture and cultural practices: the pressures exerted at the level of class or school or in public life by the most disadvantaged or those furthest from a 'normal' existence pull everything down in a general levelling. They leave no escape other than flight toward other sites (which lack of resources usually renders impossible).
>
> (Bourdieu, 1999: 129)

In the event, the most powerful groups in society maintain their positions in the social hierarchy with the aid of not only economic capital, but also the social and cultural capital embodied in their leisure lifestyles: a combination of earning power and superior taste. On top of that, the most vulnerable groups tend to be blamed for their own misfortune, since it is presumed that they lack the right social and cultural resources to determine their own lives, which in turn encourages the superior 'us' to determine what is appropriate for the inferior 'them' (Blackshaw and Long, 2005).

From social class to leisure lifestyles

Such has been Bourdieu's influence in Leisure Studies that in the mid-1980s some scholars began to argue that social class is becoming less significant to understanding leisure behaviour than individual lifestyle choices centred on patterns of consumption based on youth, gender and ethnicity. However, as Veal (2001) points out, there soon emerged a resistance to the use of the concept, mainly based on the idea that leisure lifestyles may change but social classes and their identities remain essentially the same (as coal and diamond are essentially always carbon) (e.g. Critcher, 1989). However, such accounts tended to gloss the changed climatic conditions of advanced capitalism, finding it difficult to reimagine 'workers' recast as 'consumers' – they merely saw workers consuming – who were increasingly able to occupy the place of consumption in new and imaginative ways through their leisure interests and activities.

During the 1990s the concept of leisure lifestyles continued to grow in significance, especially with more and more people rejecting lives made to the measure of social class – and even to some extent age, gender and ethnicity – for those which they perceived did not restrict other potential outlets for credulity. Leisure lifestyles today are thus seen by Bourdieu as the practical expression of the symbolic dimension of class relations based on consumption rather than production. In this view, leisure lifestyles have little to do with other significant aspects of our sense of social self either, such as national identity – except during major international sports tournaments such as the association football or rugby union world cups – rather, they are seen as identikits constructed and facilitated by global flows of consumer products and culture. The upshot is that rather than seeing leisure lifestyles as being unable to provide the kinds of stable identities associated with social class or work, leisure scholars have to come to grips with the idea that there has emerged a new kind of society – what some leisure scholars call postmodernity (see Rojek, 1995) – in which there is an increasing recognition of the notion of the quick-fix self-effacement and re-assembly, rather than some gradually shrinking, fading away, ultimately disappearing notion of fixity. In this view, the adoption of a new leisure lifestyle, then – we must accept – is often nothing more (and nothing less either) than something more, hopefully much more, potentially exciting, empowering than the last one.

The limits of Bourdieu

Bourdieu did not pursue the opportunity to apply this kind of reconceptualization of leisure lifestyles in his own work. In this regard he remained firmly within the Marxist tradition of foregrounding 'structure' at the expense of 'agency'. This has led Alexander to argue that his 'theory of practice' is 'nothing other than a theory of the determination of practice' (Alexander, 1995: 140)

Another recurring criticism of Bourdieu is that although he offers novel theories of cultural capital, social capital and body capital (embodiment), economic capital is taken for granted and remains essentially unanalysed in his sociology (Callinicos, 1999). Notwithstanding his considerable contribution to contemporary social theory, Bourdieu's re-reading of capital, arguably, supports the neoliberal argument that social inequality is not so much material (lack of money), but virtual (lack of opportunities).

A third criticism of Bourdieu is that his sociology is reductionist, deterministic and tautologous, since its overriding focus is on social stability rather than social change. 'Objective structures ... are somehow given as "cultural arbitraries", which the actions of embodied agents then reproduce' (Jenkins, 1992: 82). As Rancière explains this leads to 'a theory of the *necessary* misrecognition of social relations as the very mechanism of their reproduction' (Swenson, 2006: 642). In other words, by posing social inequality and the class divisions synonymous with social reproduction as the primary fact that needs to be explained, Bourdieu ends up explaining its necessity. In Bourdieu's sociology it would appear that individuals are all too willing to slip into the leisure identities imposed on them from above. As Rancière explains in his critique of Bourdieu's sociology as it relates to working class leisure through the life course:

> The empire of tautology; the empire of leisure. It alone creates bourgeois distance
> from the world, the 'disinterested' exercise of school, feminine investment in home

168

decorating, and half-idle, half-revolted aestheticism of the inheritor spoiled by his mother's idleness ... Like the democratic man in Plato, the adolescent smitten with the blending colors and the wanderings of insatiable leisure was the son of the industrious oligarch. The sociologist of *Distinction* only hints at his sceptical thought, that there may be no other struggles than conflicts between generations. Since *The Inheritors*, he continues his settling of scores with the same character: the inheritor who in 1964 revealed in his critique of the institution the essence of school leisure; the rebellious student who in 1970 imagined he had 'unveiled' the system while it fell to the sociologist to display its new veils. In *Distinction*, the mocking eye of the master finds him gain, older and stale, *déclassé* and aspiring to reranking [*reclassement*] through his feats in the great simile industry of the new petty bourgeoisie: the manufacture of junk jewelry or sale of symbolic services; the commerce of youth leaders, marriage counsellors, sex therapists, advertising executives, or dieticians determined to create within people the symbolic need necessary for the enlargement of their market, hence for the reconquest of their inheritance.

(Rancière, 2004: 192–193)

In other words, in Bourdieu's sociology, leisure practices have consistently been understood through their necessary misrecognition. In his obsession with imposing his own grand narrative, Bourdieu ends up with a thesis of the 'working class' with neither the leisure to think of itself in other ways (Rancière, 2004) nor alternative ways of thinking about leisure other than those imposed on them by the theorist of *Distinction*. What this suggests is that issues of self-actualization and critical self-reflection for 'working class' individuals remain largely unaddressed in Bourdieu's work. What this also means is that his sociology is limited ontologically, in the sense that it ignores the fact that *all* modern men and women are existentially individuals for whom being is itself also the performing of distinction.

There is much leisure research that demonstrates that, notwithstanding the social, economic and political context in which individuals find themselves, they will always find ways of resisting the status quo, and that this often occurs through their leisure. An example that illustrates this to good effect is Blackshaw and Crabbe's (2004) discussion of car cruising, which demonstrates how heterotopias – Foucault's (1984b) term for those sequestered places in which normal social structuring is contested and subverted – operate in modern societies. Blackshaw and Crabbe argue that car cruising is a 'deviant' leisure activity with its own kind of detached existence, of being 'in' but not 'of' the space it temporarily occupies, and which is capable of transforming ordinary life into a form of theatre. They also contend that car cruising is a 'deviant' leisure activity as much without a history as it is one without a future and that car cruises are imaginary communities, whose inspiration tends to spring from the performativity of individual cruisers: they are both events for consumption and things to be consumed by. The affiliation found at cruises is not really one of friendship, or of a community proper, but one of symbiosis, and its only glue is cruisers' insatiable appetites to connect with like-minded others.

Building on this critique, Rojek and Blackshaw (Chapter 46, this volume) argue that the bearing of 'generative principles' (Bourdieu, 1977) that produce and reproduce the social practices underpinning leisure choices in the contemporary societies is of a different order in the contemporary world than those suggested by Bourdieu. In other words, they call into question Bourdieu's tacit assumption that social structures are deeply incorporated into individuals' 'dispositions' in such a way that we can anticipate what their leisure choices are going to be over time. As they point out, drawing on the work of Bauman, liquid modern consumers prefer to wear the more informal gear of *habitat* rather than the more regimental class uniform of *habitus*. Whereas habitus is uncomplicated in the sense that it is relatively fixed because it is pre-determined by social class location, the habitat is 'a space of chaos and chronic *indeterminacy*' ... which is a schema of self-regulation subjected to competing and often contradictory meaning-conferring claims that nonetheless appear equally contingent. The ontological status of liquid moderns is for this reason not one of 'durably installed generative practices' (Bourdieu, 1977), but of under-determination, liquefaction and rootlessness.

Zygmunt Bauman and liquidity

As this last quotation shows, Bauman's work is much more alert than Bourdieu's to social contingency. This observation is reflected in his sociology, which does not in any way or form represent a particular school of thought, as in Elias's figurationalism (see Malcolm, Mansfield and Hughes, Chapter 11 in this volume). On the contrary, Bauman's sociology is full of arbitrary riches rather than engineered instruction – there are no lesson plans in the pages or in their arrangement. Bauman's books enable the reader to read dispositionally rather than methodically – he does not offer a toolkit in the way that Bourdieu does – and you build, rather, a sense of his current interests, the habits of his mind and the associative trails these take, the fragments, the jolts, new beginnings and the revisitings, in each new piece of work.

It needs to be grasped from that outset that the aim of Bauman's sociology is not to reconstruct 'the classical foundation texts of sociology as building blocks for his own comprehensive social theory' in the manner of Habermas (Pusey, 1987: 26) or to provide it with some 'new rules of sociological method' vis-à-vis Giddens (1976). Instead, Bauman merely wants to better reconcile sociology with the way in which the already existing reality actually is, but in a way that, if it needs to be 'a theory of contemporary society', is always imbued with the warmth of human life, a warmth that would fade from sociology were it to follow the intellectual trajectories suggested by Habermas and Giddens. Bauman's sociology always has the force of life in it, and to read him is to see that he is forever and always concerned with the ways in which people live today; but more than that, even, he is concerned with everyday human concerns to do with leisure, but also of love and memory and the pain and happiness they bring, the way that people exist in their own minds and the minds of others. For Bauman, being-for-others is the only authentic way a sociologist can work, can live his life. This is why he believes that it is its close attention to humankind's responsibility for the other that should give sociology its thumping heart.

In this regard, Bauman argues that what is most important in this regard is making the familiar seem strange (Bauman, 1990). This is precisely what I do with leisure in my book, which offers its own theory of liquid leisure (Blackshaw, 2010). There is something particularly apposite about the use of 'liquidity' for understanding leisure. The word 'liquid' comes from the root *liquēre* (to be fluid), which refers to substances in a physical state that cannot resist changes to their shape. Used as a metaphor for understanding the contemporary world, it makes significant flow and fluency, movement and mobility, the fragility and flimsiness of social relations, the transparency and the temporary nature of things which modernity in its formative modality 'was bent on solidifying and fixing: of human locations in the social world and inter-human bonds' (Bauman, 2004: 20).

Bauman argues that we have recently seen a shift from a 'heavy' and 'solid', 'hardware-focused' modernity to a 'light' and 'liquid', 'software-based' modernity. What sets liquid modernity apart from solid modernity is that it is a social formation that does not – couldn't, even if it so wanted – resist changes to its shape.[1] And what distinguishes our lives from those of our solid modern counterparts is their openness to change. A liquid modern life, in other words, has no solid ontological status, something that is given, is inevitable, we are pre-disposed to or firmly believe in. Some lives are no doubt more liquid than others, but anyone's identity is just something that is until further notice, or in other words, it seems to fit us as a person who chooses to live this kind of life rather than another. We are also consciously aware that no matter what our current circumstances or how certain we individually feel about their lives at the moment, things could always be different; that, for example, the identity that moves us today might be a different one tomorrow.

A life lived in this way as an individual de facto is what Agnes Heller describes as a 'contingency life', which is the opposite of the kind of life lived in the totality of a class system, for example; men and women who inhabit a contingent world, one in which they are individuals who are wholly contingent, yet make out of that very circumstance their own identities, which they may or may not choose to share with others, become contingent beings by having been stripped of that kind of innocence. As Richard Rorty (2007) suggests, people who think of themselves as contingent know that who we are is merely a matter of contingency, i.e. due to the kind of family they are born into, the city in which they are born, and everything else besides.

Living a liquid modern life, it would seem, means that the habitus into which we are born has less of a constraining influence on our lives than would have been the case even twenty or thirty years ago, which means that it is experienced as *accidental* rather than *inevitable*. Bauman knows of course that liquid modern lives are not completely free of their social class (and gender and ethnic statuses), but he knows that by now these markers of identity and difference flow into each other more than they did once upon a time in the not too distant past. He also knows that today our lives have a more in-between, DIY, ready-made feel about them, and to this extent that they are better understood as *individualized* existences. As Ulrich Beck would say, liquid modern life is best understood as a life of reflexive individualization. This alerts us to the fact that not only are we conscious of our being as individuals and that there is no external categorization powerful enough to compete with that crucial awareness, but also that in searching for some overarching narrative of meaning on which to base our lives, we are more likely to prioritize our own needs at the expense of the needs of others. To summarize, liquid modern life is the one of *Homo viator* – man and woman on the road, modern life as a search for individual meaning, a pilgrimage to the self, a search for a spiritual homeland to which we feel we can belong.

The metaphor of liquidity

Used in the way that Bauman uses it, the metaphor of liquidity is an intellectual device, not a 'thing' in the world (Beilharz, 2010: 58). It is the invocation of a reality under the spell of Bauman's sociological imagination, a world spelled out through the analytical tools that he has at his disposal. In this sense, to paraphrase Simon Critchley (2005), Bauman's sociology is a sort of sorcery, a world transformed in the language he conjures to try to understand it. What this suggests is that his sociology does not so much *reflect* the world as *illuminate* it through the idea of liquidity. In other words, Bauman constructs the world as 'ideal typical' meaning (*ideal types* are not descriptions of reality, but analytical tools that sociologists use to try to understand it). This enables him (and us) to see the world through liquid representation that he has imaginatively posed on it by using this 'ideal type'.

The image of liquidity offers Leisure Studies a fresh way of thinking about the world. This is a way of thinking that depends not on grand theory but, rather, on metaphor, which is the rhetorical tool that enables us to 'defamiliarize the familiar' and show it in a new light (Bauman, 1990). Metaphor is that part of language that enables us to practise hermeneutics. That is, on the one hand, to make meaning, i.e. make intelligible that which could not otherwise be grasped and, on the other hand, to deepen our understanding so as to make meaning even more meaningful, in the process creating some democratic operating principles as we go along. Seen in this way, Bauman presents us with an intellectual device that signals the continuation of *skholē* by an alternative means, which retrains the educated imagination into looking for both similarities and contradictions, in other words, the ambivalence of what we casually call 'reality', and to see significance and meaning in unexpected places.

This metaphorical reconstruction in intellectual work, as Bauman conceives it, is by no means a simple replacement of 'solid' modern by 'liquid' modern considerations: on the contrary, the central tenet of Bauman's sociology is the need to exhort critical analysis to constant juxtaposition. Bauman recognizes that thinking is unsurpassed when we juxtapose, when we recognize the value of bringing opposites together, when we realize that two 'realities', one posed next to the other, are in one way or another connected.

As the Wittgenstein scholar Peter Hacker (2010) points out, questions about 'what it is like to be something' require contrasts in order to make sense. In other words, when we ask 'what is it like to be liquid modern?' there is a requirement that there be a juxtaposition, and once there is, all sorts of stories are likely to follow. From this shuttling between 'solid' and 'liquid' – concepts as magic wands in and of themselves which illuminate, with an almost miraculous precision, our way of thinking by maximizing contrast – it is possible to weave a larger fabric, a sustained deliberation on some key themes, to be precise, a picture of an always unrestful modernity. What this shuttling between concepts also means is that there is a requirement to recognize that we find ourselves in a world at once strange and yet strangely familiar. *Knowing these two things at the same time is essential to understanding leisure today.*

Seeing leisure differently: the leisure life-world of 'the lads'

What should be patently obvious by now is that Bauman is a key part of my own discovery of perspective, and he gives me a particular kind of sociology that I can think with. Accordingly, in my book *Leisure Life* (Blackshaw, 2003) I make full use of the liquid metaphor in order to understand 'the lads'' leisure lives. The thesis is developed through a hermeneutic approach to make knowable the leisure life-world of a group of working-class 'lads' with whom I had grown up. This meant that the study was about their leisure life-world, my leisure life-world, but also our leisure life-world. Consequently, as a researcher I occupied a strange dual position in 'the lads'' universe – Tony Blackshaw as an insider and Tony Blackshaw the researcher as an outsider on the inside. I used this special position to not only make sense of how 'the lads' live their leisure lives, but also allow the reader to know how they and we *feel* that collective experience, individually together.

The crux of my thesis is that 'the lads' may not live in solid modernity any more – likely never have – but their collective consciousness still dwells there and the universe that is their leisure life-world is framed by a solid modern discourse, or so it seems. Even though the wider world which they individually inhabit has become liquid modern, in their leisure lives 'the lads' are still animated by their belief in an imagined community which is perceived as the cornerstone of their shared masculine, working-class existence. My central argument is that it is this shared passion for a solid modern, missing world, sometimes proudly resurrected and celebrated, sometimes merely borne out of the private burden of individuality, which gives this shared leisure life-world its depth. The book charts 'the lads'' intermittent forays into Leeds city centre on Friday and Saturday nights, which constitute a memorable vindication of this missing world. On these nights out 'the lads' do not so much relive their youth as re-create through their leisure its unheroic aftermath. Indeed, although it is the ultimate experience of a solidly modern leisure life that they desire but cannot really capture, it does not deter them from endeavouring to regain the power and certainties of its past, and seeking a realm of mutual happiness that was once upon a time theirs.

Outside the leisure life-world, resignation and disillusionment are the nearest things 'the lads' have to freedom. In the fluidity of *liquid modernity* they have to watch, powerless, as the Other invades, uninvited, their existential and material realms: women controlling their bedrooms and telling them what to do, women and black people taking their jobs, buying their houses, taking over their shops and their schools. But in the leisure life-world 'the lads' are in control. Here the features of the Other begin to elongate and liquefy, swell and then re-solidify; like Jean-Paul Sartre's *le visqueux*, they are transformed into 'the lads'' own DIY, custom-made creations. For example, women as cheerful subjects of their own lives do not exist in the discourse of the leisure life-world. Like the Jewish race in Bauman's *Modern and the Holocaust*, they have to be wiped out from a *solid modern story* in which they have no place, excluded from the leisure world that has created them. These characterizations of the Other become symbols of subjugation, power and knowledge, the luscious fruit of a *solid* leisure life lived in a *solid* version of truth. The 'universal' truth of the rationality which divides 'the lads' and others into two categories: us and them, same and other.

In the leisure life-world 'the lads' have the best of both worlds: they have their myth and are able to relativize it as a *contingent* leisure experience, which has its own monologic. Indeed, the *modus operandi* of 'the lads' leisure together always presumes this form of closure: the conformation of hegemonic masculinity and the restoration of disrupted stability, which provide intimations of a past world of communal bliss in a protected time space in which the leisure life-world attempts to impose the fixity of a masculinist, working-class myth onto the ostensible fluidity of contemporary everyday life.

Yet 'the lads'' apparently granite authenticity isn't at all what it seems. In common with other liquid modern men and women, they find it difficult to remain authentic for long because they simply have too many other choices in their lives. 'The lads' know that the weekend experience of this life-world is just a leisure break; they understand this and are resigned to their fate. In the event, it is only because of its own impossibility that the leisure life-world is possible at all. 'The lads'' may be figures carved in the past, but their identities are maintained in the present and, in common with other liquid modern men and women, they are *individuals* first and all the rest after. In the words of Bauman, it is this observation that represents the 'irreparable and irredeemable ambivalence' of the leisure life-world of 'the lads'.

Devotional leisure practice and the search for authenticity and meaning

Sociology made to the measure of a liquid modern world approaches the study of leisure as it approaches all ideas – and indeed, all human endeavours – by asking not 'What does it mean?' but rather 'What are its uses?' (Blackshaw, 2010). For leisure's meaning lies in how we make use of it. What should be clear from the foregoing discussion of the leisure life-world is that for 'the lads' the real measure of leisure is its ability to evoke the sense that life *really* is like this. This is the relationship between the 'secret centre' of leisure and life itself – a relationship that empowers leisure to a greater feeling of authenticity than ordinary, everyday existence. As my book demonstrates, it is in their leisure that 'the lads' find intimations of authenticity that they fail to find in life itself.

In the work of the existentialist philosopher Martin Heidegger (1962), authenticity is understood as that mode of human being-in-the-world (*Dasein*) of interest to those who wish to explore the existential qualities and possibilities that are uniquely their own as individuals; who cannot ignore the fact that as individuals they are 'thrown' into the world at a certain point in time and space; and who recognize that their existence has a certain distinctiveness that nonetheless transcends simple analysis, description or perception. Heidegger contrasts authenticity with inauthenticity, which is a mode of existence whereby men and women flee from their responsibility to themselves by reducing their lives to the average or the typical.

As Agnes Heller (1999) has argued, to be authentic is not only to reject the risk of alienation caused by inauthenticity, it is a way of remaining 'true to oneself' in order to achieve the single most sublime virtue of modern life. As Heller points out, authentic men and women manage to remain faithful to their choices, they are those kinds of individuals 'who are pulled and not pushed, who are personalities', which means that they are capable of achieving the sort of life as close to perfection as a modern person can get.

It is my contention that in the liquid modern world we live in, which is founded first and foremost on freedom, leisure moves steadily into its position as the principal driving force underpinning the human goal of satisfying our hunger for meaning and our thirst for giving our lives a purpose. This is the job that leisure was always cut out for, since it is that distinct realm of human activity which perhaps more than any other provides us with the thrill of the search for meaning and the exhilaration of its discovery.

To paraphrase what Agnes Heller (1999: 125) has said about culture more generally, with the onset of liquid modernity, the subsidiary, compensatory function of leisure was transformed to an interpretive function. In other words, leisure has become a hermeneutical exercise. That is, leisure has become more and more meaning. In liquid modernity, then, it is hermeneutics that deepens the meaning of leisure. It is meaning, the appeal to the *unknown known* that places *my* leisure interest at the top of the modern hierarchy of culture. It is placed high by me because it has the potential to serve for infinite interpretability – as well as giving me pleasure and happiness – again and again. In liquid modernity leisure performs a key function, then: the function of rendering meaning.

This is leisure which is an ideal pursuit and a rich source of personal and collective identity that signifies obligation, responsibility and, especially, desire. Hermeneutics presupposes that there is *something* about the leisure pertaining to our chosen devotional practice that cannot be disciplined – its 'secret centre' (its unknown known). We know that active commitment to our chosen devotional leisure practice is our duty, but its secret centre is beyond interpretation; we do not know, cannot know about its secret; rather, we *feel* its warm glow, we *sense* it. Yet knowing all this does not stop us trying to find its secret centre.[2] This is the ambivalence of devotional leisure practice. When men and women choose leisure in this way they do so with a sense of feeling, as though it were something holy, as though engaging in it were a religious function. There is more to leisure, this attitude would seem to suggest, than mere leisure pursuits; it is to live one's life in a certain way. In other words, what draws people to devotional leisure practice is, on the one hand, the hope of finding out its secret and, on the other, the promise of meaning – not to find out what our chosen leisure pursuit's secret means but the lure of the meaning of life itself.

174

What I have in mind when I use the term leisure as a devotional practice is something resembling the art of life. Foucault (1984a) suggested that a life freely chosen should use art; it is a necessity for an authentic life, not something to be admired for its aesthetic qualities. Art (and we would say leisure) should be plundered for new ideas about how to live – the 'art of life', as well as inspiration, moral lessons, comfort, and tales of the lives of others and how these might inform how we might live ourselves. Bauman (2008) goes one step further than Foucault, to suggest that because the principal force underpinning human life today is deregulation, the accelerating liquefaction of life and the shifting of social responsibilities onto individual shoulders, the art of life is the way that we all have no choice but to live now. In my view, leisure is the site par excellence of this *Bildung* (personal education), which, when practised in the way of *skholē*, acquires an artistic quality, which is also complemented by a certain ethical dimension.

To embrace the art of life is to recognize one's individual freedom. Implicit to this, as I have suggested already, is the recognition that individuals alone are responsible for their own lives; and that they can reach beyond who they are presently, because their identity, which is destined to remain forever incomplete, is a work in progress – one life, many identities. The choice to live one's life as a work of art indicates being prepared to reject the authority of former modes of existence; it also means being prepared to cope with the insecurity of a hitherto untried ontological status.

All of this would seem to suggest that the art of living is intractably an individual concern. However, once an individual recognizes the fact that she can live an authentic life, she also recognizes that, as an individual, she herself is the foundation of all values – as Agnes Heller points out, freedom itself is entirely unfit to serve this function because it is a foundation that cannot found – which also means that she is inseparable from all others, because her free choice of values determines the conditions under which others themselves choose. It is on this basis of interdependent responsibility for the self and the Other that the art of living prospers as a universalizable ethical mode of existence. It is through the art of living that the individual has the potential to be his or her own completed self, nothing less than an individual world – each individual separate and unique but still bound to one another through the felt presence of their shared humanity. This is an integral part of what the Greeks termed *eudaimonia*, meaning an authentic existence, a flourishing life, the kind of good life that Aristotle saw as the basis of ethics. The art of living, then, is a matter of living your life a certain way, which is both authentic *and* ethical.

Liquid leisure and the search for home

But why obsess with finding an authentic existence or the true life? This type of question, so suggests Hans Zehrer, is the most natural, but also the most fundamental question we can ask ourselves. For this reason it is a question that we hardly ever ask, preferring instead to assume that we know the answer. When someone asks this question, however, we can deduce that something which has hitherto given them security has been broken or has come to an end. When this 'question emerges in the historic course of a given culture, it is a sign that the foundations of the culture have become faulty, and that people are no longer unself-consciously at home in it' (Zehrer, 1952: 28).

In a world where everything is 'liquid', the question that inevitably arises is where we might find a home – a place for meaning. Yet Agnes Heller argues that although modernity is a forever starting-over world without any foundations, life need not result in one of universal homelessness; this is because modernity provides innumerable sites where contingent men and women might find a place to belong (Rundell, 2011). For Heller (2011), there are three ideal types of modern 'home-experience': spatial home-experience (the kind associated with traditional, geographically based communities); temporal home-experience (the kind that Maffesoli [1996] identifies with the 'little masses' of the uncertain and fragmenting liquid modernity, which are bound by perpetual 'disembedding and re-embedding' [Giddens, 1991]); and absolute spirit home-experience.

In my view, the latter is the most homely of liquid modernity's homes, and not only that, but its most homely territory is leisure – not just because it may offer us a personal spiritual experience, where we can find our authentic selves, but because it is a home with a social dimension that brings with it a sense of belonging and obligation to the wider social context (read: friendship, community, respect, responsibility, sincerity, trust, reciprocity, on-going conversation and so on) that makes it possible. In other words, leisure is the most homely of modernity's homes because it is not only an *experience* but also an *activity* – in acting, we actively participate with others in something bigger than ourselves.

Some caveats

As I have argued elsewhere, the trouble is that in the liquid modern society we always seem to be on the verge of moving from one devotional leisure practice to another – individuals choose their leisure; it is no longer the case that their leisure chooses them (Blackshaw, 2010). Men and women appear reluctant to embark on any one devotional leisure practice because of the fear that to give oneself to one kind of life is to close down other opportunities and, crucially, miss out on immediate happiness and pleasures. It turns out that all too often devotion is more of a love affair with the self (and the body, in a performative society like ours) rather than the leisure practice itself.

As Heller points out, the upshot of this is that hermeneutics is, as a result, removed from the continuity of its own tradition. When this happens devotional leisure practices become merely ephemeral points of attraction, which merely *feed* on the actions of others who perform the art of living for us. It would appear that devotional leisure practice in liquid modernity is often, as the philosopher James Carse (1986) would say, continued only for the purpose of continuing the play. Yet what we fail to recognize is that our individual desire to continue the play is only possible precisely because others go on with the game. What this means is that we forget that our entitlement to play (read: leisure) must be counterbalanced with actively taking responsibility for the Other. We also fail to recognize that the self-imposed constraint of learning how to live one's life as a work of art is not a one-off act, but something that needs to be mastered.

All of this is an indication that the art of living *gnothi seauton*, the ancient Greek injunction to 'know thyself', has still to be learned. And so has the yet more difficult art of grooming individuals for such a life. Yet there is available no such counsel that has *universal application* for novice artists of life, who are born free and endowed with endless possibilities, and for whom 'freedom', as the great American poet Wallace Stevens once remarked, 'is like a man who kills himself/ Each night, an incessant butcher, whose knife/ Grows sharp in blood'. Whether the future will be one in which we can individually and collectively make our chosen leisure utopias concrete will ultimately depend on whether or not we novices choose to use our freedom wisely.

Conclusion

This chapter has looked at the relative merits of the sociologies of Zygmunt Bauman and Pierre Bourdieu for Leisure Studies. It has been argued that while Bourdieu is the more studied of the two sociologists, Bauman's work is the more compelling. Where Bourdieu offers Leisure Studies a sociology that is ultimately a social theory of 'the *necessary* misrecognition of social relations as the very mechanism of their reproduction' (Swenson, 2006: 642), Bauman's sociology cracks open the contemporary world as it is in itself to expose the workings of its component parts through the metaphors of solidity and liquidity. In so doing he offers us a sociology for thinking about leisure in new ways. The brief survey of my own applications of Bauman's ideas identified the potential of his work for Leisure Studies. However, the primary aim of this chapter has been to demonstrate that if the true measure of the best sociology is the impossibility of examining and understanding leisure as it is lived just then, at that moment, before the ready-made theories and jargons of sociologists get in the way, but which nonetheless tries to make its subjects live again as well as excite interest in their lives, then Bauman's sociology succeeds better than most.

Notes

1   As Bauman points out: 'All modernity means incessant, obsessive modernization (there is no state of modernity; only a process; modernity would cease being modernity the moment that process ground to a halt)' (2004: 20). The key difference between solid modernity and liquid modernity is that the former was a progressivist, rationally arranged social formation in which its 'solids' – its material and spiritual creations, its legal statutes, its knowledge and beliefs and so on – were melted with the intention of recasting them up to the standard of a once and for all superior design, whereas the latter is a social formation in which this is no longer the case. In liquid modernity all 'solids' are viewed as temporary, to be held 'until further notice', sooner or later melted and recast as new and better versions.

2   We don't just engage in these devotional leisure interests. We want to know their secret, which is both their most convoluted aspect and what makes them most appealing. It is this secret that we want to uncover and which we will never be tired of looking for.

References

Alexander, J. C. (1995) *Fin de Siècle Social Theory: Relativism, Reduction, and the Problem of Reason.* London and New York: Verso.

Ball, S. J. (2003) 'It's Not What You Know: Education and Social Capital', *Sociology Review*, November.

Bauman, Z. (1988) 'Britain's Exit from Politics', *New Statesman and Society*, 29 July.

Bauman, Z. (1990) *Thinking Sociologically*. Oxford: Blackwell.

Bauman, Z. (1992) *Mortality, Immortality and Other Life Strategies*. Cambridge: Polity Press.

Bauman, Z. (2004) 'Liquid Sociality', in N. Gane (ed.) *The Future of Social Theory*. London: Continuum.

Bauman, Z. (2008) *The Art of Life*. Cambridge: Polity Press.

Beilharz, P. (2010) 'Zygmunt Bauman (1925–)' in J. Simons (ed.) *From Agamben to Žižek: Contemporary Critical Theorists*. Edinburgh: Edinburgh University Press.

Blackshaw, T. (2003) *Leisure Life: Myth, Masculinity and Modernity*. London: Routledge.

Blackshaw. T. (2010) *Leisure*. London and New York: Routledge.

Blackshaw, T. and Crabbe, T. (2004) *New Perspectives on Sport and 'Deviance': Consumption, Performativity and Social Control*. Abingdon: Routledge.

Blackshaw, T. and Long, J. (2005) 'What's the Big Idea? A Critical Exploration of the Concept of Social Capital and Its Incorporation into Leisure Policy Discourse', *Leisure Studies* 24 (3) 239–258.

Bourdieu, P. (1977) *Outline of a Theory of Practice*. Cambridge: Cambridge University Press.

Bourdieu, P. (1984) *Distinction: A Social Critique of the Judgment of Taste*. London: Routledge.

Bourdieu, P. (1989) 'Social Space and Symbolic Power', *Sociological Theory* 7 (1) 14–25.

Bourdieu, P. (1999) *The Weight of the World: Social Suffering in Contemporary Society.* Cambridge: Polity Press.

Bourdieu, P. (2000) *Pascalian Meditations.* Cambridge: Polity Press.

Callinicos, A. (1999) 'Social Theory Put to the Test of Politics: Pierre Bourdieu and Anthony Giddens', *New Left Review*, 236: 77–102, July/August.

Carse, J. P. (1986) *Finite and Infinite Games: A Vision of Life as Play and Possibility.* New York: Ballantine.

Critcher, C. (1989) 'A Communication in Response to Leisure, Lifestyle and Status: A Pluralist Framework for Analysis', *Leisure Studies* 8 (2) 159–162.

Critchley, S. (2005) *Things Merely Are.* London: Routledge.

Foucault, M. (1984a) 'On Genealogy of Ethics: An Overview of Work in Progress', in P. Rabinow (ed.) *The Foucault Reader: An Introduction to Foucault's Thought.* Harmondsworth: Penguin.

Foucault, M. (1984b) 'Of Other Spaces (1967), Heterotopias'. Trans. J. Miskowiec. http://foucault. info/documents/heteroTopia/foucault.heteroTopia.en.html.

Giddens, A. (1976) *New Rules of Sociological Method.* London: Hutchinson.

Giddens, A. (1991) *Modernity and Self-Identity: Self and Society in the Late Modern Age.* Cambridge: Polity Press.

Hacker, P. (2010) in J. Garvey, 'Interview with Peter Hacker', *The Philosopher's Magazine 51*, 25 October.

Heidegger, M. (1962) *Being and Time.* Oxford: Blackwell.

Heller, A. (1999) *A Theory of Modernity.* Oxford: Blackwell.

Heller, A. (2011) 'Where Are We at Home?', in J. Rundell (ed.) *Aesthetics and Modernity: Essays by Agnes Heller.* Plymouth: Lexington Books.

Jenkins, R. (1992) *Pierre Bourdieu.* London: Routledge.

Lane, J. F. (2000) *Pierre Bourdieu: A Critical Introduction.* London: Pluto Press.

Maffesoli, M. (1996) *The Time of the Tribes: The Decline of Individualism in a Mass Society.* London: Sage.

Pusey, M. (1987) *Jürgen Habermas.* London: Routledge.

Rancière, J. (2004) *The Philosopher and His Poor.* Durham, NC: Duke University Press.

Rojek, C. (1995) *Decentring Leisure: Rethinking Leisure Theory.* London: Sage.

Rorty, R. (2007) *Philosophy as Cultural Politics: Philosophical Papers Volume 4.* Cambridge: Cambridge University Press.

Rundell, J. (2011) 'Agnes Heller – Modernity, Aesthetics, and the Human Condition: An Interpretive Essay', in J. Rundell (ed.) *Aesthetics and Modernity: Essays by Agnes Heller.* Plymouth: Lexington Books.

Skeggs, B. (2009) 'Haunted by the Spectre of Judgement: Respectability, Value and Affect in Class Relations', in K. P. Sveinsson (ed.) *Who Cares about the White Working Class?* London: Runnymede Trust.

Swenson, J. (2006) 'Jacques Rancière', in L. D. Kritzman (ed.) *The Columbia History of Twentieth-Century French Thought.* New York: Columbia University Press.

Veal, T. (2001) 'Leisure, Culture and Lifestyle', *Loisir et Société/Society and Leisure* 24 (2) 359–376.

Wacquant, L. (1998) 'Pierre Bourdieu', in R. Stones (ed.) *Key Sociological Thinkers.* Basingstoke: Macmillan.

Webb, J., Schirato, T. and Danaher, G. (2002) *Understanding Bourdieu.* London: Sage.

Zehrer, H. (1952) *Man in This World.* London: Hodder and Stoughton.

16
WHAT THEY DID ON THEIR HOLIDAYS
Virilio, Baudrillard, Leisure Studies and post-theory

Steve Redhead

This chapter considers the past and potential future contribution to international Leisure Studies of two key theorists, Paul Virilio and Jean Baudrillard. Although pursuing different furrows ever since they first began to write, or photograph, Virilio and Baudrillard were friends and colleagues for many years until Baudrillard died from cancer in March 2007. Virilio is very much alive, and still writing his provocative, pithy, short books. Baudrillard, or 'post-Baudrillard' as we might describe recent ventures, lives on in some very significant books which were written in the last couple of years of his life and published posthumously. Together, over a long period since the 1950s, Baudrillard and Virilio have a huge back catalogue which is only now being properly reassessed, and radically reinterpreted, by scholars in various disciplines, including Leisure Studies. Jean Baudrillard and Paul Virilio have also both been regularly categorized as postmodernists by scholars in various different fields – for instance, Sociology, Cultural Studies, Leisure Studies, Jurisprudence, Politics, Architecture, Art. But this labelling is seen in this chapter to be fundamentally misconceived, misleading and ultimately debilitating for the utility of their legacy, either jointly or individually.

The chapter looks at ways in which the substantial legacies of both Paul Virilio and Jean Baudrillard might be better seen as singular (Paillard, 2011: 339), but related, 'post-theory'. Their long friendship and 'intersecting lives' (Dosse, 2010), similar to the intimate connections between their French social theory counterparts Gilles Deleuze and Félix Guattari (Dosse, 2010), make them worth considering, to some extent, as a duo, but equally, because of their specific differences and quite determinedly specific trajectories, they can be better considered individually. In this vein, their value for theorists and practitioners in Leisure Studies and beyond who wish to read and 'apply' the work of Paul Virilio and Jean Baudrillard can be helpfully gauged, even if ultimately the quest for applied Baudrillard and Virilio itself may be disappointing. Some of the writings of Virilio and Baudrillard which are useful to Leisure Studies are assessed anew and a more balanced conclusion is formed about their 'extreme theory' for an even more extreme world.

The reception of Baudrillard and Virilio in Leisure Studies

Leisure Studies, much like other disciplines and sub-disciplines, has long been engaged in a search for a postmodernist holy grail, especially since the 1980s. In some ways there was a lull in interest in the postmodern, postmodernism and postmodernization at various times in the subsequent years, but the general search on these lines (Blackshaw, 2010) has persisted within international Leisure Studies, albeit unevenly. For much of this thirty-year period, Jean Baudrillard, and latterly his long-time friend and colleague Paul Virilio, fitted the bill, for some critical commentators at least, as possible outriders of a postmodernist Leisure Studies – as 'hip gunslingers' of this movement, as Virilio and his architectural partner of the 1960s, Claude Parent, were once described in relation to architectural theory. However, in my view, the postmodernist labelling became a massive barrier to any long-lasting inter-pretation of Virilio and Baudrillard and required us to move 'beyond postmodernity', at least in terms of debates about concepts. Baudrillard, in particular, often endured a reading of his work which showed a fascination with a limited but linked handful of notions – most notably the concepts of 'postmodernism', 'simulation' and 'hyperreality' (Smith, Clarke and Doel, 2011: 326). As critical commentators, and subsequent re-interpreters of Baudrillard, have astutely pointed out:

> While it is perhaps understandable that this situation should have arisen, particu-larly given Baudrillard's initial reception within the English-speaking world as the 'high priest' of postmodernism, it is far from an accurate portrayal of the potential Baudrillard's work offers, or indeed, of Baudrillard himself. It is telling that the waning of interest in the postmodern since the 1990s has not, in fact, led to a corresponding decline of interest in Baudrillard. On the contrary, now that his work is no longer inter-preted in the one dimensional terms dictated by the modern/postmodern debate, a far fuller, richer, and more diverse understanding and appreciation of Baudrillard's import is beginning to emerge.
>
> (Smith, Clarke and Doel, 2011: 326)

Baudrillard's reception into the Leisure Studies field was very similar – he was hailed as the high priest of postmodernism, but, in Leisure Studies, this newer interpretation failed to displace the initial labelling, and little of the richer interpretation of Baudrillard has filtered through. Though, ironically, it may not be as productive for Leisure Studies as the modernist/ postmodernist divide, part of the 'richer, more diverse' interpretation of Baudrillard allows for a perspective rooted in what Jacques Donzelot, who himself taught with Baudrillard in the department of sociology at the University of Nanterre in France, conceives as 'patasoci-ology' (Donzelot, 2011), namechecking the interest of the young Baudrillard in pataphysics and the thought of Albert Jarry and others.

As we have seen, the whole field of Leisure Studies, from the 1980s onwards, operated with a modernist/postmodernist dichotomy in much of its theoretical discourse (Blackshaw, 2010), and Baudrillard, and to a lesser extent Virilio, fell under this rubric. This chapter attempts to move beyond the problematic division into modernist and postmodernist Leisure Studies, although such a move is not without considerable problems for utilization of the key theorists under consideration. A reconsideration of 'very late' or 'post' Baudrillard posthu-mous publications and 'later' Virilio works can give rise to a better understanding of what I have elsewhere conceived of as 'post-theory', where extreme theory for an extreme world holds sway (Redhead, 2011). In some respects, it forms part of an essay in self-criticism, as I, like many others, maintained interest in pursuing the possibilities of a postmodernist Leisure Studies (or what I once, with heavy irony, called 'popular cultural studies') and the utility of Baudrillard and Virilio for that project. There have been plenty of efforts to use Baudrillard and Virilio in the past – within this 'postmodernizing' framework. Utilizing these theorists when looking at, say, consumption, media simulation and mega events, or else the militarization or technologization of sport and leisure, has been tried with varying degrees of success (Redhead, 2011: ch. 6).

Let us take two outstanding examples of the best utilization of Jean Baudrillard and Paul Virilio in the history of Leisure Studies. Chris Rojek has been one of the foremost Leisure Studies theorists innovatively utilizing Baudrillard to shake up theoretical, and political, positions in the discipline. Rojek, over a period of twenty years (Rojek, 1990), argued strongly for seeing Baudrillard as 'one of the leading lights of postmodernist theory' (Rojek, 1990: 7) and for, in part, applying this version of postmodernist theory to 'show how Baudrillard might be located in the tradition of leisure theory' and, moreover, 'how Baudrillard's ideas might be used practically in applied research' in the everyday life of the discipline of the study of everyday life. Rojek's sophisticated perspective, derived directly from a 1990s reading of both Jean Baudrillard and postmodernist theory of the time, concluded, ultimately, that 'Baudrillard's theory is not a constructive model for Leisure Studies to follow', yet that 'as a critic of received ideas and conventional practice [Baudrillard] has much to teach us' (Rojek, 1990: 17). Most significantly of all, Rojek argued consistently over the years that 'Baudrillard challenges the positivistic assumptions of the dominant traditions in leisure studies' (Rojek, 1990: 18), and for that alone Baudrillard should be regarded as a key theorist.

In the case of Virilio, much less cited in Leisure Studies than Baudrillard but occasionally employed, with varying degrees of success, Tony Blackshaw and Tim Crabbe (Blackshaw and Crabbe, 2004) teased out pathbreaking ways of moving Leisure Studies into 'new perspectives on sport and "deviance"', using myriad theorists of the culture of the postmodern, including Paul Virilio. In their provocative and spine-tingling study of speedy, car 'cruising' youth culture, for instance, Virilio was a prominent theorist employed, alongside Michael Maffesoli, Jean-François Lyotard and Scott Lash, in their re-presentation of their research on the subject of cruising as 'performativity'. It is especially Virilio's notion of 'eye lust' that the authors found useful in their riveting analysis of what actually, ethnographically, happens at cruises. As Blackshaw and Crabbe innovatively argued:

> Take the cruise audience's faces; these too always seem staged rather than authentic. Going by 'appearances', their audiences are the best reviews cruises could have: all smiles and cheer. But looking closer, they always seem to react as one; their faces change together as if they all know what is going to happen.
>
> (Blackshaw and Crabbe, 2004: 143)

It was Virilio's idea of 'eye lust ... as a "perceptual disorder" which must be understood as a kind of mad "eye training", brought about by "the wild acceleration of ordinary, everyday representations"' (Blackshaw and Crabbe, 2004: 143) that the authors turned to for enlightenment.

There is no doubt that in these outstanding examples of Leisure Studies' use of Baudrillard and Virilio there is much to enjoy. The problem is that, I would argue, the reinterpretation of both theorists' positions which I expose in this chapter paints them differently, both in relation to other 'postmodernist' theorists used by Leisure Studies and in relation to the singular theory of each other. What I am suggesting in this chapter is that this former enterprise of utilization of Baudrillard and Virilio in Leisure Studies was flawed to some extent and needs updating alongside the reinterpretation of Baudrillard's general theoretical oeuvre now taking place. Essentially, if we look at recent published work by Virilio and Baudrillard, and their reinterpreters, a different picture emerges.

Beyond postmodernity: late Virilio

Virilio's recent work is in many ways more synchronous with the times than it has ever been. We live, as he has theorized so rigorously, in instantaneous culture. More than ever in human history we inhabit the 'now'. But it is an instant present which is catastrophic, claustropolitan, a 'university of disaster' (Virilio, 2010b) in 'the futurism of the instant' (Virilio, 2010a). A claustropolitan sociology rather than a cosmopolitan sociology may be necessary to jack into the trajectories of the catastrophic (Redhead, 2011). Moreover, the accelerated communication of the twenty-first century (smartphone, laptop computer, Twitter, Facebook, Google, Academia.edu, YouTube) which pervades much of Leisure Studies is, oddly, 'Virilian', truly a world devoid of 'solids'. It is this kind of culture of instant (140 characters) communication which Virilio discusses in conversation with Bertrand Richard (Virilio and Richard, 2010) in a series of interviews published in French in 2010. Put out by Textuel in Paris, this volume of conversations with Richard (who keeps his own words to a minimum) is full of everything from Virilio's views on Facebook to his usual diet of war technologies (for example, the Manhattan project), the spreading 'fear' of the title and the horrendous, catastrophic state of the planet we inhabit. The title originates from a play on a book title used by author Graham Greene – suitably, another confused and haunted Catholic, like Paul Virilio. At the turn of the millennium, John Armitage, editor of several influential collections of essays and interviews on and with Virilio (Armitage, 2000; 2001; 2011), hailed Paul Virilio as 'perhaps the most provocative French cultural theorist on the contemporary intellectual scene' (Armitage, 2001: 1). This statement is just as true today. John Armitage more recently stated that Virilio is 'at his finest ... one of the most thrilling and insightful cultural theorists writing today' and 'his analyses of contemporary cultural life are nothing less than first-rate' (Armitage, 2011: 25). Again, Armitage is exemplary in his judgement of Virilio's positive value for fields such as cultural theory, Leisure Studies and sociology of sport. However, Armitage also sees – much more problematically in my view – Virilio's contributions as interventions in a 'postmodern critical cultural theory' (Armitage, 2011: 25). I would argue – and seek to show here – that Paul Virilio is in no way postmodern, whatever he, and others, might have begun to say, rather late in the day, about this postmodernist labelling (Armitage, 2011).

As we face the global future, we need, in my assessment of the contemporary scene, to have in our back pocket, however difficult it may be in the application, the work and thought of Paul Virilio as our guide to what Arthur Kroker sees as the 'trajectories of the catastrophic' (Armitage, 2011: 160–161). Virilio has, at the very least, left us a lasting legacy of what he himself calls an 'accidentology', where recent events like the various global stock market crashes, Japanese earthquake/tsunami/nuclear power catastrophe, the American Midwest 'twister' devastation, the New Zealand earthquake or the Australian floods, the New York hurricane, even the experiment at the European Organisation for Nuclear Research (CERN) on the Large Hadron Collider (LHC) (Virilio, 2010c), can be put into a theoretical, cultural, political and even military perspective. *Le Grand Accélérateur* (first published in French, translated into English in 2012 [Virilio, 2012]) consists of three short essays. One is on the Credit Crunch and stock markets crash of 2008, one is on the slow death of private life in Western culture and the third, which also serves as the title of the book, considers the Large Hadron Collider.

In the title essay Virilio homes in on the idea of the LHC scientific experiment at CERN in Geneva in Switzerland, and its experimental risk to humanity, heading into a black hole. Issues such as 'what right does CERN have to cause a black hole?' have in fact already been litigated and Virilio pursues with venom and high energy the background of this 'risky' scientific experiment with 'progress'. His book has been reviewed (Poole, 2012: 8) as 'suggesting provocative parallels between high energy physics, crash-prone global finance and a fetishistic futurism'. Albert Einstein has always been a symbolic figure for Virilio, but Virilio's Catholic religious belief and his commitment to humanism in his philosophy (contrasting explicitly with Baudrillard's post-humanism) have often led him into some strange and potentially reactionary areas for a left intellectual to inhabit, and the LHC is another potentially treacherous platform for his exploration of the vagaries of scientific progress. Subsequent to Virilio's book, in 2011, researchers at CERN claimed that a neutrino beam fired from the particle accelerator near Geneva to a lab 454 miles away in Italy travelled 60 nanoseconds faster than the speed of light, thus, initially, questioning Albert Einstein's long-standing 1905 theory of relativity, a major feature in Virilio's own work since the 1960s.

Any snapshot of what I have (Redhead, 2004a) labelled accelerated culture (or Mobile Accelerated Nonpostmodern Culture – www.steveredhead.com) is dependent on key concepts created by Paul Virilio and, to some extent, the milieu of their production. For instance, for a period in the 1960s Virilio worked with architect Claude Parent in the group Architecture Principe, creating works like the 'bunker church' at Nevers in France (Virilio and Parent, 2010) and reorienting modernist architecture in the process. In the early 1960s Paul Virilio, who was a master glassmaker at the time, and architect Claude Parent, with several others, set up Architecture Principe – and in the process reoriented modernist architecture in France, though many of the grouplet's ideas never came to fruition. Perhaps the duo's most famous building to see the light of day was the 'bunker church' at Nevers. The church, Saint-Bernadette du Banlay, has sloping floors and oozes brutalism – it is a 'bunker' in appearance, modelled on Virilio's photo/textual study (1958–65) of the World War II Atlantic Wall German bunkers in France, built, in the throes of invasion, to keep the Allies out of occupied territory. A lavish book published in 2010, with French text and English translation on the same page, *Nevers* serves as a remarkable tribute to the idea of, and eventual building of, the legendary 'bunker church'. It has numerous colour and black-and-white photos, interviews with both Parent and Virilio looking back from the perspective of the twenty-first century, fifty-five years after the building of the church in 1966, documents and pictures from the construction of the project and essays and chronologies galore. Some of this book is reprinted (from Architecture Principe pamphlets in the 1960s and Virilio's recently reprinted 1975 book, *Bunker Archeology* [Virilio, 2009b]), but the majority of the 184-page hardback has never been previously widely publicized.

Paul Virilio's late friend, Jean Baudrillard (Redhead, 2008), wrote a short book in 2000 called *Mots de Passe* (Baudrillard, 2000) in which he discussed many of his own concepts – the object, value, symbolic exchange, seduction, the obscene, the transparency of evil, the virtual, the perfect crime, impossible exchange, duality and so on. Baudrillard's English publishers, Verso, called it 'simultaneously a compendium, a retrospective and a menu a la carte'. In English translation (Baudrillard, 2003) the book comprised Baudrillard's 'pass-words'. In 2010 a collective work by numerous Baudrillard scholars entitled *The Baudrillard Dictionary* (Smith, 2010) appeared in the academic market-place. The 'passwords' of 'theorist for an accelerated culture' Paul Virilio (Redhead, 2004a, 2004b) are worth considering here. Paul Virilio's near-tabloid habit of capitalizing his concepts in the middle of paragraphs lends itself to this type of dictionary on Virilio's life and work. Virilio's interviews with Bertrand Richard (Virilio and Richard, 2010), Sylvère Lotringer (Virilio and Lotringer, 2002; 2005; 2008) and Philippe Petit (Virilio and Petit, 1999) are especially recommended for supplementary reading, but because of recent developments the reader can also now make forays further into the as yet ill-defined field (Armitage, 2011) of 'Virilio Studies', complementary sub-discipline to the already established 'Baudrillard Studies' (Clarke *et al.*, 2008; Bishop, 2009; Smith, 2010), which also has its own online journal – the *International Journal of Baudrillard Studies*.

The words of Paul Virilio form part of a conceptual vocabulary of a key, if overlooked and misunderstood, theoretician of the contemporary world and the immediate future to come. In a chapter in Paul Virilio's book *The Futurism of the Instant* (Virilio, 2010a), based on earlier work completed with the photographer Raymond Depardon, there is the development, to an extent, of a sustained predictive theory of exodus from the cities, and even the planet, including forced mobilities of populations as a result of speed accidents and mega sport events such as the Olympics, soccer World Cup and so on. It could be said, following Virilio, that sport may come to be one of the biggest displacers of humanity, perhaps second only to war. Already it can be argued that two million people have had to make way for Olympic stadia in recent years, but it is Virilio's belief that things will get much worse in the near future. Virilio and Depardon have (Virilio and Depardon 2009: 184) explicitly warned that, officially, it is being estimated that 'the future environmental migrant' numbers will be 'one billion'; moreover that 'six hundred and forty five million people will be displaced from their homes over the next forty years' and that 'two hundred and fifty million will be displaced by phenomena related to climate change', all part of a demographic resettlement of the globe on a massive scale as exodus from cities (and, as I have pointed out, the planet) gathers pace in the next fifty years (Virilio 2010a). Sport mega events, in various cities around the world, will, far from regenerating the urban environment as has been the orthodoxy in the past, be a cause of part of this resettlement. As Virilio first told Sylvère Lotringer in the 1980s about the lessons of the Maracana stadium in Rio de Janeiro in Brazil (recently being rebuilt for the 2014 soccer World Cup to be held in Brazil) and the 1980 Olympics hosted in Moscow:

> the serious problem is that those present, those who participate, those for example who attend an auto race are disqualified by the absentees. The billion people who watch the Olympic Games in Moscow, or the soccer championship in Argentina, impose their power at the expense of those present, who are already superfluous. The latter are practically no more than bodies filling the stadium so that it won't look empty. But their physical presence is completely alienated by the absence of the television viewer, and that's what interests me in this situation. Once, the stadiums were full. It was a magnificent popular explosion. There were 200,000 people in the grandstands, singing and shouting. It was a vision from an ancient society, from the agora, from paganism. Now when you watch the Olympics or the soccer championship on television, you notice there aren't that many people. And even they, in a certain way, aren't the ones who make the World Cup. The ones who make the World Cup are the radios and televisions

that buy and – by favouring a billion and a half television viewers – 'produce' the championship. Those absent from the stadium are always right, economically and massively. They have the power. The participants are always wrong.

(Virilio and Lotringer, 2008)

Let us, having looked at Virilio, turn to Baudrillard.

Post Baudrillard

Jean Baudrillard has been described as 'one of the world's most influential and controversial intellectual figures' (Clarke, Doel, Merrin and Smith, 2011: 325). Baudrillard's 'very late' writings, published after his death in 2007, provide us with a number of theoretical clues to the numerous mysteries he set up in texts throughout his life. It is one of the posthumously published writings (Featherstone, 2011) of Baudrillard, *The Agony of Power* (Baudrillard, 2010a), published in English in 2010 by Semiotext(e), which I want to especially feature here, but there are also elements of the theoretical and political position taken by Baudrillard in *The Agony of Power* repeated in another of his late texts, *Carnival and Cannibal* (Baudrillard, 2010b), published in English by Seagull Press, again in 2010.

The Agony of Power is a collection of three original texts written in 2005 which were read at various conferences around the world, together with an interview with French cultural magazine *Chronic'art* from that same year. This package of late Baudrillard texts is prefaced by a substantial contextual introduction by Semiotext(e)'s Sylvère Lotringer, entitled 'Domination and Servitude'. Two years after these texts saw the light of day Jean Baudrillard died from cancer. The three texts and one interview which make up the Baudrillard part of the book are 'From Domination to Hegemony', 'The White Terror of World Order', 'Where Good Grows' and 'The Roots of Evil'. The book was published by Semiotext(e) as number 6 in its Intervention series. A photograph by Baudrillard adorns the inside of the front and back covers. Two other essays which Sylvère Lotringer was originally going to publish alongside the three papers in *The Agony of Power* were separately published by Baudrillard as another book altogether. *Carnival and Cannibal* was eventually published in 2010, comprising the essay 'Carnival and Cannibal, or The Play of Global Antagonism', a talk from 2004, and an address 'Ventriloquous Evil' from 2006. Not forgetting the other posthumously published Baudrillard book *Why Hasn't Everything Already Disappeared?* (Baudrillard, 2009) written in 2007 just before his death and published by Seagull Press in 2009, 'post-Baudrillard' is well worth taking seriously.

'Politics after that could never be the same', Sylvère Lotringer writes in the context of Baudrillard's mid-1970s work in his introduction to *The Agony of Power*. Lotringer was commenting on Baudrillard's putative mid-life epiphany in San Diego in 1975 and 1976 when, teaching with Fredric Jameson, Michel de Certeau, Jean-Francois Lyotard and others, Baudrillard came to the realization that, in Lotringer's take on it, society was losing all its moorings. Baudrillard speedily wrote his magnum opus *Symbolic Exchange and Death* (Baudrillard, 1993) and the rest is, in some sense, history. It was published in 1976 in French, but not really fully appreciated by English-speaking readers until much later. In 1976, the year zero of punk in global popular culture, Baudrillard's attitude to everything changed. In his agonizing introduction to *The Agony of Power* Lotringer claims powerfully, and in my view correctly, that Baudrillard's two key ideas throughout his work were that, firstly, reality had disappeared and became replaced by simulacra and, secondly, there was a potential symbolic challenge in this disappearance. This mid-1970s period is crucial for understanding Baudrillard's work for the rest of his life, and especially its political implications for us here in the present. Jean Baudrillard's 'post-punk' work is revealed in all its glory in *The Agony of Power*, a book hailed from within by Lotringer as nothing less than Baudrillard's intellectual testament. Baudrillard's *The Agony of Power* offers a different view of power from the myriad conflicts within the postmodernism debates. In this very late work, Baudrillard offers up a double refusal within a globalized world of integrated reality – the sovereign's refusal to dominate as well as the subject's refusal to be dominated.

In all this posthumous work, but especially in *The Agony of Power*, Baudrillard offers up a unique theory of power incorporating this 'double refusal' – the sovereign's refusal to dominate as well as the subject's refusal to be dominated. As he points out in *Carnival and Cannibal* in a passage repeated word for word from *The Agony of Power* (and partially extracted by Semiotext(e), as the quote on the back cover of *The Agony of Power*) the radicality of his thinking is in the argument that power itself has to be abolished. Baudrillard claims:

> It is power itself that has to be abolished – and not just in the refusal *to be dominated*, which is the essence of all traditional struggles, but equally and as violently in the refusal *to dominate*. For domination implies both these things, and if there were the same violence or energy in the refusal to dominate, we would long ago have stopped dreaming of revolution. And this tells us why intelligence cannot – and never will be able to – be in power: because it consists precisely in this twofold refusal.
>
> (Baudrillard, 2010b: 17–18)

The refusal to dominate, or to exercise sovereign power, according to Sylvère Lotringer, seeking to illustrate Baudrillard's theory at its most banal, can be seen in the agonies of those involved in the revolts of May 1968 or the activities of the 'post-political' Italian Autonomists in the 1970s. They were, in Baudrillard's theory, according to Lotringer's interpretation, less than confident in wanting to dominate – they agonized about power, in both their resistance to sovereignty and their unwillingness to become involved in its exercise. Indeed, as Baudrillard says emphatically, 'power itself is an embarrassment and there is no one to assume it truly' (Baudrillard, 2010a: 82).

In another of the important post-Baudrillard texts, *Carnival and Cannibal*, Baudrillard specifically recalls watching on live TV the 2006 soccer World Cup (literally 'the last World Cup' for Baudrillard, as he was to die from cancer in 2007) and, more specifically, that year's World Cup Final match, watched by billions all over the world at the same time in Virilio's city of the instant, in Munich, where France met Italy. Baudrillard conceives of his countryman Zinedine Zidane's head butt into the chest of Italy defender Marco Materazzi as a 'terrorist act' (Baudrillard, 2010b: 84). This was Zidane's last act in a long football career, of global sporting celebrity, and one which – because it meant, as he was sent off for the act, that he could not take part in the subsequent penalty shoot-out that Italy won – effectively lost France the 2006 soccer World Cup. As Baudrillard puts it:

> This is where Zinedine Zidane and his head butt come in – a stunning act of disqualification, of sabotage, of 'terrorism'. By blighting this ritual of planetary identification, these nuptials between sport and the planet, by refusing to be the idol and mirror of globalisation in such an emblematic event, he is denying the universal pact that permits transfiguration of our sad reality by Good and allows billions of unidentified human beings to find an identity in the void (the same sublimation operates in the sacred illusion of war). And it was, indeed, stigmatised as an act of desertion, but, as

such, it also became simultaneously a cult gesture: by passing from the peak of performance to the peak of dysfunction, to the thwarting of Good in all its splendour, it suddenly pointed up the Nothingness at the heart of globalisation … It is a 'blow' by which everyone can be said to have lost the World Cup. But isn't that better than having won a victory for globalisation itself. There is here the principle of a genuine event, of those singular events that challenge globalisation (hegemony) at a stroke … We might say in the same way that Zidane could have delivered his head butt or not, and there would have been valid reasons in either case. Even when there is 'chance', the event obeys the principle of Sufficient Reason … But it isn't Zidane's free will that's at issue here: though he may well have had the possibility of acting or not, the event, for its part, wasn't free not to occur. Some day or another, Zidane or no Zidane, globalisation (global power) would have found itself – finds itself right now – confronted with its success, with its extremeness, and hence faced with this automatic convulsion that has no valid reason to occur.

(Baudrillard, 2010b: 77–80)

There are many other examples of Baudrillard's personal relation to leisure practices which become part of what I call this 'post-theory'. For example, soccer-loving Baudrillard devotees can still buy, wear and read the special T-shirt made by the Philosophy Football company (self-styled London-based 'sporting outfitters of intellectual distinction', available at www.philosophyfootball.com). The shirt is 'Chelsea' blue, with the number 3 and the name Baudrillard on the back, and a Baudrillard quotation on the front. The words 'power is only too happy to make football bear a diabolical responsibility for stupefying the masses' are emblazoned on it. The full, original Baudrillard quotation is actually slightly more unwieldy: 'power is only too happy to make football bear a facile responsibility, even to take upon itself the diabolical responsibility for stupefying the masses', a typically 'singular' sentence taken from one of Baudrillard's little black books (Baudrillard, 2007), published originally in English in 1983 by Semiotext(e) but originally published in French in 1978, the year of the football World Cup in the military dictatorship of Argentina, the land of what was then the seemingly endlessly disappeared. At his wedding to his second wife, Marine, in the late 1990s, when he was well into his sixties, the ushers were kitted out with brand new Baudrillard Philosophy Football T-shirts at Jean Baudrillard's own expense!

Baudrillard's post-theory also intersects with popular music culture, but in an oblique fashion. For example, in the mid-1970s a Cleveland punk band with the name Pere Ubu emerged to globally popularize the drama of Albert Jarry from the late nineteenth century which had always fascinated Baudrillard, who produced early work on the pataphysical (Redhead, 2008). As popular music historian Clinton Heylin (Heylin, 2007) reveals, musician David Thomas, in 1975 in Cleveland, Ohio, named his band Pere Ubu after Albert Jarry's caricature king because, to Thomas, it added a texture of absolute grotesqueness, a kind of darkness descending over everything which fitted the bleak, post-Nixon mid-1970s in America. Baudrillard had never shown any awareness of this popular music culture/Ubu connection, though he did once appear in a 'punk' costume of his own (a gold lamé jacket with mirrored lapels) reading the text of his self-penned 1980s poem 'Motel-Suicide', backed by a rock band at the 'Chance Event' held at Whiskey Pete's in Las Vegas in November 1996. The only surviving photo shows the short, balding, rather 'academic' Baudrillard appearing as if he was auditioning for a place in a punk band (Redhead, 2008).

Conclusions

This chapter has looked at past and potential future contributions to Leisure Studies of two key theorists Paul Virilio and Jean Baudrillard. I have attempted to move beyond the much-utilized dichotomy of modernist and postmodernist within Leisure Studies, which has effectively been bifurcated on these lines for a long period. Baudrillard and Virilio have both been regularly categorized as postmodernists by scholars in various different fields including Leisure Studies, but this labelling has been seen here to be fundamentally misconceived, misleading and debilitating. The chapter has explored, through recent Baudrillard and Virilio writings, an alternative perspective in which the substantial legacies of both Paul Virilio and Jean Baudrillard are more productively seen outside the modernist/postmodernist bifurcation which has dominated Leisure Studies for so long.

References

Armitage, J. (ed.) (2011) *Virilio Now: Current Perspectives in Virilio Studies*. Cambridge: Polity.

Armitage, J. (ed.) (2001) *Virilio Live: Selected Interviews*. London: Sage.

Armitage, J. (ed.) (2000) *Paul Virilio: From Modernism to Hypermodernism and Beyond*. London: Sage.

Baudrillard, J. (1993) *Symbolic Exchange and Death*. London: Sage.

Baudrillard, J. (2010a) *The Agony of Power*. Los Angeles: Semiotext(e).

Baudrillard, J. (2010b) *Carnival and Cannibal*. Calcutta; Seagull Press.

Baudrillard, J. (2009) *Why Hasn't Everything Already Disappeared?* Calcutta: Seagull Press.

Baudrillard, J. (2007) *In the Shadow of the Silent Majorities*. Los Angeles: Semiotext(e).

Baudrillard, J. (2003) *Passwords*. London: Verso.

Baudrillard, J. (2000) *Mots de Passe*. Paris: Pauvert, Editions Fayard.

Bishop, R. (ed.) (2009) *Baudrillard Now: Current Perspectives in Baudrillard Studies*. Cambridge: Polity.

Blackshaw, T. (2010) *Leisure*. London: Routledge.

Blackshaw, T. and Crabbe, T. (2004) *New Perspectives on Sport and 'Deviance': Consumption, Performativity and Social Control*. London: Routledge.

Clarke, D., Doel, M., Merrin, W. and Smith, R. G. (eds) (2008) *Jean Baudrillard: Fatal Theories*. London: Routledge.

Donzelot, J. (2011) 'Patasociology at the University of Nanterre', *Cultural Politics* 7 (3) 359–369.

Dosse, F. (2010) *Gilles Deleuze and Félix Guattari: Intersecting Lives*. New York: Columbia University Press.

Featherstone, M. (2011) 'Against the Fake Empire: Utopia, Dystopia, Apocalypticism in Baudrillard's Late Works', *Cultural Politics* 7 (3) 465–476.

Heylin, C. (2007) *Babylon's Burning: From Punk to Grunge*. Harmondsworth: Penguin.

Paillard, J.-F. (2011) 'The Antidotes to the Global Lies in the Singular: An Interview with Jean Baudrillard', *Cultural Politics* 7 (3) 339–344.

Poole, S. (2012) 'Book Review of Paul Virilio: The Great Accelerator', *Guardian*, Review, 12 May, 8.

Redhead, S. (2011) *We Have Never Been Postmodern: Theory at the Speed of Light*. Edinburgh: Edinburgh University Press.

Redhead, S. (ed.) (2008) *The Jean Baudrillard Reader*. Edinburgh: Edinburgh University Press/New York: Columbia University Press.

Redhead, S. (2004a) *Paul Virilio: Theorist for an Accelerated Culture*. Edinburgh: Edinburgh University Press/Toronto and Buffalo, NY: University of Toronto Press.

Redhead, S. (ed.) (2004b) *The Paul Virilio Reader*. Edinburgh: Edinburgh University Press/New York: Columbia University Press, European Perspectives Series.

Rojek, C. (1990) 'Baudrillard and Leisure', *Leisure Studies* 9 (1) 7–20.

Smith, R., Clarke, D. and Doel, M. (2011) 'Baudrillard Redux: Antidotes to Integral Reality', *Cultural Politics* 7 (3) 325–337.

Smith, R. G. (ed.) (2010) *The Baudrillard Dictionary*. Edinburgh: Edinburgh University Press/New York: Columbia University Press.

Virilio, P. (2012) *The Great Accelerator*. Cambridge: Polity.

Virilio, P. (2010a) *The Futurism of the Instant: Stop–Eject*. Cambridge: Polity.

Virilio, P. (2010b) *The University of Disaster.* Cambridge: Polity.

Virilio, P. (2010c) *Le Grand accélérateur.* Paris: Editions Galilée

Virilio, P. (2009b) *Bunker Archeology.* New York: Princeton Architectural Press.

Virilio, P. and Depardon, R. (2009) *Native Land: Stop–Eject.* London: Thames and Hudson.

Virilio, P. and Lotringer, S. (2008) *Pure War.* Los Angeles: Semiotext(e).

Virilio, P. and Lotringer, S. (2005) *The Accident of Art.* Los Angeles and New York: Semiotext(e).

Virilio, P. and Lotringer, S. (2002) *Crepuscular Dawn.* Los Angeles and New York: Semiotext(e).

Virilio, P. and Parent, C. (2010) *Nevers: Architecture Principe.* Orléans: Hyx.

Virilio, P. and Petit, P. (1999) *Politics of the Very Worst.* New York: Semiotext(e).

Virilio, P. and Richard, B. (2010) *L'Administration de peur.* Paris: Editions Textuel.

PART III

LEISURE AS A SOCIO-CULTURAL PHENOMENON

PART III

LEISURE AS A SOCIO-CULTURAL PHENOMENON

17

THEORIZING SOCIAL CLASS, CULTURE AND LEISURE

Peter Bramham

Marx has not been alone in predicting a future society where human freedom and emancipation are possible, given the right circumstances and the right time. Indeed, from its inception in the 1970s, Leisure Studies has been grounded in optimistic assumptions about a future 'leisure society'. Forty years on, debates about the 'leisure society' still interest academic international conferences (Gilchrist and Wheaton, 2008) and provide the jumping-off point for Chris Rojek's most recent work (2010). Indeed, one of the 'founding fathers' (if one dare use that politically incorrect term) of Leisure Studies and leisure consultancy in the UK and Australia began by forecasting leisure futures. Anthony Veal (1987) stresses five major measures of leisure: participation rates, number of participants, volume of activity, time and expenditure. He then outlines nine techniques of forecasting, including trend extrapolation, scenario writing, spatial models and composite techniques. But the results of such forecasting have been poor, and even when predicting trends in the right direction have hardly been earth-shattering in their level of insight into leisure and leisure participation. One can always demand more funding for restudies, but critics see that as the devil asking for more sin or putting a vampire in charge of a blood bank. So it is not only Marxist polemics and manifestos that get predictions wrong. Yet, Eric Hobsbawm (2011) argues that Marx's analysis of capitalism is still valid and relevant today, given the global dynamic of capitalist development which generates internal contradictions of overproduction, economic concentration, crisis and change. Consequently, it is well worth exploring how key ideas have been revitalized within Marxist cultural studies, tracing how their exegesis found a reluctant and temporary presence in Leisure Studies.

Steve Rigby has argued that most Marxists mistakenly believe 'that the meaning of a text is best seen in the purposes of the author who produced it ... Critics attempt to discover what Marx "really said"' (Rigby, 1998: 1); but this approach assumes a unity and coherence in Marx's writings, while his individual texts are contradictory and interpretations are problematic. So Marxist philosophers, economists and historians can be and have been at loggerheads as to how to read Marx and Marxism and so make sense of modernity. Indeed, Marx's choice of different metaphors to understand capitalism should sensitize readers to differences, silences and contradictions within diverse publications that constitute his life's work, as well as in his many collaborations with Friedrich Engels. As Tony Blackshaw (2005) notes, the theoretical power and complexity of literary metaphors have largely been ignored by social science paradigms. Only recently have they been deployed with such powerful explanatory effect in the work of Zygmunt Bauman, and this literary thread distinguishes him from contemporary sociologists.

Marxism and modernity

One useful starting-point in Marxist analysis is to be found in Stuart Hall's (1992) view of modernity that grasps four separate, distinct formations – the economy, the polity, society and culture. Modernity is made up of four distinctive facets – the economic, the social, the political and the cultural. Such formations have their own history, institutional trajectory and momentum. Hall's loose formulation circumvents the economic determinism that has plagued debate in Marxist writings, spectacularly in relation to the primacy of the mode of production at historical stages of economic development. One should not, however, assume that all four formations move at the same pace or travel in the same direction. Traditional Marxist analysis focuses on the material world of the capitalist economy and its class relations. It theorizes the nature of society and inequality through key concepts of labour power, class, ideology and hegemony. But Hall suggests that capitalism is entering 'new times' that celebrate subjectivity or, more accurately, fragmented subjectivities, and not 'the conventional culture of the Left, with its stress on "objective contradictions", "impersonal structures" and processes that work "behind men's (*sic*) backs"' (Hall, 1988: 25). He argues (1992) that each formation has a separate domain or, to use Foucault's term (1972; 1979; 1980), discourse: the economic entails material distribution, price mechanisms, supply and demand in markets; the social is organized around face-to-face relations in families, neighbourhoods and local communities; politics is about the nature of authority and the distribution of power; and culture concerns communication and material and intellectual signification.

Notwithstanding the change in language, the question for social and historical analysis remains how to understand relations between these four domains. The fractious starting-point for Marxist theory is the primacy of economic institutions (for some 'in the last instance') over all the other three (politics, society and culture), which more or less follow over time. Hence, the most powerful metaphor in the Marxian lexicon is one of the economic base which supports the ideological superstructure: the capitalist state, media, society and religious ideas. The mode and relations of production within the economic base determine the rest. Unfortunately, it is never that straightforward, as deep schisms divide Marxist analyses, with some writers keen to stress the relative autonomy of political, social and cultural institutions from the economy. In so doing, Marxist economic analysis of historical materialism loses its functional explanatory power and becomes diluted and ambiguous in shifting historical periods or 'moments'. The challenge then for Marxist theory is to produce convincing and nuanced historical narratives on how economy shapes both the context and nature of politics, society and culture. This task is especially pressing in order to convince leisure scholars whose aphorism is that leisure is human freedom and choice.

This chapter seeks to outline the contribution of Marxist cultural studies to the understanding of free time and leisure in the period of what some now term 'postmodernity', where any analysis of social class is deemed unnecessary and alien to understanding leisure. With the postmodern turn in social theory, it is not surprising that categories of social class appear to offer little leverage on understanding processes of individualization. Ulrich Beck and Elisabeth Beck-Gernsheim (2002) dismiss 'class', along with 'family' as another 'zombie' category that sociologists cling on to but is moribund, bearing little relation to men and women's diverse ambiguous experiences of living in new postmodern times. For Bauman

(2005), the key feature of postmodernity is ambivalence, or what he and others term 'liquid modernity' (see Blackshaw, 2010a, 2010b). But the relationship between social class and leisure can be most clearly seen through the lens of culture, and Marxist theorists have been thinking about culture and its relationship with the material world of work. From the 1970s the Centre for Contemporary Cultural Studies (CCCS) at Birmingham University was at the heart of debates about the nature of class, work, community and changing patterns of consumption. Rather than accepting leisure simply as free time, Marxist writers challenged concepts both of freedom and of time under industrial capitalism. They questioned the conventional wisdoms, dominant academic disciplines and recreational managerialism that cast leisure simply as free time; as that precious time left over from work, which must be filled with serious leisure and gainful pursuit.

It is not the first time that Marxist theory has expressed concern about leisure and culture: the Frankfurt School, temporarily exiled to the USA in the 1930s and 1940s, feared the soporific and de-politicizing effects of a hedonistic consumerism fuelled by standardized mass entertainments in music, film and broadcasting. Advertising and corporate public relations were the new engines – or, as Adorno neatly phrased it, 'the cultural industries' – of modern capitalism. Their ideological task for modernity was one of both mediation and diversion: to encourage workers to acquiesce in capitalist work discipline and exploitation and to convince them that their future happiness would best be secured as willing consumers rather than as dissatisfied socialists or radical class warriors. For some Marxists, leisure was dismissed as a space in people's lives where false needs were imposed by national elites and where entertainment and recuperation would serve to compensate for alienating work. Why should Marxists study sport, comedy, literature or the mass media when there was rational revolutionary struggle amongst students and workers to organize and, of course, to theorize?

It was primarily in the late 1960s and early 1970s that the works of 'new' German Marxists, Theodor Adorno and Max Horkheimer (2002), and later Jürgen Habermas (1971; 1979), became translated into English and widely read and debated in UK universities. The writings of Marxists such as Herbert Marcuse (1991), Louis Althusser and Balibar (1970) and Nicos Poulantzas (1978), also proved very influential. As the global economy shuddered with the 1973 oil crisis and experienced seismic redistributions in the international division of labour around manufacturing, Marxist analysis took a double dose of theory as it tried to swallow unpalatable concepts of 'overdetermination' and 'hegemony', both germane to issues of control rather than to human freedom and choice.

Class, history and social control

The concept of social control became a touchstone in writing about the social history of nineteenth-century leisure and rational recreation. Peter Bailey's (1978) ground-breaking study opened up the history of leisure in the Victorian era. Gareth Stedman Jones's iconoclastic article (1977) stressed that historians, including Marxists, had passively accepted concepts from sociology without realizing that they were heuristic devices, with the result that 'social control' gradually became non-explanation and incoherence. The dominant model proffered a naive, functionalist narrative of social order, disorder and the reimposition of social order to deal with class conflict and decline in traditional recreations. It was the economic determinism of Marxist analysis that so irritated leisure scholars. Robert Storch's (1975; 1976) research suggests that the new police forces in the nineteenth century were class warriors or 'domestic missionaries' destined to control urban working-class leisure, whereas Carolyn Steedman (1983) casts the county police forces in rural areas more as 'watchers', themselves immersed in popular culture. Just as Rigby favours nuanced Marxist histories of class relations rather than categories expounded by Marxist philosophers and theoreticians, local policing studies provide a more complex picture of class relations and sustainable attempts at policing leisure. Indeed, Peter Bramham's (2005; 2006) studies of Keighley document the comfortable and pervasive localism of the night watch, Poor Law officers and magistrates and their reluctance to accept the professionalizing and centralizing policies of a more militaristic West Riding County Constabulary established in 1856.

Gareth Stedman Jones (1977) argues that moral reformers, Methodists, temperance and charity organizers were not the real agents of social control; they were distasteful to working and middle classes alike. As Hugh Cunningham (1980) argues, the domestication of the new working class was the capitalization of the leisure market and the commodification of popular culture. Stedman Jones argued that ideologies of the new working class were seen to come not from the world of work but from leisure. Rather than developing a radical or socialist consciousness from its class position and the contradictions of capitalism, the working class gradually settled for instrumental 'trade union consciousness', an accommodation with the politics of capitalist society, some following the 'cult of respectability', some not. The key issues confronting Marxism focus upon the nature of social-class relations in both production and consumption, class consciousness and political solidarity and changing class cleavages. Leisure is neither freedom nor a play space for classes to mix but, following Gareth Stedman Jones's (1983) analysis, nineteenth-century working-class leisure is defined generally as a privatized 'culture of consolation', and for earlier Marxists as a site of 'false consciousness'.

British Cultural Studies

It is more a question for the sociology of knowledge how key writers, texts or even concepts become icons of particular disciplines and how groups of writers become so influential as to galvanize and establish schools of thought or, in Max Weber's terms, to offer distinctive *Weltanschauungen*, on key questions that plague the social sciences. These epistemological and methodological problems, often framed in Kuhnian terms (1970) as 'problematics', become ever more complex when key texts or writers have transnational voices which are often delayed historically because of issues around publication, translation and copyright. Indeed, the term 'problematic' was much favoured by the CCCS, as it raised different questions from those prevalent in traditional social science disciplines. John Clarke and Chas Critcher, the most eloquent of Marxist leisure theorists, came from the intellectual hothouse of CCCS in Birmingham.

Although synthesizing the work of some continental writers, the CCCS also provided a theoretical space for feminists, Marxist feminists in particular, to question the existing sexual division of labour because Marxist writers sought to study leisure relations in the wider context of the economic, political and cultural relationships of contemporary capitalism. Nevertheless, Marxism itself faced sustained criticism from black writers, particularly Paul Gilroy (1987; 1993), as it stood accused of rendering 'race' and racism invisible.

Inspired by writers such as Raymond Williams and E. P. Thompson, British Cultural Studies sought to distance itself from the determinism of Louis Althusser. In the 1970s French structuralism was influential in a variety of disciplines, particularly anthropology, linguistics and psychoanalysis. However, it was Althusser's reading of the late Marx, his demand for scientific Marxist praxis and his analysis of ideology that proved most corrosive not only for sociology but also for more humanist and empiricist versions of Marxist analysis which stressed human agency and choice. Althusser and others influenced by his approach launched a theoretical assault on social science. Although maintaining the Marxist shibboleth of the economic base determining the superstructure 'in the last instance', Althusser suggested that the ideological superstructures could be 'relatively autonomous' from the economic base. The concept of overdetermination permitted the class contradictions of capitalism to find their expression in the ideological superstructure, or, in Althusser's terminology, the Ideological State Apparatuses (ISAs) such as the family, education or politics. Althusser therefore challenged ideas of history and human agency. English Marxism and Italian Marxism, indebted to Antonio Gramsci, were deemed equally guilty of historicism and of theoretical naivety by engaging with a false problematic. By focusing on the agency of human subjects, such analyses were deemed to be ideological. Both British and Italian theoretical traditions failed, the Althusser school argued, to develop scientific categories of Marxism which could locate and explain the structural contradictions of capitalism.

By way of contrast to Althusser, British Cultural Studies was keen to embrace Italian Marxism and, in particular, Gramsci's newly translated work on hegemony and its purchase on struggles over cultural consent in modernity. Indeed, as Stuart Hall's introduction (1980) to the theoretical problematic of Cultural Studies acknowledges, Antonio Gramsci was one crucial strand of thinking that gave shape to subsequent diverse epistemological, theoretical, methodological and practical interventions. Researchers working in the CCCS at Birmingham University were keen to map out a new field of study, a new territory or space for engagement so as to flesh out sociology, with its skeletal focus on the social, and to challenge its more traditional elitist sub-discipline, the sociology of literature, in order to broaden out its conservative Leavisite criticism of the 'Great Tradition' of English texts. In a variety of ways, the CCCS sought to raise new questions. It sought to refocus attention on class, on the mass media and on popular culture as site both for resistance and identity. By drawing on Gramsci's concept of hegemony, the CCCS defined capitalism holistically, as a totality structured in dominance, with social, political and cultural ramifications. This shift in perspective away from traditional British sociology, and the emergence of new problematics, appeared in a plethora of multi-authored publications but was most graphically illustrated in *Policing the Crisis* (Hall *et al.*, 1978), a critical study of media panic about black street crime in the UK, orchestrated in the authoritarian state response by the police and by the courts.

The devil still makes work

So when Daniel Bell (1973), Clive Jenkins and Barrie Sherman (1979) and Tom Stonier (1983) chose to celebrate the 'leisure revolution' at the beginning of the 1970s, Marxism was alive to inequality *both* at work *and* in leisure. This was not the result of ideological blindness, as by the 1980s growing numbers, particularly of young adults, experienced the oxymoron of 'enforced leisure' or unemployment as globalization tightened its grip on national economies and local lives. Marxist writers suggested that it was not simply an empirical question of mapping what free-time activities were, but more a theoretical question of why people spent their non-work time as they did.

In the field of Leisure Studies, these themes found their clearest expression with the publication of *The Devil Makes Work* by John Clarke and Chas Critcher (1985). The book sought to provide a coherent theoretical riposte to key Leisure Studies in the UK of that decade, namely the text-books of Stan Parker (1971), Ken Roberts (1978) and Robert and

Rhona Rapoport (1975). All three key texts were deemed guilty of a weak functionalist analysis which posited that market capitalism provided freedom of choice for individuals at different stages of their working lives and family cycle. *The Devil Makes Work* brought a distinctive new approach to the study of leisure, moving it away from largely untheorized empirical studies of provision and consumption and linking it explicitly to class, culture and inequality. Leisure was redefined as a site for social conflict and regulation. For Clarke and Critcher the 'conventional wisdom' of leisure research failed to acknowledge that politics and economics directly affected leisure: 'People do make choices (and not only in leisure), but their choices are made within the structures of constraint which order their lives' (Clarke and Critcher, 1985: 46). Class membership was defined as central to people's leisure experiences, and, following C. Wright Mills' work, they demanded that social theory bridge history and biography. In the late 1950s and early 1960s the 'cultural criticism' of Richard Hoggart (1957) and Raymond Williams (1965) explored the relationships between working-class culture and the dominant culture. Citing the British tradition of community studies (see, for example, the classic study of coalmining by Dennis *et al.* [1969]), Clarke and Critcher argued that leisure must still be seen as part of a collective process rather than individual choice. Leisure research, particularly in the USA, cast leisure as a free-time activity of individual consumption and/or the satisfaction of psychological needs. Ken Roberts (1978) stressed the dominance of family (not class) and leisure (not work) as key research fields. But Clarke and Critcher argued, rather, that families functioned to reproduce class relations and dependencies. In an important conference, 'Leisure and Social Control', Critcher and Clarke (1981) suggested that four main questions remained for Leisure Studies: what is the nature of the class structure? What kinds of different work experiences (especially between the sexes) are there of wage labour? How does society open up or close down leisure opportunities? Is the semi-privatized family a unity of necessity or choice? Precisely these sorts of questions were the starting-point for feminist analysis as the next wave of critical theory swept through the field of Leisure Studies (see Deem, 1986; 1999; Green *et al.*, 1990; Scraton, 1994).

Old concepts in new times

Understanding the passage of historical time, how it both shaped and was shaped by individual and collective agency, remained central questions for critical social theory, and Williams (1965) wanted cultural materialism to grasp hold of and capture 'the structure of feeling', the common culture shaped by economic, political and social forces that constituted 'the long revolution'. But, at that time, given its intellectual roots, Marxist analysis was not only interested in leisure as consumption but was naturally committed to exploring the political economy of leisure and the capitalization of leisure space and free time by global corporations. Both the commercialization and privatization of leisure have been key developments since the Second World War, and the emergence of conspicuous consumption in leisure lifestyles has become the focus of postmodern social theory.

French sociologist Pierre Bourdieu has developed gradations of Marxist categories with his discussion of tastes and distastes, cultural habitus and different circuits of economic, cultural and social capital. For some writers (Atkinson, 2007), Bourdieu is the key to strengthening Anthony Giddens' structuration theory and the reflexive project of the self in modernity by reintroducing class into his analysis. The conundrum for Marxist analysis and explanation is just how to capture the dependency relationships between the economy, society, politics and culture. This challenge remains as pressing now as it was then. It is over twenty-five years since the ground-breaking *The Devil Makes Work* was first published, and for Marxists and non-Marxists alike culture is perceived to be the bridge that links social class to leisure. Although he is a fierce critic of Marxism, keen to distance himself from the failed politics of the left, Chris Rojek's interest in leisure corporations and the processes of globalization sit comfortably within the Marxist canon. Although championing 'liquid modernity' and the 'leisure imagination', Tony Blackshaw's creative ethnography remains firmly rooted in the Marxian tradition of British Cultural Studies, following in the ground-breaking footsteps of Paul Willis's (1977) *Learning to Labour*.

Meanwhile, leisure scholars such as Tony Blackshaw (2010a) and Chris Rojek (2010) have noted, the world of leisure has moved on. In what many commentators describe as a postmodern, post-Fordist society, work is no longer felt to be central to the lives of individuals, local communities or social classes. Leisure has become an ever greater site of excess, escape, transgression, resistance and change. Rojek (2000) has spoken at one point of 'dark' or 'wild' leisure, and more recently (2005) of the need for an 'action analysis' of leisure, one which should be ideologically committed to a new, 'greenish' politics which values the care of the individual self, as well as the care of others and care of the environment.

New technologies of digitalization in computing, linked to satellite communication systems, offer diverse networks for personal information exchange as well as for data archive retrieval. These have resulted in the rapid reconfiguration of terrestrial national broadcasting, alongside innovation on the internet to realize global platforms of news and entertainment. Such digital media have simultaneously facilitated individualization, wherein resilient processes have the strength to reconfigure (at least for those with access to economic resources to buy new technologies) the immediacy of personal experiences. Face-to-face relationships (in Heidegger's terms [1962], *Dasein*) become, in one sense, more fragile, fragmentary and privatized. Intimate communications may and can be sustained by texting, e-mails, and Skyping through various media such as the telephone, iPhone, iPad, laptop and computer. Social networking sites such as Twitter and Facebook and web-based chatrooms override established and traditionally constrained family, community and neighbourhood networks. In Giddensian terms (1979), this results in 'time-space distanciation'; the disembedding of the local. Postmodernists may choose to celebrate the emergence of neo-tribes of virtual communities and the 'leisure imaginary'. Therein lie circumvention and disintegration of established, traditionally constraining contacts and class regulation. Individuals become freed from time and space, and so may choose to create avatars and new virtual identities. These may signify liberation for those involved in online dating or outright deception; for example, some adults may choose to groom children via the internet, and also in reality.

The leisure project of modernity, orchestrated by local and national policy makers in pursuit of rational recreation, has been superseded by new agendas, policy alliances and corporate forces. Alongside this there has been a pattern of deregulation in many nation-states, and growing globalization experienced through the internet, travel and new patterns of communication. In numerous cases what once was marginal and deviant has now become the basis for widely available commercial entertainment. The commercialization and commodification of leisure remains the dominant force. As chapter 4 of *The Devil Makes Work* states, 'We sell everything', and much ink has been spilt to sustain that argument (Critcher and Bramham, 2004). More recently, Peter Bramham and Steve Wagg's collection (2011) explores both change and continuity in the diverse fields of individual taste, community leisure and postmodern culture, and documents the emergence of complex new politics of pleasure, choice and desire.

Conclusion

This chapter has argued that the relationship between social class and leisure can be most clearly seen through the lens of culture and that Marxist theorists have been thinking about culture and its relationship with the material world of work. Rather than accepting leisure simply as free time, Marxist writers have challenged concepts both of freedom and of time under industrial capitalism; in so doing they have tried to take on the central debate in social science, the recursive dialectic between agency and structure. Many critics feel that the Marxist position offers a determinist theory of control with little space for human agency. So the question for Leisure Studies remains about the position of the individual at leisure, whether free or constrained. As Tony Blackshaw's, David Harris's and Anthony J. Veal's chapters on Pierre Bourdieu in this *Handbook* make clear, it is hard to avoid the salience of class position, life knowledge and social education for leisure tastes and indulgences. It is just that the Marxist gaze has shifted from production to consumption in industrial capitalism.

References

Adorno, T. and Horkheimer, M. (2002) *Dialectic of Enlightenment*. San Francisco: Stanford University Press.

Althusser, L. and Balibar, E. (1970) *Reading 'Capital'* (B. Brewster, trans.). London: New Left Books.

Atkinson, W. (2007) 'Anthony Giddens as Adversary of Class', *Sociology, 41*(3) 533–549.

Bailey, P. (1978) *Leisure and Class in Victorian England: Rational Recreation and the Contest for Control 1830–1885*. London: Routledge and Kegan Paul.

Bauman, Z. (2005) *Liquid Life*. Cambridge: Polity.

Beck, U. and Beck-Gernsheim, E. (2002) *Individualization: Institutionalized Individualism and Its Social and Political Consequences* (P. Camiller, trans., 2001). London, Thousand Oaks, New Dehli: Sage.

Bell, D. (1973) *The Coming of Post-Industrial Society: A Venture in Social Forecasting*. London: Heinemann.

Blackshaw, T. (2005) *Zygmunt Bauman*. London and New York: Routledge.

Blackshaw, T. (2010a) *Leisure*. London and New York: Routledge.

Blackshaw, T. (2010b) *Key Concepts in Community Studies*. Los Angeles, London, New Delhi, Singapore, Washington DC: Sage.

Bramham, P. (2005) 'Policing an Industrial Town: Keighley 1800–1848', *The Local Historian, 35*(4) 243–253.

Bramham, P. (2006) 'Police and Policing in Keighley 1856–1870', *The Local Historian, 36*(3) 175–184.

Bramham, P. and Wagg, S. (eds) (2011) *The New Politics of Leisure and Pleasure*. Basingstoke: Palgrave Macmillan.

Clarke, J. and Critcher, C. (1985) *The Devil Makes Work: Leisure in Capitalist Britain*. Basingstoke: Macmillan Press.

Critcher, C. and Bramham, P. (2004) 'The Devil Still Makes Work', in J. Haworth and A. Veal (eds) *Work and Leisure*. London and New York: Routledge.

Critcher, C. and Clarke, J. (1981) 'The Sociology of Leisure: Review of the Conventional Wisdom', in A. Tomlinson (ed.) *Leisure and Control* (revised format 1995 ed., Vol. 19). Eastbourne: Leisure Studies Association Publications.

Cunningham, H. (1980) *Leisure in the Industrial Revolution c1780–c1880*. London: Croom Helm.

Deem, R. (1986) *All Work and No Play? The Sociology of Women and Leisure*. Milton Keynes: Open University Press.

Deem, R. (1999) 'How Do We Get Out of the Ghetto? Strategies for Research on Gender and Leisure for the Twenty-First Century', *Leisure Studies, 18*(3) 161–178.

Dennis, N., Henriques, F. and Slaughter, C. (1969) *Coal is Our Life: An Analysis of a Yorkshire Mining Community* (2nd ed. Previous ed. published by Eyre & Spottiswoode, 1956). London: Tavistock Publications.

Dumazadier, J. (1967) *Towards a Society of Leisure*. New York: Free Press.

Foucault, M. (1972) *The Archaeology of Knowledge*. New York: Pantheon.

Foucault, M. (1979) *Discipline and Punish*. New York: Vintage Books.

Foucault, M. (1980) *Power/Knowledge*. New York: Pantheon.

Giddens, A. (1979) *Central Problems in Social Theory. Action, Structure and Contradiction in Social Analysis.* London: Macmillan.

Gilchrist, P. and Wheaton, B. (eds) (2008) *Whatever Happened to the Leisure Society?* (Vol. 102). Eastbourne: Leisure Studies Association.

Gilroy, P. (1987) *'There Ain't No Black in the Union Jack': The Cultural Politics of Race and Nation*. London: Routledge.

Gilroy, P. (1993) *The Black Atlantic: Modernity and Double Consciousness*. London: Verso.

Green, E., Hebron, S. and Woodward, D. (1990) *Women's Leisure, What Leisure?* London: Macmillan.

Habermas, J. (1971) *Toward a Rational Society: Student Protest, Science and Politics* (J. J. Shapiro, trans.). London: Heinemann Educational.

Habermas, J. (1979) *Communication and the Evolution of Society*. Boston, MA: Beacon Press.

Hall, S. (1980) 'Cultural Studies and the Centre: Some Problematics and Problems', in S. Hall, D. Hobson and P. Willis (eds) *Culture, Media, Language*. London: Heinemann.

Hall, S. (1988) 'Brave New World', *Marxism Today* (October), 24–29.

Hall, S. (1992) 'Introduction', in S. Hall and B. Gieben (eds) *Formations of Modernity* (pp. 1–16). Cambridge: Polity Press/Open University Press.

Hall, S., Critcher, C., Jefferson, T., Clarke, J. and Roberts, B. (1978) *Policing the Crisis: Mugging, the State and Law and Order*. London: Macmillan.

Heidegger, M. (1962) *Being and Time*. Oxford: Blackwell.

Hobsbawm, E. (2011) *How to Change the World. Tales of Marx and Marxism.* (First published in UK by Little, Brown) London: Abacus.

Hoggart, R. (1957) *The Uses of Literacy*. Harmondsworth: Penguin.

Jenkins, C. and Sherman, B. (1979) *Leisure Shock*. London: Eyre Methuen.

Kuhn, T. S. (1970) *The Structure of Scientific Revolutions* (2nd ed.). Chicago: Chicago University Press.

Marcuse, H. (1991) *One Dimensional Man: Studies in the Ideology of Advanced Industrial Society* (2nd ed.). Boston: Beacon.

Parker, S. (1971) *The Future of Work and Leisure*. London: MacGibbon and Kee.

Poulantzas, N. (1978) *State, Power, Socialism*. London: New Left Books.

Rapoport, R. and Rapoport, R. (1975) *Leisure and the Family Life Cycle*. London: Routledge.

Rigby, S. (1998) *Marxism and History. A Critical Introduction* (2nd ed.; 1st ed. published 1987). Manchester: Manchester University Press.

Roberts, K. (1978) *Contemporary Society and the Growth of Leisure*. London: Longman.

Rojek, C. (2000) *Leisure and Culture*. Basingstoke: Macmillan.

Rojek, C. (2005) *Leisure Theory: Principles and Practice*. Basingstoke: Palgrave Macmillan.

Rojek, C. (2010) *The Labour of Leisure: The Culture of Free Time*, available from http://ezproxy.leedsmet. ac.uk/login?url=http://www.dawsonera.com/depp/reader/protected/external/AbstractView/ S9781849204392.

Scraton, S. (1994) 'The Changing World of Women and Leisure: Feminism, "Postfeminism" and Leisure', *Leisure Studies, 13*(4) 249–261.

Stedman Jones, G. (1977) 'Class Expression versus Social Control? A Critique of Recent Trends in the Social History of "Leisure"', *History Workshop, 4* (Autumn) 162–170.

Stedman Jones, G. (1983) *Languages of Class: Studies in English Working Class History 1832–1982*. Cambridge: Cambridge University Press.

Steedman, C. (1983) *Policing the Victorian Community*. London: Routledge and Kegan Paul.

Stonier, T. (1983) *Wealth of Information: Profile of the Post-Industrial Society*. London: Methuen.

Storch, R. (1975) 'The Plague of Blue Locusts', *International Review of Social History, 20*: 61–91.

Storch, R. (1976) 'The Policeman as Domestic Missionary', *Journal of Social History, 9*: 481–501.

Veal, A. (1987) *Leisure and the Future*. London: George, Allen and Unwin.

Williams, R. (1965) *The Long Revolution*. Harmondsworth: Penguin.

Willis, P. E. (1977) *Learning to Labour: How Working Class Kids Get Working Class Jobs*. Farnborough: Saxon House.

18

LEISURE IN CULTURE

Garry Chick

In *Anthropology*, the discipline's first general text, Edward Burnett Tylor (1881) presented a remarkably prescient introduction to a field of study that was arguably only two or three decades old. While several chapters in the book are long obsolete, others are surprisingly modern in both content and organization. Chapters 8 through 11, for example, deal with the development of tools, the food quest, housing, clothing, transportation, food preparation, technology and commerce. Tylor subsumed these chapters under the general rubric 'Arts of Life'. In contrast, he titled chapter 12, the 'Arts of Pleasure'. There, he addressed poetry, music, dance, drama, art, play and games. Tylor's division of culture into the ways that humans make their livings and raise their families (the Arts of Life) and the ways in which they commonly seek enjoyment and give meaning to life (the Arts of Pleasure) was both observant and insightful. In current anthropological parlance, these are often described as utilitarian culture and expressive culture.

In an earlier book, *Primitive Culture*, Tylor (1871) provided the first modern definition of culture in its anthropological sense as 'that complex whole which includes knowledge, belief, art, morals, law, customs, and any other capabilities and habits acquired by man as a member of society' (p. 1). Two aspects of Tylor's definition have remained part of nearly all definitions of culture since then. First, he noted that, as members of human society, individuals learn culture from others. Second, because it is learned from others, it is shared. Understood in this way, culture became the key concept of anthropology and, by the middle of the twentieth century, many anthropologists thought of it as 'the most central problem of all of social science' (Malinowski, 1939: 588) and 'a foundation stone of the social sciences' (Chase, 1948: 59). In their encyclopedic review of the culture concept, the eminent American anthropologists Alfred. L. Kroeber and Clyde Kluckhohn declared 'in explanatory importance and in generality of application it [culture] is comparable to such categories as gravity in physics, disease in medicine, evolution in biology' (Kroeber and Kluckhohn, 1952: 3). These lofty claims, however, have yet to be realized.

As with other constructs, the explanatory power of culture depends on how it is defined, and most anthropological definitions can be grouped into three types on the basis of their content (Chick, 1997). First, culture can be thought of as a mental phenomenon, one that includes the knowledge, beliefs and values shared by a group. Keesing (1976: 139), for example, held that culture refers to 'systems of shared ideas, to the conceptual designs, the shared systems of meaning, that underlie the ways in which a people live'. Second, some add distinctive behaviours or behaviour patterns to the definition. Ember and Ember (1988: 167) refer to culture as 'the set of learned values, behaviours, and beliefs, that are characteristics of a particular society or population'. Finally, some include artefacts as part of their definitions. For Brown (1991: 40), for example, 'Culture is the conventional patterns of thought, activity, and artifact that are passed on from generation to generation in a manner that is generally assumed to involve learning rather than specific genetic programming'.

Basically, all definitions of culture involve some combination of knowledge, beliefs, values, behaviours or artefacts. However, the addition of the last two items creates a problem in using culture as an explanatory variable, as envisioned by Kroeber and Kluckhohn (1952), for example. The problem is that culture can no longer be used to explain behaviour or artefact, if behaviour or artefact is already part of its definition. Any effort to do so would result in a circular argument.

This has led many anthropologists to opt for cognitively oriented definitions such as that proposed by Goodenough in 1957:

> A society's culture consists of whatever it is one has to know or believe in order to operate in a manner acceptable to its members. Culture is not a material phenomenon; it does not consist of things, behaviour, or emotions. It is rather an organization of these things. It is the form of things that people have in mind, their models for perceiving, relating, and otherwise interpreting them.
>
> (p. 167)

Soon after Goodenough proposed his definition, Roberts (1964) generalized what people know and believe as 'information'. He claimed that 'It is possible to regard all culture as information and to view any single culture as an "information economy" in which information is received or created, retrieved, transmitted, and even lost' (p. 438). Thus, in order to behave in a manner acceptable to their peers, people require shared information. Using the concept of information, Richerson and Boyd (2005) defined culture as 'information capable of affecting individuals' behaviour that they acquire from other members of their species through teaching, imitation, and other forms of social transmission' (p. 5). Finally, Mesoudi, Whiten and Laland (2006) defined information as 'ideas, knowledge, beliefs, values, skills, and attitudes' (p. 331). The definitions of Goodenough (1957), Roberts (1964) and Richerson and Boyd (2005) provide a foundation for the examination of the place of leisure in culture.

Despite Tylor's pioneering work, anthropologists have shown only sporadic interest in leisure and leisure activities (e.g., games, festivals). Indeed, coverage of some expressive activities, including play and games, has actually declined over the years (Chick and Donlon, 1992). Hence, in 1998, I proposed several issues that I felt a cultural analysis of leisure should address (Chick, 1998). I will examine below how these suggestions have fared. I will also add another recent development in leisure and culture that it would have been wise to include in 1998.

Issues for the study of leisure in culture

In my 1998 article I proposed that a foundation for the study of leisure in culture should focus research attention on four areas. These include (1) the ethnography of leisure, (2) the cross-cultural validity of the leisure concept, (3) the adaptive value of leisure, and (4) the concurrent evolution of leisure and culture.

The ethnography of leisure

It remains true that most leisure research is still conducted in North America and Europe and, even more specifically, in the English-speaking regions of the world. Not surprisingly, however, leisure research, and especially research directed at tourism, is burgeoning in other areas of the world, such as China and India. It also remains true that most leisure research is conducted from a social-psychological perspective, meaning that purely descriptive, ethnographic work is rare. Indeed, it is difficult to discuss the concept of leisure in culture in any real depth because leisure has been described in detail in only a few, almost exclusively Western societies. It is difficult to see how valid theorizing and hypothesis testing can be accomplished when leisure is taken for granted to be a panhuman phenomenon, in lieu of a substantial base of cross-cultural ethnographic data. Nevertheless, it is done all the time.

But, what is ethnography? At its most basic level, ethnography is description. Furnham (2004), for example, asserted that 'Science begins with description, then taxonomy, then understanding' (p. 168). So, what is different about ethnographic description and other forms of description? Typically, ethnographies address what groups of 'people know, feel, and do' (Handwerker, 2001: 7) in particular times and places. Traditionally, anthropologists and others most frequently conducted ethnographic field research in cultural groups other than their own, but, with increased globalization, ethnographers now often work in their own or nearby communities. And anthropology is not the only field to use ethnography. Sociology in the twentieth century, for example, adopted, and adapted, ethnography as a means to examine the impacts of industrialization and urbanization in Europe and North America. A classic example is the 1929 ethnography of life in Muncie, Indiana (referred to as 'Middletown'), USA, by Robert S. and Helen M. Lynd.

An ethnography usually requires extended stays in the community of interest, generally at least a year and often longer, and involves most, and sometimes all, aspects of the lives of community members. But that has changed, with increased attention to more narrowly defined topics and/or contexts. Mini- and micro-ethnographies now focus on things such as the workings of a classroom (e.g., Smith, 2006) or a business enterprise (e.g., Hay, 1990), and may require only a few days, weeks or months (Handwerker, 2001; Bernard, 2011).

It is commonly thought that ethnography means 'qualitative', that is, research that relies solely on techniques such as participant observation and interviews. While this may be true for most ethnographies, it is demonstrably false in others. Good ethnography, according to Bernard (2011), may involve not only participant observation and interviews but also surveys, the use of archival data, field experiments and whatever other methods are necessary to find out what the ethnographer wants to know.

In 1982, Achen claimed, 'Data analysis in social science consists almost entirely in description' (p. 12). In this sense, numerous descriptive studies have been published in leisure research outlets since 1997, some of which claim to be ethnographic. Derbaix and Decrop (2011), for example, did a five-year study wherein they examined the football (soccer) subcultures of three European countries, Belgium, France and Spain. They conducted multiple interviews of 30 fans, observed and filmed games and other football-related activities and studied fan consumption of team paraphernalia. Their data illustrated how the team merchandise supports identity formation in fans.

Spracklen, Timmins and Long (2010) employed 'medium-term ethnographic research' on rugby league in northern England to show how it invents traditions linked to a 'white, working-class twentieth century culture of mills, pits, terraced houses and pubs' (p. 397). Johnson and Samdahl (2005) used what they termed 'feminist ethnography' to describe how gay men attempt to situate a gay country-western bar as a male space in response to a regular, Thursday Lesbian Night. Yarnal (2004) conducted a participant-observation study of a group cruise tour. One of her findings was that older cruise tourists use the experience to escape the social norms that accompany ageing. Clark, Hendee and Campbell (2009) used participant observation and a survey to determine problem behaviour occurring in campgrounds, formulate hypotheses and gather data on informants' knowledge and attitudes toward undesirable behaviour in public campgrounds. They found that campers and camp managers do not share the concept of environmental experience. The former felt that they could have the equivalent of a wilderness experience in a developed campground, while the latter failed to recognize the desire for such experiences among campers. Additionally, campers and camp managers differed in their perception of problem behaviours in campgrounds, with the former being more tolerant of litter and the behaviours of other campers than was the case for the latter. Brown (2007) examined shag dancing in the American Southeast (the states of North and South Carolina, Georgia and Virginia) using ethnographic methods including participant observation and interviews over a period of three years. Shag dancing developed in the 1940s among white, southern teenagers and is characterized by 'a languid sensuality and slow, casual thigh and chest contact' danced to music developed from 'early rhythm and blues, rock and roll, pop music, and gospel' (Brown, 2007: 24). Brown (2007) categorized shaggers into subtypes in terms of the level of their commitment to the activity.

After a substantial hiatus, anthropologists are also once again conducting ethnographic research on leisure and considering significant consequences of leisure, such as health and well-being, in non-Western cultures. These studies are important in alleviating what Henrich, Heine, and Norenzayan (2010) identified as the practice of making 'broad claims about human psychology and behaviour in the world's top journals based on samples drawn entirely from Western, Educated, Industrialized, Rich, and Democratic (WEIRD) societies' (p. 61). Henrich *et al.* (2010) claim that samples from WEIRD societies, often college undergraduates, are 'particularly unusual compared with the rest of the species' and 'are among the least representative populations one could find for generalizing about humans' (*ibid.*). Regrettably, the overwhelming majority of extant leisure research, including most ethnographic studies, is based on information from WEIRD samples. But there are exceptions.

In long-term ethnographic field research in Brazil and the southern United States dating to the early 1990s, Dressler and his associates (e.g., Dressler *et al.*, 1998; Dressler and Bindon, 2000; Dressler *et al.*, 2005; Dressler, *et al.*, 2007a; 2007b) have shown that lifestyle factors, including leisure, are systematically related to measures of physical and mental health. Specifically, they showed that members of cultural communities in Brazil and the southern USA share understandings of what constitutes a preferred or successful lifestyle, operationalized in terms of material possessions, leisure activities and social support. Dressler and his colleagues demonstrated that individuals who are more able to participate in this agreed-upon successful lifestyle are better adapted to the social and material conditions of their lives.

Chick and Dong (2009; Dong and Chick, 2012) produced descriptive accounts of leisure activities and constraints in six large cities in China, based on participant observation and also ethnographic techniques such as free listing and large-scale surveys. They found, for example, that leisure constraints can be categorized, based on their perceived importance to informants, into eight relatively distinct types. This work has formed the basis for additional ethnographic research currently in progress in Taiwan (e.g., Yeh *et al.*, 2010; 2011).

Given the rapidly expanding interest in leisure in China, research there is proliferating, as well. Ngai (2005), for example, examined the relationship between leisure satisfaction and quality of life in Macao, China. Important studies in China, conducted by Chinese scholars, written in Chinese and published in Chinese outlets, include Sun, Chen and Han's (2001) study of leisure among the elderly, Xu, Chen and Yang's (2008) study of leisure among university students, and Song's (2001) study of the economic aspects of leisure. Shi and Li (2010) examined leisure constraints among the elderly in three distinct parts of Beijing. Li and Chai (1999) examined patterns of leisure-time use and Sun (2008) looked at daily leisure-sport participation, including constraints, among women of three ethnic minority groups, the Uygur, Kyrgyz and Tajik, in western China. While these studies are largely descriptive and atheoretical, Qui (2007) claimed that aspects of culture, such as knowledge and religion, provide the bases for leisure constraints in China.

Leisure research in China and other rapidly developing areas of the world is in its infancy but growing quickly (see, e.g., Dong and Yi-Kook, 2010). Ethnographic research should lead the way, since, as pointed out by Furnham (2004), we need to know what exists before attempting to explain why it exists.

The cross-cultural validity of the leisure concept

Cross-cultural comparative researchers have two principal objectives. First, they use the ethnographic record in order to describe variation in cultural traits among societies. Second, they attempt to explain observed variation through hypothesis testing. While most cross-cultural studies are based on secondary data (using large databases such as the Human Relations Area Files [HRAF]) and include worldwide samples of societies, some, particularly those conducted by psychologists, involve the collection of primary data on only two or a few societies for explicitly comparative purposes (see Chick [2000] for a discussion of the HRAF, its use, and its potential for leisure research).

Unfortunately, cross-cultural researchers using secondary data have all but completely ignored leisure, partly because of its poor coverage in the ethnographic literature. Of the more than 2,000 variables already coded for the Standard Cross-Cultural Sample, only one (Broude and Greene, 1983) refers to leisure directly, although a few others deal with leisure activities, such as games, sports or festivals. The cross-cultural comparative literature contains only two studies of leisure based on data gleaned from the HRAF. Broude and Greene (1983), using data coded from the HRAF, found that where husbands and wives spend their leisure together, they also generally engage in other activities (eating, sleeping, experiencing childbirth) together. Chick (1995) examined the relationship between time allocated to leisure and cultural complexity. He showed that the amount of time devoted to leisure varied substantially among societies, but not in relationship to complexity. However, he did find that children in societies in the middle of the scale of cultural complexity (with technologically simple hunter-gatherers at one end and technologically complex civilizations at the other) were economically productive at younger ages and that women in such societies tended to have more children. It may be that children are able to shoulder part of the workload that otherwise would fall to adults in these societies.

Other comparative studies are based on cross-national data (e.g., Beatty *et al.*, 1994), while Chick and Shen (2011) examined the relationship between time allocated to leisure and population density using data from twelve small-scale societies. Still other studies examine leisure activities more generally, but in individual societies (e.g., Blanchard, 1982; Gihring, 1983; Chick, 1991; Khan, 1997). As of now, there is no comprehensive, large-sample, comparative cross-cultural study of leisure in the literature.

Several cross-cultural comparative studies of leisure involving only two societies have appeared over the last decade. These include Spiers and Walker's (2009) study of the effects of ethnicity – specifically Chinese-Canadian and British-Canadian – and leisure satisfaction on happiness and the quality of life. They found that ethnicity affected achieving in life and life as a whole, while leisure satisfaction influenced happiness and quality of life. Again using university student samples, Walker (2009) looked at the role played by culture, self-construal, often referred to as individualism and collectivism, in leisure motivation. He found that 'higher levels of some kinds of self-construal were associated, above and beyond culture, with higher levels of some types of leisure motivation' (p. 360). Walker, Jackson and Deng (2007) examined leisure constraints among Canadian and mainland Chinese university students and found that Chinese students were more constrained by intrapersonal and interpersonal factors, while Canadians were more constrained by structural factors.

While Walker (2009) acknowledges the limitations involved with using convenience samples of university students (see Henrich *et al.*, 2010), difficulties go beyond sampling. In 1961, Campbell warned that it is never possible, in two-society comparisons, to determine whether culture or some other variable is responsible for observed differences (see also Ember and Ember, 2009). Because the studies by Walker and his colleagues compare only two societies, specifically Chinese and Canadian, they can only assume that observed differences are due to culture.

There is at least one study wherein the meaning of leisure in a non-Western language is examined in detail. Liu *et al.* (2008) studied the etymology of the term most commonly used when translating the English word 'leisure' into Mandarin Chinese: *Xiu xian* (休閒 in traditional or 休闲 in simplified Chinese). While the meaning of 'leisure' and *Xiu xian* are similar, their etymologies are very different, the former being a descendant of the Latin *licēre* ('to be permitted') and the latter being derived from concepts such as 'taking a break' but with connotations of beauty and virtue, plus the idea of an opening or discontinuity in time.

While there are no formal comparative studies of terms or phrases in multiple languages that denote the concept of leisure, informal research (Chick, 1998) suggests that single terms having such a meaning are rare cross-linguistically. Instead, many languages use a term or terms denoting 'free time' when referring to leisure. The lack of comparative etymological research on terms with meanings similar to 'leisure' makes this a fertile area for future study.

The adaptive value of leisure

Anthropologists and human behavioural ecologists have long been interested in the biological and cultural adaptations that allow people to succeed in their particular environments (Laland and Brown, 2003; Richerson and Boyd, 2005). Biologically, adaptation refers to the selection of phenotypes of individuals that results in the differential replication of genetic material in the population, or 'gene pool'. For example, selection may result in a change in the shape of the beak of a population of birds, favour the adoption of migration, or both in response to changes in the kind or availability of food. Cultural adaptations are changes in the shared information of a group that influence behaviour and, ultimately, interactions with the local natural and social environments (Richerson and Boyd, 2005). As an aspect of cultural knowledge, leisure may help individuals to adapt to their environments. That is, the way in which leisure is pursued and experienced may contribute to an individual's survival or fecundity, or both.

In what remains the best study of the adaptive value of leisure, Rubin, Flowers and Gross (1986) investigated the time-allocation patterns of four culturally similar native Amazonian groups. Slash-and-burn cultivation is the primary source of food for all four groups, though each also hunts, fishes and sells handcrafts. While all four groups live in similar habitats, the

Kanela and the Bororo habitats have lower 'forest biomass and soil nutrient levels' compared to the Xavante and the Mekranoti (Rubin *et al.*, 1986: 525). Diets varied across the groups, such that 'In nutritional terms the Mekranoti are in the best position ... and the Xavante are second best ... The Bororo are in third place ... and the Kanela are in the worst position' (Rubin *et al.*, 1986: 526–527). Despite the differences in habitat and diet quality, all four groups spent about equal amounts of time per day in working.

However, Rubin *et al.* (1986) found that the Kanela and the Bororo spend substantially less of their leisure time in high-energy activities (25.3% and 33.4%, respectively) than the Xavante and the Mekranoti (47.4% and 48.6%, respectively). This pattern is most evident for children aged under 15 years. Kanela children spend more than twice as much time sleeping and resting as they do in active play, and Bororo children spend more time in inactive than active play. On the other hand, Xavante and Mekranoti children spend substantially more time playing actively than resting or sleeping. These results suggest that leisure activity levels, and therefore the energy needed for them, are adjusted according to the degree of effort required to obtain adequate nutrition. The authors regarded the observed differences in leisure energy expenditures as a 'strategy of reducing needs ... in response to resource depletion' (p. 524), a course of action favoured over the expenditure of more time on subsistence work. A similar strategy has been observed among primates living in degraded habitats. In such circumstances, the animals spend little, if any, time in play but conserve their energy resources for the food quest (Baldwin and Baldwin, 1972; Burghardt, 2005).

Reyes-García and colleagues (2009) also used time-allocation data as part of long-term ethnographic research to investigate the possible role of social leisure on happiness and well-being among the Tsimane' of the Bolivian Amazon. Over the course of a year, the researchers conducted behavioural scans and interviews to measure the well-being (defined in terms of happiness) of individuals as well as the amount of time spent in social and solitary leisure. About a third of Tsimane' time is spent in leisure, with social leisure accounting for somewhat more time (18.1%) than solitary leisure (13.7%). Results show that 'social, not solitary, leisure has a positive and statistically significant association with subjective well-being' (Reyes-García *et al.*, 2009: 432). In contrast to previous research, Reyes-García *et al.* (2009) provide important evidence from a non-Western population of the link between social leisure and well-being.

Godoy (2002) used spousal leisure sharing as a proxy for the quality of leisure and, by implication, for the quality of life. Using time-allocation data from two Tawahka communities in eastern Honduras, he found shared leisure to be unaffected by climate, season or income at low levels, but strongly affected by the age of spouses where income is higher. In a poor village, younger and older spouses spend more leisure together than do those of middle age, while the opposite pattern was true in a wealthier village. In a second study, Godoy *et al.* (2009) reported that Tsimane' informants listed 'sharing leisure time with kin and friends' (p. 564) as one of their top ten reasons for being happy.

The studies cited above provide initial indications that, in fact, leisure is an important factor in successful adaptation to one's social and physical environments. However, the concept of adaptation is largely foreign to leisure researchers, probably because it implies an evolutionary perspective, yet another foreign concept. However, there are two types of explanations for both biological and social phenomena: proximate and ultimate (Mayr, 1961; Chick, 2001). Briefly, proximate causes of behaviour are immediate and generally involve either environmental or physiological stimuli. We eat because we are hungry, for example. However, *why* do we get hungry? We get hungry because we, along with other animals, have evolved mechanisms that warn us when fuel supplies are getting low. So, ultimate explanations are evolutionary. Unfortunately, social science, in general, and leisure research, in particular, has eschewed ultimate, evolutionary explanations. As Mayr (1961) explained long ago, proximate and ultimate explanations do not compete, but are complementary, and both are required for complete understanding of behaviour.

The concurrent evolution of leisure in culture

Since 1998 there has been little or none of the grand theorizing of the 1940s and 1950s that included leisure in general as a key factor in cultural evolution (see, e.g., Chick, 1993; 1998). However, the electronic and computer revolution of the past three decades has shaped human cultures enormously in both the developed and the developing world. This is also true of the organization and individual experience of leisure (Bryce, 2001). Mannell, Zuzanek and Aronson (2005), for example, showed through time-use surveys of a sample (n = 219) of adolescents aged 12–19 that they were engaged in free-time activities about 40% of their time, with males reporting about 3% more free time than females. Sample members spent about 28.6% of their free time watching TV or videos, 6.2% playing video games, internet surfing about 5.2%, reading 5.5%, social activities 21.3% and physically active leisure 15.6%. The authors concluded that using the internet and computer/video game-playing displaces other forms of leisure for adolescents.

However, most research on the influence of electronic technology on culture, and leisure as a part of culture, has been conducted outside of the field of Leisure Studies. Many more traditional technologies, such as television, movies and aspects of the travel and print media industries, are devoted to leisure. However, computer and internet technologies are becoming primary locations for contemporary leisure through social media, online games, virtual communities, pornography, chatrooms, newsgroups, online shopping and many others. Arora (2011) has compared the development of the internet and, especially, social networking sites, to the development of the public park. He claims that early parks served as sites for socialization, and the same is now true of online social networking sites.

'Netnography' is a research tool developed to exploit internet technology. Kozinets (2010) describes netnography as the ethnography of online cultures, while Stebbins (2010) includes it under a broader category of 'exploratory internet data collection', to be used for gathering exploratory qualitative information on leisure. Such research could involve 'virtual ethnography' (Hine, 2000) conducted by communicating with informants via online surveys, blogs, newsgroups or chatrooms. Or, it can involve electronic document analysis. This would include content analysis of 'online diaries, journals or autobiographies' (Stebbins, 2010: 470), and also of websites devoted to leisure activities in general, such sites devoted to travel and tourism, amusement, gambling, music, art and other forms of entertainment. As examples, Hamilton and Hewer (2009) conducted a 'netnographic' investigation of an online salsa (i.e., dance) forum. They examined postings where participants discussed salsa music, dance, events, reviews of salsa clubs and other salsa-related topics. In other words, they did an ethnography of salsa culture. Kozinets (1997) did a netnography of X-Philes, that is, lovers of the TV series *X-Files*. To do so, Kozinets examined multiple *X-Files* websites in order to study X-Philes culture, determining what he regarded as three foundational themes that unite the diverse fans of the programme. These themes are 'The Meaning is Out There', 'I Want To Believe', and 'Trust This One' (Kozinets, 1997: 472). He concluded that X-Philes culture involves sharing of the aesthetic standards of the show, mystery and the belief in the show's sacred nature.

Nimrod (2011) used netnography to examine a year's worth of postings by senior citizens' online communities to describe what he termed *fun culture*, the posting of jokes, stories and social games. Findings indicate that online communities for seniors provide a form of casual leisure, one not demanding a high level of involvement or special training beyond understanding of how to use the internet. Additionally, participation in the online fun culture can help to maintain seniors' social networks as their offline networks shrink. The online games may also help maintain seniors' cognitive health.

If culture is viewed as information that permits individuals to behave in accord with local standards (Goodenough, 1957; Roberts, 1964), then cultural evolution involves additions to, deletions from and changes to storehouses of such information. The rise of electronic and computer technology that has occurred at an ever-accelerating pace, largely since the middle of the 1970s, has led to changes in cultural information more rapidly than in any other era in human history. Leisure, as a part of culture, has not only been changed itself but has also been an active ingredient in that change. New forms of cultural analysis, such as netnography, will be needed to keep research abreast of such change.

Leisure in culture: developing issues in culture, leisure and health

The question of how leisure, as experienced by different cultural groups, contributes to health has come to the fore in the last two decades. Iwasaki and Bartlett (2006), for example, studied stress and coping among urban aboriginal Canadians with diabetes. Their results indicate that individuals' stress involved diabetes-related aspects of their lives, but also that culturally appropriate forms of leisure, such as native arts and crafts, dancing, music and spiritual activities, were important stress-coping mechanisms.

As indicated above, Dressler and his colleagues (e.g., Dressler *et al.*, 1996; Dressler *et al.*, 1998; Dressler *et al.*, 2005; Dressler *et al.*, 2007a; 2007b) incorporated leisure in their research on 'cultural consonance', defined as 'the degree to which individuals approximate, in their own beliefs and behaviours, the prototypes for those beliefs and behaviours encoded in cultural models' (p. 1). They showed that members of cultural communities in Brazil and the southern USA share understandings of what constitutes a preferred or successful lifestyle, operationalized in terms of material possessions, leisure activities and social support. Dressler and his colleagues demonstrated that individuals who are able to participate in this preferred lifestyle are better adapted to the social and material conditions of their lives, as indicated by measures of physical and mental health, including arterial blood pressure and symptoms of stress and depression (see also McDade, 2001; 2002). According to Dressler (2009), 'low cultural consonance is a stressful experience and is likely to be associated with poor health outcomes' (p. 1). But why does consonance lead to lower stress? As noted above, studies among both humans and other social animals show that higher stress is associated with lower levels of control over one's life. People at lower levels of status hierarchies, those who have less control over their lives, show increased stress-related conditions and symptoms (Marmot, 2004; Sapolsky, 2004a; 2004b).

Building on cultural consonance theory, Chick and colleagues sought a mechanism to explain why some individuals were unable to participate in culturally salient and preferred leisure lifestyles. Leisure-constraint theory (Crawford and Godbey, 1987; Jackson, 1991) describes such a mechanism. Jackson (1991) defined leisure constraints as things that 'limit the formation of leisure preferences and ... inhibit or prohibit participation and enjoyment in leisure' (p. 279). Research in China indicates that leisure activities constitute an agreed-on cultural domain in six large cities and leisure constraints are consensus domains in two of the six (Chick and Dong, 2009). Related research in six cities in Taiwan indicates that both leisure activities and leisure constraints compose consensus domains among inform-ants. Moreover, the perceived importance of constraints is negatively correlated with leisure satisfaction, life satisfaction and perceived health (Yeh *et al.*, 2010).

Culture, leisure and sustainability

An emerging view of sustainability is of an environmentalism not only where humans must sacrifice in order to save a planet that has limited resources, but where cultural, economic and ecological perspectives operate in harmony to best use those resources in the mainte-nance of human happiness and well-being. The long-term ethnographic research by Reyes-García and her colleagues (e.g., Reyes-García *et al.*, 2009; 2010) among the Tsimane' of the Bolivian Amazon, discussed above, is about such a form of sustainability. The authors' long-term research in a largely self-sustaining community shows how leisure relates not only to health but also to happiness and well-being. In their 2010 paper, Reyes-García *et al.*, showed that 'To spend time with close family', 'To drink home-brewed beverage' (called *chicha*), 'To be visited' and 'To visit kin' were among the ten most important activities which Tsimane' informants listed as characteristic of a good lifestyle (p. 192) and which brought them happiness.

In a very different context, Snodgrass *et al.* (2011) show, based on ethnographic interviews and participation in the online game World of Warcraft (WoW), that individuals 'who report more individual "consonance" with culturally shared models of "real-life" or offline success are more likely to play in healthier ways as assessed through players' self-reports of the impact of *WoW* on their life happiness, stress relief, and patterns of problematic play' (p. 1). The authors report that extremely absorbed players 'attribute dimensions of self to in-game avatars for potential psychological benefit or harm' (p. 23).

In still other settings, Yarnal and her colleagues (Yarnal, 2004; 2006; Yarnal, Chick and Kerstetter, 2008; Yarnal *et al.*, 2009) examined, through ethnographic and survey research, how taking a group cruise tour or being a member in an older women's organization, the Red Hat Society, contributed to happiness and well-being among members of those groups. Again, sustainability in these contexts refers to the maintenance over time of the joy of living and hope for the future.

Conclusions

There have been numerous, and varied, contributions to the research areas that I suggested in 1998 for a comprehensive understanding of the place of leisure in culture, as well as the development of important new topical areas that I failed to anticipate. While few, if any, traditional ethnographies of leisure were produced in that time period, many activity-specific or context-specific mini- or micro-ethnographies were. Several new studies address the validity of the leisure concept cross-culturally, but a great deal more work is needed. Knowledge of the possible adaptive values of leisure in culture has advanced, as well, but not necessarily in the ways I anticipated. That is, the developing research areas of culture, leisure and health and culture, leisure, happiness and well-being can also be regarded as studies of leisure's culturally adaptive values and consequences.

As indicated above, the grand cultural evolutionary theorizing that characterized the 1940s and, especially, 1950s in anthropology is gone, but, instead, anthropologists, other social scientists and physical scientists and engineers have devoted substantial attention to the study of electronic technology, its use in leisure, its use as leisure and its influence on culture. Or they have used the electronic technology to conduct research on leisure forms that has frequently been ethnographic, through netnography. Unfortunately, little of this research has come from leisure researchers and, overwhelmingly, it has not been published in mainstream leisure research journals. While traditional parks and recreation and other forms of active leisure remain important, with obesity and related ills plaguing much of the developed world, it seems clear that leisure as embedded in cultures around the world is evolving most rapidly in its electronic forms. Leisure researchers need to understand this if they are to contribute to understanding and to offer guidance in the future.

References

Achen, C. H. (1982) 'Interpreting and Using Regression'. *Sage University Paper Series on Quantitative Applications in the Social Sciences* no. 07-029. Beverly Hills and London: Sage Publications.

Arora, P. (2011) 'Online Social Sites as Virtual Parks: An investigation into leisure online and offline', *The Information Society: An International Journal* 27 (2) 113–120.

Baldwin, J. D. and Baldwin, J. I. (1972) 'The Ecology and Behavior of Squirrel Monkeys (*Saimiri oerstedi*) in a Natural Forest in Western Panama', *Folia Primatologica* 18: 161–184.

Beatty, S. E., Jeon, J. O., Albaum, G., and Murphy, B. (1994) 'A Cross-national Study of Leisure Activities', *Journal of Cross-Cultural Psychology* 25: 409–422.

Bernard, H. R. (2011) *Research Methods in Anthropology* (5th ed.). Langham, MD: AltaMira Press.

Blanchard, K. (1982) *The Mississippi Choctaws at Play*. Champaign, IL: University of Illinois Press.

Broude, G. and Greene, S. J. (1983) 'Husband–Wife Relationships', *Ethnology* 22: 263–280.

Brown, C. A. (2007) 'The Carolina Shaggers: Dance as serious leisure', *Journal of Leisure Research* 39 (4) 623–647.

Brown, D. E. (1991) *Human Universals*. New York: McGraw-Hill.

Bryce, J. (2001) 'The Technological Transformation of Leisure', *Social Science Computer Review* 19 (1) 7–16.

Burghardt, G.M. (2005) *The Genesis of Animal Play: Testing the limits*. Cambridge, MA: MIT Press.

Campbell, D. T. (1961) 'The Mutual Methodological Relevance of Anthropology and Psychology', in F. L. K. Hsu (ed.) *Psychological Anthropology: Approaches to culture and personality*. Homewood, IL: Dorsey, 333–352.

Chase, S. (1948) *The Proper Study of Mankind*. New York: Harper.

Chick, G. (1991) 'Acculturation and Community Recreation in Rural Mexico', *Play and Culture* 4 (2) 185–193.

Chick, G. (1993) 'Leisure and the Evolution of Culture: Cross-cultural tests of several hypotheses', in G. Cushman, P. Jonson, and T. Veal (eds) *Leisure and Tourism: Social and environmental change*. Sydney: Centre for Leisure and Tourism Studies, University of Technology, Sydney, 293–300.

Chick, G. (1995) 'The Adaptive Qualities of Leisure: A cross-cultural survey', in C. Simpson and B. Gidlow (eds) *Proceedings of the ANZALS Conference, 1995*. Canterbury, New Zealand: Australian and New Zealand Association for Leisure Studies, 158–163.

Chick, G. (1997) 'Cultural Complexity: The concept and its measurement', *Cross-Cultural Research* 31: 275–307.

Chick, G. (1998) 'Leisure and Culture: Issues for an anthropology of leisure', *Leisure Sciences* 20 (2) 111–133.

Chick, G. (2000) 'Opportunities for Cross-Cultural Comparative Research on Leisure', *Leisure Sciences* 22 (1) 79–91.

Chick, G. (2001) 'What is Play For? Sexual selection and the evolution of play', *Play and Culture Studies* 3 (1) 3–25.

Chick, G. and Dong, E. (2009) 'An Ethnographic Analysis of Leisure Constraints in Six Chinese Cities', *The Journal of Zhejiang University* (Humanities and Social Sciences) 39 (1) 31–42. (In Chinese).

Chick, G. and Donlon, J. (1992) 'Going Out on Limn: Geertz's "Deep Play: Notes on the Balinese Cockfight" and the anthropological study of play', *Play & Culture* 5: 233–245.

Chick, G. and Shen, S. X. (2011) 'Leisure and Cultural Complexity', *Cross-Cultural Research* 45 (1) 59–81.

Clark, R. N., Hendee, J. C., and Campbell, F. L. (2009) 'Values, Behavior, and Conflict in Modern Camping Culture', *Journal of Leisure Research* 41 (3) 377–393.

Crawford, D. and Godbey, G. (1987) 'Reconceptualizing Barriers to Family Leisure', *Leisure Science* 9: 119–127.

Derbaix, C. and Decrop, A. (2011) 'Colours and Scarves: An ethnographic account of football fans and their paraphernalia', *Leisure Studies* 30 (3) 271–291.

Dong, E. and Chick, G. (2012) 'Leisure Constraints in Six Chinese Cities', *Leisure Sciences* 34: 417–435.

Dong, E. and Yi-Kook, J. (eds) (2010) *Korean Leisure: From tradition to modernity*. Japur, India: Rawat Publications.

Dressler, W. W. (2009) 'Intracultural Diversity and the Measurement of Cultural Consonance'. Presented at the 108th Annual Meeting of the American Anthropological Association, Philadelphia, PA, 20 December.

Dressler, W. W. and Bindon, J. R. (2000) 'The Health Consequences of Cultural Consensus: Cultural dimensions of life-style, social support, and blood pressure in an African American community', *American Anthropologist* 102 (2) 244–260.

Dressler, W. W., Dos Santos, J. E., and Balieiro, M. C. (1996) 'Studying Diversity and Sharing in Culture: An Example of Lifestyle in Brazil', *Journal of Anthropological Research* 52: 331–353.

Dressler, W. W., Balieiro, M. C., and Dos Santos, J. E. (1998) 'Culture, Socioeconomic Status and Physical and Mental Health in Brazil', *Medical Anthropology Quarterly* 12: 424–446.

Dressler, W. W., Balieiro, M. C., Ribeiro, R. P., and Dos Santos, J. E. (2005) 'Cultural Consonance and Arterial Blood Pressure in Urban Brazil', *Social Science and Medicine* 61: 527–540.

Dressler, W. W., Balieiro, M. C., Ribeiro, R. P., and Dos Santos, J. E. (2007a) 'Cultural Consonance and Psychological Distress: Examining the associations in multiple causal domains', *Culture, Medicine and Psychiatry* 31: 195–224.

Dressler, W. W., Balieiro, M. C., Ribeiro, R. P., and Dos Santos, J. E. (2007b) 'A Prospective Study of Cultural Consonance and Depressive Symptoms in Urban Brazil', *Social Science and Medicine* 65: 2058–2069.

Ember, C. R. and Ember, M. (1988) *Anthropology: A brief introduction*, 5th ed. Englewood Cliffs, NJ: Prentice Hall.

Ember, C. R. and Ember, M. (2009) *Cross-cultural Research Methods*, 2nd ed. Lanham, MD: AltaMira.

Furnham, A. (2004) 'Personality and Leisure Activities: Sensation seeking and spare-time activities', in R. M. Stelmack (ed.) *On the Psychobiology of Personality: Essays in honor of Marvin Zuckerman*. Amsterdam: Elsevier, 167–183.

Gihring, T. A. (1983) 'Leisure-time Activities in an Urban Nigerian Setting: Attitudes and experience', *Journal of Leisure Research* 15: 108–124.

Godoy, R. A. (2002) 'The Life Cycle, Ecological and Economic Determinants of Spousal Leisure Sharing: Panel estimations from Tawahka Amerindians, Honduras', *Human Ecology* 30: 317–337.

Godoy, R., Reyes-García, V., Gravlee, C. C., Huanca, T., Leonard, W. R., McDade, T. W., Tanner, S. and the TAPS Bolivia Study Team. (2009) 'Moving Beyond a Snapshot to Understand Changes in the Well-being of Native Amazonians', *Current Anthropology* 50 (4) 563–573.

Goodenough, W. H. (1957) 'Cultural Anthropology and Linguistics', in P. L. Garvin (ed.) *Report of the 7th Annual Round Table Meeting on Linguistics and Language Study, Monograph Series on Languages and Linguistics* 9: 167–173. Washington, DC: Georgetown University Press.

Hamilton, K., and Hewer, P. (2009) 'Salsa Magic: An exploratory netnographic analysis of the salsa experience', *Advances in Consumer Research*, 36: 502–508.

Handwerker, W. P. (2001) *Quick Ethnography*. Walnut Creek, CA: AltaMira.

Hay, F. J. (1990) 'Microethnography of a Haitian Boutique', *Social and Economic Studies* 39 (1) 153–166.

Henrich, J., Heine, S. J., and Norenzayan, A. (2010) The Weirdest People in the World?', *Behavioral and Brain Sciences* 33 (1) 1–135.

Hine, C. (2000) *Virtual Ethnography*. London: Sage.

Iwasaki, Y. and Bartlett, J. G. (2006) 'Culturally Meaningful Leisure as a Way of Coping with Stress among Aboriginal Individuals with Diabetes', *Journal of Leisure Research* 38 (3) 321–338.

Jackson, E. L. (1991) 'Leisure Constraints/Constrained Leisure: Special issue introduction', *Journal of Leisure Research* 23: 279–285.

Johnson, C. W. and Samdahl, D. M. (2005) '"The Night They Took Over": Misogyny in a country–western gay bar', *Leisure Sciences* 27 (4) 331–348.

Keesing, R. (1976) *Cultural Anthropology.* New York: Holt, Rinehart and Winston.

Khan, N. A. (1997) 'Leisure and Recreation among Women of Selected Hill-farming Families in Bangladesh', *Journal of Leisure Research* 29 (1) 5–20.

Kozinets, R. V. (1997) '"I want to believe": An ethnography of the X-Philes' subculture of consumption', in M. Brucks and D. J. MacInnis (eds) *Advances in Consumer Research*, vol. 24. Provo, UT: Association for Consumer Research, 470–475.

Kozinets, R. V. (2010) *Netnography: Doing ethnographic research online.* Thousand Oaks, CA: Sage.

Kroeber, A. L. and Kluckhohn, C. (1952) *Culture: A critical review of concepts and definitions.* Cambridge, MA: Peabody Museum.

Laland, K. N. and Brown, G.R. (2003) *Sense and Nonsense.* Oxford: Oxford University Press.

Li, Z. and Chai, Y. (1999) 'Characteristics of Citizens' Leisure Time Use on Weekends in Dalian City', *Economic Geography* 19: 80–84. (In Chinese).

Liu, H., Yeh, C. K., Chick, G. E., and Zinn, H. C. (2008) 'An Exploration of Meanings of Leisure: A Chinese perspective', *Leisure Sciences* 30 (5) 482–488.

Lynd, R. S. and Lynd, H. M. (1929) *Middletown: A study in contemporary American culture.* Oxford, UK: Harcourt, Brace.

Malinowski, B. (1939) 'Review of Six Essays on Culture by Albert Blumenthal', *American Sociological Review* 4: 588–592.

Mannell, R. C., Zuzanek, J., and Aronson, R. (2005) 'Internet/Computer Use and Adolescent Leisure Behavior, Flow Experiences and Psychological Well-being: The displacement hypothesis', Eleventh Canadian Congress on Leisure Research, Nanaimo, BC, 17–20 May.

Marmot, M. (2004) *The Status Syndrome: How social standing affects our health and longevity.* New York: Henry Holt and Company.

Mayr, E. (1961) 'Cause and Effect in Biology', *Science* 134: 1501–1506.

McDade, T. W. (2001) 'Lifestyle Incongruity, Social Integration, and Immune Function in Samoan Adolescents', *Social Science and Medicine* 53 (10) 1351–1362.

McDade, T. W. (2002) 'Status Incongruity in Samoan Youth: A biocultural analysis of culture change, stress, and immune function', *Medical Anthropology Quarterly* 16 (2) 123–150.

Mesoudi, A., Whiten, A., and Laland, K. N. (2006) 'Towards a Unified Science of Cultural Evolution', *Behavioral and Brain Sciences* 29: 329–383.

Ngai, V. T. (2005) 'Leisure Satisfaction and Quality of Life in Macao, China', *Leisure Studies* 24: 195–207.

Nimrod, G. (2011) 'The Fun Culture in Seniors' Online Communities', *The Gerontologist* 51 (2) 226–237.

Qui, Y. (2007) 'Construction on Mode of Chinese Woman's Leisure Constraint Based on Cultural Factors', *China Sport Science and Technology* 43 (1) 10–14. (In Chinese).

Reyes-García, V., Godoy, R. A., Vadez, V., Ruíz-Mallén, I., Huanca, T., Leonard, W. R., McDade, T. W., Tanner, S., TAPS Bolivian Study Team. (2009) 'The Pay-offs to Sociability: Do solitary and social leisure relate to happiness?', *Human Nature* 20 (4) 431–446.

Reyes-García, V., Gravlee, C. C., McDade, T. W., Huanca, T., Leonard, W. R., and Tanner, S. (2010) 'Cultural Consonance and Psychological Well-being: Estimates using longitudinal data from an Amazonian society', *Culture, Medicine and Psychiatry* 34 (1) 186–203.

Richerson, P. J. and Boyd, R. (2005) *Not by Genes Alone: How culture transformed human evolution.* Chicago, IL: University of Chicago Press.

Roberts, J. M. (1964) 'The Self-management of Cultures', in W. Goodenough (ed.) *Explorations in Cultural Anthropology.* New York: McGraw-Hill.

Rubin, J., Flowers, N. M., and Gross, D. R. (1986) 'The Adaptive Dimensions of Leisure', *American Ethnologist* 13 (4) 524–536.

Sapolsky, R. M. (2004a) 'Social Status and Health in Humans and Other Animals', *Annual Review of Anthropology* 33: 393–418.

Sapolsky, R. M. (2004b) *Why Zebras Don't Get Ulcers*, 3rd ed. New York: Henry Holt and Company.

Shi, S. and Li, X. (2010) 'Beijing Older Hierarchical Model of Leisure Constraints Analysis', *Proceedings of 2010 International Symposium on Tourism Resources and Management.* Retrieved 1 September 2011, from http://www.seiofbluemountain.com/search/index.php?act=allandname=+SHI+Shaohua.

Smith, L. M. (2006) 'The Micro-ethnography of the Classroom', *Psychology in the Schools* 4 (3) 216–221.

Snodgrass, J. G., Lacy, M. G., Dengah II, H. J. F., and Fagan, J. (2011) 'Cultural Consonance and Mental Wellness in the *World of Warcraft*: Online games as cognitive technologies of

"Absorption-Immersion"', *Cognitive Technology Journal* 16 (1) (online journal: http://www.cogni-tivetechnologyjournal.com/ArticleDetail.aspx?id=239)

Song, R. (2001) 'A Preliminary Study of Leisure Economy', *Journal of Guilin Institute of Tourism* 3 (1) 39–43. (In Chinese).

Spiers, A. and Walker, G. J. (2009) 'The Effects of Ethnicity and Leisure Satisfaction on Happiness, Peacefulness, and Quality of Life', *Leisure Sciences* 31 (1) 84–99.

Spracklen, K., Timmins, S. and Long, J. (2010) 'Ethnographies of the Imagined, the Imaginary and the Critically Real: Blackness, whiteness, the North of England and rugby league', *Leisure Sciences* 29 (4) 397–414.

Stebbins, R. (2010) 'The Internet as a Scientific Tool for Studying Leisure Activities: Exploratory internet data collection', *Leisure Studies* 29 (4) 469–475.

Sun, C. (2008) 'Study on Characteristics of the Daily Leisure Sports Participation of Uygur, Kirk and Tajik Women', *Journal of Chengdu Sport University* 34 (1) 20–24. (In Chinese).

Sun, Y., Chen, T., and Han, Y. (2001) 'A Study on Leisure Behavior of the Aged in Beijing', *Geographical Research* 20: 538–546. (In Chinese).

Tylor, E. B. (1881) *Anthropology: An introduction to the study of man and civilizations.* New York: D. Appleton.

Tylor, E. B. (1871) *Primitive Culture: Researches into the development of mythology, philosophy, religion, language, art, and custom.* 2 volumes. London: John Murray.

Walker, G. J. (2009) 'Culture, Self-construal, and Leisure Motivations', *Leisure Sciences* 31 (3) 347–363.

Walker, G. J., Jackson, E. L., and Deng, J. (2007) 'Culture and Leisure Constraints: A comparison of Canadian and mainland Chinese university students', *Journal of Leisure Research* 39 (4) 567–590.

Xu, X., Chen, Z., and Yang, S. (2008) 'Research on University Students' Weekend Leisure Behaviors – a Case Study of University in Guangzhou', *Yunnan Geographic Environment Research* 20 (1) 89–93. (In Chinese)

Yarnal, C. M. (2004) 'Missing the Boat? A playfully serious look at a group cruise tour experience', *Leisure Sciences* 26 (4) 348–372.

Yarnal, C. M. (2006) 'The Red Hat Society®: Exploring the role of play, liminality, and communitas in older women's lives', *Journal of Women and Ageing* 18 (1) 51–73.

Yarnal, C., Chick, G. and Kerstetter, D. (2008) '"I did not have time to play growing up … so this is my play time. It's the best thing I have ever done for myself"': What is play to older women?', *Leisure Sciences* 30 (3) 235–252.

Yarnal, C., Kerstetter, D., Chick, G. and Hutchinson, S. (2009) 'The Red Hat Society: An exploration of play and masking in older women's lives'. *Play and Culture Studies* 8: 144–165.

Yeh, C. K., Hsu, Y. C., Chick, G., Dong, E. (2010) 'Leisure, Leisure Satisfaction, and Perceived Health in Urban Mainland China and Taiwan'. Presented at the 11th World Leisure Congress, Chuncheon, Korea, 1 September.

Yeh, C. K., Hsu, Y. C., and Chick, G. (2011) 'Using Free Listing to Develop the Taiwanese Leisure Activity Inventory', *Journal of Tourism and Leisure Studies* 17 (1) 1–23.

19

RACISMS AND THE EXPERIENCES OF MINORITIES IN AMATEUR FOOTBALL IN THE UK AND EUROPE

Steven Bradbury

Introduction

Since the early 1990s there has been a steadily growing body of academic research which has focused on issues of racism in professional football in the UK and Europe. What distinguishes the approach developed in this chapter is its focus on the previously under-researched area of racism and minority experiences in amateur football. Around 21 million people are registered to take part in organized amateur football in the UK and Europe and a further 40 million people are estimated to play football recreationally without being registered at amateur clubs. To this end, amateur football can be understood to be a prominent leisure activity for a significant percentage of the populations of Europe, including large numbers drawn from minority backgrounds. This is important, since, as Carrington points out, football, in common with many other sports, 'remains a critical site for the reproduction and re-articulation of forms of racial knowledge and common-sense and is an important location in the contested struggles over ideology, politics and identity' (Carrington, 2010: 175). From this inherently sociological perspective, sporting practice does not take place in a social, cultural or political vacuum, but, rather, it is reflective of and reflects back upon a series of historically inscribed and deeply racialized power relations embedded within the societies in which it takes place. Further, the development, organization and practice of sport can be understood as a distinctly racial formation within which a series of dominant social, economic and political forces have shaped the content and importance of racial meanings and categories. To this end, sport is both receptive to and productive of racial meanings and, through the lens of sport, social relations between peoples have become structured by the signification of human biological and cultural characteristics in such a way as to define and construct differential social collectivities along distinctly racial, ethnic and cultural lines.

Sport is also a site in which old biological and new cultural racisms impinge upon and are generated by sporting practice and have become manifest in sporting arenas in explicit and more coded forms. Anthias and Yuval Davis have argued that racisms need to be recognized as a multiplicity of 'modes of exclusion, inferiorisation, subordination and exploitation that present specific and different characters in different social and historical contexts' (Anthias and Yuval Davis, 1993: 2). Referring to racisms in the plural recognizes the complexity and diversity of racisms and their often contradictory character, and supports the assertion that 'there is no one monolithic racism but numerous historical situated racisms' (Back *et al.*, 2001: 9). Recognizing the plurality of racisms provides a useful conceptual starting-point from which to examine the myriad processes and outcomes of overt, culturally coded and more institutional forms of racism and discrimination in sport. In particular, it allows for enhanced understanding of the different ways in which different minorities experience different forms of racisms in sport across a range of intersectional indices, including gender, social class, religious affiliation and national political contexts (Rowe and Champion, 2000; Scraton *et al.*, 2005; Kay, 2006; Ratna, 2007; Hylton, 2009).

This latter point is especially relevant, given the steady increase and more recent acceleration of the ethnic, cultural and religious diversity within the national populations of many European countries. Since the 1950s and 1960s, non-European in-migration trajectories to Western Europe have been underscored by the settlement of populations drawn from former colonies, and have more recently been strongly linked to the growth in numbers of asylum seekers and refugees fleeing political persecution and armed conflicts in the Middle East, Asia and Africa (Bloch and Levy, 1999; Pillai *et al.*, 2006). Since the 1990s, the Continent has also experienced significant population movements across national borders amongst cohorts drawn from European origin, following the incorporation of the Schengen Agreement into European Union law in 1997 and the increase in the number of EU member states from the mid-2000s onward. Conversely, many post-communist countries in Central and Eastern Europe appear relatively culturally homogeneous, with few 'visible' ethnic minorities, although the presence of national and religious minorities, arguably, cuts across east–west regional divides and the political construction of nation-state boundaries. Whilst it is of course the case that a range of structural, cultural and political factors have impacted differentially in shaping the parameters of societal inclusion and exclusion amongst different minority groups across a range of national contexts, it is likely, too, that minorities have some shared experiences of overt and culturally coded forms of racialized abuse and more institutionalized forms of racism and discrimination.

Here, the term 'minority' is used as a broad descriptive marker to refer to ethnically, culturally, religiously and sub-nationally distinct populations resident within nation-state boundaries. This broad conceptualization of 'minorities' includes both second- and third-generational 'settled' minority communities and more recent economic migrants and asylum and refugee groups drawn from a range of European and non-European backgrounds who presently reside in countries in which they make up a numerical minority. This broad definition of 'minorities' is premised on the recognition that minority status is both objectively ascribed (by the dominant society) and subjectively applied (by minority groups) as a means marking out ethnic, cultural, religious and sub-national difference. Whilst these differences are often applied negatively as a basis for hostility and discrimination, they are also applied positively in terms of cultural identity, group solidarity and collective resistance to racisms. This is especially the case within the cultural arena of sports, and with particular respect to professional and amateur football. This chapter will begin by illustrating the ways in which racisms have been 'played out' and conceptualized in the professional game, before providing a full examination of the practices, experiences and contestation of racisms at the amateur level of the sport. In doing so, the chapter will draw primarily on recent empirical and ethnographic research studies conducted in the UK and Europe.

217

Racisms in professional football

Much of the academic examination of racisms in sport in the UK and Europe has focused on the elite echelons of professional football. Academic inquiry in the UK initially emerged in this area in the 1980s as a response to growing public concern regarding overt forms of individual and orchestrated racist abuse from supporters which utilized a series of demeaning epithets to describe and demean black players (Cashmore, 1982; Williams, 1984; 1992). More recently, a number of authors have referenced the uneven but residual permanence of overt racism targeting black players in countries such as England, Germany and the Netherlands and have also identified the continuation of crude forms of openly anti-black sentiment at matches in Southern, Central and Eastern Europe (Back *et al.*, 2001; Van Sterkenburg *et al.*, 2005; Kassimeris, 2007; 2009a; 2009b; Llopis-Giog, 2009; Bradbury *et al.*, 2011).

Linkages between far-right political parties and the activities of spectator formations have been well documented in academic research, especially with regard to support for the English national team, where right-wing ideologies have chimed most obviously with historically embedded ideas around 'race', nation and cultural exclusivity (Williams, 1992; Garland and Rowe, 2001; Back *et al.*, 2001). Research studies in Italy and Spain have also examined connections between Ultra fan networks, racisms and hooliganism (Roversi, 1994; Spaaij and Vinas, 2005). More recently, Kassimeris (2009a) has identified the rise of new forms of politically orientated racism, xenophobia and hyper-nationalism at lower league domestic football matches in post-unification Germany. Similarly, there have been noted attempts to reassert a sense of ethno-centric (white) national identity in and through football in (re)emergent countries in Eastern Europe and the Balkans region. For example, the Ukrainian far-right political party Svoboda has actively conjoined football, anti-immigrant sentiment and nationalist ideologies and has been involved in violent confrontation with the civil and football authorities (FARE, 2010).

From the late 1990s onwards, a number of authors have alluded to the multiplicity of ways in which racisms are manifest in football spectator culture, from more obvious forms of individual and orchestrated abuse to patterns of cultural interchange and coded discourse that take place across white spectator formations. These continued expressions of racisms are premised on shared racially structured antipathies and the celebration of homogeneously white and racially closed birthplace localisms, and represent the defence of prized (white) cultural space against wider social (and multi-cultural) change (Back *et al.*, 1998; 2001; Robson, 2000; Nash, 2000). More subtle, nuanced forms of racist expression of this kind are, arguably, underpinned by strongly embedded forms of cultural racisms which prioritize and heighten perceived differences between majority and minority populations across fissures of 'race', culture and religion. This is especially evident in the reported rise in openly expressed Islamophobic sentiment and targeted abuse of Muslim players at professional matches in the UK and Europe (Van Sterkenburg *et al.*, 2005; Burdsey, 2011; Ahmed, 2011).

In recent years, there has been an increased academic focus on examining patterns of institutional racism and discrimination in professional football in the UK and Europe. In particular, these studies have focused on the ways in which a series of racially closed institutional practices embedded within the dominant and largely unchallenged white hegemonic structures of professional football impact disproportionately on levels of representation of minorities across all tiers of the game. For example, in the UK a number of research studies have highlighted a series of relatively 'closed' operational approaches to youth talent identification at professional clubs which have historically failed to incorporate a range of sites and local settings in which young minority players are present (Bains and Patel, 1996; Football

Task Force, 1998; IFC, 2003; CRE, 2004; Bains, 2005). The work of Burdsey (2004; 2007) is especially instructive in illustrating the ways in which these practices are underpinned by a series of cultural misconceptions which portray South Asian cultures as static, falsely homogeneous and culturally disinterested in football. Similar processes of cultural stereotyping which have constructed young black players as 'difficult', 'bad tempered' and 'lacking in social etiquette' have been evidenced within professional-club youth academies in Denmark and the Netherlands (Agergaard and Sorenson, 2009; Kassimeris, 2009b). Within these 'limited conditions of equality', young minority players are expected to exercise much greater adaptation to the social and cultural mores of dominant majority populations at clubs and to 'leave their cultural identity at the door'. These findings resonate strongly with the work of King (2004a; 2004b), who asserts that the upwardly mobile career trajectories of minority players are premised on the successful negotiation of dialogic, non-verbal and ritualized processes through which the attainment of 'cultural passports' and contingent inclusions are granted or withheld within the normative white spaces that define the football work-place.

Bradbury *et al.* (2011) have suggested that the under-representation of minority, especially black, coaches in the professional game is underscored by the internalization of a series of historically inscribed cultural stereotypes on the part of club owners which equate black coaches with 'physicality over intellect', 'uncertainty' and 'risk'. This research also alluded to tendencies of club owners to recruit coaches from a limited 'diversity pool' of already experienced (mostly white) applicants embedded within the social and cultural 'boys' clubs' of professional football networks. Bradbury *et al.* argue that these practices of racially inflected institutional closure are also evidenced in mechanisms of personal recommendation, sponsored mobility and patronage which underpin recruitment to senior administrative positions at professional clubs. Whilst these practices might be unconscious, unintentional and 'embodied', they nevertheless gravitate against minorities who are positioned outside of the dominant networks of mutual acquaintance of the football industry, and favour individuals drawn from recognizable (white) backgrounds with similar cultural norms, values and behaviours.

Overt and culturally coded racisms in amateur football

Long *et al.* (2009) have argued that minorities' experiences of sport and leisure are mediated by racisms and that racist expression seems especially strong at the recreational level of organized men's amateur football. For example, Long *et al.*'s (2001) study of racism in amateur football in Northern England revealed clear differences in the perceptions and experiences of racism and the continued existence of racialized tensions between players from different ethnic backgrounds. The authors concluded that 'despite some confusion as to what constitutes racist behaviour, the research team were left in no doubt that it does occur and consequently stronger measures are needed to address it' (Long *et al.*, 2001: 9). Similar research undertaken in the East Midlands of England indicated that racism was a relatively commonplace feature of the amateur game and that 'racist remarks are sometimes aimed at ethnic minority players by opposition players and spectators' (Bradbury, 2002). More recently, research studies in the UK, Germany and the Netherlands have all alluded to the continued expressions of racialized abuse, harassment and inter-ethnic tensions during competitive matches involving minority football clubs (Halm, 2005; Van Sterkenburg *et al.*, 2005; Burdsey, 2006; 2009; Kassimeris, 2009b; Bradbury, 2010). Further, research undertaken on behalf of the European Union Federal Rights Agency (EU/FRA) found that incidents of racialized abuse are not restricted to adult football venues. The study uncovered empirical and anecdotal evidence from a range of EU member states which suggested that abuse of this kind emanated from a broad spectrum of generational cohorts including coaches, parents and spectators, and often targeted children and young players from a range of minority backgrounds (FRA, 2010).

Perhaps the most common forms of overt racialized abuse reported in amateur football in the UK and Europe are those which utilize a series of racial epithets designed to describe and demean black players. Racialized abuse of this kind shares distinct parallels with that which has been more commonly apparent amongst spectator formations in professional football and which has marked out players of African and African Caribbean heritage as 'subhuman' and 'ape-like'. However, there is also a growing body of evidence which has identified overt forms of abuse targeting amateur players on the basis of their cultural, religious or national background. For example, research studies have indicated that minority players from Turkish backgrounds in Austria, Belgium and Finland, Hungarians in Romania and Slovakia, Roma in Hungary and Bulgaria and Albanians in Greece have all experienced overt forms of abuse which has drawn on ethno-nationalist, Islamophobic, anti-Semitic or anti-Gypsy sentiment (Van Sterkenburg *et al.*, 2005; Kassimeris, 2007; EU/FRA, 2010). These studies also highlight the pejorative usage of descriptive markers of cultural and religious identity such as 'dirty Turk', 'shit Moroccan', 'fucking Jew', 'Gypsy cunt' and 'backward Muslim immigrant'.

Whilst overt racialized abuse of this kind is premised on a series of biological and (imagined) cultural referents, research studies have identified the increasing practice of much more subtle, nuanced and codified forms of racisms in the amateur game. For example, research in the UK has identified the conscious utilization of deeply racialized coded insults which mark out black players as a kind of dangerous, criminal, animalistic 'other' (Bradbury, 2010). Similarly, the work of Burdsey (2004; 2007) is especially instructive in illustrating the multi-layered processes of negative stereotyping and cultural 'othering' of South Asian, especially Muslim heritage, amateur players in the UK. Research in Germany and the Netherlands has similarly identified culturally codified abuse targeting Turkish and Moroccan players as 'bag snatchers' and 'thieves' and has cited examples of opposition players and spectators imitating bleating goats and sheep (Van Sterkenburg, 2005; Kassimeris, 2009b). Similarly, players in predominantly Jewish teams in Austria, Germany, Belgium, Denmark, Austria and Hungary have all reportedly been subject to coded anti-Semitism, including comments regarding perceived physical and cultural traits, and hissing sounds in reference to the gas chambers (EU/FRA, 2010; Bradbury *et al.*, 2011).

Whilst incidences of racialized abuse in amateur football have often occurred as an immediate effect of 'heat of the moment' verbal and physical exchanges between players from different ethnic, cultural or religious backgrounds, they have also been utilized by opposition spectators and players as part of a framework of intimidating and hostile behaviours designed to 'wind up' and 'unsettle' opponents (Müller *et al.*, 2007). These more instrumental expressions of racialized abuse are viewed – and often explained away – in dominant narratives as inherently non-ideological or as one element in a wider array of physical-feature abuse which is considered to be 'part and parcel' of the game. These latter perspectives allude to a more broadly held set of norms and values within the heavily masculinized amateur (and professional) football arena which premise the acceptability of 'testing' opponents through 'trash talking' and 'banter' (Back *et al.*, 2001). However, these common-sense accounts largely extricate expressions of racialized abuse from the deeply racialized structural, cultural and national contexts in which they take place and underplay the contextual intentionality and purpose of racist expression. Whilst it is of course the case that the perception of racism on the part of those who witness or experience it is not a necessary or sufficient condition of its existence, it is important to locate the interpretation of its meaning within the contextual layers and local settings in which these racialized actions are performed and acted out (Long and McNamee, 2004). In this respect, the use of racially coded signifiers can be understood as a distinctly situated and consciously strategic response by majority-population players that is designed to reify cultural difference and encourage racialized antagonisms in a more consciously 'disguised' form. From this perspective, the continued expression of overt and culturally coded racialized abuse can be understood as offering symbolic opposition to notions of multi-culturalism as embodied within the demographic make-up of teams with significant numbers of minority players. More specifically, such behaviours can also be read as designed (and understood) to mark out some contingent parameters of belonging and cultural inclusion within the sphere of amateur football and within local (and national) societal relations more broadly.

Institutional racism and discrimination in amateur football

There has thus far been little emphasis amongst academics and policy makers on examining the processes and outcomes of institutional racism and discrimination in amateur football. Broadly speaking, where attention has been paid to this area of study it has tended to focus on two key areas. Firstly, on those more formal processes of racially inflected institutional closure emanating from the conjunctive relationship between national political models of citizenship and organizational practices and provision enacted by national governing bodies of football. Secondly, on those less formal, relatively hidden forms of racialized exclusion embedded within the everyday operations of national and regional football federations and at amateur football clubs at the local level. With reference to more formal processes of institutional closure, the recent work of the Council of Europe: European Commission against Racism and Intolerance (ECRI) and the EU/FRA report on the exclusion of migrants and minorities in sport are particularly instructive. For example, the ECRI report on combating racism and racial discrimination in the field of sport refers in its general policy recommendation No. 12 to the existence of 'legal and administrative barriers to the participation of non-citizens in local and national sports competitions in some countries' (ECRI, 2008: 7). The report goes on to say that, as a result of these barriers, both professional and amateur sports clubs have often been reluctant to admit persons who do not possess the citizenship of the country concerned. This is especially the case in a number of EU countries where national citizenship laws work in tandem with sports governing bodies' regulations to have a restricting effect on the participation of new migrants and generationally 'settled' minorities in sports, including amateur football. For example, the EU/FRA report has indicated that in one-third of EU member states fewer than between one and five citizens of other EU countries or third-country nationals are allowed to participate in amateur football teams per game. This is the case in Austria, Malta, Spain, Greece, Germany, Portugal, Slovakia, Italy and Denmark. In these latter two countries, young first- and second-generation migrants cannot legally become national citizens before the age of 18 years and football federations operate a series of quotas for national citizens in youth football. This has meant that for young new migrants and second-generation minority children and young people born in these countries to parents from different countries of origin, opportunities to play organized football remain especially limited. At the recent Sport Inclusion Network and

Football Against Racism in Europe conferences held in Vienna and Rome, respectively, in 2012, a number of academics, activists and minority representatives argued forcefully that such practices were inherently discriminatory and were perceived to be in breach of the European Charter for Fundamental Rights, which was ratified by the Lisbon Treaty in 2007 (EP/EC/EC 2007).

In addition to these deeply racialized formal legislative processes of exclusion, a number of research studies have illustrated the ways in which racially inflected patterns of institutional closure have been subtly enacted by pre-existing amateur clubs. The ethnographic studies of Burdsey (2006; 2009), Bradbury (2010; 2011) and Campbell (2011) in examining the socio-historical development of minority clubs in the UK locate the experiences of first- and second-generation minority players within the broader political context of England in the 1960s, 1970s and 1980s. These authors argue that in many major industrial areas in England during this period, rapidly changing local racial demographies engendered significant expression of resentment and hostility on the part of indigenous white communities towards newly arrived and recently settled minority communities. They go on to say that the expression of these wider societal racisms and embedded oppositions to racial integration were especially evident within the culture and practice of amateur football, where club affiliation was (and, arguably, still is) deeply rooted within heavily masculine and homogeneously white neighbourhood and kinship networks. Further, these socially constructed patterns of organization were felt to have contributed significantly to shaping the initial parameters and focus of inclusion and exclusion of young minority males in the amateur game and acted as an accelerant towards the formation of clubs from within minority kinship, community and religious networks. Other research studies have identified some comparable findings on this score with respect to the exclusion of marginalized Roma populations from mainstream amateur clubs in Central and Eastern Europe, and the lack of throughput of minority players from recreational 'street football' to more structured participation in organized amateur football settings in Denmark and the Netherlands (Halm, 2005; Agergaard and Sorenson, 2009; Bradbury *et al.*, 2011).

A number of research studies in the UK and Europe have also alluded to the historically problematic relationship between minority football clubs and regional and national football federations in the UK and Europe. In particular, these studies reference accounts of unfair treatment and unequal disciplinary procedures enacted against minority clubs and the apparent reluctance of football federations to acknowledge and then deal swiftly, effectively and transparently with incidents of racialized abuse. For example, the EU/FRA report has cited examples of discriminatory treatment in the allocation of training and match-day facilities for minority participants in Austria, Germany and Finland and alludes to the strong cultural oppositions to the greater integration of Portuguese heritage minority teams into the national competition structures of the Luxembourg football federation (EU/FRA, 2010). The work of Andersson in Sweden has drawn attention to the accounts of players at Stockholm-based minority clubs which allude to unfair treatment by referees and the greater likelihood that minority players would be booked or sent off during games for committing similar offences to indigenous Swedish players who remained unpunished (Andersson, 2009). Similarly, studies in the UK have identified the reluctance of referees to acknowledge incidents of racialized abuse and afford appropriate protection from abuse to minority players in this respect (Williams, 1994; Burdsey, 2006; 2009). Bradbury (2011) has also noted a marked discontentment amongst minority clubs in England with respect to the often lengthy, unwieldy and 'behind closed doors' approach of disciplinary procedures enacted by regional federations in the amateur game.

To some extent, the lack of action taken against racialized abuse in amateur football is informed by the residual embeddedness of some deeply held cultural stereotypes which have problematized minority players as 'troublesome' and 'hot-headed'. For example, research undertaken by Long *et al.* (2001) and Bradbury (2002) found that processes of negative stereotyping were relatively commonplace within the amateur football fraternity in the UK, with particular regard to black and South Asian players. Similarly, Turkish and Moroccan players in the Netherlands and Germany, Somali players in Denmark and players from the Balkans in Central and Eastern Europe have been comparably marked out in amateur football as having a 'bad attitude' and being 'difficult' (Agergaard and Sorenson, 2009; EU/FRA 2010; Bradbury *et al.*, 2011). Further, Andersson has noted some historical consistencies in media coverage of amateur football in Stockholm which has labelled Southern European minorities from Greece and Croatia as 'temperamental' and 'violent', in contrast to the perceived 'calmness' and 'respectful' manner of indigenous Swedish players (Andersson, 2009).

This problematization of minority players has also been extended to those who have actively spoken out against racialized abuse in the amateur game and who have invariably been accused of 'complaining' and 'being confrontational' and as 'playing the race card'. This practice has allowed football federations to deny the widespread existence and veracity of racism in the amateur game and has limited the parameters in which overt and more subtle manifestations of racialized abuse can be challenged and redressed. To this end, the work of Lusted (2009; 2011) is particularly instructive in identifying the traditional modus operandi of regional football governance in the UK and the distinctly conservative and colonialist ideologies of largely older, white males who occupy powerful positions within this voluntary and relatively autonomous infrastructure. Lusted argues that the deeply embedded hegemonic whiteness and racialized power base within amateur football governance enables a series of culturally defensive and protectionist rather than reformist philosophies and practices to be sustained over time. Further, the limited accountability of such bodies to the national ownership of the game confers significant authority on senior officials to act as key gate-keepers of the process of enabling or denying best racial equality practice at the local level. From this perspective, the non-recognition of and lack of commitment to act against racism in amateur football and the problematization of minority behaviours can be read as collective failure on the part of football federations to provide an equitable service to its broad and culturally diverse constituency of amateur players. This analysis chimes strongly with the broadly accepted notion of institutional racism outlined in the Macpherson report (1999), which suggests that discrimination of this kind can be 'detected in processes, attitudes and behaviour which amount to discrimination through unwitting prejudice, ignorance, thoughtlessness and racist stereotyping which disadvantage minority groups'.

Resisting racisms in amateur football: the case of minority clubs

Whilst the practice and experiences of myriad forms of overt, cultural and institutional racisms have been a relatively commonplace feature of amateur football in the UK and Europe, the amateur game has also been a site in which racisms of this kind have been negotiated and contested across a range of local, regional and national contexts. For example, research studies charting the socio-historical development of minority participation in organized amateur football in the UK have explicitly linked the formation of minority clubs with experiences of racial closure at pre-existing (white) amateur clubs (Bradbury, 2010; 2011; Burdsey, 2006; 2009; Campbell, 2011). The authors of these studies have argued that these minority clubs have provided a conscious physical safeguard against the on-going realities of overt racist expression and more subtle, nuanced and codified forms of cultural racisms and have provided safe and supportive leisure spaces for players from minority backgrounds. Further, a number of authors have referenced the importance of minority clubs in terms of their assumed position as a highly visible cultural resource and symbolic marker for the construction and expression of specific ethnic and religious identities (Westwood, 1990; 1991; Williams, 1994; Carrington, 1998; 1999; and Burdsey, 2006; 2007; 2009). In particular, these authors suggest that minority football (and cricket) clubs have acted as sites of cultural resistance to wider societal racism and perceived community injustice through their involvement in victories against perceived historical oppressors and the celebration of the minority sporting achievement. From these perspectives, minority clubs are understood to represent discursively constructed and distinctly racialized symbolic spaces within which participation has come to constitute a form of local community politics and community empowerment.

Research undertaken by Bradbury (2010; 2011) and Burdsey (2006; 2009) has also referenced the identifiable (and identifiably) different social, cultural and religious attachments of minority clubs in the UK. These authors suggest that the historically embedded cultural identities of clubs of this kind have helped to sustain the organizational commitment of older minority participants as club coaches and administrators and have continued to engender a strong cultural appeal to new youth cohorts. This is especially the case at South Asian clubs which have strong developmental connections to specific religious places of worship such as Sikh temples and which enable opportunities for familial, cultural and religious continuities and socialization. Further, Bradbury has argued that whilst key organizers at these South Asian clubs have made conscious attempts to avoid the kinds of racial closure which had previously impacted on their own personal experience of the game, it is likely that clubs of this kind probably have relatively limited wider appeal to players from other religious or more secular backgrounds. Also, deeply embedded racist sentiment and residual cultural stereotypes have probably gravitated away from greater sporting integration in this respect and maintained the relative demographic homogeneity of these clubs.

In contrast, other minority football clubs with less explicit cultural and religious affiliations have been a little more successful in diversifying the make-up of teams to include young players from a range of ethnic backgrounds with a strong connectedness to the everyday lived experiences of some urban multi-cultural settings. This is especially where there is a strong and highly politicized ethos regarding the social function of clubs as facilitators of multi-ethnic service provision for youth communities experiencing disproportionate levels of social, economic and cultural marginalization. Regardless of their cultural identities and make-up, minority clubs in the UK have provided valuable participation opportunities in organized football for a range of marginalized communities for whom access to local organized football has been institutionally and historically limited. Further, the conscious facilitation of inter-cultural leisure spaces at clubs has enabled young people to actively extend social connections with players from a diverse range of ethnic backgrounds. In this respect, some minority clubs have come to occupy a site in which meaningful and equitable racial integration is being positively enacted, at least within some distinctly generational, classed and highly localized settings. To this end, minority clubs can be understood to offer a practical and ideological 'third space' (Bhabha, 1990a; 1990b) in which the potential for new diverse inclusions and cross-cultural interaction might contribute to the production new, culturally hybrid identities premised on the celebration of diversity and the shared social, cultural and sporting habitus of youthful populations drawn from specific multi-ethnic locales.

Concluding comments: the limits of resistance and the centrality of hegemonic whiteness

Despite the realized efforts of minority clubs to enable collective physical and symbolic resistance to racisms, promote community empowerment and racial integration and facilitate the production of new multi-ethnic leisure spaces, their capacity to challenge and disrupt some deeply racialized hegemonic power relations embedded within the core structures of amateur football and beyond remains limited. In the first instance, the potential of minority clubs to engender increased participation opportunities and generate positive wider social outcomes for participants cannot be divorced from the wider structural dynamic and racial politics of the societies in which they are situated. In many more ethnically and culturally polarized nation-states across Europe where attitudes to 'race' have been much less malleable over time and where there exists a deeply embedded cultural resistance to the inclusion of minorities in local social relations, the likelihood of success in combating racism and enabling more equitable participation in amateur football is markedly lessened. This is, arguably, especially the case in countries in Central and Eastern Europe which exhibit rigid models of national identity and citizenship and where there is a marked defensiveness and general de-prioritization of policy interventions designed to address minority discrimination. However, it is probably also the case in many Western European countries where, in the post-9/11 period of modern history, there is a growing sense of 'democratic impatience' at the perceived lack of integration of Muslim communities and a general shift in political thinking away from multi-culturalism and towards the rhetoric and policy of integration and assimilation (Parekh, 2006; Kymlicka, 2010; Vertovec and Wessendorf, 2010).

In the second instance, there is little evidence to suggest that increased levels of minority participation in the game as players has enabled greater access to and adaptation of the presently inadequate and inequitable structures of governance at regional and national football federations. For example, research undertaken by Bradbury *et al.* (2011) indicates that fewer than 1% of officials within the senior administrative and governance tiers of national football federations in the UK and Europe were drawn from 'visible' minority populations, and that minority representation within regional structures remained marginal. Within the hierarchical pyramid structures of national and regional football federations, initial access to executive decision-making committees is often premised on the sponsored mobility, patronage and personal recommendation of more senior figures within these governing bodies. These 'promotions' are commonly perceived as a reward for individuals who have exhibited long-standing paid and/or voluntary services to football in their regions or at a national level. Given the historically inscribed power relations and limited existing demographic of older, white males within football governance infrastructures, it is hardly surprising that minority populations continue to be marginalized from the benefits and profits of these hegemonic white networks of mutual acquaintance.

Whilst the relative absence of minorities from these governance infrastructures is underpinned by processes of unconscious and indirect forms of institutional discrimination, a number of authors have suggested some deeply embedded 'cultures of resistance' to more equitable change amongst key stakeholders within the governance of the game (Bradbury, *et al.*, 2011; Hylton, 2009; 2010; Long, 2000; Long and Hylton, 2002; Long and Spracklen, 2011 ; Long *et al.*, 2005; Lusted, 2009; 2011). This resistance to change is to some extent reflective of the dominant political paradigms in certain nation-states, in which relatively closed models of national identity and citizenship underpin limited policy approaches to dealing with minorities, premised on assimilation or non-intervention. Resistance may also indicate a more general lack of 'problem awareness' or non-acknowledgement of the concept and practices of institutional discrimination and represent a reactionary response to perceived personal criticisms on this score. However, it is of course also likely that in some cases this resistance is more reflective of a general reluctance to surrender accrued rewards and decision-making powers at the personal level.

Nonetheless, in each case these practices of resistance are underscored by a series of deeply racialized hegemonic power relations embedded within the core structures and decision-making bodies of football governance. To this end, we might argue that the centrality and invisibility of whiteness which enables the 'reproduction of dominance rather than subordination, normativity rather than marginality, and privilege rather than disadvantage' (Frankenburg, 1993: 237) has maintained the status quo of social relations within the organizational tiers of amateur football. Further, the intrinsic relationship between whiteness and the processes and practices of institutional discrimination has limited the scope of minority engagement with the popular physical and cultural leisure space of amateur football and offered few opportunities for recourse against racisms in all their myriad forms. In doing so, this has rendered the experiences of minorities as marginal to and less valued than those of majority populations and has, consequently, hindered a stronger sense of cultural belonging in the sport amongst minorities in the UK and Europe. Future efforts to ensure the equal treatment of minorities in amateur football and in other sports can, arguably, be realized only through the dismantling of those deeply racialized hegemonic power relations that are embedded within the organizational make-up of sports bodies which position minorities as fit for 'doing' but not 'organizing' sports and leisure practices. This will require a significant perceptual shift towards viewing cultural diversity as a positive individual and organizational resource rather than as a problem to be dealt with. However, it is likely that the adoption of this more inclusive approach will contribute to the added value of organizations and increase their capacities to connect with and provide a more equitable service to the increasingly diverse populations of the societies in which they are situated. In this sense, in amateur football and in sport and leisure practice more broadly, it's still all to play for.

References

Agergaard, S. and Sorenson, J.K. (2009) 'The Dream of Social Mobility: Ethnic Minority Players in Danish Football Clubs', *Soccer and Society* 10 (6) 766–780.

Ahmed, A. (2011) 'British Muslim Female Experiences in Football: Islam, Identity and the Hijab', in D. Burdsey (ed.) *Race, Ethnicity and Football: Persisting Debates and Emergent Issues*. Abingdon: Routledge.

Andersson, T. (2009) 'Immigrant Teams in Sweden and the Case of Assyriska FF', *Soccer and Society* 10: 398–417.

Anthias, F. and Yuval Davis, N. (1993) *Racialised Boundaries*. London: Routledge.

Back, L., Crabbe, T., and Solomos, J. (1998) 'Racism in Football: Patterns of Continuity and Change', in A. Brown (ed.) *Fanatics! Power, Identity and Fandom in Football*. London: Routledge.

Back, L., Crabbe, T., and Solomos, J. (2001) *The Changing Face of Football: Racism, Identity and Multiculture in the English Game*. Oxford: Berg.

Bains J. with Patel R. (1996) *Asians Can't Play Football*. Birmingham: Asian Social Development Agency.

Bains, J. (2005) *Asians Can Play Football: Another Wasted Decade*. Leicester: University of Leicester.

Bhabha, H. (1990a) 'The Third Space – Interview with Homi Bhabha', in J. Rutherford (ed.) *Identity, Community, Culture, Difference*. London: Lawrence and Wishart.

Bhabha, H. (1990b) 'Interrogating Identity: The Post-Colonial Prerogative', in D. Goldberg (ed.) *Anatomy of Racism*. Minneapolis: University of Minnesota.

Bloch, A. and Levy, C. (eds) (1999) *Refugees, Citizenship, and Social Policy in Europe*. London: Macmillan.

Bradbury, S. (2002) *A Survey of Local Football Clubs Affiliated to the Leicestershire and Rutland County FA: Issues of Racism, Ethnicity and Player and Spectator Behaviour in Local Football.* Sir Norman Chester Centre for Football Research.

Bradbury, S. (2010) 'From Racial Exclusions to New Inclusions: Black and Minority Ethnic Participation in Football Clubs in the East Midlands of England', *International Review for the Sociology of Sport* 46 (1) 23–44.

Bradbury, S. (2011) 'Racisms, Resistance and New Youth Inclusions: The Socio-Historical Development and Shifting Focus of Black, Asian and Minority Ethnic Football Clubs in Leicester', in D. Burdsey (ed.) *Race, Ethnicity and Football: Persisting Debates and Emergent Issues.* Abingdon: Routledge.

Bradbury, S., Amara, M., Garcia, B., and Bairner, A. (2011) *Representation and Structural Discrimination in Football in Europe: The Case of Minorities and Women.* Loughborough: Loughborough University.

Burdsey, D. (2004) 'Obstacle Race? Race, Racism and the Recruitment of Asian Professional Footballers', *Patterns of Prejudice* 38 (3) 279–30.

Burdsey, D. (2006) 'No Ball Games Allowed? A Socio-Historical Examination of the Development and Social Significance of British Asian Football Clubs', *Journal of Ethnic and Migration Studies* 32: 477–496.

Burdsey, D. (2007) *British Asians and Football: Culture, Identity and Exclusion.* London: Routledge.

Burdsey, D. (2009) 'Forgotten Fields? Centralising the Experiences of Minority Ethnic Men's Football Clubs in England', *Soccer and Society* 10 (6) 704–721.

Burdsey, D. (2011) *Race, Ethnicity and Football: Persisting Debates and Emergent Issues.* Abingdon: Routledge.

Campbell, P. (2011) 'What is Rangers Resisting Now? "Race", Resistance and Shifting Notions of Blackness in Local Football in Leicester', in D. Burdsey (ed.) *Race, Ethnicity and Football: Persisting Debates and Emergent Issues.* Abingdon: Routledge.

Carrington, B. (1998) 'Sport, Masculinity and Black Cultural Resistance', *Journal of Sport and Social Issues* 22 (3) 275–298.

Carrington, B. (1999) 'Cricket, Culture and Identity: An Ethnographic Analysis of the Significance of Sport within Black Communities', in S. Roseneil and J. Seymour (eds) *Practising Identities: Power and Resistance.* London: Macmillan.

Carrington, B. (2010) *Race, Sport and Politics: The Sporting Black Diaspora.* London: Sage.

Cashmore, E. (1982) *Black Sportsmen.* London: Routledge.

CRE (Commission for Racial Equality) (2004) *Racial Equality in Football.* London: CRE.

ECRI (European Commission against Racism and Intolerance) (2008) *ECRI General Policy Recommendation No.12 on Combating Racism and Racial Discrimination in the Field of Sport* – adopted on 19 December 2008 CRI(2009)5 (19 December 2008).

EP/EC/EC (European Parliament, Council and Commission) (2007) *Charter of Fundamental Rights of the European Union.* 2007/C303/01.

FARE (2010) 'Ukrainian Right Wing Group Marches against "Foreign" Footballers', available at http://www.farenet.org/default.asp?intPageID=7&intArticleID=2240/sport1/hi/football/europe/9097434.stm.

Football Task Force (1998) *Eliminating Racism from Football: A Report by the Football Task Force Submitted to the Minister for Sport.* London: The Football Trust.

FRA: European Union Agency for Fundamental Rights (2010) *Racism, Ethnic Discrimination and Exclusion of Migrants and Minorities in Sport: A Comparative Overview of the Situation in the European Union.* Luxembourg: Publications Office of the European Union.

Frankenburg, R. (19939) *Displacing Whiteness.* Durham, NC and London: Duke University Press.

Garland, J. and Rowe, M. (2001) *Racism and Anti-Racism in Football.* Basingstoke: Palgrave.

Halm, D. (2005) 'Turkish Immigrants in German Amateur Football', in A. Tomlinson and C. Young (eds) *German Football: History, Culture and Society.* London and New York: Routledge.

Hylton, K. (2009) *Race and Sport: Critical Race Theory.* London and New York: Routledge.

Hylton, K. (2010) 'How a Turn to Critical Race Theory Can Contribute to Our Understanding of "Race", Racism and Anti-Racism in Sport', *International Review for the Sociology of Sport* 45 (3) 335–354.

IFC (Independent Football Commission) (2003) *Annual Report.* London: IFC.

Kassimeris, C. (2007) *European Football in Black and White: Tackling Racism in Football.* Lanham, MD: Lexington Books.

Kassimeris, C. (2009a) 'Deutschland über Alles: Discrimination in German Football', *Soccer and Society* 10 (6) 754–765.

Kassimeris, C. (2009b) 'Football and Prejudice in Belgium and the Netherlands', *Sport and Society* 12 (10) 1327–1335.

Kay, T. (2006) 'Daughters of Islam: Family Influences on Muslim Young Women's Participation in Sport', *International Review for the Sociology of Sport* 41 (3/4) 357.

King, C. (2004a) *Offside Racism: Playing the White Man*. Oxford: Berg.

King, C. (2004b) '"Race" and Cultural Identity: Playing the Race Game Inside Football', *Leisure Studies* 23 (1) 19–30.

Kymlicka, W. (2010) 'The Rise and Fall of Multiculturalism? New Debates on Accommodation and Inclusion in Diverse Societies', in S. Vertovec and S. Wessendorf (eds) *The Multiculturalism Backlash: European Discourses, Policies and Practices*. Abingdon: Routledge.

Llopis-Giog, R. (2009) 'Racism and Xenophobia in Spanish Football: Facts, Reactions and Policies', *Physical Culture and Sports Studies* 47 (1) 35–43.

Long, J. (2000) '"No Racism Here?" A Preliminary Examination of Sporting Innocence', *Managing Leisure* 5: 121–133.

Long, J. and Hylton, K. (2002) 'Shades of White: An Examination of Whiteness in Sport', *Leisure Studies* 21: 87–103.

Long, J. and McNamee, M. (2004) 'On the Moral Economy of Racism and Racist Rationalisations in Sport', *International Review of the Sociology of Sport* 39 (4) 405–438.

Long, J. and Spracklen, K. (2010) (eds) *Sport and Challenges to Racism*. Basingstoke: Palgrave Macmillan.

Long, J., Robinson, P., and Spracklen, K. (2005) 'Promoting Racial Equality within Sports Organisations', *Journal of Sport and Social Issues* 29 (1) 41–59.

Long, J., Hylton, K., Welch, M., and Dart, J. (2001) *Part of the Game: A Report Prepared for Kick It Out*. The Centre of Leisure and Sport Research at Leeds Metropolitan University. Kick It Out.

Long, J., Hylton, K., Spracklen, K., Ratna, A., and Bailey, S. (2009) *Systematic Review of the Literature on Black and Minority Ethnic Communities in Sport and Physical Recreation*. Leeds: Carnegie Research Institute, Leeds Metropolitan University.

Lusted, J. (2009) 'Playing Games with "Race": Understanding Resistance to "Race" Equality Initiatives in English Local Football Governance', *Soccer and Society* 10 (6) 722–739.

Lusted, J. (2011) 'Negative Equity? Amateurist Responses to Race Equality Initiatives in English Grass-Roots Football', in D. Burdsey (ed.) *Race, Ethnicity and Football: Persisting Debates and Emergent Issues*. Abingdon: Routledge.

Macpherson, W. (1999) *The Stephen Lawrence Inquiry: Report of an Inquiry made by Sir William Macpherson of Cluny*. London: Home Office, Cm 4262-I.

Müller, F., van Zoonen, L., and de Roode, L. (2007) 'Accidental Racists: Experiences and Contradictions of Racism in Local Amsterdam Soccer Fan Culture', *Soccer and Society* 8 (2/3) 335–350.

Nash, R. (2000) 'Contestation in Modern English Professional Football', *International Review of the Sociology of Sport* 35 (4) 456–486.

Parekh, B. (2006) *Rethinking Multiculturalism: Cultural Diversity and Political Theory* (2nd ed.). Basingstoke: Palgrave.

Pillai, R., Kyambi, S., Nowacka, K., and Sriskandarajah, D. (2006) *The Reception and Integration of New Migrant Communities*. London: Institute of Public Policy Research.

Ratna, A. (2007) 'A Fair Game? British Asian Females' Experience of Racism in Women's Football', in J. Magee, J. Cauldwell, K. Listone and S. Scraton (eds) *Women, Football and Europe: Histories, Equity and Experiences*. Oxford: Meyer and Meyer Sport Ltd.

Robson, G. (2000) *'No One Likes Us, We Don't Care': The Myth and Reality of Millwall Fandom*. Oxford: Berg.

Roversi, A. (1994) 'The Birth of the Ultras: The Rise of Football Hooliganism in Italy', in J. Williams and R. Giulianotti (eds) *Games Without Frontiers*. Aldershot: Ashgate.

Rowe, N. and Champion, R. (2000) *Sports Participation and Ethnicity in England: National Survey 1999/2000* (No. SE/1073): Sport England.

Scraton, S., Cauldwell, J., and Holland, S. (2005) 'Bend It Like Patel: Centring "Race", Ethnicity and Gender in Feminist Analysis of Women's Football in England', *International Review for the Sociology of Sport* 40 (1) 71–88.

Spaaij, R. and Vinas, C. (2005) 'Passions, Politics and Violence: A Socio-historical Analysis of Spanish Ultras', *Soccer and Society* 6 (1) 79–96.

Van Sterkenburg, J., Janssens, J., and Rijen, B. (eds) (2005) *Football and Racism: An Inventory of the Problems and Solutions in Eight West European Countries in the Framework of the Stand Up Speak Up Campaign*. Brussels: Muller Institute.

Vertovec, S. and Wessendorf, S. (2010) 'Introduction: Assessing the Backlash against Multiculturalism in Europe', in S. Vertovec and S. Wessendorf (eds) *The Multiculturalism Backlash: European Discourses, Policies and Practices*. Abingdon: Routledge.

Westwood, S. (1990) 'Racism, Black Masculinity and the Politics of Space', J. Hearn and D. Morgan (eds) *Men, Masculinities and Social Theory*. London: Unwin and Hyman.

Westwood, S. (1991) 'Red Star over Leicester: Racism, the Politics of Identity and Black Youth in Britain', in P. Werbner and M. Anwar (eds) *Black and Ethnic Leadership in Britain*. London: Routledge.

Williams, J. (1984) *On the Football Front: SNCCFR*. Leicester: University of Leicester.

Williams, J. (1992) *Lick My Boots: Racism in English Football: SNCCFR*. Leicester: University of Leicester.

Williams, J. (1994) 'Rangers is a Black Club: Race, Identity and Local Football in England', in R. Giulianotti and J. Williams (eds) *Game Without Frontiers: Football Identity and Modernity*. Aldershot: Arena.

20

FAMILY LEISURE

Maureen Harrington

Introduction

Family leisure is a rather nebulous area of leisure research, primarily because the majority of researchers conceive of leisure as an individual phenomenon (Dawson, 2000). From its inception, Leisure Studies has relied extensively on social surveys that aggregate data on individuals, which precludes the family being analysed as a social unit (Kelly, 1997). The unit of analysis is the individual, most obviously in psychological and social-psychological approaches to leisure. The same focus in the individual actor in social settings was present in the early sociological literature, in studies like those of male occupational communities and men's work–leisure relationship (Parker, 1971; Salaman, 1974). This chapter will argue that, in spite of renewed interest in the area and attempts to reconceptualize family leisure as a form of purposive leisure (Shaw and Dawson, 2001), a coherent meaning of 'family leisure' still remains elusive in Leisure Studies.

At the same time, Leisure Studies has paid little attention to negative aspects of family leisure (Shaw, 1992a). The few early works that touched on conflict in family leisure lacked empirical grounding (e.g., Orthner, 1985), or the research design measured 'leisure' inadequately as a single survey item (e.g., Strauss, Gelles and Steinmetz, 1980). More recent work acknowledges the inherent contradiction between the ideals or 'fantasy' of family leisure and how it is lived as experience within actual families. Shared leisure can lead to tensions and conflict among family members, and, when the reality falls short of expectations, parents can experience guilt, disappointment and disillusionment (Shaw, 1997; Daly, 2001a). Clarke and Critcher argued that the ambiguity and contradictions in both the work and rituals of family life highlight the conceptual limitations of 'leisure' itself; for them, 'family life is a complex mix of work and play, tension and relaxation, constraint and choice' (Clarke and Critcher, 1995: 59). Most importantly, critical researchers have pointed to tendencies within the field to reify family leisure, to ignore gender inequality as a key factor in understanding it and a lack of scrutiny of the concept itself (Shaw, 1992b). The field has also been broadly criticized by Freysinger (1997) who points out the descriptive nature of most empirical research, inconsistencies in measurement and the shallowness of theoretical formulations in family Leisure Studies.

Leisure Studies begin with the individual actor

The individual subject is, justifiably, the object of study for psychological factors such as enjoyment, satisfaction, relaxation, freedom of choice and intrinsic motivation that are commonly associated with leisure experiences (Horna, 1994; Mannell and Kleiber, 1997). For psychologists and social psychologists, leisure is conceived as a state of being that emanates from individual 'freedom of choice, intrinsic motivation and the quality of or enjoyment of the experience' (Mannell and Kleiber, 1997, cited in Shaw and Dawson, 2001: 218). Social psychologists of leisure are specifically concerned with 'how the feelings, cognitions, and behaviours of one individual are influenced by [those] of others during a period of time subjectively designated as unobligated, free, or leisure' (Iso-Ahola, cited in Horna, 1994: 48). To this extent, they study small groups, including the socialization process within the family (see Iso-Ahola, 1980a) and familial relationships (Mannell and Kleiber, 1997), so that the individual under study is considered to be part of a family.

In Leisure Studies, the family – normatively defined as a heterosexual, two-parent nuclear family – has primacy as a common leisure setting over other social groups. Ironically, as early as the 1960s, we see De Grazia bemoaning the demise of men's leisure amidst the public for the private realm of 'homeliness' and family in both Europe and the United States:

> The spread of the mass media has helped take [the man's] life out of the public or political realm and put it within the private walls of home. This is significant for several reasons. It puts his idea of freedom in the home: the home is where he really is free. It limits his free time largely to time spent with his family. It characterises free time spent elsewhere as not quite proper ... The worker in order to get to the local tavern on [Saturday] night must take his wife with him.
>
> (De Grazia, 1964: 224)

In the sociological literature on leisure, as Rojek (2000) explained, functionalist, neo-Marxist and feminist perspectives all begin with a *Homo faber* model, with many researchers assuming that 'leisure has no meaning except in relation to work' (Rojek, 2000: 115). From the beginning, the unit of analysis for examining leisure time and activity has been the individual rational actor of free will, a male person who engaged in leisure during non-work time. In the sociological literature, leisure was primarily a residual concept for discretionary time 'left over' from paid work activity, as exemplified by Ken Roberts' definition – which contrasts with de Grazia's earlier remarks:

> Leisure time can be defined as time that is not obligated, and leisure activities can be defined as activities that are non-obligatory. At work, a man's time is not his own and his behaviour is not responsive purely to his own whims. Outside work, there are certain duties that men are obliged, either by custom or law, to fulfil, such as obligations that an individual has towards his family. When these obligations have been met, a man has 'free time' in which his behaviour is dictated by his own will and preferences, and it is here that leisure is found.
>
> (Roberts, 1970: 6)

Examples of early empirical research in the area of work and leisure include the work of Parker (1971, 1983) on bank workers, businessmen, social workers and service workers; Salaman (1974) on architects and railwaymen; and Gerstl (1963) on dentists, advertising

231

agents and professors. These occupationally based studies asked men about their attitudes to work, whether or not they had work-based friendships, and determined whether their work was similar to or different from their after-work leisure pursuits. These studies did not canvass men about their family lives, although at least one researcher considered the family to be part of the leisure sphere (see Gerstl, 1963). These studies of male work and leisure implicitly assumed that there was a non-employed 'wife' at home as part of the backdrop to the scene painted of the life of railwaymen, fishermen, shipbuilders, jazz musicians and others. For example, in Salaman's study a respondent says: 'If you want to know about the railways you should ask the wife. She's the one who has had to put up with the shift work for the last twenty-five years' (1974: 82). Had any of these researchers thought to ask the wife, sociology of leisure would have advanced the study of family leisure!

Early studies on family leisure

Family leisure research emerged in the mid-1970s with the functionalist assumption that family leisure was good for both individual and family development. Orthner (1975) and Orthner and Mancini (1980; 1991) explored the role of family leisure in facilitating family interaction and bonding, particularly between the marital couple. In a comprehensive review of the family leisure literature to date, Orthner and Mancini (1991) concluded that shared leisure experiences had positive benefits for the quality of family relationships in terms of family stability, family interaction and family satisfaction, and that the family should be seen as a positive leisure context for individuals. They noted that cross-cultural studies also found a positive relationship between shared leisure and marital 'well-being and happiness' (Orthner and Mancini, 1991: 290). Couples who engaged in high levels of independent, individual activities had a lower level of marital satisfaction, particularly among wives – no surprise for feminist researchers who found male leisure activities both privileged within the family and serviced by women (e.g., Bella, 1989; Griffin, Hobson, MacIntosh and McCabe, 1982). When marital partners engaged in parallel leisure activities 'which involve sharing time but do not include substantial amounts of interaction [such as watching television or going to the movies] … [these] have a positive but modest impact on the marital satisfaction of husbands and wives' (Orthner and Mancini, 1991: 291). Interestingly, Orthner (1975) had suggested earlier that parallel activities can actually reduce family tension, by keeping negative interactions and communication to a minimal level, reducing the likelihood of conflict.

Orthner and Mancini (1991) pointed out, however, that most empirical work on leisure and the family focused on the married couple, emphasizing the relationship between leisure-activity patterns and marital satisfaction. These studies did not involve other family members, so they did not address the relationship between family satisfaction and leisure patterns involving parents and children or children alone, an important omission that was later redressed by Harrington (2001), Larson, Gilman and Richards (1997) and Shaw and Dawson (2001), among others.

A much-lauded study by Rapoport and Rapoport (1975) adopted a social-psychological approach to examine how leisure contributes to achieving developmental tasks associated with stages of the family life cycle. Griffin *et al.* criticized the Rapaports for recognizing social constraints on women's leisure in the family yet expecting these 'to be overcome through determination and individual resourcefulness' (Griffin *et al.*, 1982: 95). Wearing similarly pointed out the functionalist underpinnings of the Rapoports' developmental approach and their subscription to normative values about family life. She also dismissed the implied expectation of this study that 'it is up to the individual and the family to adapt and develop in accordance with the constraints placed upon them by the salient tasks at each stage of the life cycle' for successful family development (Wearing, 1998: 15).

There was a less well-known but more ambitious attempt by Watson (1980) to provide a broad theoretical framework for studying family leisure from his examination of the 'discrete theoretical frameworks' (Watson, 1980: 51) of prominent research in the 1970s. Watson considered two macro-level analytical approaches: the institutional, represented by Young and Wilmott (1973), and the social-system approach of Kenyon and MacPherson (1978). He also examined two micro-level approaches: the interactional perspective of Orthner (1975) and Rapoport and Rapoport's (1975) life-cycle framework. Arguing that they all presented 'testable conceptual models' (Watson, 1980: 56), he derived four propositions from a synthesis of their findings to develop an explanatory conceptual model of the family–leisure relationship. This had four main components: family status, family organization, family leisure interaction and family integration (see Watson, 1980). While Watson's concept of family integration, defined as the degree of consensus in family values, was also functionalist, his model accounted for family diversity in class, religion, residence and ethnic origin. He also identified four prominent contexts for family leisure: 'junior sports and play activities and parental participation, adolescent peer group interests, family kin and friendship relations and commercialised leisure and sports' (Watson, 1980: 59). However, Watson's work is seldom cited in the literature and his model does not appear to have been applied anywhere within the field.

Into the 1980s, most research, including the work on barriers or constraints to family leisure (Crawford and Godbey, 1987; Witt and Goodale, 1981), was at least implicitly functionalist in orientation to value consensus (see Wearing, 1998) and premised on the normative notion that 'the family that plays together, stays together'. As Shaw (1992b) argued, if family Leisure Studies reified family leisure, it also did not consider gender inequality to be a crucial factor in understanding it, nor did it conceptualize family leisure itself as problematic.

Feminist contributions to family leisure

Leisure Studies had assumed that leisure was a universal concept applicable to all, until feminist researchers began questioning the appropriateness of the concept of leisure to convey women's experience, particularly within the family context (Bella, 1989; Deem, 1986; Green, Hebron and Woodward, 1990; Wearing and McArthur, 1988). From the early 1980s, feminist researchers explored the meaning and experience of leisure for women, and particular constraints impinging on women's leisure, inside and outside the family. They were also sensitive to the implications of a pro-family, or familist, ideology for women's leisure, which arose in the 1970s and 1980s (Bella, 1989; Deem, 1986; Green, Hebron and Woodward, 1990; Harrington, Dawson and Bolla, 1992; Hunter and Whitson, 1991) and which, as we will see later, has re-emerged in some quarters of family leisure research today.

Familism is an ideology defined as a 'belief system which argues that the best way for adults to live is in nuclear families … as a socially and legally recognized heterosexual couple … who normally expect to have children[, which provides] the most stable, intimate loving relationship possible' (Luxton, 1988: 238). Familism assumes that the nuclear family is both normative and monolithic, and that all members of the family have the same positive experience of family life (Bella, 1989; Horna, 1994). Bella rejected the very notion of 'family leisure' as falling into 'the familist trap' (Bella, 1989: 163). Shaw (1992b) reiterated: 'the hegemonic view of family leisure as being exclusively positive in terms of experience and outcome may be simplistic and misleading' (p. 272), and the way that family leisure has been reified in Leisure Studies and the popular media is entirely consistent with familist ideology (Shaw, 1992b). Bella (1989, 1992) and Shaw (1992b) also queried whether family leisure really is leisure for women. They both argued that the work women do to produce positive family leisure experiences for other members of the family is rendered invisible through familism and that, as such, the contradictory negative aspects of family time are unseen (Bella, 1992; see also Green and Hebron, 1988; Hunter and Whitson, 1991; Shaw, 1992b). Other feminist researchers argued that women needed autonomous leisure away from other family members (Wearing and McArthur, 1988). As Green, Hebron and Woodward (1990) explained, 'women frequently sacrifice personal leisure in order to accommodate caring for the family, in which case their own time spaces for uninterrupted leisure become fragmented, with the attendant reduced options on how and where to spend it' (p. 23). Feminist research demonstrated that gender relations, and gender-based power differentials between individual members and among all members, shape access to leisure within the interactional context of the family.

Another important contribution to the field of family leisure, and similar to a critique of family research in general (e.g., Smith, 1993; Mandell and Duffy, 1995), was the feminist claim that family leisure research does not differentiate among types of families. Within this body of research single-parent, blended, non-custodial, childless and gay and lesbian families either were not included or were hidden (Shaw, 1992a). Shaw (1992a; 1997) questioned whether 'family leisure' was a useful concept for understanding the meaning and experience of leisure for a diverse range of families (see also Rehman, 2001; Wearing, 1998; Willming and Gibson, 2000). The message emanating from feminist researchers was unequivocal: rather than continue doing research with relatively accessible white, middle-class, heterosexual couples with children, we ought to produce more research along intersecting lines of ethnic, class, regional and sexual diversity in family life (see Bialeschki and Pearce, 1997).

Shaw (1997) and Wearing (1998) introduced a feminist poststructuralist power analysis to better inform this area of family leisure, through their reading of Foucault (1982). Wearing (1998) constructed leisure as 'personal space' where the subjectivities of men, women and children can resist, challenge and subvert what she considers hegemonic masculinity and inferiorized femininity. In her words:

> At times of social change when traditional sources of male prestige such as provider capacity falter and when women are gaining social power, men turn to sport and leisure activities for reinforcement of hegemonic masculinity. Nevertheless leisure can also be a space for men to challenge, resist and possibly loosen the grip of tough, aggressive, exclusionary masculinity ... Through repeated performative acts in leisure activities which combine individual capacities and achievements with caring, support, emotional expression, relationality and sharing, in enjoyable circumstances, it may be possible to shift the cultural construction of masculinity beyond its foundation on an opposite and inferiorized femininity. It may also allow men to enlarge their sense of self to include emotions and to allow them a vulnerability that previously needed to be covered up and protected by men and defended in many indirect ways by women.
>
> (Wearing, 1998: 100)

This passage shows that there is a slight tendency in Wearing's work to romanticize 'agency' and overemphasize an individualized notion of leisure, but it reminds us that leisure is performative, a theme that I will return to in the final part of this chapter.

Feminist scholarship in Leisure Studies has grown dramatically since the early 1990s, spurring a renewed interest in conceptualizing family leisure and refining theoretical and empirical approaches to its study. However, feminists' research on women and leisure has not been as fruitful as its promise for understanding family leisure. Arguably, their aim was theorizing women's leisure, rather than the family context of leisure and how meanings and experience may differ among women, men and children. Recent work in special issues of *Leisure Studies* (Kay, 2006) and *Annals of Leisure Research* (Pringle, Kay and Jenkins, 2011), as well as Kay's (2009) edited collection on fathers' leisure in the family holds renewed promise for a more complex understanding of family leisure.

Paradigmatic differences and the problem of 'idealization' in family leisure theory

In 1997, Shaw presented an analysis of the strengths and weaknesses of the two opposing major paradigms framing the study of family leisure. One was the dominant social-psychological approach, focusing at the micro-analytical level on family interactions, communications and relationships and emphasizing the positive benefits and outcomes of leisure time spent together as a family (Shaw, 1997). The other approach she labelled 'sociological-feminist' and described as a macro-analytical approach locating family leisure practices within broader societal gender relations, taking into account the impact of gender inequities and power differentials within the family. Shaw proposed moving toward an inclusive conceptualization of family leisure that would incorporate insights from both perspectives, while overcoming any weaknesses of each.

Shaw (1997) recognized the inherent multi-levels of contradictions in family leisure. She identified at least four levels of contradictions in family leisure warranting our attention. These contradictions occur firstly in the relationship between 'family roles and responsibilities' as social structure and 'individual freedom or action' (p. 105; see also Kelly, 1993). Secondly, on an ideological level, where there are overt or hidden contradictions between the image of happy families at leisure and the reality of families falling short of this ideal. Thirdly, she saw a contradiction between familist ideology and everyday life, where individuals' experience of family life may not measure up to their initial expectations. Finally, on the level of individual experience, she argued that family leisure can entail mutually contradictory meanings and emotions. Like Clarke and Critcher (1995), Shaw reasoned that 'family activities may be leisure and work at the same time, motivations may be a complex mix of intrinsic and obligatory factors, and both positive and negative outcomes may result from any one family leisure situation' (Shaw, 1997: 105).

Many researchers now recognize that 'family leisure' is partially an ideological construct (Shaw and Dawson, 2003; Hallman, Mary and Benbow, 2007). As Hallman, Mary and Benbow (2007: 873) explain, 'beliefs [about an ideology of togetherness] shape behaviour and can set into motion actions indicative of how conscious and deliberate a particular family is about spending time together'. Idealizations, or what Daly (2003: 171) refers to as 'the *implicit* theories that families live by' (emphasis in the original), inform everyday practices within families, including shared leisure ones. Families 'draw meaning from the cultural matrix of which they are a part and express meanings about the kind of family they wish to appear' (p. 174). This presents challenges for both surveying and, to a lesser extent, interviewing family members about family leisure. Ideological notions of how families ought to behave are implicit in what members report constitutes their family leisure practices. Parents may accentuate the positive and leave out negative aspects of family leisure, presenting the researcher with a sanitized if not idealized version of their family leisure practices. A critically minded interviewer, however, should be able to bring such contradictions to the surface (Freysinger, personal communication, 2010). An example drawn from my family leisure study (Harrington, 2001, 2006a; 2006b) shows an Australian mother's response to the question 'when the activities didn't turn out the way you wanted them', and it is worth quoting at length:

> One weekend we decided to go to the beach and [our 13-year-old son] was allowed to invite a friend who lives down the road. They wanted to go to King's Beach at Caloundra but [my husband] wanted to go to Bribie Island because he wanted to bring the dog. He wanted to go to a beach away from the surf beach and a certain area where you are allowed to bring the dog provided it is on a lead. Jake the dog knew we were going out and he had anticipated and [our son] did not want to go unless we went to King's Beach [a surf beach]. We thought right we'll just go without you [son] and it was weird we had [his friend] and [our 15-year-old daughter] in the car and had a battle to convince [our son] to get into the car but he was stubborn and wouldn't get into the car. We drove off about a kilometre up the road and I said [to my husband] this is ridiculous. Here we have [our son's] friend with us without [him] we'll go to King's Beach, take Jake the dog back. So the whole mood was just so … [our daughter] and [son] were at each other. The surf was lousy and there was hardly any surf and [my husband] knew that. We didn't have to go for the surf but to have a bit of a swim [and] basically to have a walk and a BBQ. [My husband] had a face that long and I was really peeved because [my daughter] and [son] were at each other. So it should have been a positive and enjoyable day [but] turned out to be 'RS' [i.e., ratshit, a terrible, unenjoyable] day.

This example highlights not only family leisure that went awry, it shows the reactions of different family members to the event: mother and daughter seemed to pick up on the dog's happy anticipation and glum disappointment at not going to the beach; the father had his own thoughts on what they had planned and what actually occurred; and the son has acted up in front of his friend and embarrassed everyone. As others have seen in their research, family leisure experiences vary in both relevance and quality for different family members, particularly by gender and generation, an aspect of family leisure practice that is concealed by idealization (Shaw, 1992b; Harrington, 2001; Larson, Gilman and Richards, 1997). In spite of this caution, in order to be attuned to negative and nuanced experiences in interpreting the meaning of leisure within families, research shows that overall family members derive both pleasure and purpose from what they do together for leisure. Parents tell their children nostalgic stories of family times from their own childhood, and hope that their actions will give their children happy memories of family leisure too (Daly, 1996; Harrington, 2001, 2006a).

Reconceptualizing family leisure as purposive leisure

In their study of 31 families in Ontario, Canada in which they interviewed parents, and children aged 10 years and older, about family leisure, Shaw and Dawson (2001) used the term 'purposive leisure' to refer to the meanings that parents attach to shared family leisure activity and their intentions in pursuing it. Spending leisure time with their children was highly valued by the parents in their study and they showed 'a strong sense of purpose' (p. 223) in accomplishing it. Organizing and facilitating leisure activities that both parents and children might enjoy took a lot of resolve and effort on the part of parents, but they were willing to do so for the good of their children, even at the expense of their own enjoyment. Family leisure appeared to be 'purposive' to achieving two interdependent parental goals (Shaw and Dawson, 2001). In the short term, parents saw engaging in family leisure as a way of enhancing the family as a cohesive, communicative and bonded unit, to give its members 'a sense of family' and 'memories of having good times together' (p. 224). Over the longer term, parents also wanted to provide their children with opportunities to develop healthy lifestyle patterns and to learn values that they hoped would serve them throughout life (see also Shaw and Dawson, 1998).

Indeed, shared family leisure offers teachable moments for children to learn values and life lessons 'through doing and seeing rather than being told what to do' (Shaw and Dawson, 2001: 226). As my own replication of Shaw and Dawson's study with 28 Queensland, Australia families shows, parents place a high value on family leisure as purposive leisure because it provides a social context for transmitting their values, interests and a sense of who we are as a family (Harrington, 2006a), or what Daly calls the 'family paradigm' (1996: 54). Sometimes parents talk about these values, interests and family identity as originating with previous generations (Harrington, 2001; 2006a; 2006b; 2009) and hope that the lessons learned in shared family leisure will continue to guide their children into their adult lives. Parents often say that they make the effort now in order that their children 'will want to know us' when they are grown-ups.

Purposive leisure is a useful concept for the study of family leisure; however, as a concept applied broadly across distinctive family forms and material conditions, it does not account for how family leisure may be mediated by class, ethnicity, religion and other cultural processes. Here it is important to bear in mind the performative character of purposive leisure. From this point of view, *status-positioning leisure* can be seen as a performance of family life within our pluralist performative culture (Rojek, 2000), and so how a family is positioned will shape their family leisure practices and what they purport in its engagement. I will return to this theme in the final section of this chapter. However, there is another area of family leisure research that needs to be discussed first: the faith-based pro-family research done in the US.

Resurrecting familism in family leisure research

This is a particular stream of family leisure research that is both functionalist and familist in orientation, yet embraces diversity and acknowledges purposive leisure. It comes from a band of researchers trained in educational institutions affiliated with the Church of the Latter Day Saints. Initially studying traditional families, Zabriskie and his colleagues (Zabriskie and McCormick, 2003; Agate, Zabriskie, Agate, and Poff, 2009) propose a 'Core and Balance Model of Family Leisure Functioning'. This model builds on Kelly's (1999) concepts of 'core plus balance' leisure styles and Iso-Ahola's (1984) observation that individuals' needs for stability and change are met through leisure. The model that they have elaborated is operationalized through a number of quantitative measures of family cohesion, adaptability and functioning (i.e., FACES II scale) and a Family Leisure Activity Profile (i.e., FLAP) measuring family leisure satisfaction, family leisure involvement and family life satisfaction. This model has been applied in a number of contexts, including diverse families such as those with bi-racial adoptive children (Zabriskie and Freeman, 2004); Mexican-American families (Christenson, Zabriskie, Eggett and Freeman, 2006); religious families (Agate, Zabriskie and Eggett, 2007); single-parent families (Hornberger, Zabriskie, and Freeman, 2010) and families that include children with developmental disabilities (Dodd, Zabriskie, Widmer and Eggett, 2009).

Theoretically, this research purports to be based on Klein and White's (1996) interpretation of family systems theory, but it ignores White and Klein's (2002) warning that 'systems are heuristics, not real things' (p. 123). 'The family' can be reified if you forget that you are just looking at a family *as a system* not that the family *is a system* (p. 175). Hence, to assert that 'family systems purposively facilitate family leisure activities ... to increase family functioning' (Zabriskie and McCormick, 2003: 167) assumes that the family *is* a system, something antithetical to White and Klein's meaing. It also misreads Shaw's (1997) conceptualization of family experience as replete with contradictions on multiple levels, and Shaw and Dawson's (2001) use of the term 'purposive leisure'. A second example of reification of families in this body of work is in reference to a family systems model by Olsen (1993) that 'considers communication to be the critical facilitative dimension which allows families to move back and forth along family cohesion and adaptability continua' (Poff, Zabriskie and Townsend, 2010: 368–369).

Such a family systems perspective, while providing one lens on family leisure, does not acknowledge nor account for the contradictions and conflict between and among members engaged in family leisure – nor its idealization both by subjects themselves and by those doing the research. For example, Palmer, Freeman and Zabriskie (2007) apply the concept of 'purposive leisure' to family volunteering on service expeditions where parents take their children to lesser-developed countries 'to show gratitude for the numerous blessings they had been given' (p. 447). Families who go on the kinds of expeditions entailing both service and sacrifice, I would argue, see themselves and are seen by others as doing 'good works' that 'continues to define and influence the entire identity of the family for many years to come' (Palmer *et al.*, 2007: 438). To me this illustrates the concept of family leisure as performative space, on which I shall expand below.

While the core and balance model may be intuitively attractive to some researchers interested in families' 'functioning', it does not illuminate discernible differences – arising, for example, out of gender, social class, culture – in family practices and meanings.

An alternative conceptualization: family leisure as performative space

Recently I have been working along theoretical lines suggested by Wearing's (1998) work on leisure as 'personal space' where subjectivities may be reviewed and some resisted while others are revitalized or reconstructed (p. 157). The concept of leisure as personal space leads me to thinking about family leisure as 'performative space', in which families 'do family leisure'. This also relates to temporality captured in narratives and memories of family times in which parents talk of 'always being a fishing family' or 'we just follow on [taking Sunday drives] from my parents I guess' (Daly, 2001b; Harrington, 2006a; 2006b). Rather than conceptualizing 'family' as a 'system' or as a 'form', it may be conceived as 'a distinctive social configuration that is continually brought into being through people's activities, interactions, and interpretations, situated within powerful discourses of family life' (DeVault, 2000: 487). From this perspective, family is enacted in manifold social settings in which individuals 'constitute certain actions and activities as "family" practices' (Finch, 2007: 66); they see themselves as, and can be seen by others as, doing 'family things'. Over time the narratives and memories of doing family things become markers of self- and family identity. Family leisure as performative space could include the spatial dimensions of sites of leisure practices, for example, middle-class families taking their children through the zoo, as DeVault (2000) and Hallman, Mary and Benbow (2007) observed, and the interstices between leisure spaces, for example, the walk to the public library or the drive to and from a child's sporting activity.

This notion of family leisure as performative space is consistent with Morgan's (1996) concept of 'family' as a set of activities that people 'do' rather than a social institution or structure that people belong to or 'are'. These family practices 'are often little fragments of daily life … part of the normal taken-for-granted existence' of members, and the signifi-cance of these practices 'derives from their location in wider systems of meaning' (Morgan, 1996: 190, cited in Finch, 2007: 66). Finch (2007) has argued that family practices are inherently social; they are not only 'done' but 'displayed', as their meaning 'has to be both conveyed to and understood by relevant others … to be effective as constituting "family" practices' (p. 66). From this perspective, family leisure is not only purposive to raising the kind of adults you want your children to become, but it also consists of sets of activities that show to relevant others that you are a 'good' (or not) mother or father to the children you are raising. With this conceptualization we can better make sense when parents refer to them-selves as a 'tennis family', as in Shona Thompson's (1999) study of family sport and women's labour, or simply an 'active family' or even a 'stay-at-home family'.

All families engage in family leisure practices that they not only 'do' but also 'display' the meaning of to others, even when there are some practices (refusing to play by the rules or yelling at one another) which they may wish remain hidden. Recall that Shaw (1997) implored us to follow a more critical research agenda on family leisure, cautioning us not to have a rose-tinted view of family leisure that fails to recognize the inherent contradictions in practice and meaning. By deconstructing the concept of 'family leisure' and detaching it from a normalized formation of happy families (a variant of familism) we have a better chance of understanding the performative nature of family leisure, the ways in which fami-lies 'do family' across a diversity of family forms, structures and performative spaces.

References

Agate, S., Zabriskie, R. and Eggett, D. (2007) 'Praying, playing, and successful families: The relation-ship between family religiosity, family leisure, and family functioning', *Marriage and Family Review* 42 (2) 51–57.

Agate, J.R., Zabriskie, R.B., Agate, S.T. and Poff, R. (2009) 'Family leisure satisfaction and satisfac-tion with family life', *Journal of Leisure Research* 41 (2) 205–223.

Bella, L. (1989) 'Women and leisure: Beyond androcentrism', in E.L. Jackson and T.L. Burton (eds) *Understanding Leisure and Recreation: Mapping the Past, Charting the Future* (pp. 151–179). State College, PA: Venture Publishing.

Bella, L. (1992) *The Christmas Imperative; Leisure Family and Women's Work*. Halifax: Fernwood Press.

Bialeschki, M.D. and Pearce, K.D. (1997) 'I don't want a lifestyle – I want a life': The effect of role negotiations on the leisure of lesbian mothers', *Journal of Leisure Research* 29 (1) 113–131.

Christenson, O., Zabriskie, R., Eggett, D. and Freeman, P. (2006) 'Family acculturation, family leisure involvement, and family functioning among Mexican-Americans', *Journal of Leisure Research* 38 (4) 475–495.

Clarke, J. and Critcher, C. (1995) 'Coming home to roost', in C. Critcher, P. Bramham and A. Tomlinson (eds) *Sociology of Leisure: A Reader* (pp. 55–64). London: E and FN Spon.

Crawford, D.W. and Godbey, G. (1987) 'Reconceptualizing barriers to family leisure', *Leisure Sciences* 9 (2) 119–127.

Daly, K.J. (1996) *Families and Time: Keeping Pace in a Hurried Culture*. Thousand Oaks: Sage.

Daly, K.J. (2001a) 'Deconstructing family time: From ideology to lived experience', *Journal of Marriage and Family* 63 (2) 283–294.

Daly, K.J. (2001b) *Minding the Time in Family Experience: Emerging Perspectives and Issues*. London: JAI.

Daly, K.J. (2003) 'Family theory versus the theories families live by', *Journal of Marriage and the Family* 65: 771–784.

Dawson, D. (2000) 'Social class and leisure provision', in M.T. Allison and I.E. Schneider (eds) *Diversity and the Recreation Profession: Organizational Perspectives* (pp. 99–114). State College, PA: Venture Publishing.

Deem, R. (1986) *All Work and No Play? The Sociology of Women and Leisure*. Milton Keyes: Open University Press.

De Grazia, S. (1964) *Of Time, Work, and Leisure*. New York: Anchor Books.

DeVault, M.L. (2000) 'Producing family time: Practices of leisure activity beyond the home', *Qualitative Sociology* 23 (4) 485–503.

Dodd, D., Zabriskie, R., Widmer, M. and Eggett, D. (2009) 'Contributions of family leisure to family functioning among families that include children with developmental disabilities', *Journal of Leisure Research* 41 (2) 261–286.

Finch, J. (2007) 'Displaying families', *Sociology* 41(1) 65–81.

Foucault, M. (1982) 'The subject and power', in H. Dreyfus and P. Rabinow (eds) *Michel Foucault: Beyond Structuralism and Hermeneutics*, (pp. 208–220). Brighton, NY: Harvester.

Freysinger, V. (1997) 'Redefining family, redefining leisure: Progress made and challenges ahead in research on leisure and families. Introduction to special issue', *Journal of Leisure Research* 29 (1) 1–4.

Gerstl, J.E. (1963) 'Leisure, taste and occupational milieux', in E.O. Smigel (ed.) *Work and Leisure: A Contemporary Social Problem* (pp. 146–167). New Haven, CT: College and University Press.

Green, D. and Hebron, S. (1988) 'Leisure and male partners', in E. Whimbush and M. Talbot (eds), *Relative Freedoms: Women and Leisure* (pp. 33–47), Milton Keynes: Open University Press

Green, D., Hebron, S. and Woodward, E. (1990) *Women's Leisure: What Leisure?* Basingstoke, Hampshire: Macmillan.

Griffin, C., Hobson, D., MacIntosh, S. and McCabe, T. (1982) 'Women and leisure', in J. Hargreaves (ed.) *Sport, Culture and Ideology* (pp. 88–116). London: Routledge and Kegan Paul.

Hallman, B.C., Mary, S. and Benbow, P. (2007) 'Family leisure, family photography and zoos: Exploring the emotional geography of families', *Social and Cultural Geography* 8 (6) 871–888.

Harrington, M.A. (2001) 'Gendered time: Leisure in family life' in K.J. Daly (ed.) *Minding the Time in Family Experience: Emerging Perspectives and Issues* (pp. 343–382). London: JAI.

Harrington, M. (2006a) 'Family leisure', in C. Rojek, S.M. Shaw and A.J. Veal (eds), *A Handbook of Leisure Studies* (pp. 417–432). Houndmills, Basingstoke, Hampshire: Palgrave Macmillan.

Harrington, M. (2006b) 'Sport and leisure as contexts for fathering in Australian families', *Leisure Studies* 25 (2) 165–189.

Harrington, M. (2009) 'Sports mad good dads: Australian fathering through leisure and sport practices', in T. Kay (ed.) *Fathering through Sport and Leisure* (pp. 151–172). London: Routledge.

Harrington, M.A., Dawson, D. and Bolla, P. (1992) 'Objective and subjective constraints on women's leisure', *Loisir et Société* 15 (1) 203.

Horna, J. (1994) *The Study of Leisure: An Introduction*. Toronto: Oxford University Press.

Hornberger, L., Zabriskie, R. and Freeman, P. (2010) 'Contributions of family leisure to family functioning among single-parent families', *Leisure Sciences* 32 (2) 143–161.

Hunter, P. and Whitson, D. (1991) 'Women, leisure and familism: Relationships and isolation in small town Canada', *Leisure Studies* 10: 219–233.

Iso-Ahola, S.E. (1980a) *The Social Psychology of Leisure and Recreation*. Dubuque, IA: Wm. C. Brown.

Iso-Ahola, S.E. (1984) 'Social psychological foundations of leisure and resultant implications for leisure counselling', in E.T. Dowd (ed.) *Leisure Counseling: Concepts and Applications* (pp. 97–125). Springfield, IL: Charles C. Thomas,

Kay, T. (2006) Special Issue: Fathering through Leisure, *Leisure Studies* 25 (2).

Kay, T. (ed.) (2009) *Fathering through Sport and Leisure*. London: Routledge.

Kelly, J.R. (1993) 'Leisure-family research: Old and new issues', *World Leisure and Recreation Journal* 35 (3) 5–9.

Kelly, J.R. (1997) 'Changing issues in leisure-family research', *Journal of Leisure Research* 29 (1) 132–134.

Kelly, J.R. (1999) 'Leisure behaviors and styles: Social, economic, and cultural factors', in E.L. Jackson and T.L. Burton (eds) *Leisure Studies: Prospects for the Twenty-First Century* (pp. 135–150). State College, PA: Venture Publishing.

Kenyon, G. and MacPherson, B. (1978) *The Leisure Role Socialization Project – An Overview*. Department of Human Kinetics and Leisure Studies, University of Waterloo, Waterloo, Ontario, Canada.

Klein, D.M. and White, J.M. (1996) *Family Theories; An Introduction*. Thousand Oaks, CA: Sage.

Larson, R.W., Gilman, S.A. and Richards, M.H. (1997) 'Divergent experiences of family leisure: Fathers, mothers, and young adolescents', *Journal of Leisure Research* 29 (1) 78–97.

Luxton, M. (1988) 'Thinking about the future', in K. Anderson (ed.) *Family Matters: Sociology and Contemporary Canadian Families* (pp. 237–260). London: Methuen.

Mandell, N. and Duffy, A. (1995) *Canadian Families: Diversity, Conflict and Change*. Toronto: Harcourt Brace.

Mannell, R.C. and Kleiber, D.A. (1997) *A Social Psychology of Leisure*. State College, PA: Venture Publishing.

Morgan, D. (1996) *Family Connections*. Cambridge: Polity Press.

Olsen, D. (1993) 'Circumplex model of marital and family systems: Assessing family systems', in F. Walsh (ed.) *Normal Family Processes* (pp. 104–137). New York: Guilford Press.

Orthner, D.K. (1975) 'Leisure activity patterns and marital satisfaction over the marital career', *Journal of Marriage and the Family* 37: 91–103.

Orthner, D.K. (1985) 'Conflict and leisure interaction in families', in B.G. Gunter, J. Stanley and R. St. Clair (eds) *Transitions to Leisure: Conceptual and Human Issues* (pp. 133–139). New York: New York University Press.

Orthner, D.K. and Mancini, J.A. (1980) 'Leisure behavior and group dynamics: The case of the family', in S.E. Iso-Ahola (ed.), *Social Psychological Perspectives on Leisure and Recreation* (pp. 307–328). Springfield, IL: Thomas.

Orthner, D.K. and Mancini, J.A. (1991) 'Benefits of leisure for family bonding', in B.L. Driver, P.J. Brown and G.L. Peterson (eds), *Benefits of Leisure* (pp. 289–301). State College, PA: Venture Publishing.

Palmer, A.A., Freeman, P.A., and Zabriskie, R.B. (2007) 'Family deepening: A qualitative inquiry into the experience of families who participate in service expeditions', *Journal of Leisure Research* 39 (3) 438–458.

Parker, S. (1971) *The Future of Work and Leisure*. New York: Praeger.

Parker, S. (1983) *Leisure and Work*. London: George Allen and Unwin.

Poff, R., Zabriskie, R. and Townsend, J. (2010) 'Modelling family leisure and related family constructs: A national study of U.S. parent and youth perspectives', *Journal of Leisure Research* 42 (3) 365–391.

Pringle, R., Kay, T. and Jenkins, J.M. (2011) Special Issue: Masculinities, gender relations and leisure studies: Are we there yet? *Annals of Leisure Research* 14 (2–3)

Rapoport, R. and Rapoport, R.N. (1975) *Leisure and the Family Life Cycle*. London, UK: Routledge.

Rehman, L.A. (2001) 'Using Eichler to inform family leisure research', in S. Clough and J. White (eds) *Women's Leisure Experiences: Ages. Stages and Roles* (pp. 87–97). Eastbourne, UK: Leisure Studies Association.

Roberts, K. (1970) *Leisure*. London: Longman.

Rojek, C. (2000) *Leisure and Culture*. London: Macmillan Press.

Salaman, G. (1974) *Community and Occupation; An Exploration of Work/Leisure Relationships*. Cambridge: Cambridge University Press.

Shaw, S.M. (1992a) 'Research update: Family leisure and leisure services', *Parks and Recreation* 27 (12) 13–16.

Shaw, S.M. (1992b) 'Dereifying family leisure: An examination of women's and men's everyday experiences and perceptions of family time', *Leisure Sciences* 14 (3) 271–286.

Shaw, S.M. (1997) 'Controversies and contradictions in family leisure: An analysis of conflicting paradigms', *Journal of Leisure Research* 29 (1) 98–112.

Shaw, S.M. and Dawson, D.J. (1998) *Active Family Lifestyles: Motivations, Benefits, Constraints and Participation*. Ottawa, ON: Canadian Fitness and Lifestyle Research Institute.

Shaw, S.M. and Dawson, D.J. (2001) 'Purposive leisure: Examining parental discourses on family activities', *Leisure Sciences* 23 (4) 217–231.

Shaw, S.M. and Dawson, D.J. (2003) 'Contradictory aspects of family leisure: Idealization versus experience', *Leisure/Loisir* 28 (3–4) 179–201.

Smith, D.E. (1993) 'The standard North American family: SNAF as an ideological code', *Journal of Family Issues* 14 (1) 50–65.

Strauss, M., Gelles, R. and Steinmetz, S. (1980) *Behind Closed Doors*. New York, NY: Doubleday.

Thompson, S.M. (1999) *Mother's Taxi: Sport and Women's Labor*. Albany: State University of New York Press.

241

Watson, G.G. (1980) 'The family and leisure: A sociological analysis', in D. Mercer and E. Hamilton-Smith (eds) *Recreation Planning and Social Change in Urban Australia* (pp. 47–62). Sorrett: Malvern.

Wearing, B. (1998) *Leisure and Feminist Theory*. London: Sage.

Wearing, B.M. and McArthur, M. (1988) 'The family that plays together stays together: Or does it?', *Australian and New Zealand Journal of Sex, Marriage and Family* 9: 150–158.

White, J.M. and Klein, D.M. (2002) *Family Theories: An Introduction*, 2nd ed. Thousand Oaks, CA: Sage.

Willming, C. and Gibson, H. (2000) 'A view of leisure patterns of family life in the late 1990s', *Leisure and Society* 23 (1) 121–144.

Witt, P. and Goodale, T. (1981) 'The relationship between barriers to leisure enjoyment and family stages', *Leisure Sciences* 4 (1) 29–49.

Young, M. and Wilmott, P. (1973) *The Symmetrical Family*. Penguin: Middlesex.

Zabriskie, R. and Freeman, P. (2004) 'Contributions of family leisure to family functioning among transracial adoptive families', *Adoption Quarterly* 7 (3) 49–77.

Zabriskie, R. and McCormick, B. (2003) 'Parent and child perspectives of family leisure involvement and satisfaction with family life', *Journal of Leisure Research* 35 (2) 163–189.

21

GENDERED FREEDOMS AND CONSTRAINTS FOR YOUNG WOMEN SOCIALIZING IN BARS AND CLUBS

Oona Brooks

Introduction

Although socializing and drinking in bars, pubs and clubs has traditionally been identified as a masculine leisure activity (Whitehead, 1976; Hey, 1986; Green *et al.*, 1987; Parks *et al.*, 1998), social taboos around women drinking alcohol appear to have receded in recent years (Day, Gough and McFadden, 2004). The UK has also witnessed an expansion of the night-time economy (Winlow and Hall, 2006), and bars and clubs have become more 'women friendly' through a process of feminization (Chatterton and Hollands, 2003). This cultural shift represents a stark contrast with observations from earlier studies that position drinking in pubs as a male privilege, and an expression of patriarchal society (Hey, 1986; Whitehead, 1976).

This cultural change, however, has been accompanied by gendered safety concerns relating to a rise in young women's alcohol consumption (Mathews and Richardson, 2005; McKenzie and Haw, 2006), the apparent emergence of a 'ladette' culture (Day *et al.*, 2004; Jackson and Tinkler, 2007) and concern about young women's vulnerability to drug- and alcohol-assisted sexual assault (Beynon *et al.*, 2005; Moore, 2009). These concerns have prompted a renewed interest in the development and dissemination of safety advice to women, particularly young women, who are simultaneously positioned as 'a risk' and 'at risk' when they socialize in bars and clubs (Brooks, 2009). Thus it would seem that young women are required to negotiate a myriad of tensions and expectations within the night-time economy. This raises interesting questions about both the freedoms and gendered constraints experienced by contemporary young women socializing in bars and clubs.

From a theoretical perspective, feminist structural and poststructural frameworks can be drawn upon to facilitate a nuanced understanding of these tensions in young women's use of bars, pubs and clubs. These feminist theoretical frameworks share a common concern with the concepts of gender identity, power, social control and resistance, although they offer divergent possibilities for the application of these concepts and, therefore, the way in which young women's experiences can be theorized and understood. This chapter explores these debates, drawing upon data from a qualitative study that examined young women's views, experiences and behaviours in relation to their safety while socializing in bars and clubs in Scotland.

Feminist theoretical perspectives

Despite a tendency towards viewing feminism as a homogeneous perspective, it is more accurate to acknowledge that there are *feminisms*. It is beyond the scope of this chapter to fully examine all of the diverse perspectives encompassed within feminism. However, feminist structural and poststructural perspectives are highlighted, since they incorporate some of the key tensions within contemporary feminism. For feminists, particular tensions exist between recognizing the discrimination and oppression that women encounter in their lives and the level of resistance to oppression which they have the capacity (and desire) to utilize. Feminist structural and poststructural theoretical perspectives share a common concern with power, social control and resistance, although they offer contrasting possibilities for the application of these concepts to women's lives.

Feminist theorizing about structural constraints on women's leisure formed a dominant theme within Leisure Studies in the 1980s, primarily from a socialist feminist perspective, which seeks to highlight the relationship between patriarchy and economic determinants (Deem, 1986; Green, Hebron and Woodward, 1987). Fundamental to structural theory is an appreciation of hierarchical societal structure and the way in which the interests of those in power are constructed, legitimated, normalized and reproduced through the dominant codes within society (Aitchison, 2003: 31). For feminist structural theorizing, the system of patriarchy is a central focus. Put simply, 'women's lives are seen to be *structured* by gender within a society *structured* by patriarchal relations' (Scraton, 1994: 252). Wimbush and Talbot (1988: xvi) highlight the significance of patriarchal gender relations in the realm of leisure as follows:

> Patriarchal relations, like class relations, are culturally reproduced, even magnified, within leisure and recreation. They are legitimated and sustained by a complexity of ideological and material forces which help to shape our social institutions – the family unit, the media, the education system, the legal system and so on.

Constraints on women's leisure, and women's unequal access to leisure opportunities, imposed by (capitalist) patriarchal structures, formed a significant focus of early feminist theorizing within Leisure Studies (Deem, 1986; Green *et al.*, 1987). Green *et al.* (1987) give particular consideration to women, social control and leisure; utilizing a feminist analysis, they observe that leisure is one of the areas where women's behaviour is most closely regulated. Social control is defined by Green *et al.* (1987: 79) as 'an ongoing process, one element in the struggle to maintain male hegemony which sets the limits of appropriate feminine behaviour'. Feminist theorists within Leisure Studies and beyond have argued that women's awareness of the risks associated with 'imprudent' behaviour has a profound effect on their use of public space, ultimately acting as a measure of social control over women (Deem, 1986; Green, Hebron and Woodward, 1990; Smart and Smart, 1978; Valentine, 1990; Wesely and Gaarder, 2004). Accepted standards of femininity and masculinity are hallmarks of this system; women who do not conform to these culturally accepted standards of femininity, typically characterized by passivity, modesty and restraint, risk damage to their sexual and moral reputation.

The extent to which structural arguments that were articulated around thirty years ago within Leisure Studies can explain contemporary experiences of young women is subject to debate. Modernist feminist concerns about the impact of patriarchal gender relations in structuring women's lives have been critiqued, on account of their over-reliance on structural arguments (Rojek, 1991). The 'grand narratives' associated with this type of theorizing have been accused of falsely universalizing women's experiences and, indeed, their oppression (Wearing, 1992), thus paying insufficient attention to difference, diversity and women's capacity for agency and resistance.

It is apparent, however, that some early feminist theorizing in Leisure Studies did at least attempt to address the differences *between* women in the way that they access leisure and public space, in addition to gender differences between men and women (Deem, 1986). Wimbush and Talbot (1988: 49), for example, concluded that although women's leisure opportunities are circumscribed primarily by their gender, their age, ethnic origin and class also play a significant role. Crucially, Scraton (1994: 255) argues that many of the debates central to postmodern theory are those which feminism has been engaged with for some time (e.g., rejection of the dichotomy between public and private, the need to attend to difference and diversity, and the difficulties associated with 'grand theory'). Moreover, it could be argued that critiques levelled at early feminist theorizing, due to a perceived lack of acknowledgement of women's scope for agency and resistance to patriarchal structures, are ill-founded. The potential for emancipation and change has always been at the very heart of feminist research and activism (Ramazanoglu and Holland, 2006; Skinner, Hester and Malos, 2005; Stanley, 1990).

Nonetheless, critiques of structural feminist arguments have led some feminist theorists to engage with postmodern and poststructural perspectives in search of an alternative means with which to theorize women's experiences (Aitchison, 2004; Butler, 1990; Nicholson, 1999; Wearing, 1998; Weedon, 1987). Poststructural feminism attempts to uncover the cultural codes which construct, legitimate and reproduce the gender order, rather than focusing on the political, social and economic manifestations of the gender order (Weedon, 1987). Thus, there is a shift from thinking about 'patriarchy' and the associated male domination of the structures of society (Wearing, 1996), to a concern with the way in which cultural relations serve to shape gender relations (Aitchison, 2003). This mode of theorizing attempts to accommodate 'the interrelationships between specific cultural contexts and networks of wider social structures of power' (Aitchison, 2000: 134). It is argued that this emphasis on *culture* rather than *structure* allows theorization of women as 'active agents involved in the construction of their own lives' rather than 'passive victims of overdetermined structures' (Green, 1998: 173–174). Crucially, contemporary individuals are construed as being able to utilize choice and self-monitoring to fashion identities (Green and Singleton, 2006) in a society characterized by increased reflexivity and 'individualization' (Beck and Beck-Gernsheim, 1996). In practice, drawing upon postmodern and poststructural discourses has meant that feminists have engaged in greater depth with concepts such as identity, agency and subjectivity (Green, 1998: 173).

Drawing upon a hybrid of interactionist theory and Foucault's ideas on power, subjectivity, discourse and resistance, Wearing (1998) is optimistic that contemporary women can resist directed feminine subjectivities, and that this is something which leisure can help to achieve. From this perspective, leisure can be situated as an activity which can provide young women with a means to contest and resist cultural discourses around feminine identities (Green and Singleton, 2006). For postmodern theorists, identity is fluid and there is greater scope for individual lifestyle choices (Green, 1998: 173). Belief in the ability of individual women to move beyond notions of prescribed, oppressive femininity to embrace new femininities is rooted in a sense of optimism. Wearing (1988: 144) applies this optimism to women of the 1990s:

women in the postmodern world means a diverse range of women of the 1990s who have a new self-confidence to challenge the givens of their existence, to resist what they have been told they are and to reach what they should be.

Alongside the optimism within poststructural and postmodern theorizing, it is widely recognized that postmodernism has represented a challenge to conventional feminist theorizing, hence postmodern theories have been resisted by some feminist writers (Scraton, 1994; Walby, 1992). This resistance reflects an underlying concern about the potential for postmodern discourses, with their emphasis on micro rather than macro structures, to undermine feminist work which has strived to expose gendered inequalities and discrimination with a view to improving women's social position. Scraton (1994: 255) echoes these concerns, arguing that 'one of the problems with the postmodern discourse is that political and material reality appear to be being lost in the theorizing'. Meanwhile, McNay (1992: 2) contends that tensions exist between poststructuralist perspectives and 'more politically engaged forms of critique'.

Thus, tensions exist between feminist structural and poststructural perspectives in recognizing the discrimination and oppression that women encounter in their lives and the level of resistance to oppression which they have the agency to utilize. By reflecting on the study findings in the context of the differing ideas found with feminist structural and poststructural theoretical frameworks, the extent of young women's apparent freedoms when socializing in bars and clubs is questioned within this chapter.

The study

This chapter draws upon data from a qualitative study focusing on young women's (18–25 years) safety in bars and clubs in Scotland. The main aim of the study was to understand the views, experiences and behaviours of young women socializing in bars and clubs. Individual semi-structured interviews were used to elicit participants' personal experiences and their safety concerns in bars and clubs, while focus groups were used as a contextual method (Wilkinson, 1999) to examine the way that young women discussed safety in these venues within a peer group (Bryman, 2001). The qualitative data recorded during interviews and focus groups were fully transcribed and coded using the computer-assisted qualitative data analysis software package NVivo. The analysis process followed a three-stage model comprising open, axial and selective coding (Strauss, 1987). In practice, however, this was not a linear process and the analysis moved back and forth between different stages of this model as new themes and connections within the data emerged.

Research participants (n=35) were recruited primarily through universities, colleges and youth groups. Due to the geographical spread of participants, experiences of socializing in four out of Scotland's six cities formed the main focus of discussion, although some participants also referred to their experiences of socializing in smaller towns. Participants were primarily white, heterosexual women in further or higher education. It is possible that a more diverse sample would reflect different issues according to race, class or sexuality, particularly given the construction of respectable or successful femininity through race and class (Griffin, 2004; Jackson and Tinkler, 2007; Skeggs, 1997). It is also acknowledged that sexuality impacts upon definitions of safety and the identification of safe spaces in the night-time economy (Corteen, 2002; Moran, Skeggs, Tyrer and Corteen, 2003). Nonetheless, the data generated in this study provides a valuable opportunity to examine the views and experiences of a key population within bars and clubs, since the consumption of alcohol is an acknowledged feature of student life (Gill, 2002; Piacentini and Banister, 2008) and students are a population specifically targeted by the alcohol industry (Hastings *et al.*, 2010). Moreover, young women are identified as being particularly (although by no means exclusively) vulnerable to sexual assault within licensed premises (Moreton, 2002; Schwartz, 1997; Watson, 2000) and are a key target audience for safety campaigns in these social settings.

Findings

For the young women in this study, socializing and consuming alcohol in bars and clubs was a routine and, in many cases, central leisure activity. Socializing in bars and clubs was described as fun, and contrasted with the constraints of the working week similar to the way in which the pub has conventionally been constructed as a sanctuary for the 'working man' to escape the stresses and strains of daily life (Harrison, 1971: 171). Reiterating the findings of Parks, Miller, Collins and Zetes-Zanatta (1998: 707), although drinking in bars has traditionally been a male pastime, women appear to have adopted this as a leisure activity of their own. Importantly, participants also expressed a sense of entitlement to this leisure time in a way that challenges the notion that women typically facilitate the leisure time of others, rarely perceiving themselves to have the right to take up such opportunities (Deem, 1986; Glyptis and Chambers, 1982).

However, simply looking at women's ability to access such leisure opportunities does not adequately take account of the complexities associated with *how* women access bars and clubs. As noted by Day *et al.* (2004), the mere presence of women within pubs does not necessarily constitute social acceptance. The challenges encountered by young women socializing in bar and club environments are illustrated below through consideration of their safety concerns, experiences and behaviours within these venues.

Safety concerns and experiences

None of the young women in the current study were able to describe bars and clubs as a safe space for women without some form of caveat. The following extract from Marion is typical of participants' comments in response to being asked how safe they thought bars and clubs were:

> *Marion* (INT): I generally do think they are safe places. I mean, I suppose it depends ... I think as long as you don't be silly ... you're not gonna be silly and walk off by yourself, or go home by yourself, and you keep an eye on your drinks.

Reflecting the dominant discourse of individualized responsibility within prevention literature (Brooks, 2011; Campbell, 2005; Lawson and Olle, 2005; Neame, 2003), bars and clubs were only considered to be safe spaces for women as long as they were vigilant to potential risks, engaged in safety behaviours and ensured that they were protected by other people. Further, the risks encountered by women in bars and clubs were perceived to have increased rather than decreased over time, and participants recounted experiencing sexual violence, harassment and drink spiking as a prevalent feature of their experiences of socializing in bars and clubs. Participants' understanding that women now face increased risks in bars and clubs was attributed to three perceived social and cultural changes: an increase in drink spiking; an increase in women's alcohol consumption; and a shift in social relations between men and women. The following extract from Jessica is indicative of the perceived nature of this shift:

> *Jessica* (INT): I think it [threats to safety] was always probably going on, but I think probably ... definitely like in my mum's era, and she's like fifty now, but I think when she was ... probably more guys would be a bit more reserved. Okay, still go out, but I think they would still be less in your face and a bit more 'alright love, I'll leave you alone'. Definitely I think it's changed a lot.

These perceived changes were interrelated and were understood to contribute to women's vulnerability to sexual violence and harassment. Although it is difficult to draw comparisons over time, this finding contradicts the idea that contemporary women are now substantially more liberated than those of previous generations in this regard. Almost all of the participants in the current study noted at least one safety concern which they personally had in relation to socializing in bars and clubs. Participants' safety concerns were overwhelmingly related to the fear of sexual violence. This finding resonates with earlier studies which locate the fear of sexual violence as women's primary safety concern within a range of social contexts (Myhill and Allen, 2002; Stanko, 1990; Tulloch, 2004). In keeping with research that has highlighted gendered disparities in the nature and extent of safety concerns (Stanko, 1990; Tulloch, 2004; Walklate, 2007), participants in the current study also believed that women were significantly more likely to be concerned about their safety than were men when socializing in bars and clubs. This was partly attributed to media reporting of issues relating to women's safety.

> *Suzanne* (FG02): ... in women's magazines, it's all, you know, there's all the real life stories about all the bad things that have happened, whereas boys don't have that, that they don't read about terrible like fights that they've got into, whereas we kind of read about it every week.

It does not follow, however, that the concerns of participants in the current study were irrational, as espoused by certain aspects of criminological debate (Pain, 1997; Tulloch, 2004), since participants also reported significant levels of sexual violence and harassment which they had experienced in bars and clubs. Indeed 80% of participants described at least one incident in a bar, pub or club where their personal safety had been compromised, with a total 40 incidents of rape, sexual assault, sexual harassment or drink spiking being disclosed across the sample of 35 young women. More specifically, one young woman disclosed a suspected personal experience of rape, eight reported a sexual assault and nine reported a suspected incident of drink spiking. Meanwhile, almost two-thirds of participants reported experiencing sexual harassment (e.g., being subjected to unwanted sexual comments, being followed, pulled, grabbed or flashed at). These findings suggest that incidents of sexual violence are a common feature within the accounts of participants in this study. It should be noted, however, that these findings are based on a small sample and it is not suggested that they are indicative of the prevalence of sexual violence in bars and clubs at a broader level; rather, the data presented here are intended to contextualize the accounts of young women in the current study.

Safety behaviours

A wide range of safety behaviours were adopted by young women with the intention of avoiding or preventing drink spiking, sexual violence and harassment from men. The young women did creatively resist (sometimes successfully, sometimes unsuccessfully) threats to their safety, and at times doing so was described with a sense of pride in their own strength and knowledge. While some of these behaviours were explicitly understood to be safety behaviours, other behaviours and choices, including where to go, who to go with and what to wear, were implicitly connected to safety.

Some of the safety behaviours adopted by young women reflected those advocated within safety advice directed at women (e.g., not accepting a drink you haven't seen being poured, or not leaving a bar on your own). For most of the young women in the current study, utilizing safety strategies was 'just what you do' while drinking in bars and clubs and, as such, they were described as 'common sense' precautions. Arguably, however, adopting such safety strategies are only 'common sense' measures for women, not men. This resonates with Stanko's (1990) assertion that women are expected to see the 'ordinary' as 'risky'. Some women resented and resisted this imposition on their own freedoms, although for most women taking responsibility for their own behaviour, and that of men around them, was normal and inevitable.

Participants' decisions about which bars and clubs to socialize in were influenced by their safety concerns and a desire to avoid establishments described as having a particularly drunken or sexualized environment. These undesirable venues were mainly characterized by the 'type' of person who went there, and venues which carried working-class connotations (e.g., 'rough' places with 'tarty girls', 'sleazy guys', and 'seasoned hard drinkers') were viewed as particularly unsafe by the young women in the current study. The risks associated with socializing in these undesirable venues related both to the possibility of experiencing violence or harassment and the risk of being deemed 'unrespectable' by association. This finding resonates with the work of Skeggs (2002), which highlights the construction of femininity through gender and class, whereby middle-class femininity has conventionally been regarded as the respectable ideal. Meanwhile, excessive drinking and overtly sexual or crude behaviours are associated with 'unrespectable' or problematic elements of working-class lifestyles (Jackson and Tinkler, 2007).

Participants' experiences in bars and clubs were significantly influenced by who they went to these venues with. Socializing in female-only groups meant that young women felt that they were subject to heightened male attention based on the assumption that they were open to sexual advances rather than simply enjoying a 'girls' night out'. This phenomenon, whereby women entering pubs on their own or with other women are stigmatized or subjected to sexual harassment, was documented by feminist writers in the 1980s (Hey, 1986; Stanley, 1980). Findings from the current study indicate that little has changed in this regard.

> *Sophie* (FG03): I think if girls go out, just girls, then like maybe other guys who don't know them, they take that as a sign 'oh they're going out just to pull' or 'they can't possibly be going out just because it's a night out' or anything, so it's almost like … you know, it's a signal 'oh come and talk to me' or … so they feel they have a right to make a move.

Almost all participants agreed that they felt safest when they were accompanied by a male in a bar or a club. The nature of their relationship to this 'male protector' did not appear to be particularly significant (e.g., friend, acquaintance, boyfriend, brother); this was superseded by the fact that he was male. Being accompanied by a male was deemed to offer a means of deterrence and defence against unwanted sexual attention from other males. From a radical feminist perspective, it has been argued that patriarchal ideology presents men as women's 'natural protectors' (Berrington and Jones, 2002: 309–310). The fear of rape is described as an effective mechanism of control over women, since women are manoeuvred into dependent relationships with men on the basis that those men will protect them from other men (Radford, 1987). This reliance upon 'male protectors' contradicts the notion of liberated young women who are free to act beyond gendered constraint, and draws upon patriarchal notions of chivalry, masculine strength and feminine dependence (Bosworth, 1996). It would also seem that certain taboos associated with making sexual advances towards a woman who 'belongs' to another man are still played out within bar and club environments. However, some participants did question and resist this dynamic and the associated role of 'male protector'.

> *Ruth* (FG03): But sometimes they can be a little bit too over-protective as well. Like if a guy comes up and starts talking to you they're like right behind you, 'Who's that? Who are you talking to? Are you OK?' It's like, 'I'm fine'.

While the security offered by a 'male protector' was welcomed by some, others like Ruth resented the need to rely on male acquaintances for safety and questioned the possessive nature of the protection offered by male acquaintances and boyfriends. This highlights the complex and contradictory nature of young women's relationships with men in this regard.

Self-surveillance

The young women in this study engaged in an on-going process of risk assessment, namely in relation to the intentions of men in bars and clubs. Where they were subject to sexual harassment, the young women in this study frequently expressed a desire to challenge this behaviour, although they often refrained from doing so, due to a fear making a disproportionate response or 'provoking' a more aggressive response in return.

> *Suzanne* (INT): ... but sometimes they [boys] don't listen though and that's quite, it's quite scary really, you know, when they're quite like ... once somebody's got you like that it's hard to kind of get off and say 'No, leave me alone' without being really rude 'cause you don't wanna be really rude to them and I think ... that's really difficult ... you know 'cause if they grab hold of you, how ... you don't wanna push them away 'cause that's just taking it too far then, isn't it?

> *Lorna* (INT): I'd like to think I'd got enough courage to say to them like please don't address me like that, but when people got quite a lot of drink in them then they're not gonna take no for an answer and they're probably just gonna make it worse, so ... in the long run it's easier just to be silent.

In these situations, it was at times 'easier' to draw upon passive behaviours typically associated with conventional femininity (e.g., smiling, being polite or remaining silent). Doing so had the intended effect of pacifying men and avoiding the risk of personal judgement and denigration (e.g., being viewed as frigid or lacking in a sense of humour). Participants, therefore, also attempted to pre-empt unwanted attention from men by engaging in 'self-surveillance' of their own behaviour (e.g., avoiding being 'too drunk' or giving out the 'wrong' sexual signals, and moderating their clothing choices). Participants' descriptions of their own clothing choices, and those of 'other' women when socializing in bars and clubs provided perhaps one of the most striking illustrations of the way that women performed surveillance of their own behaviour. Young women in the current study explicitly referred to 'rules' (i.e., the 'top half/bottom half' rule) which applied to their clothing choices in order to avoid appearing too 'provocative'.

> *Jessica* (INT): I think some women, obviously, dress with nothing and I think that makes them more easier as a target, like maybe they're easy. I think that targets them. But I definitely wouldn't wear a short skirt and a low cut top; I'd wear one or the other. That's just the way I am. I just sort of cover up. Wear jeans and a low cut top; that's what you usually do.

There was some suggestion that women are powerful in this regard; they have the capacity to control the nature of men's responses to them and can vary their dress according to whether or not they want male attention. However, the power women can exercise in this regard, arguably, remains within the confines of heterosexual femininity whereby women's status is defined in accordance with attractiveness to men and their perceived promiscuity or chastity.

Alcohol consumption was also a contentious issue for the young women in this study. Participants were in agreement that it was now more socially acceptable for women to partake in the conventionally masculine pursuit of alcohol consumption in bars and clubs than it was in the past. However, particular concern was articulated about the ability to remain 'in control' when consuming alcohol. These concerns related primarily to the deterioration in participants' ability to remain vigilant to potential threats to their safety, unwanted male attention and drink spiking. Young women in this study were also acutely aware of the gendered risks involved in consuming alcohol in this context. Young women's understanding of these risks relates, in the first instance, to negative perceptions attached to women who drink alcohol, particularly those who are seen to be 'drunk'. More specifically, and in keeping with earlier studies which have highlighted the connection between alcohol and a perceived lack of respectability (Green, *et al.*, 1987; Schwartz, 1997), it was understood that women who are drunk risk being viewed as unfeminine, unattractive and of questionable sexual character. However, there would appear to be some movement in this regard, since drinking in itself was not considered to be particularly problematic; negative judgements tended to be reserved for women who were seen to be drunk, particularly if they were also wearing 'revealing' clothing.

> *Eilidh* (FG02): ... if you look at it, like, historically ... women are seen as equals, on the whole, in society now, and it's not unusual for a girl to go out and get drunk, but people seem to think now it's like it's a problem, you know, women shouldn't be going out getting drunk ... it's all about women's safety and it's like kind of putting the pressure on yourself almost like if something happens to you it's your fault 'cause you were out drinking, and ... I don't know if that's right, because it doesn't seem to work the same way with men.

Being drunk was perceived to heighten women's risk of receiving unwanted sexual attention, being targeted for sexual assault by men who might view them as less likely to resist their sexual advances, or being subjected to blame in the event that they were sexually assaulted. Moreover, participants were also aware that they might be blamed by others, or indeed blame themselves, if they did experience violence, harassment or drink spiking when they had 'failed' to adopt the full range of safety behaviours recommended within the prevention literature. Watson (2000) observes that within the setting of licensed premises, women can be particularly critical of one another if they are seen to fail to look after themselves and take responsibility for their own safety. This highlights one of the negative implications of the individualized discourse inherent within much of the contemporary prevention literature targeted towards young women. In essence, it can be argued that women who fail to 'self-regulate' fail to do their gender properly (Campbell, 2005: 132).

This is not to suggest, however, that participants in the current study were merely the 'passive dupes' of repressive patriarchal power and control. Indeed, participants were 'gender aware' (McRobbie, 2004) and some participants expressed forms of resistance which reached beyond the level of employing safety strategies as individual resistance. Some participants, for example, questioned the double standards which persist in relation to the expected behaviour of men and women in the environment of bars and clubs. Certain aspects of preventive advice were also rejected by participants, particularly where adopting this advice impinged upon their capacity to have fun or where the advice invoked a victim-blaming discourse. This is indicative of a form of resistance which differs from the notion of individual resistance enacted through specific safe-keeping behaviours.

Discussion and conclusions

Reviewing findings from the current study, it is apparent that there is some movement over time in the gendered expectations of women's behaviour in bars and clubs. Indeed, young women regularly socialize in these venues and, as such, this activity forms a central aspect of their leisure. Given the conventional alignment of drinking in bars as a masculine activity this would suggest, in keeping with poststructural feminist perspectives, that there must be scope for resistance and negotiation on behalf of women in the contested social space of bars and clubs. However, it is also apparent that bars and clubs are social spaces infused with gendered expectations and risks for women. These gendered concerns impact upon which venues women feel safest in, who they feel safe with and how they behave or present themselves within these venues. Context is crucial in this regard; bars and clubs are typically sexualized environments (Parks *et al.*, 1998; Snow, Robinson and McCall, 1991), and this has particular implications for women's safety and their conduct within these venues. Echoing the findings of earlier feminist studies in this area, women's behaviour in these venues is ultimately constrained by their continual negotiation of risk, including the risk of moral judgement. This finding concurs with Campbell's (2005: 50) assertion that women engage in numerous behaviours, in order to ensure their safety in public places, which are 'a performative condition of normative femininity'. In other words, despite the apparent social acceptance of women in bars and clubs, their experiences in these venues remain significantly, although not exclusively, structured by gender.

Previous studies have described safety behaviours employed by women in the realm of leisure, such as only going out at particular times, as 'resistant practices' (Jordan and Aitchison, 2008: 343), arguing that this illustrates how women address their fears in order to participate in leisure activities (Bialeschki and Hicks, 1998; Mehta and Bondi, 1999). However, findings from the current study indicate that women's safe-keeping behaviours emanate from a sense of fear and individualized responsibility, which manifests itself in self-surveillance. When safety behaviours are synonymous with self-surveillance and self-governance, it is difficult to position these acts uncritically as resistance. Young women's sense that they should remain 'vigilant' and 'in control' resonates with the Foucauldian concepts of 'self-surveillance' and 'self-policing', which have been used to describe the ways that women regulate their behaviour in public (Mitchell, Crawshaw, Bunton and Green, 2001; Wesely and Gaarder, 2004). Thus, participants' adoption of safety behaviours may be more appropriately defined as 'accommodating techniques', a term used by Wilson and Little (2008: 181) to describe the safe-keeping practices of solo women travellers, such as modifying their clothing choices, adapting to local variations in normative femininity, avoiding places where they felt unsafe and remaining vigilant. The restrictions of occupying a state of 'hypervigilance' (Wesely and Gaarder, 2004), have been acknowledged within existing work in this area in terms of limiting women's opportunities and the mitigation of their use of leisure space for pleasure, enjoyment and relaxation (Gardner, 1990; Seabrook and Green, 2004; Snow *et al.*, 1991; Wesely and Gaarder, 2004).

These findings, alongside the individualized rhetoric of drink spiking and drug-assisted sexual assault prevention campaigns directed at young women socializing in bars and clubs, may even raise the question of whether young women's behaviour is in fact subject to greater surveillance and regulation now than it was in the past. The identification of drink spiking as a 'new' risk to women in the late 1990s, for example, would appear to have emerged at a time when there appeared to be signs of 'moral panic' (Cohen, 1972) about 'ladette' culture and troublesome young femininities (Jackson and Tinkler, 2007). In a similar vein, Jackson (2006) argues that media-driven concern about 'ladettes' is leading to greater surveillance and regulation of the behaviour of girls and young women at a time when girls are starting to gain increased freedoms and opportunities. In this regard, drinking and socializing in bars and clubs perhaps remains a 'relative freedom' (Wimbush and Talbot, 1988). Ultimately, this raises important questions about whether there really has been meaningful change in gender relations in the night-time economy or whether women are simply accommodated in bars and clubs as a result of commercial imperatives that recognize the economic power of young women as a consumer group.

References

Aitchison, C. (2000) 'Poststructural feminist theories of representing Others: a response to the "crisis" in leisure studies' discourse', *Leisure Studies 19*: 127–144.

Aitchison, C. (2003) *Gender and Leisure: Social and Cultural Perspectives*. London: Routledge.

Aitchison, C. (2004) 'From policy to place: theoretical explorations of gender–leisure relations in everyday life', in W. Mitchell, R. Bunton and E. Green (eds) *Young People, Risk and Leisure: Constructing Identities in Everyday Life*. Basingstoke: Palgrave Macmillan.

Arber, S. (2001) 'Designing samples', in N. Gilbert (ed.) *Researching Social Life*, 2nd edition (pp. 58–82). London: Sage Publications.

Beck, U., and Beck-Gernsheim, E. (1996) 'Individualization and precarious freedoms: perspectives and controversies of a subject-orientated sociology', in P. Heelas, S. Lash and P. Morris (eds) *Detraditionalization*. London: Blackwell.

Berrington, E., and Jones, H. (2002) 'Reality vs. myth: constructions of women's insecurity', *Feminist Media Studies 2* (3) 307–323.

Beynon, C., Edwards, S., Morleo, M., Anderson, Z., and McVeigh, J. (2005) *Drink Spiking Report: Executive Summary*. Liverpool John Moores University, Centre for Public Health.

Bialeschki, D. M., and Hicks, H. (1998) 'I refuse to live in fear: The influence of fear and violence on women's outdoor recreation activities'. Paper presented at the Leisure Studies Association 4th International Conference – The Big Ghetto: Gender, Sexuality and Gender, Leeds Metropolitan University.

Bosworth, M. (1996) 'Resistance and compliance in women's prisons: towards a critique of legitimacy', *Critical Criminology* 7 (2) 5–19.

Brooks, O. (2009) 'Consuming alcohol in bars, pubs and clubs: a risky freedom for young women?', *Annals of Leisure Research* 11 (3/4) 331–350.

Brooks, O. (2011) '"Guys! stop doing it!": young women's adoption and rejection of safety advice when socializing in bars, pubs and clubs', *British Journal of Criminology* 51 (4) 635–651.

Bryman, A. (2001) *Social Research Methods*. Oxford: Oxford University Press.

Butler, J. (1990) *Gender Trouble: Feminism and the Subversion of Identity*. New York: Routledge.

Campbell, A. (2005) 'Keeping the "lady" safe: the regulation of femininity through crime prevention literature', *Critical Criminology* 13: 119–140.

Chatterton, P., and Hollands, R. (2003) *Urban Nightscapes, Youth Cultures, Pleasure Spaces and Corporate Power*. London: Routledge.

Cohen, S. (1972) *Folk Devils and Moral Panics: The Creation of Mods and Rockers*. Oxford: Blackwell.

Corteen, K. (2002) 'Lesbian safety talk: problematizing definitions and experiences of violence, sexuality and space', *Sexualities* 5 (3) 259.

Day, K., Gough, B., and McFadden, M. (2004) 'Warning! Alcohol can seriously damage your feminine health', *Feminist Media Studies* 4 (2) 165–183.

Deem, R. (1986) *All Work and No Play? The Sociology of Women and Leisure*. Milton Keynes: Open University Press.

Gardner, C. B. (1990) 'Safe conduct: women, crime, and self in public places', *Social Problems* 37 (3) 311–328.

Gill, J. S. (2002) 'Reported levels of alcohol consumption and binge drinking within the UK undergraduate student population', *Alcohol* 27 (2) 109–120.

Glyptis, S., and Chambers, D. (1982) 'No place like home', *Leisure Studies* 1: 247–262.

Green, E. (1998) 'Women doing friendship: an analysis of women's leisure as a site of identity construction, empowerment and resistance', *Leisure Studies* 17: 171–185.

Green, E., and Singleton, C. (2006) 'Risky bodies at leisure: young women negotiating space and place', *Sociology* 40 (5) 853–871.

Green, E., Hebron, S., Woodward, D. (1987) 'Women, leisure and social control', in J. Hanmer and M. Maynard (eds) *Women, Violence and Social Control* (pp. 75–92). London: Macmillan Press.

Green, E., Hebron, S., and Woodward, D. (1990) *Women's Leisure, What Leisure?* Hampshire: Macmillan.

Griffin, C. (2004) 'Good girls, bad girls: Anglocentrism and diversity in the constitution of contemporary girlhood', in A. Harris (ed.) *All about the Girl: Culture, Power and Identity*. London: Routledge.

Harrison, B. (1971) *Drink and the Victorians: The Temperance Question in England 1815–1872*. London: Faber and Faber.

Hastings, G., Brooks, O., Stead, M., Angus, K., Anker, T., and Farrell, T. (2010) 'Failure of self regulation of UK alcohol advertising', *BMJ 340*: 184–186.

Hey, V. (1986) *Patriarchy and Pub Culture*. London: Tavistock Publications Ltd.

Jackson, C. (2006) '"Wild" girls? An exploration of "ladette" cultures in secondary schools', *Gender and Education 18*: 339–360.

Jackson, C., and Tinkler, P. (2007) '"Ladettes" and "modern girls": "troublesome" young femininities', *The Sociological Review 55* (2) 251–252.

Jordan, F., and Aitchison, C. (2008) 'Tourism and the sexualisation of the gaze: solo female tourists' experiences of gendered power, surveillance and embodiment', *Leisure Studies 27* (3) 329–349.

Lawson, S., and Olle, L. (2005) 'Dangerous drink spiking archetypes', *Women against Violence – An Australian Feminist Journal 18*: 46–55.

Mathews, S., and Richardson, A. (2005) *Findings from the 2003 Offending, Crime and Justice Survey*. London: Home Office.

McKenzie, K., and Haw, S. (2006) *Alcohol and Alcohol-Related Problems in Scotland: Summary and 2006 Update of Evidence*. Edinburgh: NHS Health Scotland.

McNay, L. (1992) *Foucault and Feminism: Power, Gender, and the Self*. Cambridge: Polity Press.

McRobbie, A. (2004) 'Post-feminism and popular culture', *Feminist Media Studies* 4 (3) 255–264.

Mehta, A., and Bondi, L. (1999) 'Embodied discourse: on gender and fear of violence', *Gender, Place and Culture 6* (1) 67–84.

Mitchell, W. A., Crawshaw, P., Bunton, R., and Green, E. (2001) 'Situating young people's experiences of risk and identity', *Health Risk and Society 3* (2) 217–233.

Moore, S. E. H. (2009) 'Cautionary tales: drug-facilitated sexual assault in the British media', *Crime, Media, Culture 5* (3) 305–320.

Moran, L., Skeggs, B., Tyrer, P., and Corteen, K. (2003) *Sexuality and the Politics of Safety*. London: Routledge.

Moreton, R. (2002) 'Spiked drinks: a focus group study of young women's perceptions of risk and behaviours', Central Sydney Area Health Service, Camperdown, NSW.

Myhill, A., and Allen, J. (2002) *Rape and Sexual Assault of Women: The Extent and Nature of the Problem, Findings from the British Crime Survey*. London: Home Office.

Neame, A. (2003) 'Beyond "drink spiking": drug and alcohol facilitated sexual assault', Australian Centre for the Study of Sexual Assault, Australian Institute of Family Studies.

Nicholson, L. (1999) *The Play of Reason: From the Modern to the Postmodern*. Buckingham: Open University Press.

Pain, R. (1997) 'Women's fear? Perceptions of sexual violence in public and private space', *International Review of Victimology 4*: 297–312.

Parks, K. A., Miller, B. A., Collins, L., and Zetes-Zanatta, L. (1998) 'Women's descriptions of drinking in bars: reasons and risks', *Sex Roles 38* (9/10) 701–717.

Piacentini, M. P., and Banister, E. N. (2008) 'Managing anti-consumption in an excessive drinking culture', *Journal of Business Research 62*: 279–288.

Radford, J. (1987) 'Policing male violence: policing women', in J. Hanmer and M. Maynard (eds) *Women, Violence, and Social Control* (pp. 30–46). London: Macmillan Press.

Ramazanoglu, C., and Holland, J. (2006) *Feminist Methodology: Challenges and Choices*. London: SAGE Publications Ltd.

Rojek, C. (1991) 'Leisure and recreation theory', in E. Jackson and T. Burton (eds) *Understanding Leisure and Recreation: Mapping the Past, Charting the Future*. State College, PA: Venture Publishing.

Schwartz, M. (1997) *Researching Violence against Women*. Newbury Park: Sage.

Scraton, S. (1994) 'The changing world of women and leisure: feminism, "postfeminism" and leisure', *Leisure Studies 13* (4) 249–261.

Seabrook, T. and Green, E. (2004) 'Streetwise or safe? Girls negotiating time and space', in L. Michell, R. Bunton and E. Green (eds) *Young People, Risk and Leisure: Constructing Identities in Everyday Life* (pp. 129–141). Basingstoke, UK: Palgrave Macmillan.

Skeggs, B. (1997) *Formations of Class and Gender*. London: Sage Publications.

Skeggs, B. (2002) 'Ambivalent femininities', in S. Jackson and S. Scott (eds) *Gender: A Sociological Reader* (pp. 311–325). London: Routledge.

Skinner, T., Hester, M., and Malos, E. (2005) *Researching Gender Violence: Feminist Methodology in Action*. Cullompton: Willan.

Smart, C., and Smart, B. (1978) *Women, Sexuality and Social Control*. London: Routledge and Kegan Paul.

Snow, D. A., Robinson, C., and McCall, P. L. (1991) '"Cooling out" men in singles bars and nightclubs: observations on the interpersonal survival strategies of women in public places', *Journal of Contemporary Ethnography 19* (4) 423–449.

Stanko, E. A. (1990) *Everyday Violence: How Women and Men Experience Sexual and Physical Danger*. London: Pandora Press.

Stanley, L. (1980) 'The problem of women and leisure: an ideological construct and a radical feminist alternative'. Paper presented at the 'Leisure in the 1980s' Forum, Capital Radio, 26–28 September.

Stanley, L. (ed.) (1990) *Feminist Praxis: Research, Theory and Epistemology in Feminist Sociology*. London: Routledge.

Strauss, A. (1987) *Qualitative Analysis of Social Scientists*. New York: Cambridge University Press.

Tulloch, J. (2004) 'Youth, leisure travel and fear of crime: an Australian study', in W. Mitchell, R. Bunton and E. Green (eds) *Young People, Risk and Leisure: Constructing Identities in Everyday Life* (pp. 115–128). Basingstoke, Hampshire: Palgrave Macmillan.

Valentine, G. (1990) 'Women's fear and the design of public space', *Built Environment 16* (4) 288–303.

Walby, S. (1992) 'Post-post-modernism? Theorizing social complexity', in M. Barrett and S. Phillips (eds) *Destabilizing Theory: Contemporary Feminist Debates*. Cambridge: Polity Press.

Walklate, S. (2007) *Imagining the Victim of Crime*. Buckingham: Open University Press.

Watson, J. (2000) *The Right to Party Safely: A Report on Young Women, Sexual Violence and Licensed Premises*, Melbourne, Victoria, Australia: CASA House, Centre Against Sexual Assault, Royal Women's Hospital.

Wearing, B. (1992) 'Beyond the ideology of motherhood: leisure as resistance', *Australian and New Zealand Journal of Sociology 26*: 35–58.

Wearing, B. (1996) *Gender: The Pleasure and Pain of Difference*. Melbourne, Australia: Longman.

Wearing, B. (1998) *Leisure and Feminist Theory*. London: Sage Publications.

Weedon, C. (1987) *Feminist Practice and Poststructuralist Theory*. Oxford: Basil Blackwell.

Wesely, J. K. and Gaarder, E. (2004) 'The gendered "nature" of the urban outdoors: women negotiating fear of violence', *Gender & Society 18* (5) 645–663.

Whitehead, A. (1976) 'Sexual antagonism in Herefordshire', in D. Barker and S. Allen (eds) *Dependence and Exploitation in Work and Marriage* (pp. 169–203). London: Longman.

Wilkinson, S. (1999) 'How useful are focus groups in feminist research?', in R. S. Barbour and J. Kitzinger (eds) *Developing Focus Group Research: Politics, Theory and Practice* (pp. 64–78). London: Sage Publications.

Wilson, E. and Little, D. E. (2008) 'The solo female travel experience: exploring the "geography of women's fear"', *Current Issues in Tourism 11* (2) 167–186.

Wimbush, E. and Talbot, M. (1988) *Relative Freedoms: Women and Leisure*. Milton Keynes: Open University Press.

Winlow, S. and Hall, S. (2006) *Violent Night: Urban Leisure and Contemporary Culture*. New York: Berg.

22

LEISURE AND THE LIFE COURSE

Ken Roberts

Introduction

The study of leisure and the life course is experiencing a prolonged birth: necessarily so because we have still to assemble all the evidence necessary to disentangle the effects of historical change in different age groups and birth cohorts.

Research began by studying and identifying features that characterized the leisure of specific age groups. It was subsequently noted that people built long-term leisure careers, and that their leisure in later life stages was influenced by whatever they had done and learnt earlier in life. The next complication to be noted was that early-life leisure learning varied not just cross-sectionally by gender, social class, ethnicity and place, but also according to historical period. The ideal way of disaggregating age, cohort and historical influences is through sequential birth cohort studies. The first such study commenced in Britain in 1946. Subsequently, additional British birth cohort studies have been launched in 1958, 1970, 2000 and 2012. These projects take a lifetime to mature. The oldest cohort that is still being studied (those born in 1946) are only just entering later life, enabling the long-term effects of experiences during childhood and youth to be explored. Unfortunately, as so often happens, the early waves of these studies did not collect all the evidence (about leisure during childhood and youth, in our case) that we would now like to have at our disposal. Even so, as explained below, there are good reasons to believe that current cohorts that are entering later life will exhibit different leisure profiles from those of older people in the twentieth century. There are also reasons to believe that today's children and young people will become a different leisure generation than any of their predecessors.

Age and the life course

Youth

Youth was the first age group whose leisure received sustained scrutiny. This was because it was young people's uses of free time that were most likely to be defined as a social problem. Throughout the first half of the twentieth century this problem was 'owned' by psychology.

The American psychologist G. Stanley Hall (1904) invented the psychology of adolescence (the term that remained widely used for the next fifty years) with the claim that the life stage was characterized by inner storm and stress, which could be expected to result in turbulent social relations and behaviour. By the 1950s and 1960s this view of the age group had been heavily embroidered with psychoanalytic theory (see Erikson, 1968).

However, by then the entire body of knowledge had been thrown into crisis by Margaret Mead's claim that in Samoa the transition from childhood to adulthood was free of psychological stress (Mead, 1935; 1971). Also by then, American sociologists had been investigating delinquent youth and had discovered that delinquency was typically sub-cultural, meaning that the individuals were conforming with the norms of their peer groups rather than acting out psychological problems (Thrasher, 1936; Whyte, 1943). This led to the formulation of the now classical sociological theories about the social processes that generate delinquent sub-cultures (Cloward and Ohlin, 1960; Cohen, 1955; Merton, 1938).

The years following the Second World War witnessed the formation of a series of new, flamboyant youth cultures. Initially all youth cultures were treated as delinquescent if not outright deviant (Coleman, 1961; Sugarman, 1967). However, before long, functionalist writers (functionalism was a fashionable and influential theory at that time, especially in America) were claiming that participation in youth cultures could be understood as a process of continuous socialization, with young people learning social skills that could not be acquired at home or in classrooms (Parsons, 1962; Turner, 1964).

The best-recalled intervention in these debates was by sociologists working at or associated with Birmingham University's Centre for Contemporary Cultural Studies (CCCS) (Hall and Jefferson, 1976; Mungham and Pearson, 1976). They famously insisted that youth cultures were class based, and that young people's styles had not been foisted on them by profit-seeking businesses but had been created by the young people themselves. Working-class youth were said to be taking working-class values learnt at home and reinforced in their work-places, and reworking these same values to address problems that they experienced at school, at work and in public spaces. The relevant values included solidarity and contempt for 'them', which were expressed in defiant youth styles and demeanour, and led to feelings of excitement and delight at their ability to shock and give offence. During the 1960s middle-class youth ceased to be 'straight'. University campuses were 'invaded' by beatniks and hippies (the flower people). These youth cultures will be discussed further below, but at the time they were perceived as very different from the cultures of working-class youth. Middle-class youth cultures were apparently more individualistic and more explicitly political.

During the 1980s the terms of debate shifted to whether young people's leisure had become post-subcultural. There had been an explosion of media output and a related multiplication of styles. It has been claimed that these no longer rest on any pre-existent social divisions – by class, gender, ethnicity or anything else. Rather, post-subcultural theorists argue that tastes now create their own (often short-lived) scenes, crowds and tribes which are composed of young people of both sexes and all social classes (Bennett, 1999; Maffesoli, 1994; Miles, 2000; Redhead, 1997; Thornton, 1995). Critics have queried whether this really amounts to change since the 1950s and 1960s. The claims of the CCCS theorists were based, at best, on a slender volume of research. The CCCS authors have been accused of focusing on the spectacular and neglecting 'ordinary' young people (see Muggleton, 2000; 2005). In any case, it is claimed that class divisions among youth at leisure persist in the supposed post-subcultural era (Hollands, 1995; 2002; MacDonald and Shildrick, 2007; MacRae, 2004; McCulloch *et al.*, 2006; Nayak, 2006).

Life-stage transitions

Young people's leisure has been studied mainly by sociologists and psychologists of youth. During the 1970s leisure researchers joined age-group experts in investigating the links between leisure behaviour and age or life-stage transitions. In Britain Rhona and Robert Rapoport (1975) argued that people had occupational, family and leisure careers, and that at successive life stages leisure behaviour typically expressed concerns, pre-occupations and interests arising from family and employment situations. Youth was said to be a period of exploration, forming relationships and developing interests. During family and household formation leisure became more home based and spent as a family.

Major life events (such as marriage and parenthood) have subsequently been confirmed as occasions when leisure patterns unfreeze and are reconstituted (Gershuny, 2003). Research repeatedly confirms that new family and household formation unleash a life-cycle squeeze (Estes and Wilenski, 1978) or a 'rush hour of life' (Tremmel, 2010), when demands on time and money mount.

Retirement is the other life-stage transition that has been the focus of considerable research, in this case by a combination of leisure scholars and gerontologists.

Later life

Ageing is an inevitable biological process, whereas the life course is socially constructed. For example, the life course is shaped by the ages (if any) when children are required to attend school, when young people become eligible for full adult welfare rights, and when they are allowed and when it is considered normal to marry and become a parent. Biology does not dictate answers to any of these matters, which have varied enormously by place and historical period.

Modern old age has been constructed by the nuclear family's becoming the normal residential unit, which creates an 'empty nest' life stage, and by the availability of retirement pensions. State pensions were first introduced in Germany in the 1880s by Otto von Bismarck, the first chancellor (from 1871 until 1890) of the unified Germany. Britain followed in 1909; then, before long, universally available pensions were being introduced in all industrial countries. The availability of pensions has set an age at which people can be allowed, then become expected or obliged, to retire from employment.

At the beginning of the twentieth century it was exceptional for people to live long into retirement. The pension was a reward for those who survived a full working life of employment, for men; and typically of child-bearing and child-rearing, for women. They were deemed entitled to rest for their remaining years. This 'construction' of later life survived beyond the Second World War. The initial sociological theories of later life regarded it as a time for, and a process of, gradual disengagement from adult roles. As already noted, functionalism was an influential theory at that time, especially in North American sociology. Relinquishing roles was regarded as functional for individuals whose capacities were declining, and also for the wider society, including close friends, family members and former work colleagues for whom, following years of progressive disengagement, eventual bereavement would not be hugely disruptive or distressing (Cumming, 1963).

During the first half of the twentieth century it became normal for people to survive until and beyond the retirement age. Throughout the second half of the century life expectancy continued to lengthen, and by the twenty-first century people who reached retirement age (the overwhelming majority) could expect ten, twenty or even more years of active life. This was the context in which leisure scholars, among others, became advocates of active ageing and ageing well. Post-retirement was re-imaged as a third age which presented opportunities to do more of things formerly enjoyed, to take up entirely new activities, to continue lifelong learning and continue to experience personal growth. Active leisure was shown to boost life satisfaction (for example, by Kelly *et al.*, 1987, among many others). Active leisure was also promoted as a way of changing the wider public's perceptions of the post-retirement life stage. Seniors could demonstrate that they were not 'past it' and re-image later life as a time to be anticipated eagerly (see Blaikie, 1999; Wearing, 1995).

Advocates have recognized that active ageing depends on maintaining health and fitness (which are not closely related to age among the over-60s). It also depends on people's being able to afford to continue with activities that they always enjoyed and to take up new ones. 'Woopies' (well-off older people) now constitute a significant proportion of tourists and day trippers, but they are not typical seniors. There are exceptions (church-going, volunteering, gardening and reading, plus television), but overall the trend in participation in leisure activities in later life is still downwards. Active ageing may be the ideal, but for most, disengagement is still the reality.

That said, there is a powerful tendency for people to continue with whatever has been their normal leisure for as long as they are able to do so (Atchley, 1993; 1999; Long and Wimbush, 1985). People do not suddenly abandon everything, but the general tendency following every major event in later life is to drop some activities or to do them less frequently. This occurs following retirement, when people lose regular contact with work associates and must usually adjust to a drop in their incomes. It also occurs following bereavement and the loss of someone to do things with. Failing health, which always happens at some point, leads to other things being given up (see Tokarski, 1991).

With the third age redefined in terms of opportunities to engage, gerontologists have identified a fourth age, defined by failing physical health and mental capacities. Yet even as the end of life approaches, it is claimed that it is possible for people to remain positive, to focus on what they can still do and enjoy, thus making life's closing episode a time worth living (see Hubble and Tew, 2010).

Leisure careers

Continuity

This is in fact the strongest leisure tendency within as well as between life stages. People never start afresh, but always rebuild, when required to do so, with what they already know and have experienced. Leisure may be where we enjoy the greatest relative freedom, but for most of the time most of us use this freedom to stick to routines. By far the best predictor of what people will do in any week is what they did during the previous week. This also applies from year to year. This has long been known anecdotally by personnel who work in all leisure services – sports, the arts, hobbies and crafts as well as politics and religion. They all know that if people's interests can be captured when they are young, then it is at least possible that they will remain involved for many more years. In 1981 this led Boothby and his colleagues to speculate that the extremely low rates of sport participation in the older age groups in Britain at that time could be partly due to the poverty of their earlier sport experience.

As noted earlier, the ideal way of tracing continuities and discontinuities in leisure behaviour would be through birth cohort studies, but the value of the on-going studies to leisure scholars will be limited by the limited quantity of leisure data that has been collected. An awareness of this long-term limitation led Hedges (1986) to explore people's ability to recollect their leisure biographies. His conclusion was that for structured activities – those like playing a sport, which are time and place specific, unlike listening to music, for example – most people do have sufficient ability to recall what they did in the past. The indications of participation rates in previous years look accurate. Subsequent researchers who have invited samples to recall personal histories in selected leisure activities have confirmed that continuity is indeed a powerful tendency. At any age people who play sport in one year are highly likely to continuing playing into the next year, whereas those who have lapsed at any point are unlikely ever to resume on a long-term basis (Roberts *et al.*, 1991).

Our most impressive evidence of long-term continuities in leisure behaviour has been collected opportunistically. American samples who had been surveyed nearly forty years previously, when they were students, were resurveyed during the 1980s (McGuire *et al.*, 1987; Scott and Willits, 1989; 1998). Some continuities were startling. Students who had been joining student clubs and holding office were often acting in exactly the same way when approaching and entering retirement.

Loyalty

Needless to say, people do not continue for ever with everything that they have ever done. Loyalty rates are known to vary between different kinds of leisure. Loyalty is measured by calculating the proportion of the people who have 'ever done' an activity who are 'still doing' the activity in question.

The classical arts are known to have very high loyalty rates. Children who are taken regularly to classical concerts and art exhibitions are highly likely to continue throughout adulthood (Hantrais and Kamphorst, 1987). Most sports have much lower loyalty rates. There is considerable drop-out during the transition from childhood to adulthood (Roberts *et al.*, 1991). However, there is considerable variation between different sports. Team sports which require eleven or fifteen players to attend regularly at pre-set times have much lower loyalty rates than sports that can be played more flexibility by two or four players (like golf) or that can be practised individually, as can surfing and swimming.

There are lessons in this for all leisure providers who wish to boost participation. The arts need to capture the interest and form the tastes of more children. The sports industries need to promote those sports in which loyalty is highest and then make it as easy as possible for individuals to continue to play after they have left full-time education.

Serious leisure

This concept was coined by the Canadian sociologist Robert Stebbins (1992; 2007). Everyone has a leisure biography. Career implies continuity, and an additional feature of serious leisure is career development. Any leisure activity can be practised seriously or casually. Serious participants become increasingly knowledgeable and skilled at their sports, arts, crafts, hobbies or as volunteers. This will most likely involve membership of a group. Over time, individuals can earn status and respect among co-enthusiasts. A serious career in sport may extend beyond playing, following which veterans may become referees or administrators.

There appear to be special satisfactions in a serious leisure career. Stebbins argues that a serious leisure commitment can assist people in coping with disruptive life events, such as moving between cities or being made redundant from a job, and equally during life-stage transitions such as into retirement (Stebbins, 1998). Indeed, in societies where family and occupational careers cannot be relied on to last for life, a leisure interest may be many people's most reliable asset.

Any leisure interest that is maintained throughout life, even if engagement and enjoyment are always casual – such as being a fan of a sport team, a long-running television series or a genre of music – can supply an unbroken thread linking past to present, from childhood into old age in some cases. In so far as our leisure tastes, skills and activities become part of our social identities, their lifelong retention will give ourselves and others a reliable sense of who we are.

Defending threatened identities

Leisure may enable people to maintain valued identities whose original foundations have vanished. One example is workers who have been made redundant or who have retired from main lifetime occupations. They may continue to meet, talk about former times and convince each other that they are not part of *the* unemployed or *the* retired, but that they really are still steel-men or whatever (see MacKenzie et al., 2006).

Many present-day working-class males, when younger, envisaged entering jobs in 'traditional' (as they are now described) extractive and manufacturing industries, and becoming main family breadwinners. Many of these same adults have found that these kinds of adulthood are no longer available for people like themselves. Even so, they may meet with mates who share this predicament, probably consume alcohol fulsomely, and confirm one another's identities as real, traditional, masculine men (see Blackshaw, 2003; McDowell, 2003).

Leisure generations

The baby-boomer cohort and generation

We can be confident that the cohorts currently entering later life in Western countries will exhibit different leisure profiles than their predecessors. They are the baby-boomer cohorts who became the vanguard of a baby-boomer generation.

We noted above how the youth cultures that exploded into the 1950s and 1960s were debated at that time. It took longer for their full significance to be understood. These young people were identified by Ronald Inglehart (1977), an American sociologist, as a post-scarcity generation. They had grown up in a post-war context without fear of poverty or unemployment. Real wages and salaries were rising from year to year. The expectation of those who had never experienced different conditions was that improvement would continue indefinitely. Young people in the 1950s and 1960s had unprecedented amounts of money for discretionary spending, with which they indulged their tastes in music and fashion. They wanted, and simply enacted, more personal freedom than their parents had enjoyed. The values of elders were deemed outdated. In the 1960s, first in the USA, student cultures merged with the civil rights movement, then opposition to the Vietnam War. The protests spread into Europe, then more thinly throughout the rest of the world. Their opponent became 'the system' – the entire industrial-political-military-educational complex (Roszak, 1970). This counter-culture evaporated during the 1970s but left a new generation, accustomed to rising levels of consumer spending, who were able and willing to use credit to purchase consumer durables, motor cars and flats and houses. Once in the labour market these cohorts pioneered delayed and reduced fertility. They also pioneered the dual-earner couple, thus enlarging their ability to consume. They ended the historical decline in working time and took their entire share of the benefits of economic growth in higher incomes. The careers of those who established themselves in professional and management jobs were most likely to survive the recessions of the late twentieth century (see Buchholz *et al.*, 2009). As they progressed through adulthood, these same cohorts were able to enjoy the advent of first colour, then multi-channel television. They became part of first one-car, then two- or more car households. They participated in the growth of international tourism and out-of-home dining. In mid and later adulthood they began to use the new information and communication technologies.

The same cohorts are now retiring in better health, with more wealth (mostly tied up in dwellings) and better pensions than any of their predecessors had. More are entering later life without needing to cut back on their leisure spending (see Higgs *et al.*, 2009). They may equitize their homes if necessary in order to continue to consume.

The baby-boomer cohorts led a new leisure generation of leisure consumers. 'Generation' is used here in Karl Mannheim's sense (Mannheim, 1952). There is something distinctive about the leisure tastes and experiences of every cohort of children and young people, but this does not make them a new generation. These are formed only in times of major political and economic change, like the creation of welfare states and social market economies after the Second World War. The cohorts that followed the baby boomers became part of this generation. Each cohort was able to earn somewhat more, buy more and have more than any of its predecessors, and certainly more than its own parents.

The post baby-boomer generation

The clearest sign that another new generation is currently being born, and that some of its members are aware of their position, is the arrival of the self-proclaimed €1,000 generation on the streets of Europe's major cities (see Chiotaki-Poulou and Sakellariou, 2010; Cuzzocrea and Tavani, 2010). The key feature of this generation's objective situation is that most members are unlikely to be able to obtain the types of employment that will enable them to live as well as their parents, at least in material terms. This will not apply to everyone, but the numbers who are threatened by socio-economic descent now exceed those who can confidently anticipate ascent (see Roberts, 2011, on how this situation has arisen). An implication is that leisure spending will either flatline or decline, which will challenge all the leisure industries.

The next challenges for leisure research include charting how different industries, and different sections of incoming cohorts of adults, respond to the new generation's situation.

Conclusions

The agenda for research into leisure, age and the life course is longer and more challenging than it might at first appear. The first task, of course, is to describe the leisure that characterizes each age/life-stage group, but this alone is insufficient. We also need to know:

- Are the characteristics of the age group's leisure universal or specific to a particular society or group of societies at a particular historical moment?
- Which features of an age group's leisure are due to the cohort's current circumstances, and which are due to its past experiences?
- In which leisure generation is the cohort located?

Set against this agenda, the current state of the art remains in a prolonged birth stage.

References

Atchley, R. C. (1993) *Activity and Ageing*. London: Sage.

Atchley, R. C. (1999) *Continuity and Adaptation in Ageing*. Baltimore, MD: Johns Hopkins University Press.

Bennett, A. (1999) 'Subcultures or Neo-tribes? Rethinking the Relationship between Youth Style and Musical Taste', *Sociology* 33: 599–617.

Blackshaw, T. (2003) *Leisure Life: Myth, Masculinity and Modernity*. London: Routledge,

Blaikie, A. (1999) *Ageing and Popular Culture*. Cambridge: Cambridge University Press.

Boothby, J., Tungatt, M., Townsend, A. R. and Collins, M. F. (1981) *A Sporting Chance?* Sports Council Study 22, London.

Buchholz, S., Hofacker, D., Mills, M., Blossfeld, H.-P., Kurz, K. and Hofmeister, H. (2009) 'Life Courses in the Globalization Process: The Development of Social Inequalities in Modern Societies', *European Sociological Review* 25: 53–71.

Chiotaki-Poulou, I. and Sakellariou, A. (2010) 'Youth in Greek Society and the "700 Euro Generation": The Rise of a New Generation?', paper presented at midterm conference of the European Sociological Association Youth and Generation Network, Youth, Economy and Society. Disley.

Cloward, R. and Ohlin, L. E. (1960) *Delinquency and Opportunity*. Glencoe: Free Press.

Cohen, A. K. (1955) *Delinquent Boys*. London: Routledge.

Coleman, J. S. (1961) *The Adolescent Society*. New York: Glencoe Free Press.

Cumming, E. (1963) 'Further Thoughts on the Theory of Disengagement', *International Social Science Journal* 15: 377–393.

Cuzzocrea, V. and Tavani, C. (2010) 'Superimposing Discourses on Qualified Youth: The Case of Law 7/2007 of the Autonomous Region of Sardinia', paper presented at midterm conference of the European Sociological Association Youth and Generation Network, Youth, Economy and Society. Disley.

Erikson, E. H. (1968) *Identity: Youth and Crisis*. London: Faber.

Estes, R. J. and Wilenski, H. (1978), 'Life-Cycle Squeeze and the Morale Curve', *Institute of Industrial Relations, Reprint 422*. Berkeley: University of California.

Gershuny, J. (2003) *Time, through the Lifecourse, in the Family*, ISER Working Paper 2003-3. Colchester: University of Essex.

Hall, G. S. (1904), *Adolescence*. New York: Appleton.

Hall, S. and Jefferson. T. (eds) (1976) *Resistance through Rituals*. London: Hutchinson.

Hantrais, L. and Kamphorst, T. J. (1987) *Trends in the Arts: A Multinational Perspective*. Amersfoort: Giordano Bruno.

Hedges, B. (1986) *Personal Leisure Histories*. London: Economic and Social Research Council/Sports Council.

Higgs, P. F., Hyde, M., Gilleard, C. J., Victor, C. R., Wiggins, R. D. and Jones, I. R. (2009) 'From Passive to Active Consumers? Later Life Consumption in the UK from 1968–2005', *Sociological Review* 57: 102–124.

Hollands, R. (1995) *Friday Night, Saturday Night*. Department of Social Policy. Newcastle-upon-Tyne: University of Newcastle.

Hollands, R. (2002) 'Divisions in the Dark: Youth Cultures, Transitions and Segmented Consumption Spaces in the Night-Time Economy', *Journal of Youth Studies* 5: 153–171.

Hubble, N. and Tew, P. (2010) 'Mapping Emergent Third and Fourth Age Subjectivity', paper presented at Futures of Ageing: Science, Technology and the Body, Annual Conference of the British Sociological Association Ageing Body and Society Study Group, London.

Inglehart, R. (1977) *The Silent Revolution*. New Jersey: Princeton University Press.

Kelly, J. R., Steinkamp, M. W. and Kelly, J. R. (1987) 'Later-Life Satisfaction: Does Leisure Contribute?', *Leisure Sciences* 9: 189–200.

Long, J. and Wimbush, E. (1985) *Continuity and Change: Leisure around Retirement*. London: Economic and Social Research Council/Sports Council.

McCulloch, K., Stewart, A. and Lovegreen, N. (2006) '"We Just Hang Out Together": Youth Cultures and Social Class', *Journal of Youth Studies* 9: 539–556.

MacDonald, R. and Shildrick, T. (2007) 'Street Corner Society: Leisure Careers, Youth (Sub)culture and Social Exclusion', *Leisure Studies* 26: 339–355.

McDowell, L. (2003) *Redundant Masculinities? Employment Change and White Working Class Youth*. Oxford: Blackwell.

McGuire, F. A., Dottavio, F. D. and O'Leary, J. T. (1987) 'The Relationship of Early Life Experiences to Later Life Leisure Involvement', *Leisure Sciences* 9: 251–257.

MacKenzie, R., Stuart, M., Forde, C., Greenwood, I., Gardiner, J. and Perrett, R. (2006) '"All that is Solid?" Class Identity and the Maintenance of a Collective Orientation among Redundant Steelworkers', *Sociology* 40: 833–852.

MacRae, R. (2004) 'Notions of "Us" and "Them": Markers of Stratification in Clubbing Lifestyles', *Journal of Youth Studies* 7: 55–71.

Maffesoli, M. (1994) *The Time of the Tribes*. London: Sage.

Mannheim, K. (1952) 'The Problem of Generations', in *Essays on the Sociology of Knowledge*. London: Routledge.

Mead, M. (1935) *Sex and Temperament in Three Primitive Societies*. London: Routledge.

Mead, M. (1971) *Coming of Age in Samoa*. Harmondsworth: Penguin.

Merton, R. K. (1938) 'Social Structure and Anomie', *American Sociological Review* 3: 672–682.

Miles, S. (2000) *Youth Lifestyles in a Changing World*. Buckingham: Open University Press.

Muggleton, D. (2000) *Inside Subculture: The Postmodern Meaning of Style*. Oxford: Berg.

Muggleton, D. (2005) 'From Classlessness to Subculture: A Genealogy of Post-War British Youth Cultural Analysis', *Young* 13: 205–219.

Mungham, G. and Pearson, G. (eds) (1976) *Working Class Youth Culture*. London: Routledge.

Nayak, A. (2006) 'Displaced Masculinities: Chavs, Youth and Class in the Post-Industrial City', *Sociology* 40: 813–831.

Parsons, T. (1962) 'Youth in the Context of American Society', *Daedalus* 91: 97–123

Rapoport, R. and Rapoport, R. N. (1975), *Leisure and the Family Life-Cycle*. London: Routledge.

Redhead, S. (1997) *Subculture to Clubcultures*. Oxford: Blackwell.

Roberts, K. (2011) 'The End of the Long Baby Boomer Generation', paper presented at European Sociological Association Conference, Geneva.

Roberts, K., Minten, J. H., Chadwick, C., Lamb, K. L. and Brodie, D. A. (1991) 'Sporting Lives: A Case Study of Leisure Careers', *Society and Leisure* 14: 261–284.

Roszak, T. (1970) *The Making of a Counter-Culture*. London: Faber.

Scott, D. and Willits, F. K. (1989) 'Adolescent and Adult Leisure Patterns: A 37 Year Follow-Up Study', *Leisure Sciences* 11: 323–335.

Scott, D. and Willits, F. K. (1998) 'Adolescent and Adult Leisure Patterns: A Reassessment', *Journal of Leisure Research* 30: 319–330.

Stebbins, R. A. (1992) *Amateurs, Professionals and Serious Leisure*. Montreal: McGill-Queens University Press.

Stebbins, R. A. (1998) *After Work: The Search for an Optimal Leisure Lifestyle*. Calgary: Temeron Books.

Stebbins, R. A. (2007) *Serious Leisure*. New Jersey: Transaction Publishers.

Sugarman, B. (1967) 'Involvement in Youth Culture, Academic Achievement and Conformity in School', *British Journal of Sociology* 18: 151–164.

Thornton, S. (1995) *Club Cultures: Music, Media and Subcultural Capital*. Cambridge: Polity Press.

Thrasher, F. M. (1936) *The Gang*. Chicago: University of Chicago Press.

Tokarski, W. (1991) 'Research Note: Leisure Lifestyle Careers in Old Age', *Leisure Studies* 10: 79–81.

Tremmel, J. C. (ed.) (2010) *A Young Generation under Pressure?* Heidelberg: Springer.

Turner, R. H. (1964) *The Social Context of Ambition*. San Francisco: Chandler.

Wearing, B. (1995) 'Leisure and Resistance in an Ageing Society', *Leisure Studies* 14: 263–279.

Whyte, W. F. (1943) *Street Corner Society*. Chicago: University of Chicago Press.

23

LIFESTYLE AND LEISURE THEORY

A. J. Veal

Introduction

Anthony Giddens (1991: 81) has defined lifestyle as 'a more or less integrated set of practices which an individual embraces, not only because such practices fulfil utilitarian needs, but because they give material form to a particular narrative of self-identity'. While this and other definitions emphasize individual choice, it is clear that lifestyle and self-identity are also group phenomena, as Muggleton (2000: 66) clearly demonstrates in regard to youth subcultures. Among the 'practices' which constitute a lifestyle are leisure activities, but also 'one's body, clothes, speech, ... eating and drinking preferences, home, car ... etc.' (Featherstone, 1987: 343). One school of thought also includes within the definition of life-style, individual 'beliefs, values, or norms of daily behaviour' and 'the way in which each person lives the norms of the group, class or global society to which he/she belongs' (Ruiz, 1989: 158). Furthermore, Giddens (1991: 81–2) argues that 'it would be wrong to suppose that lifestyle only relates to activities outside of work. ... choice of work and work milieu forms a basic element of lifestyle orientations'.

The field of Leisure Studies has experienced an 'on-again-off-again' relationship with lifestyle at least since the 1950s, when Havighurst and Feigenbaum (1959) used the concept in their study of the lives of middle-aged residents of Kansas City. The motivation for this involvement is both empirically pragmatic and theoretical. The empirical pragmatism arises from the desire to find succinct ways to summarize both patterns of participation in, potentially, hundreds of different leisure activities (leisure styles) and the interaction between leisure and a wide range of socio-demographic factors, including age, gender, ethnicity, parental status, income, occupation, education and geography (lifestyles). The theoretical motivation arises from a desire to understand the way patterns of leisure participation might be structured and the way explanations of such patterns might be integrated with and informed by broader social theory.

The interest in lifestyle among Leisure Studies researchers continued into the 1980s, as summarized in Veal (1993). This culminated in the publication in 1989 of a two-volume compendium of 18 papers under the auspices of Research Committee 13 (Leisure) of the International Sociological Association (Filipcova, Glyptis and Tokarski, 1989). However, in the ensuing decades interest waned. Possible reasons for this include: the resistance of neo-Marxist/cultural studies class-based perspectives (Critcher, 1989; Scraton and Talbot, 1989), which viewed lifestyle research as the product of profit-driven commercial market research which downplayed the role of class; the linking of lifestyle research with quantitative methods, in a field where qualitative methods were becoming increasingly dominant; and some confusing messages as to the nature of lifestyle, for example Roberts's (2006: 163) curious view of it as being the 'latest version of the "society of leisure" thesis' and involving only 'young singles or ... a particular section of the middle class' (p. 182). In view of the discussion of Bourdieu below and the decline in the significance of neo-Marxism in the academy, the first of these should no longer be an impediment, while the second has been overtaken by the advent of qualitative and mixed-method studies of lifestyle (e.g. Holt, 1997; Johansson and Miegel, 1992).

Just as lifestyle-related research was peaking in mainstream Leisure Studies in the late 1980s, among sociologists it became 'in vogue' (Featherstone, 1987: 55). Reimer (1995) attributes this to four developments: recognition of the increasing significance of the process of *individualization* in Western societies; recognition of the *new middle class* or *service class* (the growing class of relatively prosperous workers and their dependents, working predominantly in service industries and characterized by hedonistic lifestyles); the development of *postmodernist* ideas; and the publication in English of Pierre Bourdieu's (1984) *Distinction: A Social Critique of the Judgement of Taste*. In the last two decades, whole books have been written about lifestyle (Cahill, 2006; Chaney, 1996; Miles, 2000; Wynne, 1998) and the task of documenting the history of the concept has begun to be addressed (Bell and Hollows, 2006). Lifestyle has been recognized as 'an integral feature of the development of modernity' (Chaney, 1996: 158) and as 'closely related to some of the most central sociological questions of the twentieth century, such as the differentiation of classes and status groups, the rise of a consumer society, the process of individualization and the increasing importance of self-identity' (Johansson, 1994: 267). In the field of marketing, both academic and policy-related empirical studies of lifestyle continue to be undertaken, including general studies (e.g. Lawson, Todd and Evans, 2006; Sureda and Valls, 2004), some of which are published on a regular basis (Mintel, 2011; Strategic Business Insights, n.d.; CACI, n.d.), and studies in various sectors of leisure, including the arts (Australia Council, 2010: 44–49; Todd and Larson, 2001), tourism (Lee and Sparks, 2007) and sport (McDonald, Milne and Hong, 2002).[1] This market research activity, though varying in the extent of its theoretical underpinning, has begun to be recognized in academic reviews of the topic (e.g. Chaney, 1996: 25–40; Roberts, 2006: 168–169).

This chapter is structured by the four themes identified by Reimer, above, namely: the work of Bourdieu; individualization; the rise of the new middle class or service class; and postmodernism. However, since Bourdieu's book, *Distinction*, was designed to 'rethink Weber's opposition between class and *Stand* [status]' (Bourdieu, 1986: xiii), we first examine Max Weber's concepts of *status groups* and *style of life*.

Max Weber: status groups and lifestyle

In the 1920s, Weber posited that, in addition to stratification by class, based on wealth and/or occupation, society was stratified by *status groups* which were distinguished by the honour accorded to their members and by their distinctive lifestyle, or 'style of life'.[2] While Weber (1922/1978: 305–307) provided a lengthy definition of status group, he did not specifically define lifestyle, except in terms of its function in providing a visible indicator of membership of a status group. Furthermore, while he gave examples of status groups, such as networks of families with comparable historical lineages (e.g. the 'First Families of Virginia' in the United States, p. 933), ethnic/religious groups (e.g. the Jewish community, p. 934) and members of caste systems (e.g. as in India, p. 493), these tended to be somewhat exceptional and, apart from indicating that exclusivity of membership and behaviour codes were typically enforced, he did not explore patterns of behaviour in detail or the application of the concept across the whole of society.

The concept of status had a low profile in the following decades, although Stub (1972) presents a body of relevant American literature and Chan and Goldthorpe (2007a: 512) point out that it was used in classifying occupational groups in British industrial sociology and community studies into the 1970s, albeit while many sociologists avoided the distinction by combining status and class in measures of socio-economic status. The rise of Marxist and neo-Marxist sociology from the 1960s onwards saw an increasing emphasis on class alone (Chan and Goldthorpe, 2007a), and in the 1980s this began to influence the field of Leisure Studies (e.g. Andrews, 1981; Clark and Critcher, 1985).

Recently, however, using data on friendship patterns, Chan and Goldthorpe (2004) have developed a comprehensive 31-item occupational status order, in the Weberian sense of 'a structure of relations of perceived, and in some degree accepted, social superiority, equality or inferiority among individuals' which reflects 'the degree of "social honour" attached to certain of their positional and perhaps purely ascribed attributes (e.g. birth or ethnicity)' (Chan and Goldthorpe, 2007a: 514), and which is distinct from *class*, in the sense of relationship to the economic system. While there is a clear relationship between the 31-item occupational status order and the nine-item occupation-based class order used by Chan and Goldthorpe (2004: 393), the two systems of classification are not congruent.

Of particular relevance to leisure, Chan and Goldthorpe (2005) used this status order system in an examination of patterns of participation in various forms of cultural activity in Britain, concluding that they were clearly related to the above status order rather than to class. Further studies by Chan and Goldthorpe and others which mostly reinforce these findings internationally and across a variety of cultural forms are summarized in Table 23.1 (column A).

It should be noted that these studies, while clearly relevant to the question of the relationship between status and culture/leisure, address the issue of lifestyle in only a partial way. Thus, while status groups are typically found to have differing patterns of cultural participation, non-participants are often the largest category in all groups, and the range of cultural activities examined in any one study, even with the addition of socio-demographic variables, would not be sufficient to define a person's whole lifestyle. Furthermore, basing the definition of status groups entirely on occupation raises issues concerning people not in employment and leaves open the possibility that some status groups might be at least partly defined in terms of other variables, such as age, gender, ethnicity, religion or residential location. Even without the involvement of these variables, the initial list of 31 occupation-based status groups hardly meets the aim of Leisure Studies researchers to identify a lifestyle typology with a manageable number of categories. This does not, of course, negate the value of research using occupation-based status, but it indicates the possibilities for further research.

These studies provoked a response from researchers who sought to defend class as the key variable in the analysis of cultural participation but, since this debate also concerned the work of Bourdieu, we turn first to a consideration of his work.

Table 23.1 Studies of cultural participation related to status, class and omnivorousness

Authors	Date	Country	Cultural forms	(A) Status	(B) Omnivores
Bryson	1996	USA	Tastes in musical genres	–	✓
Van Eijck	2001	Netherlands	Tastes in musical genres	–	✓
Tomlinson	2003	UK	Food type, alcohol, pub and church going, sport, DIY participation, smoking	✗	–
Chan and Goldthorpe	2005	UK	Theatre, dance, cinema	✓	✓
Chan and Goldthorpe	2007b	UK	Opera, jazz, classical, pop/rock concerts	✓	✓
Chan and Goldthorpe	2007c	UK	Visual arts	✓	✓
Alderson *et al.*	2007	USA	Performing arts, museum/gallery, pop music, reading novels etc., cinema	✓	✓
Bukodi	2007	Hungary	Reading novels etc.	✓	–
Coulangeon and Lemel	2007	France	Tastes in musical genres	✓	✓
Katz-Gerro	2007	Israel	Tastes in musical genres	✓	–
Kraaykamp *et al.*	2007	Netherlands	Reading books, TV watching	✓	–
Torche	2007	Chile	Reading books, magazines, newspapers	✓	–
Warde *et al.*	2007	UK	Wide range of participation activities (Bennett *et al.*, 2009 survey)	–	✗
Warde *et al.*	2008	UK	As for Warde *et al.* (2007)	–	✗
Bennett *et al.*	2009	UK	Culture, media, food, sport etc.	✗	✓★★
Atkinson	2011	UK	Tastes in musical genres	–	✗

Notes

(A) ✓ = status found to be more closely related to cultural participation than class, ✗ = this finding challenged.

(B) ✓ = cultural participation found to be related to 'omnivore–univore' pattern, ✗ = this finding challenged (see under Bourdieu – below) ✓★★ true for some activities.

Bourdieu: class, cultural capital, habitus and lifestyle

In his major work, *Distinction*, based on fieldwork carried out in France in the 1960s, Bourdieu (1986: xii) sought to 'rethink Weber's opposition between class and *Stand* [estate or status]' and to add a contemporary empirical dimension to the exercise. Reimer (1995: 123) has stated that the book is 'without doubt the most influential reference and source for researchers on lifestyle; it is well-nigh impossible today to write about lifestyle without referring to *Distinction*'. Bennett *et al.* (2009: 9) go further, declaring: 'This book can fairly claim to be the single most important monograph of post-war sociology published anywhere in the world.'

In *Distinction* Bourdieu developed a theory of the relationship between class and lifestyle, based on the concepts of *economic, cultural* and *social capital, fields* and *habitus*. One of the unique features of the book is a graphical summary of the key findings of the study in the form of a two-page diagram (Bourdieu, 1986: figures 5 and 6: 128–129) in which, against the dimensions of economic and cultural capital, some 26 occupational groups are mapped onto the 'space of social position', while associated cultural tastes (for music, food etc.), patterns of consumption (food, drink, cars etc.) and leisure participation (sport, culture etc.) are mapped onto the 'space of lifestyle'. The details of just how the diagram was assembled are difficult to discern from Bourdieu's complex descriptions, but the mapping process used, in which multiple variables are plotted onto layered two-dimensional spaces ('fields'), as if on transparent sheets, is known as 'correspondence analysis' (CA) or 'multiple correspondence analysis' (MCA) (Bourdieu, 1986: 126; Le Roux and Rouanet, 2010). This is a form of 'geometrical data analysis' which can be seen as principal components analysis for categorical data and can now be conducted by computer packages.

Bourdieu's major empirical finding is that distinctive clusters of tastes and patterns of cultural consumption and participation coincide with particular occupational groups defined in terms of economic classes. The process by which this 'homology' comes about is explained by use of the concept of habitus, the set of values, sensitivities and accepted practices which are said to structure the lifestyle of a particular occupational group, or *class fraction*. The upper, or 'dominant', classes have the resources and power to exercise a high degree of choice and to cultivate their chosen activities/tastes so that they come to be seen as desirable and of high status ('legitimate culture'). At the bottom of the class system are unskilled workers and farm labourers deemed to have virtually no discretion in lifestyle choice, since their habitus is restricted to the 'taste of necessity' (Bourdieu, 1986: 177–179)[3], although, as Giddens (1991: 85–86) and Bennett (2011: 500) note, it is possible to think of numerous examples of quite varied, and sometimes influential, lifestyles among deprived groups.

Thus, in Bourdieu's schema lifestyle is securely anchored to class in a hierarchical system of both economic and cultural capital. Control of this classification system, at least in its upper reaches ('legitimate culture'), is viewed as being as significant as control over the allocation of material resources, since it reinforces class positions (Bourdieu, 1986: 13–96), and 'Position in the classification struggle depends on position in the class structure' (p. 484).[4] Bourdieu therefore challenges the Weberian notion of honour-based status as a phenomenon relatively independent of class. However, in so doing he establishes leisure activity and related tastes as not just dependent variables of class, but part of the process by which, through habitus and lifestyle, class distinctions are defined, demonstrated and maintained.

Bourdieu is not without his critics, who raise a number of issues, including: the limited generalizability of his findings from the France of the 1960s to other countries and economic and social conditions (Savage *et al.*, 1992: 101–3; Bennett *et al.*, 1999: 11–13; Reimer, 1995: 127; Van Eijck and Mommaas, 2004: 374); ignoring or downplaying factors such as the role of the state and 'household and gender relations' (Savage *et al.*, 1992: 103), popular culture, the mass media/cultural industries, gender and race/ethnicity (Bennett *et al.*, 1999: 11–13), global influences (Bennett *et al.* 1999: 201) and workplace relationships and personal networks (Erickson, 1996); treatment of the concept of class (Bennett *et al.*, 1999: 17; Frow, 1987; Reimer, 1995: 127); the questionable validity of the concepts of cultural capital (Goldthorpe, 2007) and habitus (Bennett, 2007); and the ability of MCA to account for net, as opposed to gross, effects (Chan and Goldthorpe, 2007d; Wuggenig, 2007).

These limitations notwithstanding, there has been considerable empirical research exploring Bourdieu's ideas and their application, typically focusing on leisure activity.

A significant body of research arose in response to a study conducted in America by Peterson and Simkus (1992) which found that, while the cultural participation patterns and tastes of people in lower-status socio-economic groups were quite narrowly focused and 'low brow', following Bourdieu's homology model, those in higher socio-economic groups were not narrowly focused but embraced a wide range of 'high brow' and 'low brow' tastes. The former were therefore labelled *univores* and the latter *omnivores*. In addition to exploring the issue of status as opposed to class, the research listed in Table 23.1 also addressed this issue (see column B). It can be seen that the omnivore/univore thesis was broadly endorsed for a number of cultural activities and in a number of countries. But, using qualitative techniques, Warde *et al.* (2007, 2008) and Atkinson (2011) have found support for Bourdieu's original position. As with the findings on status, it should be noted that this research cannot be seen as definitive in regard to lifestyle because of the relatively narrow range of activities covered.

A major study conducted by Bennett *et al.* (2009) and published under the title *Culture, Class, Distinction*, sought to replicate Bourdieu's research in Britain. Based on a survey of 1,800 individuals conducted in 2004–5, and supporting in-depth and focus group interviews, the study covered a range of activities and tastes similar to Bourdieu's and used MCA as well as traditional multivariate techniques. The authors are, however, critical of key aspects of Bourdieu's model, including cultural capital (pp. 28–31) and habitus (pp. 25–28, 257) and, while they share his commitment to class as the key variable, their findings in the Britain of the early twenty-first century suggest a much looser and less hierarchical relationship between class and cultural participation/lifestyle than in Bourdieu's France of the 1960s. They also note that the omnivore/univore thesis is only applicable for some types of activity and some class fractions. In including analyses of gender, ethnicity, globalization and the 'working class', Bennett *et al.* redress some of the omissions in Bourdieu's empirical work, but in so doing further undermine the rigidities of his class-based model.

From the point of view of the leisure researcher seeking a framework for presenting the complexities of leisure participation in its social context, there is little to choose between Bourdieu's schema, with some 26 class fractions and the Weberian schema using Goldthorpe's system of 31 occupation-based status groups. They are simply two ways of organizing information on occupation. As for the method used to discover lifestyle patterns empirically, while much is made of Bourdieu's use of the MCA procedure, as opposed to traditional multivariate techniques (e.g. Bennett, 2010: xxi), as Chan and Goldthorpe (2007d: 320) point out, it is a dubious proposition to argue that 'a particular theoretical position can only be empirically evaluated through one particular technique of data analysis'. Indeed, the cultural activities/lifestyles of class fractions can generally be converted into interval rather than categorical format and analysed by traditional methods, as Bennett *et al.* (2009: 80, 184) show, and those of status groups can be analysed by MCA, as shown by Chan and Goldthorpe (2007d: 322). Of particular relevance to Leisure Studies is that MCA analysis of the 'space of lifestyle' along various axes, prior to the introduction of class (see Bennett *et al.*, 2009: figures 3.1–3.4, table A2.1), is a similar process to the traditional 'leisure styles' analysis based on cluster, factor or Q analysis – a recent example of which is provided by Green *et al.* (2006) and an overview in Veal (1993). Furthermore, once identified, leisure styles are invariably analysed in terms of socio-economic group and other variables, as is the 'space of lifestyle' in Bourdieusian analysis (see Bennett *et al.*, 2009: figure 3.5). However, leisure styles are entirely empirically derived, and have hitherto been devoid of any apparent theoretical underpinning, a situation which could be remedied by the adoption of a class or status group perspective.

Individualization

The idea that a process of individualization has been taking place in Western societies, and is loosening the traditional ties of solidarity, such as class and community, is widely accepted. This has led to the suggestion that lifestyle can be studied at a number of levels, from nations, via groups to the individual (Johansson and Miegel, 1992: 23; Veal, 1993: 242–243; Muggleton, 2000: 66). In the surveys conducted as part of the British study by Bennett *et al.* (2009), 13 components of culture are examined: television; film; books; live performing arts; visual arts; music; club-going; pub-going; eating out; sport playing; sport watching; body modification (piercing, slimming etc.); and fashion. Each of these offers a wide range of choice, often the result of a mix of global, national and regional influences. While it is clear that such factors as age, gender, occupation, income, education level, ethnicity and residential location constrain and facilitate choice in many ways, it is not surprising that some theorists have argued that the processes and outcomes of individual choice, identity formation and life planning should be a major focus of social analysis in the contemporary world and that such a focus should involve the concept of lifestyle. Among these are Anthony Giddens and Ulrich Beck.

Giddens (1991) outlines his approach to lifestyles as follows:

> In modern social life, the notion of lifestyle takes on a particular significance. The more tradition loses its hold, and the more daily life is reconstituted in terms of the dialectical interplay of the local and the global, the more individuals are forced to negotiate lifestyle choices among a diversity of options. … Of course there are standardising influences too – most notably, in the form of commodification, since capitalistic production and distribution form core components of modernity's institutions. Yet because of the 'openness' of social life today, the polarisation of contexts of action and the diversity of 'authorities', lifestyle choice is increasingly important in the constitution of self-identity and daily activity (p. 5) … The notion of lifestyle sounds somewhat trivial because it is so often thought of solely in terms of a superficial consumerism: lifestyles suggested by glossy magazines and advertising images. But there is something much more fundamental going on than such a conception suggests: in conditions of high modernity, we all not only follow lifestyles, but in an important sense are forced to do so – we have no choice but to choose.
>
> (pp. 80–81)

Despite this view of lifestyle choice as a relatively autonomous process, Giddens (1991: 82) appears to endorse Bourdieu's view of lifestyle as a class-related phenomenon, but at no point in *Modernity and Self-Identity* does he make the link between lifestyle and specific class fragments as in the Bourdieu framework. Furthermore, he does not expand on types of lifestyle or the idea that lifestyle might be a group-related phenomenon; his discussion moves from individual choices to 'life politics', indeed to discussion of 'Personal lives, planetary needs' (Giddens, 1991: 221), with little in between.

In a short essay in *Risk Society: Towards a New Modernity*, Beck notes that in Germany, as a result of the rising material standard of living, and despite continuing inequalities in wealth and income:

> subcultural class identities have dissipated, class distinctions based on status have lost their traditional support, and processes for the 'diversification' and individualisation of lifestyles and ways of life have been set in motion. As a result, the hierarchical model of

social classes and stratification has increasingly been subverted. It no longer corresponds to reality.

(Beck, 1993: 91–92)

He notes that, while this is also true of some other European countries, such as Sweden and Finland (p. 96), it may not be true of others, such as France and Britain, with more entrenched class systems (pp. 101–102, n2).

Beck's focus is on the wide range of types of uncertainty and risk faced by the individual in late modernity, which call for new approaches to analysing societal workings. One of these sources of risk is that people will be '*set free* from the social forms of industrial society – class, stratification, family, gender status of men and women – just as during the course of the Reformation people were "released" from the secular rule of the Church' (Beck, 1993: 87). The risk element lies in the individual not being assigned a role in society based on birth, but being required, to a much greater extent than in the past, to take responsibility for his or her own destiny, which may include choosing alignment with a group:

> Status-based milieus and lifestyles typical of a class culture lose their lustre. The tendency is towards the emergence of individualised forms and conditions of existence, which compel people – for the sake of their own material survival – to make themselves the centre of their own planning and conduct of life. Increasingly, everyone has to choose between different options, including as to which group or subculture one wants to be identified with. In fact, one has to choose and change one's social identity as well and take the risks in doing so. In this sense, individualisation means the variation and differentiation of lifestyles and forms of life, opposing the thinking behind the traditional categories of large-group societies – which is to say, classes, estates [status groups], and social stratification.

(Beck, 1993: 88)

While he refers to 'groups and subcultures' to which individuals may belong, like Giddens, Beck does not explore their relationships to lifestyles, the individual or the wider society.

We have already noted that the three studies by Chan and Goldthorpe (2005; 2007b; 2007c) listed in Table 23.1 addressed the issue of status versus class and the omnivore/univore thesis, but they also addressed the 'individualization thesis'. Their premise was that, if the individualization thesis as put forward by Giddens and Beck was in operation, there would be no systematic relationship between cultural participation and class or status. As already noted, they do not find any relationship with class, but they do with status, and also with education, thus raising doubts about the individualization thesis. However, as noted in the earlier discussion of this research, it cannot be taken as the final word in relation to lifestyle because of the limited range of activities used.

The new middle or service class

In contrast to the traditional concern of sociology with the 'working class', a body of research, influenced to varying degrees by Bourdieu's identification of a *new petite bourgeoisie*,[5] has emerged on the lifestyles of the 'new middle class' or 'service class', since their growing numbers and relative wealth result in them being seen as significant drivers of social and cultural change, including the development of distinctive and innovative lifestyles. Four examples are reviewed below, three from the UK and one from the Netherlands.

273

Derek Wynne's (1990, 1998) study of 'life on The Heath', a new owner-occupied, relatively up-market housing estate in north-west England, identified two lifestyle groups within the broadly middle-class residents: *sporters*, who used the estate's sport/social club to play sports, and *drinkers*, who used the club primarily for socializing in the bar. These were subjected to a form of CA which located members of the two groups in the 'social space of mobility', the 'social space of lifestyle' and the 'social space of gender'.[6]

Savage *et al.* (1992: 104–131) explored lifestyles of the British middle classes based on consumption expenditure patterns revealed by the commercial 'Target Group Index' market research survey, dividing middle classes into three lifestyle groups: *ascetic* (public sector welfare professionals), *post-modern* (private sector employees) and *undistinctive* (managers and government bureaucrats).

Studies of Dutch cultural participation patterns by Van Eijck and Mommaas (2004) and Van Eijck (1999; 2001) showed that the 'new middle class', particularly those who were socially mobile, had a distinctive, more omnivorous, cultural participation pattern than had traditional middle-class groups.

Having classified more than half the British workforce as 'middle class', it is not surprising that Bennett *et al.* (2009: 177–194), in their major British study discussed above, discover considerable diversity in cultural participation patterns among such a broad grouping. While they do not delineate specific lifestyles, they conclude that 'culture matters to the middle classes, and even more so to its [*sic*] higher echelons' (p. 194). Furthermore, they note the significant but changing role of higher education in shaping cultural tastes (p. 193).

Postmodernism and postmodernity

Featherstone (1991: 83) observes that 'we are moving towards a society without fixed status groups in which the adoption of styles of life (manifest in choice of clothes, leisure activities, consumer goods, bodily dispositions) which are fixed to specific groups have [*sic*] been surpassed'. While this perspective is almost identical to those propounded by Giddens and Beck, who see it as characterizing *modernity*, for Featherstone it is indicative of a *postmodern* society. However, while he accepts that the process of lifestyle adoption has changed because of the range of options generated by the 'dynamic of consumer culture' and the growing significance of new groups (i.e. the *new petite bourgeoisie*, as discussed above), he fully endorses the decidedly modernist stance of Bourdieu in accepting that lifestyles are still firmly linked to class and class fractions.

A more thoroughly postmodern conception of the role of groups in society is advanced by Michel Maffesoli (1996), albeit under the pre-modern term *tribe* or *neo-tribe*. His book, *The Time of the Tribes*, originally published in French in 1988, has the subtitle *The Decline of Individualism in Mass Society*, clearly placing him at odds with Giddens and Beck. But what is the difference between a *lifestyle group* and a *neo-tribe*? Essentially, a tribe is seen as a group of people with a high level of personal commitment to a project. There is, therefore, some overlap with lifestyle and subculture (discussed below) and serious leisure (Stebbins, 2007). Examples help to demonstrate the distinction. In *Consumer Tribes*, in which the concept is examined from a marketing perspective, Cova, Kozinets and Shankar (2007) present a number of case studies dealing with: surfing; memorabilia collectors and highly committed followers of the British royal family; Harley-Davidson motorcycle enthusiasts; metrosexuals; the 'Stockholm Brat' enclave; cruisers (car customizers); Tom Petty and the Heartbreakers (TPATH) fans; the Sir Cliff Richard fan club; HP iTribe – online Harry Potter fans; *Star Trek* wikimedia; Warhammer gamers; Goth merchandizers; fetish groups;

an online culinary group; Hummer SUV enthusiasts; and pipe smokers. Thus, a tribe may gather around an artist or celebrity, a commercial brand, a leisure activity or a minority lifestyle. Cova *et al.* (2007: 6) note that, where commercial products or brands are concerned, a neo-tribe is typically comprised of purists who, far from being passive consumers, may actively adapt the product for their purposes and may be antagonistic towards the brand owner because of changes to the product over time; neo-tribes are seen as activators, double agents, plunderers and entrepreneurs. The measures of cultural preference and participation typically used in empirical lifestyle research have not hitherto been capable of identifying the level of commitment implied in neo-tribal membership, but, as has been shown with the growing body of research on serious leisure, this does not preclude the development of suitable measures in future.

The distinctive subcultures developed by groups of young people, particularly in the post-Second World War era, have been the focus of considerable research, which is clearly of relevance to the topic of lifestyle and leisure. In Britain, the development of the field of Leisure Studies in the 1970s and 1980s, including the study of young people's leisure, coincided with the development of the work of the Birmingham University Centre for Contemporary Cultural Studies (CCCS), which saw youth subcultures of the 1960s, such as teddy boys, mods and rockers, as forms of working-class resistance to the capitalist system (Hall and Jefferson, 1976). The basis of the approach was a neo-Marxist focus on class, in which the term 'lifestyle' had no place, since it might have been viewed as a 'Weberian deviation' (Muggleton, 2000: 9), despite its clear similarities with the concept of subculture. While the CCCS approach became the 'orthodox perspective in the British study of youth' (Roberts, 1983: 41), it was not totally dominant; for example, Hendry *et al.* (1993: 5–7) dismissed class-focused theory and completed their study of youth and leisure, conducted in Scotland from the mid-1980s, with an analysis of lifestyles.

Although foreshadowed by the work of Jenkins in 1982, a significant departure from the CCCS pattern came in the late 1990s with the emergence of the 'post-subcultural turn' (Bennett, 2011). Researchers such as Muggleton (2000) and Miles (2000) argued that in addressing the study of young people with a pre-determined structural, neo-Marxist theoretical framework, the CCCS approach had failed to engage with the lived experience of young people, while Thornton (1996: 120–22) criticized it for failing to recognize the complexities of the roles played by the media in youth subculture. Furthermore, the types of broadly based, identifiably working-class youth subcultures identified in the 1970s and 1980s no longer reflected the fragmented, postmodern, individualized environment of the youth scenes of the 1990s. Muggleton (2000: 30) concluded that, since youth subcultures were to do with 'attitudes and values, consumption practices and various leisure activities', they could 'more accurately be conceptualised as "lifestyle" groupings', while Miles (2000: 16) stated: 'it could be argued that the declining value of subculture ... demands the use of an alternative conceptual focus, and that should be *lifestyles*'. The question arises as to whether the use of the term 'lifestyle' implies a concept which is different from subculture, or whether what is involved is simply the use of a distinctive term to indicate a different approach to theorizing of the same phenomenon.

Summary and conclusions

The growing interest in lifestyle in social research over the last twenty years has made the concept of lifestyle increasingly relevant to the study of leisure, while, paradoxically, interest within the Leisure Studies community itself has declined. It has been demonstrated in this

chapter that both Weberian status-based and Bourdieusian class-based theory accommodate the concept of lifestyle, offering alternative theoretical frameworks for leisure/lifestyle
researchers. While there is a growing body of empirical evidence supporting and challenging both approaches, it is often limited in the range of activities covered or in the level of
certainty attached to conclusions, leaving substantial scope for further work. Two theoretical
developments have widened the scope of lifestyle research: first is the effect of globalization
and increasing wealth and consumer choice, which has brought to the fore the scope for
individual lifestyle choice. Second is the development of postmodern tendencies, including,
in opposition to the idea of increasing individualization, the phenomenon of the neo-tribe,
which encompasses a more active, focused approach to contemporary consumer society
linked to a more fluid concept of leisure-focused lifestyle. These trends have also led some
researchers on youth culture to turn to lifestyle as a more flexible concept through which to
view young people's lives.

Notes

1   Summaries of a number of these quantitative lifestyle and leisure style studies can be found in Veal
    (2012).
2   'Style of life' and 'lifestyle' are generally, as here, used interchangeably, although it has been
    suggested that Weber's term should be used when referring to the concept in a sociological context,
    to avoid confusion with popular and commercial usage (Scott, 2002: 34).
3   In the Routledge English translation of *Distinction* (Bourdieu, 1984), in Figure 5 (p. 129), farmers and
    farm labourers have been erroneously switched. The correct locations are shown in Bourdieu (1980).
4   I must confess to not having fully appreciated the breadth of Bourdieu's work in the brief para-
    graph on him in Veal (1989), which was based on only the short article accompanying the diagram
    of social position and lifestyle in *Media, Culture and Society* (Bourdieu, 1980). I did correct this in
    Veal (1993), but only partially.
5   The alignment of 'new middle class' and 'new petite bourgeoisie' in some studies seems quite
    loose. Thus Bourdieu (1986: 359) defines the 'new petite bourgeoisie' as comprising occupations
    involving 'presentation and representation', including 'sales, marketing, advertising, public rela-
    tions, fashion, decoration and so forth', and 'medical and social assistance', but also some nurses
    and secretaries and 'junior commercial executives' (p. 364). Of Wynne's (1998: 40) sample,
    however, over 50 per cent were from the top four managerial/professional occupational catego-
    ries. In the case of Savage *et al.* (1992: 105), who do not claim to be dealing with the *new* middle
    class, the focus is primarily on the top two 'AB' categories in the market research classifica-
    tions of social groups/occupations. Van Eijck and Mommaas (2004) covered working people
    in the top 50 per cent of occupational categories, the 'upper middle class', which they divide
    into self-employed, civil servants and private sector employees, but the relationship between
    these groups and the 'new middle class' is fluid. Bennett *et al.* (2009: 55) include in the 'middle
    classes' more than half the workforce, i.e. 'professionals, managers in large establishments and
    large employers' (24 per cent of workforce) and an 'intermediate class, which includes the lower
    managers' (30 per cent).
6   This terminology of the *social* space of mobility, lifestyles and gender is somewhat different from
    that used by Bourdieu, who refers to the 'space of lifestyle' and the 'space of social position' (or
    economic class). Wynne's (1989: 49) use of the term 'field' is also different from that of Bourdieu
    (1986: 226).

References

Alderson, A. S., Junisbai, A., and Heacock, I. (2007) 'Social Status and Cultural Consumptions in the
   United States', *Poetics* 35 (2–3) 191–212.
Andrews, E. (1981) *Closing the Iron Cage: The Scientific Management of Work and Leisure.* Montreal: Black
   Rose Books.

Atkinson, W. (2011) 'The Context and Genesis of Musical Tastes: Omnivorousness Debunked, Bourdieu Buttressed', *Poetics*, 39 (2) 169–186.

Australia Council (2010) *More than Bums on Seats: Australian Participation in the Arts*. Sydney: Australia Council.

Beck, U. (1993) 'Beyond Status and Class?', in *Risk Society: Towards a New Modernity*. London: Sage, 91–102. (Originally published in German in 1986, Frankfurt: Suhrkamp Verlag).

Bell, D., and Hollows, J. (2006) 'Towards a History of Lifestyle', in D. Bell and J. Hollows (eds), *Historicizing Lifestyle: Mediating Taste, Consumption and Identity from the 1900s to the 1970s*. Farnham, UK: Ashgate Publishing, 1–20.

Bennett, A. (2011) 'The Post-Subcultural Turn: Some Reflections 10 Years On', *Journal of Youth Studies* 14 (5) 493–506.

Bennett, T. (2007) 'Habitus Clivé: Aesthetics and Politics in the Work of Pierre Bourdieu', *New Literary History* 38 (1) 201–228.

Bennett, T. (2010) 'Introduction to the Routledge Classics Edition', in P. Bourdieu, *Distinction: A Social Critique of the Judgement of Taste*. London: Routledge, xvii–xxiii.

Bennett, T., Emmison, M., and Frow, J. (1999) *Accounting for Tastes: Australian Everyday Cultures*. Melbourne: Cambridge University Press.

Bennett, T., Savage, M., Silva, E., Warde, A., Gayo-Cal, M., and Wright, D. (2009) *Culture, Class, Distinction*. London: Routledge.

Bourdieu, P. (1980) 'A Diagram of Social Position and Life-Style', *Media, Culture and Society* 2 (3) 255–259.

Bourdieu, P. (1984) *Distinction: A Social Critique of the Judgement of Taste*. London: Routledge and Kegan Paul (originally published in French, Paris: Editions de Minuit, 1979).

Bourdieu, P. (1986) *Distinction: A Social Critique of the Judgement of Taste*. London: Routledge and Kegan Paul (paperback edition).

Bryson, B. (1996) '"Anything but Heavy Metal": Symbolic Exclusion and Musical Dislikes', *American Sociological Review* 61 (4) 884–899.

Bukodi, E. (2007) 'Social Stratification and Cultural Consumption in Hungary: Book Readership', *Poetics* 35 (2–3) 112–131.

CACI (n.d.) *ACORN (A Classification of Residential Neighbourhoods)*. London: CACI, available at: www.caci.co.uk/acorn-classification.aspx.

Cahill, D. J. (2006) *Lifestyle Market Segmentation*. New York: Haworth Press.

Chan, T. W., and Goldthorpe, J. H. (2004) 'Is there a Status Order in Contemporary British Society? Evidence from the Occupational Structure of Friendship', *European Sociological Review* 20 (5) 383–401.

Chan, T. W., and Goldthorpe, J. H. (2005) 'The Social Stratification of Theatre, Dance and Cinema Attendance', *Cultural Trends* 14 (3) 193–212.

Chan, T. W., and Goldthorpe, J. H. (2007a) 'Class and Status: the Conceptual Distinction and its Empirical Relevance', *American Sociological Review* 72 (4) 512–532.

Chan, T. W., and Goldthorpe, J. H. (2007b) 'Social Stratification and Cultural Consumption: Music in England', *European Sociological Review* 23 (1) 1–19.

Chan, T. W., and Goldthorpe, J. H. (2007c) 'Social Stratification and Cultural Consumption: the Visual Arts in England', *Poetics* 35 (2) 168–190.

Chan, T. W., and Goldthorpe, J. H. (2007d) 'Data, Methods and Interpretation in Analysis of Cultural Consumption: a Reply to Peterson and Wuggenig', *Poetics* 35 (3) 317–329.

Chaney, D. (1996) *Lifestyles*. London: Routledge.

Clarke, J., and Critcher, C. (1985) *The Devil Makes Work: Leisure in Capitalist Britain*. London: Macmillan.

Coulangeon, P., and Lemel, Y. (2007) 'Is "Distinction" Really Outdated? Questioning the Meaning of Omnivoration of Musical Taste in Contemporary France', *Poetics* 35 (1) 93–111.

Cova, B., Kozinets, R. V., and Shankar, A. (eds) (2007) *Consumer Tribes*. Oxford: Butterworth-Heinemann.

Critcher, C. (1989) 'A Communication in Response to: "Leisure and Status: A Pluralist Framework for Analysis"', *Leisure Studies* 8 (2) 159–162.

Erickson, B. H. (1996) 'Culture, Class and Connections', *American Journal of Sociology* 102 (1) 217–251.

Featherstone, M. (1987) 'Lifestyle and Consumer Culture', *Theory, Culture and Society* 4 (1) 55–70.

Featherstone, M. (1991) *Consumer Culture and Postmodernism*. London: Sage.

Filipcova, B., Glyptis, S., and Tokarski, W. (eds) (1989) *Life Styles: Theories, Concepts, Methods and Results of Life Style Research in International Perspective*. Prague: Institute for Philosophy and Sociology, Czechoslovak Academy of Sciences/Research Committee 13 of the International Sociological Association.

Frow, J. (1987) 'Accounting for Tastes: Some Problems in Bourdieu's Sociology of Culture', *Cultural Studies* 1 (1) 59–73.

Giddens, A. (1991) *Modernity and Self-Identity: Self and Society in the Late Modern Age*. Cambridge: Polity.

Goldthorpe, J. (2007) 'Cultural Capital: Some Critical Observations', *Sociologica* 2 (1) 1–23.

Green, G. T., Cordell, H. K., Betz, C. J., and DiStefano, C. (2006) 'Construction and Validation of the National Survey on Recreation and the Environment's Lifestyles Scale', *Journal of Leisure Research* 38 (4) 513–535.

Hall, S., and Jefferson, T. (eds) (1976) *Resistance through Rituals*. London: Hutchison.

Havighurst, R. J., and Feigenbaum, K. (1959) 'Leisure and Life Style', *American Journal of Sociology*, 64 (2) 396–405.

Hendry, L. B., Shucksmith J., Love, J. G., and Glendinning, A. (1993) *Young People's Leisure and Lifestyles*. London: Routledge.

Holt, D. B. (1997) 'Poststructuralist Lifestyle Analysis: Conceptualizing the Social Patterning of Consumption in Modernity', *Journal of Consumer Research*, 23 (2) 326–350.

Jenkins, R. (1982) 'Life-styles', chapter 4 in *Lads, Citizens and Ordinary Kids: Youth Life-styles in Belfast*. London: Routledge and Kegan Paul.

Johansson, T. (1994) 'Late Modernity, Consumer Culture and Lifestyles: Toward a Cognitive-Affective Theory', in K. E. Rosengren (ed.), *Media Effects and Beyond: Culture, Socialization and Lifestyles*. London: Routledge, 265–294.

Johansson, T., and Miegel, F. (1992) *Do the Right Thing: Lifestyle and Identity in Contemporary Youth Culture*. Stockholm: Almqvist and Wiksell International.

Katz-Gerro, T., Raz, S., and Meir Yaish, M. (2007) 'Class, Status, and the Intergenerational Transmission of Musical Tastes in Israel', *Poetics* 35 (2) 152–167.

Kraaykamp, G., van Eijck, K., Ultee, W., and van Rees, K. (2007) 'Status and Media Use in the Netherlands: Do Partners Affect Media Taste?', *Poetics* 35 (2–3) 132–151.

Lawson, R., Todd, S., and Evans, S. (2006) *New Zealand in the 21st Century: a Consumer Lifestyles Study*. Dunedin: Consumer Research Group, University of Otago.

Le Roux, B., and Rouanet, H. (2010) *Multiple Classification Analysis*. Newbury Park, CA: Sage.

Lee, S., and Sparks, B. (2007). 'Cultural Influences on Travel Lifestyle: A Comparison of Korean Australians and Koreans in Korea', *Tourism Management* 28 (2) 505–518.

Maffesoli, M. (1996) *The Time of the Tribes, Decline of Individualism in Mass Society*. London: Sage.

McDonald, M. A., Milne, G. R., and Hong, J.-B. (2002) 'Motivational Factors for Evaluating Sport Spectator and Participant Markets', *Sport Marketing Quarterly* 11 (2) 100–113.

Miles, S. (2000) *Youth Lifestyles in a Changing World*. Buckingham UK: Open University Press.

Mintel (2011) *Mintel's British Lifestyles Report*. London: Mintel, available at: www. mintel.com/press-centre/press-releases/746.

Muggleton, D. (2000) *Inside Subcultures: The Postmodern Meaning of Style*. Oxford: Berg.

Peterson, R., and Simkus, S. (1992) 'How Musical Tastes Mark Occupational Status Groups', in M. Lamont and M. Fournier, M. (eds), *Cultivating Differences: Symbolic Boundaries and the Making of Inequality*. Chicago: Chicago University Press, 152–186.

Reimer, B. (1995) 'Youth and Modern Lifestyles', in J. Fornäs and G. Bolin (eds) *Youth Culture in Late Modernity*. London: Sage, 120–144.

Roberts, K. (1983) *Youth and Leisure*. London: George Allen and Unwin.

Roberts, K. (2006) *Leisure in Contemporary Society*, 2nd ed. Wallingford, UK: CABI Publishing.

Ruiz, J. I. (1989) 'Life Styles and Daily Leisure', in B. Filipcova, S. Glyptis and W. Tokarski (eds) *Life Styles: Theories, Concepts, Methods and Results of Life Style Research in International Perspective*. Prague: Institute for Philosophy and Sociology, Czechoslovak Academy of Sciences/Research Committee 13 of the International Sociological Association, 156–169.

Savage, M., Barlow, J., Dickens, P., and Fielding, A. J. (1992) *Property, Bureaucracy and Culture: Middle-Class Formation in Contemporary Britain*. London: Routledge.

Scott, J. (2002) 'Social Class and Stratification in Late Modernity', *Acta Sociologica* 34 (1) 23–35.

Scraton, S., and Talbot, M. (1989) 'A Response to "Leisure, Lifestyle and Status: A Pluralist Framework for Analysis"', *Leisure Studies* 8 (2) 155–158.

Stebbins, R. A. (2007) *Serious Leisure: A Perspective of Our Time*. New Brunswick, NJ: Transaction.

Strategic Business Insights (n.d.) *VALS: Values, Attitudes and Lifestyle Survey*. Menlo Park, CA: SBI, available at: www.strategicbusinessinsights.com.

Stub, H. R. (ed.) (1972) *Status Communities in Modern Society: Alternatives to Class Analysis*. Hinsdale, IL: Dryden Press.

Sureda, J., and Valls, J.-F. (2004) 'A Comparison of Leisure Styles in Germany, France, Italy, Great Britain, Spain and Portugal', in K. Weiermair, and C. Mathies (eds) *The Tourism and Leisure Industry: Shaping the Future*. New York: Haworth Hospitality Press, 151–170.

Thornton, S. (1996) *Club Culture: Music, Media and Subcultural Capital*. Hanover: NH: University Press of New England.

Todd, S., and Larson, R. (2001) 'Lifestyle Segmentation and Museum/Gallery Visiting Behaviour', *International Journal of Nonprofit and Voluntary Sector Marketing* 6 (3) 269–277.

Tomlinson, M. (2003) 'Lifestyle and Social Class', *European Sociological Review* 19 (1) 97–111.

Torche, F. (2007) 'Social Status and Cultural Consumption, the Case of Reading in Chile', *Poetics* 35 (2–3) 70–92.

Van Eijck, K. (1999) 'Socialization, Education, and Lifestyle: How Social Mobility Increases the Cultural Heterogeneity of Status Groups', *Poetics* 26 (3) 309–328.

Van Eijck, K. (2001) 'Social Differentiation in Musical Taste Patterns', *Social Forces* 79 (3) 1163–1184.

Van Eijck, K., and Mommaas, H. (2004) 'Leisure, Lifestyle and the New Middle Class', *Leisure Sciences* 27 (4) 373–392.

Veal, A. J. (1989) 'Leisure, Lifestyle and Status: A Pluralistic Framework for Analysis', *Leisure Studies* 8 (2) 141–154.

Veal, A. J. (1993) 'The Concept of Lifestyle: A Review', *Leisure Studies* 12 (4) 233–252.

Veal, A. J. (2012) *Lifestyle and Leisure-style Studies: Summaries*. Available at: www.leisuresource.net, under 'Other papers'.

Warde, A., Wright, D., and Gayo-Cal, M. (2007) 'Understanding Cultural Omnivorousness: or The Myth of the Cultural Omnivore', *Cultural Sociology* 1 (2) 143–164.

Warde, A., Wright, D. and Gayo-Cal, M. (2008) 'The Omnivorous Orientation in the UK', *Poetics* 36 (2) 148–165.

Weber, M. (1922/1978) *Economy and Society* (edited by G. Roth and C. Wittich). Berkeley: CA: University of California Press.

Wuggenig, U. (2007) 'Comments on Chan and Goldthorpe: Pitfalls in Testing Bourdieu's Homology Assumptions Using Mainstream Social Science Methodology', *Poetics* 35 (4) 306–316.

Wynne, D. (1990) 'Leisure Lifestyles and the Construction of Social Position', *Leisure Studies* 9 (1) 21–34.

Wynne, D. (1998) *Leisure, Lifestyle and the New Middle Class*. London: Routledge.

24

THE LEISURED NATURE OF TOURISM

A sociological critique

Stephen Wearing and Alan Law

> Tourism is not just an aggregate of merely commercial activities; it is also an ideological framing of history, nature, and tradition; a framing that has the power to reshape culture and nature to its own needs.
>
> (Dean MacCannell)[1]

Introduction

The sociology of tourism encounters a wide range of possible dimensions of analysis of the essentially spatially organized social relationships between 'away' and 'home'. Key sociological themes have typically centred their attention on the kinds of identity relationships established in the networks of actors involved in tourism practices and the making of their meaning. Within the range of formulations available to interpret social engagement in tourism, the ontological distinction between 'away' and 'home' is what makes 'tourism' a thing separate from other things in our experiential repertoires and energizes the identity work that is always at stake when encountering the 'other' – constituent of 'away'. The movement of the physical body through space, and in order to reach for 'not home' (the exotic), is a key anchor-point for the work of three scholars whose ideas are canvassed here, and produces the conditions for analysis of how people engage in the touristic world at the moments of meetings with both the self and the 'other'.

The constitution of self and 'other' in the tourism context necessarily underpins theoretical and empirical work in the field, and this chapter outlines three main contemporary positions on the relationship between self and 'other' that is the foundation of a sociology of tourism and of leisure more broadly. The three main positions that have taken up the problem of how to conceive of self and 'other' in the tourism frame and which are discussed in this chapter are the symbolic interactionist approach of Dean MacCannell, the Foucauldian-inspired post-structuralism found in the work John Urry and, important to the sociology of leisure as a distinct subject field, Chris Rojek's critical and emancipatory agendas developed through his analyses of the postmodern condition which bring to light the expansion toward the infinite array of tensions at the structural and cultural levels. The chapter concludes with encouragement of more debate and a call for side-stepping the issue of 'freedom' as theoretical 'purpose' that might foster more theoretical work that simultaneously critiques and accommodates the range of social positions possible in an *opening* world in which individuals do not wait for theoretical interpretations in order to get on with their tourist lives.

MacCannell, authenticity and the social subject in active dialogue

Dean MacCannell (1979) launched the investigation of the explicitly social relations of tourism beyond the common problems of marketing by raising a number of key questions: 'What are the motivations of travellers so that we can serve them properly?' 'How many are there likely to be if we put in things that people like to see?' 'How do we cope with the issue of crowds during holiday periods?' and 'How do we balance the competing demands of different kinds of motive for tourism?' While raising these important questions (and all incidentally springing from sociological foundations), MacCannell's work sought to unpack why and how relations between tourists and hosts structure each other during precious moments of engagement. MacCannell's work is rooted in a normatively neutral American symbolic interactionist perspective and, vis-à-vis Goffman (1961), follows the main and consequential methodological route into analysis of how people manage their 'front stage' and 'backstage' (public and private) lives. In this formulation, 'actors' in the tourism 'frame' (an important dimension of symbolic interactionism that literally sets the 'stage') mutually negotiate performances of roles. The imperative to 'see behind the curtain' is an integral part of being a person so that roles can be consciously engaged, and in a playful way. The skill of an actor is how well the magic show can stay magic, or how well one can pick up the cues for what is 'really' happening, in an effort to guide effective public performance of the situated self in interaction with the situated 'other'.

MacCannell's work privileges the 'tourist' as seeker of 'backstage' in an effort to establish a more intimate relationship with a host and break through the plastic cover of the 'client/ supplier' relationship into something 'authentic', as between friends who know the *real* story but applaud the quality of what they know to be a fabrication. The point is less about whether a representation for tourist consumption is accurate, though this is the explicit platform of negotiation, and more clearly about processes by which intimacy and shared knowledge are developed, collapsing the distinction between 'self' and 'other', tourist and host, to provide a wider scope for inquiry about how people negotiate the meaning of their encountering of home/away. In this sense, the social subjects of place, visitor, host are all *active* social subjects reflexively engaging in making meaning of experience within the set frame of 'tourism', which has a particular set of roles to enact. While subjectivity in tourism is somewhat 'scripted' in this formulation (predetermined) by anticipated roles to play, the negotiation process is available as the field to deploy autonomy in negotiation.

MacCannell's later work expanded analysis beyond the play of 'front' and 'back stage' and squarely addresses the reach for authenticity as something that happens through chance encounters of the everyday kind where no *particular* narrative has to be dealt with to get through to the 'back stage' because 'traveller' is meant to *be* a 'local' sufficiently to absorb meaning and expand the self as a result. MacCannell (1992; 2000) and others (e.g. Clifford, 1997; and Horne, 1992) have highlighted the 'nomadic traveller' interested in the unknown and the unexpected as exotic from the routine manufactures laid out in modern holiday brochures, programming what we can expect. MacCannell's (1992) nomadic traveller is one who wishes to engage with the places and people met along the way in an open-endedness absent of a particular script. The nomadic traveller is interested in the unknown and the unexpected as authenticity incarnate ('I'm not a *tourist*, I'm a *traveller*'). Here the reach for authenticity remains intact and the manufactures of modernity the counterpoint for 'away'.

MacCannell (1992) also identifies the 'neo-nomad', who wants to create experiences and seeks encounters that embrace difference, but without the long journey typical of the Australian 'walkabout' nomad. That is, the open-endedness of interaction is kept intact, but a three-week Euro-rail pass or rented cottage in rural France might do the job within an annual holiday. The neo-nomad traveller, MacCannell suggests, does not travel as an invader conquering territory but in the belief that the tourist experience will be made of dialogue with those met along the way; 'they leave home not knowing where they will end up' in terms of the experiences that may arise (MacCannell, 1992: 4).

As MacCannell's work demonstrates, the importance of the 'demand for authenticity' became a major theme in tourism studies, but has been challenged on the questioning of who establishes the grounds on which anything is deemed authentic. Morris's (1995) observations on the objectification inherent in practices of cultural consumption that impose a valuation of authenticity by a colonizing culture have influenced tourism critique and expanded analysis of authenticity in tourism into one central question: 'Whose authentic is really authentic?' The question centres our attention on the battle for a legitimate 'story' that is waged by those written out of it or written into it in subordinate or passive subject positions. The critique of authenticity as 'reason' in tourism has also been influenced by Barthes' deconstruction of myths, landscapes and texts, both written and pictorial, and Foucault's theory of the relationship of power and knowledge, taken up by Urry. In these formulations, 'authenticity' is merely a colonizing discourse refusing its relationship to subversive meanings and actions generated by marginalized identities locked out of cultures rendering what is real.

MacCannell's neo-nomad is an imaginative traveller who embraces difference (1992: 4). The neo-nomad, MacCannell believes, has a freedom to be creative and interactive through understanding travel as offering chance meetings and dialogues capable of ignoring or avoiding colonizing fabrications both in self, place and 'other'. When MacCannell applies the term to describe travellers, he is proposing an enjoyment of dis-placed understanding, one that synthesizes, but does not fix or reduce, as an important contributing behaviour in travel. MacCannell (1992) contends that ways of being out-of-place that release creativity are embodied in neo-nomad travellers, who do not essentialize what or who they meet along the way. The 'other' can be met but never possessed (MacCannell, 2000). Since other-ness, MacCannell says, is precisely that which can never be possessed; the neo-nomad is freed from the grip of desire to possess and is instead animated by a desire to create (MacCannell, 2000: 169). Tribe (2008) describes such a travel moment as offering 'the possibility to abandon regular cultural baggage and explore new places, self and others' (2008: 930). MacCannell writes of the 'spiritual reach of the touristic consciousness 'through which the tourist does not try to contain everything in himself, but instead incessantly transgresses the boundaries of his own existence (2000: 175). The traveller's point of recognition of difference that occurs in the moments of awareness can lead to possibilities for extending the self (Wearing and Wearing, 1996: 240), originating new ideas and meanings. Certainly MacCannell's nomadic social subject seems to pursue the emancipatory agenda of leisure through open-ended and unscripted 'play' on the boundary of self and 'other'. To what extent though, does anything 'new' develop when 'others' meet themselves and each 'other'?

Any desire to dig beyond the surface, to make a crack in the manufacture of the 'exotic', means opening a dialogue with producers of place. In this sense, both visitor and host engage with each other's active desire for acknowledgement of difference and each moment of interaction can produce a surprise. That is, authenticity is always negotiated and fluid as desire for and knowledge of *particular* 'otherness' shifts. MacCannell's formulation suggests that the 'authentic' as exotic to the mundane is really only available through the kinds of inter-cultural negotiation produced in tourism and that the play of negotiating the authentic is the seat of personal development that can act back on 'home' self by introducing new meanings acquired elsewhere. In other words, the social subject is transformative in interaction.

This kind of American optimism about the mutually constitutive power of the autonomously negotiating social subject stands in contrast to European pessimism about the possibility of anything or anybody being autonomous through travel or much else. From this perspective, our attention is turned away from how people produce truly novel moments with profound effects on biographic agendas in interaction with each other, and toward modes of subjectivity constitution which can never truly break from scripted rules of conduct because we are, at every moment, and at every place, the outcomes of discourses within which we enact ourselves and which are produced in the range of social relations that pre-exist and formulate the meaning of encounters 'away'. Our attention is drawn to the enormous power of the 'already-constituted' as the principal dimension of tourism practice and experience (Boothroyd, in Simms, 1997), potentially rendering the touring subject somewhat passive and reduced to an actor in a consumer spectacle. At this point, 'negotiation' of subjectivity ceases, except as we work on ourselves to connect 'discourses' that interact in novel though not conscious ways.

Urry and the tourist 'gaze': knowing tourists, hosts and places

The most important work that introduced Foucault's insights to the analysis of tourism was Urry's (1990) classic book, *The Tourist Gaze*. Urry argued that the making of tourist subjectivities happens far beyond interaction between particular people, but that we are made, and participate in making of ourselves, to be responsible consumers and suppliers of experience. What counts as responsible dwells within the *narratives* of biographies for both people and places and the cultural economies that situate appropriate relationships. How we organize these plots for ourselves becomes the seat of autonomy, in the 'productive' reading of Foucault. Tourism is not about 'freedom' or open-endedness except insofar as we freely pursue desire that has its source in particular frames of the legitimate self, and this holds for both people and places. Urry's work can be considered an advance on MacCannell's insofar as dimensions of social structure beyond the immediate interaction are at stake at every moment.

Analysis of the 'see' and 'be seen' relationship takes a substantial twist in Urry's 'gaze' metaphor, developed with particular reference to Foucault's *The Birth of the Clinic* (1973) and, perhaps his most important study, *Discipline and Punish* (1977). Foucault's '*post*-structuralism' was an advance on structuralist linguistics and structuralist Marxism, which supposed that the social subject is the mere result of intersecting meanings contained in the very ways in which we structure knowledge. The structuralist, passive 'interpolated', 'determined' or even 'over-determined' subject was a mere puppet on the strings of social forces. Foucault's formulation took us a step further in analysis of identity relations, with the argument that we produce our own subjectivities within the reference grids available through knowledge authorities. That is, we work on ourselves to articulate subject positions inside of governing frames, and the identity work that we actively do on ourselves in such situations is not *just* 'negative' in the hegemonic sense of keeping something suppressed in favour of something false that might be against our emancipatory interests, or of the structuralist interpolated subject dumbly performing script, but is productive of who we are, and the 'self' is the active agent in the expression of our 'roots' as they become relevant. The important point is that we work on ourselves to be active in the 'right' way. In this view, there is no primeval autonomous subject in need of rescuing from ideological or Marxist 'hegemonic' false consciousness. There are no dark places to avoid the 'gaze' (therefore no freedom to be sought), because it is indeed everywhere, infinite in dimensions, arguably all of which intersect all of the time, including when travelling, encountering or even structuring the 'other', immersing in simple play, hedonism or even merely interpreting a beach.

Urry's analysis of 'seeing' and being 'seen' posits a reflexive relationship between visitor and host that possibly has little to do, at a fundamental level, with any kind of explicit 'negotiation', except that visitor and host can constitute each other in a mutually beneficial narrative of their meeting (e.g. client/producer, explorer/landscape, tourist/local, etc.). The 'exotic' plays an important role, but its meaning is left open to be rendered and interpreted by widely varying narratives of place and person that extend beyond the concrete moment of meeting the 'other'. Narratives that inform the action of any individual to 'be' when 'away' include all of the usual dimensions of biographical contours such as social class, ethnicity, gender and sexualities as well all of the other unlabelled dimensions of 'being' the self. The important 'Panopticon' metaphor is about being aware of how personhood should be elaborated (the 'gaze-ee') according to the dimensions of anticipation rendered by knowledge authorities (the 'gaze-er'). The tourist subject works to see and be seen in the 'right' way.

Urry highlighted the importance of language and images in his discussion of the media and their role in creating anticipation and constituting tourist subjectivity. For example, the tourist experience is interpreted post-trip in a way to reconfirm the media–images (I was there in my National Geographic photo taken by self-portrait) self inside of an exotic poster as a route to 'be' the travelling person, thereby perpetuating the cycle of the relationship between commerce and subjectivity. This hermeneutic circle (Urry, 1990; Caton and Santos, 2009) extracts power relations from the dominant/subordinate dichotomy by positioning subject and object as mutually and infinitely constitutive. That is, there is no 'cause' or 'effect' to analyse. Foucauldian theory cares less about who might be oppressing whom and more about techniques and technologies of mutually productive knowledge relations. In this sense, 'the gaze' is accomplished by visitor, host, resident, traveller, *flâneur* and so on.

In some ways, Urry's application of Foucault was seized upon as a launch-point of calls for negotiation of possible subject positions in the telling and reading of cultural stories (even the storyless pastiche of postmodern consumption) to recover subject positions obscured or mangled in representations or conditions of access to meaningful tourism. That is, we need to get at something *ideological* without the Marxist baggage. We are not 'free' because of how our identities are read to us by us inside of tourism practices, and this holds for both places and people. Critics of the apparent moral neutrality inside of the 'gaze' analysis argue that indeed particular subjectivities are written in and out or converted in some way to serve dominant/subordinate interests refusing any negotiation of interests.

Tourism, then, far from engaging an active expansion of the self through social and cultural encounters, merely produces and reproduces Western, white, gendered, sexualized and classed codes for consumption, with very little space out there for *negotiating* these as legitimate or even recognizable. However, Urry's analysis invites critique of the extent to which subject positions as 'hybridities' of varied discourses can claim voice, not as authoritative, but as present rather than simply being rendered inside of someone else's narrative. The interplay of narratives becomes important and the politics of negotiating these, the point of complaint and the target of policy action. And yet, reaching the source of the narrative to have a negotiating conversation will be difficult in the diffuseness of authorship. The emancipatory potential of 'gaze' analysis then lies in the politics of privileged 'knowledges' that distinguish self from 'other' in concrete ways. In other words, tourism *could* be a site for negotiated subjectivities, but all too often tends to get hijacked by dominant discourses reinforced in 'gaze' relations.

As explained above, MacCannell's (1979) 'demand for authenticity' became a major theme in tourism studies but, similarly, 'gaze' analysis has been challenged in the questioning of who establishes the grounds on which anything is deemed authentic. Morris's (1995) observations on the idea of objectification, inherent in the 'gaze' through practices of cultural consumption that impose a valuation of authenticity by an outside dominant culture, have had a major influence on tourism critique. The interplay of changing social constructions of work and home, alongside globalization and the continued undertaking of travel and tourism activities, challenges tourism studies to free the understanding of travel from particular histories of 'European, literary, male, bourgeois, scientific, heroic and recreational meanings' (Clifford, 1997: 31). That is, the normative neutrality of analysis of techniques and technologies of subject construction needs the social justice analysis underpinning legitimacy of 'belonging' to enable growth of the plurality of concrete lived experience as relevant to how we arrange knowledge of ourselves and others in the tourism frame.

Producing the active constitution of the 'other' via the 'gaze' is obviously a problem for those interested in disrupting knowledge power relations for identity axes such as gender, sexuality, race and social class. Some identities are enhanced and amplified, with others muted or written out of legitimacy in myriad profound and minute ways. Though Urry has not pursued implications of the 'gaze' as an emancipatory agenda, analytic space is opened for others, notably Rojek, to problematize the making of subjectivities, particularly through moral valorization, which enables some voices and disables others into a very narrow or non-existent set of choices to 'be'.

Urry's work did not explicitly engage with the governmentality literature that emerged most fully following publication of Burchell *et al.*'s (1991) book, *The Foucault Effect*, which laid out the agenda of what has become 'Governmentality Studies' – the analysis of knowledge authorities that institutionalize 'gazes' that we work on ourselves. Most of this work has been contained in analyses of the professions and the state as well as other recognizable 'institutional' practices. Work on governmentality themes as an extension of Urry's 'gaze' within the tourism frame has been taken up by scholars such as Hollinshead (1999), Feighery (2009), Hollinshead *et al.* (2009) and Werry (2008) to explore power and surveillance utilized through the institutions, organizations and agencies that regulate tourism environments and, in doing so, conduct the epistemological work to set frames of meaning and limits to action, through a range of explicit rules of practice that dominate tourism (including more subtle forms such as tourist brochures).

Certainly the regulation for the self, 'other' and place relation 'from afar' sets up neoliberalism as something to be escaped from. Tourism is also often presented as a good exit door to open up the possibility for 'wild' forms of experience. But what if today tourism is not an escape from anywhere or anybody or any 'thing'? What if there is no more exotic to be found when differences between past and present, away and home, self and 'other' all disappear in the postmodern authorless self disconnected from structured meaning? Chris Rojek takes us into forms of analysis to pose and answer these and related questions.

Rojek and the expansion of the parameters of analysis

Chris Rojek has interpreted sociological themes into the study of leisure for over 25 years, beginning with class analysis in *Capitalism and Leisure Theory* (Rojek, 1985), and continuing through main themes of cultural analysis as they have taken their turns in the sociological literature. Rojek's agenda has always been to explicitly 'sociologize' Leisure Studies by taking social theory seriously and engaging with its main debates from a position that makes the very category 'leisure' contingent on the full range of phenomena and problems located in broader programmes of theory and practice. That is, we can't take leisure seriously if we refuse the category its contingent relations to all other dimensions of experience that might have leisure as a 'border' condition, and that such border conditions (including the slippery category of 'work') are bound up in discursive practices that also shift and change with the emergence of social relations in tension.

Perhaps Rojek's main contribution to the field of tourism has been an extension of some of Urry's themes of the constitution of subjectivity in the pursuit of desire and the exotic as omnipresent in the postmodern world. In doing this he reminds us that the *reason* for travel is never fixed or monolithic and is historically constituted both in practice and in theory. The emergence of the postmodern *condition* meant an abandonment and collapsing (de-differentiation) of modernity's categories as a field of immutable practice and postmodern*ism* as an abandonment of grand-theoretical constructions of social problems. The 'de-differentiated' subject, and indeed tourist, unhooks reason and practice for travel from the exotic, because the mundane/exotic distinction disappears along with the solidity of the subject positions from whence came the discovery of 'difference' that is inherent in 'away'. Any self-actualization that might come from meeting the genuine 'other' disappears entirely when there is no 'other' as distinct from the 'self'. Subject positions (such as gender, class, race etc.) are not fixed in biographies that have to be counter-hegemonically transcended through discovery of *foreign* configurations because nothing is foreign when 'worlds' are de-differentiated by floods of popular culture that somewhat obviate physical travel as well as demand an emergent desire to 'play' with iconography, the consumption of which amplifies the radically flexible 'self'.

Pronovost (1997) criticized Rojek for somehow ignoring desire and play with an overemphasis on subjectivity constitution as a critique of the 'freedom' objective. After all, Rojek's critique of travel as a 'way of escape' renders analysis of freedoms and unfreedoms obsolete, reinforcing the position that no place, person or thing is 'free' to articulate the self because of the removal of any constraining condition, including 'place' as 'home' (not free) versus 'away' (free). As he explains:

> We confront these attractions as members of a particular class, race, nation and civilization. And were we able truly to abandon these identity values we could no longer function. Our escape attempts are therefore themselves artificial. They are encoded activities with structural parameters. There is no escape.
>
> (Rojek, 1993: 12)

Certainly the emphasis on structuring can make the social subject look more than just a bit passive and unaware of the primordial free place called 'play', unless we accept that indeed 'play' is at the heart of postmodern practices of making the pastiche of the self. In other words, that play is somehow constituted elsewhere doesn't matter so much as the proposition that personhood is play in the active and continuous game of presentation and re-presentation. The active social subject is somewhat rescued from passivity in this playful self and could be read as finally emancipated from the need to concretely situate the self in any meaning other than what is rendered in the moment of taking on and enacting a set of discursive practices. On the other hand, Rojek's position in the quote above is under no illusion that the iconographic self is already bound up with a consumerism of signs that has its roots in popular culture. The tension in this formulation is redolent of Rojek's rejection of essentialist dualisms bound up in the historical contingency of work/leisure that enables the moral foundation for traditional leisure social analysis. It is no surprise, then, that liminality (boundaries where categories uncomfortably meet) is the seat of simultaneously constraining and enabling subjectivity with the radical collision or fusion of meanings that are constituent of boundary conditions. The agency/structure debate melts away when agency and structure are mutually constitutive. Even 'freedoms' require permissions.

Rojek has won no friends in the 'old school' academy that dogmatically pushes tropes of domination/submission through lenses of Marxism, feminisms or other 'isms', since, as argued above, the unfreedoms expressed by the oppressed are situated in discourses of what counts as an unfreedom, and just as hegemonic as what is being critiqued. Rojek's treatment of criminality as 'play' meant his alienation from the healthy recreation and physical education scholarship with its quest to 'save' the oppressed from their lives of poverty, crime and servitude. Rather, Rojek takes all cultural expressions seriously and engages his analysis from the position of the 'oppressed' by ignoring the 'oppression', reconstituting it as making sense of immersion in contradictory meanings to produce something new (but not immune from knowledge in any way) in a loud and playful manner that establishes authority in ways only very narrowly comprehensible for governing institutions. Humour, desire and anger could be the more important seat of playfulness than any absence of constraint could ever hope for.

At one level, Rojek's work is subversive of the field in which it is most hungrily consumed. What do we do when the solidity of categories has gone, particularly the thing called 'leisure?' Robert Stebbins's 'Serious Leisure' also has the potential to utterly ruin the field as a distinct domain of study because 'fun' can be had anywhere, including work; and non-work can start looking like a 'career'. *Homo ludens* and *Homo faber* have passed away as separate or antagonistic subjectivities and what we are left with is an analysis of pleasure. The placing of morality as a theoretical problem to be overcome or minimally re-organized has been enormously productive for contemporary scholarship by opening up the field of possibility of questions and routes of answers. Though not all follow Rojek's bold moves into controversial positions, his work has undeniably stimulated a small army of Leisure Studies scholars to adopt European cultural and political theory as launch-points for analysis and has thoroughly destabilized who counts as the 'good guys' and the 'bad guys', the morally correct and the thoroughly bad in need of correcting in traditional 'social' theorizing in the field of the sociology of leisure. Rojek (2005) declares his positioning in the introduction to *Leisure Theory: Principles and Practice*:

Twenty years ago, I criticized Leisure Studies for coining theories of 'leisure without society'. Despite the many important contributions to leisure theory made by others in succeeding years, I find myself maintaining that this criticism holds good. That is one reason why a good deal of this book is devoted to demonstrating that leisure must be analyzed as an institution that is inextricably linked to wider, global questions of economic resource allocation, status distribution and civic regulation.

(Rojek, 2005: 15)

287

Following this advice, we are invited to examine the tourism experience as it extends far beyond the actual tourist visit, preparations or post-trip stories. In this respect, Rojek (1993: 133) raises significant questions about the relation between 'authenticity' and experience at empirical and theoretical levels. At the empirical level, the quest for authenticity and self-realization has come to an end and tourism is now equivalent to mere consumption activity. However, at the theoretical level, Rojek (1993: 126) warns us not to consume grand theories of historical change common to modernist thinkers (Marx and Durkheim, in particular), but to emphasize the 'discontinuity of change and the irregularity of association and practice enabling us to problematise universal categories of ontology and epistemology'. Rojek's suggestion that tourism can become generalized and de-differentiated places emphasis on the different meanings and elements that can and do arise in postmodernity. Is it folly, Rojek asks, in this respect, to view the tourist experience as paving the way towards self-realization or 'consciousness raising?' (Rojek, 1993: 212). Significantly here, it must be asked whether contemporary tourism offers an over-determined capitalist form of escape, a site of struggle and resistance, something that has disappeared in a postmodern mish-mash. With the 'problem' of freedom mostly relegated to irrelevance in postmodern analysis of tourist subjectivity, what then happens with ideas of leisure as 'freely chosen activity' (Roberts, 1978), or 'self-enhancing experience' (Kelly, 1982; Rojek, Shaw and Veal, 2006)? Certainly, commodification has the potential to constrain rather than enhance freedom (Cook, 2007); however, 'broader questions of freedom and control', as they say, 'have been narrowed around the right to consumer choice' (Clarke and Critcher, 1985: 232). Choices are always constituted within social and cultural configurations, and without a way to privilege subject positions perhaps the way forward is to emancipate ourselves from 'freedoms and their barriers' as the launch-point for positive theoretical growth and policy action.

Rojek (1993: 114) argues that 'travel, it was thought, led to the accumulation of experience and wisdom. One began with nothing, but through guidance, diligence and commonsense one gained knowledge and achieved self-realization.' The death of the concrete subject as author of experience inside of postmodern theory is emancipatory of responsibility to be or do anything at all, including the ability to 'self-realize'. There is 'no-self realization' in the postmodern formula. Perhaps another way forward for critical analysis might be to return to concerns with positive and negative tensions of 'belonging' and the value of ontological diversity to open-ended social change, at which point we look toward parameters and strategies of negotiating biographies as meaningful to make a way forward in recovering optimism for tourism as something mutually beneficial for self and 'other'. Perhaps by living in and learning about other people and cultures, in an environment of mutual benefit and cooperation, one is able to engage in a transformation and the development of the self in concert with the 'other'. No freedoms or unfreedoms are needed in this kind of frame for us to theorize what better kinds of tourism might look like.

Summary and conclusions

This discussion began with MacCannell's symbolic interactionist perspective, which adopts the 'front-stage/back-stage' methodological device to explore the ways in which self and other mutually negotiate in the active drama of home and away. MacCannell's formulation has produced a compelling exploration of the idea of 'authenticity'. Rather than making something problematic about authentic/fake, much work has been conducted to elaborate the negotiation of host/tourist relations within and between the facades of 'the set'.

Urry has similarly spurred a library full of analyses of ways in which we work on ourselves to be the 'right' kind of self or 'other' rendered through commercial desire that reproduces itself in our 'gaze', and the other way around. Adopting Foucault's Panopticon metaphor, the thrust of 'gaze' analysis has been to elaborate how the meanings of self and 'other' are made from governing dimensions far beyond the 'frame' of immediate interaction. Urry's work can be readily adopted in analyses of neo-liberal knowledge authorities and how we work on ourselves (as objects of the 'gaze') to be who the authoritative 'other' (holder of 'gaze') so desires. In this formulation, places are subject to the tourist's 'gaze' and make themselves as 'the tourist' would most likely consume. Here authenticity is quite irrelevant and unproblematic. The 'tourist' is also 'made' within this 'gaze' as an ensemble of 'awayness' with a set of codes elaborated when 'away'. Here tourists and the locales they go to simultaneously constitute one another in relations of production and consumption of the exotic that need no explicit negotiation because each is active in working on themselves to be and become responsible subject positions. This style of formulation is similar to the position adopted in much of the governmentality literature in search of knowledge authorities that we find ourselves made within. There are indeed no dark spaces where untainted subjectivity dwells (essential subjectivity), so there is no essential subject in need of rescuing from nasty structuring processes that would cause us to be who we are rather than the 'natural' person we would become if said structuring were not there (the 'problem' of ideology in Marxism). Tourism then allows us no release from false consciousness because there is nothing 'false' about consciousness.

The 'gaze' formulation as a descriptive mode of tourism action has been taken up by scholars with explicitly normative thrusts, absent from the original analysis. Heteronormativity, gender responsibilization and whiteness are all produced and reproduced by the 'gaze' in ways that disable expansion of legitimate subject positions and strategic action beyond what knowledge authorities (including biographical 'experience') might dish up. Here the problem becomes a political one of how subjectivities are negotiated.

The normative neutrality of both MacCannell's and Urry's work is underscored by anxieties of autonomy produced within the constraints of modernity. That, while technically, there is nothing in either formulation that points to anyone in need of rescuing from 'fakeness', desire for authentic rendering of the exotic, these could be read as a response to the mundane manufactures of modernity. Problems of the constitutive 'gaze' can also be read as anxiety over being controlled from afar, and even worse, with our own joyful participation. Rojek's work in general, and on tourism in particular, distinguished itself from that of the prior two authors through its roots in a sociology of leisure with emancipatory claims. That is, modernity caused work to become the central feature of who we are and the erosion (or extension) of modernities has meant extension of a kaleidoscopic range of possible ways that we can articulate ourselves without the need for reference to any particular biographical anchor. De-differentiation (collapsing of primordial difference between people and other objects in the tourism *field* of analysis) that comes with the postmodern condition can indeed be read as a departure from anachronistic categories that constrain choice. On the other hand, we may have left the pot to leap into the fire of malleability and vulnerability to commercial manufacture of titillation where the reach for consumption is all the meaning we really need. Tourism in this view is merely one form of consumption among others. Rojek's critique of postmodern life is that mere consumerism is no 'escape' from anything when the mundane and exotic are collapsed in a 'world-class' spectacle and become the only reasons for bothering to go somewhere.

These three authors have contributed a move into theory that suggests that we navigate social structures not of our own choosing, and that this means constantly negotiating subjectivities. In the tourism context, the distinction between home/not home means negotiating relations of otherness. If we can dispense with tourism as a dichotomy of freedom (true insight) versus unfreedom (pre-determined unawareness) it becomes possible to engage an analysis of negotiation as a critical target. Even the stereotypical package tourist can negotiate some time off from full immersion in the 'show' that is a 'European summer'. Recovery of memories is not just a marketing outcome, but also a rendering that must be interpreted within the context of the visitors' and hosts' biographies that far pre- and post-date their physical meeting. People and places have 'agency'; and theories have their own 'unfreedoms' from which we must be rescued.

Tourists 'gaze' at leisure-oriented cultural spaces such as wildlife, museums, heritage, local festivals and beaches in a way that now allows us to theorize these beyond the strictures of the market, structuralism and functionalism, creating new directions to imagine these physical spaces and their concomitant symbolic cultural signs and symbols. We are enabled with better tools to contest particular stories of ourselves and of places in ways that side-step 'freedom' as a route to productive meaning.

Side-stepping freedoms/unfreedoms as routes into new theoretical agendas in tourism research and the sociology of leisure in general might expand with Rojek's problem-oriented theoretical pragmatism that takes the play of situated meaning seriously while recognizing that 'agencies' have roots to enable and honour difference. We advocate that the future project for tourism theory is to continue to open up spaces for the 'other' to move beyond pre-determined spaces for articulation of the desire 'to be' and to envisage spaces which extend both guest's and host's horizons and provide the potential for personal and political growth. In terms of sociological perspectives of tourism, we find that they have reflected the dominant theoretical concerns extant in sociology generally and in the sociology of leisure as a professional practice.

Perhaps escape *from* the workaday world, as suggested by Rojek (1993), is an illusion, but tourism can still be a shift *to* a social space which allows for learning and growing. Nor is tourism the mere description of the passing 'gaze' at objects, either authentic or unauthentic. We can see, when looking closer, that the concept of tourism, like that of leisure (see Wearing and Wearing, 1996), needs to go beyond ideas concerning free time (away from home, in this case) and activities (available in the tourist destination) to the making of experience so that the tourist her/himself has a part to play in the active construction of the tourist experience and the host-community member is acknowledged as a person in that experience rather than a homogenized 'other'. A concentration on tourist destination as image in tourist advertising and tourist research (see Bramwell and Rawding, 1996; Cohen, 1995; Dilley, 1986; Echtner and Brent Ritchie, 1991; Gartner, 1993; Hunt, 1975; Telisman-Kosuta, 1989) tends to interpret that each individual's experience of the tourist destination will be similar and ignores the possibility of subversive subject positions (see Dann, 1995; Rowe and Stevenson, 1994). We would like to conclude that the three authors discussed in this chapter have opened a more useful perception of social relations in tourism as those which enable the possible elaboration of a diversity of subject positions as agencies from which we make the new.

Note

1   MacCannell (1992: 1).

References

Bramwell, B. and Rawding, L. (1996) 'Tourism Marketing Images of Industrial Cities', *Annals of Tourism Research* 23: 201–221.

Burchell, G., Gordon, C. and Miller, P. (eds) (1991) *The Foucault Effect: Studies in Governmentality with Two Lectures by and an Interview with Foucault.* Chicago: University of Chicago Press.

Caton, K. and Santos, C. (2009) 'Images of the Other: Selling Study Abroad in a Postcolonial World', *Annals of Tourism Research* 48 (2) 191–204.

Clarke, J and Critcher, C. (1985) *The Devil Makes Work: Leisure in Capitalist Britain.* London: Macmillan.

Clifford, J. (1997) *Routes: Travel and Translation in the Late Twentieth Century.* Cambridge, MA: Harvard University Press.

Cohen, C.B. (1995) 'Marketing Paradise, Making Nation', *Annals of Tourism Research* 22: 404–421.

Cook, D.T. (2007) 'Leisure and Consumption', in C. Rojek, A.J. Veal and S.M. Shaw (eds) *A Handbook of Leisure Studies.* Basingstoke: Palgrave Macmillan.

Dann, G. (1995) 'A Socio-Linguistic Approach towards Changing Tourist Imagery', in R. Butler and D. Pearce (eds) *Change in Tourism: People, Places, Processes.* London and New York: Routledge.

Dilley, R.S. (1986) 'Tourist Brochures and Tourist Images', *Canadian Geographer* 30: 59–65.

Echtner, C.M. and Brent Ritchie, J.R. (1991) 'The Meaning and Measurement of Destination Image', *Journal of Tourism Studies* 2: 2–12.

Feighery, W. (2009) 'Tourism, Stock Photography and Surveillance: A Foucauldian Interpretation', *Journal of Tourism and Cultural Change* 7 (3) 161–178.

Foucault, M. (1975) *The Birth of the Clinic: An Archaeology of Medical Perception.* New York: Vintage Books.

Foucault, M. (1977) *Discipline and Punish: The Birth of the Prison.* New York: Vintage Books.

Gartner, W. (1993) 'Image Formation Process', *Journal of Travel and Tourism Marketing* 2: 191–215.

Goffman, E. (1961) *The Presentation of the Self in Everyday Life.* Harmondsworth: Penguin.

Hollinshead, K. (1999) 'Surveillance of the Worlds of Tourism: Foucault and the Eye-of-Power', *Tourism Management* 20: 7–23.

Hollinshead, K., Ateljevic, I. and Ali, N. (2009) 'Worldmaking Agency – Worldmaking Authority: The Sovereign Constitutive Role of Tourism', *Touring Geographies* 11 (4) 427.

Horne, D. (1992) *The Intelligent Tourist.* McMahon's Point, NSW: Margaret Gee Publishing.

Hunt, J.D. (1975) 'Image as a Factor in Tourism Development', *Journal of Travel Research* 13: 1–7.

Kelly, J.R. (1982) *Leisure.* Illinois: Prentice Hall.

MacCannell, D. (1979) *The Tourist: A New Theory of the Leisure Class.* Los Angeles: University of California Press.

MacCannell, D. (1992) *Empty Meeting Grounds: The Tourist Papers.* London: Routledge.

MacCannell, D. (2000) 'Symbolic Capital: Urban Design for Tourism', *Journeys*, June–December: 157–183.

Morris, M. (1995) 'Life as a Tourist Object in Australia', in M. Lanfant, J. Allcock and E. Bruner (eds) *International Tourism: Identity and Change.* London: Sage.

Pronovost, G. (1997) 'A Critique of the Works of Rojek' *Loisir et Société/Society and Leisure* 20 (2) 549–554.

Roberts, K. (1978) *Contemporary Society and the Growth of Leisure.* London: Longman.

Rojek, C. (1985) *Capitalism and Leisure Theory.* London: Tavistock.

Rojek, C. (1993) *Ways of Escape. Modern Transformations in Leisure and Travel.* Basingstoke: Macmillan.

Rojek, C. (2005) 'An Outline of the Action Approach to Leisure Studies', *Leisure Studies* 24 (1) 13–25.

Rojek, C., Shaw, S.M. and Veal, A.J. (2006) 'Introduction: Process and Content', in C. Rojek, S.M. Shaw and A.J. Veal (eds), *A Handbook of Leisure Studies.* Basingstoke, UK: Palgrave Macmillan.

Rowe, D. and Stevenson, D. (1994) '"Provincial Paradise": Urban Tourism and City Imaging outside the Metropolis', *The Australian and New Zealand Journal of Sociology* 30: 178–193.

Simms, K. (ed.) (1997) *Ethics and the Subject.* Amsterdam, Atlanta: Rodopi.

Telisman-Kosuta, N. (1989) 'Tourism Destination Image', in S.F. Witt and L. Moutinho (eds) *Tourism Marketing and Managing Handbook.* New York: Prentice Hall.

Tribe, J. (2008) 'Tourism: A Critical Business', *Journal of Travel Research* 46: 245–255.

Urry, J. (1990) *The Tourist Gaze: Leisure and Travel in Contemporary Societies.* London: Sage.

Urry, J. (2002) *The Tourist Gaze: Leisure and Travel in Contemporary Societies.* 2nd ed. London: Sage.

Wearing, B.M. and Wearing, S.L. (1996) 'Refocussing the Tourism Experience: The Flaneur and the Choraster', *Leisure Studies* 16: 229–243.

Werry, M. (2008) 'Tourism, Race and the State of Nature: On the Biopoetics of Government', *Cultural Studies* 22 (3) 391–411.

PART IV

THE BIG SEVEN LEISURE PURSUITS

25

THE ANNUAL HOLIDAY

Its rise, transformations, expansion and fragmentation

John K. Walton

Delineations and definitions

The annual holiday away from home, an invented calendar custom (but increasingly also a movable feast), can be regarded as a British invention of the eighteenth century, at least in its commercial guise. It has spread and mutated across the globe, building on and incorporating local traditions as it mutates and ramifies; and as a concept it needs to be distinguished from the 'day out', the 'week-end away' and the 'short break' distributed through the recreational calendar. The 'annual holiday' should also be differentiated from the kind of pleasure regime in which several holidays are taken during the year: the concept entails the holiday as special occasion within the calendar, repeated every year, and perhaps taking on the character of ritual, calendar custom or even pilgrimage. It may involve returning annually to the same place, and is likely to be associated with people of limited resources, though sufficient for the purpose. It is not the same as the seasonal itinerancies of the leisured society of the wealthy, migrating from one fashionable location to another to observe the rituals of conspicuous consumption and display: these are the lifestyle choices of those who are able to float above the quotidian disciplines of industrial and bureaucratic labour, and for whom what to others might be 'holidays' become a way of life. For its votaries, the annual holiday, as such, was something special, to be saved for and looked forward to, a red-letter period in the calendar to be set aside, safeguarded, enhanced and enjoyed. In the late 1930s the Bolton-based anthropological research organization Mass Observation labelled the regular week at the British seaside 'the fifty-second week' and invested it with significance akin to a religious pilgrimage (Cross, 1990). Above all, the idea of the annual holiday has come to be identified with the regular rhythms of industrial society and the leisure needs of waged workers who were subjected to a measure of labour discipline: the 'leisure class' did not need annual holidays.

This chapter examines the development of the 'annual holiday' in relation to custom, invented tradition, labour relations, social policy, transport and systems of provision, adopting a global perspective looking outwards and across from British and European origins, and charting continuities and changes from the rise of the 'annual holiday' as an institution, through its heyday in Western industrial society, to its post-industrial fragmentation and complication at the turn of the millennium. We begin with the pioneering British example.

In the British setting, the annual holiday took up anything between a few days and a month or more, expanding over time at working-class level as holiday entitlements extended and living standards rose. For skilled or supervisory manual and routine clerical workers it often lasted for a week, by the end of the nineteenth century, especially in the northern factory districts (and above all in the Lancashire textile-manufacturing region). By the inter-war years, at least for the better-off in skilled and supervisory jobs, a fortnight was becoming more usual for those in work, who were benefiting from falling prices and smaller family sizes, and this trend was accentuated by the general availability of paid holidays and the extension of entitlements during the 1950s and 1960s. Even in Britain, the annual holiday never became universal: even in the most favoured districts, and the most 'affluent' years of the 1960s and 1970s, it remained out of the reach of many casual workers who were unable to budget ahead for this sort of 'lumpy' expenditure; of agricultural workers with low wages and limited access to cheap holiday public transport; and of people in the troughs of the 'poverty cycle', whether with large numbers of dependent children or the reduced earning power and physical mobility of old age. And many preferred to stay at home. But by the 1950s few urban Britons would go through their lives unable or unwilling to enjoy an annual holiday away from home, even though this might be restricted to the most prosperous periods of the family life-course.

The making of the annual holiday in Britain

Certain distinctive features of the British experience should be highlighted, and certain pervasive myths dispelled. The annual holiday as such was originally a middle-class invention. In its commercial form it originally depended on access to environments and facilities which had been created for their wealthier and more leisured social superiors, whose income came from rents and investments. Early industrialists might be slaves to the oversight of their factories, at least before the emergence of a trustworthy, techni-cally competent cadre of 'managers' (Pollard, 1968); but the emergent commercial and professional middle classes of the eighteenth century were not necessarily bound by a stultifying work ethic, and awarded themselves consecutive time for travel and pleasure, social emulation and the accumulation of cultural capital. This enabled the rapid expan-sion of spas and seaside resorts, which gathered momentum from the second quarter of the eighteenth century; of the European Grand Tour (in truncated form) as more than just an elite rite of passage; and of tourism to the Alps, the English Lake District and other areas of newly fashionable mountain scenery. On the other hand, the earliest versions of an annual holiday for working people involved temporarily returning home (domestic serv-ants returning from the city or the 'big house' to see their families, migrants returning to their villages at the local 'wakes' or fair), or varying their work routine by doing paid harvest work in hop fields or orchards (Poole, 1994).

The middle-class family holiday became the great staple business of most resorts in the eighteenth century and remained the most lucrative market in Victorian and Edwardian England, whether at the seaside or in the country. The spa or mineral-springs resort was the main exception, with its focus on routines associated with the rituals of taking the cure and the exchange of polite sociability in Assembly Rooms, pleasure gardens and theatres. The spas' lack of adaptability to the changing demographics of the market helps to explain their flagging performance after their Georgian heyday, and the growing importance of retire-ment and commuting rather than holiday-making even in expansive urban economies like those of Cheltenham or Harrogate. 'Taking the cure' was not in itself an 'annual holiday', although the amenities of a spa or hydro might make it an attractive venue for one (Durie, 2012). The spread of the family holiday through the middle classes was greatly facilitated by the 'steam revolution' in transport, to provide cheaper and more reliably timetabled journeys than by sail or stage-coach. Affluent Victorian families might spend several weeks at the coast, complete with servants, and the humorous magazine *Punch* caricatured the hazards of the journey, the development of holiday routines and the dullness of small, respectable family resorts. The week-end 'husband boat' delivering London businessmen and professionals to their families at Margate was already the butt of jokes before steam displaced sail in the 1830s, but the railway extended the opportunities for the less-affluent, including clerical workers with holiday entitlements, to take the children to the coast for a week or two. Enduring children's seaside rituals such as the donkey ride, sandcastle building and shrimping in rock-pools became familiar from the beginning of the nineteenth century, while alfresco entertainment by blackface 'minstrels', 'German' brass bands and later by *pierrot* troupes became staples of the holiday routine. From the 1860s onwards every self-respecting coastal resort acquired a pier, with steamer excursions, dancing and musical and comic entertainments punctuating the holiday and shaping the expected contours of the experience. Smaller centres, distant or otherwise insulated from major industrial centres, combined the virtues of being socially 'select' with the boredom of reiterated routines and lack of amenities (Walton, 1983).

The British seaside was the dominant destination for the annual Victorian and Edwardian middle-class holiday, but there were alternatives. The countryside, hills, lakes and mountains had their appeal, especially after the eighteenth-century revolution in attitudes to upland scenery, according to the canons of the Picturesque and Sublime, which ran parallel to the new desirability of coastal and maritime landscapes (Corbin, 1994). The Romantic movement also stimulated scenic tourism and fostered the attractions of literary landscapes associated with the works of Sir Walter Scott or William Wordsworth, while Evangelicalism engendered religious awe at the magnificence of the Creator's work (Hanley and Walton, 2010: ch. 5). The English Lake District brought all these strands together, and by the late nineteenth century a working-class 'outdoor movement' pursuing 'rational holidays' in the hills, and avoiding the commercial fleshpots of the popular resorts, was getting under way (Taylor, 1997). Moreover, just as the leisured vogue for touring within England was passed down in shortened form to make a middle-class holiday, so the aristocratic Grand Tour of Europe, where the literary landscapes were those associated with Classical authors, might be boiled down to a fortnight on the Rhine or in Northern Italy, while the 'discovery' of the Alps was similarly democratized, in processes which were already apparent before the railways were connected (Hanley and Walton, 2010: chs 5–6). The energetic lower middle-class Thomas Cook tourists of the 1860s, stretching limited means and time to soak up as many sights and cultural experiences as possible, were particularly controversial adaptors of this European dimension of the annual holiday, while by the mid-nineteenth century many middle-class British people were frequenting Western European beach resorts (Brendon, 1991). 'Where shall we go?' became an annual theme, and an immense Victorian guide-book literature, together with newspaper press coverage, began to pose questions and propose answers (Steward, 2006). Even among the comfortable Victorian middle classes, however, the annual holiday might take the form of a visit to distant 'family and friends', as in Molly Hughes' annual childhood journeys from London to Cornwall in the 1870s; and this was to remain important, though by its private and informal nature hidden from historians except via autobiography and interview (Hughes, 1977: 85–124).

The working-class holiday

The railways enabled working-class visitors in significant numbers to enter the commercial holiday market-place. At first this took the limited form of day-trips or week-end visits to established, mainly coastal venues. It is no accident that the annual holiday as a popular phenomenon first developed at the seaside, where it took enduring root (Walton, 1981). British beaches were open and accessible, and often easily divided into informally demarcated zones which allowed different classes and cultural preferences to coexist side by side, at a decorous distance (Travis, 1997). The lure of the sea, for health and play, together with the popular amusements that opened up on the beach and along the shore, was perhaps the most important driver of the emergence at working-class level of an annual holiday in surroundings that contrasted with the workaday routine, but were often shared with workmates, neighbours and family members from the same town, while at all social levels the holiday experience soon tended to develop routines of its own.

The annual holiday was invariably enjoyed in the summer. Winter holidays were 'extras' for the affluent. In its working-class guise, as it gathered momentum during the second half of the nineteenth century, it was identified with local holiday traditions, some of which were old-established religious festivals, while others were recent inventions, sometimes arising from the commercial opportunism of publicans. In Britain the most important of these were the Wakes holidays of industrial northern and midland England, which went under various local names (tides, fairs, feasts, races, thumps), together with the Glasgow Fair and other Scottish popular holidays. The annual holiday might exist alongside shorter breaks at other times, especially the great spring and summer religious festivals of Easter and Whitsuntide, which itinerated through the calendar over several weeks from year to year. The Bank Holidays Act of 1871 effectively gave Easter and Whit Mondays the status of public holidays (the latter was cut adrift from Whitsuntide and given a fixed date from 1971), and created a secular popular holiday on the first Monday in August, transferred to the last Monday of the month provisionally from 1965, and officially from 1971. Bank Holidays offered opportunities for additional short excursions to people whose main holiday took place at a different time. Over most of industrial Britain they were much less important than the Wakes holidays, which were staggered through the summer, enabling a viable popular holiday season lasting for at least two months in regional destination resorts (Walton, 1981; Barton, 2005). The emergent annual holiday also coexisted for many years with the observance of 'St Monday', an extension of the week-end for pleasure purposes which might involve an excursion by horse-drawn wagon or charabanc, train or (by the 1920s) motor-coach. This was widely observed in coal mining (especially), heavy industry and (for example) the London laundry trades, well into the twentieth century. It was in widespread decline by the mid-Victorian period, although the cutlery workshop and steelmaking economy of Sheffield was a stronghold for many years, as were the workshops of the Black Country around Wolverhampton and Dudley (Reid, 1976; Walton, 2000).

The exaggerated importance accorded to August Bank Holiday is one of several persistent myths about the history of popular holidays. The fame of August Bank Holiday Monday owes much to its identification with an individual politician, Sir John Lubbock, which provides a strong and attractive story line, and to the impact of its early metropolitan observance on the London media (Patton, 2007: 97–8, 101). Similarly, the role of the railways was more complicated than at first appears. The rapid expansion of the railway system from the 1840s made possible the great Victorian extension of the annual seaside holiday among the middle and working classes, without actually causing it: neither the provision of a system of cheap trains nor the popular preference for coastal destinations was inevitable. People had to want to use their limited leisure to travel, and to prefer the seaside as a holiday location (Walton, 1981). The penny-a-mile 'Parliamentary' trains introduced in 1844 were irrelevant: they were slow, stopped at all stations and were too expensive for long-distance leisure travel on very limited budgets. What mattered to emergent working-class demand was much faster and cheaper excursion provision, taking advantage of economies of scale at popular holiday times. This sector expanded rapidly from the 1840s, organized by paternalist employers, Sunday schools, the temperance movement, Mechanics' Institutes and private excursion agents, and increasingly by the railway companies themselves. Such day-trips helped to lay the groundwork for future extended holidays (Simmons, 1986: ch. 8; Smith, 1988; Reid, 1996). Contrary to persistent myth, Thomas Cook was never an important player in this market. His role in excursion provision for the London Great Exhibition of 1851, and in opening out Scottish and continental tours, did not extend to domestic seaside trips. These were provided mainly by regional and local operators (Brendon, 1991; Walton, 2010).

As Barton has emphasized, working-class seaside holidays were increasingly organized by the workers themselves, who took advantage of cheap commercial fares offered by the railway companies, sometimes brokered by Sunday schools, co-operatives, works committees or pubs (Barton, 2005). They often booked their own accommodation by post or sought it out on arrival, returning to the same lodging- or boarding-house (often run by someone from their home town) year after year, booking the next holiday at the end of the current one and enjoying the company of friends from the same town and work-place. A popular lodging and boarding industry developed to provide cheap, crowded holiday accommodation, especially in Blackpool and Douglas (Isle of Man). The development of a cheap, unpretentious, accessible accommodation market in popular destinations was as essential to the rise of the popular seaside holiday as were cheap fares, accessible beaches and popular entertainments (Walton, 1978; Walton, 1994; Beckerson, 2007).

The basis for the first extensions of day-trips into annual popular holidays on a large scale was the Wakes holidays of northern England, especially the 'cotton towns' of Lancashire. The 'Wakes' were a mixture of local religious holidays, customary fairs and recently invented traditions which survived early industrialization, to be extended in the better times of the 1850s onwards, enabling week-end breaks which, by the 1880s and 1890s, were extending (especially in the Lancashire weaving district) to a whole week at the seaside (Poole, 1994). Employers learned to tolerate these holidays, the gradual, piecemeal extension of which was never opposed sufficiently to become a trade union issue. The destination was predominantly the seaside, although in the popular coastal resorts attractions on dry land became more important than the beach, as Blackpool, especially, multiplied its commercial popular entertainments and built its pleasure palaces: the Tower opened for business in 1894 (Pearson, 1991). The beach was important, but more for sitting, observing and relaxing than for bathing, while there was widespread celebration of the health-giving properties of sea air (Beckerson and Walton, 2005).

Crucially, these holidays were unpaid (and remained so in the cotton industry until after the Second World War). Popular savings clubs, based on work-places, chapels, pubs, streets and local football clubs, developed to finance holidays (and holiday clothing), and the summer quarterly dividends on purchase issued by the successful local Co-operative societies made their contribution. The late-Victorian rise of the first working-class consumer society in the Lancashire cotton-spinning and weaving districts, as falling basic prices made room in budgets for sport, entertainment, fashion and holidays, was the essential context for the working-class seaside holiday. This was a high-pressure economy, founded on hard industrial work by women and adolescents as well as men, and it was not all-inclusive, even in the 'cotton towns' with their high family incomes. Young families, especially those with only one earner, and the unskilled or unemployed, were shut out, unless they could join a charity day-trip. But the growth of popular purchasing power here was essential to the growth not only of Blackpool, but also of an arc of resorts from North Wales to Morecambe, including the Isle of Man (Walton, 1983; Walton 1987: ch. 13).

Lancashire cotton (and, for example, engineering) workers were ahead of the game. West Yorkshire lagged a couple of decades behind, and Liverpool, unlike Manchester, did not send thousands of workers to the late-Victorian beaches, except on ferries across the Mersey to New Brighton. Nor did north-eastern industrial workers get beyond local day-trip range (Huggins, 1984). But seaside holiday-making was spreading among the 'labour aristocracy' in the industrial Midlands by the 1880s and 1890s. Meanwhile the Glasgow fair holiday began to make an impact on the Clyde estuary and the Isle of Man. Between the late nineteenth century and the 1960s the great 'railway factories', as at Swindon or Crewe, sent off their tens of thousands during the works holiday week, with a cut-price privilege ticket system easing the financial pain until paid holidays were introduced in 1938. For a week in July, the Cornish fishing port of St Ives became 'Swindon-by-the-sea'. Alfred Williams, the 'Hammerman Poet', described how the months from Easter to July were spent looking forward to the Swindon 'Trip', while the autumn and winter were full of post-trip gloom until the Christmas break. Such a holiday-related emotional calendar must have been common in all kinds of factory or routine work (Williams, 1915: 245, 248; Redfern, 1983: 126–7; Matheson, 2006). The huge London market was dominated by clerks and shopkeepers. Many of the former, as in the railway towns, were entitled to a fortnight's paid holiday. August Bank Holiday was more important in the south-east, and London working-class holiday-makers might use it to extend a seaside week-end at Southend or Hastings (Walton, 1981; Walton, 1983). For poorly paid workers in London's East End the annual 'holiday' often took the form of hard work in the hop fields of Kent, Sussex and adjoining counties, with squalid sanitation and sleeping accommodation, a pattern that persisted into the 1960s and had its counterparts in Black Country workers picking fruit and hops in the Vale of Evesham and Herefordshire (Samuel, 1981: 136–9).

Britain between the wars

These holiday systems persisted and spread on the established model until the transition which began in the 1960s and 1970s. There were important changes in the meantime. More middle-class people escaped from the growing working-class seaside presence in Britain by taking refuge at French coastal resorts or in the Alps, although the rise of winter sports was more about additional holidays than 'annual' ones (Barton, 2008). Mass unemployment in the old industrial areas during the inter-war depression did less damage to the annual holiday than might have been expected, as prices fell and people found ways of going on cheap holidays even when out of work. The development of 'plotland' settlements where old tramcars and railway carriages were converted into cheap accommodation offered an informal new holiday alternative, although perhaps more for week-ends than annual holidays (Ward and Hardy, 1984). Holiday camps, at first run by religious, socialist or co-operative organizations, and then commercially from the 1930s by Butlin and his rivals, were geared up to providing an 'all-in' holiday for a week or a fortnight, whether spartan or 'luxury', a relative term. They reached their peak as a regular family destination in the 1950s (Hardy and Ward, 1986). The rise of the static caravan as a cheap destination for an annual holiday, usually on the coast, was a feature of the 1950s onwards: there were 4,200 on the Lincolnshire coast in 1950, 11,000 in 1959 and 21,000 in 1974, supplemented by thousands of little holiday 'chalets' (Akhtar and Humphries, 2000; Barton, 2005: 169–71). These new, cheaper, less-inhibiting forms of holiday accommodation grew in step with the extension of paid holidays to widening sectors of the working class. This latter gathered momentum in the early 1920s, when it was pushed up the trade union agenda, and recovered traction during the 1930s, to spread further during the Second World War in the aftermath of the Holidays with Pay Act of 1938, and become general when the Act was officially brought into force. It was at this point that the democratization of popular access to the annual holiday reached its fullest development (Walton, 2000: 59–60: Barton, 2005: ch. 5).

Post-war Britain

The increasing prosperity (with full employment) of the post-war generation was accompanied by incremental extensions of paid holiday entitlements. A fortnight's paid holiday became normal from the early 1950s, and extensions to three weeks were becoming common even at working-class level by the late 1960s. This gave expanded access to short breaks and second holidays, especially for young people without children, and older people whose families were independent (Walton, 2000: 61–6). A geographically ambitious guide to European seaside resorts, published in 1959 and extending to Greece and Sweden, assumed that its (middle-class) readers would have a fortnight's main family holiday and that they would have little flexibility about when it was taken (Cooper, 1959: 1–2). From the 1950s a revolution in holiday-making began, as swelling numbers of British people took their main annual holidays abroad, building on long-standing minority middle-class attachments to (especially) the French and Belgian coast, the Rhine, the Alps and the historic cities of northern Italy, but now descending on the Mediterranean coast in ever-growing numbers in search of guaranteed sunshine, cheap alcohol and (for some) exotic encounters (Akhtar and Humphries, 2000; Barton, 2005: ch. 8). This is usually associated with the charter flight and the cheap package holiday, but prominent among its early incarnations were the international coach tour, a development of the 1930s which flourished especially in the 1950s and 1960s, and independent travel involving camping by car, hitch-hiking and backpacking by train (Hough, 1957; Walton, 2011).

The growth of new European markets for the annual holiday involved social groups which had hardly holidayed 'abroad' in the past. It gathered momentum gradually at first. Official statistics show sustained growth in British residents' holidays 'abroad' lasting more than four days, from 1.5 million in 1951 to 5 million in 1965, 5.75 in 1970 and 8.25 in 1973, on the eve of the oil crisis of the mid-1970s, which provided a temporary interruption to accelerating growth. The four-day threshold embraces a large but unknowable number of middle-class second and third holidays; and the number of holidays taken in Britain grew by at least as much as did holidays 'abroad' until 1970. Expansion during the 1960s was steady rather than spectacular, and overseas holiday travel was still mainly a middle-class market, especially for families, supplemented by young working-class people without children and by the more adventurous skilled workers. In 1966 white-collar and skilled manual workers accounted for 1,532,000 overseas holidays, out of 22 million people in those social groups, and growth among the 'semi-skilled', 'unskilled' and state pensioners was slower and later, although they accounted for 15 per cent of the market by 1972. Employers, professionals and managers dominated the statistics (Demetriadi, 1997: 52–8). This evidence challenges easy assumptions about the timing of the rise of the working-class 'sun and sand' tourist, even as the cheap airborne package tour gained ground as the favoured option; and it calls into question the uncritical application of the label 'mass tourism' to a set of phenomena which were much more complicated than this suggests (Wright, 2002).

The post-industrial holiday

At working-class level the annual holiday as a British institution, as effectively a commercialized calendar custom, was a product of industrial society, with its factories, regular work rhythms, collective bargaining and shared routines. Towards the end of the long post-war boom, fissures were beginning to appear in this long-established structure, even as the post-war welfare state appeared to consolidate it. The changes to Bank Holiday dates were straws in the wind of change. The purpose of moving August Bank Holiday to the end of the month was to reduce holiday congestion, a well-established concern of the Trades Union Congress; but the inflexibility of school holidays was the main problem here. As Peter Davies, the MP for Dover, suggested, the further extension of annual holiday entitlements would have been more beneficial than changed or additional Bank Holidays; and the comparative lack of statutory celebratory holidays in Britain, as compared with Europe and even the United States, probably helped rather than hindered the development of the annual holiday (Hansard, 4 March 1964, 30 November 1971).

The changes of the late twentieth century fragmented and dissolved the old certainties. Under the Thatcher governments the rapid rise of Mediterranean holiday-making among working-class people who still had jobs coincided with the collapse of the old mining and manufacturing industries, and the town holidays that were associated with them. Symptomatic of this was the disappearance from the calendar of the Lancashire Wakes holidays, although the decline of the cotton industry had been a much longer process. Holiday-making fragmented into shorter breaks spread through the year, with 'main' (rather than 'annual') holidays more likely to involve Mediterranean or long-haul destinations. The established British working-class resorts began to suffer from this combination of adverse changes, as the regular annual influxes no longer took place and the habitual ties between resorts and visitor hinterlands were broken by the rise of new destinations and a new generation with different expectations. The scale of the damage has sometimes been exaggerated, but it is all too visible in many traditional destination resorts, from Morecambe to Margate. The old industrial holiday patterns will never return (Browne and Walton, 2010).

Britain in comparative context

Viewed internationally, the British case is paradoxical. With an official paid holiday entitlement of 28 days per year, Britain tops the European league of holiday entitlements, more usual figures falling between 20 and 23 days; but it has fewer statutory public holidays (with eight) than anywhere else in the European Union except Holland (Renou, 2011). Britain pioneered the growth of annual holidays not only as a middle-class phenomenon, but also for the working class; but it did so without significant state or charitable intervention. After initial patronage by employers and (mainly) religious bodies, holidays were organized by the working class, for the working class, without even the initial benefit of paid holidays (Barton, 2005). Everywhere else in Europe, working-class holidays developed later and were stimulated by 'social tourism' interventions, whether promoted by the state, trade unions, religious organizations, co-operatives or collaboration between them. Such provision might include summer camps for workers and children, vouchers for cheap access to holiday services, and cheap holiday hotels for designated workers (Walton, 2012). The lack of such a structure in Britain is taken for granted, but it is remarkable when seen in wider context. It is a tribute to the agency and determination of British workers in pursuit of the annual holiday as an earned entitlement.

It is perhaps not surprising that the British were laggards in the provision of paid holidays. So much had been done without them, and international trade union campaigns were slow to make headway. The incomplete measure of 1938 came two years after the achievement of a fortnight's paid holiday in France and Belgium, for example, although many of the recipients were slow to take up the opportunities available, lacking the acculturation into holiday-making that their British counterparts had experienced over half a century (Furlough, 1998). During the 'thirty glorious years' of the post-war generation, other European countries were catching up, and the rush to the Mediterranean was a general northern European phenomenon, with Germany and Sweden also at the forefront (Kaiserfeld, 2010; Kopper, 2009). Europe, in turn, was well ahead of most of the rest of the world in developing a widespread expectation of an annual holiday as a citizen's right. Australia had a similar culture, now under threat from neo-liberalism, while the United States was always ambivalent about the morality of holiday-taking (White, 2005; Aron, 1999). Perhaps the strongest parallels, with a very strong 'social tourism' component, are the Cono Sur nations of Latin America, especially Argentina (Pastoriza, 2011). But, even within Europe, the British experience of the annual holiday has been both pioneering and unique.

References

Akhtar, M. and Humphries, S. (2000) *Some Liked It Hot.* London: Virgin Books.

Aron, C. (1999) *Working at Play.* New York: Oxford University Press.

Barton, S. (2005) *Working-Class Organisations and Popular Tourism, 1840–1970.* Manchester: Manchester University Press.

Barton, S. (2008) *Healthy Living in the Alps.* Manchester: Manchester University Press.

Beckerson, J. (2007) *Holiday Isle.* Douglas: Manx Heritage Foundation.

Beckerson, J., and Walton, J.K. (2005) 'Selling air: marketing the intangible at British resorts', in J.K. Walton (ed.) *Histories of Tourism,* Clevedon: Channel View, 55–68.

Brendon, P. (1991) *Thomas Cook: 150 Years of Popular Tourism.* London: Secker and Warburg.

Browne, P., and Walton, J.K. (eds) (2010) *Coastal Regeneration in English Resorts.* Lincoln: Coastal Communities Alliance.

Cooper, G. (1959) *The Seaside Resorts of Europe.* London: Cassell.

Corbin, A. (1994) *The Lure of the Sea.* Cambridge: Polity.

Cross, G. (1990) *Worktowners at Blackpool.* London: Routledge.

Demetriadi, J. (1997) 'The golden years, 1950–1974', in A. Williams and G. Shaw (eds) *The Rise and Fall of British Coastal Resorts.* London: Cassell, 49–74.

Durie, A. (2012) 'A fading movement: hydropathy at the Scottish hydros, 1840–1939', *Journal of Tourism History* 4: 57–74.

Furlough, E. (1998) 'Making mass vacations: tourism and consumer culture in France, 1930s to 1970s', *Comparative Studies in Society and History* 40: 247–286.

Hansard, *Parliamentary Debates,* 4 March 1964, 30 November 1971.

Hardy, D., and Ward, C. (1986) *Goodnight Campers!* London: Mansell.

Hough, G. (1957) *A Pound a Day Inclusive.* London: Hodder and Stoughton.

Huggins, M. (1984) 'Social tone and resort development in North-East England', *Northern History* 20: 187–206.

Hughes, M. (1977) *A London Girl of the 1870s.* Oxford: Oxford University Press.

Kaiserfeld, T. (2010) 'From sightseeing to sunbathing', *Journal of Tourism History* 2: 149–163.

Kopper, C.M. (2009) 'The breakthrough of the package tour in Germany after 1945', *Journal of Tourism History* 1: 67–92.

Matheson, R. (2006) *The Swindon Trip: The Annual Holiday for GWR's Swindon Works*. Stroud: The History Press.

Pastoriza, E. (2011) *La Conquista de las Vacaciones*. Buenos Aires: Edhasa.

Patton, M. (2007) *Science, Politics and Business in the Work of Sir John Lubbock*. Aldershot: Ashgate.

Pearson, L. (1991) *The People's Palaces*. Buckingham: Barracuda.

Pollard, S. (1968) *The Genesis of Modern Management*. Harmondsworth: Penguin.

Poole, R. (1994) *The Lancashire Wakes Holidays*. Lancaster: Lancashire County Books.

Redfern, A. (1983) 'Crewe: leisure in a railway town', in J.K. Walton and J. Walvin (eds) *Leisure in Britain 1780–1939*. Manchester: Manchester University Press, 117–136.

Renou, F. (2011) 'Congés payés et jours fériés: le classement européen', *Le Journal du Net*, 27 November.

Reid, D. (1976) 'The decline of St Monday, 1766–1876', *Past and Present* 71: 76–101.

Reid, D. (1996) 'The "iron roads" and the "happiness of the working classes"', *Journal of Transport History* 17: 51–73.

Samuel, R. (1981) 'Comers and goers', in H.J. Dyos and M. Wolff (eds) *The Victorian City*, Vol. 1. London: Routledge, 123–160.

Simmons, J. (1986) *The Railway in Town and Country*. Newton Abbot: David and Charles.

Smith, D.N. (1988) *The Railway and its Passengers*. Newton Abbot: David and Charles.

Steward, J. (2006) 'Spa culture in the nineteenth-century British media', in A. Cossic and P. Galliou (eds) *Spas in Britain and France in the Eighteenth and Nineteenth Centuries*. Newcastle: Cambridge Scholars Press, 375–410.

Taylor, H. (1997) *A Claim on the Countryside*. Edinburgh: Keele University Press.

Travis, J. (1997) 'Continuity and change in English sea-bathing, 1730–1900', in S. Fisher (ed.) *Recreation and the Sea*. Exeter: University of Exeter Press, 8–35.

Walton, J.K. (1978) *The Blackpool Landlady: A Social History*. Manchester: Manchester University Press.

Walton, J.K. (1981) 'The demand for working-class seaside holidays in Victorian England', *Economic History Review* 34: 249–65.

Walton, J.K. (1983) *The English Seaside Resort: A Social History, 1750–1914*. Leicester: Leicester University Press.

Walton, J.K. (1987) *Lancashire: A Social History, 1558–1939*. Manchester: Manchester University Press.

Walton, J.K. (1994) 'The Blackpool landlady revisited', *Manchester Region History Review* 8: 23–31.

Walton, J.K. (2000) *The British Seaside: Holidays and Resorts in the Twentieth Century*. Manchester: Manchester University Press.

Walton, J.K. (2010) 'Thomas Cook: image and reality', in R. Butler and R. Russell (eds) *Giants of Tourism*. Wallingford: CABI, 81–92.

Walton, J.K. (2011) 'The origins of the modern package tour? British motor-coach tours in Europe, 1930–1970', *Journal of Transport History* 32: 149–163.

Walton, J.K. (2012) 'Understanding social tourism over time and across cultures: an international historical perspective', http://www.westminster.ac.uk/_data/assets.pdf-file/0009/129477/J-Walton-Sem3-presentation.pdf accessed 1 May 2012.

Ward, C., and Hardy, D. (1984) *Arcadia for All*. London: Mansell.

White, R. (2005) *On Holidays*. Sydney: Pluto Press Australia.

Williams, A. (1915, 1980 edn.) *Life in a Railway Factory*. New York: Garland.

Wright, S. (2002) 'Sun, sand, sea and self-expression', in H. Berghoff, B. Korte, R. Schneider, and C. Harvie (eds) *The Making of Modern Tourism*. London: Palgrave Macmillan, 181–202.

26

THE DEMON DRINK

Alcohol and moral regulation, past and present

Henry Yeomans and Chas Critcher

Introduction

The consumption of alcoholic drinks is an important feature of leisure in Western societies. Pleasure in drinking can be found simply in the enjoyment of taste, but also in the way it enhances personal relaxation, sociability and recreation (Keane, 2011). Drinking permeates social rituals such as christenings, weddings and funerals. This ubiquitous enjoyment of alcohol can be problematic. Consumption eventually affects drinkers' consciousness and lessens self-control. Drinking has been blamed for diminished economic productivity, domestic disharmony and disruptions to public order. The intoxicating effects of alcohol allegedly lead to failure in social roles as worker, parent or user of public space (Room, 2011). Understandings of alcohol are thus acutely ambivalent: drinking is widely enjoyed yet frequently linked to many social problems (Gusfield, 1996).

Drink is troublesome for authority. The US government famously concluded in 1919 that the problems connected with alcohol far outweighed any individual or collective pleasure which might be derived from it. The system of prohibition that it enacted, which endured until 1933, represents one of the more extreme forms of moral regulation ever introduced. Others range from Sweden's operation of a state monopoly on off-licence sales to UK plans to introduce various minimum pricing schemes. More typical attempts to deal with the dichotomy of drink involve the legal regulation of retail licences, of drunkenness in public and of blood alcohol levels whilst driving. Regulatory regimes vary geographically and historically. Other factors intrude, such as the capacity of the drinks industry to provide employment for workers and tax for governments, the tendency for alcohol to be the focus of moral lobbying from hostile pressure groups and the ability of 'the drink question' to bestow significant electoral advantage or disadvantage.

This chapter will concentrate on how configurations of political, economic and moral factors have shaped the pleasurable use of alcohol in Britain. This issue has recently attracted attention, due to concerns about heavy episodic drinking or 'binge drinking'. Debate was sharpened by the decision of the New Labour government (1997–2010) to prioritize the de-regulation of licensing hours. New Labour also intensified other alcohol regulations by, for example, creating Drink Banning Orders, Alcohol Free Zones and 'on-the-spot' fines for disorderly conduct. Greater freedom to sell alcohol was being advocated alongside control over its consumption.

New Labour attempted to mix economic de-regulation with intensified moral regulation, in the form of rhetorical condemnation and the criminalization of undesirable drinking or drinkers. This was a reworking of a well-established historical dilemma of government: how to regulate alcohol consumption without provoking hostility from the industry or the public at large. This chapter will initially use three case studies to explore how various influences have bounded the enjoyment of alcohol through the ages: the gin craze of the eighteenth century, the temperance movement of the nineteenth century and the binge-drinking problem of the early twenty-first century. It will then analyse how the most recent forms of moral regulation involve a process of 'responsibilization'. Finally, an attempt will be made to give due recognition to the pleasures of alcohol.

Gin in Georgian England

For much of British history, alcohol was regarded as a largely non-problematic substance. In the Assize of Bread and Ale Act of 1267 beer was depicted as the 'second necessity of life'. This Act created a system of pricing designed to ensure that this essential beverage was always available at affordable prices (Burnett, 1999). Alcohol was also involved in a swathe of traditional leisure practices. Barr (1998) describes the port-drinking excesses which occurred at aristocratic Georgian dinner parties. Malcolmson (1973) notes the role of alcohol within sports, games and festivals. Thompson (1967) documents the notorious practice of 'Saint Monday', enduring well into the nineteenth century, in which the workforce would take an unscheduled day's holiday for the purposes of drinking. Taking pleasure from drink, especially beer, was a normal and acceptable part of life.

The first organized campaign about alcohol consumption occurred in the eighteenth century. Gin had arrived in Britain from the Netherlands with the ascent of the Dutch King William III to the throne after the Glorious Revolution in 1688. The British government, in the late seventeenth and early eighteenth centuries, actively promoted the manufacture and sale of gin. For the landed class, a significant influence within parliament, gin production was a useful source of revenue from surplus grain. Hence, the importation of foreign drinks was restricted while gin was permitted to be sold without a licence and taxed at a lower rate than beer (Critcher, 2011). These relaxations in the regulation of supply coincided with a growth in demand from an expanding and increasingly urbanized population. The population of London more than doubled between 1632 and 1750. Average gin consumption rose from 0.5 gallons per person per year in 1700 to 1.3 gallons in 1720 (Nicholls, 2009).

From the 1720s onwards gin drinking became the focus of moral concern amongst the rising middle classes. The Society for the Reformation of Manners highlighted the evils of gin drinking (Critcher, 2011), and Hogarth famously depicted the depravity of 'Gin Lane'. Pressure from strategically important groups such as the magistracy eventually persuaded the government to regulate the sale of gin. A succession of Gin Acts attempted to tackle the problem in 1729, 1736 and 1743 through the introduction of licensing for gin sellers and changes in the cost of a gin licence. The Gin Act 1751 eventually calmed tensions by effectively gentrifying the gin trade (Nicholls, 2009: 47). By fixing a fairly high fee for a gin licence and restricting them to premises rented for over £10 per year, the Act restricted ordinary people's access to gin and tried to make the trade 'respectable'. Warner (2004) depicts these 'gin panics' and new laws as attempts by social elites to impose order on the nation's capital. Despite the documented excesses of aristocratic men during this period, the drinking habits of women and the lower classes caused dismay. Urban social elites needed to (re)impose social order in the wake of demographic changes.

The 'gin panics' have been described as the first modern 'drug scare' (Warner 2004: 7) and 'perhaps the first drink-related "moral panic"' (Borsay, 2007: 2). They also typify the problems of regulating alcohol. The economic advantages of encouraging people to derive pleasure from gin sharply conflicted with the moral damage evident amongst the poor, and especially the female, and with the political imperative to maintain order on the streets. Not for the first or the last time, the drink question was entwined with issues of class and gender. The objection was less to the act of drinking or even to the state of drunkenness than to who was drinking what, when and where. Such hypocritical distinctions were anathema to a later generation of drink campaigners, who were at least morally consistent in their belief that all alcohol consumption was intrinsically evil.

Temperance and the Victorians

An extensive series of campaigns to reform popular leisure practices emerged in the nineteenth century. Based on convictions about the virtuous habits, including sexual purity, Sabbatarianism and hard work, as well as the immorality of practices such as gambling, animal cruelty and drunkenness, these campaigns sought to remake the means of mass enjoyment (Hunt, 1999; Roberts, 2004). Traditional games, such as derby football and cock-fighting, as well as music halls, fairs and folk festivals were all targeted by moral reformers (Harrison, 1971; Malcolmson, 1973; Storch, 1977). Since alcohol and public houses were often involved in these traditional leisure pursuits (Jennings, 2007), drinking became a target for reform partly through association. But, following the emergence of the temperance movement in the nineteenth century, alcohol consumption began to be viewed as a problem in itself. The first British temperance societies were established in 1829, and promoted moderation or abstinence from alcoholic spirits only. But the movement took a teetotal turn in the 1830s when the idea took hold that the social problems long associated with drink, such as poverty, violence and sickness, were the inevitable consequence of any form of alcohol consumption whatsoever (Yeomans, 2011). Joseph Livesey began administering teetotal pledges in 1832 and many people soon regarded even the consumption of alcohol for medicinal or religious reasons as profoundly immoral (Cook, 2006). In this climate, the recreational use of any form of alcohol, beer as well as gin, was frequently and vehemently condemned in Britain, the USA and other countries where teetotalism proved popular.

These campaigns are perhaps unsurprising. Industrialization engendered huge changes to British society and, crucially, gave middle and upper classes a vested interest in the behaviour of the working class, upon whose productivity their wealth increasingly depended. The eradication of habitual or excessive drinking, as evident in Saint Monday, would clearly increase productivity and yield financial rewards for the factory owners. Thus the early membership of temperance societies was dominated by the middle echelons of society (Shiman, 1988: 4). Some industrial leaders built 'dry' towns, such as chocolate manufacturer George Cadbury's 'Bournville' in Birmingham, to accommodate their workforces. But the temperance movement also became popular amongst the working class because it appealed to aspirations for self-betterment. Teetotalism brought respectability, and the promise of greater personal productivity might also lead to economic rewards for the worker. Its potential to alleviate working-class misery allied the temperance movement to social causes such as Chartism and the labour movement (Harrison, 1971). Although reflecting class relations in the new industrial economy, organized temperance was not simply a bourgeois attempt to discipline the workforce.

Efforts to regulate alcohol consumption had socio-economic dimensions but were also morally charged. The intermingling of temperance and Sabbatarian movements, which led to the Sunday closing of pubs becoming a key objective for some temperance societies, evidences the religious concern of many drink reformers. Specifically, organized temperance was intimately connected to evangelical Protestantism. The early movement drew much support from Nonconformists; internationally, teetotalism was strong in predominantly Protestant, non-Lutheran countries (Eriksen, 1989; Levine, 1993; Rouse and Unnithan, 1993). The beliefs of the temperance movement – individualism, routine and self-discipline – reflect Protestant worldly asceticism (Weber, 1965). Activists further believed that their cause was part of a great struggle against moral evils which would improve society (Yeomans, 2009). This pursuit of radical, societal moral advancement, manifested in efforts to achieve collective abstinence from alcohol, is rooted in the evangelical belief in the necessity of actions which strive to highlight and alleviate the depravity of human existence (Hilton, 1988; Yeomans, 2009).

Temperance groups attempted to enlist government support for their cause. Prohibitionists launched organized and well-funded campaigns which advocated radical restrictions on the drinks trade, but their demands were unfeasible, for a number of reasons. Firstly, it was difficult for governments to ignore the fact that the drinks industry was a huge source of revenue; in 1880, liquor accounted for around two-fifths of total government income through taxation (Harrison, 1971: 346). Secondly, the drinks industry itself was quick to mobilize, and groups such as the Country Brewers' Society began their own high-profile campaigns in defence of their trade (Gutzke, 1989). Thirdly, public sentiment was not particularly receptive to stricter drink controls. The Licensing Bill 1871, which proposed controversial reductions in the number of licensed premises across England and Wales, was dropped amid a vitriolic public reaction; a million people signed petitions against it (Harrison, 1971: 266; Greenaway, 2003). Fourthly, even those who sought the eradication of drunkenness had difficulty making the case for government intervention in a political culture convinced that only voluntary change was practically and ethically worthwhile (Yeomans, 2011). For compelling political and economic reasons, Victorian governments interfered with the enjoyment of drink at their peril.

Laws on drinking were tightened during this period, but often at a cost. The Licensing Act 1872 required sellers of all forms alcohol to be licensed, reduced public house opening hours and introduced new drunkenness offences. It was seen at the time as a compromise designed to appease both the drinks industry and the temperance movement. Defeated in the subsequent 1874 general election, Liberal Party leader Gladstone declared that 'we have been borne down in a torrent of gin and beer' (Gutzke, 1989: 1). The Liberal Party again lost public support in the 1890s after the failure of further attempts to strictly regulate the drinks industry (Nicholls, 2009).

Temperance efforts to achieve moral progress through collective teetotalism largely failed. Nevertheless, they did force drunkenness to be taken seriously as a social issue and, for the first time, popularized the notion that beer, as well as gin, could be responsible for intoxication and social problems (Harrison, 1971; Shiman, 1988). Popular recreation, furthermore, was remodelled during this period. Temperance groups sought to encourage teetotalism by establishing 'dry' forms of recreation, often involving tea parties, stories, hymn singing, brass bands, libraries and attempts to open parks in urban areas (Harrison, 1971; Shiman, 1988). The extinction of Saint Monday and other traditional festivities signalled the decline of alcohol's role in the rhythms of popular leisure. The demands of an industrial economy and the moral force wielded by an evangelical temperance movement certainly did not eradicate drinking. The drinks lobby and hostile public opinion prevented the dominance of the most radical, abstinence-based forms of moral regulation in this period. But laws were tighter and drink was more thoroughly moralized at the end of the nineteenth century than at the beginning.

Temperance movements always encountered popular resistance in Britain, but they have remained influential in ways often unrecognized. It is, for example, common to find due regard paid, in any British media or public debate about alcohol, to the views of the authoritative-sounding Institute of Alcohol Studies. Never is it mentioned, although it is openly stated on its website, that this organization is promoted and funded by temperance interests. The Victorian Band of Hope temperance society continues to highlight the dangers of drink; under the name Hope UK it now uses education to help children to make 'drug free choices' (Hope UK, 2011). Three of the most influential players in alcohol policy in 2010, the Chief Medical Officer of Health (Sir Liam Donaldson), the president of the Royal College of Physicians (Sir Ian Gilmore) and the chair of the parliamentary health committee (Kevin Barron), have been described by one observer of the policy process as a 'temperance triumvirate' (Reeves, 2010). Abstinence from alcohol may now otherwise be rare in modern Western societies, but the belief that alcohol consumption is immoral is still held amongst various groups, and alcohol is a prohibited substance in many Muslim states. The idea that alcohol is a physical and moral poison has many millions of subscribers worldwide. They enjoy their leisure free of alcohol.

'Binge drinking' in contemporary Britain

As Greenaway has commented, 'drink had a low political salience in mid-twentieth century Britain' (Greenaway, 2003: 150). Consumption declined from the 1890s onwards (Plant and Plant, 2006: 29), and after the First World War anxieties about drinking lessened. Mass Observation's studies, undertaken from 1937 onwards, made pubs in Bolton one of their key sites for research. They discovered that pubs were fairly inclusive; around 31 per cent of pub-goers were female, although only around 7 per cent were under the age of 25 (Barr, 1998; Nicholls, 2009). Subsequent legislative changes consolidated the pub's position. The Licensing Act 1961 extended the opening hours of pubs slightly and allowed for premises in England and Wales in which music and dancing took place to apply for licences to stay open until 2 a.m. Later, the Licensing Act 1988 abolished the war-time requirement for the afternoon closure of premises. Issues such as youth drunkenness, addiction and drink-driving were persistently seen as problematic aspects of some types of drinking but, for much of the twentieth century, alcohol itself was not viewed with the trepidation which had characterized earlier periods. Drinking began to be recognized as a broadly legitimate source of pleasure.

Nevertheless, the times and place of alcohol consumption were still heavily regulated. Unfavourable comparisons were made with more liberal licensing laws in the rest of Europe and deregulating the sale of alcohol became part of New Labour's 'modernizing' project in the early twenty-first century. The Licensing Act 2003 removed statutory limits on the opening hours of licensed premises and made it easier to obtain a licence. New Labour wanted to encourage the development of the leisure and night-time economies central to tourism and urban regeneration projects. By 2005, it was estimated that around one million people were employed in licensed premises (Department of Health, 2007), and in 2011–12 revenue from taxation of alcohol constituted 1.8 per cent of total government receipts (Browne and Roantree, 2012). These policies were electorally useful, too; on the eve of the 2001 general election, New Labour sent a text to young voters which read 'cdnt give a XXXX for lst ordrs? Vote Labour on thrsdy 4 xtra time' (Plant and Plant, 2006: 121). Powerful economic and political incentives underpinned the New Labour policies which seemed, in some respects, to mandate the enjoyment of alcohol.

Not everyone was comfortable with these apparently permissive attitudes to drinking. A 'new culture of intoxication' (Measham and Brain, 2005) emerged in Britain in the 1990s. The rave scene of the early 1990s normalized the idea of experimentation with different psychoactive states. When it declined in the mid-1990s, heavy drinking replaced drugs such as ecstasy as a route to a different psychoactive experience. The drinks industry responded: traditional pubs began to be replaced by large, modern, city-centre bars and new products, such as 'alcopops' and 'shooters', were launched. From 2004 onwards, alarm about this behavioural trend accelerated. A new term appeared, 'binge drinking', to describe what was alleged to be an epidemic of alcohol consumption that was running out of control in towns and cities. This concern peaked just when New Labour's extended opening times were implemented in November 2005 (Critcher, 2008; Yeomans, 2009). Some critics accused the government of letting market forces dictate policy (Hayward and Hobbs, 2007), while opposition politicians portrayed extended opening hours as 'madness' (Plant and Plant, 2006: 100).

The narrative is more complex than it initially seems. Firstly, while alcohol consumption did increase during much of the late twentieth century, it was declining by 2005 (Robinson and Harris, 2011; Morgan, 2011). Secondly, New Labour had also toughened up the regulation of alcohol in a number of important ways. Broader measures, such as Anti-Social Behaviour Orders, Dispersal Orders and 'on the spot' fines were introduced to discipline those whose drinking leads to crime or disorder. The Criminal Justice and Police Act 2001 enabled local authorities to designate certain areas as Alcohol-Free Zones and the Violent Crime Reduction Act 2006 allowed courts to impose Drink Banning Orders on troublesome individuals. A later mandatory code required that drink sellers ask anyone who looked as if they *might* be under 18 for proof of age and banned 'irresponsible promotions' such as 'all you can drink for £10' or 'women drink free' offers (Home Office, 2010). Thirdly, New Labour actually articulated the outrage against binge drinking. The *Safe. Sensible. Social.* (Department of Health, 2007) alcohol strategy singled out alcoholics, under-age drinkers and binge drinkers aged 18-24 as problematic.

New Labour, therefore, sought to separate responsible and moderate drinkers, whose pleasure is legitimate, from irresponsible groups, whose behaviour must be condemned, prevented and, in some cases, punished. Promoting this division of drinking types, adverts and labels on drink packaging now urge consumers to 'drink responsibly'. But defining 'responsibility' is not straightforward. The established definition entails alcohol consumption within the recommended daily limits of 3–4 units for men and 2–3 for women (Department of Health, 2012). However, this definition has been challenged by medical professionals who stress the toxic, addictive or 'risky' properties of even small quantities of alcohol. Whilst employed by the government as Chief Medical Officer, Sir Liam Donaldson used the phrase 'passive drinking' to describe the 'collateral damage' which alcohol inflicts on society (Donaldson, 2009: 5). Through violence, sickness, vandalism and a host of other means, Donaldson argued, alcohol is not just harmful to the individual drinker but 'a problem for everybody' (Donaldson, 2009: 22). From this public health perspective, no form of drinking is entirely safe, and so the political division of drinking into responsible and irresponsible forms is undermined.

The Coalition government, which came to power in 2010, has included a proposal for a minimum price per unit of alcohol, a policy of the public health lobby, in its new alcohol strategy. This measure is explicitly described by Prime Minister David Cameron as a means to tackle the 'scourge' of binge drinking but not to stop 'responsible drinking' (Home Office, 2012). The government has adopted one demand of the public health lobby groups, but not their assessment of the risks from all forms of drinking.

Binge drinking is presented as a threat to public order and decency, as an expensive nuisance for the emergency services that are required to cope with it and as jeopardizing the long-term health of those involved. And it may indeed be all, or at least some, of those things. But it is also indicative of other, historically rooted constructions of alcohol as a problem. The objections are to drunkenness in public, to the deliberate intent of drinkers to get drunk, to their apparent disregard of the peace of others and to risks posed to their own physical health. Binge drinkers, it is clear, need to be saved from themselves. Nobody else, apparently, is responsible for their condition: not the brewers and retailers who cater for their need to get drunk, nor local government, which has deliberately encouraged the growth of the night-time economy to bolster the flagging economics of city centres. Yet governments and police forces are reluctant to assume the powers that they already have to eliminate binge drinking from city centres, such as systematic enforcement of the law, involving mass arrests and instant closure of licensed premises. Politics and economics constrain the full exercise of moral outrage.

The three case studies have highlighted the factors influencing the enjoyment of drink in Britain through time. Alcohol's ambivalent status as a substance which engenders both pleasure and social problems has consistently proved difficult for the authorities. Attempts to balance or manage the pleasures and problems of alcohol are shaped by the consideration of what, at any point in time, is deemed to be economically viable, politically expedient and morally desirable. Economic viability requires considering the benefits of the contemporary drinks industry, in terms of jobs, tax and regeneration. Political expediency requires balancing the demands of pressure groups or health professionals against the unpopularity historically associated with interfering in the nation's drinking habits. Moral desirability requires prescribing how alcohol should ideally be consumed: where, when, how much and with what consequences.

Such tensions have always underlain the regulation of drink. In the eighteenth century, gin consumption and public drunkenness involving women and/or the lower social classes were vehemently condemned, while beer drinking and other forms of consumption were generally accepted. In the nineteenth century, drink laws were tightened and various alcohol-related forms of recreation were reformed partly in response to an abstinence-based temperance movement that did not accept that any pleasure can be rightly derived from such a problematic substance. In the twenty-first century, binge drinking has been widely attacked as an irresponsible form of consumption, with more responsible forms of drinking advocated instead. The case studies show that promotion of desirable forms of behaviour and the vilification of undesirable codes of drinking, through legislation, rhetorical condemnation or other means, are historically well established in Britain.

Moral regulation and responsibilization

These consistent efforts to reform the drinking habits of certain individuals and groups are best understood as forms of moral regulation, defined as 'practices whereby some social agents problematize some aspect of the conduct, values or culture of others on moral grounds and seek to impose moral regulations on them' (Hunt, 1999: ix). The main historical targets of moral regulation have been sex, gambling and alcohol – some of the principal sources of human pleasure. Such pleasure derives in part from the forsaking of control. Drink is a relaxant and disinhibitor for the individual and the group.

The exhortation to 'drink responsibly' in such a context makes sense only if alcohol is to be consumed in such a way as to deny its capacity to change consciousness. Alcohol, in this version, is to be drunk for its taste, and in such moderation that drunkenness is never achieved. But for many drinkers, occasional or regular, getting mildly or severely drunk is the whole point. It is not like food, where the taste is all. Indeed some mixers precisely seek to disguise the sharpness of alcohol with softer tastes. Alcohol is drunk for its effects. The modern regulators of alcohol would have it assume the form of another commodity to be consumed with style and in modest amounts.

But there is more involved in the slogans about responsible drinking than an invitation to middle-class respectability. The moral regulation of alcohol is a particularly transparent example of a sea change in the modes of governance in modern society. Foucauldian scholars call this 'responsibilization'. The idea is that conformity and control are to be achieved by granting citizens the right to determine their own conduct, provided that they assume responsibility for the consequences of their own actions. 'This entails a twin process of autonomization plus responsibilization – opening free space for the choices of individual actors whilst enwrapping these autonomized actors within new forms of control' (Rose, 1999: xxiii).

New Labour's alcohol policies were absolutely in line with this interpretation. Extended opening hours confirmed the autonomy of consumers, whilst moderate consumption confirmed their responsibilization. You are allowed to drink when you like, but not as much as you might like. Only thus can private and public order be maintained.

> [T]he other side of the celebration of free will, choice and self-realization through consumption is the emergence of a whole 'epidemic' of diseases of the will – failures of responsible self-control and self-management, surrender to some baser aspects of the self in compulsive consumption of drink, drugs, gambling, sex.
>
> (Rose, 1999: 266)

Drink, then, is potentially a disruptive influence. The individual out of control has to be persuaded or punished back into the fold of 'responsible' drinkers. '[A]n alcohol policy based on risk-management creates categories of moral order and disorder, defining some alcohol consumers as rational and responsible and others as irrational and irresponsible' (Järvinen, 2012: 243). Particularly sensitive is the protection of public space which has to be regulated by 'the moral rules which govern our relations in such places, defining what counts as acceptable conduct and what passes as normal interaction' (Dixon *et al.*, 2006: 187). Responsible drinking will guarantee order on the streets, good long-term health and minimal state expenditure. Such apparently laudable aims disguise another objective: the extension to drinking habits of the model of the rational consumer, who is autonomous in their exercise of choice and responsible in their conduct. Pleasure is to be derived from the exercise of control, not the abandonment of it. This is to negate the basic attraction of alcohol by de-legitimizing its unruliness and unpredictability.

Pleasure and control

Understanding modes for regulating alcohol consumption is, however, only half the story. The other half is accounting for the enduring attraction of alcohol across time and space. Official discourses proceed, as we have seen, by initially blocking out pleasure as a possible motive for drinking. They 'remain silent about pleasure as a motive for consumption, and raise instead visions of a consumption characterized by compulsion, pain and pathology' (O'Malley and Valverde, 2004: 26). More subtly, pleasure is then reconstructed around rational consumption so that it 'equates with a form of "rational" and "responsible" enjoyment' (*ibid.*: 27). However, deconstructing the discourse of neo-liberalism does not in itself deliver a definition of pleasure that is able to explain the enduring attraction of alcohol.

Academic discourses are not necessarily any better at acknowledging pleasure than are those of governing elites. The sociology of leisure offers little emphasis on or explanation of the centrality of alcohol to the pursuit of pleasure. The sociology of public health has shown more awareness of this problem. Coveney and Bunton suggest that pleasure is regarded as both self-evident and peripheral: 'Public health seems to have overlooked the point that people take drugs for the experience of pleasure, however socially defined' (Coveney and Bunton, 2003: 173). They review four constructions of pleasure in Western societies: the carnal, the disciplined, the ascetic and the ecstatic. Alcohol appeals to the carnal and the ecstatic: ingested into the body, alcohol changes the psychological state. Gin drinkers in the eighteenth century and binge drinkers today have pursued this experience. The discipline construction redefines pleasure through self-control ('responsible drinking'), while the ascetic moves beyond bodily into spiritual pleasure (logically culminating in teetotalism). Like the pleasures of sex, those of alcohol have biological roots but are always culturally channelled.

We cannot easily give expression to pleasure. We are used to experiencing it rather than describing it. Researchers into drug use have started to identify the need to recognize what is being sought through the consumption of consciousness-changing substances: 'the distinctly pleasurable elements of these moments – the corporeal and sensory joys that are experienced in and through the enhancement of sociability, closeness or confidence' (Duff, 2008: 384). Investigations of binge drinkers confirm that these are the experiences they want and get: 'having fun, conforming to peer group norms, letting yourself go, forgetting the frustrations of the day and helping confidence in a social situation ... also reducing tension, enhancing sexuality and aiding social interaction' (Szmigin *et al.*, 2008: 365). Alcohol furnishes a release from the constraints of everyday existence, enabling a 'calculated hedonism' which is 'contained by time, space and social situation' (Szmigin *et al.*, 2008: 365).

The pleasures of alcohol stem in part from this calculated loss of control. Control is also a focus of moral regulation. For those who are teetotal, any loss of control can be seen as one of the intrinsic evils of drink. Drinking only to the point where you are still wholly in control is what is advocated by the slogan to 'drink responsibly'. But binge drinkers and older drinkers who cannot resist the second bottle of wine (Järvinen, 2012) want to lose enough control to feel a different kind of person; 'certain ways of "being in the world" are inaccessible, unthinkable or just unlikely while sober' (Duff, 2008: 386).

For the moral regulator, the habitual drinker needs to exercise self-control. But alcohol consumption is a way of controlling the self by enabling a switch to another kind of self, different from but just as real as the everyday, sober self. The struggle here is not between sobriety and inebriation, order and disorder or self-indulgence and self-control. The struggle is between different kinds of self. Drink takes us out of ourselves. We might not want our selves in drink to become our permanent selves, but as occasional visitors we welcome them with open arms. Come on in: have a drink.

References

Barr, A. (1998) *Drink: A Social History*. London: Pimlico.

Borsay, P. (2007) 'Binge Drinking and Moral Panics: Historic Parallels?', *History and Policy*. Retrieved from http://www.historyandpolicy.org/papers/policy-paper-62.html.

Browne, J. and Roantree, B. (2012) *A Survey of UK Tax System*. London: Institute of Fiscal Studies. Retrieved from http://www.ifs.org.uk/bns/bn09.pdf.

Burnett, J. (1999) *Liquid Pleasures*. London: Routledge.

Cook, C. (2006) *Alcohol, Addiction and Christian Ethics*. Cambridge: Cambridge University Press.

Coveney, J. and Bunton, R. (2003) 'In Pursuit of Pleasure: Implications for Health Research and Practice', *Health: An Interdisciplinary Journal for the Social Study of Health, Illness and Medicine* 7 (2) 161–179.

Critcher, C. (2008) 'Moral Panics: A Case Study of Binge Drinking', in B. Franklin (ed.) *Pulling Newspapers Apart* (pp. 154–162). London: Routledge.

Critcher, C. (2011) 'Drunken Antics: the Gin Craze, Binge Drinking and the Political Economy of Moral Regulation', in S. Hier (ed.) *Moral Panic and the Politics of Anxiety* (pp. 171–189). London: Routledge.

Department of Health. (2007) *Safe. Sensible. Social.* London: Department of Health.

Department of Health. (2012) *Alcohol Misuse*. Retrieved from http://www.dh.gov.uk/en/Publichealth/Alcoholmisuse/index.htm

Dixon J., Levine, M., and McAulay, R. (2006) 'Locating Impropriety: Street Drinking, Moral Order and the Ideological Dilemma of Public Space', *Political Psychology* 27 (2) 187–206.

Donaldson, Sir L. (2009) *Annual Report of the Chief Medical Officer 2008*. London: Department of Health.

Duff, C. (2008) 'The Pleasure in Context', *The International Journal of Drug Policy* 19: 384–392.

Eriksen, S. (1989) 'Drunken Danes and Sober Swedes? Religious Revivalism and the Temperance Movements as Keys to Danish and Swedish Folk Cultures', in B. Strath (ed.) *Language and the Construction of Class Identities* (pp. 55–94). Gothenburg: Gothenburg University Press.

Greenaway, J. (2003) *Drink and British Politics since 1830*. Basingstoke: Palgrave.

Gusfield, J. (1996) *Contested Meanings: The Construction of Alcohol Problems*. Wisconsin: University of Wisconsin Press.

Gutzke, D.W. (1989) *Protecting the Pub: Brewers and Publicans against Temperance*. Woodbridge, Suffolk: Boydell and Brewer.

Harrison, B. (1971) *Drink and the Victorians*. London: Faber and Faber.

Hayward, K., and Hobbs, D. (2007) 'Beyond the Binge in Booze Britain: Market-led Liminalization and the Spectacle of Binge Drinking', *The British Journal of Sociology* 58 (3) 437–456.

Hilton, B. (1988) *The Age of Atonement*. Oxford: Clarendon Press.

Home Office. (2010) 'Tough New Powers to Tackle Alcohol Crime Announced'. Retrieved from http://webarchive.nationalarchives.gov.uk/+/http://www.homeoffice.gov.uk/about-us/news/powers-tackle-alcohol-crime.html.

Home Office. (2012) *Alcohol Strategy*. London: Home Office.

Hope UK. (2011) *Home*. Retrieved from http://www.hopeuk.org/.

Hunt, A. (1999) *Governing Morals: A Social History of Regulation*. Cambridge: Cambridge University Press.

Järvinen M. (2012) 'A Will to Health? Drinking Risk and Social Class', *Health, Risk and Society* 14 (3) 241–256.

Jennings, P. (2007) *The Local: A History of the English Pub*. Stroud: History Press.

Keane, H. (2011) 'Intoxication Harm and Pleasure: An Analysis of the Australian National Alcohol Strategy', in K. Bell, D. McNaughton and A. Salmon (eds) *Alcohol, Tobacco and Obesity* (pp. 107–118). London: Routledge.

Levine, H. (1993) 'Temperance Cultures: Concern about Alcohol in Nordic and English-Speaking Countries', in M. Lader, G. Edwards and D.C. Drummond (eds) *The Nature of Alcohol and Drug-Related Problems* (pp. 16–36). Oxford: Oxford University Press.

Malcolmson, R.W. (1973) *Popular Recreations in English Society 1700–1850*. Cambridge: University Press.

Measham, F. and Brain, K. (2005) '"Binge" Drinking, British Alcohol Policy and the New Culture of Intoxication', *Crime, Media, Culture* 1: 262–283.

Morgan, J. (2011, February 15). 'Why is Alcohol Consumption Falling?' *BBC News*. Retrieved from http://www.bbc.co.uk/news/magazine–12397254.

Nicholls, J. (2009) *The Politics of Alcohol*. Manchester: Manchester University Press.

O'Malley, P. and Valverde, M. (2004) 'Pleasure, Freedom and Drugs: the Uses of Pleasure in Liberal Governance of Drug and Alcohol Consumption', *Sociology* 38 (1) 27–28.

Plant, M. and Plant, M. (2006) *Binge Britain*. Oxford: Oxford University Press.

Reeves, R. (2010) 'The Worth of a Pint: It's Hard to Quantify the Social Costs – and Benefits – of Drinking', *Guardian*, 8 January.

Roberts, M.J.D. (2004) *Making English Morals*. Cambridge: Cambridge University Press.

Robinson, S., and Harris, H. (2011) *Smoking and Drinking among Adults 2009*. Newport: Office for National Statistics.

Room, R. (2011) 'Addiction and Personal Responsibility as Solutions to the Contradictions of Neoliberal Consumerism', in K. Bell, D. McNaughton, and A. Salmon (eds) *Alcohol, Tobacco and Obesity* (pp. 47–58). London: Routledge.

Rose, N. (1999) *Governing the Soul*, 2nd ed. London: Free Association Books.

Rouse, T.P., and Unnithan, N.P. (1993) 'Comparative Ideologies and Alcoholism: the Protestant and Proletarian Ethic', *Social Problems* 40 (2) 213–227.

Shiman, L.L. (1988) *Crusade against Drink in Victorian England*. Basingstoke: Macmillan.

Storch, R.D. (1977) 'The Problem of Working-Class Leisure: Some Roots of Middle-Class Moral Reform in the Industrial North, 1825–1850', in A.P. Donajgrodzki (ed.), *Social Control in the Nineteenth Century* (pp. 138–162). London: Croom Helm.

Szmigin I., Griffin, C., Mistral, W., Bengry-Howell, A., Weale, L., and Hackley, C. (2008) 'Re-framing Binge Drinking as Calculated Hedonism: Empirical Evidence from the UK', *The International Journal of Drug Policy* 19: 359–366.

Thompson, E.P. (1967) 'Time, Work-Discipline, and Industrial Capitalism', *Past and Present* 38: 56–97.

Warner, J. (2004) *Craze: Gin and Debauchery in an Age of Reason*. London: Profile.

Weber, M. (1965) *The Protestant Ethic and the Spirit of Capitalism*. London: Unwin.

Yeomans, H. (2009) 'Revisiting a Moral Panic: Ascetic Protestantism, Attitudes to Alcohol and the Implementation of the Licensing Act 2003', *Sociological Research Online* 14 (2–3).

Yeomans, H. (2011) 'What Did the British Temperance Movement Accomplish? Attitudes to Alcohol, the Law and Moral Regulation', *Sociology* 45 (1) 38–53.

27

FROM THE BACK STREET TO THE HIGH STREET

Commercial gambling and the commodification of chance

Gerda Reith

Introduction

Over the course of the late twentieth and early twenty-first centuries, commercial gambling has been transformed from a semi-deviant, largely underground pastime to a globalized, multi-billion-dollar leisure industry. This dramatic shift can be located within the broader context of changes in post-Second World War patterns of leisure and consumption, as well as the intersection of political, economic and technological forces that saw the interests of governments and big business converge around the expansion of gambling profits.

For much of their history, games of chance were regarded as a disruptive and morally dubious activity (Lears, 2003; Reith, 1999). Gambling encapsulated an orientation to rational economic enterprise that opposed the ideology of hard work, abstinence and reward, which was particularly problematic in Western societies where effort and personal merit were valued as measures of success. Reliance on capricious forces such as luck or chance to determine wealth undermined the central tenets of the Protestant work ethic, with gambling games – which deliberately courted such forces – regarded as an unproductive and potentially disruptive pastime. The fluctuations of wealth embodied in gambling were anathema to the notion of meritocracy, and were particularly disliked by the bourgeoisie, the group who most embodied the ideology of the Protestant work ethic. Throughout the nineteenth century, when industrial nations relied upon a hard-working and controllable workforce, various pieces of legislation were introduced to limit the playing of games of chance throughout the population. As with the prohibitions against other potentially disruptive forms of leisure, such as the consumption of alcohol and opium (Berridge and Edwards, 1987; Valverde, 1998), these prohibitions were directed primarily at the urban working classes, who were generally regarded as the primary carriers of 'vice'. Although they failed to erode the popularity of betting, these statutes nevertheless ensured that gambling remained a clandestine activity, consistently associated with money laundering and organized crime (Chinn, 1991; Clapson, 1992). Gambling also continued to carry negative moral connotations, emphasized by temperance reformers, of idleness, waste, greed and a 'something for nothing' mentality (Lears, 2003; Reith, 1999).

However, in the later years of the twentieth century, a range of factors came together to alter the status of gambling, transforming it from a back-street activity into a mainstream feature of the high street, enjoyed by large numbers of consumers and promoted by governments and commercial enterprises alike.

The role of the state and the commodification of chance

After the Second World War a period of increasing secularization reduced the impact of many of the temperance and anti-gambling campaigners' messages. Added to this, a consumer boom encouraged the expansion of commercial betting, while higher wages meant that the population, and especially the working classes, were more able to afford leisure activities, which in turn increased to meet the demand, with cinemas, football pools and bingo halls increasing in popularity (Dixon, 1991). In the postwar period of full employment and relative affluence, a more libertarian, consumerist ethos throughout industrial societies stimulated the growth of gambling as a legitimate – albeit still tightly regulated – form of leisure.

It was not until the last quarter of the century, however, that the conditions for large-scale expansion were met. From the 1970s an embryonic gambling industry underwent a period of dramatic liberalization as Western governments relaxed legal restrictions on promotion and expansion. Although it was still regulated by various statutory and voluntary bodies, these moves allowed the industry to expand into a global enterprise with a central place in the world economy.

This remarkable growth is intimately related to economic and political factors: notably, the shift to neoliberal political and fiscal policies that occurred in the last decades of the twentieth century. These were characterized by a general shrinking of the role of the state in public life, the promotion of free enterprise and consumer choice as the drivers of market expansion, and the emphasis on individuals' responsibility for their own welfare and well-being (Barry, Osborne and Rose, 1996; Bauman, 1998; Giddens, 1991). The reduction of state 'interference' in markets was accompanied by policies of low personal income taxation, with a concomitant reduction of revenue streams. In the revenue vacuum created by such policies, the economic utility of commercial gambling to state budgets became significant. And so, beginning with 'soft' forms of gambling such as lotteries, during the last decades of the twentieth century, states throughout North America, Australasia and Europe legislated for ever-larger and more concentrated forms of gambling, such as casinos and electronic gaming machines (EGMs), as sources of both private profit and tax revenue (Rosecrance, 1988; Volberg, 2001).

This is the process in which chance has been transformed from a source of disruption into a source of profit. As the annual brochure of the Las Vegas casino Circus Circus puts it, just like any shop, 'the casino is an entertainment merchant. It's just that we happen to merchandize playtime to our customers rather than goods' (in Spanier, 1992: 101). In this, we can see the commodification of chance as the ultimate twenty-first-century product, sold by business and purchased by the consumer – the gambler.

However, it is a problematic type of product, with the gambling industry producing a contested form of leisure. Many states now gain considerable revenues from the profits of commercial gambling, particularly lotteries, some of which are used to fund services such as education, community services and healthcare, especially in the USA. In this process, gambling has become embedded in the political structure of the state, leading to a situation in which states themselves have been described as being in 'the gambling business' (Goodman, 1995). In addition, because it tends to be the poorest social groups who spend relatively more of their income on gambling than higher ones, gambling games have been described as a 'regressive form of taxation' (Clotfelter and Cook, 2001). It is this interdependent relation between commercial profit and state revenue, as well as the inequalities of lost wealth that are embedded in the structure of gambling itself, that have stimulated criticism of its potentially harmful impacts on individuals and communities. These critical voices accompany the expansion of gambling as a form of leisure and come from a diverse range of stakeholders, from treatment organizations and religious groups to cross-party political campaigners, researchers and media lobbies (Orford, 2011; Reith, 2009).

Today the gambling industry is increasingly owned by a limited number of transnational corporations, concentrated in an oligopolistic market (Eadington, 2003). These offer a range of heterogeneous leisure experiences, from the spectacular resort casinos of Las Vegas and Macau to the ubiquitous gaming machines dispersed throughout urban communities and the 24/7 betting opportunities offered by the Internet.

Gambling corporations are organized in a similar way to other publicly owned and traded companies, utilizing the principles – identified by Ritzer (1993) as 'McDonalidization' – of calculability and control through harnessing technology to facilitate mass production of continually updated products, standardization of prices and odds, and investment in market research and advertising strategies to identify and target new markets. The industry is a global one, and is fuelled by developments in technology which see the creation of ever more appealing and sophisticated products, targeted at specific niche groups of consumers (Schull, 2005). Companies and manufacturers compete for international markets, refining their products to 'fit' national gambling habits and preferences, and colonizing both remote and terrestrial markets with an ever-changing supply of new products. The rapid spread of commercial gambling practices and new technologies has seen the proliferation of gambling throughout Europe, the Americas, Australasia, Africa and the former East European communist bloc, as well as the developing countries of South-East Asia. In post-Maoist China the historical association of gambling with individualism and capitalism gave way to a more open market in the 1980s, in which leisure and pleasure became legitimate expressions of wealth and success (Paules, 2010). Overall, the development of mass tourism and leisure industries and the spread of international financial markets have led to the incorporation of gambling into the world economy, and to the movement of gamblers across increasingly fluid national boundaries (McMillen, 1996).

As a result of these changes, in the twenty years since 1990 expenditure on commercial gambling has overtaken many other forms of leisure activity. For example, in the financial year 2007/8, global expenditure was approximately $300 billion, ranking the gambling industry roughly equivalent in size with the global pharmaceutical industry (Adams, 2007). Internationally, consumers spend more on gambling than they do on alcohol and tobacco combined (Adams, 2007). Such is the capitalist embrace of what the writer Honoré de Balzac described as 'an essentially taxable passion' (Balzac, 1977: 21).

Ritzer (1999) described the 'new means of consumption' as spectacular settings that have dramatically altered the way that leisure is produced and consumed in the post-Second World War era. These include theme parks, fast-food restaurants, shopping malls, cruise ships and, of course, casinos. Indeed Ritzer regarded the Las Vegas casino as paradigmatic of these spaces, characterized by the principles of rationalization, enchantment, simulation, implosion and surveillance. While rationalization facilitates and streamlines consumption, enchantment attracts gamblers inside, where sophisticated security surveillance follows their every move. Ritzer's Las Vegas prototype was an example of a new type of consumerism that uses immaterial signs and spectacles to enchant consumers; manipulating time and space to create environments that are more virtual than real, and that encourage the continual and ever-increasing consumption of commodities in what he terms 'hyper consumption'.

Not only in Las Vegas: urban casinos everywhere follow similar principles. Many sell themselves as 'destination' venues where a range of leisure opportunities, including shopping malls, cinemas and hotels, can be enjoyed. In many cases the casino is not the only, or even the main, highlight of a visit. Nor are the spectacular and enchanting features of modern gambling confined to casinos: racetracks, amusement arcades, televised lottery shows and bingo halls are similarly enchanting, spectacular and representative of this 'new means of consumption' (Kingma, 2010).

A significant feature in the expansion of games of chance has involved their dispersal into increasingly diverse and non gambling-specific locations, such as bars, restaurants, hotels, grocery stores and airports. Gambling technologies are disseminated throughout the spaces and communities of late modern societies, creating a phenomenon that has been described as 'McGambling' (Goodman, 1995) or 'convenience' gambling (National Gambling Impact Study Commission, 1999). These monikers describe a situation in which gambling becomes increasingly normalized, ubiquitous and constantly available through, for example, the flickering monitor of a work PC, an interactive networked television set, a hand-held mobile phone or machines in a community bar or club. As a result, it is increasingly easy for individuals to encounter high-tech, high-speed games of chance as part of the fabric of everyday life. At the same time, a range of credit and debit technologies remove the need for cash, so that individuals can play with plastic, removing the need for breaks when money runs out and allowing consumers an uninterrupted leisure experience. Contemporary Western consumer societies are now saturated by opportunities to risk money on gambling games in what are effectively gambling environments of 'hyper consumption' (Ritzer, 1993).

The games people play

Today, between 70 per cent and 80 per cent of the populations of Western nations engage in at least some form of gambling (Gerstein *et al.*, 1999; Welte *et al.*, 2002). It is, however, a heterogeneous form of leisure, with a variety of games appealing to different groups of players (Downes *et al.*, 1976). Games, and the motivations for playing them, tend to be stratified by demographic characteristics such as age, class, ethnicity and gender. For example, women have traditionally tended to favour bingo as a form of leisure that allows them to socialize in ways that can be fitted around domestic routines such as childcare and shopping (Dixey, 1996). Meanwhile, men are often drawn to the challenges of games such as race betting and poker, which allow them to display skill and establish status among peers (Bruce and Johnstone, 1996; Neal, 1998). As such, betting shops, particularly in Great Britain, are traditionally male-dominated enclaves, while bingo halls are feminized ones. Many young people engage in fruit-machine gambling to socialize with their peers, demonstrate skill and display individual and social identity (Fisher, 1993; 1995). As a legacy of their history as private members' clubs, casinos have typically appealed to higher socio-economic groups in Britain, although their more egalitarian history in, for example, the United States, has resulted in a wider, cross-class appeal in other countries (Findlay, 1986). Class and geography play a role in this patterning of behaviour, with many gambling venues such as bingo halls, fruit-machine arcades and betting shops traditionally located in working-class areas, where games are incorporated into the material and symbolic culture of working-class life (Reith and Dobbie, 2011).

Gambling is also characterized by various cultural distinctions. Although machines dominate casinos in the West, in South-East Asia, gamblers prefer table games such as cards or roulette (Nguyen, 2009). Similarly, ethnic minority groups report playing for different reasons: researchers have found that African Americans are more likely than Latinos or Whites to play for money, while Latinos more often gamble to socialize (Volberg, Toce and Gerstein, 1999). Among Asian groups, studies have suggested that gambling for money related to family obligations is more important for Samoans and Tongans than other Pacific Island groups, 'saving face' is important for Maori, while many Asians report simply gambling 'for something to do' around shift work and to relieve some of the problems associated with migration (Clarke *et al.*, 2006). For Chinese players, gambling has important oracular and predictive functions (Papineau, 2005), while among the Vietnamese the cycle of wins and losses is part of the concept of retribution or *qubao* (Ohtsuka and Ohtsuka, 2010).

Technology has a major role in the expansion of commercial gambling, and is the driver behind the constant innovation of new games, particularly electronic gaming machines, which dominate the gambling market (Schull, 2005). Machines – whether located in casinos, arcades, bingo halls or dispersed throughout the community in venues such as bars and restaurants – are estimated to account for between 50 and 60 per cent of gambling revenues worldwide (Department of Internal Affairs, 2007; Office of Economic and Statistical Research, 2007; Storer, Abbott and Stubbs, 2009). Indeed, the spread of machines, as well as the policy changes that drive them and allow gambling corporations to appeal to wider groups of consumers, has been argued to be breaking down what has traditionally been a male-dominated form of leisure and, in the process, create a 'feminization' of games of chance (Volberg, 2001).

Social and individual identity

In their many guises, games of chance can be seen as a form of leisure that embody a high degree of 'cultural capital' (Reith, 2007). Their emphasis on risk taking, hedonism and instant gratification, as well as their overt celebration of material wealth, represent key values of consumer culture. In addition, their promise of instant, vast riches regardless of effort or skill can be seen as a mirror of celebrity culture that mimics TV game shows in which ordinary viewers are turned into celebrities overnight. In both, the blind democracy of chance overrides effort and skill, undermining the values of the Protestant work ethic by rewarding risk taking and the mere participation in a game.

Consumer culture is saturated with the imagery of gambling and the values that it embodies. For example, the notions of instantaneity and escape are promoted in lottery advertisements that urge consumers to live for the present: 'forget it all for an instant' (UK scratchcard), reject work: 'work is nothing but heart attack-inducing drudgery' (Massachusetts lottery), embrace risk: 'lotto – the biggest risk of becoming a millionaire' (Netherlands lottery) and dream of a life of leisure: 'the freedom to do what you want to do, year after year' (Queensland Golden Casket) (in Reith, 2006).

Because it embodies these cultural values (and rejects others, too), as with other forms of consumption which act as sites for the creation and expression of identity, gambling can be seen as a medium for the realization of the self in late modern societies. Games of chance have been described as 'separate spheres' (Caillois, 1962; Huizinga, 1949) – leisure spaces that are separate from the rules and routines of everyday life. In them, individuals are freed from their everyday roles and obligations to explore new forms of identity. Goffman (1969) noted that games consist in becoming an illusory character and temporarily adopting a new identity which endures for the duration of the game. This fluid 'gambling identity' is one in which the everyday self is left behind and another persona – the suave high roller, the multi-millionaire lottery winner – can be considered and 'tried on'.

In this sense, games of chance have a transformative aspect: they open up a space for dreams and desires, and so embody the ultimate fantasy of reinventing the self. The possibility of winning allows engagement in fantasies of consumption which, as well as providing individualized spaces in which to imagine new ways of being, also creates social interaction through the sharing of hopes and desires in talk of 'if I won the lottery ...' (Casey, 2008).

Gambling games provide opportunities to draw on qualities and abilities not normally utilized in everyday life (Bloch, 1951; Herman, 1976; Oldman, 1974). Goffman (1969) describes the 'rules of irrelevance' which delimit the gambling situation and signify the freedom from needing to act for 'real'; the licence to 'play act' or behave out of character according to the situation at hand. In this way, gambling provides the opportunity to present an idealized identity to the self and others. It also provides the perfect arena for the testing of the self. It is tied up with taking on opponents – other players, the house and even chance itself – and trying to 'beat the system', especially in games that involve some element of skill or psychology. Through the display of skill and knowledge, gamblers in games such as horse-race handicapping or poker can become experts within their social group and so win the respect and admiration of their peers (Alvarez, 1991). Players who do this put themselves on the line and risk losing everything, displaying what Goffman calls 'face' – the ability to square up to a challenge and show qualities such as character, self-discipline and courage in the encounter with chance.

'Pathological' gambling

Ironically, at the very point when economic and political conditions created the climate for the expansion of gambling as a mass leisure pursuit, critical discourses multiplied. These have been largely couched in the language of medicine and have been levelled against the dangers of gambling 'addiction' or 'pathology' (Castellani, 2000; Collins, 1996; Reith, 2006).

The concept of 'pathological' gambling first appeared in the 1980s, when it was included in the American Psychiatric Association's *Diagnostic and Statistical Manual of Mental Disorders* (DSM). It was first classed as an 'impulse control disorder'; subsequent editions of the manual considered it a compulsion and later an addiction, characterized by a discrete set of quantifiable symptoms borrowed from physiological models of substance dependence (American Psychiatric Association, 1980, 1994, 2010). To date, dominant conceptions of problem gambling are based on a dichotomous model of a small minority of 'pathological' individuals who have lost control of their behaviour, and a larger majority of the population who gamble 'responsibly' by controlling their consumption. The former group are estimated to account for between 0.5 and 3 per cent of the populations of Western nations (Shaffer *et al.*, 1999), although, by spending far more proportionally than other players, their losses provide some 30 per cent of the profits for commercial gambling (Productivity Commission, 1999).

These discourses present a model of gamblers as 'addicts' who are psychologically or even neurologically deficient in some ways (e.g. Breiter *et al.*, 2001; Clark *et al.*, 2009; Comings, 1998; Potenza *et al.*, 2003). However, alongside these materialist models of pathology and addiction we are also witnessing a shift whereby medicalized conceptions of gambling increasingly embrace discourses based on notions of responsibility and consumer choice (Blaszczynski, Ladouceur and Shaffer, 2004). As gambling becomes more widespread, players are increasingly regarded as consumers whose freedom to choose whether and how much to engage in gambling is seen as a personal choice, with the potential risks of excessive consumption similarly regarded as a matter of individual liability. Although paying lip-service to ideas of 'responsible' industry practice and government policy, the assumptions underlying these types of discourse are still wedded to a psychological focus on the individual as the main repository of such regulated behaviour (Reith, 2008).

As opportunities to gamble increase on a global scale, discourses of pathology and irresponsibility are invoked in order to articulate the increasing experience of gambling-related harms. These reductive models individualize the problems that can be caused by excess consumption and, by focusing on the body or mind of 'aberrant' players, fail to address the fact that gambling harms tend to be experienced by the most vulnerable in society. It tends to be lower socio-economic groups, ethnic minorities, the unemployed, the under-educated and the marginalized who suffer the greatest adverse consequences from the global spread of gambling. Despite the relatively democratic appearance of participation in games of chance at the population level, the harms from this form of leisure tend to be concentrated amongst those with least to lose (Orford, 2011; Welte *et al.*, 2004).

Conclusion

Although now established as a mainstream form of leisure, gambling continues to remain contested and problematic. The requirement for constant oversight and regulation, the discursive creation of 'pathological' individuals and the consistent attraction of controversy are testimony to its troubled past. Although today the language is one of medicine, responsibility and regulation, the legacy of an activity that was once best known for vice and disorder lingers on. As with other twenty-first-century forms of excess consumption, such as binge drinking, drug addiction and obesity, we now have a population – or, more accurately, segments of populations – classified as 'pathological' or 'compulsive' gamblers, It appears, then, that alongside its considerable expansion as a form of mainstream leisure, gambling has also become the site of a new 'social pathology'.

References

Adams, P. (2007) *Gambling, Freedom and Democracy*. New York: Routledge.

Alvarez, A. (1991) *The Biggest Game in Town*. England: Oldcastle Books.

American Psychiatric Association. (1980) *Diagnostic and Statistical Manual of Mental Disorders*, 3rd ed. Washington, DC: Author.

American Psychiatric Association. (1994) *Diagnostic and Statistical Manual of Mental Disorders*, 4th ed. Washington, DC: Author.

American Psychiatric Association. (2010) *DSM–5: The future of psychiatric diagnosis*. DSM–5 development website 2010 November 26. Available from: URL: http://www.dsm5.org/Pages/Default.aspx.

Balzac, H. (1977) *The Wild Ass's Skin*, trans. H.J. Hunt. Harmondsworth: Penguin Classics.

Barry, A., Osborne, T. and Rose, N. (1996) (eds) *Foucault and Political Reason: Liberalism, neoliberalism and rationalities of government*. Chicago: University of Chicago Press.

Bauman, Z. (1998) *Freedom*. Milton Keynes: Open University Press.

Berridge, V. and Edwards, G. (1987) *Opium and the People: Opiate use in nineteenth century England*. New Haven and London: Yale University Press.

Blaszczynski, A., Ladouceur, R. and Shaffer, H.J (2004) 'A Science-Based Framework for Responsible Gambling: The Reno Model', *Journal of Gambling Studies* 20(3) 301–317.

Bloch, H. (1951) 'The Sociology of Gambling', *The American Journal of Sociology* 57(3) 215–221.

Breiter, H.C., Aharon, I., Kahneman, D., Dale, A. and Shizgal, P. (2001) 'Functional Imaging of Neural Responses to Expectancy and Experience of Monetary Gains and Losses', *Neuron* 30: 619–639.

Bruce, A.C. and Johnstone, J.E.V. (1996) 'Gender Based Differences in Leisure Behaviour: Performance, risk-taking and confidence in off-course betting', *Leisure Studies* 15: 65–78.

Caillois, R. (1962) *Man, Play and Games*, trans. M. Barash. London: Thames and Hudson.

Casey, E. (2008) *Women, Pleasure and the Gambling Experience*. Aldershot: Ashgate.

Castellani, B. (2000) *Pathological Gambling: The making of a medical problem*. Albany, NY: State University of New York Press.

Chinn, C. (1991) *Better Betting with a Decent Feller: Bookmakers, betting and the British working class 1750–1990*. Hemel Hempstead, Herts: Harvester Wheatsheaf.

Clapson, M. (1992) *A Bit of a Flutter: Popular gambling and English society 1823–1961*. Manchester: Manchester University Press.

Clark, L., Lawrence, A.J., Astley-Jones, F., Gray, N. (2009) 'Gambling Near-misses Enhance Motivation to Gamble and Recruit Win-Related Brain Circuitry', *Neuron* 61: 481–490.

Clarke, D., Tse, S., Abbott, M., Townsend, S., Kingi, P. and Manaia, W. (2006) 'Key Indicators of the Transition from Social to Problem Gambling', *International Journal of Mental Health Addiction* 4: 247–264.

Clotfelter, C. and Cook, P. (2001) *Selling Hope*. Cambridge: Cambridge University Press.

Collins, A.F. (1996) 'The Pathological Gambler and the Government of Gambling', *History of the Human Sciences* 9(3) 69–100.

Comings, D.E. (1998) 'The Molecular Genetics of Pathological Gambling', *CNS Spectrums* 3(6) 20–37.

Department of Internal Affairs (New Zealand). (2007) *Gambling Expenditure Statistics Table 1983–2007*. Retrieved 2 December 2008 from http://www.passports.govt.nz/diawebsite.nsf/wpg_URL/Resource-material-Information-We-Provide-Gaming-Statistics?OpenDocument.

Dixey, R. (1996) 'Bingo in Britain: An analysis of leisure and class', in J. McMillen (ed.) *Gambling Cultures: Studies in history and interpretation*. London: Routledge.

Dixon, D. (1991) *From Prohibition to Regulation: Bookmaking, anti-gambling and the law*. Oxford: Clarendon Press

Downes, D.M., Davies, B.P., David, M.E. and Stone, P. (1976) *Gambling, Work and Leisure: A study across three areas*. London: Routledge and Kegan Paul.

Eadington, W. (2003) 'Values and Choices: The struggle to find balance with permitted gambling in modern society', in G. Reith (ed.) *Gambling: Who wins? Who loses?* New York: Prometheus Books.

Findlay, J. (1986) *People of Chance: Gambling in American society from Jamestown to Las Vegas*. Oxford: Oxford University Press.

Fisher, S. (1993) 'The Pull of the Fruit Machine: A sociological typology of young players', *The Sociological Review* 41(3) 446–474.

Fisher, S. (1995) 'The Amusement Arcade as a Social Space for Adolescents', *Journal of Adolescence* 18: 71–86.

Gerstein, D.R., Volberg, R.A., Toce, M.T., Harwood, H., Palmer, A., Johnson, R., Larison, C., Chuchro, L., Buie, T., Engelman, L. and Hill, M.A. (1999) *Gambling Impact and Behavior Study: Report to the National Gambling Impact Study Commission*. Chicago, IL: National Opinion Research Center at the University of Chicago. Available at http://cloud9.norc.uchicago.edu/dlib/ngis.htm.

Giddens, A. (1991) *Modernity and Self-Identity*. Cambridge: Polity.

Goffman, E. (1969) *Where the Action Is: Three essays*. London: Allen Lane.

Goodman, R. (1995) *The Luck Business: The devastating consequences and broken promises of America's gambling explosion*. New York: Simon and Schuster.

Herman, R. (1976) *Gamblers and Gambling*. Lexington: Lexington Books Ltd.

Huizinga, J. (1949) *Homo Ludens*. London: Routledge and Kegan Paul.

Kingma, S. (2010) 'Introduction: Global gambling', in S. Kingma (ed.) *Global Gambling: Cultural perspectives on gambling organisations*. London: Routledge.

Lears, J. (2003) *Something for Nothing: Luck in America*. New York: Viking/Penguin.

McMillen, J. (ed.) (1996) *Gambling Cultures: Studies in history and interpretation*. London: Routledge.

National Gambling Impact Study Commission. (1999) *Final Report*. Washington, DC: Government Printing Office. Available at http://govinfo.library.unt.edu/ngisc/index.html.

Neal, M. (1998) '"You Lucky Punters!" A study of gambling in betting shops', *Sociology* 32(3) 581–600.

Nguyen, M. (2009) *The Hidden Addiction: Problem gambling amongst Southeast Asian-American youth*. Alliant International University, San Francisco Bay.

Office of Economic and Statistical Research. (2007) *Australian Gambling Statistics* (24th ed.). Queensland, Australia: Queensland Government.

Ohtsuka, K., and Ohtsuka, T. (2010) 'Vietnamese Australian Gamblers' Views on Luck and Winning: Universal versus culture-specific schemas', *Asian Journal of Gambling Issues and Public Health* 1: 34–46.

Oldman, D. (1974) 'Chance and Skill: A study of roulette', *Sociology* 8: 407–426.

Orford, J. (2011) *An Unsafe Bet? The dangerous rise of gambling and the debate we should be having*. Chichester: John Wiley and Sons.

Papineau, E. (2005) 'Pathological Gambling in Montreal's Chinese Community: An anthropological perspective', *Journal of Gambling Studies* 21: 157–178.

Paules, X. (2010) 'Gambling in China Reconsidered: Fantan in South China during the early twentieth century', *International Journal of Asian Studies* 7: 179–200.

Potenza, M., Steinberg, M., Skudlarsky, P., Fulbright, R., Lacadie, C., Wilbur, C., Rounsaville, B., Gore, J. and Wexler, B. (2003) 'Gambling Urges in Pathological Gambling: A functional magnetic resonance imaging study', *Archive of General Psychiatry* 60(8) 828–836.

Productivity Commission. (1999) *Australia's Gambling Industries*, Report No. 10. Canberra: AusInfo. Available at http://www.pc.gov.au/.

Reith, G. (1999) *The Age of Chance: Gambling in Western culture*. London: Routledge.

Reith, G. (2007) 'Gambling and the Contradictions of Consumption: A genealogy of the pathological subject', *American Behavioral Scientist* 51(1) 33–56.

Reith, G. (2008) 'Reflections on Responsibility: The neo-liberal state and the risky citizen', *Journal of Gambling Issues* 22: 49–155.

Reith, G. (2009) 'The Culture of Gambling in the United Kingdom: Legislative and social change', in C. Fijnaut, A. Littler and T. Spapens (eds) *Crime, Addiction and the Regulation of Gambling*. Leiden/Boston: Martinus Nijhoff Publishers.

Reith, G. and Dobbie, F. (2011) 'Beginning Gambling: The role of social networks and environment', *Addiction Research and Theory* 19(6) 483–493.

Ritzer, G. (1993) *The McDonaldization of Society*. Thousand Oaks CA: Pine Forge.

Ritzer, G. (1999) *Enchanting a Disenchanted World: Revolutionising the means of consumption*. Thousand Oaks, CA: Pine Forge.

Rosecrance, J. (1988) *Gambling without Guilt: The legitimation of an all-American pastime*. Pacific Grove, CA: Brooks, Cole.

Schull, N. (2005) 'Digital Gambling: The coincidence of desire and design', *Annals of the American Academy of Political and Social Sciences* 579: 65–81.

Shaffer, H.J., Vander Bilt, J. and Hall, M.N. (1999) 'Estimating the Prevalence of Disordered Gambling Behavior in the United States and Canada: A research Synthesis', *American Journal of Public Health* 89(9) 1369–1376.

Spanier, D. (1992) *All Right, O.K., You Win: Inside Las Vegas*. London: Mandarin.

Storer, J., Abbott, M. and Stubbs, J. (2009) 'Access or Adaptation? A meta analysis of surveys of problem gambling prevalence in Australia and New Zealand with respect to the concentration of electronic gaming machines', *International Gambling Studies* 9(3) 225–244.

Valverde, M. (1998) *Diseases of the Will: Alcohol and the dilemmas of freedom*. Cambridge: Cambridge University Press.

Volberg, R. (2001) *When the Chips are Down: Problem gambling in America*. New York: Century Foundation.

Volberg, R., Toce, M. and Gerstein, D. (1999) 'From Back Room to Living Room: Changing attitudes towards gambling', *Public Perspective* 10(5) 8–13.

Welte, J.W., Barnes, G.M., Wieczorek, W., Tidwell, M.-C. and Parker, J. (2002) 'Gambling Participation in the U.S.: Results from a national survey', *Journal of Gambling Studies* 18: 313–337.

Welte, J.W., Barnes, G.M., Wieczorek, W.F., Tidwell, M.-C. and Parker, J.C. (2004) 'Risk Factors for Pathological Gambling', *Addictive Behaviors* 29: 323–335.

28

LEISURE SEX

More sex! Better sex! Sex is fucking brilliant! Sex, sex, sex, SEX

Feona Attwood and Clarissa Smith

Introduction

How might we understand sex as one of the Big Seven leisure pursuits? What is sex? On an entirely functional level, sex is the physical means by which the species engages in procreation – sex is a physical activity, but it can be more than the mechanics of reproduction – and of course much is hidden (and denied) in such a definition. The term also refers to forms of physicality that have absolutely nothing to do with conception. Moreover, sex is associated with myriad intangible qualities. Sex is entwined with ideas of romance, attraction, commitment, independence, orientation, crime, identity, hygiene, waste, fantasy, confidence, despair, nature, abnormality, deviance, degradation, fulfilment, liberation, status, sin, perversion. We've deliberately avoided organizing these different conceptions within hierarchies or offering a binary list, precisely because sex is such a movable feast, varying over time and across cultures – but there is also no doubt that rules and hierarchies have existed around sex, creating limitations and opportunities. In the confines of this short chapter there simply is not the space to discuss the complex positioning of sex in Western culture across the last few centuries; instead, we are going to draw on that old chestnut of Philip Larkin's in his poem 'Annus Mirabilis' that: 'Sexual intercourse began/ In nineteen sixty-three/ (Which was rather late for me)/ Between the end of the *Chatterley* ban/ And the Beatles' first LP' (Larkin, 1967).

What Larkin's poem neatly encapsulates is the fond misbelief that every generation invents sex. But, crucially, it also links that invention to popular culture and the transgression of old certainties. Whether or not sex as a leisure pursuit is directly rooted in the permissiveness of 1960s popular culture or – to cite another myth of the liberalization of sex – was caused by the arrival of the contraceptive pill, there is no doubt that the past five decades have seen individuals encouraged to evaluate themselves and their bodies in the context of a modern, mediatized sexual culture whose symbolic resources valorize revelation and hedonism rather than discretion and self-discipline. It would, of course, be wrong to talk of sex as a singular activity or having only singular meaning – for many, sex and love are still absolutely intrinsic to kinship and to the formation of intimate relationships, but it is also clear that new forms and characteristics of sex are emerging, that sex is acquiring its own status as a recreational activity.

In modern societies, sexual consumption, experiences and practices have become ever more important to our sense of self and making the most of our lives. Sex is a source of happiness, a form of relaxation, a site of pleasure, expression of freedoms, a means of achieving spiritual wholeness and, in all its sensory potentials, sex is increasingly linked to leisure. Those processes are accelerated by the development of a range of technologies which have expanded and extended the material and mediated sources of pleasure and opportunities for sexual encounters and explorations. Even so, the common perception that Western societies have embraced an 'anything goes' view of sexual pleasure and practice is matched by intensifying drives to regulate many forms of sexual behaviour. In this chapter we examine some of the issues and contemporary contexts of leisured sex. We consider recent shifts in the definition of what sex is and could be and changing relations to commerce, leisure, self-care and relationships with others.

Sexual leisure as sexualization

According to commentators as various as the American Psychological Association, UK Prime Minister David Cameron and a broad array of activists including Abigail Bray (2009), Gail Dines (2010), and academics such as Brian McNair (2002), we are witnessing the sexualization of culture. Sex has become increasingly and insistently visible – from the endless media discussions of sexual values, practices and identities and attendant concerns about standards of morality and the prevalence of scandals; through controversies about the definitions, boundaries and proper regulation of obscenity; to the growth of sexual media of all kinds (erotica, slash fiction, sexual self-help books and porn genres), we are seeing the emergence of new forms of sexual experience (in, for example, instant message, avatar sex and sexting), made possible by developments in technology. These are all elements of a 'striptease culture' (McNair, 2002) and its cultural trends which privilege lifestyle, reality, interactivity, self-revelation and public intimacy.

In many accounts, sexualization is conceptualized as a force working on individuals and on society as a whole, but most especially on girls and women – providing scripts, moulding their bodies into particular forms of 'sexy'; and boys are 'a "guinea pig" generation … growing up addicted to hardcore pornography' (Peev, 2012: 1). What seems partly to be at stake here is the collapse of boundaries that have kept sex a part of private life, but, as Williams (2004: 166) suggests, it is nigh on impossible to define sex as 'a private matter, since it has, in effect, become so very public a matter, even to those who would argue to keep it private'.

Our understandings of sex, as orientations, practices and experiences in the twenty-first century, are shaped by changing relations of individualization which insist that sex, sexual identity and sexual health are matters for individual duty and responsibility. Being sexual is about being able to engage in the project of the self competently with due regard for one's health and well-being (Giddens, 1992), and increasingly about having sexual value (Hakim, 2011). Skills, resources and fitness are part of being a competent sexual being and taking part in sexual consumerism, sex as leisure. Young women engage in pole-dancing classes as a form of fitness (Holland, 2010), strip clubs are rebranded as gentlemen's clubs, and the spaces and places for the purchase of sexual services and the commodities which facilitate sex as forms of leisure are increasing (Attwood, 2005; Smith, 2007). For some commentators, the injunctions to enjoy oneself and to uncover one's own sexual interests simply replicate the age-old patterns of women's sexual performance for men and their servicing of men's emotional and sexual needs (Jeffreys, 2009).

Karen Boyle has suggested that it is 'important to distinguish between the commercialization of sex (the invitation to buy products to enhance our sex lives) and commercial sex (purchasing access to the bodies of others for our own gratification and independent of theirs)' (Boyle, 2010: 3). Boyle argues that porn and sex are, and should be, different things; the argument is taken up most explicitly by Gail Dines, who offers the idea of 'healthy sexuality' in comparison to what she calls 'porn sex' – sex that is 'debased, dehumanized, formulaic, and generic' (Dines, 2010: x); 'industrial strength sex' compared to sex that involves 'empathy, tenderness, caring, affection' … 'love, respect, or connection to another human being' (Dines, 2010: xxiv, xi). As Gayle Rubin wrote in 1984, such discussion of sexuality is based on the idea of a 'charmed circle' characterized by sex which is heteronormative, vanilla, procreative, coupled, taking place between people of the same generation, at home, involving bodies only, and avoiding commercial sex and pornography. Beyond this lie the 'outer limits' of sex; promiscuous, non-procreative, casual, non-married, homosexual, cross-generational, taking place alone or in groups, in public, involving sado-masochism (S/M), commerce, manufactured objects and pornography. Feminist critiques of 'sexualization' have often made clear the need to distinguish their objections from those based on moral or religious grounds, or on the offence to taste or decency. Yet recent feminist work does not seek to understand the pluralistic and shifting sensibilities around sex which embrace the postmodern elements of 'the spectacular, the popular, the pleasurable, and the immediately accessible' (Featherstone, 1991: 96).

A significant difficulty lies in the ways in which the condemnatory attitude towards the visibility of 'casual' sex, hook-up culture and so on almost always links these activities to the widespread availability of pornography, lap dancing clubs and other manifestations of the 'sex industries'. For example, Ariel Levy's invitation to readers to meet the female chauvinist pig, 'the new brand of "empowered woman" who wears the Playboy bunny as a talisman, bares all for *Girls Gone Wild*, pursues casual sex as if it were a sport, and embraces "raunch culture" wherever she finds it' (Levy, 2005, front matter) illustrates one problem in trying to maintain those distinctions. Young women's appropriations of the *symbols* of commercial sex are here held to account as indications that they are in thrall to the sex industries, that female sexuality has been commodified and repackaged back to them – that their own sexuality is buried beneath the acquisition of sex as a commodity to be packaged for men. The pessimistic views of sex being 'debased' by its contacts with 'porn sex' and 'porn culture' combine fears about child abuse, commercial sex and casual sex, as though these are all not only related but also uniformly problematic.

Despite the increasing visibility of sex, the public/private distinction may still retain its importance, drawing attention to the ways in which many people participate in 'a world of sex' without ever coming into personal contact with the 'sex industry', and indeed would reject any suggestion that their sexual practices have any connections with forms of commerce. It may not be that easy to separate out what might be understood as personal exploration and the 'simple' enhancement of one's sex life from the consumption of services which require the sexual labour of others. It may be difficult to separate out a recreational attitude to sex from that which might be conceived or experienced as sex *work*. As Jane Juffer has argued, the 'obliteration' of the public/private divide can lead to problematic assumptions of the transgression of regulation/boundaries exemplified in particular individuals such as Annie Sprinkle, where 'one performance artist's transgressive abilities begin to substitute for the conditions that determine the sexual practices of most women' (Juffer, 1998: 16). How do we give due attention to the differences while offering comprehensive and manageable groupings for research? Would filming one's sexual activities for personal contemplation constitute the production of pornography, or how might we definitively link these private productions to the widespread availability of professional porn? Is the sex toy designer a sex worker? Is there a difference between stripping for a lover and stripping in a bar? The meanings and valuations of acts/activities/practices/experiences are not so easily separated.

Sexy bodies

There are real problems with the kinds of thinking in which the body is seen as simply subject to disciplinary regimes, just as there are with the belief that sex is inevitably a force for trans-formation. Both reproduce a reductive essentialism and a rather naïve belief in bodies and pleasure as somehow outside the social. We need a space for understanding the exhortations to 'be sexy' as more than a disciplinary project and to recognize the conflicting experiences of sexual identifications and bodily sensations in the twenty-first century. Maffesoli suggests that 'the cult of the body and other forms of appearance have value only in so much as they are part of a larger stage in which everyone is both actor and spectator' (Maffesoli, 1996: 77). For those who argue that 'porn sex' involves 'using someone' and 'doing to someone', being a 'performance for others', a 'public commodity', 'separate from love', 'emotionally distant' (Malz and Malz, 2008), there is no room for understanding the ways in which new social forms of interaction, alternative sexual communities and the utilization of the body to communicate self-identity can and do offer opportunities for solidarity, recognition and sociality. It is hard to see why the characteristics of 'good sex' – as private rather than public, and clearly linked to love rather than to gratification – should be especially important for sexual politics, or why sex should be valued in terms of its capacity to develop intimacy rather than for any other reason. In fact, those characteristics of 'good sex' correspond much more clearly to a view of sex as sacred or 'special', and to the contemporary ideal of the pure relationship that Giddens (1992) describes, in which sex is anchored to emotional coherence and persistence. Casual sex, kinky sex, rough sex and even monogamous, straight, 'vanilla sex' that might be the product of routine, boredom, fun or thrill seeking does not meet these standards. A proper purpose for sex is assumed and there is little consideration of the variety of sexual practices that people engage in, their diverse understandings of what sex is or the multifarious reasons why people have sex. Despite their refutations of being 'anti-sex', writers like Dines foreclose the possibilities of sexuality as plural and in process, and the body as a significant conduit to experiences and emotions.

To fully understand the ways in which sexual interests might be changing, we also need to think about how bodies may be experienced and connected to modes of relating to one's self and to others. Lindemann (1997) describes three categories of body: the objectified, the experiencing and the experienced body. The objectified body is the one we see, it is an entity in social space and time but we cannot know how it feels. 'Just because that objecti-fied body is read … as "sexy" (or sexually attractive) does not mean it is necessarily being experienced as sexual' (Jackson and Scott, 2001: 16). The 'experiencing' body is a *sensory* one and the 'experienced' body is the specifically felt body, the one which has pain and pleasure but is also experienced as simply *there*. This becomes important in discussions of sex and sexual feeling because it is clear that there is a significant discrepancy between our stereotypical ideas of the 'sexy' body and the body which experiences sexual pleasure. Sex is not just a physiological response, a physical reaction that can be gained simply by being told what to do. The objectified body as both body in space and time and its comparator, the sexualized body or stereotypically sexually attractive body, cannot be separated from the perceptions of sexual desire, rights and possible pleasures and therefore has a relation with the experiencing and experienced body. The embodied experience of having sex is not reducible to touching, kissing, penetration, orgasm or any other associated phenomena but occurs in specific contexts as a social practice. 'Sex entails embodied selves engaged in embodied social activity and embodied interaction' (Jackson and Scott, 2001: 19).

The internet has, of course, created opportunities for networked engagement in sexual discourse, the possibilities for a more concrete sense of participation in a network of like-minded sexual subjects, and has also allowed for 'new forms of [sex] which disrupt older conceptions of its status and its place in society' (Attwood, 2006: 79). There are now online spaces in which individuals can construct communities, actions and subjectivities via message boards, blogs and hook-up sites. Increasingly, 'ordinary' individuals create their own inter-active narratives, stories, films and commentaries, posting them in forms of dialogue that were never possible within the political economies of traditional publishing or film distri-bution; moreover, sites such as gaydar.com enable the creation of sexual subcultures that are 'both physical and "virtual" ... with digital communications often structuring physical practices, identities and experiences' (Mowlabocus, 2010: 2), blurring the lines between on- and offline selves, distance and proximity, producer and consumer. In online spaces, forms of 'collectivity', 'community' and networks of sexual interactions become increas-ingly visible, though how far these are completely new phenomena or whether they will ever replace or even eradicate more traditional 'real life' interactions will require careful consideration. 'What do changing constructions of sexuality ... tell us about the way we live now in contemporary societies, about the relation between bodies and machines, or prac-tices and representations? What do they suggest about the way we envisage and organize the public and private worlds, or about changes in the management of intimate relationships?' (Attwood, 2006: 79).

Sex as leisure

In an important but functionalist division of forms of leisure activity Stebbins (1982; 1997) characterizes sex as a form of 'casual leisure' focused on sensory stimulation and sharing characteristics with eating, drinking and sight-seeing – all forms of what he sees as non-productive activity centred on 'immediately, intrinsically rewarding, relatively short-lived' pleasure 'requiring little or no special training to enjoy it' (Stebbins, 2001: 305). Casual leisure is understood in Stebbins' account as an essentially consumerist preoccupation with play, entertainment, stimulation – all those activities which are less substantial, and without a sense of future purpose, than their opposite, 'serious leisure': forms of activity which are 'important to the wellbeing of the individual and society' (Rojek, 2000: 18). Whether or not that categorization of sex as 'casual' was *ever* an adequate understanding of the multiplici-ties of previous generations' sexual cultures is beyond the scope of this chapter, but it seems entirely inadequate as a means of comprehending the reach, scope and meaningfulness of sex in the twenty-first century. We wouldn't want to deny that sex can be playful, entertaining, stimulating and experienced in the here-and-now, but Stebbins' 'scornful' (Blackshaw, 2010) dismissal of casual leisure fails to recognize the ways in which even the avowedly hedonistic pursuit of sex may be more than *just* frivolous, that it might, like forms of 'serious leisure' have significant benefits (and costs) for individuals and society, offering consider-able potential for productivity, development of skills and knowledge, and thereby might engender self-confidence, identity and community through achievement. The placing of sex within a serious/casual leisure dichotomy confirms Rojek's suggestion that the concept of serious leisure is underpinned by moral foundations and seeks to valorize particular forms of social behaviour – such as the development of heteronormative companionship and community. As Rojek suggests: 'Serious leisure' can be understood as 'a vehicle for the cultural and moral reaffirmation of communities as places in which the individual recognizes relations of belonging' (Rojek, 2000: 18). Even so, while recognizing the hierarchical and potentially regressive designations, we also feel that the term 'serious leisure' may have resonances and application for our understandings of sex in the twenty-first century.

First, the designation of 'sex' as 'casual leisure' fails to acknowledge the role that sex has played in official and non-institutional discourses of marriage and romance, of the sexual revolution, of identity formation, identity politics, religious moral revivalism, campaigns against pornographication (pornification) and sexualization. In each of these, though to varying degrees, impacts and effects, sex has acted as a driver, motivator, consolidator and important means towards intimacy, community, social cohesion and, for pessimistic observers, the most potent destroyer of all those 'pro-social' effects. The importance that sex assumes in these variously motivated conceptualizations surely undermines the idea that it is *simply* hedonistic and purposeless (though it can be those things). For example, anti-porn author Robert Jensen suggests that 'good' sex is private rather than public, and clearly linked to love rather than to gratification, that sex should involve 'a sense of connection to another person, a greater awareness of one's own humanity and sometimes, even a profound sense of the world that can come from meaningful and deep sexual experience' (in Boulton, 2008: 257).

Second, sex is, of course, socially constructed within contextual frameworks of competing cultural norms. Sex is experienced in intensely personal ways – for some, as we have already seen, it is a conduit to the most wonderful sensations and a means by which long- and/or short-term intimacies are fostered, but for others it is a tiresome chore, a painful imposition or simply tedious. Sex can be understood as an everyday activity, not particularly important to the individual, pleasurable as and when it is indulged in but having little further meaning – a functional way of keeping oneself healthy and in touch with a partner. For others, sex may most nearly connect with forms of communality where social belonging and social relationships beyond normative or monogamous relationships are important to identification and possession of one's 'sexuality', for example in gay, lesbian, bisexual or open relationships. For yet others, sex may be more like an 'extreme sport', where orgasm (temporary pleasure) is less important than as a side-effect of testing the body's limits, or creating new and exciting forms of intimacy with one or more partners, of acquiring skills and knowledges, of thrill seeking and risk taking, sought as pleasures in their own right. Of course, it is easiest to see these other sensations in relation to activities occurring within sexual subcultures such as swinging or BDSM (bondage and discipline; dominance and submission; sadism and masochism), which, with their focus on initiation, mentoring and community, may most effectively display qualities of serious leisure, providing a fulfilling leisure experience – restorative, resourceful and enhancing participants' quality of life (Newmahr, 2010). As Mark Brendon comments of his swinging lifestyle: 'Here I can fall in love and truly love my fellows, give and take in equal measure and walk away, having learned from them, shared with them and feeling more integrated with my world, whereas in every other form of casual – or, still worse, pseudo-committal – sex, I feel diminished.' (Brendon, 2008: 303).

Thinking about sex as leisure we draw here on Csikszentmihalyi's definition of leisure as a crossover of free time, activity and attitude (1975); 'leisured sex' isn't simply about having sex, clashing genitals or some other body parts in pursuit of orgasm, it is about having the time to give to exercise one's interests in sex, to engage in sex as a form of relaxation, entertainment, self-realization, self-gratification and gratification of others, and personal development. The experience of 'time-crunching' means that while people may have gained additional free time, their subjective sense is of having much less (Robinson and Godbey, 1997), and in the modern construction of sex it is important to *make time* for sex – an element explored in some depth in sex manuals which exhort readers, particularly long-term partners and couples who have just become parents, to ensure that they make time for sex as a key means of keeping their relationship healthy and intimate.

This functional and heteronormatively romantic ideal has increasingly been marked by a middle-class 'fun ethic' (Bourdieu, 1984) which incorporates a hedonistic and 'liberated' sexuality. Articles in magazines as diverse as *Cosmopolitan*, *GQ*, *Good Housekeeping* and *Nerve* are written by the cultural intermediaries of 'striptease culture' (McNair, 2002), a new service class (Lash and Urry, 1987) of 'sexiterati' – journalists, designers, PR practitioners, advertisers, sex therapists, marriage counsellors, and dieticians whose knowledge about the 'symbolic goods and services' (Nixon and du Gay, 2002: 496) necessary to a good sex life are on seemingly constant display. Women's magazines, advice manuals, videos such as *The Lovers' Guides* have, for decades, focused on the ways in which sex ought to be pleasurable and fun and can be learned. Interestingly, for an aspect of human life which is seemingly so important, its purpose and intentions are often conceptualized in limited ways – we have swapped procreation for recreation and therefore FUN, but the notion of 'fun' is limited by concerns that sex should, however wild, remain within the boundaries of adult, consensual and sane and be, above all, pleasurable.

Lifestyling sex

Magazines and self-help programmes like the *Sex Inspectors* and *The Lovers' Guides* exhort heterosexual couples to bring a kind of work ethic into this most personal sphere of everyday life – with the application of techniques, tools and toys to enhance sexual pleasure and get over the 'trauma' of lack of orgasms etc. Efficiency, investments and rewards are all part of the leisure of sex (Harvey and Gill, 2011). But self-help can also be seen as more than exhortations to get more from your sex life: the *Lovers' Guides* videos of the 1990s, for example, may be seen as an interesting response to the problem of AIDS and the ways in which the possibilities of infection problematized 1960s discourses of sexual liberation and sexual satisfaction through multiple partners. The *Guides* offered a way of reinvigorating the long-term romance and sexual pleasures of monogamy, part of the broader projects of sex as a leisure pursuit but also of an understanding of sex as a form of skilled practice whose pleasures come at least partly from according it significance within the routines of daily life. From this viewpoint it is not enough to have sex, much better to be able to demonstrate skill, imagination and practice, and in the *Guides* this became a possibility within mature and long-term relationships where the domestic space became a playground, sexing up the home. With their emphasis on dispelling ignorance and shame, their avowed intent to speak to couples attempting to deepen levels of intimacy and pleasure in their relationships, the *Guides* offered themselves to interested couples seeking ideas and practical steps for improving skills within a sophisticated but domestic arrangement. Individuals need to negotiate competing and often conflicting social pressures to be sexual, and to conform to ideas of 'normality' (Barker, 2012), particularly the emphasis on maintaining the body as a desiring body in the sense of leisure, but also putting in the work to make that happen. Sexuality is something that we possess, innately, but also is something to be worked at, practised and improved – it is to be both disciplined and enjoyed as a form of pleasure, relaxation and as access to the true self.

Contemporary sexualities may often be constructed as forms of consumer lifestyle, requiring the necessary therapeutic and commercial products which give access to proper sex. Certainly, new forms of sex-cultural production are partly aimed at meeting the 'extension of sexual consumerism' (McNair, 2002: 87), which can be traced not only in the expansion and diversification of the 'pornosphere', but more broadly in the emergence of a 'striptease culture'. Striptease culture embodies a widespread preoccupation with 'self-revelation' (McNair, 2002: 81) and 'public intimacy' (ibid.: 98), evident in reality TV and other types of first-person media, as well as in the development of new technologies for self-publishing and social networking. Sex also figures more visibly than ever before in forms associated with high culture. Since the early 1990s, erotica have been sold in large bookstore chains, but, with the publishing phenomenon of E.L. James's *Fifty Shades of Grey*, supermarkets have now begun to stock tales of lust and leather beside the check-out. Sex is a recurring theme in contemporary art, and more recently in design, possibly because both 'offer a realm of sexual pleasure and hedonism ... are treated as recreational activities ... and ... are viewed in openly self-preoccupied, consumerist terms' (Poynor, 2006: 7–8). We are, Poynor argues, 'in the process of designing a pornotopia' (2006: 9). Key to the development of a 'pornotopia' has been the rise of sexual consumerism centred on 'feminine' sensibilities, for example, the visibility of chic sexual products – expensive lingerie and luxury sex toys – sold in glamorous sex shops modelled on stylish boutiques that emphasize their designer credentials and reaffirm nostalgic ideas of 'secrecy' and 'privacy' wrapped up in 'affordable luxury' (Juffer, 1998).

The expressions of young women's sexual interests that are condemned as deriving from pornified culture are more complex than the 'effects' complaints might suggest; there is no doubt that sexual freedom has not consigned sexism to the bin and the emotional outfalls of casual relationships are as painful as they ever were, but the idea of these interests as simply an effect of sexualization is one which cannot find anything positive in more open attitudes and more aggressively expressed interests in sex. How can we open up debate about active female sexualities and their materialization in culture, how do we understand the complexities of sexualization, commodification, objectification and, crucially, subjectification in the expressions of new sexual sensibilities and their hedonistic pursuits?

Sexual cultures

Although increasingly mainstream, this new sexual hedonism draws on some previously quite marginal sexual sensibilities. The first of these is derived from sex-positive and sex-radical writing and practice devoted to the reclaiming of sexual pleasure and to a revaluation of reviled practices such as masturbation, S/M, the use of pornography and sex work. The second is drawn from gay cultures, emphasizing the celebration of diversity and the creation of communities based around sexuality. The third is a 'playboy' sensibility, embodied in the development of media and leisure spaces focused on straight men's entertainment.

While quite different in many ways, these share a view of sex as a valid source of effort, play and work, and all have become more visible in contemporary popular culture. If *Playboy* can be understood as the forerunner of much of the lifestyle media and the mainstream leisure venues that are currently aimed at men, most obviously in men's magazines and the 'gentlemen's clubs' (Osgerby, 2001), then it has also had significant impact on the ways in which women might view sex. A sex-positive/sex-radical stance is evident in the sexy form of mainstream post-feminism embodied by performers such as Madonna and Lady Gaga. Gay lifestyles have been mainstreamed as a form of cosmopolitan leisure and conspicuous consumption.

If sexual cultures originate within the contexts of dominant heteronormative culture, some can be understood as positive responses to the demands of structures such as marriage, monogamy etc., and then there are those that are in negative response (Jenks, 2005: 10) or forms of 'delinquent' sexualities. As with other subcultures, sexual subcultures are often non-normative, non-mainstream, 'deviant', marginalized and even criminal groups (Jenks, 2005: 121) offering their own sources of identity and signifying differences – modes of inclusion – even as dominant culture might be 'disapproving' or 'repulsed'. Subcultures are often valued positively because they are actively produced: a means for people to express their differences from the 'mainstream', creating 'cultures' that are defined by their 'authenticity' (Hollows, 2003: 36). In relation to mainstream culture, some sexual cultures may appear deviant, resistant and transgressive, but they are also expressions of alternate identities and forms of community.

While deviant sexual activity is often understood as the result of 'forces' which must be halted, regulated or medicated away, the sensuous pleasures of these acts are not acknowledged. Just as gay couplings occurred while such liaisons were criminalized, so we have to think about the reasons why people might commit acts that are criminalized today – because they want to, they like it, find pleasure, find fulfilment. Risk also needs to be understood as part of the thrill. The conception of 'risky sexual practice' too often contributes to a pathologizing of non-normative sexual practices as 'evidence' of an inability to make sound assessments or rational judgements about what constitutes 'safe sex'. Participants in unusual sexual activities may have uneven levels of understanding of the health implications of individual acts but also make calculations about those relative risks and their possible pleasurable outcomes – indeed risk taking can produce or intensify pleasure. Instead, sexual activity should be understood as sets of intense experiences linked to the wider norms of sexual culture. Work on participants in extreme sports has highlighted the very different understandings of the vocational habitus that characterizes, for example, competitive bodybuilding or its polar opposite, ballet, demonstrating that the requirements for specific body types, regimes of discipline and training, expectations of hard work and mental toughness 'impact on the ideals, aspirations and conduct ... influenc[ing participants'] perception and understanding of risk, pain and injury' (Probert *et al.*, 2007: 273). The pleasures and dangers of any pursuit are not absolute; they are socially and culturally bounded and may be understood quite differently by those within the particular milieu and those outside. As Probert *et al.* indicate, 'risk may be construed ... as an essential, routine part of activity ... a sensation which can be embraced and valued ... a means to test skill and self-mastery ... and/or an element ... to be managed, minimized and downplayed' (Probert *et al.*, 2007: 273).

For example, 'intensive sex partying' practised by some gay men can involve 'high risk' behaviours, including multiple partners, sexual adventurism, drug taking and higher incidences of 'unsafe' sexual activities such as 'fisting', but Hurley and Prestage (2009) caution against pathologizing this kind of partying precisely in order to understand the place of risk in some gay men's lives and how such risk is mitigated by knowledge and shared expertises, the development of sexual repertoires and practical sexual literacies. Far from engaging in risky practices in dangerous ways without due regard for one's own or others' safety, sex-party participants take pleasure both in the sexual sensations *and* in each other's well-being. For many people there are gains to be made in terms of mastering sexual techniques: increasing one's sexual capital, engaging in and cementing relationships, acquiring the proper physical prowess, developing skills and opportunities for orgasm, reducing risk and, if we take to heart Naomi Wolf's (2012) recent claims about the possibilities for creativity derived from the vagina's capacity for orgasm, then capacities for joy, pleasure and creativity. If 'being sexy' is a form of leisure, a form of engaging with the aspects of the social in particular ways, then reading the how-to techniques in women's magazines, being good at sex, taming elements of the masculinized pornosphere (Juffer, 1998) in order to enjoy participation in sexual cultures are all pursuits sought for their own pleasures and for the connections they enable to one's own body, experiences, emotions and to those of others. In this sense sex as leisure might be understood as 'delight in a surplus beyond the satisfaction of basic need' (Inglis, 2000: 59)

What are the ways in which intimacy might be understood more precisely and understood as a social good, and a shared aim beyond the traditional and heteronormative dyad? What commonalities can we theorize? Traditionally, proper intimacy in sex has been predicated on exclusivity (monogamy), but various sexual cultures, from wife-swapping through to swinging, may produce intimacy, and offer opportunities for intimacy via variation, community, sharing, etc. As Newmahr (2010) illustrates, 'skills' may not be limited to physicality and technicalities (although those do seem to be a major concern within sex manuals); skills may have emotional dimensions, imaginative dimensions and important social capital can be derived from those. Sexual pleasures may be pleasures which are sought for their own sake, but also on an experiential level enable a sense of belonging to a community in which others are also exploring the possibilities of sex. There are varieties of acts, identities, behaviours and a variety of sub-cultures which are products of their interactions, sometimes organized around orientations or identifications, specific acts, fashions or performances – young people's sexual cultures may be very different from those of older individuals, differentiated as well by attitudes towards religiosity, gender, ethnicity etc.. Thus, socio-cultural norms and values and their specifics influence sexual behaviour and may be unique to the individual, while at the same time shared. 'Atmosphere', 'knowledge', 'environment', self-confidence, value systems, perception of safety, understandings of risk, social skills, ability to compromise or readjust to circumstances, may have considerable influence on what an individual feels inclined to pursue. As Deleuze and Guattari have argued, 'we know nothing about a body until we know what it can do, in other words what its affects are, how they can or cannot enter into composition with other affects, with the affects of another body' (Deleuze and Guattari, 1987: 257). This spirit of experimentation/exploration may be the defining characteristic of many modern sexualities.

Conclusions

The emergence of modern recreational sexualities is linked to – and can be seen as emblematic of – a broad range of contemporary concerns with image, lifestyle and self-exposure, which have become means of self-care, self-pleasure and self-expression. In this sense, sex increasingly overlaps with other important spheres of contemporary life, and in particular that of leisure. Sexual practices in the West have become matters of personal taste and lifestyle – even that most sanctioned of sexual relationships, the heterosexual marriage, has become a site of playfulness where long-term intimacy is to be fostered through recognition of the importance of sex. Other kinds of sexual encounters – the affair, the one-night stand, 'pleasing oneself' through the use of pornography and sex toys, forms of commercial and virtual sex have also become more acceptable and a 'sexy' persona is now often expressed through a set of performances accompanied by consumption of sexual commodities. It is in this commodification of sexuality that we have seen the development of a new 'recreational' sexuality focused on self-pleasure and fun: characterized by 'adventurism', 'experimentation', 'choice', 'variety' and 'sensation' (Illouz, 1999: 176). Recreational sex has become part of what has been described as the 'ethical retooling' of consumer capitalism and its promotion of a 'morality of pleasure as a duty' (Bourdieu, 1984: 365–71).

Alongside this, we also see growing irritations with the sexualization of culture and a sense that sex has become the big story at the expense of more politicized conceptions of sexual freedoms, choices, individualism and community. Even so, any examination of the ethics or politics of sexual leisure will need to engage with the particular commitments and engagements of specific sexual cultures (including those most ordinary and supposedly 'natural' heterosexual couplings). Of course, sex is an intensely topical issue, subject to many opposing views and 'strong opinions'. And, for many people, the only important considerations are the moral or political issues related to sex (who, and in what contexts, is having sex?), its practice (is it 'healthy' for the individual, for their partners, for society? Is it premised on 'equality' or 'authentic' values?), and its 'effects' (what 'harms' might come to individuals and to society at large). Even as we consider ourselves to live in liberated times, too often the practices, cultures and identities that are constructed around sexual desire are measured against a standard of 'regular' heterosexuality. Sexual practices and experiences and their roles and significances in everyday life continue to be contested, the focus of new struggles over the definitions of healthy sex, work and play. Capturing the meanings of recreational sex and the varying importance of sex in everyday life will need research which proceeds with recognition of the multiplicities of rights and responsibilities, pleasures and displeasures, interests and issues for individuals and sexual communities. If the limits of 'sex' are undergoing significant revision, research will need to engage with the wheres and hows of its modifications, what modes of representation, what technologies, strategies and practices, and by whom the boundaries of sex are being redrawn.

References

Attwood, F. (2006) 'Sexed Up: Theorizing the Sexualization of Culture', *Sexualities* 9(1) 77–94.

Attwood, F. (2005) 'Fashion and Passion: Marketing Sex to Women', *Sexualities* 8(4) 392–406.

Barker, M. (2012) *Rewriting the Rules: An Integrative Guide to Love, Sex and Relationships*. London: Routledge.

Blackshaw, T. (2010) *Leisure*. London and New York: Routledge.

Boulton, C. (2008) 'Porn and Me(n): Sexual Morality, Objectification, and Religion at the Wheelock Anti-Pornography Conference', *The Communication Review* 11(3) 247–273.

Bourdieu, P. (1984) *Distinction: A Social Critique of the Judgement of Taste*. London: Routledge.

Boyle, K. (ed.) (2010) 'Introduction', *Everyday Pornographies*. London: Routledge.

Bray, A. (2009) 'Governing the Gaze: Child Sexual Abuse Moral Panics and the Post-Feminist Blindspot', *Feminist Media Studies* 9(2) 173–191.

Brendon, M. (2008) *Swinging: The Games Your Neighbours Play*. London: The Friday Project.

Csikszentmihalyi, M. (1975) *Beyond Boredom and Anxiety*. San Francisco: Jossey-Bass.

Deleuze, G. and Guattari, F. (1987) *A Thousand Plateaus*. Minneapolis: University of Minnesota Press.

Dines, G. (2010) *Pornland: How Porn has Hijacked Our Sexuality*. Boston, MA: Beacon Press.

Featherstone, M. (1991) *Consumer Culture and Postmodernism*. London: Sage.

Giddens, A. (1992) *The Transformation of Intimacy: Sexuality, Love and Eroticism in Modern Societies*. Cambridge: Polity Press.

Hakim, C. (2011) *Erotic Capital: The Power of Attraction in the Boardroom and the Bedroom*. New York: Basic Books.

Harvey, L. and Gill, R. (2011) 'The Sex Inspectors: Self-help, Makeover and Mediated Sex', in K. Ross (ed.) *Handbook on Gender, Sexualities and Media*. Oxford: Blackwell.

Holland, S. (2010) *Pole Dancing, Empowerment and Embodiment*. Basingstoke: Palgrave Macmillan.

Hollows, J. (2003) 'The Masculinity of the Cult', in M. Jancovich, A.L. Reboll, J. Stringer and A. Willis (eds) *Defining Cult Movies: The Cultural Politics of Oppositional Taste*. Manchester: Manchester University Press.

Hurley, M. and Prestage, G. (2009) 'Intensive Sex Partying amongst Gay Men in Sydney', *Culture, Health and Sexuality* 11(6) 597–610.

Illouz, E. (1999) 'The Lost Innocence of Love: Romance as a Postmodern Condition', in M. Featherstone (ed.) *Love and Eroticism*, London: Sage.

Inglis, F. (2000) *A Delicious History of the Holiday*. London: Routledge.

Jackson, S. and Scott, S. (2001) 'Putting the Body's Feet on the Ground: Towards a Sociological Reconceptualization of Gendered and Sexual Embodiment', in K. Backett-Milburn and L. McKie (eds) *Constructing Gendered Bodies*. London: Palgrave.

Jeffreys, S. (2009) *The Industrial Vagina: The Political Economy of the Sex Trade*. London: Routledge.

Jenks, C. (2005) *Subculture*. London: Sage.

Juffer, J. (1998) *At Home with Pornography: Women, Sex and Everyday Life*. New York and London: New York University Press.

Larkin, P. (1967) 'Annus Mirabilis', *High Windows*. London: Faber & Faber.

Lash, S. and Urry, J. (1987) *The End of Organized Capitalism*. Cambridge: Polity.

Levy, A. (2005) *Female Chauvinist Pigs: Women and the Rise of Raunch Culture*. New York and London: Free Press.

Lindemann, G. (1997) 'The Body of Gender Difference', in K. Davis (ed.) *Embodied Practices: Feminist Perspectives on the Body*. London: Sage

Maffesoli, M. (1996) *The Time of the Tribes*. London: Sage.

Malz, W. and Malz, L. (2008) *The Porn Trap: The Essential Guide to Overcoming Problems Caused by Porn*. New York: HarperCollins.

McNair, B. (2002) *Striptease Culture: Sex, Media and the Democratization of Desire*. London and New York: Routledge.

Mowlabocus, S. (2010) *Gaydar Culture: Gay Men, Technology and Embodiment in the Digital Age*. Farnham: Ashgate.

Newmahr, S. (2010) 'Rethinking Kink: Sadomasochism as Serious Leisure', *Qualitative Sociology* 33(3) 313–331.

Nixon, S. and du Gay, P. (2002) 'Who Needs Cultural Intermediaries?', *Cultural Studies* 16(4) 495–500.

Osgerby, B. (2001) *Playboys in Paradise: Masculinity, Youth and Leisure-style in Modern America*. Oxford and New York: Berg.

Peev, G. (2012) 'Children Grow Up Addicted to Online Porn Sites', *Daily Mail*, 19 April.

Poynor, R. (2006) *Designing Pornotopia: Travels in Visual Culture*. London: Laurence King Publishing.

Probert, A., Palmer, F. and Leberman, S. (2007) 'The Fine Line: An Insight into "Risky" Practices of Male and Female Competitive Bodybuilders', *Annals of Leisure Research* 10(3–4) 272–290.

Robinson, J.P. and Godbey, G. (1997) *Time for Life: The Surprising Ways Americans Use Their Time*. State College, PA: The Pennsylvania State University Press.

Rojek, C. (2000) *Leisure and Culture*. Basingstoke: Palgrave Macmillan.

Rubin, G. (1984) 'Thinking Sex: Notes for a Radical Theory of the Politics of Sexuality', in C.S. Vance (ed.) *Pleasure and Danger: Exploring Female Sexuality*. Boston, MA: Routledge and Kegan Paul.

Smith, C. (2007) 'Designed for Pleasure: Style, Indulgence and Accessorized Sex', *European Journal of Cultural Studies* 10(2) 167–184.

Stebbins, R. A. (2001) 'The Costs and Benefits of Hedonism: Some Consequences of Taking Casual Leisure Seriously', *Leisure Studies* 20: 305–9.

Stebbins, R. A. (1997) 'Casual Leisure: A Conceptual Statement', *Leisure Studies* 16(1) 17–25.

Stebbins, R. A. (1982) 'Serious Leisure: A Conceptual Statement', *Pacific Sociological Review* 25: 251–272.

Williams, L. (2004) 'Second Thoughts on *Hard Core*: American Obscenity Law and the Scapegoating of Deviance', in P. Church Gibson (ed.) *More Dirty Looks: Gender, Pornography and Power*. London: BFI.

Wolf, N. (2012) *Vagina: A New Biography*, London: Virago.

29

TELEVISION AND CULTURAL CITIZENSHIP

Nick Stevenson

One of the most interesting developments in Leisure Studies since the early 1970s has been the fragmentation of general awareness into specific interest. Nowhere is this trend more well established that in the critical study of television. The topic of this chapter, that the way we understand television has wider implications for questions of cultural citizenship, is well established amongst media scholars. The development of a genuinely mass medium that was able to beam into people's homes a sense of the wider world has obvious implications for how we understand questions of rights, obligations and a shared sense of cultural identity. However, if we want to understand the shifting role of television in contemporary life we need to do so historically. During the 1960s, as we shall see, many radical democratic writers saw the arrival of mass television as potentially strengthening a shared civic identity. Much of the contemporary argument around new media (especially the Internet, mobile phones and blog sites) now carries the burden of radical hope for building a more civically engaged society. Television is now increasingly written about as the domestic medium, or through notions of the commodified spectacle. In current debates about the ability of media to help citizens imagine political alternatives to the present, television has seemingly a rapidly diminishing presence. Here I want to investigate how we might understand the civic role of television, given its continued power to help to inform the subjectivities of modern citizens. I aim to avoid the tendency within some work to juxtapose mass television to the more 'liberating' quality of new media. Television remains important as a common mass-mediated experience that is able grant modern citizens access to a plurality of narratives, stories and perceptions that communicates to them a shared and differential sense of their shifting identities.

Questions of cultural citizenship

The idea of cultural citizenship has provoked a considerable amount of debate in recent times (Couldry, 2006, Hermes and Dahlgren, 2006, Stevenson, 2003). Largely these debates have sought to develop the notion of citizenship to include the role that popular culture plays in developing the civic identities of citizens. More specifically, by cultural citizenship I mean an approach that seeks to investigate questions of cultural respect, learning and democracy. Here I seek to explore the extent to which democratic spaces and places can interrogate, make meaningful and understand wider processes of social change. In particular I have been critical of those who simply locate the idea of cultural citizenship as being exclusively concerned with the 'uses' of commercial culture. For instance, John Hartley (1999: 155) locates television as 'a transmodern teacher' that offers daily lessons on a number of aspects of the wider world. This includes moral and ethical aspects and, more significantly, surface impressions of others in an increasingly pluralistic society. What television actually 'teaches' is the acceptance of difference and DIY citizenship. If television was once part of a 'fourth estate' being expected to tell truth to power, then more recently it has become centrally concerned with questions of identity. Hartley (1999: 161) illustrates this view by commenting upon the way that television mixes together plural tribes and taste communities and offers us the tools for 'semiotic self-determination'. Television through its evolution has democratized knowledge and learning through the progressive fragmentation of audiences, allowing for the explosion of new kinds of civility and the exploration of difference largely through a commercial setting. From the point of view of the critique developed in the chapter these features are at least partially suggestive, but taken together they are deeply misleading. What is missing is the location of the consumption of television in the wider setting of the partial historical erosion of more democratic spaces and sensibilities by neoliberalism.

Jacques Rancière (2006) has identified a central paradox evident in democratic regimes that on one level defines itself against tyrannous states, while at the same time seeking to restrict the spread of democratic ways of life internally. In other words, democratic regimes seek to curtail the 'excess of democratic vitality' (Rancière, 2006: 7). Ruling elites restrict the role of democracy, as they fear that embedded in the ideal is hostility to those who are 'entitled' to govern. Rancière (2006: 56) talks of the movement for democracy and an active civic life as 'a double movement'. This involves the attempt to extend equal forms of citizenship to all citizens and opposition towards those who would seek to utilize wealth and power in order to secure special privileges. The struggle for democracy is the struggle to bring everyone into common forms of citizenship while simultaneously preventing unchallenged rule by elected or unelected elites. Democratic citizenship should be continually questioning exclusions from citizenship entitlement and be wary of the rule of elites. However, the rule of capital and political elites more generally has a tendency to restrict the expression of democracy in spaces and places outside of their direct control. This means that politics is increasingly being taken over by unelected elites, the most important of which being the rich and powerful. As the welfare state is downgraded, inequalities increased, multiculturalism displaced and the rule of capital enhanced, meaningful forms of democracy go into decline. What matters, then, is the extent to which the media (or, in this case, television) are able to constitute discordant publics full of different voices, critical perspectives and a diversity of experiences. This, as we shall see, is not simply a matter of plurality, but of the freedom to move between different stories and narratives while recognizing our commonality as well as our difference (Silverstone, 2007: 40). Given the emergence of mass television within a post-war society, we can expect many of its features to have been determined by the politics of the time. The dominance of social democracy in the Western European context meant that television was regulated in the public interest in ways that could never be said of the press. However, as we shall see, more recently the rise of neoliberalism has meant that in more contemporary times television is now inflected with a more market-driven sensibility. In terms of questions of citizenship, television is a medium that is still defined by democratic possibility, but whose content is now more governed by the market than by the state.

If Raymond Williams (1962) argued for the civic development of television and media and communication in the 1960s he did so in the context of a struggle for a learning and communicative democracy. A genuinely participatory democracy could come into being for the vast majority of ordinary people only if the labour movement was able to resist capitalism, education became less concerned with passing exams and a new generation of artists offered public spaces to communicate with the wider citizenry. Similarly, radical educationalist Henry Giroux (2004) locates wider questions of culture within a wider democratic crisis. Leisure Studies has a responsibility to promote a wider culture of questioning, criticism and democracy. Here we need to recognize the extent to which democratic spaces that promote different kinds of understanding are currently being marginalized by the dominant practices of neoliberal capitalism. Especially significant is Giroux's identification of free market doctrines as fostering 'competitive, self-interested individuals vying for their own material and ideological gain' (Giroux, 2004: 106). Neoliberalism is a form of domination that introduces certain identities and cultural identifications as a way of driving out more democratic concerns. This is why the story of television is one of civic and democratic possibility.

Public service television and its discontents

In the British context, key to understanding the development of television in relation to mainstream society has been the idea of public service broadcasting. Paddy Scannell (1989) describes how public service broadcasting's emphasis upon quality, equality of access and diversity sought to create a common civic culture. The educative role played by broadcasting aimed to create not only a shared national identity but the possibility of participating within a common community. Television and radio helped to create the possibilities of an informed citizenry, providing people with quality forms of information in order to act as citizens. However, since the development of a mass television society from the 1950s, the dominance of public service television has been progressively diluted. Especially significant here was the 1986 Peacock Report, which argued that new opportunities in technology could have a dramatic effect upon the pluralization of consumer choice. Television from this point on became increasingly more driven by the needs of consumers and the expansion of markets than it was by a need to maintain a shared civic culture.

During the 1960s many cultural critics argued that television maintained a progressive potential that was not evident in the national press. This was largely due to the ideas of public service values that had governed the emergence of television. Raymond Williams (1962) developed a radical critique of public service broadcasting, accurately describing it as paternalistic, given the way that it sought to define mass tastes and pleasures. In particular, Williams wanted to offer new rights to radical artists and to democratize public broadcasting so as to give more ordinary people a voice in shaping the medium. In particular, Williams had been encouraged by the development of 'Play for Today' on the BBC during the 1960s producing radical realist theatre, particularly around questions of class. Dramatists such as Ken Loach, Dennis Potter and others made their mark on the mass audiences during this period. We also need to remember that the 1960s was also the period of radical innovation in respect of film, especially in terms of the representation of class (Rowbotham and Beynon, 2001). However, film has remained a place where different class identities can be explored in ways that are now less true for television. The radical realist experiments within film and television of the 1960s continue to find a resonance through more contemporary cinema like *Fish Tank* and *The Arbor*.

These dramatic forms could also be linked to the working-class novels of the period, offering the possibility of previously excluded voices being heard by masses of people for the first time. Television could be further democratized only if it continued to offer public spaces of experimentation that maintained a sense of autonomy from the direct rule of the market or the state. Williams notably resisted an analysis of television that sought to dismiss it as a form of crass commercialism. If this line of argument was followed, then the BBC would simply become the preserve of more traditionally defined 'high' culture, leaving mass tastes to be defined by commercial television. Instead, Williams perceptively recognized that it was the role of the public service broadcaster not only to communicate to large publics, but to refuse simple divisions between high and low culture. A democratic culture, Williams felt, would act as a bridge between different sections of the audience. Television, to remember Williams's (1968) great novel, was capable of persuading the audience to become border crossers. As a mass medium, television offered the possibility of creating genuinely democratic, plural and critical publics. When it was at its most radical it did not simply reconfirm a taste community, but introduced more critical ways of seeing and thinking for wider audiences. However, as Mulgan and Worpole (1986) argued, in practice, public service broadcasting tended to uphold elite tastes, whereas the more populist-driven commercial channels offered less earnest programming. A more democratically inspired cultural policy would need to question this division while providing democratic spaces that enabled aesthetic innovation and genuinely popular as well as critical programming.

It was probably Richard Hoggart (2001) who best understood the educative role of broadcasting. This was not only because he wrote about media and education, but because he recognized the importance of developing critical literacy. If media were to perform their civic role they could do so only if they were formally regulated and citizens had educated expectations of television and radio. This requires an education system that offers more than the technical or functional literacy demanded by the labour market. Instead, educated citizens need to be mindful of attempts to convert them into being consumers of poor-quality media texts. Hoggart's work is particularly clear in pointing to the connection between low levels of literacy amongst the population and commercially exploitative media. Indeed Hoggart's writing is representative of the labour movement's desire to articulate a common civic culture through broadcasting as well as education that talked a language of learning, critical engagement and voice that has become absent from more contemporary debates.

The prospects for democracy and a reformed public service model were intimately linked, and preoccupied many on the progressive left. Later, John B. Thompson (1990) offered an updated model of public service television that he described as regulated pluralism. In particular, Thompson was concerned about the concentration of power within certain media organizations like News International and the tie between the BBC and state power. Thompson proposed to empower independent producers in a way that was similar to Williams's arguments of the 1960s. Similarly John Keane (1991) argued that the increase in market-driven communication meant that public service broadcasting had become more, not less relevant. However, like Thompson, Keane wanted to expand the possibilities of more independent voices within civil society by offering them access to state funding. Here Keane and Thompson are following an argument that public television is important to the extent to which it helps to bolster civic communication, rather than simply being an end in itself

Missing from these accounts is a more critical treatment of the idea of pluralism. If television is to provide critical and democratic content, then this pushes the argument beyond simple plurality. Here we need to defend the idea that broadcasting (and education) might have a role in developing critical literacy as a form of border crossing. This would seek to expand the possibilities of citizens in relation with publics thinking across a number of narratives and perspectives. The idea of border crossing resists the idea that publics could or should be a unified voice, but provides narratives, stories and perspectives that allow citizens in educated and media settings to move between them. As Henry Giroux (1993: 367–368) writes, critical literacy depends upon the 'importance of acknowledging that meaning is not fixed and that to be literate is to undertake to dialogue with others who speak from different histories, locations, and experiences'. We need to recognize that mediation (like education) is about the continued process of translation and interpretation that asks questions about meaningfulness, inclusion and exclusion, and who has the ability to cross borders.

However, there were other voices beginning to be developed in the 1990s that saw that the writing was on the wall for the idea of public service television. Richard Hoggart (1995) and Pierre Bourdieu (1996) both warned that the move towards a more commercially driven culture had resulted in the progressive cultural impoverishment of television. The dominance of the market was having a corrupting effect upon journalism as the search for audience ratings and sensation drove cultural tastes and standards downwards. If the 1950s and 1960s had seen television dominated by the idea that it was the role of broadcasters to raise the standards of the audience, by the 1990s television was dominated by the already tried and tested. If, as Graham Murdock (1999) notes, the right to participate within a common civic space was crucial to cultural citizenship, then public service broadcasting remains central, given that its main address is to the public as citizens and not consumers. The main argument here is that while commercial channels may well contribute to civic debate, their main concern remains selling space to advertisers. Despite the emphasis that commercial broadcasters have placed upon lifestyle programmes and cultural diversity, questions of citizenship continue to require common forms of public space.

This position was openly challenged by Elizabeth Jacka (2003), who sought to argue that the connection between democracy and public service provision was increasingly open to question in changed circumstances. In this new age of pluralistic television and technological media we need to rethink our assumptions in order to make them relevant for a postmodern democracy. Here Jacka (drawing heavily upon the arguments of Hartley [1999] that I reviewed earlier) argues that those who defend public service television reproduce certain assumptions about the low and degraded nature of commercial culture. This position is problematic, as it rests upon a desire to regulate the tastes and passions of ordinary people. This is a familiar argument within cultural studies and has been used to reveal the levels of disgust and strategies of distinction made by elites in respect of the cultures of the lower orders. However, what it misses is any discussion about questions of cultural value or, indeed, quality. If those who wish to defend public service broadcasting are doing so simply because they don't want to be swamped by 'vulgar' commercialism, then this is clearly problematic. More often, however, the defence of public service television is connected to the need to maintain public values, genuinely public spaces and critical thinking. Here the concern is less about cultural barbarism and more to do with the possibility of democratic debate, exchange and complex forms of cultural production. As John Mepham (1990) argues, talking about quality does not necessarily imply a defence of high culture. If we are to defend questions of 'quality' we need to do so in a culturally pluralist society. Citizens require a variety of stories and narratives in order to highlight complex ethical and moral problems that come with living in diverse, violent and exploitative societies. In this respect, there are a variety of narratives available through television, from soap operas to news and from documentaries to films. It is misleading simply to be 'against soap operas'; rather, we need to identify the virtues of these cultural forms. We can then make judgements about different soap operas in terms of how successful they are in dramatizing everyday life and providing the audience with access to a diversity of narratives and questions. The problem being, of course, that there is also a long tradition of simply judging popular culture from the position of high or literary culture. However, this does not have to be the case and suggests that questions of value and critique can be as much part of popular culture as they can of anything else. Neither Jacka nor Hartley takes these questions seriously enough. Instead they wrongly position the argument to speak up for public service television as either a form of nostalgia or simply distaste for a more pluralistic age. Yet, if we are to defend the idea of public television (as I think we must), then we need to do so with a stronger idea of the changed cultural conditions that now dominate the twenty-first century.

Neoliberal television and cultural citizenship

Toby Miller (2007) has argued that much of the debate in respect of cultural citizenship and television has missed the extent to which the medium is now overwhelmingly driven by the needs of capital and commerce rather than of diverse publics. The recent 'make-over' of television means that cultural criticism needs to respond to new televisual realities. If television in the 1950s and 1960s provided a common gathering place for diverse publics, then this world seems to be disappearing. Roger Silverstone's (1994) classic study of television emphasizes its role in suburban and family life. Viewed in this way, it rests upon a certain gendered division of labour in the home and its role in making distant conflict 'safe' for suburban consumption. Here we might also consider the ways in which the time of television fits into the structuring of the day and the assumptions that are made by broadcasters as to who is watching. While these concerns are still present, Silverstone's reflections now evoke a less technologically sophisticated and fragmented age. The rise of a more individualized medium is taking place in the context of more 'self-determined programming schedules' (Lotz 2007: 14). The shift from a society where viewers had little choice in terms of what they watched to one where, since the 1980s, viewers' viewing patterns are now less organized centrally, due to the impact of technology and multi-channel television, has meant that television's role in society needs to be reconsidered. Increasingly, television is one option amongst many in terms of home entertainment, with many ordinary citizens having a number of technological devices at their disposal. If, as Castells (2009: 59) argues, the number of hours that citizens spend viewing television is still expanding (on average about 57 hours a week in the USA), this is happening in an environment where audience size is considerably fragmenting and where media are increasingly becoming interactive. If television is still a genuinely mass medium we need to recognize the extent to which the ways in which we engage in its content have been transformed. As Castells (2009: 195) also mentions, if the media have been pluralized they have been corporatized at the same time. Many of the new channels that have been developed are linked to large media corporations and are run primarily as businesses whose job it is to bring people entertainment and news (and sometimes infotainment).

Here we might note the ways in which ideas of the televisual spectacle have made a return to more recent forms of critical analysis than had previously been apparent. Douglas Kellner (2003) argues that media spectacles have become a key organizing principle of the dominant capitalist society. For Kellner, updating Debord's (1994) original reflections, in the society of the spectacle fashion models, celebrities and icons become increasingly important. Culture is increasingly dominated by the power of certain images and brands. Society's central feature is the dominance of a new form of techno-capitalism whereby capital accumulation, the knowledge revolution and new technology have combined to produce a new kind of society. The culture of the spectacle instigates a new form of domination of mass distraction, profit and the continuing expansion of social and cultural domains that fall under its sway, from politics to sport and from music to the news media. The problem with these reflections, as Raymond Williams (1974) identified, is that an analysis driven by technological or commercial criteria tends to neglect the complexity of audiences and more specific meanings and to underestimate how the same technologies could have alternative, more civic uses. Further, Williams (1974: 131) was aware that television could have unpredictable effects. The search for sensation and spectacle not only serves the dominant interests of elites, but in other circumstances could lead in other directions. The television images of the British student protests in 2010 were ultimately driven by the spectacle, but also helped to translate a sense of young people as active citizens who were unwillingly to stand passively by and accept the way in which the government was seeking to restructure higher education in the interests of the rich. Of course, the main driving force of the spectacle is anti-democratic, but it can have unpredictable effects.

The development of the politics of the televisual spectacle has not been the only notable trend of an increasingly market-driven television. The other has been the development of reality television. Nick Couldry (2008) has argued that the cruelty of much reality television stems from the way in which it ideologically seeks to prepare the audience for life under neoliberalism. The demand by employers for greater flexibility, malleability and longer hours has a strong family resemblance, perhaps, to the ways in which participants on reality television have to submit to an external authority. Further, the explicit regulation of conduct by reality television, and cruel forms of punishment of those who deviate from the norms of the programme, have a great deal in common with the intensified surveillance that many citizens can expect at work. Similarly, others have noted the ways in which 'reality television' seeks to work on the subjectivity of the television viewer through notions of empowerment (Ouellette and Hay, 2008). Here the invitation issued by much reality television is to become an enterprising self. The enterprising self is upwardly mobile, learns to live 'the right way' and refuses 'state dependency'. A number of reality television programmes have focused upon the failing lifestyles of poorer people, suggesting that they have simply made the wrong choices.

Similarly, other programmes being pioneered by well-known celebrities act as moral entrepreneurs who explicitly promote certain lifestyle choices on the part of audiences (Hollows and Jones, 2010). A common problem is that television, rather than seeking to democratically provide a plurality of narratives allowing for critical reflection, explicitly seeks to make an intervention into the way that the world is constituted. Politically, this usually involves an agenda which talks of 'empowering' ordinary people with access to a celebrity brand that mostly fails to ask wider questions related to power, democracy and citizenship. These trends are also evident in more explicitly entrepreneurial programming like the *Dragons' Den* and *The Apprentice*, where television is explicitly involved with the fostering of certain lifestyles rather than others. The normative value of a life of upward mobility, wealth and market-driven success is of course also a prime part of the constitution of other more overtly populist programming, such as the *X Factor* and other talent shows that now dominate television schedules. Of course we need to remember that much lifestyle television, or what Frances Bonner (2003) calls 'ordinary television', is focused on mundane matters like gardening, food, clothing, holidays and the home, but this does not prevent it from becoming imbricated with neoliberal ideals. However, some celebrity reality television can raise more problematic questions beyond the frames of neoliberalism. More recently *Jamie's Dream School* (broadcast on Channel 4 in 2011) raised a number of questions about an increasingly authoritarian school system that fails so many young people. The programme offers a contradictory text based on well-known celebrities that at least partially demonstrates how difficult it is to teach young people, and how many of them fail to gain a sense of their own worth and creativity from the education system. Of course this stops short of what we might ask of more democratic forms of culture, but the dominant hegemony around schooling has at least been subtly contested in the way that it is not in more 'formal' news items.

Finally, we should also recognize that our globally mediated television culture is far from ushering in a homogeneous culture of neoliberalism. If the dominant discourses of the war on terror sought to divide humanity into the camps of good and evil, then television has also made available a more mutable world (Buck-Morss, 2003). Our discordant visual culture has recently brought into full view that fact that the West arms dictatorships, but also the lie that democracy has to be imposed from the outside or that Arab nations were simply not suited for democracy. Notably, the recent televised uprisings in countries such as Egypt and Libya could also yet play a role in encouraging protests closer to home against the anti-democratic system pursued by neoliberal governments. If television under neoliberalism is continually imposing thinking within certain borders and frameworks, it is also commonly involved in their questioning as well.

Cultural citizenship and the future of television

If television was seen as holding out the possibility of a common civic identity necessary for democracy, this has now been partially displaced by more neoliberal and less predictable definitions. Notably, many of the more recent publications on issues related to media and democracy have been more concerned with the potential of the Internet than of television. The possibility of audiences producing their own content, the development of radical blogs and the increased possibility of civic movements for making an intervention have all, not surprisingly, attracted a considerable amount of attention (Hands, 2011). However, often missing from these reflections is a recognition that many of the more 'radical' websites are still quite marginal, in the way that television is not. Here we need to know more about how radical websites become translated into wider publics (Fenton, 2008). This is not intended to undermine their civic importance, but suggests that television is still hugely significant in the way in which it shapes the horizons and practices of the majority of citizens.

Georgina Born (2004) argues that public television remains significant in an age of audience fragmentation, commercialism and Internet provision. This is largely because of its ability to articulate common and trusted meeting-points for a plurality of its citizens. Public service television remains significant, due to its commitment to 'no other imperative than the public interest' (Born, 2004: 514). This perhaps remains an overly rosy view of the current state of health of public service television in an era of dramatic cuts, down-sizing and its participation in what I called neoliberal television. However, media scholars need to be careful not to give up on the significance of public service broadcasting even in the Internet age. That public service television still has a role to play in providing a critical public space for what I have termed border crossing remains significant. Here the argument has perhaps moved beyond the need to provide a common national civic culture through public service broadcasting. More to the point is how public service broadcasting becomes a common meeting-point, joining together a number of discordant publics of which new media are only a part. Zygmunt Bauman (2007: 86) argues that, rather than this being the age of intermixing, as it is commonly understood by some of the globalization literature, it might be best understood as one of 'mixophobia'. Contemporary public spaces are better understood through a fear of difference and Otherness than the common ability to border-cross. The drive towards communities of sameness is the desire to eliminate the stranger from our screens, cities or common places. If the idea of the common school within education is increasingly being replaced by increasingly specialized, market-driven and segregated schools, then something similar can be discerned within public communication. If, as Williams and Hoggart had hoped, public service broadcasting could be the place of civic engagement that crossed borders, this has become harder to achieve. However, despite those who have looked to the Internet as a means of providing a focus for democratic sentiment, I remain concerned about the way that it fosters micro as opposed to expansive publics unless it becomes linked to other media. Cultural citizenship, alternatively, seeks to articulate a form of democratic politics that is concerned not only with the mobilization of sentiment, but with the transformation of larger publics as well. Despite attempts by neoliberal media and education systems to both exclude and close the minds of citizens, we need to retain a sense of hope and possibility of other publics being formed beyond radical enclaves.

References

Bauman, Z. (2007) *Liquid Times*. Cambridge: Polity Press.

Bonner, F. (2003) *Ordinary Television*. London: Sage.

Born, G. (2004) *Uncertain Vision: Birt, Dyke and the Reinvention of the BBC*. London: Vintage.

Bourdieu, P. (1996) *On Television*. New Press: New York.

Buck-Morss, S. (2003) *Thinking Past Terror*. London: Verso.

Castells, M. (2009) *Communication Power*. Oxford: Oxford University Press.

Couldry, N. (2006) 'Culture and citizenship', *European Journal of Cultural Studies* 9 (3) 321–339.

Couldry, N. (2008) 'Reality TV, or the secret theatre of neoliberalism', *The Review of Education, Pedagogy, and Cultural Studies* 30 (3) 3–13.

Debord, G. (1994) *The Society of the Spectacle*. New York: Zone Books.

Fenton, N. (2008) 'Mediating hope: new media, politics and resistance', *International Journal of Cultural Studies* 11 (2) 230–248.

Giroux, H. (1993) 'Literacy and the politics of difference', in C. Lankshear and P. McLaren (eds) *Critical Literacy: Politics, Praxis and the Postmodern*. Albany: New York Press, pp. 367–378.

Giroux, H. (2004) *The Terror of Neoliberalism*. London: Paradigm.

Hands, J. (2011) *@ is for Activism*. London: Pluto Press.

Hartley, J. (1999) *Uses of Television*. London: Routledge.

Hermes, J. and Dahlgren, P. (2006) 'Cultural studies and citizenship', *European Journal of Cultural Studies* 9 (3) 260–265.

Hoggart, R. (1995) *The Way We Live Now*. London: Pimlico.

Hoggart, R. (2001) *Between Two Worlds*. London: Aurum Press.

Jacka, E. (2003) 'Democracy as defeat: the impotence of arguments for public service broadcasting', *Television and New Media* 4 (2) 177–191.

Hollows, J. and Jones, S. (2010) '"At least he is doing something": moral entrepreneurship and individual responsibility in Jamie's Ministry of Food', *European Journal of Cultural Studies* 13 (3) 307–322.

Keane, J. (1991) *The Media and Democracy*. Cambridge: Polity Press.

Kellner, D. (2003) *Media Spectacle*. London: Routledge.

Lotz, A.D. (2007) *The Television Will Be Revolutionized*. New York: New York University Press.

Mepham, J. (1990) 'The ethics of quality in television', in G. Mulgan (ed.) *The Ethics of Quality in Television*. London: BFI Publishing, pp. 56–72.

Miller, T. (2007) *Cultural Citizenship: Cosmopolitanism, Consumerism, and Television in a Neoliberal Age*. Philadelphia: Temple Press.

Mulgan, G. and Worpole, K. (1986) *Saturday Night and Sunday Morning*. London: Comedia.

Murdock, G. (1999) 'Rights and representations; public discourse and cultural citizenship', in J. Gripsrud (ed.) *Television and Common Knowledge*. London: Routledge, pp. 7–18.

Ouellette, L. and Hay, J. (2008) *Better Living through Reality Television: Television and Post-welfare Citizenship*. Oxford: Blackwell.

Rancière, J. (2006) *Hatred of Democracy*. London: Verso.

Rowbotham, S. and Beynon, H. (eds) (2001) *Looking at Class*. London: Rivers Oram Press.

Scannell, P. (1989) 'Public service broadcasting: the history of a concept', in A. Goddwin and G. Whannel (eds) *Understanding Television*. London: Routledge, pp. 11–29.

Silverstone, R. (1994) *Television and Everyday Life*. London: Routledge.

Silverstone, R. (2007) *Media and Morality*. Cambridge: Polity Press.

Stevenson, N. (2003) *Cultural Citizenship*. Basingstoke: Open University Press.

Thompson, J.B. (1990) *Ideology and Modern Culture*. Cambridge: Polity Press.

Williams, R. (1962) *Communications*. London: Penguin.

Williams, R. (1968) *Border Country*. London: Chatto and Windus.

Williams, R. (1974) *Television: Technology and Cultural Form*. New York: Schocken Books.

30

RECREATIONAL DRUG USE AND THE CLUB SCENE

Margaretha Järvinen

Introduction

In the late 1980s and early 1990s, recreational use of illegal drugs (cannabis, ecstasy, amphetamine, LSD, cocaine etc.) started to increase dramatically in many Western countries and is now regarded as an integrated part of night life in modern societies. Recreational drug use may be defined as occasional and limited use of drugs in specific settings, and as controlled and predictable drug intake without severe physical, mental or social consequences (Measham et al., 2000; Parker, 2005).

Since the mid-1990s, recreational drug use has been analysed from a variety of theoretical angles: in terms of normalized behaviour, controlled loss of control, calculated hedonism, commercialized illicit pleasure and as drug-induced time out from the stresses and strains of the modern world. These approaches stand in sharp contrast to more conventional understandings of illegal drugs as substances that in the first place 'trick' people, then 'trap' them and finally 'entomb' them (Manderson, 2005). Indeed, much of today's research on recreational drug use has developed in response to the previously all-dominant pathology paradigm which depicted drug users as psychological and/or social delinquents. With this development, research on illegal drug use has moved from being part of the sociology of deviance to being one of the 'Big Seven' research areas within Leisure Studies.

This chapter is structured as follows. First, the most important developments within the field of illegal drug use in (some) Western countries are described – not least the gradual mainstreaming of the dance drug scene and the inclusion of determined intoxication into the night-time economy of urban landscapes. Second, some of the central theoretical approaches to recreational drug use are discussed. Third, the chapter focuses its attention on drug-use careers among recreational users and the question of what happens when occasional use becomes regular, and potentially uncontrolled, use. The final part of the chapter discusses the limits of extant research approaches and their ideological and theoretical agendas.

From underground to mainstream clubs

The expansion of illegal drug use started in the mid-1980s with the emergence of dance scenes centred on specific styles of electronic music. In the USA, the dance culture called 'house' originated in Chicago (named after The Warehouse Club) and was accompanied by the New York variant, garage (after the Paradise Garage Club) and Detroit techno (Ter Bogt *et al.*, 2002). From here, house music spread to Europe, where it was combined with the electronic dance music from countries such as Germany and the Netherlands. The ideals of this new dance and drug culture were sensitivity, community and hedonism, and, with a reference to the 1960s, the year 1988 was called 'the second summer of love' (Collin and Godfrey, 1997). With another reference to the 1960s, the new clubbers transformed the hippie slogan 'make love, not war' into 'drop pills, not bombs' (*ibid.*).

By the late 1980s, house had become a mass movement. Young people around the Western world gathered at raves in hangars, abandoned factory buildings or open-air settings. The location of the parties was often held secret until the last minute when organizers revealed the address to potential participants. Due to the combination of mass participation and widespread use of illegal drugs, the public soon turned against these events, and legislation reduced the number of large-scale unlicensed venues. In parallel with this, the dance scene and its associated drug use moved into traditional night-club settings (Measham *et al.*, 1998; Riley *et al.*, 2001). In the first half of the 1990s the house and drug-use scene was professionalized and commercialized and the accompanying music disintegrated into a variety of styles: techno, hard-core, trance, tribal etc. (Measham *et al.*, 1998; Ter Bogt *et al.*, 2002). With this, the use of new dance drugs moved from the underground to mainstream venues.

Dancing on drugs

The dance revolution (Measham *et al.*, 1998; 2000) brought about an unprecedented increase in drug use among youths and young adults in the Western world. In Britain, the proportion of young people who had ever tried an illegal drug almost tripled from the mid-1980s to the mid-1990s (Measham *et al.*, 1998). Cannabis remained the favourite drug among young Britons, but dance drugs such as ecstasy, amphetamine and LSD showed the biggest increases.

Of all the new dance drugs in the 1990s and the beginning of the new millennium, ecstasy (MDMA) received most attention, both in the media (largely due to ecstasy-related deaths) and in research. Studies of ecstasy users preliminarily showed three things. First, and in accordance with the mainstreaming of the club scene described above, that ecstasy users did not come from marginalized and disadvantaged groups but from all parts of the youth population. Second, that ravers and clubbers did not use just ecstasy (although this was the drug achieving most of the media and research attention) but a variety of legal and illegal drugs. And third, that most of the users were able to control their drug intake and restrict it to weekend and party settings.

Hammerslay *et al.* (1999), for instance, interviewed around 200 ecstasy users in Glasgow, showing that most of the users took ecstasy seldom and that daily or almost daily use was extremely rare – the heaviest user group took the drug about once a week. Ecstasy users in Glasgow were typically multi-substance users, combining ecstasy with LSD, amphetamines, cocaine and cannabis. The interviewees in Hammerslay *et al.*'s study came from a broad range of socio-economic backgrounds and included almost equal proportions of men and women. A weak social gradient was found in relation to the frequency and quantity of ecstasy use. Light users were most likely to be students, medium users were more likely than the others to be in work and heavy users were most likely to be unemployed.

Another example of studies from the dance scene in the 1990s is Lenton *et al.*'s (1997) research on ravers in Perth, Australia. Three-quarters of the 83 ravers interviewed in the study reported that they had used ecstasy, but other illegal drugs were even more popular, especially LSD, with which 96 per cent had experience. Lenton *et al.* explain the popularity of LSD by the unreliable quality and availability of ecstasy in Australia and the high cost of the drug compared with the UK and other European countries. The Perth study showed that ravers were an unremarkable group when it came to social background, being similarly connected to family, school, work and community as were their non-drug using peers.

Although the house dance scene originally came from the USA, 'the rave rage', with its associated large-scale use of ecstasy and other dance drugs blew back to North America only in the early 1990s (Bahora *et al.*, 2009). Bahora *et al.* interviewed 112 ecstasy users in Atlanta, Georgia, showing that most study participants were able to take the drug without interference with their everyday functioning in society (work, studies, social relationships). The interviewees did not associate ecstasy use with symptoms of withdrawal or craving or serious negative health effects. Ecstasy was seen as a means to unwind, relax and connect with other people. A small minority reported daily ecstasy use and many of these participants also used other drugs such as cocaine, methamphetamine or heroin (Bahora *et al.*, 2009).

Cocaine has been an important drug for recreational users, both before, during and after the 1980/90s epoch of ecstasy. In some dance scenes in the late 1980s the ascent of ecstasy happened as a rebellion against cocaine, which was seen as a 'cold' and 'egoistic' drug – as opposed to the 'warm' and 'social' drug ecstasy (Nabben and Korf, 1999). From the late 1990s until today, the use of cocaine has been rising in many European countries, especially in the UK and Spain, but also in Denmark, Ireland and Italy (EMCDDA, 2011; Ilse *et al.*, 2006). In the USA, where club use of ecstasy developed later than in Europe, cocaine has again become the most widely used drug in the club scene (Kelly *et al.*, 2006; Ramo *et al.*, 2010). Interviewing 400 clubbers in the New York dance scene, Ramo *et al.* (2010) demonstrated the importance of cocaine: 40 per cent used cocaine and no other illegal drugs; 44 per cent mixed cocaine with other drugs, especially ecstasy, and 14 per cent engaged in an extensive and relatively indiscriminate poly-drug use.

The typical pattern of cocaine use in the club scene in Europe and the USA is to combine it with intense drinking in order to achieve a sharper and more controlled intoxication than alcohol alone provides. The increased popularity of cocaine seems to be related to a quest for self-control and self-regulation, and to the negative experiences that some clubbers have had with ecstasy (zombie behaviour, poor quality of ecstasy tablets on the market). On cocaine (or coke, cola), clubbers feel more normal and more sober than on ecstasy, and they are less afraid of losing track of what is happening (Nabben and Korf, 1999; van der Poel *et al.*, 2009). Cocaine in combination with alcohol is seen by many clubbers as the perfect mix 'when energy, sociability and intense excitement are required' on long weekend nights (Williams and Parker, 2001; see also Demant, 2010; Järvinen *et al.*, 2010).

Recent studies of clubbers in different European countries reveal that multi-substance use is the most common form of illegal drug use (EMCDDA, 2011). Hence, dance drug use in the twenty-first century has been described as a 'cocktail of celebration' which includes alcohol, cannabis, cocaine, amphetamines, methamphetamine, ecstasy, fantasy (GHB), ketamine and magic mushrooms, a cocktail the exact contents of which varies with region, leisure venue and individual preferences (Measham, 2004).

According to the clubbers themselves, dance drugs bring about a range of positive effects: they enhance vitality within milieus of sociality; they kick-start emotions and make it possible for the user to stay alert for long hours; they increase the user's ability to perform in more socially desirable ways by making him or her happy, outgoing, calm and self-assured

(Olsen, 2009). Different drugs of course have different effects on users. Boys *et al.* (2001) asked a large number of poly-drug users in Britain for what purposes they took various legal and illegal drugs. The participants described the most important functions of cannabis and alcohol as being 'relaxation' and 'getting stoned/intoxicated'; amphetamine and ecstasy were associated with the ability to 'keep going', 'stay awake', 'enhance activity' and 'elation/euphoria'; and cocaine with the ability to 'keep going', 'stay awake', 'increased confidence' and 'feeling better when down or depressed' (Boys *et al.*, 2001). Hence, cocaine was comprehended as having some functions (confidence, consolation) that the other stimulants, amphetamine and ecstasy did not have to the same extent; a difference that may be part of the explanation for cocaine's popularity.

Drug use as a leisure lifestyle

Theoretically, research on clubbers and their recreational drug use may be seen as a reaction to a deviancy perspective on drug users. Since the mid-1990s, club studies have depicted drug users as mainstream young people, typically by referring to their involvement in the educational system and work-life (Parker *et al.*, 1998; Lenton *et al.*, 1997). Because experimentation with illegal drugs is so widespread, drugs users can no longer (if they ever could) be regarded as 'abnormal' individuals or as representatives of delimited subcultures, they 'cannot be written off as delinquent, street corner "no hopers"' (Parker *et al.*, 1998: 2). In the decade of dancing (beginning in the late 1980s), drug use moved from the exception of the norm to a (more or less) mainstream youth phenomenon, a process that called for new theoretical approaches (South, 2004).

Especially in Britain, research on recreational drug use developed in opposition to structuralist approaches to youth and their cultures. In the 1990s, British dance and drug scholars depicted their own research as an alternative to the subcultural studies at the Birmingham Centre for Contemporary Cultural Studies (CCCS), which they criticized for being too preoccupied with social class. Dancers and clubbers should not be seen as underprivileged youths struggling against the socio-economic circumstances of their existence, as subcultural research would have it. The concept of subculture was problematic, the critics said, because it imposed rigid lines of division between deviant youth groups and a dominant mainstream culture (Bennett, 1999). Instead of structuralist interpretations, club researchers used the concept lifestyle, understood as a game in which individuals took part, 'choosing certain commodities and patterns of consumption and articulating these cultural resources as modes of personal expression' (Bennett, 1999: 607). 'Neotribe' (Maffesoli, 1996) was another concept adopted by dance and drug researchers who wanted to describe the shifting and unstable social affiliations of youths experimenting with certain lifestyles, and the consumption-based 'tribal' identities created through them. Typical of the new drug research, then, was that clubbers/dancers were seen not as locked into particular ways of being, determined by their class (or gender or ethnicity), but as active consumers and pleasure seekers whose choices reflected self-constructed notions of identity (Bennett, 1999; Parker *et al.*, 1998).

In line with this reasoning, Parker *et al.* coined their 'normalization thesis' on illegal drug use (Parker *et al.*, 1998; Measham *et al.*, 1994, 1998; Williams and Parker, 2001; Parker, 2005). Normalization is about stigmatized and deviant groups becoming included in mainstream society whereby 'their identities or behaviour become increasingly accommodated and perhaps eventually valued' (Parker, 2005: 205). Building on research on the club scene in Manchester, Parker and his co-workers demonstrated that recreational drug use had become extremely widespread among *ordinary* youths (Parker and Egginton, 2002). An important part of the normalization process was that the changes in drug-use rates were accompanied by a social accommodation of illegal drug use. Hence, Parker and his co-workers showed that drug attitudes had become more accepting, not only among the users themselves, but also among their non-using peers and in society at large. In the twenty-first century, Parker (2005) concluded, 'sensible' drug use is so common and socially accommodated in Britain that it may be regarded as normalized, not in the sense that a majority of young people use illegal drugs on a regular basis, but in the sense that drug use is a non-stigmatized and, in some settings, even normative activity.

One reason for the spread of 'normal' recreational drug use is, according to Parker *et al.* (1998), individualization and increased contingency in late-modern times, meaning that today's youths have to navigate through a more uncertain and rapidly changing world, which requires flexibility and makes risk taking necessary (Williams and Parker, 2001). Drug use has, in this perspective, become more common because the world is increasingly stressful, because uncertainties are always present and because the route to independent adulthood has been prolonged (young people stay longer in the educational system, their working careers are more insecure, they postpone marriage or stay single etc.). Illegal drug use is part of a 'work hard – play hard' lifestyle which is typical for young people's life today, and cannot be explained with reference to the users' psychological or social make-up (Williams and Parker, 2001).

Drug users as rational risk managers

Another and related characteristic of the research on recreational drug use is that it regards clubbers as rational subjects who weigh the pros and cons of drug use and deliberately choose what relationship they want to have to drugs. Parker (2005: 210) talks about 'drug wisdom' among youths, stating that most drug users apply a cost–benefit assessment to drugs which acknowledges that there are risks and downsides to psycho-active substance use, as well as pleasure and other positive experiences. In this perspective, recreational drug users are autonomous and reflexive subjects who make reasoned choices about drugs consumption, rational subjects who assess their self-regulated substance use as functional and consistent with other aspects of their life. Measham (2004: 319) discusses the intoxication sought by these rational subjects in terms of a 'controlled loss of control', describing a self-regulated consumption pattern that is kept within the boundaries of time (weekends), space (clubs or private parties) and company (supportive friends). For clubbers with a controlled drug intake, illegal drugs are a normal feature of their 'life management' (South, 2004: 536). The goal of these users is to live successful lives in relation to conventional work and family values and at the same time to 'be in heaven every weekend' (*ibid*). 'Calculated hedonism' is yet another term used of club drug use (Featherstone, 1991). The term refers to drug consumers who are committed to career success and achievements in society but regard drug-related pleasure as a reward for their everyday struggles and as an integrated part of their leisure.

In research on clubbing, drug users are typically depicted as consumers who are free, and should be left free, to make their own choices and take responsibility for them. This is a neoliberal approach to drug use, an approach that regards drug users as autonomous and self-reflective subjects who seek the pleasures that illegal drugs may provide but also strive to avoid the harms with which drug use may be associated. In this perspective, drug use is a calculated risk activity and, contrary to more conventional understandings, drugs are not regarded as inherently dangerous – if handled sensibly and responsibly (Duff, 2004; Riley *et al.*, 2010). As many studies have shown, this is also the way that clubbers look upon their drug use. Analysing the Swedish drug scene, Rödner (2006) found that recreational drug users situated the risks of drug use not in the pharmacological characteristics of the substances, but in the people who use them and in the circumstances of use. The participants in Rödner's study described themselves as being in full control of their drug intake, which they restricted to special occasions, avoiding drug use that had a negative impact on work or study time. Equally important, they tried to control the context and process of drug intake by using drugs in safe settings and together with people whom they knew; by avoiding drug purchases from unknown sellers; and by looking after their bodies (e.g. eating healthily before and after drug intake). Participants also tended to create a psychological distance between themselves and 'risk groups' of drug users, i.e. people with 'weak personalities' or 'poor upbringing', whom they regarded as being in danger of developing drug addiction and other problems (Rödner, 2006).

Hedonism and the night-time economy

A third approach in research on recreational drug use is to focus not on the drug consumers but on the settings that facilitate drug use (Hobbs *et al.*, 2000; Laidler *et al.*, 2006; Sanders, 2006; Silverstone, 2006). Here, drug scholars analyse the interrelationship between the consumption and the production of drug- and alcohol-related pleasure. While the night-time economy used to be a marginal zone of space and time, it is now promoted as central to the image of modern Western cities (Hobbs *et al.*, 2000). As Hobbs *et al.* point out, regulation of the night-time zone (e.g. alcohol and entertainment licensing) has fallen increasingly out of step with market forces. Instead of controlling and trying to curb the disorderliness of urban night life, modern cities seek to promote the growth of their night-time economies by inviting customers to hedonism and excessive consumption. Intoxication is the norm in these night-time zones of the city (Hobbs *et al.*, 2000; Measham and Brain, 2005).

Goulding *et al.* (2008) analyse clubbing as a market-place culture tied to urban spaces in which the often alienating and individualizing aspects of late modern life can be temporarily ameliorated 'in favour of the effervescent excitement and energy of ritualistic, communal sociality' (p. 759). As opposed to the unauthorized rave parties of the 1980s, today's clubbing and dance drug use may be seen as a form of 'contained illegality' where drug users are included in a commercialized, sanitized and domesticated pursuit of leisure and pleasure (*ibid.*).

It is important to note that alcohol – the discussion of normalized use of *illegal* drugs notwithstanding – is still the most important drug in the night-time economy. As Measham and Brain (2005) have demonstrated, the increase in illegal drug use in the 1990s came together with an unprecedented growth of binge drinking among clubbers. The 'big bang' in sessional alcohol consumption was, according to Measham and Brain, promoted by the alcohol industry. One aspect of this development was the introduction of a range of new alcohol products in the 1990s targeting young people: alcopops, high-strength beers, ready-to-drink spirit mixers, shots etc. (Measham and Brain, 2005: 267). Another aspect was the systematic transformation of urban drinking establishments – 'a move from "spit and sawdust" working–class back street pubs to modern "chrome and cocktails" city centre café bars', aimed at the 18- to 35-year-old customer group (*ibid*). This was an invitation to people 'not just to go out drinking but to get drunk', an invitation to calculated hedonism and time out (Measham and Brain, 2005: 273). The night-time economy beckons potential customers, promising them pleasure, exciting experiences and a sense of community that is lacking from the humdrum rhythms of everyday life. Hobbs *et al.* (2000) call this 'the allure of liminal opportunities': people are invited to take part in a weekend celebration that is self-generating, revitalizing and ostensibly liberating – yet this celebration is thoroughly standardized, commercialized and staged (pp. 701–711).

Purcell and Graham (2005) describe the development of the nightclub scene in Toronto. Just like in European cities, club culture has become the dominant form of entertainment in Toronto, and many of the traditional taverns and pubs have been displaced by nightlife environments that target young, rich, urban adults. Characteristic of the new establishments is an 'ethic of aggressive hedonism and sexuality' (*ibid*: 161). Referring to Hobbs *et al.*'s (2000) UK studies, Purcell and Graham conclude that the dominant nightclubs in Toronto, like their British counterparts may be described as 'large impersonal disco bars that feature an undercurrent of heightened sexuality, dimmed-down lighting rig, booming sound system, and always the necessary cast of bouncers on the door' (Hobbs *et al.*, 2000: 707; Purcell and Graham, 2005: 161). Sanders' (2006) depiction of life at a London club, where he worked as a bouncer while also doing ethnographic research, is worth quoting at some length:

> In a space where the legal limit was 750 people, these Saturday nights often topped 1000 [...] The use of ecstasy and cocaine was blatant [...] On the dance floor, people are 'having it large': hands in the air, whooping and yelling, boogieing in a sweaty drug fuelled mass [...] Clubbing is carnival, and carnival licenses fun, play, 'losing' oneself and being intoxicated. From the pounding rhythmic music and hooked electronic samples, to the lasers and smoke, bells and whistles, lights and images, the club atmosphere encouraged [drug] use.
>
> (Sanders, 2006: xi and 132)

From recreational to regular use

As shown above, research on recreational drug use has developed in opposition to research approaches regarding drug use as a problem, whether individual or societal. Research on ravers and clubbers has analysed drug users who are able to control their drug intake and (more or less) restrict it to the weekends and leisure settings. In this type of research there is very little focus on clubbers who are unsuccessful in their risk management, clubbers who escalate their drug intake and experience adverse effects of their hedonistic lifestyle.

One of the few studies analysing heavy recreational users is South's (2004) Essex study. As South points out, the cultural perspective on drug use (characteristic of most studies quoted in this chapter) sometimes needs to be combined with a more structurally oriented approach. Choices in relation to drug use are not altogether free but are affected by social circumstances, and sometimes by habituation and dependence. The participants in South's study reported different kinds of drug-induced problems, for instance related to their working life – they experienced problems such as tiredness, concentration problems, absenteeism, lateness and accidents at work. The daily lives of these heavy users often blurred the lines of legal and illegal. Many participants were involved in drug dealing and other criminal activities, which provided an alternative to their low incomes and made it possible for them to maintain their drug habit.

Vervaeke and Korf (2006) followed a group of long-term ecstasy users in Amsterdam, also focusing on their occupational careers. The participants were first-generation ecstasy users who had started to take the drug in the late 1980s and who were now in their forties and fifties. Nearly all had been regular users, taking ecstasy several times a week in their peak period of use. They were also poly-drug users who typically took several different drugs in combination or in sequence. A relatively large proportion of them reported career interruptions due to illness or unemployment. In general, participants were not particularly career minded. They seemed to adapt their work life to their social life, rather than the other way round, for instance by seeking out jobs that were compatible with a partying lifestyle and ecstasy use. Some long-term users were successful in this and held jobs that could be combined with an intense or more occasional drug use; other users were less lucky and ended up in unemployment. The participants with the highest ecstasy consumption levels were also those who were most likely to be currently unemployed (Vervaeke and Korf, 2006).

Järvinen and Ravn (2011) used Becker's career concept to analyse the trajectories of drug use in a group of Danish clubbers with regular and problematic drug use (as defined by the clubbers themselves). The drug-use careers of regular users had some distinct characteristics. First, the development of heavy drug use was typically associated with a change in partying forms. Participants went from taking drugs at one-night parties to taking them in binges at all-weekend parties that started on Thursday or Friday and continued to Sunday afternoon. In parallel with this, gatherings in private homes became more important because participants felt that they could not take all the drugs they wanted in club settings. Second, the clubbers' circle of friends increasingly came to consist of other drug users, party friends, whom they spent more and more time with at the expense of the time spent with non-drug-using friends, family etc. Third, the clubbers started to use drugs for other reasons than before: stimulants, for instance, which were originally used in party settings, were now taken for relaxation at home, also when the participants were alone. Furthermore, intoxication tended to become a goal in itself, and not a means to achieve other things (self-confidence, enhanced activity, feelings of community). Finally, this transformation was for many clubbers related to the fact that they came to occupy new positions in the drug-supply network. Some acted as drug sellers (on a smaller or larger scale, for a shorter or longer period), others were in a relationship with a person who was selling, which meant that they had more or less unlimited access to drugs (Järvinen and Ravn, 2011).

Although the participants in the Danish study experienced problems with drugs, none of them said that they wanted to give up their drug use altogether (Järvinen and Ravn, 2011). The strategy they had chosen was rather to roll back their drug-use career in the direction of the recreational drug-use pattern that they had started out with. When describing their attempts to leave their problematic drug use, they focused on the same dimensions – but in a reversed direction – that had transformed them from recreational to regular drug users. They tried to leave the pattern of all-weekend parties, resume contact with their non-drug-using friends, restrict their drug use to weekends, use 'drugs for the right purposes' (stimulants for elation and activity; sedatives for relaxation) and they all claimed that they had now stopped selling drugs and that their drug intake had diminished in consequence. What they all wanted was to leave the phase of intensive drug use behind and return to a controlled drug-use pattern that did not interfere with their everyday functioning in relation to health, personal relationships, work, school and the like (Järvinen and Ravn, 2011).

Discussion

It is standard procedure for scholars writing within the cultural tradition of drug research to describe their own approach as an alternative to the comprehensive epidemiological and medical research traditions on illegal drugs (not covered in this chapter). Within these traditions, cultural researchers often say, research is one-sidedly focused on the problems of illegal drug use and not on the pleasurable aspects, without which no human being would ever become a drug user. Representing a public-health rationale, epidemiological research focuses on the quantity and frequency of drug use and its associated physical and psychological risks. Club and dance studies, on the other hand, often based in ethnography, strive to analyse illegal drug use in its socio-cultural context, paying a lot of attention to the experiences and understandings of the drug users themselves. Some cultural researchers have been participants in club and drug-use settings, which means that they have insider knowledge about the club scene and its people, and also often hold relatively positive attitudes to illegal drug use (see Measham and Moore, 2006, and Bennett, 2002, for a discussion of the advantages and disadvantages of the insider position).

As has been shown above, this research is often neoliberal in its conceptualization of drug users and their drug use: dancers/clubbers are not seen as delinquent individuals, but as well-functioning, autonomous consumers who are willing and able to control their drug intake if only they are entrusted with this responsibility. Illegal drug use is not necessarily problematic, according to these researchers, although it is certainly constructed as such in drug policies, in the traditional drug treatment system and by observers who think that drugs should be eradicated from society. Cultural drug researchers often point to excessive alcohol (and sometimes tobacco) use as a more serious threat to the welfare of youths and young adults than illegal drug use. By depicting illegal drugs as similar to legal drugs, or even as more safe than them, cultural researchers have attempted to rehabilitate illegal drug users from their stigmatized position as irrational 'others' in society. Part of their project has also been to question national and international drug policies, which are often ineffective and, according to some observers, do more harm than good.

In recent years the wave of dance and drug studies seems to have reached a saturation point. It is today widely accepted that most people who experiment with illegal drugs in, e.g., club and dance settings do not get trapped in drug habits and develop addiction. It is also evident, however, that some clubbers escalate their drug intake and become regular users whose drug intake impacts on their commitment to work, school, family etc. So far there is very little research on heavy recreational users; we do not know who they are (in terms of individual characteristics, social networks and socio-economic background) and why they develop an excessive drug-use habit. When addressing these and other questions related to drug problems it is possible that we will experience a return to more structural approaches to drug use, approaches that have been more or less absent in cultural drug research since the mid-1990s. The odds are that the neoliberal, rational actor approach of much club research, with its focus on free, considered consumer choices, will have to be supplemented with other theoretical understandings.

References

Bahora, M., Sterk, C.E. and Elifson, K.W. (2009) 'Understanding Recreational Ecstasy Use in the United States: A Qualitative Inquiry', *International Journal of Drug Policy* 20 (1) 62–69.

Bennett, A. (1999) 'Subcultures or Neo-Tribes? Rethinking the Relationship between Youth, Style and Musical Taste', *Sociology* 33 (3) 599–617.

Bennett, A. (2002) 'Researching Youth Culture and Popular Music: A Methodological Critique', *British Journal of Sociology* 53 (3) 599–617.

Boys, A., Marsden, J. and Strang, J. (2001) 'Understanding Reasons for Drug Use among Young People: A Functional Perspective', *Health Education Research* 16 (4) 457–469.

Collin, M. and Godfrey, J. (1997) *Altered State: The Story of Ecstasy Culture and Acid House.* London: Serpent's Tail.

Demant, J. (2010) 'Kokain og alkohol – en kontrollabel cocktail?' (Cocaine and alcohol – a controllable cocktail?), in M. Järvinen, J. Demant and J. Østergaard, J. (eds) *Stoffer og natteliv* (Drugs and Night Life). Copenhagen: Hans Reitzels Forlag, 146–164.

Duff, C. (2004) 'Drug Use as a "Practice of Self": Is there Any Place for an "Ethics of Moderation" in Contemporary Drug Policy?', *International Journal of Drug Policy* 15 (5) 385–393.

EMCDDA (2011) *Annual Report*. Lisbon: European Monitoring Centre for Drugs and Drug Addiction.

Featherstone, M. (1991) 'The Body in Consumer Culture', in B. Turner (ed.) *The Body: Social Process and Cultural Theory*. London: Sage, 170–196.

Goulding, C., Shankar, A., Elliot, R. and Canniford, R. (2008) 'The Marketplace Management of Illicit Pleasure', *Journal of Consumer Research* 35 (5) 759–771.

Hammerslay, R., Ditton, J., Smith, I. and Short, E. (1999) 'Patterns of Ecstasy Use by Drug Users', *British Journal of Criminology* 39 (4) 625–647.

Hobbs, D., Lister, S., Hadfield, P., Winlow, S. and Hall, S. (2000) 'Receiving Shadows: Governance and Liminality in the Night-Time Economy', *British Journal of Sociology* 51 (4) 701–717.

Ilse, J., Prinzleve, M., Zurhold, H., Haasen, C. and Cocaine EU-team (2006) 'Cocaine and Crack Use and Dependence in Europe – Experts' View on an Increasing Public Health Problem', *Addiction Research and Theory* 14 (5) 437–452.

Järvinen, M. and Ravn, S. (2011) 'From Recreational to Regular Use: Qualitative Interviews with Young Clubbers', *Sociology of Health and Illness* 33 (4) 554–569.

Järvinen, M., Demant, J. and Østergaard, J. (2010) (eds) *Stoffer og natteliv* (Drugs and Night Life). Copenhagen: Hans Reitzels Forlag.

Kelly, B.C., Parsons, J.T. and Wells, B.E. (2006) 'Prevalence and Predictors of Club Drug Use among Club-Going Young Adults in New York City', *Journal of Urban Health* 83 (5) 884–895.

Laidler, K.J., Hunt, G., Mackenzie, K. and Evans, K. (2006) 'The Emergence of Clubs and Drugs in Hong Kong', in B. Sanders (ed.) *Drugs, Clubs and Young People. Sociological and Public Health Perspectives*. Aldershot: Ashgate, 107–121.

Lenton, S., Boys, A. and Norcross, K. (1997) 'Raves, Drugs and Experience: Drug Use by a Sample of People Who Attend Raves in Western Australia', *Addiction* 92 (10) 1327–1337.

Maffesoli, M. (1996) *The Time of the Tribes: The Decline of Individualism in Mass Society*. London: Sage.

Manderson, D. (2005) 'Possessed: Drug Policy, Witchcraft and Belief', *Cultural Studies* 19 (1) 36–63.

Measham, F. (2004) 'The Decline of Ecstasy, the Rise of "Binge" Drinking and the Persistence of Pleasure', *Probation Journal. The Journal of Community and Criminal Justice* 51 (4) 309–326.

Measham, F. and Brain, K. (2005) '"Binge" Drinking, British Alcohol Policy and the New Culture of Intoxication', *Crime, Media, Culture* 1 (3) 262–282.

Measham, F. and Moore, K. (2006) 'Reluctant Reflexivity, Implicit Insider Knowledge and the Development of Club Studies', in B. Sanders (ed.) *Drugs, Clubs and Young People: Sociological and Public Health Perspectives*. Aldershot: Ashgate, 13–25.

Measham, F., Newcombe, R. and Parker, H. (1994) 'The Normalization of Recreational Drug Use amongst Young People in North-West England', *British Journal of Sociology* 45 (2) 287–312.

Measham, F., Parker, H. and Aldridge, J. (1998) 'The Teenage Transition: From Adolescent Recreational Drug Use to the Young Adult Dance Culture in Britain in the Mid-1990s', *Journal of Drug Issues* 28 (1) 9–32.

Measham, F., Aldridge, J. and Parker, H. (2000) *Dancing on Drugs: Risk, Health, and Hedonism in the British Club Scene*. London: Free Association Books.

Nabben, T. and Korf, D.J. (1999) 'Cocaine and Crack in Amsterdam', *Journal of Drug Issues* 29 (3) 627–652.

Olsen, A. (2009) 'Consuming E: Ecstasy Use and Contemporary Social Life', *Contemporary Drug Problems* 36 (1) 175–191.

Parker, H. (2005) 'Normalization as a Barometer: Recreational Drug Use and the Consumption of Leisure by Younger Britons', *Addiction Research and Theory* 13 (3) 205–215.

Parker, H. and Egginton, R. (2002) 'Adolescent Recreational Alcohol, and Drug Careers Gone Wrong: Developing a Strategy for Reducing Risks and Harms', *International Journal of Drug Policy*, 13 (5) 419–432.

Parker, H., Aldridge, J. and Measham, F. (1998) *Illegal Leisure: The Normalization of Adolescent Recreational Drug Use*. London: Routledge.

Purcell, J. and Graham, K. (2005) 'A Typology of Toronto Nightclubs', *Contemporary Drug Problems* 32 (1) 131–167.

Ramo, D.E., Grov, C., Delucchi, K., Kelly, B.C. and Parsons, J.T. (2010) 'Typology of Club Drug Use among Young Adults Recruited Using Time-Space Sampling', *Drug and Alcohol Dependency* 107 (2–3) 119–127.

Riley, S., Thompson, J. and Griffin, C. (2010) 'Turn On, Tune In, But Don't Drop Out: The Impact of Neo-liberalism on Magic Mushroom Users' (In)ability to Imagine Collectivist Social Worlds', *International Journal of Drug Policy* 21 (6) 445–451.

Riley, S., James, C., Gregory, C., Dingle, H. and Cadger, M. (2001) 'Patterns of Recreational Drug Use at Dance Events in Edinburgh, Scotland', *Addiction* 96 (7) 1035–1047.

Rödner, S. (2006) 'Practicing Risk Control in a Socially Disapproved Area: Swedish Socially Integrated Drug Users and Their Perception of Risks', *Journal of Drug Issues* 36 (4) 933–952.

Sanders, B. (2006) (ed.) *Drugs, Clubs and Young People. Sociological and Public Health Perspectives.* Aldershot: Ashgate.

Silverstone, D. (2006) 'Pub Space, Rave Space and Urban Space: Three Different Night-Time Economies', in B. Sanders (ed.) *Drugs, Clubs and Young People. Sociological and Public Health Perspectives.* Aldershot: Ashgate, 141–152.

South, N. (2004) 'Managing Work, Hedonism and "the Borderline" between the Legal and the Illegal Markets: Two Case Studies of Recreational Heavy Drug Use', *Addiction Research and Theory* 12 (6) 525–538.

Ter Bogt, T., Engels, R., Hibbel, B., van Wel, F. and Verhagen, S. (2002) '"Dancestasy": Dance and MDMA Use in Dutch Youth Culture', *Contemporary Drug Problems* 29 (1) 157–181.

van der Poel, A., Rodenburg, G., Dikstra, M., Stoele, M. and van de Mheen, D. (2009) 'Trends, Motivation and Settings of Recreational Cocaine Use by Adolescents and Young Adults in the Netherlands', *International Journal of Drug Policy* 20 (2) 143–151.

Vervaeke, H. and Korf, D.J. (2006) 'Long-Term Ecstasy Use and the Management of Work and Relationships', *International Journal of Drug Policy* 17 (6) 484–493.

Williams, L. and Parker, H. (2001) 'Alcohol, Cannabis, Ecstasy and Cocaine: Drugs of Reasoned Choice amongst Young Adult Recreational Drug Users in England', *International Journal of Drug Policy* 12 (5) 397–413.

31

HOW SHOPPING CHANGED LEISURE

Tony Blackshaw

This chapter is a critical essay underpinned by an idea which is intuitively true: namely, that there are certain goals which can be achieved only as a by-product of aiming for something else. There are plenty of examples in the leisure domain that illustrate this. As is well known to all leisure scholars, we find happiness when we are absorbed by a meaningful leisure activity – what Csikszentmihalyi (1974) calls a state of 'flow'. As Pascal Bruckner (2010) suggests (in his highly influential book *Perpetual Euphoria: On the Duty to be Happy*), the nature of happiness is to be an enigma – trying to be happy is a recipe for unhappiness. It is with such an idea in mind that this chapter deals with its subject. In order to get to grips with the significance of shopping for Leisure Studies, we must understand the pervasive reach of consumerism in the contemporary world, whose stamp is the *market-mediated mode of life* (Bauman, 1990), and which appears to be the way we live today. In this way the chapter deals with the notion of leisure as consumerism rather than of shopping as a specific leisure activity.

The ideas presented below constitute a theory both in the sense of a conceptual schema and in the sense of a set of propositions about consuming as the way of life in contemporary societies. The impetus to the construction of this theory has its roots in my dissatisfaction with the unsophisticated character of the discussion of shopping (and, by default, consuming) in Leisure Studies, which is best characterized by the statement 'It is different here than elsewhere'. One firm generalization emerges from the discussion developed in this chapter: in the contemporary world there exist no leisure activities or pursuits that are immune from consumerism.

There are two main reasons for the failure of generalizations of this sort to emerge in Leisure Studies. First, the discursive formation known as Leisure Studies has only imperfectly taken to itself the influence of shopping as a significant area of interest, generally at second hand through the work of sociologists and market researchers. Part of the reason for this relative absence seems to be a concern that shopping is in some way an inauthentic leisure activity. The second, more important, reason lies in the inadequacy of social theory, which all too often tends to see consumerism in a wholly negative light, especially relating to issues of freedom and social control in leisure. This inadequacy is perhaps best summed up in Ritzer's (1993) social theory of McDonaldization (see Rojek, 2005). Despite the many studies of consumerism that have been developed in sociology and cultural studies, we are still lacking a conceptual scheme in Leisure Studies that specifies with some degree of clarity what are the important elements of consumerism and what these mean for understanding contemporary leisure.

In this chapter it is argued that these can be found in the shift from a 'solid' producer-based modernity to a 'liquid' consumer-based modernity, which sees individuals as 'shaped and trained' as shoppers first and foremost (Bauman, 2004). However, as consumerism makes leisure increasingly take the form of shopping, this chapter argues, we should start to think of its different manifestations, especially as they are incarnated in the fast pace of liquid modern life, as calling forth different kinds of relationship with consumerism. To this end, and contrary to the dominant view in Leisure Studies, this chapter argues that, if today shopping is *the* way of life, it is because it offers us the right to a 'thoroughly individual' choice, while supplying the social approval for that choice (Bauman, 1990), which suggests that its principal driving force is IKEAization (and freedom) rather than McDonaldization (and social control) (Blackshaw, 2010).

To help achieve this goal of understanding, what follows is divided into four sections. As the discussion developed so far has hopefully made clear, the focus of this chapter is on leisure as consumerism rather than shopping as a specific leisure activity. Section two explains the marketization of social and cultural life that aimed to save capitalism from stagnation at the end of the post-war consumer boom, based on the redistribution of wealth through the welfare state and mass production. Sections three and four discuss the relative merits of Ritzer's (1993) McDonaldization thesis and my own IKEAization thesis for explaining this societal shift towards the marketization of the world, and what this means for leisure. In the first instance, however, it is necessary to put some flesh on the idea of shopping as a leisure activity. This is important, since not only does it demonstrate why shopping is for many people an important leisure activity and that they spend a good deal of their free time (and money) trying to amplify the pleasures and happiness that it brings, but also that it has helped to redraw the boundaries of socialization, which today consists of *offers* rather than *norms*, and seduction rather than normative regulation (Bauman, 2010: 73).

Shopping as a leisure activity

In ordinary use, shopping refers to the process of examining products or services presented by retailers, with the intent to make a purchase. However, sociologists of shopping have argued that it is important to consider the various reasons why people shop (see for example Miller, 1998; Zukin, 2004). In some contexts shopping may be considered a strictly utilitarian activity, but in others it is clearly a leisure pursuit. Market researchers recognize that shopping is often purely task orientated, with product or service acquisition as the central goal. However, they are also aware that shopping clearly is for many people a pleasure-seeking activity that appeals to desire, fantasy and the affecting experiences we have with products or services.

This distinction is often brought to bear in discussions of gender differences in shopping. In their study *Men Buy, Women Shop* (Knowledge@Wharton, 2007), for example, researchers at Wharton's Jay H. Baker Retail Initiative and the Verde Group, a Toronto market-research company, found that whereas for men shopping is 'a mission' – they tend to target what they are looking for, buy it and then immediately leave the store – for women it has a special kind of pleasure all of its own. As Walter Benjamin might have said, the 'event' of the shopping experience, at the moment of its realization, is for women everything, since it incorporates pleasure, such pleasure that 'pleasure' is not a word capable of identifying with the kind of pleasure that shopping brings – or so it would seem.

Don DeLillo's novel *White Noise*, at once mocking and applauding, provides a useful counterpoint and corrective to the view that men do not shop for pleasure in the same ways that women do. The book's main protagonist, Jack Gladney, is galvanized into shopping mode by one of his colleagues at the 'College-on-the-Hill', Eric Massingdale, whom he meets for the first time outside work in the Mid-Village Mall. Eric, who is intrigued by Jack's off-campus choice of clothing, tells him, 'with a grin turning lascivious, rich with secret meaning', that he has the look of a 'big, harmless, aging, indistinct sort of guy'. This encounter awakens Jack to the significance of his own invisibility and this puts him 'in the mood to shop':

> I found the others and we walked across two parking lots to the main structure in the ... Mall, a ten-story building arranged around a center court of waterfalls, promenades and gardens ... into the elevator, into the shops set along the tiers, through the emporiums and department stores, puzzled but excited by my desire to buy. When I could not decide between two shirts, they encouraged me to buy both. When I said I was hungry, they fed me pretzels, beer, and souvlaki. The two girls scouted ahead, spotting things they thought I might want or need, running back to get me, to clutch my arms, plead with me to follow. They were my guides to endless well-being ... We smelled chocolate, popcorn, cologne; we smelled rugs and furs, hanging salamis and deathly vinyl. My family gloried in the event. I was one of them, shopping, at last ... I shopped with reckless abandon ... I shopped for its own sake, looking and touching, inspecting merchandise I had no intention of buying, then buying it ... I began to grow in value and self-regard. I filled myself out, found new aspects of myself, located a person I'd forgotten existed ... I traded money for goods. The more money I spent, the less important it seemed ... Brightness settled around me ... we ate another meal.
>
> (DeLillo, 1985: 83–84)

Jack Gladney finds out that shopping is what makes his life palpable; it not only makes him feel visible, but has the ability to show him what happiness looks like. In this sense Jack recognizes that consumer goods are not simply objects; that he can see himself in them. As Linda Grant observed in another context, he learns that shopping can be 'something so mysterious, complex and potentially transformative that it is almost metaphysical' and that buying something like a 'new coat can induce not only happiness but a radically revised sense of who you are. You can call this by some piece of jargon if you wish, you can invoke phrases such as "self-esteem", but they don't encompass the whole vast empire of the self. The new coat makes things possible. It casts you in a new light to yourself' (Grant, 2004).

What Grant is referring to here is the phenomenon called the 'looking glass self', which was the term coined by Charles Horton Cooley (1902) to explain how our attitudes about ourselves are shaped on the basis of the perceptions of significant others. What this tells us is that not only is shopping psychologically important to some people's sense of self but also it must be understood as a socio-cultural phenomenon.

What this means is that we must recognize that the shopping process is inevitably bound up with status differentiation. That is, shopping demands not only economic capital but also, crucially social capital and cultural capital. In this regard we need to recognize that shopping 'stands for production, distribution, desiring, obtaining and using, of symbolic goods' (Bauman, 1992: 223), involving a kind of symbolic rivalry over the meaning of products and services and the differences and distinctions that they signify. Extending this idea empirically to explore the actual shopping practices, Miller concludes his own study by suggesting that the foremost purpose of 'shopping is not so much to buy things that people want, but to strive to be in a relationship with subjects that want these things' (Miller, 1998: 108). In other words, we reconcile our relationships with other people through the ways in which we shop and it is through this process that shopping reproduces both status differentiation as well as the social inequalities that it represents.

What this brief discussion of our key concept tells us is that for many people today shopping – whether it is experienced actually, in malls and other retail outlets, or virtually, online – is an important leisure pursuit which is pivotal to helping them to express themselves, realize new social identities and improve their social statuses (Zukin, 2004). What it does not tell us is anything about the changing configuration of social, cultural, economic and ideological arrangements associated with capitalist accumulation that have been underway since the early 1970s and which have been of crucial importance for explaining the ways in which leisure has become more shopping-like.

The rise of consumerism and the consumer society

It takes someone special to come along and point out what we don't know that we think we know about the here and now; and that it can always bear reimagining. Those readers who are familiar with Zygmunt Bauman's work will be aware that his approach to understanding shopping is different in that it suggests that any attempt to elevate it as a specific realm of socio-cultural activity falls short, since it misses the true target, which is the rise of consumer society.

The new reach of the market and concomitant hyper-consumerism had its roots in the social, political, economic and ideological contradictions that were at work in Western democracies at the end of the 1960s and in the early 1970s and which came together to give modernity a new specific and distinctive liquid shape. Between the end of the Second World War and the start of the 1970s the reach of the market extended to such a degree that Western democracies were fundamentally transformed. They changed so rapidly and radically that it can be reasonably interpreted that by the onset of the 1980s the *longue durée* of modernity had entered a new conjuncture in which the contradictions underpinning social class inequality, revealed during the Industrial Revolution, moved decisively away from a specific and distinctive producer 'heavy' and 'solid', 'hardware-focused' shape to take the form of a more uncertain but distinctively consumer 'light' and a 'liquid', 'software-based' one (Bauman, 2000a). If solid modernity was one of the rationalization of objects (and human subjects) through standardization, abstraction and Fordist mass production, Bauman asserts, the liquid modernity that superseded it was one of rationalization through cultural difference, reflexive individualization and consumerism.

In the immediate post-war period Western democracies had witnessed two decades of uninterrupted economic growth and full employment, which had marked the shift from 'needing' to 'wanting' and had seen the comforts of home and consumerism at last come within the reach of the majority of working people. This period had been dominated by public ownership and wealth redistribution through the welfare state. However, by the middle of the 1970s there were clear signs that this world was coming to an end, especially with the economic predicaments sparked by the 1974 oil crisis, which saw the stagnation of the world economy, growing worker unrest and the emergence of what Habermas (1975) termed a legitimation crisis.

Capitalism needed a solution. As that most perceptive interpreter of this period, Wolfgang Streeck, explains, it found this in a wave of profound restructuring of both production processes and product lines. Worker militancy was vanquished, not least through a secular expansion of labour supply, first by mass entry of women into paid employment, and then by the internationalization of production systems … firms were busy re-engineering their products and processes, with the help of new micro-electronic technologies capable of dramatically shortening production cycles; making manufacturing machinery less dedicated, thereby lowering the break-even point for their products; and rendering much manual labour dispensable, or at least enabling firms to relocate to other parts of the world where it was cheaper and more deferential … In short, capital's answer to the secular stagnation of markets for standardized goods at the end of the Fordist era included making goods less standardized … As mass production gave way to something like large-scale boutique production, customers were increasingly spared the compromises they had had to make when purchasing the standardized goods of old – where there always remained a gap between what different buyers might ideally have liked and the one-size-must-fit-all product that producers were able to provide.

(Streeck, 2012: 30–31)

As Lyotard (1979) was to argue at the time, this collapse of the standardization of consumer goods was reflected in the collapse of all grand narratives. Basically, in keeping with the other social, cultural, economic and ideological changes that were occurring at this time, there was a conspicuous shift in the way in which knowledge-claims came to be legitimated. In a nutshell, Lyotard's argument was that by the late 1960s and early 1970s science (like religion and leisure) had been turned into yet another commodity. In turn, *truth* was now determined, like everything else, not by its ability to tell the *Truth*, but by its exchange value.

If early industrial modernity had stood for the language game of denotation (the difference between true or false), post-industrializing modernity now stood for an alternative, 'technical' game of efficiency versus inefficiency. As a result, performativity became the new criterion of the legitimacy of knowledge-claims. All of a sudden it appeared that everybody seemed to have a view about what constitutes the *truth* and as a result various 'language games' or knowledge-claims were now played out through the 'techniques and technologies' of performativity. For Lyotard, this plurality of competing voices was made possible by the 'performativity criterion', which invokes an 'incredulity to metanarratives' – in short scepticism towards any idea or theory which posits universal truth-claims.

For Lyotard, this period proved to be a watershed in the history of Western democracies, which saw this new, reoriented capitalism become so pervasive that it appeared that there was nothing left that could not be commodified. The status of knowledge had altered and performativity had come to represent a kind of hyper-capitalist efficiency which was able to bring the 'pragmatic functions of knowledge clearly to light and elevate all language games to self-knowledge' (Lyotard, 1979: 114). In Austin's (1962) terminology, truth was now performative rather than constative, and the most convincing truth-claims were those which the market would determine as the most performatively efficient.

In short, everything was now to be judged by its market value; if it doesn't sell, it isn't what is wanted, pure and simply. Truth now had to be exercised and measured in the manner of its performance. The upshot was that if branding was once upon a time solely the language of the market, it had now become *the* language of humankind as a whole.

As we have seen already, Bauman (2010) was subsequently to argue, we can say that now, in our liquid modern world, that culture no longer consists of any *norms* but, rather, of *offers*, and to this extent is governed by a 'consumer attitude' which refers the whole of life to the market; it orients every desire and each effort in the search for a tool or an expertise one can buy. It dissolves the problem of control over the wider setting of life (something most people will never achieve) in the multitude of small shopping acts that are – at least in principle – within your reach. It *privatizes*, so to speak, issues so that they are not perceived as *public*; it *individualizes* tasks so that they are not seen as *social*. It now becomes my duty (and, as I am encouraged to hope, also a task I can perform) to improve myself and my life, to culture and refine, to overcome my own shortcomings and other vexing drawbacks to the way I live.

(Bauman, 1990: 204)

As he points out in the same publication, the emergence of this 'consumer attitude' produced not only a quite specific form of subjectivization in humankind, but one that also displays a quite specific outlook on the world, which first of all entails

perceiving life as a series of problems, which can be specified, more or less clearly defined, singled out and dealt with. It means, secondly, believing that dealing with such problems, solving them, is one's duty, which one cannot neglect without incurring guilt or shame. It means, thirdly, trusting that for every problem, already known or as may still arise in the future, there is a solution – a special object or recipe, prepared by specialists, by people with superior know-how, and one's task is to find it. It means, fourthly, assuming that such objects or recipes are essentially available; they may be obtained in exchange for money, and shopping is the way of obtaining them. It means, fifthly, translating the task of learning the art of living as the effort to acquire the skill of finding such objects and recipes, and gaining the power to possess them once found: shopping skills and purchasing power.

(Bauman, 1990: 203–204)

If the major accomplishment of the centred 'roots of order' underpinning solid modernity was to turn life into a regimentality in which the work of *Homo faber* and the leisure of *Homo ludens* were divided (Rojek, 2005), the major accomplishment of the decentred disorder sustaining liquid modernity has been its ability to turn the attention of *Homo faber* and *Homo ludens* to the life of *Homo consumens* (Bauman, 2007). Indeed, as Bauman argues, it is the instantaneity of consumer culture and its ability to 'take the waiting out of wanting' in delivering *Homo consumens'* hopes and dreams that is today what is imagined as the measure of the success of a life worth living.

The scale of this all-pervasive societal shift towards rationalization through cultural difference, reflexive individualization and consumerism and what this means for leisure is perhaps best illustrated by drawing on a Weberian critique. As is well known, Weber argued that the incessant drive to the accumulation of knowledge and wealth is what underpins modern capitalism. This is because in modern societies rationality and rationalization become all pervasive, and leisure, like all other distinct realms of human activity, is increasingly rationalized – what Weber called the 'iron-cage of rationalization' – for the major needs of modern society are 'cumulative, quantified and quantifiable' (Heller, 1999).

Weber's ideas were developed over one hundred years ago. In the next section, I critically discuss George Ritzer's (1993; 2003) contribution to this debate, and in particular his metaphor of McDonaldization. With this Ritzer provides one of the most up-to-date and perhaps the most compelling of applications of Weber's ideas, which recognizes Streeck's (2012: 34) observation that mass production 'did not disappear but became much more sophisticated, characteristically developing a market niche of its own, and this becoming another instance of niche production'. Importantly, what Ritzer also provides us with is a theory with which to test the conceptual power of Weber's original putative insights as they apply to the commodification of leisure. As the following discussion demonstrates, however, in so doing he massively oversimplifies both the meaning and the purpose of consumerism in the lives of modern men and women and what this tell us about the relationship between leisure and freedom and control. In developing this critique, the McDonaldization thesis is juxtaposed with my own alternative IKEAization thesis.

The McDonaldization of leisure and its limits

The first thing to point out is that McDonaldization is not a description of reality, but an *ideal type* or analytical tool that we might use to try to understand those aspects of the world which remain for most of us agonizingly confused, contradictory and incoherent (Bauman, 2007). It can be defined as the process by which the principles of the global fast-food restaurant McDonald's are progressively dominating more aspects of society – including leisure – as well as having a significant bearing on the way that globalization works. McDonaldization has often been depicted as a contemporary version of Max Weber's rationalization thesis involving the organization of society by bureaucratic means. The key distinction between McDonaldization and Weber's original thesis is that Ritzer argues that the principal form of rationalization is assumed by the flexible, global corporation, best exemplified in the fast-food giant. However, Ritzer draws on the key aspects of Weber's work to demonstrate how rationality and rationalization through McDonaldization pervade everyday life, to the extent that they are little by little producing, out of the world we have to live in, a 'disenchanting' world that we might not want to live in, but appear not to be able to do much about. Ritzer's thesis is well known and here I shall merely summarize its key principles.

According to Ritzer (2003: 138) the essence of the McDonaldization process is distinguished by five essential dimensions. The first of these is efficiency, 'or the effort to discover the best possible means to whatever end is desired'. A McDonaldizing society is a speeded-up, time-conscious and consumption-based society and consumers expect to be served promptly and efficiently. In order to make this possible, McDonald's and its customers strike a deal. The fast-food corporation puts into place an inventory of norms, rules, regulations and structures to ensure that its employees perform as efficiently as possible and its customers react by dining in a similar manner. The 'drive-thru' window is the example that Ritzer usually uses to illustrate this dimension.

The second dimension concerns calculability. This emphasizes quantity – perhaps best personified in the 'Big Mac' burger – which is often accompanied with the loss of quality. Time is of the essence here. Just as the efficiency of McDonald's staff is measured by the speed with which they can produce food and serve it to customers, so McDonald's restaurants are designed to coerce customers not stay around for too long after they have finished eating. As we have seen, the expectation is that, ideally, they will buy 'drive-thru' and not come into the restaurant at all.

The third dimension is predictability. Not only is it expected that McDonald's products and services will be the same the world over – a Big Mac is always a Big Mac – but so also will be the McDonaldization experience. In another book, Ritzer (2004) likens the predictability found in McDonald's restaurants to what Marc Augé (1995) calls non-places, which, in marked contrast to places (those topographical sites loaded with substance), are merely repositories of liquid flows, or what he call 'nullities', globally conceived and controlled and lacking the distinctive substance – conversation, flexibility, localism, humanity – that make experiences, products and services real. In other words, McDonaldization is too superficial to be authentic.

The fourth dimension of McDonaldization is control. In explaining this Ritzer turns to technology and the example of french-fry machines: just as McDonald's employees are controlled by the bell that rings to tell them when the fries are cooked to just the right colour and texture, so customers are controlled by their inability to choose well-cooked fries.

The final aspect of McDonaldization is the irrationality of rationality, which also affects both employees and customers. Basically, in the process of rationally organizing its business, McDonald's ends up removing all the things that make work rewarding and eating (read: leisure) a pleasurable experience. The upshot of this is dehumanization: 'Employees are forced to work in dehumanizing jobs and customers are forced to eat in dehumanizing settings and circumstances. The fast-food restaurant is a source of degradation for employees and customers alike' (Ritzer, 2003: 141).

Ritzer himself often refers to the package holiday as the exemplary application of McDonaldization to leisure (Harris, 2005), but, as Rojek (2005: 208) demonstrates, the scope of this metaphor is far reaching in its application and 'McLeisure' encompasses a broad range of leisure activities, including:

- *Shopping centres/malls*: provide an 'assembly line' experience of shopping based in predictability, uniformity and standardization.
- *Convenience foods*: offer a streamlined, predictable, efficient experience of food consumption. Microwave foods 'mechanize' and 'quantify' the process of food preparation by timing the process of cooking.
- *Theme parks*: control and monitor the consumption of leisure space and time. Theme parks employ systems of queuing that are akin to a 'conveyor belt' system. Seeing sights is based in the principle of efficiency, which discourages lingering or wandering off on your own.
- *Television*: schedules and, increasingly, programme content are driven by the ratings war. This involves the predominance of calculability and quantitative over qualitative criteria.
- *Sports*: measuring and monitoring sports performance is now a standard feature of sports organization. Sports stadia increasingly utilize standards of predictability as a feature of design. For example, domes and artificial turf aim to minimize disruption caused by the weather. Processes of queuing and seating adopt 'assembly line' standards of efficiency and predictability.

Ritzer's metaphor is significant for a number of reasons. Two are especially worth mentioning for our purposes. First, McDonaldization is not just another cunning business model. As Bauman (2000b: 234) points out, 'there must have been a fertile soil for the seed, once sown, to grow so quickly – resonance (indeed, a degree of mutual adequacy) between the changes in the existential conditions of postmodern individuals and the escape-from-uncertainty-through-designed-standards which McDonaldization is all about'. Second, McDonaldization shows us that the difference between consuming and leisure is 'getting more blurred by the day and for many practical purposes has been already obliterated'.

Ritzer's metaphor has been much debated and there are a number of *general* criticisms of it that can regularly be found in the literature. This is not the place to provide an exhaustive discussion of these criticisms, as the inventory is much too long, encompassing the full range of social, economic, cultural, political and ethical implications and connotations of Ritzer's work (see, for example, Alfino, Caputo and Wynyard, 1998). Here we will discuss only some *general* criticisms of McDonaldization in so far that they highlight its main deficiencies *specifically* for understanding leisure.

The idea of McDonaldization is – just like Weber's original thesis – in large measure depressing. It is a highly speculative metaphor, and its incorporation of (post)modernity into the ideal type just described is dubious, to say the least. This has led a number of commentators to criticize Ritzer for failing to provide solid empirical evidence for his theorizing. That is, like many other people, Ritzer has obviously spent some time in McDonald's, observing how its business concept works in action, in order to build his evidence, but he doesn't appear to have researched in any great depth the relationships between 'the changes in the existential conditions of postmodern individuals and the escape-from-uncertainty-through-designed-standards which McDonaldization is all about', identified by Bauman above.

McDonaldization emphasizes the point that not only is our leisure circumscribed by rational systems that we have little control over, but also the cultural standardization and normalization of experience that these present us with is inevitable (Rojek, 2005). If, in Foucault's language, McDonaldization expresses a particular combination of power and knowledge, then this does not vary between different national configurations; this is because it is able to cater efficiently for needs that, as Weber explained, are 'cumulative, quantified and quantifiable'. The upshot of rationalization through McDonaldization is the *homogenization* of leisure. Those who want to be themselves in their leisure have to overcome the feeling of 'disenchantment', throw off 'the iron cage' mentality pressing down on them and find their own authentic voices – but this is unlikely, since the progressive accumulation of McDonaldization is an infinite process.

However, the notion that employees and customers simply acquiesce in the roles ascribed to them by McDonaldization is open to theoretical reductionism; that is, Ritzer reduces practical knowledge to theoretical knowledge and ignores the fact that, whatever its dark side, leisure, like culture, is praxis (Bauman, 1999). Ritzer seems to assume, on the one hand, that we do not have the necessary skills to outwit McDonaldization and that we passively accept its authoritarian powers and, on the other, that we do not want products and services with a human face. He also ignores the possibility that people might seek alternatives to the irrational, antisocial and dehumanizing effects of McDonald's.

This leads us on to the two foremost criticisms of Ritzer. First, just like Weber, he assumes that modernity is a 'disenchanted' world which is characterized by a *deficit of meaning*. However, by turning away from everyday life to theory, both Weber and Ritzer choose not to focus on the freedoms and the opportunities that modernity offers us, by focusing instead on its ostensible deficits. Contrary to what Weber and Ritzer suggest, liquid modernity, especially, is characterized by a *surplus of meaning*. Indeed, since the early 1980s we have witnessed an exponential growth in leisure, and, importantly, not just the kind that is provided for our consumption through rational expert systems. Most of these new leisure opportunities might not be entirely divorced from commercialization, but many of them are marked with a significant degree of meaning – vocation, innovation and devotional practice – rather than merely reflecting cynical attempts by rational systems to 're-enchant' a modern world that has lost its aura by 'adding leisure values' (Harris, 2005). Examples that fit this trend include brewing real ale, growing fruit and vegetables in allotments, ecotourism and much else besides. What is also significant about these new leisure trends is the way in which people work to create through their leisure interests new synergies that carry both the weight and the meaning of culture. To take just one example, the traditional Punjabi musical and dance form of bhangra has been taken up by many young Asian musicians in Britain, who have fused it with a vast range of other musical forms (often hybrids themselves) such as disco, techno, house, raga, jungle and hip-hop, to create new sounds and dance forms that are now being re-exported back to Asia.

Second, McDonaldization is simply not sophisticated enough to be the principal driving force of the consumer society. It appears to be because Ritzer tells us everything that matters about consumerism for McDonaldization. But he never gets far with saying what matters about consumerism for ordinary men and women. Contrary to what Bauman suggests (2000b: 234), it is the global home-furnishing corporation, IKEA, not McDonaldization, that 'is most seminal of the many present-day trends since it augurs, or brings in its wake, a thorough revolution in business practice as well as in the most essential aspects of daily-life culture' (Baumann, 2000b: 234), because this is the metaphor that truly reflects our actual experiences of leisure.

The IKEAization of leisure

Since the early 1980s IKEA has had a massive influence on the development of the business of the home-furnishing market, turning furniture into a fashion item, while making it affordable and disposable (Simmons, 2005). As Simmons points out, the designation 'IKEA' stands for Ingvar Kamprad Elmtaryd Agunnaryd. Ingvar Kamprad is the name of the man who founded the company in the 1940s, who grew up on a farm called Elmtaryd, in a village in Sweden called Agunnaryd. IKEA's corporate identity is a simple one, ostensibly based on Kamprad's philosophy of wanting to 'create a better everyday life for the majority of people' through a commitment to good design at a price that suits its customers; while promoting a sound social and environmental image, it simply recognizes the fact that consumers operate with the entitlement to enjoy the products of someone else's labour.

The IKEA brand is a good example of what Rojek (2010) refers to as *neat capitalism*. Through this term Rojek identifies the knowing, deliberate attempts by entrepreneurs such as Ingvar Kamprad to offer clever but cool solutions to pressing social, cultural and economic questions. His use of the term 'neat' here is intended to express the self-aggrandizing manner in which neat capitalism is promulgated and practised, especially the way it which it sells itself as offering 'savvy *stateless solutions*' to the problems of society and the world by drawing on the sentiments of popular imagination.

There is no better example of the success of neat capitalism than IKEA. At the time that Simmons wrote his book in 2005, IKEA had 202 shops in over 32 countries and was printing 145 million catalogues in 48 editions and 25 languages; it had 410 million customers worldwide, 1 million of whom visit its shops every day; and employed 84,000 staff. Between 1994 and 2005 its income increased from $4.3 billion to $19.4 billion, representing a growth of more than 400 per cent (Bailly, Caudron and Lambart, 2006); this occurred while the company reduced its prices by between 15 and 20 per cent during the 5-year period 2000–5. In achieving this success, contrary to McDonald's, IKEA has not had to sacrifice its integrity, undermine its brand or alienate its customers.

Notwithstanding its axiomatic power as the liquid modern business model *par excellence*, what is hardly commented on, however, is that during its 60-odd years' existence, and particularly over the last 15 years or so, IKEA has become the paradigm for understanding changes in all areas of contemporary life. IKEAization has changed the way that people shop. It has helped to realign our economic social class system. It has changed the way we interact. It has become part of our social and cultural fabric. Let us consider its key dimensions and how we might apply the metaphor to contemporary leisure.

First, IKEAization emphasizes the essence of the notion of home in a modern world in which it cannot help but be missing (Bauman, 2001). It answers the ultimate question that modernity poses to us: how can one find a home when the things that make it so – continuity, warmth, comfort, safety – are always on the cusp of being taken away? The essence of the IKEA brand is the idea that feeling at 'home' is a nourishing antidote to a thoroughly individualized modern life. The wonder and the warmth of a home – you can't beat it. This is what makes IKEAization so absorbing: in this metaphor men and women can find a ready-made solution for subtracting themselves from the exhausting experience of being alone in the world. In other words, with IKEAization the world becomes homely. You might say that the core business philosophy of IKEA is to give people a home as they have never experienced it before. To this extent IKEAization stresses the significance of the experience of intimate places for human beings, identifying the interior spaces of the house – bedrooms, living rooms, kitchens, attics, stairs – and the small spaces contained within it – drawers, sideboards, chests and wardrobes, as our 'first world'. As Bachelard puts it:

> Before he is 'cast into the world', as claimed by certain hasty metaphysics, man is laid in the cradle of the house [sic]. And always, in our daydreams, the house is a large cradle. A concrete metaphysics cannot neglect this fact, this simple fact, all the more, since this fact of value, an important value, to which we return in our daydreaming. Being is already a value. Life begins well, it begins enclosed, protected, all warm in the bosom of the house.
>
> (Bachelard, 1994/1964: 7)

We also see the 'home' in a different way through IKEAization: as a source of self, an enriching collective world. But the products of IKEAization are much more than lifestyle accessories. In IKEA stores shoppers find what middle-class fans find in the working-class game of association football: a sense of home.

Another one of the primary dimensions of IKEAization is its democracy. Unlike McDonaldization, which seeks uniformity by trying to absorb disparate personalities, IKEAization recognizes that this is an impossible task. Here lies IKEAization's moral aspect: not only is it keen to promote its social and environmental image, but that it is democratic. No *apparent* stratification as such; no fixity of social class, no patriarchal, racial or age hierarchies: it is open to all comers. As Donald Sassoon puts it: IKEA is the place where 'workers and burghers alike buy the contents of their homes' (Sassoon, 2005: 147). Questionable though it may be, it is the assertion that it includes everyone that gives IKEAization its sting. It knows exactly what it stands for, and it is not for the social class society of the past – even if, as we have seen, it offers its customers the warmth and comfort of that past if they wish to purchase it.

Third, as we have seen already, contrary to McDonald's, great importance is given to incalculability and unpredictability. IKEAization emphasizes 'affordable solutions for better living', but not to the detriment of quality ('Who needs a new kitchen with more than good looks?': IKEA kitchens come with a 25-year 'everyday quality guarantee'), diversity ('Everyone's welcome in an IKEA kitchen') and innovations in style, but not with an expensive price ('Big on style. Not on price'). Not only does IKEA have its own teams of product designers ('Why do designers work for us?' IKEA asks. 'Because they are passionately mad') to come up with the goods that it stacks on its warehouse shelves, but it also offers its customers prefabricated furniture arrangements which are both 'jaw-dropping' and made to measure in its very own 'have-it-all-approach to affordable design'. IKEAization does what McDonaldization could only dream of: it outstrips the imagination of any consumer. It also fits very nicely the requirements of individual men and women who have little time for waiting at check-out counters and who want to exchange any faulty goods they have purchased with the minimum of fuss.

To briefly apply this dimension to leisure. The transformation of fashion is a good example. Retailers, such as the British billionaire owner of the Arcadia group and Topshop, Sir Philip Green, another *neat* capitalist, have been very successful at offering their own IKEA-type innovations in fashion by making luxury and style 'accessible' to everyone. What Green does better than most other retailers in the fashion business is offer 'individualized' products that mirror the aura of designer clothes on the high street at cheap prices; the trick being to offer luxury and style on the cheap without stripping away what makes it special. He also has an eye for a new market, and not only that, but an acute awareness that people have little time and patience when they shop these days. Anyone who has recently walked into a Topman store will also be aware of its proclivity for playing cool, up-to-the-minute 'indie' music. Topman has recently struck a deal with Rough Trade records to sell 'indie' music in its stores (Bray, 2009). The message is a clear one: come to Topman and find the coolest clothes and coolest new sounds before either hit the mainstream.

Fourth, IKEA may be a global brand, but, unlike McDonald's, there is something inherently provincial about its character, and this is a cause for celebration. Its lack of USA hegemony is a key part of the appeal of IKEAization. It anthropomorphizes its products by giving them Swedish names that charm its customers and which they can relate to: Aneboda (chest of drawers), Ektorp (armchair), Grimen (bed), Mysa Rönn (quilt cover), Pax Ådal (wardrobe), Tuvull (travel rug) and much else besides. In so doing it offers its customers a shopping experience with a homespun, European feel about it, rooted in the experience of the IKEA 'family' and delivered by 'co-workers' who are expected to care. Unlike McDonaldization, IKEAization is warm, intimate and enchanting.

IKEAization is also unlike McDonaldization in another key way. Fifth, its roots lie not in the hegemony of the cultural practices of USA free-time activity, but in the Protestant work ethic (Simmons, 2005). Ingvar Kamprad knows that the satisfaction that comes through giving your home an IKEA make-over cannot just be bought: it has to be earned, learned and worked at. As Simmons points out, IKEA's customers recognize that the way in which IKEA operates is largely to do with lowering costs, and that there is complicity between them and the company to make this business model work. The upshot of this is that IKEA's customers have developed a disciplined and diligent commitment to picking up their own furniture, carrying it home and making it themselves. As Simmons puts it:

> the ideas of 'flat-pack' and 'IKEA' are inseparable. The practicality of the invention meant that transportation costs for furniture could be greatly reduced – and the assembly costs of putting the furniture together could be passed on to the customer. In a sense, this seems an enormous cheek. Yet IKEA customers participate willingly because they understand their role in reducing the price they pay for furniture.
>
> (Simmons, 2005)

Yet, at the same time, and what goes unnoticed by Simmons, is that IKEAization offers the tantalizing prospect of maximum Puritanism for the minimum of sacrifice – another underlying irony.

Crucially, IKEAization also caters for consumers who are looking for something that is a tad more challenging than the straightforwardly 'off the peg': self-assembly can be a bit tricky, and everyone struggles a bit, but with a bit of effort you get there in the end. IKEAization recognizes that the real pleasure of consuming lies in its ambivalence: the enthralment of the search and the exhilaration of discovery. IKEA customers not only get excited about acquiring stylish new furniture but also relish the anticipation and thrill of gaining new knowledge and skills in the process of putting together their acquisitions. As we have already seen, what also makes IKEA attractive to its customers is that its products are as elastic as the tales of its marketing spinners and extendable enough to fulfil whatever dreams they have in mind.

Weber famously identified the Protestant work ethic as the crucial cultural feature in the development of industrial capitalism. The way in which the Protestant work ethic becomes discernible with IKEAization is also in the productive use of leisure time. To this extent IKEAization blurs the distinction between serious and casual leisure (Stebbins, 2006). In other words, even when leisure is commodified it does not rule out the fact that it provides men and women with the enthralment and satisfaction that is assumed by Stebbins to accompany only serious leisure activities. This can be seen in Baudrillard's (1989; 1990) idea of the 'into', which suggests that the point is not just to have a leisure interest, but to be 'into' leisure, which he suggests is a new form of 'voluntary servitude'. This dimension of IKEAization can be seen in the imposition of the strict and punishing regimes in sport, exercise and keep fit which provide us with a broad range of elaborate ways for refashioning the body. In these ways we assert our freedom, refuse poor physical limits and transform our bodies (just like our homes) into what we want them to be.

It is in these ways that IKEAization also emphasizes the idea of cool. Most readers of this chapter will be so familiar with the idea of cool that they will probably think that it barely needs to be explained. After all, it is difficult to imagine anything people do today that is not robed in the idea. Yet, for all its popularity, and any ostensible certainty about its origins, cool is at best an elusive disposition. If ice and fire are binary extremes, cool is a zombie category somewhere in between. It is a way of being-in-the-world which is 'defined by that quality of being simultaneously with-it and disengaged, in control but nonchalant, knowing but ironically self-aware, and above all inscrutably undemonstrative' (Filler, 2012). The cool attitude is the mind-set of IKEAization.

The cult of cool, of cultivating a cool appearance, criss-crosses all aspects of IKEAized leisure: rappers justify their lyrical extremities with it; some football fans found their identities on it; consumers always seem to be on the look-out for guides to living that tell them the coolest ways to live and how to pose and what is the coolest music to listen to and where to shop for the coolest clothes and what to eat and drink in the coolest restaurants and where to go for the coolest holidays.

What this suggests is that the technologies associated with IKEAization facilitate freedom rather than control. Shopping has by now replaced work as the backbone of the reward system and it is only the losers in the liquid modern board game of Snakes and Ladders – the 'flawed consumers' (Bauman, 1998) – who are still controlled through the work ethic. As we have seen, IKEAization redraws the boundaries between social class divisions as a relationship between those with different abilities to shop. In an IKEAizing society control is barely noticeable, because there is always something to fit even the smallest budget and the shallowest commitment. It is this last dimension which perhaps best exemplifies why it is *precarized* IKEAization rather than progressive McDonaldization that is 'the most seminal of the many present-day trends'. To tweak what Bauman said of consumerism generally and what can be applied to IKEAization specifically:

> What makes the freedom offered by [IKEAization] more alluring still is that it comes without the blemish which tainted most other forms [for example, public sector leisure facilities]: the same market which offers freedom offers certainty. It offers the individual the right to a 'thoroughly individual' choice; yet it also supplies social approval for such choice, thereby exorcizing that ghost of insecurity which … poisons the joy of the sovereign will. In a paradoxical way [IKEAization] fits the bill of the 'fantasy community' where freedom and certainty, independence and togetherness live alongside each other without conflict. People are thus pulled to [IKEAization] by a double bind: they depend on it for their individual freedom; and they depend on it for enjoying their freedom without paying the price of insecurity.
>
> (Bauman, 1988: 61–62)

Conclusion

To sum up, this chapter has presented a conceptual scheme which provides a way of classifying shopping in Leisure Studies. It began by discussing the emergence of shopping as a specific kind of leisure activity. More importantly, though, it tried to explain the pervasive nature of consumerism in contemporary societies and the implications of this for leisure. It did this by arguing that the mantle of the principal driving force of consumer society is assumed by IKEAization. An IKEAized existence is a compelling one. McLeisure and IKEALeisure share the family resemblance of being consumerist. However, the key difference between the two is that where in the former consuming is firmly located in the *fixed* 'design-standards which McDonaldization is all about', in IKEAization the relationship is not one-way: the reason for consuming is located in a cultural discourse between our own aspirations and the *fluid* and *flexible* design-standards of IKEAization. Richard Hoggart (1973) offers an approach to classifying leisure which suggests that if we are going to make distinctions these should be made between family resemblances – distinctions which make qualified *active* judgement, rather than the application of a fixed scale. In other words, you can judge leisure only within its own kind, e.g. rock climbing is a category of leisure that is different from ballroom dancing. What this suggests is that, notwithstanding the critique developed in this chapter it is clearly the case that some kinds of leisure remain more consumerist than others. What we can also conclude is that IKEALeisure should be understood as 'good of its kind'. McLeisure should not. The utility of this conceptual scheme obviously requires some appropriate empirical investigation, but the hope is that it will serve the purpose of providing some impetus for further study of consumerism in Leisure Studies.

References

Alfino, M., Caputo, J. and Wynyard, R. (1998) (eds) *McDonaldization Revisited*. Westport, CT: Greenwood Press.

Augé, M. (1995) *Non-Places: Introduction to an Anthropology of Supermodernity*. Trans. J. Howe. London: Verso.

Austin, J.L. (1962) *How to Do Things with Words*. Edited by J.O. Urmson. Oxford: Clarendon.

Bachelard, G. (1994/1964) *The Poetics of Space*. Boston, MA: Beacon Press.

Bailly, O., Caudron, J.-M. and Lambart, D. (2006) 'Secret Hidden behind IKEA's Wardrobes', *Le Monde Diplomatique*, December.

Baudrillard, J. (1989) *America*. London: Verso.

Baudrillard, J. (1990/1983) *Fatal Strategies*. London: Pluto.

Bauman, Z. (1988) *Freedom*. Buckingham: Open University Press.

Bauman, Z. (1990) *Thinking Sociologically*. Oxford: Blackwell.

Bauman, Z. (1992) *Intimations of Postmodernity*. London: Routledge.

Bauman, Z. (1998) *Work, Consumerism and the New Poor*. Buckingham: Open University Press.

Bauman, Z. (1999) *Culture as Praxis*. London: Sage.

Bauman, Z. (2000a) *Liquid Modernity*. Cambridge: Polity Press.

Bauman, Z. (2000b) 'Book Review of the McDonaldization Thesis: Explorations and Extensions by George Ritzer', *Journal of Contingencies and Crisis Management* 8 (4) 234.

Bauman, Z. (2001) *Community: Seeking Safety in an Insecure World*. Cambridge: Polity Press.

Bauman, Z. (2004) *Identity: Conversations with Benedetto Vecchi*. Cambridge: Polity Press.

Bauman, Z (2007) *Consuming Life*. Cambridge: Polity Press.

Bauman, Z. (2010) *44 Letters from the Liquid Modern World*. Cambridge: Polity Press.

Blackshaw, T. (2010) *Leisure*. London and New York: Routledge.

Bray, E. (2009) 'The New Link between Music and Fashion', *Independent*, 21 August.

Bruckner, P. (2010) *Perpetual Euphoria: The Duty to be Happy*. Trans. S. Rendall. Princeton: Princeton University Press.

Cooley, C.H. (1902) *Human Nature and the Social Order*. New York: Scribner's.

Csikszentmihalyi, M. (1974) *Flow: Studies of Enjoyment*. Chicago: University of Chicago Press.

DeLillo, D. (1985) *White Noise*. London: Picador.

Filler, M. (2012) 'Real Cool', *New York Review of Books*, 21 June.

Grant, L. (2004) 'She's Gotta Have It', *Guardian G2*, 21 September.

Habermas, J. (1975) *Legitimation Crisis*. Trans. and with an introduction by T. McCarthy. Boston, MA: Beacon Press.

Harris, D. (2005) *Key Concepts in Leisure Studies*. London: Sage.

Heller, A. (1999) *A Theory of Modernity*. Oxford: Blackwell.

Hoggart, R. (1973) *Speaking to Each Other. Volume One: About Society*. Harmondsworth: Penguin.

Knowledge@Wharton (2007) *'Men Buy, Women Shop': The Sexes Have Different Priorities when Walking Down the Aisles*. Retrieved from http://knowledge.wharton.upenn.edu/article.cfm?articleid=1848.

Lyotard, J.-F. (1979) *The Postmodern Condition: A Report on Knowledge*. Minneapolis: University of Minnesota Press.

Miller, D. (1998) *A Theory of Shopping*. Ithaca, NY: Cornell University Press.

Ritzer, G. (1993) *The McDonaldization of Society*. Newbury Park: Pine Forge Press.

Ritzer, G. (2003) *Contemporary Social Theory and Its Classical Roots: The Basics*. New York: McGraw Hill.

Ritzer, G. (2004) *The Globalization of Nothing*. London: Pine Forge Press.

Rojek, C. (2005) *Leisure Theory: Principles and Practice*. Basingstoke: Palgrave Macmillan.

Rojek, C. (2010) *The Labour of Leisure: The Culture of Free Time*. London: Sage.

Sassoon, D. (2005) 'From Buddenbrooks to Babbitt?', *New Left Review* 36: 141–148.

Simmons, J. (2005) 'IKEA – Brand of Many', *Observer*, 12 June.

Stebbins, R.A. (2006) *Serious Leisure: A Perspective for Our Time*. New Brunswick, NJ: Aldine/ Transaction.

Streeck, W. (2012) 'Citizens as Consumers', *New Left Review* 76: 27–47 (July/August).

Zukin, S. (2004) *Point of Purchase: How Shopping Changed American Culture*. London and New York: Routledge.

PART V

USES OF LEISURE

32

ABNORMAL LEISURE AND NORMALIZATION

Chris Rojek

There are three main types of abnormal leisure: invasive, mephitic and wild (Rojek, 2000). Simply put, invasive leisure refers to forms of behaviour situated in leisure time that involve self-harm. The most common examples are alcohol and drug abuse. Mephitic leisure is a type of leisure conduct that involves doing harm to others. Examples include sexual harassment, physical, emotional and verbal aggression, hate crime, prostitution and mugging. Wild leisure consists of forms of illicit leisure practice that involve acts of opportunist behaviour. Examples include joy riding, looting, illegal downloading, illegal trading, hacking, street crime and trespass.

We know from cultural criminology that it is a mistake to regard crime as an intrinsic quality of acts. Rather, following labelling theory, crime depends upon the meaning assigned to acts (Ferrell, Hayward and Young, 2008; Hall, 2012).

At first sight, this may seem a bit skew-whiff. After all, common sense dictates that if you threaten to kill someone, or preside over an organization that might murder others, you are nothing but a common or garden criminal, meriting the mobilization of the full force of the law.

To be sure, this was exactly the response of the apartheid state in South Africa to Nelson Mandela, leader of the ANC armed wing Umkhonto we Sizwe (Spear the Nation). In 1962 Mandela was arrested, charged with terrorism and sentenced to life imprisonment (1964). He served 27 years. Upon his release he resumed leadership of the ANC. In 1994 he was elected President of South Africa.

We need not delve into the complicated political details behind this *volte face* here.[1] The point to grasp is that the label applied to Mandela was utterly transformed after the context of social and political relations in South Africa moved from an apartheid to a post-apartheid system. From the moral label of a dangerous, merciless terrorist, Mandela was eventually redefined, and generally has been revered, as the father of the new nation.

Through fastening upon the *meaning* assigned to the act, as opposed to the legal label affixed to it, the cultural reaction to illicit behaviour is elucidated, i.e. the meaning that it carries for the perpetrators themselves and the social groups to whom they are attached. It has generally been presumed that for non-perpetrators, the social reaction to illegal leisure is admonitory. By definition, illegal leisure consists of meanings that are incommensurate with, or depart from, legally defined orthodoxy. For example, illegal recreational drug use involves the exchange and consumption of goods that are legally prohibited.

Leaving aside the controversial question of the effects of drugs on drug users, law enforcement agencies acknowledge that the consequences of the consumption of illegal drugs are severe for the organization and operation of international crime. Procurement does not merely break the law. It also perpetuates international drug cartels and gangs that operate globally to produce and distribute illegal drugs. It therefore directly perpetuates and magnifies organized crime.

For example, there are well-documented connections between illegal drug trade and human trafficking. That is, profits from the drug trade finance the trafficking of victims for various forms of sexual exploitation. In addition, developing an addiction to drugs is a strategy used by drug barons and brothel keepers, to subdue illegal sex workers and regiment labour (Shelley, 2012).

Drug and human trafficking gangs and cartels are concentrated in Mexico, Turkey, Russia, North Africa and the Balkans. They supply markets in the affluent metropolitan centres of Western Europe, North America and Southern Asia (Cengiz, 2011; Bosco *et al.*, 2009). So, some forms of illicit leisure practice pump-prime organized crime and support the diversification of criminal activities in some cartels and gangs.

For the student of leisure, what is perhaps more noteworthy, because it is more enigmatic, is the complex process through which leisure behaviour that offends criminal law is regarded as inoffensive by practitioners and passes without admonition among their circle and those attached to it. That is, some forms of illegal leisure that have become institutionalized in society do not trigger the social reaction of admonition. On the contrary, they are regarded as acceptable practice.

Consider: illegal downloading of intellectual property, fare dodging and the recreational use of illegal drugs are rife. Yet the majority of participants do not regard their behaviour as criminal activity. Far from violating the law, these practices are widely perceived as considerations first and foremost of identity and lifestyle rather than of moral scruple.

Traditionally, we have analysed these questions through the filter of subcultures; that is, durable social networks that develop codes of practice that are antithetical to what might be called the culture of conventional leisure behaviour.[2] Within these subcultures practices that are officially labelled as illegal are condoned by the members of the group. This applies to all three categories of abnormal leisure.

My typology of invasive, mephitic and wild forms partly reinforced this subcultural perspective. However, I am now self-critical of this tendency of conceptualizing illegal leisure forms only, or even primarily, in terms of subcultures. I am now struck by the prevalence of illegal leisure practice that passes without admonition, not so much among practitioners, *but in society at large.* What I am referring to is not a new category of 'abnormal leisure'. On the contrary, despite unequivocally breaking the law, the leisure behaviour at issue is mostly viewed and practised as entirely normal and unexceptional. I have in mind the commerce in counterfeit or stolen goods, the illegal downloading of intellectual property, the 'responsible' use of illegal drugs, fare dodging etc. These illegal activities have become *normalized* in society. Generally, they pass without censure and, to a large degree, with the collusion of the authorities.[3]

I propose to introduce the umbrella term *inoffensive forms of illegal leisure* to refer to these practices. Unlike abnormal forms, they are defined by a broadly *tolerant* social reaction from those who come into contact with them. Later, I will examine the cases of counterfeit commerce and illegal downloading in detail in order to throw light on the mechanics of the phenomenon. Before coming to this, it is necessary to remind ourselves of the characteristics of abnormal forms.

The abnormal forms and why a rethink is necessary

Invasive forms of leisure involve illicit leisure practices that are predicated in private consumption and exchange, necessitating a spatial withdrawal from society. This is, of course, compatible with solely individual practice. There are many among us who spend at least part of our leisure in the consumption of banned narcotics, the illegal downloading of intellectual property, child pornography etc.

Collaterally, invasive leisure involves social networks that isolate themselves from society and participate in covert illegal leisure conduct. In the Prohibition (1920–33) era in the USA, illegal dens and clubs, where liquor was openly sold and consumed, were numerous. Colloquially, they were known as 'speakeasies'. Although illegal, their location and means of access were matters of common knowledge (Coffey 2008; Okrent 2011). They were periodically subject to clamp-downs, but, on the whole, the police acquiesced in their presence. In the 1920s and 1930s, especially as the Great Depression hit, with negative effects on employment and real wages, speakeasies became woven into the fabric of American life, but of course their contours in everyday relations were oblique and under-stated.

It would be a mistake to view invasive leisure networking as purely a historical phenomenon. Recreational drug use is also often network based. Studies of crack drug use clearly establish that distribution and use is based in underground social networks organized around vibrant drug subcultures (Johnson *et al.*, 1995; Elsie *et al.*, 2012).

Studies of illegal gambling in Vietnam and Israel have revealed similar patterns of illegal invasive networking based in subcultural formation and underground settings (Israeli and Mehrez, 2000; Nguyen, 2004). As with the speakeasies of the American Prohibition era, illegal gambling circuits are clandestine, yet involve folk knowledge of settings and means of access that, while not exactly 'common', are widely distributed.

In both individual and network forms, invasive leisure assumes the shape of subcultural practice. That is, conduct is relatively divorced from mainstream social life and, while it passes without admonition among participants, it provokes a negative social reaction in society. These traits are replicated in the remaining two abnormal forms.

Turning to mephitic practice, as with the invasive category, this type of leisure practice is compatible with individual behaviour. Intimidation, violence, hate crime and sex abuse by individuals in leisure time and space are habitual and commonplace (Philpot, 2009; Gerstenfeld, 2011).

In contrast to invasive forms, mephitic leisure behaviour is often public, since it is based in physically, verbally and emotionally confronting and harassing others. Studies of client violence against legal and illegal sex workers demonstrate a variety of network abuse syndromes and the full array of risk factors (Shah, 2004; Brents *et al.*, 2010).

One of the lessons of this work is that it quickly shows that to conceive of mephitic forms exclusively in terms of individual practice is invalid. Social networks that engage in mephitic forms as a regular feature of leisure practice are entrenched in society. Studies of hate groups engaging in hate crime, ritual abuse, child sex rings and gang intimidation demonstrate the participation of organized subcultures with clear patterns of recruitment and codes of practice (Burgess, 1984; Scott, 2001; Miller *et al.*, 2006; Valdez, 2008; Ryan and Leeson, 2011).

Further, it is perfectly appropriate to cite the centrality of subcultural structures in these forms of leisure practice. For example, research into adolescent gangs shows that violence against others, via intimidation and physical assault, is seminal in subcultural integration, self-esteem and group status (Stretesky and Pogrebin, 2007). Research into male and female adolescent gangs in South Carolina argues that an under-examined dimension in this area is the dynamics of victimization *within* gang subcultures (Gover *et al.*, 2009).

Mephitic forms based in network practice are remarkably difficult to uproot and banish from society. Ever since Thrashers' (1927) classic study of adolescent gangs, politicians and the police have been privy to the essentials of this form of mephitic subcultural formation as well as research-based remedies to tackle the problem. Despite this, adolescent gangs have been adept at redefining themselves inter-generationally and taking on new forms to reinforce the old goals of group integration and status enhancement.

Gang subcultures also figure in wild leisure forms. These types of leisure refer to random, opportunistic and 'casual' (in Bob Stebbins's 2001 sense of the term) instances of leisure practice.[4] The classic study is the dynamics of collective conflict at the Bathurst Bike Races (Cunneen *et al.*, 1989). This involved extensive rioting at the Australian Motor Cycle Grand Prix. The incident involved subcultures but is more accurately classified as an example of crowd disorder. This subcategory of wild leisure is usually based in the perception of specific cases of injustice that are employed to build a bigger case against authority. Typically, they take the form of aggressive eruptions that disrupt social order and provoke police interventions. The pre-Olympic rioting and looting in the UK in August of 2011 has been interpreted as a reaction to the lavish funds spent on the London Olympics (2012) at a time when youth unemployment, especially in the provinces, was producing widespread distress.

Wild forms are not, of course, confined to subcultural or network activity. Individuals engage in trespass, petty larceny, hacking and illegal downloading on an opportunistic and casual basis. The notion of wild leisure was originally developed to capture illicit leisure practice that does not necessarily involve the formation of illegal leisure subcultures or the development of leisure 'careers'.[5] Modern life produces countless opportunities for rule breaking and illicit leisure.

The category of wild leisure was devised to capture these forms. Looking back, it was a half-way house to register my dissatisfaction with bracketing illegal leisure exclusively with subcultural organization. In a preliminary way, it sought to challenge the polarization between legal leisure (practised by scrupulously law-abiding citizens) and illegal leisure (practised by criminal or emergent criminal types). What it was driving at is that illegal practice is also a *normal* part of leisure conduct. I suggested that David Matza's (1964) concept of 'drift' ought to be revived in order to explore the affinities between abnormal leisure and crime (Rojek, 2000).

To continue, Matza (1964) queries the common-sense notion that the criminal is morally and socially segregated from the rest of society. This distinction operates with the notion that the criminal is set apart from the upstanding moral majority by reason of some form of socio-economic 'strain' or moral inadequacy. Matza submits that while some crimes take the form of planned conduct committed by career criminals, many other types are related to sheer opportunism. He coins the concept of 'drift' to communicate the idea that where external circumstances provide for low rates of detection and punishment, the propensity of individuals to evaluate that criminal acts carry low levels of risk is optimized. In such circumstances, some individuals 'drift' into illegal conduct without fully developing a criminal career or forming the structure of a genuine criminal character. Examples include pilfering, trespass, road rage, petty theft, hate crime, illegal downloading, illegal trading, hacking and fiddling.

Matza's objective is to demonstrate the ordinary, non-exceptional character of many types of crime. To expand, the commonplace notion that the criminal is separate from the rest of society is dismantled. Instead, the analytic focus switches to consider why some individuals drift into trajectories of illegal activity that result in detection and punishment. The tacit assumption behind Matza's thought is that in certain circumstances anyone can commit a criminal act.

Because leisure is associated with a relaxation of social controls and general dis-inhibition, it supports drift practice (Elias and Dunning, 1986). Thus, the majority of criminal incidents take place outside work time and in non-work settings. The home, the community, the street and recreation spaces are the main arenas for crime. Wild leisure argued that complexity, change and flexibility in modern life multiplies opportunities for rule breaking and criminal conduct in leisure practice.

I now believe that the category of wild leisure did not go far enough to solidify the point. The drift in leisure practice that legally breaks the law without admonition is far more engrained in culture than I originally realized. Indeed, it is institutionalized in the fabric of social life. Twinning wild leisure with opportunistic, casual conduct fails to embrace this dimension of leisure practice.

It does not follow that the three categories of abnormal leisure need to be jettisoned. I remain of the opinion that they refer to real forms of leisure practice and, as such, remain relevant. However, the need to add to them with a category that captures the 'normalization' of illegal leisure must now be addressed. This requires a fourth category, *inoffensive forms of illegal leisure*, the details of which I shall come to presently.

Before that, we must turn to the matter of what is exactly meant by the term 'normalization', since this is the foundation of the proposal that a fourth category of illegal leisure practice needs to be differentiated.

Illegal leisure: the normalization thesis

The origins of the term 'normalization' lie in the late 1950s in Denmark. It emerged in relation to the practical project of creating 'normal' living conditions for people with learning difficulties. Since then, the concept has gone through several iterations (Emerson, 1992; Wolfensberger, 1984).

Within the field of illegal leisure the most influential contribution has been made in relation to recreational drug use (Parker, Aldridge and Measham, 1998; Parker, Williams and Aldridge, 2002). They define normalization as,

> stigmatized or deviant individuals or groups (and to some degree their social behaviour) becoming included in as many features of conventional everyday 'normal' life as possible.

> (Parker, Williams and Aldridge, 2002: 942)

In their longitudinal study of adolescent drug users, Parker *et al.* (1998) trace a multitude of pathways in drug use. They propose that in the UK 'responsible' adolescent substance abuse is now 'normalized'. That is, the responsible recreational use of drugs is popular and widely accepted among youth groups. Further, it is generally tolerated by family and kinship networks, community workers, social workers and key health personnel.

The normalization thesis demonstrates how a deviant recreational practice (illegal substance abuse) is informally institutionalized in social networks so that it is redefined in time as acceptable. That is, it does not provoke censure, nor is it referred to the police.

The normalization thesis is of great interest to students of leisure. It refers to the rendering of legally offensive abnormal, law-breaking behaviour as not subject to admonition. Hence, some forms of deviant subculture are tolerated at the level of open culture and some types of criminal organization are legitimated. In a word, normalization makes legal offences culturally *inoffensive*. Normalization alerts us to the proposition that illegal forms of practice are *commonplace* in leisure relations and that leisure is the means through which normalization crystallizes. Far from being repudiated as criminal behaviour, these forms are defended and respected as acceptable, even 'well judged', 'fit' practice.

In order to substantiate these arguments, it will be helpful to briefly examine a couple of case studies of leisure practice that offends the law but which is socially regarded as inoffensive. The case studies I have selected are the consumption of counterfeit goods and the illegal downloading of intellectual property. I have done so in order to highlight the wholly 'normal' character of illegal conduct in some forms of leisure practice.

The consumption of counterfeit goods

Counterfeit goods are illegal duplications of legitimate brands that use identical forms of design, packaging and trademarks without authorization. They are sold at a fraction of the legitimate retail or online price (Ang *et al.*, 2001). They differ from *pirated* and *knock-off* products.

A pirated product is an imitation designed to be recognized as an inexact brand replica. A knock-off product is an item that resembles the brand but is not identical to the copyrighted item.

The World Trade Organization (1994) holds that:

> 'counterfeit trademark goods' shall mean any goods, including packaging, bearing, without authorization, a trademark that is identical to the trademark validly registered in respect of such goods that cannot be distinguished in its essential aspects from such a trademark, which thereby infringes the rights of the owner of the trademark in question under the law of the country of importation.

The counterfeit trade violates registered copyright over brand names, patents and trademarks. It is estimated to account for approximately 5–7 per cent of global commerce, i.e. $600 billion (Norum and Cuno, 2011: 27; Lee and Workman, 2011: 289).

More recently, these figures have been challenged as a gross under-estimate. Wiedmann *et al.* (2012) maintain that the counterfeit trade accounts for 10 per cent of global consumer transactions. In other words, one in ten of all commodity transactions are illegal.

Strictly speaking, there is nothing new about the trade in counterfeit products. In 27 BC there were cases of French counterfeiters forging the seal of wines so as to pass them off as more expensive Roman imports (Phillips, 2005). Similarly, Pliny the Elder (AD 23–79) complained of the inflationary consequences of the trade in counterfeit coins (Chen *et al.*, 2005).

Counterfeiting also has a long history in international statecraft. During the American War of Independence, the British government forged the American dollar and exported it into the American economy with the deliberate intention of triggering hyper-inflation (Baack, 2001).

Similarly, during the Second World War prisoners in Sachsenhausen concentration camp were forced to forge English currency. The plan behind the so-called 'Operation Bernhard' was to drop the forgeries from aeroplanes and so cripple the British economy (Robertson, 2005).

Whatever the true figure, there is little doubt that counterfeit consumption is a significant part of the global economy and rapidly multiplying in scale. Estimates suggest that since the early 1990s the trade has expanded 10,000 times (Norum and Cuno, 2011: 27).

The expansion is the result of a mixture of factors, namely more efficient supply chains, better design values, deregulation of border controls, the spread of access to copyright design data through hacking, direct/low-risk internet sales provision, various types of intellectual property theft and escalating consumer demand for point-of-sale price advantage. The most common counterfeit goods worldwide are clothing, cigarettes, shoes, watches, cosmetics, leather goods, jewellery and pharmaceuticals (Lee and Workman, 2011).

Counterfeit trade extends over the whole range of age, gender and socio-economic categories. It is routine in consumer culture (Rutter and Bryce, 2008). Sourcing is concentrated among manufacturers in South-East Asia (principally China, South Korea, Taiwan), West Africa and the former Soviet bloc economies (Riston, 2007).

Chow's (2003) research into the counterfeit trade in China revealed strong links with organized crime, and the collusion of local populations through various forms of protectionism. Following an escalation in enforcement effects against illicit recreational drugs, such as cocaine and heroin, there is evidence that organized crime syndicates such as the Russian mafia, Mexican drug gangs, Chinese Triads and Colombian drug cartels have transferred resources to counterfeit pharmaceuticals (McEwen and Strauss, 2009: 253).

With the rise of the digital economy, the internet is becoming fundamental to the global expansion of the trade. It is calculated that 'cybersquatting' (using a domain name that capitalizes on an established brand) accounts for 1.7 million websites (Wotherspoon and Cheng, 2009: 32). The digital economy supports many pathways for expanding the trade from direct junk mail shots to auction sites. Most auction sites, such as eBay, are self-policed and hence attractive to counterfeit suppliers. Servers can exchange identities rapidly, thus making it difficult for authorities to trace supply chains and finance flows. Additionally, although supply chains are global, anti-counterfeiting legislation is national and often disjointed. The lack of binding, uniform global policies hampers the efforts of the authorities to combat the trade. Producers who encounter an escalation of policing in one country simply switch operations to regions where anti-counterfeiting provisions are less sophisticated.

In recent years, anti-counterfeiting legislation has intensified. In the USA, the Counterfeit Drug Prevention Act (CDPA, 2007) and the Intellectual Property Enhanced Criminal Enforcement Act (IPECEA, 2007) provide for harsher sentencing for trafficking in counterfeit goods and knowingly supplying counterfeit goods to at-risk groups. The IPECEA criminalizes the intent to commit copyright infringement and assigns $12 million to create a special organizations unit within the Federal Bureau of Investigation (FBI) to coordinate investigation of intellectual property theft.

International cooperation has also increased. In 2007, the US Trade Representative, Susan Schwab, announced that the USA had commenced talks with key trading partners to implement the Anti-Counterfeiting Trade Agreement (ACTA). The ACTA aims to bolster information sharing between law enforcement agencies; increase criminal and civil enforcement of intellectual property rights violation; upgrade border controls; and reform the international law regarding the enforcement of intellectual property rights (Somers and Kilaru, 2008).

In response, host nations where supply is concentrated have taken measures to counteract the trade, in a bid to enhance their international standing. Russia and East Africa have intensified enforcement against copyright violation (Von Braun and Munyi, 2010;

Charlton, 2012). However, the European Parliament refused to ratify the ACTA in 2012, on the grounds that the proposed legislation threatens individual liberties by infringing personal privacy. As of June 2012, the USA, Australia, Canada and Japan are among countries that have signed ACTA, but none has yet ratified it in national legislation. The difficulties illustrate the problems facing anti-counterfeiting law enforcers, who struggle to combat crime, but face resistance from civil liberties groups who maintain that blanket legislation curtails individual rights to duplicate and exchange for private use.

The trade is associated with job losses in both the manufacturing and retail sectors. The treasury is also deprived of revenue because counterfeit production and exchange acknowledges no fiscal disciplines. It also involves leakage on the margins of legitimate companies, since they are required to produce advertising and educational campaigns about the risks associated with counterfeit products. The counterfeit trade, especially in auto-parts, beverages, fake foods and pharmaceuticals, carries health risks, since imitations, pirated goods and knock-offs are not subject to regulatory provision (deKieffer, 2006).

Counterfeiters exploit and manipulate the association among consumers of feeling daring, liberated and infallible by purchasing reproductions at a fraction of brand-name cost on the street, in car boot sales or on the internet. In this way purchasing counterfeit goods becomes a marker of consumer esteem and bargain hunting.

Research into attitudes and practices indicates that most consumers are willing accomplices in counterfeit trade (Karpova and Hyejeong, 2010; Lee and Workman, 2011). Partly, this reflects the status of counterfeit transactions as victimless crimes. That is, the consumption of counterfeit goods takes the form of an offence against an abstraction (the corporation), rather than an individual. Consumers are therefore usually less inhibited in engaging in counterfeit trade, since it seems to harm nobody. What of the reasons given for engaging in the consumption of counterfeits?

The motivations of consumers are varied. In most consumer surveys bargain hunting and value for money are the main reasons given. There is no strong evidence that the consumption of counterfeit goods is related to strong anti-capitalist values or that it is perceived as criminal activity. On the contrary, counterfeiting is wholly capitalistic in orientation. It aims to supply duplicates of luxury brands at affordable prices. By competitive cost cutting, the counterfeiter exposes the super-profits of the producers of luxury brands and benefits the consumer (who could not otherwise afford to consume them).

Pushing this further, one might even assert that counterfeiting involves a Robin Hood principle. Just as legitimate luxury suppliers buy resources of production in the low-cost markets in order to sell output in high-cost markets, the counterfeiter takes the design and trademark and widens access to it. But few consumers of counterfeit goods see themselves as modern-day Robin Hoods. Their primary motivation is to accumulate, usually, luxury commodities that they would otherwise be unable to afford. The durability of the counterfeit as compared with that of the original luxury commodity does not seem to figure significantly in consumer calculations.

The decisive thing is to acquire and exhibit the brand. To own a counterfeit Omega watch or Gucci sunglasses, even if it is done tongue-in-cheek, is a mark of self-esteem and status enhancement.

The illegality and amorality of counterfeiting do not seem to weigh heavily with ordinary consumers. Typically, buying counterfeit goods is not perceived as a criminal act associated with deviant subcultures. It simply realizes the market potential to acquire high-status goods at fractional cost and enjoy the 'delight' of bargain hunting (Rutter and Bryce, 2008: 1158).

Illegal downloading

Illegal downloading of intellectual property refers to duplicating material that is formally protected by copyright law. Peer-to-peer (P2P) file sharing applications (e.g. Bit Torrent, eMule, Gnutella, Rapidshare and Soulsearch) have become staple providers of leisure resources, especially among the young. P2P networks allow users to download files from connected computers without going through centralized servers. The gifting of copyright material through these means is creating a haemorrhage in cash flow from copyright holders.

In 2005 copyright piracy of sound recordings, motion pictures, software and entertainment media produced a combined loss to US copyright holders and retailers of $25.6 billion (Siwek, 2007). Research in Spain discovered that 91 per cent of music consumption among a cross-representative sample was illegal (Sandulli and Martin-Barbero, 2007: 74). Similarly, one estimate puts the quantity of illegal files currently available on unauthorized file-sharing sites at 800 million (David and Kirkhope, 2004: 441). The International Federation of the Phonographic Industry (IFPI) estimates that today 95 per cent of tracks are downloaded without payment to rights holders (IFPI Digital Music Report, 2009: 5). Even allowing for the likelihood that this is an exaggeration designed to paint the industry in a parlous state so as to court protective legislation, there is no doubt that illegal downloading is producing significant market contraction.

It is generally accepted that college students constitute the biggest group of unauthorized downloaders. Some estimates suggest that one in three of US college students download music illegally (Sheehan, Tsao and Yang, 2010: 241).

The representatives of content copyright holders, such as the Recording Industry Association of America (RIAA) and Motion Picture Association of America (MPAA), have responded by launching legal actions against pirates and demonizing illegal file sharers (Cenite *et al.*, 2009: 206). From the rise of Napster to the end of 2007, it is estimated that over 20,000 copyright infringement actions were initiated globally against file sharers (Fisher, 2007).

Litigation has concentrated upon three target groups: randomly selected individuals, known servers and known high-offender groups. The RIAA and MPAA have announced a zero-tolerance policy against unauthorized individual file sharers. It produced a mixed response. In some industry circles it is now accepted that litigation against individuals produces more trouble than it is worth. Most obviously, legal action addresses only the tip of the iceberg, since policing measures are unable to comb the full range of illegal users nationally (to speak nothing of a global basis). Further, zero tolerance does not differentiate between the strong and the weak. Litigation against children, adolescents and the elderly has the effect of creating damaging publicity for industry plaintiffs by turning unauthorized users into victims.

Turning to the question of litigation against servers, the industry gained one high-profile scalp with the closure of Napster (2001).[6] More recent campaigns against Gnutella and Kazaa have also achieved restraint of P2P exchange objectives. Notwithstanding this, servers have been effective in avoiding detection by shifting to new site locations and launching counter-suits against plaintiffs, based upon the First Amendment of the US Constitution (which protects the freedom of religion, speech and the press). Plaintiffs are increasingly deterred from legal action because litigation against servers can be protracted and costly and the results are often uncertain and inconclusive.

Coming to the topic of targeting high-offender groups, in 2007 the RIAA sent letters to the 25 US universities in which the worst offenders are enrolled. The action followed a move in Senate to eliminate illegal file sharing. This was a measure of *moral force*, appealing to the sense of responsibility of university authorities and the better nature of students. Although it gained a good deal of publicity, it was strictly limited in successfully deterring unauthorized exchange. As with shopping for counterfeit goods, the practice of illegal file exchange has become engrained in routines of leisure behaviour. It does not automatically and indelibly carry the stigma of criminal conduct.

Whether they be individuals, servers or high-risk groups, defendants have responded that the legal actions of copyright holders and their representatives fail to grasp the transformation in the gift economy that is elicited by the ease of access afforded by digital technology. They accuse plaintiffs of using a pre-digital logic to achieve just remedies in a digital age. As such, it is no surprise that the results of litigation have been mixed. Plaintiffs use a sling-shot in the age of mobile downloading and the iCloud. There is some justice in this line of argument.

If one looks at the history of non-commercial digital gifting, it is rapidly apparent that Digital Rights Management (DRM) legislation, designed to protect copyright, is of comparatively recent provenance. Under American law, before 1997, the distribution of copyright-infringing material for non-commercial purposes carried no legal penalty. The No Electronic Theft Act (1997) made file users sharing P2P networks for non-commercial purposes liable in civic and criminal courts. It was the agitation of industry rights holders and their representatives that culminated in the Digital Millennium Copyright Act (1998). This criminalizes the production and distribution of technologies and services designed to prohibit access, or duplication that infringes copyright. These legal measures have opened up a stream of copyright-control initiatives collectively known as DRM. These include the application of encryption technology, policing and further legislation to defend copyright infringement. DRM seeks to delineate and enforce clear, unambiguous lines around the digital gift economy and the wider set of relations linked to unauthorized downloading.

However, most commentators agree that DRM is a crude and inefficient approach (Burkart and McCourt, 2006; David, 2010; Kusek and Leonhard, 2005). No fool-proof encryption technology exists, and unauthorized servers and consumers have proved themselves adept in mitigating the risks of policing and legal punishment.

The main motivation of file sharers is to acquire content for free (Lessig, 2004). However, researchers into unauthorized downloading have cautioned against stereotypes. Research into illegal downloading among college students has revealed wide variation in ethical attitudes. High ethical tolerance of unauthorized downloading among consumers correlates with two unexamined presumptions (Cenite *et al.*, 2009; LaRose *et al.*, 2006).

Firstly, that rights leakage is insignificant to the revenue stream of artists and music corporations. The logic here seems to support the position that many illegal consumers hold fast to the model of the sovereign consumer. That is, the rights of the consumer to buy in the cheapest market are paramount. Individual consumers take the view that the unauthorized contents of their iPod or MP3 player is not going to dent the balance sheets of Universal Music, the Warner Music Group or Sony-BMG. There seem to be inhibitions or a lack of interest which prevent individuals who hold the sovereign consumer model from developing a perspective on the effects of aggregate consumer behaviour. At any rate, their code of ethics does not include provision for the argument that the action of unauthorized downloading damages artists/music corporations.

Secondly, there is some evidence that a significant number of illegal downloaders regard file sharing as a legitimate component of the digital gift economy. That is, illegal downloading simply realizes the latent potential in the web and the laptop/mobile phone/iPad to widen access.

Although there is no denying the profound costs to copyright holders that are caused by illegal downloading, there is also reason to believe that the sovereign consumer model is far from being universal. Cenite *et al.* (2009: 215) discovered that unauthorized downloaders are mostly cognizant and respectful of rights issues. They engage in illegal downloading because of access problems with traditional commercial retail outlets or a belief that recordings are over-priced, and they possess a sense of building intimations of digital community through P2P networks. The challenge for rights holders is to provide ease of access at the right price to expand legal consumption (Cenite *et al.*, 2009: 219).

Although the industry has made strenuous efforts to demonize illegal downloaders, the digital consumption of music (whether via purchase or unpaid downloads) is complex. Deterrence policies are not a simple matter because consumers do not fall into a straight binary divide between Good Guy (legal purchase) and Bad Guy (illegal downloading) behaviour. Rather, it appears that individuals alternate between good- and bad-guy behaviour according to circumstance (Andersen and Frenz, 2010). That is, they engage in drift practice without developing a full-bodied 'career' in illegal leisure conduct.

The argument that consumer responses to digitalization are complex is strengthened by business data on *legal* digital music sales since the P2P challenge. For example, in 2001 Apple launched iTunes as a legal online service to provide musical resources in order to boost sales of the iPod. By 2010 iTunes sales accounted for 28 per cent of turnover in the US music market and 70 per cent in the legitimate download market. Apple has sold 10 billion songs through the iTunes store and holds a back catalogue of 12 billion tracks (Rutter, 2010: 412).

These figures further weaken the kneejerk response of the music industry that digitalization is a threat. The financial performance of iTunes suggests that digitalization produces new business opportunities that carry the potential to expand market share. Indeed, some researchers submit that file sharing offers opportunities for sampling products that translate into purchases that will eventually work to the benefit of artists and music corporations. Through sampling, consumers access music that they would not otherwise hear, and go on to legally consume it for their record collections (Giesler and Pohlmann, 2003; Lessig, 2004). While there may be some truth in this argument it surely applies only to the margins of consumer behaviour.

If the iTunes performance indicates that digitalization is not necessarily a bitter pill, it remains the case that unauthorized downloading has severely disrupted the traditional profit line of the music and film majors, plunging many music corporations and retailers into financial difficulties and outright bankruptcy. It is no less clear that most illegal downloaders do not see their behaviour as 'criminal'. It is more in the nature of applying technology to seize competitive market advantage.

Conclusion: the logic of inoffensive forms

The chief reason why some forms of illegal leisure are regarded as inoffensive is that the social reaction to the law relating to them is of a particular non-conformist type. Conformity with the law may be assumed as a given of social order. But since law is always a matter of meaning it follows that, at the level of social interaction, revision and reframing are constant (Ferrell, Hayward and Young, 2008; Hall, 2012). In general, social reactions that treat illegal leisure practice as inoffensive and not worthy of admonition stem from two causes.

In the first place, tolerant social reactions to illegal leisure practice reflect the judgement by the *polis* that the law in question is *invalid*. Such was clearly the case with respect to the Jim Crow (segregation) laws in the USA between 1876 and 1965 and the Pass laws in apartheid South Africa. Both restricted the mobility and public access of non-white groups.[7] The state designated and policed areas for eating, playing, studying and even drinking. This produced direct consequences upon the gestation and development of minority-group leisure forms, since it justified and reproduced strict rules of spatial access and social inclusion and exclusion.

Social reactions that define a law as invalid generally lead in time to questioning the authority of the individuals and groups that formulate and implement the law. They may take the form of protests and rioting which, in themselves, go beyond non-observance of the law and create new opportunities for challenge and protest. These responses may translate from political resistance to straightforward, violent incidents of wild leisure.

The second general type of non-conformist reaction tolerates illegal leisure practice on the basis that the laws relating to it are *unenforcable*. It is perfectly acceptable to propose that if you buy a counterfeit Mulberry bag from a high street kiosk or a replica of a product with the (fake) L'Oreal brandmark on eBay, you may be fully conscious of committing a criminal act.

However, the inhibition against doing so is mediated by the acknowledgement that the risk of detection is negligible. To be sure, it is widely recognized that the resources that society invests in order to mitigate counterfeit trade, illegal downloading, illegal parking and the like are disproportionate to the scale of the problems. If one in ten transactions in the world involve the consumption of counterfeit goods, a zero-tolerance policy implies levels of public investment in surveillance, policing and judicial process that are dismissed by society as unacceptable. Not unreasonably, involvement in illegal leisure is multiplied if participants believe that they run low risks of detection. The same is no less true for the illegal downloading of copyright material and for fare dodging.

The original model of abnormal forms of leisure sought to demonstrate that specific types of illegal leisure practice are not regarded as 'criminal' by participants. It presupposed that practice takes the forms of subcultural interaction in which practitioners see themselves as divorced from the rest of society. What the model failed to capture was institutionalized illegal leisure forms that do not elicit social reactions of admonition or censure. These forms are normalized in society. They do not presuppose the eventual crystallization of a criminal identity.

The social candour and persistence of these practices suggest that the concept of 'normal leisure' practice needs to allow for orientations and behaviours in which ethical ambivalence is manifest. The polarization between legal and illegal practice, normal and abnormal conduct, cannot be taken at face value. Society itself allows for conditional latitude around legal provisions that demarcate some forms of leisure practice as formally illegal. Among the tasks facing the study of leisure is the examination of the relationships between illegality, conditional latitude and ethical ambivalence. The 'normalization' of illegal leisure practice is far more deep rooted and widespread than perhaps most of us assume.

Notes

1   Note that it is not confined to the case of Mandela and South Africa. There are many examples of individuals who have been labelled as 'terrorists' or 'seditionaries' who are subsequently pardoned by the state or awarded offices of power, honour and privilege. For example, the late Vaclav Havel, who was imprisoned as a dissident during the communist era in Czechosolovakia, was elected President of the nation in 1989. Similarly, Martin McGuinness, who was convicted in 1973 for activity with the Provisional IRA (holding explosives and ammunition), eventually became Deputy First Minister of the Northern Ireland Assembly.

2　There are inherent difficulties with the notion of 'normality': 'Normal, from whose perspective?'; 'Normal under what conditions?'; 'Normal in relation to what erasure of history?' etc. These difficulties do not prevent the term's being used ubiquitously in everyday interaction relating to leisure practice.

3　Periodically, the authorities crack down on the counterfeit trade, illegal downloading, fare dodging etc. But they do not exactly practise a policy of zero tolerance. Hence, the illegal forms prosper.

4　For Stebbins (2001), casual leisure involves practices that do not possess a sense of 'career', i.e. investment of time, money and other resources to achieve higher skills. According to Stebbins (2001: 58), 'casual leisure can be defined as immediately, intrinsically rewarding relatively short-lived pleasurable activity requiring little or no special training to enjoy it'.

5　Invasive and mephitic forms are perfectly compatible with the notion of serious leisure 'careers'. That is, following Stebbins (2001: 3), 'an amateur, hobbyist or volunteer activity that participants find so substantial and interesting that, in the typical case, they launch themselves on a career centred on acquiring or expressing its special skills'. Strictly speaking, there is no moral privilege in the concept of serious leisure. It can involve the acquisition and expression of skills that are illegal and amoral.

6　Napster was a peer-to-peer system set up by Shawn Fanning, John Fanning and Sean Parker. It operated between 1999 and 2001. During this period its ease of use was a high-profile thorn in the side of intellectual property copyright holders, especially record labels.

7　Palestinians in Israel are subject to similar punitive restrictions on mobility and social gathering (Sacco, 2001).

References

Andersen, B. and Frenz, M. (2010) 'Don't Blame the P2P File-sharers: The Impact of Free Music Downloads on the Purchase of Music CDs in Canada', *Journal of Evolutionary Economics* 20(5) 715–40.

Ang, S.H., Cheng, P., Lim, E. and Tambyah, S.K. (2001) 'Spot the Difference: Consumer Responses towards Counterfeits', *Journal of Consumer Marketing* 18(3) 219–35.

Baack, B. (2001) 'Forging a Nation-State: The Continental Congress and the Financing of the American War of Independence', *The Economic History Review* 54(4) 639–56.

Bosco, F., di Cortemiglia, V. and Serojitdinov, A. (2009) 'Strategies against Trafficking Patterns', in C. Friesendorf, C. (ed.) *Strategies against Human Trafficking*. Vienna: National Defence Academy and Austrian Ministry of Defence and Sport, 35–82.

Brents, L., Rochelle, L., and Williamson, C. (2010) 'Violence and Legalized Brothel Prostitution in Nevada', *Journal of Interpersonal Violence* 20(3) 270–95.

Burgess, A.W. (1984) *Child Pornography and Sex Rings*. New York: Free Press.

Burkart, P. and McCourt, T. (2006) *Digital Music Wars*. Lanham, MD: Rowman and Littlefield.

Cengiz, M. (2011) *Turkish Organized Crime from Local to Global*. Saarbrücken: VDM Verlag.

Cenite, M., Wang, M., Peiwen, C. and Chan, G.S. (2009) 'More than Just Free Content: Motivations of Peer-to-Peer File Sharers', *Journal of Communication Inquiry*, 33: 2006–221.

Charlton, J. (2012) 'IFLA Raises Concerns about ACTA, *Information Today* 29(6) 14–15.

Chen, Y., Kivanc, M. and Kirovski, D. (2005) 'Certifying Authenticity via Fibre Induced Paper', *ACM SciGecom Exchanges* 5(3) 29–37.

Chow, D.K. (2003) 'Organized Crime, Locals, Protectionism, and the Trade in Counterfeit Goods in China', *China Economic Review* 14(4) 473–84.

Coffey, T. (2008) *The Long Thirst*. New York: Norton.

Cunneen, C., Findlay, M., Lynch, R. and Tupper, C. (1989) *Dynamics of Collective Conflict: Riots at the Bathurst 'Bike Races'*. North Ryde: Law Book Co.

David, M. (2010) *Peer to Peer and the Music Industry*. London: Sage.

David, M. and Kirkhope, J. (2004) 'New Digital Technologies: Privacy/Property Globalization and Law', *Perspectives on Global Development and Technology* 3(4) 437–49.

deKieffer, D. (2006) 'The Internet and the Globalization of Counterfeit Drugs', *Journal of Pharmacy Practice* 19(4) 215–20.

Elias, N. and Dunning, E. (1986) *The Quest for Excitement*. Oxford: Blackwell

Elsie, R., Arruda, N., Vaillancourt, E., Boivin, J.F., Morisette, C., Leclerc, P., Alary, M. and Bourgois, P. (2012) 'Drug Use Patterns in the Presence of Crack in Downtown Montreal', *Drug and Alcohol Review* 34(1) 72–80.

Emerson, E. (1992) 'What is Normalization?', in H. Brown and H. Smith (eds) *Normalization: A Reader for the Nineties*. London: Routledge, 1–18.

Ferrell, J., Hayward, K. and Young, J. (2008) *Cultural Criminology: An Invitation*. London: Sage.

Fisher, M. (2007) 'Download Uproar: Record Industry Goes after Personal Use', *Washington Post*, 30 December.

Gerstenfeld, P. (2011) *Hate Crimes: Causes, Controls and Controversies*. London: Sage.

Gover, A.R., Jennings, W. and Tewksbury, R. (2009) 'Adolescent Male and Female Gang Members' Experience with Violent Victimization, Dating Violence and Sexual Assault', *American Journal of Criminal Justice* 34(1) 103–15.

Giesler, M. and Pohlmann, M. (2003) 'The Anthropology of File Sharing', *Advances in Consumer Research* 30: 273–79.

Hall, S. (2012) *Theorizing Crime and Deviance*. London: Sage.

IFPI Digital Music Report (2009) *The Business Model for a Changing Environment*. http://www.ifpi.org/content/library/dmr2009.pdf

Israeli, A.A. and Mehrez, A. (2000) 'From Illegal Gambling to Legal Gambling: Casinos in Israel', *Tourism Management* 21(3) 281–91.

Johnson, B., Golub, A. and Fagan, A. (1995) 'Careers in Crack, Drug Use, Drug Distribution and Nondrug Criminality', *Crime and Delinquency* 41(3) 275–95.

Karpova, E. and Hyejeong, K. (2010) 'Consumer Attitudes toward Fashion Counterfeits', *Clothing and Textiles Research Journal* 28(2) 79–94.

Kusek, D. and Leonhard, G. (2005) *The Future of Music: Manifesto for the Digital Music Revolution*. Boston, MA: Berklee Press.

LaRose, R., Lai, Y., Large, R., Love, B. and Wu, Y. (2006) 'Sharing or Piracy?', *Journal of Computer Mediated Communication* 11(1) 1–21.

Lee, S.H. and Workman, J. (2011) 'Attitudes toward Counterfeit Purchases and Ethical Beliefs among Korean and American Students', *Family and Consumer Sciences Research Journal* 39(3) 289–305.

Lessig, L. (2004) *Free Culture: How Big Media Uses Technology and the Law to Lock Down Culture and Control Creativity*. London: Penguin.

Matza, D. (1964) *Delinquency and Drift*. New Brunswick: Transaction Publishers.

McEwen, A. and Strauss, L. (2009) 'Counterfeit Tobacco in London', *Trends in Organized Crime* 12: 251–59.

Miller, K., Merrill, J., Farrell, M., Sabo, P., Donald, F. and Grace, M. (2006) 'Jocks, Gender, Binge Drinking and Adolescent Violence', *Journal of Interpersonal Violence* 21(1) 105–20.

Nguyen, T. (2004) 'The Business of Illegal Gambling: An Examination of the Gambling Business of Vietnamese Cafes', *Deviant Behaviour* 25(5) 451–64.

Norum, P. and Cuno, A. (2011) 'Analysis of Demand for Counterfeit Goods', *Journal of Fashion and Marketing*, 15(1) 27–40.

Okrent, D. (2011) *Last Call: The Rise and Fall of Prohibition*. New York: Scribner.

Parker, H., Aldridge, J. and Measham, F. (1998) *Illegal Leisure*. London: Routledge.

Parker, H., Williams, L. and Aldridge, J. (2002) 'The Normalization of "Sensible" Recreational Drug Use', *Sociology* 36(4) 941–64.

Phillips, T. (2005) *Knock Off: The Deadly Trade in Counterfeit Goods*. London: Kogan Page.

Philpot, T. (2009) *Understanding Child Abuse: The Partners of Child Sex Offenders Tell Their Stories*. London: Routledge.

Riston, M. (2007) 'Fakes Can Genuinely Aid Luxury Brands,' *Marketing* 21–22, 25 July.

Robertson, F. (2005) 'The Aesthetics of Authenticity: Printed Banknotes as Industrial Currency', *Technology and Culture* 46(1) 31–50.

Rojek, C. (2000) *Leisure and Culture*. London: Macmillan.

Rutter, J. (2010) 'Consumers, Crime and the Downloading of Music,' *Prometheus* 28(4) 411–18.

Rutter, J. and Bryce, J. (2008) 'The Consumption of Counterfeit Goods: "Here Be Pirates?"', *Sociology* 42(6) 1146–64.

Ryan, M. and Leeson, P. (2011) 'Hate Groups and Hate Crime', *International Review of Law and Economics* 31(4) 256–62.

Sacco, J. (2001) *Palestine*. London: Jonathan Cape

Sandulli, F. and Martin-Barbero, S. (2007) '68 Cents per Song: A Socio-Economic Survey on the Internet', *Convergence* 13(1) 63–78.

Scott, S. (2001) *The Politics and Experience of Ritual Abuse*. Milton Keynes: Open University Press.

Shah, S. (2004) 'Prostitution, Sex Work and Violence: Discursive and Political Contexts of Five Texts on Paid Sex, 1987–2001', *Gender and History* 16(3) 794–812.

Sheehan, B., Tsao, B. and Yang, S. (2010) 'Motivations for Gratifications of Digital Music Piracy among College Students', *Atlantic Journal of Communication* 18(5) 241–58.

Shelley, L. (2012) 'The Relationship of Drug and Human Trafficking: A Global Perspective', *European Policy on Criminal Policy and Research* 18(3) 241–53.

Siwek, S. (2007) *Copyright Industries in the US Economy: The 2003–07 Report*. Washington DC: International Intellectual Property Alliance.

Somers, M. and Kilaru, N. (2008) 'Counterfeit Culture', *IP Litigator* 14(1) 41–2.

Stebbins, R. (2001) *New Directions in the Theory and Research of Serious Leisure*. New York: Edwin Mellen Press.

Stretesky, P. and Pogrebin, M. (2007) 'Gang-Related Gun Violence: Socialization, Identity and Self', *Journal of Contemporary Ethnography* 36(1) 85–114.

Thrasher, F. (1927) *The Gang*. Chicago: Chicago University Press.

Valdez, A. (2008) *Mexican American Girls and Gang Violence*. Basingstoke: Palgrave.

Von Braun, J. and Munyi, P. (2010) 'New Enforcement Mechanisms Challenge the Legality of Generics in the Name of Public Health', *African Journal of International and Comparative Law* 18(2) 238–53.

Wiedmann, K.-H., Hennings, N. and Klarmann, C. (2012) 'Luxury Consumption in the Trade-Off between Genuine and Counterfeit Goods,' *Journal of Brand Management* 19(7) 544–66.

Wolfensberger, W. (1984) 'A Reconceptualization of Normalization as Social Role Valorization', *Mental Retardation* 34(7) 22–25.

World Trade Organization (1994) http://www.wto.org/english/docs_e/legal_e/legal_e.htm.

Wotherspoon, D. and Cheng, M. (2009) 'Web of Deceit,' *Risk Management* 56(8) 32–36.

33

BEHIND THE NET-CURTAIN

Home-based work and leisure spaces

Jon Dart

> What really goes on in most people's homes remains a mystery, an intriguing and frustrating mystery.
>
> (Hunt, 1995: 301)

> Of all concepts, that of leisure is the most intractable. Like the concept of time, in the words of St Augustine, we know what it is when no-one asks us, but when they ask what it is, we find it hard put to find an answer. It is a polar concept to be sure. That is, it is contrasted with something else – work is the usual candidate. But when we try to define work we find ourselves begging questions about leisure.
>
> (Barrett, 1989: 9)

In Leisure Studies there has been a long tradition in which people have sought to address the relationship between leisure and work (the 'work–leisure couplet'). However, the emergence of *flexible* (post-Fordist, post-industrial, neoliberal) work arrangements has led some to question the relevance of employing paid *work* to help understand *leisure*. In these altered conditions home-based work can be seen as a highly flexible form of employment, from an employer's viewpoint, whilst for an individual such new working arrangements may be said to offer a better work–life balance, with an emphasis placed on their leisure lives. This had led some to suggest that *leisure* is better served by exploring notions of lifestyle choice, identity and consumption.

For most people, the home represents an important place for leisure and remains a significant site in terms of the amount of time and money spent there. However, traditional notions of 'the home' can prove problematic for those who undertake paid work in their home environment and it is this observation that forms the critical focus of this chapter. Beginning with an outline of the relationship between work and leisure, a brief account of home-based working (from 'sweating to telework') is given. The discussion then moves to the importance of the home as a place for, and of, leisure, before it reflects on the specific experiences of two groups of home-based workers: traditional, manual workers and middle-class professional 'teleworkers'. The chapter focuses on their experiences of their home as a leisure space and the impact of paid home-based work upon their leisure.

The relationship between work and leisure

Leisure has often been seen as the antithesis of paid work, with the link between work and leisure a long-standing debate within the discipline, Mills (1959: 12) noting how the 'problems of leisure ... cannot be even stated without considering the problems of work'. This relationship can be located in the particular Western conception of work which emerged during the Industrial Revolution. This saw leisure coming to be understood as a specific historical and social construction primarily equated with free time.

Originally an offshoot of the sociology of work, a distinct leisured theme began to emerge in the class-based community studies of the 1950s and 1960s (Young and Willmott, 1957; Dennis, Henriques and Slaughter, 1956). Following these early studies were a series of reports commissioned by the Joint Sports Council (SC) and Social Science Research Council (SSRC) Panel on Leisure and Recreation in the 1970s and 1980s. In what might now be seen as a golden age of large-scale leisure research, a substantial amount of empirical data were collected, which raised standards in the theoretical and methodological study of leisure. The final report in this series (SC/SSRC, 1985: 1) recommended that future research address 'work in the domestic / black economy'. Although home-based work was not referred to specifically, there were allusions to how technological development might impact on work patterns, with 'it being important to understand whether these effects have any impact on the type and range of the workers' leisure choices' (ibid.: 20).

Preceding the SC/SSRC reports and providing the first specific sociological analyses of leisure were Roberts (1970) and Parker (1971). Their focus was concerned with questions such as: 'How much leisure do people have?'; 'How might they use it?'; 'How do they in fact use it, why, and what are the consequences?' (Roberts, 1997). The central concerns of Parker (1971; 1983) were the ways in which paid work, conditions of employment, rationale for work and work status might impact upon the quality of leisure. Although Parker (1983: 9) noted that research into the possibilities and problems associated with 'flexible lifestyles' (including working patterns) was needed, his model was criticized for its weak functionalism, with leisure seen as a function of work (Bacon and Pitchford, 1992). Deem (1986) suggested that the different aspects of freedom and choice discussed in Parker's (1971) research were significantly different for women, whilst Clarke and Critcher (1985) criticized the pluralist and formalistic approaches presented, and the work–leisure couplet, de-contextualized from wider social relations. The absence of gender from the early studies and subsequent 'add and stir' approaches to women's experiences were criticized by Griffin *et al.* (1982), who saw this as constituting a masculine hegemony. Subsequent research showed that for many mothers, leisure activities were often diluted with (unpaid) housework and childcare duties (Deem, 1986; Green, Hebron and Woodward, 1990; Wimbush, 1987; Wimbush and Talbot, 1988; Thompson, 1990; Shaw, 1992). Authors such as Shaw (1994) and Kelly and Kelly (1994) went on to recommend an approach which combined home and unpaid housework, so as to offer a more complete understanding of leisure. As Green *et al.* (1990: 40) stated, 'the changing nature of employment is fundamental to the development of our understanding of leisure', and

> Work and leisure are no longer regarded as separate spheres but instead as a complex set of experiences involving degrees of freedom and constraint. When the 'grey' areas between work and play become a major focus of research instead of being tacked on as an afterthought to the main model, it becomes easier to site leisure in context.
>
> (Green *et al.*, 1990: 19)

Given that the original research in these areas was conducted some 40 years ago, questions have been asked as to why the work–leisure couplet remained such an obsession for many sociologists of leisure (Clarke and Critcher, 1985; Veal, 1987). Rojek (1993; 1995) has repeatedly suggested that the gradual collapse of the distinction between work and leisure has allowed for a wider and more searching investigation into the historical and social mechanisms which enable and regulate leisure practice. Tracking the history of Leisure Studies and the work–leisure relationship reveals a shift from a class and gender focus to a more individualistic lifestyle approach to leisure. The so-called 'cultural turn' (McLennan, 1998) that has taken place across much of the social sciences has led to increased attention on cultural and ideological influences and those areas neglected by traditional approaches (Rojek, 1995). The suggestion is that more attention be given to leisure as a complex commodity in post-modern culture and to replace the work–leisure couplet with a leisure identity based on cultural populism, patterns of consumption and non-work factors. Rojek (1993; 1995) has been a standard bearer of many of these ideas and has questioned the modernist approach to the polarization of work and leisure in an increasingly post-modern world. For Rojek, the 'old school' have been 'put out to grass' by the arrival of the prophets of the post-modern. Contra such prophets are those who see leisure as fully integrated within a capitalist system into which people are born, work, play and die, and a society shaped by class relations. However, as Rojek (1995) also notes, capitalism prioritizes work over leisure, privileges individual experience over collective experience and tends to reduce human relationships to monetary (exchange) values. It will be argued here that the structure and dynamic of capitalism provides the key to understanding modern society, including leisure.

Flexible home working: from 'sweating' to 'telework'

The great Victorian cities (Briggs, 1963), with their concentrated housing and centralization of labour, contributed to the physical separation between the home and paid work and the institutionalization of 'public' and 'private' spheres. Despite this growing separation, there remained the existence of paid work in the home (also known as putting out, slop work, outwork or sweating). 'Sweating', identified by Charles Booth, was specifically applied to journeymen tailors, who were subject to long hours, low rates of wages, unsanitary conditions and irregularity of employment (Blackburn, 1997). Sweated home-based labour evaded the emerging factory legislation, but did attract the attention of Victorian philanthropists and social investigators from the mid-1800s onwards, much of the historical material coming from the Webbs, Cadbury, the Rowntrees, the Fabians and other benevolent middle-class social reformers (Rowbotham, 1994). Many of these social investigators attributed sweating to the unregulated sector and identified it as primarily a gendered issue, leading campaigners to highlight links between women and welfare policies. However, as Blackburn (1997) and Lewenhak (1977) identified, these reformers failed to recognize or accept that low pay was a cause of sweating, coupled with a lack of trade union organization and an oversupply of labour, which led to instability in the labour market.

Although there was a widespread assumption that home-based work disappeared after the First World War, Allen and Wolkowitz (1987) used local history projects, anecdotal evidence and personal recollections to show the persistence of homeworking throughout the twentieth century. This suggests that home-based work merely reverted to its traditional invisibility from public view. During the 1970s, as part of a wider debate on women and employment, interest refocused on the home-based worker (Brown, 1974), with much of the literature on home-based working identifying low-paid, female workers. Recent literature on home-based working has shifted to the developing world, especially India and the Far East, Central and South America, recording the impact of supply chains and export zones on the edge of developed countries (Jhabvala, 1994; Pollert, 1996; Rosa, 1994; Rowbotham and Mitter, 1994; Tate, 1996).

In recent years, with the rise of information and communication technology (ICT), there has been increased public awareness of people undertaking different forms of paid work in their home.[1] Niles *et al.* (1976) are credited with first using the term 'telework' to describe an arrangement that would reduce the need to commute to work, helping to make the savings required by the oil shortages in the early 1970s. Teleworking was heralded as a win–win situation for all concerned, with Toffler's (1980) 'third wave' seeing telework and the 'electronic cottage' realize a number of gains for family life. At the time, the politician and Member of Parliament (MP) Shirley Williams suggested that 'microelectronics offers the opportunity of reuniting the family' (cited in Huws 1991: 24). Futurologists, utopians and other science fiction writers predicted that 'electronic cottages' could act as 'community centres' for employment and leisure, production and consumption (for example, see Seabrook, 1988). Robertson (1985) suggested that home working could lead to the decentring of work, while Jenkins and Sherman (1979) considered a future in which people's emphasis had shifted away from work and onto leisure. The suggestion that a computer and a connection to the internet can free an individual from having to attend a centralized work location continues to be a regular theme in the popular media.

Recent discussion on home-based work has tended to concentrate on self-employed professionals and those making a 'lifestyle choice' to 'downsize' their work obligations. Many of the advocates of home-based working are companies seeking to reduce organizational overhead costs such as office rental, internet connection, cleaning, electricity, heating and lighting, all of which would be transferred to the home-based individual. Popular discussion on new forms of home-based work typically contains an uncritical endorsement of this new, flexible and beneficial style of working, and neglects the historical experiences of home-based working; this is somewhat surprising, given the spatial and temporal similarities.

The need for 'flexible work practices' has long been promoted by politicians and business leaders and is a key ideological expression of neoliberal capitalism. Most of the literature on flexible home-based work is located in one of two camps: the first camp see employers and employees mutually benefiting, with the latter having the opportunity to balance work with other commitments that might otherwise exclude them from paid work altogether; in the other camp one finds an insecure and vulnerable workforce, with a neoliberal ideology promoting labour market deregulation which typically leads to poor conditions of employment, more part-time work, temporary employment, sub-contracting and self-employment. The term 'flexible' is often portrayed as a positive word, with its antonyms including terms such as obstinate, stubborn and rigid (Harvey, 1990), with Pollert (1988b) suggesting that 'flexibility is functional, whilst rigidity is dysfunctional'. Thus, the neoliberal call for 'greater flexibility for all' is part of an ideological offensive which celebrates casualization and cost cutting whilst seeking to ensure that the changes being sought are inevitable. It is therefore important to continue to question the language being used to legitimate an array of policy practices that can been seen as reactionary and anti-worker (Brocklehurst, 1989; Gordon, 1988; Pollert, 1988a, 1988b).

Having outlined the relationship between work and leisure and offered a brief outline of the history of home-based work, discussion now moves on to consider the home as a leisure space. The chapter will then examine the presence of paid work in the home space and how it impacts upon an individual and their family's leisure.

The home as a leisure space

The period before the Industrial Revolution found the overwhelming majority of people working in their own homes or villages (Bolton, 1975), with the domestic system of manufacture dominating in England. During the 1700s and 1800s domestic manufacture was usually supported by a small-holding, with the household acting as the central unit of production and households involved in a complex variety of task work and waged labour. The demarcation of the public and private domains can thus be seen as historically specific and socially constructed (Davidoff and Hall, 1995; Hall, 1990). As productive work began to be banished from the home the space began to be used for sleeping, eating, cooking and washing (all allocated distinct spaces), and separate from polite social intercourse. Whilst shopkeepers and artisans might have 'lived above the shop', a growing number amongst the petite-bourgeoisie (e.g. builders, lawyers, notaries, civil servants) began treating their houses as solely places of residence (Rybczynski, 1986).

With this separation, the home became a place of privacy, intimacy, domesticity, sanctuary and comfort. Such notions were first evident in seventeenth-century Dutch bourgeois society, and spread to English, French and other northern European societies by the eighteenth century (Rybczynski, 1986). It was the new urban middle class who were the most zealous in promoting the separation of the domains (Davidoff and Hall, 1995), with their homes no longer being places of trade, but instead becoming places of leisure. Contributing to the need for more segregated living spaces was the growth in home-based leisure activities (such as reading, writing and music), made possible by an increased amount of time free from subsistence needs, albeit a situation limited to the middle classes (Davidoff and Hall, 1995). By contrast, many in the working class saw this spatial separation take place more slowly and with much less applicability, due primarily to a lack of physical space (Davidoff and Hall, 1995). However, by the second half of the nineteenth century those in the working class began to see their dwelling place as a home with rooms holding different functions, and family life started to acquire the characteristics of privacy, child centredness and leisure. Since the rise of industrial capitalism, the spatial and temporal separation of the home and paid work has become more distinct. Thus, the home has become a place in which to rest and relax and an important site for family leisure (Samdahl and Jekubovich, 1993), with Harvey (1990: 292) noting how the home has often acted as 'a private museum to guard against the ravages of the time-space compression'.

Philosophical discussion of the home has explored it in terms of its physical space and its links with family, community, leisure and work (Bourdieu, 1984; Heidegger, 1971; Honig, 1994). While house means shelter and can 'be anywhere', it has traditionally involved bricks, timber, mortar and trowel, doors and windows (Douglas, 1991; Rykwert, 1991). Just as a home is a space for consumption and an expression of taste, it is also not necessarily a fixed space and can 'be anywhere'. One therefore needs to be attentive when using the related, but different, ideological terms of the home and house, household and family (Somerville, 2007). The suggestion of the home as a place of comfort and safety, and as a bastion against the modern, aggressive, external public world has currency, especially amongst men. Thus, conceptualizing the home as 'a haven in a heartless world' (Lasch, 1977) neglects the experiences of many women within the home environment. Despite such androcentrism, many people continue to make considerable financial and emotional investment in the concept of the home.

The input of social geographers has long informed the study of leisure, yet, despite its importance as site of leisure activity, investigation of leisure in the home remains an under-researched area (Roberts, 1999: 129). In part, this is due to the difficulty in accessing the home space, with Rice (1981) noting the 'there is hardly a window in any family house which is not curtained effectively to obscure the view of the inquisitive passer-by'. This adds to the mystery and compounds the challenge that Hunt (1995) identifies in the quotation at the beginning of this chapter. However, this is not necessarily because people are unwilling to talk about their lives (Glyptis *et al.*, 1987), which makes the lack of investigation on home leisure even more surprising. It may be as Roberts (1999: 129) suggests, that unless the leisure-orientated research findings on the home are unusual (e.g. sexual or intimate), the data collected can often appear quite mundane, with the banality of findings often proving a challenge to explain. It is also the case that leisure research has primarily been policy driven, with less interest on what happens with the privacy of the home space.

The SC/SSRC Panel indicated that of all the projects carried out in the 'golden age' of leisure research, the area which was seen to fill the biggest empirical gap was that of leisure and the home. The study by Cherry (1982) found that although homes were well equipped with leisure items, people often experienced a lack of time to use them. Cherry's study was a precursor to the major report on *Leisure and the Home* carried out by Glyptis *et al.* (1987). The researchers sought to address the paradox that whilst the home is the place where most leisure time is spent, and where much investment is made financially, it generated very little interest amongst leisure researchers. This was evidenced by Glyptis *et al.*'s (1987) succinct review of the fragmentary empirical literature on 'what goes on in the home'. The authors acknowledge that the principal concern of the report was to present some statistics on home life: types of housing, the space available and its allocation, room counting, the exterior spaces (e.g. garage, garden), leisure equipment in the house (e.g. television, sports gear, crafts, musical instruments), the type and range of activity, the patterning of time use and the locations and social contexts of activity.

Glyptis *et al.*'s (1987) study incorporated a time-space analysis, recording what people did, with whom and where, how the space in the home was used and the subject's perception of whether an activity was work or leisure. A clear pattern emerged that confirmed the home as an important centre of activity. On average, the home accommodated 86 per cent of all events and 74 per cent of all leisure events, with the lounge and the kitchen accounting for 52 per cent of all home-based events. Due to the mass of data collected, the authors admit that they selected themes to inform policy and to highlight areas for future research. Annual studies by the UK Office for National Statistics show a steady rise in overall leisure spending, with an increasing percentage of household income being spent on in-home leisure entertainment. Most significant has been the increasing awareness of and greater affordability of leisure-orientated in-home technologies, such as television, computer and internet connection and access to social media.

Home-based working contains many contradictory images associated with work and home (Nippert-Eng, 1996), and thus offers a valuable case study to explore the relevance of the relationship between work and leisure, space and time. What is significant is not only the home as a physical entity but also the activities that take place within it. As Graham (1983: 135) has suggested, 'places remain constant while definitions of their social space change'. Similarly, Goffman (1969) noted how the same region at different times can act as both a 'front' and 'back region', with the 'performance' often more important than the location. The lack of distinction between the home, work and leisure, between temporal and spatial boundaries, has been a central theme in the studies of women and house/work (Deem, 1986; Green, Hebron and Woodward, 1990; Wimbush and Talbot, 1988). In the remaining part of this chapter, the lived experiences of home-based workers are discussed, exploring what the home space meant to different people, given the impact of paid work.

Raising the roof on the home: leisure and paid work

The following discussion is based on my own research that involved two groups of home-based workers. The first, a group of traditional home workers engaged in industrial manual work; and a second group of professional home-based workers ('teleworkers'). Using data generated from 38 semi-structured interviews, the concepts of space, time and leisure were discussed and these were found to be clearly shaped by gender and the levels of choice and constraint that the home-working individuals experienced (see Dart, 2001; 2006).

Bringing paid work into the home space created a number of problems for the home-working individuals and their families. Those who worked in their lounge or kitchen did not always feel the necessity, or have the option, to pack away the (paid) work when they finish for the day. It was common to find a family watching television in the evening surrounded by half-full boxes and packaging, with the ability to relax, to 'switch off', compromised by the visible presence of paid work. The continued visibility of paid work in the home raises important issues about the nature of the home space: with the identification of a space (for example, the lounge or the bedroom) remaining constant, its definition as a social space was under constant threat. With the bedroom traditionally seen as the most private space within the home and the ultimate sanctuary against the outside world, the introduction of paid work crossed a boundary and made complete the penetration of the public into the private. What was evident was that many of the home-based workers, especially those who had to share home and work space, faced difficulties in creating and maintaining a sense of a constant or precise meaning attached to certain locations within the home. So whilst a physical space might remain the same (for instance, 'the lounge'), the meaning and perception of this space for the individual was often different, even if the appellation remained unchanged.

Amongst the most significant issues identified was the sustained sense of isolation, which individuals contrasted to their previous work experience in a centralised work-place, one which had acted as an important place for friendships and related leisure opportunities. Conversely, individuals found that being at home during the day time was often interpreted by their friends that they were available for social visits, with such visits ('interruptions') causing paid work to be rescheduled, which would then impact upon other activities. It was evident that the presence of paid work confused for the host, their family and visitors any sense of the traditional image of the home as a social leisure space. Employing traditional conceptions of the home revealed that there were complex and diverse meanings in operation, with these layers creating multiple contradictions for the home-based worker. Only where there existed a separate and distinct space for the paid work was it felt that there existed an opportunity to secure a sense of stability in meaning and a level of control over the home environment and leisure activities. It can thus be concluded that the dualistic nature of the 'public and private' did not provide a useful model for those who work at home.

The research showed that the industrial workers had very little control over their work time, with 'time-crunched' days leaving little time available for leisure. Traditional expectations associated with female gender roles result in double shifts becoming triple shifts, leaving many of the women too tired from their paid and unpaid work to enjoy any leisure. It was the industrial home-based women, as distinct from the professional home-working women, who were least able to cushion the negative effects caused by this time crunch. Although the professional women had a greater level of freedom in their paid work than did the industrial home-based women, they still experienced constraint, due to the temporal and spatial demands of childcare.

Indeed, adopting a class-based analysis reveals differences between the industrial and the professional home-based workers in the degree of control over their work and non-paid work. For the professional women, their exercise of power was more self-defined, with greater control over their paid work and a higher level of income, which allowed a greater degree of choice. The professional women, although primarily responsible for childcare and household duties, did have the opportunity to buy in help, whereas the industrial home-based women had no such opportunity. Whilst all the home-based workers were selling their labour power, they were doing so under different circumstances.

It is suggested that temporal flexibility, often highlighted as a benefit for home-based workers in terms of their leisure opportunities, was only realized when a rigid timetable had been established. Clearly, this was a contradiction and went against the inherent meaning of flexibility and those definitions of leisure which see it as spontaneous and freely chosen. Where no such timetable, was possible then little or no leisure activity took place. 'Leisure' had to be purposefully built into an individual's busy schedule, and subsequently protected; otherwise it was rare for any of the home-based workers to identify examples of personally enjoyable leisure activities. The collapse of traditional temporal boundaries and the emergence of scattered hours (Breedveld, 1996; 1998) meant that, for many, their paid work was dispersed throughout the day, evening and night and across the week. The positive flexibility often associated with home-based work was illusory (except for the suppliers of the work) and rarely equated with greater levels of control or choice. The flexibility of home-based working saw few tangible leisure benefits for the individual, with, as a consequence, the rejection of any equating of flexible work time with increased levels of control or sovereignty.

What was central in the research was the extent to which the industrial and professional home-based workers were able to make choices; choices that were orientated towards, or at least which facilitated, an increased role for leisure in their everyday lives. It was the recurring themes of choice and constraint that were inseparable for those working in their home space. In exploring whether home-based work was undertaken as a short-term practical measure, or was a long-term career and lifestyle choice, it was necessary to employ a wider perspective when assessing the workers' levels of choice, control and constraint. My research found that for the industrial home-based women it was the decision to have a child that resulted in a highly restricted range of choice. Many of those interviewed identified it was their decision to have and look after young children which was the catalyst to begin paid home work. Even when the children had grown up and left home, the consequences of this decision remained.

The changing nature of paid work in advanced industrial society has led some to question the value of the work–leisure couplet and to argue that it is no longer sufficiently sensitive to account for the multiple interpretations of 'work' found in contemporary society. Exploring the experiences identified by the home-based workers, it was the overriding impact of paid work which was unmistakable. Where there existed a lack of clearly defined spatial and temporal boundaries between work and non-work, there was a manifest tension for the individual and their family. Those who sought to manage the work–life balance were able to do so primarily through their ability to establish clear boundaries between paid-work space and time. Very few of the home-based individuals interviewed had been able to achieve what could be perceived as a successful integration of their paid work and family life. It was no coincidence that it was the level of control over their work that was linked to their class position and to the presence (or absence) of children.

For many of the home-based workers the anticipation of leisure was better than their actual leisure experience; for some, even anticipation lay beyond their horizon. The potential for leisure as an enriching experience typically failed to live up to expectations. This was because paid and unpaid work dominated daily life and left little time, space or money available for leisure. What was significant was how poor work often equated with poor leisure. The impact of the intrusion of paid work into a space traditionally seen as private should not be underestimated. For the individuals discussed here, the home no longer acted as a retreat from an outside world of paid work, with the absence of temporal and spatial boundaries often intensifying the time-space compression. The study found numerous examples of the low priority accorded to leisure, which was seen as 'recuperation rather than recreation', and 'leisure as left-overs'.

Closing the door?

What these findings suggest is that hearing and listening to what home workers have to say about their leisure experiences is important for the production of responsible knowledge in Leisure Studies. With this in mind I would like to propose a research agenda, based on empirical evidence (notwithstanding the methodological challenge of 'getting in the front door'), to explore what is happening in this important but neglected leisure space. The lack of research is more evident, given the increasing amount of time spent in the home space, brought about by computer technology, the internet and social media. The home should be where one starts, given that it remains the primary space for leisure. However, the home is not a fixed space, but it is one where people can (should?) expect to have a degree of control. For many people, the importance of the 'private realm' of the home remains as one of the few constants in late modernity. However, as this study found, for those who 'take in' paid work, the orientating sense of the home was disrupted by the presence of paid work, which impacted upon their capacity to construct a constant sense of space.

What is suggested is a strong, sustained relationship between work and leisure and the importance of control over space and time. The industrial home-based workers were too busy raising a family to be concerned with creating a leisure-orientated lifestyle. They sought flexibility in their paid work – not with the intention of going to the gym, or cinema or some other leisure activity – but, rather, to look after their children and their home. By contrast, the home-based professional women were more likely to emphasize personal fulfilment from their paying work. This suggestion offers a stark contrast to some postmodern accounts, which see leisure as conspicuous consumption, hedonistic or as a kind of identity expression. What is required is more empirical research; when leisure researchers neglect historical, material and structural influences, their conclusions are likely to be weaker as a consequence. The study of leisure is best served by striking a balance between the more enduring and underpinning political economy and a constantly changing society and culture.

In conclusion, it is work in all its guises which needs to be resurrected and reinstated as the cornerstone when researching leisure. Theoretical challenges in defining work ought not to allow the pretext to dominate that everything requires a 'post-modern gaze'. Important debates on the nature of work continue to take place, for example, 'What counts as work?' 'Who does the counting?' and 'How is work to be categorized?' Technological advances continue to de-standardize work and expand flexible work practices. Given the emergence of new patterns and styles of work, the need remains to employ the work–leisure couplet. As Roberts (1997) has suggested, some of the old questions remain the best and require continual and sometimes more subtle answers; the degree of control over space and time remain amongst the most significant. It is evident that the work–leisure couplet should not be made redundant but, rather, is in need of regular modification and re-grounding in order to understand the specificities of lived experience. Leisure Studies has become fascinated, at times bedazzled, by the bright lights and 'sizzle' of consumption, resulting in a leisure theory that is far removed from the influences of paid work and employment. At times, so immersed are we in the capitalist system that we become preoccupied with conspicuous consumption and its identity/lifestyle sibling. One needs to challenge the paralysing effects of the spectacular and its alternate celebration and pessimism that there are no alternatives.

Note

1   The term *work* is subject to constantly shifting meanings, which, when coupled with 'home-based', creates a multitude of possible definitions. Thus, home-based work is not a universal term, but has different meanings attached in different circumstances. Amongst the terms that have been applied in recent times to those doing paid work in the home are location-independent workers, electronic remote workers, electronic cottagers, telecommuters, teleworkers, remote workers, moonlighters, outworkers, distance workers, freelancers, the self-employed, small businesses, those providing personal services (childcare, private teachers), and those who live in a different part of the same building from where the paid work is located (e.g. publicans, hotel workers, shopkeepers).

References

Allen, S. and Wolkowitz, C. (1987) *Homeworking – Myths and Realities*. Hong Kong: Macmillan.

Bacon, B. and Pitchford, A. (1992) 'Managerial Work in Leisure: A Deconstruction', in J. Sugden and C. Knox (eds) *Leisure in the 1990s: Rolling Back the Welfare State*. LSA Publications, No. 46.

Barrett, C. (1989) 'The Concept of Leisure: Idea and Ideal', in T. Winnifrith and C. Barrett (eds) *The Philosophy of Leisure*. London: Macmillan.

Blackburn, S. (1997) '"No Necessary Connection with Homework": Gender and Sweated Labour 1840–1909', *Social History* 22 (3) 269–285.

Bolton, B. (1975) *An End to Homeworking*. London: Fabian Society.

Bourdieu, P. (1984) *Distinction: A Social Critique of the Judgement of Taste*. London: Routledge.

Breedveld, K. (1996) 'Post-Fordist Leisure and Work', *Leisure and Society* 19 (1) 67–90.

Breedveld, K. (1998) 'The Double Myth of Flexibilisation', *Time and Society* 7 (1) 129–143.

Briggs, A. (1963) *Victorian Cities*. Penguin: Harmondsworth.

Brocklehurst, M. (1989) 'Homeworking and New Technology: The Rhetoric and the Reality', *Personnel Review* 18 (2) 1–70.

Brown, M. (1974) *Sweated Labour: A Study of Homework*. London: Low Pay Unit.

Cherry, G. (1982) *Leisure and the Home. A State of the Art Review*. Sports Council/Social Science Research Council Joint Panel on Sport and Leisure Research, Centre for Urban and Regional Studies, University of Birmingham.

Clarke, J. and Critcher, C. (1985) *The Devil Makes Work: Leisure in Capitalist Britain*. Basingstoke: Macmillan.

Dart, J. (2001) *'Raising the Roof' – Leisure and the Home-based Worker*. Unpublished PhD thesis. Leeds Metropolitan University.

Dart, J. (2006) 'Settee or Work-Station? Home-based Work and Leisure Spaces', *Leisure Studies* 25 (3) 313–328.

Davidoff, L. and Hall, C. (1995) 'My Own Fireside: The Creation of the Middle Class Home', in S. Jackson and S. Moores (eds) *The Politics of Domestic Consumption*. Hemel Hempstead: Prentice Hall/ Harvester Wheatsheaf.

Deem, R. (1986) *All Work and No Play?* Milton Keynes: Open University Press.

Dennis, N., Henriques, F. and Slaughter, C. (1956) *Coal is Our Life: An Analysis of a Yorkshire Mining Community*. London: Eyre and Spottiswoode.

Douglas, M. (1991) 'The Idea of a Home: A Kind of Space', *Social Research* 58 (1) 287–307.

Glyptis, S., McInnes, H. and Patmore, A. (1987) *Leisure and the Home*. London: Sports Council/ESRC.

Goffman, E. (1969) *The Presentation of Self in Everyday Life*. Penguin: Harmondsworth.

Gordon, D. (1988) 'The Global Economy: New Edifice or Crumbling Foundations?', *New Left Review* 168: 24–65.

Graham, H. (1983) 'Do Her Answers Fit His Questions? Women and the Survey Method', in E. Gamarnikow, D. Morgan, J. Purvis, and D. Taylorson, (eds) *The Public and the Private*. London: Heinemann.

Green, E., Hebron, S. and Woodward, D. (1990) *Women's Leisure – What Leisure?* London: Macmillan.

Griffin, C., Hobson, D., McIntosh, S. and McCabe, T. (1982) 'Women and Leisure', in J. Hargreaves (ed.) *Sport, Culture and Ideology*. London: Routledge.

Hall, C. (1990) 'Private Persons versus Public Someones: Class, Gender and Politics in England 1780–1850', in T. Lovell (ed.) *British Feminist Thought*. Oxford: Blackwell.

Harvey, D. (1990) *The Condition of Postmodernity*. Oxford: Blackwell.

Heidegger, M. (1971) *Poetry, Language, Thought*. New York: Harper and Row.

Honig, B. (1994) 'Difference, Dilemmas and the Politics of the Home', *Social Research* 61 (3) 563–597.

Hunt, P. (1995) 'Gender and the Construction of Home Life', in S. Jackson and S. Moores (eds) *The Politics of Domestic Consumption*. Hemel Hempstead: Prentice Hall/Harvester Wheatsheaf.

Huws, U. (1991) 'Telework: Projections', *Futures* (January/February) 19–31.

Huws, U. (1994) *Key Results from a National Survey of Homeworkers*. Leeds: National Group on Homeworking, Report No. 2.

Jenkins, C. and Sherman, B. (1979) *The Collapse of Work*. London: Eyre Methuen.

Jhabvala, R. (1994) 'Self-Employed Women's Association: Organising Women by Struggle and Development', in S. Rowbotham and S. Mitter (eds) *Dignity and Daily Bread*. London: Routledge.

Kelly, J. and Kelly, J. (1994) 'Multiple Dimensions of Meaning in the Domains of Work, Family and Leisure', *Journal of Leisure Research* 26 (3) 250–274.

Lasch, C. (1977) *Haven in a Heartless World*. New York: Basic Books.

Lewenhak, S. (1977) *Women and Trade Unions: An Outline History of Women in the British Trade Unions Movement*. London: Ernest Benn.

McLennan, G. (1998) 'Sociology and Cultural Studies: Rhetoric of Disciplinary Identity', *History of Human Science* 11 (3) 1–17.

Mills, C.W. (1959) *The Sociological Imagination*. Oxford: Oxford University Press.

Niles, J., Carlson, R., Gray, P. and Hanneman, G. (1976) *The Telecommunications–Transportation Trade-off: Options for Tomorrow*. New York: Wiley.

Nippert-Eng, C. (1996) *Home and Work: Negotiating Boundaries through Everyday Life*. London: University of Chicago Press.

Parker, S. (1971) *The Future of Leisure*. London: McGibbon and Kee.

Parker, S. (1983) *Leisure and Work*. London: Unwin Hyman.

Pollert, A. (1988a) *Farewell to Flexibility?: Restructuring Work and Employment*. Oxford: Blackwell.

Pollert, A. (1988b) 'Dismantling Flexibility', *Capital and Class* 34: 42–75.

Pollert, A. (1996) 'Gender and Class Revisited: Or the Poverty of Patriarchy'. *Sociology* 30 (4) 639–659.

Rice, M. (1981) *Working Class Wives*. London: Virago.

Roberts, K. (1970) *Leisure*. London: Longman.

Roberts, K. (1997) 'Why Old Questions are the Right Responses to New Challenges: The Sociology of Leisure in the 1990s', *Society and Leisure* 20 (2) 369–381.

Roberts, K. (1999) *Leisure in Contemporary Society*. Oxon: CABI.

Robertson, J. (1985) *Future Work*. London: Gower Press.

Rojek, C. (1993) *Ways of Escape*. London: Macmillan.

Rojek, C. (1995) *Decentring Leisure: Rethinking Leisure Theory*. London: Sage.

Rosa, K. (1994) 'The Conditions and Organisational Activities of Women in Free Trade Zones', in S. Rowbotham and S. Mitter (eds) *Dignity and Daily Bread*. London: Routledge.

Rowbotham, S. (1994) 'Strategies against Sweated Work in Britain, 1820–1920', in S. Rowbotham and S. Mitter (eds) *Dignity and Daily Bread*. London: Routledge.

Rowbotham, S. and Mitter, S. (eds) (1994) *Dignity and Daily Bread*. London: Routledge.

Rybczynski, W. (1986) *Home: A Short History of an Idea*. London: Heinemann.

Rykwert, J. (1991) 'House and Home', *Social Research*, 58 (1) 51–62

Samdahl, D. and Jekubovich, N. (1993) 'Patterns and Characteristics of Adult Daily Leisure', *Society and Leisure* 16 (1) 129–149.

Seabrook, J. (1988) *The Leisure Society*. London: Blackwell.

Shaw, S. (1992) 'Dereifying Family Life: An Examination of Women's and Men's Everyday Experiences and Perceptions of Leisure Time', *Leisure Sciences* 14 (4) 271–286.

Shaw, S. (1994) 'Gender, Leisure and Constraint: Towards a Framework for the Analysis of Women's Leisure', *Journal of Leisure Research* 26 (1) 1–7.

Somerville, P. (2007) 'Home Sweet Home: A Critical Comment on Saunders and Williams', *Housing Studies* 4 (2) 113–118.

SC/SSRC (Sports Council/Social Science Research Council) (1985) *Proposals for the Continuing Development of Leisure Research. A State of the Art Review.* Sports Council/Social Science Research Council Joint Panel on Sport and Leisure Research, Centre for Urban and Regional Studies, University of Birmingham. September.

Tate, J. (1996) 'Making Links: The Growth of Homeworker Networks', in E. Boris and E. Prugel (eds) *Homeworkers in Global Perspective.* Routledge: London.

Thompson, S. (1990) 'Thank the Ladies for Their Places: The Incorporation of Women into Sport', *Leisure Studies*, 19 (2) 135–143.

Toffler, A. (1980) *The Third Wave.* London: Collins.

Veal, A. (1987) *Leisure and the Future.* London: Unwin.

Wimbush, E. (1987) *Mothers with Young Children – Understanding Their Leisure.* Leisure Studies Association Newsletter Supplement: Women's Leisure, Constraints and Opportunities. Brighton: LSA Publication.

Wimbush, E. and Talbot, M. (eds) (1988) *Relative Freedoms: Women and Leisure.* Milton Keynes: Open University Press.

Young, M. and Willmott, P. (1957) *Family and Kinship in East London: A Study of Work and Leisure in London.* Harmondsworth: Penguin.

34

CONSUMERISM AS SHAPED BY THE PURSUIT OF LEISURE

Robert A. Stebbins

Consumerism, according to the *Oxford English Dictionary*, is the 'emphasis on or preoccupation with the acquisition of consumer goods'. This chapter examines how our leisure interests guide our acquisition of consumer goods and services. It is the obverse of an equally current intellectual concern revolving around how the contemporary, widespread desire to acquire goods, also known as 'the work-earn-and-spend ethic', influences our consumptive choices. This second question, which has been explored from various angles by, for example, Herbert Marcuse (1968), Juliet Schor (1998) and Zygmunt Bauman (2007), is not necessarily a leisure-related matter. Though it will be mentioned here from time to time, it will not be discussed in any detail.

Intellectual background

Scholarly interest in how consumerism shapes the pursuit of leisure has a long, albeit spotty, history. In the modern era it began with Thorstein Veblen (1857–1929), an American economist who wrote mostly between 1899 and 1923 and who is generally credited with having pioneered the idea of conspicuous consumption. In his celebrated work, *The Theory of the Leisure Class* (Veblen, 1899), he argued that leisure can be used to demonstrate status and power in modern industrial society, such that this practice results in a distinctive leisure class. Nevertheless, use of wealth in this way is of relatively recent origin. Historically, societies were unable to produce a level of material goods beyond that needed for subsistence. But eventually parts of some societies – the main examples being the industrial and post-industrial societies of today – came to enjoy a surplus of these goods, which raised questions about how the surplus should be controlled, distributed, and used. Control, distribution, and use refer, in effect, to sets of options, one of which is conspicuous consumption. This kind of use is manifested in the publicly visible purchase and hence ownership of distinctive goods and services available only to people who have the money (control) to buy them (distribution).

The leisure class for whom conspicuous consumption was a mark of membership also embraced the value of being exempt from all necessary remunerated employment. Not having to work for a living is honorable and meritorious – the very essence of a decent person. This orientation toward work has ancient roots, most notably in the writings of

Plato and Aristotle. In Veblen's theory, leisure connotes the non-productive use of free time. Nevertheless, leisure for the leisured class was often, in accord with the perspective presented later in this chapter, of the serious variety, exemplified in learning ancient languages, studying occult science, breeding show horses, and going in for equestrian sports. Good manners and refined tastes were considered the *sine qua non* of the properly cultured and leisured gentleman, which, however, like all serious leisure, took time and perseverance to learn and perfect.

Much later, working by analogy to George Ritzer's (1993) treatise on McDonaldization, Alan Bryman endowed the term Disneyization (probably coined by Gill, 1991, and applied chiefly to American architecture) with some theoretic substance. He did so by extending the idea of Disneyitis beyond urban architecture, to argue that aspects of our society are increasingly exhibiting features associated with Disney theme parks. Bryman defines Disneyization as 'simply the process by which the principles of the Disney theme parks are coming to dominate more and more sectors of American society as well as the rest of the world' (Bryman, 2004: 1). He holds that 'Disneyization' is characterized by four aspects, or dimensions, which may be observed not only in Disney's theme parks but also, with growing frequency, in many other spheres of modern Western life. They are:

- *theming* – clothing institutions or objects in a narrative that is largely unrelated to the institution or object to which it is applied, such as a casino or restaurant with a Wild West narrative;
- *hybrid consumption* – a general trend whereby the forms of consumption associated with different institutional spheres become interlocked with each other and increasingly difficult to distinguish;
- *merchandising* – the promotion and sale of goods in the form of or being copyright images and/or logos, including such products made under license;
- *performative labour* – the growing tendency for front-line service work to be viewed as a performance, especially one in which the deliberate display of a certain mood is seen as part of the labour involved in service work.

(Bryman, 2004: 2)

Two of Bryman's dimensions need further explanation. Hybrid consumption refers to purchasing a good or service that involves two or more different ways or, in Bryman's words, 'forms' of consuming it, a process that blurs the conventional distinction between the forms. Shopping, visiting a theme park, eating in a restaurant, staying at a hotel, patronizing a museum, going to a cinema, gambling at a casino, and so on exemplify various ways of consuming. Hybrid consumption occurs, for example, when people go to a museum, visit its gift shop, and enjoy a meal in its restaurant, all accomplished within the same establishment during the same session of leisure.

Performative labour is so named because it resembles a theatrical performance. That is, workers serving the public are increasingly also performers, a main component being what Bryman has labelled 'emotional work'. Such work refers to 'employment situations in which workers as part of their work roles need to convey emotions and preferably to appear as though these emotions are deeply held' (Bryman, 2004: 104). In Disneyization the emotions are generally positive. Workers are supposed to smile, look patrons in the eye, and in this manner convey genuine attachment to their job and the people they serve. It is hoped that the client-observers of such histrionics will then feel good about the workers and the organization in which they are employed. The driving force behind Disneyization is a vast public desire for particular kinds of leisure experiences, for which they are willing to pay and from which the providers of these experiences profit.

Bryman (2004: 5–10) also distinguishes Disneyization from the related idea of Disneyfication. Richard Schickel (1986) was one of the first to use the latter term. He said that we 'Disneyfy' when we transform an object into something superficial, often done by simplifying or trivializing it. The intention is to render objects understandable to the lowest common denominator of patron, a formula that Disney routinely followed with historical events, fairy tales, traditional stories, and the like. In this adulterated state, it was believed, the material would be optimally entertaining, or, in the language of this chapter, it would generate a casual leisure experience for the largest possible segment of the target population.

Meanwhile, overlying the mass consumption of today is a trend toward shaping leisure activities and their availability to meet the interests of particular categories of consumers (Godbey, 2004). Mass leisure has always had a clear sense of equality about it – it is for everyone. But now, though mass leisure is still enjoyed, another kind of leisure is growing in parallel with it. This leisure is 'appropriate'; it is customized by or for special categories of society. And the emergence of these categories reflects some of the recent transformations to postmodern society. Godbey explains how these groups emerge in the wake of today's brisk pace of social change.

First, he notes the explosive population growth in the West. It is fuelled substantially by international migration, which brings different sets of leisure-related customs. The efflorescence of 'ethnic' restaurants and grocery stores is evidence of this, as is the demand for special recreational facilities for Muslim women (VandeSchoot, 2005). Films shown in cinemas catering to particular nationalities constitute another sign of customization along lines of immigrant tastes. How many immigrants from Germany, Italy, Japan, or Korea, for example, buy cars in their new country that were made in the old country, cars used for leisure and for work and other obligations? Now we find video and CD shops catering for certain ethnic tastes in film and music. In the area of illegal deviant leisure, roosters are raised and sold for cockfighting in North America by immigrants from Asia and Latin America, where this practice is legal (Pynn, 2008).

Second, composition of the family has changed considerably, with greater diversity: reconstituted families, many more single-parent units, multi-ethnic and multi-racial groups and gay and lesbian unions. With regard to the latter, the increasing extension of legal recognition has resulted in changes in the way that gay and lesbian families are now treated. For example, in most Western countries today a number of hotels operate according to a 'gay friendly' policy.

Third, the world's population is ageing. This has been paralleled by an increase in leisure programmes and services for the elderly, exemplified in their own exercise programmes, musical performances, dance sessions, and local tours. Crafts are popular with older people, which leads some of them to take courses in this area and many of them to patronize stores supplying relevant material and the tools to work it with.

Fourth, work is, for many people, different now from what it used to be. Today the typical worker is always learning something new. Part-time jobs are now more common, as is work at home. Some seniors continue working part time. Writing on new leisure, I observed (Stebbins, 2009) that part-time employment opens up workers to free-time opportunities as diverse as making up languages and practising money slavery (where males make monetary payments to women in exchange for being humiliated and degraded over the Internet). And for those in the workforce suffering from a time famine, they may now play with dispatch the new 'express' board games.

Fifth, Godbey holds that today's economy is, in many respects, an experience economy. Evidence for this trend is ubiquitous. Thus, the rich may have the expensive though highly unusual experience of spaceflight, as provided by the Russian Space Agency. Nowadays people pay to ride on a luge run or a zip line, be pulled in a dog sled, go rafting on a raging river, eat at a fine restaurant, enjoy a spa, ride a helicopter to a mountain top, and similar thrills. All this for the distinctive experience that each can bring.

Sixth, religion is also becoming more diverse in the West, thereby forcing customization of leisure services to accommodate the diverse free-time interests that are commensurate with religious principles. The example above of special recreational services for Muslim women fits here, too, as do some of the ethnic restaurants and grocery stores, their ethnicity in this instance being religious (e.g., those vending vegetarian cuisine; kosher food; special meat, fish, or fowl for sacred holidays). Religion and custom also lead people to different leisure while celebrating their own special days. Ramadan, Ukrainian Christmas, and the Chinese New Year illustrate these practices.

In conjunction with these social changes identified by Godbey, there are a number of technological innovations that we can also identify. A good example is the 'galactic city' (Lewis, 1995), which is an increasingly common urban phenomenon. This kind of 'community' – it spreads over considerable territory toward the outer edge of a larger metropolitan area, while having no clear center – encourages use of the automobile and involvement in local leisure. This situation helps to explain the popularity of, for example, neighbourhood conversation cafés. These casual-leisure sociable conversations operate, often fortnightly, on a no-charge basis, and are held in a public setting, usually a local café. Anyone may participate, which is done by speaking in turn on a mutually agreed-upon subject. This session is followed by open dialogue. A skilled host leads the session.

Leisure and consumption

Leisure is, among other things, *doing* something, engaging in an activity, while consumption aims at *having* something, with that good or service possibly constituting a leisure activity or being used in one (Stebbins, 2009). In the present chapter consumerism refers to *having* something that is leisure in itself (e.g., purchasing a CD or a massage or purchasing entry to a museum or cinema), or having something that facilitates leisure (e.g., purchasing a violin or piece of sports equipment or purchasing an air ticket to a holiday resort, or a computerized search service for a genealogical project). In other words, sometimes leisure and consumption occur in the same breath – the having and doing are literally or virtually simultaneous – whereas at other times the two are separate – having facilitates doing and therefore precedes it.

Let us start by observing that a substantial amount of consumption today has little or nothing to do with leisure, as exemplified in buying toothpaste, life insurance, accounting services, natural gas for home heating, transit tickets for getting to work, and the like. Such consumption, call it *obligatory consumption*, however important for consumers, lies beyond the scope of this chapter. As for the other areas of consumption, the relationship of this process with leisure is often complicated.

In these other areas – in *leisure-based consumption* – a critical distinction to make is whether the leisure component of a particular activity is directly and solely dependent on the acquisition of a thing or service (e.g., buying a CD, concert ticket, or a session of massage) or whether purchase of something is but a prerequisite to a set of conditions that, much more centrally, shape the activity as a leisure experience (Stebbins, 2009). In other words, is consumption an initiator of a leisure experience or a facilitator of such experience? In *initiatory leisure-based consumption* a person buys, for instance, a ticket enabling entrance to a cinema, a CD enabling listening to recorded music, a new sporty car enabling pleasurable motoring, or a club membership enabling fine drinking and dining with valued members. In such consumption the purchaser proceeds more or less directly to use of the purchased item. Here leisure and consumption do seem to be inextricably linked – an identity – even while sense of the initial consumption may fade as the owner replays for the tenth time the CD or drives six months later the flashy new automobile.

Not so with *facilitative leisure-based consumption*. Here the acquired item only sets in motion a set of activities which, when completed, enable the purchaser to use the item in a satisfying or fulfilling leisure experience. As an example, note that amateur violinists, if they are to play at all, must first rent or purchase a violin – an act of acquisition. Yet their most profound leisure experience is competently and artistically playing music and, earlier, practising to accomplish this, all of which costs nothing, though, obviously, it is certainly facilitated by using the acquired instrument (a consumer product). Moreover, this profound leisure experience might be further facilitated by buying music lessons and paying for public transit tickets to get to a teacher's studio.

In this last example, one or more consumer purchases or rentals are necessary steps to experiencing the leisure being sought. Still, leisure activities exist for which no facilitative consumption whatsoever is needed for participation in them. There are areas in free time where consumption and leisure are clearly separate spheres. It is in the free-time sphere that we find *non-consumptive leisure* (examples presented later). As a basis for exploring this complicated relationship between leisure and consumption, let us review some concepts in Leisure Studies which, together, show in detail where leisure and consumption are sometimes simultaneously having and doing (consumption as initiator of leisure) and where, at other times, the having and doing are separate processes (consumption as facilitator of leisure).

The serious leisure perspective

Consumption as initiator of leisure or as a facilitator of it varies across the three forms of the serious leisure perspective. This perspective (Stebbins, 2007) may be described, in simplest terms, as the theoretical framework that synthesizes three main forms of leisure, showing, at once, their distinctive features, similarities, and interrelationships. The three forms – serious leisure, casual leisure, and project-based leisure – may be briefly defined as follows:

- serious leisure: systematic pursuit of an amateur, hobbyist, or volunteer activity sufficiently substantial, interesting, and fulfilling for the participant to find a (leisure) career there acquiring and expressing a combination of its special skills, knowledge, and experience;
- casual leisure: immediately, intrinsically rewarding, relatively short-lived pleasurable activity, requiring little or no special training to enjoy it;
- project-based leisure: short-term, reasonably complicated, one-off or occasional, though infrequent, creative undertaking carried out in free time, or time free of disagreeable obligation (Stebbins, 2005a).

The idea of core activity is a further conceptual tool of use in our effort to explore the relationship between leisure and consumption. A *core activity* is a distinctive set of interrelated actions or steps that must be followed in order to achieve the outcome or product that the participant finds attractive (e.g., enjoyable, satisfying, fulfilling). This activity carries with it a substantial, positive emotional component. It lies at the centre of what Dubin (1992) calls a 'central life interest'. In the preceding example, playing the violin is a core activity for the amateur, whereas buying music and rosin, arranging for instrumental repairs, travelling to music lessons, and even purchasing the violin are, by comparison, peripheral activities.

Casual leisure

Much of casual leisure may be qualified as initiatory consumption, even while some kinds of play, relaxation, and sensual stimulation, for instance, are not at all consumptive. The examples presented earlier of buying a CD, a cinema ticket, and the like open the door to casual leisure activities. Considering the eight types of casual leisure allows us to see where initiatory consumption is most likely to occur in this form (Stebbins, 2007: 38–39):

- play (including dabbling, dilettantism);
- relaxation (e.g., sitting, napping, strolling);
- passive entertainment (e.g., through TV, books, recorded music);
- active entertainment (e.g., games of chance, party games);
- sociable conversation (e.g. gossip, 'idle chatter');
- sensory stimulation (e.g., sex, eating, drinking, sight-seeing);
- casual volunteering (e.g., handing out leaflets, stuffing envelopes);
- pleasurable aerobic activity.

The last and newest addition to this typology – pleasurable aerobic activity – refers to physical activities that require effort sufficient to cause marked increase in respiration and heart rate. Here I am referring to 'aerobic activity' in the broad sense, to all activity that calls for such effort, which, to be sure, includes the routines pursued collectively in (narrowly conceived of) aerobics classes and those pursued individually by way of televised or video-taped programmes of aerobics (Stebbins, 2004). Yet, as with its passive and active cousins in entertainment, pleasurable aerobic activity is, at bottom, casual leisure. That is, to do such activity requires little more than minimal skill, knowledge, or experience. Examples include the game of 'hashing' (a type of treasure hunt held in the outdoors which is derived from the activities associated with the Hash House Harriers), kickball (described in *The Economist*, 2005, as a cross between soccer and baseball), and such children's games as hide-and-seek.

People consume on an initiatory basis mainly in passive and active entertainment and, to a lesser extent, in relaxation and sensual stimulation. Much of our entertainment is commercial; it is bought, for example, with subscriptions to cable television and tickets to shows, as well as with instruments of entertainment such as board games, iPods, and DVDs. We may relax after paying the fee for a session at a spa or the price for a drink at a bar. Additionally, some sensory stimulation may be experienced only with the purchase of something: a bag of marijuana, the services of an illegal bookmaker, or a ticket, say, to ride a tour bus, take a scenic cruise on a lake, or go by cable car up the side of a mountain.

Elsewhere in the vast realm of casual leisure, non-consumptive leisure reigns. Some people can relax, without financial outlay, while sitting on their front porch, strolling in a nearby park, or taking a nap. Consensual sexual relations, unless purchased through prostitution or in-kind favours, are free of charge. And so is all of casual volunteering. The same may be said for some of the pleasurable aerobic activities (e.g., kickball, the treasure hunts of the Hash House Harriers).

Serious leisure

Many serious leisure pursuits require one or more prerequisite purchases, but here participants accent the highly appealing core activities of their leisure. This was illustrated above in the vignette about purchasing a violin and then learning to play it. Moreover, here too there are pursuits, including much, if not all, of volunteering, where consumption is negligible, if nonexistent. Here there is no need to acquire something, to buy it or rent it. The same is true for a variety of hobbies, among them the liberal-arts reading hobbies (e.g., reading a kind of history or science), some collecting hobbies (e.g., leaves, seashells, insects), and some outdoor sport and activities (e.g., playing soccer or touch football, walking in nature, swimming in a lake).

Moreover, some interesting exceptions come to mind. Sometimes consumption, though peripheral to the core activity of the serious leisure in question, may nevertheless be quite a momentous act. Thus, buying an expensive, fine violin is a memorable event for the committed amateur violinist, as would be the purchase of a pure-bred dog for a hobbyist dog breeder or a top-class sailboat for a hobbyist sailor.

In fact the complex relationship between consumption and leisure becomes still more involved when the act of acquisition is itself complicated. This complexity, among the serious leisure activities, appears to be most common in the hobby of collecting. Consider the efforts that a coin collector has to make in order to locate and buy a rare specimen. This person must learn where to look for the item, travel to this place to acquire it, and perhaps bargain with its owner for an affordable price. This is, in fact, a core activity of all collecting – acquisition of collectibles – though there are typically other such activities, among them, cataloguing the collectibles acquired and preserving them. Collectors of fine art, old cars, and antique furniture, and possibly other objects, also commonly experience in these complex terms acquisition of their collectibles. Furthermore, the violinist and dog breeder exemplified in the preceding paragraph, even though they are not collectors, may undertake acquisitions at this level of complexity. Given that, in these instances, consumption is itself a core leisure activity, I will refer to such activities as *core facilitative consumption*. They occur during the first phase of consumption, culminating in one or more purchases.

By the way, all that has just been said here about serious leisure and consumption also applies to 'devotee work'. The latter may be conceived of as pleasant obligation, in that such workers, though they must make a living by performing their work, do this in a highly intrinsically appealing activity. Work of this sort is also essentially leisure, recently analysed with serious leisure under the heading of 'serious pursuits' (Stebbins, 2012).

Project-based leisure

Before discussing the relationship of project-based leisure and consumption, let us look at a typology of the first. Whereas systematic exploration may reveal others, two types have so far been identified: one-off projects and occasional projects. These are presented next, using a classificatory framework for amateur, hobbyist, and volunteer activities developed earlier (see Stebbins, 1998, chaps. 2–4).

One-off projects

In all these projects people generally use the talents and knowledge which they have at hand, even though for some projects they may seek certain instructions beforehand, including reading a book or taking a short course. And some projects resembling hobbyist activity participation may require a modicum of preliminary conditioning. Always, the goal is to undertake successfully the one-off project and nothing more, and sometimes a small amount of background preparation is necessary for this. It is possible that a survey would show that most project-based leisure is hobbyist in character, and next most common, a kind of volunteering. First, the following hobbyist-like projects have so far been identified:

- Making and tinkering:
  - interlacing, interlocking, and knot-making from kits
  - other kit-assembly projects (e.g., stereo tuner, craft store projects)
  - do-it-yourself projects done primarily for fulfilment, some of which may even be undertaken with minimal skill and knowledge (e.g., build a rock wall or a fence, finish a room in the basement, plant a special garden). This could turn into an irregular series of such projects, spread over many years, possibly even transforming the participant into a hobbyist.

- Liberal arts:
  - genealogy (not as ongoing hobby)
  - tourism: special trip, not as part of an extensive personal tour programme, to visit different parts of a region, a continent, or much of the world.

- Activity participation:
  - long back-packing trip, canoe trip
  - one-off mountain ascent (e.g., Fuji, Rainier, Kilimanjaro).

One-off volunteering projects are also common, though possibly somewhat less so than hobbyist-like projects. And less common than either are the amateur-like projects, which seem to concentrate in the sphere of theatre.

- Volunteering
  - volunteer at a convention or conference, whether local, national, or international in scope
  - volunteer at a sporting competition, whether local, national, or international in scope
  - volunteer at an arts festival or special exhibition mounted in a museum
  - volunteer to help restore human life or wildlife after a natural or human-made disaster caused by, for instance, a hurricane, earthquake, oil spill, or industrial accident.

- Arts projects (this new category replaces Entertainment Theatre, see Stebbins, 2011):
  - entertainment theatre: produce a skit or one-off community pageant; prepare a home film, video or set of photos
  - public speaking: prepare a talk for a reunion, an after-dinner speech, an oral position statement on an issue to be discussed at a community meeting
  - memoirs: therapeutic audio, visual and written productions by the elderly; life histories and autobiographies (all ages); accounts of personal events (all ages) (Stebbins, 2011).

Occasional projects

The occasional projects seem more likely to originate in or be motivated by agreeable obligation than are their one-off cousins. Examples of occasional projects include the sum of the culinary, decorative, or other creative activities undertaken, for example, at home or at work for a religious occasion or someone's birthday. Likewise, national holidays and similar celebrations sometimes inspire individuals to mount occasional projects consisting of an ensemble of inventive elements.

Project-based leisure may be consumer based. Thus most, if not all, one-off projects require preliminary purchases, though not, however, of the momentous variety, as seen in the example of the expensive violin given earlier. The same may be said for the liberal arts projects, with the possible exception of constructing a genealogy. Although computer programs may be bought for this purpose, some people prepare their genealogies by writing and telephoning relatives and writing up their results by hand (Lambert, 1996). Finally, activity participation seems to invariably involve purchase of equipment and travel services. Indeed, getting to some of these activities, itself often a major commercial undertaking, may be quite involved and not especially pleasant (e.g., international travel to the base of Mount Everest). But this is still not a core activity of the sort described above in acquiring certain collectibles.

By contrast, one-off volunteering projects, with one possible exception, can be qualified as non-consumptive leisure. That is, unless we count as acquisitions the costs of transportation, clothing, and food borne by the volunteer while engaging in the altruistic activity and the festival, museum, or sporting organization does not reimburse these. Nonetheless, some disaster volunteers may have to spend a great deal of money on transportation, lodging, and meals in order to help at the site of a hurricane or oil spill.

Occasional projects seem, much of the time, to require buying something in order to make them possible. Holding a surprise birthday party will have its costs, as will decorating the house and yard for the Christmas season. Here, too, there are exceptions, among them, the research that some people conduct to buy a new car, which they carry out on the Internet and at certain dealers (this example assumes that they are not coerced into making this purchase). Another exception is evident in those who plan a major holiday in a faraway place, which they do by consulting the Internet, certain print media, and, possibly, knowledgeable friends and relatives. Here they engage in a sort of core facilitative consumption.

Conclusions

Much of what has been said here may be summarized in the generalization that consumption in relation to leisure, to the extent that the first is either initiatory or facilitative, is, in part, a practical process: to be able to engage in the leisure, depending on its nature, the participant will have to buy a particular thing or service. A second generalization follows, namely, that the heart of the consumption-based leisure experience, which is found in participating in the core activity or activities, lies outside this practical expenditure. This was discussed earlier as the second phase of consumption. Furthermore, for some kinds of leisure, such monetary outlays, I have argued, are more or less flatly unnecessary; they are non-consumptive leisure.

Two exceptions to the first generalization are, however, also highly important. One of them has already been treated of earlier, namely, core facilitative consumption in Phase One. The other is the role of conspicuous consumption in leisure. Conspicuous consumption elevates significantly the importance for the consumer of the commercial side of this person's leisure. Purchasing expensive, dazzling goods and services earns the buyer a special cachet in the eyes of the other people in his or her circle.

Note, too, that some types of serious leisure, gained through facilitative consumption, can also be conspicuous. For example, someone with the money might purchase season tickets for the best seats in the house for the opera or a major league sport. This would be conspicuous casual leisure, were the buyer a mere consumer of the art or sport, but would be conspicuous serious leisure, were this person a buff. *Consumers*, or *fans*, more or less uncritically consume, for instance, restaurant fare, sports events, or displays of art (concerts, shows, exhibitions) as pure entertainment and sensory stimulation, whereas *buffs* participate in these same situations as more or less knowledgeable, albeit non-professional, experts (Stebbins, 2005b: 6). The latter have been classified as a kind of liberal arts hobbyist (Stebbins, 2007: 28–29).

In sum, it seems that, whereas economists see the act of purchasing a good or service as lying at the heart of consumption, a Leisure Studies-based understanding of the consumptive process puts the accent elsewhere. The latter stresses the first and second phases of consumption, minimizing, in doing this, the demarcating act of acquiring something. To be sure, purchases relate in major ways to the economy, as felt in wages earned, businesses sustained, taxes collected, goods and services purchased, to mention a few. But the motivational and socio-cultural context behind these ways is lost in this kind of analysis. In this respect a Leisure Studies perspective sheds important new light on modern-day acquisition and consumption.

References

Bauman, Z. (2007) *Consuming Life*. Cambridge: Polity Press.

Bryman, A.E. (2004) *The Disneyization of Society*. London: Sage.

Dubin, R. (1992) *Central Life Interests: Creative Individualism in a Complex World*. New Brunswick, NJ: Transaction.

The Economist (2005) 'Up Off the Couch', 22 October.

Gill, B. (1991) 'The Sky Line: Disneyitis', *New Yorker*, 19 April.

Godbey, G. (2004) 'Contemporary Leisure Patterns', in G.S. Cross (ed.) *Encyclopedia of Recreation and Leisure in America*, vol. 1. Detroit, MI: Charles Scribner's Sons.

Lambert, R.D. (1996) 'Doing Family History', *Families* 35 (1) 11–25.

Lewis, P. (1995) 'The Urban Invasion of Rural America: The Emergence of the Galactic City', in E. Castle (ed.) *The Changing American Countryside: Rural People and Places*. Lawrence, KA: University of Kansas Press.

Marcuse, H. (1968) *One-Dimensional Man: Studies in the Ideology of Advanced Industrial Society*. London: Routledge

Pynn, L. (2008) '1,300 Birds Killed in B.C. Gambling Busts', *Calgary Herald*, 1 March.

Ritzer, G. (1993) *The McDonaldization of Society: An Investigation into the Changing Character of Contemporary Social Life*. Thousand Oaks, CA: Pine Forge Press.

Schickel, R. (1986) *The Disney Version: The Life, Times, Art, and Commerce of Walt Disney*, rev. ed. London: Pavilion.

Schor, J. B. (1998) *The Overspent American: Upscaling, Downshifting and the New Consumer*. New York: Basic Books.

Stebbins, R.A. (1998) *After Work: The Search for an Optimal Leisure Lifestyle*. Calgary, AB: Detselig.

Stebbins, R.A. (2004) 'Pleasurable Aerobic Activity: A Type of Casual Leisure with Salubrious Implications', *World Leisure Journal*, 46 (4) 55–58 (also available at www.seriousleisure.net – Digital Library, Other Works).

Stebbins, R.A. (2005a) 'Project-based Leisure: Theoretical Neglect of a Common Use of Free Time', *Leisure Studies* 24 (1) 1–11.

Stebbins, R.A. (2005b) *The Role of Leisure in Arts Administration*. Occasional Paper Series, Paper No. 1. Eugene, OR: Center for Community Arts and Public Policy, University of Oregon (published online at: http://aad.uoregon.edu/icas/documents/stebbins0305.pdf).

Stebbins, R.A. (2007) *Serious Leisure: A Perspective for Our Time.* New Brunswick, NJ: Transaction Publishers.

Stebbins, R.A. (2009) *Leisure and Consumption: Common Ground, Separate Worlds.* New York: Palgrave Macmillan.

Stebbins, R.A. (2011) 'Personal Memoirs, Project-based Leisure and Therapeutic Recreation for Seniors', *Leisure Studies Association Newsletter*, 88 (March): 29–31 (also available at www.seriouslei-sure.net – Digital Library, Leisure Reflections No. 26).

Stebbins, R.A. (2012) *The Idea of Leisure: First Principles.* New Brunswick, NJ: Transaction Publishers.

VandeSchoot, L. (2005) *Navigating the Divide: Muslim Perspectives on Western Conceptualizations of Leisure.* Master's thesis, Wageningen University, Social Spatial Analysis Chair Group.

Veblen, T. (1899) *The Theory of the Leisure Class: An Economic Study of Institutions.* New York: Macmillan.

35

LEISURE AND HIGHER EDUCATION

David Harris

Introduction

Elite education has long been associated with a leisurely lifestyle, from ancient Greece, through Confucian China to post-war France (Bourdieu *et al.*, 1994). In *Pascalian Meditations*, Bourdieu (2000) reminds us that Plato valued *skholē*, an activity (and later a place, a school) where philosophers could congregate away from the demands of everyday necessity and work, and engage in pleasurable speculation. Such speculation, about the nature of Being and its relationships with ideas and language, combined leisure and philosophizing. The ability to delegate dealing with the necessities of life to others (slaves, plebeians, women) enabled philosophers to develop arguments for their own sake, but there was a clear elitism in the practice. Scholastic philosophy was also notoriously unconcerned with scientific or social-scientific accounts of the world. Plato's account of the after-dinner discussions of philosophy involving Socrates and his companions displays the playful and sometimes competitive qualities of the debates in ancient Greece beforehand (Lee, 1964). Socrates' fate – execution after he had annoyed too many members of the Athens elite – also showed the wisdom of a degree of withdrawal from the public gaze, into the groves of Academe.

Modern leisure has usually been compared with paid work, which loses this connection with academic discourse. Classically, leisure helps to 'recreate' suitable stances towards work, with leisure extending as well as contrasting with work, as in Parker (1995). More recently, leisure and work offer similar moments of the same humanizing and pleasurable activities, such as 'flow' (Csikszentmihalyi, 1997). However, the ancient connection between leisure and academic discourse is still present in important ways, for Bourdieu especially, as we shall see. Bourdieu's analysis sketches out the relationships between the leisure pursuits of elite groups and the kind of academic practices favoured in French elite universities in the 1960s.

Bourdieu on elite education

The work on education came first, despite the misleading publication dates for the English editions, and it might be less familiar to students specializing in leisure. Bourdieu's analyses showed that actual lectures in French universities in the 1960s were awash with references to European literature, historical knowledge, and classical cultures. Academic languages dealt in a 'second order language of allusions and cultural complicities' (Sociology Research Group, 1980: 46). This is seen as 'second nature to intelligent and gifted individuals', leading to seemingly 'natural' divisions among students. However, 'academic judgments ... in reality consecrate cultural privilege' (Sociology Research Group, 1980: 46). There is, however, 'a fiction that there is no misunderstanding' (Bourdieu, Passeron and Saint Martin, 1994: 13).

Pedagogy was dominated not by careful attempts to explain concepts but by 'Professorial charisma ... The display of virtuosity, the play of laudatory allusions or depreciatory silences' (Bourdieu and Passeron, 1979: 42). The lectures that Bourdieu and his associates observed were characterized by 'verbal acrobatics, hermetic allusion, disconcerting references, or peremptory obscurity ... technical tricks ... such as the concealment of sources, the insertion of studied jokes ... the avoidance of compromising formulations [which might prove to be wrong]' (Bourdieu and Passeron, 1990: 125). Approaches involving seriousness and hard work were not seen as a properly academic approach. For example, students and many professors would consider any kind of practical instruction about coping with university life – like how to draw up a bibliography – as demeaning, the act of a 'vulgar schoolmaster' (Bourdieu and Passeron, 1979: 3). Instead, upper-class students and professors adopted a romantic image of free, inspired creation. Successful students learned to reproduce the same style in their essays, as a kind of echo of the professorial lecture. Tests administered by Bourdieu and his associates in their own research questioned the myth of effective, transparent communication, however: they revealed 'imperfect comprehension of academic language, and even of common language' (Sociology Research Group, 1980: 81).

It was not the fault of the students. Academic pedagogy is about status rather than efficiency. It expresses values, codes, and notions of who is worthy to receive it (Bourdieu and Passeron, 1990). It produces a 'distinguished distance, prudent ease, and a contrived naturalness'. By contrast, working-class language is expressive and particularistic, moving from case to case, from 'illustration to parable', avoiding fine words (Bourdieu and Passeron, 1990: 116). In elite universities, manners contaminate all practice. It is important to demonstrate natural ease, casual delivery, and 'stylistic understatement', and never to be too demonstrative, which will only lead to a suspicion of 'self-interested vulgarity' (Bourdieu and Passeron, 1990: 119). It is far more effective to go along with the fiction of an egalitarian exchange with one's assessors.

Why was the particular elite and scholastic curriculum content and pedagogic style seen as so obviously relevant and of such universal interest? There are no technical reasons. Bourdieu argues that curriculum contents and pedagogical approaches represent a 'cultural arbitrary', a set of values and tastes embodied in an elite group: this is represented to other groups as naturally right, in a form of 'symbolic violence', although this is misrecognized again. Thus, universities seem neutral in any struggle between classes and groups, able to protect science and critique as above petty conflicts, as the embodiment of 'the Utopian vision of the "critical university"' (Bourdieu and Passeron, 1990: 65). In practice, social class origin plus uneven career possibilities 'transmute a social inequality into a specifically educational inequality' (Bourdieu and Passeron, 1990: 158). For many participants, these processes of transmutation are 'the strategies of the habitus ... more unconscious than conscious' (Bourdieu, 1988: 91). There is no need to actually calculate the best route through a university career – the effective path just seems natural to elite students. In this way 'capital breeds capital' (Bourdieu, 1988: 91).

Some systems made the link especially clear, Bourdieu tells us – in Mandarin China candidates had to pass an examination before they were admitted to the elite civil service, but the test was based on knowledge of Confucian texts. This equally arbitrary curriculum, seen as perfectly sensible and natural, no doubt, confined admission in practice only to those members of a cultivated elite who had had the leisure time free from necessity to devote years to the study of the texts. With the cult of the British amateur gentleman, the same features applied, albeit in a less explicit form, and gentlemanly leisure interests, manners and dispositions were the basis of selection for the elite ranks of the UK civil service too, even after formal admissions.

Bourdieu on leisure and taste

Explicit links between leisure preference and elite status emerged from Bourdieu's (1984) study of leisure in France. This used some extensive empirical analysis which showed definite patterns of preferences in leisure and cultural matters between the social classes, between various other social groups such as the genders, and between Parisians and provincials. These patterns can be explained in terms of underlying tastes. Briefly, popular tastes reflect an 'aesthetic' involving an interest in immediate participation, based on easy emotional identification with events or objects. Elite tastes, posing as a 'pure aesthetic' are set up in opposition to popular versions, and value emotional distance, calm contemplation, and the formal qualities of the work or the technical analysis of the effects.

To take an example, people varied in their reactions to being shown photographs, including one of an old woman's work-worn hands. A manual worker expressed sympathy with the suffering represented by the gnarled fingers, whereas a Parisian (elite) engineer showed 'An aestheticising reference to painting, sculpture, or literature ... [which indicates] ... the neutralization and distancing which bourgeois discourse about the social world requires and performs. "I find this a very beautiful photograph ... It puts me in mind of Flaubert's old servant-woman"' (Bourdieu, 1984: 45).

What this shows is that the structure of tastes has a major political function in closing off barriers to entry to elite groups: only those with the right cultural tastes can fully belong. It is not even easy to learn what is culturally acceptable later in life, since much learning goes on during childhood and the results are stored in the unconscious, in the form of a 'habitus'. Children growing up in elite families, especially Parisian ones, are taken to visit museums and art galleries, and the opera, they read and discuss 'quality' newspapers, and indulge in 'educated' talk about philosophy and literature. Those who have developed such a habitus are able without conscious thought to produce effortless commentary on any emerging cultural matters, and to immediately distinguish 'good' and 'bad' taste, in a way which is recognized by other members of the elite, and which signals that they belong. In other words, the upbringing of elite children, including the provision of suitable leisure, provides them with a store of 'cultural capital' which can be used to gain social advantage.

British leisure: the case of Bourdieu and Bennett *et al.*

Whether the foregoing analysis applies to contemporary leisure practices, especially in the UK, is more debatable. A substantial study by Bennett, Savage, Silva, Warde, Gayo-Cal and Wright (2009), set out to test Bourdieu (1984) with reference to modern British leisure interests, and found a rather different picture. There still were class differences in both taste for and participation in leisure pursuits, but this varied quite widely across the different fields. Music and the visual arts, for example, featured substantial class divisions, but in fields like sport, age and gender differences were more apparent. Ethnicity also emerged as a significant factor in producing significant clusters of preferences (for example in music).

Those clusters indicate some sort of general patterning (so that those who like opera also like eating in French restaurants), but nothing like a general class outlook. Intensity of interest and participation also varies, and with them the ability for cultural activities to involve the process of making social distinctions. Thus contemporary music is more intense than, say, watching television, so it can generate social tensions 'to some extent along the lines of class and educational qualifications, but more importantly on the basis of age and ethnicity' (Bennett *et al.*, 2009: 93). As one curious example shows, eating in Italian restaurants specifically seems to have no social significance at all. In sport, class seems to affect rates of participation mostly, and there is little social significance in preferences. However, body types are still very significant in social terms, and especially important is the 'exercised and cultivated body … Bodies display the insignia of unequal possession of cultural capital' (Bennett *et al.*, 2009: 169).

The complexity that emerges is enough for Bennett and his colleagues to break with Bourdieu's schema. Cultural capital must be disaggregated rather than tied to class. Leisure fields themselves vary in their internal organization, offering an 'assemblage of personal, technical and institutional forms' (*ibid*: 171), and in their social significance. It is more common for people to develop tastes for different sorts of culture across the 'low' and 'high' divide, as in 'cultural omnivorousness'. This will lead to different types of cultural capitals which are mobilized in different combinations.

In the midst of complexity, it is surprising to find Bennett and his colleagues occasionally insisting that social class is still important, though: 'Despite only limited evidence for a self conscious middle class, a pervasive and powerful middle class cultural dominance exists' (*ibid*: 179); members of the middle-class groups talk of their own hybridity or mobility, but still 'require and reproduce the classifications and idioms of class' (*ibid*: 193); overall there are still 'subtle boundaries', despite 'reflexive appropriation' (*ibid*: 194); knowledge of elite culture conveys some career advantages 'personal introductions … jobs after retirement, invitations on the social circuit … access to positions in voluntary associations' (*ibid*: 190). There is no apparent snobbishness, though, no contempt for popular leisure pursuits, and thus no active role for these class perceptions, no attempts at class closure based on them.

However, we might question the sincerity of some of the responses to the research questions. The problem is that apparent toleration of popular culture may be 'an insincere affectation' (*ibid*: 189). Turner and Edmonds (2002: 237), in their study of Australian elites, discover a tactical element, too, 'a cultural strategy that we have called the distaste of taste', which helps to avoid unnecessary attention and thus a challenge to the legitimacy of privilege.

Further methodological differences between Bourdieu and Bennett *et al.* also make any simple comparisons difficult. For example, Bourdieu is drawn by theoretical and political commitments to focus on class and minimize the effects of gender, Bennett *et al.* insist, while he was simply legally unable to ask about ethnicity in his 1984 study (Bennett *et al.*, 2009: 38). However, Bourdieu discusses several mediating effects on the basic division between the aesthetics produced by distributions of cultural capital, including the influence of other types of capital (economic, social, and educational), and the different opportunities to convert one type into the others. This explains some of the important details of taste in certain class fractions – the petite bourgeoisie, for example tend to have good stocks of educational and cultural capital but poor stocks of economic and social capital, which leaves them unable to be fully incorporated into the elite, but culturally distant from the masses. Hence their cultural restlessness and their liking for the artistic avant-garde. It is worth adding that Bennett *et al.* seem not to discuss conversion of capitals at all and prefer to see leisure and education as separate, as in the usual academic division of labour in Britain. For them, educational diplomas are now an important part of claims to privilege, replacing leisure, but, unlike Bourdieu, they do not inquire about the links between educational success and elite leisure pursuits in the first place.

Additional differences, turning on the technicalities of the types of statistical analysis involved in the two studies, can be left aside here. The general differences involve notions of the role of empirical research. For Bourdieu, the interest is in formulating underlying theoretical models which explain empirical complexity, while for Bennett *et al.* the discovery of complexity is an important finding in its own right. This is not a simple division between French theorists and British concerns with 'facts', however, since a preference for complexity is itself based on a theoretical position embracing a particular picture of modernity with no classic social divisions and much greater distance between culture and the economy.

One item in the dispute is of particular interest here, though. Bourdieu suggests that at the heart of the high aesthetic is a focus on form rather than content. In the Postscript to Bourdieu (1984), he controversially suggests that formal philosophical aesthetics, especially Kant's, have enshrined formalism as a key to understanding 'the sublime', but that Kant's categories themselves really just reproduce elite tastes. In Bennett *et al.* the 'Kantian aesthetic' issue becomes further operationalized as a split between bourgeois disinterestedness in cultural matters versus a taste for the necessary among the masses. Indeed, Bennett and his colleagues find no interest in formalism, or in any philosophical analysis of the beautiful and the sublime in Britain. This specifically explains the absence of a taste for the avant-garde, and more generally casts doubt on Bourdieu's entire schema.

In what follows, it might be possible to revive Bourdieu's analysis by reconsidering the taste for the formal, but of a more technical type. Technical competence in analysing cultural activities seems to be associated with the cultural omnivores, for example, and to lie behind the cultural confidence of the middle-class individuals in managing participation in the different forms of leisure activity: some films might be classified as 'realist', for example. Taking a technical stance implies a certain neutralization, a disinterestedness, and an interest in matters beyond what is dictated by 'the necessary' or the immediate, it could be argued. It also requires a certain security which can underpin any cultural adventures. This stance still pays dividends in higher education, it can be argued.

British higher education

Whether this sort of realization of cultural capital takes place in the UK sector is harder to establish. Although Halsey, Heath and Ridge (1980) found few cultural problems facing working-class entrants to elite universities, some other studies of working-class women undergraduates (e.g. Plummer 2000) report many cases of cultural ill-ease, usually focused on matters such as managing academic language, coping with the style of argument or dealing with the embarrassment of verbal presentations.

After the emergence of a mass university system, these cultural styles might be diminishing. Plain speech and new teaching methods involving objectives, presentations, electronic teaching, and demands for transparent and accountable forms of assessment could be seen as signs of dilution. However, elite styles are still present, at least in written forms. To take a recent example, the work of the French philosopher Gilles Deleuze seems to be becoming popular in British circles, even though he was writing in the classic French elite style in the 1960s and 1970s. The challenges presented to current British students by Deleuzian work can be seen by considering one small sample:

417

The body without organs is like the cosmic egg, the giant molecule swarming with worms, bacilli, Lilliputian figures, animalcules, and homunculi, with their organization and their machines, minute strings, ropes, teeth, fingernails, levers and pulleys, catapults: thus in Schreber the millions of spermatazoids in the sunbeams, or the souls that lead a brief existence as little men on his body. Artaud says: this world of microbes, which is nothing more than coagulated nothingness.

(Deleuze and Guattari, 1984: 281)

Anyone unable to recognize the reference to a famous Freudian case – that of Dr Schreber – to Lacan's account of that case, which Deleuze and Guattari wish to criticize, or to the work of the schizophrenic poet and playwright Antonin Artaud, or anyone unattuned to playful French avant-garde literary style might be expected to struggle even more with this sort of discourse. Yet they would skip at their peril, because the 'body without organs' is a major figure in Deleuzian philosophy and it is hard to proceed very far without considering its implications. The literal implications of Freud's or Artaud's works are not really the issue, though, since Deleuze wants to encourage intellectual curiosity and allude to his position, before eventually developing a model of reality. In the process, other metaphors, allusions, and analogies abound, which helps to avoid any schoolmasterly directness or vulgarity. The works actually require a leisured reading, one which feels secure enough not to have to demonstrate understanding in exchange for a grade, one which can take its time, reflect on arguments, enjoy puzzles, and acquire clues to meanings through the slow accumulation of insights.

There are limited studies of how cultural capital might affect aspects of an educational career, but there is no systematic study of British higher education and its academic discourses to compare with Bourdieu's. Perhaps the nearest was the SOMUL (the Social Mediation of University Learning) study of student experience which argued that the UK higher education system is now quite diverse, in terms of student intake, courses on offer, and organizational arrangement for teaching and learning. However, 'the class composition of participants is proving resistant to change' (Houston and Lebeau, 2006: 5). Given the empirical nature of the study, it is not surprising that the familiar discovery of complexity ensued. There is the same ambivalence about Bourdieu as in the Bennett *et al.* study discussed above, possibly for the same reasons. For example, quoting Bourdieu and Passeron: 'We would not object to Bourdieu's view on the role the school system plays in "ratifying, sanctifying and transforming the cultural inheritance that comes from the family as scholastic merit"', yet the main effect of different stocks of cultural capital seems to be to affect 'the lives of students and their interactions with others', rather than their academic performance (Houston and Lebeau, 2006: 7). The SOMUL study did not attempt to theorize about matters like the role of elite leisure tastes and did not examine teaching styles in order to demonstrate the effects of cultural capital on academic discourse: it would probably be unethical now to do so.

There are some smaller studies on the possible effects of cultural capital at different stages in the system, often offering ingenious attempts to measure cultural capital in various ways. For example Noble and Davies (2009) have designed a short questionnaire to test the effects of low levels of cultural capital on application to university. They tested levels of cultural capital by asking about participation in elite leisure interests, including attending art galleries and museums, and going to classical concerts. They found that students' own levels of cultural capital did have an effect separate from that of their parents. At the other end of a career, Stempel (2006) suggests a link between cultural capital acquired while playing sport and subsequent employment. In a systematic analysis of American data, Stempel shows that it is not that sport 'builds character' or offers 'transferable skills', but, rather, that talking about sport helps applicants to bond with employers, confirming what Bennett *et al.* said about networking (above).

There is a less direct area that also might be worth exploring – the work on study skills. In some of the work, there is a recognition of the aesthetics of contemporary academic culture (Arksey and Harris, 2007). Here we might return to the issues of form and disinterestedness stressed by Bourdieu as a constituent of elite tastes, although with a technical emphasis. At their most specific, assessment regulations often indicate the importance of being 'objective' or 'critical', for example, which requires the sort of emotional detachment and interest in form (of arguments in this case) that seem characteristic of elite aesthetics. The classificatory interests and management strategies of the leisure omnivores in the Bennett study can also be seen as compatible with academic work, and some of the omnivores were actually engaged in higher education. More generally, the widespread claimed benefits of a 'deep' approach are usually introduced as a matter of orientations to learning, but the early work sometimes expressed matters of taste, such as an open distaste for 'surface' engagement with educational material and assignments (see Harris, 1995). Given the psychological orientations of the studies, there is no specific interest in any social origins of these approaches to study, however.

Higher education as leisure

The final set of possible links between higher education and leisure involves a reversal of the connections we have been discussing so far. Higher education might have an impact on subsequent leisure activities. After all, higher education can provide stocks of cultural capital itself, and this can be converted back into leisure. Bourdieu is sceptical about whether educational experiences can cancel out family advantage altogether, when it comes to social closure, but there still might be some relative personal benefits. Kjølsrød's (2003) examination of 'specialised play' involves people finding particular significance in activities such as collecting various objects. Such play provides not only its own kind of excitement and pleasure but also an opportunity to experiment with personal identity, to find personal meaning in leisure activities. These pleasures are enhanced if people are able to bring to the task educational capital, having learned about the history of their particular interest, for example, or being able to classify specimens or research particular topics. These pleasures can be extended to other kinds of activities too, of course, as when knowledgeable football fans are particularly able to develop allegories (Guttmann, 1986), which links the success of their team to the success of themselves, their town or their nation.

There is also an argument that higher education itself can be conceived as a leisure activity in its own right. A more extensive discussion is available in Harris (2012), but, briefly, this is seen best, perhaps, in those engaged in lifelong learning. Jones and Symon (2001) say that their activities can be well described using the familiar term 'serious leisure'.

Even conventional contact with higher education at the undergraduate level can yield pleasure characteristic of leisure activities. Several analysts (for example Cohen, 2004) have argued that higher education is in fact being colonized by the values and processes of work, showing themselves in the form of rational organization, bureaucratic management, quality-control regimes, the audit culture and so on. Leisurely engagements with text of the kind suggested above are being squeezed out of the system. Nevertheless, some pleasures still seem necessary, if motivation is to be maintained, for staff and students.

Certainly, the pleasures of flow, for example, still seem available. There is still that ability to engross oneself in academic work in order to experience that avoidance of mundane problems, to be able to balance competence and challenge in meaningful ways. Some pedagogues have even attempted to build the experience of flow into the design of assignments for their students (Shin, 2006). There are even pleasures in taking risks and overcoming them in a way which leads to some personal insight about oneself and one's capabilities. We are accustomed to analysing this kind of pleasure in areas such as extreme sports, using concepts such as 'edgework' (Lyng, 1990), but there could be equivalents in learning to enjoy the risks of academic life – risking a low grade or the mortification of a poor presentation and coming through.

Finally, there are still pleasures of escape, detachment and speculation, just as with the ancient Greek example that we began with, suitably modified, of course. Thus Quinn (2007) describes the pleasures of being able to think subversive thoughts, pursue personal projects, and gain an element of detachment from and mastery over routine patterns of thinking. The challenge for modern mass education could well be to block the further intrusion of work-like practices and make higher education more like leisure for all.

References

Arksey, H. and Harris, D. (2007) *How to Succeed in Your Social Science Degree*. London: Sage.

Bennett, T., Savage, M., Silva, E., Warde, A., Gayo-Cal, M. and Wright, D. (2009) *Culture, Class, Distinction*. London: Routledge.

Bourdieu, P. (1984) *Distinction: A Social Critique of the Judgement of Taste*. London: Routledge.

Bourdieu, P. (1988) *Homo Academicus*. Cambridge: Polity Press.

Bourdieu, P. (2000) *Pascalian Meditations*. Cambridge: Polity Press.

Bourdieu, P. and Passeron, J.-C. (1979) *The Inheritors: French Students and Their Relation to Culture*. Chicago: University of Chicago Press.

Bourdieu, P. and Passeron, J.-C. (1990) *Reproduction in Education, Society and Culture*, 2nd ed., London: Sage Publications.

Bourdieu, P., Passeron, J.-C. and Saint Martin, M. (1994) *Academic Discourse*. Cambridge: Polity.

Cohen, P. (2004) 'A Place to Think? Some Reflections on the Idea of the University in the Age of the "Knowledge Economy"', *New Formations* 53 (12) 12–27.

Csikszentmihalyi, M. (1997) *Finding Flow: The Psychology of Engagement with Everyday Life*. New York: Basic Books.

Deleuze, G. and Guattari, F. (1984) *Anti-Oedipus: Capitalism and Schizophrenia*. London: The Athlone Press.

Guttmann, A. (1986) *Sports Spectators*. New York: Columbia Press.

Halsey, A., Heath, A. and Ridge, J. (1980) *Origins and Destinations. Family, Class and Education in Modern Britain*. Oxford: Clarendon Press.

Harris, D. (1995) 'Still Seeking the Audience?', in F. Lockwood (ed.) *Research and Development in Distance Education*. London: Routledge.

Harris, D. (2012) 'Work and Leisure in Higher Education', *British Journal of Sociology of Education* 33 (1) 115–132.

Houston, M. and Lebeau, Y. (2006) *The Social Mediation of University Learning*. SOMUL Working Paper 3, available from: http://www.open.ac.uk/cheri/documents/somul_wp03.pdf

Jones, I. and Symon, G. (2001) 'Lifelong Learning as Serious Leisure: Policy, practice and potential', *Leisure Studies* 20: 269–283.

Kjølsrød, L. (2003) 'Adventure Revisited: On structure and metaphor in specialized play', *Sociology* 37 (3) 459–476.

Lee, H. (1964) *Plato: The Republic*. Harmondsworth: Penguin.

Lyng, S. (1990) 'Edgework: A social psychological analysis of voluntary risk-taking', *American Journal of Sociology* 95 (4) 851–886.

Noble, J. and Davies, P. (2009) 'Cultural Capital as an Explanation of Variation in Participation in Higher Education', *British Journal of Sociology of Education* 30 (5) 591–605.

Parker, S. (1995) 'Towards a Theory of Work and Leisure', in C. Critcher, P. Bramham and A. Tomlinson (eds) *Sociology of Leisure: A Reader.* London: E & F Spon.

Plummer. K. (2000) *Failing Working Class Girls.* Stoke-on-Trent: Trentham Books.

Quinn, J. (2007) 'Welcome to the Pleasure Dome: Women taking pleasure in the university', in P. Cottrill, S. Jackson and G. Letherby (eds) *Challenges and Negotiations for Women in Higher Education.* Dordecht, Netherlands: Springer.

Shin, M. (2006) 'Online Learners' "Flow" Experience: An empirical study', *British Journal of Educational Technology* 37: 705–720.

Sociology Research Group in Cultural and Education Studies (eds) (1980) *Melbourne Working Papers 1980.* University of Melbourne.

Stempel, C. (2006) 'Gender, Social Class, and the Sporting Capital–Economic Capital Nexus', *Sociology of Sport Journal* 23: 273–292.

Turner, B. and Edmonds, J. (2002) 'The Distaste of Taste: Bourdieu, cultural capital and the Australian postwar elite', *Journal of Consumer Culture* 2 (2) 219–240.

36

LEISURE, NATIONAL IDENTITY AND CELEBRATING NATIONAL DIFFERENCE

Alan Bairner

Introduction

Central to debates about the origins, characteristics and implications of globalization has been the widespread belief that cultural differences are disappearing under the weight of global forces. Amongst those cultural forms that are deemed to be threatened with eventual extinction are those closely associated with national identity. This chapter touches on the main elements of that argument before developing the thesis that in response to globalization, many national cultures are fighting back, resulting in the widespread celebration of what makes people nationally distinct (Bairner, 2005). Empirical evidence in support of this position can be found in a wide range of apparently diverse leisure experiences, including sport, eating and drinking, and domestic life. It is argued here that, whilst some leisure activities are more susceptible than others to global forces, often with complex consequences, it is still possible to identify close links between national identity and various cultural forms in numerous parts of the world. Indeed, to fully understand leisure practices wherever they occur, it is vitally important that questions relating to national identity are addressed.

The global and the national

It has frequently been argued that the various processes that have come to be known collectively as globalization pose a major threat to nations and to identities created and supported by the concept of the nation. The argument is perfectly straightforward even though it is commonly expressed in far from accessible language. Put simply, economic, political, cultural and ideological trends, supported by a pervasive and all-powerful global media industry, must inevitably destroy the distinctiveness upon which nations, nationalism and national identities depend for their very existence. For some this means the triumph, at least temporarily, of what Tom Nairn (2002: 147) describes as 'the dissemination of a secular faith, the new monotheism of cure-all Free Trade, or marketolatry'. For other commentators, globalization understood in this way will inevitably culminate in something even more specific, namely the universal acceptance of a peculiarly American way of doing things – ironic, given that part of the argument aims to prove that all nations are doomed (Ritzer, 2004). Others are more precise on this point and suggest that all nation-states and national cultures are in danger of being subsumed within a new global order accompanied by its own homogeneous culture. Indeed, John Urry has challenged the very notion that what has emerged has been a struggle between the national and the global, with the latter being characterized as a new region. This 'territorial trap', as Urry (2003: 43) calls it, ignores the fact that global systems are by their nature entropic and challenge the very notion of the bounded region.

Specifically in relation to sport, Miller *et al.* (2001: 59) argue that the global exchange of sporting bodies 'has made it increasingly difficult for the nation-state to be represented by conventional corporeal symbols, as the spread of schooling, commodification, scientization, medicalization, and surveillance as part of the NICL [New International Division of Cultural Labor] has reorganized sporting bodies'. Maguire *et al.* (2002: 4) suggest that 'modern sport is bound up in a global network of interdependency chains that are marked by uneven power relations'. The consequence is a set of global power networks within which 'the practice and consumption of elite modern sport can best be understood' (Maguire *et al.*, 2002: 4). 'Given this growth in the multiplicity of linkages and networks that transcend nation-states', they continue, 'it is not surprising that we may be at the earliest stages of the development of a transnational or global culture, of which sport is a part' (Maguire *et al.*, 2002: 7).

Elsewhere, however, Maguire (1994) presents a subtler and altogether more seductive version of the globalization thesis to argue that the concept describes a process in which there is considerable exchange of cultural values and modes of expression. According to this interpretation, the nation as we have known it may well be about to disappear, but it will do so not because of the triumph of a single and unidirectional tendency – e.g. Americanization – but, rather, because all national cultures borrow and will continue to borrow from each other. For Maguire, the result is a world that is characterized by 'diminishing contrasts', but also by 'increasing varieties'. The prognosis remains, however, that distinctive national identities, as traditionally understood, will still disappear. Against the cultural convergence thesis of globalization, indeed, stands the argument that 'globalization does not necessarily imply homogenization or integration' (Waters, 1995: 136). As Robertson (1995: 34) contends, for example, 'it makes no sense to define the global as if the global excludes the local'.

There is, of course, another approach that argues even more forcefully that the demise of the nation and the concomitant triumph of a global order have both been greatly exaggerated. As Anthony D. Smith (1995: 2) points out, 'in the era of globalization and transcendence, we find ourselves caught in a maelstrom of conflicts over political identities and ethnic fragmentation'. Indeed, it can be claimed that the forces associated with the idea of globalization have actually created political and cultural space in which historically submerged nations and nationalities have been reawakened and infused with new vitality. According to Smith (1995: 7), 'only by grasping the power of nationalism and the continuing appeal of national identity through their rootedness in pre-modern ethnic symbolism and modes of organization is there some chance of understanding the resurgence of ethnic nationalism at a time when "objective" conditions might appear to render it obsolete'. In terms of understanding the precise nature of nations and nationalism, the crucial debate, as we shall see in the next section, has been between those who argue that the nation is a natural phenomenon founded on tangible material factors and those who emphasize the invented, manufactured or even imagined character of nationhood. In the discussion that follows we shall see evidence that supports both of these positions. In addition, and particularly relevant to the subject matter of this chapter, is the claim that the idea of the nation often resides in those seemingly banal aspects of everyday life (Billig, 1995; Edensor, 2002). Indeed, there is, arguably, no better way to test the validity of rival perspectives on globalization and on the idea of the nation than to examine activities that are part of everyday human existence and are central to the ways in which people see themselves and are seen by others. To this end, the chapter examines sport, eating and drinking, and design, with specific reference to the production and reproduction of national identities.

Sport

In recent years, there has emerged a considerable and growing literature on the relationship between sport, nations and national identities (Cronin, 1999; Cronin and Mayall, 1998; Hargreaves, 2000; Bairner, 2001; Smith and Porter, 2004; Silk *et al.*, 2005). This is scarcely surprising, given Billig's (1995: 93) assertion that 'nationhood is near the surface of contemporary life' and the fact that sport is similarly visible, not least through the media. At times, there is some terminological and conceptual slippage in the resultant debates, as seen in the interchangeable use of the concepts of nation-state and nation and of nationality and national identity. Nevertheless, as Allison (2000: 345) argues, 'whether we are talking about nationalism or patriotism or the development and expression of national identity ... it is clear that a national dimension is an important part of sport'. For Miller *et al.* (2001: 31), 'the sporting body bears triumphant national mythologies in a double way, extending the body to encompass the nation and compressing it to obscure the social divisions that threaten national unity'. These claims can be amply supported by evidence drawn from a wide variety of countries and an array of different sporting contexts. For most sportsmen and -women, even in an era when money is a major incentive for sporting success, representing the nation still matters. Of course, it is not inconceivable, and is becoming more common, that athletes might represent more than one nation, with neither ethnic origins nor even well-established civic connections being necessary for a move from one to another. Thus, Ticher (1994: 75) refers to 'an increasing number of international players, across a whole range of sports, whose apparently "obvious" nationality conflicts with the country they represent'. Nevertheless, for the overwhelming majority of athletes engaged in international sport today, the matter is still relatively clear cut. For fans, moreover, things are, arguably, even more straightforward. Following one's 'proxy warriors' (Hoberman, 1984) into international competition is perhaps one of the easiest and most potentially gratifying ways of underlining one's sense of national identity, one's nationality or a combination of the two. As a consequence, it is worth examining some of the underlying factors that help to make nations matter in the world of sport.

As prefigured earlier, it is relatively standard practice in sociological and political studies of nations and nationalisms to differentiate between primordialist (or ethno-symbolist) and modernization perspectives (Smith, 1998). Central to the former is the belief that nationalist attachments or relations are associated with the significance attributed to criteria that are perceived to be objective – language, ethnicity, geography, religion – and which are almost certain to predate the emergence of the modern nation-state and of nationalism as a modern political ideology. As Machin (2007: 12–13) notes, 'today, this idea is considered deeply suspect'. The more popular perspective, on the other hand, focuses on nations and nationalisms as modern inventions or imaginings which emerge in response to new social and economic challenges (Anderson, 1991; Hobsbawm and Ranger, 1992, and see Blackshaw, 2010). However, as Machin (2007: 13) observes, this rationalist, modernization thesis 'reveals the contingency of the nation but struggles to understand its apparent inevitability and its common potency'. Somewhere between those two extreme positions are various assertions that, whilst nations and nationalism may indeed be modern and nation-states most certainly are, their existence and resilience rely heavily on the presence of certain historic criteria, both real and imagined, upon which nationalists themselves consistently draw.

In relation to the primordialism–modernization debate, Lefebvre (1991: 112) asserts, 'both of these approaches to the question of the nation, the argument from nature and the argument from ideology, leave space out of the picture'. However, this is less true of the primordialist or ethno-symbolist position than of the modernist perspective. For example, Grosby (2007: 110) refers to the importance of 'a bounded, territorial focus that distinguishes the collective consciousness of a nation from that of other social relations'. It is on that basis that we can argue that a discussion of the possibility that modern sports can generate support for a qualified primordial perspective is far less absurd or irrational than initial reactions might suppose. More specifically, it is argued here that the relationship between national sports and the landscapes with which they are commonly associated assists greatly in helping us to understand the reproduction of certain readings of the nation. Indeed, according to Hechter (2000: 14), '*territoriality* is one objective criterion that does seem to be a necessary characteristic of the nation'. Thus, it is vitally important, as Sörlin (1999: 103) advocates, to understand 'the different processes of articulation and re-articulation of landscapes in the context of shaping national and regional images and identities'. One such conduit is sport (see Bairner, 2009).

The significance of landscape in relation to the representation of nations is seldom more apparent than in the lyrics of national anthems. Whilst some national songs refer to former battles, to leaders and to heroes, and even to the nation as a largely abstract entity, many focus on a national landscape, with Croats celebrating their 'beautiful homeland', Danes their 'lovely land' and Swedes their 'loveliest land on earth'. Given that major international sporting events have become amongst the most regular and prominent settings for renditions of such anthems, the relationship between sport, nation and landscape already begins to emerge. But there is more to this relationship than a coincidental coming together of related phenomena, not least because, as Sörlin (1999: 109) has it, 'People belong to nations and provinces and towns and villages, to a large extent because of that acquired sense of having been connected to place and memory'.

There are numerous criteria that can be invoked in attempting to define what constitutes a national sport (Bairner, 2009). However, it can surely be demonstrated that national sports and games are in some sense linked to what is thought to be the essence of specific nations, even though their actual origins may be pre-national or at least prior to the emergence of nation-states. They represent the nation symbolically, despite the fact that they may well have demonstrably failed to capture the interest of a majority of the people who comprise the civic nation and/or the nation-state. They are played and watched by people who, at least in the eyes of nationalists, truly belong, rather than by those whose authenticity as national beings is open to question. In addition, activities of this type may well be used by those whose role it is to promote the nation, its products and its tourism industry precisely because these national sports testify to what are projected as unique characteristics of the nation and, more specifically, of the national landscape – cricket in England, ice hockey in Canada, skiing in Austria, golf in Scotland and so on. The landscapes that are intimately bound up with defining certain sports as 'national' are real enough. Benedict Anderson (1991) is regularly invoked in discussions on the relationship between sport and national identity formation (Smith and Porter, 2004). One wonders, however, to what extent the 'imagined communities' thesis is in danger of becoming overused, such that it comes to represent nothing other than the claim that national identity is all in the mind, with no material basis, whereas it was initially intended to help us understand the complex nature of national identity formation, weaving together as it does both objective and subjective factors. Blackshaw (2010: 119) argues that 'there is more "imagined" than "community"' in Benedict Anderson's imagined communities. This is almost certainly true. Nevertheless, the national communities that are 'imagined' are not simply the idealized products of fertile nationalist imaginations. On the other hand, only on rare occasions are they unique to any particular nation, and hardly ever are they typical of the nation in its entirety. These are real landscapes which become inscribed in the imagination of many, perhaps most, members of the national community and, most notably, they are largely unaffected by globalization except where the extraction of natural resources is crucial to the global economy.

Some sports, of course, cannot so easily be linked to the material essence of specific nations. A global game such as association football, for example, whilst given its first modern formulation on the playing fields of English public schools, is no longer associated in the popular imagining with any specific landscape, national or otherwise. Yet there is arguably no other sport which has been so regularly linked to specific nations through reference to the evolution of playing styles (Wilson, 2009). As Wilson (2009: 6) demonstrates, 'globalization is blurring national styles, but tradition, perpetuated by coaches, players, pundits and fans, is strong enough that they remain distinguishable'. As indeed do the fans who, in apparent defiance of homogenizing trends, go to greater and greater lengths with face painting and *faux* national dress to identify themselves as culturally different. In various ways, therefore, sport offers us examples of how the real and the imagined combine to foster a sense of national identity. A similar process is discernible in other areas of social life, not least the activity of eating and drinking.

Eating and drinking

Food is often cited as an example of how globalization makes connections between people, cultures and places (Hannerz, 1996). Indeed, arguably the most extreme version of the concept of globalization is that which charts the course of cultural convergence not simply towards homogenization in general but, more specifically, as mentioned earlier, Americanization. Whilst this may not have occurred in the sense of the global adoption of American sports, the ubiquity of Coca-Cola, Starbucks and McDonald's may offer incontrovertible proof for such a claim. To sit in a Starbucks in Derby is not the same as sitting in a Starbucks in Seattle, even though it involves partaking of the same global phenomenon. For Jean Baudrillard, one of the distinguishing features of modern societies is their entry into and acceptance of the 'hyperreal', both simulated and 'realer than real' (Baudrillard, 1983). To that extent, eating a Big Mac is a simulated American experience, even if one is sitting in a McDonald's in Europe or Asia. Whether it can be described as an authentically American experience is a different matter. Whatever one's conclusion, however, this consideration begs the additional question as to whether or not this type of apparently homogenizing experience, also exemplified by the proliferation of Chinese restaurants throughout the world (Wu and Cheng, 2002), undermines national identity and, in particular, its association with food and drink.

According to Bell and Valentine (1997: 165), 'a nation's diet can have a key role to play in nationalistic sentiments, with threatened invasions of "filthy foreign food" being seen as dangerous to the whole fabric of national identity'. However, as Cwiertka (2006: 178) argues, 'the national cuisine emerges as a result of negotiation between the local and the foreign'. Furthermore, the 'filthy foreign food' that arrives with globalization is generally different, to varying degrees, from the food that is eaten in that particular cuisine's nation of origin, modified as it is to suit the tastes of the host nation. For example, although Roberts (2002: 216) asserts that 'the spread of Chinese food throughout the world is undoubtedly one of the most remarkable examples of the globalization of food', what are we to understand, in this context, by the term 'Chinese food'? Commenting on the early diffusion of Chinese cuisine, Roberts (2002: 217) recognizes that 'what was being sold purported to be an authentic example of an exotic dish, and this was being reinforced by messages imparted by the décor and other features of the location in which the food was served'. In fact, what was taking place was simulation. Moreover, given the diversity of regional cooking in China, the very idea of a generic Chinese cuisine was itself a lie. This is not to deny that authentic Chinese regional cooking – from Szechuan, Hunan, Dongbei and so on – can be found outside China. For example, the small market town of Loughborough in the English Midlands is home to two restaurants offering authentic Szechuan cooking. It comes as little surprise, however, that the overwhelming majority of their customers are Chinese students from the local university, whilst English diners continue to patronize those Chinese restaurants which cater for the traditional British palate, or else a large Thai restaurant where neither the ingredients nor the flavours are as challenging to the conventional British taste.

In the case of Japan, we may be more inclined to accept the idea of a national cuisine. However, this has been possible only since the 1920s, when, as Cwiertka (2006: 79) reports, reforms in military catering 'largely contributed to the moulding of a nationally homogeneous taste'. Thereafter, 'throughout the twentieth century, owing to urbanization, rising standards of living and a shift towards industrialized mass manufacture, not only did soy sauce become the dominant flavouring for the ever increasing number of Japanese, but its taste was becoming increasingly standardized' (Cwiertka, 2006: 81). Subsequently, the concept of Japanese cuisine has been fetishized both by the Japanese themselves and by its enthusiasts abroad. As with Chinese food, however, the globalization of Japanese food has resulted in different consequences depending on the tastes of those for whom the dishes are intended. For example, the presence of a sizeable Japanese community in California helped to inspire a Japanese food trend with some claim to authenticity (Cwiertka, 2006). This is a far cry from global restaurant chains such as Wagamama or YO! Sushi, where, according to Cwiertka (2006: 196), 'authenticity and ethnic appropriateness seem to be the last things that mattered'. Similar thoughts are prompted by that other highly visible global catering phenomenon – the Irish pub.

As Slater (2000: 247) observes, 'the Irish pub has truly gone global'. That these institutions generally possess characteristics that make them seem more Irish or 'Oirish' than the overwhelming majority of pubs in Ireland itself makes them potentially ideal examples of what Baudrillard meant by hyperreality. According to Muñoz *et al.* (2006: 223), 'Irish pubs allow consumers to be immersed into Irish culture, past and present'. For Slater (2000: 247), however, 'if the Irish pub is to travel it can only do so as a simulated entity'. All of this can be linked to a wider process through which 'themed environments have become enmeshed in consumers' daily experiences' (Lego *et al.*, 2002: 61). Even in Dublin, Ireland's capital city, where themed bars associated with specific foreign cultures have emerged (Slater, 2000), 'pubs are revamped to look like the "Irish" bars which have been exported worldwide' (McManus, 2001: 116), with inevitable consequences for the construction of Irish identities (Mays, 2005). One of the most prominent features of themed Irish bars is that they are specifically designed to appear Irish, or at least to appear Irish in ways that the non-Irish, and increasingly the Irish themselves, regard as Irish. In part, of course, this is achieved through the sale of Irish consumables, such as Guinness, whiskey and meals including cooked breakfasts, wheaten bread and stew. It is also essential to decorate the interior with an array of

Irish memorabilia. Finally, all of this is then presented to the customer in a setting that is intended to be redolent of Irish design. Whilst the latter may in fact be more imagined than real, this is by no means always its role in relation to constructions of national identity, as the next section reveals.

Design

According to Edensor (2002: 103), 'Despite the fact that all human societies surround themselves with instrumental, decorative, religious and symbolic objects, dominant sociological theories have tended to conceive them as either associated with their relation to labour – in Marxist readings – or as vehicles for status.' Yet, he goes on, 'people grow up relating to things'. Activities such as playing and watching sport, eating and drinking allow people to step out of their domestic lives at least temporarily. Furthermore, despite the attractions offered by the world outside, 'in industrialized societies', as Miller (2001: 1) observes, 'most of what matters to people is happening behind the closed doors of the private sphere'. Moreover, it is here that we are most likely to encounter what Turner and Khondker (2010: 74) describe as 'the strong aesthetic condition of (national) resistance'. Just as we are able to 'read' landscapes, so too can we 'read' dwelling places (Bachelard, 1969). Countless nations throughout the world are recognized as having their own distinctive approach to interior design. This in turn means distinctive contexts in which the peoples of the world, even those places most subject to the pressures of globalizing consumer culture, live their lives.

One such nation is Japan, where the resistance to globalization has, arguably, been more successful than in most countries, and nowhere more so than in relation to interior design. Writing in the mid-1930s, Junichirō Tanizaki (2001: 29) observed, 'the beauty of a Japanese room depends on a variation of shadows heavy shadows, against light shadows – it has nothing else'. At the time, others were quick to argue that Japan was rather more anxious to imitate the United States in matters of taste. In the West, however, according to Tanizaki (2001: 58), 'light is used not for reading or writing or sewing but for dispelling the shadows in the farthest corners, and this runs against the basic idea of the Japanese room'. Thus, 'a Japanese room might be likened to an inkwash painting, the paper-paneled shoji being the expanse where the ink is thinnest, and the alcove where it is darkest' (Tanizaki, 2001: 32). Further understanding is to be found in the Japanese concept of *wabi sabi* – 'an aesthetic ideal and philosophy that is best understood in terms of the Zen philosophy that has nurtured and molded its development over the last thousand years' (Juniper, 2003: 1). Whilst many modern living spaces lack the intimacy associated with a philosophy that sees beauty in imperfection, 'wabi sabi provides an alternative to these poorly designed and mass-produced environments' (Juniper, 2003: 105). Here, perhaps, lies the secret of distinctively Japanese design.

Much has changed, of course, in Japan as elsewhere since the 1930s, when Tanizaki was writing. Indeed, it has been argued that 'the discourse surrounding the Japanese dwelling draws on an aesthetic and social ideal of order associated with the elite in feudal Japan' (Daniels, 2001: 225). Nevertheless, as Aldersey-Williams (1990: 69) argues, 'there is no doubt that design that takes account of cultural identity [is] growing in importance as designers become cautious that global design is not all … good'. The challenge, though, is 'how to find meaningful expression at a time when each of our identities is becoming more complicated' (Aldersey-Williams, 1990: 70). In a highly competitive age, characterized initially by the rise of the so-called tiger economies of East and South-East Asia and, more recently, by the economic growth of Brazil, Russia, India and China, the 'national aesthetic', ironically, becomes an important marketing agent.

An outstanding example of distinctive branding is to be found close to Beipu township in Hsinchu County, Taiwan, where Hakka brothers, Fan Yang-tien and Fan Yang-wu, make wooden furniture (Hwang, 2008). Although the Fans are the third generation of their family's wood-related business, by the early 1990s the domestic furniture industry was in crisis, due to cheap imports and higher production costs. As one commentator expressed it, 'to upgrade Taiwan's economic status, the island needs to move away from OEM [original equipment manufacture]-oriented industries and start manufacturing products that carry domestically created brand names and original designs' (Wu, 1997). It was in those circumstances, as Hwang (2001: 2) notes, that 'local culture and history began to gain more attention'. The Fan brothers decided to focus on their own designs and, by 2007, their Smangus Workshop had become a recognized brand name in the local furniture market. Why? Perhaps, above all, because it offers distinctive designs in an era in which they are most needed. According to Hwang (2008: 58), the Fan brothers occupy three chairs – 'the first for family heritage, the second for the woodworking tradition, and the third for a unique design philosophy'.

In other parts of the world, wood plays a similar role in the persistence of the national aesthetic. Writing about Romania, for example, Drazin (2001: 197) makes the more widely applicable point that 'people participate in their environment through wood and imbue their environment with emotionality'. As with the relationship between national identity and sport, the significance of the natural landscape should not be ignored. On the other hand, as with cuisine, there is always room for invention, for example in 'the deliberate search for a national design sensibility in Australia' (Jackson, 2002: 14).

Further evidence if the importance of interior design for the reproduction of national identities is to be found in the countless outdoor museums in which dwellings from earlier eras serve to provide insights to natives and foreign visitors alike into the way in which a particular national people has experienced domestic life over the years. With specific reference to Stockholm's version of this phenomenon, Crang (1999: 451) writes, 'Skansen illustrates an alternative framing of national heritage by means of its temporality and its articulation of a national project through folk cultures'. Again, this type of institution undeniably contributes to 'the idea of regional types and distinctive cultural landscapes' (Crang, 1999: 452–3). Nevertheless, the sheer number of Swedish visitors to Skansen is evidence of the degree to which life behind closed doors (now open to the public) is recognized, rightly or wrongly, as part of the national fabric.

Conclusions

As Turner and Khondker (2010: 32) note, 'Globalization does not mean the removal or erasure of local culture.' This is clearly demonstrated in a wide range of activities, including music and dance. This chapter has focused on sport, eating and drinking, and design. All of the major approaches to the study of nations, nationalism and national identities – primordialism, ethno-symbolism, modernization theory, imagined community and invented tradition – are useful in trying to understand each of these aspects of human experience. There is no need to believe without reservation in the naturalness of nations in order to appreciate that certain natural features can play a role in the nationalizing of particular activities. At the same time, it is important to acknowledge, when necessary, the influence of invention, fusion and the imagination in the construction of what purport to be authentic national cultures. No matter how one interprets the presence of the national in leisure activities, however, all interpretations ultimately point towards the conclusion that national identity and the celebration of difference continue to be central components of the leisure experience.

References

Aldersey-Williams, H. (1990) 'Design and Cultural Identity', *International Journal of Technology and Design Education* 1 (2) 69–74.

Allison, L. (2000) 'Sport and Nationalism', in J. Coakley and E. Dunning (eds) *Handbook of Sports Studies*. London: Sage.

Anderson, B. (1991) *Imagined Communities. Reflections on the Origin and Spread of Nationalism*, 2nd ed. London: Verso.

Bachelard, G. (1969) *The Poetics of Space*. Boston, MA: Beacon Press.

Bairner, A. (2001) *Sport, Nationalism and Globalization. European and North American Perspectives*. Albany, NY: State University of New York Press.

Bairner, A. (2005) 'Sport and the Nation in the Global Era', in L. Allison (ed.) *The Global Politics of Sport. The Role of Global Institutions in Sport*, London: Routledge.

Bairner, A. (2009) 'National Sports and National Landscapes: In Defence of Primordialism', *National Identities* 11 (3) 223–239.

Baudrillard, J. (1983) *Simulations*. New York: Semiotext(e).

Bell, D. and Valentine, G. (1997) *Consuming Geographies. We Are What We Eat*. London: Routledge.

Billig, M. (1995) *Banal Nationalism*, London: Sage.

Blackshaw, T. (2010) *Sage Key Concepts in Community Studies*. London: Sage.

Crang, M. (1999) 'Nation, Region and Homeland: History and Tradition in Dalarna, Sweden', *Ecomene* 6 (4) 447–470.

Cronin, M. (1999) *Sport and Nationalism in Ireland. Gaelic Games, Soccer and Irish Identity since 1884*. Dublin: Four Courts Press.

Cronin, M. and Mayall, D. (eds) (1998) *Sporting Nationalisms. Identity, Ethnicity, Immigration and Assimilation*, London: Frank Cass.

Cwiertka, K. J. (2006) *Modern Japanese Cuisine. Food, Power and National Identity*. London: Reaktion Books.

Daniels, I. M. (2001) 'The "Untidy" Japanese House', in D. Miller (ed.) *Home Possessions. Material Culture behind Closed Doors*. Oxford: Berg.

Drazin, A. (2001) 'A Man *Will* Get Furnished: Wood and Domesticity in Urban Rumania', in D. Miller (ed.) *Home Possessions. Material Culture behind Closed Doors*. Oxford: Berg.

Edensor, T. (2002) *National Identity, Popular Culture and Everyday Life*. Oxford: Berg.

Grosby, S. (2007) 'The Successor Territory', in A. S. Leoussi and S. Grosby (eds) *Nationalism and Ethnosymbolism. History, Culture and Ethnicity in the Formation of Nations*. Edinburgh: Edinburgh University Press.

Hannerz, U. (1996) *Transnational Connections, Culture, People, Places*. London: Routledge.

Hargreaves, J. (2000) *Freedom for Catalonia? Catalan Nationalism, Spanish Identity and the Barcelona Olympic Games*. Cambridge: Cambridge University Press.

Hechter, M. (2000) *Containing Nationalism*. Oxford: Oxford University Press.

Hoberman, J. (1984) *Sport and Political Ideology*. London: Heinemann.

Hobsbawm, E. J. and Ranger, T. (eds) (2012) *The Invention of Tradition*, reissue edition. Cambridge: Cambridge University Press.

Hwang, J. (2001) 'Back to the Grass Roots', *Taiwan Review*, January. Available at: http://taiwanreview.nat.gov.tw/fp.asp?xItem=677&ctNode=1342. Accessed 19 January 2012.

Hwang, J. (2008) 'Harmony in Opposites', *Taiwan Review*, January: 54–59.

Jackson, S. (2002) 'The "Stump-jumpers": National Identity and the Mythology of Australian Industrial Design in the Period 1930–1975', *Design Issues* 18 (4) 14–23.

Juniper, A. (2003) *Wabi Sabi. The Japanese Art of Impermanence*, Rutland, VT: Tuttle Publishing.

Lefebvre, H. (1991) *The Production of Space*. Oxford: Blackwell.

Lego, C. K., Wood, N. T., McFee, S. L. and Solomon, M. R. (2002) 'A Thirst for the Real Thing in Themed Retail Environments', *Foodservice Business Research* 5 (2) 61–74.

Machin, A. (2007) 'Language-Games of the Nation', *CSD Bulletin* 14 (1/2) 12–14.

Maguire, J. (1994) 'Sport, Identity Politics and Globalization: Diminishing Contrasts and Increasing Varieties', *Sociology of Sport Journal* 11 (4) 389–427.

Maguire, J., Jarvie, G., Mansfield, L. and Bradley, J. (2002) *Sport Worlds. A Sociological Perspective*. Champaign, IL: Human Kinetics.

Mays, M. (2005) 'Irish Identity in an Age of Globalization', *Irish Studies Review* 13 (1) 3–12.

McManus, R. (2001) 'Dublin's Changing Tourism Geography', *Irish Geography* 34 (2) 103–123.

Miller, D. (2001) 'Behind Closed Doors', in D. Miller (ed.) *Home Possessions. Material Culture behind Closed Doors*, Oxford: Berg.

Miller, T., Lawrence, G., McKay, J. and Rowe, D. (2001) *Globalization and Sport*. London: Sage.

Muñoz, C. L., Wood, N. T. and Solomon, M. R. (2006) 'Real or Blarney? A Cross-Cultural Investigation of the Perceived Authenticity of Irish Pubs', *Journal of Consumer Behaviour* 5: 222–234.

Nairn, T. (2002) *Pariah. Misfortunes of the British Kingdom*. London: Verso.

Ritzer, G. (2004) *The McDonaldization of Society*, rev. ed. Thousand Oaks, CA: Sage.

Roberts, J. A. G. (2002) *China to Chinatown. Chinese Food in the West*. London: Reaktion Books.

Robertson, R. (1995) 'Globalization: Time-Space and Homogeneity-Heterogeneity', in S. Lash and R. Robertson (eds) *Global Modernities*. London: Sage.

Silk, M. L., Andrews, D. L. and Cole, C. L. (eds) (2005) *Sport and Corporate Nationalisms*. Oxford: Berg.

Slater, E. (2000) 'When the Local Goes Global', in E. Slater and M. Peillon (eds) *Memories of the Present. A Sociological Chronicle of Ireland, 1997–1998*, Dublin: Institute of Public Administration.

Smith, A. and Porter, D. (2004) *Sport and National Identity in the Post-War World*. London: Routledge.

Smith, A. D. (1995) *Nations and Nationalism in a Global Era*. Cambridge: Polity Press.

Smith, A. D. (1998) *Nationalism and Modernism*. London: Routledge.

Sörlin, S. (1999) 'The Articulation of Territory: Landscape and the Constitution of Regional and National Identity', *Norsk Geografisk Tidsskrift* 53: 103–112.

Tanizaki, J. (2001) *In Praise of Shadows*. London: Vintage Books.

Ticher, M (1994) 'Notional Englishmen, Black Irishmen and Multicultural Australians: Ambiguities in National Sporting Identity', *Sporting Traditions* 11 (1) 75–91.

Turner, B. S. and Khondker, H. H. (2010) *Globalization East and West*. London: Sage.

Urry, J. (2003) *Global Complexity*. Cambridge: Polity Press.

Waters, M. (1995) *Globalization*. London: Routledge.

Wilson, J. (2009) *Inverting the Pyramid. The History of Football Tactics*. London: Orion.

Wu, D. Y. H. and Cheng, S. C. H. (2002) *The Globalization of Chinese Food*. London: Routledge Curzon.

Wu, W. Y. (1997) 'Upgrading Taiwan's Industrial Design', *Taiwan Review*, January. Available at: http://taiwanreview.nat.gov.tw/fp.asp?xItem=348&ctNode=1342. Accessed 19 January 2012.

37

SOCIAL CAPITALISM
AND LEISURE POLICY
RECONSIDERED

Tony Blackshaw

In a journal article, 'What's the Big Idea? A Critical Exploration of the Concept of Social Capital and Its Incorporation into Leisure Policy Discourse', published in *Leisure Studies* in 2005, Blackshaw and Long identified the triumphant march of social capitalism into social policy circles and critically discussed its relative merits for examining and understanding the role for leisure in policy strategies. The argument underpinning their analysis was that at the cusp of the new millennium the idea had taken hold in political circles in the UK that we needed an alternative way of dealing with social inequality that didn't involve the state[1] taxing those in work and then blowing the proceeds on undeserving recipients. A new consensus seemed to have emerged which was now inclined to believe that social inequality is no longer so much material (lack of money) as virtual (lack of opportunities).

As they wrote at the time, this new consensus chimed nicely with Tony Giddens' (1998) 'Third Way', which claimed to offer a political response to altered societal conditions that had emerged on two fronts. On the first, the combination of social, cultural, economic and political changes, relating to de-industrialization, individualization, consumerism, information technology-driven globalization and the emergence of 'life politics' at the expense of 'class politics'; on the second front, the collapse of state socialism in the Soviet Union and the rest of the Eastern bloc – both of which, according to Giddens, had undermined the viability of post-war social democratic politics and social policies.

Giddens proposed that social policy for these new times needed to be underpinned by a radical centre-left politics embodied with a 'utopian realist' outlook. If capitalism and communism had been central to the world order for most of the second-half of the twentieth century, at the start of the new millennium it was now time for an alternative political ethic in its own right, defensible in its own terms and self-supporting – what Nikolas Rose (1999: 167) describes as a sort of 'natural, extra-political zone of human relations ... [that in its] ... "natural-ness" is not merely an ontological claim but implies affirmation, a positive evaluation' – which would provide the necessary impetus for renewing social democracy, especially by encouraging a more active civil society.

With this 'utopian realism', the end of ideology in social policy was visualized, and what this meant in policy terms was two things. On the one hand, that it was no longer conceivable for the state to think that it should corner the 'market' for dealing with social inequality; and on the other, that the state should also be guarded against throwing more material resources at poverty because this might serve to frustrate the accomplishment of a more active civil society – or even directly negate it, by making the poor dependent.

Giddens' work on the 'Third Way' had drawn him into the inner circle of New Labour politics and this led to his appointment at the London School of Economics in 1997. Once the Labour administration was elected into office in the same year, this 'utopian realism' became its new vision. For almost fifty years after the Second World War, the Labour Party's battle against social inequality had centred on the welfare state of Attlee, Bevan and Beveridge, but a landslide victory under the leadership of Tony Blair signalled the beginning of the heyday of the 'Third Way', when Labour visibly put on a 'new' coat of paint. For the better – or so it seemed at the time – 'welfarism' had to give way to 'social capitalism', and this was underpinned – inevitably – by an attempt to install an alternative political, ethical and self-determined community centred in and governed by the state.

Looking back just eight years to when this article was published, the preoccupations of UK central government seem markedly different from those of today. If social capitalism was the big idea in social policy then, it is so-called 'big society' that rules the roost now. The Conservative–Liberal Coalition, elected in 2010, champions traditional values of personal responsibility, respect and local sovereignty, while actively undermining state solutions to social policy challenges, instead preferring to mobilize Edmund Burke's 'little platoons' by removing funding in order to 'encourage' a sense of ownership of ourselves and our communities.

Not surprisingly, centre-left critics have been quick to argue that the idea that social policy challenges can be met by ordinary people acting alone, volunteering in their communities – while the market corrects itself – is pure fantasy. If we are really to rise to the challenge of eliminating social inequality, the centre-left argument goes, we are going to need more than 'little platoons' to get us there. All the same, what I shall argue in this chapter is that the fundamental premises underpinning social policy for social capitalists and for aficionados of the 'big society' actually overlap,[2] and this is not because they each seek to conjoin increased public participation with more individual responsibility, but as a result of a more fundamental ideological shift in which every corner of social policy – including leisure policy – has come to absorb neoliberalism, the political doctrine that developed in earnest from the close of what Hobsbawm (1995) calls the 'short twentieth century' (1914–91) onwards, involving the ostensible denial of ideology, the affirmation of entrepreneurship in the light of the opportunities arising from capitalism in the period of intensified globalization, and the substitution for the social state of the market state (Bauman, 2012), which appropriates the idea of community voraciously for its own political ends.

The foremost aim of this chapter, then, is to provide a revised interpretation of the relative merits of social capitalism for examining and understanding the role for leisure in social policy strategies. The chapter begins by identifying and briefly outlining the key insights developed by Blackshaw and Long (2005) concerning the conceptual basis of Putnam's social capital thesis. The chapter subsequently argues that, contrary to received wisdom, it is not functionalism and the politics of civic communitarianism that really underlie social policy in the UK but, rather, neoliberalism. The arguments developed are interpreted in terms of the vital roles given to 'community' and 'leisure' in current neoliberal social policy strategies.

Social capitalism, civil society and leisure

Social capitalism attained its popularity in New Labour circles through its use in the US political scientist Robert Putnam's article 'Bowling Alone: America's Declining Social

433

Capital', which appeared in the *Journal of Democracy* in 1995 and was subsequently published as a book with the title *Bowling Alone: The Collapse and Revival of American Community*, in 2000. At the time of its appearance, Putnam's social capital thesis presented a direct challenge to received ideas about civil society in contemporary American society.

Civil society is an imprecise and often contradictory term which Adam Ferguson, a leading philosopher of the Scottish Enlightenment, described as the processes by which humankind developed out of its 'rude' condition into a state of civilization. In Putnam's usage the term approximates to that realm of sociability and public participation outside the structures of the state which incorporates both *informal* activities, such as going down to the local for a pint and a game of darts, dining out with friends and so on, and more *formal* organized activities, which are based on shared 'enthusiasm, pleasure and enjoyment' (Bishop and Hoggett, 1986). What this demonstrates is three significant things about the relationship between leisure and civil society. First, leisure is a pillar of civil society. Second, leisure is of political significance because it is, to paraphrase John Keane, 'an aggregate of institutions whose members are engaged primarily in a complex of non-state activities – economic and cultural production, household life and voluntary associations – and who in this way preserve and transform their identity by exercising all sorts of pressures and controls upon State institutions' (Keane, 1988: 14). Third, leisure rests on a complex foundation that state action can either fortify or undermine.

Although the antecedents of Putnam's interest in social capital can be traced back to the leisure pursuits that he followed in his youth, theoretically it is tied to the political and social thought of Alexis de Tocqueville (1969) and the sociology of Emile Durkheim (1933; 1961), whose analyses of the problems associated with an emerging modernity have recently been revived by political scientists so as to shed some light on some of our own. As Blackshaw and Long demonstrate, the success and popularity of Putnam's social capital thesis is undoubtedly located in its assumption that, notwithstanding the processes of change by which society achieved modernity, localism is still a significant principle of social organization. In other words, his thesis works with the civic communitarian assumption that community, with its emphasis on social networks, kinship ties, face-to-face social relations, shared identity, values and spirit of belonging, not only serves certain societal functions but also continues to be a meaningful social formation for individuals. In this view, social capital is the social cement of human society. If not unambiguously explicating the communitarian roots of his work, Putnam acknowledges that 'social capital is closely related to what some have called "civic virtue"' (Putnam, 2000: 19). Delanty (2003: 81) takes this observation further when he suggests that there is a 'civic tradition within communitarianism [that] has made social capital and participation in public life central', and he identifies the work of Putnam as central to this strand of political theorizing. As Delanty points out, civic communitarianism is by and large a 'Tocquevillian discourse of the loss of community'. Indeed, it is Tocqueville's most famous expression, 'habits of the heart', that both Putnam (1993; 1995) and, notably, Bellah *et al.* (1987) endorse in their discussions of the civic associations necessary for healthy social democracy.

The critique underpinning Putnam's social capital thesis is that we are currently witnessing the deterioration of those social networks and relationships associated with civic virtue and social responsibility, which involve communities and other social groups establishing common values, trust and cooperative ways of being and working together for mutual benefit. In his book, where he observes that the bowling leagues of his youth, with their legions of teams, are no longer a dominant form of civic leisure participation in the USA and that people now tend to 'bowl alone', Putnam builds his own version of this decline of civic virtue and community, laced with some inevitable nostalgia:

the last several decades have witnessed a striking diminution of regular contacts with friends and neighbours. We spend less time in conversation over meals, we exchange visits less often, we engage less often in leisure activities that encourage casual social interaction, we spend more time watching (admittedly some of it in the presence of others) and less time doing. We know our neighbours less well, and we see old friends less often. In short it is not merely 'do good' civic activities that engage us less, but also informal connecting.

(Putnam, 2000: 115)

Obviously, people don't actually bowl alone, but in small, closed groups, such that the activity does not involve dealings with people beyond the immediate social group. Insisting that this concern with the decline of social capital is not just a hankering for the nostalgia of the community of his youth, Putnam presents a wealth of research data, contending that there is a positive relationship between social capital and education, economic prosperity, health and well-being, and the democratic process overall, and uses this to make the case that through social capitalism the problems of civil society are resolved more easily: sociability (like business transactions) is less costly; personal coping is facilitated; information flows are better; and increased mutual awareness between individuals, communities and organizations promotes tolerance, as well as challenging ignorance and distrust.

In Putnam's account social capital is not merely a good idea; it is the conceptual basis of a thesis. He argues that it represents sets of actions, outcomes or social networks (relations and ties) that allow people and civic associations to operate more effectively when they act together. Social capital, from Putnam's perspective, then, is functional for civil society. Social capital tends to be accompanied by two kinds of reciprocity: bonding ties, which signify interaction between 'like people' whose social networks are inward looking and exclusive; and bridging ties or inter-group links, which are more outward looking and inclusive. At the same time, social capital has some further important characteristics: it is both a public and a private 'good' in that, just as individuals benefit from their contribution to social capital, so do others; it is evidenced in many different kinds of social networks – family, neighbours, church groups, personal social circles, civic organizations, e-groups. Some of these networks are repeated and intensive, some involve strong ties, while others involve weak ties; some are episodic and casual; some are formal, some informal; and its networks and reciprocity are largely positive for those inside particular communities and social groups, but its external effects are by no means always positive – some of the most robust communities and organizations are the same ones that have cultivated social networks that are exclusive and reproduce both inequality and/or what Field (2003: 88) calls 'perverse goals'. Despite these negative or dysfunctional aspects, Putnam suggests that the real value of social capital lies in its positively functional capacity to transform itself 'from something realized by individuals to something possessed (or not possessed) by either individuals or groups of people' (DeFilippis, 2001: 785).

The above points notwithstanding, Putnam's thesis is far more than just functionalism (Blackshaw and Long, 2005). As has been suggested already, it is an attempt to elaborate a civic communitarian philosophy in a way that offers some practical solutions for dealing with the decline in civil relations where a much more itinerant, anonymous life has taken shape, where people no longer know or care about their fellow citizens and find themselves oppressed, or at least detached from the society of which they are ostensibly a part.

The limits of social capitalism

Yet, as compelling as these arguments are, the picture that social capitalists paint of civil society broken by neoliberalism, and the solutions that they proffer for piecing it back together, do not stand up to critical scrutiny. In particular, social capitalism holds no panacea for dealing with that major public issue with which it is mostly associated: the poverty and the different forms of social exclusion that encumber the poorest communities where people eke out an existence with a pervasive sense of diminished possibilities resulting from the restructuring of global capitalism.

In 'What's the Big Idea?' Blackshaw and Long develop an analysis of Putnam's understanding of social capital that brings attention to three other critical problems: the limitations of the research underpinning the thesis; the ideological implications of social capitalism; and the limitations of the theoretical basis of social capital. They begin their article by arguing that not only are Putnam's own research and the secondary research that he tends to rely on hampered by a positivist orientation, but he also uses it in ways that are vague and misleading, as well as evincing a tendency to ignore what the 'data' tells him about how social networks operate in the real world. For example, Putnam asserts that changes in work patterns, principally women's increased involvement in full-time employment, have contributed 10 per cent to the fall in social capital. This idea is based on the observation that women are responsible for much social interaction and civic engagement at the community level through entertainment at home, volunteering, or running community groups, and that, with less disposable time available, these have suffered. However, this overlooks the massive injection of social interaction that is provided to women by involvement in the workplace.

Blackshaw and Long also point out that Putnam pays little or no attention to the feminist theoretical critique that argues that 'communities' often make claims on their members which are based on extant and often insidious hierarchies of patriarchal domination and subordination. As pointed out, the problem is that Putnam is intent on bending the 'data' to fit his thesis that the biggest single cause of the decline in social capital is the departure of his long civic generation and he uses this taken-for-granted ideological assumption to form his research, rather than the other way round.

In the event, Blackshaw and Long argue that in Putnam's work ideology operates at two broad levels: as an ideology-as-culture, which is a body of civic communitarian political ideas, and as an ideology-in-process, whose symbolic action (symbolic exchange, symbolic power and symbolic violence) operates in tandem with the more explicitly material effects of the former. In terms of thinking about the symbolic nature of Putnam's own project – that is, the way in which it generates for Putnam and other like-minded communitarians their own social capital – Blackshaw and Long point out that the greater part of what Putnam offers is rhetorical rather than substantive, more an imaginary construction than a solution for the pains that it claims to cure. They demonstrate that through the idea of social capital Putnam is navigating far from the use of language as a set of uninformed conventions, subsumed within the realm of an ideology of word and world realism, a discourse whose virtual effects verge on the real, but, ironically, in terms of the real world, bears little relevance to the worlds of those people whom it purports to take care of. In other words, Putnam, in reputing his values before the fact, legislates the present and future by nostalgically reimagining the past and using it ideologically to maintain capitalistic (and hegemonic) ways of dealing with the defeat of inequality, injustice and the humiliation of poverty.

As a result, Blackshaw and Long argue, Putnam overlooks Bourdieu's theoretically important point that what he calls 'the profits of membership' of civic associations and social networks are not available to everybody. Indeed, the point of all 'capitals' – not just social capital – is that they are resources to be exploited and it is their exclusivity that gives them their value (Ball, 2003). In a nutshell, people are able to realize social capital through their social networks precisely because they are able to exclude others. This ostensible failing of Putnam's thesis is normally presented as a bonus, in that some aspects of social capital are seen not as positional goods in a zero-sum game; those contributing to trust, support and security might be seen to be strengthened if shared; moreover, in using it, social capital is seen to grow. However, Putnam ignores the fact that the 'profits' of community life are not things that you can so easily cost, measure or bank on.

Blackshaw and Long conclude 'What's the Big Idea' by arguing that social capital has two decisive (and divisive) features: on the one hand, it is a tangible resource made by advantage of social networks, and on the other, like all forms of capital, it has a symbolic dimension, which contrives to hide networks of power woven into the fibres of familiarity. In the event, they suggest, following Bourdieu, that in understanding social capital we must take into account the extent, quality and quantity of social actors' networks *and* their ability to mobilize these, which is always governed by the mutual understanding that any given field is an arena of struggle. In other words, and as Bourdieu (1984) would have said, it is the battle for *distinction* that gives social capital its ostensible qualities.

Social capitalism and leisure policy revisited

In the final part of 'What's the Big Idea?' Blackshaw and Long conceive that it might be more 'profitable' to recast social policy interventions, drawing on leisure in ways that develop a central interpretive role for cultural intermediaries which involves trying to breathe life into the cross-fertilization of cultures which might have taken place, had it not been for ignorance, intolerance or distrust. Underpinning this approach is the recognition that we need to pay people the compliment of taking them seriously as individuals and communities with moral intelligence. They also conclude that leisure has a key role to play in this type of intervention, because it has the potential to communicate across those cultural boundaries that divide different social and cultural groups in a way that is at the same time respectful of the differences that separate them.

There is no doubt that the idea of developing this kind of third space, which seeks to conjoin increased public participation, is massively important for tackling issues of social inequality, and that leisure has a definite role to play in this process. As Axel Honneth (2002) shows us very clearly, how we realize our identities as modern individuals depends a great deal on the ways in which we develop self-confidence, self-respect and self-esteem through our 'intersubjective, symmetrical and reciprocal' relationships with others. However, the challenge of breathing life into the cross-fertilization of cultures addresses only one of the two important problems that we know about in the social policy war against structural inequality. The other, and even bigger problem is the one below the tip of the visible iceberg: the substitution for the social state of the market state, which appropriates community for its own political ends. Indeed, the rhetoric of 'community' surrounding social capitalism (and the so-called 'Third Way' and 'big society') may be suggestive of a warm, cosy bed of a social policy world, but the truth is that it feeds on and into a neoliberal discourse that has not only individualized structural inequalities as consumer inadequacies, but has also down-graded all current social policy interventions to market solutions.

One of the key reasons for this is that politicians of both the centre-left and the right feel unthreatened by 'community' because, unlike that word of the same family resemblance, communism, it is a political ideology without socialism. As we shall see below, however, the 'Third Way' owes a great deal more to the ideology of neoliberalism and free market economics than of community, not least because, as a result of the failures of communism, there has emerged an almost fundamentalist belief in the market and the view that markets offer universal remedy to all societal ills. Indeed, everything in neoliberalism has to be judged by its market value and if it doesn't sell, it is not what is wanted, purely and simply. 'Community' matters to neoliberals because it sells. As we shall see below, the appropriation of 'community' is seen by all 'Third Way' adherents as a smart political strategy, creating a new kind of hegemony that money cannot buy: Community plc: gilt edged. This has been accompanied by the hugely successful creation of 'Brand Community', much copied in social policy circles.

Indeed, the idiom of 'community' has become a symbol of a certain kind of neoliberal social policy interventions, at least those directed at the poorest denizens of society. The cast is a familiar one: 'community leisure', 'community sport', 'community health', 'community policing', 'community housing' and so on. In living on a contemporary council estate, for example, you cannot be anything but intensely aware of the pressure of 'community' around you, the cacophony of need and want is hard to escape; and it feels like everybody is forced to feel the same experience of 'community', which is stultifying because it is to be imprisoned in the iron cage of other people's thoughts and judgements. However, what is most tellingly neoliberal is the phraseology of 'community' policy discourse: 'social capitalism', 'capacity building', 'community empowerment', 'entrepreneurial values', 'efficiency', 'targets', 'evidence'.

In short, 'community' is about investing in social capital as a kind of welfare consumerism, i.e. self-actualized welfare, which is shorthand for more individual 'choice' and 'selectivity', with the hope of engendering marketwise 'community' values in a modern setting through a form of managerialism and, where possible, the decentralization of services. The way that 'community' is used here is plainly and simply as a family-friendly mechanism for mobilizing neoliberal values. This is community policy markedly at odds with that defined by Butcher *et al.* (1993), which associates it with the policy goals, outcomes and processes explicitly aimed at the realization of the community values such as solidarity, social justice and democracy by encouraging participation from all sections of the general public, in particular the socially disadvantaged and other marginalized groups.

For 'Third Way' adherents – centre-left or right: social capitalism or 'big society' – the recipe is repetitive, additive, more community, impressing with its inexhaustible quality of power and plunder. The basic line is: more community – and more – still more community – still more. The major attraction of 'community' social policies is of course that they promise the kinds of social intervention that are 'bottom up', rather than 'top down', and which, in the process of delivery, are more reflective of the interests of local communities. Indeed, typical philosophies about political community put about by high-minded politicians tend to offer the following kinds of 'benefits':

> Virtue regenerated – crime reduced – public safety enhanced – institutionalization banished – dependency transformed to activity – underclass included – democratic deficit overcome – idle set to work – political alienation reduced – responsive services assured – economy reinvigorated by seating it, as it were, within networks of trust and honour – the Gordian knot of the State versus individual not cut but untied, all by a simple idea of politics: community.

> (Rose, 1999: 187)

However, as Bauman points out, social policy recast as 'community' policy tends to rest on a promise of simplification which

> brought to its logical limit ... means a lot of sameness and a bare minimum of variety. The simplification on offer can only be attained by the separation of differences: by reducing the probability of their meeting and narrowing the extent of communication. This kind of communal unity rests on division, segregation and keeping of distance. These are the virtues figuring most prominently in the advertising leaflets of communitarian shelters.
>
> (Bauman, 2001: 148)

As Jean Baudrillard (2005) might say, these shelters are most effective in depriving their clients of their 'right of revenge' and their capacity to take reprisals. To use an analogy from popular culture, 'all the rage' 'community' initiatives work just like those 'all the rage' comedy television shows, such that, by affecting a self-deprecating ironic tone in the delivery of their services, they effectively short-circuit our opportunities for criticizing them. As that most acerbic political commentator Peter Preston (2005) put it:

> Try community charge in poll-tax mode and it's a spoonful of sugar to help the medicine go down. Try care in the community and it's somebody over there calling on poor Mrs Bloggs once a week if she's lucky. Try America's community colleges and we mean comprehensives not city academies. Try community service orders, and the guy over there clearing rubbish could find himself in prison next time.

All of which suggests that 'community' policy, as well as being limited to a game of second-best in which there is the tacit assumption that the market is the clear winner – community support officers as second-rate police officers employed to do policing on the cheap or NHS dentists abandoning the health and hygiene side of their profession for the more lucrative but less publicly oriented one of beautification – also tends to exacerbate the conditions that it promises to rectify by intensifying the kinds of social and cultural separateness, human suffering, social disruption and the break-up of local communities. The idea of 'community' is undoubtedly most attractive to the neoliberal adherents of the 'Third Way' because not merely does it speak the brand confident, popular and stylish, in a 'do-what-the-manual-tells-you' kind of way – stakeholding and capacity building, bridging capital and bonding capital, bottom up and grass roots – but it also gives every appearance of having managed to embrace the ethos of community practice and its attendant values. Yet, 'community' is most appealing, first and foremost, because it offers social policy interventions 'managed' on neoliberal lines, but delivered with the kind of warmth and homeliness that welfarism always struggled to achieve. 'Community' is used, at best, as a sop to the limitations of market forces. In other words, it effectively occupies a space in the public sector that might otherwise have been filled with something much less desirable – a public service.

As Tim Crabbe (2007: 39) points out in his perceptive critique of 'Third Way' community leisure interventions based on welfare consumerism, which attempt to mobilize the 'power of sport' to tackle social problems such as crime and anti-social behaviour, community sport is

> seen to provide a means of educating the 'flawed' or 'illegitimate' consumers in 'our way of doing things'. It emphasises the legitimate rules of consumer society, which have

often proven beyond the community youth worker, probation officer and educational welfare officer who lack the cache of social and cultural capital that goes with contemporary sport. What this kind of social intervention represents for the mainstream then is an extension of the seductive appeal of its own consumer society ... part of the attraction of these forms of community sports work to the mainstream is their lack of any ideological critique of the consumerism, which contributes to the young people's ghettoisation. Indeed the offer of a 'passport' or gateway 'out' is premised upon the mediated appeal of one of the most rabidly commercialised industries on the planet ... the funding representatives or agents of those who are 'legitimate' members of consumer society, the socially 'included', are happy to sponsor the endeavours of community sports agencies because of their presumed capacity to 'reach' and 'manage' a constituency of the 'excluded', who have proven increasingly troublesome for more traditional interventionist agencies.

As that most astute observer of the current political scene Ross McKibbin (2006: 3) puts it, the UK is governed by an increasingly narrow political elite who, no matter what their formal political allegiances, 'are all the same kind of people who think the same way and know the same things' and who are committed to this 'model of market-managerialism [which] has largely destroyed alternatives, traditional and untraditional'. As McKibbin goes on to point out, these politicians might not have conceded, contra Margaret Thatcher, that there is such a thing as '"society", a "we" as well as a "me"', but they nonetheless tacitly adopt the neoliberalist mantra that ours is a 'highly privatised society increasingly shaped by "social entrepreneurs", charities, do-gooders, people with axes to grind, and our old friend "faith groups": in other words, a society based on the model of a market and restored social hierarchies.'

Dean MacCannell extends these critical observations to conclude that the community concept in its orthodox sociological understanding has ceased to be of any use in the public sphere, suggesting that the intention of social policy today is nothing less than an ambition

> to get every thought and action onto a balance sheet, to extend commercial values into every space of human relationship, the central problem ... will be to create ersatz 'communities' to manufacture and even sell a 'sense' of community, leaving no free grounds for the formation of relations outside the corporation. The complexity of this feat of social engineering – that is, the construction of believable sense of community where no community exists – should not be underestimated, nor should the drive to accomplish this feat be underestimated.
>
> (MacCannell, 1992: 89)

For MacCannell, any substance that community might once have had has been swept away by its *appropriation*, which has turned it into a spectacle of fictions intent on making the *illusion* of community real to itself and to others. To paraphrase what Terry Eagleton (1990: 209) said of commodities, 'as pure exchange-value, it's as if community has erased from itself every particle of matter; as alluring auratic object, it parades its own unique sensual being in a kind of spurious show of materiality'.

The upshot of this state of affairs is that social policy rarely has anything to do with 'community'. Indeed, there is frequently not anything remotely 'community' about the many so-called initiatives on offer other than what's in their labelling, namely because they do not have the essential conditions or purpose that sustain an actual community.

Community merged with the market as social policy – endlessly appropriated, endlessly used to give credence to yet another strategy, another make-over – restricts real innovation and alternative thinking about a new route to social justice by keeping ideas bound in mental manacles that bind even tighter than the old dichotomy of welfarism versus the market.

This neoliberal marketized version of 'community' is nothing less than the false face of social policy. It has become the exemplar of a kind of postmodern aesthetic, embraced by policy makers for its discourse of pulling-togetherness as well as its social-control function, and not least its overall family-friendly appeal. Yet, at both the popular and the political level, 'community' is little more than a feel-good label employed to give creditability to variety of otherwise often mutually contradictory social policy phenomena. Like Prospero, policy makers sprinkle social policy problems with community fairy dust and the spell is enchanting. However, we have seen that, with the ideology of neoliberalism, not only politics but also the market dominates. To reiterate, neoliberal social policy merely appropriates 'community' and then pushes it aside, its values and goals substituted by market ones.

Conclusions

We can conclude that, for all the rhetoric, community values do not provide any compelling basis for the dominant contemporary version of social policy. What we have instead is social capitalism, which is a kind of aesthetical 'community' policy that is ideologically determined by neoliberalism and centred in and governed by the market state. This entails that the fundamental nature of social policy is not underpinned by community values at all, but a parody of those values. In other words, and to paraphrase Jean Baudrillard, we are deep in a masquerade, where social capitalism is really a game of marketing (2010: 62). In his words, the *coup de force* of neoliberal ideology 'is to make everything dependant [*sic*] on the economic order, to subject all minds to a single mental dimension' (*ibid*: 86–87).

In the light of this conclusion, it would be tempting to conclude that the immediate future of social policy is bleak. It might also be tempting to conclude that there is no longer any role for community in social policy, other than its appropriation, or leisure, other than its vital role as a 'means of educating the "flawed" or "illegitimate" consumers in "our way of doing things". However, there is no compelling reason to suggest that this should necessarily always be the case from now on. As has been suggested by plenty of commentators, one of the major lessons of the short twentieth century was that the political fundamentalism of communism leads humanity nowhere but the graveyard. Yet very few commentators to date have mustered a comparable critique of that alternative fundamentalism that has hitherto been the *idée fixe* of the twenty-first century, and which leads nowhere but to human suffering, social disruption and the break-up of local communities: neoliberalism. Any new rendition of social policy which draws on both community and leisure must include not only such a critique, but also an urgent impetus to think *socially* about structural inequalities: to make human (read: socialism) rather than monetary value (read: social capitalism) the goal of social policy. This is about collective responsibility and the duty of us all to each other to be committed to putting ourselves in the shoes of the so-called 'socially excluded' in order to really know 'them' and 'their' worlds, or, in other words, to empathize with those at the brunt end of social inequality, and not only that, but also to be embarrassed with and for them.

Notes

1 The state is defined here as a 'union of power (that is, the ability to have things done) and politics (that is, the ability to decide which things need to be done)' (Bauman, 2012: 110).
2 In this chapter both social capitalists and aficionados of the 'big society' are referred to as adherents of the 'Third Way'.

References

Ball, S. J. (2003) 'It's Not What You Know: Education and Social Capital', *Sociology Review*, November.
Baudrillard, J. (2005) *The Intelligence of Evil or the Lucidity Pact*. Oxford: Berg.
Baudrillard, J. (2010) *The Agony of Power*. Los Angeles: Semiotext(e).
Bauman, Z. (2001) *Community: Seeking Safety in an Insecure World*. Cambridge: Polity Press.
Bauman, Z. (2012) *This Is Not a Diary*. Cambridge: Polity Press.
Bellah, R., Madsen, R., Sullivan, W., Swidler, A. and Tipton, S. (1987) *Habits of the Heart*. Berkeley: University of California Press.
Bishop J. and Hoggett, P. (1986) *Organizing around Enthusiasms: Mutual Aid in Leisure*. London: Comedia.
Blackshaw, T. and Long, J. (2005) 'What's the Big Idea? A Critical Exploration of the Concept of Social Capital and Its Incorporation into Leisure Policy Discourse', *Leisure Studies* 24 (3) 239–258.
Bourdieu, P. (1984) *Distinction: A Social Critique of the Judgement of Taste*. London: Routledge and Kegan Paul.
Butcher, H., Glen, A., Henderson, P. and Smith, J. (1993) (eds) *Community and Public Policy*. London: Pluto Press.
Crabbe, T. (2007) 'Reaching the "Hard to Reach": Engagement, Relationship Building and Social Control in Sport Based Social Inclusion Work', *International Journal of Sport Management and Marketing* 2 (1–2) 27–40.
DeFilippis, J. (2001) 'The Myth of Social Capital in Community Development', *Housing Policy Debate* 12 (4) 781–806.
Delanty, G. (2003) *Community*. London: Routledge.
Durkheim, E. (1933) *The Division of Labour in Society*. Glencoe, IL: Free Press.
Durkheim, E. (1961) *Moral Education: A Study in the Theory and Application of the Sociology of Education*. Glencoe, IL: Free Press.
Eagleton, T. (1990) *The Ideology of the Aesthetic*. Oxford: Blackwell.
Field, J. (2003) *Social Capital*. London: Routledge.
Giddens, A. (1998) *The Third Way: The Renewal of Social Democracy*. Cambridge: Polity Press.
Hobsbawm, E. (1995) *Age of Extremes: The Short Twentieth Century 1914–1991*. London: Abacus.
Honneth, A. (2002) 'An Interview with Axel Honneth: The Role of Sociology in the Theory of Recognition'. Interviewed by A. Peterson and R. Willig. *European Journal of Social Theory* 5 (2) 265–277.
Keane, J. (1988) *Democracy and Civil Society*. London: Verso.
MacCannell, D. (1992) *Empty Meeting Grounds: The Tourist Papers*. London: Routledge.
McKibbin, R. (2006) 'The Destruction of the Public Sphere', *London Review of Books* 28 (1) January.
Putnam, R. D. (1993) 'The Prosperous Community: Social Capital and Public Life', *The American Prospect* 4 (13) 11–18.
Putnam, R. D. (1995) 'Bowling Alone: America's Declining Social Capital', *Journal of Democracy* 6 (1) 65–78.
Putnam, R. D. (2000) *Bowling Alone: The Collapse and Revival of American Community*. New York: Simon & Schuster (Touchstone).
Preston, P. (2005) 'There is No Such Thing as Community', *Guardian*, 18 July.
Rose, N. (1999) *Powers of Freedom: Reframing Political Thought*. Cambridge: Cambridge University Press.
Tocqueville, A. de (1969) *Democracy in America*. New York: Doubleday.

38

SERIOUS LEISURE

The case of groundhopping

David Bauckham

Introduction

Despite the considerable amount of academic literature devoted to football, football culture and football fandom, comparatively little attention has been given to the subculture of football fans known as 'groundhoppers' (aka 'hoppers'), or the activity of 'groundhopping' (aka 'hopping'). There is no agreed definition, but this leisure pursuit can broadly be described as the 'collecting' of experiences of watching a complete ninety minutes of football at as many different grounds or stadia as possible, with the ultimate aim being to 'tick off' the complete set of visits in a particular league. In other words, if groundhopping is about collecting football experiences, it is concerned with the venue rather than the match.

This chapter discusses hopping within the context of Robert Stebbins' 'Serious Leisure Perspective' (Stebbins, 2007), incorporating data gathered from a series of interviews conducted with fifteen 'football grounds enthusiasts' (to use the author's own preferred descriptor). In particular, it explores the extent to which the subculture of groundhopping meets the criteria for classification as a serious leisure pursuit. In so doing, the chapter also tries to answer the following questions: Does groundhopping represent a homogeneous subculture? Does it constitute as set of sub-worlds? Or it is best understood as a marginal 'tourist' activity pursued by individuals (and mainly men) with a similar taste for new football experiences?

Unpacking serious leisure

Stebbins identifies three distinct forms of leisure synthesized into a common 'Serious Leisure Perspective', namely the interrelated concepts of 'serious', 'casual' and 'project-based' leisure.[1] This chapter is concerned with the former. Serious leisure involves the 'systematic pursuit of an amateur, hobbyist, or volunteer core activity that people find so substantial, interesting and fulfilling that, in the typical case, they launch themselves on a (leisure) career centred on acquiring and expressing a combination of its special skills, knowledge, and experience' (Stebbins, 2007: 5). Serious leisure pursuits are often shaped by individuals as a 'subjective career' through which they are motivated to continue and persist with a specific leisure activity. With regard to development of such a career, Green and Jones (2005) cite Levine and Moreland (1995), who identify four general career stages whereby a sport-related identity may be developed, namely: pre-socialization, recruitment, socialization, and acceptance. Stebbins also notes a fifth and final stage: decline.

There is not the scope within this chapter to explore Stebbins' thesis in any depth. For the purposes of the following discussion, however, we should note that serious leisure is subdivided into three ideal types: amateur pursuits, hobbyist activities, and career volunteering. Stebbins also identifies 'six distinguishing qualities' of serious leisure: perseverance; the sense of a career; significant personal input which draws on acquired knowledge, experience and skill; durable benefits; identification with the chosen leisure pursuit; and the development of a 'unique' or distinctive ethos or culture amongst participants. Perhaps what Stebbins sees as the most important of these is 'durable benefits', which often encapsulates the following kinds of expression: self-actualization; personal enrichment; self-expression; personal regeneration or renewal; a sense of accomplishment; enhancement of self-regard; a sense of community; and lasting physical products.

Stebbins also identifies the personal and social rewards of being involved in serious leisure pursuits. Notwithstanding the 'seriousness' of serious leisure, Stebbins acknowledges that thrill-seeking activity forms an important part of this reward system and contributes substantially to the motivation to stick with the pursuit in the hope of finding similar experiences again and again. Thus, thrills tend to predominantly be associated with the rewards of self-enrichment. As Stebbins notes, the intensity with which some participants approach their leisure suggests that they may, at times, be in 'psychological flow', where experiencing the activity becomes its own reward (Csikszentmihalyi and Robinson, 1990).

Although Stebbins' thesis has received considerable plaudits in Leisure Studies, it is not without its critics. Rojek (2000), for example, has suggested that the term 'serious' carries with it strong moralistic connotations. He also argues that the definition could apply just as well to the construction of deviant leisure identities and careers. Blackshaw and Crabbe (2004) agree that the notion of serious leisure might well be more widely applied than Stebbins originally anticipated, and that the integrative elements might be associated with the commitment found within any number of 'deviant subcultures' which extend beyond the morally laden cultures originally defined. For his part, Stebbins (1997, 2007) has acknowledged the existence of both serious and casual deviant leisure practices, but notes that the latter are probably the more common and widespread of the two.

These observations notwithstanding, it is the dichotomous nature of the thesis that appears to be the central focus for much of the critique surrounding the Serious Leisure Perspective. This is perhaps surprising, given that early on in its development Stebbins himself noted that casual and serious leisure 'are merely the poles of a complicated dimension along which individuals may be ranked by their degrees of involvement in a particular activity', suggesting that, given further research, it was likely that a research-informed conception that conveyed continuousness would replace what he referred to as a 'primitive dichotomy' (Stebbins, 1992: 6).

The problem appears to be that, as most researchers tend to look at either serious or casual leisure, there is a tendency to inadvertently stress the existence of a dichotomy. That having been said, it is perhaps Stebbins' own emphasis on serious leisure and apparent dismissal of casual leisure – at least in his early work – that is partly to blame. Nevertheless, Blackshaw (2010) considers that Stebbins sets up serious leisure as the 'champion' of the depth and substance of demanding leisure against the shallow superficiality of 'consumerist' casual leisure. For Stebbins, people are either fundamental about their leisure or they approach it without any quantifiable passion. This, argues Blackshaw, further ignores other serious leisure pursuits such as 'extreme leisure' that are not amateur, hobbyist or voluntary.

Rather than a polar dichotomy, Patterson (2001) describes a leisure continuum, from 'casual forms of leisure' to serious leisure. Other studies have demonstrated that participants progress and regress between serious and casual leisure (Brown, 2007), and sometimes 'zig-zag' between the two poles of such a continuum (Heuser, 2005). Taking a slightly different view, Shen and Yarnal (2010) propose a 'Leisure Experience Characteristic' framework, locating individuals on a continuum of leisure experiences, with casual and serious leisure representing the extremes at either end of that continuum. In addition, these authors feel that the continuity between the two can be viewed more clearly by examining the behavioural commitment of participants, as this conveys the kind of continuity suggested in Stebbins' notion of a 'leisure career'. Stebbins himself recognizes such an overlap, and has suggested that it is ultimately the attitude of a participant towards an activity that distinguishes whether it is casual or serious leisure, noting the existence of 'dabblers' in every serious leisure field that he has studied (Stebbins, 1997).

Getting to grips with groundhopping

Although there appears to be no agreed definition of 'groundhopping', what is fairly certain is that the term was used in print for the first time by Lenton (1979: 11), writing under the pseudonym of 'The Rover' in the now defunct magazine *Netstretcher*:

> Surely the number one groundhopper is Gerry Shepherd, who, having got through 92 Football League grounds is now well on his way through the Non-League circuit. To get to the Gainsborough Trinity v. Marine match recently he had to catch a train, bus, and ferry from Scarborough before hitching five lifts to arrive spot on time for an evening kick-off. Can anyone beat that?

As Crabbe *et al.* (2006) point out, this 'trainspotting' mind-set resides in the mind of many a football fan. But, as the above example demonstrates, it is often an extreme form of consumption among hoppers. Take the example of hopper Brian Buck (*Daily Mail*, 2011), who has visited 3,000 different grounds in the UK and recently celebrated his 10,000th game milestone. This illustrates perfectly why hoppers are invariably looked upon with bewilderment by the majority of football supporters. To them, travelling many miles to an unfamiliar ground, often alone, in some cases by public transport, to watch two clubs play, even though there is no vested interest in the outcome of the game, is incomprehensible. In this regard it can be argued that the practice of groundhopping represents a form of football fandom distinct from that of fans of football clubs, in that for hoppers the *actual activity* of football as a sport, and the *setting* in which it takes place, are often more important than supporting a particular club – even though many profess a specific allegiance and some hold season tickets. For hoppers, viewing a football match *in situ* is central to the activity, most often as a neutral. Hoppers are first and foremost fans of *football*, even that played at the lowest levels, and therefore might accurately be described as 'soccerphiles'. As Marchant (2011) observes in a BBC radio documentary about the activity: 'Going to see teams you don't want to see is all part of the job for a groundhopper.'

The earliest written account of 'groundhopping' is almost certainly by Easterbrook (1959), who, in describing himself as a 'collector' of football grounds, describes many of the components of contemporary hopping. Yet it is perhaps Grillo (2007) who provides the most compelling description, stating that many hoppers view the label as derisory and prefer to be known as 'football travellers'. Photographer Mike Floate, who describes himself as a 'visual historian' rather than a hopper, suggests that there might be different factions of the 'traveller', but they are united by one thing, which is often the catalyst for the start of many a hopping career: the desire for multi-stadia experience.

> For some, seeing a photo of a ground is enough, but for others the desire to know exactly what else there is at each ground is just too much – a visit must be made.
>
> (Floate, 1997: 4)

Certainly, many hoppers describe the thrill of visiting a 'new' ground or stadium for the first time, and, arguably, no one has described this experience better than Inglis (2001: 19–20), who in the following quotation relates his passion to his childhood experience of looking through a fence into a football ground (Chelmsford City), aged five or six:

> From our side of the fencing, we could hear vague rumblings from a crowd. As we moved nearer, through gaps in the fence I caught glimpses of an expanse of turf ... I am certain that at that moment something clicked. This was my first experience of a football ground ... That sensation of standing on the outside of a secret paradise, of desperately wanting to go in, has never left me. Nor has the memory of that Chelmsford ground; turf on the outside, turf on the inside; public space and private space, separated by a humble, green, corrugated fence.

Focusing his attention on the more celebratory-oriented aspects of groundhopping, Schwier classifies its adherents as an example of what he terms 'the fun-oriented fan faction'. Drawing his analysis from web pages, he describes the 'mixture of adventure, expedition, passion for football, pioneer romanticism and party culture' (Schwier, 2006: 174) of groundhopping.

These basic insights notwithstanding, academic discourse related to groundhopping has been sparse, with newspaper and magazine features tending to focus on the eccentricity exhibited by a minority of stereotypical hoppers, often with a comedic emphasis (Incenzo, 1997; Fischer, 2004). Wilson (2012), however, while referring to hoppers as 'an odd and eccentric bunch', nevertheless highlights the initiative demonstrated, and extraordinary logistical feats that some will accomplish in order to tick off a 'new' ground, particularly when they are prepared to travel overseas to do so.

Groundhopping as serious leisure and sport tourism

Elements of hopping appear to fit several of the five categories of hobbyist activities described by Stebbins: collectors, activity participants and hobby enthusiasts who become knowledgeable experts in their field. With regard to the latter category, Stebbins notes that this can be extended to include 'cultural tourism'. Green and Jones (2005) consider that tourism may become part of the unique ethos of the serious leisure participant and easily fits into Stebbins' definition of a 'leisure career'. These authors consider that collecting this kind of 'tourist' experience enhances the career path any serious leisure participant. Such experiences also serve as an important source of subcultural capital (Thornton, 1995). Within the hopping subculture such capital might be measured in the number of grounds visited, with the greatest value to be found in grounds that no longer exist, or those of relatively obscure clubs in leagues low down in the football pyramid. Thus, knowledge of places, events and attractions, of stories and lore, of the ritual and ceremony of the subculture's experience with the place, all contribute to the status of the serious sport tourist. When objectified, such cultural capital takes the form of souvenirs and/or photos from the activity and/or the destination.

Whilst convincingly demonstrating that sports tourism meets Stebbins' six distinctive qualities of serious leisure, Green and Jones also consider that 'serious sport tourism', which they define as 'travel to participate in serious leisure', is able to help individuals to develop a positive sense of social identity. For the majority of hoppers, whose travel to and from a match can often be accomplished within a twenty-four hour period without the need for an overnight stay, such tourism might be more properly defined as 'excursionist' (Weaver and Oppermann, 2000). Nevertheless, some hoppers undertake more ambitious and lengthy trips. Such travel – known by some as organized 'hops' (Metcalf, 1998) – puts them in extended contact with other participants.

Bammel and Burrus-Bammel (1996) consider that tourism is best understood as a matter of collecting experiences. This certainly appears to be a common interest shared by many hoppers, who, as previously noted, are essentially collectors of football grounds, ticking them off as they are visited. Collecting may also manifest itself through the acquisition of artefacts, such as programmes, pin badges and photographs relating to their visit to a new ground. Virtually all hoppers record their visit in some form, and with varying degrees of detail. *Groundhoppers*, a documentary film by Norwegian film-maker Eivind Tolås about a groundhopping tour of the UK by brothers Bjarte and Kjell Hjartøy, shows one of the brothers assiduously entering details of each game (and pubs visited) onto his computer spreadsheet (Tolås, 2005).

McIntosh and Schmeichel (2004) consider that collecting is notable for the fact that many of the motives offered as central to collecting revolve around self-identity, and especially the development of a more positive sense of self. These authors suggest that collectors are drawn to collecting as a means of bolstering the self by setting up goals that are tangible and attainable, and provide the collector with concrete feedback of progress made. Interestingly, if one is to draw comparisons with the 'collecting' of football grounds, they note that 'the hunt', the action of finding an item and making it one's own, is frequently considered the most enjoyable aspect of the collecting process.

Tankel and Murphy (1998) define 'a collectible' as an artefact that is acquired because its presumed monetary value will increase over time. Whilst this certainly applies to some hoppers' collections of programmes and pin badges, it does not apply to the 'collecting' of football grounds; this merely seems to be a never-ending quest towards acquiring a 'set' such as 'The 92' (every one of the grounds in the Premier League and Football League). In their study of collectors of comic books, these authors concluded that the acquisition, compilation and preservation of such books resembles the activities of museums and libraries and forms the basis for what they term 'curatorial consumption'. Such motivations for curatorial behaviour, as in fandom in general, do not derive from qualities uniquely inherent in the artefact, but rather from the value received from the collectors' interactions *with* the artefacts and, equally, the curatorial behaviours themselves. These insights can readily be applied to the collection of match-day programmes, in particular, where some hoppers purchase an additional copy, to be kept in mint condition. It might also apply to the taking and preservation of images as a photographic archive of football grounds, which for some enthusiasts clearly has a curatorial dimension.

Groundhopping as an achieved subculture

Even cursory examination demonstrates that groundhopping meets a number of the characteristics of what Donnelly (2007) describes as an 'achieved subculture'. To use an expression from Donnelly, hopping is associated with a package of 'cultural characteristics', which sees many of its adherents employing similar artefacts and symbols, engaging in similar forms of behaviour and adhering to a set of norms and values specific to a subculture. However, the key word here is 'similar', and it might be argued that within the subculture of groundhopping there exists a definable set of sub-worlds which are distinct from one another. What this suggests is that there is an important distinction to be drawn between separate subcultures, and separate units of the same subculture (Gordon, 1947). For example, whereas the majority of hoppers may be little more than 'collectors' of football grounds, and have to physically witness ninety minutes of football (and even a goal) at that ground for it to 'count', others may have a principal interest such as photography or the study of the socio-cultural history of the ground or stadium. For this category of hopper, if indeed they *are* hoppers, there is often an aesthetic and/or romantic motivation, and not necessarily a requirement to actually watch a football match.

Within this context, it is important to acknowledge that the development of a leisure career is a consequence of gradual immersion and 'recreational specialization' (Bryan, 1977; Scott and Schafer, 2001) for those who are motivated to want to pursue a deeper involvement than mere 'simple' participation. It might be argued that the different variants of hopping described above might be considered forms of such specialization. Similar analogies may be drawn with the activities of railway enthusiasts (Worthington, 2006) and birdwatchers (Scott *et al.*, 2005), both of which contain identifiable sub-worlds within their own subculture.

Donnelly (2007) further describes the membership of a subculture as being accommodated within a series of five concentric circles, which reflect different levels of commitment. In hopping terms, the innermost circle represents those likely to attend a match when and wherever possible, even if it means travelling substantial distances, while at outer circle are those occasional participants – 'dabblers' – with only a cursory knowledge of the meanings associated with the subculture. The circles in between these two extremes are more fluid and dynamic, allowing for movement in both directions.

The attitudes, beliefs and behaviours of climbers are used by Donnelly to further illustrate the distinguishing features of a subculture, many of which are also recognizable within groundhopping. In Donnelly's view, 'scope' and 'potential' are two aspects that must be present for the cycle of subcultural development to occur; this is clearly evident through hoppers' search for ever more obscure football grounds to 'conquer', if one chooses to appropriate Donnelly's climbing analogy. Certainly, many strive for greater challenges once 'The 92' has been achieved; whilst others eschew the professional game altogether and instead focus their attention on the many non-League and overseas clubs available for exploration.

Jones (2000) considers that, by its very nature, serious leisure provides a strong sense of social identity to the participant, which in turn has a positive influence on the individual's self-concept and self-esteem. In this regard, hoppers appear to find 'safety' within their own subculture, in which they perceive that they are understood and accepted. This might be seen as a safety net that shelters them from other groups of football supporters that may not accept or understand or may even deride their hopping activities. Even the most solitary of hoppers might perceive that he is a member of something bigger than himself, even if he has no direct interaction with others within the group. Nevertheless, it should be noted that, in accordance with Stebbins' category of 'identification', the development of social identity as a serious leisure participant is dependent upon the individual's being able to recognize himself as a group member.

Groundhopping in the words of groundhoppers

What is missing from the discussion generated so far is any direct reference to research carried out with groundhoppers. Between May and August 2009, the author carried out a combination of fifteen face-to-face interviews and asynchronous online questioning with groundhoppers. Each interview was based on twenty-nine questions largely formulated around Stebbins' categories of serious leisure, which were designed to elicit interviewees' own perceptions of groundhopping subculture.

Those initially approached were either personally known by the author as keen hoppers and/or 'familiar names' through their groundhopping activity. Some were authors of groundhopping blogs; others were publishers of groundhopping-related journals, and/or photographers of football grounds. This methodology was developed in order to obtain a rich variety of responses that it was hoped might also demonstrate a variety of attitudes, motivations and sub-worlds within groundhopping subculture. Further interviewees were identified through snowball tactics.

All interviewees were males aged between 37 and 61 years, with a mean age of 47. Two-thirds were either married or 'in a relationship'. Two were divorced. All but one, who was semi-retired, were in full-time employment (including one self-employed individual). Interestingly, four were employed as accountants, whilst a further three were postal workers.

This was a small-scale study and therefore it is difficult to generalize data gained from the research to the wider population of groundhoppers. A further potential limitation was the 'purposive' nature of the research sample itself; however, this enabled the author to generate richer and more meaningful responses than might otherwise have been obtained from a random sample of similar size.

Despite the limitations of sample size, data gathered from those who took part in the study suggests very strongly that groundhopping is best understood as a serious leisure pursuit. It was possible to code a significant number of responses from those interviewed against Stebbins' six distinguishing qualities. In all cases the presence of a leisure career was evident; and, in one case, the apparent 'decline' of such a career. All the interviewees demonstrated varying degrees of perseverance and personal effort, and in addition reported feelings that generally mirrored the eight 'broad outcomes' described by Stebbins as 'durable benefits'. For some, there were clearly elements of 'thrill and psychological flow' in their activity, particularly a sense of deep, focused involvement and requirement of concentration (although it could be argued that such emotions are similar for many football fans who are not necessarily hoppers). Others expressed the anticipation of visiting a ground for the first time, especially when it surpassed expectations:

> If you turn up at a ground and it's better than you thought, you feel ... I feel quite elated.
>
> (Interviewee 1)

Anecdotes of perseverance and overcoming adversity were expressed in a number of interviews, many of which centred on the desire to find a game, preferably at a 'new' ground, even when inclement weather had resulted in wholesale postponements.

There have been times where I've been in London and made five or six phone calls to try and find which games are going to be on and when I haven't I've been gutted, absolutely gutted. And when I find out there was one on that I didn't manage to find out about, I'm even more gutted.

(Interviewee 3)

Another interviewee declared that he felt 'suicidal' if on a Saturday he had not been able to find a game to go to. Whilst such feelings of despair are probably exaggerated, they do nevertheless suggest a psychological dimension of addiction, dependence and withdrawal amongst some 'hardcore' hoppers. A number of interviewees related ultimately futile stories of perseverance in the face of adversity, and it would appear that hoppers seem to enjoy recounting glorious failures as much as their successes.

In general there was a significant sense of accomplishment amongst those interviewed. Most often such feelings related to visiting a 'new' ground for the first time and 'ticking it off', thereby reinforcing the perception of groundhopping as essentially a collecting-based hobby whereby acquiring a 'set' of grounds is the principal goal.

There is a definite feeling of satisfaction gained from 'ticking' a new ground. If that feeling were to leave me, then that might be the time to stop.

(Interviewee 12)

Interestingly, however, one hopper admitted that the feeling of accomplishment in hopping was for him becoming increasingly diminished as more and more targets were met, perhaps indicating that he was reaching the end-stage of his 'hopping career' and entering the final stage of decline described by Stebbins:

I did feel good on completing 'The 92' … the subsequent sense of achievement in completing the non-League divisions gives an increasingly diminished return. It's just a routine now; it's an ongoing plod.

(Interviewee 8)

Many of the interviewees reported that the sports tourism aspect of hopping, together with knowledge gained through visiting places that they might not otherwise have experienced, was a powerful reward gained through hopping. Some intentionally planned a route to visit places of interest, and for a number of those interviewed, this served as a greater motivator than simply ticking off a ground from a list.

That's the one thing you look forward to on a Saturday. Choosing somewhere to go: a part of the country maybe you haven't been to before; finding out a little about it and then going there.

(Interviewee 7)

Indeed, far from being merely 'tickers off', some of those interviewed expressed a far deeper interest in football culture, both within the UK and abroad. International hopping is clearly associated with more complex logistical problems to be surmounted, not only with the booking of transport and flights, but also acquiring tickets and ensuring that a match is actually happening on a specific date. In such cases, even the Internet can have its limitations, especially when the text is in an unfamiliar language.

International groundhopping appears to have also resulted in the acquisition of knowledge through experience for many hoppers, thus indirectly fulfilling self-actualizing needs:

> I did go to the Ukraine to see Dynamo Kiev, which motivated me to attempt to learn the Cyrillic alphabet. While I can't claim to know all of it, I can now recognize words and am able to speak some of them.
>
> (Interviewee 10)

Even those who did not appear particularly interested in the more holistic aspects of hopping admitted to enjoying the experience of a match more at a particularly scenic ground, even if there was not much in the way of facilities. Thus, some hoppers appear to be not only collectors of grounds but collectors of both football experiences and football knowledge.

> I do come to these places to discover that our country is full of fantastic variety and colour, and that going to watch the same team from the same debenture seat once a fortnight does not allow the typical fan that opportunity of discovery.
>
> (Interviewee 8)

When asked to describe 'costs', not surprisingly a number of interviewees cited the financial costs incurred, particularly those regularly travelling large distances and/or watching games in Europe or even further afield; whilst one expressed concern over the carbon footprint he was creating. Several commented that such costs had made them more circumspect when considering hopping trips. Time and effort were also considered a cost by some, who also admitted that the travel was exhausting at times. Another confessed that on occasions he felt that the activity was a 'millstone' that he felt obliged to maintain.

Others commented that there was also a cost incurred in respect of difficulties in maintaining relationships and other leisure pursuits, due to their commitment to groundhopping. Some acknowledged that in order to experience the rewarding aspects of hopping, other, less rewarding experiences sometimes had to be endured, occasionally making them question the activity:

> It's crossed my mind a few times … you know, a field in the middle of nowhere and it starts chucking it down with rain and there's no cover. You think 'what am I doing? I'd rather be doing something else'.
>
> (Interviewee 1)

Overall, though, the rewards outweighed such costs, and optimism of future, more rewarding experiences invariably prevailed.

Whilst there was a generally broad correlation amongst the responses that fulfilled Stebbins' various criteria, those that referred to the 'unique ethos' of hopping, and by inference its culture and social world, were less uniform. Responses indicated that whilst hoppers value the benefits of social interaction that the activity brings, a shared spirit of community manifested in shared attitudes, practices, values, beliefs and goals was not always present. Certainly, it was less homogeneous than had been anticipated by the author. Many of those interviewed stated that they valued the small circle of friends and acquaintances made through hopping but didn't necessarily feel part of, or *want* to be part of other cliques within the subculture.

Ironically, it appears that the Internet, and particularly discussion forums and bulletin boards that ostensibly function to bring like-minded communities together, have been in some way responsible for some of the divisions that have developed in the hopping world. Several of those interviewed cited the message board of the late Tony Kempster (Tony's English Football Site) as a valuable networking tool, but equally, some were contemptuous of what they perceived as the bragging and 'one-upmanship' displayed by posters writing about visiting ever more obscure grounds that were little more than recreation ground pitches. To some degree the reason for such extreme or 'hardcore' hopping is that the more grounds (or pitches) one visits, the greater the challenge is to find more. However, it might equally be described as an example of 'serious leisure taken too far' (Lawrence 2006):

> There are degrees of severity for people who can't leave it alone. For instance the football season has ended and these hoppers all going to Summer Leagues. I mean they're just fields in the middle of nowhere.
>
> (Interviewee 1)

> I think some people like to sort of boast ... if they can get one up on a fellow ground-hopper where they've been, you know somewhere remote ... [it] makes their day to know they've been there and the other people haven't.
>
> (Interviewee 7)

Far more divisive is the debate on what groundhopping actually is, and in particular what should *count*. One thing most agreed on is that, because there are no specific 'rules' related to what actually *counts* as a 'new' ground, and because participants essentially have their own criteria, it is difficult to arrive at a universally agreed definition. Thus there are inevitable disputes over tallies between the more serious and competitive hoppers. Scott *et al.* (2005) describe how division occurs within social worlds because people fundamentally disagree over what constitutes appropriate activity, and this certainly seems to apply within the social world of groundhopping.

This was something that became apparent during the course of the interviews, and especially in responses to the question whether hoppers had any particular rules or rituals attached to their activity. One interviewee, for example, stated that he would not visit grounds where there was no stand or floodlights. In his view, these were merely pitches and not grounds. Another said that he could not 'count' a ground if he arrived after kick-off, unless it was only a matter of minutes and he had been delayed by no fault of his own. If he had miscalculated the journey time, then that was another matter. There were also differences in opinion as to whether a ground had to be visited twice if two separate clubs were sharing it, or whether a Premier League or Football League ground could 'count' if it was being visited for an international match.

As an extension to the question of identification, interviewees were also asked whether they believed a 'stereotypical hopper' really existed. A number stated that one hopper could usually spot another hopper, and all agreed that there were some eccentric, obsessive personalities – the *'comedy hoppers'*, in the words of one interviewee. These are hoppers who take the activity to extremes, are generally lacking in social skills, and whose exploits, some of which are probably apocryphal, have passed into hopping 'folklore'. Equally, however, all maintained that such stereotypes were largely in the minority.

This debate was also reflected in responses to the question whether those interviewed identified themselves as groundhoppers. Whilst the majority had little hesitation in answering an unequivocal 'yes', others were more circumspect and sought to clarify what the label actually signified. These individuals were loath to describe themselves as hoppers, stating that although they were collectors of football grounds, they were far more interested in the ground for its own sake: its architectural fabric and social-cultural significance, rather than purely witnessing a game there as a means to the end of ticking it off a list.

> I think groundhoppers have actually the wrong name because they're not bothered about the ground; they're bothered about what goes on *in* the ground.
>
> (Interviewee 2)

Conclusions

The activity and subculture of groundhopping sits broadly within the definition of serious leisure. The applicability of Stebbins' model holds out the possibility of incorporating the complexity of this subculture into its explanations of the 'six distinguishing qualities'. However, the applicability of Stebbins' model may also be limited by the paucity of research on groundhopping. In this author's study it was found that the applicability of the distinguishing quality of 'unique ethos' requires further research involving a larger sample, or possibly an ethnographic study. Central to this aspect of serious leisure, the term 'ground-hopper' needs to be properly defined and agreed upon, along with clear guidelines that stipulate what 'counts' and what doesn't. This is not an impossible task since, to take one example, 'The Ninety-Two Club' (www.ninetytwoclub.org.uk) already lays down some very precise guidelines that many individuals appear happy to comply with. However, at present groundhopping is too informal and lacking in any structure for it to be termed an achieved subculture. Further research involving a larger sample would also be required in order to develop a taxonomy of sub-worlds. The research underpinning this chapter has demonstrated that the two most obvious ones would be, on the one hand, those who primarily 'collect' and 'count' grounds for the sake of completing leagues and who have to witness a complete game; and, on the other hand, those who have a more social historical interest as, for example, photographic archivists, who do not keep a score and do not have to necessarily witness a game – a visit is all that is necessary.

Note

1 Casual leisure is considerably less substantial than serious leisure and offers no sense of career. In Stebbins' (1997) view it is intrinsically hedonistic, 'immediately, intrinsically rewarding, relatively short-lived core activity, requiring little or no special training to enjoy it' (Stebbins, 2007: xii). Project-based leisure, on the other hand, refers to the more short-term, often one-off, projects requiring considerable planning and effort; these often take the form of celebratory or commemorative events.

References

Bammel, G. and Burrus-Bammel, L.L. (1996) *Leisure and Human Behaviour*, 3rd ed. Madison, USA: Brown & Benchmark.

Blackshaw, T. (2010) *Leisure*. London and New York: Routledge.

Blackshaw, T. and Crabbe, T. (2004) *New Perspectives on Sport and Deviance: Consumption, Performativity and Social Control*. Abingdon: Routledge.

Brown, C.A. (2007) 'The Carolina Shaggers: Dance as Serious Leisure', *Journal of Leisure Research* 39 (4) 632–647.

Bryan, H. (1977) 'Leisure Value Systems and Recreational Specialization: The Case of Trout Fishermen', *Journal of Leisure Research* 9: 174–187.

Crabbe, T., Brown, A., Mellor, G. and O'Connor, K. (2006) *Football: An All Consuming Passion.* Manchester: EA Sports Research/Substance.

Csikszentmihalyi, M. and Robinson, R.E. (1990) *The Art of Seeing: An Interpretation of the Aesthetic Encounter.* Los Angeles: J. Paul Getty Museum.

Daily Mail (2011) 'Is This Britain's Biggest Football Fan? Spurs Supporter Brian Has Watched 10,000 Games and Visited 3,000 grounds', 2 April. Retrieved from: http://www.dailymail.co.uk/sport/football/article-1372635/Is-spurs-fan-Brian-Buck-Britains-biggest-football-fan.html.

Donnelly, P. (2007) 'Toward a Definition of Sport Subcultures', in A. Tomlinson (ed.) *The Sport Studies Reader.* London: Routledge.

Easterbrook, B.V. (1959) 'Collectors' Corner', *FA News*, December, 158–161.

Fischer, D. (2004) 'The Craziest Fans in the World', *FIFA Magazine*, 6 June: 56–59.

Floate, M. (1997) *Grounds Frenzy.* Swanley: Newlands Printing Services.

Gordon, M.M. (1947) 'The Concept of the Sub-culture and its Application', in K. Gelder and S. Thornton (1997) (eds) *The Subcultures Reader.* London: Routledge.

Green, B.C. and Jones, I. (2005) 'Serious Leisure, Social Identity and Sport Tourism', *Sport in Society* 8 (2) 164–181.

Grillo, R. (2007) *Anoraknophobia: The Life and Times of a Football Obsessive.* Stroud: Stadia Publishing.

Heuser, L. (2005) 'We're Not Too Old to Play Sports: The Career of Women Lawn Bowlers', *Leisure Studies* 24 (1) 45–60.

Incenzo, T. (1997) 'Fan's Eye View: No 222 Groundhopping', *Independent*, 6 September. Retrieved from: http://www.independent.co.uk/sport/fans-eye-view-no--222--groundhopping--1237748.html.

Inglis, S. (2001) *Sightlines: A Stadium Odyssey.* London: Yellow Jersey Press.

Jones, S. (2000) 'A Model of Serious Leisure Identification: The Case of Football Fandom', *Leisure Studies* 19 (4) 283–298.

Lawrence, L. (2006) 'To Obsessively Go … Exploring Serious Leisure and the "Other" Side of Leisure in Cult Fandom', in S. Elkington, I. Jones and L. Lawrence (eds) *Serious Leisure: Extensions and Applications.* Brighton: University of Brighton, Leisure Studies Association.

Lenton, B. (1979) 'The Rover: Netstretcher', *The Non-League Soccer Magazine* 11 (18 September).

Levine, J. and Moreland, R. (1995) 'Group Processes', in A. Tedder (ed.) *Advanced Social Psychology.* New York: McGraw-Hill.

Marchant, I. (Presenter), and Everett, P. (Producer) (2011) *The Completists* [Radio Broadcast]. London: BBC Radio 4, 30 January.

McIntosh, W.D. and Schmeichel, B. (2004) 'Collectors and Collecting: A Social Psychological Perspective', *Leisure Sciences* 26: 85–97.

Metcalf, R. (1998) 'Football: Groundhoppers Invade Devon Again', *Independent*, 10 April. Retrieved from: http://www.independent.co.uk/sport/football-groundhoppers-invade-devon-again--1155513.html#.

Patterson, I. (2001) 'Serious Leisure as a Positive Contributor to Social Inclusion for People with Intellectual Disabilities', *World Leisure Journal* 43 (3) 16–24.

Rojek, C. (2000) *Leisure and Culture.* Basingstoke: Palgrave Macmillan.

Schwier, J. (2006) 'Fandom and Subcultural Media', in A. Tomlinson and C. Young (eds) *German Football: History, Culture, Society.* London: Routledge.

Scott, D. and Schafer, C.S. (2001)'Recreational Specialization: A Critical Look at the Construct', *Journal of Leisure Research* 33 (3) 319–343.

Scott, D., Cavin, D., Cronan, M. and Kerins, A.J. (2005) 'Hardcore Leisure: A Source of Division within Leisure Social Worlds'. Paper presented at the Eleventh Canadian Congress on Leisure Research, Nanaimo, B.C.

Shen, X.S. and Yarnal, C. (2010). 'Blowing Open the Serious Leisure–Casual Leisure Dichotomy: What's in There?', *Leisure Sciences* 32 (2) 162–179.

Stebbins, R.A. (1992) *Amateurs, Professionals, and Serious Leisure.* Montreal and Kingston: McGill-Queen's University Press.

Stebbins, R.A. (1997) 'Casual Leisure: A Conceptual Statement', *Leisure Studies* 16 (1) 17–25.

Stebbins, R.A. (2007) *Serious Leisure: A Perspective for Our Time*. New Jersey: Transaction Publishers.

Tankel, J.D. and Murphy, K. (1998). 'Collecting Comic Books. A Study of the Fan and Curatorial Consumption', in C. Harris and A. Alexander (eds) *Theorizing Fandom: Fans, Subculture and Identity*. New Jersey: Hampton Press, Inc.

The Ninety-Two Club. http://www.ninetytwoclub.org.uk/nineq.htm/ [online].

Thornton, S. (1995) *Club Cultures: Music, Media, and Subcultural Capital*. Cambridge: Polity.

Tolås, E. (Director) (2005) *Groundhoppers* (documentary film). Bergen, Norway: Flimmer Film.

Tony's English Football Site. http://www.tonykempster.co.uk/ [online].

Weaver, D. and Oppermann, M. (2000) *Tourism Management*. Brisbane: John Wiley.

Wilson, J. (2012) 'ACoN Diary 3: David Dein, Visas and the Art of Groundhopping. FourFourTwo' (25 January). Retrieved from: http://fourfourtwo.com/blogs/africacupofnations2012/archive/2012/01/25/acon-diary–3-david-dein-visas-and-the-art-of-groundhopping.aspx.

Worthington, B. (2006) '"Getting Steamed Up about Leisure": Aspects of Serious Leisure within the Tourism Industry', in S. Elkington, I. Jones and L. Lawrence (eds) *Serious Leisure: Extensions and Applications*. Brighton: University of Brighton, Leisure Studies Association.

39

VOLUNTEERING AS LEISURE, LEISURE AS VOLUNTEERING

Geoff Nichols and Kirsten Holmes with Tom Baum

Introduction

Volunteering and leisure are closely linked. Researchers have argued that some forms of volunteering are also leisure, and many leisure organizations rely on the contributions of volunteers. Yet both are also contested concepts, as is apparent in the discussions developed by the contributors to this volume (e.g. Blackshaw, Bramham, Rojek, Roberts, Spracklen, Stebbins, *et al.*) and their writings elsewhere. Likewise, there are divergent views with respect to how both leisure and volunteering are changing. A further common thread engages with debates about how an increasingly fragmented and fluid society (Bauman, 2005) is reflected in both leisure and volunteering.

This chapter first reviews theoretical concepts and public perceptions of volunteering. Second, it considers overlaps between leisure and volunteering; and third, it discusses contemporary changes in volunteering. It is important to note that understandings of leisure, volunteering and the relationship between them will vary between cultures (Meijs *et al.*, 2003). Much literature and theory draws strongly on the Western European/North American/ Australasian experience. By contrast, Hustinx *et al.* (2010) note that in some cultures there is no specific term for volunteering. For example, in Russian there is no single word that encapsulates what is generally understood to be volunteering in the 'Western' literature. In India, by contrast, the term appears to be interpreted as synonymous with social work. There is also a different emphasis between Europe and North America, where volunteering is, respectively, within a strong tradition of small organizations led by volunteers themselves, or is located within large non-profit organizations in which volunteers are managed by paid employees.

What is volunteering?

A recent review (Hustinx *et al.*, 2010) has concluded that volunteering is challenging to define, firstly because it is a social construct and secondly because it is studied across a range of disciplines which attribute different meanings and functions to it. Hustinx *et al.* also articulate a further difficulty in that theoretical accounts of volunteering are biased towards methodological approaches in which the variable 'volunteering' is explained by a causal relationship with other variables, such as age, gender, etc., and this has tended to ignore the complexity of the concept.

Unpaid work, activism and leisure

A common theoretical conception of volunteering is as three overlapping categories of activity: unpaid work or service, activism and leisure (Billis, 1993 in Rochester *et al.*, 2010) (see Figure 39.1). First, unpaid work has been the dominant paradigm for policy makers and management theory. Second, activism is association around a set of shared values (with some debate over whether this needs to be expressed in a delivery or campaigning organization [Musick and Wilson, 2008: 23]). Third, volunteering as leisure has drawn on Stebbins' typologies of 'serious leisure', casual volunteering and project-based leisure (Stebbins, 2007). An example of unpaid work might be volunteers working in a hospital alongside employees doing the same work (O'Donohue and Nelson, 2009), or volunteers at major sporting events (Ralston *et al.*, 2004). Activism might be represented by 'knocking on doors in a voter registration drive in the segregated South (of the United States) in the 1960s' (Musick and Wilson, 2008: 19). Serious leisure has been used to understand steam engine-museum enthusiasts (Hagan, 2008) and leaders in the UK Guide Association (Nichols and King, 1999), among numerous other examples.

The three-perspective model (Figure 39.1) is useful because each type of volunteering has characteristic motivations, areas of activity and roles. Thus, it gives insights for volunteer management (see Schulz *et al.*, 2011). However, Billis provides an academic construct which has not been empirically tested to see if it accords with the views of volunteers themselves. Culturally speaking, the unpaid-work paradigm has dominated in Anglo-Saxon countries – that is, North America, Australasia and the UK – whereas the activism model more widely operates in Northern Europe.

Importantly, volunteering should not be confused with membership of 'non-profit' organizations or organizations led by volunteers. Countries with a large number of voluntary associations tend to have a larger number of volunteers; however, membership of such an association does not automatically imply active volunteering (Musick and Wilson, 2008).

Figure 39.1 A three-perspective model of volunteering (Rochester *et al.*, 2010: 15)

Dimensions of volunteering

A conceptualization of volunteering in English-speaking Western countries as unpaid work suggests that it should involve a net cost to the volunteer, and thus implies a degree of altruism. Cnaan *et al.* (1996) analysed definitions of volunteering and concluded that there were four common dimensions:

- *free choice*, which ranged from free to obligated;
- *remuneration*, which ranged from none to a stipend/low pay;
- *structure*, which ranged from formal to informal;
- *intended beneficiaries*, which ranged from complete strangers, to friends or relatives, to oneself.

Thus, a *pure* definition of a volunteer would be at one end of these scales, with a high personal net cost, i.e. free will, unpaid, formal structure and benefiting strangers; but a *moderate*, or even a *broad*, definition would also be possible. The validity of these scales was tested in a survey of 514 volunteers in Pennsylvania and Delaware. The public perception of net cost to the volunteer was the overriding concept, and this was judged relative to the perception of how much this net cost was felt by the volunteer. Thus, two volunteers might incur identical costs, but the one who experiences a greater relative loss will be regarded as a 'purer' form of volunteer. This implies that perceived altruism is important. The notion of a scale of volunteer 'purity' and how this may be changing is discussed later with reference to changes in society (Hustinx and Meijs, 2011).

While Cnaan's ongoing work was in the United States, surveys have found the 'net cost' concept of volunteering to be the common denominator of all four dimensions of volunteering across Canada, Israel, Belgium, India, the Netherlands, Germany, Italy and the United States (Meijs *et al.*, 2003). Across all these countries 'remuneration and less free will have a definitive negative impact on people's perception of who is a volunteer' (p. 32). However, net cost to the volunteer appears to be more important in defining a volunteer than are free will and free choice of activity.

Economic theory (Weisbrod, 1978; Hustinx *et al.*, 2010: 415) has also been employed to explain an apparent paradox of volunteering in which individuals motivated by self-interest (as in economic models) incur an apparent net cost. Such costs can be substantial, as is the case with volunteer tourists, paying substantial sums to volunteer (Tomazos and Butler, 2012). Explanations are that a volunteer receives private or intrinsic benefits such as marketable work experience or a 'warm glow' of satisfaction. The volunteer may also value the 'public goods' they produce, which can be shared by everyone. Thus a certain degree of altruism would be represented by the provision of a public good, but, on the other hand, a volunteer would also benefit themselves. For example, a volunteer helping to run a sports club may do so partly for their own benefit, to allow them to play the sport and gain the other rewards of club membership; and partly to create opportunity for others to play sport. Researching altruism is made difficult by the impossibility of avoiding socially acceptable responses (Rochester *et al.*, 2010: 121). For example, while Smith (1994) noted that altruism is often given as a reason for volunteering, in his earlier work (Smith, 1981) he argued that there was little pure altruism in participation, since people gain some pleasure for themselves even when acting 'altruistically'. Volunteers' motivations are best understood as a balance between self-interest and altruism. Motivation could, in turn, offer a fifth dimension to Cnaan *et al.*'s volunteerism construct. Alternatively, motivation could be considered as an attitude underlying the 'intended beneficiaries' dimension; from an economic perspective, the main beneficiaries are the volunteers themselves.

Leisure, work and freedom, and what these mean for volunteering

Leisure has also been delineated along a series of dimensions. These usually include perceived freedom, intrinsic motivation or satisfaction, competence or mastery, discretionary time and spontaneity (Esteve *et al.*, 1999; Iso-Ahola, 1979; Unger and Kernan, 1983). However, as with volunteering, there are different perceptions of what leisure is or may be. Leisure dimensions have also been empirically tested; however, unlike volunteering, there are no similar cross-cultural studies and, as a consequence, there appears to be less consensus on the meaning of leisure.

While relative freedom, in that 'individuals can ... feel that they have scope for choice' (Roberts, 1978: 5) has always been a central criterion of leisure, the degree and nature of choice has been fiercely debated, and recently reflects different views on how society is changing, with implications for both volunteering and leisure. As elucidated by Spracklen (2011: 193–198; Snape, 2012), contrasting views of leisure are as a relatively free activity; as an activity constrained by structure; and as freedom in a post-modern society in which structural constraints are less relevant. Debates between these positions are a matter of degree and are amply developed elsewhere in this book. These positions imply a different role for leisure in the task of establishing and maintaining a personal identity – which we shall return to in discussing changes in volunteering.

The positions in the debate above depend as much on the perspective of the commentator, and the evidence they choose to draw on, as on the experience of the general public. It is interesting to compare the proponents of modernist and post-modernist positions. For Roberts (2011: 14–15), 'leisure cannot be a source of our basic identities'. These are 'based on occupations, ethnicity/nationality, sex and family roles'. Identity is based on traditional structural variables – 'we do not change our basic identities every time we shop and purchase new outfits or refresh our music libraries'. By contrast, Bramham and Wagg (2010) claim to show, through case studies, that class and gender 'is (in the commodified, corporatized West, at least) being replaced by a more fluid identity politics' (Spracklen, 2011: 196). Similarly, for Crouch (2010), 'space is in a constant flux and people make their way through their lives and the act of creativity is fundamental to the construction of fleetingly real, solid identities and senses of space' (cited in Spracklen, 2011: 195). For Blackshaw (2010: 120), 'in the liquid modern world we live in, which is founded first and foremost on freedom, leisure moves steadily into its position as the principal driving force underpinning the human goal of satisfying our hunger for meaning and our thirst for giving our lives a purpose'. Although including inconsistencies (Veal, 2011), Blackshaw draws heavily on Bauman's notion of 'liquid modernity' to argue that Western society is less structured, and so the individual is free to pursue leisure, particularly through consumption; although this appears to ignore the possibility that the ability to consume is unevenly distributed and conspicuous consumption is itself a positional good (Nichols, 2009).

The point of this foray into leisure theory is that relative 'freedom' is a common dimension of volunteering and leisure. But debated points include: how 'free' leisure is, how important leisure is as a site of identity construction and expression, and whether leisure is becoming more important as a site of identity construction in a 'liquid modernity'.

Relating leisure to volunteering

How, then, do we compare leisure and volunteering? Leisure and volunteering intersect through Stebbins' concept of serious leisure; through the dimension of relative freedom, through the quality of the experience, and through the relation of both to available time. Where is the overlap? Not all forms of volunteering are leisure. Parker (1997), for example, identified four types of volunteering based on the individual's motivation, of which only one form is leisure volunteering. The role of freedom and obligation within the volunteer experience is particularly problematic for leisure researchers and leads to marginal forms of volunteering. One example of this is where young people are required to volunteer in order to gain work experience leading to paid employment. This is particularly common in museums in the UK, where it is generally considered a requirement for aspiring museum professionals to work unpaid for considerable lengths of time (Holmes, 2006).

A key aspect of volunteering is that it can provide leisure opportunities for others. This might be in organizations led by paid staff – for example, National Trust historic properties in England. It might be through organizations completely led by volunteers: for example, there are about 100,000 sports club run by volunteers in England, each relying on about twenty volunteers (Nichols, forthcoming), and sports and physical recreation organizations accounted for 37 per cent of all volunteering in Australia (Australian Bureau of Statistics, 2011).

In organizations led by volunteers an important implication is that the core volunteers not only provide opportunities for others' leisure, but also maintain the structure of voluntary organizations in which others can volunteer. For example, in UK sports clubs, 20 per cent of volunteers contribute about 80 per cent of the work (Nichols, 2005). If, as a consequence of a trend towards episodic volunteering, discussed below, it were to become impossible to replace these 'stalwarts', the infrastructure of volunteer-led organizations would collapse.

Leisure, work and volunteering

Leisure and volunteering are also related to each other through the relationship of both to paid work. This influences the quality of the experience of leisure and volunteering, and the availability of time for both activities.

While the relationship between work and leisure is no longer a 'hot topic' in Leisure Studies, early Leisure Studies in the UK was strongly influenced by industrial sociology and was initially preoccupied with this relationship. Parker's (1976) text-book on the topic had a chapter devoted to the subject, and Roberts (1978) similarly discussed leisure as non-work on the third page of his volume. The very idea of work and leisure as measured and delimited by time, and taking place in different spaces, has been argued to reflect a hegemony imposed by industrialization (Thompson, 1968). This is related to discussion about freedom: particularly drawing on a neo-Marxist perspective in that work and leisure have been contrasted by degrees of freedom. However, as Parker pointed out, and Beatty and Torbert (2003) have recently reiterated in their crash-course introduction to Leisure Studies for managers, another way of conceptualizing both leisure and work is in terms of 'quality of activity' (Parker, 1976: 18). This could be defined in relationship to moral judgements (as in a religious-based definition), or in psychological terms (for example, a sense of 'flow'), or, as Beatty and Torbert (2003: 249) suggest, as an attitude of mind: 'the ability to experience both at the same time is an indicator of personal development and is therefore a skill that ... can be cultivated'. This fails to acknowledge that, whatever one's attitude of mind and personal development, the opportunity to achieve personal satisfaction in paid work is unevenly distributed between jobs; and there is a tendency for management theorists to gloss over this. However, the main point is that there may be a false dichotomy between leisure and work in terms of the quality of the experience. In this respect, the experiences of work, leisure and volunteering could overlap.

Leisure and volunteering are also affected by the distribution of time in paid work. The distribution of this time, within the population and between jobs, has changed since the 1970s. As Roberts described as early as 1998, 'working life has been changed by the decline of occupational communities and long-term occupational careers, the normalisation of non-standard hours, the end of the formerly long-term decline in hours, and the spread of unemployment' (Roberts, 1998: 21). As leisure spending has grown, so have the service industries, to meet the new demand, and thus patterns of work become less standardized. It is important to add to this the considerable increase in female employment.

Changes in availability of time have affected leisure. The destandardization of working hours appears to have been reflected in sports participation as a trend away from team sports and towards more casual participation between 1987 and 1996 (Coalter, 1999), continued between 2005 and 2010; when growth sports have been athletics (including all forms of running), gym and cycling; whereas golf, badminton, tennis, cricket, rugby union and rugby league have all experienced a decline (Gratton *et al.*, 2011). Later in this chapter we also note a trend from regular volunteering to episodic volunteering which may be due to similar changes in working patterns.

Changes in availability of time will also affect who volunteers. The considerable increase in numbers of females in the labour market may reduce their propensity to volunteer. On the other hand, larger numbers of the retired and unemployed will potentially increase the supply of volunteers, although with quite different motives.

Changes in availability of time will affect how much people volunteer. It appears that time at work has increased for some people, although it is not easy to distinguish between time pressures arising from a 'real' increase in working hours (Schor, 2006) and from a perception of a time famine arising from an exponentially increasing bombardment of opportunities, especially those in the congested leisure time (Robinson and Godbey, 1999). Whether real or perceptual, a lack of time is the first reason given in surveys asking people why they do not volunteer (Cabinet Office, 2008; Atwood *et al.*, 2003) and why they do not volunteer in sport (Taylor *et al.*, 2003).

A further factor influencing leisure could be widening social inequalities. Replicating Wilkenson and Pickett's (2009) influential analysis of a negative relationship between income inequality and well-being, Gratton *et al.* (2011) have also shown that sports participation appears to be lower in countries with greater social inequality, such as the UK. It is highest in the Nordic countries, which are the most equal. This may be because in more unequal societies people think that they have less time to devote to sport. It may be that the opportunity cost of time devoted to sport, or volunteering, is greater in more unequal societies, measured in relation to the time required to maintain relative status position. Thus, if UK society continues to become more unequal, we would expect volunteering to decline.

Thus the relation between leisure and work has several implications for volunteering. Some lucky people may be able to achieve the same satisfying quality of experience in all three activities. A move from standardized working times will affect when time is available for leisure. A change in the distribution of work will affect who is available to volunteer. And a real or perceptual reduction in leisure time, whether due to increased time at work or not, will reduce the perceived time available to volunteer.

461

Changes in volunteering

The preceding discussion has hinted at changes in leisure and volunteering, which this section will consider in more detail, starting with volunteering and relating this back to leisure.

Traditionally, volunteering commitments have been seen as sustained or continuous, with volunteers working for the same organization over an extended period of time, developing significant leisure careers in the process (Stebbins, 1996). In this way, volunteering mirrors traditional long-term working relationships between employer and employee in the main-stream remunerated economy. More disparate forms of commitment and volunteering have gained in popularity (Brudney, 2005; Merrill, 2006), perhaps reflecting wider short-termism in employment and leisure relationships generally, or what Watson *et al.* (2003) describe as fragmentation in working and personal life. Current trends overwhelmingly suggest that work–life balance issues and the demands they place on people's time, from employment, family and leisure, affect the hours that people can commit to volunteering (Gaskin, 2003; Merrill, 2006). Indeed, in Western countries there has been a pattern of decreasing hours devoted to voluntary activity since the 1990s (Grimm *et al.*, 2006; Australian Bureau of Statistics, 2007; Cabinet Office, 2008).

The remainder of this chapter will consider four aspects of change: a decline in volunteering; the growth of episodic volunteering; reflexivity in volunteering; and changes in perceptions of volunteering.

A decline in volunteering

Notwithstanding the political impetus to encourage volunteering activity as part of the notion of 'The Big Society' in the UK (Kisby, 2010), the UK National Citizenship survey reported a decline in volunteering: 'twenty-five per cent of people reported that they volunteered formally at least once a month in 2010–11, a lower rate than at any point between 2001 and 2007–08 (when it ranged between 27 per cent and 29 per cent), but unchanged on 2008–09 and 2009–10 levels' (National Statistics, 2011: 1). This decline may reflect less available time, or a reduction in perceived time, or the greater opportunity cost of time as society becomes more unequal. It is possible that it reflects a more individualistic society in which commit-ment to active citizenship to promote the common good has diminished. In Australia, a decline in volunteer hours has been noted which coincides with an increase in volunteer participation (Australian Bureau of Statistics, 2007). More Australians are volunteering, but for less time, which suggests that the nature of volunteer participation is changing.

Episodic volunteering

Macduff (1991) first coined the term 'episodic volunteering' to refer to one-off volunteering assignments which offer a flexible relationship with an organization, such as that evident with respect to event volunteering. Hustinx and Lammertyn (2003: 568) use 'distant' to describe volunteer participation that is characterized by loose, infrequent, short-term and activities-based involvement. More recently, it has been recognized that, whilst the volunteering activities may be short term, the volunteers may return or re-engage with a single organization in a series of episodic relationships (Handy *et al.*, 2006; Macduff, 2005). This may also be considered a form of project-based leisure, where participants engage in a serious leisure activity for a finite period of time (Stebbins, 2005). Returning to Watson *et al.*'s (2003) analysis, the volunteering episode, therefore, may be seen as a fragment within a series of disjointed life experiences, also reflecting, in part, Bauman's (2005) concept of liquidity in contemporary living that is part of an increasing trend in all forms of life, including work and leisure.

While there have been numerous papers identifying the episodic volunteering phenomenon (for example, Merrill, 2006), evidence of trends has been harder to find. It is suggested in England by an increase in the percentage of the population volunteering at least once in the previous twelve months, between 2001 and 2003, but a static rate of regular volunteering, defined as at least once a month for the last twelve months (Evans and Saxton, 2005); and responses from volunteer organizations (Ellis Paine *et al.*, 2007). It has been identified in trends in Australian sport participation (Cuskelly, 2005) and, as noted above, more Australians are volunteering, but for less time (Australian Bureau of Statistics, 2007), which suggests a move to episodic volunteering. Hustinx *et al.* (2010: 426) understand this as reflecting 'the changing living conditions and biographies of contemporary individuals, and through this ... the changing availability and willingness to volunteer'. The simplest explanation is that the changing distribution of available time has affected volunteering in the same way as it has affected leisure. A more complex explanation, offered by Hustinx *et al.* (2010) is that there has been 'a shift from group based practices to self-monitoring of individual live narratives' as part of a process of 'modernization and individualization' (p. 426). This argument accords with Blackshaw's (2010) view of changes affecting leisure.

Reflexivity in volunteering

A third trend in volunteering has been postulated as 'reflexive volunteering', which means that 'present day volunteering is entrenched in the active (re-)design of individualized biographies, identities, and lifestyles' (Hustinx *et al.*, 2010: 426). This corresponds exactly to Blackshaw's (2010) view of the role of leisure, although we noted above that this was fiercely debated and, in particular, not shared by Roberts (2011). Interestingly, a study of volunteers who stopped volunteering found no evidence that this was a means of 'coping with biographical uncertainty' (Hustinx, 2010: 238) but, rather, it was because of changes in personal circumstances. The transition from traditional to modern styles of volunteering has been questioned, with Hustinx and Lammertyn (2004: 575) cautioning against 'too strong focus on grand modernization narratives' to explain the shift from collective to more individualistic forms of volunteering.

Changes in perceptions of volunteering

It has been argued that, in response to changes in society, particularly the fragmentation of available time and individualization, not only has there been a trend towards episodic volunteering, but there has to be willingness on the part of volunteer managers to modify pure definitions of volunteering (Hustinx and Meijs, 2011).

However, there is no longitudinal research to show that public perceptions of volunteering have changed, and the 'net cost' principle may still be paramount. Nevertheless, in order to attract volunteers, managers may have to change their traditional perceptions of volunteering. For example, it may be acknowledged that a major reason for young people choosing to volunteer is because it is perceived to offer direct benefits to themselves, in terms of work experience leading to paid employment, for example, in museums (Holmes, 2006). Volunteering opportunities could be 'sold' to retired people by emphasizing the social rewards. Normative expectations of volunteering as an obligation of membership in an organization could be established on joining. Volunteering opportunities could be packaged with personal rewards, targeted towards specific groups; for example, the opportunity to meet mid-life singles could be combined with volunteering to maintain a local park. The point is that volunteer managers need to be prepared to adapt the 'pure' form of volunteering in order to attract volunteers in changed circumstances. Further, the concept of volunteering is a social construction and so is open to change, and will change in response to social factors.

Re-embedding volunteering

Hustinx and Meijs argue that alongside the 'dis-embedding' of traditional volunteering is a 're-embedding' process where collective ground is reclaimed through interventions to promote volunteering by third parties, together with organizational strategies that allow for more individual and flexible management of volunteers. In concluding their article, Hustinx and Meijs (2011) suggest that this re-embedding of volunteering may challenge people's view of who are volunteers and what is volunteering. The authors go on to note that 're-embedding often involves some level of obligation, and makes more explicit the returns and rewards for the volunteer. As a consequence, the re-embedding of volunteering may lead to changes in our common perceptions of volunteering' (p. 16). Over time, as re-embedding continues it is likely that the purist view of volunteering as the unselfish altruist, contributing to a worthy cause or organization on a sustained basis for no personal, obvious reward, will continue to relax, giving greater validity to volunteering that involves a certain level of obligation and remuneration and is temporally constrained. If this is the case, leisure volunteering; distinguished from other forms of volunteering by the absence of obligation and participant free will; is likely to lose ground in an increasingly compressed time poor world to more obligatory forms.

Conclusions

Thus, leisure and volunteering are both socially constructed concepts. Common ground and the identification of potential characteristics which overlap between the two lie in: the concept of serious leisure; the dimension of relative freedom; the quality of the experience; and the relation to available time. It is interesting to consider the extent to which both leisure and volunteering are changing in parallel ways. The trends in volunteering suggest that it is in flux and possibly under threat from the fluidity of work and leisure lives and the growth in individuality, and needs to be re-embedded by reinforcing normative behaviour around societal expectations. This could have significant implications for leisure organizations that are dependent on volunteers. A further research gap is that, while we know that the very idea of volunteering varies across cultures, we have little of idea of this variation in conceptions of leisure. This is indeed a 'black hole' in Leisure Studies, revealing the Western-centric underpinning of academic and policy discourse in this field.

References

Atwood, C., Singh, G., Prime, D., Creasey, R. *et al.* (2003) *2001 Home Office Citizenship Survey: People, Families and Communities*. Home Office Research Study 270. London: Home Office.

Australian Bureau of Statistics. (2007) *Voluntary Work Australia, 2006*. Canberra: Australian Bureau of Statistics.

Australian Bureau of Statistics. (2011) *Voluntary Work Australia, 2010*. Canberra: Australian Bureau of Statistics

Bauman, Z. (2005) *Liquid Life*. Cambridge: Polity Press.

Beatty, J. and Torbert, W. (2003) 'The False Duality of Work and Leisure', *Journal of Management Inquiry* 12 (3) 239–252.

Blackshaw, T. (2010) *Leisure*. London: Routledge.

Bramham, P. and Wagg, S. (2010) *The New Politics of Leisure and Pleasure*. Basingstoke: Palgrave Macmillan.

Brudney, J. (ed.) (2005) *Emerging Areas of Volunteering*. ARNOVA Occasional Paper Series 1(2).

Cabinet Office. (2008) *Helping Out. A National Survey of Volunteering and Charitable Giving*. Available at: http://www.cabinetoffice.gov.uk/third_sector/Research_and_statistics/third_sector_research/helping_out.aspx (accessed 7 February 2008).

Cnaan, R., Handy, F. and Wadsworth, M. (1996) 'Defining Who is a Volunteer', *Nonprofit and Voluntary Sector Quarterly* 25: 364–383.

Coalter, F. (1999) 'Sport and Recreation in the United Kingdom: Flow with the Flow or Buck the Trends?', *Managing Leisure* 4 (1) 24–39.

Crouch, D. (2010) *Flirting with Space: Journeys and Creativity*. Farnham: Ashgate.

Cuskelly, G. (2005) 'Volunteer Participation Trends in Australian Sport', in G. Nichols, and M. Collins (eds) *Volunteers in Sports Clubs*. Eastbourne: LSA.

Ellis Paine, A., Malmersjo, G. and Stubbe, W. (2007) 'Kortdurend Vrijwilligerswerk: Zegen of vloek?' [Short-term Volunteering: A Curse or a Blessing?], *Vrijwillige Inzet Onderzocht* [Voluntary Effort Studied], 4, supplement, 101–110.

Esteve, R., San Martin, J. and Lopez, A.E. (1999) 'Grasping the Meaning of Leisure: Development of a Self-Report Measurement Tool', *Leisure Studies* 18: 79–91.

Evans, E. and Saxton, J. (2005) The 21st Century Volunteer: A Report on the Changing Face of Volunteering in the 21st Century. nfpsynergy: http://www.nfpsynergy.net/includes/documents/cm_docs/2008/2/21st_century_volunteer.pdf (accessed 16 April 2009).

Gaskin, K. (2003) *A Choice Blend: What Volunteers Want from Organisation and Management*. London: Institute for Volunteering Research.

Gratton, C., Rowe, N. and Veal, A.J. (2011) 'International Comparisons of Sport Participation in European Countries'. An Update of the COMPASS Project. *European Journal of Sport and Society* 8 (1–2) 99–116.

Grimm, R., Dietz, N., Foster-Bey, J., Reingold, D. and Nesbit, R. (2006). *Volunteer Growth in America: A Review of Trends since 1974*. Washington, DC: Corporation for National and Community Service.

Hagan, J. (2008) *The Volunteer and the Professional – Presence, Development, Policy and Management*. Dissertation completed as part of requirement for the degree of MSc Heritage Tourism Development at the University of Sunderland, Reproduced in *LSA Newsletter* 84 (November 2009) 48–62.

Handy, F., Brodeur, N. and Cnaan, R. (2006) 'Summer on the Island: Episodic Volunteering', *Voluntary Action* 7 (3) 31–46.

Holmes, K. (2006) 'Experiential Learning or Exploitation? Volunteering for Work Experience in the UK Museums Sector', *Museum Management and Curatorship* 21: (3) 240–253.

Hustinx, L. (2010) 'I Quit, Therefore I Am? Volunteer Turnover and the Politics of Self-Actualization', *Nonprofit and Voluntary Sector Quarterly* 39 (2) 236–255.

Hustinx, L. and Lammertyn, F. (2003) 'Collective and Reflexive Styles of Volunteering: A Sociological Modernization Perspective', *Voluntas* 14 (2) 167–187.

Hustinx, L. and Meijs, L.C.P.M. (2011) 'Re-Embedding Volunteering: In Search of a New Collective Ground', *Voluntary Sector Review* 2 (1) 5–22.

Hustinx, L., Cnaan, A.R. and Handy, F. (2010) 'Navigating Theories of Volunteering: A Hybrid Map for a Complex Phenomenon', *Journal of the Theory of Social Behaviour* 40 (4) 410–434.

Iso-Ahola, S.F. (1979) 'Basic Dimensions of Leisure', *Journal of Leisure Research* 11 (1) 28–39.

Kisby, B. (2010) 'The Big Society: Power to the People', *The Political Quarterly* 81 (4) 484–491.

Macduff, N. (1991) *Episodic Volunteering: Building the Short-Term Volunteer Program*, Walla Walla, WA: MBA Publishing.

Macduff, N. (2005) 'Societal Changes and the Rise of the Episodic Volunteer', in J. Brudney (ed.) *Emerging Areas of Volunteering*. ARNOVA Occasional Paper Series 1 (2).

Meijs, L., Handy, F., Cnaan, R., Brudney, J., Ascoli, U., Ranade, S., Hustinx, L., Weber, S. and Weiss, I. (2003) 'All in the Eyes of the Beholder? Perceptions of Volunteering Across Eight Countries', in P. Dekker and L. Halman (eds) *The Values of Volunteering: Cross Cultural Perspectives*. New York: Kluwer Academic/Plenum Publishers.

Merrill, M. (2006) 'Global Trends and the Challenges for Volunteering', *The International Journal of Volunteer Administration* 24 (1) 9–14.

Musick, M.A. and Wilson, J. (2008) *Volunteers: A Social Profile*. Bloomington: Indiana University Press.

National Statistics. (2011) *Citizenship Survey: April 2010–March 2011, England*. Available at: http://www.communities.gov.uk/publications/corporate/statistics/citizenshipsurveyq4201011 (retrieved 8 November 2011).

Nichols, G. (2005) 'Stalwarts in Sport', *World Leisure* 2: 31–37.

Nichols, G. (2009) 'Inequality and Positional Consumption – a Fresh Insight into Debates in Leisure Studies on Time Pressures on Leisure and Volunteering, Choosing a Work/Life Balance and the Nature of a "Leisure" Society', *Journal of Policy Research in Tourism, Leisure and Events* 1 (3) 270–275.

Nichols, G. (forthcoming) 'Voluntary Sports Clubs and Sport Development', in K. Hylton (ed.) *Sports Development: Policy, Process and Practice*, 3rd ed. London: Routledge.

Nichols, G. and King, L. (1999) 'Redefining the Recruitment Niche for the Guide Association in the United Kingdom', *Leisure Sciences* 21 (4) 307–320.

O'Donohue, W. and Nelson, L. (2009) 'The Psychological Contracts of Australian Hospital Volunteer Workers', *Australian Journal on Volunteering* 14 (9) 1–11.

Parker, S. (1976) *The Sociology of Leisure*. London: George Allen and Unwin.

Parker, S. (1997) 'Volunteering: Altruism, Markets, Careers and Leisure', *World Leisure and Recreation* 39 (3) 4–5.

Ralston, R., Downward, P. and Lumsdon, L. (2004) 'The Expectations of Volunteers Prior to the XVII Commonwealth Games 2002: A Qualitative Study', *Event Management* 9 (1–2) 13–26.

Roberts, K. (1978) *Contemporary Society and the Growth of Leisure*. London: Longman

Roberts, K. (1998) 'Work and Leisure: The Recent History of a Changing Relationship and the Related Leisure Issues', *Vrijetijdstudies* 16 (1) 21–34.

Roberts, K. (2011) 'Leisure: The Importance of Being Inconsequential', *Leisure Studies* 30 (1) 5–20.

Robinson, J. and Godbey, G. (1999) *Time for Life: The Surprising Ways Americans Use Their Time*. College Park: Pennsylvania State University Press.

Rochester, C., Ellis Paine, A. and Howlett, S. with Zimmeck, M. (2010) *Volunteering and Society in the 21st Century*. Basingstoke: Palgrave Macmillan.

Schor, J. (2006) 'Overturning the Modernist Predictions: Recent Trends in Work and Leisure in the OECD', in C. Rojek, S. Shaw and A.J. Veal (eds) *A Handbook of Leisure Studies*. Basingstoke: Palgrave.

Schulz, J., Nichols, G. and Auld, C. (2011) 'Issues in the Management of Voluntary Sports Organisations and Volunteers', in B. Houlihan and M. Green (eds) *Handbook of Sports Development*. London: Routledge.

Smith, D.H. (1981) 'Altruism, Volunteers, and Volunteerism', *Journal of Voluntary Action Research* 10: 21–36.

Smith, D.H. (1994) 'Determinants of Voluntary Participation and Volunteering: A Literature Review', *Nonprofit and Voluntary Sector Quarterly* 23: (3) 243–263.

Snape, B. (2012) Book Review: 'The Meaning and Purpose of Leisure: Habermas and Leisure at the End of Modernity, 2009, by Karl Spracklen', *Leisure Studies* 31 (1) 126–128.

Spracklen. K. (2011) *Constructing Leisure: Historical and Philosophical Debates*. Basingstoke: Palgrave Macmillan.

Stebbins, R.A. (1996) 'Volunteering: A Serious Leisure Perspective', *Nonprofit and Voluntary Sector Quarterly*', 25 (2) 211–224.

Stebbins, R.A. (2005) 'Project-Based Leisure: Theoretical Neglect of a Common Use of Free Time', *Leisure Studies* 24 (1) 1–11.

Stebbins, R. (2007) *Serious Leisure: A Perspective for Our Time*. New Brunswick, NJ: Transaction.

Taylor, P., Nichols, G., Holmes, K., James, M., Gratton, C., Garrett, R., Kokolakakis, T., Mulder, C. and King, L. (2003) *Sports Volunteering in England*. London: Sport England.

Thompson, E.P. (1968) 'Time, Work-Discipline and Industrial Capitalism', *Past and Present* 38: 56–97.

Tomazos, K. and Butler, R. (2012) 'Volunteer Tourists in the Field: A Question of Balance?', *Tourism Management* 33 (1) 177–187.

Unger, L.S. and Kernan, J.B. (1983) 'On the Meaning of Leisure: An Investigation of Some of the Determinants of the Subjective Experience', *Journal of Consumer Research* 9 (4) 381–392.

Veal, A.J. (2011) Review of 'Leisure', by Blackshaw. *Managing Leisure* 16 (2) 169–173.

Watson, I., Buchanan, J., Campbell, I. and Briggs, C. (2003) *Fragmented Futures: New Challenges in Working Life*, Sydney: Federation Press.

Weisbrod, B.A. (1978) *The Voluntary Non-Profit Sector*. Lexington, MA: Lexington Books, in C. Gratton and P. Taylor (1991) (eds) *Government and the Economics of Sport*. London: E and F Spon.

Wilkenson, R. and Pickett, K. (2009) *The Spirit Level: Why More Equal Societies Almost Always Do Better*. London: Allen Lane.

40

YIN AND YANG

The relationship of leisure and work[1]

Joy Beatty and William R. Torbert

In common vernacular, work and leisure are framed as polar opposites: what is work cannot be leisure. Indeed, leisure is often construed as the 'left-over time' – time not spent at work, or on other obligations, time for doing anything ... or nothing. By contrast, we will argue and offer various forms of evidence for a very different appreciation of work and leisure. In our view, leisure is the primary source of activity, inquiry, freedom, and love, while work is a secondary derivative, but one that can be chosen voluntarily and done in a leisurely fashion (e.g., to offer some obvious examples, piano playing, writing, video-game testing, experiential mathematics, etc.). Thus, in our view, work and leisure intertwine with one another and sometimes lose their boundaries altogether, more like the Yin-Yang symbol with mirror-opposite black and white embryos, each pregnant with its emergent other.

In this chapter we explore this sinuous, interdependent relationship, offering the Taoist *taijitu* symbol – more commonly known as the Yin and Yang – as an organizing metaphor. *Taijitu* is roughly translated as 'the diagram of ultimate power'. Yin and Yang are the polar energies represented by interlaced swirls enclosed in a circle (Figure 40.1). The dot in each swirl represents each energy, at its highest stage of realization, pregnant with the seed of its complement, into which it is about to transform (Fischer-Schreiber, 1996). The concepts are illustrated as a series of seemingly polar opposites, such as moon/sun, black/white, cold/hot, feminine/masculine, passive/active, and weak/strong (Robinet, 1997), although they are actually a whole octave of music or rainbow of colours.

The *taijitu* symbol provides an effective metaphor for the relationship of leisure and work because it illustrates the interdependence of opposites; neither can exist alone and each needs the other to show its contours. The conception of work and leisure as antonyms has created an artificial division that has impoverished our understanding of both terms. Our definition of leisure does not measure an amount of time or a kind of activity but, rather, focuses on an inner dialogue with the source of our own experiencing and being. We propose that, at their best, both work and leisure can be intrinsically motivated. Leisure allows us to discover the qualities of the good life and of our own particular calling, while work allows us to 'real-ize' the calling. Together, such complementary leisure and work can provide us with a lifetime sense of sustainable involvement, development, and satisfaction. We first discuss leisure and work separately, then offer some comparisons. Understanding the characteristics of leisure

Figure 40.1 Yin/Yang symbol

and cultivating 'good' leisure is important, we argue, at both the individual and societal level. In our conclusion, we advocate that educating for leisure is critical.

Yin: leisure

Management scholars and lay persons may see leisure as trivial and inconsequential, as little more than free time to re-create energy for work. In contrast, leisure scholars see it as a product of more fundamental social structures and suggest that changes in the institutions of work, family, and education all fundamentally influence leisure (Coalter, 1989). Roberts (2011) distinguishes between 'little leisure' and 'big leisure', noting that individuals' leisure choices are relatively inconsequential (i.e., little leisure); but that 'big leisure', meaning the larger social and cultural implications of leisure, is highly consequential. For individuals, the main functions of participating in leisure are well-being and identity construction (Blackshaw, 2010). Socially, the benefits are economic, as leisure inevitably and increasingly involves consumption, which fuels major sectors of the economy. It doesn't matter which specific leisure activities people pursue, as these benefits apply on the aggregate.

Leisure may be framed as an economic choice regarding the investment of free time (Hunnicutt, 1988), a psychological attitude or state of mind (Csikszentmihalyi, 1975), or a location for identity development (Rojek, 2000). Topics of study range widely from quilting (Stalp, 2006), to volunteering (Lockstone-Binney *et al.*, 2010) and fitness (Maguire, 2008); Scottish whiskey tourism (Spracklen, 2011) and illegal drug use (Shinew and Parry, 2005) have also been considered leisure topics. So what is leisure, that it can be all these things?

We find three major approaches to the definition of leisure, based upon either: (1) time (how much time are people not-working?); (2) activity (what do people do when they are not-working?); and (3) intent (what kind of an intention is the intent to act in a leisurely manner?). The first and most common approach is time based. Leisure is understood as 'free time', encompassing basically everything one does when one is not at work, nor under obligation to family or social constraints. One's leisure is calculated by subtracting the hours given to work and other obligations from the 24 hours of the day. Large-scale data come from statistical analysis of time-use diaries, and the criterion is the quantity of time.

This view reflects an industrialized view of the world in which work is scheduled first and everything else is then 'free time' (Robinson and Godbey, 1997). Indeed the historical conditions of the Industrial Revolution provided the opportunity and necessity to divide time into clearly defined parcels dedicated to work and not-work. Leisure and paid holidays were seen as compensatory for increasingly specialized and tedious work, and were used primarily to recuperate in preparation for more (tedious) work (Cross, 2005). In this view, more time spent away from work and/or obligations equals more leisure, regardless of the activity engaged in or the attitude one has at the time.

The relationship with work-time was emphasized in early notions of leisure, as presented by Veblen's (1899) 'leisure class' and Dumazedier's (1967) 'leisure society' thesis. Both wrote that as societies become more advanced, less time would be required for basic survival. With basic needs met, the assumption was that people would naturally opt for more free time. Indeed, Dumazedier warned of a potential 'leisure crisis' – of people not knowing how to spend their leisure time in developmentally beneficial ways.

Using the time-based definition of leisure, some sources report encouraging results: research shows that since the mid-1960s, overall time spent working has decreased, and therefore leisure time (interpreted as 'left-over' time) has increased for both men and women (Aguiar and Hurst, 2007; Gershuny, 2003). Other researchers using time-diary research offer a more complicated view of a gender gap in leisure, with women doing more unpaid work (Bittman and Wajcman, 2000; Jacobs and Gerson, 2001; Mattingly and Bianchi, 2003).

The main advantage of a time-based approach to defining leisure is that it provides an objective and easily quantified measure, freeing researchers from the task of assessing and categorizing specific leisure-time activities. But the time-based definition of leisure lacks an intrinsic character of its own (Allen, 1989; De Grazia, 1962; Neulinger, 1981); it is simply defined by what it is not. Further, the quality of the experience is overlooked, and leisure is nothing if not 'experienced quality'.

The second approach to defining and measuring leisure is behavioural or activity based. Here, leisure is associated with categories of activities often done while one is at leisure. This view reflects the development of modern leisure and the growth of cultural industries like radio, film, and television. Tourism, recreation and sport, hobbies, volunteering, etc. are all classified as leisure, and the person who engages in any of these activities is concomitantly 'doing' leisure.

It offers a convenient formula for aspiring 'leisurites' who can efficiently buy their leisure experiences from a set menu of leisure packages (e.g., 'Let's see … A Disney vacation or golf tour?'). An activity-based approach has been convenient because it is more objective, and it is easier to measure and compare observed behaviours.

Actually, the earliest definitions of leisure in the West also had an action focus. Both Plato and Aristotle emphasized the importance of activity in their discussions of leisure. But 'active' in Plato's and Aristotle's terms means something different from the 'activities' that are now categorized as leisure, such as watching TV or spectator sports. Aristotle explicitly distinguished leisure from idleness and *acedia*, which translates as 'sloth' and generally means apathy and disinterest in voluntary action (Ciulla, 2000). Watching TV (especially when someone else in the family is managing the remote) is about as passive, listless, and inactive as waking life gets (Torbert and Rogers, 1973). In the original Aristotelian definition of leisure, an inner attitude of voluntary engagement and inquiry is the core of leisure, not the particular outer activity (Aristotle lists but two true leisure activities: meditation and music).

With Aristotle, the third approach to defining leisure addresses the inner experience of leisure. Leisure is defined as a reflective attitude or state-of-being experienced when one is voluntarily and inquiringly engaged in an activity. Only amidst such activities are we likely to experience a developmentally capacity-expanding outcome. Six hundred years and more after Aristotle, the early church fathers wrote of *otium sanctum*, or 'holy leisure', which referred to a sense of balance in life, the ability to be at peace through the activities of the day, and an ability to rest and pace oneself (Foster, 1978).

This approach to leisure includes a reflective and spiritual aspect. Leisure is an attitude emphasizing a capacity for active silence, intentional listening, and receptivity (Pieper, 1998). It is for the cultivation of the self, and the self in relation to friends under the sign of inquiry. Leisure is seen not as a time free from work (the empty, negative sense), but as time free to determine what the good life is, what is really worth doing, and how to do it with moment-to-moment integrity, mutuality, and sustainability (Torbert and Associates, 2004).

We advocate that the third approach has the most definitional power, because it specifies the core concepts implicit in the other two: people often experience an *attitude* of leisure in their *time* spent away from work, doing particular types of *activities* commonly associated with leisure. Yet this attitude can also be experienced during portions of time spent at work, doing activities not commonly recognized as leisure activities. What distinguishes this attitude of leisure, and how is it distinct from other concepts?

The attitude of leisure

The attitude of leisure – leisureliness – is distinguished by its intrinsic motivation, its inquiring, awareness-enhancing quality, and its transforming, developmental outcome. Leisure becomes leisurely from the inside out, not the outside in. In this chapter, we define leisure as an attitude or state of being that is intrinsically motivated, actively inquiring, and developing toward more inclusive awareness. An example of a leisurely activity would be a regular meeting for friendly conversation among diverse peers who exercise mutual influence within a community dedicated to ongoing inquiry. Discovering a calling through spiritual, political, musical, and scientific modes of inquiry and turning it into one's life work (all performed voluntarily as a 'living inquiry') is another example (Torbert, 1991).

Doing what one *wants* to do is a condition of leisure, and leisurely activities must be intrinsically motivated. As Plato said, leisure is the 'eternally optional task' that one chooses for its own sake, not for any instrumental purpose. Neulinger (1981) offers a spectrum of leisure experiences ranging from 'pure leisure' to 'pure job'. In pure leisure, the motivation is only intrinsic, with satisfaction ideally coming from the activity itself; 'pure job' is only extrinsically motivated, done for the money and the boss. However, extrinsic rewards, such as receiving compensation for a behaviour, do not automatically eliminate the potential for a leisure attitude. In practice, we often settle for less 'pure' versions of leisure. To illustrate, consider tasks which you perform in your own life that are not exactly work, but sometimes do not feel like leisure either: walking the dog, working out, cooking a meal for one's family, or reading a very dry academic journal. While there may be aspects of these tasks that are intrinsically enjoyable, they are also done for instrumental purposes. This ambiguity of leisure makes it especially mysterious. Leisure can only be self-defined, and is therefore idiosyncratic. Walking the dog on a sunny day can be leisure; on a raw, rainy day, the same person may experience walking the dog as work. But another person may view the very changes of weather as a pleasure because they 'break' the taken-for-grantedness of her daily experience, reminding her that she can engage now in broad meditative inquiry – whether about the aesthetics of the puddles, the sensations of walking, or the essay on leisure to which she will return in a few minutes.

471

Leisure is associated with personal development because it supports 'open space' for reflection and inquiry. This open space may at first look like residual time to do nothing, but it is actually much more than that. Although this space is not being 'used' in a physical way, it offers balance and perspective similar to Yin and Yang. Two twenty-minute periods of Transcendental Meditation each day, at the beginning of one's lunch break and just before one's evening begins, can have this effect; so can five Islamic prostrations per day; etc.

The experience of leisure can lead to personal development via active intellectual, emotional, and/or physical engagement. Leisure can educate us and develop new tastes and interests for us if we take initiative and invest time in them (Dumazedier, 1967). An example of developmental leisure is the notion of 'serious leisure' (Stebbins, 1992), the systematic pursuit of an amateur, hobbyist, or volunteer activity – dancing, butterfly photography, sculpting, yoga – that we may find so substantial and interesting that we launch ourselves into a career centred on acquiring and expressing those special skills, knowledge, and experience. Serious leisure requires significant personal effort; the rewards are personal enrichment, self-actualization, self-expression, enjoyment, recreation, and sometimes even financial return (Stebbins, 1997). Here, we see Yang and Yin, leisure and work, complementing one another, with work completing the leisurely aim. This personal development aspect incorporates the three dimensions of leisure definitions: it requires an investment of time, and typically has as its focus some type of activity that creates the conditions for us to experience the attitude of leisure. However, the distinguishing concept of serious leisure is the attitude one experiences while doing it.

Here is one concrete example of a person's self-examination, upon completion of an autobiographical writing exercise (in a course she has voluntarily chosen), about the leisure commitments she now wishes to make. We use this passage with the author's permission to illustrate how leisure is related to personal developmental goals.

- I recently phoned a therapist. I have realized that I never really processed the events that occurred in Michigan, and by seeking counselling, I hope to gain peace.
- I will continually seek to broaden my perspective by seeking friendships with people from diverse backgrounds, reading a wider variety of literature, travelling, and meditating.
- Perhaps most immediate is my goal to overcome my own insecurities, which is of course really a lifetime project. If I am to advance developmentally, I must be able to spend more time contemplating life beyond myself. To a certain degree, we are what we think about, and I do not spend enough time thinking about others. In order to cultivate patience, wisdom, empathy, compassion, honesty, and a giving and forgiving heart, both in my professional and personal life, I believe the best method of attainment is through my spiritual life. After writing my autobiography, I realize that most of what I am proud of in life was obtained because of my character, which, for me, has grown through my relationship with God. Also, however, I believe that meditation, and an exploration of Buddhism will also expand my awareness.
- Finally, I want to start coaching soccer again. When I felt a surge of emotions brought on by writing the autobiography, I spoke with one of the girls who I coached. We had not spoken in four years, and yet she told me that she and several of the other girls who I had coached were talking about me just a few days prior, agreeing that they enjoyed their soccer experience with me and that their enjoyment diminished after I left. I truly believe that I have a gift for coaching and I must be sure not to neglect it. Therefore, I will obtain my national 'B' license this summer.

Leisure is associated with personal development in another way, too: developmental theorists have found that, as people transform to later developmental stages, they incorporate more leisurely, inquiring perspectives across their life domains (Kegan, 1994; Torbert, 1996; Wilber, 2000). Each stage is marked by a different action logic, which is an internally coherent system of beliefs that we may not be fully aware of ourselves, but that directly shapes our actions and is difficult to transform (Argyris and Schon, 1974; Bacharach, Bamberger, and McKinney, 2000). In early developmental action-logics the focus is on external standards and conventional social norms, and people with these action-logics have dichotomous worldviews (win/lose; work/leisure; action/inquiry, etc.). In later stages, people move toward more mutual, more playful, more paradoxical perspectives that integrate economic, political, and spiritual elements of life through a creative reshaping of roles, tasks, and relationships. Leisurely inquiry among friends becomes a priority in shaping their time and vocation (Torbert, 1996): work and leisure cease to be dichotomous. They recognize that they themselves play a key role in framing and reframing the meaning of each activity and in determining the role it plays in their life as a whole.

Some leisure scholars find this idea of personal development elitist, prescriptive, and normative. Who is to judge one form of leisure as serious and another as not serious? We rebut that it is at least as prescriptive and elitist for a third-party social scientist embracing a modernist research approach to impose a supposedly 'neutral' definition of what activities constitute leisure from the outside, without reference to the internal state of the acting person. To fully understand leisure, the empirical 'objective' approach must be combined with the 'subjective' approach of determining the meaning of the activity for the person engaging in it. One person's leisure is another's torture, as the following example illustrates: Frederick W. Taylor, the Father of Scientific Management, was ordered by his doctor to play golf, and he hated it. He apparently compared his time at the sport with visits to the dentist (Andrew, 1981).

The important methodological question is whether a leisurely internal state can be validly and reliably measured, and the empirical question is whether the resulting measure correlates with other significant social variables. A number of empirical studies (Fisher, Rooke, and Torbert, 2001; Rooke and Torbert, 1998; Torbert and Fisher, 1992) using different measures of persons' inner-state leisureliness have shown strong relationships with the degree of decision-making responsibility of a person's job, the degree of success with which a person leads organizational transformation, and in the extent to which regular, long-term, voluntary collaborative inquiry leads to developmental progression.

When leisure is understood as an aggregate experience that combines time, activity, and intent, it is a quality of being that one can cultivate. It is not merely something one does (like going to a movie) or acquires (like purchasing a holiday cruise package), although either of these *may* be done in a leisurely manner. Because leisure is intrinsically motivated, the objective is not to meet others' norms but to develop one's own taste for inquiry, beauty, and ethical action; this requires action and vigilance about our leisure pursuits.

Yang: work

In different historical periods, work has been imbued with religious and political themes, seen variously as a curse, a duty to God, and as a symbol of alienation and subjugation. For the Greeks, work was a curse and was best done by slaves (Parker, 1983), and Virgil referred to work as *labor improbus*, which translates to 'wicked toil' (De Grazia, 1962). Hebrew and early Christian traditions also viewed work as a curse that was the product of original sin; through work one could atone for one's sins.

Later, Protestantism established work as the key of life. The best way to serve God, according to Luther, was to do most perfectly the work of one's calling (Parker, 1983). Calvin declared that all men must work because it is the will of God, but they must not lust after the fruits of their labour. This paradox is at the core of the Protestant work ethic. The tenets of the work ethic evolved, including diligence, deferment of pleasure, and scrupulous use of time. Time and pleasure were carefully metered: for example New England Puritan settlers increased their number of work days by avidly striking long-standing religious holidays (including Christmas) from their calendars (Alesina, Glaeser, and Sacerdote, 2005). In contrast to earlier periods, when one's social status was fixed at birth, working people gradually realized that by working more they could improve their material condition (Rose, 1985). They now had a motivation to sacrifice leisure time so as to get ahead. Gradually, work evolved from a religious and moral undertaking – a means to redemption – to a secular and materialist one, as a way to fuel consumption.

The propensity to conceptualize leisure as 'not work' is premised upon a specific framing of work. Questioning this view of work may help to free us from the false dichotomy of work and leisure. Work is seen as necessary and required drudgery, and it requires effort. In some languages, the word for 'labour' is closely associated with pain – as in the Greek *ponos*, the French *travail*, and the German *Arbeit* (Meilaender, 2000), not to mention an English-speaking woman's labour as she delivers nature's greatest miracle, a new child. Often represented as a unitary concept of 'wage labour' (Karlsson, 1995), it is seen as debasing, and as a sign of subjugation to a master (Veblen, 1899). According to Marx (2010/1844), industrialized work has commodified labour and caused alienation when the workers were unable to determine their own actions or reap the rewards of their labour. Work and leisure become contested elements of the capitalist social structure (Rojek, 2009), with contested power and class structures. For example, some have predicted that, as technology increases, the workforce will polarize into a core of overworked elites and a larger group of precariously employed or unemployed workers (Granter, 2008).

This framing of work paints an unduly negative view and denies us the possibility of any intrinsic motivation at work. While it is true that some jobs fit these negative descriptions, there is variation in the motivating potential of jobs. Work can satisfy personal needs for competence and esteem and social needs for discipline, connectedness, regularity, and self-efficiency (Wilson, 1996).

Further, people are not entirely powerless and can proactively shape their work, as the job-crafting literature tells us (Wrzesniewski and Dutton, 2001). In job crafting, employees shape the task boundaries of the job, the relational boundaries of the job, or both. These proactive steps change the social environment of their work, generating greater meaning and building work identity. Even routine, monotonous work can be reframed by workers to include aspects of leisure and play (for example, Roy, 1959). When work is meaningful, it allows one to be creative, use and develop skills, and take responsibility and initiative (Gamst, 1995; Parker, 1983). It can also provide a venue to experience sustainable involvement and development that is intrinsically motivating – similar to leisure.

Indeed, as mentioned earlier in this chapter, developmental theory offers a 'ladder' of action-logics from the most externally defined, coercive, and alienating to the most internally defined, mutual, and fulfilling. This developmental ladder can distinguish not only alienating labour from fulfilling leisure, but also broadly different types of work. There is a world of difference in each rung up the ladder from:

1   chain-gang or assembly-line work, to
2   clerical work, to
3   craft work (manual, service-oriented, or intellectual), to
4   managerial work, to
5   strategic, more widely empowering, leaderly work, to
6   power-and-paradigm-transforming work, 'called' by voluntary, leisurely contemplation.

Given the centrality of work in our culture, and given this developmental ladder towards increasingly leisurely work, we should not be surprised to learn that Juster (1986) has found that the intrinsic satisfaction that people receive from work in our culture is greater than the intrinsic satisfaction they get from their free time. Nor should we be surprised that Csikszentmihalyi and LeFevre (1989) have found that flow occurs more than three times as often in work as in free time.

For some of the richest people in the world who work by choice, there is no distinction between work and leisure. Rojek (2000) explores the leisure choices of billionaires Bill Gates, Warren Buffet, and Richard Branson. These men could stop working any time they like, but they continue to work and report great pleasure from working long, 16-hour days. Paradoxically, they work longer hours than average people. This work ethic does not have the characteristics of routine and monotony that social critics ascribe. But, let us pause and inquire critically into this conflation of work and leisure. Just how leisurely is a life in which the pleasures of work altogether eclipse one's desire for free time?

The blurring of work and leisure, Yin and Yang

Despite modern developments of reduced working hours, increased leisure time, and increasing productivity, we as a society are more harried than ever (Glorieux *et al.*, 2010; Linder, 1970). Instead of experiencing the portended 'leisure crisis', we have invested our productivity dividend into more work. We live in a culture in which 'busy-ness' is a virtue that socially displays our importance and success (Gershuny, 2005). People who work the hardest to earn the most money, ironically, lack the time to enjoy it.

We are migrating toward a fusion of work and leisure, with people bringing work attitudes to their leisure tasks. For example, some people adopt 'time-deepening' behaviour (Robinson and Godbey, 1997) to make their leisure more efficient. Examples of this are doing more than one thing at a time, substituting less time-intensive leisure activities for more time-intensive ones, and setting leisure activities within precise time goals. Given our limited time, we face competing leisure demands, and may even have 'inconspicuous consumption' (Sullivan and Gershuny, 2004) – a situation in which people purchase expensive leisure goods with the intent of using them, but never actually get the time to do so; the hope and promise of leisure is tucked away in storage with their ski and scuba equipment. We know that, in the USA at least, workers are not taking all the vacation days to which they are entitled (Expedia.com, 2011) (although this seems to be less of a problem in European countries). All this contributes to feelings of time pressure.

Contemporary developments such as increasing professionalization, service sector jobs, and technologies that invade the home have all blurred the boundaries of work and leisure. Many of us have willingly sacrificed a firm boundary between work and leisure in exchange for the flexibility of accessing texts and e-mails 24/7. Technology has decreased our daily labour requirements and spurred the growth of inactive leisure (i.e., surfing the internet, spending time on video games or social media) (Albrechtsen, 2001). The ubiquity of electronic devices offers the affordance of multi-tasking in both work and leisure contexts, accompanied by ever-diminishing contacts with live human beings and nature.

Increasing mechanization and bureaucratization of work has also shaped the character of leisure, away from active leisure to more passive consumption of mass commercial entertainment. Time spent in the most enjoyable and engaging leisure activities such as socializing with friends, pet care, worshipping, reading, and listening to music has gone down since the mid-1960s – findings which come from Krueger's (2007) study using affective data measuring respondents' feelings while engaged in activities.

So what activities are people doing instead? Data shows that TV watching has gone up significantly (Aguiar and Hurst, 2007; Jacobs and Gerson, 2001; Krueger, 2007). Robinson and Godbey (1997) estimate that the average American spends 40 per cent of his or her free time watching television, and more recent time-diary data from Glorieux *et al.* (2010) using a Flemish sample show that 43 per cent of total weekly leisure time is spent watching TV. Ironically, these studies also report that people do not enjoy watching TV, as compared to other leisure alternatives; however, people do it because it's cheap and easy.

In response to the increasing time demands of the work-place, we see some people creating their own solutions by downshifting their career aspirations and reclaiming intrinsic motivation for their work. For example, Ravenscroft and Gilchrist (2009) write of the working society of leisure. Here leisure is composed of self-determined work, and instead of the compartmentalization of work and leisure, the two are intentionally merged into a 'single labour project' (Ravenscroft and Gilchrist, 2009: 24). Adherents to this practice receive limited extrinsic reward in their work, but enjoy the intrinsic rewards once reserved for leisure activities. However, this path is not available to all, as it requires cultural and economic capital, coming generally from higher levels of specialized training and the ability to be mobile.

As Robinson and Godbey explain (1997), 'voluntary' implies that you have a choice among alternatives *and* that you give some up in order to enact or consume the one you want. They further note that the time-deepening described above lures us into thinking that we can multi-task, and thereby avoid sacrificing anything. But what we thereby in fact sacrifice is everything: voluntary control over the pace and quality of our moment-to-moment experiencing. We increasingly define ourselves by our accomplishments and our acquisitions. This means that we have to be 'on the go', achieving and doing all the time – because to do nothing is to be nothing.

Both work and leisure constructs are suffering from a narrowing (Allen, 1989) or 'flattening out' (Quarrick, 1989) of their meanings. The risk is that we, as a culture, have virtually forgotten what it means to cultivate leisure, through which we develop the freedom and integrity to question assumptions.

Leisure education

Leisure must be acknowledged as legitimate: to consume or enjoy leisure does not make one lazy. Workers have been encouraged to develop life skills to give them maximum flexibility in the labour market, and education has shifted towards training for vocational and social roles. It should also educate for leisure skills, to help people reach their true potential through active leisure and self-improvement.

Educating for leisure is the process of helping people to develop appreciation and skills to use their leisure in personally rewarding ways (Brightbill, 1960). A distinction is made between educating for serious or active leisure, which may be unfamiliar to people, versus casual (passive) leisure, for which no special skills are needed. Leisure education can increase awareness of both serious and casual leisure, their benefits, and the importance of having a balanced set of both kinds (Cohen-Gewerc and Stebbins, 2007). People can be exposed to different kinds of leisure and ways to embark on serious leisure careers. Students of leisure need to learn how to observe fresh opportunities, and to be present in the moment. Part of the leisure experience is to allow time for reflection and contemplation, with time bounded from outside distractions. People can develop a more leisurely attitude by learning mindfulness practices, to recover ethical and spiritual ground (Levy, 2007).

Our recommendations suggest that developing a leisure attitude is an individual's responsibility, but we admit that some features of leisure are shaped by cultural norms. Research by Alesina, Glaeser, and Sacerdote (2005) studies the differences in leisure consumption between Europeans and Americans. From an economic perspective, they note that the marginal tax rate in Europe is much higher, which makes it less attractive for people to work more hours. They found that legally mandated holidays can explain 80 per cent of the difference in weeks worked between the USA and Europe, and they note the significance of labour regulation and unionization in bringing this about. They find a social multiplier effect, meaning that the utility of time off goes up as more people are also taking time off – resulting in Europeans' summer vacation en masse. This mass culture of leisure likely leads to better leisure infrastructures in Europe. Therefore organizational and government policies do set some limitations on the leisure opportunities, and these policies matter.

Drawing from this, the suggestion for the US market could be that in order to get more and better leisure experiences we need higher taxes and more unions. But remember that the notion of vacations as leisure is rooted in the time perspective of leisure. We have advocated in this article that leisure is about an attitude, not just the amount of time one has off. Similarly, we might suggest that organizations create Chief Leisure Officers to support their employees' leisure pursuits – a radical thought that is unlikely to sit well with capitalist philosophy, but interesting to consider, given that organizations are major social actors with the resources and efficiency to launch such an effort. More supportive cultural and organizational infrastructures could help as individuals take steps to build their diversity skills; but exercising one's leisure skills requires individual initiative. Responsibility for and control of leisure is best left to the individual and not yoked for organizational gain.

Our crisis of leisure is not that we have too much. We've managed to fill all the available time doing *something*, so the question instead is about the quality of the leisure we have. Our crisis of leisure is that we generate virtually none and can't quite imagine what we are missing. Can we rediscover the active, erotic intertwining of the Yin and Yang of work and leisure in our lives?

Note

1   An earlier version of this paper has been published in *Journal of Management Inquiry*, Vol. 12 No. 3 September 2003, by Sage Publications. All rights reserved. ©

References

Aguiar, M. and Hurst, E. (2007) 'Measuring Trends in Leisure: The allocation of time over five decades', *Quarterly Journal of Economics* 122 (3) 969–1006.

Albrechtsen, S. J. (2001) 'Technology and Lifestyles: Challenges for leisure education in the new millenium', *World Leisure Journal* 43 (1) 11–19.

Alesina, A. F., Glaeser, E. L. and Sacerdote, B. (2005) 'Work and Leisure in the US and Europe: Why so different?', *Harvard Institute of Economic Research Discussion Paper No. 2068*. Retrieved from http://ssrn.com/abstract=706982

Allen, R. T. (1989) 'Leisure: The purpose of life and the nature of philosophy', in T. Winnifrith and C. Barrett (eds) *The Philosophy of Leisure*. New York: St. Martin's Press.

Andrew, E. (1981) *Closing the Iron Cage: The scientific management of work and leisure*. Montreal: Black Rose Books.

Argyris, C. and Schon, D. (1974) *Theory in Practice: Increasing professional effectiveness*. San Francisco: Jossey Bass.

Bacharach, S., Bamberger, P. and McKinney, V. (2000) 'Boundary Management Tactics and Logics of Action: The case of peer-support providers', *Administrative Science Quarterly* 45: 704–736.

Bittman, M. and Wajcman, J. (2000) 'The Rush Hour: The character of leisure time and gender equity', *Social Forces* 79 (1) 165–189.

Blackshaw, T. (2010) *Leisure*. Abingdon: Routledge.

Brightbill, C. K. (1960) *The Challenge of Leisure*. Englewood Cliffs, NJ: Prentice-Hall.

Ciulla, J. B. (2000) *The Working Life: The promise and betrayal of modern life*. New York: Times Books.

Coalter, F. (ed.) (1989) *Freedom and Constraint: The paradoxes of leisure*. London: Routledge.

Cohen-Gewerc, E. and Stebbins, R. A. (2007) *The Pivotal Role of Leisure Education: Finding personal fulfillment in this century*. State College, PA: Venture Publishing.

Cross, G. (2005) 'A Right to Be Lazy? Busyness in retrospective', *Social Research* 72 (2) 263–286.

Csikszentmihalyi, M. (1975) *Beyond Boredom and Anxiety*. San Francisco: Jossey Bass.

Csikszentmihalyi, M. and LeFevre, J. (1989) 'Optimal Experience in Work and Leisure', *Journal of Personality and Social Psychology* 56: 815–822.

De Grazia, S. (1962) *Of Time, Work, and Leisure*. New York: Twentieth Century Fund.

Dumazedier, J. (1967) *Toward a Society of Leisure* (S. E. McClure, trans.). Toronto: Collier-Macmillan. (Original work published in 1962).

Expedia.com (2011) *Vacation Deprivation Study*. Retrieved from http://www.expedia.com/p/info-other/vacation_deprivation.htm.

Fischer-Schreiber, I. (1996) *The Shambhala Dictionary of Taoism*. Boston, MA: Shambhala.

Fisher, D., Rooke, D. and Torbert, W. (2001) *Personal and Organizational Transformation: Through action inquiry*. Boston: Edge\Work Press.

Gamst, F. (1995) 'Considerations of Work', in F. Gamst (ed.) *Meanings of Work: Considerations for the twenty-first century*. Albany, NY: State University of New York Press.

Gershuny, J. (2003) *Changing Times: Work and leisure in a post-industrial society*. Oxford: Oxford University Press.

Gershuny, J. (2005) 'Busyness as the Badge of Honor for the New Superordinate Working Class', *Social Research* 72 (2) 287–314.

Glorieux, I., Laurijssen, I., Minnen, J. and Van Tienoven, T. P. (2010) 'In Search of the Harried Leisure Class in Contemporary Society: Time-use surveys and patterns of leisure consumption', *Journal of Consumer Policy* 33: 163–181.

Granter, E. (2008) 'A Dream of Ease: Situating the future of work and leisure', *Futures* 40 (9) 803–811.

Foster, R. (1978) *Celebration of Discipline*. New York: Harper & Row.

Hunnicutt, B. K. (1988) 'Work, Leisure, and Labor Supply: An analysis of the 1980 U.S. Census Data', *International Review of Modern Sociology* 18 (1) 31–55.

Jacobs, J. A. and Gerson, K. (2001) 'Overworked Individuals or Overworked Families? Explaining trends in work, leisure, and family time', *Work and Occupations* 28 (1) 40–63.

Juster, F. T. (1986) 'Preferences for Work and Leisure', *Economic Outlook USA*, First Quarter, 15–17.

Karlsson, J. C. (1995) 'The Concept of Work on the Rack: Critique and suggestions', in R. L. Simpson and I. H. Simpson (eds) *Research in the Sociology of Work: The meaning of work*. Greenwich, CT: JAI Press.

Kegan, R. (1994) *In Over Our Heads: The mental demands of modern life*. Cambridge, MA: Harvard University Press.

Krueger, A. B. (2007) 'Are We Having More Fun Yet? Categorizing and evaluating changes in time allocation', *Brookings Papers on Economic Activity* 2: 193–217.

Levy, D. M. (2007) 'No Time to Think: Reflections on information technology and contemplative scholarship', *Ethics and Information Technology* 9: 237–249.

Linder, S. B. (1970) *The Harried Leisure Class*. New York: Columbia University Press.

Lockstone-Binney, L., Holmes, K., Smith, K. and Baum, T. (2010) 'Volunteers and Volunteering in Leisure: Social science perspectives', *Leisure Studies* 29 (4) 435–455.

Maguire, J. S. (2008) 'Leisure and the Obligation of Self-Work: An examination of the fitness field', *Leisure Studies* 27 (1) 59–75.

Marx, K. (2010) *Essential Writings of Karl Marx*. St. Petersburg, FL: Red and Black Publishers.

Mattingly, M. J. and Bianchi, S. M. (2003) 'Gender Differences in the Quantity and Quality of Free Time: The U.S. experience', *Social Forces* 81 (3) 999–1030.

Meilaender, G. C. (ed.) (2000) *Working: Its meaning and its limits*. Notre Dame, IN: University of Notre Dame Press.

Neulinger, J. (1981) *To Leisure: An introduction*. Boston, MA: Allyn and Bacon.

Parker, S. (1983) *Leisure and Work*. London: George Allen and Unwin.

Pieper, J. (1998) *Leisure: The basis of culture* (G. Malsbary, trans.). South Bend, IN: St. Augustine's Press. (Original work published in 1952).

Quarrick, G. (1989) *Our Sweetest Hours: Recreation and the state of mental absorption*. Jefferson, NC: McFarland & Company.

Ravenscroft, N. and Gilchrist, P. (2009) 'The Emergent Working Society of Leisure', *Journal of Leisure Research* 41 (1) 23–39.

Roberts, K. (2011) 'Leisure: The importance of being inconsequential', *Leisure Studies* 30 (1) 5–20.

Robinet, I. (1997) *Taoism: Growth of a religion* (P. Brooks, trans.). Stanford, CA: Stanford University Press. (Original work published in 1992).

Robinson, J. and Godbey, G. (1997) *Time for Life: The surprising ways Americans use their time*. University Park, PA: Pennsylvania State University Press.

Rojek, C. (2000) *Leisure and Culture*. Basingstoke: Macmillan.

Rojek, C. (2009) *The Labour of Leisure*. London: Sage.

Rooke, D. and Torbert, W. (1998) 'Organizational Transformation as a Function of CEOs' Developmental Stage', *Organizational Development Journal* 16 (1) 11–28.

Rose, M. (1985) *Re-working the Work Ethic*. New York: Schocken.

Roy, D. (1959) 'Banana Time: Job satisfaction and informal interaction', *Human Organization* 18: 158–168.

Shinew, K. J. and Parry, D. C. (2005) 'Examining College Students' Participation in the Leisure Pursuits of Drinking and Illegal Drug Use', *Journal of Leisure Research* 37 (3) 364–386.

Spracklen, K. (2011) 'Dreaming of Drams: Authenticity in Scottish whisky tourism as an expression of unresolved Habermasian rationalities', *Leisure Studies* 30 (1) 99–116.

Stalp, M. C. (2006) 'Negotiating Time and Space for Serious Leisure: Quilting in the modern U.S. home', *Journal of Leisure Research* 38 (1) 104–132.

Stebbins, R. A. (1992) *Amateurs, Professionals, and Serious Leisure*. Montreal: McGill-Queen's University Press.

Stebbins, R. A. (1997) 'Serious Leisure and Well Being', in J. T. Haworth (ed.) *Work, Leisure, and Well-being*. London: Routledge.

Sullivan, O. and Gershuny, J. (2004) 'Inconspicuous Consumption', *Journal of Consumer Culture* 4: 79–100.

Torbert, W. (1991) *The Power of Balance: Transforming self, society, and scientific inquiry*. Thousand Oaks, CA: Sage.

Torbert, W. (1996) 'The "Chaotic" Action Awareness of Tranformational Leaders', *International Journal of Public Administration* 19 (6) 911–939.

Torbert, W. and Associates (2004) *Action Inquiry: The secret of timely and transformative leadership*. San Francisco: Berrett-Koehler.

Torbert, W. and Fisher, D. (1992) 'Autobiographical Awareness as a Catalyst for Managerial and Organizational Development', *Management Education and Development* 23 (3) 184–198.

Torbert, W. and Rogers, M. P. (1973) *Being for the Most Part Puppets*. Cambridge, MA: Schenkman Publishing Company.

Veblen, T. (1899) *The Theory of the Leisure Class*. London: Allen and Unwin.

Wilber, K. (2000) *Integral Psychology: Consciousness, spirit, psychology, therapy*. Boston, MA: Shambhala.

Wilson, W. J. (1996) *When Work Disappears: The world of the new urban poor*. New York: Alfred A. Knopf.

Wrzesniewski, A. and Dutton, J. E. (2001) 'Crafting a Job: Revisioning employees as active crafters of their work', *Academy of Management Review* 26: 179–201.

PART VI

NEW DIRECTIONS

41

CULTURAL TOURISM

Greg Richards

Introduction

Cultural tourism is, arguably, one of the most important segments of tourism and is increasingly a major channel for cultural consumption in general. As leisure time becomes more pressured (or is perceived to be), so traditional forms of cultural recreation undertaken at home tend to spread into holiday time, the one remaining substantial block of leisure time for many people (Richards, 1998). Cultural tourism is particularly significant as a leisure activity, not just because of this displacement, but also because it provides a laboratory in which to study key aspects of leisure consumption and production.

Cultural tourism has become a particular focus of research in recent decades as the growing links between culture and tourism have been recognized (OECD, 2009). The cultural tourism market is frequently seen as a particularly rapid growth area, even though empirical evidence suggests that the growth of cultural tourism is linked to the general expansion of tourism consumption (de Haan, 1997). What has probably increased the visibility of cultural tourism is the growing diversity of forms of cultural consumption by tourists, which in turn can be linked to the increase in cultural supply and the widening definition of 'culture' (Richards 2007). Arguably, cultural tourism now accounts for around 40 per cent of international tourism (UNWTO 2004), although those travelling for specific cultural motives probably account for only 5–10 per cent of global tourism flows (Richards, 2001).

Although the volume and economic value of cultural tourism has tended to attract the attention of policy makers, the academic significance of cultural tourism lies in what it reveals about wider social practices, and the nature of leisure practices in particular. Cultural tourism unites two areas of enquiry that have traditionally been relatively separate: the productive world of tourism (linked to business and management) and cultural consumption practices (a focus for Leisure Studies and sociology). The growth of tourism in the latter half of the twentieth century turned cultural consumption on holiday from an elite preserve into a mass phenomenon, creating a distinct sector of 'cultural tourism' (Richards, 1996a). This rapidly expanding market quickly revealed the links between cultural consumption and the production of culture for tourism through the expansion of cultural consumption spaces and the rise of 'heritage' (Hewison, 1987; Richards, 1996b). The increased interweaving of production and consumption revealed by cultural tourism presaged more recent concepts of 'co-creation' (Prahalad and Ramaswamy, 2004).

In the field of Leisure Studies, the two decades since 1990 have seen an increase in the attention paid to tourism, and particularly to the cultural aspects of the phenomenon (e.g. Stebbins, 1996; Aitchison *et al.*, 2001). Part of the explanation for this, arguably, lies in the growing de-differentiation of tourism and everyday life, which has brought tourism closer to the central concerns of leisure scholars. But there has also been a shift in the focus of tourism scholars as well, particularly in the increased attention paid to the cultural aspects of travel. As attention shifted from the purely economic significance of cultural tourism towards consideration of its socio-cultural meaning, analyses of the search for authenticity and the role of museums and monuments in the production of meaning for tourists proliferated (MacCannell, 1976; Horne, 1984). Many early analyses of cultural tourism were linked to notions of 'high' culture, but the increasing de-differentiation of cultural consumption evident from the 1960s onwards began to question this positioning of cultural tourism consumption. As cultural tourism gradually spread to include many different cultural forms, including folk culture, traditions, popular culture and creative activities, so cultural tourism became a less rarefied and separate realm of tourism consumption. The expansion of cultural forms consumed by tourists also heightened the view of culture and tourism being in 'conflict' with each other, a situation which can be seen as 'inevitable' in view of the cultural differences between hosts and guests and the different objectives of the tourism and cultural 'industries' (Robinson and Boniface, 1999).

Many saw (cultural) tourism as being at the forefront of processes of commodification, which they felt tended to rob local culture of meaning and authenticity. Most notable perhaps is Greenwood's (1977) critical assessment of the relationship between a Basque cultural festival and tourism. He emphasized the commodifying role of tourism and the changes that it wrought on 'authentic' local culture as performances were adapted to suit the needs of tourists. As Pereiro (2013) has emphasized, however, the anthropological views on tourism have evolved to embrace different viewpoints, ranging from the optimistic view prevalent in the 1960s (de Kadt, 1978) to the more critical views on commodification espoused in the 1980s and 1990s to a more recent 'adaptive approach' that emphasizes the ability of local communities to adapt to and to use tourism for their own ends.

Cultural tourism has therefore integrated a growing range of theoretical perspectives from sociology, anthropology, cultural studies, economics and other disciplines. A range of these approaches can be found in the *Routledge Handbook of Cultural Tourism* (Smith and Richards, 2013). Growing multidisciplinary perspectives and theoretical cross-fertilization have facilitated more rigorous analysis of cultural tourism, but they have also increased the contribution of cultural tourism to the development of tourist studies and the contribution of tourism studies to wider theory. As Johnson (2009) has underlined, cultural tourism research has done much to uncover links between the production and consumption of places in recent years (e.g. Frey, 2009; Russo, 2002). This has been increasingly taken up in studies of urban leisure and tourism, such as Miles (2010), Maitland's (2007) 'new tourist areas' and the rise of 'creative clusters' related to the growing attractiveness of everyday leisure for tourists (Pappalepore, 2010).

To date, these developments have attracted relatively little attention from leisure scholars, probably because holidays still tend to be viewed as a specific form of leisure time removed from 'everyday' leisure (Gratton, 1995). This problem of the isolation of Leisure Studies and tourism is compounded by the nature of available data. Leisure activities are measured in everyday, home-centred contexts, whereas tourism is usually studied as an activity removed in both time and space from the home context (Binkhorst *et al.*, 2010).

However, this isolation is gradually reducing as studies in cultural tourism make a greater contribution to wider social science debates (Johnson, 2009) and as leisure scholars become more interested in tourism. This is reflected, for example, in the increasing number and range of tourism contributions found in the journal *Leisure Studies*. Recent issues have featured research on whisky tourism (Spracklen, 2011), music tourism (Snape, 2012), wine tourism (Lee and Chang, 2012), the tourism legacies of mega events (Dansero and Puttilli, 2010) and holiday meals (Heimtun, 2010), all of which could broadly be seen as 'cultural tourism'.

This chapter explores some of the areas of cross-fertilization that have emerged between Leisure Studies and cultural tourism in recent years, including the relationships between production and consumption, leisure as extension or compensation for work, omnivorous modes of consumption and serious leisure.

What is cultural tourism?

Before entering into a detailed discussion of the relationship between leisure and cultural tourism, it is useful to look at how cultural tourism can be defined. A comprehensive review of cultural tourism definitions has recently been provided by Buczkowska (2011). This indicates that there is a wide range of definitions designed to serve different purposes. In broad terms, however, most definitions can be characterized as technical definitions, designed to measure cultural tourism quantitatively, or conceptual definitions, more concerned with what cultural tourism is.

This division was concretized in the Association for Tourism and Leisure Education (ATLAS) Cultural Tourism Project (Richards, 1996a; 2011), which adopted two different definitions designed to encapsulate both of these functions. The 'conceptual definition' saw cultural tourism as involving

> The movement of persons to cultural attractions away from their normal place of residence, with the intention to gather new information and experiences to satisfy their cultural needs.
>
> (Richards, 1996a: 24)

The 'technical definition' was more concerned with the problem of determining where cultural tourists might be found, in order to quantify different types of cultural tourism consumption and production. This involved 'All movements of persons to specific cultural attractions, such as heritage sites, artistic and cultural manifestations, arts and drama outside their normal place of residence' (Richards, 1996a: 24).

The conceptual definition of cultural tourism shows the important link between cultural tourism and leisure, particularly in the focus on motivation and cultural consumption. Although there have been many attempts to produce definitions of cultural tourism over the years, the essence remains fairly simple: cultural tourism involves cultural consumption by people while travelling. However, this still leaves room for a wide range of leisure activities which can be regarded as falling under the umbrella of cultural tourism. This at least partly explains why there have been many areas of overlap between cultural tourism research and leisure research over the years.

Links between leisure consumption and production

One of the problematic issues in Leisure Studies has been dealing with the links between production and consumption. Traditionally, leisure scholars tended to view leisure as a consumption-based activity, contrasted to the productive area of work. This began to change as the leisure boom underlined the productive role of the 'leisure industries' (Mommaas, 2000) and as tourism began to be considered as a site of consumption and identity formation as well as a productive 'industry'. As Rojek (2009) has pointed out, it has become increasingly difficult to view leisure and work as dichotomous categories, and therefore also to separate production from consumption. Cultural tourism provides copious illustrations of this argument.

For example, there has been growing attention paid to the work of 'doing tourism' (Smith, 2012) – in cultural tourism this work entails a successful replication of the ritual of cultural consumption and/or a performance of the cultural role expected of the tourist (Edensor, 2000). There is also considerable evidence to suggest that as well as simply performing cultural tourism, consumers are also increasingly involved in the production of that which they consume.

In studies of the production of cultural tourism the role of the 'new cultural intermediaries' (Bourdieu, 1984) became a particular focus of attention. Given the status of cultural tourism as a relatively specialized niche within the broader field of tourism, the role of intermediaries in organizing tourism consumption became particularly clear. A specific mechanism suggested by Bourdieu was the substitution of cultural capital for economic capital. This process became very visible in cultural tourism, where a large number of art historians, archaeologists and other cultural intermediaries utilized the growing interest in heritage (Hewison, 1987) to develop new careers in tourism (Richards, 2001).

These intermediaries were similar not just in terms of their source of cultural capital, but also in their own cultural preferences. A study in Amsterdam showed that the 'new producers' involved in cultural tourism tended to live in the historic city centre, exactly the type of areas also being developed for heritage and city tourism (Richards, Goedhart and Herrijgers, 2001). The spatial coincidence of consumption and production tends to strengthen the kind of specialization of tourism and leisure functions in city centres that has been noted by authors such as Zukin (1995) and Hannigan (1998).

The realization that culture was increasingly being shaped by cultural intermediaries for tourist consumption focused attention on processes by which authenticity was produced for and by tourists (MacCannell, 1976). The role of intermediaries was seen as one not simply of production, but increasingly of co-production of tourist experiences. The very nature of 'authentic' cultural tourism experiences was questioned as it became obvious that authenticity was a mediated, subjective phenomenon. For example Ex and Lengkeek (1996) related the role of authenticity to Cohen's typology of tourists, arguing that the need for authenticity, and the type of authenticity desired, would vary by individual. McKercher and du Cros (2002) emphasized the different types of experiences sought by cultural tourists, ranging from 'deep' purposeful experiences to casual, serendipitous encounters. This reflects the discussion about 'serious' and 'casual' modes of leisure (see below).

Perhaps not surprisingly, therefore, a strand of recent work has also developed the perspective of the tourist as an active performer who can also help to produce or 'co-create' the (cultural) tourism experience (e.g. Binkhorst, 2007; Binkhorst and den Dekker, 2009). In seeking to develop their own creativity, consumers utilize the raw materials provided by local and global culture to create their own experiences, while producers increasingly adopt an enabling role. The tourism experience becomes much more of a co-production between 'tourists' and 'locals'. This presents a subtle but important shift away from the concept of the tourist gaze (Urry, 1990), which sees the gaze primarily as something externally imposed on tourists. Stylianou-Lambert (2011) found that even though cultural tourists may adopt a tourist gaze during travel, they do not abandon other gazes or perceptual 'filters' carried from home, and they use these to produce new cultural experiences.

Extension or reversal?

The discussion of the production and consumption roles of tourists is also linked to the debate about whether leisure activities provide a reversal of, or a compensation for, work, or if leisure acts more as an extension of work (e.g. Miller and Weiss, 1982). Much tourism research has centred on the compensatory thesis, seeing tourism as something different from everyday life and therefore providing difference or rest from daily routines (Urry, 1990). However, other authors have pointed out the tendency for tourism to develop its own (daily) rhythms and practices (Bargeman and van der Poel, 2006), which have an integral connection with life at home. Studies in cultural tourism have also tended to favour the extension hypothesis. For example, Thrane (2000) found that the cultural consumption of cultural tourists is actually very like their consumption at home. He concludes that cultural tourism is far more a process of extension of work in leisure time, rather than a reversal.

Results from the ATLAS surveys also indicated that 'normal' or 'everyday' leisure consumption patterns were in fact repeated on holiday. There was also a tendency for certain professionals to engage in 'busmen's holidays', where, for example, museum staff would visit other museums during their holiday time.

Not only do people tend to follow similar patterns of cultural behaviour at home and on holiday, but those who consume more culture at home also consume more on holiday. Patterns of extension are increasingly supported by information technology and global information networks that allow us to take our own practices with us when we travel. Instead of being guided by the authoritative texts of guide books, we increasingly act as bricoleurs of our own information streams, carried with us by the same technology that we use at home (smartphones, iPads, laptops). In carrying our practices with us on holiday, there is also more chance that holiday leisure will tend towards an extension of 'normal' leisure.

Omnivorous consumption by cultural tourists

The view that cultural tourists were often engaging in an extension and even an intensification of everyday cultural consumption on holiday provided a natural link to the emerging concept of omnivorous cultural consumption (Peterson and Kern, 1996). Peterson and his collaborators have suggested that cultural consumers can be categorized in terms of their tendency to stick to a single type of culture, such as pop music or classical music (cultural univores), or else to mix different cultural forms, such as opera (traditional 'high' culture) and football ('popular' culture) in a form of 'omnivorous' consumption.

Measuring omnivorous consumption in leisure is complicated by the tendency to spread different types of consumption over long periods of time, requiring data to be collected over long time spans. In tourism, however, the concentrated 'cultural laboratory' provided by the holiday allows a more focused study of the extent to which different cultural forms are mixed. The ATLAS research has been used as one means of testing the omnivore hypothesis in tourism. The ATLAS research is interesting in this context because it provides a measure of consumption across a range of different cultural fields. The study of omnivorous consumption requires 'data on a broad range of cultural practices and preferences (music, reading, television viewing, film attendance, sport, etc.) and not just data bearing on one cultural sector' (van Rees *et al.*, 1999: 350). The omnivore thesis is also based on data about general tastes and preferences, rather than on specific choices made in specific contexts. The identification of omnivorous consumption is therefore usually based on household surveys and similar research that covers consumption over a relatively long time period. The study of cultural tourism experiences thus offers the possibility to develop a laboratory for the study of omnivorousness, asking questions about the extent to which mixing of cultural styles occurs in different situations and with different individuals.

Toivonen (2006) tested the omnivore hypothesis in relation to cultural tourism using the ATLAS data. He found that there was relatively strong omnivorousness in attending cultural events and visiting cultural attractions on holiday, particularly for those aged 50 years or over and highly educated tourists. Omnivorous tourists tended to be omnivorous not only because they visited popular attractions more frequently than other tourists but especially because they visited less-popular attractions more often. More recent work by Richards and van der Ark (2013) based on the ATLAS data indicates that omnivorous consumption is particularly pronounced in city-break tourism, as compared with other types of holidays. Barbieri and Mahoney (2010: 493) pointed to a similar pattern in their study of omnivorous cultural tourism behaviour:

> cultural omnivorous behaviour extends beyond arts consumption and is relevant to cultural tourism products and behaviours. Omnivores are more frequent tourists and are attracted to destinations with more diverse cultural and heritage attractions and experiences, including historical sites, museums, natural centres, live performances and festivals.

The idea that omnivores are particularly attracted to (cultural) tourism experiences also fits with the idea of the 'voracious' omnivore (Sullivan and Katz-Gerro, 2007), which also offers a possible explanation why cultural tourism exhibits patterns of work extension:

> The voracious activity pattern may perhaps be one way to reconcile the contradiction between the 'increasingly overworked' contention and the 'increase in leisure time' contention, if we maintain that discretionary time can be devoted to work and to leisure alike by means of voracious cultural participation.

(p. 134)

Cultural tourism as serious leisure

Another way that leisure scholars have viewed cultural tourism is as a form of 'serious leisure' (Stebbins, 1996). Stebbins suggests that some leisure activities are pursued as a serious form of personal development or learning, motivations that are often ascribed to cultural tourists (Richards, 1996a). Serious leisure is contrasted with 'casual leisure', which is related to relaxation or 'fun'. One might, following Stebbins, characterize cultural tourists as engaging in serious leisure, while many other tourists, such as beach tourists, are engaging in shallow forms of fun and sun seeking.

However, a body of cultural tourism research indicates that the distinctions proposed by Stebbins are difficult to maintain. May (1996), for example, identified motivations of authenticity seeking among 'mass' tourists as well as more 'elite' travellers. Learning is a motivation for almost all cultural tourists, independent of their apparent level of 'seriousness' (Richards, 2001).

More recent development of specific niches within the field of cultural tourism seems to touch more closely on Stebbins' ideas. As cultural tourism has grown and developed into a mass market (Russo, 2002), so an increasing range of cultural tourism niches have emerged: gastronomic tourism (Hjalager and Richards, 2002), heritage tourism (Timothy and Boyd, 2003), indigenous tourism (Pereiro, 2013), dark tourism (Stone, 2006) etc.

One recent niche to be identified has been 'creative tourism' (Richards, 2011; Wurzburger *et al.*, 2009). Richards and Raymond (2000: 18) provided the following definition of creative tourism: 'Tourism which offers visitors the opportunity to develop their creative potential through active participation in courses and learning experiences which are characteristic of the holiday destination where they are undertaken.'

In some senses the development of creative tourism can be seen as a reaction to the growth of cultural tourism. People used to classic modes of cultural tourism have begun to seek out more interactive forms of engagement with culture that avoid mass cultural tourism. Rather than the classic high cultural sights of a destination, it seems that many cultural tourists are now seeking engagement with 'everyday' culture that is integrated into the daily lives of local people. This trend is being catered for with a growing array of creative tourism products that allow tourists to interact creatively with local people and learn new skills as they do so. This underlines the point that leisure is increasingly the creative space that people use to support the social ties that underpin acquisition of relational capital in the network society (Richards, 2010). (Cultural) tourism is emerging as a creative space in which significant blocks of leisure are used as a means of personal and creative development, building capital for use in 'everyday' leisure and work.

This development is becoming increasingly visible in the area of events, which now increasingly function as a means of developing the co-presence necessary for the maintenance of social networks. Richards and Palmer (2010) have identified the rise of 'eventful cities' that attract visitors and residents to the creative spaces provided by major events such as the Edinburgh Festival or the European Capital of Culture. The event serves as a temporal and spatial accelerator, creating interactions between large numbers of people over a short period of time, adding to the atmosphere of the city as well as providing 'hot spots' for creative interaction and innovation. In this way, cultural tourism functions as a way not just of consuming culture, but of producing it.

Conclusions

The growing body of research on cultural tourism indicates an increasingly complex and rich relationship between the consumption of culture through tourism and the wider field of Leisure Studies. As the divisions between tourism, culture and leisure become increasingly indistinct, so leisure scholars are also discovering cultural tourism as a fruitful area of enquiry.

Emerging work in the field of cultural tourism casts interesting light on the debate about 'what is leisure?' Holidays, in particular, have traditionally been viewed as an area of almost 'pure' leisure – a compulsory inversion of work. More recent analyses of the work of doing tourism, and cultural tourism in particular, call this traditional view into question. In fact, the boundaries of leisure may not be so important as the 'leisure lens' that is used to view specific practices. The use of a leisure-practice perspective in the ATLAS Cultural Tourism

Project, for example, has prevented this research from being swallowed up in the production- and management-related view that has tended to dominate the tourism literature. At the same time, the position of cultural tourism as a space and time apart from 'everyday' leisure has allowed the research to move beyond the traditional restrictions of the leisure debate.

Cultural tourism has also emerged as an interesting laboratory for leisure research. The work done on issues such as inversion, omnivorousness and serious leisure illustrates how the concentrated lens of the 'holiday' is a useful device for examining leisure and, in particular, the boundaries of leisure.

References

Aitchison, C., MacLeod, N.E. and Shaw, S.J. (2001) *Leisure and Tourism Landscapes: social and cultural geographies*. London: Routledge.

Barbieri, C. and Mahoney, E. (2010) 'Cultural tourism behaviour and preferences among the live-performing arts audience: an application of the univorous–omnivorous framework', *International Journal of Tourism Research* 12: 481–496.

Bargeman, B., and van der Poel, H.J.J. (2006) 'The role of routines in the vacation decision-making process of Dutch vacationers', *Tourism Management* 27 (4) 707–720.

Binkhorst, E. (2007) 'Creativity in tourism experiences: the case of Sitges', in G. Richards and J. Wilson (eds) *Tourism, Creativity and Development*. London: Routledge, pp. 124–144.

Binkhorst, E. and den Dekker, T. (2009) 'Agenda for co-creation tourism experience research', *Journal of Hospitality Marketing and Management*, 18: 311–327.

Binkhorst, E., den Dekker, T. and Melkert, M. (2010) 'Blurring boundaries in cultural tourism research', in G. Richards and W. Munsters (eds) *Cultural Tourism Research Methods*. Wallingford: CABI, pp. 41–51.

Bourdieu, P. (1984) *Distinction: a social critique of the judgement of taste*. London: Routledge.

Buczkowska, K. (2011) *Cultural Tourism – Heritage, Arts and Creativity*. Poznań: AWF w Poznaniu.

Dansero, E. and Puttilli, M. (2010) 'Mega-events tourism legacies: the case of the Torino 2006 Winter Olympic Games – a territorialisation approach', *Leisure Studies* 29: 321–341.

de Haan, J. (1997) *Het Gedeelde Erfgoed*. Rijswijk: SCP.

de Kadt, E. (1978) *Tourism: passport to development*. Oxford: Oxford University Press.

Edensor, T. (2000) 'Staging tourism: tourists as performers', *Annals of Tourism Research* 27: 322–344.

Ex, N. and Lengkeek, J. (1996) 'Op zoek naar het echte?' *Vrijetijdstudies* 14: 21–46.

Frey, O. (2009) 'Creativity of places as a resource for cultural tourism', in G. Maciocco and S. Serreli (eds) *Enhancing the City, Urban and Landscape Perspectives*. Berlin: Springer, pp. 135–154.

Gratton, C. (1995) 'A cross-national/transnational approach to leisure research: the changing relationship between work and leisure in Europe', in G. Richards (ed.) *European Tourism and Leisure Education: trends and prospects*. Tilburg: Tilburg University Press, pp. 215–232.

Greenwood, D.J. (1977) 'Culture by the pound: an anthropological perspective on tourism as cultural commoditization', in V.L. Smith (ed.) *Hosts and Guests*. Philadelphia: University of Pennsylvania Press, pp. 129–139.

Hannigan, J. (1998) *Fantasy City: pleasure and profit in the postmodern metropolis*. London and New York: Routledge.

Heimtun, B. (2010) 'The holiday meal: eating out alone and mobile emotional geographies', *Leisure Studies* 29: 175–192.

Hewison, R. (1987) *The Heritage Industry: Britain in a climate of decline*. London: Methuen.

Hjalager, A.-M. and Richards, G. (2002) *Tourism and Gastronomy*. London: Routledge.

Horne, D. (1984) *The Great Museum*. London: Pluto Press.

Johnson, L.C. (2009) *Cultural Capitals: revaluing the arts, remaking urban spaces*. Farnham: Ashgate.

Lee, T.H. and Chang, Y.S. (2012) 'The influence of experiential marketing and activity involvement on the loyalty intentions of wine tourists in Taiwan', *Leisure Studies* 31: 103–121.

MacCannell, D. (1976) *The Tourist: a new theory of the leisure class*. New York: Schocken Books.

McKercher, B. and du Cros, H. (2002) *Cultural Tourism*. New York: Haworth Press.

Maitland, R. (2007) 'Conviviality and everyday life: the appeal of new areas of London for visitors', *International Journal of Tourism Research* 10: 15–20.

May, J. (1996) 'In search of authenticity off and on the beaten track', *Environment and Planning D: Society and Space* 14 (6) 709–736.

Miles, S. (2010) *Spaces for Consumption*, London: Sage.

Miller, L.E. and Weiss, R.M. (1982) 'The work–leisure relationship: evidence for the compensatory hypothesis', *Human Relations* 35: 763–771.

Mommaas, J.T. (2000) 'De opmars van de vrijetijdsindustrie', *Landelijk Contact* 48 (5) 7–8.

OECD (2009) *The Impact of Culture on Tourism*. Paris: OECD.

Pappalepore, I. (2010). 'Tourism and the development of "creative" urban areas: evidence from four non-central areas in London'. PhD thesis, University of Westminster, School of Architecture and the Built Environment. Available at: http://westminsterresearch.wmin.ac.uk/8880/ (accessed 14 April 2011).

Pereiro, X. (2013) 'Understanding indigenous tourism' in G. Richards and M. Smith (eds) *Handbook of Cultural Tourism*. London: Routledge.

Peterson, R.A. and Kern, R.M. (1996) 'Changing highbrow taste: from snob to omnivore', *American Sociological Review* 61: 900–907.

Prahalad, C.K. and Ramaswamy, V. (2004) *The Future of Competition: co-creating unique value with customers*, Cambridge, MA: Harvard Business School Press.

Richards, G. (1996a) *Cultural Tourism in Europe*. Wallingford: CABI.

Richards, G. (1996b) 'Production and consumption of European cultural tourism', *Annals of Tourism Research* 23 (2) 261–283.

Richards, G. (1998) 'Time for a holiday? Social rights and international tourism consumption', *Time and Society* 7: 145–160.

Richards, G. (ed.) (2001) *Cultural Attractions and European Tourism*. Wallingford: CABI.

Richards, G. (ed.) (2007) *Cultural Tourism: global and local perspectives*. New York: Haworth Press.

Richards, G. (2010) Leisure in the Network Society: from pseudo-events to hyperfestivity? http://www.academia.edu/1271795/Leisure_in_the_Network_Society

Richards, G. (2011) 'Creativity and tourism: the state of the art', *Annals of Tourism Research* 38 (4) 1225–1253.

Richards, G. and Palmer, R. (2010) *Eventful Cities: cultural management and urban revitalization*. London: Routledge.

Richards, G. and Raymond, C. (2000) 'Creative tourism', *ATLAS News* 23: 16–20.

Richards, G., Goedhart, S. and Herrijgers, C. (2001) 'The cultural attraction distribution system', in G. Richards (ed.) *Cultural Attractions and European Tourism*. Wallingford: CABI, pp. 71–90.

Richards, G., and van der Ark, L.A. (2013) Dimensions of cultural consumption among tourists: Multiple correspondence analysis, Tourism Management, http://dx.doi.org/10.1016/j.tourman.2013.01.007

Robinson, M. and Boniface, P. (1999) *Tourism and Cultural Conflicts*, Wallingford: CABI.

Rojek, C. (2009) *The Labour of Leisure: the culture of free time*. London: Sage.

Russo, A.P. (2002) 'The "vicious circle" of tourism development in heritage cities', *Annals of Tourism Research* 29: 165–182.

Smith, L. (2012) 'The cultural work of tourism', in L. Smith, E. Waterton and S. Watson (eds) *The Cultural Moment of Tourism*. London: Routledge.

Smith, M. and Richards, G. (2013) *Routledge Handbook of Cultural Tourism*. London: Routledge.

Snape, B. (2012) 'Turning the tune: traditional music, tourism, and social change in an Irish village', *Leisure Studies* 31: 258–259.

Spracklen, K. (2011) 'Dreaming of drams: authenticity in Scottish whisky tourism as an expression of unresolved Habermasian rationalities', *Leisure Studies* 30: 99–116.

Stebbins, R.A. (1996) 'Cultural tourism as serious leisure', *Annals of Tourism Research* 23 (4) 948–950.

Stone, P.R. (2006) 'A dark tourism spectrum: towards a typology of death and macabre related tourist sites, attractions and exhibitions', *TOURISM: An Interdisciplinary International Journal* 52 (2) 145–160.

Stylianou-Lambert, T. (2011) 'Gazing from home: cultural tourism and art museums', *Annals of Tourism Research* 38 (2) 403–421.

Sullivan, O. and Katz-Gerro, T. (2007) 'The omnivore thesis revisited: voracious cultural consumers', *European Sociological Review* 23: 123–137.

Thrane, C. (2000) 'Everyday life and cultural tourism in Scandinavia: examining the spillover hypothesis', *Leisure and Society* 23: 217–234.

Timothy, D.J. and Boyd, S.W. (2003) *Heritage Tourism*. London: Pearson Education.

Toivonen, T. (2006) 'Happy time: three papers on national and international trends in leisure time'. *Turku School of Economics Discussion and Working Papers No. 5.*

UNWTO (2004) *Tourism Market Trends*. UNWTO: Madrid.

Urry, J. (1990) *The Tourist Gaze*. London: Sage.

van Rees, K., Vermunt, J. and Verboord, M. (1999) 'Cultural classifications under discussion: latent class analysis of highbrow and lowbrow reading', *Poetics* 26: 349–365.

Wurzburger, R., Pattakos, A. and Pratt, S. (eds) (2009) *Creative Tourism: a global conversation*. Santa Fe: Sunstone Press.

Zukin, S. (1995) *The Cultures of Cities*. Malden, MA: Blackwell.

42

EVENT MANAGEMENT

Chris Rojek

Since the early 1990s Event Management modules have ballooned in proportion, to become a major element in Leisure and Recreation education. To be sure, lately they have developed their own degree programmes, publication outlets and research networks. These courses of study now enrol many students who, twenty years ago, would have opted for Leisure and Recreation Studies. The development in the curriculum represents more than a change in tone and emphasis. Event Management purports to be a new area of study, hot-wired to popular culture, effective revenue generation and the needs of the digital age. It would be going too far to propose that Event Management is the future, and Leisure and Recreation Studies is the past. The latter field is too well established, with strong employment pathways to public leisure and recreation departments and private providers, to wither away.

That having been said, there is no doubt that Event Management has emerged as the undisputed market leader, delivering training for the labour market in Meetings, Incentives, Conventions and Exhibitions (MICE). There is a widespread, almost entirely unsubstantiated, sense in which the knowledge base and skills repertoire of Event Management is asserted to be more relevant to the central challenges of leisure and recreation today. It is, hence, held to be more congruent with prevailing market conditions. It is as if Leisure and Recreation Departments belong to the old, pre-wired world in which employment opportunities were concentrated in the public sector, markets were assumed to be primarily national and work was presupposed to be the central life interest. The hype surrounding Event Management presents it as serving the mixed, global economy with job prospects in the private and public sectors and a flexible, post-work orientation.

In this chapter I want to explore three questions in order to throw these considerations into sharper relief and greater detail: What is Event Management? Why are Events prominent? What are their consequences? The backdrop to these questions is the belief that Event Management reflects an approach to the provision of leisure and recreation that is driven by a mixture of market logic and communitarian sentiments.[1] Further, the prominence of Global Events in popular culture reflects the ubiquitous influence of communication power and has emerged as a significant element in moral regulation.[2] The Public Relations–Media hub portrays Global Events as the reflection of spontaneous, invincible 'people power'.[3] In reality, Events (at least at the global level) are part of the battery of media-dependent instruments that *invisible government* employs to control network publics.[4] I will elaborate these points later. Let me turn to the three questions.

What is Event Management?

Event Management is a specialized branch of project delivery pertaining to the organization of conferences, festivals, expositions and symposia. The knowledge and skills base is concentrated in three interlinked spheres of learning and operation: Event Planning, Event Leadership and Post-Event Evaluation. This covers a wide range of technical issues encompassing, Event logistics, content creation, organizing locations/venues, crowd control, transport flows, accommodation support, working with stakeholders, operating with regulatory agencies, risk management, regional and/or global coordination, media targeting, social capital strategy, merchandizing and post-Event evaluation arrangements.

The discipline draws on traditions of academic enquiry and management experience in Hospitality Management Studies, Tourist Studies, Business Studies, Organization Studies, Risk Analysis and Leisure and Recreation Studies. The central outward purpose of Events is twofold: to raise funds and to develop social consciousness.

Events fall into three sub-categories: Minor, Major and Mega (Roberts, 2004: 108–20). Minor Events refer to local projects that are usually designed to fulfil neighbourhood or workforce needs.

Major Events refer to metropolitan or regional festivals (the Hay Festival of Literature and the Arts, the Munich Oktoberfest, the Coney Island Mermaid Parade). A notable sub-branch is Hallmark Events. These are fairs, festivals, expositions, cultural and sporting events designed to showcase a host community, usually a city, in the tourist market (Hall, 1989: 263).

Mega Events refer to large-scale, non-governmental, global cultural events that adopt a spectacular form of presentation, seek large sponsorship deals and aim at mass appeal (Roche, 2000). Typically, they presuppose syndicated rights with corporate and state media networks and merchandizers.

This chapter focuses overwhelmingly upon Mega (Global) Events. I do not mean to imply that Minor and Major Events are of no consequence. Both are expressions of human compassion. As such, they do credit to their organizers and participants. The reason for addressing Mega Events is that this high-profile and increasingly prominent form of Event Management throws into relief some of the inherent contradictions in the form.

A distinction must be made between *Single Issue* and *Cyclical Events*. As the term implies, a Single Issue Event is of limited duration and focuses upon a specific social, economic or political problem or upheaval of nature. Examples include famine in Ethiopia (Live Aid, 1985), relief for the victims of Hurricane Katrina ('A Concert for Hurricane Relief', 2005) and support for the victims of the earthquake in Haiti ('Hope for Haiti Now' concert, 2010). Single Issue Events are non-recurring. They aim to raise social awareness and generate funds to address one-off incidents and emergencies.

Cyclical Events are calendarized celebrations of individual and team prowess. They espouse messages of unity and brotherhood. Typically they are organized around sporting skill (the FIFA World Cup, the Olympics) or artistic accomplishment (the Edinburgh Arts Festival, the St Tropez Film Festival, the Stratford Shakespeare Festival).

Event Management presents itself as a stateless solution to the question of responsible citizenship. While it may entail partnerships between voluntary associations, state departments and corporate interests, it regards itself pre-eminently to be a spontaneous expression of 'people power'. As such, Event Management draws explicitly on elements of 1960s/1970s counter culture, in particular, the emphasis on direct expression, display, justice, consumer subjectivity and non-conformity. Single Issue Mega Events are not orthodox approaches to fund generation and relief. They carry with them the aura of non-conformity and outlaw justice.

As a corollary, emotionalism is a pivotal feature of publicity and fund-raising campaigns. This is accentuated by the use of high-profile celebrities to humanize the event concept. For example, the Live 8 (2005) concert which was designed to be the climax of the Make Poverty History campaign made extensive use of Sir Bob Geldof and Bono as advocates and diplomats for the cause of forcing the economically developed countries to make a real difference in managing global inequality and injustice (Cooper, 2008).

Global humanitarian Events have produced an 'A' list of celebrity 'Big Citizens' (Angelina Jolie, Brad Pitt, Madonna, George Clooney, Michael Stipe, Sean Penn) who operate as the unelected, largely unaccountable, conscience of the world. They transfer the glamour of celebrity into the charity sector and international statecraft.

In all types of Events, the ethos of self-help and making a difference is strongly accented. Events are presented as offering direct, concrete, popular solutions to problems, incidents and emergencies around which established social institutions, notably the state and corporations, fail to deliver. They afford extra-parliamentary, non-corporate options for the articulation of compassion and practice of constructive activism. As such, they offer extra-parliamentary gateways of power to ordinary people. They exploit and develop the rhetoric of the active citizen as the crux of robust civic culture. A 'town hall' model of democracy is invoked in which every citizen's voice counts and everyone is equal. The strain of populist sentiment is evident in the rhetoric that 'team world' is organized and mobilized to 'make a difference'. The notion of what 'team world' constitutes and what kind of difference is being made by invoking its operation is largely unexamined. The accent is upon direct, emotionally fuelled rapid action. The inflation of emotional content and the lack of precision about the ends of fund distribution are a cause for concern among many specialists in Development Studies (Easterly, 2007; 2010; Moyo, 2010).

Evidently, Events of this type work on the basis that a new type of politics has been born and is being practised. Nash (2008: 168) observes that global humanitarian Events operate with the tacit acceptance of extra-territorial obligations that invoke the idea of cosmopolitan citizenship. That is, the realization by citizens in the economically advanced countries that they have duties and responsibilities to those living on or below the poverty line in the developing world. The key to this is the data flows on poverty, injustice and inequality provided by communication networks. Communication power equips inquisitive citizens with broad ambitions. By the same token, it frames episodes, incidents and emergencies in ways that are designed to privilege favoured types of reading (Castells, 2009; Curran, 2010; 2011).

Cosmopolitan citizenship presumes informed citizens who recognize the world (rather than their nation) as their 'homeland'. This is dramatically expressed in Global Events where individuals in the wealthy countries display support and make pledges on behalf of the nameless, invisible, suffering communities in the world. Cosmopolitan citizenship aims to

> create a new imagined political community to put pressure on the cosmopolitanizing state ... it [is] a matter of transforming the dominant frame of 'national interest' to conceive of justice more broadly, as concerning those with whom national citizens are connected *outside the nation*.
>
> (Nash, 2008: 172)

Critics have noted that cosmopolitan citizenship is somewhat deceptive, for it refers to illusory communities (since they have no defined, measurable presence or legal delineation). Illusory communities are extremely useful publicity tools. The Event Management team behind Live Aid (1985) claimed that the Event was watched by 2 billion viewers. This is equivalent to almost one in two of the world's population at the time. The organizers of Live Earth (2005) also claimed an 'estimated' audience of 2 billion. The Live 8 (2005) website, carrying the Event concept strapline 'The Long Walk to Justice', posted an 'estimated' viewing audience for the Live 8 concerts of 3 billion.

These estimates grab headlines, but they have no scientific standing. At best, they are guesses based upon syndication rights data. Yet they legitimate celebrity advocacy and bolster public perceptions of the indisputable value of Mega Events.

Additionally, the division between 'active citizens' in the West and 'recipients of aid' in dependent nations is objectionable because it suggests a skewed, problematic version of citizenship. The binary divide between a stricken world and an advantaged world is over-simplistic and complicates programmes of global citizenship because it implies preordained divisions (Yrjola, 2009). Nash (2008: 177) herself refers to the 'narcissistic sentimentalism' of cosmopolitan citizens and Global Event planners. Global Events mask psychological and social outputs that have as much to do with 'us' (in the donor countries) as with 'them' (in recipient countries). I shall return to develop this point later.

Why have Events become so prominent?

Live Aid (1985) set the bar for Event Management. It was the first Single Issue Mega Event to fully exploit global corporate network power. In the Event planning stage television was used to raise social consciousness of famine and disease in Ethiopia. The Event lasted for 16 hours, featuring world headline acts on two stages in London and Philadelphia. It was broadcast live to 160 countries. Live Aid drew extensively on the notion that television offers an unprecedented window on the world. Investigative TV journalism was credited with exposing the real level of suffering in Ethiopia. The tacit implication was that elected government and big business either wilfully or negligently disguised the full extent of the humanitarian crisis in Ethiopia.

It is often forgotten today that at the time, the world's leading aid donors – Britain and the USA – refused to give financial assistance to Ethiopia (Polman, 2010; Trilling, 2011). In contrast, Live Aid was presented as an alliance between people power and the media spotlight to blame and shame political and business leaders into making a decisive intervention while persuading the people to exercise responsible citizenship.

It imposed its stamp on subsequent mega, major and minor projects in Event Management. All command ordinary people to make their voice heard and to stand up and be counted. Even non-humanitarian Event Management stresses the value of informality, flexibility and querying conventional wisdom. Events carry a pedagogic dimension in which the workforce or the general public are taken into the confidence of Event planners and educated about issues that are not openly or widely discussed in the office, on the shop floor or in wider civil society. Because they challenge orthodoxy and routine they are often portrayed as expressions of righteous dissent, permeated with a palatable, festive quality. Events allow ordinary people to speak their mind and let their hair down. Frankness is revered as a mark of authenticity. Caution and emotional withholding are deplored.

Furedi (2004: 173) submits that modern resistance movements use a bio-medical idiom rather than a collectivist model to register criticism and challenge the status quo. Physical, vocal and visual display and exhibitionism have replaced collective agitation and organization. Earlier generations expressed radicalism around the edict that 'the personal is political'. In a weightless, wired-up world, where communication network power is ubiquitous, this has been replaced with visual and emotional codes that convey 'resistance through representation' (Castells, 2009; Curran, 2011).

Furedi (2004) relates these developments to the post-war ascendance of therapy culture. The fear of shame about expressing emotions has been transformed into an obligation to make your feelings known. Ernest Gellner (1994) once speculated that as urban-industrial societies become more productive and generate more wealth, the struggle for survival makes way for a struggle for approval and acceptance.

Event Management certainly reflects emotionalism, the need for display and the requirement for approval and acceptance. Structurally speaking, it is a combination of market principles and neo-communitarianism. The market in emotions, as well as economic resources, is identified as the mechanism for optimal goal achievement. Along with this goes a fastidious distaste for bureaucracy and red tape. Global humanitarian projects are portrayed as involving 'team world' in relief programmes. Again, it is notable that 'team world' is, in reality, an illusory community. Yet the rhetoric surrounding it is pivotal in the advocacy and diplomacy roles of celebrity 'Big Citizens' and Event Management activists.

The heavy dependence upon public relations expertise and network power (the PR–Media hub) is presented as the most effective way of getting the message (the Event concept) across. However, it is also compatible with indoctrination and emotional manipulation.

The political philosophy underlying Event Management is ultimately conservative. It seeks reform rather than revolution. Echoing the communitarian belief system, it calls upon citizens to be responsible, active and *realistic* about what they can achieve (Etzioni, 1993; Putnam, 2000; Barber, 1984). Social problems are defined as incidents and emergencies requiring urgent, direct, rapid responses. Scant attention is paid to the structures and causal chains that underlie and link public incidents and emergencies. Instead the emphasis is upon immediate, decisive action, not system-wide progressive reconstruction (Easterly, 2007; Moyo, 2010).

The communitarian belief system takes the notion of the moral majority seriously. It purports to speak for the common man, although it is not elected to do so, nor, strictly speaking, is it accountable. While it is dismissive of neo-liberal solutions to public ills, it is deeply sceptical of state control. Empowerment and activism are viewed as obligations of the community. A middle path to social and economic problems is favoured. This is substantiated by an appeal to 'naturalistic' values of common sense and decency.

The PR–Media hub is dedicated to Event concepts that are automatically understood and easy to digest. 'Feed the World' and 'Make Poverty History' are catchy and media friendly. Precisely because of this, they over-simplify social problems and inflate the power of stateless solutions.[5] They allow Event advocates and diplomats to occupy the moral high ground and preach to others that if they are not part of the solution they are part of the problem.

In 2010, when Sir Bob Geldof was subject to severe media criticism that a proportion of Live Aid money had been appropriated by rebel forces of the Tigray Liberation Army, he responded with indignant, uncompromising ferocity. He insisted that 'not a single penny' of Live Aid funds had been appropriated. Yet Band Aid's own Field Director in Ethiopia, John James, is reported as estimating that between 10 and 20% of Live Aid was seized by rebel groups to buy arms and supplies (Brennan, 2010).

Other commentators have alleged that the hard-line Communist government in Ethiopia of the day, headed by the dictatorial Colonel Menguistu Haile Mariam, commandeered significant Live Aid cash to fund the war effort (Polman, 2010). Mariam headed the largest standing army in black Africa (Vallely, 1985: 12). His party insisted on overseeing charity fund distribution, controlling media access and enforcing regulations. The junta was accused of using Live Aid money to engineer food shortages in the rebellious northern provinces while, needless to say, maintaining the masquerade of even-handed fund distribution (Polman, 2010; Trilling, 2010).

Suzanne Franks (2010) submits that a leaked Live Aid memo proves that the organization was aware of distribution irregularities committed by the military junta. But it refrained from challenging the Mariam regime because it saw its chief responsibility as relieving want and suffering. However, as Franks (2010: 55) observes, the irony in this is that charity funds were inadvertently supplied to prolong armed conflict in Ethiopia and so *increase* the want and suffering of the people. This lends support to the argument that there is an under-examined and poorly understood relationship between some types of charity fund raising and warmongering (Polman, 2010).

Events cater to the compassionate need of people to do something, to do anything, to help victims of natural disaster, armed conflict and injustice. They are perfectly suited to corporate communication power and digitally connected public networks. However, post-Event evaluation systems often lack the power to ensure that fund distribution is bound by proper standards of regulation and probity. The sheer scale of revenues generated by Mega Events invites corruption. Money laundering, theft and creative accounting are tried and tested methods of fund appropriation. Global Event Management teams lack the infrastructure and workforce to combat these threats. They are at the mercy of embezzlement sharks and bent regulators.

What are the consequences of Events?

A peculiar myopia afflicts the professional Event Management literature (Getz, 2007; Bowdin *et al.*, 2011; Shone and Parry, 2010). There is no mention of Kracauer's (1995) work on 'the mass ornament' in Weimar Germany.[6] The Situationist perspective on the spectacle, and its role in disciplining social behaviour, is seldom referenced (Debord, 1967).[7] This enhances the cosy professional self-image in Event Management of offering a novel contribution to the field of human endeavour. But it is awfully presumptuous.

Boiled down to essentials, what the professional literature says is that Events provide three key benefits, economic, social and civic (Getz, 1994; Arcodia and Reid, 2004; Bowdin *et al.*, 2011).

On the economic level it is claimed that they have a clear and incontrovertible multiplier effect. Major and Mega Events boost income streams by increasing tourist flows, engendering recapitalization programmes and attracting inward investment.

In social matters, Events are said to elicit integration and facilitate harmony. Major and Mega Cyclical Events are credited with promoting brotherhood and unity. The goodwill produced by the Olympics or the FIFA World Cup is implied to have a halo effect on work, schooling and business.

Finally, at the civic level Major and Mega Events are credited with enlarging publicity and building civic pride. Hosting global Cyclical or Single Issue Events is regarded as building the brand of the nation. This, together with the supposed strong economic multiplier effect, explains the intensely competitive nature of bidding wars to host the Olympics or FIFA World Cup. Similarly, large-scale ceremonies like royal weddings and funerals are credited with 'bringing the nation together' and strengthening bonds of unity (McGuigan, 2000).

Each of these benefits is open to criticism and none of them should be accepted at face value. On the question of the supposed multiplier effect of Events, many researchers argue that short-term investment gains are often offset by longer-term post-Event legacy costs such as underused stadia, empty hotel space and a contraction in tourist flows produced by tourist fears of congestion, overcrowding, terrorism and overpricing (Whitson and Horne, 2006). The 1976 Olympics in Montreal left the city with a compound debt of Ca$2 billion, in capital and interest costs (Levine, 1999).

Wider analysis of the costs–benefits ratio of the Olympics over the last twenty years suggests that economic gain is, at best, ambivalent. Where the balance sheets of host nations go into the black immediately after the Event, there are often serious run-on costs relating to the rehousing of evicted populations, compensation for urban and environmental clearance programmes and service fees for support corporations. Furthermore, Mega Events produce a series of inflationary effects on building costs, real estate values and risk management (Coates and Humphreys, 1999; Teigland, 1999; Owen, 2002).

A good example of the inflationary effect of Cyclical Mega Events and run-on fees is security. Post 9/11, security issues have become ever more prominent (and expensive) in Event planning and general policing. As Western leaders obsess about the so-called 'war on terror' the business opportunities for so-called 'homeland security' firms have been significantly ramped up.

The run-up to the Athens Olympics (2004) involved intensive and extensive lobbying by the security and surveillance industry, especially from Israel and the USA. The industry alleged that Greek risk management was unrealistic and under-prepared. It successfully gained contracts for the installation of high-tech CCTV surveillance and related information-gathering equipment and enhanced security policing. The security and surveillance cost of the Sydney Olympics (2000) were $180 million. The planning committee for the Athens Olympics (2004) was estimated to have been in the region of $1 billion. The security bill for the Beijing Olympics (2008) came in at $6.5 billion. These figures suggest that risk control is a rapidly escalating component of Mega-Event budgeting.

Critics have argued that the international security and surveillance industry deliberately exaggerates risk so as to drive up orders (Samatas, 2007: 35). In the London Olympics (2012), lobbying by the security and surveillance industry doubled security costs from £282 million to £563 million.

There are related concerns about the threat to civil liberties posed by surveillance and security upgrades. Many of the policing provisions and technologies (drones, helicopters, data mining, biometrics, security zones) used by homeland security corporations to regulate sporting Mega Events like the Olympics owe their origin to the field of war. The security and surveillance industry has exploited the desire of host communities to present themselves as safe havens for major Global Event investment. From the standpoint of national government, the outlay can be partly recouped by post-Event reallocation of surveillance equipment to monitor and address domestic threats associated with multi-culturalism, multi-ethnicity and religious divides.

In London, more troops were deployed (13,500) than fought in the war in Afghanistan. The London Games were defended by an aircraft carrier moored in the Thames and air missile systems (including unmanned drones over the stadia and opening and closing ceremonies). A city-wide system of scanners, disease-tracking systems, new police control centres and checkpoints was installed. The security cost of hosting and protecting 17,000 athletes for 17 days has been priced at £59,000 per competitor (Graham, 2010; 2012).

The short-term economic effects of Cyclical and Single Issue Mega Events are no rule of thumb to the long-term economic consequences for the host community. Inflationary effects may take years to show. Yet the cost in policing bills, the elimination of affordable housing and transferring essential (low-paid) workers to the urban periphery may impose heavy economic disadvantages to the host community. Mega Events command high global publicity. But their economic profile supports the old adage that not everything that glisters turns to gold. The cost of the Olympic Games in Athens (2004) is regularly cited as leaving the Greek economy with long-term structural weaknesses that contributed to the profound crisis after the global financial crash of 2008.

Moving on to the question of the purported social effects of Events, there is certainly evidence that Mega Events elicit goodwill, integration and harmony. But the evidence that this is a durable legacy effect is not tenable (Whitson and Horne, 2006). Social benefits are more accurately described as episodic and are tied to the immediate pre-Event, Event proper and immediate post-Event cycle.

The legacy of Events on policing, enforced resettlement programmes and real estate values is more powerful and demonstrable. Shaw (2008) argues that the International Olympic Committee engaged in profiteering and was a catalyst for the unacceptable infringement of civil liberties (movement and assembly) during the planning and administration of the Vancouver Olympics (2010). Programmes of infrastructural upgrade and gentrification led to evictions and the contraction of affordable housing in the downtown Eastside area. Additionally, the ecologically sensitive Eagleridge Bluffs was bulldozed in order to provide new highway access to ski slopes. Shaw (2008) concludes that the Games inflated real estate values. The principal beneficiaries were property developers, not the local population.

City fathers often use Mega Events as a pretext to introduce schemes of gentrification and urban cleansing projects so as to generate media-friendly representations of the host venue. In November 2011, 3,000 troops were deployed in the Rocinha favella in Rio de Janeiro to 'clean up' an urban hot spot. This is part of a long-term strategy by the municipal and national government to produce an image of Rio that will sit well with media corporations and boost pre-Event inward investment flows.

The strong messages of camaraderie and brotherhood engineered by Event Management teams have precipitated ripples of dissent and counter-cultural protest (Juris, 2008; Gorringe and Rosie, 2008; Routledge, 2011). Grassroots opposition groups like No Games 2010 and the Olympic Resistance Network attacked the Vancouver Olympics (2010) (Kennelly and Watt, 2011; Hiller and Wanner, 2011). This ruffled the feathers of media corporations primed (and paid) to present the Games in an overwhelmingly positive light. It highlighted that Mega Events are not just about brotherhood, but develop issues relating to power that provoke dissent.

Unease about the economic cost of Events and the added powers given to police are not confined to so-called 'anti-social' elements. On the contrary, they are shared by rank and file members of society who object to national and municipal governments imposing *their* brands of the community upon the people and rubbing the noses of the people in it by asking them to also pick up the bill for holding the Event.

To come now to the question of civic pride, there is little doubt that hosting global Events is a major mark of international status. The Beijing Olympics (2008) and the Rio FIFA World Cup (2014) and Rio Olympics (2016) were pursued as trophies of global standing by the host cities and their national governments. Yet the evidence of durable national pride is weak. Most Greeks enthusiastically celebrated the Athens Olympics (2000), but they have gone on to rue the cost and its part in contributing to the economic collapse in the country after 2008.

Increasingly, Global Cyclical Events are being targeted by counter-culture and opposition groups for demonstration and protest (Juris, 2008; Gorringe and Rosie, 2008; Routledge, 2011). Cyclical Events provide a world stage serviced by the global corporate media power in which issues of social inclusion, disempowerment, inequality and limited citizenship can be turned into prime-time news.

Conclusions

By definition, Events break routine. To this extent, Event Management exploits and develops erstwhile associations between a break in routine and escapism and transcendence. The ancient Greek Olympic Games, the Roman Games and Carnival in the Middle Ages all carry powerful overtones of escapism and transcendence (Bakhtin, 1968; Fagan, 2011; Suttard, 2012).

Yet Global Event Management claims to do something more. It purports to combine ludic energy with moral energy. The play form is enlisted as an instrument of healing the world. Its novelty lies in the proposition that mass entertainment transmitted through the global media to various network publics has the power to transform social consciousness and raise funds to change the world. The moral energy behind the Live Aid (1985) concert was to end famine in Ethiopia and feed the world. Live 8 (2005) and Live Earth (2005) were, respectively, morally committed to end poverty and to solve the global environmental crisis.

However, the evidence that Global Events achieve their moral goals is weak. Unpublished research by Bengry-Howell suggests that most who attend an Event or pledge donations privilege ludic energy over moral energy (Tickle, 2011). That is, they are drawn to the Event as a means of escapism and conjuring up a ritual sense of transcendence. The moral commitment to social transformation is highly conditional and generally ephemeral.

These research findings are reinforced by the work of social commentators on the effect of Global Events in reducing the development gap (between the economically advanced and developing countries). Easterly (2007), Moyo (2010) and Sachs (2011) argue convincingly that the publicity value of Global Events is transient and the funds that they generate are hopelessly disproportionate to the scale of problems of global inequality and hunger. For these authors, Global Events are a red herring. They distract public consciousness from necessary fiscal reforms in the West and the re-engineering of social and economic investment from the core economic nations to those situated on the periphery.

To give a concrete example, aid arrangements from the economically advanced nations to the developing countries are not straightforward. Overseas aid is often offset by unfair trade arrangements. The International Energy Agency (2012) reported that in 2011 sub-Saharan Africa received about $15.6 billion in aid. However, over the same period the region spent $18 billion on importing oil (Harvey 2012). Developing countries are locked into high economic investment in infrastructure and manufacturing capacity. The legacy of this is a high dependence upon fossil fuels. One option is to develop renewable sources of energy. However, this is resisted by lobbyists for the petroleum companies who want to maintain their grasp on the sub-Saharan energy market. Without enforceable regulation, overseas aid money designed to improve education, health and welfare is diverted into the coffers of Western suppliers of energy, manufacturing capacity and infrastructural resources. Western aid therefore becomes a disguised form of recycling funds from one budget in the West to another.

If it is right to conclude that ludic energy is stronger and, in the long run, outdistances moral energy in Event consciousness, the question of the structure of Event consciousness must be addressed. This consciousness cannot be divorced from the representations of the media, since Global Event Management is inextricably entwined with network power and the interests behind it.

Event Management and the corporate media claim to be a window on the world. However, the world that they present is sensory rather than analytical. It appeals to the emotions above and beyond the mind. The world is portrayed as a parade of incidents and emergencies. The media mostly cocoon the structures and causal chains behind them in a conspiracy of silence. Instead they present the world as a series of disjointed events, emergencies and incidents. They are wedded to a form of consciousness that might be called 'Event Consciousness'. That is, a perspective that concentrates on data and phenomena as *emotional impressions*. What this obscures is, in Kantian terms, the noumena, i.e. the forces underlying observable data which, of course, have profound causal significance upon not only *what* is observed, but *how* it is observed.

Television coverage of the crisis in Ethiopia shocked Sir Bob Geldof and thus directly led to Live Aid (1985). Yet this coverage concentrated on images of dying, hungry Africans, rather than on the causes of the civil war in Ethiopia and the reasons for the quiescence of the Western powers. Event consciousness is emotional, festive (in the sense of using agency to make a difference) and primal (in the sense of bringing isolated individuals in the West back into touch with their common humanity). Yet its after-effects are fragmentary, episodic and susceptible to appropriation by separate interests which use them for conventional political ends.

Global Events have the power to seize global air time, generate large sums of money in the short term and briefly raise consciousness about issues or emergencies. The results of this are not insignificant. Live Aid, Live 8 and Live Earth produced substantial sums of money for aid and the war against pollution. Yet the Event Managers behind them were unable to protect all of the funds from various types of racketeering. Further, while the funds raised alleviated *some* suffering, they left the basic systems of global inequality firmly intact (Easterly, 2007; Polman, 2011).

In part, Global Events are popular because they allow populations in the West to name and shame leaders and governments who do not contribute enough to global aid. In doing so they make us feel better about ourselves. Following on from Furedi's (2004) account of the rise of therapy culture in the West, Global Events have an analgesic function in making citizens in the West feel that they can 'make a difference'. For a brief moment our sense of incredulity and powerlessness about the problems facing the world lifts, and we gain the pleasurable momentum that goes with 'doing something' and experiencing a sense of belonging with a wider global community of cosmopolitan citizens.

In reality, the escapism and powerful feeling of transcendence that Global Events achieve are largely the product of media corporations. In conjunction with Global Event planners and managers, they orchestrate the public response to famine, natural disaster and injustice. Incidents and episodes are matched with humanitarian concerts and dollars. But the real difference to the world's problems that Global Events make is negligible, and the cosmopolitan communities that they appear to generate are phantoms.

Event Management uses a combination of free market economics and communitarianism to address social, economic and political issues. It perpetuates a doctrine of piecemeal, limited reform rather than significant, durable material change. Although it makes a virtue of non-conformity, Event Management presents the fundamentals of a historically determined distribution of global resources as 'obvious' and fundamentally unchangeable. Accordingly, it confines itself to little more than tinkering at the margins.

Charity answers to the human need for compassion, but it is incapable of making a deci-sive contribution to overturning global inequality, ending hunger or combating injustice. To do that requires the mobilization of the resources of the state, operating through bilateral and multilateral alliances with other nation-states and corporations to regulate business interests for the purposes of global empowerment, distributive justice and social inclusion. Global Event Management does not take this step and, for the most part, regards itself to be pursuing a separate agenda. Where more radical objectives are flagged, as with the Make Poverty History Campaign and Live 8 (2005) concert, they are watered down by the political and economic establishment and turned into ploughshares (Nash, 2008; Elavsky, 2009; Harrison, 2010).

Global Events are as much about providing emotional gratification to Western popula-tions (who are mostly powerless to have an effect on global matters on a day-to-day basis) as about acting as a contribution to global inequality and injustice. They afford solace for those who feel guilty that they do not strive hard enough to do good in the world in their daily lives. Via corporate media, the live action, round-the-world display of doing good undoubtedly delivers ego gratification and contributes to the façade of social integration. This dispels the intimation that Global Events are conducted and managed in the name of illusory communities. In reality, these uncoordinated, anonymous communities have no genuine power to change the structure of poverty, injustice or environmental degradation. The image of them that is conjured up by corporate media networks enables us to chant and to believe that, for a moment, 'we are the champions'.

Yet we forget that the delusion of individual potency in the midst of organized collective impotence is the cocktail of choice in late capitalist power structures. They leave individuals drunk on their supposed power and fertility, while making sure that, at the corporate and state levels, business as usual is the order of the day. Slowly, reluctantly, we are starting to see Global Events for what they are: not the unstoppable expressions of 'people power', but televisual accessories in the moral regulation of populations who believe themselves to be free, but who are, in reality, captive in a cage which supports vested interests and which is not of their own devising.

Notes

1　It is undeniable that Event Management is a child of neo-liberalism. The whole thrust of the enter-prise is based in the arguments that the state and corporations have both failed to tackle the ills of the world. Global Event Management presents a media-savvy 'third way'. It allows for partnerships with the state and business, but insists on the condition of popular independence.

2　'Live Aid' (1985) set the bar for Global Event Management's application of the media to raise social consciousness and generate funds. Global Events are intertwined with communication power (Castells, 2009). The power of the media, rather than of any constitutional foundation, is the real basis for the claims of cosmopolitan citizenship that are often made in connection with Global Events.

3　People power is entirely a rhetorical device. Global Events are not beholden to any form of plebi-scitary power.

4　The term 'invisible government' comes from the so-called 'father of public relations', Edward Bernays (1928). Somewhat controversially, he argued that modern democracies require a govern-ment of human relations experts whose tasks are (a) to discover the real interests of the people; (b) attach these interests to progressive goals; and (c) fashion leaders and policies to facilitate the marriage of popular interest and progress.

5　Stateless solutions arise and are developed outside the parameters of organized (parliamentary) politics. They claim to reflect the will of the people and seek to enlist governments and states to join in partnership with them. However, their key characteristic is that they are subject to neither party politics nor corporate logic.

6   Kracauer (1985) was one of the first modern commentators to argue that industrial democracy required spectacle to distract workers from the injustice of the surplus value arrangement. The displays and parades of Weimer and Hitler Germany were a modern form of bread and circuses.

7   Debord (1967) argues that modern communication takes the spectacle and distraction to a level of terrible perfection. His work does not give much solace to anyone interested in changing the system of exploitation and mystification that is capitalism, for it suggests that the system has become self-perpetuating and that co-optation is the fate of all forms of resistance.

References

Allen, J. (2000) *Event Planning*. Toronto: Wiley.

Arcodia, C. and Reid, S. (2004) 'Event Management Associations and the Provision of Services', *Journal of Convention and Event Tourism* 6 (4) 5–25.

Bakhtin, M. (1968) *Rabelais and His World*. Cambridge, MA: MIT Press.

Barber, B. (1984) *Strong Democracy*. Berkeley: University of California Press.

Bernays, E.L. (1928) *Propaganda*. New York: Ig Books.

Bowdin, G., Allen, J., O'Toole, W., Harris, R., and McDonnell, L. (2011) *Event Management*, 3rd ed. Oxford: Butterworth-Heinemann.

Brennan, Z. (2010) 'Sorry Bob, Band Aid Millions DID Pay for Guns: Charity's Man in Ethiopia Tells His Disturbing Story', *Daily Mail*, 19 March. http://www.dailymail.co.uk/news/article-1259061/Sorry-Bob-Geldof-Band-Aid-millions-DID-pay-guns.html#ixzz2Icjppens.

Castells, M. (2009) *Communication Power*. Oxford: Oxford University Press.

Coates, D. and Humphreys, D. (1999) 'The Growth Effects of Sport Franchises, Stadia and Events', *Journal of Policy Analysis and Management* 16 (1) 601–24.

Cooper, A.F. (2008) *Celebrity Diplomacy*. London: Paradigm Publishers.

Curran, J. (2010) *Entertaining Democracy*. London: Routledge.

Curran, J. (ed.) (2011) *Media and Democracy*. London: Bloomsbury.

Debord, G. (1967) *Society of the Spectacle*. Cambridge: Zoon.

Easterly, W. (2007) *The White Man's Burden: Why the West's Efforts to Aid the Rest Have Done So Much Ill and So Little Good*. Oxford: Oxford University Press.

Easterly, W. (2010) 'Lennon the Rebel, Bono the Wonk', *Washington Post*, 12 December.

Ecclestone, D. (2011) 'Bob Geldof: Live Aid and Myth' *Mojo*, 4 January.

Elavsky, C. (2009) 'United as ONE: Live 8 and the Politics of the Global Music Spectacle', *Journal of Popular Music Studies* 21 (4) 384–410.

Etzioni, A. (1993) *The Spirit of Community*. New York: Touchstone.

Fagan, G. (2011) *The Lure of the Arena: Social Psychology and the Crowd at the Roman Games*. Cambridge: Cambridge University Press.

Franks, S. (2010) 'Why Bob Geldof Got It Wrong', *British Journalism Review* 21 (2) 51–6.

Furedi, F. (2004) *Therapy Culture*. London: Routledge.

Gellner, E. (1994) *Conditions of Liberty: Civil Society and Its Rivals*. Harmondsworth: Penguin.

Getz, D. (2007) *Event Studies*. Oxford: Butterworth-Heinemann.

Gorringe, H. and Rosie, M. (2008) 'The Polis of "Global Protest"', *Current Sociology* 56 (3) 691–710.

Graham, S. (2010) *Cities under Siege*. London: Verso.

Graham, S. (2012) 'Olympics 2012 Security: Welcome to Lockdown London', *Guardian*, 12 March.

Hall, C.M. (1989) 'Hallmark Events and the Planning Process', in G. Sym, B. Shaw, D. Fenton, and W. Mueller (eds) *The Planning and Evaluation of Hallmark Events*. Aldershot: Avebury.

Harrison, G. (2010) 'The Africanization of Poverty: A Retrospective on "Make Poverty History"', *African Affairs,* 109 (436) 391–408.

Harvey, F. (2012) 'Overseas Aid to Africa Being Outweighed by Hefty Costs of Importing Oil', *Guardian*, 2 April. http://www.guardian.co.uk/world/2012/apr/01/overseas-aid-africa-oil-imports-costs.

Hiller, H. and Wanner, R. (2011) 'Public Opinion in the Host Olympic Cities: The Case of the 2010 Vancouver Winter Games', *Sociology* 45 (5) 883–99.

International Energy Agency (2012) *Key World Energy Statistics*. Paris: International Energy Agency.

Juris, J. (2008) 'Performing Politics: Image, Embodiment and Affective Solidarity during Anti-Corporate Globalization Protests', *Ethnography* 9 (1) 61–97.

Kennelly, J. and Watt, P. (2011) 'Sanitising Public Space in Olympic Host Cities: The Spatialised Experiences of Marginalized Youth in Vancouver (2010) and London (2012)', *Sociology* 45 (5) 765–81.

Kracauer, S. (1995) *The Mass Ornament*. Cambridge, MA: Harvard University Press.

Levine, M. (1999) 'Tourism, Urban Development and the "World Class" City: The Cases of Baltimore and Montreal', in C. Andre, P. Armstrong and A. Lapiere (eds) *World Class Cities: Can Canada Pay?*. Ottawa: Ottawa University Press.

McGuigan, J. (2000) 'British Identity and "the People's Princess"', *Sociological Review* 48 (1) 1–18.

Moyo, D. (2010) *Dead Aid*. London: Penguin.

Nash, K. (2008) 'Global Citizenship as Show Business: The Cultural Politics of Make Poverty History', *Media, Culture & Society* 30 (2) 167–81.

Owen, K. (2002) 'The Sydney 2002 Olympics and Urban Entrepreneurialism', *Australian Geographical Studies* 40 (3) 563–600.

Polman, L. (2010) *War Games*. London: Penguin.

Putnam, R. (2000) *Bowling Alone*. London, Simon and Schuster.

Roberts, K. (2004) *The Leisure Industries*. Basingstoke: Palgrave-Macmillan.

Roche, M. (2000) *Mega-Events and Modernity*. London: Routledge.

Routledge, P. (2011) 'Sensuous Solidarities: Emotions, Politics and Performance in the Clandestine Insurgent Rebel Clown Army', *Antipode*, online version, 1–29.

Sachs, J. (2011) *The Price of Civilization*. London: Bodley Head.

Samatas, M. (2007) 'Security and Surveillance in the Athens 2004 Olympics', *International Criminal Justice Review* 17 (3) 220–38.

Shaw, C.A. (2008) *Five Ring Circus*. Gabriola Island, BC: New Society Publishers.

Shone, A. and Parry, B. (2010) *Successful Event Management: A Practical Handbook*. 3rd ed. London: Cengage Learning.

Suttard, D. (2012) *Power Games: Ritual and Rivalry at the Ancient Greek Olympics*. London: British Museum Press.

Teigland, J. (1999) 'Mega-Events and Impacts on Tourism', *Impact Assessment and Project Appraisal* 17 (4) 305–17.

Trilling, D. (2011) 'The Art of Listening: Live Aid,' *New Statesman*, 8 July.

Vallely, P. (1985) 'Bureaucrats Take Note,' *The Times*, 24th July.

Whitson, D. and Horne, J. (2006) 'Underestimated Costs and Overestimated Benefits? Comparing the Outcomes of Sports Mega-Events in Canada and Japan', *Sociological Review* 54: 71–89.

Yrjola, R. (2009) 'The Invisible Violence of Celebrity Humanism', *World Political Science Review* 5 (1) 272–9.

43

EXTREME LEISURE

The case of extreme sporting activities

Victoria Robinson

Introduction

Extreme leisure activities are of all sorts. They have been defined as those activities in which individuals experience leisure differently, due to their being taken to the limit of their resources. These activities can range from 'abnormal' leisure, such as unprotected anal intercourse, to extreme sports. They have been seen as allowing the individual to experience transcendence beyond the mundane and everyday, with a suggestion that such pursuits afford a particular glimpse into the human condition (see Blackshaw, 2009). For those of us seeking new directions in this area of Leisure Studies, extreme sports are a rich resource. The focus in this chapter, therefore, is on extreme sporting activities, on which, since the 1980s, there has been theoretical and empirical work on the more established alternative sports such as skateboarding, rock climbing and surfing, whilst activities such as windsurfing, snowboarding, BMX biking, extreme ironing, extreme skiing, ultimate Frisbee, kitesurfing, in-line skating, parkour, whitewater kayaking and adventure racing have also been defined as alternative sports as the category has both expanded and diversified.

There are different terms used to define such activities, and debates about which terms best describe these sports and capture the diversity of participants' experiences. For example, Wheaton (2000 and 2004a) uses the term 'lifestyle sports'; 'extreme sports' is preferred by Rinehart and Sydnor (2003) and Robinson (2008; 2013), whilst 'whiz sports' is used by Midol and Broyer (1995); and Lyng (1990; 2005) utilizes the term 'edgework' to describe a number of diverse, high-risk activities, including sport, and these are seen as sites where traditional norms and boundaries are transgressed. Other terms employed in debates about these sports include the categories of 'risk sports' (Breivik, 1999), 'panic sports', 'alternative sports' and 'new sports' (see also Laviolette, 2007). These sports, which increasingly have grown globally in popularity, have been analysed from a range of academic disciplines, including sociology, gender studies, philosophy, cultural geography, psychology, anthropology, architecture and urban planning, amongst others (Wheaton, 2010).

Wheaton (2004a) has argued that it is the meaning of these terms, not the terms themselves, which is of most relevance. In her research on male windsurfers, she uses the term 'lifestyle' because it is a description used by the participants about themselves. She also argues that this term embodies the cultures and identities integral to a specific sport, and shows the importance of the socio-historical context for such activities. Wheaton asserts that the alternative definition of 'extreme' has been incorporated into popular and media discourses, and defining sports in this way works to co-opt any radical elements of alternative sports. However, in later work (Wheaton, 2007) she acknowledges that the term 'extreme' can be useful to describe dominant aspects of the participants' experience, for example, their 'extreme' commitment to a particular activity.

Others have chosen to consciously employ the term 'extreme' when analysing diverse alternative sports, although they problematize its use. Rinehart and Sydnor (2003: 3) argue: 'Though the cultural pop of a term like "extreme", when linked to sports, gives those sport forms a certain faddish panache, many participants are in for the long haul.' Many extreme sports participants reject media-fuelled representations of them as needless risk takers and adrenaline-fuelled junkies, thus confirming Rinehart and Sydnor's (2003: 12) view that extreme sports athletes are not 'lunatics' or 'daredevils', but 'meticulous performers, giving themselves to some lofty art form'.

Furthermore, rather than overstating the importance of these differences in terminologies to describe and analyse a range of new sports, Wheaton makes a useful point: 'Despite differences in nomenclature, many commentators are agreed in seeing such activities as having presented an "alternative", and *potential* challenge to traditional ways of "seeing", "doing" and understanding sport' (Wheaton, 2004a: 3).

Alternative, extreme or lifestyle sports have been differentiated from traditional sports such as football, cricket and rugby as being less competitive, institutionalized and rule bound, as well as being less exclusive on gender grounds, for example. However, this rather neat traditional/new sports dichotomy has been problematized. For instance, Beal (1995: 54), when discussing skateboarding as a potential challenge to capitalist ideologies, allows that 'numerous individual and daily resistances occur in mainstream sport'. Conversely, Connell (1987) expounds the view that the combination of force and skill involved in organized sports such as baseball, football and cricket also occurs in more individualized sports such as surfing.

Different extreme sports participants often feel that their particular sport is the most exciting, risky or unique. Farrell illustrates this with free diving (the sport of breath-hold diving where some divers can hold their breath for 9 minutes and dive beyond 200 metres): 'No other sport has the potential to take you to the limits of your own mortality so quickly' (Farrell, 2007: 33). In a similar vein, Browne, when discussing in-line skaters, found that the 'riders' did not like being lumped together 'with stunt acts and freaks, not to mention skydivers, bungee jumpers or rock climbers' (Browne, 2004: 11). Therefore, groups of extreme sports enthusiasts have sought to differentiate themselves from each other. This can partially be explained by sporting participants' desire to maintain authenticity.

The issue of authenticity itself is a pertinent one to consider in relation to different alternative sports. Le Breton (2000), for instance, has the view that participation in extreme sports affords the individual redemption and a new significance for themselves, through displaying the will-power to overcome pain and suffering that such sports entail. Moreover, Wagg *et al.* (2009) note in respect of the 'real' or 'authentic' which is often defined in relation to how an activity is performed that: 'The *meaning* of participation is articulated around personal expression and gratification, such as the "thrill of vertigo", and the natural high experienced in an adrenaline rush. As Rinehart (2000) suggests, the posers and "pretenders" in lifestyle sports are soon revealed' (Wagg *et al.*, 2009: 71).

However, this notion of authenticity has been problematized. Blackshaw (2009) cites Baudrillard's concern with hyperreality, where a contemporary postmodern focus on wanting experiences to be 'more real than real' is, in reality, 'the allure of the spectacle of the consumer society performing itself through anything from extreme sport to extreme cuisine to extreme pornography' (p. 76). He also notes that this analysis can be extended to a critique of extreme leisure pursuits which, it is argued, do not necessarily allow people to experience a changed or 'authentic self'. Further, theoretical accounts of such activities arguably focus on the 'edge' of everyday existence, and ignore what there is at life's centre. Additionally, we know more from studies about the so-called 'authentic' participant at the centre of such sports, but less about those considered 'inauthentic', itself a term which is both subjective and context specific.

Another angle on authenticity is suggested by Beal and Smith (2010) in their focus on 'Maverick' a surf break in the USA, which claimed the life of the professional surfer Mark Foo. As Wheaton (2010) argues, their concern is with Ritzer's analysis of the perceived tensions between both increased rationalization and distinctions in current global cultural processes, and with Ritzer and Stillman's notion of re-enchantment to explore how such a sporting lifestyle is sold and repackaged for a mass audience. Their case study of surfing is seen to reveal that it is through discourse that something is produced which focuses on the 'authentic' aspects of a break such as Maverick, therefore challenging rationality, but simultaneously does so through rationalization, and with a view to packaging the sport for consumer profit.

Lifestyle/extreme sports: globalization, consumerism and defining features

As well as a consideration of terminology/authenticity, another aspect which has concerned those interested in extreme sport has been the effects of globalization and the impact and complex interaction of this process on sports at the local level, including on national and regional identities and the effects on the consumption and organization of different sports.

Global processes have been seen as characterized by the organization of diversity and not uniformity, '[n]ew sports such as windsurfing, hang-gliding and snowboarding have emerged and "extreme sports" have become the cutting edge for some devotees of peak experiences' (Maguire, 1999: 87). Moreover, extreme sports have been viewed as evidence of resistance to globalization/Americanization due to this pluralization process. Such processes are evident with the emergence of a world media system and an international sport system which gives sport a global character, including the rise of the celebrity sports star, such as David Beckham and others (see Cashmore, 2004, and Smart, 2005). Extreme sports increasingly do not escape such processes; witness the high media profile of extreme sports activists such as Tony Hawks. Further, Wagg *et al.* (2009) outline how, though each sport has its own identity, history and development trajectory, there remain commonalities in their ideologies and ethos and, in more recent times, 'the transnational consumer industries that produce the commodities that underpin their cultures' (Wagg *et al.*, 2009: 69).

Wheaton (2000; 2004a; 2005; 2007; 2010) characterizes lifestyle/extreme sports as non-aggressive activities, yet embracing of danger and risk, predominantly white, middle-class and Western in composition and individualistic in form and attitude. Rinehart and Sydnor (2003) also argue that they are exclusionary, on the grounds of participants needing funds, access and leisure time to pursue these activities. Fletcher (2008) argues that these sports appeal especially to the middle classes' desire to escape a class habitus need for both disciplined labour and deferred gratification. In addition, these sports are usually individualistic, and not team sports, though team-based new sports exist – for example, ultimate Frisbee (Wheaton, 2004a) and adventure racing (Rinehart and Sydnor, 2003).

Wheaton (2010) makes the point that these sports originated in North America, where they had their roots in the counter-cultural movements of the 1960s and 1970s, and then were imported into Europe. (Though it must be noted that some sports, for example, rock climbing, have a pre-existing, rich European historical tradition [Robinson, 2013].) However, the remarkable growth of participation in extreme sports is extending from Western countries, including New Zealand, the UK and the USA to Africa, South America and China. For example, Knijnik, Horton and Cruz (2010) explore the experiences of Brazilian elite women surfers, whilst in the same collection, from a Foucauldian perspective, Spowart, Burrows and Shaw (2010) interrogate surfing mothers in New Zealand, asking in the process if surfing offers different ways of 'doing' motherhood.

Diverse characteristics help to define 'lifestyle sports' (Wheaton, 2004a). Some activities, such as windsurfing, snowboarding and ultimate Frisbee, could be seen as new sports, while others, such as rock climbing and surfing, have been revitalized through the involvement of newer generations. All these sports, however, are characterized by the active, rather than passive, involvement of participants, although they are usually non-aggressive and non-contact in nature. Participants have been classed into different categories, which include those who participate irregularly, 'poseurs' and those who are fully committed and possess the most technical skills and investment. Inherent to the sports is the consumption of new gear and equipment, such as boards/bikes and the involvement of new technology (for example, in rock climbing, with new and improved gear such as safer and stronger climbing harnesses or new protection devices and technologically improved climbing boots). Furthermore, Wheaton (2004a) argues that such new sports call for a commitment in time and/or money and a lifestyle constructed around social identities, attitudes, collective expression and a sense of hedonistic freedom. Institutionalization, commercialization and regulation are often denounced or sometimes resisted, and the sports are usually further indicative of creative, performative and aesthetic factors. However, Rinehart and Sydnor (2003) and others since are of the opinion that extreme sports are increasingly becoming commercialized.

Moreover, Wheaton (2004a) details that such lifestyle sports take place in new or appropriated outdoor spaces, mostly without fixed or limited boundaries. Participants often express nostalgic thoughts of a past rural life, where nature is revered; for example, Lewis (2000) has explored the climbing body in relation to nature and modernity. It has also been argued that new sports, such as wilderness sports or skateboarding, afford different opportunities for empowerment around demonstrations of skill and strength (Whitson, 1990).

Further, Dant and Wheaton (2007), in relation to these sports, express the view: 'The experience of whiz and flow, the buzz and excitement can be appreciated both internally, as emotions are stimulated by physical sensation, and externally, within a social context in which such experiences are shared' (Dant and Wheaton, 2007: 12). Therefore, in extreme sports, experiencing pain or fear in a sporting activity can induce a chemical reaction, which can then produce intense emotional and social responses (see also Robinson, 2013).

Csikszentmihalyi (1975) argues that certain leisure pursuits, including climbing, can produce a sense of flow, through a person's becoming detached and, so, objective about the activity in hand. Furthermore, this provides a space which is separate from everyday anxieties. Such a state also sometimes grants people a significant glimpse into themselves and their self of identity (Harris, 2005). Yet, Le Breton (2000) has discussed participation in such sports as being characterized by an escape back *into* the body, through engaging with danger and, so, with risk. Thus, extreme pursuits are not necessarily 'balanced' kinds of activity, ones which can be seen to facilitate 'flow', when defined as the pleasurable loss of self (Harris, 2005).

Extreme sporting identities and modernity

Wheaton (2004a) makes an argument that a destabilization of social categories and increased fluidity of social relationships have caused a theoretical interest in fragmented identities. She cites Bauman (1992), who contends that lifestyle has overtaken class as the social relation of production, as well as Maffesoli (1996), who argues that collectivities based around new forms of identification and interests, such as alternative lifestyle and sporting interests, are more fluid than subcultures and so are not determined by class background. Alongside new and increasingly privatized consumption patterns and lifestyle choice identities, as well as the importance of lifestyle sports, this indicates a shift to an advanced capitalist/postmodern culture. Further, postmodern sporting identities are increasingly seen as self-reflexive, fragmented and fluid, which parallels a view that sport and leisure are important sites for both identity construction and individualization, and the development of the sports themselves can be seen to be in a 'post modern' phase (Wheaton, 2004a).

Further, Borden contends that loss of identity is an issue for new sports participants faced with the dissolution of past reference points. Skateboarders, he argues, create their own subculture, which is 'a social world in which self-identifying values and appearances confront conventional codes of behaviour' (Borden, 2001: 137). Meanwhile, Robinson (2008) found, with UK male climbers, a refusal of a binary of childhood and traditional adulthood which meant that they did not always want to put away the 'childish things' of a sporting passion upon being in a settled job or having children of their own, thus leading to relationship or career difficulties. In addition, her data on male sporting identities revealed that these are complex and variable across age, ability and status. Wheaton (2007) argues that climbers, windsurfers and skaters have a more shared or secure sense of status and identity, one which is seen to cut across perceived internal differences. But Robinson's (2008) climbers' anxiety over sporting performance in relation to others, in respect of any subsequent and potential loss of reputation, revealed that these differences were not always resolved.

Borden (2001), in his work on skateboarders and the urban environment, argues that young skateboarders reject both society as a whole and the normative patterns of the family, particularly 'the work-leisure, workplace-home socio-spatial routines of the traditional nuclear family' (Borden, 2001: 151). This shares similarities with Robinson's (2008) and Wheaton's (2000 and 2004a) recognition that age and life-course experiences and a heterosexual lifestyle were key in terms of how extreme sports participants competed with and related to each other, as well as providing a context for how they conceptualized and made sense of their own sporting identity and achievements.

Building on issues of gender and identity

Alternative sports, as opposed to traditional organized sports, seemingly offer greater possibilities for resistance to and disruption of traditional relationships, of which gender, to date, has been the most theorized. This is particularly due to the high numbers of women entering such sports in recent years (see, for example, Barkham, 2006). For instance, Midol and Broyer (1995) argue that new sports may liberate participants from traditional gender roles because of the blurred boundaries they create. In relation to skateboarding, Beal (1995) states: 'sport has also been analysed as a place where dominant values and norms are challenged and where alternative norms and values are created' (Beal, 1995: 252). Thus, the possibility of more fluid gender identities and relationships, the relative lack of emphasis on competition, and the potential for women to achieve sporting success in these new sports have received theoretical attention. The presence of women in such sports is also seen to weaken popular associations between sport and masculinity, so broadening the recognized boundaries of traditional masculinities (see Borden, 2001; Robinson, 2008; Wheaton, 2004b).

However, the question of whether lifestyle/extreme sports do afford meaningful challenges to traditional gender identities has been scrutinized. These leisure pursuits can still position women participants as more 'passive' than men in specific sporting contexts as well as construct discourses which posit women as less 'physical' or less able than men, or less competitive, because of their biology. As Horne *et al.* (1999) note, 'fashionable' new sports are not necessarily classless or genderless. In skateboarding, Beal (1999), for instance, found that only four women made up the forty-one skateboarders interviewed, and other women associated with the sport were inactively defined as 'skate betties'. Similarly, Wheaton (2000) identified 'windsurf widows', female non-participants who remained at home, and Robinson (2008) highlighted the existence of climbing 'belay bunnies', women who don't often climb but who hold the ropes of their male partners, allowing them to be active. More recently, Atencio, Beal and Wilson (2009) found in urban skateboarding that women's habituses were considered as lacking in skill and aversive to risk taking. Women, therefore, came to be positioned as inauthentic participants in the street skateboarding social field, and so largely excluded from accessing symbolic capital.

Such contradictory attitudes to gender relations in skateboarding were highlighted by Borden (2001) in a study of skateboarders in relation to urban and public space and how participants use and appropriate such spaces for their own (sporting) ends. Young men in their teens and twenties had 'broadly accommodating dispositions towards skaters of different classes and ethnicity' (p. 263), but female skateboarders were actively discouraged by convention, including being objectified. Older skateboarders were discriminated against and a homosocial masculinity and homophobia were also apparent, whilst gender relations were complex, in that views on women ranged from acceptance to the view women that should not be participating (p. 144).

Yet, across a range of alternative sports, an increasingly older participatory demographic indicates that such age-based discrimination may undergo changes as the sports change in this way. However, overall, if new sports are viewed as a site in which to actively fight gender oppression and where gender relations are contested, then Kay and Laberge's (2004) viewpoint, that this promise is not always substantiated at the level of practice in specific sports, is still pertinent. As Wheaton (2013 forthcoming) points out: 'Studies have demonstrated the complex and shifting ways in which different structural, material and ideological factors operate in excluding different groups of women and girls in these activities. Nevertheless there are clear differences *between* activities as well as spatial, temporal, and cultural variations'.

In relation to masculinity specifically, Wheaton's (2000) research demonstrates that windsurfing cannot be considered a sport which embodies any radical 'new' masculine identification, but instead, men's relationships with women and other men here are both variable and complex. Robinson (2008), in empirical research on male rock climbers' identities, found evidence both of climbers challenging traditional/dominant notions of gender roles, identity and power, and of participants merely appearing to reinvent them, while in reality reconstructing traditional gender roles. Meanwhile, Kusz (2003; 2004) found that in media representations of extreme sports in North America, norms and values of individualism and risk taking were linked closely to a white masculinity, which therefore gave both white masculinity and the values associated with it cultural hegemony over other groups. (See also

Huybers-Withers and Livingstone [2010] for an analysis of masculinity in mountain biking media, where hegemonic masculinity is still much in evidence.)

Wagg *et al.* (2009) call for further research on the participants in such new sports other than the global core of the white male. How, then, do variables such as race and ethnicity, sexuality, class, disability and age interact in these sports? It is this increasing emphasis on intersectionality which is characterizing work on extreme leisure pursuits. For example, Wheaton (2013 forthcoming) emphasizes the need to focus on an absence of race and ethnicity in theorizing around alternative leisure pursuits (and the methodological difficulties in doing this), as well as a pressing need to explore ageing participants' experiences. She also highlights how previous concerns with lifestyle sports and space, via Lefebvre (1991), have viewed space not just as a physical or geographical phenomenon or location, but that it is socially created and sustained, and reflects and maintains the interests of dominant groups, and has been explored in concepts such as localism in relation to surfers (or, for parkour, see Bavinton, 2007). Thus, in this way, she reveals how an imaginative way forward for researchers on alternative sport is, as van Ingen (2003) suggests, to 'develop more nuanced inquiries into the intersection of gender, sexuality, and race *in place*' (van Ingen, 2003: 210).

Extreme commercialization

Globalization has affected both public perception of extreme sports and the opportunities available to extreme sports' participants. This can be seen in the way the media hijack extreme sports to sell everything from soft drinks to cars to deodorants, the range of lifestyle sport publications that are available for different sports and the way in which gear and clothing intended initially for activists have entered the mainstream, with, for example, the products of outdoor companies such as North Face and Patagonia being sold on the high street.

Therefore, any possibility of liberating or transformatory scripts for sporting participants needs to be seen in the context of the current commercialization and professionalism of a range of extreme sports which has accompanied globalization (see Booth, 2011; Rinehart and Sydnor, 2003; Robinson, 2013; Thorpe, 2012; Wheaton, 2004a). The worldwide dominance of an international Americanized culture can lead to homogeneous sporting cultures, but extreme sports can also display challenges to such a dominant culture when sport is seen as a field in which ideologies, values and meanings may be contested/resisted. With French 'whiz sports', such as surfing, windsurfing and snowboarding, Midol and Broyer (1995: 208) argue: 'We are far from the patriarchal rigidity of control when the attitude is one of "make or break".' But they also state that such sports, on initially becoming official and organized, produce innovative forms in opposition to existing ones, and later receive official recognition or are absorbed into the existing traditional organizations.

But how do we conceive of this in current times when types of rock climbing such as sport climbing and bouldering are being considered for inclusion in the 2020 Olympic Games, when skateboarding is being considered as an Olympic sport at the 2012 Games and when snowboarding, previously adopted by sporting participants as an alternative to skiing, which was viewed as a 'safe' sport in its traditional form, is already an official Winter Olympics sport? (See also Edwards and Corte [2010] on BMX and the relationship of the sport to the Entertainment and Sports Programming Network's X games, which attract global audiences in their millions.)

Regarding globalization of the media, Hargreaves and McDonald (2004: xi) ask: 'In what ways has the media industry specifically, and the culture industries in general, sought to embrace lifestyle sports?' The issue of whether such sports represent superficial, even nihilistic, materialistic cultural forms increasingly appropriated by transnational media corporations to be sold as a package to passive consumers has also been considered (see Wheaton, 2004a); whilst Rinehart and Sydnor (2003) cite the Disney Corporation, MTV and the Discovery Channel, as well as corporate giants such as Pepsi and Coke, as having appropriated and determined the electronic imaging of extreme sports globally. The related issue raised by Hargreaves and McDonald (2004), of whether lifestyle sports are a rejoinder to the commercially exploitative world of more mainstream/dominant sport, can also be explored by asking if and how extreme sports participants work such commercialism to their best advantage, and whether they are still able to maintain a personal and sporting ethical stance if they do so.

This is contemplated by Barkham, when he writes regarding surfing: 'Brands, advertising, image, peer pressure, transport and the leisure society may bring people to pick up a board. But the thing that drives so many to return is surfing's intrinsic pleasure' (Barkham, 2006: 9). Thus, this view also substantiates Beal and Wilson's (2004) research, that for the US skaters in their study, commercialization was becoming more accepted, including sponsorship, as they saw advantages in these changes for both the sport and themselves. As Thorpe (2006: 221) reveals in her discussion of female snow-, skate- and surfboarders, though their 'radical potential' disappeared when boarding became commercialized by the late 1990s, 'commercialization is not solely a co-opting force'. In addition, Rinehart and Sydnor (2003) note the subterranean existence of videos, films and sporting 'zines which attempt to prevent the corruption of these alternative sports by the mainstream, as well as being self-reflective about the history they are making in the process.

Wheaton (2004a) argues for the need to move beyond the dichotomy of either incorporation or resistance in relation to these sports by, for example, more empirical work being done on how people negotiate identities in respect of their consumption choices and the associated tensions. More recently, Coates, Clayton and Humberstone (2010) reflect on the culture of Canadian snowboarding to assess how participants engage with the mainstream snowboarding industry and media in order to attempt to gain control of it from an organizational level, and not necessarily through style or symbolism, resulting in their definition of 'resistance agency', as illustrated by the snowboarders' everyday attempts to take control; whilst in relation to surfing, Stranger (2010) identifies the difficulty of easily identifying, in postmodernization, a mainstream against which subcultures can be viewed. As Wheaton (2010: 1066) asserts in her review of Stranger, he views large surfing companies who moved into the global mainstream from the margins as 'products of postmodern aestheticization and their movement towards incorporation as part of a broader aestheticization/postmodernization of the mainstream'. However, subcultural sporting participants are able, through a grassroots-based culture, to share moments of transcendence, and such companies are still able to maintain a cachet of 'insider' authentic status in the sport. (See also Nelson [2010] on the increasing importance of virtual media for the progress of the sport of BMX.) Such developments ensure that Wheaton's (2005) call for acknowledgement of the importance of the move beyond cross-cultural comparisons to an exploration of the impact of global flows on, between and within local subcultures and their medias and industries is still relevant.

Risk

Even though high-risk 'extreme' sports have grown in popularity, Stranger (1999) has pointed out that there remains a lack of empirical work on the meanings that people give to *voluntary* risk taking (see also Tulloch and Lupton, 2003). Though more studies have occurred in recent years, Stranger's view, that voluntary risk taking is done for a variety of reasons, ranging from a desire for thrills and excitement to overcoming personal fears to exercising personal agency, as well as for emotional engagement, control and self-improvement, is still pertinent. Tulloch and Lupton (2003) highlight Lash's (1993; 2000) call for an investigation into how members of subcultural groups respond differently to risk in aesthetic and emotional ways, including being ambivalent and contradictory. They also point to the importance of Lash's idea that risk judgements are ultimately about the fear of the 'terrible sublime' of death and argue that 'fine grained empirical analysis, which is able to explore people's ideas and experiences of risk' (Tulloch and Lupton, 2003), can be utilized to explore where, and how, the reflexivity that challenges modernity occurs and how it is expressed.

Risk sports and other leisure activities have also been conceptualized using the term 'edgework'. Milovanovic (2005) argues, in relation to modern society, that it is in the spaces of 'edgework' that the expression of emotions can occur, as opposed to the focus on rationality and reason when seen as features of a post-Enlightenment society. Lyng (2005), when discussing the concept of 'edgework', asks the question why people risk their lives when there are no material rewards for doing so, and concludes that people are drawn to extreme sports and other edgework activities because of the seductive and playful character of the experiences involved. Lyng (2005) also observes that risk-taking experiences are best understood as undertaken to escape contemporary life, including aspects such as institutionalized routines, alienation and over-socialization.

The view that risk is actively sought by extreme sports enthusiasts is substantiated by theorists who have analysed people's behaviour across a range of risk activities. For instance, Smith, in discussing financial trading as a high-risk activity, compares this to risk sports, where the people involved in them are seen to maximize, rather than minimize, risk activity: 'Most skydivers … and other leisure risk takers fervently embrace the risk factors of their sport' (Smith, 2005: 188). However, the risks that enthusiasts take can be conceptualized in diverse ways; for instance, by risking injury, they confirm Harris's (2005) contention that extreme sports participants knowingly gamble with their bodies. Alternatively, risk sports participants can risk their lives and/or their family's well-being, as illustrated by Tulloch and Lupton's (2003) findings, which document people starting to take fewer physical risks in sporting activities, when starting a family.

A different view is given by West and Allin (2010), whose research on rock climbers, utilizing Beck and Giddens, questioned the idea that extreme sports activists necessarily court risk, rather than manage it reflexively. Humberstone (2009) highlights a need to consider adventure sports in a global context, given that Westerners pursue their activities increasingly in more 'exotic' natural locations, thus providing apparently 'authentic' adventure experiences, and so the nexus of local cultural understandings and practice of adventure, and Western perceptions of adventure risk are crucial to explore. In addition, the globalization of a sport such as climbing has seen climbers now travelling outside their own country to destinations such as Thailand, China, Patagonia, Vietnam, Peru, Australia and New Zealand, to name but some. The ethical implications of pursuing extreme sports in countries, where, for example, low wages and poverty exist, is something that Western participants will increasingly have to grapple with as the visiting of these destinations increases (Robinson, 2013). Also, the impact of extreme sports on biodiversity conservation has been studied. Arlettaz *et al.* (2007) found that disturbance by snow sport free-riders appears to elevate stress on declining bird species, which potentially represents a new serious threat for wildlife in Alpine habitats. (See also Mansfield and Wheaton [2011] for a collection of articles exploring different leisure activities and the environment.)

In empirical research with Australians and Britons, Tulloch and Lupton aptly ask, 'Is risk perceived as "democratizing" in its universal effects, as Beck sees it, or do the old, "modernist" categories of age, gender, social class and so on still play an important role in the ways people understand and deal with risk?' (Tulloch and Lupton, 2003: 11). As an example, empirical and theoretical work has been carried out on risk in relation to rock climbing, and has found differences in how men and women respond to risk as they become parents or enter the elite levels of the sport, and inequality in media treatment of famous women mountaineers, such as the UK's Alison Hargreaves (see Coates, 2012; Robinson, 2008; 2013; Summers, 2007).

From a different perspective, psychologists Brymer and Oades (2009) examined a range of sports, including base jumping, waterfall kayaking and extreme skiing, and found that risk taking was combined with a wish to show courage and humility in the face of a powerful nature. In contrast to this, Kay and Laberge discuss the sport of extreme skiing, finding that skiers think that taking increased risks will avenge those who have already died: 'It apparently gives solace to those left alive that death is noble in the name of freedom ... or a steeper descent' (Kay and Laberge, 2003: 392). Further, risk taking does not always have such noble intentions. In mountaineering, recent deaths on Everest, it has been argued, could have been avoided if those passing other climbers not yet dead were not so focused on summitting (Malley, 2006). In this context, Beaumont and Douglas (2006) feel that Everest has been reduced to a 'playground', not to mention the environmental aspects of the pursuit of extreme leisure sports. Hence, the pursuit of extreme sports raises complex moral and ethical issues.

Therefore, it is only by locating the concept of risk and how it shifts in terms of what is considered a 'risky pursuit' in a wider political, social and economic context, for example, how governments legislate against risk, that we can see how extreme sports connect to new social movements such as environmentalism. Wagg *et al.* (2009) cite Jarvie (2006), who is concerned to see if extreme/alternative leisure pursuits can move outwards from such hedonistic/individual pursuits to link to progressive social change or political activism, asking, in effect, if such sports are a site for a new politics and an antidote to global capitalism. In this potential context, Laviolette (2006) uses a case study of UK surfing culture in Cornwall and the concerns that surfers had over sewage, resulting in the forming of a pressure group 'Surfers Against Sewage' to safeguard the local environment and public health.

In his most recent work, Laviolette's aim is 'to explore how adventurous practices have become activities which are germane to the dawning of new forms of individual and social imaginations where a different world becomes possible' (Laviolette, 2011: xii). Furthermore, he links 'adventurous pleasures' with a moral responsibility towards both the environment and what he terms 'egalitarian social thought', and activities such as extreme sports and the landscape within which they are enacted are 'existentially grounded within the socially somatic imagination' (*ibid.*). As Booth (2012) argues, it is in Laviolette's example of such sports as cliff jumping that we can see the two main principles of his somatic imagination thesis, which are the sensual body, and social narratives of heroism and how they connect. Booth outlines that Laviolette's embodied imagination thesis is both powerful and provocative (if ignoring of the biological realm of the senses), in that it contends that new versions of society can be created through the 'shared narratives' based on the embodied experiences of participants in such sports, which create different models of things such as respect, courage and heroism to those which already exist in society.

Therefore, for some theorists, in response to these social contexts individuals engage with a range of extreme sports and so enter a world based on the transgression and reformulation of boundaries which have been conceived of as: 'life versus death, consciousness versus unconsciousness, sanity versus insanity, ordered sense of self and environment versus disordered sense of self and environment' (Lyng, 1990: 864).

Conclusions

A framework for the theorizing of extreme sporting activities is becoming established across disciplinary boundaries and theoretical positions. Giulianotti's wish to 'encourage the abandonment of sectional division and to embrace theoretical diversity among communities of sports scholars from different disciplinary backgrounds' (Giulianotti, 2004: 1) is increasingly a theoretical reality for such sports.

Subcultural theories have had prolific and resonant implications for the study of extreme sporting collectivities, identification and identity politics (see Beal, 1999; Wheaton, 2004a; Atkinson and Young, 2008). Atkinson and Young (2008) chart how skateboarders and snowboarders were two of the most studied subcultural groups of the 1990s as part of the cultural resistance 'analytical meta-narrative' of sports studies, but also reveal how later theorists were concerned with how such sports both contained elements of the mainstream sports that they were positioned against and, later, came to resemble such sports. Theoretically, there was then a move to assessing just how much such resistance in youth sporting cultures had been romanticized.

Subcultural perspectives have also been critiqued by the anthropologist Dyck (2000), who argues that a notion of subcultures in relation to sport can ignore sporting phenomena or relationships and argues instead for ethnographic enquiry into the activities, relationships and meanings of sport. Thorpe (2006) has offered further critique of the concept, in that subcultural theory can be seen to be unconcerned with the dimension of change, whilst Robinson (2008) has pointed out a lack of attention to structural, material constraints on individual agency. However, Wheaton (2010) has identified how recent analysis of extreme sports has connected these activities to the structural context of a predominantly neo-liberalist economic-cultural system, where values such as individualism which are inherent in these sports further such a system, given that they are integral to its maintenance. (See also Young and Atkinson [2008] on the neo-liberalist discourse.)

Further, post-subcultural theory, though useful to studies of extreme sports because of an emphasis on difference, resistance, multiple and fluid identities and contradiction, still continues to exclude issues of race, ethnicity (see Wheaton, 2007; 2013 forthcoming) and heterosexuality (Robinson, 2008), or, indeed, age and disability. However, there are new theoretical insights emerging from fields such as cultural geography and youth studies, with an emphasis on the social policy implications of extreme sport participation; for example, on issues such as child obesity or inclusion, and well-being (see West and Allin, 2010; Wheaton, 2010).

Wheaton's earlier argument that work on sporting subcultures needs to 'borrow from, and integrate with, theorizing in other areas of sport and mainstream sociological work' (Wheaton, 2007: 15) can be seen in how feminist theoretical and empirical approaches to lifestyle sports now include a diverse range of theoretical perspectives, including hegemonic masculinity, Bourdieusian scholarship, third wave feminism and Foucauldian and Deleuzian post-structuralist approaches (Wheaton, 2013 forthcoming). Other recent theoretical concerns have involved a consideration of the emotional, sensual and aesthetic dimensions of extreme sports (Booth, 2012; Thorpe and Rinehart, 2010), as well as a consideration of the wider contexts that participants engage with in extreme sport, for example as parents, colleagues and in heterosexual relationships across the life course (see Coates, 2012; Dilley and Scraton, 2010; Robinson, 2007; 2008 for a case study of rock climbing).

Lastly, how we conduct work methodologically into extreme sports has started to receive further innovative theoretical attention (see Robinson [2008] for a discussion of the insider/outsider location of a female researching male climbers, Coates [2010] on the use of ethnographic fiction in researching rock climbers, Wheaton [2013 forthcoming] on issues of whiteness and race/ethnicity, Thorpe [2011] on snowboarding, and Brown, Dilley and Marshall [2008], who explore understanding the social worlds and experiences of extreme sports participants through using a head-mounted video camera, specifically mountain bikers' and walkers' embodied, multi-sensory ways of knowing and experiencing landscapes, thus offering interpretative and reflexive approaches to social research on extreme sports). In effect, therefore, the methodological and epistemological issues in how we know what we know about extreme sporting leisure activities, as well as the theoretical concerns outlined above, need to come more to the forefront of the extreme leisure agenda in the twenty-first century.

References

Arlettaz, R., Patthey, P., Baltic, M., Leul, T., Schaub, M., Palme, R. and Jenni-Eiermann, S. (2007) 'Spreading Free-Riding Snow Sports Represent a Novel Serious Threat for Wildlife', *Proceedings B of the Royal Society Biological Sciences* 274 (161) 1219–1224.

Atencio, M., Beal, B. and Wilson, C. (2009) 'The Distinction of Risk: Urban Skateboarding, Street Habitus and the Construction of Hierarchical Gendered Relations', *Qualitative Research in Sport and Exercise* 1 (1) 3–20.

Atkinson, M. and Young, K. (eds) (2008) *Tribal Play: Subcultural Journeys through Sport*. Research in the Sociology of Sport, Vol. 4, UK: JAI Press.

Barkham, P. (2006) 'A Bigger Splash, A Lot More Cash', *Guardian*, 17 July, 6–9.

Bauman, Z. (1992) *Intimations of Postmodernity*. London: Routledge.

Bavinton, N. (2007) 'From Obstacle to Opportunity: Parkour, Leisure, and the Reinterpretation of Constraints', *Annals of Leisure Research* 10 (3–4) 391–412.

Beal, B. (1995) 'Disqualifying the Official: An Exploration of Social Resistance through the Subculture of Skateboarding', *Sociology of Sport Journal* 12 (3) 252–267.

Beal, B. (1999) 'Skateboarding: An Alternative to Mainstream Sports', in J. Coakly and P. Donnelly (eds) *Inside Sports*. London: Routledge.

Beal, B. and Smith, M. M. (2010) 'Maverick's: Big-wave Surfing and the Dynamic of "Nothing" and "Something"', in B. Wheaton (ed.) Special Issue: The Consumption and Representation of Lifestyle Sports, *Sport in Society: Cultures, Commerce, Media, Politics* 13 (7–8) 1102–1116.

Beal, B. and Wilson, C. (2004) '"Chicks Dig Scars": Commercialisation and the Transformations of Skateboarders' Identities', in B. Wheaton (ed.) *Understanding Lifestyle Sports: Consumption, Identity and Difference*. London: Routledge.

Beaumont, P. and Douglas, E. (2006) 'Has Mighty Everest Been Reduced to a Playground?', *Observer*, 21 May, 24–25.

Blackshaw, T. (2009) 'Extreme Leisure', in T. Blackshaw and G. Crawford *The Sage Dictionary of Leisure Studies*. London: Sage.

Booth, D. (2012) 'Extreme Landscapes of Leisure: Not a Hap-hazardous Sport, *Sport in Society: Cultures, Commerce, Media, Politics* 15 (9) 1315–1318.

Booth, R. (2011) *Surfing: The Ultimate Guide*. Greenwood Guides to Extreme Sports. Westport, CT: Greenwood Press.

Borden, I. (2001) *Skateboarding, Space and the City: Architecture and the Body*. Oxford: Berg.

Breivik, G. (1999) *Empirical Studies of Risk Sport*. Norges idrettshøgskole: Institutt for samfunnsfag.

Brown, K., Dilley, R. and Marshall, K. (2008) 'Using Head-mounted Video Camera to Understand Social Worlds and Experiences', *Sociological Research Online* 13 (6), http://www.socresonline.org.uk/13/6/1/1.pdf

Browne, D. (2004) *Amped: How Big Air, Big Dollars, and a New Generation Took Sports to the Extreme*. London: Bloomsbury.

Brymer, E. and Oades, L. G. (2009) 'Extreme Sports: A Positive Transformation in Courage and Humility', *Journal of Humanistic Psychology* 49 (1) 114–126.

Cashmore, E. (2004) *Beckham*. Cambridge: Polity.

Coates, E. (2010) 'A Personal Journey Through "Moments": Doctoral Research into Parents Who Rock Climb', *Journal of Adventure Education and Outdoor Learning* 10 (2) 147–160.

Coates, E. (2012) 'A Fine Balance: Stories of Parents Who Climb'. Unpublished PhD Thesis, University of Buckinghamshire, UK.

Coates, E., Clayton, B. and Humberstone, B. (2010) 'A Battle for Control: Exchanges of Power in the Subculture of Snowboarding', *Sport in Society* 13 (7) 1082–1101.

Connell, R. W. (1987) *Gender and Power: Society, the Person and Sexual Politics*. Cambridge: Polity.

Csikszentmihalyi, M. (1975) *Beyond Boredom and Anxiety*. San Francisco: Jossey-Bass.

Dant, T. and Wheaton, B. (2007) 'Windsurfing: An Extreme Form of Material and Embodied Interaction', *Anthropology Today* 23 (6) 8–12.

Dilley, R. and Scraton, S. (2010) 'Women, Climbing and Serious Leisure', *Leisure Studies* 29 (2) 125–141.

Dyck, N. (ed.) (2000) *Games, Sports and Cultures*. Oxford: Berg.

Edwards, B. and Corte, U. (2010) 'Commercialization and Lifestyle Sport: Lessons from 20 Years of Freestyle BMX in "Pro-Town, USA"', in B. Wheaton (ed.) Special Issue: The Consumption and Representation of Lifestyle Sports, *Sport in Society: Cultures, Commerce, Media, Politics* 13 (7–8) 1135–1151.

Farrell, E. (2007) 'Into Blue', *Holland Herald, KLM*, November: 30–39.

Fletcher, R. (2008) 'Living on the Edge: The Appeal of Risk Sports for the Professional Middle Class', *Sociology of Sport Journal* 25 (3) 310–330.

Giulianotti, R. (ed.) (2004) *Sport and Modern Social Theorists*. London: Palgrave.

Hargreaves, J. and McDonald, I. (2004) 'Series Editors' Foreword', in Wheaton, B. (2004) *Understanding Lifestyle Sport: Consumption, Identity and Difference*. London: Routledge.

Harris, D. (2005) *Key Concepts in Leisure Studies*. London: Sage.

Horne, J., Tomlinson, A. and Whannel, G. (1999) *Understanding Sport: An Introduction to the Sociological and Cultural Analysis of Sport*. London: Routledge.

Humberstone, S. (2009) 'Inside/Outside the Western "Bubble": The Nexus of Adventure, Adventure Sports and Perceptions of Risk in UK and Mauritius', in J. Ormrod and B. Wheaton (eds) *On the Edge: Leisure, Consumption and the Representation of Adventure Sports*. Eastbourne, UK: Leisure Studies Association.

Huybers-Withers, S. M. and Livingstone, L. A. (2010) 'Mountain Biking is for Men: Consumption Practices and Identity Portrayed by a Niche Magazine', in B. Wheaton (ed.) Special Issue: The Consumption and Representation of Lifestyle Sports, *Sport in Society: Cultures, Commerce, Media, Politics* 13 (7–8) 1204–1222.

Jarvie, G. (2006) *Sport, Culture and Society: An Introduction*. London: Routledge.

Kay, J. and Laberge, S. (2003) 'Imperialistic Construction of Freedom in Warren Miller's *Freeriders*', in R. Rinehart and S. Sydnor (eds) *To the Extreme: Alternative Sports, Inside and Out*. Albany, NY: State University of New York Press.

Kay, J. and Laberge, S. (2004) '"Mandatory Equipment": Women in Adventure Racing', in B. Wheaton. (ed.) *Understanding Lifestyle Sports: Consumption, Identity and Difference*. London: Routledge.

Knijnik, J. D., Horton, P., and Cruz, L. O. (2010) 'Rhizomatic Bodies, Gendered Waves: Transitional Femininities in Brazilian Surf', in B. Wheaton (ed.) Special Issue: The Consumption and Representation of Lifestyle Sports, *Sport in Society: Cultures, Commerce, Media, Politics* 13 (7–8) 1170–1185.

Kusz, K. (2003) 'BMX, Extreme Sports, and the White Male Backlash', in R. Rinehart, and S. Sydnor (eds) *To the Extreme: Alternative Sports Inside and Out*. Albany, NY: State University of New York Press.

Kusz, K. (2004) 'Extreme America: The Cultural Politics of Extreme Sports in 1990s America', in B. Wheaton (ed.) *Understanding Lifestyle Sports: Consumption, Identity and Difference*. London: Routledge.

Lash, S. (1993) 'Reflexive Modernization: The Aesthetic Dimension', *Theory, Culture and Society* 10, 1–23.

Lash, S. (2000) 'Risk Culture', in B. Adams, U. Beck and J. Van Loon (eds) *The Risk Society and Beyond*. London: Sage.

Laviolette, P. (2006) 'Green and Extreme: Free-flowing through Seascape and Sewer', *World Views: Environment, Culture, Religion* 10 (2) 178–204.

Laviolette, P. (2007) 'Hazardous Sport?', *Anthropology Today* 23 (6) 1–2.

Laviolette, P. (2011) *Extreme Landscapes of Leisure: Not a Hap-Hazardous Sport*. Farnham: Ashgate.

Le Breton, D. (2000) 'Playing Symbolically with Death in Extreme Sports', *Body and Society* 6 (1) 1–11.

Lefebvre, H. (1991) *The Critique of Everyday Life*. Volume 1 (J. Moore, trans.). London: Verso. (First published in France, 1947.)

Lewis, N. (2000) 'The Climbing Body, Nature and the Experience of Modernity', *Body and Society Journal* 6 (3–4) 58–80.

Lyng, S. (1990) 'Edgework: A Social Psychological Analysis of Voluntary Risk-taking', *American Journal of Sociology* 95: 851–886.

Lyng, S. (2005) 'Edgework and the Risk-Taking Experience', in S. Lyng (ed.) *Edgework: The Sociology of Risk-Taking*. London: Routledge.

Maffesoli, M. (1996) *The Time of the Tribes: The Decline of Individualism in Mass Society*. London: Sage.

Maguire, J. (1999) *Global Sport: Identities, Societies, Civilizations*. Cambridge: Polity.

Malley, J. (2006) 'Italians Passed Us By, Says Everest Rescuer', *Guardian*, 9 June.

Mansfield, L. and Wheaton, B. (eds) (2011) Special Issue: Leisure and the Politics of the Environment, *Leisure Studies* 30 (4).

Midol, N. and Broyer, G. (1995) 'Toward an Anthropological Analysis of New Sport Cultures: The Case of Whiz Sports in France', *Society of Sport Journal* 12: 204–212.

Milovanovic, D. (2005) 'Edgework: A Subjective and Structural Model of Negotiating Boundaries', in S. Lyng (ed.) *Edgework: The Sociology of Risk-Taking*. London: Routledge.

Nelson, W. (2010) 'The Historical Mediatization of BMX-freestyle Cycling', in B. Wheaton (ed.) Special Issue: The Consumption and Representation of Lifestyle Sports, *Sport in Society: Cultures, Commerce, Media, Politics* 13 (7–8) 1152–1169.

Rinehart, R. (2000) 'Emerging Arriving Sport: Alternatives to Formal Sport', in J. Coakley and E. Dunning (eds) *Handbook of Sport Studies*, London: Sage.

Rinehart, R. and Sydnor, S. (2003) 'Proem', in R. Rinehart and S. Sydnor (eds) *To the Extreme: Alternative Sports, Inside and Out*. Albany, NY: State University of New York Press.

Robinson, V. (2004) 'Taking Risks: Identity, Masculinities, and Rock Climbing', in B. Wheaton (ed.) *Understanding Lifestyle Sports: Consumption, Identity and Difference*. London: Routledge.

Robinson, V. (ed.) (2007) Introduction, Special Issue of *Sheffield Online Papers in Social Research*, Gender and Extreme Sports: The Case of Climbing, August, Issue 10.

Robinson, V. (2008) *Everyday Masculinities and Extreme Sport: Male Identity and Rock Climbing*. Oxford: Berg.

Robinson, V. (2013) *Rock Climbing: The Ultimate Guide*. Greenwood Guides to Extreme Sports. Westport, CT: Greenwood Press.

Smart, B. (2005) *The Sports Star: Modern Sport and the Cultural Economy of Sporting Celebrity*. London: Sage.

Smith, C. W. (2005) 'Financial Edgework: Trading in Market Currents', in S. Lyng (ed.) *Edgework: The Sociology of Risk-Taking*. London: Routledge.

Spowart, L., Burrows, L. and Shaw, S. (2010) '"I Just Eat, Sleep and Dream of Surfing": When Surfing Meets Motherhood', in B. Wheaton (ed.) Special Issue: The Consumption and Representation of Lifestyle Sports, *Sport in Society: Cultures, Commerce, Media, Politics* 13 (7–8) 1186–1120.

Stranger, L. (1999) 'The Aesthetics of Risk: A Study of Surfing', *International Review for the Sociology of Sport* 34 (3) 265–276.

Stranger, M. (2010) 'Surface and Substructure: Beneath Surfing's Commodified Surface', in B. Wheaton (ed.) Special Issue: The Consumption and Representation of Lifestyle Sports, *Sport in Society: Cultures, Commerce, Media, Politics* 13 (7–8) 1117–1134.

Summers, K. (2007) 'Unequal Genders: Mothers and Fathers on Mountains', in V. Robinson (ed.) Special Issue of *Sheffield Online Papers in Social Research*, Gender and Extreme Sports: The Case of Climbing, August, Issue 10.

Thorpe. H. (2006) 'Beyond "Decorative Sociology": Contextualising Female Surf, Skate and Snow Boarding', *Sociology of Sport Journal* 23: 205–228.

Thorpe, H. (2011) *Snowboarding Bodies in Theory and Practice*. Global Culture and Sport Series. London: Palgrave Macmillan.

Thorpe, H. (2012) *Snowboarding: The Ultimate Guide*. Greenwood Guides to Extreme Sports. Westport, CT: Greenwood Press.

Thorpe, H. and Rinehart, R. (2010) 'Alternative Sport and Affect: Non-representational Theory Examined', in B. Wheaton (ed.) Special Issue: The Consumption and Representation of Lifestyle Sports, *Sport in Society: Cultures, Commerce, Media, Politics* 13 (7–8) 1268–1291.

Tulloch, J. and Lupton, D. (2003) *Risk and Everyday Life*. London: Sage.

van Ingen, C. (2003) 'Geographies of Gender, Sexuality and Race: Reframing the Focus on Space in Sport Sociology', *International Review for the Sociology of Sport* 38: 201–216.

Wagg, S., Brick, C., Wheaton, B. and Caudwell, J. (2009) *Sports Studies*. London: Sage.

West, A. and Allin, L. (2010) 'Chancing Your Arm: The Meaning of Risk in Rock Climbing', in B. Wheaton (ed.) Special Issue: The Consumption and Representation of Lifestyle Sports, *Sport in Society: Cultures, Commerce, Media, Politics* 13 (7–8) 1234–1248.

Wheaton, B. (2000) '"New Lads"? Masculinities and the "New Sport" Participant', *Men and Masculinities Journal* 2 (4) 434–456.

Wheaton, B. (ed.) (2004a) *Understanding Lifestyle Sports: Consumption, Identity and Difference*. London: Routledge.

Wheaton, B. (2004b) '"New Lads"? Competing Masculinities in the Windsurfing Culture', in B. Wheaton. (ed.) *Understanding Lifestyle Sports: Consumption, Identity and Difference*. London: Routledge.

Wheaton, B. (2005) 'Selling Out? The Commercialisation and Globalization of Lifestyle Sports', in L. Allison (ed.) *The Global Politics of Sport*. London: Routledge.

Wheaton, B. (2007) 'After Sport Culture: Rethinking Sport and Post-Subcultural Theory', *Journal of Sport and Social Issues* 31 (3) 283–307.

Wheaton, B. (ed.) (2010) 'Introducing the Consumption and Representation of Lifestyle Sports', Special Issue: The Consumption and Representation of Lifestyle Sports, *Sport in Society: Cultures, Commerce, Media, Politics* 13 (7–8) 1057–1081.

Wheaton, B. (2013 forthcoming) *The Cultural Politics of Lifestyle Sport*. Routledge: London.

Whitson, D. (1990) 'Sport in the Social Construction of Masculinity', in D. Sabo and M. Messner (eds) *Sport, Men and the Gender Order*. Champaign, IL: Human Kinetics.

44

LEISURE, COMMUNITY, AND POLITICS

Erin K. Sharpe

Introduction: definitions and theoretical framework

This chapter focuses on the ways that politics play out in the myriad social worlds that unfold in the community sphere. It begins from the standpoint that there is nothing natural about leisure; that leisure is 'always, and already political' (Rojek, 2005: 24). By focusing on leisure in the community sphere, the author provides a forum in which to put some flesh on this argument. To lightly sketch out to what 'leisure in the community sphere' refers, it might be said that it tends to be those forms of leisure that unfold in spaces that are open to the public, that we engage in collectively, and through which we inhabit or construct a subject positioning as a 'community member'. Some of what comes to mind as finding a home within this definition includes the kinds of leisure activities that we find in public parks, markets, squares, or playgrounds, and community events, such as sports tournaments, festivals, fairs, or carnivals. This definition excludes leisure that unfolds in private spaces such as the home, or is untied to collective or community experience. To this extent it has resonance with Thibault's (2008) concept of 'civil sphere' leisure, which he describes as that realm of leisure that stands apart from the private sphere of home and the parochial sphere of work. What this tells us is that in leisure in the community sphere there is always the potential for people to meet strangers (Sennett, 1993) and have unmediated interactions (Mitchell, 1996). These observations notwithstanding, this chapter operates with the caveat that the edges of all such definitions are fuzzy and porous, as they exist in degrees rather than absolutes.

Understanding the ways that politics play out in leisure that unfolds in the community sphere involves exploring, unveiling, and considering the political processes that work on and are produced in such contexts. Oftentimes the politics is overt; community leisure spaces such as the street, the park, the mall, or the café have long been important sites for groups to engage in the politics of representation and participation. Furthermore, marginalized groups that have been denied participation in the public have used leisure-based events such as festivals or carnivals as a vehicle to voice concerns and be seen and heard (Jackson, 1992). What such observations tell us is that power is regularly exerted on leisure practices in the community, as authorities attempt to regulate and enforce what leisure can be practised where and by whom. At other times the politics are embedded in the dominant values, power structures, ideologies, and histories of the community, and it is through interrogations into leisure that takes place in the community sphere that the processes underlying collective identity, belonging, exclusion, or marginality become more apparent.

The intention of this chapter is to identify and illustrate the varied ways that politics play out in leisure that takes place in such contexts. However, the scope is narrowed to focus primarily on the relationships between leisure, community and politics as they are manifest in community leisure *space* and community leisure *events*. Spaces that are ostensibly publicly accessible are often highly controlled or regulated, and an examination of community leisure space can reveal the ways in which power is exerted as well as raise questions about who constitutes 'the public' and who might be excluded. Similarly, events that are constructed as celebrations and affirmations of community also offer insight into the ways in which power dynamics operate, as well as the ways in which 'community' identity is built and contested.

In order to develop this critique, the chapter draws primarily on two theoretical perspectives that are particularly relevant to the study of leisure, community, and politics: the sociospatial approach (Gottdiener and Hutchison, 2000) and the performance paradigm (Conquergood, 1991).

Emerging out of geography, the sociospatial approach emphasizes 'spatiality', or the socially produced and interpreted nature of space (Soja, 1985). Marking a move beyond spatial determinism in which space is treated as a 'container' for social activities, the sociospatial approach instead contends that spaces are not 'fixed' or 'done' but instead are in 'a constant state of transition as a result of continuous, dialectical struggles of power and resistance among the diversity of landscape providers, users and mediators' (Aitchison, 1999: 29). The sociospatial approach thus provides us with a way of thinking 'in terms of the ever-shifting geometry of social/power relations ... It is a view of space that is opposed to that which sees it as flat, immobilized surface, as stasis ... which is to see it as depoliticized' (Massey, 1994: 4). Thus, the aim of the sociospatial approach is to reveal the ways that power is exerted in material spaces, particularly in terms of how difference and hierarchy become 'built in' to everyday places and spaces and 'concretized' through routines and practices (Gieryn, 2000). It also involves exploring the construction of our thinking in regard to how spaces are to be used and interpreted, and thus our ideas regarding what acts are 'out of place' in certain locations (Cresswell, 1996). The work that is undertaken from within a sociospatial perspective can unfold at different levels of analysis. For example, it can involve exploring the 'close-up' struggles of power and resistance among the diversity of actors invested in a space (Aitchison, 1999), as well as how local struggles articulate with broader political, social, and economic forces from beyond their boundaries (Gottdiener and Hutchison, 2000).

As its nomenclature suggests, the performance paradigm draws attention to the performative dimension of social life, and especially the relationship between performance and power. As a theoretical framework, this perspective originated with the work of anthropologist Victor Turner on ritual and social drama (Guss, 2001). Turner's (1982) argument was that by being set apart from the normative and the everyday, cultural performances were important dramatizations that enabled participants to understand, criticize, and even change the worlds in which they live (Guss, 2001). For Turner, cultural performances were 'not simple reflectors or expressions of culture or even of changing culture but may themselves be active agencies of change', in that through the performances actors were able to 'sketch out what they believe to be more apt or interesting "designs for living"' (Turner, 1982: 24).

The performance paradigm has led to a shift in perspective, from seeing leisure events as expressions or representations of community, to understanding them as performances that construct and produce community. Whereas Turner focused primarily on the socially trans-formative potential of events, work within the performance paradigm contends that cultural performances offer a context in which sociopolitical struggles are enacted, the result of which can involve contestation, transgression, affirmation, as well as deeper entrenchment of the current social order.

Landscapes of control: the politics of community leisure space

Probably one of the most dominantly held ideas about the relationship between leisure, community, and politics is the role that community leisure space is thought to hold in the formation of an active citizenry. The idea that community leisure spaces such as the streets, parks, squares, meeting houses, and other shared spaces play a central role in the formation of an active and participatory community began with de Tocqueville and has been held by 'urbanists' and public space advocates ever since (Amin, 2006). In this perspective, shared community spaces are seen as 'symbols of collective well-being and possibility … sites of public encounter … and spaces for political deliberation' (Amin, 2006, para. 1). However, Amin (2006) and others have begun to ask if this reading of public spaces as sites for the formation of an active citizenry is still valid. Critics, for example, point to the myriad of pathways for participation to the citizenry, which, in broadening options for participation weaken the significance of community space in the process (Goheen, 1998). Thus, in this light, the relationship between community leisure space and an active citizenry may be called into question. However, the political nature of community leisure space certainly is not.

One way that politics interpellates community leisure space is through the processes of control and exclusion that unfold in the community sphere. One way that power exerts itself in community leisure space is through disciplinary practices that control the movement of bodies in specific ways. As Foucault (1977) describes in his work on discipline, control can be exerted through a variety of disciplinary techniques, including temporalization (control-ling when spaces can be used), containment (establishing boundaries), or regulation (estab-lishing rules for how movement should unfold), and further enforced through surveillance and policing. Although certainly all community spaces would have some form of discipline, these forms of discipline need to be scrutinized in terms of whom they are being applied to and on what basis. For example, Andrew, Harvey and Dawson (1994) conducted a review of the regulations of public parks in Toronto and found that the regulations were more oriented toward ease of maintenance than they were around social engagement or freedom of move-ment. However, more significant concerns arise when disciplinary practices are found to be excluding certain groups of users.

The case study of skateboarding in New York City by Chiu (2009) aptly illustrates the ways in which processes of discipline and control can unfold in community leisure space. Chiu traced the ways that the power structures of the city were brought to bear to address the growth in popularity of street skateboarding in the 1990s. Chiu argues that as skate-boarding grew in popularity it was designated as an urban issue; efforts to control and contain boarding emerged as a result, and skateboarders contested these attempts. Laws prohibiting skateboarding were passed and signage was placed in parks and plazas where skateboarding was designated as problematic. Officers of the Department of Parks and Recreation were authorized to expel skaters, issue tickets, and confiscate equipment. Some sites were also refurbished to make them less appealing to skaters by building bumps and bars into skateable surfaces such as railings and ledges. In order to contain the 'problem' the city also designated eighteen 'skate parks' across the city, which attempted to reform and discipline skateboarding according to the logic of youth sport activity. Chiu noted that this discourse of constructing skateboarders as a disorderly and risky group was sustained by changing attitudes toward surveillance in the light of 9/11, which normalized and justified such policing practices.

These observations notwithstanding, power is not exerted solely by the overt actions of legitimated authorities; to a wide extent we regulate our own actions in community leisure space based on our own normative expectations regarding who and what is allowed in that specific leisure site. In other words, in all spaces 'people have a strong feeling regarding how to behave, which kinds of behaviour are out of place and what is "normal" and unobtrusive' (Peters and de Haan, 2011). Cresswell (1996) uses the metaphors of 'in place' and 'out of place' to capture the way that ideology shapes behaviour in spatial experience. Cresswell also contends that an examination of who or what is 'in place' and 'out of place' can reveal the power dynamics that are in play within the community more broadly. Although disheartening, it is perhaps not surprising that the literature on spatiality contains copious reports of community leisure spaces as constructed according to the normative expectations of dominant identities, including adult (Green and Singleton, 2006; Travlou, 2004), white (Haluza-Delay, 2006; Lashua, 2006; Scraton and Watson, 1998; Thomas, 2005), heterosexual (Brickell, 2000; van Ingen, 2004), and consumer (Zukin, 1995). The consequences of these constructions are that the behaviours or characteristics of dominant identities carry on unremarked, whereas behaviours or characteristics that differ are viewed as threatening, inappropriate, or outside the boundaries of public acceptability (Iveson, 1998). In other words, 'in place' and 'out of place' are marginalizing processes.

Power also circulates at a micropolitical level among different actors or groups within the leisure spaces of the community. Spaces may become territorialized, whereby different spaces become associated with specific social identities (Robinson, 2000), and access to and use of that space becomes open only to those associated with the relevant characteristics. In some cases, territorialization can result in exclusion. For example, a study of youth in rural communities revealed significant conflict and exclusion resulting from groups of different ages and identities claiming ownership of different public leisure spaces such as the recreation centre, park, and playground (Tucker and Matthews, 2001). Territorialization can emerge as the result of habitual practices or patterns of use (Amin, 2006), or it may result through more aggressive acts of groups claiming spaces as their own and systematically excluding others through various rituals and practices of 'purification' (Sibley, 1995). For example, in his study of race relations in Thunder Bay, Ontario, Haluza-Delay (2006) described a range of exclusionary practices against Aboriginal Canadians in city leisure spaces, including blatant discrimination, marginalizing interaction, and subtle racializing. For those subjected to these practices, common responses were spatial separation and withdrawal from community space.

Although this section of the chapter has focused primarily on the ways in which power is exerted in controlling or exclusionary ways, it is important to note that exclusion is never complete, and further, that those who are subjected to these processes do not always acquiesce. Actors demonstrate resistance to social control in a variety of ways, enacted at both an individual and a collective level. For example, in Chiu's study of skateboarding, it was found that skaters contested the strategies of social control primarily by persisting in their practice of street skating. In addition, spaces are always contested and the meanings ascribed to them are never fixed.

Performance of community: the politics of community leisure events

In the popular imagination, and increasingly in cultural policy, community leisure events, such as festivals, sporting events, or fairs, are seen as enjoyable occasions that provide residents with an opportunity to socialize as well as to celebrate the character, value, history, and continuity of local life (De Bres and Davis, 2001; Clarke and Jepson, 2011). Community events identify a key aspect of local culture, and provide a time and place for people in the community to gather in shared celebration (Smith, 1993). As a collective experience, festivals and other community events are noted for their *communitas* – the expression used by Turner (1982) to capture the feeling of unity and closeness that often emerges in collective rituals. These feelings of community pride and cohesion are also enhanced by the act of successfully 'pulling off' a complex event like a community festival, which serves as a source of pride as well as building identity as a cooperative and 'can-do' community (Ziakas and Costa, 2012).

However, performance theory reminds us that the process of celebrating community is not a politically benign process; a performance is not a mere reflection of community-as-is; the performance itself contributes to the construction *of* community. Community events set out to celebrate community, which is a process that involves 'employing a collection of symbols that define the community and represent it to the outside world' (Bonnemaison, 1990: 25, in Quinn, 2003). In other words, the event serves as a 'summarized pronouncement and manifestation of what is known, through which local people celebrate and parade their identity'. More importantly, events are occasions for 'the intensification of what social order knows itself to be and for the validation of this knowledge' (Ziakas and Costa, 2012: 31). As Quinn (2003: 332) notes, the political dimension becomes manifest when researchers begin asking, 'which symbols are selected to represent the community? Who chooses the symbols and what interests/values are being promoted?' The challenge to festival scholars is that there is no generalizable answer to these questions, as each event can be understood only within its own local history and context. Each event is its own site of struggle where competing interests intersect, and different viewpoints and voices get articulated. At some times, events reproduce or legitimate ideology, whereas at other times they critique and subvert it (Conquergood, 1991).

At a micropolitical level, power plays out through the festival-production process. Typically, festivals and events that are run by local authorities, with the intent of celebrating community, are more likely to conserve and maintain the overt values, power relations, and received histories of the community (Clarke and Jepson, 2011; Smith, 1993; Waterman, 1998; Ziakas and Costa, 2012). Clarke and Jepson (2011) have noted that festival planning is largely an undemocratic process that involves little community consultation. Thus, the events are produced to express the interests and values of socially and politically dominant groups (Waterman, 1998). For example, in their study of a historical festival in England, Clarke and Jepson (2011) were able to show how the festival was dominated by a small group of 'cultural power brokers' who exerted control over defining what stood as the 'culture' to be celebrated and were able to maintain control over the festival through claims of superior cultural knowledge. Overall, these processes, in reinforcing a definition of valued 'culture' as the culture of the elite, contribute to the disenfranchisement of community members whose culture takes different forms. Others have similarly noted the tendency for events to be organized around an art form that caters to the values of the cultural elite (e.g., opera, classical music, fine art) or to be directed by individuals who represent the interests of the socially and politically privileged members of the community (Jeong and Santos, 2004; Quinn, 2003; Waterman, 1998).

However, festivals are also a vehicle for groups who perceive themselves to be marginalized to counter this marginality and claim cultural, ideological, and political space within the broader community sphere. In fact, the practice of marginalized groups using festivals, events, and other forms of public performance as a way to resist and contest social order has a long history, although it is only recently that they have received scholarly attention. Some studies emphasize the local character of the struggle, and specifically the relationship between 'claiming space' on the ground and 'creating space' in the public imagination to assert identity and resist oppression (Smith, 1993). Examples include analyses of events such as Caribana festival in Toronto (Jackson, 1988), Notting Hill Festival in London (Cohen, 1982), and Lesbian and Gay Pride Festivals (Kates and Belk, 2001). For example, the Caribana festival, a festival of Caribbean culture, dance and music, is analysed by Jackson as a vehicle for the Caribbean diaspora in Toronto to raise issues of ethnic and cultural marginalization (Jackson, 1988). In a similar vein, Lesbian and Gay Pride Festivals emerged in cities across North America as a protest at the ongoing dominance of heterosexist culture (Kates and Belk, 2001). These analyses emphasize the intersections of culture and politics, as well as the role that fun, frivolity, and festivity play in the political process.

Other scholarly work on festivals has captured events in which the political dynamics and social relations are not as clear cut as either 'domination or 'resistance'. For example, the study by Furniss (1998) of the participatory role of First Nations in the Williams Lake Stampede is an illustrative case in point. Williams Lake Stampede, a western Canadian rodeo festival, began in 1919. Alongside traditional rodeo events such as roping competitions and horse races, the festival also includes various dramatic re-enactments of scenes that retell the frontier myth of history, including re-enactments of Indian–White conflict on the frontier. Clearly, these re-enactments are problematic for how they valorize a colonialist history, subject First Nations culture to the gaze of white spectators, and potentially reaffirm cultural stereotypes that contribute to the disempowerment of First Nations. However, Furniss found that although participation has continued through the seventy-year history of the festival, many First Nations felt deeply ambivalent about the festival, and that participation was framed as a form of 'strategic essentialism', whereby the risk of engaging in an essentializing performance was outweighed by the opportunity that the festival provided to command public attention and become more visible, thus potentially opening the door to raising issues and addressing cultural misunderstandings.

Smith (1995) has also critiqued the resistance framework. In his view, while it repositions the centre and its boundaries, the implicit end-point of any resistance framework is 'to replace one type of boundary with another. This means that, while inequality may effectively be challenged, the fact of having a boundary – signifying simultaneously the facts of belonging and exclusion, entitlement and disenfranchisement – goes unquestioned' (p. 148). Smith advocates instead an analytical approach that focuses on identifying the boundary-making processes that underlie community events, and the complex ways that various resistances related to local identity, historical context, ideology, and social relations come into play in these processes. To illustrate, she offers the case of the Beltane Festival, a celebration of Victorian revival in a small town in Scotland that in 1991 faced – and then refused to address – accusations of racism due to the use of black face in one of the long-standing festival activities. Smith noted in her analysis that racism certainly accounted for part of the reason for this decision, but she also contended that there were other ways to understand the community's actions, including as a form of resistance to outside interference, as well as resistance to the intrusion of English racial politics into Scottish affairs (Smith, 1993).

Scholars have also explored alternative analytical frameworks that attend to the multiplicity of resistances to (and affirmations of) dominance that become manifest in the context of community events. For example, Watson and Ratna (2011) took an intersectional approach to considering how 'race', ethnicity, gender, and class were performed, contested, and negotiated in the context of a 'Bollywood' festival in northern England. Their introduction of the concept of 'space for leisure' also draws attention to the boundary-making process as it emphasizes being and belonging as a process of active and ongoing negotiation that is contextual and relational. This approach shows promise, and the field is encouraged to explore other theoretical and analytical approaches that are able to come to terms with the ambiguity, complexity, and polysemy of contemporary festivals and community events.

The future of leisure, community, and politics

This chapter has explored the way that politics play out in leisure that unfolds in the community sphere as it stands now. But what is on the horizon for the future? There are two trends worth noting, as they both promise to have a significant impact on the community leisure sphere. The first is the ongoing shift of cities from spaces of production to spaces of consumption (Zukin, 1991), which has resulted in new economic models that have begun to frame leisure events such as festivals, theatre, and sport events as vehicles for the expansion of economic interests (Waterman, 1998). Increasingly, cities and municipalities are looking at leisure spaces and events as economic opportunities and catalysts for urban renewal and cultural tourism (Quinn, 2003). It is a common occurrence, for example, for municipal authorities to 'invent' festivals in an effort to expand off-season tourism and local economic development (Hughes, 1999). This new frame has raised the stakes to ensure that leisure spaces are predictable and aligned with the image that the community aims to project, and in the process tremendous power is exerted upon those bodies and behaviours that disrupt the image-making or consumption process. Overall, this process is appearing to depoliticize the event sphere, as it limits and restricts the forms of cultural expression that are deemed acceptable (Quinn, 2003). This process also appears to be intensifying social exclusion, as it encourages exclusionary spatial practices based on economic standing or purchasing power (Silk, 2007), whereby it is the (dirty, loitering, unpredictable) lower-class residents who are 'managed' out of leisure spaces, in favour of high-value others (Mordue, 2007; Zukin, 1991).

However, a second trend has emerged which suggests that community leisure is currently in a process of intensified politicization, due to shifts within the political activism and social movement fields. In recent years, for example, the social movement literature has documented a shift toward a prefigurative model of activism with a similar festive style (Heartfield, 2003). As Duncombe (2002: 1) noted, with the growing tendency for political events to incorporate music, dance, play, puppetry, and other creative elements, 'social protests these days seem to have much more in common with arts fairs and theatre festivals than with the more traditional models of march, rally, and civil disobedience'. Day (2004) has characterized the shift from protest politics to prefigurative politics as a move from a 'politics of demand' to a 'politics of the act'. In a politics of demand, the vision of social change is embedded in a hegemonic conception of the political, and social actions are oriented towards reform or the eradication of power, with the goal of emancipation. In a 'politics of the act', the attempt is to 'refuse, rather than rearticulate' hegemonic structure and break out of the loop of the endless perpetuation of desire for emancipation (p. 734). One of the central reasons for this shift is the growing feeling among activists that the traditional model of politics is outdated and ineffective. The new 'politics of the act', based in festivity and leisure, makes the work participatory, productive, and possibly more effective. For activists, this more festive and creative style of activism is also easier to sustain because it is imaginative, visionary, but, perhaps most of all, because it fun to be involved in.

References

Aitchison, C. (1999) 'The New Cultural Geography: The Spatiality of Leisure, Gender, and Sexuality', *Leisure Studies 18* (1) 19–39.

Amin, A. (2006) Collective Culture and Urban Public Space. Downloaded 12 December 2011 from http://www.publicspace.org/es/texto-biblioteca/eng/b2003-collective-culture-and-urban-public-space.

Andrew, C., Harvey, J., and Dawson, D. (1994) 'Evolution of Local State Activity: Recreation Policy in Toronto', *Leisure Studies 13* (1) 1–16.

Brickell, C. (2000) 'Heroes and Invaders: Gay and Lesbian Pride Parades and the Public/Private Distinction in New Zealand Media Accounts', *Gender, Place, and Culture: A Journal of Feminist Geography 7* (2) 163–178.

Chiu, C. (2009) 'Contestation and Conformity: Street and Park Skateboarding in New York City Public Space', *Space and Culture 12* (1) 25–42.

Clarke, A. and Jepson, A. (2011) 'Power and Hegemony within a Community Festival', *International Journal of Festival and Event Management 2* (1) 7–19.

Cohen, A. P. (1982) 'A Polyethnic London Carnival as a Contested Cultural Performance', *Ethnic and Racial Studies 5*: 23–41.

Conquergood, D. (1991) 'Rethinking Ethnography: Towards a Critical Cultural Politics', *Communication Monographs 58*: 179–194.

Cresswell, T. (1996) *In Place/Out of Place: Geography, Ideology and Transgression.* Minnesota, MN: University of Minnesota Press.

Day, R. (2004) 'From Hegemony to Affinity: The Political Logic of the Newest Social Movements', *Cultural Studies 18* (5) 716–748.

De Bres, K. and Davis, J. (2001) 'Celebrating Group and Place Identity: The Case of a New Regional Festival', *Tourism Geographies 3* (3) 326–337.

Duncombe, S. (2002) 'Introduction', in S. Duncombe (ed.) *Cultural Resistance Reader.* London: Verso.

Foucault, M. (1977) *Discipline and Punish: The Birth of the Prison.* London: Allen Lane.

Furniss, E. (1998) 'Cultural Performance as Strategic Essentialism: Negotiating Indianness in a Western Canadian Rodeo Festival', *Humanities Research 3*: 23–40.

Gieryn, T. (2000) 'A Space for Place in Sociology', *Annual Review of Sociology 26*: 463–496.

Goheen, P. G. (1998) 'Public Space and the Geography of the Modern City', *Progress in Human Geography 22* (4) 479–496.

Gottdiener, M. and Hutchison, R. (2000) *The New Urban Sociology* (2nd ed.). Boston, MA: McGraw-Hill.

Green, E. and Singleton, C. (2006) 'Risky Bodies at Leisure: Young Women Negotiating Space and Place', *Sociology 40* (5) 853–871.

Guss, D. M. (2001) *The Festive State: Race, Ethnicity, and Nationalism as Cultural Performance.* Berkeley, CA: University of California Press.

Haluza-Delay, R. (2006) 'Racialization, Social Capital, and Leisure Services', *Leisure/Loisir 30* (1) 263–285.

Heartfield, J. (2003) 'Capitalism and Anti-capitalism', *Interventions 5* (2) 271–289.

Hughes, G. (1999) 'Urban Revitalization: The Use of Festive Time Strategies', *Leisure Studies 18*: 119–135.

Iveson, K. (1998) 'Putting the Public Back into Public Space', *Urban Policy and Research 16* (1) 21–33.

Jackson, P. (1988) 'Street Life: The Politics of the Carnival', *Environment and Planning D: Society and Space 6*: 213–230.

Jackson, P. (1992) 'The Politics of the Street: A Geography of Caribana', *Political Geography 11* (2) 130–151.

Jeong, S. and Santos, C. A. (2004) 'Cultural Politics and Contested Place Identity', *Annals of Tourism Research 31* (3) 640–656.

Kates, S. M. and Belk, R. W. (2001) 'The Meanings of Lesbian and Gay Pride Day: Resistance through Consumption and Resistance to Consumption', *Journal of Contemporary Ethnography* 30 (4) 392–429.

Lashua, B. D. (2006) '"Just Another Native?" Soundscapes, Chorasters and Borderlands in Edmonton, Alberta, Canada', *Cultural Studies Critical Methodologies* 6: 391–410.

Massey, D. B. (1994) *Space, Place, and Gender*. Minneapolis, MN: University of Minnesota Press.

Mitchell, D. (1996) 'Political Violence, Order, and the Legal Construction of Public Space: Power and the Public Forum Doctrine', *Urban Geography* 17: 158–178.

Mordue, T. (2007) 'Tourism, Urban Governance and Urban Space', *Leisure Studies* 26 (4) 447–462.

Peters, K., and de Haan, H. (2011) 'Everyday spaces of inter-ethnic interaction: the meaning of urban public spaces in the Netherlands', *Leisure/Loisir* 35(2) 169–190.

Quinn, B. (2003) 'Symbols, Practices and Myth-Making: Cultural Perspectives on the Wexford Festival Opera', *Tourism Geographies* 5 (3) 329–349.

Robinson, C. (2000) 'Creating Space, Creating Self: Street-frequenting Youth in the City and Suburbs', *Journal of Youth Studies* 3 (4) 429–443.

Rojek, C. (2005) 'An Outline of the Action Approach to Leisure Studies', *Leisure Studies* 24 (1) 24–35.

Scraton, S. and Watson, B. (1998) 'Gendered Cities: Women and the Public Leisure Space in the Postmodern City', *Leisure Studies* 17 (2) 123–137.

Sennett, R. (1993) *The Fall of Public Man*. London: Faber and Faber.

Sibley, D. (1995) *Geographies of Exclusion: Society and Difference in the West*. New York: Routledge.

Silk, M. L. (2007) 'Come Downtown and Play', *Leisure Studies* 26 (3) 253–277.

Smith, S. (1995) 'Where to Draw the Line: A Geography of Popular Festivity', in A. Rogers and S. Vertovec (eds) *The Urban Context: Ethnicity, Social Networks, and Situational Analysis*. Oxford: Berg Publishers.

Smith, S. J. (1993) 'Bounding the Borders: Claiming Space and Making Place in Rural Scotland', *Transactions of the Institute of British Geographers* 18 (3) 291–308.

Soja, E. (1985) 'The Spatiality of Social Life: Towards a Transformative Retheorization', in D. Gregory and J. Urry (eds) *Social Relations and Spatial Structures*. Basingstoke: Macmillan.

Thibault, A. (2008) *Public and Civil Leisure in Quebec*. Trois-Rivières, PQ: University of Quebec Press.

Thomas, M. E. (2005) '"I Think It's just Natural": The Spatiality of Racial Segregation at a U.S. High School', *Environment and Planning A* 37: 1233–1248.

Travlou, S. (2004) 'A Teenager's Guide to Public Spaces in Edinburgh: Mapping Teenage Microgeographies', *Proceedings of Open Space/People Space: An International Conference on Inclusive Environments, Edinburgh, UK*. Retrieved 18 September 2007 from http://www.openspace.eca.ac.uk/conference/proceedings/PDF/Travlou.pdf.

Tucker, F. and Matthews, H. (2001) '"They Don't Like Girls Hanging Around There": Conflicts over Recreational Space in Rural Northamptonshire', *Area* 33 (2) 161–168.

Turner, V. W. (1982) *From Ritual to Theater: The Human Seriousness of Play*. New York: Performing Arts Journal Publications.

van Ingen, C. (2004) 'Therapeutic Landscapes and the Regulated Body in the Toronto Front Runners', *Sociology of Sport Journal* 21: 253–269.

Waterman, S. (1998) 'Carnivals for Elites? The Cultural Politics of Arts Festivals', *Progress in Human Geography* 22 (1) 54–74.

Watson, B. and Ratna, A. (2011) 'Bollywood in the Park: Thinking Intersectionally about Public Leisure Space', *Leisure/Loisir* 35 (1) 71–85.

Ziakas, V. and Costa, C. (2012) '"The Show Must Go On": Event Dramaturgy as Consolidation of Community', *Journal of Policy Research in Tourism, Leisure and Events* 4 (1) 28–47.

Zukin, S. (1991) *Landscapes of Power: From Detroit to Disneyworld*. Berkeley: University of California Press.

Zukin, S. (1995) *The Culture of Cities*. Cambridge, MA: Blackwell.

45

ETHNICITY, RACISM AND THE REAL SOCIAL VALUE OF SPORT

Grant Jarvie

Introduction

Studies of the relationship between leisure and racism have not dominated the fields of Leisure Studies, Race Relations, Ethnic and Racial Studies, Sociology or other bodies of knowledge but they have made a contribution to what we know about racism, how it pervades many cultures, takes many different forms and must remain a focus of any social or progressive twenty-first-century political agenda. It is not necessary here to argue whether the challenge of racism has been one of the political successes or failures of Leisure Studies and other fields, but it is necessary for both studies of racism and forms of advocacy that challenge racism to be much more prominent in the international field of Leisure Studies.

The issue of racism and ethnicity in sport is complex. Sport has the potential to make an enormous difference but it is also a fertile ground for the expression of violence and racism. Various countries expressed concerns about potential incidents of violence and racism in football in the run-up to the 2012 European Football Championships in Ukraine and Poland. One popular way for developing nations to announce to the world that they have made it onto the global stage in the early twenty-first century is to host a major international sporting event: from China's Beijing Olympics in 2008, to Russia's Sochi Winter Games of 2012, South Africa's World Cup stewardship in 2010 and Brazil's double coup of the 2014 World Cup and 2016 Summer Olympics, staging a spectacle of this magnitude is a clear signal to the world that you are now a country of note (Hancox, 2012). This was certainly the motivation for Poland and Ukraine's joint bid to host the Euro 2012 soccer championships. But the event that was supposed to be a measure of Ukraine's post-Soviet development ran the danger of highlighting a host of national shortcomings, from virulent racism to an oppressive, dysfunctional political system. A relatively successful football festival in some ways helped to mask deeper structural issues, while at the same time providing a platform for government messages.

Racism has long been a stain on European football. Racist taunts and gestures aimed at non-white players are all too common at football matches; there have even been instances of rowdy fans throwing bananas onto the field at players of African descent. But according to a recent piece in the *New York Times*, that racism is perceived to be more virulent in the football stadiums of Eastern Europe, where fans have also been known to aim Nazi-style salutes and chants of 'Sieg Heil!' at non-white players. The concern over racism at Euro 2012 was stoked when the BBC's *Panorama* documentary series did a report on racist incidents at football matches across Eastern Europe, including video from a recent Premier League match in Ukraine that showed Ukrainian fans savagely beating a group of Indian spectators. The racism issue seemed to reach a crescendo when the families of two black players in England's national team publicly announced that they would not be attending matches in Ukraine because of concerns for their safety (BBC News, 2012). Ashley Walcott, the brother of English player Theo Walcott, announced via Twitter that the Walcott family would be skipping matches in Ukraine 'because of the fear of possible racist attacks/confrontation. Some things aren't worth risking.' Walcott's statement was echoed by the former England defender Sol Campbell, another black player, who, after watching the *Panorama* footage, urged English fans to 'stay at home, watch it on TV. Don't even risk it ... because you could end up coming back in a coffin' (http://www.bbc.co.uk/news/world-europe-18286941). Italy's star striker Mario Balotelli, the son of immigrants from Ghana, added to the litany, saying that he would walk off the pitch during Euro 2012 if he heard any racist taunts from the crowd; Balotelli also said that he had once had bananas thrown at him in a bar in Rome (http://www.bbc.co.uk/news/world-europe-18286941).

European legislation is clear, in that Article 21 of the Charter of Fundamental Rights of the European Union asserts that 'any discrimination based on any ground such as sex, race, colour, ethnic or social origin, genetic features, language, religion or belief, political or any other opinion, membership of a national minority, property, birth, disability, age or sexual orientation shall be prohibited' (Kjaerum, 2012: 11). The issue of racism in sport continues periodically to make newspaper headlines. In England the legal case involving the alleged racial remarks made by the Chelsea and England defender John Terry against the Queens Park Rangers defender Anton Ferdinand was still on-going at the time of this writing, while towards the end of 2011 Luis Suarez, the Liverpool footballer, was found guilty of racially abusing Manchester United player Patrick Evra (Barnes, 2012: 59; Barrett, 2012: 58; Taylor, 2012: 10). Such examples remind us that sport continues to contribute to both ethnic tensions and racism within contemporary society.

The year 2011 also marked the passing away at the age of 80 of the South African-born cricketer Basil D'Oliveira, who left an indelible mark upon the struggle to bring about change in apartheid South Africa (Wilde, 2011: 15). By helping to change the face of South African cricket, D'Oliveira also helped to change the face of sport internationally. In 1965 the Anti-Apartheid Movement organized low-key placard-carrying protests outside each ground of the South African cricket tour to Britain, but the issue of both apartheid South Africa and racism in sport was elevated in 1968 over the question whether the coloured South African Basil D'Oliveira, by then a top and regular First Test player, should be selected for England's cricket tour to South Africa that year. The anti-apartheid campaigner Peter Hain (2012: 49) noted that D'Oliveira was offered £40,000 by a South African-based representative of the cigarette company Rothmans to declare himself unavailable. The English cricket selectors omitted him from the touring party, prompting the journalist John Arnott to observe 'That no one of an open mind will believe that he was left out for valid cricket reasons', and, as it transpired, the South African authorities had informed the Marylebone Cricket Club that D'Oliveira would not be welcome.

What the D'Oliveira episode did was educate the international public about the brutality and ugliness of racism. The strong links between the British and South African cricket establishments were fractured and it is perhaps ironic that in 1992 it was a further rebel cricket tour to South Africa, led by the former England captain Mike Gatting, that was

531

implicated in the downfall of apartheid South Africa and the induction of the first African National Congress (ANC) government, led by Nelson Mandela. D'Oliveira's impact in South Africa was recognized in his meeting with Mandela in 1989. D'Oliveira was the first captain of South Africa's non-white side when it faced Kenya in 1956 (Wilde, 2011: 15) – a fact that probably gave D'Oliveira a stronger case than Owen Dunnell, who led the first all-white South African test team in 1889, to be recognized as the first to lead a representative South African national team. The above case has been used to illustrate the potential of sport to play a part in bringing about social change, provide a resource of hope, and be part of a broader social and political campaign that impacted upon racism and ethnicity in one society. The objective of any public intellectual or activist working in the area of sport, racism and ethnicity should be to provide not evidence and explanation but, ultimately, interventions aimed at making and bringing about change.

This chapter is divided into several sections: (i) the first part is necessarily lengthy in order to outline issues of definition, key arguments that have been used to explain racism and ethnicity and to illustrate these where possible by using examples from sport; (ii) the second part acknowledges a body of work arising out of the study of post-colonialism and 'other' communities, as it is important to emphasize that the relationship between sport, racism and ethnicity must be considered not solely in socio-economic terms but also in geo-political terms; (iii) the third and fourth parts of this consider questions of identity and the search for common ground – the former because it has dominated so much of the explanations behind sport, racism and ethnicity, and yet it is argued here that it is necessary to move beyond identity politics, not least because of its tendency to be divisive; the latter because it is the search for common ground that helps to bind humanity together during times of conflict. The work of Amartya Sen (2009) and Nancy Fraser (2003) has helped with this exercise. This leads us to the final part of the chapter, which considers the role of sport in supporting movements for social change and, in particular, the place of sport, racism and ethnicity in struggles not only to progress society but also to value sport's social contribution.

Sport, racism and ethnicity

Enquiries into sport and racism have taken a number of starting-points, and contained within them their own politics of difference. Arguments about the relationship between sport, racism and ethnicity have tended to rely upon a particular set of arguments (Carrington, 2010; Eitzen, 2003; Jarvie, 2002; Jarvie and Thornton, 2012; Kjaerum, 2012; Markovits, 2003; Spaaij, 2011; Wigginton, 2006), These have included that sport (i) is inherently conservative and helps to consolidate patriotism, nationalism and racism; (ii) has some inherent property that makes it a potential instrument of integration and harmonious ethnic and race relations; (iii) as a form of cultural politics has been central to processes of colonialism, imperialism and post-colonialism in different parts of the world; (iv) has contributed to unique political struggles which have involved black and ethnic political mobilization and the struggle for equality of and for black peoples and ethnic minority groups; (v) is an important facet of ethnic and racial identities; (vi) has produced stereotypes, prejudices and myths about ethnic minority groups which have contributed both to discrimination against and an under-representation of ethnic minority peoples within certain sports; (vii) faces race and ethnicity as factors influencing choices that people make when they choose to join or not to join certain sports clubs; and (viii) needs to develop a more complex set of tools for understanding the limits and possibilities that influence sport, racism and ethnicity and, in particular, the way that such categories historically articulate with other categories and social divisions.

There is no simple answer to what constitutes racism. It is important not to confuse the terms *racism* and *ethnicity*. Even those who argue that ethnic minorities are united by a common experience of racism often fail to be sufficiently alert to the diverse ways in which racism has an impact on different social divisions in sport. An ethnic group is theoretically one in which association with both a particular origin and specific customs is adopted by people themselves to establish a shared identity (Platt, 2011). Ethnic groups are therefore self-conscious and claimed identities. There is often a perceived link between ethnic identity and national identity. Ethnicity and nationality are also often regarded as interchangeable concepts. The extent to which ethnicity, race and nation should be treated together rather than separately is also debated, but there are strong interconnections between them, including a common connotation of origin-based groupness (Aspinall, 2012). The terms *racism* and *ethnicity* are used throughout this chapter, but the question of identity will be returned to towards the end of this study.

Individuals, groups and communities often read events from a particular perspective. The case of Hassiba Boulmerka may be illustrative, in that the Arab-African sportswoman was forced at a particular point in her career to leave Algeria for France in order to escape a backlash from Muslim zealots (Jarvie and Reid 1997: 215). Winner of the women's 1500 metres final at the 1991 World Athletic Championships, Boulmerka became the first Algerian, first Arab and first African woman to win a gold medal at any World Athletic Championships. On her return to Algeria, the then President Chadli Benjedid greeted her as a national heroine. But Muslim zealots denounced her from the pulpit for baring her most intimate parts (her legs) before millions of television viewers. President Benjedid was himself publicly denounced for embracing a woman in public. At the time, the row underscored the clash between modernity and Islamic fundamentalism. It was a clash that was all the more surprising, given Algeria's position in the Arab world at the time as the torch-bearer of modernism and socialism and its successful struggle for independence from colonial rule. Hassiba Boulmerka moved to France, and the Islamicists lost an opportunity to promote national unity in Algeria during the early 1990s. However, how should such a case be approached by a researcher or public intellectual, or by an activist or sports enthusiast? Would it be from the standpoint of ethnicity, gender, colonialism or racism? Each of these perspectives would provide only a partial explanation. It is therefore important to be alert in identifying ethnic differences and inequalities and to ask to what extent the category of ethnicity helps to understand or compound any explanation that may be located elsewhere. In the end, while evidence and explanation are important so too are the questions of change and intervention and what tactics might be used to make the world a better place.

The term *racism* is used widely, and in many cases loosely, in accounts of world sport. It is often associated with many other terms, most notably, *race, racial, ethnicity, multiculturalism, multiracial,* and *discrimination* (Alleyne, 2002; Akilade, 2012; Aspinall, 2012; Braham, Rattansi and Skellington, 1995; Nussbaum, 2000). The literature and research on racism in sport is also dominated by the use of certain terms such as *black, white, Afro-Caribbean, African, African-American, Asian, people of color,* and many other terms that are used in campaigns to symbolize and assert differences between people in sport and in other areas of life (Bass, 2002; Carrington, 2010; Markovits, 2003; McRae, 2003; Wigginton, 2006). The terminology is in constant flux, and historically the generic term *black* has at times included and excluded different groups of people. There is also instability in the capitalized 'Black' and 'White' that have served as a reminder of the historical and social fluidity of the terms, while at the same time being used to distance discussions of racism in sport from the logical and historical fallacy of treating 'racial' terms as if they were natural categories. In the literature on racism and sport, the term *racism* often specifically refers to a belief system or systems that sustain racialism, often linking certain characteristics with negatively valued social, psychological or physical traits. Racism in sport is often closely linked to notions of prejudice and the unequal distribution of power resulting from racist behaviour. It is crucial not to generalize, and in this sense it is important to be aware of *racisms*.

The popularity and social significance of sport have meant that it often has been influenced by a multitude of racial contexts and tensions at different points of time in different parts of the world. Sport itself has had to address and think about challenging specific problems emanating from at least three forms of racism. *Structural racism* refers to racism embedded within the history of societies and the extent to which this structural racism has had an impact on sport. Factors commonly associated with structural racism include gaps between different racial and ethnic groups in terms of income, education, health and employment. *Institutional racism* refers to the practices and procedures within sport that discriminate against people. Areas commonly associated with institutional racism in sport include the gaps between different discriminated-against groups in terms of holding positions of influence and power in sport, or the extent to which tensions between different groups become visibly crystallized at sports events because of institutionally racist practices and procedures. *Individual racism* refers to the actions and attitudes of individuals toward members of ethnic or racial groups. Such actions and attitudes support and often reproduce discrimination and racism through sport.

Enquiries into sport and ethnicity have covered similar terrain, but with some notable differences. The language of ethnicity itself is not unproblematic, and dangers exist when it is used to substitute for the language of race, racism, nationality and/or nationalism. The lack of clarity over the concept of ethnicity and its closeness to nationality much of the debate about sport has focused upon the way in which sport has tended to contribute to ethnic or civic forms of nationalism or identity. Discussions of sport and ethnicity and sport and nationality often overlap, on the basis that once a person is away from their country of origin, their nationality may be taken to be their ethnicity, because of both the acknowledged commonality within a group and acknowledged differences from others. Thus the discussion of sport in Polish, Italian or Scottish communities outside of Poland, Italy and Scotland often clings to the ideas of belonging and identity with these countries, but also to that which differentiates such ethnic communities from other ethnic communities within any host country. Membership of any ethnic group need not be fixed in time, and a people's sense of identity may wax or wane. Ethnicity, like other categories such as sect, tribe, clan, town or even region often helps to explain questions such as who am I, who else is like me, whom should I trust and who am I not. Sport contributes to answering many of these questions for many ethnic communities, particularly where there is a close relationship with traditional or indigenous sports and games.

When asking about the value of social and political theory in explaining sport, racism and ethnicity, it is tempting to suggest that (i) asking theoretical questions is crucial to allowing us to explain or generalize about sport, racism and ethnicity; (ii) theoretical or hypothesis testing is a necessary part of approaching or organizing research into sport, racism and ethnicity; (iii) theory is capable of illuminating circumstances or, equally, of destroying certain cherished myths that are often taken for granted; (iv) theory stimulates new ideas and is fruitful in terms of generating further areas of research or studies into sport, racism and ethnicity; and (v) theory helps to frame and illuminate the process of decision making and why some decisions take the form that they do and others are rejected. Studies that place the concepts of racism or ethnicity at the heart of the enquiry are not neutral, in the sense that they prioritize certain questions over others.

Drawing upon some of the thinking presented in Carrington (2010: 5), it is worth mentioning, in relation to some aspects of race, sport and politics, that he recognizes that shifts between what he refers to as human freedom and unfreedom, and the history of racial signification in sport, can be used to mark both change and stasis. *Race, Sport and Politics* is, at the time of writing, one of the most sustained and fresh arguments around this area, and in this sense the intervention is to be welcomed. The key arguments are straightforward in that it is asserted that: (i) sport has become an important if somewhat overlooked arena for the making and remaking of race beyond its own boundaries (p. 3); (ii) the influence of sport upon black politics and, more widely, African diasporic people, how they understand themselves and how such communities are viewed by others is significant (p. 4); and (iii) what the author refers to as the deeply priapean nature of modern sports, and in particular its white colonial framing, needs to be exposed (p. 4). It is a trans-disciplinary study and an attempt to reframe the question of race and sport despotically that makes this a timely intervention.

The notions of racism and ethnicity remain important to our understanding of contemporary life, and they do so in at least two senses. In a socio-economic sense, anti-racism and ethnic relations, policies and practices serve to remind us that racism and ethnicity remain central to a complete social and political understanding of social inequality, social division and social policy. Socio-economic relations between and within different cultures and groups of people provide but one dimension to any contemporary understanding of the politics of sport, racism and ethnicity. In a geo-political sense, the ideas of racism and ethnicity and the continuing conflict between different states, nations and communities also serve to remind us that racial and ethnic mobilizations both within and between different countries also have a geo-political dimension, as well as a socio-economic dimension. The body of research on sport and post-colonialism or sport and 'others' has helped to sensitize researchers to just such a geo-political dimension.

Sport and post-colonialism

In drawing attention to the fact that indigenous Australians grew up in historical contexts of racism both inside and outside of sport, Gardiner (2003: 43) concludes that indigenous players have to confront a sports culture in which traditionally white codes attempt to dictate order and define black bodies. The texts that have emerged from indigenous people's lives in Australia have begun to produce an 'other' history of Australian football codes. In reality there is also a rich substantive terrain of women's sport in Africa, Asia and the Middle East, but, as Hargreaves (2004: 197) points out, there is a dearth of feminist sport literature from outside the West. She draws our attention to the need to develop multiple complex accounts of women in sport, and also to the *vital* point that too many homogeneous accounts of sporting identity for women tend to conceal many hidden forms of injustice, discrimination and activism in other worlds. This holds true for work on the body and identity, as much as it does for sport. Anne Leseth (2003: 243), talking of dance, sport and the body in Dar-es-Salaam, contrasts the notion of a Western body image with 'other' points of view, and in doing so draws upon the words of Betty, a 25-year-old woman living in a squatter area of Dar-es-Salaam, who explains: 'it is not important whether you have a body shape like a bodybuilder, a beauty queen or a traditional figure, the crux of the matter is how this person moves when it comes to speed and style' (Leseth, 2003: 242). This powerful piece of ethnography illustrates how the use of sport and dance in Tanzania can produce fundamentally different ways of thinking about bodily practice that take us beyond the traditional way of thinking about colonial sport and the body. It vividly illustrates the power of sport and dance as a means of developing, changing and reshaping lives in a post-colonial Tanzania.

Sport, identity and recognition

It is often argued that it is not identity that colonized nations, developing countries or ethnic groups want, but recognition and a redistribution of resources (Jarvie, 2009). The usual contemporary approach to identity politics in sport tends to start from the idea that identity is constructed dialogically. The proposition is that identity is forged by virtue of the fact that one becomes an individual subject only by virtue of recognizing and being recognized by another subject or group or nation. Recognition is seen as being essential to developing a sense of self, and being mis-recognized involves suffering a sense of distortion of one's relation to one's self, and consequently feeling an injured sense of identity (Fraser, 2003). This logic is transferred onto the cultural and political terrain. As a result of repeated encounters with the stigmatizing gaze and the resultant internalizing of negative self- or group-images, the development of a healthy cultural identity is affected. Within this perspective the politics of recognition through sport is mobilized as a potential strategy in the repair of self- or group-dislocation by affirmative action that challenges derogatory or demeaning pictures of the group. The argument is that members of mis-recognized groups or national groups suffering from a lack of identity can jettison such images in favour of self-representations of their own making, and collectively produce a self-affirming culture of recognition. Add to this public assertion the gaining of respect and esteem from society at large and a culture of distorted mis-recognition changes to being one of positive recognition.

This model of how identity politics in sport may operate contains some genuine insights into the effects and practice of racism, colonization, nationalism, imperialism and other forms of identity politics that operate through sport, and yet the model is both theoretically and politically problematic, in that such an approach leads to both the reification of group identity and the displacement of resource distribution. The problems of displacement and the reification of social and political identities in sport are serious insofar as the politics of recognition displaces the politics of redistribution and may actually promote inequality. To promote identity politics in sport as opposed to the politics of recognition runs the danger of encouraging separatism, intolerance, chauvinism, authoritarianism and forms of fundamentalism. This, then, is the problem of reification and identity politics in sport. What is needed is to develop accounts of recognition in sport that can accommodate the full complexity of social identities, including racial and ethnic identities, instead of promoting reification and separatism. This means developing accounts of recognition in sport that allow for issues of redistribution rather than displacing or undermining such concerns in relation to sport, racism and ethnicity.

Moving beyond identity in the search for common ground and capability

There also exists the explicit argument that what binds people together in terms of a common humanity is just as important as the power or weaknesses of a singular identity, ethnic or otherwise. Forcing people into boxes of singular identity is a feature not only of many high theories of culture and civilization but also of a mass of studies that have sought to explain the relationship between sport and national identity. Lovelock *et al.*'s recent exploration of immigrant experiences of belonging in nature-based settings reflects not only upon studies that have linked nature to national identity, but also that embodied belonging is something, it is argued, that all humans have in common (Lovelock *et al.*, 2011: 527). There is a useful suggestion here that the environment or nature can help assist with providing a sense of common belonging or common ground – but that some new immigrants to New Zealand may never realize embodiment in relation to national or regional parks (*ibid.*). There are very real dangers, as has been recently argued, with any identity politics that it may become reified or a badge of belonging or a claim to insurgency (Jarvie, 2009).

Seeing people in their environmental or social context can run the danger of classifying people as a member of one group, for example, a national group, whether it be New Zealand, Scotland, China, Canada or elsewhere. The solitarist illusion has implications for the way that global identities are seen and invoked. If a person can have only one ethnic identity, then the choice between the national and the global can become an all or nothing contest, which can be dangerous. It is crucial that reified or solitarist models of identity through sport are questioned, their authority and coherence examined and alternative more socially orientated models of intervention that search for common ground are provided. Thus, it is seen as important, within a capability approach to sport, racism and ethnicity, to confirm what Klein (2001) initially referred to as a reclaiming of the commons, but which Sen (2006) has addressed as the search for common ground. There is an important role not only for any effective global justice movement but also for any effective politics of sport. They may all belong to a series of different alliances and coalitions based upon different issues, while not giving up on the important search for common ground. There is a compelling need for the contemporary world to ask questions not just about identity politics, but also about the common ground that invokes the richness of the many identities and capabilities of human beings.

In 2009, when the then Labour Chief Secretary to the UK Treasury, Liam Byrne, gave a speech on public sector reform, he declared that social justice meant capability and power for everyone (Derbyshire, 2009). In support of the argument, Byrne drew heavily upon Sen, who argued that responsible adults must be in charge of their own well-being but that the capabilities upon which a person can draw to actually make a difference to their own life or situation invariably depend upon the very nature of the social arrangements in which the individual or community find themselves; in other words, their environment.

Sen's contributions to political discourse serve to remind us that when political parties talk about equality and inequality the first question to ask is often 'equality of what?' Redistribution of income and resources certainly matters, but so does what people can do with these resources in order to improve individual and other capabilities. This may apply to individuals, communities and countries. Sen makes the following key distinctions:

- Functioning: a functioning is an achievement of a person, what she or he manages to do or be. Achieving a functioning with a given bundle of commodities depends on a range of personal and social factors. A functioning refers to the use a person makes of the commodities at his or her command.
- Capability: a capability reflects a person's ability to achieve a given functioning
- Capability set: the capability set describes the set of attainable functioning that can be achieved.

The issues of multiculturalism, ethnicity and racism and the link to people's lives, freedoms and capabilities are clearly explained in *The Ideas of Justice* (Sen, 2009). First it is argued that the environment cannot be thought of just in terms surroundings. It must also consider the opportunities or possibilities for development that it offers people. Thus the impact of the environment on human lives and communities must be amongst the primary considerations in assessing its value. Second, the environment is a matter not only of passive preservation but also of active pursuit. It is within human power to enhance the environment in which we live. The power to intervene with effectiveness and reasoning may enhance the process of development itself. Seeing development in terms of increasing the effective freedoms won for and by human beings brings the constructive agency of people engaged in sport within the domain of developmental achievements.

A capability set helps to describe a set of attainable factors that a person can achieve (Sen, 2005). The emphasis on a set of capabilities acquired by an individual, but also by a community or place, reflects opportunities to win further positive freedoms or further choices over lifestyles. This moves us beyond simple dichotomous or singular identity approaches to sport. It adds a new dimension to thinking about sport, politics, ethnicity and racism. The interaction between sport, racisms and ethnicities may certainly be viewed in socio-economic terms or geo-political terms, but in either case what is required is a consideration of how the environment also helps the development of human functions, life chances, choices and further freedoms. One of the strengths of Sen's framework is that it is flexible and exhibits a considerable degree of freedom for researchers to apply and develop it in different ways.

Clearly, Sen is not alone in thinking that matters of freedom won and social justice need to move beyond elements of material existence. Others would include Nussbaum (2000) and Stiglitz (2006). What matters here is that for both the individual and communities, opportunities must exist to consider development as freedom, and that these necessitate an understanding that to be genuinely free you need a capability set that goes beyond material capability. There is here cogency in thinking about sport, racisms and ethnicity that are about sustaining, extending or winning further freedoms for people or communities. In many cases these further freedoms need to be fought for and won, and therefore in the last section of this chapter issues of sport, racism and ethnicity in the age of activism are considered.

Sport, racism, and ethnicity in an age of activism?

During 2011 a local activist by the name of Parhat Ablat organized a joint Han-Uighur baseball team at Xinjiang University, China. The first part of this section opens with his story. Parhat notes:

> Little did I know that the Xinjiang University baseball team, which I led, would have such an unexpected impact. When I took charge, my only intention was to share my love of baseball with the community. But it went beyond that, giving people a chance to interact with someone from a different ethnic background for the first time and create lasting bonds of camaraderie.

Describing the social make-up of the team, Parhat explains:

> The players all come from different towns and various ethnic groups in Xinjiang, China. They come from rural and urban locales – some are Uighur, some are Han – while others are Kazakh and other smaller ethnic minorities. For many, it is the first time they have ever talked to someone whose life experience was radically different from their own. The team became a platform where bonds of friendship were built not just on the field, but off the field as well.

He goes on:

> If there is one way sports made this possible, it's by serving as a unifier and giving a group of people a common goal, which in our case was the China National College Baseball Tournament championship.

He explains the significance:

> When given the chance to work together, people learn to understand one another. In its own small way, sports can build a more harmonious society. As baseball did in our case, sports in other countries and regions can help build bridges between different groups of people within one country.

Such examples are many, but the role of sport in developing, at least impacting upon, human capabilities and social relationships is often unrecognized, described as unsustainable and lacking a substantive evidence base to inform any real impact upon social policy. Yet such stories are not unusual and should not be dismissed simply because they do not constitute any particular milestone or event in the struggle either for sport or through sport in terms of racism and ethnicity. Sport's capacity to be a resource of hope for many groups of people is wrongly dismissed, and yet it is not as if sport has not figured in attempts to make different societies and places increasingly free from racism and ethnic struggle.

Table 45.1 identifies some milestones (far from exhaustive) in the emergence of changing sets of race relations in sport. It is crucial to acknowledge that the experience of racism in 1881 would be entirely different from the experience of racism in sport in today. Precisely because the context, time period and comparative physical cultures are different, it is important to remember that any explanation of sport, racism and ethnicity is complex. Nonetheless, sporting milestones such as those in Table 45.1 allow researchers to comment upon both continuity and change in relation to racism in sport and to enter not just a debate about explanation but an opportunity for activism in relation to social change and intervention.

Sport has been involved with campaigns, activism, policies and protests aimed at discrediting explicit racism and the power of colonialism (Bass, 2002; Bloch, 2012; Eitzen, 2003; James, 1963; Plowden, 1996; Remnick, 2000; Wigginton, 2006). The struggle for sport has involved drawing attention to the fact that, until the 1960s, many black and other peoples of colour in the United States were still denied human and civil rights. The de-colonization of Africa, the attempt to defeat institutional racism in the United States, the overthrow of apartheid in South Africa and the defeat of US imperialism in Cuba and Vietnam have all implicated sport as an area of activism, if not of policy intervention. The publication of *Outside In* by Labour Party activist, Member of Parliament and anti-apartheid campaigner Peter Hain serves as a reminder of the part played by sport in bringing about change in South Africa (Hain, 2012).

Some of the most prominent areas of legislation and injustice in sport have grown out of struggles over racism: (i) the period of *apartheid* sport in South Africa from 1948 to 1992, when specific racial legislation which separated the practice of sport by racial groupings gave rise to the international slogan 'You cannot have normal sport in an abnormal society'; (ii) the practice of *colonialism* in many parts of the world, which formed the backcloth to sporting relations between many countries. During the 1960s and 1970s the cricket rivalry between England and the West Indies reflected racial tensions and racism rooted in years of colonial struggle. Terms such as White Wash and Black Wash were used to refer to English or West

Table 45.1 Milestones in changing race relations in sport

Year	Event
1881	Guyanese-born Andrew Watson captains Scotland, becoming the first black international footballer.
1936	Jesse Owens wins four gold medals for the USA at the Olympics in Berlin.
1947	Jackie Robinson becomes the first black Major League Baseball player of the modern era, debuting for the Brooklyn Dodgers.
1971	Evonne Goolagong wins the French Open and Wimbledon, becoming the first Aborigine to win a tennis grand slam.
1977	Commonwealth leaders agree to discourage sporting links with apartheid South Africa.
1977	Laurie Cunningham becomes the first black footballer to play for England.
1982	During World Cup finals, the National Front actively recruits at England matches.
1999	Foundation of Football Against Racism in Europe.
2006	England bowler Monty Panesar becomes the first Sikh to represent any nation except India in test match cricket.
2011	Emmanuel Adebayor resigned to racism. Real Madrid striker says racism is still 'part of life' in and out of football.
2011	Luis Suárez of Liverpool found guilty of racially abusing Patrice Evra of Manchester United.

Indian victories while at the same time sport took on the mantle of symbolic colonial/ anti-colonial struggle both between the two teams and also in the selection of the West Indian team, as is explained in C. L. R. James's (1963) classic period account of West Indian cricket; (iii) the popularity and worldwide coverage of sport has meant that *sport as vehicle for protest* has been a successful medium for drawing attention to the treatment of Black Americans as second-class citizens in the United States of America and in American sport, as evidenced by the Black Power protests at the 1968 Mexico Olympic Games. The extent to which Aborigine or Inuit peoples have also been marginalized in mainstream Australian or Canadian sport has also been a target for sporting activists. For example, much of the coverage of the 2000 Sydney Olympic Games revolved around the performances of the 400 metres Olympic Gold Medallist Cathy Freeman and the plight of Aborigine people living in contemporary Australia; and (iv) *legislation* such as the UK Race Relations Acts of 1976 and 2004 and various amendments provide the machinery of the law to investigate and act against racism in all walks of life in Britain, including sport. The UK Equalities Act of 2010 lays out employment rights to which workers, including sports workers, are entitled under the racial discrimination provisions within the Act.

There have been important historical moments that can often symbolize a prejudice, a protest, an ideology or the breaking down of barriers. Sport has been racist, but has also provided some of the most poignant anti-racist moments. In 1881 Andrew Watson became the first black player to play for Scotland at football/soccer. In August 1936 Jesse Owens won an unprecedented four gold medals at the Olympic Games in Berlin, in Nazi Germany. In 1938 Joe Louis crushed Max Schmeling, signalling the end of a period of white supremacy in boxing. In 1967 Muhammad Ali, the World Heavyweight boxing champion, condemned the war in Vietnam, arguing that he did not have any quarrel with the Vietcong. In October 1968 American black athletes protested, on the Olympic medal rostrum, against the treatment of black people in America and elsewhere, notably South Africa. Evonne Cawley

(Goolagong) became the first aboriginal Australian to play in a Wimbledon tennis final in 1971, while Arthur Ashe became the first black American to win the Wimbledon Men's Tennis Championship in 1973. In 1995 Nelson Mandela, following South Africa's victory in the Rugby World Cup, talked of sport as a force that could mobilize the sentiments of a people in a way that nothing else could. In 1998, when Zinedine Zidan lifted the Football World Cup for France, the French President talked of the French football team as being symbolic of the new, multi-racial, integrated France. In 2001 Pele, arguably the world's greatest footballer, endorsed a worldwide anti-racist campaign in football with the words that racism is cowardice that comes from fear, a fear of difference. In February 2002 Vonetta Flowers became the first African American to win a gold medal at the Winter Olympic Games. In 2011 England bowler Monty Panesar became the first Sikh to represent any nation except India in Test Match cricket.

In 1997, when Tiger Woods won the golf Masters and donned the green jacket that accompanied the winning of the coveted title, golf became thrilling to watch for an entirely new audience. On the hallowed putting greens of Augusta, where Woods would not have been allowed membership a few years earlier, history had been made. Social change through sport occurred, and at the time America did not have the language to deal with the change. Not since Lee Elder squared off against Jack Nicklaus in a sudden-death play-off at the American Golf Classic in 1968 had a black golfer gained so much televised attention (Bass, 2002). The sports press cast the feat of Woods as breaking a modern colour line, yet no one, including Woods himself, could fully describe exactly what colour line had been broken. The press conveyed his parental heritage as variously African American, Asian and Native American; overwhelming numbers of others portrayed Woods as a black athlete, a golfer who had brought about change in the same way that had been attributed to the likes of Jesse Owens, Tommie Smith, John Carlos, Muhammad Ali, Tydie Pickett, Louise Stokes, Vonetta Flowers and Alice Cochrane. Woods did not consider himself in such terms, but embraced a more nuanced racial heritage that was more representative of the melting pot imagery associated with American history and a determining demographic factor of the so-called Generation X (Bass, 2002: xvi).

In times of hardship and scarce resources the potential for conflict between groups of people is often highlighted. The economic and financial crisis from 2008 to the present has left deep scars that will take a long time to heal and that will shape policy making for years to come. Lower potential output, higher total and long-term unemployment, vast public and private debt, and volatile capital markets are just some features of the new reality that policy makers face. Income inequality has widened further, too, which is not helpful for long-term growth. Invariably, certain groups of people are often disproportionately affected. These challenges are daunting and sport is not the answer, but it has a part to play and can often be part of a process or a platform to build upon and develop those human capabilities and further freedoms mentioned by Sen and others.

Conclusions

While it is important to explain and understand sport, racism and ethnicity, the more important questions emanate from questions relating to social change. It is certainly important to ask: What empirical evidence can we draw upon to substantiate aspects of sport, racism and ethnicity? (What is happening?) What theories, ideas and concepts can we draw upon to explain and analyse this substantive evidence? (How can we make sense of what is happening?) What capacity does sport have to produce social change? (What can be done to produce change?) What is the contemporary role of the student, intellectual or researcher in the public arena? (What are you going to do about it?). *Yet it is the interplay between these questions that is perhaps more important.* It is the constant interplay between theory, explanation, evidence and intervention that is one of the hallmarks of the best research into sport, racism and ethnicity. We need evidence in order to combat racism in sport, but we also need advocacy.

This chapter has attempted to do several things: (i) it has demonstrated that racism in aspects of leisure remains a contemporary problem in many parts of the world; (ii) it has outlined some key concepts, definitions and legislation that have been used to explain the relationship between sport, racism and ethnicity; (iii) it has recognized the impact of post-colonialism and other bodies of work that have highlighted that racism should be considered in both a socio-economic and a geo-political sense; and (iv) it has rejected the argument that identity in sport is enough and suggested that future studies of sport, racism and ethnicity might consider the way in which sport potentially helps to develop human and economic capabilities, and also a sense of common ground.

At the beginning of the chapter it was suggested that studies of the relationship between leisure and racism have not dominated the fields of Leisure Studies, Race Relations, Ethnic and Racial Studies, Sociology or other bodies of knowledge, but they have made a contribution to what we know about racism, how it pervades many cultures, takes many different forms and must remain a focus of any social or progressive twenty-first-century political agenda. The question was also asked as to whether the challenge of racism has been a political success or failure for Leisure Studies. The answer to such a question must remain open, and yet the opportunity to do more is also open to any genuinely progressive political party, university, journal or society, to name but a few potential drivers of change.

References

Akilade, A. (2012) 'How Racist is Scotland?', *Sunday Herald*, 15 January, 38–39.

Alleyne, B. (2002) *Radicals against Race: Black Activism and Cultural Politics.* Oxford: Berg.

Aspinall, P. (2012) 'Answer Formats in British Census and Survey Ethnicity Questions: Does Open Response Better Capture Superdiversity?' *Sociology* 46 (2) 354–364.

Barnes, S. (2012) 'Suarez Comedy Finds Tragedy on the Overlap', *The Times*, 6 January.

Barrett, T. (2012) 'Liverpool and Dalglish Should be Charged, Says Anti-racism Body', *The Times*, 6 January.

Bass, A. (2002) *Not the Triumph but the Struggle: The 1968 Olympics and the Making of the Black Athlete.* Minneapolis: University of Minnesota Press.

BBC News (2012) 'Ukraine's President Downplays Euro 2012 Racism Fears', 21 May, http://www.bbc.co.uk/news/world-europe-18286941 (accessed 18 June 2012).

Bloch, C. (2012) 'Racism in Sport: Some Progress to be Confirmed', *Sport and Discriminations in Europe.* Paris: Sport and Citizenship, pp. 13–16.

Braham, P., Rattansi, A., and Skellington, R. (1995) *Racism and Anti-Racism.* London: Sage Publications.

Carrington, B. (2010) *Race, Sport and Politics: The Sporting Black Diaspora.* London: Sage.

Derbyshire, J. (2009) 'The New Statesman Profile on Amartya Sen', *New Statesman*, 27 July: 32–35.

Eitzen, D. (2003) *Fair and Foul: Beyond the Myths and Paradoxes of Sport.* New York: Rowman and Littlefield.

Fraser, N. (2003) 'Social Justice in the Age of Identity Politics', in N. Fraser and A. Honneth (eds) *Redistribution or Recognition.* London: Verso, 97–119.

Gardiner, G. (2003) 'Black Bodies – White Codes: Indigenous Footballers, Racism and the Australian Football League's Racial and Religious Vilification Code', in J. Bale and M. Cronin (eds) *Sport and Post-Colonialism.* Oxford: Berg, 29–45.

Hain, P. (2012) *Outside In.* London: Bite Back Publishing.

Hancox, E. (2012) 'Offsides: Racism and Political Division Taint Euro 2012', *World Policy Institute Blog*, 7 June (accessed 18 June 2012).

Hargreaves, J. (2004) 'Querying Sport Feminism: Personal or Political', in R. Giulianotti (ed.) *Sport and Modern Social Theorists*. Basingstoke: Palgrave, 187–207.

James, C. L. R. (1963) *Beyond a Boundary*. London: Stanley Paul.

Jarvie, G. (2002) 'Sport, Racism and Ethnicity', in J. Coakley and E. Dunning (eds) *Handbook of Sports Studies*. London: Sage, 334–344.

Jarvie, G. (2009) 'Identity, Recognition or Redistribution through Sport?' in J. Harris and A. Parker (eds) *Sport and Social Identities*. Basingstoke: Palgrave Macmillan: 15–28.

Jarvie, G. and Reid, I. (1997) 'Race Relations, Sociology of Sport and the New Politics of Race and Racism', *Leisure Studies* 16 (4) 211–219.

Jarvie, G. and Thornton, J. (2012) *Sport, Culture and Society*. London: Routledge.

Kjaerum, M. (2012) 'Sport and Discrimination in Europe', *Sport and Citizenship* 17 (December) 11–12.

Klein, N. (2001) 'Reclaiming the Commons', *New Left Review* 9 (May/June) 81–90.

Leseth, A. (2003) 'Michezo: Dance, Sport and Politics in Dar-es-Salaam, Tanzania', in N. Dyck and E. P. Archetti (eds) *Sport, Dance and Embodied Identities*. Oxford: Berg, 231–247.

Lovelock, K., Lovelock, B., Jellum, C. and Thompson, A. (2011) 'In Search of Belonging: Immigrant Experiences of Outdoor Nature-Based Settings in New Zealand', *Leisure Studies* 30 (4) 513–529.

Markovits, B. (2003) 'The Colors of Sport', *New Left Review* 22 (July/August) 151–160.

McRae, D. (2003) *In Black and White: The Untold Story of Joe Louis and Jesse Owens*. London: Scribner.

Nussbaum, M. (2000) *Women and Human Development: The Capabilities Approach*. Cambridge: Cambridge University Press.

Platt, L. (2011) *Understanding Inequalities*. Cambridge: Polity Press.

Plowden, M. (1996) *Olympic Black Women*. Gretna, LA: Pelican Publishing Company.

Remnick, D. (2000) *King of the World: Muhammad Ali and the Rise of an American Hero*. London: Picador.

Sen, A. (2005) 'Human Rights and Capabilities', *Journal of Human Development* 6 (2) 151–166.

Sen, A. (2006) *Identity and Violence: The Illusion of Destiny*. London: Allen and Unwin.

Sen, A. (2009) *The Idea of Justice*. London: Allen and Unwin.

Spaaij, R. (2011) *Sport and Social Mobility: Crossing Boundaries*. London: Routledge.

Stiglitz, J. (2006) *Making Globalization Work*. New York: W.W. Norton.

Taylor, D. (2012) 'Suarez Could have Caused a Riot', *Observer*, 12 February, 10–11.

Wigginton, R. (2006) *The Strange Career of the Black Athlete*. Westport, CT: Praeger.

Wilde, S. (2011) 'A Quiet Dignity', *Sunday Times*, 20 November, 15.

46

THE LABOUR OF LEISURE RECONSIDERED

Chris Rojek and Tony Blackshaw

The twinning of labour with leisure is fit to raise hackles in the community of scholars that specialize in Leisure Studies.[1] Because labour is generally linked to pecuniary activity it is automatically associated with coercion, rigidity and lack of fulfilment. In contrast, leisure is associated with freedom, flexibility, choice and pleasure (Page and Connell, 2010: 11–34). The best reason for being wary of this polarized way of thinking is that it does not conform to general observation or experience. There is no essential reason to connect toil, alienation and restraint with labour. Just as freedom, flexibility, choice and pleasure are not necessarily universal characteristics of leisure.

Sean Sayers (2007), in an insightful philosophical account of the concept of labour, follows Marx in observing that labour is the seat of creativity. This is a far cry from regarding labour as the source of woe and dissatisfaction. Sayers wants to reclaim for labour characteristics of joy and self-fulfilment. But what does it mean to propose that labour is the seat of creativity?

According to Sayers (2007), part of the species character of humankind is to seek self-realization through creative endeavour. By acting upon Character, Nature and Society, humans grow and progress. Labour freely given to a cause dear to the heart and that engages with the brain of the worker is a source of pleasure and the real basis for the wealth of society. Hence, Sayers (2007: 168) asserts that 'human productive power is the avenue to the development of human nature and thus a primary human and social value'.[2]

If this is the case, the question of why toil, dissatisfaction and restraint are so commonly associated with labour begs to be answered. True to his Marxist colours, Sayers (2007) recognizes no great difficulty in dealing with these matters. The reason why labour has negative connotations for many is that it is expressed in a social and economic system that nominally extends freedom to all, but which is based, in reality, in organized class inequality. As Marx (1959) maintains, by reframing the fundamentals of this system through the socialization of wealth, society will achieve 'the free and full development' of the individual.

That the reform of capitalism through greater state involvement in wealth distribution has not accomplished this end poses no great obstacle for Sayers (2007). In his view, the real socialization of wealth has not transpired. That is, economic, social and political resources are still concentrated in the hands of the ruling class. For this reason, under presently existing conditions, it is absurd to speak of the free and full development of the individual. Even those who consider themselves free, or at least 'freer' than others (in the sense of having more wealth and life chances), are part of a global system of organized inequality that supports, among other things, sweatshop labour, intolerance of unionization and child labour. What is it that makes the majority submit to unfulfilling labour and a regime of personal freedom that is subject to the defence and perpetuation of class interests? There have been many attempts within the Marxist tradition in Leisure Studies to answer this question in terms of class domination, ideology, false consciousness, hegemony and the like. They come with their own strengths and weaknesses.

A new concept from political science, *inverted totalitarianism*, has yet to make headway in the study of leisure. Although the concept clearly bears traces of Marxist thought, it carries none of the baggage of positing class rule or privileging class action as the only progressive force capable of transcending capitalism. It offers a more nuanced understanding of how 'freedom', co-optation and, by implication, leisure operate in contemporary consumer culture. Before returning to the issues raised by Sayers' account of labour, and considering them in relation to leisure practice, we should consider the contribution of inverted totalitarianism.

Inverted totalitarianism

The term 'inverted totalitarianism' was coined by the political theorist Sheldon Wolin (2008). As the adjective implies, it is the converse of totalitarianism. The latter refers to a system of control based upon an authoritarian leader and the cadre structure around him. Totalitarianism is intolerant of dissent and non-conformity. It applies punitive measures against them. In contrast, inverted totalitarianism guarantees freedom of speech, media and religion, while at the same time it intensively employs lobbying, cronyism, clientism and other forms of *invisible government* to produce what Wolin (2008: 7) calls the 'co-optation' of the individual.[3]

The decisive agents running the show are the state and the corporation. However, they have assembled a phalanx consisting of sympathetic intelligentsia in the media and universities to defend and advance their ascendancy. What counts as freedom is not a matter of the opinion of individual men and women. Rather, it springs automatically, and generally operates in ways that are unquestioned, from the framing devices, especially in the media, that shape social consciousness of public issues (see also Castells, 2009: 142–3, 155–65).

Inverted totalitarianism requires a major revision of Habermas's (1989) classic concept of 'the public sphere'. In Habermas, the latter is the zone in civil society in which discussion of incidents, episodes, patterns and 'drifts' (of opinion or behaviour) may be pursued without let or hindrance. As such, it is the first line of defence in democracy against elected and unelected forms of authority. Why this must be revised is that Wolin's work suggests that the public sphere is already compromised by the various devices applied by inverted totalitarianism.

Through lobbying, cronyism and clientism the public possesses a take on incidents, episodes, patterns and drifts that is rigged. It is rigged to exploit and develop the position of the vested interests that control society. While there are class interests at play in the higher state, Marxism makes a mistake in coalescing all social and economic characteristics of the powerful into one category. Corporations like Virgin and Apple are not the same as BP or General Motors. They pioneered social responsibilities, environmental concerns and encouraged a culture of informality that eventually had repercussions on the business practices of more traditional corporations (Frank, 1997; McGuigan, 2009). Wolin argues that the nexus of power rests between corporations and elements of the state system. Following the rise of neo-liberalism in the 1980s, the welfare settlement that used to govern the state has been destabilized in favour of an ethos of management defined by the benchmarks of corporate culture.

Contra Marxism, Wolin argues that the labour process and ownership of the means of production are not the correct foundation for examining inverted totalitarianism. Instead, he concentrates upon institutional regimes in business and government. These operate through complex alliances, deals and feedback loops to 'manage democracy'.

The vested interests in inverted totalitarianism constitute an invisible government that seeks the consent of the people through the parliamentary system. However, both economically and ideologically, they operate outside the parliamentary system to counter policy trends that are contrary to their (corporate) interests. Through lobbyists, cronyism and other connections with media network power they shape social consciousness. This applies not only to specific social policies but to wider categories that influence personal conduct, such as 'freedom', 'civic responsibility', 'tolerance' and 'justice'. Central to Wolin's case is that these interests are profoundly undemocratic. While they are linked to public figures in business and politics, they operate as a clandestine directorate that is not subject to duties of public transparency or the responsibility of public accountability.

The argument allows for more diversification and friction within the category of the vested interests than is allowed for in the Marxist conception of the ruling class. In the Marxist tradition, the ruling class acts in consort to enhance ascendancy. Economically, in hard times those who constitute the ruling class permit inefficient agents from within their own number to fall by the wayside, while they accumulate and intensify power. In contrast, Wolin's concept allows for some elements of the vested interests to make concessions to the propertyless strata and to communicate commitment to eradicating poverty and injustice. To remind ourselves: in the Marxist tradition these concessions and commitments would be regarded as part of the strategy for achieving class hegemony, i.e. the consolidation of class rule through making concessions to the propertyless strata. Against this tradition, inverted totalitarianism points to cleavages in the power base of the vested interests that are enduring and, in some instances, support genuine resistance.

For Wolin, rather more is involved here than conceding that Richard Branson, the late Steve Jobs or Warren Buffett are not the same as Frederick Goodwin, the Koch Brothers or Rupert Murdoch.[4] The cleavages within the ranks of the powerful are substantial. By adopting strategies to engineer consent in what Butsch (2008) calls 'the citizen audience', they produce conflicting messages and zones of ethical and spatial ambiguity that can be seized upon as resources in dissent and non-conformity. Listening to the consumer, paying attention to the consequences of industry on the environment and being responsible and creative about job losses were all central messages of the Occupy movement (Gitlin, 2012). Occupy sought to transcend the system of stratified exploitation based around property ownership that is the linch-pin of capitalism. But it did so using many of the arguments that Warren Buffett or Richard Branson, in developing 'cool capitalism', would condone.

Under inverted totalitarianism, the consumer metaphysic ('you are what you own') breeds conformity and regimentation.[5] At the same time, the labour devoted to consumption is widely appreciated as dead labour, since it does not create value but uses values created by others for self-esteem or competitive advantage. The weight of dead labour pressing upon the living is one of the issues highlighted by Occupy. The consumer metaphysic has become a social, economic and environmental threat not just to elements within the power base, but to the viability of the entire system. For it is socially divisive, economically wasteful and environmentally unsustainable.[6] So having more is actually gaining less, since to possess more fans the flames of social unrest, economic crisis and environmental collapse.

Wolin does not directly go into the relationship between inverted totalitarianism and leisure practice. Despite this, conceptually, he lays the ground for examining how the consumer metaphysic both advances and divides the vested interests behind inverted totalitarianism. This is the prerequisite for turning his arguments onto the sphere of leisure practice. It demonstrates the *programmed* nature of leisure practices that do harm to you, while at the same time pinpointing the relationship between these practices and the vested interests. Because it recognizes cleavages within the powerful, it also allows for zones of ethical and spatial ambiguity through which the ascendancy of power can be resisted and challenged. Incidentally, it also highlights the pivotal importance of *labour* in eliciting resistance and change through leisure. This brings us back to Sayers' (2007) account of creativity as the seat of labour.

However, before returning to this theme, it is necessary to give an example of how inverted totalitarianism elicits mediated responses to personal freedom in leisure practice.

Inverted totalitarianism and tobacco consumption

Consider the case of products that have been scientifically proven to be harmful to us. For instance, take the case of tobacco. The US Surgeon General's initial report on smoking was published in 1964. It led to publicity campaigns, government health warnings and taxes designed to discourage consumption.

Despite this, global consumption has been steadily rising since 1960. It is estimated that 1.6 billion people (nearly one fifth of the world's population) are smokers and that this is set to rise to over 1.6 billion by 2025 (Srinivas and Rao, 2009).

Consumption in nations with active health movements and high levels of literacy has generally declined. In the USA sales have declined by around 21% since 1998. The 378 billion cigarettes sold in 2005 was the lowest figure since 1951 (Dobson, 2006). In the UK in 1948 82% of men smoked some form of tobacco and 65% smoked cigarettes. By 1970 the percentage of male smokers had fallen to 55%. It is currently 21%. For women the rate actually rose from 41% to 44% between 1948 and 1970. Thereafter it dropped to around 20%. Currently, it is estimated that around 10 million adults in the UK smoke cigarettes (Office of National Statistics, 2012).

This sounds like a success story for public health education. However, this holds up only if the rest of the world is excluded. As we have already noted, the global rise in tobacco consumption since 1960 has been steady. Rates of consumption in the developing world, where health education campaigns are not strong and where literacy rates are lower, have

Table 46.1 Global production and consumption of cigarettes (in billions)

Year	Production	Consumption
1965	2150	–
1970	3112	3075
1980	4388	4328
1990	5419	5256
2000	5609	5489
2003	5662	5453

Source: US Department of Agriculture (USDA)

increased, while rates in the affluent countries with high literacy rates have, on the whole, declined. One third of cigarettes smoked worldwide are consumed in China (Dobson, 2006). In Russia, between 1992 and 2003, smoking prevalence rose from 57% to 63% among men and from 6% to 15% in women (Wade, Merrill and Lindsay, 2010). When adjustments are made for age there is evidence of a rapidly increasing rate of smoking among young people. The World Health Organization estimated that prevalence of tobacco smoking among young people (15 to 25 years) was 70% in males and 28% in females (WHO 2008).

In Pakistan cigarette consumption is estimated to have grown by 30% between 2003 and 2009 (Mushtaq, Mushtaq and Beebe, 2011: 431). In Asia as a whole, around 700 million, mostly men, smoke. The habit is estimated to kill approximately 2.3 million Asians per year, that is, almost half of the world's smoking victims. Rates of cancer and other tobacco-related diseases are rising rapidly (*Economist*, 2007).

The cigarette multinationals that have encountered trade barriers (notably anti-smoking health education campaigns and high taxes) in affluent *per capita* markets simply switch resources to lower *per capita*, more trade-friendly markets. The same economic necessity that drives the corporations onward in the first place is reproduced in the next place. Advertising campaigns in the new markets underplay health risks and foreground smoking with economic independence (since to smoke regularly you must be rich enough to literally burn money away) and high status. Young women are a strong target group because smoking is said to be associated with sexual freedom and weight loss.

Hardly any serious medical commentator challenges the proposition that smoking is associated with a variety of avoidable diseases that contribute to increasing mortality. Yet, on the supply side, industry multinationals have sought to enhance the position of this physically harmful practice in global leisure practice. Health questions have been met with enhanced branding exercises that link tobacco with liberation, affluence and – for women – sexual independence. The links with liberation and affluence are especially appealing to young people. They are one reason for the alarming rise in cigarette consumption in Asia and former Soviet bloc nations. In the midst of low-wage economies, with poor rates of unionization, smoking is an activity that encourages distraction and builds status.

What is the quality of personal 'freedom' extended here? Wolin (2008: 140–5) makes it painfully clear that town hall models of democracy have no real purchase for macro-political processes in Western society. These processes are dominated by a managed form of democracy, 'steeped in corporate culture' and intent on profit maximization above protecting the common good. By fusing smoking with liberation and success, tobacco multinationals are increasing the propensity, especially of young people in the developing world, to take on the habit. They are certainly contributing to ill-health and higher rates of mortality through smoking and secondary inhalation. While warnings against tobacco use have become widespread, they are countered by images that associate smoking with glamour, achievement and independence. Since smoking is now banned from public settings in many countries, it is safe to submit that it is overwhelmingly a leisure practice. But if medical opinion is overwhelmingly solid in proposing that smoking is harmful, the freedom extended by the tobacco industry to develop the practice is very dubious indeed.

Smoking, then, is a case of a leisure practice that literally kills you, which is permitted as a legitimate business for multinational corporations like Reynolds American, Philip Morris (Altria) and Lorillard. It is not only a matter of the effects on tobacco users or the people surrounding them, who are subject to the risk of secondary smoking. The people employed in these corporations are actively engaged in defending and extending (globally) a leisure practice that is known to risk health and life itself. They labour to promote a leisure activity that produces illness, premature mortality, pollution and adds to the burden of general taxation through health-care costs.

One wonders how they reconcile this with older notions of responsible citizenship and care for the other.

Resistance to smoking is not just a gut feeling. It is based upon the accumulation and dissemination of medical data which unequivocally demonstrates the link between smoking and health risk. Historically speaking, considerable labour has been devoted to these tasks. Even today, the citizen audience engages in personal research on the internet, in newspapers and on television programmes about the effects of smoking on health.

So the case of smoking reveals a dual process of labour expenditure. On the supply side, it entails workers producing wants and needs in consumers to expand the consumption of cigarettes in leisure time. On the demand side, it involves the citizen audience developing appetites for consuming cigarettes and, conversely, accumulating medical and health data to resist tobacco.

Was Veblen right?

When reference is made to the *labour of leisure*, then, it is partly the activity of resistance that one is driving at. That is, voluntary labour focused in leisure settings oriented to accumulating data on health and well-being. By definition, this is 'creative' in Sayers' (2007) sense of the term. For it uses self-directed energy and mental power against risk to prolong life. Modern life carries the requirement to be flexible and open to new data and new wants. As we shall see presently, Bauman (2007) refers to a 'liquid' quality in contemporary life. Basic to this is the notion that individuals are receptive to new information and impressionable.

Indeed, contemporary life abounds with stimuli upon individuals, concentrated in leisure relations, to equip themselves with information and learning to improve self-esteem, reduce personal risk and enhance social impact. In a society motored by network communication power the information that we get about health, diet, grooming, cultural and aesthetic literacy, ethical responsibility etc. is provided around the clock. Capitalizing on it requires individuals to expend a great deal of *labour*.

It is as well to acknowledge that the proposition that labour is expended in the service of leisure is not new. Thorstein Veblen (1934 [1899]) famously argued that urban-industrial society has a tendency to produce and sustain a leisure class who make a public show of avoiding any form of pecuniary labour. Of course, one could find plenty of examples in this class of the idle rich. However, according to Veblen, they are the exception to the rule. He argues that exemption involves a great deal of display. Further, in order to be *automatically convincing* and *beyond reproach*, display involves considerable labour. So the leisure class devotes time to pre-industrial pursuits (such as equestrianism or hunting), learning dead languages (Ancient Greek and Latin), engaging in charitable functions and throwing lavish entertainments (balls, sporting contests). The common denominator in all of these events is that they are no longer required by urban-industrial society. By cultivating them, the leisure class signals its freedom from the need to work. The display of this status differentiation is *labour intensive*. Hence, Veblen's (1934 [1899]) insistence that it is a mistake to regard the leisure class as idle. To be sure, it might be said that, functionally speaking, it provides a service to society in defending the standards of old-fashioned repose, courtliness and decorum that urban-industrial civilization drives down.

It is scarcely the case that this form of labour has disappeared from contemporary leisure practice. The rich have not abandoned pre-industrial forms (equestrianism, hunting, throwing lavish entertainment); while celanthropy – the bountiful charitable donation of money and time by the private power base – continues to be revered as a favoured mark of high social status (Bishop and Green, 2008). The ascent of self-made celanthropists based in the entertainment sector (Bono, Elton John, Angelina Jolie, Brad Pitt, Madonna, Celine Dion, Avril Lavigne, Jay Z) suggests that the adoption of charitable duties is now a precondition of true super-star status (Rojek, 2012).

Yet the ripples of investing labour in leisure are not confined to those who dress in ermine or reside in gated communities. Veblen (1934 [1899]) worried that the practice of conspicuous consumption indulged in by the leisure class would be aped by the succeeding social orders. If the elevation of waste exceeds the rate of production in society, the result is economic crisis and eventual collapse.

Veblen wrote before our knowledge of the environmental crisis caused by over-production and over-consumption solidified. Today, environmental collapse, centring on the unsustainable consumption of fossil fuels, probably poses a more serious long-term threat to the economy and society than do financial irregularities or liquidity. Nonetheless, conspicuous consumption has played a full role in creating environmental instability.

It is inappropriate to take this question on here, since it takes us away from the prime concerns of the current chapter. It is clear that, as Western society has become more affluent, and the system of network mass communications has become ubiquitous, the labour of leisure has multiplied.

The labour of leisure and the syndrome of consumerism

Accumulating status-enhancing data and cultivating practices to boost self-esteem and social impact are within the reach of anyone with a television or hand-held communication device. A routine and extensive component of ordinary leisure practice takes the form of absorbing data about status differentiation and commodity enhancement fit to increase self-esteem and social impact. Reality TV make-over shows, like *What Not to Wear*, *Extreme Makeover* and *Ambush Makeover*, are extreme examples. In addition to making celebrities of presenters like Trinny Woodall and Susannah Constantine, they enforce a strict discipline of received ideas about fashion, cosmetics and self-presentation onto a public that is directly addressed as inferior or, at least, wanting in these respects.

Make-over shows are one front of a vast leisure-based industry that concentrates upon saturating spectators with all kinds of make-over information relating, *inter alia*, to topics of health, diet, grooming, exercise, emotional management, cosmetics, romance, etiquette, child rearing and sexual practice. Entire satellite TV channels are dedicated to diet, exercise and self-improvement. Mainstream television and film deal with the same issues. Characters and presenters operate as informal life coaches, developing plots and narratives designed to re-orientate the citizen audience to accomplish a better, more fulfilling life. The consumption metaphysic has become intertwined with a complex narrative of self-help. The social consciousness of personal defects and qualities of character and embodiment that are *lacking* is so widespread as to be described as 'normal'. The consumer framework is dictated by the vested interests behind inverted totalitarianism. The agenda of self-improvement and social impact that it sustains coincides with the business and government requirements of the power base. By forcing people to see themselves as lacking, the power base naturally bewitches the citizen audience into developing consumer wants and needs in order to heal the lack.

In a series of works, Zygmunt Bauman (1990; 1998; 2007) has been concerned to demonstrate how modern life is afflicted with what he calls the *syndrome* of consumerism. While he seldom refers explicitly to leisure practice, it is clear that he regards leisure to be consolidated by consumption. There are many aspects to his argument. At its core is the proposition that consumer culture is not at all about choice or freedom. To be sure, outwardly it appears to provide a cornucopia of options and life possibilities. So much so that consumers have the illusion of gaining truly novel experiences and commodities. This confirms Wolin's (2008) standpoint that inverted totalitarianism demands that consumers believe that they are free, in order to pacify and regiment them.

Bauman (2000; 2005) uses the metaphor of 'liquid life' to convey how consumers sail in and out of a range of experiences that were formerly regarded as bounded and delineated. It is characterized by 'the feebleness, weakness, brevity and frailty of bonds and [the] inability to keep shape for very long' (Bauman in Rojek, 2004: 301).

In Bauman's sociology there is a heavy psychological price to pay so as to impose order on life. Indeed, it is not too much to state that, for him, the drive to control social and physical processes is the mother of melancholia. For in modern life every wall and every demarcation line is fated to fall down or be swept away by the irrepressible tendency to turn all solid things into liquid. The individual must be constantly open to new data and information, but it is our common fate to feel our security abandoned as new waves of data and information flow over us and sweep aside our old certainties.

This line of thinking applies directly to the question of leisure and consumer culture.

Consumer goods are designed to be purchased, enjoyed and discarded as new products come online. For Bauman, the ephemeral nature of consumption means that it can never be a genuine source of lasting fulfilment or satisfaction. Everything consumed presupposes its replacement: this is the ambivalence of consumer culture. As a result, the consumer is trapped on a treadmill of ever-changing wants and desires.

Again, from Wolin's (2008: 139) standpoint this suits the requirements of inverted totalitarianism because devoting energy to ceaseless consumption contributes to 'political demoralization and langour'. The consumer metaphysic privileges the notion that you are what you own and therefore shuts down options of cooperation and non-self-aggrandizement. It also creates the backlash of dead labour weighing upon the living, as we mentioned earlier. But the point to stress at this juncture of the discussion is the huge role that the consumer metaphysic/consumption syndrome plays in the necessary task (for the interests behind inverted totalitarianism) of political cynicism.

By the same token, to say that there is a design behind consumption suggests that the activity is governed by discernible ends. The chief end in question is, of course, the maximization of wealth for the interests that own and control the instruments of production, exchange and consumption. Here too, modernity's irrepressible tendency to turn solids into liquid eventually comes into play. The attempt to wring more wealth out of the earth and labour creates resistance in the form of dissenting social movements critical of environmental melt-down and economic crisis.

To come back centrally to the question of leisure and consumer culture, liquid life suggests an absence of anchors, moorings and guide ropes. To be truly liquid is to be rudderless and all at sea. Yet, while the modern experience of consumption truly shows that nothing lasts, it also expresses the adjoining tendency of seeking to impose order upon things by constantly being open to new data and information.

One irony of this, savoured by Bauman, is that the pell-mell rush to be personally relevant and personally differentiated conceals a standardizing drive. Inverted totalitarianism constantly conspires to fill everyone with the zest of difference and individuality but uses *the same means* to do so. Consider the case of fashion. It is subject to the law of perpetual change. At the same time its *raison d'être* is to make a personal statement. The force of this is mitigated when one realizes that everyone who buys and wears the same fashion is making the *same statement*. Nevertheless, while this statement is, in the nature of things, understood to be not everlasting, it affords finite shape and order in a sea of shapelessness and disorder.

This means that consumer culture under inverted totalitarianism is not akin to an 'anything goes' set of encounters. The goal of capitalist wealth accumulation canalizes experience to follow preferred directions, especially in relation to questions of personal expenditure and social conformity. The fixation on the commodity form means that consumers can never enjoy real fulfilment or enduring satisfaction. They are addicted to possessing commodities and experiences that are predicated on the enforced labour and low pay of others throughout the world. To submit to the world of commodities is to condemn oneself to the realization that consumption can never deliver replete experience. This is why Bauman (in Rojek, 2004) selects the noun 'syndrome' as an apposite description of modern consumer culture. It is also why the forms of leisure that are organized around this culture are incapable of delivering genuine fulfilment or satisfaction. To repeat, everything consumed presupposes its replacement.

The metaphor of liquid life suggests a lack of permanence and a fluid orientation to things and relationships. Because of this it may seem perverse to offer a solid connection between liquid life and the labour of leisure. For the latter term suggests discipline and dedication. We need only to remind ourselves of Stebbins's (2007) concept of serious leisure, with its insistence upon self-directed, goal-oriented behaviour, to see that a large sector of leisure relationships are not 'liquid' in the sense of going anywhere and mixing freely with whatever comes to pass.

However, there is a real connection between liquid life and the labour of leisure. It has to do with the business of making a statement and drawing a line, even in the midst of the full awareness that life is no longer solid and nothing lasts. To go into it is necessary in order to clarify and elucidate some of the main qualities that define leisure experience today. What are the issues here?

Liquid life: from habitus to habitat

The basic feature of liquidity is openness to experience. The questions of how we learn and exchange elements of exchange and develop standards of conduct are complex. What might explain this complexity? Sociologists have conventionally drawn on the concept of *habitus*, which, as they point out, is designed to convey the mental maps and ground rules of social conduct that we learn through socialization (Bourdieu, 1977). This equips individuals with a conscience and schema of self-regulation that operate automatically in social encounters. However, it is inflected by social factors of class, gender, religion, status and other social divisions. This is one source of complexity.

Another is that the conscience and schema of self-regulation that we acquire through socialization are not static. Automatic responses to situations and encounters may be compromised by common or garden influences such as new technologies or inter-generational change. An example may help to clarify what we mean here. In the 1990s, the use of sexist and racist language in rap and hip-hop was offensive to many humanists and democrats. However, in the under-25 demographic rap and hip-hop are now the most popular forms of music for both sexes and among all Western-based ethnicities (Rentfrow and Gosling, 2007; Rentfrow *et al.*, 2009). Now that the music is mainstream, the sexist, racist lyrics are prosaic.

The change in social mores, then, is another source of complexity. Social change brings its own challenges. What is taken for granted in one area may be reversed in another. What these conventional approaches tend to underestimate is that living a liquid modern life means that not only does habitus have a less constraining influence on us than it might have had in the past, but also today we are faced with some social changes that are monumental in their scope. What might explain this? One compelling answer lies in the idea that with the emergence of liquid modernity we have also witnessed a major shift in human consciousness.

What distinguishes human lives today from those of not so long ago is their utter contingency: no matter what our current circumstances or how certain we individually feel about our lives at the moment, things could always be different. We might have an experience in a couple of hours, next week or twenty years from now that will place us squarely in a new and previously unimagined place. One experience at the right moment might change everything. A liquid life might not always feel like a freely chosen one, and when considered over a period of time probably looks like a fairly stable existence; however, depending on our individual state of affairs, and who we might happen to meet, all of this can suddenly and unexpectedly change.

In other words, liquid modernity would appear to have converted *necessity* into *contingency-awareness*, which means that habitus is experienced as accidental rather than inevitable. Of course, liquid modern lives are not completely free of their social class, gender and ethnic statuses, but these markers of identity and difference flow into each other more than they did once upon a time in the not-too-distant past. The upshot of this is that today our lives have a more in-between, DIY ready-made feel about them, and to this extent that they are better understood as *individualized* existences. A liquid modern life, in other words, has no solid ontological status, something that is given, is inevitable, we are predisposed to or firmly believe in. Some lives are no doubt more liquid than others, but anyone's habitus is just something that is until further notice. In other words, it seems to fit us as a person who chooses to live this kind of life rather than another.

The bearing of 'generative principles' (Bourdieu, 1977) that produce and reproduce social practices is of a different order in liquid modernity. In Bauman's view, liquid modern consumers prefer to wear the more informal gear of *habitat* rather than the more regimental class uniform of habitus. Whereas habitus is uncomplicated in the sense that it is relatively fixed because it is predetermined by social class location, the habitat is 'a space of chaos and chronic *indeterminacy*' (Bauman, 1992: 193), which is a schema of self-regulation subjected to competing and often contradictory meaning-conferring claims that nonetheless appear equally contingent. The ontological status of liquid moderns is for this reason not one of 'durably installed generative practices' (Bourdieu, 1977), but one of under-determination, liquefaction and rootlessness. What this means is that our identities are neither given nor can they ever be confirmed once and for all.

As Bauman (2002) points out, casting society's members as individuals is the trademark of modernity. As he argues, though, this casting is no longer understood as a once-in-a-lifetime act; today casting ourselves is something that has to be re-enacted on a daily basis. Under inverted totalitarianism, Wolin (2008) holds that the state and corporations are the central casting agents. This 'positions' individuals, but it does not exactly deprive them of consciousness. Unlike previous generations, it is now left to us as individuals to carry the weight of the world on our shoulders; it is individuals who are first and foremost responsible for the world and for themselves. In other words, we are today compelled to decide the *meaning* of our own being and what we would like to do with our lives. In the process individualization has transformed human identity from a 'given' into a 'task'.

Lacking any inherited system of social norms, liquid modern lives are not so much guided by 'classificatory schemes' and 'ultimate values' (Bourdieu, 1977) as by the mission to find meaning in the world of consumers outside themselves: 'Information becomes a major resource, and experts the crucial brokers of all self-assembly' (Bauman, 1992: 196). For Wolin (2008), under inverted totalitarianism the distribution of media is rigged to favour the vested interests. Self-assembly varies from individual to individual, depending mostly on the social, cultural and economic capital that a given individual commands, but there is one motivation that binds all of us together. This is not Socrates' immense undertaking – 'how to live?'– but 'how to be happy?' In liquid modernity, the desire to be happy is ubiquitous and insatiable; it becomes not just a possibility or even choice but a 'requirement and a duty' (Bruckner, 2010). The consumer metaphysic equates happiness with consumption.

So the injunction to be happy reinforces inverted totalitarianism by strengthening the drive to consume.

In order to be regarded as competent, relevant social actors need to recognize and effectively manage the complexities identified above. The concepts of emotional intelligence and emotional labour have emerged as ways of understanding how we identify and handle complexities. Emotional intelligence refers to the knowledge, skills and other capabilities involved in practising suitable behaviour according to social context. In order to be seen as competent, relevant and credible, humans need to present in social settings in ways that are regarded to be appropriate. This requires a good deal of knowledge and work.

The technologies and people skills involved here are referred to as emotional labour. By technologies, we mean the presentation of embodiment, including grooming, cosmetics, dress sense, diet, manners and decorum, designed to communicate the impression of appropriate behaviour in social settings.

By people skills, we mean forms of address, informal gestures designed to put people at their ease and confidence-building measures of various sorts.

These social attributes have grown more significant as post-war society has moved into a condition in which emotional disclosure, showing that you are in touch with your deep feelings, is highly valued. Avoiding denial and acknowledging vulnerability have become significant markers of competence, credibility and relevance. Empathy and flexibility are cherished more preciously than emotional autonomy and intransigence.

The notion that the self is fragile and vulnerable is now part of common currency. Efforts to discount or devalue it are scorned. In education, health management, community work, policing and government, personal vulnerabilities and the socio-economic context behind behaviour are transparent. Severe parenting, uncaring employers and governments that do not listen are repudiated. Instead, the accent is upon displaying responsible, balanced parenting, articulating care and governments that listen.

This connects up with keeping in touch with issues of health, diet and risk assessment. Part of emotional intelligence and emotional labour is looking good, feeling confident about yourself and making the most of your life in order to find happiness. In a culture that is increasingly organized around visual cues and data flows, impression management possesses keen value. The exhibition of responsibility, care and listening are the cornerstones of effective self-presentation and productive social encounters.

Yet all of these competences are constantly being challenged by the existential situation of individuals, which, as we have seen, is fast and fluid. Identity needs to be self-constituted continually, largely on the basis of trial and error (Bauman, 1992: 193). In the search for meaning, identity becomes palimpsest and permanently changing but not developing in any clear direction. At any given time, the constitution of identity involves the 'disassembly' of some existing elements and the 'self-assembly' of new ones.

The only constant in all of this is the body – our 'friend, our sole skiff on Earth, a loyal companion that we should support and care for' (Bruckner, 2010: 30) – to whom we have to devote continual attention. The labour that this involves might still 'performed as if it is an absolute end in itself', as Max Weber suggested, but it is no longer *interiorized* in the consciousness through the work ethic. To expand some basic insights outlined by Debray (2007), unbending reflexive individualization has led to a shift in the subjective centre of gravity from human consciousness to the realm of the corporeal, which is valued in and for itself and has a *material* significance to which we feel a sense of moral obligation. In other words, the legitimating reference for the work ethic is no longer *spiritual* (i.e. God tells me it is sacred) or an *ideal* (i.e. my consciousness tells me it is true) but *effective* (i.e. my body shows me it works).

The point today is to be 'into' your body which is a 'scenario' (Baudrillard, 1989) to be maximized through a series of self-controlling and self-enhancing activities (jogging, aerobics, dieting) that would surely have been resented had they been imposed by some external agency. Accordingly, these fitness regimens are 'not perceived as externally imposed, cumbersome and resented necessities, but as manifestos of the [individual's] freedom. Their heteronomy, once blatant through coercion, now hides behind seduction' (Bauman, 1992: 194). What this suggests is that the *work ethic* is better expressed as the *labour of leisure*, which is an individualized phenomenon (rather than a mass social one) *exteriorized* onto the body and performed for no other reason than that it is *effective*.

What it also demonstrates is that leisure is the pivotal setting in which emotional intelligence grows and emotional labour skills are learned. Television, listening to recorded music, using the internet and reading magazines are primary leisure pursuits (Page and Connell, 2010). Even casual interaction with them invests individuals with hints and tips about effective people skills, grooming, deportment and discourse. Indeed, lacking a pre-designed life-project, we crave orientation points to guide us through the life course. These are provided by celebrities who have emerged as *informal life coaches*, equipping us with role models and laying down standards of interpersonal etiquette that are emulated from the living room or browsing a hand-held device (Rojek, 2012). These forms of leisure are best seen as neither rest nor relaxation. Rather, they exert a *pedagogic* function over the individual. Effective emotional intelligence and emotional labour require cultural literacy. Leisure is a setting in which exposure to cultural stimuli is maximized. It is here that people assemble the building blocks of knowledge and acquire the skills that enable them to construct a persona that is valued as competent, credible and relevant. Leisure, it might be said, is the power-house for expanding cultural literacy. Through it, we submit to pedagogies that improve emotional intelligence and enhance emotional labour.

Morally, these influences supply people with a horizon of emotional achievement to which they are encouraged to aspire, and socially, they elicit conformity. Informal counselling and informal life coaching contribute to an atomized view of humanity in which individuals are portrayed as having 'their' isolated problems, quite separate from wider structural questions in society. Informal networks of emotional support have been displaced and devalued by the triumph of professional life coaching and diagnosis. The concept of power structures beyond the family, and destructive chains of interdependence that injure and mortify people, are obscured by the strong focus upon universal emotional vulnerability and the worth of subjective responsibility (Furedi, 2004).

Conclusion

There is a central paradox at the core of pedagogic leisure. Using leisure to advance emotional competence and self-control is practised as a form of self-improvement in a liquid modern setting where discontent with the world is tied intimately to personal discontent, and the sense of 'defects' or a general 'lack' in oneself is strongly reinforced by the corporate–state nexus (Wolin, 2008). By acquiring this type of emotional intelligence and developing the accomplishments of effective emotional labour we aim to make ourselves credible, worthwhile, relevant individuals. However, in doing so, we follow step-by-step programmes that have a homogenizing effect. The more 'individual' we become in following them, the more we end up like everyone else pursuing the same track. Moreover, while informal (and formal) life coaching and counselling encourage individuals to believe that they find their own way to solving the personal problems that prevent them from being happy, in reality, pedagogy is directed learning. Individuals do not reach their solutions through self-directed emotional intelligence and emotional labour. Instead, they are encouraged to 'make up their own minds' in approved and guided ways. Again, this suits the interests of inverted totalitarianism because it gives the illusions of individual freedom and personal growth while nailing down individuals to political demoralization and languor.

However, central to Wolin's (2008) account of inverted totalitarianism is the proposition that there are always cleavages and divisions in the power base that support resistance and opposition. To come back to Sayers' (2007) position, creativity is the seat of human labour. Inverted totalitarianism's attempt to close down creativity by the double process of spreading alienated labour and the consumer metaphysic has structural limits.

When these limits are reached, the conflicts and fissures in the power base become more well defined. Given the depth of the financial crisis that has beset the system since 2008, there is every reason to suppose that one set of structural limits has been reached. In the words of Barbara Ehrenreich (2009: 8):

> The consumer culture encourages individuals to want more – cars, larger homes, television sets, cell phones, gadgets of all kinds – and positive thinking is ready at hand to tell them they deserve more and can have it if they really want it and are willing to make the effort to get it. Meanwhile, in a competitive business world, the companies that manufacture these goods and provide the paychecks that purchase them have no alternative but to grow. If you don't steadily increase market share and profits, you risk being driven out of business and swallowed by a larger enterprise. Perpetual growth, whether of a particular company or entire economy, is of course an absurdity.

Upon the bricks of this absurdity, over three decades of deregulation, de-unionization, privatization and free trade agreements have unfurled, with the assent of both right- and left-wing governments. Free market principles have conquered universities, hospitals, the post office, museums, art galleries, national utilities provision and national transport systems.

Many liberal and middle-ground pundits predicted that the 2008 crash would profoundly and irrevocably discredit the arguments of the New Right. As Tom Frank (2012) cogently submits, precisely the opposite is the case. The New Right has not abandoned market logic. On the contrary, it has re-energized around the thesis that the 2008 crash happened because the doctrine of the New Right was not pursued with sufficient exactitude. The solution is to redouble the essentials of the New Right case and to extend them with unfaltering determination.

The result is likely to be an intensification of the economic crisis. The power grab will be restricted to the already hugely privileged power base. The have-nots will get what the New Right believes they deserve: less.

Leaving aside New Right bluster and mindless ballyhoo that, especially in the USA, accompanies the cry of 'individual liberty', the days of over-production and over-consumption are drawing to a natural close because the resources of the planet are dangerously depleted. Liquid life (and inverted totalitarianism) is coming up against structural barriers that cannot be redefined and recast to make people happy. The 'smile or die' philosophy that has put inverted totalitarianism in good stead in the post-war period loses credibility in a global scenario where oil prices are volatile, food prices are rising and the effects of climate change are unpredictable (Ehrenreich, 2009).

Pedagogic leisure teaches you how to consume, but it can also teach you how to resist. Our hope for the future lies in the role that the labour of leisure can play in making people understand better how the world really works and act accordingly. On the whole, we think that the progressive claims for the Occupy movement are exaggerated (Gitlin, 2012). We are dubious that a social force that purports to be 'leaderless', 'structureless' and makes a fetish of discarding anything that resembles 'traditional politics' is capable of anything more than an emotional outburst. At the same time, we maintain that the emotional outburst does have good pedagogic consequences. The lesson that Occupy taught society is that *we are us*.[7] That message of interconnectedness in our shared condition and fate is timely. It is the pretext for directing the labour of leisure to expose how inverted totalitarianism draws lines around popular notions of freedom, choice and self-determination. Freedom is for the birds, but learning the place of entrapment and mystification in leisure practice is a task for humans. We entreat more and more to join us in the practical and theoretical taking on of this task. Only then will the study of leisure move from a position in which questions of common interest and a shared future cease to be matters of presumed intimacy and become concrete reality.

Notes

1   The old message of 'the leisure society' theorists of the 1960s and 1970s is that automation and scientific management will produce the end of work and leisure for all. This has not come to pass, but the residue of this thinking covers Leisure Studies even today – especially in the most powerful concentration of power in the discipline: the USA.

2   In the Marxist tradition the productive power of labour is not experienced as alienation if its means and ends are the common interest. In Marx's (1959: 820) original discussion of the realms of necessity and freedom, it is absolutely clear that necessary labour is a prerequisite of all forms of society. However, when it is devoted to the common interest, rather than the sectional interests of the ruling class, it loses its character of being 'forced' and externally 'dictated'. For Marx, the creativity that is absent in general labour under capitalism would be regained if the labour of each were given for the well-being of all.

3   The term 'invisible government' is borrowed from Edward Bernays (1928). Bernays is the acknowledged 'father of public relations'. He introduced the term to apply to the backroom staff of professional opinion makers and developers of people skills. Their task is to combine the interests of the people with political representatives capable of directing society into directions of mutual benefit. He had in mind mass-opinion researchers, economists, image makers, communication analysts and, of course, public relations experts. There is almost a complete absence of interest in Bernays in inequalities and power differences in society which make the notion of 'mutual interest' inherently problematic. His meaning of invisible government is innocent and technocratic. Nonetheless, if one turns it around and uses it to apply to the clandestine relations of lobbying, cronyism and clientism among the financial, corporate and political power base, the term is invested with a new, more disturbing meaning. For this reason, we have used it in this chapter.

4   Why are there no sociological studies of these public opinion makers? They present themselves as the champions of the common man, yet express no mandate, do not put themselves forward for election and are essentially unaccountable (in the way that billionaires can be essentially unaccountable to the needs and interests of ordinary people). It is odd that the individual agents who do most to frame the horizons of the world that we inhabit remain as enigmatic and remote as the veritable Houses of Plantagenet and Bourbon.

5   The term 'consumer metaphysic' is of course an adaptation of C. Wright Mills' famous criticism of the New Left that identified labour (the proletariat) as the key agent of historical change. We are using the term 'consumer metaphysic' here to refer to the process through which inverted totalitarianism bewitches the consumer to think of life as commodity culture. You *are* what you *own*.

6   Of course, the movement is much more than that. It is anti-war, anti-racism, anti-sexism, anti-capitalist, pro-environment and pro-equal sexual rights. It regards itself as a populist movement. The 'Declaration of the Occupation of New York City' (2011) stated that it was dedicated to ending mass injustice, guaranteeing civil and workers' rights, spreading co-operation, opposing the power of what came later, to be called 'the 1%' (Lang and Lang Levitsky, 2012: 49–51).

7   On a visit to Melbourne in November of 2011, one of us (Rojek) saw the words 'We Are Us' chalked on the pavement on Spring Street adjoining old Parliament House and the Treasury Gardens. The Gardens were partly inhabited by Occupy protesters. In our minds the phrase memorably encapsulates the triumph and illusions of Occupy. The triumph rests in the conviction that the system must change for the good of 'the 99%'. The illusion is that it will combust spontaneously. The conquest of the vested interests requires more than agitation and action. It requires organization and leadership, not least because the 1% are unlikely to surrender their privilege without armed resistance.

References

Baudrillard, J. (1989) *America*. London: Verso.

Bauman, Z. (1990) *Thinking Sociologically*. Oxford: Blackwell.

Bauman, Z. (1992) *Intimations of Postmodernity*. London: Routledge.

Bauman, Z. (1998) *Work, Consumerism and the New Poor*. Buckingham: Open University Press.

Bauman, Z. (2000) *Liquid Modernity*. Cambridge: Polity Press.

Bauman, Z. (2002) 'Foreword: Individually, Together', in U. Beck and E. Beck-Gernsheim *Individualization*. London: Sage.

Bauman, Z. (2005) *Liquid Life*. Cambridge: Polity Press.

Bauman, Z. (2007) *Consuming Life*. Cambridge: Polity Press.

Bernays, E. (1928) *Propaganda*. New York: Ig Books.

Bishop, M. and Green, M. (2008) *Philanthrocapitalism*. London: A&C Black.

Bourdieu, P. (1977) *Outline of a Theory of Practice*. (Trans. R. Nice). Cambridge: Cambridge University Press.

Bruckner, P. (2010) *Perpetual Euphoria: The Duty to be Happy*. (Trans. S. Rendall). Princeton: Princeton University Press.

Butsch, R. (2008) *The Citizen Crowd*. London: Routledge.

Castells, M. (2009) *Communication Power*. Oxford: Oxford University Press.

Debray, R. (2007) 'Socialism: A Life-Cycle', *New Left Review* 46 (July/August): 5–28.

Dobson, R. (2006) 'US Cigarette Consumption Falls to Lowest Point since 1951,' *British Medical Journal* 332 (7543): 687, 25 March.

Economist (2007) 'Asia: Can't Kick the Habit; Smoking in Asia', 22 September.

Ehrenreich, B. (2009) *Smile Or Die: How Positive Thinking Fooled America and the World*. London: Granta.

Frank, T. (1997) *The Conquest of Cool*. Chicago, Chicago: University Press.

Frank, T. (2012) *Pity the Billionaire: The Hard-Times Swindle and the Unlikely Comeback of the Right*. New York: Metropolitan Books.

Furedi, F. (2004) *Therapy Culture*. London: Routledge.

Gitlin, T. (2012) *Occupy Nation*. New York: itBooks.

Habermas, J. (1989) *The Structural Transformation of the Public Sphere: An Inquiry into a Category of Bourgeois Society*. Cambridge: Polity Press.

Lang, A. S. and Lang Levistky, D. (eds) (2012) *Dreaming in Public. Building the Occupy Movement*. Oxford: New International.

Marx, K. (1959) *Capital*, Volume 3. London: Lawrence & Wishart.

McGuigan, J. (2009) *Cool Capitalism*. London: Pluto.

Mushtaq, N., Mushtaq, S., and Beebe, L. (2011) 'Economics of Tobacco Control in Pakistan', *Tobacco Control* 20: 431–435.

Office of National Statistics (UK) (2012) *General Lifestyle Overview: A Report on the 2010 General Lifestyle Survey*. London: HMSO.

Page, S. and Connell, J. (2010) *Leisure: An Introduction*. London: Prentice-Hall.

Rentfrow, P. J. and Gosling, S. D. (2007) 'The Content and Validity of Stereotypes about Fans of 14 Music Genres', *Psychology of Music* 35: 306–326.

Rentfrow, P. J., McDonald, J. A., and Oldmeadow, J. A. (2009) 'You Are What You Listen To: Young People's Stereotypes about Music Fans', *Group Processes and Intergroup Relations* 12: 329–344.

Rojek, C. (2004) 'The Consumerist Syndrome in Contemporary Society: An Interview with Zygmunt Bauman', *Journal of Consumer Culture* 4 (3) 291–312.

Rojek, C. (2012) *Fame Attack: The Inflation of Celebrity and its Consequences*. London: Bloomsbury Academic.

Sayers, S. (2007) *Marxism and Human Nature*. London: Routledge.

Srinivas, K. and Rao, B. (2009) 'Explaining Cross-Country Variation in Cigarette Consumption', *Tobacco Induced Diseases* 5 (1) 1.

Stebbins, R.A. (2007) *Serious Leisure: A Perspective for Our Time*. New Jersey: Transaction Publishers.

Veblen, T. (1934 [1899]) *Theory of the Leisure Class: An Economic Study in the Evolution of Institutions*. New York: Modern Library.

Wade, B., Merrill, R., and Lindsay, G. (2010) 'Cigarette Pack Warning Labels in Russia: How Graphic Should They Be?', *European Journal of Public Health* 21 (3) 366–372.

WHO (2008) *Convention on Tobacco Control*. Geneva: WHO.

Wolin, S.S. (2008) *Democracy Incorporated*. Princeton: Princeton University Press.

47

VIRTUAL LEISURE

Garry Crawford

Over recent decades the word 'virtual' has been a common prefix, placed in front of many activities to suggest that computers, or other information communication technologies, are involved in mediating a particular experience. However, this has undoubtedly been most commonly seen in relation to leisure practices, such as where playing sport-related video games becomes commonly labelled as 'virtual sports' (e.g. Leonard, 2009), online gambling as 'virtual gaming' (e.g. thevirtualgames.com), or online social networking sites and persistent worlds (e.g. Second Life) as providing links to our 'virtual friends' (e.g. Merchant, 2001). This chapter provides an introduction to key debates and literatures on the role of the 'virtual' within contemporary leisure practices. It begins with a brief consideration of the origins of the prefix 'virtual' and, in particular, its derivation from the concept of 'virtual reality', and the development of associated leisure technologies, such as the Internet and video games. The chapter then considers key debates that highlight the impact that information communication technologies have had on the nature of society, and both the benefits and dangers that these potentially bring. Finally, the chapter questions the validity of technologically deterministic accounts that seek to either praise or question the impact of technology, and suggests instead that a more profitable way forward is to consider the role of these (increasingly mundane) technologies as embedded within the patterns of everyday life.

Considering the virtual

'Virtual reality' (or VR) is generally defined as the idea of occupying spaces or personas outside of the 'real world'. However, the concept of 'virtual reality' is not a new idea. The origins of the term are usually attributed to the French playwright Antonin Artaud and his 1938 book *The Theatre and Its Double* (Davis, 1998). In this book Artaud describes the theatre as 'la réalite virtuelle', or a virtual reality in which the drama of the theatre creates a world beyond the ordinary and the everyday.

The central role of technology in creating virtual reality emerges most notably in the cyberpunk fiction of the early 1980s. Of course, the theme of technology in literature is not new. The eponymous hero of Miguel de Cervantes' 1605 *Don Quixote* famously faced off against a mechanical, clanking windmill, while Mary Shelley's *Frankenstein* is a stark warning against the excesses of scientific advancement; amongst countless other examples.

However, it was the cyberpunk genre that most vividly explored and popularized a techno-logically advanced dystopian future which blurred the boundaries between the 'real' and the 'unreal' as 'cyborgs' (human–machine hybrids) stretched the limits of our known world and the possibilities within this (Longhurst *et al.*, 2008). In particular, it is Damien Broderick's 1982 science fiction novel *The Judas Mandala* that is frequently attributed with being the first book to utilize the term 'virtual reality' to describe technology-enabled presence. Ideas of technology-enabled alternative realities have since become a popular and ever-present theme in modern science fiction literature, as well as being popularized in films such as *Brainstorm* (1983), *The Lawnmower Man* (1992), *eXistenZ* (1999) and, probably most famously, *The Matrix* trilogy (1999; 2003; and 2003).

As with most science 'fiction', there are elements of science 'fact' that feed into and inform these fantasy worlds, and certainly the late 1980s and early 1990s saw the emergence of many new technologies that were firing the imaginations of novelists, filmmakers, social commentators and academics alike. In particular, in the 1980s 'virtual reality' technologies were advanced greatly and popularized by the work of the American computer scientist Jaron Lanier, whose company, VPL Research Inc., was the first to sell VR goggles and gloves, which allowed users to interact with a multi-sensory computer-generated environ-ment (see Burdea and Coiffet, 1994). But of course Lanier was not alone in developing and advancing high-end technologically mediated environments, and there continues to be very active research in both the commercial and academic sectors in developing and advancing forms of VR technologies.

Of notable importance here is also the advent of the Internet. It is generally accepted that the origins of the Internet can be found in the loose conglomerate of computer networks that developed around the Advanced Research Projects Agency Network (ARPANET), created by the Defense Advanced Research Projects Agency (DARPA) of the United States Department of Defense in the late 1960s (Gere, 2008). This was helped further by the development of a number of Internet protocols for the transmission of data in the 1970s, and most notably 'Ethernet', developed at Harvard University in 1974 (Crawford *et al.*, 2011). However, it seems that, whenever and wherever possible, people will always strive to find ways of playing with, and gaining pleasure from, new technologies. Even the most 'serious' of technologies, such as weapons, become utilized as the basis of sport, leisure and fun, such as target shooting. As it seems was the case for the early days of the Internet; initially devel-oped for military purposes, it was social networking, video gaming, and then, later, music, video and pornography, that were crucial in cementing the significance of the Internet within contemporary leisure patterns (Crawford *et al.*, 2011).

Largely concurrent, and often interlinked with the development of the Internet, is the rise of video games. What are generally seen as the first video games, such as William Higinbotham's *Tennis for Two* and Steve Russell and colleagues' *Spacewar!*, were in the late 1950s and 1960s similarly being developed in university computer laboratories, and then distributed to others over fledgling computer networks (Crawford *et al.*, 2011). Of particular note here is the development of the game *MUD*. *MUD* (which gave its name to a genre of games) was a text-based adventure game, that is to say, players were presented with written descriptions of an environment, which they responded to by typing in a number of pre-set options – such as 'go west' or 'look'. Though not the first text-based adventure game (that mantle is normally attributed to the game *Adventure*, developed a few years earlier in 1975 by Will Crowther), *MUD* was the first multiplayer online adventure game, and T.L. Taylor (2006: 23) describes this game as signalling 'a new turn in which multi-user spaces were to become one of the most innovative developments within internet technologies and certainly a genre that excited many computer users'. Importantly, *MUD* also paved the way for the closely linked phenomena of multi-user 'persistent' (sometimes called 'virtual') worlds, such as the hugely popular Second Life.

Today, new[1] information communication technologies have grown to play an increasingly central role within contemporary social and cultural life and, consequently, have become an important area of social and academic debate.

Understanding new technologies

Discussions of the impact of technology on society are far from new. For example, Karl Marx, writing in the mid-1800s, argued that the 'mode of production', in other words technologies of production (e.g. factories), was crucial in shaping the social relations and culture within that particular society. Likewise, Heidegger (1977) expands upon the work of Marx, but suggests that the techniques and knowledge associated with technologies also play a significant role in shaping the nature of society and culture (Longhurst *et al.*, 2008). But of course, the impact of technology on society predates even the Industrial Revolution; as the ability to craft and use tools, construct dwellings, the invention of the wheel, gunpowder and the printing press, along with an almost endless list of historical and ancient technologies, have all significantly shaped human culture.

However, from around the late 1950s and 1960s the idea began to emerge that we were shifting into a new historical period, characterized by new forms of society and culture based around new information communication technologies and the importance of the transfer and ownership of information and knowledge. In particular, the Austrian economist Fritz Machlup in 1958 suggested that we were witnessing a shift towards a new economy, based around 'knowledge industries'. Similarly, a few years later Peter Drucker (1968) noted the shift in employment trends away from 'manual' labour towards 'knowledge work' (Longhurst *et al.*, 2008), and Manuel Castells, in his three-volume work *The Information Age: Economy, Society and Culture* (Castells, 1996; 1997; 1998), argues that since the 1980s a new type of economy and society has developed. For Castells, while societies remain capitalist in nature, what has changed is a shift away from an 'industrial mode of development' and towards an 'informational mode of development'. At the centre of this informational mode of development are global networks, and Castells terms the development of this new social structure a 'network society' (Longhurst *et al.*, 2008).

A key factor in this societal development is processes of 'digitalization' (Flew, 2002). Digitalization can be understood as a shift away from analogue technologies, towards the storage, delivery and reception of information in digital forms – that is to say, in binary code. The simplest illustration of the difference between analogue and digital technology is radio. Analogue radios carry information on radio waves, which modulate (vary up and down) either in strength (AM) or in frequency (FM). However, there is only a limited range of frequency or strength variations that can be used to carry information. Hence, digital radio, though still using modulation, sends information in binary code, which allows for the transmission of more information (Longhurst *et al.*, 2008).

Digitalization has played a key role in the transformation of many leisure forms, such as radio, photography, music and film (to give but a few examples), but more profoundly it has greatly increased our access to information. Media, and their messages, are no longer restricted to a solitary voice, of, say, the BBC as it was in 1950s Britain, but rather, audiences have access to an almost endless stream of media and information, across a multitude of television and radio channels, billions of websites and a constantly shifting and growing mediascape beyond. Hence, Lyotard (1984) argues that in an information age there has been a decline in the belief of one truth or one knowledge – a decline in grand or metanarratives.

For many writers, like Howard Rheingold (1991; 1994), Sherry Turkle (1995), George Gilder (1990), Jonathan Emord (1991) and Nicolas Negroponte (1995), to name but a few, this new information age is seen as heralding new opportunities for experiences and participation beyond the everyday and the mundane, and beyond the social power structures that constrain them. For example, in 1995 the American sociologist Sherry Turkle argued that the Internet has allowed people to play with their identities and personas, providing a new opportunity to project their fantasies and ideas into this 'virtual reality'. As Kerr *et al.* (2004: 15) write:

> New media ... allow for and foster the users' experimentation with alternative identities (Turkle 1995). This is true for computer games as well as internet chat rooms etc. The pleasure [is] of leaving one's identity behind and taking on someone else's ...
>
> (Kerr *et al.*, 2004: 15 cited in Crawford, 2012: 78)

Similar arguments can also be seen in the work of Pierre Lévy (1997), who suggests that users of new information communication technologies are becoming part of a participatory and democratic 'knowledge community' – networking, communicating, sharing ideas and knowledge online.

Lévy (1997) argues there has been a decline in the power and pull of what he terms 'organized' social groups, such as nation and religion, as well as 'organic' groups, such as the family and clans, which have been replaced by 'self-organized' groups. These self-organized groups, Lévy suggests, are held together by shared patterns of production and mutual knowledge, or what he terms a 'collective intelligence'. These ideas have been picked up most notably by the media scholar Henry Jenkins (2006a: 140), who argues that Lévy's collective intelligence is not the same as the dystopian image of the 'hive mind', where individual thought and voices are suppressed, but, rather, this is more egalitarian, and 'far from demanding conformity, the new knowledge culture is enlivened by mutual ways of knowing'. For Jenkins, key examples of this include video gamers, bloggers and cult media fans, who are no longer content with simply consuming media, but instead are active participants in seeking out 'niche' interests and are creative and co-productive through their gameplay, surfing and blogging. To illustrate his argument, Jenkins (2006a) provides a number of examples of the creative input of video gamers, such as how LucasArts included would-be players in the development process of its new *Star Wars* massively multiplayer online role-playing game *Star Wars Galaxies*, how Maxis encourages 'grassroots' production of game skins and add-ons for its *The Sims* game series, and also the (often cited) example of the 'player-created' game modification (of the Valve game *Half-Life*) *Counter-Strike*.

Certainly, it is evident that new information communication technologies, such as the Internet and video games, do allow users new forms of leisure, new ways of gathering information and new opportunities for social networking and interacting (both with technologies and with others). In particular, the evolution of the Internet has seen the rapidly expanding popularity of websites that revolve primarily around user-generated content, such as YouTube, Facebook, Twitter and 'blogs' (short for 'web-logs', which are online diaries). This has led some to suggest that the Internet has now evolved into what is sometimes referred to as the 'Web 2.0'. This refers to the evolution of the nature and architecture of the web to incorporate more sites such as social networking sites, blogs and wikis (websites that allows users to edit and add to content, such as online encyclopaedias like

Wikipedia), as well as a growth in a more participatory form of media use (as outlined by Jenkins 2006a; 2006b).

Similarly, many writers have argued that video games have changed the way that individuals interact with and use media.[2] In particular, many early writers on video games, such as Chris Crawford (1982) and Loftus and Loftus (1983), suggest that video games have provided new modes of engagement. In this argument, audiences of older media forms such as television and books are cast as passive recipients of media texts, while video gamers are portrayed as key participants, if not co-authors, in their gaming experience. For example, as Loftus and Loftus (1983: 41) argue, 'when we watch a movie or read a book, we passively observe the fantasies. When we play a computer game, we actively participate in the fantasy world created by the game' (cited in Newman 2004: 94). Similarly, Douglas Rushkoff (1999) describes video games as a revolution in youth culture; where once audiences simply received media, now gamers can be seen as actively shaping what they see on the screen. For Rushkoff, video gaming is about 'world creation', which subverts traditional hierarchies of control.

It is also the case that new information communication technologies are having a profound effect on other forms of leisure and entertainment. For example, video game technologies have expanded the possibilities and realms of sports participation and sports spectating. For instance, Atkinson (2007) highlights how leisure establishments have been set up which allow golfers to hit a ball toward large screens and see the flight of the ball continue on, while similar machines allow people to bat against simulated Major League Baseball pitchers, or participate in numerous other sporting activities. Similarly, Syed and Miah (2006) talk about the near-future possibilities of being able to play sports 'Matrix-style': in other words, where the player is plugged into a full sensory-immersed (VR) environment. Electronic readers, such as Amazon's Kindle and Apple's iPad are transforming the world of publishing. Though the death of print publishing, which has been forecast by many (see, for example, Mims, 2010), may still not be here, it is evident that many publishers, particularly newspapers and magazines, have sought to make their periodicals more 'interactive' and to offer greater video content in order to appeal to the growing market of people who browse these on tablet computers and e-book readers. Also, video games have heavily influenced the style and nature of many films. In that, not only have we seen a plethora of films based upon video games, such as *Max Payne* and *Resident Evil*, but other films have very obviously drawn on video game themes, such as utilizing the 'beat 'em up' format in *Scott Pilgrim versus the World*, or films like *Sucker Punch* closely conform to video game aesthetics, narratives and character types (Crawford, 2012). The examples could go on and on, as the ways in which new media and technologies are changing leisure practices and patterns are an almost endless list.

However, equally, it is important not to get too carried away in the euphoria for new information communication technologies that is expressed by many writers, nor to seek to ignore patterns of continuity in an attempt to highlight all that is 'new' about 'new' media and technologies. Certainly, many writers, such as Henry Jenkins and Pierre Lévy, have been criticized for being overly optimistic and celebratory of the role of new technology in empowering users; and Ross and Nightingale (2003: 148) go as far as to describe Jenkins as 'utopian' in his outlook. For example, Jenkins' (2006a) use of the creation of *Counter-Strike* as a key illustration of participatory video game culture is highlighted by Dovey and Kennedy (2006) as a very much over-romanticized case which usually portrays the game as the product of one lucky and plucky Canadian student, Minh 'Gooseman' Le. However, *Counter-Strike*, as with most examples of so-called 'amateur' produced software, such as most share- and freeware, was created by an organized and highly skilled team of programmers.

May (2002) argues that this form of 'gift-giving', that is to say, producing goods such as software for free, is not an example of an increasing democratization but, rather, a key feature of a new capitalist economy. It is through the production of cultural products such as video game modification and add-ons that amateur and semi-professional producers demonstrate and audition their skills in an increasingly competitive corporate market-place. This productivity, May (2003: 98) argues, is largely driven by the 'promotion of self-interest'. It is, moreover, also a culture readily exploited by media corporations, who are happy to select and use, free of charge, the fruits of the labour of 'amateur' producers, and occasionally elevate some to positions within their companies once they have proved their worth; such as happened with Minh Le.

The heralding by authors such as Jenkins and Lévy, and the early work of Turkle, of the opportunities of an information age, has frequently been countered by more sceptical or even at times dystopian readings of the impact of contemporary and future technologies. One of the most cited considerations of the negative consequences of a new information age is the work of Neil Postman. Postman in 1993 suggested that contemporary society could be seen as 'Technopoly'; that is to say, a society dominated and controlled through new technological forms. This is a society dominated by a blind faith in science and technology, yet without any purpose or meaning. This is 'progress without limits', where we are producing increasingly vast quantities of information, but without any means of evaluating this. The prime example of this is the computer, which Postman sees as undermining education. The computer has merely increased our reliance upon it, which perpetuates the creation of more and more information but undermines and replaces group learning, cooperation and social reasonability. As Postman (1993: 71) wrote: 'Technopoly is a state of culture. It is also a state of mind. It consists in the deification of technology, which means that the culture seeks its authorization in technology, finds its satisfactions in technology, and takes its orders from technology.'

New information communication technologies, such as the Internet, have also been criticized as both a consequence of and a contributor to the individualization of society. In particular, the later work of Sherry Turkle (2011) shifts somewhat away from her early enthusiasm, towards a much more cautionary tone which highlights the anti-social nature of new technology usage. Turkle's key argument in her 2011 book, *Alone Together*, is summed up by its subtitle: *why we expect more from technology and less from each other*. For Turkle, we have become too reliant on machines, and too commonly seek connections with people online rather than with those in front of us. In a recent interview she argued that 'we have inspiring and enhancing technologies, yet we have allowed them to diminish us' (Harris, 2011: 17).

Many of these arguments appear to reflect the concerns of Raymond Williams (1974), who suggested that individuals living in Western consumerist nations had undergone a 'mobile privatization', which sees their primary connection to the world as existing through media outlets, such as television. Moreover, Schell (2010) suggests that, increasingly, new information communication technologies are seeking to address people's disconnection with the world by offering them more 'authentic' experiences. For example, terms such as 'realistic' and 'authentic' have become synonymous with the marketing of video games; where games such as *Wii Sports* seek to replicate the movements and actions of sports such as tennis, bowling and boxing, and football management games such as *Football Manager* become more complex each year, attempting to get closer to what it is like to be a *real* manager of a professional football team – all of which is summed up most succinctly by the sports game division of Electronic Arts (EA Sports), which declares its games' authenticity with the motto 'if it's in the game, it's in the game'.

However, it is equally important not to get too caught up in arguments as to whether new information communication technologies invariably bring with them either negative or positive consequences for society, as both sides of this debate can be accused of being overly technologically deterministic. What such technological deterministic arguments fail to acknowledge is that social change is never simply the result of technological innovation but, rather, part of a complex process of social interactions that involve many different social and technological actors (Flew, 2002). In particular, this is the argument made by advocates of an Actor Network Theory approach (or 'ANT' for short) and, most notably, Bruno Latour (e.g. Latour, 2005). This seeks to understand social order as consisting of networks, linking together human agents, technologies, objects, animals and 'anything at all that is connected' (Kirkpatrick, 2008: 102). In this approach technologies, objects and so forth are understood as social actors (or 'actants'), which act alongside, and with, human beings. From this perspective, then, the social is understood simply as a particular arrangement of networks of actants, and the object of the ANT analysts is to seek out and follow these social links, wherever they may lead.

ANT has not been that widely embraced within Cultural, Media or Leisure Studies (Couldry, 2008), and it has been criticized by many, particularly as it is seen as largely descriptive, in that it does not seek to identify power relations within networks and seems to assume parity between all actors (see Kirkpatrick, 2008). However, ANT is useful, as it recognizes complex webs of interactions and focuses attention on the everyday social networks and links between humans and their physical world.

Leisure technologies and everyday life

Probably as a consequence of the cyberpunk literature, the film industry and technological evangelists, too often, new information communication technologies have been seen as 'spectacular'; an escape and a place away from the mundane and everyday 'real' world; or offering an even better 'hyperreal' version of it. For example, Murray and Jenkins (no date: 2) wrote that the pleasure of playing a video is in 'being transported to another place, of losing our sense of reality and extending ourselves into a seemingly limitless, enclosing, other realm' (cited in Crawford, 2012: 77). Similarly, there has been a tendency to prioritize the direct and focused engagement of users with a particular technology. For example, Bryce and Rutter (2001) suggest that the heightened concentration and focus of video gamers can be understood as a state of 'flow' (Csikszentmihalyi, 1988), similar to that entered into by high-level athletes. Such priorities have tended to lead many writers to highlight the high levels of 'active participation' and 'interaction' of new information communication technology users (see Shaw, 2010). However, it is evident that using new information communication technology, such as playing video games, surfing the Internet or texting friends on a mobile telephone, can be for many individuals, for much of the time, a relatively ordinary, if not mundane, activity, often undertaken in a state of distraction (Benjamin, 1931) or, as Highmore (2011: 115) describes it, 'absentminded' media consumption. In particular, this can be seen in Enevold and Hagström's (2008) research on mothers who game, which suggests that many women play video games while undertaking other tasks – such as their example of mothers playing *World of Warcraft* in the early hours of the morning while nursing the baby. This is also a point made by Lally (2002: 107) in her research on the use and location of computers within the home, which suggests that 'some study participants frequently play a computer game while simultaneously doing something else, either computer-based or non-computer-based'.

Lally's work fits into an area of research known as the 'domestication of technology' literature. This is a body of work by a group of academics that emerged in the 1990s, most notably inspired and led by the British media scholar Roger Silverstone and his colleagues at Brunel University. One of its key writers, Leslie Haddon (2004), suggests that the main feature of this literature is an understanding how information communication technologies enter the home, the meanings they have, and the relationship that technologies have with individual and group identities. However, though initially this literature focused primarily on the domestication of technologies within the home, Morley (2006) suggests that there later developed an interest in the 'de-domestication' of technologies as well. That is to say, with an increasing trend towards small and mobile technologies, researchers began to become interested in how information communication technologies not only were located in the home, but also were being carried and used outside of the home.

The presence of new information communication technologies in our everyday lives has undoubtedly been advanced greatly by how small and mobile many advanced technologies have become. Mobile telephone systems have been available since the 1940s, and hand-held radios long before that. Similarly, mobile video games machines have been popular since the 1960s, with the introduction of games such as Cragstan's battery-powered hand-held game *Periscope Firing Range* (Crawford, 2012). However, mobile technologies have advanced greatly over previous decades, and have increasingly 'converged' to link together many once-separate technologies into small, pocket-sized equipment. For example, most modern 'smartphones' not only allow users to make calls and access SMS (short message services or 'texts'), they also commonly include the capability to take high-quality pictures, surf the web, send and receive e-mails, create and edit documents, play complex video games and much more beyond.

Furthermore, it is important to recognize that the location of new information communication technology within patterns of everyday life does not stop at the direct interaction with a piece of technology. Technologies, such as video games and the Internet, have a much wider impact on the nature of our social and cultural lives. As Burn (2006) argues, video games have become a regular source of conversation between friends, while Internet sites such as Wikipedia provide common sources of knowledge and social networking sites like Facebook and Twitter provide key mechanisms for keeping in touch with people – to name but a few examples.

New information communication technologies offer new and exciting forms of leisure, as well as resources for the building of friendships, knowledge and identities. However, as with all, once 'new', technologies their presence and location becomes quickly slotted into the routines and patterns of everyday life, such as playing a Nintendo DS game while commuting on a bus, sending an e-mail on an iPad while waiting for a train, discussing *Football Manager* team tactics with friends in the pub or gaming preferences displayed on the T-shirt by a commuter on the tube. If we are to understand the role and importance of new information communication technology in shaping patterns and forms of contemporary leisure, it is important that we leave behind the baggage associated with concepts such as the 'virtual', which casts new technologies as a break from the 'real' world, and, rather, seek to understand how technologies are used, played with, talked about and often ignored by many of us in the routines of our daily lives.

Conclusions

The idea of 'virtual reality' has often been sold to a technology-eager public as an (almost) achievable escape from our ordinary lives and personas into a world of endless possibilities.

Science fiction writers, social commentators and academics have heralded a new information age which is bringing new social forms and opportunities. Conversely, others have warned against an overreliance on new information communication technologies, which only perpetuates the creation of new technologies and the circulation of greater volumes of information, with no real purpose or discernible benefits. Undoubtedly, new information communication technologies have impacted on the nature of contemporary social and cultural life, probably nowhere more visibly than in terms of leisure patterns and practices – by introducing new ways of playing and relaxing, while simultaneously changing for ever how other leisure practices are experienced and encountered. However, if we are to fully understand the social and cultural significance of new information communication technologies, including their role in contemporary patterns of leisure, it is not the real world that we need to escape but, rather, technologically deterministic and science-fiction inspired concepts such as ideas of the 'virtual'. Video games do not 'transport' gamers to 'another place', nor are users of the Internet living out 'virtual' lives in online persistent worlds. They, and we, are all locating and integrating technologies into our everyday (and very 'real') lives in increasingly mundane ways, and it is here that we need to consider the changing patterns of contemporary leisure.

Notes

1 The prefix 'new' is frequently used to describe media and technologies, such as the Internet and video games, which are seen to have developed in the latter part of the twentieth century. However, establishing what is 'new' about 'new' media and technologies is problematic; as supposedly 'new' technologies, such as the Internet, can be understood as largely recombinants of pre-existing media forms, such as images, texts, video and audio – and this is a debate that I explore more fully in the chapter on consumption and information communication technologies in Longhurst *et al.* (2008).

2 The question of whether 'new' information technologies can be considered as media is a complex and on-going debate. For example, certain writers such as Lantz (2009) argue that video games cannot be considered as *media*, as, unlike media forms (such as books and television shows), video games are not a passive conveyor of a media message. For Lantz, and others, video games are better understood as interactive *games*, the nature of which is shaped by their participants (the gamers). However, in Crawford (2012) I argue that this is a rather problematic argument, which does not take into consideration that technologies, such as the Internet and video games, still only allow users to make certain (often limited) choices of what they can do and where they can go, and, to a large extent, users are still an audience to others' content.

References

Atkinson, M. (2007) 'Virtual Sports', in G. Ritzer (ed.) *Encyclopaedia of Sociology*. Boston, MA: Blackwell.

Benjamin, W. (1931) 'A Small History of Photography', in W. Benjamin (1979) *One Way Street and Other Writings*. London: Verso.

Bryce, J. and Rutter, J. (2001) 'In the Game – In the Flow: Presence in Public Computer Gaming', poster presented at Computer Games and Digital Textualities, IT University of Copenhagen, 1–2 March. Online at: http://digiplay.info/Game.php.

Burdea, G. and Coiffet, P. (1994) *Virtual Reality Technology* (2nd ed.). London: Wiley-Interscience.

Burn, A. (2006) 'Reworking the Text: Online Fandom', in D. Carr, D. Buckingham, A. Burn and G. Schott (eds) *Computer Games: Text, Narrative and Play*. Cambridge: Polity.

Castells, M. (1996) *The Rise of Network Society*, Vol. 1 of *The Information Age: Economy, Society and Culture*. Oxford: Blackwell.

Castells, M. (1997) *The Power of Identity*, Vol. 2 of *The Information Age: Economy, Society and Culture*. Oxford: Blackwell.

Castells, M. (1998) *End of the Millennium*, Vol. 3 of *The Information Age: Economy, Society and Culture*. Oxford: Blackwell

Couldry, N. (2008) 'Actor Network Theory and Media: Do They Connect and on What Terms?', in A. Hepp, F. Krotz, S. Moores, and C. Winte (eds) *Connectivity, Networks and Flows: Conceptualizing Contemporary Communications*. Cresskill: Hampton Press.

Crawford, C. (1997) *The Art of Computer Game Design*. New York: McGraw-Hill (originally 1982).

Crawford, G. (2012) *Video Gamers*. London: Routledge.

Crawford, G., Gosling, V.K. and Light, B. (2011) 'The Social and Cultural Significance of Online Games', in G. Crawford, V.K. Gosling and B. Light (eds) *Online Gaming in Context: The Social and Cultural Significance of Online Games*. London: Routledge.

Csikszentmihalyi, M. (1988) *Optimal Experience: Psychological Studies of Flow in Consciousness*. Cambridge, MA: Cambridge University Press.

Davis, E. (1998) *Techgnosis: Myth, Magic and Mysticism in the Information Age*. London: Serpent's Tail.

Dovey, J. and Kennedy, H. (2006) *Games Cultures: Computer Games as New Media*. Maidenhead: Open University Press.

Drucker, P. (1968) *The Age of Discontinuity: Guidelines to Our Changing Society*. New York: Harper and Row.

Emord, J. (1991) *Freedom, Technology, and the First Amendment*. San Francisco: Pacific Research Institute.

Enevold, J. and Hagström, C. (2008) 'My Momma Shoots Better than You! Who Is the Female Gamer?', *[Player]* conference proceedings, IT University of Copenhagen, Copenhagen, 26–29 August, 144–167.

Flew, T. (2002) *New Media*. Melbourne: Oxford University Press (Australia).

Gere, C. (2008) *Digital Culture* (2nd ed.). London: Reaktion.

Gilder, G. (1990) *Microcosm: The Quantum Revolution in Economics and Technology*. New York: Touchstone.

Haddon, L. (2004) *Information Communication Technologies in Everyday Life: A Concise Introduction and Research Guide*. Oxford: Berg.

Harris, P. (2011) 'Social Networking under Fresh Attack as Tide of Cyber-Scepticism Sweeps US', *Observer*, Society, 23 February.

Heidegger, M. (1977) *The Question Concerning Technology and Other Essays* (trans. W. Lovitt). New York: Harper and Row.

Highmore, B. (2011) *Ordinary Lives: Studies in the Everyday*. London: Routledge.

Jenkins, H. (2006a) *Fans, Bloggers and Gamers: Exploring Participatory Culture*. New York: New York University Press.

Jenkins, H. (2006b) *Convergence Culture: Where Old and New Media Collide*. New York: New York University Press.

Kerr, A., Brereton, P., Kücklich, J. and Flynn, R. (2004) *New Media: New Media Pleasures?* STeM Working Paper: Final Research Report of a Pilot Research Project. Online at: http://www.stem. dcu.ie/reports/NMNP.pdf.

Kirkpatrick, G. (2008) *Technology and Social Power*. Basingstoke: Palgrave Macmillan.

Lally, E. (2002) *At Home with Computer*. Oxford: Berg.

Lantz, F. (2009) 'Games Are Not Media', *Games Design Advance*. Online at: http://gamedesignad-vance.com/?p=1567.

Latour, B. (2005) *Re-Assembling the Social: An Introduction to ANT*. Oxford: Oxford University Press.

Leonard, D. (2009) 'An Untapped Field: Exploring the World of Virtual Sports Gaming', A.A. Raney and J. Bryant (eds) *Handbook of Sports and Media*. London: Routledge.

Lévy, P. (1997) *Collective Intelligence: Mankind's Emerging World in Cyberspace*. Cambridge: Perseus.

Loftus, G.R. and Loftus E.F. (1983) *Mind at Play: The Psychology of Video Games*. New York: Basic Books.

Longhurst, B., Smith, S., Bagnall, G., Crawford, G. and Ogborn, S. (2008) *Introducing Cultural Studies* (2nd ed.). London: Prentice-Hall.

Lyotard, J.F. (1984) *The Postmodern Condition: A Report on Knowledge*. Minnesota: University of Minnesota Press.

May, C. (2002) *The Information Society: A Sceptical View*. Cambridge: Polity.

Merchant, G. (2001) 'Teenagers in Cyberspace: An Investigation of Language Use and Language Change in Internet Chatrooms', *Journal of Research in Reading* 24 (3) 293–306.

Mims, C. (2010) 'Predicting the Death of Print', *Technology Review*, http://www.technologyreview. com/blog/mimssbits/25642/.

Morley, D. (2006) 'What's Home Got to Do with It? Contradictory Dynamics in the Domestication of Technology and the Dislocations of Domesticity', in T. Berker, M. Hartmann, Y. Punie, and K.J. Ward (eds) *Domestication of Media and Technology*. Maidenhead: Open University Press, 19–36.

Murray, J.H. and Jenkins, H. (no date) *Before the Holodeck: Translating Star Trek into Digital Media*. Online at: http://web.mit.edu/21fms/wwww/faculty/henry3/holodeck.html.

Negroponte, N. (1995) *Being Digital*. New York: Hodder and Stoughton.

Newman, J. (2004) *Videogames*. London: Routledge.

Postman, N. (1993) *Technopoly: The Surrender of Culture to Technology*. New York: Vintage Books.

Rheingold, H. (1991) *Virtual Reality*. London: Summit Books

Rheingold, H. (1994) *The Virtual Community: Finding Connection in a Computerized World*. London: Secker and Warburg.

Ross, K. and Nightingale, V. (2003) *Media Audiences: New Perspectives*. Maidenhead: Open University Press.

Rushkoff, D. (1999) *Playing the Future: What We Can Learn from Digital Kids*. New York: Riverhead Trade.

Schell, J. (2010) 'Design Outside of the Box'. Presentation at annual DICE (Design Innovate Communicate Entertain) Conference. Online at: http://www.g4tv.com/videos/44277/dice-2010-design-outside-the-box-presentation/.

Shaw, A. (2010) 'What Is Video Game Culture? Cultural Studies and Game Studies', *Games and Culture* 5 (4) 403–424.

Syed, M. and Miah, A. (2006) 'Digital Era Taking Fans Closer to Action', *Times* (London). Retrieved 1 September 2008 from http://andymiah.wordpress.com/category/cyber- sport/.

Taylor, T.L. (2006) *Play between Worlds: Exploring Online Game Culture*. London: MIT Press.

Turkle, S. (1995) *Life on the Screen: Identity in the Age of the Internet*. New York: Simon and Schuster.

Turkle, S. (2011) *Alone Together: Why We Expect More from Technology and Less from Each Other*. New York: Basic Books.

Williams, R. (1974) *Television: Technology and Cultural Form*. London: Fontana.

48

YOUTH CULTURE, LEISURE AND LIFESTYLE

From subcultures to post-subcultures

Andy Bennett

The sociological study of youth culture has been characterized by two distinctive paradigms of theoretical and empirical enquiry. From the late 1960s through to the late 1990s, the concept of subculture dominated the field of youth culture research. A central tenet of this approach was a focus on class as a basis for understanding the cultural practices of youth. During the early 2000s, the field of youth cultural studies experienced what several researchers have referred to as a 'post-subcultural' turn (Bennett, 2011a; 2011b). This term has been used to explain a shift from rigid, class-based 'subcultural' theories of youth culture to new approaches that posit youth culture as comprising more fluid and transient youth groupings, variously referred to as scenes, lifestyle groups and neo-tribes. In contrast to subcultural theory, much of the work associated with the 'post-subcultural' turn has broadened its scope to focus upon a broader range of youth consumption and leisure, notably in relation to sport, tourism and various forms of digital media. Arguably, there is much to be learned from opening up the study of youth culture to such dimensions of leisure. The purpose of this chapter will be to consider what an examination of the broader terrains of youth leisure and lifestyle reveals about the nature of contemporary youth cultural practice in both a local and a global sense.

Situating youth culture

As noted above, research on youth culture was initially dominated by the concept of subculture. Subculture acquired ready usage in research on patterns of youth leisure and style through the work of the Birmingham Centre for the Study of Contemporary Culture (CCCS) (see Hall and Jefferson, 1976). Borrowing 'subculture' from the Chicago School, where it had been used to construct a sociological explanation of youth deviance (see, for example, Merton, 1957; Becker, 1963), the CCCS adapted the concept as a means of providing an interpretation of the stylistic responses of young working-class males in post-Second World War Britain. According to the CCCS, post-war British youth subcultures, by dint of their quasi-gang structure, were illustrative of continuing expressions of class-based solidarity among working-class youth. Such continuing manifestations of working-class consciousness, argued the CCCS, undermined the comments of observers who suggested that post-war affluence was creating a classless society. This position is effectively summed by Clarke *et al.*, who argue:

There is no 'subcultural solution' to working-class youth unemployment, educational disadvantage, compulsory miseducation, deadend jobs, the routinisation and specialisation of labour, low pay and the loss of skills. Sub-cultural strategies ... 'solve', but in an imaginary way, problems which at the concrete material level remain unresolved.

(Clarke *et al.*, 1976: 47–48)

Key to the theory of subcultural resistance developed by the CCCS was the cultural Marxism of Italian neo-Marxist Antonio Gramsci. While Gramsci (1971) believed that social change on the scale envisaged by Marx was unlikely to occur in the advanced capitalist societies, he also argued that social control in any absolute sense became more difficult to maintain, the social relations of late capitalism being characterized by a constant struggle between conflicting class interests. The result, contended Gramsci, was a shift in the basis of power in capitalist society. The ruling class was no longer able to maintain power purely on the basis of its economic dominance but also had to exercise it 'in moral and intellectual terms' (Bennett *et al.*, 1981: 198). Gramsci refers to this process as 'hegemonic rule', hegemony expressing the dominant system of ideas and beliefs through which the ruling class is able to exert power over society. According to Gramsci, the hegemonic order is susceptible to challenges from below. Although such challenges are in themselves incapable of usurping the ruling class from its dominant position they can, nevertheless produce a 'crisis of authority' (Bennett *et al.*, 1981: 199).

Drawing on this idea, the CCCS suggested that working-class youth subcultures represented pockets of resistance to the ruling hegemonic order. Through appropriating the stylistic resources of the burgeoning youth fashion market (see Chambers, 1985) and using them as visual markers of collective group identities based on traditional working-class sensibilities such as neighbourhood and 'territory', or 'turf', subcultures issued challenges to dominant institutions such as law-enforcement agencies and educational institutions, subcultural style being a clear indicator of resistance against the conformity demanded by the latter. Moreover, according to Cohen (1972), subculture also symbolized a defence of working-class community per se in the face of the break-up of traditional working-class communities due to post-war slum clearance and the relocation of residents to new housing estates.

As this brief account of subcultural theory suggests, although certain domains of youth leisure were acknowledged and investigated by researchers, the forms of leisure that featured in subcultural studies were both restricted and subject to a specific form of interpretation. In effect, subcultural theory focused almost exclusively on the stylistic qualities of youth cultural groups, style in this sense being largely restricted to a semiotic reading of fashion items, hairstyle and, in some few cases, body modification.

A classic case in point here is Hebdige's (1979) reading of punk style. Using Lévi-Strauss's (1966) concept of bricolage and Barthes' (1977) concept of signifying practice, Hebdige considered how the visually spectacular image of punk rock in late 1970s Britain resonated with the socio-economic climate of an industrial nation in decline. According to Hebdige, punk's appropriation of domestic items such as safety pins and lavatory chains from their normal everyday contexts and reassembly on the surface of the body, combined with the subversion of conventional norms of fashion – for example, the ripping of clothes for effect and the positioning of zip fasteners on the outside of garments – signified the socio-economic dislocation of Britain at this time.

Hebdige's interpretation of punk has been criticized on a number of accounts, including its lack of attention to manifestations of punk outside of London – and specifically in the provinces (Clarke, 1981) and its failure to take into account the role of women (McRobbie, 1980). A further problem with Hebdige's (1979) work, and indeed the broader subcultural studies field in which the work is situated, is a lack of attention to the range of leisure and lifestyle preferences that underpinned punk. Laing (1985) has accurately pointed to Hebdige's wholesale lack of attention to the importance of music in punk – this in itself is a significant oversight, given the sheer impact of punk music as a sonic and lyrical statement that visibly challenged the rock establishment of the late 1970s. Indeed, punk was a watershed moment for youth culture in a variety of ways, many of which were never satisfactorily recorded, if represented at all, in the subcultural literature. The DIY (do-it-yourself) ethos, which had been nominally evident in previous forms of youth culture, notably the hippie movement, became more prominent during the punk era both in terms of attitudes towards music production and in other media such as literature. A key example of this is the now legendary punk fanzine *Sniffin' Glue*, initiated by Manchester-based punk fan Mark Perry in July 1976. Reference to such broader patterns of DIY cultural production and consumption in punk rarely registered in subcultural studies of the punk genre and style, largely because of the latter's reliance on textual and semiotic analysis of the most obvious items – the spectacular fashion – of the punk regalia.

Similar oversights can be seen in relation to other examples of post-war youth culture. The CCCS's take on mod culture, perhaps the most celebratory element of early 1960s youth in terms of its cultural consumption practices, is once again primarily restricted to an analysis of lower middle-class youth's appropriation of fashion items in a symbolic show of resistance against the mundane clerical and other low-status white-collar jobs that occupied mods' lives during the week (see Hebdige, 1976). In addition to being a largely male-centric reading of mod, this approach once again restricted itself to a relatively narrow reading of mod style. This becomes clearly evident when contrasted with Feldman's (2009) *We Are the Mods*. Published some thirty years after the CCCS work, and much less invested in the cultural Marxist approach of theorists associated with CCCS subcultural theory, Feldman's work presents a far broader picture of mod culture in which various aspects of the cultural consumption through which mod culture was fashioned are considered.

In addition to looking at aspects of fashion and style, Feldman also focuses on the literature, television and films favoured by the mods, as well as other consumption preferences – drugs, alcohol, cigarettes and so on. Important attention is also given to the various technologies available to mods – transistor radios, plastic 45 records, instamatic cameras and the like became important commodities through which mods were able to make important statements concerning their lifestyle and aesthetic preferences. Although it would be inaccurate to describe Feldman's work as post-subcultural, at the same time its interpretation and understanding of mod culture draws on a range of approaches – particularly in relation to its ethnographic engagement with the everyday enactment and articulation of cultural consumption – reflects an approach to the study of youth culture that is rooted in the post-subcultural turn.

The post-subcultural turn

During the late 1990s and early 2000s, a new generation of youth cultural researchers challenged subcultural theory, claiming that its structural determinist approach and reliance on theoretical abstraction at the expense of ethnographic enquiry rendered it ineffective as a framework for understanding the actual everyday cultural practices of youth. Thus, as Muggleton observes: 'Style is read as text, and only the semiotician is entrusted to crack the code. There is, in other words, an academic "elitism" implicit in this method' (Muggleton, 2000: 13). Similarly, Bennett argues that a key problem with the CCCS subcultural theory is the

> contention that such styles were uniformly used by working-class youth in a strategy designed to resist the structural changes taking place around them. This is because such a contention rests on the rather tentative notion that, having gained an element of freedom to pick and choose between an increasing range of consumer items, working-class youth were somehow driven back to the fact of class as a way of articulating their attachment to such commodities. It could rather be argued that post-war consumerism offered young people the opportunity to break away from their traditional class-based identities, the increased spending power of the young facilitating and encouraging experimentation with new, self-constructed forms of identity.
>
> (Bennett, 1999: 602)

The post-subcultural turn, as the new era in youth cultural research came to be known, drew on a variety of existing concepts – scene, lifestyle and neo-tribe – as a means of re-theorizing youth. What each of these concepts had in common was a capacity for critical enquiry into youth culture that transcended the confines of class-based explanations to consider youth cultural formations as more reflexively grounded and based around common articulations of taste. Scene had already been conceptualized by Straw (1991) as a model that looked beyond notions of class and community in its understanding of how music was appropriated in an everyday context. According to Straw, clusters of common taste for particular genres of music were more likely to manifest themselves at the trans-local level, due to the global flows of music and associated cultural resources. Neo-tribe, originally adapted by Shields (1992) from Maffesoli's (1996) concept of *tribus*, was incorporated into the work of youth researchers such as Bennett (1999) and Malbon (1999) as a means of critically engaging with the notion of youth cultures as stable and relatively self-contained entities. On the contrary, it was argued, youth cultural groups often exhibited more fluid boundaries, with memberships that were free floating.

The concept of lifestyle was originally introduced by Weber (1978/1922) and emerged again during the early 1990s in the work of sociologists such as Giddens (1991) and Chaney (1996). From there it was adopted by youth culture researchers such as Miles (2000) in studies of young people's everyday cultural consumption practices. Key to lifestyle theory is the notion that late modernity has produced new forms of cultural association based on patterns of common taste for particular forms of cultural goods and resources. This argument has significant implications for our understanding of youth culture, as it shifts the focus from previous subcultural interpretations of youth, in which the everyday appropriation of cultural resources is cast in a relatively narrow sense of class-based forms of symbolic resistance, to one in which cultural consumption is understood as a cross-class practice with a more multifarious range of meanings and significance.

To put this observation another way, in the context of post-subcultural studies of youth, the interpretation and understanding of youth consumption and leisure practices was significantly broadened beyond the resistance thesis, offering potential for new and different understandings of these practices. The broader scope applied in post-subcultural studies was also informed by a more empirically grounded approach, with research routinely drawing on ethnographic data. Thus, in addition to offering new theoretical angles on the importance of everyday leisure and consumption practices for youth, post-subcultural studies also speaks more directly to the perceptions and understandings of young people themselves. As Bennett notes:

> The structuralist narratives produced by the CCCS served to render fieldwork redundant in social settings deemed to be underpinned by irremovable socio-economic determinants which, it was argued, fundamentally shaped the consciousness of social actors.
>
> (Bennett, 2002a: 453)

In response to the theoretical stance adopted in subcultural theory, post-subcultural research took a more empirically grounded position. Indeed, in moving from text as a primary mode of analysis to a consideration of the local contexts in which texts and other forms of cultural consumption were actively appropriated and used by young people, a much richer account of young people as agents active in the production of their own cultural sphere began to emerge (Bennett, 2000). Rather than cultural consumption and resultant patterns of leisure being regarded as a simple reflection of structural circumstances which youth resisted but had no real control over, the post-subcultural turn moved far beyond such straitjacketed interpretations of youth culture. At the same time, a broader range of cultural practices began to be considered by youth researchers as integral to the everyday production of youth cultural groups. The remainder of this chapter focuses on a selection of contemporary studies of youth cultural consumption and leisure practices that illustrate some of the new directions in which youth culture research is currently developing.

Although not all of the following studies fall squarely within the remit of post-subcultural studies, they do reflect a more open engagement with the everyday cultural sensibilities of youth and their reflexive engagement with space and place. Increasingly such work is also highly sensitive to ways in which global flows are creating new trans-local (Peterson and Bennett, 2004) connections between youth cultural groups through media such as travel and new technology.

Music

Since the mid-1950s and the advent of rock and roll, popular music has been packaged and marketed primarily as a 'youth' music (Shumway, 1992). As noted earlier, subcultural theory paid little attention to the significance of popular music beyond paying lip-service to it as an aspect of youth style.[1] Indeed, it was initially in the field of popular music studies, notably in the work of Simon Frith, that much of the early important work on the relationship between youth and music appeared. Frith offered an early acknowledgement of the need to distinguish between different types of youth fans for popular music, including among those who seemed to be the most stylistically committed to various popular music genres. Thus, observed Frith:

> The problem is to reconcile adolescence and subculture. Most working-class teenagers pass through groups, change identities, play their leisure roles for fun; other differences between them – sex, occupation, family – are much more significant than distinctions of style. For every youth 'stylist' committed to a cult as a full-time creative task, there are hundreds of working-class kids who grow up in a loose membership of several groups and run with a variety of gangs. There's a distinction here between a vanguard and a mass, between uses of leisure *within* subcultures.
>
> (Frith, 1983: 219–20)

Since Frith offered this observation, the field of youth and music research has grown exponentially, effectively mapping the series of genres and subgenres that have emerged since the post-Second World War era and considering a range of ways in which music becomes significant for young people in the context of their everyday lives. In this respect, work utilizing the concept of scene has been of pivotal importance in terms of developing a broad range of insights regarding how young people engage with popular music in their everyday lives. As Stahl (2004) observes, a critical value of the scene's perspective is its unlocking of the microcosmic levels at which music works for young people, who may simultaneously write, perform, promote and consume music. Due to the rise of what could be termed the 'post-Fordist' music industry (Smith and Maughan, 1998), the boundaries between music as leisure and music as work and employment have to some extent been blurred; many of those involved in music consumption are simultaneously involved in music production at some level and are, in effect, 'prosumers' (Ritzer and Jurgenson, 2010). The digital revolution (discussed in more detail below) has been a key facilitator here, providing opportunities for music composition and recording to high quality standards, with the internet offering avenues for the promotion and dissemination of music that side-step the mainstream music industry.

Many popular music researchers now argue that all music scenes, including local, relatively obscure scenes, are locked into trans-local networks by virtue of the way in which digital technology has opened up new opportunities for online communication between members of scenes in different geographical spaces. For example, Kahn-Harris (2004) illustrates how the global extreme metal scene is highly dependent on the commitment of small-scale promoters and similar informal networks who work together to facilitate the touring of bands whose music-making activities are largely reliant on shoe-string budgets and the goodwill of fans to provide accommodation, meals and so on. In addition to facilitating new forms of music promotion and the organization of tours for groups and artists (Rogers, 2008), music fans have also utilized such technologies in highly creative ways. Kibby (2000), for example, notes how fans of cult US country-folk singer-songwriter John Prine have constructed and used online fan sites to discuss and evaluate the work of Prine. Bennett (2002b) similarly notes how fans of the Canterbury scene have effectively revived the latter as a 'virtual' scene through using online communication as a means of collectively debating the definition and historical significance of what has come to be known as the Canterbury Sound.

The concept of neo-tribe has also been extensively used in research on popular music as a means of discussing the significance of popular music-based consumption and leisure beyond the confines of subcultural theory. Malbon (1999) and Bennett (1999) have each argued that in the case of electronic dance music (EDM), the highly eclectic soundscapes typical at EDM events, combined with the more relaxed and tolerant atmosphere (at least initially) attracted crowds from different, in some cases stylistically and aesthetically opposed, youth cultural groupings. According to both Malbon and Bennett, the spontaneous and relatively fluid nature of EDM events led to a new neo-tribal sensibility among attendees, for whom the experiential nature of the setting acted as a common draw for individuals who would travel to designated spots to temporally engage in a shared, highly liminal moment.

Neo-tribal characteristics have also been associated with other types of music event, notably music festivals. As Dowd *et al.* observe, the liminality of the festival setting, combined with the way in which the space of the festival often draws like-minded people together from their mundane everyday settings, produces a particular kind of collective dynamic:

Drawn together from geographically dispersed locations and away from the expectations of everyday life, fans and performers can immerse themselves in a particular culture and experiment with different identities.

(Dowd *et al.*, 2004: 149)

Cummings (2005) extends this perspective on festivals in her work on indie music festivals in Australia. According to Cummings, the neo-tribal quality that manifests itself in the physical gathering of fans at indie music festivals is further articulated through fans' online engagement during periods between festival gatherings. As Cummings argues, given the relative infrequency of indie music festivals, most of which occur on an annual basis, fans who are dispersed across different geographical regions are driven to find new ways of connecting with each other, so as to keep in touch and to consolidate their sense of themselves as a 'scene'.

Sport

Significantly, while popular music has often been a key focus in post-subcultural research, little attention has been focused on what some authors have referred to as sporting subcultures (Wheaton, 2007). This is a critical oversight, given the sheer number of sporting activities that now align with youth cultural consumption and leisure, including skateboarding, snowboarding and surfing to name but three examples. The extent to which any of these activities, or other associated sports, could be referred to as subcultural is debatable, for reasons specifically related to the subculture/post-subculture debate already discussed in the first part of this chapter. In beginning to consider this point, surfing serves as a good example. Although admittedly a niche sport, surfing has received less attention than other forms of youth (and post-youth) leisure, despite its longevity. When it has been a topic for academic research, surfing has typically been referred to as a subculture (see, for example, Reed, 1999; Stedman, 1997). However, such a categorization is, arguably, flawed at a number of levels. At the very least, there exists no obvious structural basis for such a description. As a form of sport-leisure, surfing could hardly be described as class, gender, race or even age specific. On the contrary, surfing ranges across such demographic categories (Baker *et al.*, 2012). What bonds surfers together is not so much a structurally ingrained rejection, or resistance, of mainstream values (however these may be construed). Rather, surfing culture is bonded by a widely shared enthusiasm for the activity, grounded in the quest for technique, knowledge of the ocean's behaviour and the challenges that this brings. In many respects, then, the term 'lifestyle' is, arguably, far better suited to surfing, given the lifestyle sensibilities that cohere and underpin surfing culture as this is engaged in by individuals from many different walks of life.

Skateboarding is another field of youth leisure-sport activity that, despite the existence of relatively little research on this popular youth activity, has been conveniently labelled a subculture (Beal, 1995). Key to the use of this term is the notion that, through its appropriation of urban space, skateboarding resists the authority and regulation of official civic and law enforcement agencies. Related to this is the argument that, due to its DIY origins, skateboarding continues to embody a strong level of resistance to consumer capitalism.

The first major study of skateboarding was the work of Borden (2000). Focusing particularly on the physical appropriation of urban space by skaters, Borden noted how the latter are transformed into meaningful sites similar to what Chatterton and Hollands (2002) refer to as playscapes in their instructive work on the regulation of the urban night-time economy. Significantly, however, rather than invoking the rhetoric of subculture to explain the collective motivations of skaters, Borden concentrates instead on the creative strategies employed by skaters in imposing their own meanings on cityscapes and architecture. Indeed, integral to Borden's work is the interpretation of skating culture not as locally situated pockets of resistance but, rather, as a trans-locally connected lifestyle community whose potent use of digital technology functions to link skaters together across the globe. Thus, writing in the early 2000s, Borden observed that many skaters posted video clips of their skating moves on websites, the latter being accompanied by 'textual descriptions, choreographic codes using the ASCII character set [and] still photographs' (Borden, 2000: 118–19).

Clearly, the technologies now used by skaters will have advanced significantly. But the basic tenets of Borden's argument remain current in that, through the use of such technology, skaters both illustrate their individual prowess and pass on their skill and abilities to others. Borden suggests that use of the internet by skaters in this way also acts as an important community-building device: 'The overall effect [of the internet] is to make it easier for skaters to disseminate material globally, certainly compared to their access to commercial magazines or videos' (Borden, 2000: 119). By dint of this, argues Borden, skateboarding is an inherently 'trans-local' phenomenon. Skaters exchange images and information about skating style and technique on the internet but operationalize these resources in the context of their own local environment. As such, local groups of skaters experience an on-going dialogue between their own creative synergy and a global skating community. According to Borden:

> [The skating] community is knitted through a continual exchange and re-experiencing of a lexicon of skate moves. The image becomes not only a locally lived but, simultaneously, a globally reproduced and exchanged phenomenon, part of modernity's intensification of global communication and simultaneity.
>
> (Borden, 2000: 126)

As these two examples illustrate, although the post-subcultural approach has not widely embraced the field of sport-leisure, the types of discourse employed do not align with subcultural theory either. On the contrary, the perspectives applied are broadly indicative of the arguments currently being deployed by post-subcultural theorists.

Digital media

Borden's work demonstrates one way in which digital media is being used by youth culture in ways that help young people to connect with others at a trans-local level while simultaneously allowing them to creatively subvert oppressive aspects of their everyday environments. Such is the centrality of digital media now in many forms of youth cultural practice that it has been argued that it has become a primary platform for the articulation of youth cultural sensibilities and must be acknowledged as centrally significant for our understanding of the ways in which contemporary youth cultural formations are shaped. Thus, as Bennett observes:

> we can no longer take it for granted that membership of a youth culture involves issues of stylistic unity, collective knowledge of a particular club scene or even face-to-face interaction. On the contrary, youth cultures may increasingly be seen as cultures of

'shared ideas', whose interactions take place not in physical spaces such as the street, club or festival field but in the virtual spaces facilitated by the internet.

(Bennett, 2004a: 163)

In recent work on youth and digital media on Australia's Gold Coast, Robards and Bennett (2011) examine how online social networking sites such as MySpace and Facebook give rise to heightened modes of identity construction and articulation in which shared tastes in music, sport, food and so on have critical resonances. Through moving beyond the subculture–dominant culture binary and embracing Chaney's (2002) notion of fragmented culture, Robards and Bennett illustrate how digital media's capacity for enhancing young people's capacity for choosing and 'managing' social identities is clearly anchored in an era of what Giddens (1991) has referred to as reflexive modernity. Atton considers the importance of digital media for youth as a form of political empowerment, with reference to new social movements which, as Atton observes, regularly utilize the internet 'as the primary channel for autonomous communication' (Atton, 2002: 133). Through side-stepping traditional media, the internet offers new social movements the potential 'for sociality, community, mobilization, knowledge construction and direct political action' (*ibid*). According to Atton, in addition to facilitating global communication between locally dispersed movements and action groups, the internet also provides a vehicle for more equal participation in debate and decision-making processes.

A similar position is argued by Baker in her work on contemporary youth culture and net-radio, which she describes as 'a form of alternative-radical media ... internally organized by taste (music) distinctions, power over production practices, and the degree of resistance to traditional radio formats' (Baker, 2012: 409). Although Baker refers to the youth net-radio phenomenon as a subculture, it is clear from her data that a wide range of young people are drawn to the opportunities offered by net-radio to transcend traditional media. Again, then, it seems reasonable to suggest that such qualities of net-radio use are less subcultural than related post-subcultural trends in which young people are motivated to use net-radio to articulate a range of different lifestyle sensibilities and related aesthetic and political outlooks.

Finally, Light *et al.* (2012) examine the relationship between digital technologies and what they refer to as 'vernacular creativity'. Using the example of graffiti art, Light *et al.* suggest that online social networking sites, as opposed to merely facilitating forms of sociality and communication, are also a platform for engaging in and supporting creativity. Through utilizing YouTube, observe Light *et al.*, graffiti artists are able to subvert dominant media discourses that routinely cast graffiti using discourses of moral panic. In their place, artists offer alternative discourses of graffiti as powerful and genuine statements of vernacular creativity; a means through which young, disempowered members of local communities are able to re-empower themselves: 'YouTube has facilitated a remediation of vernacular creativity, in the area of youth leisure with respect to common activities such as "colouring in", painting and an engagement with the arts more generally' (Light *et al.*, 2012: 352).

Tourism and travel

Another aspect of youth cultural practice that has grown significantly since the early 1990s is international travel. During the mid–late 1960s stories of the hippie trails to Morocco and India became an iconic aspect of the counter-cultural aesthetic underpinned by a desire to escape the technocracy of the world (Roszak, 1969; Bennett, 2001). However, international travel among youth cultures largely remained limited until the 1990s, when travel became cheaper and particular trans-local scenes began to flourish. A case in point here is the dance tourism that has grown up around the electronic dance music scene. As Melechi (1993) notes, the origins of dance tourism are rooted in the mid-1980s, when young British holiday-makers on the Spanish island of Ibiza discovered the Balearic Beat being played by DJs in the clubs of Ibiza Town.

From there, the little-known style made its way back to the clubs of UK cities such as Manchester, while Ibiza itself become known as a global dance music capital attracting thousands of young dance tourists every year. As Bennett (2004b) observes, through its reputation Ibiza has become subject to a form of 'musicalised' tourist gaze (Urry, 1990). Thus, in the same way that fans of blues and country flock to Chicago and Nashville to experience the 'authentic' sites for these musics, so devotees of dance music often visit Ibiza with the express purpose of paying homage to the clubs and spaces where 'Balearic Beat' was first created. The mystique of Ibiza is further enhanced by virtue of the fact that it has served as an important nodal point for a trans-national community of DJs (see Laing, 1997) whose paths inevitably crossed in the island's dance clubs. Ibiza's 'tourist gaze' is further enhanced by the regular release of CD collections, comprising music featured in the island's dance clubs. The packaging of such CDs often features stereotypical images of the 'island paradise' – palm trees, empty beaches, golden sunsets – while the titles of collections, such as 'Chilled Ibiza', add to the seductive quality of the Ibiza experience.

Dance tourism has also become intertwined with other forms of tourist experience, particularly related to remote areas of natural beauty and natural phenomena. Luckman's (2003) work on the rural rave scene in Australia focuses on the emphasis that young ravers place on rave as a distinctly 'tribal' experience and one that allows a reconnection with the natural world. A similar point is made by Hetherington, who observes how the hippie festivals staged around Stonehenge, the ancient megalith in the English county of Wiltshire, create an entirely different experience of the space from that promoted by the official tourism industry. Thus, according to Hetherington, while the tourist's and the festival-goer's inter-pretations of Stonehenge began by using the same basic knowledge about the megalith, each interpretation works this knowledge in different ways to 'legitimize different sets of practices and individualized lifestyles' (Hetherington, 1992: 89). Thus, for the tourist the significance of Stonehenge lies in the clues it is seen to provide concerning the culture and customs of ancient Britain. By contrast, for the festival-goer, Stonehenge's perceived links with ancient Britain connect with and sustain a 'neo-pagan spiritual revival' (*ibid*.: 88). Such neo-pagan sensibilities also mesh with dance tourism at eclipse festivals, that is, music and cultural festivals organized to coincide with total eclipses of the sun as these occur in different parts of the world. As St. John (forthcoming, 2013) notes, such festivals accommodate a global scene of 'eclipse chasers', who travel the globe in order to experience the remarkable natural phenomenon whereby the sun is completely eclipsed by the moon, plunging the earth at that particular point into darkness. According to St. John, eclipse chasers comprise an eclectic group of individuals, including hippies, EDM fans, pagans, spiritualists and so on. In many ways, then, the eclipse festival constitutes a distinctly neo-tribal gathering, as individuals from characteristically different cultural and lifestyle contexts converge in liminal space to experience an extraordinary but short-lived natural event.

Conclusion

This chapter has examined various aspects of youth cultural leisure. It began with an account of the transition that has taken place in youth cultural research since 2000, from subcultural theory to what is now often referred to as the post-subcultural turn. The point was made that, due to its primary focus on class and structural explanations of youth culture, subcultural theory remained highly insensitive to both the variety and the plurality of different patterns of cultural consumption both among and within youth cultures. It was subsequently argued that, with the shift to post-subcultural explanations of youth and its reliance on alternative theoretical concepts – scene, neo-tribe and lifestyle – a broader variety of consumption and leisure practices among youth culture have been acknowledged. The remainder of the chapter considered some of the key studies of youth consumption and leisure to have emerged as a result of this conceptual shift in the study of youth culture.

Note

1   Important exceptions here are studies by Murdoch and McCron (1976) and Willis (1978). However, neither of these studies is strictly a part of the subcultural theory canon.

References

Atton, C. (2002) *Alternative Media*. London: Sage.

Baker, A. (2012) 'Exploring Subcultural Models of a Discursive Youth Net-radio Hierarchy', *Continuum: Journal of Media and Cultural Studies* 26(3) 409–421.

Baker, S., Bennett, A. and Wise, P. (2012) 'Living "the Strip": Negotiating Neighbourhood, Community and Identities on Australia's Gold Coast', in H. Skott-Myhre and J. Richardson (eds) *Habitus of the Hood*. London: Intellect Books.

Barthes, R. (1977) 'The Third Meaning', in S. Heath (ed.) *Image, Music, Text*. London: Fontana.

Beal, B. (1995) 'Disqualifying the Official: An Exploration of Social Resistance through the Subculture of Skateboarding', *Sociology of Sport Journal* 12 (3) 252–267.

Becker, H.S. (1963) *Outsiders: Studies in the Sociology of Deviance*. New York: Free Press.

Bennett, A. (1999) 'Subcultures or Neo-Tribes? Rethinking the Relationship between Youth, Style and Musical Taste', *Sociology* 33 (3) 599–617.

Bennett, A. (2000) *Popular Music and Youth Culture: Music, Identity and Place*. Basingstoke: Macmillan.

Bennett, A. (2001) *Cultures of Popular Music*. Buckingham: Open University Press.

Bennett, A. (2002a) 'Researching Youth Culture and Popular Music: A Methodological Critique', *British Journal of Sociology* 53 (3) 451–466.

Bennett, A. (2002b) 'Music, Media and Urban Mythscapes: A Study of the Canterbury Sound', *Media, Culture and Society* 24 (1) 107–120.

Bennett, A. (2004a) 'Virtual Subculture? Youth, Identity and the Internet', in A. Bennett and K. Kahn-Harris (eds) *After Subculture: Critical Studies in Contemporary Youth Culture*. Basingstoke: Palgrave.

Bennett, A. (2004b) 'Chilled Ibiza: Dance Tourism and the Neo-Tribal Island Community', in K. Dawe (ed.) *Island Musics*. Oxford: Berg.

Bennett, A. (2011a) 'The Continuing Importance of the "Cultural" in the Study of Youth', *Youth Studies Australia* 30 (3) 27–33.

Bennett, A. (2011b) 'The Post-Subcultural Turn: Some Reflections Ten Years On', *Journal of Youth Studies* 14 (5) 493–506.

Bennett, T., Martin, G., Mercer, C. and Woollacott, J. (eds) (1981) *Culture, Ideology and Social Process*. London: Open University Press.

Borden, I. (2000) *Skateboarding, Space and the City: Architecture and the Body*. Oxford: Berg.

Chambers, I. (1985) *Urban Rhythms: Pop Music and Popular Culture*. Basingstoke: Macmillan.

Chaney, D. (1996) *Lifestyles*. Routledge: London.

Chaney, D. (2002) *Cultural Change and Everyday Life*. Basingstoke: Palgrave.

Chatterton, P. and Hollands, R. (2002) 'Theorising Urban Playscapes: Producing, Regulating and Consuming Youthful Nightlife City Spaces', *Urban Studies* 39 (1) 153–173.

Clarke, G. (1981) 'Defending Ski-Jumpers: A Critique of Theories of Youth Subcultures', in S. Frith and A. Goodwin (eds) (1990) *On Record: Rock, Pop and the Written Word*. London: Routledge.

Clarke, J., Hall, S., Jefferson, T. and Roberts, B. (1976) 'Subcultures, Cultures and Class: A Theoretical Overview', in S. Hall and T. Jefferson (eds) *Resistance through Rituals: Youth Subcultures in Post-War Britain*. London: Hutchinson.

Cohen, P. (1972) *Subcultural Conflict and Working Class Community*, Working Papers in Cultural Studies 2. Birmingham: University of Birmingham.

Cummings, J. (2005) 'Australian Indie Music Festivals as Scenes', in R. Julian, R. Rottier and R. White (eds) *TASA Conference 2005. Community, Place, Change*, University of Tasmania. The Australian Sociological Association: 1–9.

Dowd, T.J., Liddle, K. and Nelson, J. (2004) 'Music Festivals as Scenes: Examples from Serious Music, Womyn's Music and SkatePunk', in A. Bennett and R.A. Peterson (eds) *Music Scenes: Local, Translocal and Virtual*. Nashville, TN: Vanderbilt University Press.

Feldman, C.J. (2009) *'We Are the Mods': A Transnational History of a Youth Subculture*. New York: Peter Lang.

Frith, S. (1983) *Sound Effects: Youth, Leisure and the Politics of Rock*. London: Constable.

Giddens, A. (1991) *Modernity and Self Identity: Self and Society in the Late Modern Age*. Cambridge: Polity.

Gramsci, A. (1971) *Selections from the Prison Notebooks*. London: Lawrence and Wishart.

Hall, S. and Jefferson, T. (eds) (1976) *Resistance through Rituals: Youth Subcultures in Post-War Britain*. London: Hutchinson.

Hebdige, D. (1976) 'The Meaning of Mod', in S. Hall and T. Jefferson (eds) *Resistance through Rituals: Youth Subcultures in Post-War Britain*. London: Hutchinson.

Hebdige, D. (1979) *Subculture: The Meaning of Style*. London: Routledge.

Hetherington, K. (1992) 'Stonehenge and Its Festival: Spaces of Consumption', in R. Shields (ed.) *Lifestyle Shopping: The Subject of Consumption*. London: Routledge.

Kahn-Harris, K. (2004) 'Unspectacular Subculture? Transgression and Mundanity in the Global Extreme Metal Scene', in A. Bennett and K. Kahn-Harris (eds) *After Subculture: Critical Studies in Contemporary Youth Culture*. Basingstoke: Palgrave.

Kibby, M.D. (2000) 'Home on the Page: A Virtual Place of Music Community', *Popular Music* 19 (1) 91–100.

Laing, D. (1985) *One Chord Wonders: Power and Meaning in Punk Rock*. Milton Keynes: Open University Press.

Laing, D. (1997) 'Rock Anxieties and New Music Networks', in A. McRobbie (ed.) *Back to Reality: Social Experience and Cultural Studies*. Manchester: Manchester University Press.

Lévi-Strauss, C. (1966) *The Savage Mind*. London: Weidenfeld and Nicolson.

Light, B., Griffiths, M. and Lincoln, S. (2012) '"Connect and Create": Young People, YouTube and Graffiti Communities', *Continuum: Journal of Media and Cultural Studies* 26 (3) 343–355.

Luckman, S. (2003) 'Going Bush and Finding One's "Tribe": Raving, Doof and the Australian Landscape', *Continuum: Journal of Media and Cultural Studies* 17 (3) 318–332.

Maffesoli, M. (1996) *The Time of the Tribes: The Decline of Individualism in Mass Society* (trans. D. Smith). London: Sage.

Malbon, B. (1999) *Clubbing: Dancing, Ecstasy and Vitality*. London: Routledge.

McRobbie, A. (1980) 'Settling Accounts with Subcultures: A Feminist Critique', in S. Frith and A. Goodwin (eds) (1990) *On Record: Rock, Pop and the Written Word*. London: Routledge.

Melechi, A. (1993) 'The Ecstasy of Disappearance', in S. Redhead (ed.) *Rave Off: Politics and Deviance in Contemporary Youth Culture*. Aldershot: Avebury.

Merton, R.K. (1957) *Social Theory and Social Structure*. London: Collier-Macmillan Ltd.

Miles, S. (2000) *Youth Lifestyles in a Changing World*. Buckingham: Open University Press.

Muggleton, D. (2000) *Inside Subculture: The Postmodern Meaning of Style*. Oxford: Berg.

Peterson, R.A. and Bennett, A. (2004) 'Introducing Music Scenes', in A. Bennett, and R.A. Peterson (eds) *Music Scenes: Local, Translocal and Virtual*. Nashville, TN: Vanderbilt University Press.

Reed, M.A. (1999) 'Waves of Commodification: A Critical Investigation into Surfing Subculture'. Unpublished MA thesis, San Diego State University, USA.

Ritzer, G. and Jurgenson, N. (2010) 'Production, Consumption, Prosumption: The Nature of Capitalism in the Age of the Digital "Prosumer"', *Journal of Consumer Culture* 10 (1) 13–36.

Robards, B. and Bennett, A. (2011) 'My Tribe: Postsubcultural Manifestations of Belonging on Social Network Sites', *Sociology* 45 (2) 303–217.

Rogers, I. (2008) '"You've Got to Go to Gigs to Get Gigs": Indie Musicians, Eclecticism and the Brisbane Scene', *Continuum: Journal of Media and Cultural Studies* 22 (5) 639–649.

Roszak, T. (1969) *The Making of a Counter Culture: Reflections on the Technocratic Society and its Youthful Opposition*. London: Faber and Faber

Shields, R. (1992) 'The Individual, Consumption Cultures and the Fate of Community', in R. Shields (ed.) *Lifestyle Shopping: The Subject of Consumption*. London: Routledge.

Shumway, D. (1992) 'Rock and Roll as a Cultural Practice', in A. DeCurtis (ed.) *Present Tense: Rock and Roll and Culture*. Durham, NC: Duke University Press.

Smith, R.J. and Maughan, T. (1998) 'Youth Culture and the Making of the Post-Fordist Economy: Dance Music in Contemporary Britain', *Journal of Youth Studies*, 1 (2) 211–228.

St. John, G. (forthcoming, 2013) 'Techno-Paganism and Totality: Psytrance Festivals and the Total Solar Eclipse', in D. Weston and A. Bennett (eds) *Pop Pagans*. London: Equinox.

Stahl, G. (2004) '"It's Like Canada Reduced": Setting the Scene in Montreal', in A. Bennett and K. Kahn-Harris (eds) *After Subculture: Critical Studies in Contemporary Youth Culture*. Basingstoke: Palgrave.

Stedman, L. (1997) 'From Gidget to Gonad Man: Surfers, Feminists and Postmodernisation', *Journal of Sociology* 33 (1) 75–90.

Straw, W. (1991) 'Systems of Articulation, Logics of Change: Communities and Scenes in Popular Music', *Cultural Studies* 5 (3) 368–388.

Urry, J. (1990) *The Tourist Gaze: Leisure and Travel in Contemporary Societies*. London: Sage.

Weber, M. (1978/1922) 'The Distribution of Power within the Political Community: Class, Status, Party', in *Economy and Society: An Outline of Interpretive Sociology*. Berkeley, CA: University of California Press.

Wheaton, B. (2007) 'After Sport Culture: Rethinking Sport and Post-Subcultural Theory', *Journal of Sport and Social Issues* 31: 283–307.

Willis, P. (1978) *Profane Culture*. London: Routledge and Kegan Paul.

49

THE MEANING OF LIQUID LEISURE

Johan Bouwer and Marco van Leeuwen

Introduction

In recent years, scholars in the field of Leisure Studies have claimed that their discipline is in a state of crisis. One explanation for this is that the orthodox leisure science paradigm, based as it is on outdated sociological insights, fails to accommodate the theoretical and methodological necessities that the study of leisure in the so-called 'postmodern' era demands. In addition, and significantly, the question has also arisen about the extent to which leisure activities are not merely economically valid entities, but also meaningful and value based. Several scholars have proposed ways out of the impasse that Leisure Studies supposedly is in. Fred Coalter, for instance, pointed out more than a decade ago that both British and North American scholars of leisure largely ignore issues of individual meaning (Coalter, 1997: 255). Another notable leisure scholar, Karla Henderson, recently suggested that we should embrace pluralism within Leisure Studies, arguing for continuous change, while at the same time articulating a collective identity within the Leisure Studies field (Henderson, 2010: 397). A third scholar, Tony Blackshaw – whose work is the primary focus of this chapter – addresses the crisis by attempting to integrate Coalter's and Henderson's positions into a coherent position of his own. Taking Zygmunt Bauman's analysis of modernity as a jumping-off point, he generates a vast array of relevant philosophical and socio-cultural claims and ideas from his base metaphor 'liquid leisure'. Relevantly for the current discussion, he investigates how leisure can be used to design an authentic, artful existence – where such an existence would focus on infusing meaning into our lives in ways that befit the variety and ambiguity of human experience.

This chapter engages in dialogue with Blackshaw's claim that leisure is the key domain within which people nowadays find and create meaning by expressing and exploring their freedom. He holds that leisure is the driving force for 'our human goal of satisfying our hunger for meaning and our thirst for giving our lives a purpose' (Blackshaw, 2010: 120). His expansion of leisure has 'liberated an age-old search for pleasure, happiness and freedom' (Roberts, 2011: 12). This interesting hermeneutical break with orthodox critical sociology of leisure, more specifically, calls for an exploration of the conceptual interconnections between 'liquid leisure' and individual meanings of leisure. Moreover, within this postmodern conceptual cauldron the role of creative freedom – and its counterpart responsibility

– in forgoing one's identity floats to the surface. Two themes: meaning (spirituality) and freedom (morality), will be at the centre of reflection in this chapter. The chief aim is to explore both the nature of these two concepts and their implications for getting to grips with the crisis in Leisure Studies.

The route to be followed in exploring these conceptual interconnections is the following: firstly, the so-called crisis in Leisure Studies will be mapped. Secondly, a brief overview will be given of the main arguments conveyed for addressing the 'crisis'. Thirdly, Blackshaw's solution for moving beyond the 'crisis' will be analysed specifically. Fourthly, a conceptual analysis will be made of the two mentioned main pillars undergirding his argument, namely meaning (spirituality) and freedom (morality), which, fifthly, will be followed by a section that critically weighs Blackshaw's position by exploring the interrelationships between the key concepts that are at stake in this chapter, namely 'liquid leisure', 'meaning' and 'freedom'.

The 'crisis' of Leisure Studies

The 'crisis' that Leisure Studies is purported to be in has been identified and addressed by leisure scholars for quite some time now. Mommaas, for instance, noted as early as 1997 that although a lot of research is being done on issues such as time, consumption, play and pleasure, they are no longer connected to the concepts of leisure or free time (Mommaas, 1997: 241). That is, the *public* significance of leisure has changed, which has resulted in a 'pluralization' in the academic study of leisure, making the existing barriers between Leisure Studies and other socio-cultural academic disciplines more permeable. Mommaas claims that the collective foundation which undergirds public participation in a common culture seems to have been dissolved. The challenge for Leisure Studies, in his mind, lies in searching for a new alignment with the 'plurality' of themes and issues mentioned above and in developing a new 'collective project of leisure' (Mommaas, 1997: 252).

Another scholar who addressed the crisis in the study of leisure – also in 1997 – is Coalter. He focuses on the manifestation of the 'crisis' in the two main scholarly traditions, Leisure Studies (UK) and Leisure Sciences (US). Regarding the former, he relates the reason for the 'crisis' to the 'close relationship' of Leisure Studies to the socio-theoretical impact of academic disciplines such as sociology and social policy. Their 'collectivist, welfarist and liberationist analyses' are increasingly challenged by the divergent forces inherent to post-modernism, which manifest themselves in an attitude that questions the pretentions of positivist methodology in leisure research. The idea, then, is that positivist analyses fail to take individual meaning (of leisure activities or attitudes) into consideration.

Proponents of the USA-centred Leisure Sciences tradition take a slightly different tack, but also arrive at the conclusion that the study of leisure is out of date. They view the statement that leisure has 'a unique set of meanings [...] or is the sole proprietor of freedom and intrinsic meaning' as an 'oversimplification' (Coalter, 1997: 255–256). Putting these two streams of criticism together, Coalter states that analyses so far have failed to address social and cultural meanings of leisure in a satisfactory manner. Coalter concludes that neither Leisure Studies, nor Leisure Sciences has adequately addressed the 'nature of leisure meanings and their relationship to wider sources of meaning and identity' (Coalter, 1997: 265).

Summarizing, we can say that Mommaas defined the need for a new collective 'project' in the study of leisure, and that Coalter identified the fundamental denominator of that project, namely 'meaning'. Several scholars have since then suggested ways out of the 'crisis'. In the following section, the views of three of them will be explicated: Coalter, Henderson and Blackshaw.

Reactions to the 'crisis'

Coalter's idea to combat the crisis in the academic study of leisure is, as noted above, to focus on 'meaning'. He challenges Leisure Studies and Leisure Sciences to explore the lived experience of the everyday life of individuals. The main inroad into this realm should be, he claims, the 'meanings of activities and the relationships supporting activity and given expression through activity'. Analysing this phenomenon will help to generate insight into the ways in which individuals are building on a common culture around leisure in a post-modern context (Coalter, 1997: 266). Scholars are invited to look for both the potential and limitations of leisure in a changing culture and to consider the interrelationships between leisure meaning and other sources of meaning and identity, to adopt 'methodological modesty' when researching leisure and to search for understanding 'ontological issues' as well (Coalter, 1997: 266).

Where Coalter suggests zooming in thematically, Henderson rather pleads for a *pluralist* point of view, accommodating a diversity of concepts, theories, methods and specialties (Henderson, 2010: 399). This, of course, aligns quite well with the main reason for the crisis in Leisure Studies, namely its inability to absorb postmodern diversity and multiplication. She finds support for her ideas in the views of Stebbins: he also values 'fragmentation', one of the hallmarks of postmodernity, as a productive guiding principle for the study of leisure (Henderson, 2010: 396). Henderson is a firm believer in the maxim that leisure can never be separated from its context, thus implying that the value of leisure for society should be at the centre of the scholarly attention. As a more concrete suggestion towards overcoming the 'crisis' in the study of leisure, she volunteers a four-tiered approach. Her suggested strategy involves (1) embracing and anticipating change, because it is the 'new normal' for leisure and society and, as scientists, we should be appreciative of our field of study involving objects, perspectives and contexts that are in a continuing state of transmutation; (2) articulating a clear and flexible collective identity for Leisure Studies, in which leisure is seen as a basic value, e.g. as a phenomenon that contributes to the enhancement of human lives through positive experiences; (3) contributing to analysis and 'affirmation of what makes life meaningful' and communicating its value to society in an inter-, multi- and transdisciplinary way; and (4) collaborating actively with others across disciplinary boundaries and on different levels, with the intent of generating 'co-created knowledge' (Henderson, 2010: 397–398).

Blackshaw, the third scholar who offers a solution to the 'crisis' in the academic study of leisure, introduces the concept 'liquid leisure'. In this, he follows in the slipstream of Zygmunt Bauman. Defining leisure as 'liquid' draws into focus the flow and fluency, movement and mobility, and brittleness and breakability of social relations. More generally, it highlights the transparency and the temporary nature of things, which modernity in its formative modality was bent on solidifying and fixing. It takes us beyond conceptualizing human locations in the social world and inter-human bonds as static, and instead views them in their appropriate organic situatedness (Bauman, 2004: 20). This idea of fluidity is in concordance with the assessments of all three scholars mentioned above (Mommaas, Coalter and Henderson). In addition, as stated earlier, Blackshaw takes special care to focus on the human search for meaning and authenticity within this 'liquid' modern context, based as it is on freedom and the exploration thereof by social agents. In this sense, leisure can be viewed as a 'facilitator' of meaning and a domain for individual freedom. The contours of Blackshaw's ideas, our main partner of this discussion's solution for addressing the 'crisis', will be explored further in the next section.

Blackshaw's solution: liquid leisure, meaning and freedom

For Blackshaw, leisure is dynamic and fluid not merely because of its instantiation in a multimodal context: it is itself a process rather than a thing. Leisure, he claims, has become a *hermeneutical exercise*: it has ceased to be defined by 'its good or bad aspects [...], work against leisure, serious leisure against casual leisure, leisure as freedom against leisure as constraint'. Rather, the essence of leisure lies in the search for pleasure, happiness and freedom, and its meaning has deepened into an appeal to 'the unknown known' – the secret of leisure that is uncovered in the search (Blackshaw, 2010: 141–142). In this light, we could interpret leisure as a *devotional* practice, because the conscious choice for one's own leisure practice is based on a feeling that deems that practice as something 'holy', as 'though engaging in it were a religious function' (Blackshaw, 2010: 142).

Blackshaw proposes that we should understand this devotional practice as a central feature of modern life, and he characterizes it as 'reflexive individualization' (Blackshaw, 2010: 102). This feature is especially necessary today, for the 'postmodern imagination' provides individuals with a vast array of possibilities for making (a kind of) meaning that, in face of the lack of solid ontologies or a grand theory, has its own authority. Echoes of the Aristotelian *skholē* concept seem to resound in these individual leisure practices by alternative means: this 'liquid leisure'-style *skholē* involves not only cognitive development, but also the moral and social development of individuals (Blackshaw, 2010: 5). For the study of leisure as a discipline, this means, according to Blackshaw, that the fading demarcation lines between current academic disciplines that study and interpret leisure necessitate an integrative approach that also takes into account the 'imaginative world' – the realm where we dream of the things that we want to do and can do in order to pursue our personal cognitive, moral and social evolution. The study of leisure therefore becomes more than simply describing or analysing social developments along positivistic lines, but starts to absorb imaginative and creative properties of *art*.

This implies that leisure practice as an *artistic* endeavour establishes the possibility conditions for an individual *art of life*. Furthermore, 'To embrace the art of life is to recognize one's individual freedom', Blackshaw says (2010: 145–148). This recognition rests on grasping one's responsibility in choosing the way of living one's own life, *and* on being aware that one's identity is being formed in a continuous, dynamic process. It is then important to realize that no individual is completely free; the freedom of others constrains one's own freedom. Blackshaw states that it is 'on this basis of interdependent responsibility for the self and the Other that the art of living prospers as a universalizable ethical mode of existence' (Blackshaw, 2010: 150). The art of living, then, is a matter of living your life a certain way, which is both personally authentic and socially ethical. This artful existence is something that has to be learned.

By unpacking 'liquid leisure' into a dynamic of finding *meaning* in the exploration and exploitation of *freedom*, Blackshaw intends to establish a coherent way of looking at Leisure Studies as a discipline. This is an agenda that demands additional critical analysis. In the remaining sections, we will take a closer look at 'freedom' and 'meaning' as they manifest themselves within 'liquid life', and the way in which the interplay of these domains might offer new insights into leisure as a practice. By doing this, we extrapolate and refine some of the notions still left implicit in Blackshaw's theory, in a way that we feel points the way towards a more effective, interdisciplinary and modern form of Leisure Studies.

Freedom, identity, ethics and the body

In Blackshaw's theory, the regenerative, meaning-giving power of leisure stems from its role as a context for freedom and playfulness (Blackshaw, 2010: 152). In the case of leisure, 'freedom' indicates the underdetermined life space within which we can choose what we want to do and who we want to be. This immediately calls into question three other inter-locking concepts: identity, ethics and the body. We will address each of these four concepts in turn.

(a) *Freedom*, and in particular its corollary, 'free will', is a philosophically tricky concept. The good news for the current discussion is that the metaphysical details are not debilitating. Of course leisure is not free in a metaphysical sense. Every leisure activity is about a subjuga-tion to rules – but *different* rules than the ones we are normally required to follow. When we play a game of football, for instance, we are free of caring for our family, or of any concerns related to work, but we are bound to follow the rules of the game.

A well-known account of free will within a deterministic context is due to the philosopher Harry Frankfurt (1971), who understands the freedom of the will to be neutral regarding determinism: someone can be called free if he wants the things he is causally determined to want. Transposing this insight to the leisure context, we can say that leisure-as-subjugation-to-rules obviously is not free. But: what if you *want* that subjugation? What if playing a game (e.g. football), defined by its characteristic constraints (e.g. you cannot pick up the ball) and possibilities (e.g. strategy, teamwork), allows a person to express who he wants to be (e.g. an active, youthful person, a good team player and friend)?

For a leisure activity to be effective in generating a sense of freedom, it does not really matter whether that activity or the decision chain leading up to it was *really* free in a strong sense. What matters is that the agent has the appropriate feeling of freedom; and whether that feeling is metaphysically genuine or whether it is the universe, the brain or whatever entity playing tricks on the agent, his mind, soul or whatever else is supposed to experience that freedom is not our primary concern. We want to claim that this is 'free enough': leisure offering the space to express who we are or want to be – our personal identity – is what it means for something to be free in a *phenomenal* sense.

(b) This brings us to the next important step in our analysis: indulging in leisure activities feels free, in part, because it helps us to shape our *personal identity*.

This, in a circumspect way, is one of the implications of liquid modernity/postmodernity, the context within which Blackshaw defines his notion 'liquid leisure'. That is, the liquidity he speaks of can be found on two levels, the social and the psychological. *Social* fluidity is expressed in extensive variety between groups or individuals: where once society was structured along divisions of gender, class and race, our current leisure options are much less rigid (even though the old divisions still have not been discarded completely). Leisure today, as has been noted several times before, is defined by individual freedom. The other kind of fluidity, *psychological* fluidity, involves variety within individuals: opinions, experiences and categorizations that we make are generally contingent, hence dynamic.

The implication, then, is that if both society and identity are liquid, we are forced, either by design (humans are social animals) or by necessity (today's society is built on co-depend-ence), to organize ourselves in social structures.

Leisure provides a psychologically salient context in which to train our ability to navi-gate the social and psychological fluidity that we find ourselves in. In that sense, leisure is a *normativity game*, offering us insight into how people play with norms. That is, utilizing the playful freedom inherent in leisure (there's the *game*-aspect), we can explore alternative behavioural scripts and contexts (hence *normativity*), to explore different ways of constructing our personal narrative. To claim that liquid leisure is a normativity game is to say that leisure is characterized by a context-dependent malleability of experiential and social normative dynamics. Leisure, therefore, provides the playground on which to 'practise' who you want to be in different situations, each with its own legislative dynamics (see the football example above), and express that in the rest of your life choices.

In the background of this conception of leisure is an idea of what personal identity is, or at least how it can emerge: assuming different roles within various leisure contexts (different rule systems) presents opportunities to diversify behavioural/psychological 'scripts' (experiences). A consistent (social) enaction of specific psycho-behavioural traits across different contexts then establishes a narrative sequence, from which a description of one's personal identity can be extracted (e.g. as a *leitmotif*). This explanation serves to highlight an idea that we wish to defend, namely that personal identity is constituted by placing new experiences in a narrative context, i.e. the behavioural and cognitive 'jurisprudence' that we build up by living and acting, seeing other agents doing the same and remembering effective behavioural profiles for application at a later date in similar situations (see e.g. Van Leeuwen, 2009).

Leisure is especially relevant in the shaping of our narrative identity because of the centrality of experience: many of the best stories that form our sense of self are connected to leisure activities, such as significant sports victories, holidays and outings that served to strengthen family bonds, major aesthetic experiences and so on. In these instances of being exposed to something of transcendental importance (joy, pride, love, beauty), leisure opens us up to self-creation (i.e. self-management, 'conscious, deliberate self-shaping'), which can otherwise be explained as the autonomous writing of self-narratives (i.e. how you understand yourself, your identity and how you wish to present yourself to others).

(c) The third concept to be analysed is '*ethics*'. Earlier, when discussing Blackshaw, the notion 'art of life' emerged. Understanding self-creation as an artful way of writing self-narratives implies an ethical dimension – due to the normative claims encapsulated in the word 'art'. Now, interestingly enough, Blackshaw (2010) says relatively little about the ethics of liquid leisure, but there are some leads in his book.

For instance: 'leisure itself does not include ethics of any kind, but when people freely engage in leisure together they establish their own ethics' (Blackshaw, 2010: 47). The term 'freely' is extremely important here. If we are free in our leisure time, even in the non-metaphysical sense as discussed earlier, where in the postmodern Petri dish of liquid leisure can we find solid ground for a workable ethics?

Reading between the lines, there are some usable ideas in Blackshaw's liquid leisure paradigm. One of them is the 'art of life' idea: leisure has the potential to be a domain within which to practise the art of life: looking for beauty, love and fulfilment. That, of course, is a beautiful ideal, but it does not yet tell us how that art is to be practised in an ethical sense. After all, a potential's being present does not mean that it will actually be realized. Leisure offers just as many opportunities to indulge in the ugly aspects of life (hooliganism, vandalism, child pornography etc.).

(d) A more solid clue to understanding the ethical implications of the art-of-life idea can be found in the central position that Blackshaw awards to *bodily* experience – a Nietzschean principle if ever there was one. Blackshaw (2010: 113–115) suggests that the caricature of postmodernism (extreme cultural relativism) is not helpful in studying leisure. We agree that leisure today is no longer to be categorized a priori according to gender, race, social stature or any other kind of rigid designation, but there is a guiding principle at work here, after all: personal experience, and, in particular, the primacy of the body in it.

Cokal (2010), for instance, illustrates the primacy of personal bodily experience when discussing horror movies: a confrontation with something grotesque/monstrous/shocking can elicit revulsion – often a bodily reaction, a *visceral* sensation – exactly because it takes us beyond the safety of our everyday routine. In doing so, this sensation sparks glimpses of the sublime – remember this for when we discuss spirituality as a component of leisure as the art of life.

Many of the most common leisure pursuits are activities that connect, at least in some sense, to this basic end of the spectrum, meaning that they involve chiefly visceral sensations. This embodied character is, however, exactly the source of their power. A viscera-based drive towards creative expression or sensational experience can serve as a way to feel alive and inspired. Brymer and Gray (2009: 135), for instance, note that 'for veteran adventure athletes the natural world acts as a facilitator to a deeper, more positive understanding of self and its place in the environment'. The overriding power of these activities derives exactly from their visceral properties: they involve strong, basic sensations that are real and feel true, and at the same time serve to weave the agent and what he does into a broader tapestry of meaning and purpose.

Before we touch upon the specifics of that meaning – by addressing the spiritual dimension, in the section below – we need to take a brief detour into ethics. The problem here, in the light of our earlier promise to work our way towards a stand on ethics, is obvious: using viscera-based sensations as a source of subjective/fabricated ethical insights is likely to result in convictions that are not in alignment with extant socio-cultural expectations. In other words: ethical pandemonium.

Luckily, in the past decade or so, there have been some significant advances in body-based ethical theories with a strong pedigree not just in phenomenology (which has a long and rich history in the Continental, chiefly anti-positivist philosophical tradition, e.g. Bergson, Nietzsche, Husserl), but also in biology and neuroscience. One of the most famous modern proponents of the notion that bodily sensations inform cognition is Antonio Damasio (1999).

Two of the philosophers working within the embodied and embedded cognition paradigm (within which it is claimed that psychological states are not restricted to information processing in the brain, but fundamentally involve input from the entire body, and cannot be divorced from a meaningful interrelatedness with the environment) and who have also devised a coherent ethical system are Jesse Prinz and Shaun Nichols. The position that they defend can be called Naturalistic Sentimentalism, which claims that morality should be seen as a byproduct of particular biological predispositions. In other words: moral norms are sentimental norms.

Nichols (2008) extrapolates this idea into a cultural ethical theory by noting that 'emotions played a role in determining which norms survived throughout our cultural history. In particular, norms prohibiting actions likely to elicit *negative* affect will have enhanced cultural fitness.' This is called the affective resonance hypothesis: 'Norms that prohibit actions to which we are predisposed to be emotionally averse will enjoy enhanced cultural fitness over other norms' (Nichols, 2008).

In this light, the drive, found in almost all cultures, to experience the sublime via sensory stimulation – drug use by mystics or youths out on the town on Saturday night, Western society's predilection for everything and anything involving sex, martyrs attempting to achieve transcendence through pain, extreme athletes pushing their bodies to the limit, monks fasting etc. – makes a lot of sense. Even in less extreme cases, the centrality of experience in leisure and the understanding of leisure as 'art of life' highlights the connectedness of bodily sensations and 'higher', spiritual pursuits.

The very notion 'art of life', with or without leisure as the context within which this art can be practised, juxtaposes ethics with the *spiritual*. The 'art' aspect combines creativity and playfulness in what is essentially a devotional practice – a spiritual striving towards everything that is beautiful, truthful and good. The 'life' aspect points towards human existence as a potentiality – a space to explore and give shape, direction and purpose – which implies ethical responsibility as a major source of contextual constraints.

We have discussed the interplay between the concepts of freedom, personal identity, ethics and embodiment. Before we tie meaning, (narrative) identity and spirituality together in a coherent view of the role of leisure, we first need to explore the 'spirituality' aspect.

Leisure as devotional practice: spiritual meaning

Blackshaw adapts a statement by the German philosopher Josef Pieper, that leisure fundamentally is an attitude of mind, a condition of the soul, by saying that 'the meaning of life is the meaning of leisure' (Blackshaw, 2010: 152). In this sense, the concept 'meaning' does not refer to everyday meaning-making, but to ultimate or ontological meaning. He holds that leisure has a secret centre, that it can be seen as a 'devotional practice', a 'spiritual practice' and can be sensed as something 'holy' (Blackshaw, 2010: 142–143).

This idea aligns with empirical findings on the meanings of leisure (Watkins and Bond, 2007: 287–307). Respondents in this study indicated, for instance, that leisure is about achieving fulfilment 'through a deeply felt emotional response and experience of happiness', which 'reinforces one's identity and is related to pleasure, mental and spiritual relaxation, choice, satisfaction, mastery and self worth' (Watkins and Bond, 2007: 295–299).

Now, 'spirituality' is a term with a long and chequered history. It is important, therefore, to shed more light on the nature of spirituality as we wish to describe it – which is not necessarily in its familiar religious form. We will do so by providing brief conceptual descriptions from the perspectives of (a) theology and religious studies, (b) psychology, (c) philosophy and (d) sociology.

(a) In religious studies and theology, there are different views on how spirituality and religion can be differentiated. For many, these two concepts are synonyms. For others, they are antonyms. As far as the study of spirituality is concerned, two approaches can be identified in the discussions that developed over the twentieth century. One approach, a deductive one, is strongly theologically oriented. The other, an inductive one, starts from the lived experience. Waaijman's research on the phenomenology of Christian spirituality shows three basic forms: (1) the established schools of spirituality (defined as historical syntheses, displaying a great diversity of forms, like the monastic system, Benedictine, Jesuits, Reformational spirituality etc.), (2) primordial spiritualities such as lay (everyday) spirituality, indigenous spirituality and secular spirituality (it is closely related to life as it is directly lived) and (3) counter spirituality, which offers opposition against established power configurations (Waaijman, 2006: 5–12). His analysis of the fundamental structures of spirituality pointed towards three elements, namely (1) a relational process between God (divine pole) and man (human pole), (2) a gradual process from awe to love and (3) transformation in/of human existence (on personal, social and socio-cultural levels).

(b) Within *psychology*, spirituality has emerged as a domain of study opposite to religion. It represents an individual's striving to reach sacred or existential goals in life, such as meaning or wholeness, exploring one's inner potentials to the best of one's ability, or connecting with fellow human beings in an uplifting way. Spirituality, in recent years, is understood more and more as an attitude of relatedness to the world, something that gives meaning to life.

Analysis of the commonalities and differences between religion and spirituality brought Zinnbauer to define spirituality as 'a personal or group search for the sacred', and religiosity as a 'personal or group search for the sacred that unfolds within a traditional sacred context' (Zinnbauer and Pargament, 2005: 35): he defines spirituality as the broader construct. Pargament holds religion to be the broader construct by relating spirituality to the 'search for the sacred' and religion to the 'search for significance in ways related to the sacred' (Zinnbauer and Pargament, 2005: 36). Whatever the case may be, the common denominator between spirituality and religion is the *sacred* – be it within traditional communal contexts of religious exercise, based on an articulated set of convictions and rituals, or outside this context in the domains of everyday life as experienced by individuals.

(c) Spirituality has also been studied in *philosophy* – Robert Solomon looked at it as a source of inspiration for sceptics. He advocates a 'natural' spirituality that embraces the material world, the desires, sex and sensuality, the body and, perhaps, fast cars, money and luxury goods as well – all in the right proportions (Solomon, 2004: 51). Such a 'natural' spirituality depicts a broader consciousness of life. It embraces both rationality and emotionality and seeks to discover a bigger 'I' – not unlike the way in which extreme athletes look for the sublime in pushing their body to extremes. Extrapolating these Romanticist ideals, Solomon isolates love (compassion), awe and (cosmic) trust as the most important passions of spirituality (Solomon, 2004: 62–71). These properties are all seen as forms of acceptance. Roothaan (2007) designed a spirituality 'for the future' based on four coordinates. These are (1) the definition of what life is, (2) orientation towards life, (3) life in the spiritual Western tradition and (4) openness towards the future. Inspired by the thought of Hannah Arendt, Roothaan advocates a spirituality that should be able to show a way of dealing with dilemmas surrounding the vulnerability of human life. Puchalski, a medical doctor, defines spirituality as 'the aspect of humanity that refers to the way individuals seek and express meaning and purpose, and the way they experience their connectedness to the moment, to self, to others, to nature and to the significant or sacred' (Puchalski, 2009: 1). As such, spirituality often gives people a sense of well-being, improves quality of life and provides social support.

(d) Sociology, the discipline that is usually most closely associated with 'classical' Leisure Studies, got interested in spiritually as a social phenomenon fairly recently. Within this context, spirituality focuses on the connection between the personal experience and the institution, and their collective relationship with the sacred. Leisure, from a sociological perspective, is understood as an activity which expresses the freedom of the individual, and obedience to an external authority is no longer a dominant factor (Flanagan, 2010: 16). In this postmodern context, leisure requires a way of infiltrating secular domains of social life (Holmes, 2005: 34). If engaged in freely, spirituality opens up the sacred for the individual, and this is how he can find meaning in life. Thus, the search for meaning and self-actualization has also captured a place within the field of sociology.

What this very brief overview shows is that 'spirituality' has some distinct characteristics. It involves a direct and personal experience of what is deemed to be sacred or transcendental, resulting in a broader consciousness of life, with a specific focus on compassion or love, and inspired by awe and cosmic trust. The psychological and, in a sense, ethical implications are that spiritual experiences evoke a sense of meaning, purpose and connectedness (relationality) and instigate a process of transformation in/of human existence. In this sense (to make good on the promise made at the beginning of this section), we can see that spirituality is to be distinguished from the concept of 'religion', which involves a more narrow application of spirituality, namely within a communal setting and based on a set of (communal) beliefs and rituals.

Interestingly, and relevantly to the purposes of the present chapter, some of the characteristics of 'spirituality' as outlined above have been confirmed by studies executed by leisure scholars. Multidisciplinary research done by Willson on the conceptualization of 'spirituality' in the context of tourism has identified spirituality's core commonalities as (1) the search for personal meaning and purpose in life, (2) transcendence and (3) connectedness (Willson, 2010: 236). Heintzman formulates spiritual well-being as 'a high level of faith, hope, and commitment, in relation to a well-defined worldview or belief system that provides a sense of meaning and purpose to existence in general, and that offers an ethical path to personal fulfillment, which includes connectedness with self, others and a higher power or larger reality' (Heintzman, 2009: 423). He identifies sacralization, sense of place and repression avoidance as specific spiritual functions of leisure.

Schmidt, in Heintzman's wake, relates spirituality to the human capacity and inclination of transcending existing knowledge, expressing belief in a higher power and to a mystical state. It includes a frame of reference wider than the immediate, the material and the everyday and leads the believer to seek or experience a personal meaning in their own life (Schmidt, 2007: 174–175; Schmidt and Little, 2007: 224). Strikingly, Schmidt holds that the 'sacred' dimension of spirituality – as explicated in the conceptual analysis above – is not primary. However, he does identify a 'transcendence' dimension, but apparently the respondents in his research did not see that as identical with 'sacred'. This aligns with Willson's position as described above. This aspect – the non-synonymity of these two varieties of spirituality in a leisure context – demands additional conceptual exploration. In particular, such an investigation might help us to make better sense of Blackshaw's reference to leisure as something 'holy': which kinds of spirituality should we connect to leisure experiences? Are they two separate dimensions of a certain kind of (primordial) spirituality, or is there conceptual 'confusion' in play? And: what is the relevance of this apparent duality for the initial statement in this section that the meaning that Blackshaw ascribes to leisure is of an ultimate or ontological nature?

Liquid leisure: co-creating meaning

In this last section the key concepts that are at stake in this chapter, namely liquid leisure, freedom and meaning, will be tied together in an attempt to create a more coherent and concrete idea of what leisure is and does.

Specifically, we are now in a position to see that in leisure the following conceptual clusters are important:

1   *Freedom and normativity*: the (relative) freedom in leisure time to choose activities and attitudes implies a differentiation in (and possible conflicts due to) normative/ethical styles, depending on the leisure context.
2   *Creativity and inspiration*: the freedom to choose in leisure is, to a large extent, the freedom to look for inspiring ideas and experiences, to be creative or to stimulate creativity, to look for spiritual fulfilment.
3   *Identity, experience and meaning*: expressing creativity and exploring inspiring activities can result in meaningful experiences, which can help to constitute someone's intended/ desired personal identity. That is, in leisure time people can exploit the aforementioned freedom to construct particularly salient parts of a personal narrative.

Note the interrelatedness/impredicativity of the clusters: someone's identity will determine the norms that they wish to implement in their life, and the specific kinds of freedom that they desire in their leisure time.

The overall drive of leisure in this sense is to improve personal and communal well-being. Here we also see an impredicative loop. That is, the search for things that we *want* to do in leisure – i.e. pursuing positive experiences – can inspire a self-stimulation effect. The causal chain here is that positive emotion stimulates creativity, which facilitates co-creation, which can stimulate positive emotions.

There is ample empirical evidence for the beneficial effect of positive emotions on overall – and long-term – well-being. Gable and Haidt (2005) refer to two empirical studies: 'Harker and Keltner (2001) coded the emotional expressions of women in their college yearbook photos and correlated them with outcomes such as marital satisfaction and psychological well-being 30 years later. Women who expressed more positive emotion in their photos at 22 years of age had significantly more favorable outcomes in their 50s.' And: 'Danner, Snowdon, and Friesen (2001) found that autobiographies of Catholic nuns written in their early 20s predicted survival in old age. Specifically, nuns whose essays contained positive emotional content lived longer than nuns whose essays lacked such content. Astoundingly, there was a 2.5 risk-ratio difference between the lowest and highest quartiles of positive emotional expression!' As Stevenson and Wolfers (2008: 5) show, there is also a strong bodily component involved – in line with our earlier idea about visceral sensations in leisure: 'a variety of evidence points to a robust correlation between answers to subjective well-being questions and more objective measures of personal well-being. For example, answers to subjective well-being questions have been shown to be correlated with physical evidence of affect such as smiling, laughing, heart rate measures, sociability, and electrical activity in the brain.'

Now, a general state of well-being, reflected in a positive mood, is claimed to enhance creative ideation (Davis, 2009). In the social arena, a positive inclination ameliorated with creative ability – call it a benign inventiveness – can assist in smoothing out any social stress that might emerge. We will even venture the stronger claim that leisure tools (i.e. meaningful experiences by way of art, events and other creative interactive encounters) can facilitate meaning-directed attunement processes, resulting in the co-creation of shared values in a social/collaborative/interactive network.

This co-creation process is the process of adhesion to something bigger, something collectively formed in the creative acts that leisure offers so much room for. These processes can result in spiritual experiences, in experiences of partaking in something that transcends the immediately personal – and sometimes this is *not* a metaphor in leisure. Examples: visiting a dance event and celebrating deep into the night can evoke strong *physical* sensations of togetherness and love (even without the use of illegal substances); an important game by the national football team can erase political and cultural demarcations and truly unite a country's inhabitants, if only for a while; a masterful performance by an inspired and inspiring artist can spark a momentary glimpse of the infinite, the transcendent. These experiences are *co-creative* because they emerge in the coming together of different components, each of which is necessary for the transcendent to exist: dancers and musicians meet in a context of engineered imagination (the dance event); athletes act out a battle and supporters invest themselves emotionally (the sports game); the observer allows himself to be touched by the artist's technical skill and/or emotive power (the aesthetic experience).

These are the kinds of experiences that enhance one's life, that underline specific meaningful events and place explanation marks after the events that have a particularly meaningful role to play in the narrative of one's life. We express who we are or who we want to be through the choices we make, freely, in our leisure time, and those impressive experiences in turn determine who we interpret ourselves as being.

Conclusions

In this chapter, we have unpacked some of the most fertile ideas in Blackshaw's 'liquid leisure' idea, and added some of the depth and breadth that we feel these notions need so as to form a viable contribution to a new Leisure Studies. In particular, understanding leisure within the framework of artful living immediately establishes the need for a workable ethical perspective: life as art implies standards to be met or ideals to be realized. These standards tend to be of a particular kind because human beings are social animals: humans being 'social' means that they establish workable interaction dynamics through mutual dependence, and humans being 'animals' means that the rules and regulations that they collectively gravitate towards tend to be informed, at least partially, by bodily sensations (pleasure, pain, revulsion, grief and so on).

Leisure is an important context within which these social interaction systems are created, tested and developed, and the most impressive formative experiences are, we wish to claim, spiritual in kind. The 'spiritual' moniker is much broader than merely religious, for it also involves profound intellectual insight and overwhelming aesthetic experience. Through these spiritual experiences, a person can place meaningful markers in his life; he can make sense of what he experiences.

In this brief recapitulation lies the road ahead for Leisure Studies as we see it. In order to make sense of leisure as artful living we need an interdisciplinary approach that explicitly includes embodied psychology, philosophy and ethics, and the broad concept of spirituality as explained above. This opens up leisure as a domain for the co-creation of meaningful experiences – that is, the social construction of beauty and collective well-being.

'What is the meaning of life?' is a perennial potboiler of a question that is, at best, pretentious and, most likely, rather meaningless. After all, it demands a singular act of explanation (*the* meaning) to justify (the *meaning*) a poorly defined concept (*life*) that is intended to signify the totality of existence – more or less. It is perhaps surprising, and even quite heartening, then, to find, as we suggest that we have in the preceding pages, that leisure does appear to be able to give us at least some portion of an answer that will satisfy us, even if we don't know exactly what the question is supposed to mean.

Blackshaw's artful living – part of which means choosing the leisure activities that make us and our dearest companions happy – refers to creating our own meaningful truths. Giovanni Battista Vico (1668–1744) already said: 'Veri criterium est id ipsum fecisse' (the criterion of truth is: having made it yourself). Immanuel Kant (1724–1804) agreed when he said 'Denn nur das, was wir selbst machen können, verstehen wir aus dem Grunde'. A very loose translation in line with the current chapter's theme could be: if, in leisure time, we create the life that we want to lead, we might, for a moment here and there, understand life, the universe and ourselves a little bit better.

References

Bauman, Z. (2004) *Identity: Conversations with Benedetto Vecchi.* Cambridge and London: Harvard University Press.

Blackshaw, T. (2010) *Leisure.* London and New York: Routledge.

Brymer, E. and Gray, T. (2009) 'Dancing with Nature: Rhythm and Harmony in Extreme Sport Participation', *Journal of Adventure Education and Outdoor Learning* 9 (2) 135–149.

Coalter, F. (1997) 'Leisure Sciences and Leisure Studies: Different Concept, Same Crisis?', *Leisure Sciences* 19 (4) 255–268.

Cokal, S. (2010) 'Hot with Rapture and Cold with Fear: Grotesque, Sublime and Postmodern Transformations in Patrick Süskind's Perfume', in T. Fahy, (ed.) *The Philosophy of Horror*. Lexington: University Press of Kentucky.

Damasio, A. (1999) *The Feeling of What Happens: Body and Emotion in the Making of Consciousness*. London: Random House.

Davis, M.A. (2009) 'Understanding the Relationship between Mood and Creativity: A Meta-Analysis', *Organizational Behavior and Human Decision Processes* 108: 25–38.

Flanagan, K. (2010) 'Introduction', in K. Flanagan and P.C. Jupp (eds) *A Sociology of Spirituality*. Farnham/Burlington: Ashgate.

Frankfurt, H.G. (1971) 'Freedom of the Will and the Concept of a Person', *The Journal of Philosophy* 68 (1) 5–20.

Gable, S.L. and Haidt, J. (2005) 'What (and Why) is Positive Psychology?', *Review of General Psychology* 9 (2) 103–110.

Heintzman, P. (2009) 'The Spiritual Benefits of Leisure', *Leisure/Loisir* 33 (1) 419–445.

Henderson, K.A. (2010) 'Leisure Studies in the 21st Century: The Sky is Falling?', *Leisure Sciences* 32 (4) 391–400.

Holmes, P.R. (2005) *Becoming More Human: Exploring the Interface of Spirituality, Discipleship and Therapeutic Faith Community*. Bletchley: Paternoster.

Mommaas, H. (1997) 'European Leisure Studies at the Crossroads? A History of Leisure Studies in Europe', *Leisure Sciences* 19 (4) 241–254.

Nichols, S. (2008) 'Sentimentalism Naturalized', in W. Sinnott-Armstrong (ed.) *The Psychology and Biology of Morality*. Cambridge, MA: MIT Press.

Puchalski, C.M. (2009) 'Ethical Concerns and Boundaries in Spirituality and Health', *Virtual Mentor* 11 (10) 804–815. http://virtualmentor.ama-assn.org/2009/10/pdf/oped1-0910.pdf (retrieved 28 December 2012).

Roberts, K. (2011) 'Leisure: The Importance of Being Inconsequential', *Leisure Studies* 30 (1) 5–20.

Roothaan, A. (2007) *Spiritualiteit Begrijpen: een Filosofische Inleiding* [Spirituality Understood: A Philosophical Introduction]. Amsterdam: Boom.

Schmidt, C. (2007) 'The Lived Experience of the Spiritual Potential of Leisure', *Annals of Leisure Research* 19 (3) 173–193.

Schmidt, C. and Little, D.E. (2007) 'Qualitative Insights into Leisure as a Spiritual Experience', *Journal of Leisure Research* 39 (2) 222–247.

Solomon, R. (2004) *Spiritualiteit voor Sceptici* [Spirituality for the Skeptic]. Baarn: Ten Have.

Stevenson, B. and Wolfers, S. (2008) *Economic Growth and Subjective Well-Being: Reassessing the Easterlin Paradox*, Brookings Papers on Economic Activity, Spring.

Van Leeuwen, M. (2009) 'Thinking Outside the Box – A Theory of Embodied and Embedded Concepts'. PhD thesis, Radboud University Nijmegen, http://repository.ubn.ru.nl/handle/2066/74392.

Waaijman, K. (2006) 'What is Spirituality?', *Acta Theologica Supplementum* 8: 1–18.

Watkins, M. and Bond, C. (2007) 'Ways of Experiencing Leisure', *Leisure Sciences* 29 (3) 287–307.

Willson, G.B. (2010) 'Exploring Travel and Spirituality: The Role of Travel in Facilitating Life Purpose and Meaning within the Lives of Individuals'. PhD thesis, University of Waikato, http://researchcommons.waikato.ac.nz/bitstream/handle/10289/4030/thesis.pdf?sequence=3 (retrieved 14 May 2012).

Zinnbauer B.J. and Pargament, K.I. (2005) 'Religiousness and Spirituality', in R.F. Paloutzian and C.L. Park (eds), *Handbook of the Psychology of Religion and Spirituality*. New York: The Guilford Press.

INDEX